THE *Gourmet* COOKBOOK

A RUX MARTIN BOOK
HOUGHTON MIFFLIN HARCOURT BOSTON NEW YORK

THE *Gourmet* COOKBOOK

More Than 1,000 Recipes

Edited by

RUTH REICHL

hmhco.com

Library of Congress Cataloging-in-Publication Data is available.

ISBN 978-1-328-53477-4

For permissions, see page 1040.
Book design by Anne Chalmers

Printed in China

C&C 10 9 8 7 6 5 3 2 1

ACKNOWLEDGMENTS

If we had understood how huge a project this would be, I don't think any of us would have had the courage to begin. If we had realized how many thousands of recipes we would have to test, and retest, and retest again, to choose the ones in this book, we would have had the sense to walk away.

In retrospect, I'm grateful that we didn't. For me it was a fascinating learning experience. I had the good fortune to have Zanne Stewart and Kemp Minifie as my partners; their combined tenure at *Gourmet* spans more than sixty years, and selecting recipes with them was like becoming part of an ongoing history lesson. Zanne, our executive food editor, can tell you the origin of each recipe—who produced the prototype in 1973, who improved on it ten years later, and how it was updated just last year. Kempy, senior food editor and the chocolate maven to end all chocolate mavens, can talk in painstaking detail about why one cake is better with high-class chocolate and another one is not. The hours I spent choosing the recipes for this book with them truly enriched my life.

This book owes an enormous debt to the many people who have contributed recipes to *Gourmet* magazine over the years. They include famous chefs, former food editors, and, most important, our readers. Without them, the magazine—and the book—would not exist.

Once the recipes were chosen, our fabulous food editors went to work. If Lillian Chou, Ruth Cousineau, Allison Ehri, Gina Marie Miraglia Eriquez, Paul Grimes, Ian Knauer, Robynne Maii, Katy Massam, Amy Mastrangelo, Lori Powell, Melissa Roberts-Matar, Maggie Ruggiero, Tracey Seaman, Alexis Touchet, and Shelley Wiseman had not been willing to roast chickens and time tortes early in the morning and in lieu of lunch each day, this book would not exist. Their able assistants, Maria Bravo, Rafael Payano, and Margarita Sanabria, were also invaluable. Their combined efforts were heroic, and I am truly grateful.

Throughout the testing, Jane Daniels Lear was standing in the kitchen, taking notes as we tasted and pelting the cooks with questions about what they were doing and why. Jane has been writing *Gourmet*'s "Kitchen Notebook" and "Cook's Corner" for almost fifteen years, and she probably knows more about the ingredients we buy and the mechanics of cooking than anyone else alive. She has artfully combined her own knowledge with the wisdom of the cooks and that of Zanne and Kempy. Add to that the entire history of *Gourmet*, and what you get in the recipe headnotes is a very good idea of what has been taking place in America's kitchens over the past sixty years.

John Willoughby was the other invaluable partner in this project; every time we were up against a wall, his wisdom and deep cooking knowledge pulled us through. This book belongs very much to him.

Diane Abrams, the director of Gourmet Books, and associate editors Linda Immediato and Kate Winslow were the doctors who delivered this tome, cheering us on and keeping us on track. And it was Diane who had the great good sense to ask Nina Berkson to enhance the book with her lovely illustrations.

Thanks to Barry Estabrook, for his early encouragement, excellent advice, and ongoing assistance. And to Cheryl Brown, Hobby Coudert, Margie Dorrian, Roopa Gona, John Haney, Margo Leab, Nanette Maxim, Nichol Nelson, Robin Pellicci, Natalie Radolinski, Stephanie Stehofsky, and Hollis Yungbliut, without whom the book would never have gone forward.

For help with history, science, and ethnic ingredients, we relied on a vast array of learned friends outside the magazine. Anne Mendelson's advice and counsel were crucial. Jon Rowley, a fount of information on all things piscatorial, was enormously helpful with seafood information. Thanks too to Jean Anderson, Elizabeth Andoh, Caroline Bates, Shirley and Arch Corriher, Bruce Cost, John T. Edge, Maureen Fant, Bruce Feiler, Jessica Harris, David Karp, Lynne Rossetto Kasper, Jill Norman, Fred Plotkin, Maricel Presilla, Nina Simonds, John Martin Taylor, Nach Waxman, William Woys Weaver, Paula Wolfert, and all who gave generously of their time and knowledge.

Many thanks to Anne Chalmers, for her elegant design, and to Michaela Sullivan, for the striking jacket. Thanks as well to Judith Sutton, who worked tirelessly to fine-tune the book, and to Liz Duvall, Houghton Mifflin's production manager for this project. And one final bow to our agent, the endlessly wise and unflappable Doe Coover, and our editor, the eagle-eyed and extremely precise Rux Martin, for whom good enough is never adequate.

You've been quite a team, and we are forever in your debt.

Contents

INTRODUCTION

The book that taught me to cook was a big brown leather-covered tome with *The Gourmet Cookbook* stamped in gold on the front. I called it "the Book," but to a little girl in the fifties, it was more than that. It was the doorway to a magic land where sophisticated men sipped drinks with names like angel's dream (brandy topped with cream) while beautiful women nibbled on truffled chicken. Dreamily I turned the pages, perusing recipes for lobster Newburg, apricot soufflé, and *niu moa ai*. The last was a recipe for leftover chicken that casually began, "Saw the tops off six small fresh coconuts and scrape out half the coconut meat."

The fact that I had never seen a fresh coconut, much less a truffle, a duck, or any kind of soufflé, troubled me not at all; I liked knowing that such things were out in the world and that people were eating them. It gave me hope that one day I too would have a chance to taste such exotic dishes.

A few years ago, I came across *niu moa ai* once again. It was on the occasion of *Gourmet*'s sixtieth anniversary, which we had decided to celebrate with a retrospective issue. In pursuit of the past, I spent the better part of a year leafing through back issues of the magazine. I was stunned by what I uncovered. Through the years, *Gourmet* chronicled every food trend that our country has embraced, and during that time every important food authority contributed recipes to the magazine. James Beard was one of *Gourmet*'s very first writers, and before long M.F.K. Fisher, Elizabeth David, Jane Grigson, and Clementine Paddleford all joined him.

In the early years, most Americans who considered themselves gourmets looked to France for inspiration, but that soon began to change. The history of American cooking is the history of immigration, and as new arrivals reached our shores, they changed the way we ate. The transformation of our national cuisine was clearly reflected in the magazine, which began reporting on Indian spices, Mexican food, and the cooking of Asia. Before long, *Gourmet*'s editors were asking experts like Madhur Jaffrey, Diana Kennedy, Claudia Roden, Marcella Hazan, and Nina Simonds to show us how to re-create the true flavors of faraway places. As our horizons expanded, we invited more experts into our kitchens, and the pages of the magazine filled up with recipes by authors as diverse as Elizabeth Andoh, Rick Bayless, and Paula Wolfert. *Gourmet*'s writers visited restaurants in the four corners of the world and returned with recipes. Meanwhile, a new group of young American chefs were eagerly inventing dishes and showing off their latest creations in *Gourmet*'s pages. What I had discovered was a treasure trove of extraordinary recipes, a history of American cooking in its most exciting years. It was far too much for a single issue of the magazine, and the idea for this book began to take shape.

The concept was straightforward: we would look through all the recipes we had ever published, select the best, and retest them. Then we would gather the cream of the crop into a book.

Pleased with the simplicity of this plan, we set out to create a master list. That was when the enormity of the project began to dawn on us: we had more than fifty thousand recipes! Even after we had whittled them down, the master list was huge. We had no choice: the only sensible way to proceed was to sit down and go through the recipes one by one.

It took about a year. I chafed at the slowness of the process, but as I look back, I realize that it has been the most valuable lesson in my entire culinary career. The editors engaged in this project have, all together, been cooking for more than three hundred years, and our collective memory is the soul of this book. We remember how the food processor, which was introduced in *Gourmet*'s pages in 1975, changed the way America cooked. We witnessed the advent of

California cooking and the southwestern food movement and watched as the Cajun food craze of the early eighties ratcheted up Americans' appreciation for spicy food. We saw the growth of farmers markets and applauded as ethnic herbs, vegetables, and spices became more readily available. As we talked through these recipes, I found myself going home, night after night, eager to cook some long-forgotten recipe.

There was, for instance, the day we found the scallop mousse. Looking at the recipe, I found myself thinking that it sounded too easy: it contains nothing but scallops, cream, and egg white. *Does this really work?* I wondered.

"This was one of the first real breakthroughs we had with the food processor," said our executive editor, Zanne Stewart. "We discovered that when you purée scallops, they seem to have a magical ability to hold together almost by themselves." I tried the recipe that very night—and I've made it a dozen times since then. It's so extraordinary that it's become my favorite first course.

Every day I learned something new. A discussion of chicken terrines led to a discourse on "glove boning," which led to a reminiscence about the day Jacques Pépin arrived in the test kitchen to demonstrate this method of removing a bird's bones without cutting into the flesh. The technique, which mirrors the way ladies used to don elbow-length kid gloves, requires a great deal of practice. I thought it might be nice to include instructions for glove boning, but after quite a bit of discussion, we decided against it. This is not, after all, a historical document, but a book that wants to live in your kitchen.

We did, however, put in hundreds of recipes for nights when you need to get dinner on the table in a matter of minutes. The truth is that these are the recipes we use most often ourselves. I'd be embarrassed to tell you how frequently I make oven-braised beef with tomato sauce and garlic, which takes fifteen minutes of active time, over the weekend, just so I can reheat it for a weeknight dinner. Or how many nights I come rushing in from the office to make pasta with capers, garlic, and bread crumbs, a dish I love, in twenty minutes flat. I can put seared sea bass with fresh herbs and lemon on the table in less than half an hour, and I'd be sorry if my family discovered how little effort goes into that chocolate caramel sauce they're so fond of.

We have updated every recipe so that you will never be required to engage in complicated and old-fashioned practices. We have updated the ingredients as well. Reading through spicy stir-fried beef with tangerine and cinnamon, I discovered that this wonderful Chinese recipe called for Scotch whisky. Why? Well, twenty-five years ago, when *Gourmet* published Nina Simonds's series on Chinese cooking, it was almost impossible to get Shaoxing rice wine in the United States. Nina experimented and found that Scotch was a better substitute than the sherry most cooks were then calling for. Since rice wine is now readily available, we simply call for it.

Our original goal was to select a thousand recipes, but in the end even that wasn't enough. Too many recipes were too good to eliminate. Consider, for example, the case of the cassoulet. You'll find that this book contains two versions. After a cook-off among the many we have published over the years, we selected the most recent recipe, from the Paris issue of 1999. It is, as befits the great bean dish of southwestern France, a serious project best attempted over a couple of days. It is not the sort of dish a casual cook will be tempted to try, so we decided to include as well a recipe for a quick cassoulet that can be put together in a few hours.

As we continued testing and tasting, we uncovered many surprises. There was, for example, a terrine from the late seventies that was fondly remembered as the best we'd ever published. It was a major effort, which required most of a day to prepare. When it was finally ready to taste, we gathered around with high anticipation. I watched as faces fell. Is it our tastes that have changed, or the ingredients?

I think it is a bit of both. Americans are more demanding diners now than we were thirty, forty, and fifty years ago, and we have developed much more sophisticated palates. Our taste for rich food has become more moderate; rivers of cream and butter are no longer enough to make us happy.

At the same time, kitchen tools and the ingredients themselves have been constantly changing. Today's home cook has access to better equipment, hotter stoves, and more professional tools than previous cooks did. Meanwhile, meat has become leaner and less tasty, while supermarket vegetables have become prettier and less flavorful. Once hard-to-find ingredients are now available in the grocery store, and those that aren't can be ordered over the Internet. Is it any wonder we found that any recipe more than five years old needed to be updated?

The testing process was grueling. At the magazine, we rarely develop a recipe in fewer than eight tries, and once a recipe has been tested and retested, it undergoes a final check to make sure that it will work perfectly for you. For this book, our standards became even more rigorous. Serious negotiation enabled us to pare the hundreds of

chocolate cake recipes we have published over the years down to an essential nine. These are no ordinary chocolate cakes, and we wanted to be certain you would not be disappointed with the results. That is why we baked each cake with a variety of chocolates, from super-premium brands to supermarket basics. For several wonderful weeks, we ate chocolate cake three times a day.

Then there were the sticky buns. It took nine different tries—in different-sized pans—to develop the perfect recipe. But then, on the retest, we decided that we might be able to do even better. So we went back to the drawing board. I'm pretty sure this is the world's best sticky bun recipe, one you will use again and again.

Our goal was to give you a book with every recipe you would ever want. Each time we considered eliminating one, we imagined you standing in your kitchen, thinking about what to cook. Perhaps you're searching out a dinner-party dish—rib-eye steak with wild mushrooms, for instance—or maybe you just need something simple and satisfying, like a really great macaroni and cheese. We wanted everything you might need to be in this book. So while we were able to eliminate *niu moa ai* (sawing those coconuts is just too much trouble), we thought a fancy for lobster Newburg might strike you every once in a while. The one here, incidentally, is so delicious that it could bring this gloriously old-fashioned dish back into fashion. And the apricot soufflé? Pure heaven on a spoon.

As I hold this new book in my hands, I am seven years old again, standing in my mother's kitchen, enthralled with the romance of cooking, dreamily flipping though the pages of "the Book." I know that there are still people out there eager for adventure in the kitchen—and I know that this is the perfect place to find it.

—Ruth Reichl

THE *Gourmet* COOKBOOK

HORS D'OEUVRES AND FIRST COURSES

It's too bad we're stuck with this snooty French word. That's what we kept thinking as we chose the recipes for this chapter. As we were spinning through the decades, watching the metamorphosis of hors d'oeuvres, it became clear that they are the most American part of the meal.

They may sound inconsequential, but if you look through the recipes in this chapter, you'll soon realize that hors d'oeuvres are much more than festive little tidbits. They are the archetypal American food. If you want to see where American food has been or predict where it is going, hors d'oeuvres will show you the way.

These are the entry point, the place where unfamiliar international flavors are invited into the culture for the very first time. Guacamole made an appearance at cocktail parties long before tamales ever turned up on the table, and people who wouldn't dream of attempting a full-blown Turkish meal will happily offer stuffed grape leaves to their guests. And if fried calamari had not become a classic American first course, the squid population would be considerably larger.

For most cooks, hors d'oeuvres are an invitation to adventure—an opportunity to try new tastes without much risk. That's undoubtedly why *Gourmet* has had such a long love affair with the first part of the meal; over the years we've published tens of thousands of recipes for everything from simple clams casino to complex hundred-corner shrimp balls.

Limiting ourselves to the nearly one hundred recipes you find here was excruciatingly difficult, since between us we had enough favorites to fill an entire book. But we were very demanding; as we tested, tasted, and retested, we kept asking ourselves if each was the very best version of the dish we had ever tried. If not, it did not make the cut.

Some of these dishes are like deviled eggs: anyone can make them. Others, like the rabbit terrine with green olives and pistachios, present a serious challenge. We were especially exacting when it came to the difficult ones: when we create a recipe that takes a great deal of your time, we want to be certain that you'll be very happy with the result. Trust us, you will.

In fact, you will be happy with all the hors d'oeuvres (or appetizers, nibbles, or tidbits) in this chapter. Every one of them came into the world intent on turning an ordinary meal into a party.

How to Throw a Cocktail Party

Parties celebrate life's joyous events. But cocktail parties, in particular, can be the source of a great deal of angst on the part of the host. Here are a few tips for success.

MAKE COPIOUS LISTS. Go through each recipe you're using and write down all the things you need. List ingredients and other items, such as napkins, sealable plastic bags, and heavy-duty trash bags. Make another list of the food you're serving and what you're serving it on or with — utensils, trays, little bowls for discarded wooden picks or olive pits. Collect all of these in one place and clean them. When it's time to tuck them away again, make a cheat sheet. That way, the next party will be a snap.

GET HELP. If you'll be hosting sixteen or more people, hire a bartender and someone to pass around the finger food. It's money well spent. And renting glassware and plates will make your life much easier (serve all drinks, including wine, in the same kind of glass). If a friend volunteers to pitch in, be grateful for both the help and the company: assembling dumplings or *arepas* for a crowd is a great excuse to visit with an old pal.

DO THE MATH. Think about the variety of dishes you want and the richness of each one. Here are some very general, and very generous, guidelines: For eight to ten guests, serve at least four types of hors d'oeuvres; each person will eat three or four of each type. For fourteen to sixteen guests, serve five or six hors d'oeuvres; each guest will have two or three of each one. For twenty to thirty guests, serve seven or eight hors d'oeuvres; each guest will have one or two of each.

THE FOOD SHOULD SERVE THE PURPOSE OF THE PARTY. Don't serve food that is messy or too participatory at a formal soirée: make the nibbles neat and bite-sized. Save something like steamers for a casual get-together after a day at the beach.

SERVE SIMPLE THINGS WITH HIGH DRAMA. Admittedly, some party food can be time-consuming to prepare. Pick and choose the recipes that catch your fancy, then fill in the gaps with, for instance, an enormous bowl of cherry tomatoes. Shop for shortcuts: good olives, pâté, cheeses, baguettes. What you're after is abundance with minimal effort.

TIMING IS EVERYTHING. Figure out how many hors d'oeuvres (or components thereof) can be made ahead, then devise a game plan.

YOU CAN NEVER HAVE TOO MUCH ICE. Running out of the all-important cubes is mortifying, so buy tons. Let the leftover stuff melt and use it to water the plants.

MAXIMIZE SPACE. Remove everything you don't need from the kitchen. Clean out the fridge and freezer. Keep cold drinks and bags of ice in an ice chest or the bathtub. Trays or baking sheets of canapés can be stacked if you use juice glasses as pillars to separate them.

MIX UP BATCHES OF ONE PARTICULAR COCKTAIL. It's festive, and guests will have one and then most likely switch to wine or beer. Order plenty of liquor. (Unopened bottles can be saved for the next party or, in some states, returned.)

SO GUESTS START ARRIVING AND YOU'RE NOT READY. It's kind of a metaphor for life, isn't it? Stop. Take a deep breath. Go mingle for fifteen minutes. Then slide back into the kitchen. (No one will notice.) You're giving a party, and everyone is thrilled to be there.

Hors d'Oeuvres

Candied Walnuts

MAKES 2 CUPS
ACTIVE TIME: 10 MINUTES ■ START TO FINISH: 1 HOUR

■ Cindy Pawlcyn's creative verve has enlivened a handful of California restaurants, including Mustards Grill. She simmers her walnuts in water first to draw out any bitterness, then coats them with sugar before frying. The sugar caramelizes, leaving a crisp coating. Serve with tangy cheeses and dates, with drinks, or in salads. ■

2 cups (about 8 ounces) walnut halves
½ teaspoon salt, or to taste
⅛ teaspoon cayenne, or to taste
¾ cup confectioners' sugar
About 9 cups vegetable oil for deep-frying
SPECIAL EQUIPMENT: a deep-fat thermometer

Combine walnuts with water to cover in a saucepan, bring to a simmer, and simmer until slightly softened, about 5 minutes. Drain, then transfer to paper towels to dry completely, 40 to 50 minutes.

Stir together salt and cayenne in a small bowl. Stir together walnuts and sugar in another bowl. Heat 2 inches oil in a 4-quart heavy saucepan over moderately high heat until it registers 350°F on thermometer. Scoop up about ⅔ cup sugared walnuts with a slotted spoon or wire skimmer, shaking off excess sugar, and fry, stirring frequently, until brown and crisp, 1 to 2 minutes. Transfer to a baking sheet and fry remaining nuts in 2 batches. (Return oil to 350°F between batches.) Sprinkle salt mixture over nuts while they are warm and let them cool completely. Transfer to a flattened brown paper bag to drain off excess oil, spreading nuts in a single layer.

COOK'S NOTES

- Don't be tempted to line the baking sheet with paper towels—the sugar will make the nuts stick to it.
- The candied walnuts can be kept for up to 3 days in an airtight container, in layers separated by wax paper, at room temperature.

Rosemary Walnuts

MAKES 2 CUPS
ACTIVE TIME: 10 MINUTES ■ START TO FINISH: 25 MINUTES

■ You can't ever make enough of these walnuts, and they're as good at the end of a meal as at the beginning. They were brought to us by the late Laurie Colwin. She was principally known as a novelist, but to us she was quite simply one of the best food writers on the planet: honest, engaging, and energetic. This is one of her most popular recipes. ■

2½ tablespoons unsalted butter
2 teaspoons dried rosemary, crumbled
1 teaspoon salt
½ teaspoon cayenne
2 cups (about 8 ounces) walnut halves

Put a rack in middle of oven and preheat oven to 350°F.

Melt butter in a baking sheet with sides in oven. Stir in rosemary, salt, and cayenne. Toss walnuts in butter until well coated and spread out into one layer.

Bake for 10 minutes. Serve warm or at room temperature.

COOK'S NOTE

- The walnuts can be kept for up to 3 days in an airtight container at room temperature.

Roasted Pumpkin Seeds

MAKES 1½ CUPS
ACTIVE TIME: 8 MINUTES ■ START TO FINISH: 20 MINUTES

■ Roasted green pumpkin seeds, or pepitas, are the fastest hors d'oeuvre we know, and people can't stop eating them. Buy the seeds (make sure they're unroasted) at a place with a high turnover—they can turn rancid quickly—and keep them in the freezer until you're ready to roast them. They're a terrific garnish for soups and salads as well. ■

1½ cups (6 ounces) green (hulled) pumpkin seeds
1 teaspoon olive oil
¼ teaspoon fine sea salt

Roast pumpkin seeds in a 10- to 12-inch heavy skillet, preferably cast-iron, over moderately low heat, stirring constantly, until puffed and lightly browned, 5 to 7 minutes. Drizzle with oil and sprinkle with sea salt, then stir to coat. Serve warm or at room temperature.

COOK'S NOTE

- The roasted pumpkin seeds can be kept for up to 3 days in an airtight container at room temperature.

Baked Potato Chips

MAKES ABOUT 50 CHIPS
ACTIVE TIME: 10 MINUTES ■ START TO FINISH: 40 MINUTES

■ These flat, crisp chips are reason enough to buy an adjustable-blade slicer such as a Japanese Benriner or mandoline, and reason enough never to go near store-bought baked potato chips again. Delicious and delicate on their own, they are also sturdy enough to make a great vehicle for dips and toppings. For really elegant chips, embellish each one with half a teaspoon of crème fraîche and a teaspoon of caviar. Or top with half a teaspoon of sour cream and a small piece of (skinless) smoked peppered mackerel. ■

3 tablespoons olive oil
1 (8-ounce) russet (baking) potato, scrubbed
½ teaspoon kosher salt
SPECIAL EQUIPMENT: a mandoline or other adjustable-blade slicer, such as a Japanese Benriner

Put racks in upper and lower thirds of oven and preheat oven to 375°F.

Generously brush two large baking sheets with sides with some of olive oil. Cut potato into very thin (1/16-inch-thick) slices with slicer and arrange in one layer on baking sheets. Lightly brush slices with remaining oil and sprinkle with salt.

Bake, switching position of sheets after 5 minutes, until golden, 10 to 20 minutes total (check frequently after 10 minutes). Transfer chips as baked to a rack to cool.

COOK'S NOTE

- The chips can be kept for up to 3 days in an airtight container at room temperature.

VARIATIONS

- SALT AND PEPPER POTATO CHIPS: Sprinkle potatoes with ¼ teaspoon coarsely ground black pepper before baking.
- ROSEMARY POTATO CHIPS: Sprinkle potatoes with 1½ teaspoons minced fresh rosemary before baking.

Sweet Potato Chips with Lime Salt

MAKES ABOUT 200 CHIPS
ACTIVE TIME: 15 MINUTES ■ START TO FINISH: 25 MINUTES

■ A bowl of these long chips—a beautiful tangle of orange shards sprinkled with tart lime salt—will be devoured by party guests in no time. ■

1 teaspoon finely grated lime zest
1½ teaspoons kosher salt
2 large sweet potatoes (1½ pounds total)
About 8 cups vegetable oil for deep-frying
SPECIAL EQUIPMENT: a deep-fat thermometer

Stir lime zest together with salt in a small bowl.

Peel sweet potatoes. Using a vegetable peeler, shave as many long strips as possible from potatoes.

Heat 2 inches oil in a 3- to 4-quart wide heavy saucepan over moderately high heat until it registers 375°F on thermometer. Fry potato strips in 6 batches, stirring frequently, until chips are lightly browned and bubbling stops, 1 to 1½ minutes. Transfer chips to paper towels to drain and sprinkle with lime salt. (Return oil to 375°F between batches.)

COOK'S NOTE

- The chips can be made up to 1 hour ahead.

Seeded Crisps

MAKES 40 CRISPS
ACTIVE TIME: 25 MINUTES ■ START TO FINISH: 25 MINUTES

■ Deep-fried wonton wrappers with a seeded coating on one side are a revelation: unusual, dramatic, and delicious. Have fun with this recipe by coming up with your own mix of seeds—cumin and fennel, perhaps, or black and white sesame seeds. ■

- 3/4 cup sesame seeds
- 2 tablespoons poppy seeds
- 2 tablespoons mustard seeds
- 1 tablespoon kosher salt
- 3/4 teaspoon cayenne
- 6 tablespoons water
- 2 tablespoons cornstarch
- About 4 cups vegetable oil for deep-frying
- 40 wonton wrappers

SPECIAL EQUIPMENT: a deep-fat thermometer

Stir together seeds, salt, and cayenne in a small shallow bowl. Stir together water and cornstarch in a small bowl until smooth.

Heat 1 inch oil in a 3-quart heavy saucepan over moderate heat until it registers 360°F on thermometer. Working quickly (do not let oil overheat), brush one side of each of 2 wonton wrappers with cornstarch mixture and gently press coated sides into seed mixture. Shake off any excess seeds and fry wrappers, turning once, until golden, 30 to 40 seconds total (some seeds will fall off during frying). Transfer crisps to paper towels to drain. (If desired, remove seeds from oil with a small fine-mesh sieve to avoid burned seeds.) Make more crisps 2 at a time in same manner. (Return oil to 360°F between batches.)

COOK'S NOTE

■ The crisps can be kept for up to 3 days in an airtight container at room temperature. Before serving, recrisp them on a baking sheet in a 225°F oven for 10 to 15 minutes.

VARIATION

■ SESAME WONTON CRISPS: Substitute 1 cup toasted sesame seeds (see Tips, page 939) for the seed mixture. Add wrappers to oil and fry, turning once, until golden, about 10 seconds per batch.

Pita Toasts

MAKES 48 TOASTS
ACTIVE TIME: 10 MINUTES ■ START TO FINISH: 25 MINUTES

■ What did we do for toasts before pitas came along? Toast points, obviously, but these days they come across as a little fussy. Pocket pitas work so well because they split into thin halves that can easily be cut into wedges that have an attractive natural curl to them. Pitas can be found in most supermarkets as well as Middle Eastern markets, but be aware that there are wide variations among brands. Some are thick and bready; here you are looking for the very thin ones. Feel free to use the whole wheat variety. ■

- 4 (6-inch) pita breads (with pockets)
- About 1/4 cup olive oil
- Kosher salt (optional)

Put racks in upper and lower thirds of oven and preheat oven to 375°F.

Split pitas horizontally to make 8 rounds. Lightly brush rough sides with oil. Sprinkle with salt, if using, and cut each round into 6 wedges.

Arrange wedges in one layer on two baking sheets. Bake, switching position of sheets halfway through baking, until golden and crisp, about 12 minutes total. Transfer toasts to a rack to cool.

COOK'S NOTE

■ The toasts can be kept for up to 1 week in an airtight container at room temperature.

Benne Seed Pita Toasts

MAKES 64 TOASTS
ACTIVE TIME: 20 MINUTES ■ START TO FINISH: 35 MINUTES

■ These toasts are especially good with the Crab and Coconut Dip on page 21, but they are also delicious with soups or crumbled over a salad. The name benne derives from the West African word for sesame; it was from there that slave ships took the seeds to the Americas. ■

- 1 tablespoon cornstarch
- 3/4 stick (6 tablespoons) unsalted butter, melted and cooled
- 3/4 teaspoon salt
- 1/3 cup sesame seeds, toasted (see Tips, page 939)
- 4 (6- to 7-inch) pita breads (with pockets)

Put racks in upper and lower thirds of oven and preheat oven to 375°F.

Whisk together cornstarch and 2 tablespoons butter in a small bowl until smooth. Whisk in salt, remaining 4 tablespoons butter, and sesame seeds.

Split pitas horizontally to make 8 rounds. Brush rough sides of pita halves with butter mixture, stirring mixture well before brushing. Cut each pita half into 8 wedges and arrange in one layer on two baking sheets.

Bake toasts, switching position of sheets halfway through baking, until golden, 10 to 12 minutes total. Transfer toasts to a rack to cool.

COOK'S NOTE

■ Like other seeds, sesame seeds have a high oil content and become rancid easily, so buy them from a shop with a quick turnover (a natural foods store is often your best bet) and smell them before using. Store them in the freezer.

Liptauer Cheese

MAKES ABOUT 1 CUP
ACTIVE TIME: 10 MINUTES ■ START TO FINISH: 9 HOURS (INCLUDES CHILLING)

■ The seasoned spread called Liptauer takes its name from a fresh sheep's milk cheese made in Liptó, Hungary. When our first recipe was published in the 1940s, it was made with cream cheese, most likely because sheep's milk cheese was unavailable. Another sign of the times was that the dish, originally made with one-eighth teaspoon of garlic, was considered spicy. Recently we tried the spread with both sheep's milk cheese and a mild goat cheese and found that we preferred the latter. ■

- 6 ounces mild goat cheese or cream cheese, softened
- 1/2 stick (4 tablespoons) unsalted butter, softened
- 1 teaspoon paprika, preferably Hungarian
- 1 teaspoon drained capers
- 2 flat anchovy fillets, rinsed, patted dry, and minced
- 2 tablespoons minced shallots
- 1/2 teaspoon caraway seeds
- Salt and freshly ground black pepper

ACCOMPANIMENT: crackers, toasted baguette slices, or toasts

Beat together cheese and butter in a medium bowl with an electric mixer at medium speed until well combined. Add paprika, capers, anchovies, shallots, caraway, and salt and pepper to taste and beat until well combined.

Pack cheese into a small bowl and refrigerate, covered, for at least 8 hours to allow flavors to develop.

Bring cheese to room temperature before serving with crackers or toasts.

COOK'S NOTE

■ The cheese spread can be refrigerated, tightly covered, for up to 3 days.

Everyday Pimento Cheese

MAKES ABOUT 3 CUPS
ACTIVE TIME: 25 MINUTES ■ START TO FINISH: 2½ HOURS (INCLUDES CHILLING)

■ When the writer James Villas shared his mother's recipe with us, he explained that the origin of pimento (as it is often spelled in the South) cheese remains a mystery. But he did know that many folks raised south of the Mason-Dixon Line keep a crock of this "southern pâté" on hand. The cheese must be the finest sharp or extra-sharp Cheddar available, and the mayonnaise must be Duke's, Hellmann's (or Best Foods), or homemade. Other ingredients are hotly contested. Serve with crackers or celery sticks, or use as a filling for finger sandwiches. ■

- ½ pound extra-sharp Vermont white Cheddar
- ½ pound extra-sharp New York orange Cheddar
- 1 (7-ounce) jar pimientos, drained and finely chopped
- Salt
- ½ teaspoon freshly ground black pepper
- Cayenne to taste
- ⅔ cup mayonnaise

Finely grate cheeses into a large bowl. With a fork, stir in pimientos, salt to taste, black pepper, and cayenne, then stir in mayonnaise, mashing mixture until fairly smooth. (It should be flecked with small pieces of pimiento.) Scrape into a small bowl or jar and refrigerate, covered, for at least 2 hours to allow flavors to develop.

Bring cheese to room temperature before serving.

COOK'S NOTE

■ Pimento cheese can be refrigerated, tightly covered, for up to 4 days.

Guacamole

MAKES ABOUT 3½ CUPS
ACTIVE TIME: 20 MINUTES ■ START TO FINISH: 20 MINUTES

■ Guacamole is one of the easiest Mexican dishes to make. There are dozens of variations, and we give a few of our favorites on page 10. The fall-winter fruit version is similar to one we learned from Diana Kennedy, the doyenne of Mexican cooking. (She uses peaches and pomegranate seeds, fruits that are in season at the same time in Mexico.)

Guacamole is traditionally made with a *molcajete y tejolote,* a mortar and pestle made of volcanic rock. In this recipe, we've simply mashed all the ingredients together in a bowl with a fork. (A large ceramic mortar and pestle works well too.) If you find you make guacamole often, though, you might want to get authentic and track down a *molcajete* (see Sources). It's awfully satisfying to use one of the oldest pieces of kitchen equipment in the New World, and it makes a dramatic serving vessel. If using a *molcajete* or other mortar, mash the onion, chiles, and salt together into a rough paste before adding the avocados. In any case, keep the avocados chunky; don't overmash them into a purée. ■

- 4 ripe California avocados (2 pounds total), halved, pitted, and peeled
- ½ cup finely chopped white onion
- 3–4 serrano chiles, minced, including seeds
- 2½ tablespoons fresh lime juice, or to taste
- 1¼ teaspoons kosher salt, or to taste

ACCOMPANIMENT: tortilla chips

Combine avocados, onion, chiles, lime juice, and salt in a bowl and mash with a fork until avocado is mashed but still somewhat chunky. Stir until blended. Serve with tortilla chips.

COOK'S NOTE

■ The guacamole can be made up to 1 hour ahead and refrigerated, covered with plastic wrap placed directly against its surface.

VARIATIONS

- GUACAMOLE WITH TOMATO: Stir 1 tomato, cut into 1/3-inch dice, into the basic mixture.
- RADISH AND CILANTRO GUACAMOLE: Mash the guacamole with 1/2 cup chopped fresh cilantro, then stir in 4 medium radishes cut into 1/4-inch-thick matchsticks.
- FALL–WINTER FRUIT GUACAMOLE: Stir a diced Fuji apple and 3/4 cup quartered seedless red grapes into the guacamole. If you like, stir in 1/2 cup pomegranate seeds and sprinkle a few more on top.
- SUMMER FRUIT GUACAMOLE: Stir 3/4 cup quartered seedless green grapes and a diced firm but ripe peach into the guacamole. You could use 2/3 cup raspberries in place of the peach: add them to the guacamole and mash lightly, then stir in the grapes.

Charred Tomatillo Guacamole

MAKES ABOUT 3 1/2 CUPS
ACTIVE TIME: 30 MINUTES ■ START TO FINISH: 30 MINUTES

■ The fruity, tangy tartness of tomatillos, an Aztec and Mayan staple native to Mexico and Guatemala, works wonders in this guacamole. The recipe came from Susan Feniger and Mary Sue Milliken, of Santa Monica's Border Grill. As they became household celebrities with their *Too Hot Tamales* cooking show, fresh tomatillos went from a hard-to-find item in specialty produce stores to one sold in supermarkets across America. Even though they are sometimes labeled "Mexican green husked tomatoes," they're only distantly related to backyard beefsteaks. Like their cousin the Cape gooseberry, tomatillos are enclosed in a papery husk; pull it off and rinse the fruit if it's sticky. ■

- 6 ounces tomatillos (about 6), husked and rinsed
- 1/2 small red onion, finely chopped
- 3–4 serrano chiles, seeded (see Cook's Note) and finely chopped
- 1/2 cup finely chopped fresh cilantro
- 1 teaspoon salt
- 1/2 teaspoon freshly ground black pepper
- 2 large firm but ripe California avocados (1 pound total)

ACCOMPANIMENT: tortilla chips

Preheat broiler. Broil tomatillos in a shallow baking pan about 4 inches from heat until tops are charred, 7 to 10 minutes. Turn tomatillos over with tongs and broil until charred on bottoms, about 5 minutes more.

Stir together onion, chiles, cilantro, salt, and pepper in a large bowl (or use a large mortar and pestle). Add tomatillos 2 at a time, mashing with a fork (or pestle) to form a coarse paste.

Pit and peel avocados. Add avocados to mixture and mash until incorporated but still chunky. Serve with tortilla chips.

COOK'S NOTES

- For moderately spicy guacamole, seed about half of the chiles; for a milder version, seed all of them.
- The guacamole can be made up to 8 hours ahead and refrigerated, covered with plastic wrap placed directly against its surface. Bring to room temperature before serving.

Roasted Red Pepper and Eggplant Dip

MAKES ABOUT 2 3/4 CUPS
ACTIVE TIME: 45 MINUTES ■ START TO FINISH: 26 3/4 HOURS (INCLUDES CHILLING)

■ Roasted eggplant has the most beautiful silky texture, and so do roasted red peppers. That's one reason we combined the two to make this Mediterranean-inspired dip. The other reason is color, for no matter how you cook eggplant, it turns gray and dingy. We roast the vegetables to add depth of flavor, then purée them and simmer the purée to get rid of the excess liquid. For a spicier dip, include the seeds from the jalapeño. ■

- 1 (3/4-pound) eggplant
- 2 pounds red bell peppers
- 1/4 cup extra-virgin olive oil, plus additional for coating vegetables
- 4 large garlic cloves, minced (1 1/2 tablespoons)
- 3 tablespoons fresh lemon juice, or to taste
- 1 small jalapeño chile, seeded if desired and minced
- 1 teaspoon salt
- 1/2 teaspoon freshly ground black pepper

ACCOMPANIMENT: pita breads, cut into wedges

Put a rack in upper third of oven and preheat oven to 400°F.

Rub eggplant and bell peppers lightly with oil and arrange on a baking sheet with sides. Roast, turning once or twice, until eggplant is very soft and bell peppers are lightly charred, 30 to 40 minutes. Transfer peppers to a bowl, cover tightly with plastic wrap, and let stand for 15 minutes. Let eggplant cool slightly.

Peel, core, and seed bell peppers and pat dry. Halve eggplant, scoop out flesh, and put flesh in a food processor. Add bell peppers, oil, garlic, lemon juice, jalapeño, salt, and pepper and coarsely purée.

Transfer purée to a heavy saucepan and simmer, stirring frequently, until reduced to about 2¾ cups and excess moisture has evaporated, 15 to 20 minutes. Let cool.

Refrigerate dip, covered, for at least 1 day for flavors to develop.

Serve with pita wedges.

COOK'S NOTE

- The dip can be refrigerated for up to 1 week.

Olive and Eggplant Spread

MAKES ABOUT 1 CUP

ACTIVE TIME: 15 MINUTES ■ START TO FINISH: 1¼ HOURS

■ This is very similar to the Provençal olive condiment known as tapenade, but it's beefed up with eggplant, which gives it a more luxurious texture and, not incidentally, makes it less expensive to prepare. ■

- 1 (1-pound) eggplant, halved lengthwise and flesh scored in a crosshatch pattern
- 4 tablespoons extra-virgin olive oil
- ¼ cup Kalamata or other brine-cured black olives, rinsed, patted dry, and pitted
- 1 tablespoon drained capers, rinsed
- Salt and freshly ground black pepper

ACCOMPANIMENT: Pita Toasts (page 7) or lightly toasted baguette slices

Put a rack in middle of oven and preheat oven to 375°F.

Rub eggplant all over with 2 tablespoons oil. Place cut sides down in a small baking pan and bake until flesh is browned and very tender, about 50 minutes. Let cool slightly.

Scoop flesh from eggplant into a food processor; discard skin. Add olives, capers, remaining 2 tablespoons oil, and salt and pepper to taste and purée until smooth.

Transfer to a bowl and serve with pita toasts or baguette slices.

COOK'S NOTE

- The spread can be made up to 3 days ahead and refrigerated, covered. Bring to room temperature before serving.

Eggplant "Caviar"

MAKES ABOUT 4 CUPS

ACTIVE TIME: 20 MINUTES ■ START TO FINISH: 7 HOURS (INCLUDES CHILLING)

■ This thick purée of eggplant, tomato, olive oil, and seasonings came into being in the 1940s. Its origins are lost, but the food historian William Woys Weaver wouldn't be surprised if the concept were medieval or Byzantine. He notes that *aubergínia*, an eggplant paste, was made in the lodgings of St. John of Jerusalem as a substitute for fish paste, which was forbidden during Lent.

This is a great vegetarian dip, especially in August and September, when eggplants and tomatoes are at their peak. It's best when made at least six hours ahead so the flavors have a chance to meld. ■

- 2 medium eggplants (2 pounds total)
- 2 large tomatoes (1 pound total)
- 3 tablespoons olive oil
- 1 large onion, chopped
- 1 large green bell pepper, cored, seeded, and chopped
- 2 large garlic cloves, chopped
- 2 tablespoons fresh lemon juice
- 1½ teaspoons salt
- ½ teaspoon sugar
- ½ teaspoon freshly ground black pepper

ACCOMPANIMENT: crackers or baguette slices

Preheat broiler. Halve eggplants lengthwise. Score flesh of each half ½ inch deep in a crosshatch pattern to make 1-inch squares (do not cut through skin). Arrange eggplants, cut sides up, and tomatoes on a baking sheet with sides. Broil 4 to 6 inches from heat, turning once, until eggplants are very soft and skin of both vegetables is charred, 20 to 25 minutes. Let cool slightly.

Meanwhile, heat oil in a 12-inch heavy skillet over moderate heat. Add onion, green pepper, and garlic and cook, stirring occasionally, until onion is pale golden, 15 to 20 minutes. Remove from heat.

When eggplants are cool enough to handle, remove and discard skin. Peel tomatoes.

Transfer onion mixture to a food processor, add eggplant, tomatoes, lemon juice, salt, sugar, and pepper, and pulse until coarsely puréed. Let cool to room temperature, then refrigerate, covered, for at least 6 hours.

Serve cold or at room temperature, with crackers or baguette slices.

COOK'S NOTE

- The eggplant caviar can be refrigerated for up to 2 days.

Toasted Walnut, Roasted Red Pepper, and Cumin Spread

Muhammara

MAKES ABOUT 2 CUPS
ACTIVE TIME: 15 MINUTES ▪ START TO FINISH: 30 MINUTES

▪ We think this Turkish spread is so delicious it deserves to be better known. Bread crumbs give it body, and the roasted red peppers make it rosy. A touch of sweetness comes from pomegranate molasses, a secret ingredient in a number of Turkish and Middle Eastern dishes. Its syrupy, savory pungency is not dissimilar to that of aged balsamic vinegar, and you'll be surprised what a useful condiment it can be. (Try drizzling it over grilled vegetables or meaty fish steaks.) ▪

2–4 garlic cloves (to taste)
½ teaspoon salt, or to taste
1 (7-ounce) jar roasted red peppers, drained and patted dry
⅔ cup fine fresh bread crumbs
⅓ cup walnuts, lightly toasted (see Tips, page 938) and finely chopped
1 tablespoon fresh lemon juice, or to taste
2 teaspoons pomegranate molasses (see Glossary)
1 teaspoon ground cumin
½ teaspoon red pepper flakes
½ cup extra-virgin olive oil

ACCOMPANIMENT: Pita Toasts (page 7) or crudités

Using a large knife, mince and mash garlic to a paste with salt, then transfer to a food processor. Add red peppers, bread crumbs, walnuts, lemon juice, pomegranate molasses, cumin, and red pepper flakes and purée until smooth. With motor running, add oil in a slow stream and process until well blended.

Transfer spread to a bowl and serve with pita toasts or crudités.

COOK'S NOTE

- The spread can be made up to 1 day ahead and refrigerated, covered. Bring to room temperature before serving.

Tzatziki

Cucumber Yogurt Dip

MAKES ABOUT 5 CUPS
ACTIVE TIME: 25 MINUTES ▪ START TO FINISH: 4½ HOURS (PLUS OVERNIGHT DRAINING)

▪ In Greece, this refreshing dip is eaten all sorts of ways: as a *meze,* or hors d'oeuvre, along with good black olives, hummus, and baba ghanouj; as part of a main course, served as an accompaniment to everything else; as a sauce for gyros and other sandwiches; and as a salad. Greek yogurt is so thick you can stand a spoon in it. Unless you can find good, thick farmhouse yogurt (a Greek market is your best bet), you'll need to drain the yogurt in a sieve for a day. It will thicken to the right consistency. ▪

3 pounds (6 cups) plain low-fat yogurt
2 seedless cucumbers (usually plastic wrapped), peeled, halved lengthwise, seeded, and finely chopped (3¾ cups)
5 garlic cloves, minced

2 tablespoons extra-virgin olive oil, preferably Greek
1½ tablespoons chopped fresh dill
1 tablespoon finely chopped fresh mint
1 tablespoon white wine vinegar
1 teaspoon salt
½ teaspoon freshly ground black pepper

ACCOMPANIMENT: Pita Toasts (page 7)
SPECIAL EQUIPMENT: cheesecloth

Put yogurt in a large sieve or colander lined with a double thickness of cheesecloth and set over a large bowl. Let yogurt drain, covered and refrigerated, for 24 hours.

Transfer yogurt to a clean bowl; discard whey. Stir in remaining ingredients. Refrigerate, covered, for at least 4 hours.

Serve tzatziki chilled or at room temperature, with pita toasts.

COOK'S NOTE

- The tzatziki can be refrigerated for up to 3 days.

Asparagus with Wasabi Mayonnaise Dip

MAKES ABOUT 80 HORS D'OEUVRES
ACTIVE TIME: 15 MINUTES ■ START TO FINISH: 25 MINUTES

■ Blanching asparagus turns it a vibrant green that's the color of spring. We love the barely cooked stalks with this spicy mayonnaise. If you enjoy sushi, then you know the pale green condiment called wasabi. It comes from the root of an Asian plant that is similar to horseradish and is pungent and fiery in flavor. ■

3 pounds thin to medium asparagus, trimmed
1 cup mayonnaise
4 teaspoons soy sauce
1½ teaspoons sugar
2 teaspoons fresh lemon juice
2 teaspoons wasabi paste (see Cook's Note)

Blanch asparagus in 2 batches in a 6- to 7-quart wide pot of boiling salted water (1 tablespoon salt per every 4 quarts water) for 1 minute per batch. Transfer to a colander and rinse under cold water to stop the cooking. Drain well and pat dry.

Whisk together remaining ingredients in a small bowl until sugar is dissolved.

Serve asparagus with dip.

COOK'S NOTES

- You can substitute wasabi powder for the wasabi paste, but we find that the paste imparts a fresher flavor. If you opt for the powder, see Glossary for more information. Wasabi paste and powder are available at Asian markets and many supermarkets.
- Both the asparagus and the dip can be prepared up to 1 day ahead. Refrigerate separately, covered.

Roasted Pepper and White Bean Spread

MAKES ABOUT 1⅓ CUPS
ACTIVE TIME: 10 MINUTES ■ START TO FINISH: 10 MINUTES

■ The great thing about a well-stocked pantry is that it enables you to be spontaneous. For this quick spread, for instance, all you need is a jar of roasted red peppers, a can of white beans, and an anchovy fillet. The anchovy isn't strictly necessary, but it does give a background to the beans, without the slightest fishy flavor. The roasted red peppers contribute a little sweetness and a pretty pink cast. ■

1 cup (8 ounces) drained bottled roasted red peppers, rinsed
1 cup rinsed canned white beans
½ cup coarse fresh bread crumbs (from 1 slice firm white bread)
1½ teaspoons chopped flat anchovy fillet (optional)
¼ cup extra-virgin olive oil
½ teaspoon salt
¼ teaspoon freshly ground black pepper

ACCOMPANIMENT: Pita Toasts (page 7) or lightly toasted baguette slices

Combine all ingredients in a food processor and purée until smooth. Serve with pita toasts or baguette slices.

COOK'S NOTE

- The spread can be made up to 3 days ahead and refrigerated, covered. Bring to room temperature before serving.

White Bean Purée with Garlic Vinaigrette and Croûtes

SERVES 6

ACTIVE TIME: 30 MINUTES ■ START TO FINISH: 1¾ HOURS PLUS SOAKING TIME FOR BEANS

■ There are bean dips that are made with canned beans in the food processor, and then there is this. It's a great example of the way the French embellish a humble ingredient: a garlicky vinaigrette and a bit of cream turn the beans into something sophisticated. Using beans that have been soaked, cooked, and then put through a food mill rather than a food processor makes a difference in texture—they are lighter, fluffier, and less starchy than canned beans. ■

FOR BEAN PURÉE

- ½ pound (1¼ cups) dried small white beans, such as navy or pea, picked over and rinsed
- 1 fresh thyme sprig
- 2 slices firm white sandwich bread, crusts discarded
- ⅓ cup heavy cream
- 2 tablespoons extra-virgin olive oil
- Salt and freshly ground black pepper

FOR GARLIC VINAIGRETTE

- 2 garlic cloves, peeled
- 1 teaspoon Dijon mustard
- 1 tablespoon red wine vinegar
- 3 tablespoons extra-virgin olive oil
- Salt and freshly ground black pepper

ACCOMPANIMENT: toasted baguette slices

SPECIAL EQUIPMENT: a food mill

SOAK AND COOK THE BEANS: Soak beans in water to cover by 2 inches, refrigerated, for at least 8 hours (or see page 267 for quick-soaking procedure); drain.

Combine beans, thyme, and water to cover by 2 inches in a 3- to 4-quart saucepan and bring to a simmer. Simmer, partially covered, until beans are very tender, about 1¼ hours (some beans will fall apart). Scoop out and reserve 1 cup cooking liquid. Drain beans and discard thyme.

MEANWHILE, MAKE THE GARLIC VINAIGRETTE: Blanch garlic in a small saucepan of boiling water for 3 minutes. Drain and finely chop.

Transfer garlic to a small bowl and whisk in mustard and vinegar. Add oil in a slow stream, whisking until well blended. Season with salt and pepper.

MAKE THE BEAN PURÉE: Crumble bread into a large bowl and stir in cream. Force beans through food mill into moistened bread, then stir in oil. Add reserved cooking liquid 1 tablespoon at a time until purée is spreadable. Season generously with salt and pepper.

Transfer purée to a plate and arrange toasts around it. Serve warm, with vinaigrette spooned over purée.

COOK'S NOTE

- The purée can be made up to 1 day ahead. Cover with plastic wrap placed directly against its surface and refrigerate. To serve, bring to room temperature and then reheat over low heat, stirring. Add water if necessary to make the purée spreadable and season with salt and pepper again if necessary.

Hummus with Toasted Pine Nuts, Cumin Seeds, and Parsley Oil

MAKES ABOUT 4 CUPS

ACTIVE TIME: 40 MINUTES ■ START TO FINISH: 40 MINUTES

■ Hummus is so common these days it's become almost pedestrian. Not this version. The starchiness of the chickpeas is counteracted by the sharpness of the parsley oil and the cumin seeds. Those additions also make for an attractive presentation: served on a platter with a drizzle of bright green oil and a scattering of toasted cumin seeds, this is just the thing for a hot summer's night. As with other nuts, pine nuts have a high oil content and go rancid easily, so buy them from a shop with a quick turnover, store them in the freezer, and smell them before using. ■

- 1/4 cup packed fresh flat-leaf parsley sprigs, plus 2–3 additional sprigs
- 3/4 cup extra-virgin olive oil
- 3 tablespoons pine nuts
- 1 teaspoon cumin seeds
- 2 (19-ounce) cans chickpeas, drained and rinsed
- 4 garlic cloves
- 2/3 cup well-stirred tahini (Middle Eastern sesame paste)
- 2/3 cup water
- 5 tablespoons fresh lemon juice, or to taste
- 1 teaspoon salt

ACCOMPANIMENT: Pita Toasts (page 7)

Put a rack in middle of oven and preheat oven to 350°F.

Purée 1/4 cup parsley with 1/4 cup oil in a blender or small food processor. Pour through a fine-mesh sieve into a bowl, pressing hard on solids; discard solids.

Toast pine nuts and cumin seeds in a small baking pan in oven, stirring occasionally, until golden, about 10 minutes. Let cool.

Combine 1/2 cup chickpeas with garlic in a food processor and process until garlic is finely minced. Add tahini, water, lemon juice, salt, remaining chickpeas, and remaining 1/2 cup olive oil and purée until smooth.

Strip leaves from remaining parsley sprigs. Divide hummus between two shallow dishes and smooth tops. Drizzle with parsley oil and scatter parsley, pine nuts, and cumin seeds over tops. Sprinkle with salt to taste. Serve with pita toasts.

COOK'S NOTES

- For hummus with a silky texture, remove the skins from the chickpeas by squeezing the beans from them.
- The parsley oil and hummus can be made up to 3 days ahead and refrigerated separately, covered. Bring the oil to room temperature before using.
- The pine nuts and cumin seeds can be toasted up to 3 days ahead and kept in an airtight container at room temperature.

Herbed Lima Bean Hummus

MAKES ABOUT 4 CUPS
ACTIVE TIME: 25 MINUTES ■ START TO FINISH: 1 HOUR

■ Lima beans give this dip a beautiful celadon color, and mint and dill make it sparkle. Our inspiration was a recipe for *bissara*, a garlicky purée from Egypt made from dried broad beans, in Claudia Roden's *Mediterranean Cookery*. Even those who don't like limas will be won over by this dip. ■

- 2 (10-ounce) packages frozen baby lima beans
- 1 large onion, chopped
- 5 garlic cloves, smashed
- 1 teaspoon salt
- 1/4 cup chopped fresh cilantro
- 1/4 cup chopped fresh flat-leaf parsley
- 1 teaspoon ground cumin
- 1/4 teaspoon cayenne, or to taste
- 3 tablespoons fresh lemon juice, plus additional to taste
- 5 tablespoons extra-virgin olive oil
- 2 tablespoons chopped fresh dill
- 2 tablespoons chopped fresh mint
- Freshly ground black pepper

ACCOMPANIMENT: Sesame Wonton Crisps (page 7) or Pita Toasts (page 7)

Combine beans, onion, garlic, salt, and 2 cups water in a 3-quart saucepan and bring to a simmer. Simmer, covered, until beans are tender, about 8 minutes. Stir in cilantro and parsley, then remove from heat and let stand, uncovered, for 5 minutes. Drain.

Transfer bean mixture to a food processor, add cumin, cayenne, lemon juice, 4 tablespoons (1/4 cup) oil, dill, and mint, and purée until smooth. Transfer to a bowl and cool to room temperature, stirring occasionally.

Season dip with salt, pepper, and lemon juice to taste. Mound in a serving bowl and drizzle with remaining 1 tablespoon oil. Serve with crisps or toasts.

COOK'S NOTE

- The dip can be made up to 3 days ahead and refrigerated, covered. (Drizzle with the remaining oil before serving.)

Exotic Mushroom Pâté

MAKES ABOUT 40 HORS D'OEUVRES
ACTIVE TIME: 1 HOUR ■ START TO FINISH: 10½ HOURS (INCLUDES CHILLING)

■ This pâté is neither easy nor inexpensive, but when you are looking for a tour de force, it is a gorgeous thing. If you feel the urge to simplify, omit the topping, but the pâté won't be as impressive, and you won't have the exquisite contrast of the parsley and the almonds. ■

FOR PÂTÉ

- 1½ cups chicken stock or store-bought low-sodium broth
- 1 ounce (1 cup) dried porcini mushrooms (see Sources)
- 1 stick (8 tablespoons) unsalted butter
- ¾ cup minced shallots (5 ounces)
- 2 garlic cloves, minced
- ¼ cup dry sherry
- ¾ pound shiitake mushrooms, stems discarded and caps thinly sliced (6 cups)
- ¾ pound oyster mushrooms, stems trimmed and thinly sliced, caps thinly sliced (3¾ cups)
- 1 cup heavy cream
- 4 large eggs
- ¼ cup (1 ounce) whole almonds with skins, toasted (see Tips, page 938), cooled, and finely ground in a food processor
- ¼ cup chopped fresh flat-leaf parsley
- 2 teaspoons chopped fresh thyme
- ⅓ cup fine fresh bread crumbs
- 1½ tablespoons fresh lemon juice
- 2 teaspoons salt
- ½ teaspoon freshly ground black pepper

FOR MUSHROOM TOPPING

- 2 tablespoons unsalted butter
- 1 tablespoon olive oil
- 1 cup (3 ounces) shiitake mushrooms, stems discarded and caps quartered
- 1 cup (2¾ ounces) oyster mushrooms, stems discarded and caps quartered
- ¾ cup (3½ ounces) whole almonds with skins, toasted and coarsely chopped
- ¼ cup fresh flat-leaf parsley leaves
- ⅛ teaspoon salt
- ⅛ teaspoon freshly ground black pepper

ACCOMPANIMENT: assorted toasts and/or crackers

SPECIAL EQUIPMENT: a 12-by-3-by-2¾-inch loaf pan or terrine (see Sources); parchment paper

MAKE THE PÂTÉ: Butter loaf pan, then line bottom and sides with parchment paper and butter paper.

Bring stock to a boil in a small saucepan. Remove pan from heat, add porcini, and let soak in hot stock until softened, about 30 minutes.

With a slotted spoon, transfer porcini to a medium-mesh sieve set over a bowl. Press on porcini with back of a spoon to remove excess liquid, then add this to soaking liquid and reserve. Rinse porcini to remove any grit. Pat dry, chop, and put in a large bowl.

Strain reserved soaking liquid through a fine-mesh sieve lined with a coffee filter or dampened paper towel into another small saucepan. Bring to a brisk simmer over moderate heat and simmer until reduced to about ¼ cup, about 10 minutes. Add to porcini.

Put a rack in middle of oven and preheat oven to 350°F. Heat 2 tablespoons butter in a large nonstick skillet over moderate heat until foam subsides. Add shallots and garlic and cook, stirring, until softened, about 6 minutes. Add sherry and cook, stirring, for 1 minute. Transfer mixture to a blender. Heat 2 more tablespoons butter in skillet over moderately high heat until foam subsides. Add one third of shiitake and oyster mushrooms and cook, stirring, for about 2 minutes. Transfer to a bowl and cook remaining mushrooms in 2 batches, adding 2 more tablespoons butter to skillet for each batch. Add 2 cups sautéed mushrooms to shallot mixture in blender, and add remaining mushrooms to porcini mixture.

Add cream, then eggs and almonds to blender and purée until mixture is very smooth, about 1 minute. Add purée to porcini mixture and stir in parsley, thyme, bread crumbs, lemon juice, salt, and pepper until well combined. Pour mixture into loaf pan and cover with foil.

Put loaf pan in a larger baking pan and add enough boiling water to reach halfway up sides of loaf pan. Bake until set ½ inch from edges, about 50 minutes (pâté will not be completely set in center). Remove loaf pan from baking pan and let cool to room temperature on a rack. Refrigerate pâté in loaf pan, covered, for at least 6 hours. Bring pâté to room temperature (this may take 1 to 2 hours) before adding topping.

WHILE THE PÂTÉ COMES TO ROOM TEMPERATURE, MAKE THE TOPPING: Heat butter and oil in a large skillet over moderately high heat until foam subsides. Add mushrooms and almonds and cook, stirring, until mushrooms are tender and liquid they give off has evaporated, 6 to 8 minutes. Transfer to a heatproof bowl and let cool, then add parsley, salt, and pepper and toss to combine.

To unmold pâté, run a thin knife between parchment and loaf pan. Invert a large plate over loaf pan and invert pâté onto plate; peel off paper. Mound topping on pâté, and spread on toasts and/or crackers.

COOK'S NOTE

- The pâté, without the topping, can be refrigerated, covered, for up to 5 days. Bring to room temperature before serving.

Fresh Fig, Mascarpone, and Pesto Torte

MAKES ABOUT 32 HORS D'OEUVRES
ACTIVE TIME: 45 MINUTES ■ START TO FINISH: 5¾ HOURS (INCLUDES CHILLING)

■ An elegant hors d'oeuvre at a buffet-style party, this spreadable torte shows off two glories of late summer: figs and pesto. Because sliced fresh figs have a natural beauty, the fig topping that covers the torte makes it appealing even after guests have made inroads. Served cut into thin wedges, the torte also makes a wonderful first course. ■

FOR CRUST

- 1 cup finely ground wheat crackers, such as Wheat Thins (about 60)
- ½ cup pine nuts, toasted (see Tips, page 938), cooled, and pulsed in a food processor until finely ground
- 1 tablespoon unsalted butter, melted and cooled
- ¼ teaspoon salt
- ⅛ teaspoon freshly ground black pepper

FOR FILLING

- 1¼ pounds cream cheese, softened
- ½ cup mascarpone or sour cream
- 3 large eggs
- Salt
- ¼ teaspoon freshly ground black pepper
- 1¼ cups Pesto (page 889) or store-bought pesto
- 2 pounds firm but ripe fresh figs (16 large), stems discarded, half of figs cut into ¼-inch-thick slices
- ½ cup fig preserves (see Sources)
- 1½ tablespoons white wine vinegar

ACCOMPANIMENT: thin baguette slices

SPECIAL EQUIPMENT: a 10-inch springform pan

MAKE THE CRUST: Put a rack in middle of oven and preheat oven to 325°F. Butter springform pan.

Stir together ingredients with a fork in a bowl. Press mixture into bottom of buttered pan. Bake until lightly browned, about 10 minutes. Let cool on a rack. (Leave oven on.)

MEANWHILE, MAKE THE FILLING: Combine cream cheese, mascarpone, eggs, ½ teaspoon salt, and pepper in a medium bowl and beat with an electric mixer until very smooth, about 2 minutes.

Pour half of filling into crust. Drop dollops of pesto (using it all) over filling and spread evenly (some filling may show through). Top pesto with sliced figs, overlapping them slightly. Pour remaining filling over figs, spreading it evenly.

Bake torte until top is golden and set, 50 minutes to 1 hour (don't worry if it cracks). Cool in pan on a rack, about 1 hour (filling will deflate slightly), then refrigerate, loosely covered, for at least 3 hours.

If preserves are very chunky, finely chop in a food processor. Bring preserves and vinegar to a simmer in a small saucepan; remove from heat and let cool. Stir in a pinch of salt.

Slice remaining figs lengthwise into ¼-inch-thick slices. Run a thin knife around edge of pan and remove side. Spread torte with preserves mixture, leaving a ½-inch border all around, then top decoratively with fig slices.

Transfer torte to a serving plate with two large metal spatulas and let come to room temperature before serving. Serve with baguette slices.

COOK'S NOTE

- The baked torte, without the fig topping, can be refrigerated, covered, for up to 2 days.

Salmon Rillettes

MAKES ABOUT 4½ CUPS
ACTIVE TIME: 30 MINUTES ■ START TO FINISH: 4¾ HOURS (INCLUDES CHILLING)

■ Like classic rillettes, an unctuous paste with savory tendrils of pork or rabbit, this spread of fresh and smoked fish has an appealing coarse texture. It's equally rich, but easier—and faster—to prepare. ■

1 pound skinless salmon fillet
1 pound thinly sliced smoked salmon, finely chopped
1 stick (8 tablespoons) unsalted butter, softened
¾ cup minced shallots (5 ounces)
⅓ cup chopped fresh flat-leaf parsley
2 tablespoons fresh lemon juice
2 teaspoons Dijon mustard
2 teaspoons drained capers
2 teaspoons Cognac or other brandy
2 teaspoons finely grated lemon zest
¼ teaspoon salt
½ teaspoon freshly ground black pepper
ACCOMPANIMENT: toasted sliced baguette or Italian bread

Bring 3 cups water to a boil in a deep 12-inch skillet. Add fresh salmon, reduce heat, and poach at a bare simmer, turning once, until just cooked through, 8 to 10 minutes total. With a slotted spatula, transfer salmon to a bowl and let cool slightly.

Flake poached salmon with a fork. Add smoked salmon, butter, shallots, parsley, lemon juice, mustard, capers, Cognac, zest, salt, and pepper and stir until well combined. Pack into a 1-quart terrine or bowl. Refrigerate, covered, for at least 4 hours.

Bring rillettes to room temperature before serving with toasts.

COOK'S NOTE

- The rillettes can be refrigerated, covered, for up to 24 hours. (Bring to room temperature before serving.)

Brandade

MAKES ABOUT 3½ CUPS
ACTIVE TIME: 25 MINUTES ■ START TO FINISH: 45 MINUTES PLUS 1 TO 3 DAYS FOR SOAKING COD

■ One taste of this purée of salt cod, olive oil, and cream will take you to the South of France. It gives you the green light to drink rosé. Serve the brandade with crudités—raw fennel and carrots, for instance—and boiled potatoes, or as a topping for our Baked Potato Chips (page 6). ■

½ pound choice-grade, center-cut, skinless, boneless salt cod, rinsed well
2 large russet (baking) potatoes
1 cup heavy cream
6 large garlic cloves, thinly sliced
2 Turkish bay leaves or 1 California bay leaf
2 fresh thyme sprigs
2 whole cloves
¼ cup extra-virgin olive oil
Salt
¼ teaspoon white pepper
ACCOMPANIMENTS: garlic toasts or crusty bread and/or vegetables (including artichokes) for dipping

Soak cod in a large bowl of water to cover by 2 inches, refrigerated, for 1 to 3 days, changing water three times a day to remove excess salt. Drain well and refrigerate until ready to use.

Peel potatoes, cut into 1-inch pieces, and put in a 2- to 3-quart saucepan with well-salted water to cover by 1 inch. Bring to a boil, then reduce heat and simmer until potatoes are very tender, 12 to 15 minutes. (Do not drain until ready to beat.)

Meanwhile, combine cream, garlic, bay leaves, thyme, and cloves in a small heavy saucepan, bring to a simmer, and simmer gently, partially covered, until garlic is tender, about 8 minutes. Discard bay leaves, thyme, and cloves. Purée garlic with cream in a blender until smooth.

Place cod in 2-quart saucepan. Add water to cover, bring just to a simmer, and remove from heat. (Cod will just flake; do not boil, or it will become tough.)

Drain cod and potatoes in a colander. While still

warm, transfer to a large bowl, add cream mixture, and beat with an electric mixer at low speed until well combined. Add oil in a slow stream, beating at low speed, and add salt to taste and white pepper.

Transfer to a bowl and serve with toasts or bread and/or vegetables.

COOK'S NOTE

- The brandade can be refrigerated, covered, for up to 1 week. To serve, reheat, uncovered, in a 350°F oven for about 20 minutes.

Smoked Salmon Mousse with Salmon Roe and Crudités

MAKES ABOUT 5 CUPS
ACTIVE TIME: 25 MINUTES ■ START TO FINISH: 8½ HOURS (INCLUDES CHILLING)

■ This fish mousse is just perfect, silky and satisfying. Canned salmon really works best here. ■

Salt Cod

We've experienced a tremendous variation in the quality of salt cod we buy. "You have to start with a true cod from the waters of the North Atlantic, not one of its cousins, like cusk, hake, or pollack, which are sometimes passed off as salt cod," explains Roy Christiansen, the retired owner of World-Wide Fish, an importer and wholesaler of salted and dried fish. "Then quality depends on how it's handled on the boat, at the processing plant, by the importer or wholesaler, and finally by the retailer."

Salt cod is graded by size (jumbo to medium for skinless, boneless fillets, extra-large to small for bone-in cod with the skin on) as well as quality: "choice" or "standard." ("Select" is a fine but rarely seen grade for bone-in cod.)

You're most likely to find salt cod fillets packed in plastic bags or wooden boxes at fish markets and some specialty foods shops and supermarkets. Bone-in salt cod, preferred by the Spanish, Portuguese, and Italians, can often be found at ethnic markets. We use choice-grade fillets in our test kitchens and prefer buying them loose or packed in plastic bags so we can see what we're getting. Look for thick pieces that feel firm yet give slightly when gently squeezed. Also look at the color: the whiter, the better. And check for salt: a light film or coating is desirable; too much, and the fish will take longer to rehydrate. Wrapped in plastic and stored in the refrigerator, salt cod will keep for at least six months.

Because salt cod differs in degree of saltiness depending on the producer, a less salty version may need only one day of soaking, while another can require up to three. To test it, simply taste a small piece after one day; you want it to be pleasantly salty but not overwhelming.

Fresh cilantro leaves for decoration
- 2 tablespoons cold water
- 1 tablespoon fresh lemon juice
- 2¾ teaspoons unflavored gelatin (from two ¼-ounce envelopes)
- ⅓ cup boiling water
- ½ pound thinly sliced smoked salmon
- 1 (7¼-ounce) can salmon, drained and any tough pinbones and skin discarded
- 1½ cups sour cream
- ¼ teaspoon Tabasco, or to taste
- ¼ cup finely chopped scallions
- ½ teaspoon salt
- ½ teaspoon freshly ground black pepper
- 1 cup very cold heavy cream
- ¼ cup (2 ounces) salmon roe

OPTIONAL GARNISH: celery leaves

ACCOMPANIMENTS: assorted crudités, such as cucumber, celery, jicama, daikon, and blanched snow peas

SPECIAL EQUIPMENT: a 5-cup charlotte mold or soufflé dish

Lightly oil mold, line bottom with a round of wax paper, and oil paper. Arrange cilantro leaves decoratively face down on paper and press gently on leaves.

Combine cold water and lemon juice in a small bowl. Sprinkle gelatin over mixture and let stand for 1 minute to soften. Add boiling water and stir until gelatin is dissolved.

Combine smoked salmon, canned salmon, sour cream, and Tabasco in a food processor and blend until smooth. Add gelatin mixture, scallions, salt, and pepper and pulse until well combined.

Beat heavy cream in a large bowl with an electric mixer until it holds soft peaks. Add to salmon mixture and pulse until just combined. Pour mousse into prepared mold, smooth top, and refrigerate, covered, for at least 8 hours.

Dip mold into a large pan of hot water for 5 to 10 seconds, then run a thin knife around edge. Invert a platter over mold and invert mousse onto platter. Spoon salmon roe around edges of mousse.

Garnish with celery leaves, if desired, and serve with crudités.

COOK'S NOTE

- The mousse can be refrigerated, in the mold, covered, for up to 1 day.

Chunky Clam and Bacon Dip

MAKES ABOUT 2 CUPS

ACTIVE TIME: 30 MINUTES ■ START TO FINISH: 30 MINUTES

■ Clams and bacon are a natural combination. Clam dip on its own is on the homely side, so we prettied this one up with chopped red pepper, scallions, and fresh basil. We like to serve it with pita toasts, but crudités or potato chips are great too. ■

- ¼ pound bacon (4 slices), chopped
- 2 (6½-ounce) cans minced clams
- 8 ounces cream cheese, softened
- ¼ cup sour cream
- ⅓ cup finely chopped red bell pepper
- 3 scallions, finely chopped
- 2 tablespoons finely chopped fresh basil
- 1 teaspoon drained bottled horseradish
- 1 teaspoon fresh lemon juice, or to taste
- ¾ teaspoon Worcestershire sauce

Tabasco to taste

ACCOMPANIMENT: Pita Toasts (page 7), crudités, or potato chips

Cook bacon in a 12-inch heavy skillet over moderate heat, stirring, until golden and crisp, about 6 minutes. With a slotted spoon, transfer to paper towels to drain.

Drain clams in a large sieve set over a bowl; reserve clam juice. Whisk together cream cheese and sour cream in another bowl. Whisk 2 tablespoons reserved clam juice into cream cheese mixture, along with clams, bacon, and remaining ingredients.

Serve with pita toasts, crudités, or potato chips.

COOK'S NOTE

- The dip can be made up to 1 day ahead and refrigerated, covered. Bring to room temperature before serving.

Hot Crab and Artichoke Dip

SERVES 8

ACTIVE TIME: 1 HOUR ■ START TO FINISH: 1¾ HOURS

■ Hot dips were considered the mark of sophistication back in the 1970s. Here we meld two wildly popular ones, and guess what: those Junior League cooks were on to something. A little red bell pepper adds some welcome color, and chiles spice it up. ■

- 1 (9-ounce) package frozen artichoke hearts
- 3 tablespoons unsalted butter
- 1 red bell pepper, cored, seeded, and finely chopped
- 2 tablespoons all-purpose flour
- 1¼ cups half-and-half
- 3 scallions, thinly sliced
- ½ cup finely grated Parmigiano-Reggiano
- 1½ teaspoons fresh lemon juice, or to taste
- 1½ tablespoons minced drained pickled jalapeño chiles
- ½ teaspoon salt
- ¼ teaspoon celery salt
- ¾ pound jumbo lump crabmeat, picked over for shells and cartilage

ACCOMPANIMENT: Benne Seed Pita Toasts (page 8), Pita Toasts (page 7), or crackers

Put a rack in middle of oven and preheat oven to 375°F. Butter a 1½-quart shallow baking dish.

Cook artichoke hearts according to package instructions; drain well and finely chop.

Melt 1 tablespoon butter in a 2- to 3-quart heavy saucepan over moderately low heat. Add bell pepper and cook, stirring occasionally, until softened, about 5 minutes. Stir in artichokes and transfer to a bowl.

Melt remaining 2 tablespoons butter in cleaned saucepan over moderately low heat. Add flour and cook, stirring, for 3 minutes, to make a roux. Add half-and-half in a slow stream, whisking constantly, and bring to a boil, whisking. Reduce heat and simmer, whisking, for 3 minutes.

Remove from heat and stir in artichoke mixture, scallions, ⅓ cup Parmesan, lemon juice, jalapeños, salt, and celery salt. Gently stir in crab. Transfer to buttered baking dish and sprinkle with remaining Parmesan.

Bake dip until bubbling, 20 to 25 minutes. Serve warm with pita toasts or crackers.

COOK'S NOTE

■ The dip can be assembled, but not baked, up to 1 day ahead and refrigerated, covered.

Crab and Coconut Dip with Plantain Chips

SERVES 6

ACTIVE TIME: 20 MINUTES ■ START TO FINISH: 20 MINUTES

■ We all know and love crab dip, but this rendition is sexy. The coconut milk both lightens it up and gives it a lush tropical undercurrent. You can serve this with any plain chips, but plantain chips take the whole thing home. ■

- ⅓ cup well-stirred canned unsweetened coconut milk
- 3 scallions, chopped
- 1 teaspoon chopped jalapeño chile, including seeds
- ½ cup chopped fresh cilantro
- ½ cup mayonnaise
- 3 tablespoons fresh lime juice, or to taste
- 1 pound jumbo lump crabmeat, picked over for shells and cartilage and coarsely shredded
- Salt

ACCOMPANIMENT: Plantain Chips (recipe follows)

Combine coconut milk, scallions, jalapeño, and ¼ cup cilantro in a blender and blend until smooth. Pour into a bowl. Whisk in mayonnaise, lime juice, and remaining ¼ cup cilantro until just combined. Stir in crab and salt to taste. Serve spooned onto plantain chips.

COOK'S NOTE

■ The dip can be made up to 6 hours ahead and refrigerated, covered. Stir before serving.

Plantain Chips

MAKES ABOUT 35 CHIPS
ACTIVE TIME: 30 MINUTES ■ START TO FINISH: 30 MINUTES

■ Plantains are related to bananas, but unlike their cousins, they are not eaten raw. Instead, this starchy tropical staple is cooked much like potatoes. Although plantains can be used in all stages of ripeness, hard green ones are best for frying. Of course, you can substitute store-bought plantain chips from the local bodega, but the addition of lime zest and the long, dramatic slices make these homemade ones far more satisfying. ■

- 1½ teaspoons finely grated lime zest
- 1½ teaspoons salt
- ¼ teaspoon cayenne
- About 6 cups vegetable oil for deep-frying
- 4 green plantains (1½ pounds total)

SPECIAL EQUIPMENT: a deep-fat thermometer

Stir together zest, salt, and cayenne in a small bowl.

Heat 2 inches oil in a 5-quart heavy pot over moderate heat until it registers 375°F on thermometer. While oil is heating, cut off ends of plantains. Score skin of each plantain 5 times lengthwise, avoiding ridges. Soak in a bowl of hot water for 5 minutes; drain.

Peel plantains and slice lengthwise with a Y-shaped peeler or adjustable-blade slicer into very thin strips (about 1/16 inch thick).

Fry strips 6 at a time, turning frequently, until golden, 30 to 45 seconds. Transfer to paper towels to drain and sprinkle immediately with salt mixture.

COOK'S NOTE

■ The plantain chips can be made up to 2 days ahead and kept in an airtight container at room temperature.

Brandied Chicken Liver Pâté

MAKES ABOUT 1½ CUPS
ACTIVE TIME: 25 MINUTES ■ START TO FINISH: 6½ HOURS (INCLUDES CHILLING)

■ Reading down the list of ingredients, you'll find everything you would expect in a simple, classic pâté—until you reach the currants, which are a delightful surprise. Their sweetness brings out the sweetness of the chicken livers and cuts the richness at the same time. You might also serve this pâté in individual little ramekins for a first course. ■

- ½ stick (4 tablespoons) unsalted butter
- ¾ cup finely chopped onion
- 1 large garlic clove, finely chopped
- 1 pound chicken livers, trimmed and rinsed
- Salt and freshly ground black pepper
- ¼ cup Cognac or other brandy
- ¼ teaspoon freshly grated nutmeg
- Pinch of ground allspice
- ⅓ cup dried currants

ACCOMPANIMENT: toasted baguette slices or crackers

Melt butter in a 12-inch heavy skillet over moderate heat. Add onion and garlic and cook, stirring occasionally, until softened, 6 to 8 minutes. Pat chicken livers dry and season with salt and pepper. Add to skillet and cook, stirring and turning occasionally, until almost cooked through but still slightly pink inside, about 10 minutes. Add Cognac and simmer until most of it has evaporated, about 2 minutes. Transfer mixture to a food processor.

Add nutmeg, allspice, ¼ teaspoon salt, and ¼ teaspoon pepper to processor and purée until very smooth, about 1 minute. Transfer pâté to a bowl and let cool. Season with salt and pepper.

Meanwhile, cover currants with boiling water in a heatproof bowl and soak until plumped, about 6 minutes. Drain and pat dry.

Stir currants into pâté. Pack pâté into a crock (or a few small crocks), cover surface with plastic wrap, and refrigerate for at least 6 hours.

Bring pâté to room temperature (this will take about 1½ hours) before serving with toasts or crackers.

COOK'S NOTE

■ The pâté can be refrigerated, covered, for up to 3 days.

Rabbit Terrine with Green Olives and Pistachios

MAKES ABOUT 48 HORS D'OEUVRES
ACTIVE TIME: 1½ HOURS ■ START TO FINISH: 11½ HOURS (INCLUDES CHILLING)

■ People tend to think of pâtés and terrines as heavy and full of fat, but this one is quite the opposite: clean, light, and virtually fat-free. It has finesse and delicacy yet manages to be deeply satisfying as well. Have your butcher cut up the rabbit. If you don't have terrine molds, you can make the terrines in two baking pans; see Cook's Note. ■

FOR RABBIT AND BROTH

- 1 (3-pound) rabbit, cut into 8 pieces
- 4 shallots, thinly sliced
- 2 carrots, thinly sliced
- 3 fresh parsley sprigs
- 2 fresh thyme sprigs
- 1 leek (green part only; white reserved for another use), rinsed well
- 1 head garlic, halved horizontally
- ½ teaspoon salt
- ½ teaspoon black peppercorns, cracked
- 6¼ cups cold water
- 2 large egg whites, shells reserved and crushed
- 4 teaspoons unflavored gelatin (from two ¼-ounce envelopes)
- 3 tablespoons Sercial (dry) Madeira

FOR ASSEMBLING TERRINES

- ½ teaspoon fennel seeds, toasted (see Tips, page 939)
- ½ cup (3 ounces) Picholine or other brine-cured green olives, pitted and coarsely chopped
- ⅓ cup shelled salted natural pistachios (not dyed red), coarsely chopped
- 3 tablespoons finely chopped fresh chives
- 1 teaspoon chopped fresh thyme
- ½ teaspoon salt
- ¾ teaspoon freshly ground black pepper

FOR TOASTS

- Unsalted butter, softened
- 24 very thin slices firm white sandwich bread

SPECIAL EQUIPMENT: two 12-by-2-inch tapered narrow rectangular terrines (3 cups; see Sources); kitchen string; an electric coffee/spice grinder; two 11½-by-1½-inch strips of corrugated cardboard, wrapped tightly in foil; two 10- to 11-inch rolling pins or high-shouldered full wine bottles

COOK THE RABBIT: Remove fat, kidneys, and liver from rabbit if necessary. Put rabbit, shallots, carrots, parsley, thyme, leek, garlic, ¼ teaspoon salt, peppercorns, and 6 cups water in a 6-quart heavy pot and bring to a boil, skimming froth. Reduce heat and gently simmer, partially covered, until rabbit is tender, about 1 hour. Let rabbit cool in broth, uncovered, for 30 minutes.

CLARIFY THE BROTH: Remove rabbit from broth and set aside. Pour broth through a fine sieve into a bowl; discard solids. Whisk egg whites in a large bowl until foamy; add eggshells. Whisk in warm broth in a stream and return mixture to cleaned saucepan. Heat over moderate heat, stirring and scraping bottom constantly with a wooden spoon to prevent egg whites from sticking, until broth comes to a simmer (this will take about 10 minutes). Reduce heat and gently simmer, without stirring, until impurities rise to surface and form a crust and broth underneath is clear, about 10 minutes.

Meanwhile, coarsely shred rabbit meat, being careful to remove all small bones, and put in a large bowl.

Pour broth through a sieve lined with a double thickness of dampened paper towels into a bowl; let stand until all broth drains through. (If necessary, tap edge of sieve repeatedly with metal spoon to help broth drain.) Discard solids. Broth should be completely clear; if not, repeat procedure with clean dampened paper towels.

If clarified broth measures more than 2½ cups, boil to reduce and remove from heat. If it measures less, add water to make 2½ cups, pour into a saucepan, and bring just to a simmer; remove from heat. Sprinkle gelatin over remaining ¼ cup cold water and let soften for 1 minute, then whisk into hot broth until dissolved. Stir in Madeira and remaining ¼ teaspoon salt, or to taste.

ASSEMBLE THE TERRINES: Lightly oil terrines (to anchor plastic wrap) and line each one with a sheet of plastic wrap large enough to drape over edges. Place terrines on a tray. Cut four 18-inch pieces of kitchen string and place 2 crosswise under each terrine, about 2 inches from each end (these will be used to secure rolling pins or bottles to terrines).

Grind fennel seeds in coffee/spice grinder. Toss rabbit with ground fennel, olives, pistachios, chives, thyme, salt, and pepper. Divide mixture between terrines. Stir broth well and pour slowly into terrines, filling to 1/4 inch from top. Cover and refrigerate any remaining broth. Place a foil-wrapped cardboard strip on top of each terrine, rest a rolling pin or bottle on top of cardboard, and tie to terrine, creating just enough pressure to press cardboard about 1/2 inch into terrine (some broth will spill over onto tray). Chill terrines, on tray, for 3 hours.

Remove string, weights, and cardboard from terrines. Heat any reserved jelled broth, plus spillover from tray, just until it becomes liquid. Add to terrines. Cover with overhanging plastic wrap and refrigerate for at least 6 hours more.

WHILE THE TERRINES CHILL, PREPARE THE TOASTS: Put a rack in middle of oven and preheat oven to 350°F.

Butter bread and cut each slice into 2 pieces the shape of terrine slices. Place on two baking sheets and toast in batches until golden, about 10 minutes. Let cool.

To unmold terrines, unfold plastic wrap and invert molds onto a long narrow platter; pull slightly on plastic to release terrines from molds, then remove it. With a serrated knife, gently cut terrines into 1/2-inch-thick slices. Arrange on a platter and serve with toasts.

COOK'S NOTES

- The terrines can be refrigerated (after removing weights) for up to 3 days.
- If you don't have terrine molds, you can make the terrine in a baking pan and then serve it already cut and on the toasts. You'll need two 13-by-9-inch pans, or one pan and a foil-wrapped cardboard rectangle just slightly smaller than the inside dimensions of the pan. Line one pan as directed above (use two lengths of plastic wrap, overlapping them generously in the center of the pan) and spread all of rabbit mixture evenly in pan. Pour broth over. Cover with more plastic wrap and gently press the second 13-by-9-inch pan on top, or put the cardboard directly on the plastic wrap. Distribute 3 pounds of weight (such as three 1-pound cans) in the pan or on the cardboard and chill the terrine until completely firm, at least 4 hours.

  Remove the weights, top pan or cardboard, and top layer of plastic wrap and invert the terrine onto a cutting board. Remove the remaining plastic wrap and cut the terrine into 1 1/4-inch squares with a long sharp knife.

Classic Foie Gras Terrine

SERVES 10
ACTIVE TIME: 1 1/4 HOURS ■ START TO FINISH: 1 1/2 DAYS (INCLUDES CHILLING)

■ Ariane Daguin of D'Artagnan, the foremost supplier of foie gras and game meats in America, grew up in Gascony, where her father was an eleventh-generation chef. By age ten, she was working in his Michelin two-star kitchen. When we were creating this recipe (adapted from one in *D'Artagnan's Glorious Game Cookbook,* by Daguin, George Faison, and Joanna Pruess), we wondered about the difference between duck and goose livers. Gascons prefer duck foie gras, said Daguin, because it has a richer, fuller flavor. The liver is a more manageable size and loses less fat as it cooks. But other people prefer goose foie gras, which is subtler and slightly creamier—less rustic, in other words. Note that a foie gras terrine is intended to have a layer of lovely, delicious yellow fat. Save any remnants of the fat for sautéing potatoes or wild mushrooms.

Foie gras, which comes in a Cryovac package, is available at many specialty foods shops and butchers and by mail from D'Artagnan (see Sources). ■

- 1 (1 1/2-pound) whole raw Grade A duck or goose foie gras, at room temperature, cleaned and deveined
- 4 teaspoons kosher salt
- 1/2 teaspoon white pepper
- 1/4 cup Sauternes or 3 tablespoons Armagnac

ACCOMPANIMENT: toasted slices of *pain de mie* (dense white sandwich loaf) or baguette

SPECIAL EQUIPMENT: a 3- to 4-cup ceramic or enameled terrine, 2 1/2 to 3 inches deep (preferably oval and with a lid; see Sources); an instant-read thermometer; a piece of cardboard trimmed to fit just inside top of terrine, wrapped well in plastic wrap; a 3-pound weight (1 or 2 large soup cans)

Put a rack in middle of oven and preheat oven to 200°F. Line a small roasting pan with a folded kitchen towel or six layers of paper towels (this will provide insulation so bottom of terrine won't cook too quickly).

Sprinkle each lobe and any loose pieces of foie gras on both sides with salt and white pepper. Sprinkle one third of Sauternes into terrine and firmly press large lobe of foie gras, smooth side down, into bottom. Wedge any loose pieces of foie gras into terrine to make lobe fit snugly. Sprinkle with another third of Sauternes. Put smaller lobe of foie gras smooth side up in terrine and firmly press down to create a flat surface and snug fit. Sprinkle with remaining Sauternes. Cover surface of foie gras with plastic wrap, then cover terrine with lid or foil.

Put terrine (with plastic wrap and lid) in a roasting pan and fill roasting pan with enough hot water to reach halfway up sides of terrine. Bake until thermometer inserted diagonally into center of foie gras registers 120°F, 1 to 1½ hours (see Cook's Note).

Remove terrine mold from roasting pan. Pour out water and remove towel. Return terrine to roasting pan and remove lid. Put wrapped cardboard directly on surface of foie gras and set weight on cardboard (this will force fat to surface; don't worry if fat overflows). Let stand at room temperature for 20 minutes.

Remove weight and cardboard and spoon any fat that has dripped over sides of terrine mold back on top (fat will seal terrine). Refrigerate, covered with plastic wrap, until solid, at least 1 day.

To unmold terrine, run a hot knife around edges of mold. Invert onto a plate and reinvert, fat side up, onto a serving dish. Cut into slices with a hot sharp knife and serve with toasts.

COOK'S NOTES

- In her cookbook, Daguin sticks to the traditional French method and cooks foie gras to 120°F, but the USDA recommends cooking it to an internal temperature of 160°F to be sure any harmful bacteria are killed. We tried both methods and prefer Daguin's; to our tastes, it results in the perfect degree of doneness. However, if you are concerned, bake the terrine until it reaches 160°F, about 3½ hours.

CLEANING AND DEVEINING FOIE GRAS

The appeal of foie gras (pronounced "fwah grah"; it means "fat liver" in French) lies in its sumptuous texture and flavor, which derive mostly from fat. When buying foie gras, look for one marked Grade A—it should be firm to the touch and unblemished. As with all liver, trim away any green spots—they're bitter. Rinse the foie gras briefly before removing any large veins that run through it. Let it come to room temperature (about 20 minutes) before you devein it, though, or it may break into pieces. Ariane Daguin told us that "it's important to keep each lobe in one piece—better not to devein enough than to devein too much. The more fat that escapes during cooking, the drier the liver. But don't worry if the crooked piece between the lobes comes off or breaks—you can tuck it into the terrine later."

1

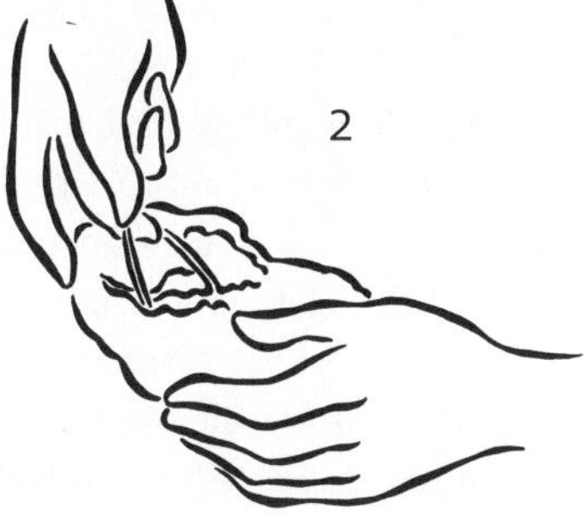

2

1. Work with one lobe at a time. Put each lobe smooth side down and, starting at the larger end, look for the main vein. With your fingers, carefully lift up the vein, anchoring the foie gras with your other hand.
2. Ease the vein up and out, pushing the foie gras apart slightly if necessary, and follow the vein toward the other end of the lobe. You will begin to feel smaller veins branching out. Pull those out too, but stop when they break off. Finally, peel off any loose surface membrane.

- If the weight of your foie gras differs from ours by more than half a pound (goose liver tends to be larger than duck), use a larger or smaller terrine, increase or decrease the weight as appropriate, and adjust the amount of seasoning accordingly.
- If you don't have an oval terrine (the word refers both to the cooking vessel and to the meat inside it), you can use a soufflé dish or a glass loaf pan that's just large enough to hold the foie gras snugly.
- The terrine can be refrigerated in the mold, its surface covered with plastic wrap, for 3 to 5 days. Once unmolded, the terrine will keep, tightly wrapped in plastic wrap and refrigerated, for another 3 days.
- Hot terrine lids can be hard to grasp with oven mitts; sturdy metal tongs are great for grabbing the handle.

BL-Tomatoes

MAKES 14 HORS D'OEUVRES
ACTIVE TIME: 30 MINUTES ■ START TO FINISH: 45 MINUTES

■ You won't miss the toast. ■

- 14 (1-inch-diameter) cherry tomatoes
- 3/8 teaspoon salt
- 1/4 pound lean bacon (4 slices)
- 2 tablespoons thinly sliced scallions
- 1/4 cup finely chopped romaine or iceberg lettuce
- 2 tablespoons mayonnaise
- 1/8 teaspoon freshly ground black pepper

SPECIAL EQUIPMENT: a melon ball cutter (optional)

Cut a 1/8-inch-thick slice from bottom of each tomato with a serrated knife, so tomatoes will stand upright. Cut a 1/8-inch-thick slice from stem ends and gently scoop out pulp and seeds with melon ball cutter or a small spoon; discard. Sprinkle tomato shells with 1/4 teaspoon salt and invert on paper towels to drain for 15 minutes.

Meanwhile, cook bacon in a 12-inch skillet over moderate heat until crisp, about 10 minutes. Transfer to paper towels to drain and cool, then finely crumble.

Stir together bacon, scallions, lettuce, mayonnaise, remaining 1/8 teaspoon salt, and pepper in a small bowl until well combined. Divide mixture evenly among tomato shells and arrange in a serving dish.

Vodka-Spiked Cherry Tomatoes with Pepper Salt

MAKES ABOUT 60 HORS D'OEUVRES
ACTIVE TIME: 45 MINUTES ■ START TO FINISH: 1 3/4 HOURS

■ What makes these tomatoes special is the fact that they are peeled. Don't worry; after you blanch them, their skins slip right off, and you are rewarded with tender little orbs. They're given a serious kick by the vodka. ■

- 3 pints firm small red and yellow cherry or grape tomatoes
- 1/2 cup vodka
- 3 tablespoons white wine vinegar
- 1 tablespoon superfine sugar
- 1 teaspoon finely grated lemon zest
- 3 tablespoons kosher salt
- 1 1/2 tablespoons coarsely ground black pepper

Cut a small X in bottom of each tomato. Blanch tomatoes 5 at a time in a 2-quart saucepan of boiling water for 3 seconds, then immediately transfer with a slotted spoon to a bowl of ice and cold water to stop the cooking. Drain tomatoes and peel. Transfer to a large shallow dish.

Stir together vodka, vinegar, sugar, and zest in a small bowl until sugar is dissolved. Pour over tomatoes and gently toss to coat. Marinate, covered and refrigerated, for at least 30 minutes.

Stir together salt and pepper in a small bowl. Serve with tomatoes for dipping.

COOK'S NOTES

- The tomatoes can be peeled up to 1 day ahead and refrigerated, covered.
- The marinade can also be prepared up to 1 day ahead and refrigerated, covered.
- The tomatoes can marinate for up to 1 hour.

Jicama and Cucumber Chile Spears

SERVES 4
ACTIVE TIME: 10 MINUTES ■ START TO FINISH: 10 MINUTES

■ Jicama spears with lime juice and chili powder are a popular street snack in Mexico. Crunchy, tangy, tart, and spicy all in one bite, they are refreshing on a hot day and have the bonus of being fat-free. This recipe can easily be doubled. ■

- 2 (½-pound) pieces jicama, peeled and cut into 2½-by-⅓-inch spears
- 1 seedless cucumber (usually plastic wrapped), halved lengthwise, seeded, and cut into 2½-by-⅓-inch spears
- 4 teaspoons fresh lime juice
- ¼ teaspoon chili powder
- Pinch of cayenne
- 1 teaspoon kosher salt, or to taste

Toss all ingredients together in a bowl and serve.

Deviled Eggs

MAKES 12 HORS D'OEUVRES
ACTIVE TIME: 15 MINUTES ■ START TO FINISH: 1 HOUR

■ Whether at a homey backyard barbecue or a fancy cocktail party, deviled eggs are always one of the first things to disappear. Make these your own by embellishing them with your favorite herbs or spices—tarragon or chervil, for instance—or a little chopped sweet pickle. Here we chose to garnish with paprika. Supermarket paprika works fine, of course, but if you want to take this classic to a whole new level, try smoked paprika, an age-old ingredient that somehow seems very twenty-first century. Paprika chiles aren't dried in the sun in Spain, as they are in Hungary, but instead are roasted over smoldering oak fires before being ground to a velvety powder. We like La Chinata brand, which comes in three strengths (sweet, bittersweet, and hot). It's available at many specialty foods shops, or see Sources for mail-order information. ■

- 6 large eggs
- ¼ cup mayonnaise
- 1 teaspoon Dijon mustard
- ⅛ teaspoon cayenne
- Salt and freshly ground black pepper

OPTIONAL GARNISHES: smoked or regular paprika and chopped fresh chives

SPECIAL EQUIPMENT: a pastry bag fitted with a ½-inch star tip (optional)

Put eggs in a 3-quart heavy saucepan, cover with cold water by 1½ inches, partially cover pan, and bring to a rolling boil. Reduce heat to low, cover completely, and cook eggs for 30 seconds. Remove from heat and let stand, covered, for 15 minutes.

Transfer eggs to a bowl of ice and cold water and let stand for 30 minutes; drain.

Peel eggs and halve lengthwise. Carefully remove yolks and mash in a bowl with a fork. Add mayonnaise, mustard, and cayenne and stir with fork until smooth. Season with salt and pepper.

Fill pastry bag, if using, with yolk mixture and pipe (or spoon) into egg whites. Sprinkle yolk mixture with paprika and chives, if desired.

COOK'S NOTE

■ The deviled eggs can be made up to 4 hours ahead and refrigerated, covered.

VARIATION

■ The plain mayonnaise can be replaced with a tangy mixture of 2 tablespoons mayonnaise mixed with 2 tablespoons plain yogurt.

Prosciutto- and Parmesan-Stuffed Mushrooms

MAKES 24 HORS D'OEUVRES
ACTIVE TIME: 20 MINUTES ■ START TO FINISH: 40 MINUTES

■ People love stuffed mushrooms as much as they love deviled eggs. This rendition, with prosciutto and Parmesan, is especially good. ■

24 large (1½- to 2-inch-wide) mushrooms (about 1 pound)
4 tablespoons olive oil
1 large garlic clove, minced
½ cup finely chopped onion
½ cup finely chopped prosciutto (3 ounces)
¼ cup fine dry bread crumbs
3 tablespoons minced fresh flat-leaf parsley
¾ cup finely grated Parmigiano-Reggiano
1 large egg, lightly beaten
¼ teaspoon salt
¼ teaspoon freshly ground black pepper

Put a rack in middle of oven and preheat oven to 400°F. Lightly grease a shallow baking dish large enough to hold mushroom caps in one layer.

To remove stems from mushrooms, hold each mushroom stem side up in palm of one hand and use other hand to push stem gently sideways until it pops out. If any stem remains in cap, gently scoop it out with a small spoon. Trim off and discard bottoms of stems and finely chop stems.

Heat 2 tablespoons oil in a 10- to 12-inch heavy skillet over moderate heat. Add mushroom stems, garlic, and onion and cook, stirring, until stems are very tender, about 8 minutes. Transfer to a bowl, add prosciutto, bread crumbs, parsley, ½ cup Parmesan, egg, salt, and pepper, and stir to combine well.

Divide filling among mushroom caps, mounding it slightly, and arrange in one layer in greased baking dish. Sprinkle mushrooms with remaining ¼ cup Parmesan and drizzle with remaining 2 tablespoons oil. Bake until mushroom caps are tender, about 20 minutes.

Parmesan Walnut Salad in Endive Leaves

MAKES ABOUT 25 HORS D'OEUVRES
ACTIVE TIME: 25 MINUTES ■ START TO FINISH: 3½ HOURS

■ Endive leaves are a popular vehicle for dips, and their subtle bitterness is a wonderful foil for the nutty sweetness of the Parmigiano-Reggiano and walnuts. We adapted this recipe from a salad made with butter lettuces at Restaurant Cibrèo, in Florence. It is worth the effort to purchase an excellent Parmigiano for it. ■

1 small garlic clove
½ teaspoon salt
1 tablespoon mayonnaise
2 tablespoons fresh lemon juice
2 tablespoons olive oil
1 (6-ounce) piece Parmigiano-Reggiano, sliced ⅛ inch thick and cut into ⅛-inch dice
½ cup finely chopped celery
1 cup (3½ ounces) walnuts, lightly toasted (see Tips, page 938) and finely chopped
¼ cup finely chopped fresh flat-leaf parsley
4 Belgian endives, trimmed and leaves separated

Using a large knife, mince and mash garlic to a paste with salt. Whisk together garlic paste, mayonnaise, lemon juice, and oil in a medium bowl. Stir in cheese and celery, then stir in walnuts, parsley, and salt to taste. Refrigerate, covered, for at least 3 hours to allow flavors to develop.

Mound 1 tablespoon salad onto wide end of each endive leaf.

COOK'S NOTES

- The endives can be trimmed and leaves separated up to 1 day ahead. Refrigerate, wrapped in dampened paper towels, in a sealed plastic bag.
- The salad mixture can be refrigerated for up to 8 hours.

Baked Cheddar Olives

MAKES 20 HORS D'OEUVRES
ACTIVE TIME: 20 MINUTES ■ START TO FINISH: 40 MINUTES

■ These standbys of 1950s bridge club hostesses are worth resurrecting. They're *good*—crisp on the outside with a briny surprise inside. And they can be made with ingredients no kitchen should lack. ■

1 cup coarsely grated sharp Cheddar (about 4 ounces)
½ cup all-purpose flour
⅛ teaspoon cayenne

2 tablespoons unsalted butter, softened
20 small pimiento-stuffed green olives (from a 3-ounce jar), drained and patted dry

Put a rack in middle of oven and preheat oven to 400°F.

Stir together cheese, flour, and cayenne in a bowl. Blend in butter with your fingertips until a dough forms.

Drop tablespoons of dough onto a sheet of wax paper and place 1 olive on each piece of dough. Lightly flour your hands and wrap dough around olives, enclosing each one completely. Transfer olives to a baking sheet with sides and bake until pastry is golden, about 15 minutes. Serve warm.

COOK'S NOTE

■ The dough-wrapped olives can be prepared up to 2 hours ahead and refrigerated on the baking sheet, covered with plastic wrap. Bring to room temperature before baking.

Cheddar Pecan Crackers

MAKES ABOUT 50 CRACKERS
ACTIVE TIME: 15 MINUTES ■ START TO FINISH: 1 HOUR

■ These cheese crackers are wonderful to have on hand, especially during the holidays, and you'll find that every guest will want the recipe. They are thin but not too fragile. ■

1 stick (8 tablespoons) unsalted butter, softened
2 cups coarsely grated Cheddar (about 8 ounces)
1 large egg yolk
½ teaspoon salt
½ teaspoon cayenne
⅔ cup all-purpose flour
⅔ cup pecans, finely chopped

Put a rack in middle of oven and preheat oven to 350°F. Butter two baking sheets with sides.

Beat together butter and Cheddar in a large bowl with an electric mixer until smooth. Beat in remaining ingredients.

Roll rounded teaspoons of dough into balls and arrange about 3 inches apart on buttered baking sheets. Flatten each ball into a 1½-inch disk. Bake, one sheet at a time, until golden, 15 to 18 minutes per batch. Transfer crackers to a rack to cool.

COOK'S NOTE

■ The crackers can be made up to 1 day ahead and kept in an airtight container at room temperature.

Fricos

Parmesan Crisps

MAKES 12 CRISPS
ACTIVE TIME: 15 MINUTES ■ START TO FINISH: 30 MINUTES

■ Delicate, crisp, lacy—these are the best cheese wafers you've ever had. ■

1 (3-ounce) piece Parmigiano-Reggiano
1 tablespoon all-purpose flour
¼ teaspoon freshly ground black pepper
SPECIAL EQUIPMENT: a nonstick baking sheet liner, such as a Silpat (see Sources)

Put a rack in middle of oven and preheat oven to 375°F. Line a large baking sheet with nonstick liner.

Using largest holes on a box grater, coarsely shred enough cheese to measure 1 cup.

Stir together cheese, flour, and pepper in a small bowl. Arrange tablespoons of cheese mixture 4 inches apart on baking sheet, stirring mixture after each tablespoon to keep flour evenly distributed. Flatten each mound slightly with a metal spatula to form a 3-inch round.

Bake fricos until golden, about 10 minutes. Cool on baking sheet on a rack for 2 minutes, then carefully transfer crisps (they are very delicate) with metal spatula to rack to cool completely. Repeat with remaining cheese mixture to make more fricos.

COOK'S NOTE

■ The fricos can be kept, layered between sheets of wax paper, in an airtight container at room temperature for up to 3 days.

How to Organize a Cheese Tasting

A cheese tasting is a versatile entertainment. You can make it as simple or as elaborate as your imagination, your cheese shop, and your wallet allow, and you can serve it before a meal, as a course before dessert, or as a buffet for a party. Part of the fun is the planning. Do you want to showcase the products of a particular country — regional classics of Italy, for instance, or hand-crafted cheeses of the United States? Or would you rather home in on a specific type, such as Cheddars or blues, or perhaps the kind of milk used (cow's, sheep's, goat's)? You can also compare different soft cheeses or hard cheeses.

We love putting together an eclectic assortment of cheese types and textures; see the list below for some suggestions. Display the cheeses with small labels affixed to help out guests (make little flags with toothpicks if you want). We recommend eating the cheeses in "flights," or one group at a time, an enlightening way to compare and contrast different examples of the same kind of cheese. It's best to start with the lighter goat cheeses, then progress through the soft, creamy cheeses to the more piquant hard cheeses, and end with the blues. (As with tasting wines, if you begin with more powerful flavors, your palate won't be able to appreciate the subtler ones.)

Good cheeses deserve the best breads you can find — a crusty baguette, an honest multigrain, a tangy sourdough, a walnut-studded whole wheat. Other accompaniments that can give balance to a menu of rich cheeses are a few salads (one of soft butter lettuces with a light vinaigrette, say, and another of celery, fennel, and red pear), sweet dates, California walnuts, and the most beautiful grapes you can find.

STORAGE AND SERVING TIPS: Wrap cheese *loosely* in wax paper — it needs to "breathe" in order to ripen further — and then in foil, and store in the bottom of the refrigerator. Cheese should never be frozen, because freezing ruins the texture. Bring it to room temperature before serving; if it is served too cool, much of the flavor will be lost and the texture will be off. Leave it wrapped while it stands so that cut surfaces don't dry out. We suggest serving six ounces of cheese per person. (For producers of artisanal cheeses, see Sources.)

GOAT CHEESES: Chabichou du Poitou, Picandine chèvres, Pouligny-Saint-Pierre, Valençay, Coach Farm

SOFT CHEESES: Hudson Valley Camembert, Muenster, Pierre Robert, Taleggio

FIRM/HARD CHEESES: Dry Jack, farmhouse English Cheddars such as Keen's and Montgomery (rich, buttery, and more complex than American mass-produced Cheddars), Parmigiano-Reggiano

BLUE CHEESES: Cabrales, Gorgonzola dolce, Maytag Blue, Roquefort

Special Implements for Cutting and Serving Cheese

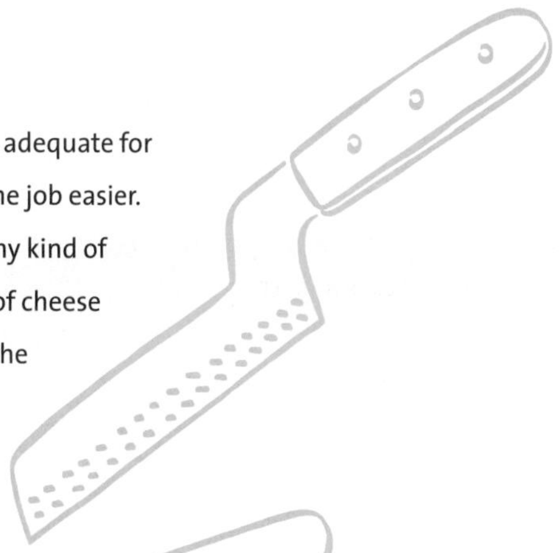

A clutch of well-sharpened, good knives, preferably one for each cheese, is perfectly adequate for a cheese tasting. But cookware shops stock some specialized tools that can make the job easier. A hard-cheese knife, which comes in a variety of sizes, is actually great for almost any kind of cheese. Its offset straight-edge blade allows you to cut a slice from a wheel or slab of cheese without rapping your knuckles on the cutting board, and the etched sides prevent the cheese from sticking, tearing, or dragging the blade off course. The kind of cheese knife with upswept prongs at the pointy end is a popular gift item. Similar in design to a tomato knife, its blade is scalloped for ease of cutting, and the forked tip is used to spear slices.

For prizing a morsel from a wedge of Parmigiano-Reggiano, nothing works better than a knob-handled Parmesan knife, with its distinctive arrowhead-shaped blade. The sharp tip easily digs into the hard, crumbly cheese, and if you twist the handle and rock the short blade back and forth, the cheese breaks evenly along the grain. (Save some of that inedible hard rind — it adds great flavor when simmered in a pot of minestrone.)

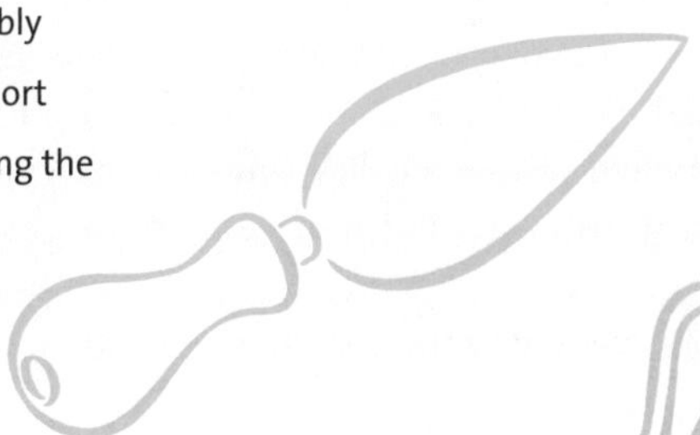

If you're a big fan of very soft, fresh cheeses, you might want to invest in a lyre- or hacksaw-shaped cheese wire, which will cut cleanly through the youngest, creamiest chèvre with the greatest of ease. This prosaic tool acquires a certain lethal elegance when reconfigured into a Roquefort cutter, a foot-tall, guillotine-like implement that consists of a marble base sized to fit the classic seven-inch cheese cylinder. Above the base is poised the taut cutting wire, of a gauge so fine it will slice cleanly through the blue-green veins without smearing the soft white cheese into them. A spring-loaded quick-action handle delivers surgically precise cuts. The perfect plaything for the cheese lover who has everything . . .

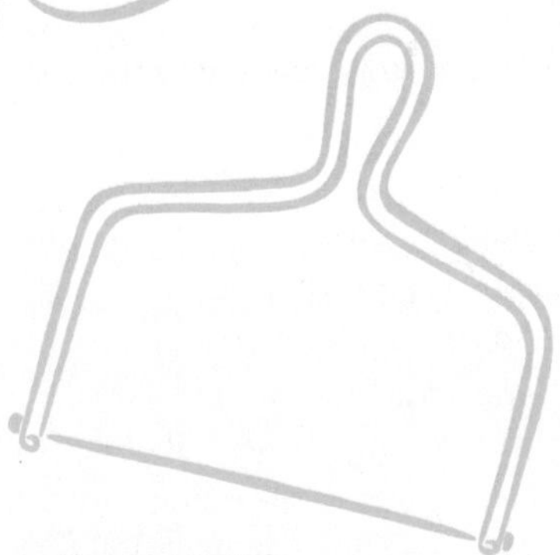

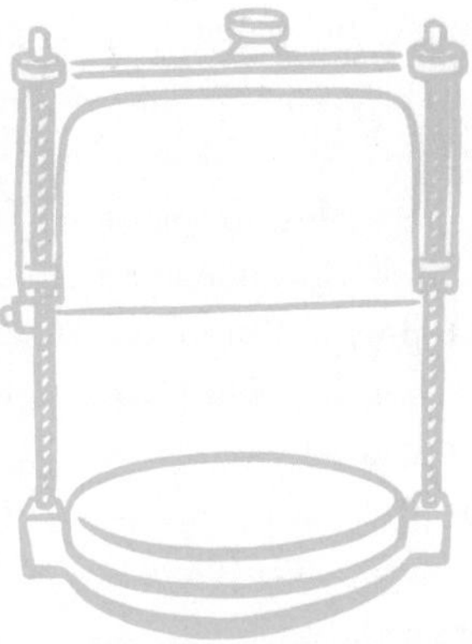

Cheese Pastries

MAKES ABOUT 60 HORS D'OEUVRES
ACTIVE TIME: 1½ HOURS ■ START TO FINISH: 3½ HOURS (INCLUDES CHILLING DOUGH)

■ These miniature sandwiches—flaky, crisp Cheddar crackers with a filling of Gruyère—melt in your mouth. ■

- 1½ cups all-purpose flour
- ½ teaspoon salt
- ⅛ teaspoon cayenne
- 1 cup coarsely grated sharp Cheddar (about 4 ounces)
- ¾ stick (6 tablespoons) cold unsalted butter, cut into ½-inch cubes, plus 3 tablespoons butter, softened
- 6 tablespoons heavy cream
- 1 large egg, lightly beaten
- 1½ cups finely shredded Gruyère (about 4 ounces)

SPECIAL EQUIPMENT: a 1½-inch round cookie cutter

Sift together flour, salt, and cayenne into a medium bowl. Blend in Cheddar and cold butter with your fingertips or a pastry blender until mixture resembles coarse meal. Add cream and stir until a dough forms. Press dough into a ball, flatten into a 5-inch disk, and refrigerate, wrapped in plastic wrap, until firm, about 2 hours.

Put a rack in middle of oven and preheat oven to 450°F.

Roll out dough on a lightly floured surface with a lightly floured rolling pin into a 16- to 17-inch round. Cut out as many rounds as possible with lightly floured cutter and transfer to ungreased large baking sheets. Reroll scraps and cut out additional rounds. (If you have only two large baking sheets, chill the scraps, then reroll, cut out more rounds, and put on cooled baking sheet after first batch has baked.)

Brush top of each round lightly with egg. Bake, one sheet at a time, until lightly browned, 5 to 7 minutes. Transfer rounds to a rack to cool. (Leave oven on.)

Beat together Gruyère and softened butter in a bowl with an electric mixer at medium speed until well combined, about 1 minute.

Arrange half of Cheddar rounds upside down on baking sheets. Divide Gruyère mixture among them, using about ¼ teaspoon per round. Top with remaining Cheddar rounds, right sides up, and press together lightly. Bake in batches in upper and lower thirds of oven until cheese is just melted, about 4 minutes per batch. Serve warm.

COOK'S NOTES

- The pastry rounds can be baked up to 2 days ahead and kept in an airtight container at room temperature.
- The Cheddar rounds can be sandwiched with Gruyère up to 4 hours ahead and kept, loosely covered, at room temperature until ready to bake.

Cheese Straws

MAKES 24 HORS D'OEUVRES
ACTIVE TIME: 20 MINUTES ■ START TO FINISH: 45 MINUTES

■ Frozen puff pastry, like frozen homemade chicken stock, is money in the bank, because you can use it to whip up something delicious in no time. Take cheese straws: there is something classic, and classy, about them. They are thin and elegant, and one *feels* thin and elegant when nibbling them. These are best if not made too far ahead. ■

- 1 sheet frozen puff pastry (from a 17¼-ounce package), thawed
- 1 large egg lightly beaten with 2 teaspoons water, for egg wash
- 1 cup finely grated extra-sharp Cheddar (about 4 ounces)
- Coarse sea salt

Put a rack in middle of oven and preheat oven to 425°F. Generously butter two baking sheets.

Roll out pastry on a lightly floured surface with a lightly floured rolling pin into a 14-by-12-inch rectangle. Cut crosswise in half to form two 12-by-7-inch rectangles. Brush both rectangles with some egg wash. Sprinkle cheese evenly over one rectangle and top with other rectangle, egg wash side down. Press firmly on pastry to force out any air pockets, then roll out gently to make layers adhere (rectangle should be about 12½ by 7½ inches). Brush pastry with egg wash and sprinkle evenly with coarse salt.

With a pastry wheel or sharp knife, cut pastry crosswise into twenty-four 1/2-inch-wide strips. Holding one end of a strip in each hand, twist strip two or three times and place on a buttered baking sheet, pressing ends onto sheet to keep strip twisted. Repeat with 11 more strips, placing strips 1 inch apart on baking sheet.

Bake strips until golden, 10 to 12 minutes.

Meanwhile, shape remaining strips in same manner and arrange on second baking sheet. Loosen baked strips with a metal spatula and transfer to a rack. Bake remaining cheese straws in same manner. Serve warm or at room temperature.

COOK'S NOTE

- The straws can be formed up to 2 weeks ahead. Freeze on the baking sheets until solid, then transfer to sealable plastic bags and keep frozen until ready to bake.

VARIATIONS

- CHEDDAR CUMIN CHEESE STRAWS: Toss cheese with 1/2 teaspoon ground cumin before sprinkling over pastry, then top with other pastry rectangle. Brush with egg wash and sprinkle with 2 teaspoons cumin seeds before cutting.
- SPICY PARMESAN CHEESE STRAWS: Use 1 cup finely grated Parmigiano-Reggiano (about 2 ounces) in place of Cheddar and toss with 1/4 teaspoon cayenne before sprinkling over pastry.

Gougères

MAKES ABOUT 55 HORS D'OEUVRES
ACTIVE TIME: 20 MINUTES ■ START TO FINISH: 1 1/4 HOURS

■ Gougères are one of the simple glories of French cuisine, as much at home in an elegant setting as in a rustic one. Think of them as savory cream puffs, because the dough, *pâte à choux* ("paht-ah-*shoo*"), is exactly the same. The pronounced nutty flavor of Gruyère is important, as is the nutmeg—just the littlest bit of the spice rounds out the flavors beautifully. (Try some in macaroni and cheese or a potato gratin.) Note that we specify freshly grated nutmeg; pregrated nutmeg in a tin is a pallid version of the real thing. ■

1 cup water
1 stick (8 tablespoons) unsalted butter, cut into tablespoons
1/2 teaspoon salt
1 cup all-purpose flour
4–5 large eggs
1 1/2 cups finely grated Gruyère (about 4 ounces)
2 tablespoons finely grated Parmigiano-Reggiano
Rounded 1/4 teaspoon freshly grated nutmeg
1/4 teaspoon freshly ground black pepper
SPECIAL EQUIPMENT: parchment paper (optional); a pastry bag fitted with a 1/2-inch plain tip (optional)

Put racks in upper and lower thirds of oven and preheat oven to 375°F. Line two large baking sheets with parchment paper or lightly butter them.

Combine water, butter, and salt in a 3-quart heavy saucepan and bring to a full boil over high heat, stirring until butter is melted. Reduce heat to moderate, add flour all at once, and cook, stirring vigorously with a wooden spoon, until mixture pulls away from sides of pan, about 30 seconds. Continue to cook and stir to remove excess moisture for about 1 1/2 minutes. Remove from heat and let cool slightly, about 3 minutes.

Add 4 eggs, one at a time, beating well with wooden spoon after each addition; batter will appear to separate but will become smooth once beaten. Mixture should be glossy and just stiff enough to hold soft peaks and fall softly from a spoon. If it is too stiff, beat remaining egg in a small bowl and add to batter 1 teaspoon at a time, beating and then testing batter after each addition until it reaches desired consistency. Stir in cheeses, nutmeg, and pepper.

Fill pastry bag, if using, with batter and pipe fifteen 1-inch-diameter mounds 1 inch apart onto each baking sheet, or spoon level tablespoons of batter onto sheets. Bake, switching position of sheets halfway through baking, until puffed, golden, and crisp, about 30 minutes total. Make more gougères in same manner with remaining batter. Serve warm.

COOK'S NOTES

- If you spoon the batter onto the baking sheets rather than piping it, the active time will be about 15 minutes longer. It is helpful to use a regular teaspoon to scoop the batter out of the measuring spoon onto the baking sheets.

- The gougères can be baked up to 2 days ahead and refrigerated in sealable plastic bags. They can also be frozen for up to 1 week. Reheat, uncovered, on baking sheets in a 350°F oven for about 10 minutes if refrigerated or 12 to 15 minutes if frozen.

Onion Parmesan Toasts

MAKES 14 HORS D'OEUVRES
ACTIVE TIME: 10 MINUTES ■ START TO FINISH: 15 MINUTES

■ We have reader Hope Mihalap, from Norfolk, Virginia, to thank for reminding us of this classic, which couldn't be easier—all you need is an onion, mayonnaise, Parmesan, and bread. The result is surprisingly wonderful; even people who don't like raw onions tend to love this combination. Feel free to substitute any supermarket bread (whole wheat would be nice) for the cocktail rye or pumpernickel. As for the onion, sweet varieties such as Vidalia and Walla Walla are becoming more widely available, but we've even used a regular yellow onion in a pinch. In fact, it seems as if regular onions are growing sweeter all the time—tears while chopping are almost a thing of the past—which is not necessarily a good characteristic in general but one that works here. ■

- 3/4 cup chopped sweet onion, such as Vidalia or Walla Walla
- 1/2 cup mayonnaise
- 14 slices party (cocktail) rye or pumpernickel bread
- 1/4 cup finely grated Parmigiano-Reggiano
- Freshly ground black pepper

Preheat broiler. Stir together onion and mayonnaise in a small bowl.

Arrange bread in one layer on a baking sheet and broil 6 inches from heat, turning once, until lightly toasted, 1 to 2 minutes per side (watch carefully). Remove from oven and turn toasts over. Spread evenly with onion mixture and sprinkle with cheese and pepper to taste. Broil until topping is bubbling and lightly browned, 1 to 2 minutes (watch carefully to prevent burning). Serve warm.

Stilton Tart with Cranberry Chutney

MAKES 32 HORS D'OEUVRES
ACTIVE TIME: 1 HOUR ■ START TO FINISH: 4 1/2 HOURS
(INCLUDES MAKING DOUGH AND CHILLING)

■ You've heard of slice-and-bake cookies? Well, this is a bake-and-slice hors d'oeuvre, made by cutting a big rectangular or round tart into finger food for a crowd. It is *much* easier than making hors d'oeuvres one by one. Cranberry chutney is a wonderful Christmasy accompaniment, but any fruit chutney will do. ■

- Basic Pastry Dough for a single-crust pie (page 790)
- 1 cup heavy cream
- 1 large egg
- 2 large egg yolks
- 1/4 teaspoon salt
- 1/4 teaspoon freshly ground black pepper
- 1 1/2 cups chilled crumbled Stilton (any rind removed; 5 ounces)

ACCOMPANIMENT: Cranberry Chutney (recipe follows)
SPECIAL EQUIPMENT: a 13 1/2-by-4-by-1-inch rectangular fluted tart pan with a removable bottom (see Cook's Note)

BAKE THE TART SHELL: Roll out dough on a lightly floured surface with a floured rolling pin into a 17-by-8-inch rectangle. Fit dough into tart pan and trim excess dough to a 1/2-inch overhang. Fold overhang inward and press against sides of pan to reinforce sides of shell. Refrigerate until firm, about 30 minutes.

Put a rack in middle of oven and preheat oven to 350°F.

Lightly prick bottom and sides of tart shell all over with a fork. Line shell with foil and fill with pie weights, dried beans, or raw rice. Bake until sides are set and edges are golden, about 20 minutes. Carefully remove foil and weights and bake until golden all over, 10 to 15 minutes more. Let shell cool in pan on a rack for 20 minutes. Reduce oven temperature to 325°F.

MAKE THE FILLING: Whisk together cream, egg, yolks, salt, and pepper in a small bowl until combined.

Put tart shell (still in pan) on a baking sheet and scatter cheese evenly over bottom of shell. Slowly pour cream mixture into shell. Bake until filling is golden around edges and just set, 30 to 35 minutes. Cool tart completely in pan on rack.

Cut tart into 32 rectangles and serve topped with chutney.

COOK'S NOTES

- The tart can also be made in a 9-inch fluted round tart pan with a removable bottom; roll the dough into an 11-inch circle.
- The tart can be made up to 1 day ahead and refrigerated, covered. Crisp pastry in a 350°F oven, then cool before serving.

Cranberry Chutney

MAKES ABOUT 2 CUPS
ACTIVE TIME: 20 MINUTES ■ START TO FINISH: 20 MINUTES

■ This chutney is a natural with roast turkey (or on a turkey sandwich, preferably at midnight), but it's also great with duck or pork. ■

1 tablespoon vegetable oil
2/3 cup coarsely chopped shallots
1 (12-ounce) bag fresh or frozen (not thawed) cranberries
2/3 cup sugar
3 tablespoons cider vinegar
1 teaspoon minced garlic
1 teaspoon minced peeled fresh ginger
1/2 teaspoon salt
1/8 teaspoon red pepper flakes

Heat oil in a 3-quart heavy saucepan over moderate heat. Add shallots and cook, stirring occasionally, until softened, about 3 minutes. Stir in remaining ingredients and simmer, uncovered, stirring occasionally, just until berries pop, 10 to 12 minutes. Let cool.

COOK'S NOTE

- The chutney can be made up to 1 week ahead and refrigerated, covered.

Roasted Garlic–Pea Purée on Sourdough Croûtes

MAKES 24 HORS D'OEUVRES
ACTIVE TIME: 15 MINUTES ■ START TO FINISH: 2 1/4 HOURS

■ Because we're often disappointed by the starchiness of the "fresh" peas we find in the markets, we're big fans of frozen peas. We were thrilled when they worked so perfectly in this spread. It was inspired by an Italian fava bean purée, but the frozen peas are much less labor-intensive. ■

1 sourdough baguette, cut diagonally into 24 (1/4-inch-thick) slices
5 tablespoons extra-virgin olive oil
Salt and freshly ground black pepper
2 large heads garlic
1 (6- to 8-ounce) piece Parmigiano-Reggiano
2 (10-ounce) packages frozen peas, thawed
2 teaspoons fresh lemon juice, or to taste
OPTIONAL GARNISH: 24 small arugula leaves

Put a rack in middle of oven and preheat oven to 400°F.

Arrange baguette slices in one layer on a large baking sheet. Lightly brush tops of slices with 2 tablespoons oil and season with salt and pepper. Bake until golden, about 8 minutes. Transfer to a rack to cool.

Meanwhile, wrap each head of garlic tightly in foil and roast until tender, about 50 minutes. Carefully unwrap garlic and let cool for 10 minutes.

Separate cloves and squeeze garlic out of skins into a bowl. Finely grate enough cheese to measure 1/2 cup.

Cook peas in 3 tablespoons water in a medium saucepan over moderate heat, stirring occasionally, until just tender, about 3 minutes. Transfer peas to a food processor, add garlic, grated cheese, lemon juice, 1 tablespoon oil, 1/2 teaspoon salt, and 1/4 teaspoon pepper, and purée until smooth. Transfer purée to a bowl and let cool completely.

Using a vegetable peeler, shave 24 small thin slices from remaining piece of cheese. Spread 1 heaping tablespoon purée on each toast and, if desired, top with an arugula leaf. Top each with a cheese shaving and drizzle toasts with remaining 2 tablespoons oil.

COOK'S NOTE

- The purée can be made up to 1 day ahead and refrigerated, covered. Bring to room temperature and season with salt and pepper before serving.

Slow-Roasted Tomato Bruschetta

MAKES ABOUT 45 HORS D'OEUVRES
ACTIVE TIME: 30 MINUTES ■ START TO FINISH: 6½ HOURS

■ Every summer we fall in love. Juicy tomatoes, mounded in bushel baskets at roadside farm stands, are the objects of our affection, and we can't help buying more than we really need. But we don't even think of refrigerating them, because chilling is the quickest way to turn a perfect tomato into a flavorless, mushy one. Immediate action is crucial, yet few of us have the time for a canning spree. So we've turned to slow roasting, a cooking method that concentrates the tomato flavor by slowly evaporating the juices in a low-temperature oven. The results are incredible—meaty, silken tomatoes that are a great thing to have around, infinitely better than so-called sun-dried tomatoes, which are often oversalted and leathery. And the technique requires only fifteen minutes of active effort on the cook's part.

The tomatoes are delicious after they are roasted for six hours. Here we put them on crusty bread with a drizzle of good olive oil. If you want to serve them with pasta, the flavor needs to be a little more intense: cook them for an additional two hours and they'll be perfect. ■

4 pounds plum tomatoes (20–25), halved lengthwise
6 garlic cloves, minced
8 tablespoons extra-virgin olive oil
1½ teaspoons salt
Freshly ground black pepper
1 (22- to 26-inch-long) baguette, cut into 40–50 (½-inch-thick) slices

Position racks in upper and lower thirds of oven and preheat oven to 200°F.

ROAST THE TOMATOES: Put tomatoes cut sides up on two large baking sheets with sides. Stir together garlic and 5 tablespoons oil and spoon over tomatoes. Sprinkle with 1 teaspoon salt and season with pepper. Roast, switching position of sheets halfway through roasting, for 6 hours; tomatoes will shrink but retain their shape. Let cool slightly. Increase oven temperature to 350°F.

MAKE THE TOASTS: Arrange bread in one layer on two large baking sheets with sides and brush with remaining 3 tablespoons oil. Sprinkle with remaining ½ teaspoon salt and season with pepper.

Bake, switching positions of sheets halfway through baking, until pale golden and crisp, 10 to 12 minutes.

Place a tomato half on each slice of toast and arrange bruschetta on two platters. Serve warm or at room temperature.

COOK'S NOTES

- The roasted tomatoes can be refrigerated in an airtight container for up to 2 weeks. Bring to room temperature before using.
- The toasts can be made up to 1 week ahead and kept in an airtight container at room temperature.

Sesame Rice Balls with Red Pepper Dipping Sauce

MAKES ABOUT 40 HORS D'OEUVRES
ACTIVE TIME: 2 HOURS ■ START TO FINISH: 2 HOURS

■ This is vegetarian sushi made simple—no seaweed, no bamboo rolling mat—but still beautiful. The procedure for making the rice balls might look involved, but it is actually very straightforward, and you'll get the hang of it in no time. For more information about these Asian ingredients, see Glossary; they can be found at Japanese markets and, more and more, at supermarkets, or see Sources for mail-order information. ■

FOR DIPPING SAUCE
1 red bell pepper, cored, seeded, and coarsely chopped
¾ cup seasoned rice vinegar
2 tablespoons sugar
½ teaspoon red pepper flakes

FOR RICE BALLS
2 cups Japanese short-grain rice
2 cups water

¼ cup seasoned rice vinegar
⅓ cup minced Japanese pickled ginger
1 tablespoon wasabi paste, or 1½ tablespoons wasabi powder stirred to a paste with 2 teaspoons water
20 frozen edamame (soybeans) in the pod, thawed
¼ cup black sesame seeds, toasted (see Tips, page 939)

MAKE THE DIPPING SAUCE: Combine bell pepper, vinegar, and sugar in a blender and purée until smooth. Transfer to a small heavy saucepan and stir in red pepper flakes. Simmer, uncovered, for 5 minutes. Pour through a fine-mesh sieve into a small bowl, pressing on solids; discard solids.

MAKE THE RICE BALLS: Rinse rice in a bowl in several changes of cold water until water is almost clear, then drain well in a large sieve. Combine rice and 2 cups water in a 3-quart heavy saucepan and let stand for 10 minutes.

Cover pan with a tight-fitting lid and bring to a boil over high heat. Cook at a rapid boil (lid will be rattling and foam may drip down outside of pan) until water is absorbed, about 5 minutes. Remove from heat and let stand, covered, for 10 minutes.

Transfer warm rice to a large wooden bowl. Sprinkle vinegar over it a little at a time while gently tossing with a flat wooden paddle or spoon so vinegar is absorbed and rice begins to cool, then let cool to room temperature.

Stir together ginger and wasabi paste in a small bowl. Remove edamame from pods.

Hold a 12-inch square of doubled plastic wrap in palm of one hand and put an edamame bean in center, then invert 1 packed tablespoon of rice on top of bean. Gather plastic up around rice and twist tightly to form a ball (bean should still be visible). Unwrap, leaving plastic in your hand, and, going in from side opposite bean, poke a dampened finger into center of ball and fill hole with ¼ teaspoon ginger mixture. Close rice over mixture and twist plastic tightly to re-form ball, then flatten slightly. Remove rice ball from plastic and sprinkle some sesame seeds over top and sides, pressing lightly so they adhere; do not coat bean with seeds. Place rice ball bean side up on a plate. Make more rice balls in same manner (dip tablespoon in a bowl of warm water as necessary so grains of rice don't stick).

Serve rice balls with dipping sauce.

COOK'S NOTES

- If you prefer to use fresh edamame, cook the pods briefly in boiling water.
- The dipping sauce can be made up to 1 day ahead and refrigerated, covered. Bring to room temperature before serving.
- The rice balls can be made up to 4 hours ahead and refrigerated, tightly covered with plastic wrap. Bring to room temperature before serving.

Tuna Empanaditas

MAKES ABOUT 50 HORS D'OEUVRES
ACTIVE TIME: 1 HOUR ■ START TO FINISH: 1½ HOURS

■ You might say these *empanaditas* are the ultimate rainy-day hors d'oeuvre: all you need to make them is a few pantry staples—canned tuna, pimiento-stuffed olives, and capers—and frozen puff pastry. A little Spanish-inspired tapa, they are great with a glass of dry sherry. ■

FOR FILLING
1 (6-ounce) can light tuna in olive oil (not drained)
½ cup finely chopped onion
½ cup finely chopped pimiento-stuffed green olives
2 tablespoons drained capers, rinsed and chopped
Salt and freshly ground black pepper

FOR PASTRY
1 (17¼-ounce) package frozen puff pastry sheets, thawed

SPECIAL EQUIPMENT: a 2¼-inch round cookie cutter

Put a rack in middle of oven and preheat oven to 400°F.

MAKE THE FILLING: Pour oil from tuna into a medium skillet. Add onion and cook over moderate heat, stirring occasionally, until softened, 3 to 4 minutes. Remove from heat.

Mash tuna in a bowl with a fork, then stir in onion, olives, and capers. Season generously with pepper and very lightly with salt.

MAKE THE *EMPANADITAS*: Roll out 1 pastry sheet on a lightly floured surface with a lightly floured rolling pin into a 13-inch square. Cut out 25 rounds with floured cookie cutter; discard trimmings.

Put 1/2 teaspoon filling in center of each round. Hold 1 filled round in palm of your hand and moisten edges with a finger dipped in water, then cup your hand and fold dough over to form a half-moon; pinch edges to seal. Transfer *empanadita* to an ungreased large baking sheet and press tines of a fork around sealed edge to crimp and seal. Form more *empanaditas* with remaining rounds. Bake *empanaditas* until golden, 20 to 25 minutes. Cool on baking sheet on a rack for about 10 minutes.

Meanwhile, make more *empanaditas* with remaining pastry sheet and filling. Bake in same manner. Serve warm.

COOK'S NOTE

- The *empanaditas* can be formed (but not baked) up to 1 week ahead. Freeze in one layer on a baking sheet until firm, then transfer to sealable plastic bags and freeze. Bake, unthawed, for about 30 minutes.

Sherried Mushroom Empanaditas

MAKES ABOUT 50 HORS D'OEUVRES
ACTIVE TIME: 1 HOUR ■ START TO FINISH: 2½ HOURS

■ We love the sweetness of cream sherry with the mushrooms, but any kind (except cooking sherry) will do. Spanish Serrano ham deserves to be more popular: the deep rose–hued slices have a more substantial texture than prosciutto, which can sometimes be tender unto flabbiness. Luckily, it's available by mail (see Sources). ■

FOR FILLING

- 2 tablespoons unsalted butter
- 1/2 cup finely chopped onion
- 1/2 pound mushrooms, trimmed and finely chopped in a food processor
- 1/2 cup finely chopped red bell pepper
- 2 ounces Serrano ham (see above), finely chopped (1/2 cup)
- 2 tablespoons sherry
- 2 tablespoons finely chopped fresh flat-leaf parsley
- 1 tablespoon fine dry bread crumbs
- 1/4 teaspoon salt
- 1/4 teaspoon freshly ground black pepper

FOR PASTRY

- 1 (17-ounce) package frozen puff pastry sheets, thawed

SPECIAL EQUIPMENT: a 2¼-inch round cookie cutter

FOR THE FILLING: Melt butter in a 12-inch heavy skillet over moderate heat until foam subsides. Add onion and cook, stirring occasionally, until softened, about 3 minutes. Add mushrooms and red bell pepper and cook, stirring occasionally, until vegetables are tender and liquid mushrooms give off has evaporated, about 5 minutes. Add ham and sherry and cook, stirring, until sherry evaporates, 1 to 2 minutes.

Transfer mixture to a bowl. Stir in parsley, bread crumbs, salt, and pepper. Let filling cool to room temperature, about 30 minutes.

MAKE THE *EMPANADITAS*: Prepare pastry, fill, and bake *empanaditas* following instructions in recipe for Tuna Empanaditas, above.

Rye Crispbread Crackers with Pepper-Dill Crème Fraîche and Smoked Salmon

MAKES ABOUT 24 HORS D'OEUVRES
ACTIVE TIME: 35 MINUTES ■ START TO FINISH: 2¾ HOURS

■ It might seem strange to give the crackers top billing here, but they're that delicious, and that easy. They are made in big, crisp sheets, so you can break them off in dramatic shards. They're wonderful against the buttery smoked salmon, and, happily, you'll have twice as many as you need for this recipe. ■

FOR CRISPBREAD CRACKERS

- 1 teaspoon active dry yeast (from a ¼-ounce package)
- 1 cup warm water (105°–115°F)
- 1/8 teaspoon sugar
- 1 tablespoon caraway seeds, toasted (see Tips, page 939)
- 1⅔ cups unbleached all-purpose flour

1 cup rye flour
1½ teaspoons kosher salt

FOR CRÈME FRAÎCHE

½ cup crème fraîche
2 tablespoons chopped fresh dill
¼ teaspoon salt
½ teaspoon freshly ground black pepper

FOR TOPPING

¼ pound thinly sliced smoked salmon, cut into 1-inch pieces
1 teaspoon finely grated orange zest

OPTIONAL GARNISH: small fresh dill sprigs

SPECIAL EQUIPMENT: a stand mixer with paddle attachment and dough hook (optional); an electric coffee/spice grinder

MAKE THE CRISPBREADS: Stir together yeast, warm water, and sugar in bowl of a stand mixer fitted with paddle attachment (if you don't have a stand mixer, see Cook's Note) and let stand until foamy, about 5 minutes. (If mixture doesn't foam, discard and start over with new yeast.)

Finely grind caraway seeds in coffee/spice grinder. Add caraway, 1 cup all-purpose flour, rye flour, and salt to yeast mixture and beat at medium speed until incorporated. Switch to dough hook and gradually beat in remaining ⅔ cup flour at medium speed. Beat dough until it begins to pull away from sides of bowl, then beat for 5 minutes more.

Gather dough into a ball, put in a lightly oiled large bowl, and turn to coat with oil. Cover bowl with plastic wrap and let dough rise in a warm, draft-free place until doubled in bulk, about 1½ hours.

Put racks in upper and lower thirds of oven and preheat oven to 400°F. Lightly oil two large baking sheets.

Punch down dough and divide in half. Flatten each piece with lightly floured fingers into a 6-by-4-inch rectangle and let stand for 3 minutes.

Roll out each piece of dough on a floured surface into a 15-by-10-inch rectangle (⅛ inch thick). Transfer each rectangle to an oiled baking sheet and trim any overhang. Cover each rectangle loosely with a dampened kitchen towel or plastic wrap and let stand for 15 minutes.

With tines of a fork, make lengthwise and crosswise perforated lines in each rectangle about 2 inches apart to facilitate breaking crispbreads into crackers. Bake, switching position of sheets halfway through baking, until golden brown and crisp, about 20 minutes total. Transfer to racks to cool.

Break each crispbread into about 24 crackers.

MAKE THE CRÈME FRAÎCHE AND ASSEMBLE THE HORS D'OEUVRES: Stir together crème fraîche, dill, salt, and pepper in a bowl. Spoon ½ teaspoon crème fraîche onto each cracker, then drape a piece of salmon on top and sprinkle with zest. Garnish each hors d'oeuvre with a dill sprig, if desired.

COOK'S NOTES

- If you don't have a stand mixer, stir together the yeast, warm water, and sugar in a bowl and let stand until foamy. Add 1 cup all-purpose flour, rye flour, caraway, and salt and mix with a wooden spoon until incorporated. Turn the dough out onto a work surface and gradually knead in the remaining ⅔ cup flour, then continue to knead until smooth, about 8 minutes.
- The crackers can be made up to 3 days ahead and kept in an airtight container at room temperature.
- The crème fraîche can be made up to 2 days ahead and refrigerated, covered.

Blini with Three Caviars

MAKES ABOUT 30 HORS D'OEUVRES
ACTIVE TIME: 1¼ HOURS ■ START TO FINISH: 4¼ HOURS (INCLUDES RISING AND CHILLING TIMES)

■ Blini are small, thin Russian buckwheat pancakes that are leavened with yeast rather than baking soda. They are a classic accompaniment to caviar. The three different caviar types—black, golden, and salmon—offer a variety of flavors, and they look pretty arranged on a platter. These also make a striking first course for a fancy dinner: serve three blini per person, each topped with a different caviar. ■

1 (1/4-ounce) package (2 1/2 teaspoons) active dry yeast
1/4 cup warm water (105°–115°F)
4 teaspoons sugar
1 cup whole milk
1 tablespoon unsalted butter
1/2 cup buckwheat flour (see Sources)
1/2 cup all-purpose flour
1/2 teaspoon salt
1 large egg, separated
6 tablespoons very cold heavy cream
1–2 tablespoons unsalted butter, melted, for brushing griddle
1 cup sour cream
2 ounces black caviar
2 ounces golden caviar
2 ounces salmon roe

MAKE THE BATTER: Stir together yeast, warm water, and 1 teaspoon sugar in a large bowl. Let stand until foamy, about 10 minutes. (If mixture doesn't foam, discard and start over with new yeast.)

Meanwhile, heat 1/2 cup milk and butter to lukewarm (105°–115°F).

Add buckwheat flour, remaining 1 tablespoon sugar, and heated milk mixture to yeast mixture and beat vigorously with a wooden spoon for 1 minute. Cover tightly with plastic wrap and let rise in a warm, draft-free place for 2 hours, or refrigerate overnight. (Chilling overnight produces a tangier flavor; let batter come to room temperature before proceeding.)

Heat remaining 1/2 cup milk to lukewarm (105°–115°F). Add to batter along with all-purpose flour, salt, and egg yolk and whisk for 1 minute; batter will be thin. Let rise, covered with plastic wrap, in a warm, draft-free place until doubled in bulk and bubbly, about 1 hour.

Beat cream in a medium bowl with an electric mixer until it holds soft peaks, then fold into batter. Beat egg white with cleaned beaters in a small bowl until it just holds stiff peaks. Gently but thoroughly fold into batter.

COOK THE BLINI: Preheat oven to 200°F.

Heat a griddle or 10- to 12-inch heavy skillet over moderate heat until hot and brush lightly with melted butter. Working in batches of 4 to 6, spoon 2 tablespoons batter per blini onto griddle, spreading with spoon to form 3-inch rounds. Cook blini, turning once, until golden, about 2 minutes total. Transfer to a platter and keep warm in oven, loosely covered with foil. Brush griddle lightly with butter as needed between batches.

Serve each blini topped with sour cream and one kind of caviar.

COOK'S NOTES

- The blini can be wrapped in foil packages of 8 to 12 and refrigerated for up to 2 days or frozen for up to 1 month. Reheat, still in the foil, in a 350°F oven until heated through, 10 minutes if refrigerated, 20 if frozen.
- The blini recipe can be doubled, but use only 1 package of yeast.

Fresh Corn Madeleines with Sour Cream and Caviar

MAKES ABOUT 36 HORS D'OEUVRES
ACTIVE TIME: 25 MINUTES ■ START TO FINISH: 45 MINUTES

■ The batter of these miniature madeleines contains fresh corn, which makes them extra moist. Corn and caviar are a natural combination (maybe because corn always benefits from a little salt), but you don't really need the caviar; try topping the madeleines with sour cream and a dab of salsa, or eat them perfectly plain with tomato soup. ■

FOR MADELEINES

1 tablespoon unsalted butter, melted, plus additional for brushing molds
1/3 cup yellow cornmeal (not coarse)
2 tablespoons all-purpose flour
1/2 teaspoon sugar
1/4 teaspoon baking soda
1/4 teaspoon salt
1/8 teaspoon freshly ground black pepper
1 large egg
1/3 cup well-shaken buttermilk
1/2 cup fresh corn kernels, chopped

FOR TOPPING

About 1/3 cup sour cream
50 grams (1 3/4 ounces) caviar, preferably sevruga

OPTIONAL GARNISH: chopped fresh chives

SPECIAL EQUIPMENT: a miniature madeleine pan with 20 (½-tablespoon) molds, preferably nonstick (see Sources); a small pastry bag fitted with a small star or leaf tip (optional)

MAKE THE MADELEINES: Put a rack in middle of oven and preheat oven to 400°F. Brush molds with melted butter.

Whisk together cornmeal, flour, sugar, baking soda, salt, and pepper in a medium bowl. Whisk together egg, buttermilk, 1 tablespoon melted butter, and corn in another bowl, then add to dry ingredients, stirring just until combined.

Spoon 1 teaspoon batter into each mold. Bake until madeleines are golden around edges and spring back when pressed lightly, 5 to 6 minutes. Turn madeleines out onto a rack to cool completely. Repeat with remaining batter.

TOP THE MADELEINES: Put sour cream in pastry bag, if using, and pipe (or spoon) about ½ teaspoon onto each madeleine. Top each with a rounded ¼ teaspoon caviar and sprinkle with chives, if desired.

Caviar

Because real Caspian caviar is a diminishing resource, sturgeon roe is extremely expensive and should be purchased with caution. You can find bargain caviar, but it usually costs less for a reason: often it is old, with a musty or even mildewed flavor. Buy fresh, unpasteurized caviar from a reputable dealer. If you're going to order in any quantity, purchase a small amount first and taste it to make sure you're getting what you want. Caviar varies from batch to batch.

BELUGA, the largest, mildest, and most expensive, comes from huge sturgeon that weigh about 1,800 pounds and reach 20 feet in length. The best roe, which is called triple zero (000), is light gray and has a buttery flavor. Beluga is a little darker than the other caviars; the fragile eggs are soft and sweet, with a slightly creamy taste.

OSETRA sturgeon weigh only 80 to 100 pounds, and their eggs are a bit smaller, with a golden streak and a fruity, almost nutty flavor that sets the caviar apart from the others. The finest golden osetra, which was once reserved for the czars, is especially beautiful, with a complex range of flavors.

SEVRUGA, from the smallest sturgeon, is the smallest-grained of all the caviars, with the most powerful flavor. The color can vary from light gray to black, the flavor from delicate to quite strong. Because the roe is smaller, you rarely get the "pop" you do from beluga.

PRESSED CAVIAR is a good option if you like your caviar on blini, slathered with crème fraîche and all the accoutrements. Thick, almost sticky, and jamlike, it is made from sevruga and osetra roe that is too fragile to maintain its integrity. The roe is blended and heated, then pressed through fabric bags. Because it takes four pounds of roe to produce one pound of pressed caviar, the flavor is very strong, but if you love caviar, you will undoubtedly love pressed caviar.

Caspian sturgeon is under increasing pressure from pollution, habitat loss, and overfishing, but take heart: your caviar dreams don't have to countenance an environmental nightmare. In tasting several farm-raised domestic caviars, we found Sterling Classic white sturgeon caviar from Stolt Sea Farm delicious and fresh-tasting, with a great texture. And the rainbow trout caviar from Sunburst Trout Company elicited raves, even from those who don't like salmon roe. (See Sources.)

COOK'S NOTE

▪ The madeleines are best baked no more than 6 hours ahead. Once they are cooled, keep in an airtight container at room temperature until ready to top and serve.

Virginia Ham and Melon Apple Chutney on Corn Bread Rounds

MAKES 24 HORS D'OEUVRES
ACTIVE TIME: 1¼ HOURS ▪ START TO FINISH: 2 HOURS

▪ Virginia is for history and ham. At least, that's what Eugene Walter wrote in the classic *American Cooking: Southern Style,* one of the best in the Foods of the World series published by Time-Life. A Virginia country ham is cured with salt, smoked, and aged according to a centuries-old method. When served with biscuits, it should be sliced paper-thin. Instead of the usual biscuits, though, we use thin corn bread rounds, which manage to be sturdy and delicate at once. ▪

FOR CORN BREAD ROUNDS
- ⅔ cup yellow cornmeal
- ⅓ cup all-purpose flour
- 2 tablespoons sugar
- ½ teaspoon baking powder
- ½ teaspoon salt
- 5 tablespoons unsalted butter, melted and cooled
- 2 tablespoons whole milk
- 1 large egg

FOR TOPPING
- About 2 tablespoons Dijon mustard
- ¼ pound sliced cooked Virginia country ham (see Sources), cut into 1½-by-⅓-inch strips
- ½ cup Melon Apple Chutney (recipe follows)

SPECIAL EQUIPMENT: a 1½-inch round cookie cutter

MAKE THE CORN BREAD ROUNDS: Put a rack in middle of oven and preheat oven to 350°F. Generously grease a 13-by-9-inch baking pan.

Whisk together cornmeal, flour, sugar, baking powder, and salt in a medium bowl. Whisk together butter, milk, and egg in a small bowl, then add to cornmeal mixture and stir just until combined. Spread, preferably with an offset spatula, or pat out batter in a very thin, even layer in greased baking pan.

Bake until firm and pale golden, 20 to 25 minutes. Cut out 24 rounds from hot corn bread with cookie cutter and transfer rounds to a rack to cool. (Reserve remaining corn bread for another use.)

ASSEMBLE THE ROUNDS: Spread each round with a thin layer of mustard, then top with a few strips of ham and about 1 teaspoon chutney.

COOK'S NOTE

▪ The corn bread rounds can be made up to 1 day ahead. Cool, then keep in an airtight container at room temperature.

Melon Apple Chutney

MAKES ABOUT 1 CUP
ACTIVE TIME: 20 MINUTES ▪ START TO FINISH: 1¼ HOURS

▪ This recipe makes more chutney than you'll need for the corn bread rounds, but it's a great condiment for cheese and crackers or roasted meats. ▪

- 1 (1½-inch) piece cinnamon stick
- 2 whole cloves
- 5 allspice berries
- ¾ cup diced (¼-inch) cantaloupe or honeydew, or a combination
- 1 Granny Smith apple, peeled, cored, and cut into ¼-inch dice
- ½ cup sugar
- 6 tablespoons distilled white vinegar
- 3 tablespoons dried currants
- 2 tablespoons minced peeled fresh ginger
- Pinch of salt

SPECIAL EQUIPMENT: cheesecloth; kitchen string

Wrap cinnamon stick, cloves, and allspice in a 6-inch square of cheesecloth and tie with string to form a bag. Crush spices gently in bag with a rolling pin or the bottom of a heavy skillet.

Combine melon, apple, sugar, vinegar, currants, ginger, salt, and cheesecloth bag in a 1½-quart heavy saucepan and bring to a boil. Reduce heat and simmer, uncovered, stirring occasionally, until syrup is thick and most of liquid has evaporated, 30 to 35 minutes. (Syrup will continue to thicken as it cools.)

Discard cheesecloth bag and let chutney cool.

COOK'S NOTE

- The chutney can be made up to 2 days ahead and refrigerated, covered. Bring to room temperature before using.

Fried Zucchini Blossoms

MAKES 18 HORS D'OEUVRES
ACTIVE TIME: 25 MINUTES ■ START TO FINISH: 25 MINUTES

■ These taste like summer. Whether you pick blossoms from your garden or buy them at the farmers market, choose male flowers. Recognizable by their long, straight stems and the unmistakably male-looking stamen in the center of each blossom, the males don't produce a vegetable but exist to pollinate the females. Some chefs like to fry female blossoms with tiny baby zucchini still attached, but Mexican and Italian purists wouldn't hear of it. Other chefs like to remove the stamen of the male flowers, but it isn't necessary. What *is* necessary is a quick peek inside each blossom to check for bugs before frying. ■

2/3 cup all-purpose flour
2/3 cup club soda or beer (not dark)
1/4 teaspoon salt
About 4 cups vegetable oil for deep-frying
18 zucchini blossoms
SPECIAL EQUIPMENT: a deep-fat thermometer

Whisk together flour, club soda, and salt in a bowl until smooth.

Heat 1 inch oil in a 3-quart wide heavy saucepan over moderate heat until it registers 375°F on thermometer. Working in batches of 3, dip blossoms in batter to coat, brushing them against side of bowl to remove excess batter, and fry, turning occasionally with a slotted spoon, until golden, 1 to 2 minutes per batch. Transfer to paper towels to drain and sprinkle lightly with salt. (Return oil to 375°F between batches.) Serve warm.

COOK'S NOTES

- The batter can be made up to 2 hours ahead and refrigerated, covered. Bring to room temperature and whisk again before using.
- The first batches of fried blossoms can be kept warm on a baking sheet in a 350°F oven until all the blossoms are fried.
- The blossoms can also be panfried, but they will not be as crisp and three-dimensional as the deep-fried ones. Instead of making batter, stir together 1/2 cup all-purpose flour and 1/2 teaspoon salt and toss the blossoms in the flour, shaking off the excess. Heat 2 tablespoons unsalted butter in a 12-inch heavy skillet over moderately high heat until the foam subsides. Add the blossoms in batches and cook, stirring, until they just begin to wilt, 1 to 2 minutes.

Fried Eggplant Sticks

MAKES ABOUT 36 HORS D'OEUVRES
ACTIVE TIME: 30 MINUTES ■ START TO FINISH: 1 HOUR

■ Coating the eggplant sticks in seasoned flour and bread crumbs before you fry them causes them to become crisp on the outside and almost custardy on the inside, a great contrast in texture. But then there's the unusual trick of dipping them in confectioners' sugar, which is how they're served at the restaurant McKinnon's Louisiane, in New Orleans. It may sound a little wacky, but it really works. These are good dipped in coarse salt too. ■

1 (1-pound) eggplant, peeled, cut lengthwise into 1/2-inch slices, and then into 3-by-1/2-inch sticks
1 teaspoon salt
2 cups all-purpose flour
1/4 teaspoon freshly ground black pepper
2/3 cup evaporated milk
2 cups fine dry bread crumbs
About 4 cups vegetable oil for deep-frying
ACCOMPANIMENT: confectioners' sugar or kosher salt
SPECIAL EQUIPMENT: a deep-fat thermometer

Toss eggplant sticks with 1/2 teaspoon salt in a colander. Let stand in sink or on a plate for 30 minutes.

Line a baking sheet with wax paper. Combine flour, pepper, and remaining 1/2 teaspoon salt in a large bowl or paper bag. Pour milk into a shallow dish and put bread crumbs in another shallow dish.

Pat eggplant dry and toss in flour mixture until well coated, then put in a coarse sieve and shake off excess flour. Dip eggplant sticks a few at a time in milk, letting excess drip off, dredge them in bread crumbs, shaking off excess, and transfer to lined baking sheet, arranging them in one layer.

Heat 1 inch oil in a 4-quart heavy saucepan over moderate heat until it registers 350°F on thermometer. Fry eggplant sticks in batches of 12, turning, until golden brown, about 2 minutes per batch. Transfer to paper towels to drain. (Return oil to 350°F between batches.) Serve warm with a small bowl of confectioners' sugar or kosher salt for dipping.

Sesame Tempura Green Beans with Soy Dipping Sauce

SERVES 6

ACTIVE TIME: 20 MINUTES ■ START TO FINISH: 20 MINUTES

■ Tempura is one of Japan's great gifts to the culinary world. Though you might not think of green beans as party food, when dressed up in lacy tempura, they're a knockout. The sesame seeds in the batter add both flavor and crunch. ■

About 7 cups vegetable oil for deep-frying
2 tablespoons soy sauce
2 teaspoons fresh lime juice
1 teaspoon superfine sugar
1 cup all-purpose flour
1/4 cup sesame seeds
1 cup beer (not dark)
3/4 pound green beans, trimmed
Salt

SPECIAL EQUIPMENT: a deep-fat thermometer

Heat 2 inches oil in a 4-quart heavy saucepan over moderate heat until it registers 365°F on thermometer. Meanwhile, make dipping sauce by stirring together soy sauce, lime juice, and sugar in a small bowl until sugar is dissolved. Make batter by whisking together flour and sesame seeds in another small bowl, then add beer and whisk until smooth.

When oil is hot, toss about 10 beans in batter until coated, then add to oil one at a time (to keep them separate) and fry, turning, until golden, about 1 1/2 minutes. Transfer to paper towels to drain and sprinkle with salt. Coat and fry remaining beans in same manner. (Return oil to 365°F between batches.)

Serve beans with dipping sauce.

COOK'S NOTE

■ Like other seeds, sesame seeds have a high oil content and become rancid easily, so buy them from a shop with a quick turnover (a natural foods store is often your best bet) and smell them before using. Store them in the freezer.

Hundred-Corner Shrimp Balls

MAKES ABOUT 45 HORS D'OEUVRES

ACTIVE TIME: 1 HOUR ■ START TO FINISH: 5 HOURS (INCLUDES DRYING)

■ We think this recipe, from Nina Simonds, the Chinese cooking authority and longtime contributor to our pages, is one of the greatest hors d'oeuvre recipes we've ever published. Think of it as a fancy version of shrimp toast: balls of shrimp filling are rolled in little cubes of bread, then twice-fried to a burnished golden brown. The faceted corners of the diced bread give this hors d'oeuvre an unusual and elegant shape. If the Museum of Modern Art exhibited food, this would be a gallery draw. (For more about the Asian ingredients, see Glossary.) ■

20 slices very thin firm white sandwich bread, crusts discarded, cut into 1/4-inch dice
1/2 cup drained canned whole water chestnuts
18 ounces large shrimp in shells (21–25 per pound), peeled and deveined

1 large egg white, lightly beaten
2 tablespoons finely chopped pork fat or lard
1 tablespoon Chinese rice wine or sake
1½ teaspoons minced peeled fresh ginger
1½ teaspoons minced scallion
¾ teaspoon salt
1½ tablespoons cornstarch
About 8 cups peanut oil or corn oil for deep-frying
3 tablespoons kosher salt
1 tablespoon crushed Sichuan peppercorns, lightly toasted (see Tips, page 939), or 1 teaspoon *sansho* (Japanese pepper) plus ½ teaspoon freshly ground black pepper

SPECIAL EQUIPMENT: a deep-fat thermometer

Spread bread cubes in one layer on a baking sheet and let dry at room temperature for at least 4 hours.

Blanch water chestnuts in boiling water for 1 minute. Drain and rinse under cold water. Pat dry and finely chop.

Purée shrimp in a food processor. Transfer to a medium bowl and stir in water chestnuts, egg white, pork fat, rice wine, ginger, scallion, salt, and cornstarch. Beat shrimp mixture vigorously with a wooden spoon, throwing it against side of bowl to combine well and compact it. Dip your hands in cold water and form a rounded teaspoon of mixture into a ball, then roll ball in bread cubes, pressing cubes in lightly. Place on a baking sheet and make more shrimp balls in same manner, arranging in one layer on baking sheet.

Heat 2 inches oil in a 5- to 6-quart heavy pot over moderate heat until it registers 375°F on thermometer. Fry shrimp balls in batches of 8, turning several times, until golden, 1 to 2 minutes per batch. Transfer to paper towels to drain. (Return oil to 375°F between batches.)

Heat oil until it registers 375°F again. Fry shrimp balls again in 4 batches, turning frequently, until deep golden, about 1 minute per batch. Transfer shrimp balls to fresh paper towels to drain.

Stir together kosher salt and peppercorns in a small bowl. Serve shrimp balls with peppercorn mixture for dipping.

COOK'S NOTE

- The bread dice can be left to dry for up to 12 hours.

Spicy Lemon-Marinated Shrimp

MAKES ABOUT 20 HORS D'OEUVRES
ACTIVE TIME: 1 HOUR ■ START TO FINISH: 9 HOURS (INCLUDES MARINATING)

■ We've taken a southern classic, pickled shrimp, and added a new flavor that is actually very old. Dried Aleppo chile flakes are from the Aleppo province of northern Syria. Their earthy, robust flavor, with more richness than heat, is famous throughout the Middle East. If you substitute New Mexico chile flakes or plain old red pepper flakes, you will have something a little different yet still excellent. ■

1 large lemon
1½ teaspoons coriander seeds
3 tablespoons white wine vinegar
1 tablespoon olive oil
1 tablespoon water
1 tablespoon sugar
1½ teaspoons Aleppo or New Mexico chile flakes (see Glossary) or a rounded ¼ teaspoon red pepper flakes
1 tablespoon plus 2½ teaspoons kosher salt
2 tablespoons pickling spices
1 pound large shrimp in shells (21–25 per pound), peeled, tail and first shell segment left intact, and deveined

SPECIAL EQUIPMENT: an electric coffee/spice grinder

Remove zest from lemon with a vegetable peeler and remove any white pith from zest strips with a sharp paring knife. Halve lemon and squeeze 3 tablespoons juice.

Finely grind coriander in coffee/spice grinder. Whisk together coriander, zest, juice, vinegar, oil, water, sugar, chile flakes, and 2½ teaspoons salt in a large bowl until sugar and salt are dissolved.

Fill a 3- to 4-quart saucepan with water, add pickling spices and remaining 1 tablespoon salt, and bring to a boil. Add shrimp and boil until just cooked through, about 1½ minutes. Drain well, then add warm shrimp to marinade and toss to coat. Let cool slightly.

Transfer shrimp and marinade to a large sealable plastic bag. Marinate shrimp, refrigerated, turning bag occasionally, for at least 8 hours.

Drain shrimp before serving.

COOK'S NOTE

- The shrimp can marinate for up to 3 days.

Cilantro Lime Shrimp

MAKES ABOUT 24 HORS D'OEUVRES
ACTIVE TIME: 30 MINUTES ■ START TO FINISH: 35 MINUTES

■ This is ridiculously simple and really refreshing. The citrus, cilantro, and red pepper flakes make for a beautiful balance of hot and sour. ■

- 3 large garlic cloves
- 1⅛ teaspoons salt
- ½ cup fresh lime juice
- ¼ cup sweet orange marmalade
- ¼ cup finely chopped fresh cilantro
- 4 tablespoons olive oil
- 1 tablespoon soy sauce
- ½ teaspoon red pepper flakes
- ½ teaspoon freshly ground black pepper
- 1 pound large shrimp in shells (21–25 per pound), peeled, tail and first segment of shell left intact, and deveined

OPTIONAL GARNISH: fresh cilantro sprigs

Using a large knife, mince and mash garlic to a paste with 1 teaspoon salt. Whisk together garlic paste, lime juice, marmalade, cilantro, 3 tablespoons oil, soy sauce, red pepper flakes, remaining ⅛ teaspoon salt, and pepper in a small bowl. Transfer ⅓ cup mixture to another small bowl or ramekin and reserve for dipping sauce. Combine shrimp with remaining mixture in a large sealable plastic bag and seal bag, pressing out excess air. Marinate shrimp, refrigerated, turning bag once, for 15 minutes.

Drain shrimp and gently pat dry. Heat 1½ teaspoons oil in a 12-inch nonstick skillet over moderately high heat. Add half of shrimp and cook, turning occasionally, until golden brown and just cooked through, about 3 minutes total. Transfer shrimp to a platter and cook remaining shrimp in remaining 1½ teaspoons oil in same manner.

Garnish shrimp with cilantro, if desired, and serve with dipping sauce.

Coconut Shrimp with Tamarind Ginger Sauce

MAKES ABOUT 48 HORS D'OEUVRES
ACTIVE TIME: 1 HOUR ■ START TO FINISH: 1 HOUR

■ Coconut shrimp can sometimes be too sweet or the coating too thick, but these are just perfect. Tamarind gives the sauce a deep, sophisticated tang. The combination of the two is a real taste of the Caribbean. ■

FOR SAUCE

- 1 teaspoon tamarind concentrate (see Glossary)
- 1½ tablespoons fresh lime juice
- ⅔ cup mayonnaise
- 1½ tablespoons mild honey
- 2 teaspoons Dijon mustard
- 1 teaspoon finely grated peeled fresh ginger
- ¼ teaspoon salt

FOR SHRIMP

- 4 cups (about 10 ounces) sweetened flaked coconut, coarsely chopped
- 1 cup all-purpose flour
- ¾ cup beer (not dark)
- ¾ teaspoon baking soda
- ½ teaspoon salt
- 1 teaspoon cayenne
- 1 large egg
- About 7 cups vegetable oil for deep-frying
- 1½ pounds medium shrimp in shells (31–35 per pound), peeled, tail and first segment of shell left intact, and deveined

SPECIAL EQUIPMENT: a deep-fat thermometer

MAKE THE SAUCE: Whisk tamarind concentrate into lime juice in a small bowl until dissolved. Stir in remaining sauce ingredients.

PREPARE THE SHRIMP: Spread half of coconut in a shallow soup bowl or pie plate. Whisk together flour, beer, baking soda, salt, cayenne, and egg in a small bowl until smooth.

Heat 2 inches oil in a 4- to 5-quart deep heavy pot over moderately high heat until it registers 350°F on thermometer. While oil is heating, coat shrimp: Hold 1 shrimp by tail and dip into batter, letting excess drip off, then dredge in coconut, coating completely and pressing gently to help it adhere. Transfer to a plate and coat remaining shrimp in same manner, adding remaining coconut to bowl as needed.

Fry shrimp in batches of 8, turning once, until golden, about 1 minute per batch. Transfer to paper towels to drain and season lightly with salt. (Skim any coconut from oil and return oil to 350°F between batches.)

Serve shrimp with sauce.

COOK'S NOTE

- The sauce can be made up to 6 hours ahead and refrigerated, covered. Bring to room temperature before serving.

Miniature Crab Cakes with Tomato Ginger Jam

MAKES ABOUT 36 HORS D'OEUVRES
ACTIVE TIME: 1¾ HOURS ■ START TO FINISH: 5 HOURS (INCLUDES CHILLING AND MAKING JAM)

■ We love these crab cakes because they are baked, not sautéed, which makes things easy. The cornflake coating adds crunch and a little sweetness. ■

- ½ cup mayonnaise
- 1 large egg
- 1 tablespoon Dijon mustard
- ¾ teaspoon Old Bay Seasoning
- 1½ teaspoons fresh lemon juice
- ¼ teaspoon salt
- ⅛ teaspoon freshly ground black pepper
- ⅛ teaspoon Tabasco
- 1 pound jumbo lump crabmeat, picked over for shells and cartilage
- 4 cups cornflakes

OPTIONAL GARNISH: thinly sliced fresh cilantro leaves
ACCOMPANIMENT: Tomato Ginger Jam (recipe follows)

Whisk together mayonnaise, egg, mustard, Old Bay, lemon juice, salt, pepper, and Tabasco in a medium bowl. Gently stir in crabmeat. Refrigerate, covered, for 2 hours.

Butter two baking sheets. Pulse cornflakes in a food processor until coarsely ground. Spread in a shallow dish. Form 1 heaping teaspoon crab mixture into a 1½-inch-diameter cake (mixture will be very moist), then gently dredge in cornflakes and transfer to a buttered baking sheet. Make more crab cakes in same manner. Refrigerate, covered, for at least 1 hour.

Put a rack in middle of oven and preheat oven to 400°F.

Bake crab cakes in two batches until crisp and golden, 8 to 10 minutes. Transfer with a spatula to a platter, top each with about ½ tablespoon jam, and garnish with cilantro, if desired.

COOK'S NOTE

- The unbaked crab cakes can be refrigerated, covered, for up to 4 hours.

Tomato Ginger Jam

MAKES ABOUT 1¼ CUPS
ACTIVE TIME: 30 MINUTES ■ START TO FINISH: 1 HOUR

■ Slightly Indian in its flavors, this condiment is also delicious with shrimp or scallops, or with cheese—Cheddar, goat cheese, or even cream cheese on a cracker. ■

- 2 tablespoons unsalted butter
- ¼ cup minced shallots
- 1 tablespoon finely grated peeled fresh ginger
- 1 large garlic clove, minced
- ¾ teaspoon salt
- ¼ teaspoon freshly ground black pepper
- ⅛ teaspoon red pepper flakes
- 1 tablespoon sugar
- 1½ pounds plum tomatoes, halved, seeded, and finely chopped
- 1½ tablespoons fresh lime juice
- 2 tablespoons finely chopped fresh cilantro

Melt butter in a 10-inch heavy skillet over moderately low heat. Add shallots, ginger, garlic, salt, black pepper, and red pepper flakes and cook, stirring, until shallots are softened, about 5 minutes. Add sugar and cook, stirring, until dissolved. Add tomatoes, increase heat to moderate, and simmer, stirring occasionally, until thickened, 10 to 15 minutes.

Let jam cool to room temperature, then stir in lime juice and cilantro. Serve at room temperature.

COOK'S NOTE

- The jam can be made up to 2 days ahead, without the lime juice and cilantro, and refrigerated, covered. Stir in the lime juice and cilantro just before serving.

Panko Scallops with Green Chile Chutney

MAKES 60 HORS D'OEUVRES
ACTIVE TIME: 1¼ HOURS ■ START TO FINISH: 1¼ HOURS

■ As evidenced by this recipe, the Japanese bread crumbs called panko make the best possible coating for seafood, turning a beautiful golden brown and holding their crunchiness. The accompanying chutney has classic Indian flavors, but it is easily made because it uses packaged dried coconut rather than the fresh coconut called for in traditional recipes. ■

FOR CHUTNEY

2 cups chopped fresh cilantro
½ cup chopped scallions
¼ cup sweetened flaked coconut
2–3 serrano or jalapeño chiles (to taste), chopped, including seeds
3 tablespoons vegetable oil
1½ tablespoons finely grated peeled fresh ginger
2½ tablespoons fresh lime juice, or to taste
2 tablespoons water
Salt and freshly ground black pepper

FOR SCALLOPS

60 small sea scallops (3½ pounds), tough side muscle removed from each if necessary
Salt and freshly ground black pepper
2 large eggs
¼ cup whole milk
3 cups panko (Japanese bread crumbs) or coarse dry bread crumbs
About 1 cup vegetable oil

MAKE THE CHUTNEY: Combine all ingredients except salt and pepper in a blender and purée until smooth. Transfer to a bowl and season with salt and pepper. Refrigerate, covered.

PREPARE THE SCALLOPS: Pat scallops dry and season with salt and pepper. Whisk together eggs and milk in a shallow bowl. Put panko in another shallow bowl. Dip scallops one at a time in egg mixture and then in panko, turning to coat, and transfer to a tray.

Put a rack in middle of oven and preheat oven to 400°F.

Heat 3 tablespoons oil in a 12-inch nonstick skillet over moderate heat until hot but not smoking. Cook scallops in 5 batches, turning once, until just cooked through and golden brown, about 3 minutes per batch. Transfer to a rack set in a shallow baking pan, arranging scallops in one layer. Wipe skillet clean with paper towels between batches and add more oil as needed.

PANKO

Bread has been big stuff in Japan ever since the Portuguese took their bread-baking knowledge to the country around 1600. The bread crumbs called panko might more accurately be called bread *shards;* a sweet, spongy, squared-off loaf is dried, then grated, which gives the crumbs their unique texture. After frying, the fluffy, crisp flakes turn a lovely golden brown, and they stay crunchy longer than ordinary bread crumbs because they absorb less grease. Panko is available at Japanese and other Asian markets, many fish stores, and the seafood departments of many supermarkets, and by mail (see Sources).

Transfer pan of scallops to oven and heat through, about 3 minutes. Serve scallops topped with chutney.

COOK'S NOTES

- The chutney can be made up to 3 days ahead. Season again with salt and pepper before serving.
- The scallops can be coated with panko up to 4 hours ahead and refrigerated, loosely covered.
- The scallops can be fried up to 1 hour ahead and kept at room temperature. Reheat in the oven before serving.

Salt Cod Fritters

MAKES ABOUT 70 HORS D'OEUVRES
ACTIVE TIME: 1 HOUR ■ START TO FINISH: 1½ HOURS PLUS 1 TO 3 DAYS FOR SOAKING COD

■ We are big fans of these fritters (who doesn't love fried food?), especially in cold weather, when one bite makes you think of the sunny Caribbean. Because they're sturdy enough to be made ahead and reheated, they're great party fare. ■

- ½ pound choice-grade, center-cut, skinless, boneless salt cod (see page 19), rinsed well and cut into 2-inch pieces
- 1 cup all-purpose flour
- ¼ cup whole milk
- 1 large egg
- ¾ teaspoon baking powder
- Rounded ¼ teaspoon ground allspice
- 2 garlic cloves, minced
- 1 large fresh hot red or green chile, such as New Mexico (see Glossary), seeded if desired and minced
- 3 scallions, finely chopped
- 1 tablespoon finely chopped fresh cilantro
- About 6 cups vegetable oil for deep-frying

SPECIAL EQUIPMENT: a deep-fat thermometer
ACCOMPANIMENT: Caribbean Spicy Dipping Sauce (recipe follows)

Soak cod in a large bowl of water to cover by 2 inches, refrigerated, for 1 to 3 days, changing water three times a day to remove excess salt. Drain well and refrigerate until ready to use.

Grind cod as fine as possible in a food processor. Add flour, milk, egg, baking powder, allspice, and garlic and blend well. Transfer to a bowl and stir in chile, scallions, and cilantro.

Preheat oven to 300°F.

Heat 1½ inches oil in a 4- to 5-quart heavy pot over high heat until it registers 360°F on thermometer. Working in batches of 10, drop teaspoons of fish mixture into oil and fry, stirring and turning, until golden and cooked through, 1 to 2 minutes per batch. With a slotted spoon, transfer fritters to paper towels to drain, then keep warm in a baking sheet with sides in oven. (Return oil to 360°F between batches.)

Serve fritters with sauce for dipping.

COOK'S NOTE

- The fritters can be made up to 2 hours ahead and refrigerated, covered. Reheat on a baking sheet with sides in a 450°F oven for about 5 minutes.

Caribbean Spicy Dipping Sauce
Sauce Chien

MAKES ABOUT 1 CUP
ACTIVE TIME: 15 MINUTES ■ START TO FINISH: 45 MINUTES

■ In the Caribbean, the colorful and etymologically mysterious *sauce chien* ("dog sauce") is as common as ketchup is in the United States. The sauce is supposed to be on the watery side. We like to think of it as a spicy wash for almost anything; try it on shellfish, grilled fish, or pork. ■

- ½ small onion, minced
- 1½ scallions, minced
- ¼ cup minced red bell pepper
- 1 garlic clove, minced
- ½ Scotch bonnet or habanero chile (see Glossary), seeded and minced, or ½ teaspoon Scotch bonnet pepper sauce (see Sources)
- ½ teaspoon salt
- ⅛ teaspoon dried thyme, crumbled
- ½ cup water
- 1 tablespoon white wine vinegar

2 tablespoons fresh lime juice
1 tablespoon vegetable oil
1 tablespoon chopped fresh cilantro, or to taste
OPTIONAL GARNISH: fresh cilantro sprigs

Stir together onion, scallions, bell pepper, garlic, chile, salt, and thyme in a small heatproof bowl. Bring water and vinegar to a boil in a small saucepan. Pour over vegetables and let cool.

Stir lime juice and oil into sauce, then stir in cilantro and transfer to a serving bowl. Garnish with cilantro sprigs, if desired.

COOK'S NOTE

- The sauce, without the cilantro, can be made up to 2 days ahead and refrigerated, covered. Bring to room temperature and stir in the cilantro before serving.

Italian Fried Salt Cod

MAKES ABOUT 25 HORS D'OEUVRES
ACTIVE TIME: 30 MINUTES ■ START TO FINISH: 30 MINUTES PLUS 1 TO 3 DAYS FOR SOAKING COD

■ Right off Rome's "food and flower square," the Campo de' Fiori, is a stand that's famous for its fried salt cod, *baccalà fritto*. It is sublime. The next best thing is this recipe. Fried in large pieces, the salt cod stays moist and delicious. ■

1 pound choice-grade, center-cut, skinless, boneless salt cod (see page 19), rinsed well
About 4 cups vegetable oil for deep-frying
1 cup all-purpose flour
½ teaspoon salt
2 tablespoons olive oil
½ cup plus 3 tablespoons water
¼ cup finely chopped fresh flat-leaf parsley
1 teaspoon coarse sea salt or kosher salt
ACCOMPANIMENT: lemon wedges
SPECIAL EQUIPMENT: a deep-fat thermometer

Soak cod in a large bowl of water to cover by 2 inches, refrigerated, for 1 to 3 days, changing water three times a day to remove excess salt. Drain well and refrigerate until ready to use.

Heat vegetable oil in a 5- to 6-quart heavy pot over moderate heat until it registers 385° to 390°F on thermometer. While oil is heating, whisk together flour, salt, olive oil, water, and parsley in a bowl. Pat cod dry, then cut into 3-by-½-inch strips.

Working in batches of 4, coat strips in batter, transfer to oil with tongs, and fry, turning, until golden, 1½ to 2 minutes per batch. Transfer to a paper towel–lined baking sheet to drain. (Return oil to 385° to 390°F between batches.)

Sprinkle cod with sea salt and serve immediately, with lemon wedges.

COOK'S NOTE

- If your sea salt is very coarse, you may want to crush it lightly with a mortar and pestle or the side of a large heavy knife.

Clams Casino

MAKES 24 HORS D'OEUVRES
ACTIVE TIME: 35 MINUTES ■ START TO FINISH: 1 HOUR

■ This concoction of baked clams with butter, shallots, and bacon was a favorite dish at the casino at Narragansett Pier, in Rhode Island; hence its name. The casino was built in 1883 by the famous New York architectural firm of McKim, Mead, and White, and the landscaping was by Frederick Law Olmsted, who designed Central Park. The main building is long since gone, but the Gilded Age lives on in these delicious morsels. On the East Coast, littlenecks are the clams of choice; a great alternative on the West Coast is Manilas. Don't be tempted to substitute sweet red bell pepper for the more pedestrian green bell pepper called for; the flavor of the green pepper, simultaneously racy and familiar, provides background and balance for the other flavors. ■

2½ cups kosher salt (for stabilizing clamshells)
24 small (about 2 inches wide) hard-shelled clams, well scrubbed
2 bacon slices, finely chopped
2 tablespoons unsalted butter

- 1/3 cup finely chopped shallots
- 1/2 cup finely diced (1/8-inch) green bell pepper
- 1 tablespoon finely chopped fresh flat-leaf parsley
- 1 teaspoon fresh lemon juice
- 1 tablespoon finely grated Parmigiano-Reggiano
- 1/8 teaspoon salt
- 1/8 teaspoon freshly ground black pepper

SPECIAL EQUIPMENT: a clam knife

Put a rack in middle of oven and preheat oven to 425°F. Spread 1½ cups kosher salt on a baking sheet with sides.

To shuck clams, grip one in a kitchen towel, with its hinge nearest you. Slide clam knife between the two shells at a point opposite hinge and rotate clam, sliding knife between shells, until knife reaches hinge (1). Cut through hinge, being careful to avoid center of clam (2). Open shells, sliding knife along underside of top shell to detach clam. Pull top shell off and discard. Slide knife under clam to detach it from bottom shell (3) and transfer clam to a bowl; reserve bottom shell. Repeat with remaining clams. Scrub reserved shells inside and out, then dry. Return clams to shells and nestle shells in salt on baking sheet to keep them stable.

Cook bacon in a 10-inch heavy skillet over moderate heat, stirring occasionally, until fat is rendered but bacon is not yet crisp, 3 to 5 minutes. With a slotted spoon, transfer bacon to paper towels to drain. Pour off and discard all but 2 teaspoons fat from skillet. Add butter and heat until foam subsides, then add shallots and green pepper and cook, stirring occasionally, until softened, about 5 minutes. Transfer to a small bowl, add bacon, parsley, lemon juice, cheese, salt, and pepper, and stir to combine.

Top each clam with a scant teaspoon of vegetable topping.

Bake clams until juices are bubbling and tops are golden, about 12 minutes. Meanwhile, spread remaining 1 cup kosher salt on a platter.

Serve clams hot, nestled in salt on platter.

HOW TO SHUCK CLAMS

1

2

3

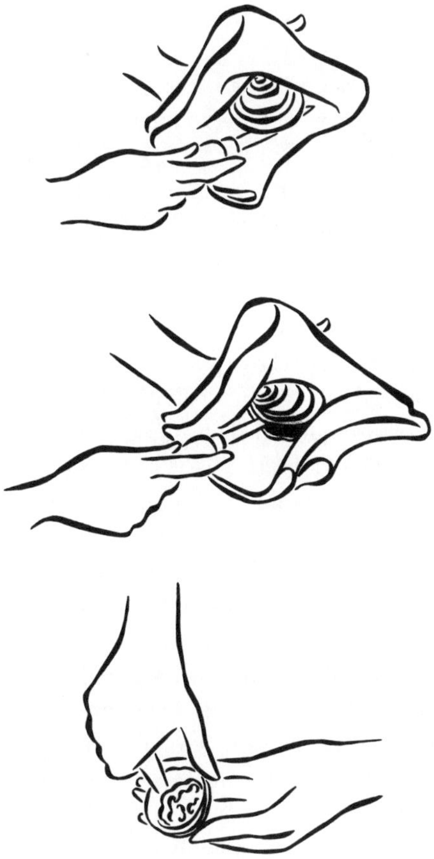

COOK'S NOTE

- The vegetable topping can be made up to 1 day ahead. Cool completely, uncovered, then refrigerate, covered.

Clams Perce

MAKES 24 HORS D'OEUVRES

ACTIVE TIME: 50 MINUTES ■ START TO FINISH: 50 MINUTES

■ This recipe is delicious and incredibly easy; essentially, all you need besides kitchen staples are the clams and a package of poultry stuffing (we like Pepperidge Farm). The most common small hard-shelled clam on the East Coast is the littleneck; cooks on the West Coast might want to use Manilas. These baked clams are the creation of Perce (pronounced "Percy") Goodale, the owner of a Manhattan watering hole that was frequented by publishing types. ■

24 small (about 2 inches wide) hard-shelled clams, well scrubbed
1½ cups kosher salt (for stabilizing clamshells)
1 cup packaged dry poultry stuffing, larger pieces crushed
¼ cup finely grated Parmigiano-Reggiano
3 bacon slices, each cut into 8 pieces
Worcestershire sauce

ACCOMPANIMENT: lemon wedges

Bring 1 cup water to a boil in a 4-quart heavy saucepan. Add clams, cover, and cook, stirring occasionally, until clams just open wide, 4 to 8 minutes; check frequently after 4 minutes and transfer clams as they open with a slotted spoon to a bowl. Discard any clams that have not opened.

Preheat broiler. Spread kosher salt on a baking sheet with sides.

Slide a paring knife or a clam knife under each clam to detach it from bottom shell and reserve 24 half shells. Scrub reserved shells inside and out, then dry thoroughly. Return clams to shells and nestle shells in salt on baking sheet to keep them stable. Divide stuffing and cheese among clams. Top each with a piece of bacon and a drop of Worcestershire sauce.

Broil clams 5 to 6 inches from heat until bacon is cooked and stuffing is golden brown, 2 to 3 minutes. Serve immediately, with lemon wedges.

Oysters Rockefeller

MAKES 36 HORS D'OEUVRES
ACTIVE TIME: 40 MINUTES ■ START TO FINISH: 2 HOURS

■ New Orleans, 1899. The restaurant? Antoine's. The dish of the moment? Oysters Rockefeller, so named because it was very rich, very . . . fin de siècle. Antoine's has never given out the recipe but says that oysters were a last-minute substitution for snails and the kitchen used whatever greens were available, with the exception of spinach—which, ironically, has become part of the dish. There have been many permutations over the years. This version is so good that authenticity seems irrelevant. ■

36 large oysters, scrubbed and shucked, ¼ cup liquor and bottom shells reserved
¼ pound Boston lettuce, trimmed and finely chopped (2 cups)
3 ounces baby spinach, coarse stems discarded, finely chopped (2 cups)
½ cup minced scallions
1¼ cups fine dry bread crumbs
¼ cup minced fresh flat-leaf parsley
2 tablespoons minced celery
1 garlic clove, minced
1 stick (8 tablespoons) unsalted butter
1 tablespoon Pernod or other anise-flavored liqueur
1½ teaspoons anchovy paste
Pinch of cayenne, or to taste
¼ teaspoon salt
¼ teaspoon freshly ground black pepper
6 lean bacon slices
3–4 cups kosher salt (for stabilizing oyster shells)

OPTIONAL GARNISH: fresh flat-leaf parsley sprigs
ACCOMPANIMENT: lemon wedges

Scrub reserved bottom oyster shells again to remove any grit or bits of oyster and dry thoroughly; set aside. Refrigerate oysters and reserved liquor separately, covered.

Stir together lettuce, spinach, scallions, ¼ cup bread crumbs, parsley, celery, and garlic in a large bowl. Heat butter in a 12-inch heavy skillet over moderate heat until foam subsides. Add lettuce mixture and cook, stirring, until greens are wilted, 1 to 2 minutes. Stir in Pernod, anchovy paste, cayenne, salt, and pepper. Spread mixture in a baking pan to cool to room temperature quickly, then refrigerate, covered, until cold, about 45 minutes.

Put a rack in middle of oven and preheat oven to 450°F.

Cook bacon in a large skillet over moderate heat until crisp, about 8 minutes. Transfer to paper towels to drain and cool, then crumble.

Spread kosher salt on two large baking sheets with sides. Place an oyster in each reserved shell and moisten oysters with some of reserved oyster liquor. Place a heaping teaspoon of vegetables on each oyster and sprinkle bacon over vegetables, then top bacon with remaining vegetables and sprinkle each oyster with a heaping teaspoon of remaining 1 cup bread crumbs. Nestle oysters, as you finish them, in salt on baking sheets to keep them upright.

Bake until edges of oysters begin to curl and bread crumbs are browned, 16 to 18 minutes. Spread kosher salt on a platter. Transfer baked oysters to platter and nestle in salt. Garnish oysters with parsley sprigs, if desired, and serve with lemon wedges.

Rumaki

Chicken Livers and Water Chestnuts Wrapped in Bacon

MAKES 24 HORS D'OEUVRES
ACTIVE TIME: 20 MINUTES ■ START TO FINISH: 1½ HOURS

■ We can thank Vic Bergeron, the owner of the original Trader Vic's restaurant, in San Francisco, for bringing rumaki into mainstream dining culture. He claimed that this hors d'oeuvre, with Chinese roots and a Japanese name, came from Hawaii. ■

- ¼ pound chicken livers, trimmed and rinsed
- ¼ cup soy sauce
- 1 tablespoon finely grated peeled fresh ginger
- 2 tablespoons packed light brown sugar
- ½ teaspoon curry powder
- 12 canned water chestnuts, rinsed, drained, and halved crosswise
- 8 bacon slices (½ pound), cut into thirds

SPECIAL EQUIPMENT: 24 wooden picks, soaked in cold water for 1 hour

Cut chicken livers into 24 (roughly ½-inch) pieces. Stir together soy sauce, ginger, brown sugar, and curry powder in a small bowl. Add livers and water chestnuts and toss to coat. Marinate, covered and refrigerated, for 1 hour.

Preheat broiler. Remove livers and chestnuts from marinade; discard marinade. Place a piece of bacon on a work surface and put a piece of liver and a chestnut half in center. Wrap bacon around liver and chestnut and secure with a wooden pick. Make more rumaki in same manner.

Broil rumaki on rack of broiler pan 2 inches from heat, turning once, until bacon is crisp and livers are cooked but still slightly pink inside (unwrap one to check for doneness), 5 to 6 minutes. Serve immediately.

SHUCKING OYSTERS

Arm yourself with a short, sturdy oyster knife (available at cookware shops and most fish markets) and a sturdy glove—almost any kind will do, even a gardening glove. Scrub the oysters thoroughly with a stiff brush under cold running water. Holding an oyster flat side up, so as not to lose any of the salty juices, or liquor, insert your oyster knife into the narrow hinged end and twist until the shell loosens and pops open (1). Don't be shy; this requires a certain amount of force. If the shell crumbles and will not open at the hinge, take it through the front door: aim your blade for the wide end of the shell. Slide the knife blade against the flat upper shell to cut the large muscle and free the oyster. After prying off the lid, slide your knife along the bottom shell to loosen the oyster from its mooring (2).

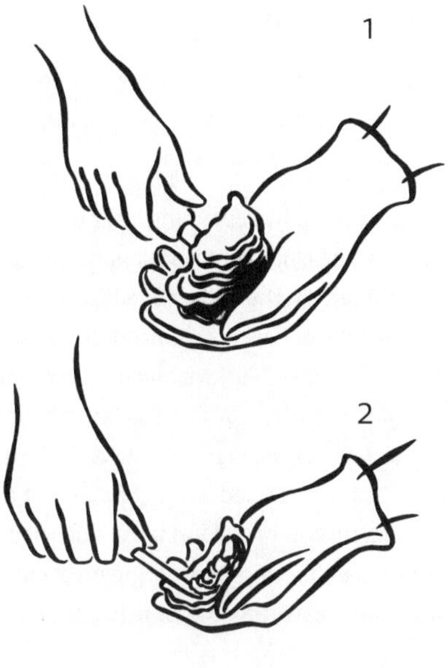

Buffalo Chicken Wings

MAKES 24 TO 28 HORS D'OEUVRES
ACTIVE TIME: 1 HOUR ■ START TO FINISH: 1¾ HOURS

■ Though common to cuisines around the world, chicken wings didn't really take off in the United States until the early 1960s. Their flight to fame is credited to Teressa and Frank Bellissimo, the owners of the Anchor Bar in Buffalo, New York. Mrs. Bellissimo, in an ingenious attempt to use up an overabundance of wings at the restaurant, deep-fried them, tossed them in her husband's hot sauce and melted butter, and served them with celery sticks and blue cheese dressing on the side—a cool, creamy antidote to the spicy blaze of the wings. Their bar food eventually spread across the country. You can deep-fry our wings à la Anchor Bar, but we think they're just as delicious grilled. ■

FOR BLUE CHEESE DIP

- ½ cup mayonnaise
- ¼ cup plain yogurt
- 2 ounces blue cheese, crumbled (½ cup)

FOR CHICKEN WINGS

- 3 pounds chicken wings, split at joint and wing tips discarded
- 2 tablespoons vegetable oil if grilling, about 6 cups vegetable oil if deep-frying

Salt

Table salt, kosher salt, and rock salt all come from salt mines, whereas sea salt is obtained by evaporating seawater. Some manufacturers add iodine to salt, for nutritional reasons, as well as free-flowing agents to prevent the crystals from clumping together.

TABLE SALT has small crystals. When iodine has been added, it's called iodized salt. In our recipes, when we call for just "salt," we mean table salt.

KOSHER SALT is preferred by many chefs because it's easy to grab when making a dish and doesn't dissolve on the fingers. It may or may not have additives, depending on the brand. When applied to salt, the word *kosher* doesn't mean kosher in the usual sense of conforming to Jewish dietary laws. (All salt, coarse or fine, is considered pareve — neither animal nor dairy.) Rather, it means that the salt is of a coarseness suitable for koshering meat and poultry. (One part of the koshering process is salting the meat to remove as much blood as possible. If the salt is too fine, it dissolves on the surface; if it is too coarse, the flakes or pellets won't draw out enough blood.)

ROCK SALT, usually found in hardware stores and used for melting snow, is very coarse grayish salt. Because it isn't manufactured under the same standards as table, kosher, and sea salts, it isn't FDA-approved for culinary use.

SEA SALT, available in coarse or fine crystals, comes from seawater that has been allowed to evaporate naturally. Depending on the brand, iodine and free-flowing agents may have been added. Most of the sea salt sold in the United States is imported. The most famous kind is from France's Brittany region. According to Mark Kurlansky, the author of *Salt: A World History,* Brittany's *sel gris* acquires its distinctive color when salt crystals sink to the gray earth at the bottom of the salt ponds. *Fleur de sel* is not *sel gris* washed white; it's lightweight crystals that float to the ponds' surface and are skimmed off. Other sea salts include Maldon, harvested in England since the Middle Ages; Anglesey, from Wales; Sicilian salt, from the huge salt flats at Trapani; Korean salt, which is roasted in bamboo cylinders; pink Hawaiian salt, harvested from clay salt pools; and black Hawaiian salt, from lava-lined pools.

Sea salt can add not just flavor but a spiky crunch to food, so it is best used as a garnish or condiment. Big, almost shardlike crystals of Maldon salt are delicious, for example, sprinkled on a tomato sandwich or grilled fish. If you do want to cook with sea salt (for some reason, greens seem especially delicious when cooked with *fleur de sel*), be aware that you can't substitute measure for measure (particularly in baking) if a recipe calls for table or kosher salt, so err on the cautious side.

Salt
½ stick (4 tablespoons) unsalted butter
3–4 tablespoons hot sauce, such as Frank's or Goya
1½ tablespoons cider vinegar

ACCOMPANIMENT: celery sticks, soaked in a bowl of ice and cold water for 30 minutes and drained

SPECIAL EQUIPMENT: a deep-fat thermometer if frying

MAKE THE DIP: Whisk together mayonnaise and yogurt in a small bowl, then stir in blue cheese (dip will not be smooth).

TO GRILL THE WINGS: Prepare a charcoal or gas grill: If using a charcoal grill, open vents in bottom of grill, then light charcoal. Fire is medium-hot when you can hold your hand 5 inches above rack for just 3 to 4 seconds. If using a gas grill, preheat on high, covered, for 10 minutes, then reduce heat to moderately high.

Pat wings dry and put in a bowl. Rub 2 tablespoons oil onto wings and season with salt. Lightly oil grill rack and grill wings, uncovered, turning once, until cooked through and golden brown, 16 to 20 minutes total. Transfer to a platter.

TO DEEP-FRY THE WINGS: Heat 1½ inches oil in a 5- to 6-quart deep heavy pot over high heat until it registers 380°F on thermometer. Pat 6 or 7 wings dry, carefully lower into oil, and fry, stirring occasionally, until cooked through, golden, and crisp, 5 to 8 minutes. Transfer to paper towels to drain. Fry remaining wings in same manner. (Return oil to 380°F between batches.)

COAT THE WINGS: Melt butter in a 12-inch skillet over moderately low heat. Stir in hot sauce, vinegar, and salt to taste. Add grilled or fried wings and toss to coat.

Serve wings warm or at room temperature, with dip and celery sticks.

COOK'S NOTE

- The dip can be made up to 8 hours ahead and refrigerated, covered.

"La Brea Tar Pit" Chicken Wings

MAKES 48 HORS D'OEUVRES
ACTIVE TIME: 15 MINUTES ■ START TO FINISH: 2 HOURS

■ It's easy to understand why chicken wings are so popular (as if all that crisp skin weren't enough of a reason). Economical and sold in just about every market, they capture the essence of relaxed entertaining: it's hard to stand on ceremony while eating with your fingers. Anyone who has ever visited the La Brea tar pits in Los Angeles will understand how this great-tasting hors d'oeuvre got its name. The recipe came to us from reader Metta Miller, from Boston, and it's a staff favorite. ■

4 pounds chicken wings, split at joint and wing tips discarded
1 cup soy sauce
½ cup dry red wine
½ cup plus 1 tablespoon sugar
¼ teaspoon ground ginger

Put a rack in middle of oven and preheat oven to 400°F.

Arrange wings in one layer in a large roasting pan.

Combine remaining ingredients in a small saucepan and heat over moderately low heat, stirring, until sugar is dissolved. Pour evenly over wings.

Bake for 45 minutes. Turn wings over and bake until sauce is thick and sticky, 1 hour to 1 hour and 10 minutes more. Transfer wings to a platter.

Chicken Saté with Peanut Curry Sauce

MAKES ABOUT 10 HORS D'OEUVRES
ACTIVE TIME: 25 MINUTES ■ START TO FINISH: 1½ HOURS

■ All the ingredients for these Southeast Asian skewers of grilled chicken are easy to find. We particularly love the sauce. It's not made in the usual way, with peanut butter, but with coconut milk and ground-up peanuts, which give it a coarser texture. You can broil the chicken (see Cook's Note) if you are unable to grill outdoors. ■

1½ cups well-stirred canned unsweetened coconut milk
1 tablespoon soy sauce
1½ teaspoons curry powder
¾ teaspoon ground coriander
2 teaspoons cornstarch
1 (¾-pound) whole skinless, boneless chicken breast
¾ cup salted dry-roasted peanuts, finely ground in a food processor
1 teaspoon fresh lime juice
¼ teaspoon red pepper flakes, or to taste
Salt

GARNISH: 1 teaspoon minced fresh cilantro

SPECIAL EQUIPMENT: about ten 8-inch bamboo skewers, soaked in cold water for 30 minutes

MARINATE THE CHICKEN: Whisk together coconut milk, soy sauce, curry powder, and coriander in a small bowl until well combined. Transfer ½ cup to another small bowl and stir in cornstarch until smooth. Cover and refrigerate remaining coconut mixture.

Cut chicken lengthwise into ½-inch-thick slices (about 10). Add to cornstarch mixture, stirring to coat. Marinate, covered and refrigerated, for at least 1 hour.

MAKE THE DIPPING SAUCE: Stir together reserved coconut mixture, peanuts, lime juice, and red pepper flakes in a small heavy saucepan and bring to a simmer. Simmer, stirring occasionally, until thickened, 8 to 10 minutes. Stir in salt to taste. Transfer to a small bowl and let cool.

GRILL THE CHICKEN: Prepare a charcoal or gas grill. If using a charcoal grill, open vents in bottom of grill, then light charcoal. Fire is medium-hot when you can hold your hand 5 inches above rack for just 3 to 4 seconds. If using a gas grill, preheat on high, covered, for 10 minutes, then reduce heat to moderately high.

While grill is heating, thread a strip of chicken onto each skewer. Lightly oil grill rack and grill chicken, uncovered, turning once, until cooked through, about 6 minutes total.

Sprinkle dipping sauce with cilantro and serve with chicken saté.

COOK'S NOTES

- The chicken can marinate for up to 24 hours.
- The chicken can also be cooked on the rack of a broiler pan under a preheated broiler. Broil 3 to 4 inches from the heat, turning once, for about 6 minutes total.

Ginger-Hoisin Beef and Scallions on Crispy Noodle Cakes

MAKES ABOUT 35 HORS D'OEUVRES
ACTIVE TIME: 40 MINUTES ■ START TO FINISH: 3 HOURS

■ The beauty of rice noodles is that they become really crisp when fried, so the noodle cakes serve as handy vehicles for the beef tenderloin. These fancy little bites are easy to eat and an appealing change from the usual toasts. ■

1 (1-pound) piece center-cut beef tenderloin (3 inches thick)
¼ cup fresh lime juice
¼ cup hoisin sauce
2 tablespoons soy sauce
2 tablespoons finely grated peeled fresh ginger
¼ pound rice stick noodles (rice vermicelli)
About ½ cup vegetable oil
8 thin scallions

Pat tenderloin dry. Cut lengthwise in half, then cut each piece lengthwise in half, to make 4 long strips in all.

Whisk together lime juice, hoisin, soy sauce, and 1 tablespoon ginger in a bowl. Put beef and hoisin mixture into a sealable heavy-duty plastic bag, seal, and turn to coat beef with marinade. Marinate beef, refrigerated, turning bag once or twice, for at least 1 hour.

Cook noodles in a 4-quart saucepan of boiling water (unsalted) until tender, about 3 minutes; drain in a colander. Toss with 1 tablespoon oil in a bowl.

Finely chop white and pale green parts of scallions. Cut remaining scallion greens lengthwise into thin 1½-inch-long strips. Wrap strips in a dampened paper towel and refrigerate. Add chopped scallions and remaining 1 tablespoon ginger to noodles and toss until well combined.

Heat 3 tablespoons oil in a 12-inch nonstick skillet over moderate heat. Working in batches of 6 to 8, drop heaping tablespoons of noodles into skillet, spacing them evenly, and arrange with a fork into 1½-inch rounds. Cook cakes, turning once, until golden and crisp, about 4 minutes per batch. Transfer to paper towels to drain. Add more oil to skillet as needed, heating it before adding noodles.

Put a rack in middle of oven and preheat oven to 450°F.

Transfer beef to a plate and pour marinade into a small saucepan. Bring to a brisk simmer and simmer for 2 minutes. Let cool.

Heat 1 tablespoon oil in a 12-inch heavy ovenproof skillet over moderately high heat. Pat beef dry and brown, one piece at a time, on all sides, about 3 minutes; transfer to a clean plate. Return all beef to skillet, then transfer skillet to oven and cook beef for 6 to 8 minutes for medium-rare. Transfer beef to a cutting board and let stand for 20 minutes.

Cut beef into ¼-inch-thick slices and put one slice on each noodle cake. Top each beef slice with about ¼ teaspoon sauce and a few strips of scallion greens.

COOK'S NOTES

- The noodle cakes can be made up to 1 day ahead and kept in an airtight container at room temperature.
- The scallion greens can be refrigerated for up to 1 day in a sealable plastic bag.
- The beef can marinate for up to 6 hours.
- The beef can be cooked and the sauce simmered up to 1 day ahead. Cool completely, then refrigerate separately, covered. Bring to room temperature before serving.

Korean Barbecued Beef in Lettuce Cups

MAKES 60 HORS D'OEUVRES
ACTIVE TIME: 1 HOUR ■ START TO FINISH: 1½ HOURS

■ We make this Korean dish with skirt steak rather than the more typical short ribs, because skirt steak is juicier and tenderer—qualities you want in a beef hors d'oeuvre. Slivers of mango and crisp apple are a vibrant contrast to the beef. ■

- ½ cup soy sauce
- ¼ cup rice vinegar (not seasoned)
- ⅓ cup chopped scallions
- 2 tablespoons sugar
- 2 tablespoons minced garlic
- 2 tablespoons minced peeled fresh ginger
- 1 tablespoon Asian sesame oil
- 2½ teaspoons Asian chili sauce (see Glossary)
- 1¾ pounds skirt steak
- 2 small red apples, such as Gala
- 1 firm but ripe mango
- 2 tablespoons fresh lime juice
- Salt and freshly ground black pepper
- 60 (3- to 4-inch-long) Bibb lettuce leaves (from about 8 heads)

OPTIONAL GARNISH: sesame seeds, toasted (see Tips, page 939)

Stir together soy sauce, vinegar, scallions, sugar, garlic, ginger, oil, and 1½ teaspoons chili sauce in a bowl. Transfer one quarter of marinade to a medium bowl and set aside.

Put steak and remaining marinade in a glass dish and turn steak to coat. Cover and marinate at room temperature, turning once, for 30 minutes.

Meanwhile, cut apples into ¼-inch-thick 1-inch-long sticks. Peel and pit mango, then cut into strips the same size. Toss apples and mango with lime juice, remaining 1 teaspoon chili sauce, and salt to taste in a medium bowl.

Preheat broiler. Transfer steak to lightly oiled rack of broiler pan (discard marinade) and broil 2 to 3 inches from heat, turning once, until slightly charred, 4 to 6 minutes total for medium. Let steak stand for 5 minutes.

Cut steak diagonally against the grain into ¼-inch-thick slices and halve slices crosswise. Toss beef in reserved marinade with salt and pepper to taste. Divide among lettuce leaves, top with fruit, and sprinkle with sesame seeds, if desired.

COOK'S NOTE

- The fruit mixture can be made up to 1 day ahead and refrigerated, covered.

Swedish Meatballs

MAKES ABOUT 50 HORS D'OEUVRES
ACTIVE TIME: 20 MINUTES ■ START TO FINISH: 1 HOUR

■ Although many people think Swedish meatballs must be served with a gravy, at a Christmas Eve smorgasbord they are simply drizzled with pan juices, wrote reader Birgitta Tegelberg, of Piedmont, California. Her version of this dish is light, delicate, moist, and tender—the epitome of what meatballs should be. ■

- 3/4 cup fine fresh bread crumbs
- 1/4 cup heavy cream
- 1/4 cup club soda
- 3/4 pound ground beef round
- 1/2 pound ground veal
- 1/4 pound ground pork
- 1 medium onion, finely chopped
- 1 large egg, lightly beaten
- 2 teaspoons salt, or to taste
- 1/2 teaspoon freshly ground black pepper

Stir together bread crumbs, cream, and club soda in a small bowl. Let stand for 20 minutes.

Put racks in upper and lower thirds of oven and preheat oven to 400°F. Oil two large baking sheets with sides.

Combine beef, veal, and pork in a large bowl. Add onion, bread crumb mixture, egg, salt, and pepper and blend with your hands just until well combined; do not overmix.

Form level tablespoons of mixture into meatballs and arrange about 1 inch apart on oiled baking sheets. Bake, turning meatballs over and switching position of sheets halfway through baking, until browned, about 20 minutes total.

With a slotted spoon, transfer meatballs to a platter. Set baking sheets on top of stove or a heatproof surface. Divide 1/3 cup water between pans and deglaze, off heat, stirring and scraping up brown bits with a wooden spoon.

Drizzle pan juices over meatballs. Serve with wooden picks.

Stuffed Grape Leaves with Merguez Sausage

MAKES ABOUT 75 HORS D'OEUVRES
ACTIVE TIME: 2 3/4 HOURS ■ START TO FINISH: 5 1/4 HOURS (INCLUDES CHILLING)

■ Merguez is a spicy beef sausage from North Africa. It adds punch and brightness to these stuffed grape leaves. The currants lighten the sausage-rice mixture and lend a hint of sweetness. ■

- 2 (1-pound) jars brine-packed Greek or California grape leaves
- 2 cups water
- Salt
- 1 cup long-grain white rice
- 3 large lemons
- 6 tablespoons olive oil
- 3/4 pound merguez or hot Italian sausage, casings discarded
- 1 1/2 cups finely chopped red onions
- 1/2 cup pine nuts, toasted (see Tips, page 938)
- 1/4 cup chopped fresh dill
- 1/4 cup chopped fresh flat-leaf parsley
- 1/2 cup dried currants
- 1/2 teaspoon freshly ground black pepper
- About 3 1/2 cups chicken stock or store-bought low-sodium broth

PREPARE THE LEAVES: Unfurl stacks of grape leaves, keeping leaves stacked. Put in a large bowl of water and gently agitate, without separating leaves, to rinse. Blanch stacks of leaves in 5 batches in a 3- to 4-quart saucepan of boiling water for 3 minutes per batch. Transfer blanched leaves, in batches, to a colander and rinse under cold running water to stop the cooking.

MAKE THE FILLING: Bring 2 cups water and 1/2 teaspoon salt to a boil in a 2-quart saucepan. Stir in rice, cover tightly, and cook over low heat until rice is tender and water is absorbed, about 20 minutes. Let stand for 5 minutes, covered, then fluff with a fork and transfer rice to a large bowl.

Meanwhile, finely grate zest from lemons and squeeze enough juice to measure 1/4 cup.

Heat 1 tablespoon oil in a 12-inch heavy skillet over moderate heat. Add sausage and cook, stirring to break up lumps, until no longer pink, about 5 minutes. Transfer to a bowl and cool to room temperature.

Wipe out skillet, add 1½ tablespoons oil, and heat over moderate heat. Add onions and cook, stirring, until softened but not browned, about 8 minutes. Stir into rice, along with zest, 2 tablespoons lemon juice, nuts, dill, parsley, currants, 1¼ teaspoons salt, and pepper. Crumble cooled sausage into ¼-inch pieces and stir into rice.

FILL AND ROLL THE GRAPE LEAVES: Lay 1 grape leaf smooth side down on a kitchen towel. Trim stem flush with leaf (if leaf is very large, trim to about 5½ inches wide, saving trimmings). Spoon 1 tablespoon filling onto leaf near stem end. Fold bottom of leaf over filling and tightly roll up filling in leaf, folding in sides and squeezing roll to pack filling (roll should be about 3½ inches long). Make more rolls using remaining filling in same manner.

COOK THE GRAPE LEAVES: Heat stock just to a simmer. Keep warm, covered.

Line bottom of a 4- to 5-quart heavy pot with any leaf trimmings and remaining whole leaves. Arrange rolls seam sides down and close together in layers in pot, seasoning each layer with salt. Drizzle with 2 tablespoons oil and remaining 2 tablespoons lemon juice, cover with an inverted heatproof plate slightly smaller than pot, and press down gently.

Add just enough stock to reach rim of plate and bring to a boil. Reduce heat, cover pot with a lid, and cook rolls at a bare simmer for about 50 minutes; leaves should be tender and filling should be soft. Remove from heat, transfer rolls to large trays to cool, and brush with remaining 1½ tablespoons oil.

Cover cooled rolls with plastic wrap and refrigerate until cold, 2 to 3 hours.

COOK'S NOTES

- The filling can be made up to 1 day ahead and refrigerated, covered.
- The stuffed grape leaves can be refrigerated in an airtight container for up to 5 days.

Shrimp Dumplings with Dipping Sauce

MAKES 18 HORS D'OEUVRES
ACTIVE TIME: 40 MINUTES ■ START TO FINISH: 40 MINUTES

■ Quick dumplings made with supermarket ingredients—shrimp, canned water chestnuts, wonton wrappers—satisfy a craving for something Chinese. They aren't shaped in the traditional way, just folded into triangles and crisped on both sides before a brief steaming to cook the filling. ■

- ½ pound large shrimp in shells (21–25 per pound), peeled and deveined
- ½ cup canned water chestnuts, rinsed, drained, and finely chopped
- 1 tablespoon lightly beaten egg white
- 2 tablespoons finely chopped scallion greens
- 1 tablespoon finely grated peeled fresh ginger
- 3 tablespoons soy sauce
- 18 wonton wrappers
- ½ teaspoon sugar
- 2 tablespoons vegetable oil
- ¾ cup boiling water

Purée 3 shrimp in a food processor and transfer to a medium bowl. Finely chop remaining shrimp in food processor and add to bowl. Add water chestnuts, egg white, two thirds of scallion greens, two thirds of ginger, and 1 tablespoon soy sauce and stir until combined.

Put 6 wonton wrappers on a dry work surface (keep remaining wrappers in package) and lightly brush edges with cold water. Mound about 1 tablespoon filling in center of each wrapper, then fold each wrapper over filling to form a triangle, pressing down around filling to force out excess air and seal edges well. Make more dumplings with remaining wrappers and filling in same manner.

Stir together sugar and remaining scallion greens, ginger, and 2 tablespoons soy sauce in a small bowl to make dipping sauce.

Heat 2 teaspoons oil in a 12-inch nonstick skillet over moderately high heat. Brown dumplings in 3 batches, turning once, for 3 minutes per batch (add 2 teaspoons more oil to skillet between batches). Transfer to a plate. After browning final batch, return all dumplings to skillet, add boiling water, and cook, covered, until filling is cooked through (open one dumpling to check), 3 to 5 minutes.

Serve dumplings with dipping sauce.

Steamed Pork and Jicama Dumplings

Siu Mai

MAKES 60 HORS D'OEUVRES
ACTIVE TIME: 1½ HOURS ■ START TO FINISH: 1¾ HOURS

■ *Siu mai,* classic Chinese dumplings found on many dim sum menus, are one of the easiest kinds to form because of their open tops. We tend to think of jicama as a Mexican ingredient (it's native to Central America), but the tuber has been appreciated in Asia for centuries. It's crunchy, like a water chestnut, but sweeter. Don't try to make these ahead and keep them warm, because they'll turn leathery. Steam them a batch at a time and send them out of the kitchen. ■

- 1 large egg white
- 2 tablespoons minced peeled fresh ginger
- 1 tablespoon minced garlic
- 1 tablespoon peanut oil or vegetable oil
- 1 tablespoon Asian sesame oil
- 1 tablespoon soy sauce
- 1 tablespoon cornstarch
- 2 teaspoons sugar
- ½ teaspoon salt
- 1 cup diced (¼-inch) peeled jicama
- ½ cup minced scallions
- 1½ pounds ground pork (not lean)
- 60 wonton wrappers (from two 12-ounce packages) or gyoza skins
- 2 tablespoons black sesame seeds, toasted (see Glossary and Tips, page 939)
- 2 tablespoons white sesame seeds, toasted

ACCOMPANIMENT: Dipping Sauce (recipe follows)

SPECIAL EQUIPMENT: a 2½-inch round cookie cutter if using wonton wrappers; a pasta pot with a deep perforated colander/steamer insert (see Cook's Note)

MAKE THE FILLING: Lightly whisk egg white in a large bowl, then whisk in ginger, garlic, peanut oil, sesame oil, soy sauce, cornstarch, sugar, and salt. Add jicama, scallions, and pork and mix with your hands until well combined.

ASSEMBLE THE DUMPLINGS: If using wonton wrappers, separate wrappers and restack in piles of 10. Cut through each stack with cookie cutter; discard trimmings. Arrange 6 wonton or gyoza wrappers in one layer on a work surface (keep remaining wrappers covered with plastic wrap) and mound a scant tablespoon filling in center of each. Lightly moisten edge of wrappers with a finger dipped in water. Working with one at a time and leaving dumpling on work surface, gather edge of wrapper around side of filling, pleating wrapper to form a cup, leaving dumpling open at top, and pressing pleats against filling (1). With wet finger, flatten filling so it is flush with edge of wrapper, and transfer dumpling to a tray. Make more dumplings in same manner with remaining wrappers and filling.

STEAM THE DUMPLINGS: Generously oil bottom of colander/steamer insert. Bring a few inches of water to a boil in pot (bottom of insert should be above water). Arrange 10 dumplings about ½ inch apart in insert and steam over moderate heat,

SIU MAI

1

2

covered, until dough is translucent and filling is just cooked through, about 6 minutes.

Stir together black and white sesame seeds. Sprinkle seeds over dumplings (2) and serve immediately with dipping sauce. Cook remaining dumplings in same manner.

COOK'S NOTES

- The dumplings, without the sesame seeds, can be formed and steamed up to 1 day ahead. Cool completely, then refrigerate, covered. The dumplings can also be frozen for up to 1 week. Freeze in one layer on a plastic-wrapped tray until firm, then transfer to a sealable plastic bag, force out excess air, and seal the bag. Steam the dumplings (do not thaw if frozen) over simmering water until heated through, about 6 minutes.
- These dumplings are traditionally cooked in stacked bamboo or metal steamers, but we use a pasta pot with a deep perforated colander/steamer insert. If your pot has a second shallow insert, you can steam two batches of dumplings at the same time. Or use a bamboo steamer if you have one. If using a bamboo steamer, line two steamer trays with parchment paper and poke holes in the paper. Arrange the dumplings 1/4 inch apart in steamer trays. Fill a wok with enough water to reach the bottom edge of a steamer tray and bring to a boil. Stack the trays in the wok, cover, and steam for 6 minutes, reversing the position of the trays after 3 minutes.

Dipping Sauce

MAKES ABOUT 1 CUP
ACTIVE TIME: 5 MINUTES ■ START TO FINISH: 5 MINUTES

■ You can use plain soy sauce for dipping, but rice vinegar and sugar round out the flavor. ■

- 1/2 cup soy sauce
- 1/4 cup water
- 3 tablespoons seasoned rice vinegar
- 2 teaspoons sugar
- 2 tablespoons thinly sliced scallions

Stir together soy sauce, water, vinegar, and sugar in a small bowl until sugar is dissolved. Just before serving, stir in scallions.

COOK'S NOTE

- The dipping sauce, without the scallions, can be made up to 3 days ahead and refrigerated, covered. Stir in the scallions and bring to room temperature before serving.

Pot Stickers

MAKES 45 HORS D'OEUVRES
ACTIVE TIME: 2 HOURS ■ START TO FINISH: 2 1/4 HOURS

■ These little dumplings owe their texture—fluffy-tender on the pleated top, crispy-crunchy on the bottom—to the fact that they are fried and then steamed, and they couldn't be more emblematic of traditional home cooking. Chinese New Year is the time when many families gather around a table to make (and eat) dozens of pot stickers. It may take a while to get the hang of forming the pleats, but they don't have to be perfect. This is intended not as an exercise in frustration but as a communal activity with people you love. ■

FOR POT STICKERS

- 3/4 cup minced Napa cabbage
- 1/2 teaspoon salt
- 6 ounces ground pork (not lean)
- 1/2 cup minced garlic chives or regular chives
- 1 tablespoon Asian sesame oil
- 1 tablespoon soy sauce
- 1 1/2 teaspoons Chinese rice wine or sake
- 1 teaspoon cornstarch
- 3/4 teaspoon minced peeled fresh ginger
- 1/2–3/4 teaspoon minced garlic
- 45 wonton wrappers or gyoza skins
- 6 tablespoons vegetable oil

FOR SAUCE

- 1/4 cup soy sauce
- 1/4 cup rice vinegar (not seasoned), or to taste
- 1 tablespoon Asian chili paste (see Glossary)

SPECIAL EQUIPMENT: a 3-inch round cookie cutter if using wonton wrappers

MAKE THE POT STICKERS: Stir together cabbage and salt in a colander. Let stand for 20 minutes.

Squeeze cabbage to remove excess moisture. Stir

together cabbage, pork, chives, sesame oil, soy sauce, rice wine, cornstarch, ginger, and ½ teaspoon garlic if using garlic chives, or ¾ teaspoon if using regular chives, in a large bowl, throwing mixture lightly against side of bowl to combine and compact it.

Sprinkle bottom of a shallow baking pan with flour or cornstarch. If using wonton wrappers, separate wrappers, restack in piles of 9, and cut through each stack with cookie cutter; discard trimmings. Work with one wonton or gyoza wrapper at a time, keeping remaining wrappers covered with plastic wrap. Put a teaspoon of filling in center of wrapper (1) and fold it over filling to form an open half-moon shape (2). With a wet finger, moisten border along inner edge of dumpling skin farthest from you. Using thumb and forefinger of one hand, form 10 to 12 tiny pleats along unmoistened edge of dumpling skin closest to you (3), pressing pleats against moistened border to enclose filling. The moistened border will stay smooth and will automatically curve in a semicircle (4). Put in flour-dusted baking pan and make more pot stickers in same manner, arranging them ½ inch apart.

MAKE THE SAUCE: Stir together all ingredients in a small bowl.

COOK THE POT STICKERS: Heat 2 tablespoons vegetable oil in a 9-inch nonstick skillet over moderately high heat. Add half of dumplings, pleated edges up (skillet will be crowded), and fry until golden on bottom, 1 to 2 minutes. Add ¾ cup cold water, cover skillet, and reduce heat to moderate. Cook dumplings until most of liquid has evaporated, 7 to 10 minutes. Pour off any excess liquid, drizzle 1 tablespoon vegetable oil around edge of skillet, and cook dumplings, uncovered, until bottoms are crisp and golden brown, 1 to 2 minutes more. Transfer dumplings to a serving plate and keep warm, loosely covered with foil. Cook remaining dumplings in same manner with remaining 3 tablespoons oil and another ¾ cup cold water.

Serve dumplings with sauce.

COOK'S NOTE

- The pot stickers, assembled but not cooked, can be frozen for up to 2 weeks. Freeze in one layer on a plastic wrap–covered tray until firm, then transfer to a sealable plastic bag, force out excess air, and seal. Do not thaw before cooking.

HOW TO MAKE POT STICKERS

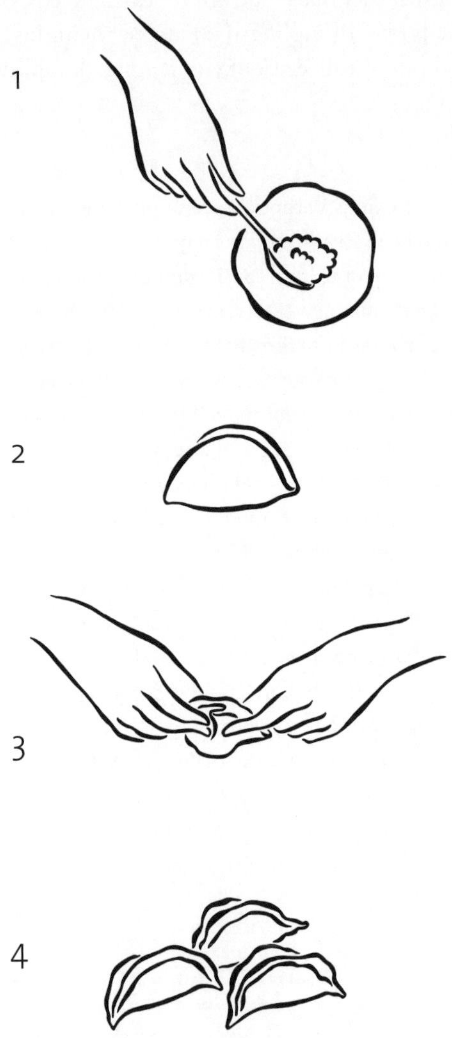

Arepas with Yucatecan Pulled Pork and Pickled Onion

MAKES ABOUT 60 HORS D'OEUVRES
ACTIVE TIME: 2 HOURS ■ START TO FINISH: 12½ HOURS (INCLUDES PICKLING ONIONS)

■ The Colombian fried cakes called *arepas* are becoming increasingly popular in the United States. They have a wonderful roasty-toasty flavor from the flour they're made with, which is more like fine cornmeal than the masa harina used for tortillas. Pork and corn are a natural combination, so we've topped these *arepas* with shredded pork from Mexico as well as pickled onion, one of our all-time favorite condiments. ■

FOR PICKLED ONION

- 1 medium red onion, cut into 3/4-inch-wide wedges, wedges very thinly sliced crosswise
- 1–2 habanero or Scotch bonnet chiles (to taste; see Glossary), stemmed, seeded, and very finely chopped
- 1/2 cup distilled white vinegar
- 1/2 teaspoon dried oregano, preferably Mexican (see Sources), crumbled
- 1/2 teaspoon salt, or to taste

FOR PORK

- 1/2 teaspoon cumin seeds
- 1/4 teaspoon allspice berries
- 1/2 teaspoon black peppercorns
- 2 tablespoons achiote (annatto) seeds (see Glossary)
- 6 large garlic cloves, coarsely chopped
- 1 1/2 teaspoons salt
- 1 teaspoon dried oregano, preferably Mexican, crumbled
- 1/3 cup fresh orange juice
- 1/3 cup distilled white vinegar
- 3 pounds pork shoulder chops (3/4 inch thick)

FOR *AREPAS*

- 3 cups whole milk
- 1/2 stick (4 tablespoons) unsalted butter, cut into pieces
- 1 1/2 cups white *arepa* flour (see Glossary)
- 1 tablespoon sugar
- 1 teaspoon salt
- 1 cup coarsely grated mozzarella (about 5 ounces)
- 2 1/2 tablespoons vegetable oil

SPECIAL EQUIPMENT: an electric coffee/spice grinder

PICKLE THE ONION: Stir together all ingredients in a bowl. Refrigerate, covered, for at least 12 hours.

MEANWHILE, MARINATE THE PORK: Combine cumin seeds, allspice berries, and peppercorns in a dry small heavy skillet and toast over moderate heat, stirring occasionally, until spices are fragrant and seeds are a shade or two darker. Let cool.

Finely grind cumin, allspice, peppercorns, and achiote in coffee/spice grinder. Mash garlic to a paste with salt in a mortar with a pestle, or mince and mash to a paste with a heavy knife. Transfer garlic paste to a 2 1/2- to 3-quart shallow glass or ceramic baking dish. Stir in spice mixture, oregano, juice, and vinegar. Add pork and rub meat all over with marinade. Marinate pork, covered and refrigerated, for at least 2 hours.

COOK THE PORK: Bring pork to room temperature. Put a rack in middle of oven and preheat oven to 325°F.

Add 1/2 cup water to baking dish and cover tightly with foil. Bake pork until very tender, 1 3/4 to 2 hours. Uncover and let cool slightly.

MEANWHILE, MAKE THE *AREPAS*: Bring milk to a simmer in a small saucepan. Remove from heat and pour 1/2 cup into a small bowl; set aside. Add butter to hot milk remaining in pan and stir until melted.

Toss together *arepa* flour, sugar, salt, and mozzarella in a large bowl. Add hot milk with butter and stir until combined. Let mixture stand until milk is absorbed enough to form a soft dough, 1 to 2 minutes (dough will continue to stiffen as it stands).

With palms of your hands, form 1 tablespoon dough into a ball. Flatten ball on wax paper to a 1 1/2- to 1 3/4-inch disk. Transfer to a wax paper–lined tray and cover with plastic wrap. Form disks with remaining dough in same manner, stirring in some of reserved milk as necessary if dough becomes too stiff and edges of disks crack when flattened.

SHRED THE PORK AND COOK THE *AREPAS*: When pork is cool enough to handle, transfer to a cutting board, reserving cooking juices in baking dish. Shred pork, discarding bones and excess fat. Return meat and any juices accumulated on cutting board to baking dish.

Heat 1 1/2 teaspoons oil in a 12-inch nonstick skillet over moderately low heat until hot. Cook *arepas* in batches of 10 to 12, turning once, until cooked through and golden in patches, 8 to 12 minutes per batch (add more oil to pan between batches as needed). Transfer *arepas* to a platter and cover to keep warm. Top *arepas* with pork and pickled onion. Serve warm.

COOK'S NOTES

- The pickled onion can be made up to 2 days ahead.
- The pork can marinate for up to 1 day.
- The pork can be cooked and shredded up to 1 day ahead and refrigerated, covered. Reheat, covered, in a 350°F oven for 10 to 15 minutes.

- The *arepas* can be cooked up to 1 day ahead. Cool completely, then wrap in foil packages in one layer (10 per package) and refrigerate. Reheat, in foil, in a 350°F oven for 10 to 15 minutes. The *arepas* can also be frozen for up to 2 weeks. Thaw for 30 minutes at room temperature before reheating.

First Courses

Asparagus Salad with Celery Leaves, Quail Eggs, and Tarragon Vinaigrette

SERVES 4
ACTIVE TIME: 45 MINUTES ■ START TO FINISH: 1 HOUR

■ This is an impressive springtime first course, beautiful with the various shades of green from the asparagus, tarragon, and celery leaves. It's a good reminder, too, that celery leaves are worth saving and adding to salads. Dainty quail eggs add to the elegance of this dish. They are available from specialty foods shops, butchers, Asian markets, and even some supermarkets, or see Sources. ■

8 quail eggs
1 pound asparagus, preferably thin, trimmed
Kosher salt
2 tablespoons tarragon white-wine vinegar or white wine vinegar
2 teaspoons whole-grain mustard
1 teaspoon Dijon mustard
1/3 cup safflower oil or grapeseed oil
1 small shallot, thinly sliced into rings
1 tablespoon coarsely chopped fresh tarragon
Freshly ground black pepper
1 cup pale green celery leaves (from center of bunch)

Cover eggs with cold water in a very small saucepan, bring to a simmer, and cook, covered, for 5 minutes. Rinse eggs under cold running water to stop the cooking, then peel while still warm and quarter.

Cut asparagus on a very sharp diagonal into 1/8-inch-thick slices, leaving 2-inch tips. Halve tips lengthwise if thicker than slices. Arrange asparagus in a steamer rack and sprinkle with salt. Steam, covered, over boiling water until just tender, 2 to 3 minutes. Transfer to a bowl of ice and cold water to stop the cooking. Drain well and pat dry.

Whisk together vinegar and mustards in a medium bowl. Add oil in a slow stream, whisking constantly until well blended. Stir in shallot, 2 teaspoons tarragon, and salt and pepper to taste.

Toss asparagus and celery leaves with half of vinaigrette and mound on four plates. Tuck quail eggs decoratively into salads. Drizzle remaining vinaigrette over and around salads and sprinkle with remaining 1 teaspoon tarragon.

COOK'S NOTES

- The quail eggs can be cooked up to 1 day ahead (peel them while still warm) and refrigerated, covered.
- The asparagus can be blanched up to 6 hours ahead and refrigerated, covered.

Mesclun Salad with Goat Cheese–Stuffed Figs Wrapped in Bacon

SERVES 4
ACTIVE TIME: 45 MINUTES ■ START TO FINISH: 45 MINUTES

■ Figs in bacon rest easy on a bed of mesclun. We stuff the figs with aged goat cheese, which is firmer than fresh and has a dry rind. Bûcheron and aged Pouligny-Saint-Pierre have just the right amount of tang, but ask at the cheese counter for a comparable substitute if you have trouble finding either of them. Café Pasqual's, in Santa Fe, serves a version of this dish—"pigs 'n' figs"—with blue cheese. ■

8 bacon slices (1/2 pound)
8 firm but ripe fresh figs, trimmed and halved lengthwise
1/4 pound aged goat cheese, such as Bûcheron or Pouligny-Saint-Pierre
3 tablespoons packed light brown sugar
1/2 teaspoon ground cumin
1/2 teaspoon kosher salt
4 ounces mesclun (4 cups)
1 teaspoon fresh lemon juice, or to taste

Freshly ground black pepper
1½ tablespoons extra-virgin olive oil

SPECIAL EQUIPMENT: a melon ball cutter; wooden picks

Cook bacon in a large heavy skillet over moderate heat, turning occasionally, until most of fat is rendered but bacon is still pliable, about 10 minutes. Transfer to paper towels to drain.

Preheat broiler. Remove 1 scoop of flesh from each fig half with melon ball cutter and discard. Scoop up cheese with melon ball cutter and just fill each fig half. Press fig halves together to form whole figs.

Stir together brown sugar, cumin, and salt and rub onto one side of each bacon slice. Wrap a bacon slice, sugared side out, around each fig and secure with a wooden pick.

Lay figs on their sides on rack of broiler pan and broil about 3 inches from heat, turning frequently, until bacon is browned, about 2 minutes. Let cool slightly, then discard picks.

Toss mesclun with lemon juice and salt and pepper to taste, then gently toss with oil. Arrange greens on plates and top each with 2 figs.

Goat Cheese and Walnut Soufflés with Watercress and Frisée Salad

SERVES 8

ACTIVE TIME: 30 MINUTES ■ START TO FINISH: 1 HOUR

■ American goat cheese made in the French tradition has enjoyed widespread popularity since the late twentieth century. Both artisanal and commercial goat cheeses are available nearly everywhere today. These individual soufflés make a wonderful herb-scented first course for Easter dinner. ■

FOR SOUFFLÉS

3 tablespoons unsalted butter
¾ cup (3 ounces) walnuts, lightly toasted (see Tips, page 938), cooled, and finely chopped in a food processor
¼ cup all-purpose flour
1 cup whole milk
4 large eggs, separated, left at room temperature for 30 minutes
6 ounces mild goat cheese, crumbled
1 teaspoon fresh thyme leaves or ¼ teaspoon dried thyme, crumbled
¼ teaspoon salt
¼ teaspoon freshly ground black pepper
Pinch of cream of tartar

FOR SALAD

3 tablespoons sherry vinegar
¾ teaspoon Dijon mustard
½ teaspoon salt
¼ teaspoon freshly ground black pepper
¼ cup walnut oil
2 tablespoons olive oil
10 ounces watercress, coarse stems discarded (5 cups)
6 ounces frisée, torn into bite-sized pieces (5 cups)

SPECIAL EQUIPMENT: eight 4-ounce ramekins

MAKE THE SOUFFLÉS: Put a rack in upper third of oven and preheat oven to 400°F. Butter ramekins with 1 tablespoon butter, then coat bottom and sides of each ramekin with about 1 tablespoon walnuts. Place ramekins on a baking sheet.

Melt remaining 2 tablespoons butter in a small heavy saucepan over moderately low heat. Whisk in flour and cook, whisking, for 3 minutes to make a roux. Add milk in a steady stream, whisking constantly, and bring to a boil over moderate heat, whisking. Boil, whisking, for about 2 minutes; sauce will be very thick. Transfer to a bowl to cool slightly.

Whisk yolks one at a time into sauce, then whisk in goat cheese, thyme, salt, and pepper until well combined.

Beat whites with a pinch of salt in a large bowl with an electric mixer at medium-high speed until frothy. Add cream of tartar and beat until whites just hold stiff peaks. Whisk one third of whites into cheese mixture to lighten it, then fold in remaining whites gently but thoroughly.

Divide soufflé mixture among ramekins and sprinkle each soufflé with about 1½ teaspoons of remaining walnuts. Bake until puffed and golden, about 20 minutes.

MEANWHILE, MAKE THE SALAD: Whisk together vinegar, mustard, salt, and pepper in a small bowl, then add oils in a slow stream, whisking until well blended. Toss watercress and frisée with dressing in a large bowl. Divide salad among eight plates, arranging it to one side.

Transfer a ramekin to each plate and serve immediately.

COOK'S NOTES

- The soufflés can be baked up to 1 day ahead and served as fallen soufflés. Cool, uncovered, then refrigerate, covered. Reheat in a 350°F oven, uncovered, until heated through, 10 to 15 minutes.
- The dressing can be made up to 1 day ahead and refrigerated, covered.

Tomato Tatins

SERVES 4

ACTIVE TIME: 15 MINUTES ■ START TO FINISH: 40 MINUTES

■ Like tarte Tatin, the famous French upside-down apple dessert created by the Tatin sisters, these savory stacks of roasted tomato slices and pesto are topped with a crisp crust that ultimately becomes the bottom. ■

- ⅓ cup olive oil
- 6 medium tomatoes (2 pounds total)
- Salt
- 4 (½-inch-thick) slices country-style bread
- 1 garlic clove, halved crosswise
- Freshly ground black pepper
- 8 teaspoons store-bought basil pesto

SPECIAL EQUIPMENT: one 4-inch round cookie cutter or ramekin; four 8-ounce ramekins

Put racks in upper and lower thirds of oven and preheat oven to 450°F. Lightly brush two baking sheets with sides with some of oil.

Cut tomatoes into ½-inch-thick slices, discarding tops and bottoms (you will need 16 slices). Arrange tomato slices in one layer on baking sheets and season with salt.

Roast tomatoes, switching position of sheets halfway through roasting, until just tender but not falling apart, about 15 minutes total. Let cool slightly on sheets on racks. (Leave oven on and put one rack in middle of oven.)

Cut out one round from each slice of bread with cookie cutter, or use upside-down ramekin as a guide and cut out rounds with a sharp knife. Brush rounds on both sides with remaining oil, then sprinkle lightly with salt. Arrange in one layer on a baking sheet. Toast rounds until golden brown, about 5 minutes. Immediately rub both sides of toasts with cut sides of garlic and season with salt and pepper. (Leave oven on.)

Stack 2 tomato slices in bottom of each ramekin and spread with 1 teaspoon pesto. Repeat layering once and top each tatin with a toast round.

Arrange ramekins on a baking sheet and bake tatins just until hot, about 5 minutes. Wearing oven mitts, invert a plate over each ramekin, invert ramekin onto plate, and carefully lift off ramekin. Serve immediately.

Morels in Cream on Brioche

SERVES 4

ACTIVE TIME: 45 MINUTES ■ START TO FINISH: 1 HOUR

■ Treating fresh morels this way allows this seasonal delicacy to sing. Toasted bread and a cream sauce carry the earthy, nutty flavor of the mushrooms. Spring doesn't get any more delicious than this. ■

- 3 tablespoons unsalted butter
- 1 pound morel mushrooms, trimmed, washed well, and patted dry (see Cook's Notes)
- 1 tablespoon all-purpose flour
- 1 cup heavy cream, heated until hot
- Salt and white pepper
- 5 (½-inch-thick) slices from a large rectangular brioche loaf or challah, toasted, crusts discarded, and each slice cut into 4 triangles

Heat butter in a 12-inch heavy skillet over moderately high heat until foam subsides. Add morels and cook, stirring frequently, until beginning to brown, 6 to 8 minutes. Sprinkle in flour and cook, stirring, for 1 minute. Add hot cream in a slow stream, stirring constantly, and bring to a boil, stirring constantly. Reduce heat to low, cover, and simmer gently, stirring once, until morels are tender, 10 to 15 minutes. Season with salt and white pepper.

Arrange 5 toasts on each of four plates and spoon morels and sauce on top. Serve immediately.

COOK'S NOTES

- You can substitute 1 ounce ($1\frac{1}{3}$ cups) small dried morels for the fresh. Soak in $2\frac{1}{2}$ cups warm water until softened, 10 to 30 minutes. Lift from the soaking liquid, rinse well, and pat dry with paper towels. Pour the soaking liquid through a paper towel–lined sieve into a bowl. Add ½ cup soaking liquid with the cream (dried morels will absorb more liquid than fresh).
- See Sources to find both fresh and dried morels.

Mushroom Charlottes with Port and Currant Sauce

SERVES 8

ACTIVE TIME: $1\frac{3}{4}$ HOURS ■ START TO FINISH: 2 HOURS

■ These mushroom-filled mounds of crisp, buttery, golden toast look beautiful and are sensational as a first course for Christmas dinner or as a Sunday night supper with just a simple salad to follow. This dish is fairly labor-intensive but not in the least bit prissy; the toast lends the charlottes a rustic quality. ■

FOR FILLING

- 2 tablespoons unsalted butter
- 2 medium onions, finely chopped
- 3 garlic cloves, minced
- $1\frac{1}{2}$ pounds mushrooms, trimmed and chopped
- 1 teaspoon salt
- ½ teaspoon freshly ground black pepper
- ¼ teaspoon dried thyme, crumbled
- 1 large egg
- 4 ounces cream cheese, softened
- ¼ cup heavy cream
- ¼ cup minced fresh flat-leaf parsley
- ½ cup finely grated Parmigiano-Reggiano

FOR CRUSTS

- 1 (1-pound) loaf very thinly sliced white sandwich bread
- 1 stick (8 tablespoons) unsalted butter, melted and cooled slightly

FOR SAUCE

- ½ cup plus 1 tablespoon tawny port
- ¼ cup dried currants
- ½ cup beef stock or store-bought broth
- 2 tablespoons currant jelly
- 2 teaspoons red wine vinegar
- 2 teaspoons arrowroot
- Salt and freshly ground black pepper

OPTIONAL GARNISH: fresh flat-leaf parsley sprigs

SPECIAL EQUIPMENT: eight 4-ounce charlotte molds (see Sources) or ramekins; a $2\frac{1}{4}$-inch round cookie cutter; a $2\frac{3}{4}$-inch round cookie cutter

MAKE THE FILLING: Melt butter in a 6-quart heavy pot over moderately low heat. Add onions and garlic and cook, stirring, until softened, about 3 minutes. Add mushrooms, salt, pepper, and thyme, increase heat to moderate, and cook, stirring occasionally, until most of liquid mushrooms give off has evaporated, 12 to 15 minutes. Cool for 15 minutes.

Transfer mixture to a kitchen towel and squeeze out 1 cup liquid into a small bowl. Reserve liquid for sauce and transfer mushrooms to another bowl. Blend egg, cream cheese, and cream in a food processor until smooth. Stir into mushrooms, along with parsley, Parmesan, and salt and pepper to taste.

ASSEMBLE AND BAKE THE CHARLOTTES: Put a rack in middle of oven and preheat oven to 425°F.

Cut rounds from 8 slices of bread with $2\frac{1}{4}$-inch cookie cutter. Brush rounds lightly on both sides with butter, then fit into bottoms of molds. Cut rounds from 8 more slices of bread with $2\frac{3}{4}$-inch cutter and reserve for tops. Trim crusts from 10 more slices and cut each slice into 4 squares. Brush lightly on both sides with butter and line sides of each mold with 5 slices, overlapping them slightly and pressing gently against sides of mold to keep in place. Spoon filling into molds, pressing it down lightly and filling molds just to top of bread lining. Brush both sides of reserved rounds lightly with remaining butter and top each mold with a round, pressing it down firmly to cover filling completely.

Put charlottes on a baking sheet and bake until bread is golden, 15 to 20 minutes.

MEANWHILE, MAKE THE SAUCE: Combine ½ cup port and currants in a 1- to $1\frac{1}{2}$-quart saucepan and boil until liquid is reduced to about 3 tablespoons, 3 to 5 minutes. Add stock and reserved mushroom liquid and boil until reduced to about 1 cup, 8 to 10 minutes.

Whisk in jelly and vinegar and boil, whisking, until jelly is dissolved. Stir together remaining 1 tablespoon port and arrowroot in a small bowl, then whisk into sauce. Boil sauce, whisking, for 1 minute. Whisk in salt and pepper to taste. Remove from heat and partially cover to keep warm.

Invert a plate over each charlotte, then invert charlotte onto plate. Spoon sauce around charlottes and garnish with parsley sprigs, if desired.

COOK'S NOTES

- Since there are a lot of mushrooms in this recipe, you might want to pulse them in your food processor instead of chopping them by hand.
- The mushroom filling can be made up to 1 day ahead and refrigerated, covered. (Refrigerate the reserved mushroom liquid too, covered.) Bring to room temperature before proceeding.

Green Chile Cheesecake with Papaya Salsa

SERVES 16 AS A FIRST COURSE, 32 AS AN HORS D'OEUVRE
ACTIVE TIME: 1¼ HOURS ■ START TO FINISH: 4 HOURS (INCLUDES COOLING)

■ This savory cheesecake is so rich and intensely flavored that you need to serve each person only a sliver. The sweet papaya salsa counteracts the spiciness of the fresh green chiles. This combination of flavors and textures is the creation of reader Sondra Wilson, of Kennewick, Washington. ■

FOR CRUST

- 1½ cups finely ground blue corn chips (from a 9-ounce bag)
- 1 tablespoon unsalted butter, melted and cooled

FOR FILLING

- 1½ cups sour cream
- 2 large eggs
- 1 pound cream cheese, softened
- 2 tablespoons unsalted butter, softened
- 8 green chiles, such as New Mexico or poblano (1¾ pounds total; see Glossary), roasted (see Tips, page 941), peeled, and finely chopped
- 1 cup grated Monterey Jack (about 4 ounces)
- 1½ cups grated sharp Cheddar (about 6 ounces)
- 1 tablespoon minced fresh dill
- ¼ cup chopped fresh cilantro
- ½ teaspoon salt

FOR SALSA

- 1 (1-pound) firm but ripe papaya
- 2 garlic cloves, minced
- 1 medium red onion, finely chopped
- 1 red bell pepper, cored, seeded, and finely chopped
- 2 tablespoons chopped fresh cilantro
- ¼ cup rice vinegar (not seasoned)
- ½ teaspoon salt
- ¼ teaspoon freshly ground black pepper

SPECIAL EQUIPMENT: a 10-inch springform pan

MAKE THE CRUST: Put a rack in middle of oven and preheat oven to 350°F.

Stir together corn chip crumbs and butter in a bowl until evenly moistened. Press onto bottom of springform pan. Bake until fragrant, about 10 minutes. Cool on a rack. Reduce oven temperature to 325°F.

MAKE THE FILLING: Blend together sour cream and eggs in a food processor. Add cream cheese and butter and blend until smooth, about 1 minute. Transfer to a medium bowl and stir in chiles, remaining cheeses, dill, cilantro, and salt.

Pour filling over crust. Bake until center is just set, 40 to 45 minutes. Cool in pan on rack, about 2 hours.

AN HOUR BEFORE SERVING, MAKE THE SALSA: Peel, halve, and seed papaya, then coarsely chop (you will have about 2 cups). Stir together papaya with remaining ingredients in a bowl.

Serve slivers of cheesecake with salsa on small plates.

COOK'S NOTES

- The chiles can be roasted and peeled up to 1 day ahead. Refrigerate, covered.
- The cheesecake can be made up to 1 day ahead. Cool completely, uncovered, then refrigerate, covered. Bring to room temperature before serving.

Chestnut Ravioli with Sage Brown Butter

SERVES 8

ACTIVE TIME: 1 HOUR ■ START TO FINISH: 1 HOUR

■ Now that wonton wrappers are available at most supermarkets, making ravioli is quick and easy. This is an elegant and unusual wintry first course, especially when served with a crisp white wine to cut the richness. ■

- 7 tablespoons unsalted butter
- 2 ounces sliced pancetta or 2 bacon slices, finely chopped
- 1/4 cup finely chopped onion
- 1 large garlic clove, smashed
- 7 ounces bottled whole cooked chestnuts (see Cook's Note), coarsely chopped
- 1/4 cup water
- 1 Granny Smith apple
- 2 tablespoons finely grated Parmigiano-Reggiano
- 1 tablespoon finely chopped fresh flat-leaf parsley
- Salt and freshly ground black pepper
- 1 tablespoon fresh lemon juice
- 48 wonton wrappers
- 1 tablespoon finely chopped fresh sage

SPECIAL EQUIPMENT: a 2 3/4-inch round cookie cutter

Melt 3 tablespoons butter in a large heavy saucepan over moderate heat. Add pancetta and cook, stirring, until crisp on edges, about 5 minutes. Add onion and garlic and cook, stirring, until onion is softened, about 3 minutes. Add chestnuts and water and simmer, stirring, until liquid is reduced by half, about 2 minutes.

Transfer mixture to a bowl and discard garlic. With a fork, mash chestnuts to a coarse paste. Peel half of apple and cut enough of peeled half into 1/4-inch dice to measure 3 tablespoons. (Reserve remaining unpeeled apple.) Stir peeled apple into chestnut mixture, along with Parmesan, parsley, and salt and pepper to taste.

Cut enough of unpeeled apple into 1/4-inch dice to measure 3 tablespoons. Toss with lemon juice in a small bowl. Set aside.

Put 1 wonton wrapper on a work surface (keep remaining wrappers covered with plastic wrap) and mound 1 scant tablespoon filling in center. Lightly brush edges of wrapper with water and top with a second wrapper, pressing down around filling to force out air. Cut ravioli into a round with cookie cutter and seal edges well, pressing them together with your fingertips. Transfer ravioli to a dry kitchen towel and make more in same manner.

Heat remaining 4 tablespoons butter in cleaned saucepan over moderate heat until foam subsides and butter begins to turn brown. Add sage and cook, stirring, until sage is crisp and butter is golden brown, 1 to 2 minutes. Remove from heat and season with salt and pepper. Set pan aside.

Add ravioli to a 6-quart pot of boiling salted water (1 tablespoon salt per every 4 quarts water) and cook at a slow boil, occasionally stirring gently, until tender, 3 to 5 minutes. With a slotted spoon, carefully transfer ravioli to a colander to drain, then slide ravioli into pan of sage butter and heat over moderate heat, stirring gently, for 1 minute.

Divide ravioli among eight plates and sprinkle with diced apple and pepper to taste.

COOK'S NOTE

■ Bottled chestnuts are more reliable than fresh, which can sometimes be moldy or rotten. They are available in specialty foods shops and some supermarkets, or see Sources.

Crispy Artichoke "Flowers" with Salsa Verde

SERVES 6

ACTIVE TIME: 40 MINUTES ■ START TO FINISH: 55 MINUTES (INCLUDES MAKING SALSA)

■ This traditional Roman Jewish dish, now emblematic of Roman food in general, is something you find all over the city in the spring, when artichokes are in season and piled high on market tables. These *carciofi alla giudia* are twice-fried. The first frying is done at a low heat to cook the artichokes. The second frying, in hotter oil, causes the leaves to spring open and gives them their crisp look. Because of the last-minute nature of frying, you'll want to follow the artichokes with a simple main course or something that can be at the ready. ■

- 2 lemons, halved
- 6 small (not baby) artichokes (4 ounces each)
- About 4 cups olive oil for deep-frying
- Salsa Verde (page 890)

SPECIAL EQUIPMENT: a melon ball cutter (optional); a deep-fat thermometer

TRIM AND FRY THE ARTICHOKES: Fill a large bowl with 6 cups cold water. Squeeze juice from 2 lemon halves into bowl.

Cut off artichoke stems and discard. Bend back outer leaves of 1 artichoke until they snap off close to base; remove and discard several more layers of leaves in same manner until you reach pale yellow leaves with pale green tips (see illustrations, page 518). Cut off pale green tips. Carefully spread leaves and scrape out purple leaves and hairy choke with melon ball cutter or a sharp spoon. Trim dark green fibrous parts from base, then rub artichoke all over with a lemon half and drop into lemon water. Trim remaining artichokes in same manner.

Drain artichokes well, stem ends up. Heat 1½ inches oil in a 2-quart deep heavy saucepan over moderate heat until it registers 200°F on thermometer. With tongs, transfer artichokes to oil, stem ends down, and simmer until tender, about 10 minutes. Transfer to paper towels to drain.

Heat oil until thermometer registers 365°F. Spear 1 artichoke through center of stem end with a long kitchen fork, immerse in oil (still on fork), and fry until leaves are spread open, browned, and crisp, 30 to 40 seconds. Drain well, stem end up, on paper towels. Fry remaining artichokes in same manner. (Return oil to 365°F for each artichoke.)

Serve artichokes hot, warm, or at room temperature with salsa verde.

Pissaladière

Provençal Onion, Tomato, and Anchovy Tart

SERVES 6

ACTIVE TIME: 1 HOUR ■ START TO FINISH: 4 HOURS (INCLUDES MAKING PUFF PASTRY)

■ This classic French pizza, made with pastry rather than bread dough, is simultaneously sophisticated and rustic. Eat it sitting outside, with a glass of rosé or, if you want to be ultra-traditional, the anise-flavored liqueur called pastis. ■

- Quick Rich Puff Pastry (recipe follows), chilled as directed
- 2 tablespoons plus 1 teaspoon olive oil
- 1 pound onions (3 medium), halved lengthwise and sliced crosswise
- 1½ teaspoons minced fresh basil or ½ teaspoon dried basil, crumbled
- 1½ teaspoons minced fresh thyme or ½ teaspoon dried thyme, crumbled
- 1½ teaspoons minced fresh rosemary or ½ teaspoon dried rosemary, crumbled
- ½ teaspoon salt
- ½ teaspoon freshly ground black pepper
- 1 (14½-ounce) can whole tomatoes in juice, drained and chopped
- 1 head Roasted Garlic (page 935), halved crosswise and flesh squeezed out
- 2 tablespoons finely chopped fresh basil or flat-leaf parsley
- ⅓ cup finely grated Parmigiano-Reggiano
- 2 medium tomatoes, halved, seeded, and cut crosswise into ⅛-inch-thick slices
- 1 (2-ounce) can flat anchovy fillets, drained, patted dry, and each cut lengthwise into 4 thin strips
- 20 Niçoise or Kalamata olives, pitted, quartered if using Kalamata olives

OPTIONAL GARNISH: mixed minced fresh basil, thyme, and rosemary

Rinse a baking sheet with cold water, letting excess run off (do not dry). Roll pastry into a 16-by-12-inch rectangle ($\frac{1}{8}$ inch thick) on a lightly floured surface with a lightly floured rolling pin. Loosely roll pastry around rolling pin, then unroll on dampened baking sheet. Chill dough, loosely covered, for 30 minutes.

Heat 2 tablespoons oil in a 10- to 12-inch heavy skillet over moderate heat. Add onions, minced herbs, salt, and pepper and cook, stirring occasionally, until onions are golden, about 12 minutes. Add canned tomatoes and cook, stirring and scraping up brown bits, until tomatoes are soft, about 3 minutes. Stir in garlic and chopped basil. Remove from heat.

Put a rack in middle of oven and preheat oven to 400°F.

Brush edges of pastry with water, fold them over to form a 1-inch-wide border, and press firmly to seal. Score all 4 edges with tines of a fork and prick interior of tart shell all over at $\frac{1}{4}$-inch intervals. Bake pastry until lightly golden, about 20 minutes (prick center if it puffs excessively during baking). Remove from oven. Increase oven temperature to 425°F.

Sprinkle 2 tablespoons cheese evenly in tart shell, then scatter onion mixture evenly over it. Sprinkle onions with 2 more tablespoons cheese, then top with sliced tomatoes, overlapping them slightly. Brush tomatoes with remaining 1 teaspoon oil. Scatter anchovies and olives over tart. Bake until pastry is golden and crisp, 25 to 30 minutes. Sprinkle warm tart with remaining cheese and serve warm or at room temperature, garnished with herbs, if desired.

Quick Rich Puff Pastry

MAKES ENOUGH FOR A 15-BY-11-INCH TART
ACTIVE TIME: 15 MINUTES ■ START TO FINISH: 2½ HOURS

■ In a pissaladière, the dough is as important as the filling. Our homemade quick rich puff pastry results in a delicious, buttery crust, and it is much easier and less time-consuming to make than regular puff pastry. (We tried using store-bought frozen puff pastry, one of our favorite standbys, but this one works better here.) ■

- 2 cups all-purpose flour
- ½ teaspoon salt
- 2 sticks (½ pound) cold unsalted butter, cut into ½-inch cubes
- ½ cup ice water

Whisk together flour and salt in a large bowl. Blend in butter with your fingertips or a pastry blender until mixture resembles coarse meal. Stir in ice water with a fork, then form dough into a ball.

Turn dough out onto a work surface, flatten into a 6-by-4-inch rectangle, and lightly dust with flour. Wrap in plastic wrap and refrigerate for 1 hour.

Roll out dough on a floured surface with a floured rolling pin into a 12-by-6-inch rectangle, dusting it with flour if it sticks to rolling pin. Turn dough, if necessary, so a short side is nearest you, then fold dough into thirds like a letter: bottom third up and top third down. Brush off any excess flour and turn dough so a short side is nearest you. Roll out dough into a 12-by-6-inch rectangle again, then fold into thirds again. Refrigerate, wrapped in plastic wrap, for 20 minutes.

With a short side nearest you, roll out dough a third time into a 12-by-6-inch rectangle, then fold like a letter again. Refrigerate, wrapped in plastic wrap, for 20 minutes.

With a short side nearest you, roll out dough into a 12-by-6-inch rectangle, then fold like a letter again and refrigerate, wrapped in plastic wrap, for at least 30 minutes.

COOK'S NOTE

- The finished dough can be refrigerated, wrapped in plastic wrap, for up to 1 day.

Onion and Bacon Tart

SERVES 8
ACTIVE TIME: 45 MINUTES ■ START TO FINISH: 6 HOURS (INCLUDES RISING)

■ This tart, which also makes a light lunch, is something like a German pizza. Onions are cooked down until they caramelize and become golden, then mixed with caraway seeds and bacon. A tiny amount of crème fraîche binds the flavors and gives the tart its tender texture. The food writer Kay Rentschler shared this recipe with us. ■

FOR DOUGH

- 1 cup lukewarm water (105°–115°F)
- ½ teaspoon honey
- ¼ teaspoon active dry yeast
- 2 cups high-gluten all-purpose flour (not bread flour; see Sources)
- ½ teaspoon salt

FOR TOPPING

- 5 ounces slab bacon (without rind), cut into ¼-inch-thick slices, slices cut crosswise into ¼-inch-wide strips
- 2 tablespoons unsalted butter
- 2 pounds small onions, halved and cut into ¼-inch-thick slices
- ¼ teaspoon caraway seeds
- ¾ teaspoon salt
- ½ teaspoon freshly ground black pepper
- 2 tablespoons crème fraîche
- 1 tablespoon minced fresh thyme

SPECIAL EQUIPMENT: a stand mixer with paddle attachment and dough hook; a pizza stone (see Sources); a small offset spatula

MAKE THE DOUGH: Stir together lukewarm water, honey, and yeast in bowl of mixer and let stand until foamy, about 5 minutes. (If mixture doesn't foam, discard and start over with new yeast.)

Add flour and salt and beat with paddle attachment at medium speed until a dough forms. Switch to dough hook and knead dough at medium speed until it no longer sticks to sides of bowl, 10 to 15 minutes. Cover bowl tightly with plastic wrap and let dough rise in a warm, draft-free place until doubled in bulk, about 4 hours. (Dough will be sticky.)

Put pizza stone on bottom rack of oven and preheat oven to 450°F; allow about 1 hour for stone to heat.

MEANWHILE, MAKE THE TOPPING AND SHAPE THE DOUGH: Sprinkle bacon into a 12-inch heavy skillet and add 3 tablespoons cold water. Cook over moderate heat, stirring occasionally, until bacon renders its fat and is translucent, about 6 minutes. With a slotted spoon, transfer to paper towels to drain.

Pour 1 tablespoon bacon fat into a 15-by-10-inch baking sheet with sides and grease pan with your fingers. Discard remaining bacon fat and set skillet aside.

With greased fingers, transfer dough to baking sheet and stretch into a small rectangle, then continue to stretch at intervals, while onions are cooking, until dough is a 10-by-8-inch rectangle. (Dough will become more malleable as it rests.)

Heat butter in reserved skillet over moderate heat until foam subsides. Add onions, caraway seeds, ½ teaspoon salt, and pepper and cook, stirring occasionally, until onions are golden, about 20 minutes. Spread onions on a baking sheet and let cool completely.

Stir together crème fraîche, thyme, and remaining ¼ teaspoon salt in a small bowl.

ASSEMBLE AND BAKE THE TART: Spread crème fraîche mixture evenly over dough, all the way to edges, with offset spatula. Scatter bacon and onions on top.

Bake tart in baking pan on pizza stone until edges of crust are golden, 20 to 25 minutes. Cool in pan on a rack for 10 minutes, then cut into squares and serve warm.

COOK'S NOTE

- The tart can be made up to 1 day ahead, cooled completely, and refrigerated, covered. Reheat in a 350°F oven until heated through, 10 to 15 minutes.

Cheese Fondue

SERVES 6

ACTIVE TIME: 30 MINUTES ■ START TO FINISH: 30 MINUTES

■ Whether you're serving this as a first course or as a meal, you'll want to take advantage of the great artisanal breads available today and accompany it with toasted cubes of walnut or pancetta bread or another favorite. The mixture of Emmental and Gruyère is important for flavor as well as texture. And even though most cooks won't get through a bottle of kirsch in their lifetime, it's worth buying for a fondue. We're not really sure why just two teaspoons enhance the flavor of the cheese; perhaps it just makes it taste authentic. Follow all this richness with a chopped salad or a leafy green salad, some charcuterie—thinly sliced sausage, perhaps—and a fruity dessert. ■

- 1 garlic clove, halved crosswise
- 1½ cups dry white wine, preferably Swiss
- 1 tablespoon cornstarch

2 teaspoons kirsch
2 cups coarsely grated Emmental (about 8 ounces)
2 cups coarsely grated Gruyère (about 8 ounces)

ACCOMPANIMENT: cubes of French or other bread

SPECIAL EQUIPMENT: a fondue pot and fondue forks or long wooden skewers

Rub inside of a 4-quart heavy saucepan with cut sides of garlic, then discard garlic. Add wine to pan and bring just to a simmer over moderate heat. Stir together cornstarch and kirsch in a cup.

Gradually add cheese to pot and cook, stirring constantly in a zigzag pattern, not a circular motion, to prevent cheese from clumping, until cheese is just melted and creamy; do not let boil. Stir cornstarch mixture again and stir into fondue. Bring fondue to a simmer and cook, stirring, until thickened, 5 to 8 minutes.

Transfer to fondue pot set over a flame and serve with bread for dipping.

WASTE NOT, WANT NOT

Fromage fort (literally, "strong cheese") is a blend of cheeses flavored with wine or herbs. It's a terrific way to use up leftover pieces of cheese. Remove and discard the rinds, if any, from 1 pound of assorted cheeses. Grate hard cheeses and cut softer cheeses into 1-inch pieces. In a food processor, blend cheeses with 3/4 stick (6 tablespoons) softened unsalted butter and 3 tablespoons dry white wine until very smooth, about 1 minute. Transfer to a small bowl. *Fromage fort* can be served immediately, when the consistency is soft; if a firmer consistency is desired, refrigerate, covered, for at least 2 hours. Serve with bread or crackers.

Gefilte Fish

SERVES 8

ACTIVE TIME: 40 MINUTES ■ START TO FINISH: 2 HOURS (INCLUDES MAKING STOCK)

■ Gefilte fish accompanied by horseradish is the traditional first course of the Passover seder in Ashkenazic (Eastern European) households; it's often served on other holidays and the Sabbath as well. The word *gefilte* means "stuffed" in Yiddish, and it refers to an old form of the recipe, in which the mousse is stuffed into a carp and poached. Store-bought gefilte fish cannot compare with homemade, and almost every Jewish family has its own recipe for these fish-mousse dumplings. Our version is particularly light and fresh-tasting. ■

1 tablespoon vegetable oil, plus additional for brushing skillet
4 cups Fish Stock (page 930)
4 cups water
1 pound skinless whitefish fillets, any bones discarded, finely chopped (not in a food processor)
2 medium carrots, finely chopped
1 medium onion, grated
2 tablespoons finely chopped fresh flat-leaf parsley
1 large egg, lightly beaten
1/3 cup matzo meal
1 teaspoon sugar
1 1/4 teaspoons salt
1/4 teaspoon freshly ground black pepper

ACCOMPANIMENT: bottled horseradish

Line a baking sheet with wax paper. Lightly brush bottom of a deep 12-inch skillet with vegetable oil. Combine fish stock and water in skillet and bring to a boil.

Meanwhile, stir together whitefish, carrots, onion, parsley, egg, 1 tablespoon oil, matzo meal, sugar, salt, and pepper in a large bowl until well combined.

With wet hands, form 1 1/2 tablespoons of fish mixture into torpedo-shaped dumplings and put on lined baking sheet.

Poach dumplings in 3 batches in simmering stock mixture, turning occasionally, until just cooked through, about 4 minutes per batch (break one open to check). With a slotted spoon, transfer to a plate lined with paper towels to drain. Serve warm or at room temperature, with horseradish.

Scallop Mousse with Ginger-Infused Velouté

SERVES 6

ACTIVE TIME: 1¾ HOURS ■ START TO FINISH: 2¼ HOURS (INCLUDES MAKING STOCK)

■ Ginger and star anise add sparkle and zing to this creamy mousse, and if you want even more of an Asian touch, serve a head of steamed baby bok choy alongside each mousse. ■

FOR HERB MIXTURE

- 1 tablespoon finely chopped fresh chives
- 1 tablespoon finely chopped fresh flat-leaf parsley
- 1 tablespoon finely chopped fresh cilantro
- 1½ teaspoons finely chopped fresh tarragon

FOR SAUCE

- ¼ cup finely chopped leek (white and pale green parts only)
- 2 tablespoons unsalted butter
- ½ cup finely chopped shallots
- ¼ cup finely chopped fennel bulb
- ¼ cup finely chopped carrot
- ¼ cup finely chopped celery
- 4 star anise
- ¼ cup finely chopped peeled fresh ginger, plus 1 tablespoon very thin (1-inch-long) matchsticks
- 1 cup dry white wine
- 1 cup Fish Stock (page 930)
- 1 cup heavy cream
- ½ teaspoon salt
- ¼ teaspoon freshly ground black pepper
- ½–1 teaspoon fresh lemon juice, or to taste

FOR MOUSSE

- ⅓ pound sea scallops, tough side muscle removed from each if necessary
- 1 tablespoon lightly beaten egg white
- Rounded ¼ teaspoon salt
- ⅛ teaspoon white pepper
- 1 cup very cold heavy cream

SPECIAL EQUIPMENT: six 2-ounce ramekins

MAKE THE HERB MIXTURE: Stir herbs together in a small bowl.

MAKE THE SAUCE: Wash chopped leek in a bowl of cold water; lift out and drain well.

Melt butter in a 2-quart heavy saucepan over moderate heat. Add leek, shallots, fennel, carrot, celery, star anise, and chopped ginger and cook, stirring, until vegetables are softened, about 5 minutes. Add wine, bring to a simmer, and simmer briskly until liquid is reduced to 2 tablespoons, about 5 minutes.

Add fish stock, bring to a boil, and boil until liquid is reduced to ½ cup, about 10 minutes. Add cream, salt, pepper, and 2 tablespoons herb mixture and bring to a simmer. Remove pan from heat and let sauce steep with herbs, uncovered, for 15 minutes.

Pour sauce through a fine-mesh sieve into a bowl, pressing on solids; discard solids.

Return sauce to cleaned pan, add ginger matchsticks, and bring just to a simmer. Simmer gently, uncovered, until reduced to 1 cup, about 10 minutes. Stir in lemon juice and salt and pepper to taste. Remove from heat and cover to keep warm.

MEANWHILE, MAKE THE MOUSSE: Put a rack in middle of oven and preheat oven to 325°F. Butter ramekins, line bottoms with rounds of parchment or wax paper, and butter paper.

Combine scallops, egg white, salt, and white pepper in a food processor and purée until smooth. With motor running, add cream in a steady stream and process just until well incorporated. Divide mousse among ramekins, smoothing tops with back of a small spoon.

Put ramekins in a baking pan and add enough boiling water to pan to come halfway up sides of ramekins. Bake until a tester inserted into center of a mousse comes out clean, 10 to 12 minutes.

Meanwhile, gently reheat sauce.

TO SERVE: Run a small thin knife around edge of each mousse, then invert mousse onto paper towels to blot excess moisture. Discard parchment paper. Using a metal spatula, transfer mousse to plates. Spoon sauce over and around mousse and sprinkle with remaining 1½ tablespoons mixed herbs.

COOK'S NOTES

- The mousse can be made (but not baked) up to 1 day ahead. Fill the ramekins and refrigerate, covered with plastic wrap.

- The sauce can be made up to 1 day ahead. Cool, uncovered, then refrigerate, covered. Reheat gently before serving.

Escargots à la Bourguignonne

SERVES 4

ACTIVE TIME: 30 MINUTES ■ START TO FINISH: 30 MINUTES

■ For many people, the best thing about snails is the hot butter, heady with garlic, shallot, and parsley, spilling out of the shells. Snail butter is delicious on grilled meats as well as almost any seafood. Snails served this way are a classic bistro teaser. Pass the baguette, please. ■

- 1 stick (8 tablespoons) unsalted butter, softened
- 1½ teaspoons minced shallot
- 1 garlic clove, minced
- 1 tablespoon finely chopped fresh flat-leaf parsley
- ½ teaspoon salt
- ¼ teaspoon freshly ground black pepper
- 1 tablespoon dry white wine
- 2 (4½-ounce) cans escargots (see Cook's Note)
- 3 cups kosher salt (for stabilizing snail shells)

SPECIAL EQUIPMENT: 24 sterilized escargot shells (see Cook's Note)

Put a rack in middle of oven and preheat oven to 450°F.

Beat butter, shallot, garlic, parsley, salt, and pepper in a small bowl with an electric mixer until well combined. Beat in wine until well combined.

Divide half of garlic butter among snail shells. Stuff 1 snail into each shell and top snails with remaining butter. Spread kosher salt on a large baking sheet with sides and nestle shells, butter sides up, in salt.

Bake until butter is melted and sizzling, 2 to 3 minutes. Serve immediately.

COOK'S NOTES

- Escargots (and escargot shells) are available in specialty foods shops and many supermarkets, or see Sources.
- The escargots can be prepared up to 30 minutes ahead and kept at room temperature until ready to bake.

Fried Calamari with Peperoncini Mayonnaise

SERVES 4

ACTIVE TIME: 45 MINUTES ■ START TO FINISH: 45 MINUTES

■ Most Americans learn to appreciate squid in the form of tempting little bites of fried calamari. We decided to revisit the old favorite, this time with a peperoncini-spiked mayonnaise for dipping. Keep in mind that quick cooking makes for tender squid. Rice flour (found at Asian markets, natural foods stores, and in the ethnic foods section of some supermarkets) is the secret to a delectably light, crisp coating. ■

- 6–8 drained bottled peperoncini (Italian hot green peppers)
- ½ cup mayonnaise
- 1 pound cleaned squid, preferably small
- About 6 cups vegetable oil for deep-frying
- ¾ cup rice flour
- ¾ teaspoon salt
- ½ teaspoon freshly ground black pepper

SPECIAL EQUIPMENT: a deep-fat thermometer

Halve peperoncini lengthwise and discard stems and seeds. Rinse and pat dry, then mince enough to measure ¼ cup. Stir into mayonnaise in a small bowl.

Rinse squid under cold running water. Lightly pat dry between paper towels, leaving some moisture so rice flour will stick. Leave tentacles whole. Cut bodies (including flaps, if attached) crosswise into ⅓-inch-wide rings. Set aside, separately, on paper towels.

Put a rack in middle of oven and preheat oven to 200°F.

Heat 2 inches oil in a 4- to 5-quart heavy pot over high heat until it registers 390°F on thermometer. Meanwhile, whisk together flour, salt, and black pepper in a shallow bowl. Set a medium-mesh sieve in another shallow bowl.

Dredge a small handful of squid rings in flour mixture, tossing to coat well. Transfer to sieve and shake to remove excess flour; return excess flour to first bowl. Fry floured rings in oil, stirring to separate, until golden, about 1 minute. Transfer to dry paper towels to drain, arranging in one layer. Coat and fry remaining rings in about 3 more batches in same manner. (Return oil to 390°F between batches.) Transfer fried and drained rings to a shallow baking pan, in one layer, and keep warm, uncovered, in oven.

Coat and fry tentacles in 2 or 3 batches until golden, about 1½ minutes per batch. Transfer to paper towels to drain, then transfer to baking pan. (Return oil to 390°F between batches.)

Serve calamari with peperoncini mayonnaise for dipping.

Crabmeat, Apple, and Mango Salad on Cumin Apple Chips

SERVES 6
ACTIVE TIME: 40 MINUTES ■ START TO FINISH: 2½ HOURS (INCLUDES MAKING CHIPS)

■ Parchment-thin apple chips, made savory with a little cumin, form crackling layers on which the salad is stacked, to make a first course that resembles napoleons. Apple and mango together might sound a bit much for the crab, but the diced apple provides crunch, and the mango contrasts with its rich smoothness. You could also mound this salad in halved avocados for a lunch main course, to serve four. ■

FOR DRESSING

- 1 medium Granny Smith apple, cored and chopped (1 cup)
- 2 tablespoons chopped shallots
- 1 large garlic clove, chopped
- 2 tablespoons cider vinegar
- ¾ teaspoon salt
- ⅔ cup extra-virgin olive oil

FOR SALAD

- 1 pound jumbo lump crabmeat, picked over for shells and cartilage
- ½ large, firm, but ripe mango, peeled, pitted, and cut into ¼-inch dice (½ cup)
- 1 medium Granny Smith apple, cut into ¼-inch dice (¾ cup)
- ⅓ cup chopped fresh cilantro
- Salt
- 18 Cumin Apple Chips (recipe follows)

MAKE THE DRESSING: Combine apple, shallots, garlic, vinegar, and salt in a blender and purée until very smooth. With motor running, add oil in a slow stream, blending until very smooth, about 30 seconds.

PREPARE THE SALAD: Gently stir together crab, mango, apple, cilantro, and 6 tablespoons dressing in a bowl. Season with salt.

Just before serving, put 1 apple chip on each of six plates and top each chip with about 3 tablespoons crab salad. Top each with another chip and another 3 tablespoons crab salad, then top each stack with another chip. Drizzle plates with some of remaining dressing and serve immediately.

COOK'S NOTE

■ The dressing can be made up to 1 day ahead and refrigerated, covered.

Cumin Apple Chips

MAKES 18 CHIPS
ACTIVE TIME: 10 MINUTES ■ START TO FINISH: 1¾ HOURS

■ You'll want to make these crunchy, sweet-tart chips as a snack. Their preparation is especially easy with a Silpat or other reusable nonstick baking sheet liner. (For more about nonstick baking sheet liners, see Sources) ■

3 tablespoons confectioners' sugar
1 teaspoon ground cumin
1 medium Granny Smith apple

SPECIAL EQUIPMENT: a nonstick baking sheet liner, such as a Silpat, or parchment paper; a wide (3¾-inch) mandoline or other adjustable-blade slicer, such as a Japanese Benriner

Put a rack in middle of oven and preheat oven to 200°F. Line a large baking sheet with nonstick liner or parchment.

Sift together confectioners' sugar and cumin, then sift together again. Sift half of cumin sugar evenly onto liner (or paper).

Cut apple crosswise into very thin slices (about 1/16 inch thick) with slicer. Arrange 18 of largest slices nearly touching each other on liner. (Reserve remaining apple slices for another use.) Sift remaining cumin sugar evenly over apples.

Bake slices until pale golden and beginning to crisp, about 1½ hours. Immediately peel chips off liner and let cool on a rack.

COOK'S NOTES

- The apple chips can be kept in an airtight container at room temperature for up to 1 week.
- If you use parchment paper, be prepared for some chips to stick to it. When they do, return them to the oven for 3 minutes to soften.

Scallion, Mushroom, and Shrimp Custards

SERVES 4
ACTIVE TIME: 20 MINUTES ■ START TO FINISH: 40 MINUTES

■ These custards are steamed, which gives them a delicate, almost ethereal texture. They're inspired by the Japanese egg custard called *chawan mushi,* made with *dashi* broth (a stock based on dried bonito flakes). We've used chicken stock for simplicity's sake, but any delicate stock or broth you have on hand will work as well. ■

3 large eggs
1½ cups chicken stock or store-bought low-sodium broth
2 teaspoons mirin (Japanese sweet rice wine; see Glossary)
1 teaspoon soy sauce
2 teaspoons finely grated lemon zest
Pinch of salt
4 medium shrimp in shells, peeled, deveined, and chopped
1 scallion (white part only), minced
1 large mushroom, trimmed and chopped

SPECIAL EQUIPMENT: four 6-ounce custard cups or ramekins

Lightly beat eggs in a medium bowl with a fork. Skim any fat from broth, then add to eggs, along with mirin, soy sauce, zest, and salt, and stir to combine well. Let stand at room temperature for 10 minutes, then pour through a fine-mesh sieve into another bowl.

Divide shrimp, scallion, and mushroom among custard cups or ramekins. Pour in custard mixture and cover each tightly with foil.

Arrange cups in a steamer rack set over boiling water and steam, covered, over high heat for 2 minutes. Reduce heat to moderate and steam custards until set, about 10 minutes more.

Serve immediately.

Pork and Bell Pepper Pie

Empanada de Lomo de Cerdo

SERVES 12
ACTIVE TIME: 45 MINUTES ■ START TO FINISH: 7¾ HOURS (INCLUDES MARINATING TIME AND MAKING DOUGH)

■ In Spain's Galicia region, innumerable tapas bars serve small plates of seafood in vinaigrettes, tiny green peppers, and portions of big round fish or meat *empanadas.* This Galician tapa was created by Penelope Casas, a renowned authority on Spanish food. It makes a great first course, and it would be a terrific addition to a buffet party as well. ■

- 1/4 teaspoon dried thyme, crumbled
- 1/4 teaspoon dried oregano, crumbled
- 1 tablespoon sweet paprika, preferably Spanish
- 1/8 teaspoon saffron threads, crumbled
- 2 tablespoons minced fresh flat-leaf parsley
- 1 garlic clove, minced
- 1 1/4 teaspoons kosher salt, or to taste
- 6 tablespoons olive oil, preferably Spanish
- 1 (3/4-pound) piece boneless lean pork loin, trimmed, cut into 1/8-inch-thick slices and then into 1/8-inch-wide strips
- 2 medium onions, quartered and thinly sliced into strips
- 2 green bell peppers, cored, seeded, and cut into 1/2-inch-wide strips
- 2 tablespoons dry white wine
- 1/4 teaspoon freshly ground black pepper
- Empanada Dough (recipe follows)
- 1 large egg lightly beaten with 1 teaspoon water, for egg wash

Combine thyme, oregano, paprika, saffron, parsley, garlic, 1 teaspoon salt, and 4 tablespoons (1/4 cup) oil in a medium bowl. Add pork and toss to coat. Marinate pork, covered and refrigerated, for at least 3 hours.

Heat remaining 2 tablespoons oil in a large heavy skillet over moderately high heat until hot but not smoking. Add onions and bell peppers and cook, stirring, for 2 minutes. Reduce heat to moderately low, cover, and cook, stirring occasionally, until vegetables are tender, about 15 minutes. With a slotted spoon, transfer vegetables to a plate.

Increase heat to moderately high, add pork and marinade to skillet, and cook, stirring, until pork is no longer pink, 2 to 3 minutes. Add wine and cook, stirring, for 1 minute. Remove from heat and stir in vegetables, remaining 1/4 teaspoon salt, and pepper. Let cool for 30 minutes.

Put a rack in middle of oven and preheat oven to 400°F.

Roll out dough on a lightly floured surface into a 15-by-10-inch rectangle. Turn it over and brush off any excess flour. Position dough with a short side nearest you and fold into thirds like a letter to form a rough 10-by-5-inch rectangle. Cut rectangle crosswise in half. Turn both squares of dough over and brush off excess flour. Roll out each piece into a 14-inch square and, using a platter or large lid as a guide, cut out a 14-inch round from each square of dough.

Lightly brush a baking sheet with water. Transfer 1 dough round to baking sheet and top it with pork mixture, leaving a 1/2-inch border all around. Put remaining round on top and press edges together to seal. Crimp edges decoratively. Cut several slits in top of pastry with a small sharp knife and lightly brush pastry with egg wash.

Put *empanada* in oven, reduce heat to 350°F, and bake until golden, about 45 minutes. Transfer baking sheet to a rack to cool for 5 minutes. Cut *empanada* into wedges and serve warm or at room temperature.

COOK'S NOTE

- The pork can marinate for up to 8 hours.

Empanada Dough

MAKES ENOUGH FOR ONE 14-INCH *EMPANADA*
ACTIVE TIME: 25 MINUTES ■ START TO FINISH: 2 1/2 HOURS

■ This is a very tender, flaky dough. It's made by repeatedly spreading a flour-and-egg dough with shortening or lard, folding it, and rolling it out like puff pastry. ■

- 3 cups all-purpose flour
- 1 1/2 teaspoons salt
- 2 large egg yolks
- 3/4 cup cold water
- 5 teaspoons red wine vinegar
- 1 cup vegetable shortening or lard, softened

Stir together flour and salt in a large bowl. Lightly beat yolks in a small bowl, then stir in water and vinegar. Stir into flour mixture.

Turn out mixture onto a lightly floured surface and knead gently with heel of your hand until it forms a dough, then shape into a ball. Let dough stand at room temperature, wrapped in plastic wrap, for 30 minutes.

Roll out dough on lightly floured surface into a 15-by-10-inch rectangle. If necessary, turn dough so a short side is nearest you. Spread 1/3 cup shortening evenly over it with a rubber spatula, then fold into thirds like a letter to form a rough 10-by-5-inch rectangle. Wrap in plastic wrap and refrigerate for 15 minutes.

Roll out dough into a 15-by-10-inch rectangle again, then spread half of remaining shortening evenly over it and fold dough in same manner. Refrigerate again for 15 minutes.

Repeat procedure a third time with remaining 1/3 cup shortening and refrigerate dough, wrapped in plastic wrap, for at least 1 hour.

COOK'S NOTES

- This dough is very soft, but it can tighten during the final rolling and become difficult to work with. If that happens, put it on a baking sheet lined with parchment or wax paper and refrigerate for 15 minutes before rolling.
- The dough can be refrigerated for up to 2 days. It can also be frozen, wrapped well in plastic wrap, then foil, for up to 3 months. Thaw in the refrigerator for 24 hours, still wrapped, before using.

SOUPS

In the early years of *Gourmet*, soup often seemed like just an excuse to put another plate on the party table, an opportunity to show off an extra sterling spoon. It went by fancy names—*potage, consommé, crème de la* this or that. Nothing better exemplifies that particular age of soup than vichyssoise, which was nothing that its name implied. It was not hot, not French, and not complicated. It could not even boast about its ancient pedigree, since it was invented early in the twentieth century in America by Louis Diat, the chef at New York City's Ritz-Carlton (he later became *Gourmet*'s in-house chef). None of this really mattered, though, because what vichyssoise had going for it, like many of its contemporaries, was that it was rich and it was delicious.

American soups soon tumbled off their pedestal, though. When we developed into a can-opener culture, soup lost much of its cachet. In its purest form, it became what children ate for lunch; in its more elaborate guises, soup was an indispensable ingredient in the ubiquitous casseroles of the fifties and sixties. Later, thanks to dehydration, it also became the basis of the dips that went with the chips at college parties.

But as Americans began to discover the foods of other cultures, soup lost its bland demeanor and underwent a transformation. It got spicy, it got substantial, it moved to the center of the meal. No longer the overture that introduced the production, soup took center stage and became the starring act.

Here you will find soup in all of its fascinating incarnations, from the classic lobster bisque that began the fancy dinner parties of the forties to the feisty tortilla soup that took America by storm in the nineties. This extraordinary selection encompasses the comfort of matzo ball soup, the elegance of cream of lentil and chestnut soup with foie gras custards, and the hearty goodness of black bean soup laced with rum. There are thin soups (lemon broth dotted with ravioli) and thick ones (*soupe au pistou* laden with vegetables), purées and gumbos. There are old-fashioned soups (clam chowder) and newfangled ones (chilled lemongrass tomato). Our soups span the globe, from the *pho* of Vietnam to the *harira* of Morocco and the *fanesca* of Ecuador. And our chefs' offerings begin with Louis Diat's vichyssoise, go through the bongo-bongo of Trader Vic, and end up with a hot-and-sour pumpkin soup that was recently bestowed on us by Ming Tsai, the chef-owner of Blue Ginger, in Wellesley, Massachusetts.

Different though these soups may be, they all share a few qualities: they offer comfort and sustenance, fill the house with wonderful aromas, and can make a single dish seem like a meal. We love them all, and we think you will want to offer each of them a permanent place at your table.

Crème Vichyssoise

SERVES 8 TO 10 (MAKES ABOUT 11 CUPS)
ACTIVE TIME: 40 MINUTES ■ START TO FINISH: $3\frac{1}{2}$ HOURS (INCLUDES CHILLING)

■ Everything you want in a cold soup is right here. The leek and potato combination has a sweet succulence all its own. We love the way two peasant ingredients—leeks were once called "poor man's asparagus"—puréed and smoothed out with cream, turn into something so elegant. Vichyssoise was invented by the formidable French chef Louis Diat, who joined the New York Ritz-Carlton as chef de cuisine in 1910; this is one of his variations. In 1947 he became the in-house chef at *Gourmet*. ■

- 4 medium leeks (white and pale green parts only), halved lengthwise and coarsely chopped ($2\frac{1}{2}$ cups)
- 2 tablespoons unsalted butter
- 1 medium onion, chopped
- $1\frac{1}{2}$ pounds russet (baking) potatoes (2 medium), peeled, diced, and reserved in 4 cups water
- 2 teaspoons salt
- 2 cups whole milk
- 2 cups half-and-half or light cream
- 1 cup heavy cream
- White pepper

OPTIONAL GARNISH: thinly sliced fresh chives

Wash leeks in a bowl of cold water; lift out and drain well. Melt butter in a 6- to 8-quart heavy pot over low heat. Add leeks and onion, cover, and cook, stirring occasionally, until softened, about 10 minutes. Add potatoes, with water, and salt and simmer, covered, until potatoes are tender, 30 to 40 minutes.

Add milk and half-and-half and bring just to a boil, stirring, then remove from heat.

Purée mixture in batches in a blender (use caution) and force through a fine-mesh sieve into a large bowl, pressing hard on solids; discard solids. Stir in cream and white pepper to taste.

Place bowl in a larger bowl of ice and cold water and stir until soup is cold. Refrigerate, covered, until very cold.

Season with salt before serving and sprinkle with chives, if desired.

VARIATION

■ VICHYSSOISE WITH SORREL: Decrease the leeks to 1 cup chopped (about 2 leeks) and add $\frac{3}{4}$ pound sorrel, stems discarded and leaves coarsely chopped (10 cups), to the butter along with the onion.

SORREL

We tend to think of lemony-tart sorrel as a harbinger of spring, but in cool climates it flourishes throughout the summer and into fall. To use it cooked, as in the classic *potage germiny* (cream of sorrel soup) or, as we do here, to punctuate a variation on vichyssoise, purchase a generous amount, since sorrel cooks down even more than spinach. Though it isn't possible to preserve its bright color — it turns a muddy olive green when cooked — its flavor remains vibrant. A sparkly salad green, sorrel can also be used as an herb. Its astringency will offset the richness of smoked salmon, eggs, or a creamy cheese.

Chilled Pea Soup with Lemon Cream

SERVES 6 (MAKES ABOUT 6 CUPS)
ACTIVE TIME: 30 MINUTES ■ START TO FINISH: 8½ HOURS (INCLUDES CHILLING)

■ In an antithesis to a hefty, rib-sticking pea soup, we play up the sweetness of sugar snaps in this intensely flavored, bright green broth. Chill it well, add sour cream, lemon zest, and (just for fun) lacy pea shoots, and you have a superb hot-weather soup. If you want the lemon cream to float like a little cloud on top of the soup, make sure the soup is really cold first. ■

- 3 tablespoons olive oil
- 2 medium onions, chopped
- 2 pounds sugar snap peas, cut into ½-inch-wide pieces
- 1 teaspoon sugar
- 6 cups plus 2½ tablespoons water
- 2 teaspoons salt, or to taste
- 3 tablespoons sour cream
- 1 teaspoon finely grated lemon zest

OPTIONAL GARNISH: young pea shoots (see page 556)

Heat oil in a 6-quart wide heavy pot over moderately low heat. Add onions and cook, stirring occasionally, until softened, 5 to 7 minutes. Add sugar snaps and cook, stirring occasionally, until crisp-tender and bright green, 6 to 8 minutes. Add sugar and cook, stirring, for 1 minute.

Purée pea mixture with 6 cups water in 6 batches in a blender until very smooth, about 30 seconds per batch, then pour through a fine-mesh sieve into a large bowl; do not press on solids (discard solids). Stir in salt. Refrigerate, covered, until very cold, about 8 hours. (Note: Long chilling is necessary if you want the lemon cream to float. But do not chill longer, or soup will discolor.)

Whisk together sour cream, zest, and remaining 2½ tablespoons water in a small bowl. Pour through fine-mesh sieve into another small bowl (to remove air bubbles).

Serve broth topped with lemon cream and garnished with pea sprouts, if desired.

Sieves

Straining a soup might seem to be an unnecessary extra step if your soup is already puréed, but it will give it a silkier, smoother texture — exactly what you want in an elegant soup. When you're aiming for the essence of flavor without any pulp, you'll need a fine-mesh sieve. (The tighter the mesh, the more solids it removes from liquid.) When you want to remove vegetable skins but keep the pulp in a soup (to give it body), as in Fresh Corn Soup (page 99), use a medium-mesh sieve and push the pulp through the wire mesh with a flexible rubber spatula. Regardless of which sieve you are using, press down hard, forcefully scraping the spatula back and forth across the mesh, and don't forget to scrape the sediment from the underside of the sieve. Sieves come in handy for all sorts of kitchen tasks, so when buying them get large ones so you can work efficiently, and save that tiny one for straining tea leaves.

Cold Tomato and Sour Cream Soup

SERVES 6 (MAKES ABOUT 6 CUPS)
ACTIVE TIME: 40 MINUTES ■ START TO FINISH: 1¾ HOURS (INCLUDES CHILLING)

■ Celebrate the end of summer—and the height of the tomato season—with this soup. Nothing is cooked (all you need is a blender), yet it is vivid in both appearance and taste. We love the contrast between the clean, clear tomato flavor and the sour cream topping. Enjoy every mouthful, and think, *Same time next year.* ■

3 pounds tomatoes, quartered
2 teaspoons finely grated lemon zest
2–4 tablespoons fresh lemon juice (to taste)
1 tablespoon finely chopped scallion greens
1 teaspoon sugar
Pinch of dried thyme, crumbled
Pinch of dried marjoram, crumbled
1 teaspoon salt
1/4 teaspoon freshly ground black pepper
1 cup sour cream

Purée tomatoes in batches in a blender until smooth, then force purée through a medium-mesh sieve into a large bowl; discard solids. Stir in lemon zest, juice, scallion greens, sugar, thyme, marjoram, salt, and pepper.

Refrigerate, covered, until cold, at least 1 hour.

Ladle soup into bowls and top with dollops of sour cream.

COOK'S NOTE

- The soup can be refrigerated for up to 1 day.

Cold Avocado Corn Soup with Cilantro Oil

SERVES 6
ACTIVE TIME: 50 MINUTES ■ START TO FINISH: 2½ HOURS (INCLUDES CHILLING)

■ This suave avocado soup is an homage to the flavors of Mexico. We get all the corn has to give by first roasting the whole ear, then using the kernels and the cob itself to make a broth. Finish the soup with a drizzle of cilantro oil and *crema*, a Mexican cultured heavy cream similar to sour cream, which adds tangy richness and ties everything together. ■

FOR SOUP
1 ear corn, shucked
4 cups plus 2 tablespoons water
1¼ cups chopped white onions
1 garlic clove, smashed
1½ teaspoons salt
1 serrano chile, stemmed and coarsely chopped (including seeds)
2 firm but ripe California avocados (1–1¼ pounds total)
3 tablespoons fresh lime juice
1/4 cup *crema* (see Glossary) or sour cream

FOR CILANTRO OIL
1 cup coarsely chopped fresh cilantro
1/4 cup olive oil
1/2 teaspoon salt

SPECIAL EQUIPMENT: a 3/4-inch melon ball cutter

MAKE THE SOUP: Roast corn on grate of a gas burner over high heat, turning occasionally, until kernels are charred in spots, 4 to 5 minutes. (Alternatively, heat a dry, well-seasoned cast-iron skillet over moderately high heat and roast corn, turning occasionally, for about 10 minutes.) Transfer corn to a cutting board. When cool enough to handle, cut kernels from cob with a sharp knife, then cut cob into thirds.

Combine kernels, cob, 4 cups water, 1/2 cup onions, garlic, and salt in a 3-quart saucepan, bring to a boil, and boil until liquid is reduced to about 3 cups, about 20 minutes. Remove from heat and cool, uncovered. Discard cob.

Purée corn mixture with chile and remaining 3/4 cup onions in a blender. Pour through a fine-mesh sieve into a large bowl, pressing hard on solids; discard solids. Return broth to cleaned blender.

Halve, pit, and peel 1 avocado. Add to blender along with 2 tablespoons lime juice and purée until smooth. Transfer soup to bowl and cover with plastic wrap placed directly on surface. Refrigerate soup until cold, at least 1 hour.

MEANWHILE, PREPARE THE OIL: Combine cilantro, oil, and salt in cleaned blender and purée, scraping down sides several times. Pour oil into cleaned fine-mesh sieve set over a bowl and let drain for 15 minutes (do not press on solids). Discard solids.

ASSEMBLE THE SOUP: Halve and pit remaining avocado. Scoop small balls from flesh with melon ball cutter and toss gently with remaining 1 tablespoon lime juice in a bowl.

Whisk together *crema* and remaining 2 tablespoons water in a small bowl until smooth.

Season soup with salt and ladle into six shallow soup bowls. Divide avocado balls among bowls, then drizzle with *crema* and cilantro oil.

COOK'S NOTES

- The soup can be refrigerated for up to 1 day.
- The cilantro oil can be made up to 3 hours ahead and refrigerated, covered. Bring to room temperature before using.

Jellied Borscht

SERVES 4 (MAKES ABOUT 4 CUPS)
ACTIVE TIME: 15 MINUTES ■ START TO FINISH: 5 HOURS (INCLUDES CHILLING)

■ Staggeringly simple and good, this is a perfect starter, or even a light lunch, on a sultry day. And it's beautiful too, served in cool white soup plates. This recipe is from Karen Hanauer of New York City, who acquired it from her aunt. The main ingredient, a jar of borscht with shredded beets, is available in many supermarkets year-round; otherwise, look for it during the Jewish holidays. Stock up on a few jars during Passover and you'll be set for the summer. ■

- 1 (32- to 33-ounce) jar borscht with shredded beets
- ¼ cup fresh lemon juice
- ¼ teaspoon salt
- 5 teaspoons unflavored gelatin (from two ¼-ounce envelopes)

ACCOMPANIMENTS: finely diced radish or cucumber, chopped fresh dill, and sour cream

Pour borscht through a large sieve into a 3-quart saucepan; reserve beets for another use. Stir in lemon juice and salt, then sprinkle with gelatin. Let stand for 1 minute to soften.

Bring soup to a boil, stirring. Pour into a 9-inch glass or ceramic baking dish. Cool for 20 minutes, then refrigerate, covered, until set, at least 4 hours.

Cut jelled soup into ⅓-inch dice and serve in bowls, with accompaniments on the side.

COOK'S NOTE

- The soup can be refrigerated for up to 4 days.

Chilled Buttermilk Soup with Beets, Cucumber, Radishes, and Dill

Chlodnik

SERVES 4 (MAKES ABOUT 5 CUPS)
ACTIVE TIME: 15 MINUTES ■ START TO FINISH: 30 MINUTES

■ This Polish soup, called *chlodnik* (pronounced "hu-*wohd*-neek"), is a refreshing, restorative first course for a summer meal. It's creamy, yes, and it has an earthy sweetness from the beets, a peppery bite from the radishes, and a cooling crunch from the cucumber. ■

- 3 cups well-shaken, very cold buttermilk
- ½ cup sour cream
- ½ teaspoon salt
- 1 cup chopped bottled pickled beets, plus ¼ cup pickled beet liquid
- 1 cup chopped seedless cucumber (usually plastic wrapped)
- ½ cup chopped radishes
- 2 tablespoons chopped fresh dill

Whisk together buttermilk, sour cream, and salt in a large bowl, then stir in remaining ingredients. Refrigerate, covered, until cold, at least 15 minutes.

COOK'S NOTE

- The soup can be refrigerated for up to 8 hours.

Cold Buttermilk and Shrimp Soup

SERVES 4 TO 6 (MAKES ABOUT 5 CUPS)
ACTIVE TIME: 20 MINUTES ■ START TO FINISH: 3¼ HOURS (INCLUDES CHILLING)

■ A soothing, rejuvenating supper after a long, hot summer day, this soup has a venerable pedigree: it has appeared in our pages from time to time since the 1940s, and M.F.K. Fisher offers a rendition in her classic *How to*

Cook a Wolf. The combination of tangy buttermilk and chopped shrimp is elusive and quite delicious. ■

- 1/2 pound medium shrimp in shells (31–35 per pound)
- 1 quart well-shaken, very cold buttermilk
- 1–2 teaspoons dry mustard (to taste)
- 1 teaspoon salt
- 1 teaspoon sugar
- 1/2 pound cucumbers, peeled, seeded, and finely chopped
- 2 tablespoons finely chopped fresh chives

OPTIONAL GARNISH: cucumber slices

Cook shrimp in boiling salted water (1 tablespoon salt per every 4 quarts water) until just cooked through, about 1 minute. Drain.

When shrimp are cool enough to handle, peel and devein. Reserve 2 or 3 shrimp for garnish, covered and refrigerated, and chop remainder.

Whisk together buttermilk, mustard, salt, and sugar in a large bowl. Add chopped shrimp, cucumbers, and chives and stir until well combined. Refrigerate, covered, until very cold, about 3 hours.

Chop reserved shrimp. Ladle soup into bowls and garnish with shrimp and cucumber slices, if using.

COOK'S NOTE

- The shrimp can be cooked up to 1 day ahead and refrigerated, covered.

Cucumber Soup with Wasabi Avocado Cream

SERVES 6 (MAKES ABOUT 6 CUPS)
ACTIVE TIME: 25 MINUTES ■ START TO FINISH: 25 MINUTES

■ This soup is a quick, luxurious first course. The astringency of cucumbers, the buttery richness of avocado, and the pungent, pure heat of Japanese wasabi contrast with and complement one another. ■

- 3 seedless cucumbers (usually plastic wrapped), peeled, seeded, and sliced
- 1/2 cup cold water
- 1/2 teaspoon distilled white vinegar
- 1 tablespoon kosher salt
- 1 ripe California avocado, halved, pitted, and peeled
- 1/2 teaspoon fresh lime juice
- 1 (8-ounce) container plain yogurt
- 1 teaspoon wasabi paste (see Glossary), or 1 1/2 teaspoons wasabi powder mixed with 1/2 teaspoon water, or to taste
- 2 tablespoons finely chopped fresh chives
- Freshly ground black pepper
- 1 1/2 cups ice cubes

OPTIONAL GARNISH: finely chopped fresh chives

Purée cucumbers with water, vinegar, and 2 teaspoons salt in batches in a blender until very smooth. Transfer to a bowl.

Mash together avocado, lime juice, and remaining 1 teaspoon salt in a small bowl with a fork until smooth. Whisk in yogurt, wasabi, chives, and pepper to taste.

Just before serving, blend cucumber soup with ice in batches until smooth. Serve topped with wasabi avocado cream and sprinkled with chives, if desired.

COOK'S NOTES

- The soup can be made (but not blended with the ice) up to 1 day ahead; refrigerate, covered.
- The wasabi avocado cream can be made up to 1 day ahead. Cover with plastic wrap placed directly on its surface and refrigerate.

Mexican Corn Soup

SERVES 6 (MAKES ABOUT 6 CUPS)
ACTIVE TIME: 1 1/4 HOURS ■ START TO FINISH: 2 1/2 HOURS PLUS ADDITIONAL TIME IF MAKING STOCK

■ We love corn and often turn to Mexico for inspiration. Here is a chunky, lusty soup that's alive with cilantro and cumin. It can be eaten hot, but its rounded flavors really bloom when it's served at room temperature. ■

- 3 tablespoons olive oil
- 1 1/2 teaspoons minced garlic
- 1 medium onion, chopped
- 2 jalapeño chiles, stemmed and seeded

2 teaspoons ground cumin
1½ teaspoons ground coriander
1 teaspoon salt
¼ teaspoon freshly ground black pepper
1 carrot, thinly sliced (½ cup)
1 celery rib, thinly sliced (½ cup)
3½–4½ cups (28–36 ounces) chicken stock or store-bought low-sodium broth
2½ cups water
8 ears corn, shucked, kernels cut off cobs, and kernels and cobs reserved separately
1 red bell pepper, roasted (see Tips, page 941), peeled, seeded, and finely chopped
2–3 tablespoons minced fresh cilantro or flat-leaf parsley, or to taste
Pinch of cayenne, or to taste (optional)

Heat oil in a 3- to 4-quart heavy saucepan over moderately low heat. Add garlic and cook, stirring, for 1 minute. Add onion and jalapeños and cook, stirring, until onion is softened, about 4 minutes. Add cumin, coriander, salt, and pepper and cook, stirring, for 2 minutes. Add carrot and celery, increase heat to moderate, and cook, stirring, for 5 minutes. Add 3½ cups stock, water, and corncobs and simmer, uncovered, for 15 minutes.

Add all but 1 cup of corn kernels and simmer, covered, until kernels are very tender, 12 to 15 minutes. Remove and discard corncobs.

Purée mixture in batches in a blender (use caution) until very smooth, at least 1 minute per batch. (For an even smoother soup, force blended mixture through a fine-mesh sieve into a large bowl, pressing hard on solids.) Cool to room temperature, uncovered.

Cook reserved 1 cup corn kernels in a small saucepan of boiling water until tender, 2 to 4 minutes. Drain in a colander and rinse under cold water to stop the cooking.

Stir corn into soup, along with bell pepper, cilantro, cayenne (if using), and salt and pepper to taste. Thin soup with additional stock, if desired. Serve at room temperature.

COOK'S NOTE

- The soup can be made up to 1 day ahead. Cool, uncovered, then refrigerate, covered. Bring to room temperature before serving.

Chilled Lemongrass Tomato Soup

SERVES 6
ACTIVE TIME: 30 MINUTES ■ START TO FINISH: 16½ HOURS
(INCLUDES MAKING AND CHILLING TOMATO WATER)

■ Tomatoes and watermelon have an amazing affinity for each other, which is set off nicely by the citrusy, clean aroma of lemongrass, a dramatic, long-leaved tropical herb (see page 160). This soup will surprise you: it is thin, because it's made with "tomato water," and not brightly colored, but it is just packed with flavor. A small amount of gelatin thickens the soup slightly, causing it to linger on the palate. The San Francisco chef Alain Rondelli provided the inspiration for this recipe. ■

3 stalks lemongrass, root ends trimmed and tough outer leaves discarded
6 cups Tomato Water (recipe follows)
1½ teaspoons unflavored gelatin (from a ¼-ounce envelope)
1 (1-inch-thick) watermelon slice
GARNISH: 1 tablespoon finely chopped fresh chives; 2 teaspoons finely chopped fresh mint

Finely chop enough of lower 6 inches of lemongrass stalks to measure ¼ cup. Discard remainder.

Combine lemongrass and 1 cup tomato water in a small saucepan, bring to a simmer, and simmer, uncovered, for 10 minutes.

Pour through a fine-mesh sieve into another small saucepan; discard solids. Stir in gelatin and heat over low heat, stirring, until gelatin is dissolved. Stir together gelatin mixture and remaining 5 cups tomato water in a large bowl. Refrigerate, covered, for at least 8 hours. (Soup will not jell, just thicken slightly.)

Remove rind and seeds from watermelon and discard. Finely chop enough melon to measure ¾ cup. Divide soup among six bowls and garnish with chives, watermelon, and mint.

COOK'S NOTE

- The soup can be refrigerated for up to 1 day.

Tomato Water

MAKES ABOUT 6 CUPS
ACTIVE TIME: 15 MINUTES ■ START TO FINISH: 8¼ HOURS

■ This pale liquid may not look assertive, but its spunky flavor is the very essence of tomato. If you have any extra after making the soup base, splash it, like lemon juice, into summer recipes that need a little brightening. ■

- 5 pounds tomatoes (10 medium), quartered
- 1½ tablespoons kosher salt

SPECIAL EQUIPMENT: four 18-inch squares cheesecloth; kitchen string

Purée tomatoes with salt in a food processor until smooth. Line a large sieve with layered squares of cheesecloth and set over a very tall nonreactive pot. Carefully pour tomato purée into center of cheesecloth. Gather edges of cheesecloth up over purée to form a large sack, then, without squeezing purée, gently gather together enough cheesecloth to form a neck and tie neck securely with string. Tie sack to a wooden spoon longer than diameter of pot, lift sack out of sieve, and lay spoon across top of pot, suspending sack; there should be enough room underneath sack so that it will not sit in tomato water as it accumulates. Let purée drain, refrigerated, for 8 hours.

Without squeezing it, remove and discard sack. Transfer tomato water to a bowl.

Cold Curried Carrot and Coconut Milk Soup

SERVES 6 TO 8 (MAKES ABOUT 8 CUPS)
ACTIVE TIME: 45 MINUTES ■ START TO FINISH: 7½ HOURS (INCLUDES CHILLING) PLUS ADDITIONAL TIME IF MAKING STOCK

■ Coconut milk gives this Southeast Asian–inspired soup a nondairy creaminess without making it taste overwhelmingly of coconut. It's a satiny purée of bold flavors. ■

- 2 tablespoons unsalted butter
- ¾ cup finely chopped scallions (about 1 bunch)
- 1 small onion, chopped (about ⅔ cup)
- 1 tablespoon finely grated peeled fresh ginger
- 1 tablespoon curry powder
- ¼ teaspoon salt
- Freshly ground black pepper
- 1½ pounds carrots, thinly sliced
- 2½ cups (20 ounces) chicken stock or store-bought low-sodium broth
- 1 cup well-stirred canned unsweetened coconut milk
- 1 tablespoon fresh lime juice, plus additional to taste
- About 2 cups ice water

OPTIONAL GARNISH: thinly sliced scallions

Melt butter in a 3- to 4- quart heavy saucepan over moderately low heat. Add scallions, onion, and ginger, along with curry powder, salt, and pepper to taste, and cook, stirring occasionally, until softened, about 4 minutes. Add carrots and stock and simmer, covered, until carrots are very soft, about 15 minutes. Remove from heat.

Purée mixture in batches with coconut milk in a blender (use caution) until very smooth; transfer to a bowl. Stir in 1 tablespoon lime juice and cool, uncovered. Refrigerate soup, covered, until cold, at least 6 hours.

Just before serving, thin soup to desired consistency with ice water and season with additional lime juice, salt, and pepper. Ladle soup into bowls and sprinkle with sliced scallions, if desired.

COOK'S NOTE

■ The soup can be refrigerated for up to 2 days.

Gazpacho Cordobés

SERVES 4 TO 6 (MAKES ABOUT 6 CUPS)
ACTIVE TIME: 30 MINUTES ■ START TO FINISH: 12 HOURS (INCLUDES CHILLING)

■ Good olive oil can give flavor and body to a soup. One spoonful of this and you will understand what we mean. In a sophisticated departure from the more common "toss everything into a blender" kind of gazpacho, this one calls for roasting the tomatoes and peppers to concentrate their flavors, and it uses fresh tarragon as an aromatic. The recipe is from Lawrence Saez, of San Francisco, who wheedled it out of his grandmother, a successful restaurateur in Córdoba, Spain. Try it with a glass of Manzanilla sherry. ■

- 2 pounds tomatoes
- 2 red bell peppers
- 2 Kirby (pickling) cucumbers, peeled and chopped
- 4 garlic cloves, finely chopped
- 2 tablespoons sherry vinegar, or to taste
- ½ cup extra-virgin olive oil
- 4 (½-inch-thick) slices from a round country-style loaf (9 inches in diameter), crusts discarded
- ½ teaspoon minced fresh tarragon
- 2 teaspoons salt
- 1 teaspoon freshly ground black pepper

SPECIAL EQUIPMENT: a food mill fitted with a medium disk

Put a rack in upper third of oven and preheat oven to 350°F.

Arrange tomatoes and bell peppers in one layer in a foil-lined shallow baking pan. Roast for 30 minutes.

Transfer tomatoes to a large glass or ceramic bowl and continue to roast peppers until lightly charred, about 15 minutes more. Transfer peppers, including any juices in pan, to another glass or ceramic bowl and let stand, covered, until cool enough to handle, 20 to 30 minutes.

Holding them over bowl to catch juices, peel tomatoes and tear flesh into pieces. Holding them over their bowl to catch juices, peel peppers, discarding stems and seeds, and tear peppers into pieces; add to tomatoes. Pour pepper juices through a fine-mesh sieve into tomato mixture. Stir in cucumbers, garlic, vinegar, and oil.

Cut bread into 1-inch pieces. Soak in a small bowl of water for 10 minutes. Drain bread (do not squeeze out excess liquid) and stir into tomato mixture, along with tarragon, salt, and pepper. Refrigerate, covered, for at least 8 hours.

Purée mixture, in batches if necessary, in a food processor, and return to bowl. Chill, covered, for 2 hours. Force gazpacho through food mill into another large bowl. Season, if desired, with more vinegar, salt, and pepper.

COOK'S NOTE

■ The tomato and bread mixture can be refrigerated for up to 1 day.

Watermelon Gazpacho

SERVES 4 TO 6 (MAKES ABOUT 6 CUPS)
ACTIVE TIME: 30 MINUTES ■ START TO FINISH: 30 MINUTES

■ This is not a fruit soup, to be served as dessert, but a savory one with a subtle, teasing flavor (no one will be able to guess what it is) and great color. It makes a terrific summertime first course. ■

- 1 (4-pound) piece watermelon, rind discarded and flesh cut into large chunks (7 cups)
- 1½ cups ice cubes
- ¾ cup (3 ounces) whole almonds with skins
- 3 garlic cloves, coarsely chopped
- 8 slices firm white sandwich bread, crusts discarded and bread torn into pieces
- 2 tablespoons red wine vinegar
- 2 teaspoons kosher salt
- Freshly ground black pepper
- ¼ cup extra-virgin olive oil

Seed 1 cup watermelon chunks and cut into small dice.

Purée remaining watermelon in a blender, in batches if necessary. Pour purée through a medium-mesh sieve into a large bowl, pressing on solids; discard solids.

Blend juice with ice, almonds, and garlic, in batches if necessary, until smooth. Add bread, vinegar, salt, and pepper to taste and blend. With motor running, add oil in a slow stream, blending until smooth.

Ladle soup into bowls and serve topped with diced watermelon.

Mango-Spacho

SERVES 4 (MAKES ABOUT 5 CUPS)
ACTIVE TIME: 30 MINUTES ■ START TO FINISH: 1 HOUR

■ Here is a tomato-free gazpacho that relies on the voluptuous, creamy texture of mango. Crisp cucumber and the heat of chiles cut the sweet richness. This recipe comes from La Mère Michelle restaurant, in Saratoga, California. ■

- 1 large, firm, but ripe mango, peeled, pitted, and cut into ¼-inch dice
- 1 cucumber, peeled, seeded, and cut into ¼-inch dice (1¼ cups)
- ½ serrano chile, seeded and minced
- ½ jalapeño chile, seeded and minced
- ⅓ cup fresh corn
- 2 scallions, thinly sliced
- 1 garlic clove, minced
- 1 tablespoon chopped bottled roasted red pepper
- 1 tablespoon chopped fresh basil
- 1 tablespoon chopped fresh cilantro
- ½ cup cold water
- ½ cup mango nectar
- 2 tablespoons distilled white vinegar
- 2 tablespoons fresh orange juice
- 1 tablespoon fresh lemon juice
- 1 tablespoon fresh lime juice
- 1 teaspoon salt
- ¼ teaspoon sugar (optional)

Stir together all ingredients in a large bowl. Refrigerate, covered, for at least 30 minutes.

COOK'S NOTE

■ The soup can be refrigerated for up to 2 days.

Beef Consommé with Tiny Choux Puffs

SERVES 8 (MAKES ABOUT 6 CUPS)
ACTIVE TIME: 2¼ HOURS ■ START TO FINISH: 2¼ HOURS PLUS ADDITIONAL TIME IF MAKING STOCK

■ Consommé is pure essence of beef—simple, elegant, nourishing on many different levels. It's not hard to make, but it does require time and effort. And is it ever worth it. Because of the natural gelatin from the bones, this clear soup has a wonderful body and gloss. Tiny *choux* puffs—baby profiteroles, that is—are there for crisp, chewy texture as well as adornment. ■

- 20 black peppercorns
- 4 large egg whites, shells reserved and crushed
- 1 pound plum tomatoes, quartered
- 1 pound celery (5–6 large ribs), cut into 1-inch pieces
- ½ pound lean ground sirloin
- 1 tablespoon kosher salt
- 6 cups Veal Stock (page 929) or store-bought broth
- Salt

OPTIONAL GARNISH: celery leaves and diced, seeded, peeled tomatoes

ACCOMPANIMENT: Tiny Choux Puffs (recipe follows)

Crack peppercorns with a mortar and pestle or wrap in a kitchen towel and crack with the bottom of a heavy skillet.

Whisk egg whites in a large bowl until foamy. Add eggshells. Pulse tomatoes and celery separately in a food processor until coarsely chopped, then add to egg whites. Whisk in beef, kosher salt, and peppercorns.

Put veal stock in a 4-quart heavy saucepan, and if it is jelled, heat until it becomes liquid. Whisk in beef mixture. Heat over moderately high heat, stirring and scraping bottom of pan constantly with a wooden spoon to prevent egg whites from sticking, until stock comes to a simmer (about 20 minutes). Reduce heat and gently simmer, without stirring, until all impurities rise to surface and form a crust and broth underneath is clear, about 30 minutes.

Ladle broth, with crust, into a large sieve lined with a double thickness of dampened paper towels set over a large bowl, and let all liquid drain through.

(If liquid doesn't drain completely, tap edge of sieve with a metal spoon to help drain.) Broth should be completely clear; if not, strain again, using clean dampened paper towels. Discard solids.

Bring consommé to a boil in a 3-quart saucepan and season with salt. Ladle into bowls and top with tiny *choux* puffs. Sprinkle with celery leaves and diced tomatoes, if using.

COOK'S NOTE

- The consommé can be made up to 1 day ahead. Cool, uncovered, then refrigerate, covered. It can also be frozen for up to 1 month.

Tiny Choux Puffs

MAKES ABOUT 90 TINY PUFFS

ACTIVE TIME: 20 MINUTES ■ START TO FINISH: 40 MINUTES

■ You will need only about one third of these baby profiteroles for the consommé, but the *choux* dough doesn't work if you cut the recipe down, so freeze the extras. Sprinkled with Parmesan and heated in the oven, they make great hors d'oeuvres. Or stuff them with ice cream and drizzle with chocolate sauce for irresistible little dessert bites. ■

- ½ cup water
- ½ stick (4 tablespoons) unsalted butter, cut into small pieces
- ¼ teaspoon salt
- ½ cup all-purpose flour
- 2 large eggs

SPECIAL EQUIPMENT: a pastry bag fitted with a ⅜-inch plain tip

Put a rack in middle of oven and preheat oven to 425°F. Grease two large baking sheets.

Combine water, butter, and salt in a 2-quart heavy saucepan and bring to a boil over high heat. Reduce heat to moderate, add flour all at once, and cook, stirring vigorously with a wooden spoon, until mixture pulls away from sides of pan, about 2 minutes. Remove from heat and cool slightly.

Add eggs one at a time, stirring vigorously after each addition until mixture is smooth.

Transfer dough to pastry bag and pipe ⅓-inch-diameter mounds about ½ inch apart on baking sheets. Gently flatten tips of mounds with a fingertip dipped in water. Bake, one sheet at a time, until golden brown and cooked through, 12 to 15 minutes. Cool on a rack.

COOK'S NOTE

- The puffs can be made up to 2 days ahead. Cool completely, then store in an airtight container at room temperature. They can also be frozen for up to 1 month. Thaw, then heat in a 350°F oven for 5 minutes to recrisp.

Miso Soup

SERVES 6

ACTIVE TIME: 10 MINUTES ■ START TO FINISH: 20 MINUTES

■ Subtly flavored miso soup—smoky, salty, sweet—is a mainstay of breakfast in Japan and is also served for lunch and dinner. Made from *dashi,* a simple, delicate stock, and thickened with the white fermented soybean paste called *shiro miso,* it's a particularly calming way to start the day. The specialty ingredients used in this recipe are available at Japanese markets; for mail-order information, see Sources. ■

- ½ cup dried wakame (a type of seaweed; see Glossary)
- ¼ cup white miso (fermented soybean paste)
- 6 cups Dashi (recipe follows)
- ½ pound soft tofu, drained and cut into ½-inch cubes
- ¼ cup thinly sliced scallion greens

PREPARE THE WAKAME: Soak the wakame in warm water to cover by 1 inch in a bowl until softened, about 15 minutes. Drain in a sieve.

MAKE THE SOUP: Stir together miso and ½ cup *dashi* in a bowl until smooth. Heat remaining 5½ cups *dashi* in a saucepan over moderately high heat until hot, then gently stir in tofu and softened wakame. Simmer for 1 minute and remove from heat. Immediately stir in miso mixture and scallion greens and serve.

Dashi
Japanese Sea Stock

MAKES ABOUT 6 CUPS
ACTIVE TIME: 5 MINUTES ■ START TO FINISH: 10 MINUTES

■ This basic stock, made with dried kelp (konbu) and dried bonito flakes, is used extensively in Japanese cooking. Full of delicate flavor, it doesn't contain a drop of fat. Don't be put off by the specialty ingredients (see Sources if you don't have a Japanese market handy)—the stock is quick to make and very nutritious. Konbu comes packaged in lengths that are most easily cut with scissors. ■

1 ounce (30 grams) konbu (dried kelp; see Glossary)
6 cups cold water
1 cup tightly packed dried bonito flakes (*katsuobushi;* see Glossary)
SPECIAL EQUIPMENT: cheesecloth (optional)

Wipe any sand or salt from konbu with a dampened cloth. Combine konbu and cold water in a 4-quart heavy saucepan and bring just to a boil over high heat. Remove from heat and remove konbu (reserve for another use, if desired). Sprinkle bonito flakes over liquid and let stand for 3 minutes, then, if necessary, stir to make flakes sink.

Pour stock through a cheesecloth-lined sieve or a coffee filter into a large heatproof bowl. Reserve bonito flakes for another use.

COOK'S NOTES

- The stock can be made up to 4 days ahead. Cool completely, uncovered, then refrigerate, covered.
- The dried bonito flakes can be saved to sprinkle over cooked rice. Keep them refrigerated in an airtight container.

Lemon Broth with Green Pea Ravioli

SERVES 6
ACTIVE TIME: 35 MINUTES ■ START TO FINISH: 35 MINUTES PLUS ADDITIONAL TIME IF MAKING STOCK

■ Spring tastes like this. In this recipe, peas are transformed into a creamy, ethereal filling for ravioli. Their skins are removed with a food mill instead of being ground up by a food processor, making the soup especially smooth. Wonton wrappers, available in most supermarkets, make tender, delicate ravioli that can be put together in no time flat. ■

1 cup frozen baby peas, thawed
1 small shallot, finely chopped
1½ teaspoons olive oil
3 tablespoons finely grated Parmigiano-Reggiano
3 tablespoons fine fresh bread crumbs
Salt and freshly ground black pepper
18 wonton wrappers
4 cups (32 ounces) chicken stock or store-bought low-sodium broth
1 garlic clove, smashed
1 teaspoon finely grated lemon zest
OPTIONAL GARNISH: fresh chervil or parsley leaves and cooked frozen peas
SPECIAL EQUIPMENT: a food mill fitted with a fine disk

MAKE THE FILLING: Force peas through food mill into a bowl to remove skins.

Cook shallot in oil in a small skillet over moderately low heat, stirring occasionally, until softened, about 3 minutes. Remove from heat and stir into pea purée, along with cheese and bread crumbs. Season with salt and pepper.

FILL THE RAVIOLI: Put 1 wonton wrapper on a lightly floured surface (keep remaining wrappers in package). Mound a level teaspoon of filling in center of wrapper (1), lightly dampen edges of wrapper with a fingertip dipped in water, and fold over to form a triangle, pressing down around filling to force out air. Press edges together firmly to seal (2). Moisten one end of long side of triangle and fold opposite end over, creating a little hat shape, then pinch together to seal (3).

Transfer to a dry kitchen towel and make 17 more ravioli in same manner.

COOK THE RAVIOLI: Combine the stock, garlic, zest, and salt and pepper to taste in a saucepan and bring to a simmer.

Meanwhile, cook ravioli in a large pot of boiling salted water (1 tablespoon salt per every 4 quarts water) until al dente, 2 to 3 minutes; drain.

Divide ravioli among six soup plates and ladle broth over them; discard garlic. Garnish with chervil or parsley and peas, if desired.

COOK'S NOTE

- The ravioli can be assembled up to 1 day ahead and refrigerated, covered, in a baking pan lined with a dry kitchen towel.

HOW TO MAKE GREEN PEA RAVIOLI

1

2

3

Quick Hot Borscht

SERVES 4

ACTIVE TIME: 15 MINUTES ■ START TO FINISH: 1 HOUR

■ Even people who hate beets sometimes love borscht, especially a hot version on a bitterly cold, snowy night. Here is a quick version, made with pickled beets (for that sweet-sour tang) and canned beef broth, that can be put together practically before you can say "Dr. Zhivago." ■

4 medium boiling potatoes, peeled and halved
1 tablespoon vegetable oil
2 carrots, coarsely chopped
2 celery ribs, coarsely chopped
1 medium onion, chopped
1 (14- to 15-ounce) can beef broth
Salt and freshly ground black pepper
1 (16-ounce) jar sliced pickled beets
GARNISH: 1/4 cup sour cream; 3 tablespoons chopped fresh dill

Put potatoes in a 3- to 4-quart saucepan, cover with cold well-salted water by 1 inch, and bring to a boil. Reduce heat and simmer until potatoes are tender, 20 to 25 minutes; drain and cover to keep warm.

Meanwhile, heat oil in a 3-quart heavy saucepan over high heat. Add carrots, celery, and onion and cook, stirring frequently, until beginning to brown, about 5 to 6 minutes. Add broth and salt and pepper to taste and bring to a boil, then reduce heat and simmer, covered, until vegetables are tender, about 13 minutes.

Stir in beets, including liquid, and simmer, covered, for 8 minutes more.

Ladle borscht into four bowls and add potatoes. Top with sour cream and sprinkle with dill.

How to Cool Soups (and Stocks) Quickly

Clever you: while you were putting supper on the table and enjoying the meal, you had chicken soup simmering gently away on a back burner. But if you cover your finished soup and put it away when it's still hot, it may sour, and all your lovely, resourceful work will be ruined. The trick is to cool it down fast so you can put it in the fridge and consider your day's work done. The path of least resistance is to ladle the soup into smaller, preferably shallow containers and let them sit, uncovered, until the soup is at room temperature. You can also speed things along by chilling the pot quickly in a larger bowl of ice and cold water. (If you have only a small amount of soup—a quart, say—and you're in a rush, you can refrigerate it, uncovered, without bringing down the temperature of the refrigerator.) This applies to any soup that has animal protein or a meat, poultry, or fish stock in it.

5 large egg yolks
3/4 cup finely grated Parmigiano-Reggiano
3 tablespoons extra-virgin olive oil
Freshly ground black pepper
1/4 loaf country-style bread

SPECIAL EQUIPMENT: an instant-read thermometer

Combine water, garlic, thyme, bay leaf, and salt in a 2-quart heavy saucepan and bring to a boil. Reduce heat and simmer, covered, for 45 minutes.

Discard thyme and bay leaf. Force mixture through a medium-mesh sieve into a large bowl, then return to saucepan. Whisk together yolks, cheese, and 2 tablespoons oil in same bowl until well combined. Add 1/2 cup hot garlic broth in a slow stream, whisking, then add yolk mixture to remaining hot garlic broth, whisking.

Cook soup over moderately low heat, whisking constantly, until it is slightly thickened and registers 170°F on thermometer, about 5 minutes; do not let boil. Stir in pepper to taste.

Tear bread into bite-sized pieces and divide among four soup bowls. Ladle soup over bread and drizzle with remaining 1 tablespoon oil.

Rustic Garlic Soup

SERVES 4 (MAKES ABOUT 4 CUPS)
ACTIVE TIME: 25 MINUTES ■ START TO FINISH: 1 1/4 HOURS

■ A certain rough-hewn elegance is apparent here: the garlic is mellow and sweet, the broth enriched with egg yolks. This classic peasant soup works as a first course as well as a Sunday night supper around the kitchen table. In Italy, it's called *aquacotta,* or "cooked water." Making something out of nothing can really be something. ■

5 cups water
1 large head garlic (about 3 inches in diameter), separated into cloves, smashed, and peeled
2 fresh thyme sprigs
1 Turkish bay leaf or 1/2 California bay leaf
1 1/2 teaspoons salt

Chinese Egg Drop Soup with Noodles

SERVES 4
ACTIVE TIME: 25 MINUTES ■ START TO FINISH: 25 MINUTES PLUS ADDITIONAL TIME IF MAKING STOCK

■ Although egg drop soup is not traditionally made with noodles, they add texture and substance, turning this into more of a meal. So you can look at this either as a Chinese take on Mom's chicken noodle or Mom's take on a Chinese classic. ■

5 cups (40 ounces) chicken stock or store-bought low-sodium broth
2 tablespoons medium-dry sherry
1 teaspoon soy sauce
1 (2-inch) piece fresh ginger, thinly sliced
1 large garlic clove, smashed

1 ounce (1 cup) dried fine egg noodles
2 large eggs, lightly beaten
1–2 scallions, thinly sliced (to taste)
1 teaspoon Asian sesame oil, or to taste
Salt

Combine stock, sherry, soy sauce, ginger, and garlic in a 2-quart heavy saucepan and bring to a boil. Remove ginger and garlic with a slotted spoon and discard. Stir in noodles, then reduce heat and simmer, uncovered, until tender, about 4 minutes.

Stirring soup in a circular motion, add eggs in a slow, steady stream. Simmer, undisturbed, until strands of egg are cooked, about 1 minute. Remove from heat and stir in scallions and sesame oil. Season with salt and serve.

Shiitake–Bok Choy Soup with Noodles

SERVES 4
ACTIVE TIME: 20 MINUTES ■ START TO FINISH: 20 MINUTES

■ This quick Asian soup gets depth of flavor and a smoky sweetness from *katsuobushi,* or dried bonito flakes (made from a fish related to mackerel and tuna). You can use Chinese wheat noodles or thin Japanese wheat or buckwheat noodles, which can all be found in natural foods stores and some supermarkets as well as Asian markets (or see Sources for mail-order information). Contributed by *Gourmet* reader Beth Nicholson, of Ashland, Massachusetts, this soup won instant approval in our test kitchens. ■

6 cups water
2/3 cup (one 8-gram package) dried bonito flakes (*katsuobushi;* see Glossary)
1/2 pound bok choy, cut into 1/4-inch-thick slices
1/2 pound shiitake mushrooms, stems discarded and caps thinly sliced
6 ounces thin Asian wheat or buckwheat noodles (see headnote)
1/4 teaspoon salt
1/4 teaspoon freshly ground black pepper
6 scallions, cut diagonally into thin slices (1 cup)

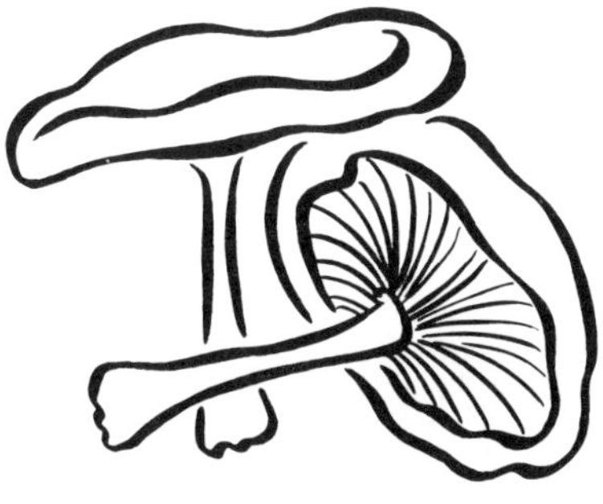

Combine water and bonito flakes in a 5- to 6-quart pot, bring to a boil, and boil for 1 minute. Pour stock through a fine-mesh sieve into a large bowl; discard bonito flakes or reserve for another use (see Cook's Note on page 92).

Return stock to pot and add bok choy, mushrooms, and noodles. Bring to a simmer and simmer, uncovered, until noodles are tender, 2 to 5 minutes, depending on type of noodle. Stir in salt, pepper, and scallions and serve.

Tortilla Soup with Crisp Tortillas and Avocado Relish

SERVES 8 (MAKES ABOUT 9 CUPS)
ACTIVE TIME: 40 MINUTES ■ START TO FINISH: 1 HOUR PLUS ADDITIONAL TIME IF MAKING STOCK

■ Earthy and elemental, this is comfort food, Mexican style—and anything but pedestrian. Fried corn tortillas are used as a flavoring and a thickener, and roasted vegetables add great flavor. Ancho chiles (deep, rich, fruity) and guajillos (spicy and sweet) are both workhorses of the Mexican kitchen. This soup, offset beautifully by a crisp fried tortilla garnish and a cool, bright avocado relish, is from the masterful Robert Del Grande, of Café Annie, in Houston. ■

FOR SOUP

½ white onion, coarsely chopped
1 pound plum tomatoes
6 garlic cloves, peeled
2 dried guajillo chiles (see Glossary), stemmed, seeded, and ribs discarded
2 dried ancho chiles (see Glossary), stemmed, seeded, and ribs discarded
About 1½ cups peanut oil or vegetable oil for deep-frying
10 (5- to 6-inch) white corn tortillas, cut into ¼-inch-wide strips
8 cups (64 ounces) chicken stock or store-bought low-sodium broth
½ teaspoon dried oregano, crumbled
1 teaspoon kosher salt
Freshly ground black pepper

FOR AVOCADO RELISH

2 firm but ripe California avocados
1 small tomato, finely chopped
⅔ cup finely chopped white onion
1–2 serrano chiles (to taste), seeded if desired and finely chopped
2 tablespoons chopped fresh cilantro, plus 8 fresh cilantro sprigs
2 teaspoons fresh lime juice
1 teaspoon kosher salt
½ teaspoon coarsely crushed black peppercorns

ACCOMPANIMENT: lime wedges

SPECIAL EQUIPMENT: a deep-fat thermometer

MAKE THE SOUP: Preheat broiler.

Arrange onion, tomatoes, and garlic in one layer in a baking pan and broil about 2 inches from heat, turning occasionally with tongs, until tomato skins are blistered and lightly charred, 10 to 15 minutes. Let cool.

Heat a dry griddle or heavy skillet over moderate heat until very hot but not smoking. Toast chiles 1 or 2 at a time, pressing down with tongs, until more pliable, a few seconds on each side. Transfer to a bowl. Add hot water to cover chiles and soak until soft, about 20 minutes.

Drain chiles and transfer to a blender. Add vegetable mixture and purée until smooth.

Heat ½ inch oil in a 9-inch heavy skillet until it registers 375°F on thermometer. Fry tortilla strips in 5 batches, turning, until crisp and pale golden, 30 seconds to 1 minute per batch. Transfer to paper towels to drain. (Return oil to 375°F between batches.)

Put two thirds of tortilla strips in a plastic bag and finely crush with a rolling pin.

Combine stock and chile purée in a 5-quart heavy pot and bring to a boil, stirring. Stir in crushed tortilla strips, oregano, and salt and simmer, uncovered, whisking occasionally, until tortillas are soft and soup is slightly thickened, 30 to 45 minutes. If necessary, season soup with salt and pepper.

MEANWHILE, MAKE THE RELISH: Quarter avocados. Pit, peel, and cut into ¼-inch dice. Gently stir together avocados, tomato, onion, chiles, chopped cilantro, lime juice, salt, and crushed peppercorns in a bowl until well combined.

Divide relish, remaining tortilla strips, and cilantro sprigs among eight soup plates and ladle soup over mixture. Serve with lime wedges.

French Pea Soup

Potage Saint-Germain

SERVES 6 (MAKES ABOUT 8 CUPS)
ACTIVE TIME: 35 MINUTES ■ START TO FINISH: 45 MINUTES PLUS ADDITIONAL TIME IF MAKING STOCK

■ Dinner guests will presume you spent hours making this sublime soup, but in fact *potage Saint-Germain* is French food fast. Lettuce is often paired with peas because it adds a fresh, almost grassy sweetness. ■

FOR CROUTONS

1 baguette or loaf Italian bread, crusts discarded if desired and cut into ½-inch cubes (1½ cups)
2 tablespoons unsalted butter, melted
Salt

FOR SOUP

1½ cups chopped leeks (white parts only; 2 large leeks)
2 tablespoons unsalted butter
3 cups (24 ounces) chicken stock or store-bought low-sodium broth
2 cups water
2 (10-ounce) packages frozen peas, thawed, or 4 cups shelled fresh peas

4 cups chopped Bibb or Boston lettuce
1/2 cup fresh mint leaves
Salt and freshly ground black pepper
1/4 cup heavy cream (optional)

MAKE THE CROUTONS: Put a rack in middle of oven and preheat oven to 350°F.

Drizzle bread cubes with butter in a shallow baking dish, tossing to coat well, and bake, stirring occasionally, until golden and crisp, 10 to 15 minutes. Season with salt.

MAKE THE SOUP: Wash leeks well in a bowl of cold water; lift out and drain well. Melt butter in a large saucepan over moderately low heat. Add leeks and cook, stirring occasionally, until softened, 6 to 7 minutes. Add stock and water and bring to a boil. Add peas and lettuce and simmer, partially covered, until peas are tender, 6 to 10 minutes. Stir in mint.

Purée soup in batches in a blender (use caution) until very smooth. Return soup to pan, season with salt and pepper, and reheat over moderately low heat, stirring, until hot.

Beat cream, if using, in a small bowl until slightly thickened but still pourable. Season with salt. Ladle soup into six bowls. Drizzle drops of cream, if using, on each serving and draw a skewer or knife through drops to form a decorative pattern. Serve with croutons.

COOK'S NOTES

- The croutons can be made up to 1 day ahead and kept in an airtight container at room temperature.
- The soup can be made (without the cream) up to 1 day ahead. Cool completely, uncovered, then refrigerate, covered. Reheat before serving.

Asparagus Soup with Parmesan Custards

SERVES 6
ACTIVE TIME: 45 MINUTES ■ START TO FINISH: 2 1/2 HOURS PLUS ADDITIONAL TIME IF MAKING STOCK

■ This is a lovely asparagus soup, but the custards really set it apart and make it unforgettable. They are infused with the salty, nutty flavor of the cheese, which is then strained out, leaving them silky smooth. The subtle play between the silkiness of the custards and the velvety soup makes this a wonderful special-occasion dish. ■

USE CAUTION WHEN BLENDING HOT LIQUIDS

When it comes to transforming hot broth and soft vegetables into a perfect puréed soup, an old-fashioned blender is hard to beat. But be careful. The hot steam escaping from the soup gets trapped between the liquid and the lid, creating a sort of combustion chamber. When the steam expands under pressure, a blender can literally flip its lid, spattering its searing cargo over the kitchen and the cook. Since soups must be puréed while they are still hot in order to become as smooth as possible, it's best to blend them — and other hot liquids — in batches, filling the blender jar no more than halfway and starting the blending on low speed. It also helps to open the small center cap in the blender's lid slightly, to decompress the contents. Drape the blender jar with a kitchen towel, press the button, and stand back.

FOR CUSTARDS

- 1¼ cups coarsely grated Parmigiano-Reggiano (about 2½ ounces)
- 1 cup heavy cream
- ½ cup whole milk
- 1 large egg
- 2 large egg yolks
- ⅛ teaspoon salt
- Pinch of white pepper

FOR SOUP

- 1 large leek (white and pale green parts only), finely chopped (1¼ cups)
- 2 tablespoons unsalted butter
- ½ cup finely chopped shallots
- ¾ teaspoon salt
- ¼ teaspoon freshly ground black pepper, or to taste
- 2½ pounds asparagus, trimmed and cut into 1½-inch-long pieces
- 3½ cups (28 ounces) chicken stock or store-bought low-sodium broth
- 1½ cups water
- ¼ cup heavy cream

OPTIONAL GARNISH: Parmigiano-Reggiano curls (shaved from a wedge with a vegetable peeler)

SPECIAL EQUIPMENT: six 2-ounce ramekins

MAKE THE CUSTARDS: Combine cheese, cream, and milk in a small heavy saucepan and bring just to a boil over moderate heat, stirring occasionally. Remove from heat and steep, covered, for 30 minutes.

Put a rack in middle of oven and preheat oven to 300°F. Generously butter ramekins.

Pour cream mixture through a fine-mesh sieve into a bowl, pressing lightly on cheese solids, then discard them. Whisk together egg, yolks, salt, and white pepper in another bowl. Add cream in a slow stream, whisking until smooth. Divide among ramekins.

Set ramekins in a baking pan. Carefully add enough boiling water to pan to come halfway up sides of ramekins. Bake until centers of custards are completely set, 40 to 45 minutes. Transfer ramekins to a rack and cool for just 5 minutes (do not allow to cool longer, or custards will stick to ramekins).

WHILE THE CUSTARDS BAKE, MAKE THE SOUP: Wash chopped leek in a bowl of cold water; lift out and drain well. Melt butter in a 4- to 6-quart heavy pot over moderately low heat. Add leek, shallots, ½ teaspoon salt, and pepper and cook, stirring, until leek is softened, about 3 minutes. Add asparagus, stock, and water and bring to a boil. Reduce heat and simmer, covered, until asparagus tips are crisp-tender, 2 to 4 minutes. Remove 6 asparagus tips and set aside to cool. Continue to simmer soup, covered, until stalks are just tender, 6 to 8 minutes longer. Meanwhile, halve cooled tips lengthwise and reserve for garnish.

Purée soup in batches in a blender until smooth (use caution) and transfer to a large bowl. Pour through a fine-mesh sieve into cleaned pot. Stir in cream, remaining ¼ teaspoon salt, and pepper to taste and heat over moderately low heat until hot.

SERVE THE SOUP: Run a thin knife around edge of each custard to loosen it, then invert a soup bowl over ramekin and invert custard into bowl. Ladle soup around custards and garnish with reserved asparagus tips and Parmesan curls, if using.

COOK'S NOTE

- The soup can be made up to 1 day ahead. Cool, uncovered, then refrigerate, covered.

Roasted Tomato Soup with Rajas and Queso Fresco

SERVES 4 (MAKES ABOUT 5 CUPS)
ACTIVE TIME: 45 MINUTES ■ START TO FINISH: 1 HOUR PLUS ADDITIONAL TIME IF MAKING STOCK

■ This deep-flavored soup represents Mexican cooking at its most sophisticated. Its complexity belies the fact that it's relatively simple to put together. The thing that makes it so extraordinary is the addition of *rajas,* which are chile strips, usually roasted poblanos. *Rajas* are a real treasure, as is Rick Bayless, the creator of this soup and the chef-owner of Frontera Grill, in Chicago. *Queso fresco* is a mild, salty, crumbly, fresh cow's milk cheese, and Mexico oregano is fresher-tasting and not as harsh as the regular kind (which will certainly work too). ■

- 1 pound tomatoes
- 1 tablespoon olive oil
- 1 medium white onion, halved lengthwise and cut lengthwise into ¼-inch-thick slices
- 1 large garlic clove, finely chopped

½ teaspoon dried oregano, preferably Mexican (see Sources)
½ pound poblano chiles (3 medium-large), roasted (see Tips, page 941), peeled, seeded, and cut into ¼-inch-wide strips
4 cups (32 ounces) beef stock or store-bought broth
Salt
¼ pound *queso fresco* (Mexican fresh white cheese; see Glossary) or salted farmer cheese, cut into ½-inch cubes (1 cup)

Preheat broiler. Broil tomatoes in a shallow baking pan about 4 inches from heat until blackened on top, about 6 minutes. Turn tomatoes and broil until blackened on bottom. Cool.

Peel tomatoes over a bowl to catch juices. Transfer tomatoes and juice to a blender or food processor and blend until coarsely puréed.

Heat oil in a 3-quart heavy saucepan over moderately high heat until hot but not smoking. Add onion and cook, stirring occasionally, until browned at edges but still firm, about 5 minutes. Add garlic and oregano and cook, stirring, for 1 minute. Stir in chiles and cook, stirring occasionally, until hot. Add tomato purée and simmer, stirring frequently, until very thick, about 7 minutes.

Stir in stock and bring to a boil. Boil, uncovered, stirring frequently, until slightly thickened, about 3 minutes. Season soup with salt. Divide among four bowls and scatter cheese over top.

Fresh Corn Soup

SERVES 6 (MAKES ABOUT 7 CUPS)
ACTIVE TIME: 20 MINUTES ■ START TO FINISH: 40 MINUTES

■ Pure simplicity, creamy without cream, this soup is all about corn—good, fresh farm-stand corn, mind you, nothing less. Like succotash, it's perfect for September, when enthusiasm for corn on the cob begins to wane the tiniest bit. And it's equally good served hot or cold. ■

8 cups corn kernels (from 10–14 ears)
6 cups water
1 tablespoon kosher salt or coarse sea salt
GARNISH: ¼ cup chopped fresh chives

Combine corn, water, and salt in a 4- to 5-quart pot and bring just to a boil. Reduce heat and simmer, covered, until corn is very tender, about 20 minutes.

Purée soup in batches in a blender until very smooth (use caution) and pour through a large medium-mesh sieve, pressing on solids, into a saucepan if serving hot or a metal bowl if serving cold; discard solids.

Reheat soup, stirring, until hot; or chill it by setting bowl of soup in a larger bowl of ice and cold water and stirring. If soup is too thick, thin with water.

Serve sprinkled with chives.

COOK'S NOTES

- The soup can be made up to 3 days ahead and cooled, uncovered, then refrigerated, covered. Reheat gently before serving, or serve chilled.
- You've got a small mountain of corn to deal with for this recipe, and here is the most efficient, least messy way to remove the kernels: After shucking, lay each ear on its side and slice the kernels off with a large sharp knife. Then stand each ear on end and scrape it down with the back of your knife blade to remove the juicy good stuff that's left.

Creamless Creamy Squash Soup

SERVES 6 (MAKES ABOUT 6 CUPS)
ACTIVE TIME: 30 MINUTES ■ START TO FINISH: 1 HOUR

■ Butternut squash is a wonderful base for a soup. The texture of this one is particularly beautiful and silky, because of the puréed potatoes and carrot (not a drop of cream is used). Those vegetables give the soup roundness, finesse, an extra dimension that is enriched with olive oil. Perhaps the most unusual thing about this soup (to Americans, anyway) is the garnish: crisp crumbs of amaretti, Italian almond macaroons. In Italy, amaretti are often incorporated into winter squash and pumpkin ravioli fillings to play up the sweetness of the vegetables. Here that sweet, nutty crunch puts the soup right over the top. The recipe, from Faith Heller Willinger's cookbook *Red, White, and Greens,* was inspired by chef Fabio Picchi, at Cibrèo, in Florence. He prefers meat stock in the soup, but Willinger finds the flavor almost as rich with water. ■

2 tablespoons extra-virgin olive oil, preferably Tuscan, plus additional for drizzling
1 celery rib, chopped
1 medium carrot, chopped
1 medium onion, chopped
½ pound boiling potatoes
1 pound winter squash, such as butternut, peeled, seeded, and cut into ½-inch cubes
1 fresh peperoncino (small Italian hot green pepper) or ⅛ teaspoon red pepper flakes
2 teaspoons coarse sea salt
3½ cups boiling water, plus additional for thinning
GARNISH: 1 crisp amaretto (Italian almond macaroon), finely crushed (2 tablespoons)

Heat oil in a 3-quart heavy saucepan over low heat. Add celery, carrot, and onion and cook, stirring occasionally, until tender but not browned, 10 to 12 minutes. Meanwhile, peel potatoes and cut into ½-inch cubes.

Stir squash, potatoes, peperoncino, and sea salt into onion mixture, then stir in 3½ cups boiling water and simmer, covered, until vegetables are very tender, about 20 minutes.

Remove and discard peperoncino, if using. Purée soup in batches in a blender (use caution), adding more water as necessary to thin to desired consistency.

Serve soup drizzled with additional oil and sprinkled with amaretto crumbs.

Hot-and-Sour Pumpkin Soup

SERVES 6 TO 8 (MAKES ABOUT 10 CUPS)
ACTIVE TIME: 40 MINUTES ■ START TO FINISH: 1½ HOURS (PLUS ADDITIONAL TIME IF MAKING STOCK)

■ Pumpkins are amazingly versatile in the kitchen, and this soup will get you to think about the vegetable in a whole new way. Don't expect the dark hot-and-sour soup found in Chinatown, thick with shreds of bean curd and vegetables. This looks like a typical creamy pumpkin soup, but here the pumpkin makes a gaily colored, slightly sweet background for an explosion of lively flavors: lemongrass, kaffir lime leaves (which have an intense lemon-lime fragrance), and galangal, a rhizome closely related to ginger that has a more pungent sharpness.

This recipe is adapted from one created by the chefs Ming Tsai and Tom Berry at Blue Ginger, in Wellesley, Massachusetts. They serve the soup with shrimp toasts, but it is delicious on its own. ■

2 tablespoons vegetable oil
1 large onion, coarsely chopped
1 tablespoon chopped garlic
1 tablespoon chopped peeled fresh ginger
1 (3-pound) sugar or cheese pumpkin, peeled, seeded, and cut into 1-inch cubes (6 cups)
1 cup dry white wine
8 cups (64 ounces) chicken stock, or 4 cups (32 ounces) store-bought low-sodium broth plus 4 cups water
6 stalks lemongrass, root ends trimmed and tough outer leaves discarded
1 (1-inch) piece galangal (see Glossary), thawed if frozen, peeled, and coarsely chopped
3–5 (1½-inch-long) fresh Thai chiles (see Glossary) or 2 jalapeño chiles (to taste), seeded if desired and coarsely chopped
4 fresh or frozen kaffir lime leaves (see Glossary)
⅓ cup fresh lime juice
¼ cup Asian fish sauce
1 tablespoon sugar
Salt and freshly ground black pepper
OPTIONAL ACCOMPANIMENT: Shrimp Toasts (recipe follows)

Heat 1 tablespoon oil in a 5-quart heavy pot over moderate heat. Add onion, garlic, and ginger, cover, and cook, stirring occasionally, until onion is softened, about 4 minutes. Add pumpkin and wine, bring to a boil, and boil, uncovered, until wine is reduced by about half, about 5 minutes. Stir in stock and bring to a boil. Reduce heat and simmer, covered, until pumpkin is tender, about 20 minutes.

Meanwhile, coarsely chop lower 5 inches of lemongrass stalks; discard remainder. Heat remaining 1 tablespoon oil in a 10-inch heavy skillet over moderately high heat until hot but not smoking. Add lemongrass, galangal, and chiles and cook, stirring, until lightly browned, about 1 minute. Remove from heat.

Purée pumpkin mixture in batches (use caution) in a blender and return to pot. Stir in lemongrass mixture, lime leaves, lime juice, fish sauce, and sugar and simmer, uncovered, for 20 minutes.

Force soup through a medium-mesh sieve into a bowl; discard solids. Season well with salt and pepper.

Serve toasts on the side, if desired.

COOK'S NOTE

- The soup can be made up to 2 days ahead. Cool, uncovered, then refrigerate, covered.

Shrimp Toasts

MAKES 24 TOASTS
ACTIVE TIME: 45 MINUTES ■ START TO FINISH: 45 MINUTES

■ Paired with the hot-and-sour pumpkin soup, these toasts make a clever soup-and-sandwich combo. Although they have to be prepared at the last minute, the soup can be made ahead and simply reheated. Jicama gives a tender crunch to this shrimp paste. ■

- ½ pound shrimp in shells, peeled and deveined
- 1 tablespoon finely chopped peeled fresh ginger
- 1 tablespoon Asian sesame oil
- 1 tablespoon rice wine or medium-dry sherry
- 1 large egg white
- ¼ cup diced (⅛-inch) peeled jicama
- 2 tablespoons chopped fresh cilantro
- 2 scallions, thinly sliced
- Salt and freshly ground black pepper
- About 6 cups vegetable oil for deep-frying
- 12 very thin slices firm white sandwich bread, crusts discarded
- ¼ cup sesame seeds

SPECIAL EQUIPMENT: a deep-fat thermometer

Combine shrimp, ginger, sesame oil, rice wine, and egg white in a food processor and pulse until a coarse paste forms. Transfer to a bowl. Stir in jicama, cilantro, scallions, and salt and pepper to taste.

Heat 2 inches vegetable oil in a 3-quart saucepan over moderately high heat until it registers 375°F on thermometer. While oil is heating, spread shrimp paste over bread slices, using about 2 tablespoons per slice and spreading it evenly to edges. Sprinkle with sesame seeds, then gently press seeds into paste to help them adhere.

Add 2 bread slices, shrimp sides down, to the hot oil and fry until shrimp paste is browned, about 1 minute. Turn over with a slotted metal spatula and fry until undersides are golden, about 30 seconds. Transfer to paper towels to drain. Fry remaining slices 2 at at time in same manner. (Return oil to 375°F between batches.)

Cut each toast diagonally into 2 triangles and serve immediately.

Fresh Mushroom Soup

SERVES 4 (MAKES ABOUT 4 CUPS)
ACTIVE TIME: 15 MINUTES ■ START TO FINISH: 30 MINUTES PLUS ADDITIONAL TIME IF MAKING STOCK

■ In the late 1920s, a young Russian widow named Katish escaped from the Russian Revolution and eventually settled in Los Angeles, where she became the housekeeper and cook for a large family. Wanda L. Frolov first wrote about this emigré and her honest home cooking in the pages of *Gourmet*, and her stories were gathered into a book in 1947 (*Katish: Our Russian Cook* is currently available in a Modern Library series about food). Katish did many delicious things with mushrooms, including a creamy soup. We've adapted the recipe slightly. All you need is a loaf of crusty bread with some good butter to make this a meal. ■

- 2 cups half-and-half
- 1 medium onion
- ½ stick (4 tablespoons) unsalted butter
- ¾ pound mushrooms, trimmed and thinly sliced
- 4 teaspoons all-purpose flour
- 1 cup beef stock or store-bought broth
- ½ Turkish bay leaf or ¼ California bay leaf
- ¼ teaspoon salt
- ⅛ teaspoon freshly ground black pepper
- 2 teaspoons fresh lemon juice

Bring half-and-half just to a boil in a heavy saucepan, then remove from heat and cover to keep warm.

Meanwhile, cut a ¾-inch-thick crosswise slice from center of onion; reserve remainder for another use. Heat butter in a 6-quart wide heavy pot over moderately high heat until foam subsides. Add mushrooms and cook, stirring, until golden brown, 8 to 10 minutes. Add onion slice, then sprinkle mushrooms with flour and cook, stirring, for 2 minutes. Add stock in a slow stream, stirring constantly, then add half-and-half, bay leaf, salt, and pepper. Reduce heat to low and cook, uncovered, stirring occasionally, for 10 minutes.

Discard onion and bay leaf and stir in lemon juice.

Celery Root Bisque

SERVES 12 (MAKES ABOUT 9 CUPS)
ACTIVE TIME: 45 MINUTES ■ START TO FINISH: 1 HOUR

■ This refined soup is delicious on its own and even better when crispy bits of duck confit (duck leg slowly cooked and preserved in its own fat) and cracklings made from the skin add their crisp, salty, gamy counterpoint to the satiny bisque. Prepared confit is increasingly available at specialty foods shops, or see Sources for mail-order information. ■

- 1 confit duck leg (optional)
- ½ stick (4 tablespoons) unsalted butter
- 1 (1½-pound) celery root (celeriac), peeled with a sharp knife and cut into ½-inch cubes (4 cups)
- ½ pound shallots (6 large), thinly sliced
- 2 celery ribs, chopped (1¼ cups)
- 1½ teaspoons salt
- Freshly ground black pepper
- 8 cups water
- 1 tablespoon fresh lemon juice, or to taste
- ¼ cup heavy cream (optional)

If using duck leg, peel off skin and reserve it. Remove meat from bones. Discard bones and shred meat.

Cut duck skin into thin strips. Cook in a small nonstick skillet over moderate heat until fat is rendered and skin is crisp and golden brown, 3 to 4 minutes. With a slotted spoon, transfer cracklings to paper towels to drain, and season with salt. Discard fat in skillet and set skillet aside.

Melt butter in an 8-quart heavy pot over moderately high heat. Add celery root, shallots, celery, salt, and pepper to taste and cook, stirring occasionally, until vegetables are golden, about 12 minutes. Add water, bring to a boil, and boil, uncovered, until celery root is very tender, about 15 minutes.

Purée mixture in batches in a blender (use caution) until smooth and transfer to a large saucepan. Stir in lemon juice and, if necessary, more water to thin to desired consistency. Season with salt and pepper and keep warm, covered.

Heat duck meat in same nonstick skillet over moderate heat, stirring, just until hot, 2 to 3 minutes. Season with salt and pepper.

Whisk cream, if using, in a bowl until it just holds stiff peaks.

Reheat bisque if necessary. Serve topped with duck, cracklings, and a dollop of whipped cream.

COOK'S NOTE

■ The soup can be made and the duck prepared up to 2 days ahead. Cool the soup completely, uncovered, then refrigerate, covered; refrigerate the duck meat and cracklings separately. Bring the cracklings to room temperature before proceeding.

Shrimp Bisque with Pernod

SERVES 8 (MAKES ABOUT 8 CUPS)
ACTIVE TIME: 30 MINUTES ■ START TO FINISH: 2 HOURS

■ You'll notice that very little cream is used in this luxurious soup. The bisque is thickened with rice (one traditional way to give a soup body). Herbaceous, anise-tinged Pernod is a classic Gallic touch. It mysteriously intensifies the shrimp flavor. ■

- ½ stick (4 tablespoons) unsalted butter
- 1¼ pounds medium shrimp in shells (31–35 per pound), peeled (shells reserved) and deveined
- ½ cup Pernod
- 8 cups water
- 1 Turkish bay leaf or ½ California bay leaf
- 3 medium carrots, chopped
- 2 celery ribs, chopped

- 1 medium onion, chopped
- 2 tablespoons long-grain white rice
- 2 tablespoons tomato paste
- 1/8 teaspoon cayenne
- 2 teaspoons salt
- 1/3 cup heavy cream
- Fresh lemon juice to taste

OPTIONAL GARNISH: chopped fresh chives

Melt 1 tablespoon butter in a 4-quart saucepan over moderately high heat. Add shrimp shells and cook, stirring frequently, until golden. Add Pernod and boil, stirring frequently, until most of liquid has evaporated, about 4 minutes. Add water and bay leaf and bring to a boil. Reduce heat and simmer, uncovered, for 20 minutes. Pour shrimp stock through a fine-mesh sieve into a bowl, pressing on shells; discard shells.

Meanwhile, melt 1 tablespoon butter in a 6-quart heavy pot over moderate heat. Add shrimp and salt to taste and cook, stirring frequently, until shrimp are just cooked through, 3 to 4 minutes. With a slotted spoon, transfer to a bowl. Add remaining 2 tablespoons butter to pot, then add carrots, celery, and onion and cook, stirring, until softened, about 10 minutes.

Stir in rice, tomato paste, cayenne, salt, and shrimp stock and simmer, covered, until rice is tender, about 20 minutes.

Set aside 12 shrimp and stir remainder into bisque. Purée bisque in batches in a blender (use caution) until very smooth, then pour through a fine-mesh sieve into another pot. Add cream and cook over low heat, stirring, until heated through; do not let boil. Stir in lemon juice and salt to taste.

Cut reserved shrimp into 1/4-inch dice.

Ladle soup into eight bowls and top with diced shrimp and chives, if using.

COOK'S NOTE

- The bisque can be made up to 2 days ahead. Cool, uncovered, then refrigerate, covered.

Lobster Bisque

SERVES 8 (MAKES ABOUT 8 CUPS)
ACTIVE TIME: 1 3/4 HOURS ■ START TO FINISH: 3 1/2 HOURS

■ Rich, delicious, and possessing the mineral, deep-sea brininess that only lobster can bring, this upmarket soup is a pull-out-all-the-stops first course. It is also enormously practical. The recipe calls for only two lobsters, but because you are using them shells and all, soup for eight is the result. (See page 339 for more about lobster.) ■

BAY LEAVES

Bay leaves are among the most influential culinary aromatics. They bring subtle nuances and background notes to many dishes. Of the two bay leaves dried for culinary use, however, we try to avoid the California variety. Its long, skinny, pointed leaves possess a strong, one-dimensional, camphorlike odor and flavor that can flat-out ruin things. We prefer the more rounded, almost squat Turkish bay leaves, the true *Laurus nobilis* of antiquity. Their flavor manages to be deep and bright at the same time. In fact, almost all our recipes that call for the seasoning are written with the imported leaves in mind. They are packaged and sold by the leading spice companies McCormick and Spice Islands (look closely at the shape of the leaves when buying them, because the variety isn't always specified) as well as the mail-order spice merchant Penzeys (see Sources). And don't forget to remove a bay leaf before serving: its sharp edges can scratch the throat.

- 3 quarts water
- 1 cup dry white wine
- 3 fresh tarragon sprigs
- 1 Turkish bay leaf or 1/2 California bay leaf
- 1 1/2 teaspoons salt
- 2 (1- to 1 1/4-pound) live lobsters
- 1 pound carrots, cut into 2-inch pieces
- 2 celery ribs, cut into 2-inch pieces
- 2 medium onions, quartered
- 2 garlic cloves, peeled
- 1/2 stick (4 tablespoons) unsalted butter
- 3 tablespoons Cognac or other brandy
- 1 tablespoon tomato paste
- 1/4 teaspoon cayenne
- 2 tablespoons cornstarch
- 1/2 cup heavy cream
- 1/2 teaspoon fresh lemon juice

OPTIONAL GARNISH: chopped fresh tarragon

COOK THE LOBSTERS: Combine water, wine, tarragon sprigs, bay leaf, and salt in an 8- to 10-quart pot and bring to a boil over moderately high heat. Plunge lobsters headfirst into boiling liquid, loosely cover pot, and cook for 9 minutes. With tongs, transfer lobsters to a shallow baking pan to cool. Pour cooking liquid into a large bowl.

Crack lobster shells and remove meat from claws, joints, and tails. Transfer all juices and tomalley to a bowl and reserve shells; discard lobster bodies. Cut meat into 1/2-inch pieces; refrigerate, covered. Wrap claw shells in a kitchen towel and pound with a mallet (they are usually too tough to cut with shears). With kitchen shears, cut remaining shells into 1/2-inch pieces.

MAKE THE BISQUE: Pulse carrots, celery, onions, and garlic in a food processor until finely chopped. Melt butter in cleaned pot over moderate heat, add chopped vegetables, and cook, stirring occasionally, until softened, 8 to 10 minutes. Add lobster shells and cook, stirring occasionally, for 5 minutes. Stir in Cognac and simmer until it has evaporated, about 3 minutes. Stir in tomato paste, cayenne, lobster cooking liquid, and reserved juices and tomalley. Bring just to a boil, then reduce heat and simmer, stirring occasionally, until liquid is reduced by about half, 1 1/4 to 1 1/2 hours. Discard bay leaf.

With a slotted spoon, transfer solids (including shells) in small batches to food processor and purée until as smooth as possible (shells will still be in large pieces). Force solids through a fine-mesh sieve into a large bowl, pressing hard on them. Then pour some cooking liquid through sieve to help push as much of solids through as possible; discard remaining solids. Return soup to cleaned pot.

Stir together 1/2 cup soup and cornstarch in a small bowl until smooth. Bring soup to a boil, then stir cornstarch mixture and whisk into soup. Simmer, whisking constantly, until slightly thickened, 1 to 2 minutes. Add cream, lemon juice, lobster meat, and salt to taste and heat through, 1 to 2 minutes; do not let boil.

Serve garnished with tarragon, if desired.

COOK'S NOTE

- The bisque can be made up to 2 days ahead. Cool, uncovered, then refrigerate, covered. Reheat, stirring, over low heat; do not let boil.

Bongo-Bongo

Puréed Oyster and Spinach Soup

SERVES 4 (MAKES ABOUT 4 CUPS)
ACTIVE TIME: 15 MINUTES ■ START TO FINISH: 20 MINUTES

■ This strange but sublime concoction of puréed oysters and creamed spinach is from Trader Vic, the man who brought the world mai tais, Ruby Rangoons, and bongo-bongo's sister soup, boula-boula—all fancifully named signature creations. The original Trader Vic's restaurant (now one of twenty-five worldwide), in San Francisco, is still going strong, a welcome reminder to everyone that none of us should take ourselves too seriously. Although the original recipe called for baby-food creamed spinach, we prefer the fresher flavor of frozen creamed spinach. ■

- 1/2 cup shucked small oysters (about 26 oysters), drained, 3/4 cup liquor reserved
- 1/4 cup thawed frozen creamed spinach
- 2 1/2 cups half-and-half
- 2 tablespoons unsalted butter
- 1 garlic clove, minced
- 1 1/2 teaspoons bottled steak sauce, preferably A1

3/4 teaspoon salt
1/4 teaspoon freshly ground black pepper
Pinch of cayenne
2 teaspoons cornstarch mixed with 2 teaspoons cold water
2/3 cup heavy cream

SPECIAL EQUIPMENT: 4 flameproof soup bowls

Preheat broiler.

Combine oysters and oyster liquor in a 3-quart saucepan and bring just to a simmer. Poach oysters at a bare simmer until they are plump and edges curl, 2 to 3 minutes. Transfer to a blender, add spinach, and purée until smooth (use caution).

Bring half-and-half to a simmer in a 4-quart heavy saucepan over low heat. Stir in oyster-spinach purée, butter, garlic, steak sauce, salt, pepper, and cayenne and bring just to a simmer, stirring. Stir cornstarch mixture, then add to soup, stirring, and boil, stirring, for 2 minutes.

Ladle soup into soup bowls and put in a shallow baking pan. Beat cream with an electric mixer until it holds soft peaks. Spread cream over surface of soup. Broil 5 inches from heat until cream is lightly browned, about 3 minutes.

Cream of Lentil and Chestnut Soup with Foie Gras Custards

SERVES 6

ACTIVE TIME: 45 MINUTES ■ START TO FINISH: 1 1/2 HOURS

■ This is the most voluptuous lentil soup you'll ever find. One taste and you'll have to put your spoon down, sit back, and take it all in. Utterly French in concept and execution, it proves that lentils and cream are an unbeatable combination. The exquisite foie gras custards, baked in the bottom of the soup plates themselves, are a wonderful little surprise. The recipe is adapted from one by Yves Camdeborde, the chef-owner of La Régalade bistro, in Paris.

French green lentils, *lentilles du Puy*, are more delicate than other varieties and also hold together better. They are available in specialty markets and some well-stocked supermarkets, or by mail (see Sources). ■

FOR CROUTONS

About 1 1/2 cups vegetable oil
4 very thin slices firm white sandwich bread, crusts discarded and bread cut into 1/4-inch dice

FOR SOUP

4 fresh thyme sprigs
4 fresh parsley sprigs
4 fresh chives
2 Turkish bay leaves or 1 California bay leaf
1 cup (7 ounces) French green lentils (*lentilles du Puy*), picked over and rinsed
1/2 pound (1 1/2 cups) bottled whole cooked chestnuts (see Sources)
10 cups cold water
1 1/2 teaspoons kosher salt
Freshly ground black pepper
1/2 cup heavy cream

FOR CUSTARDS

100 grams (3 1/2 ounces) cooked goose foie gras (see Sources)
2 large eggs
2 large egg yolks
1 teaspoon kosher salt
1 cup heavy cream

GARNISH: 1/3 cup sliced almonds, toasted (see Tips, page 938)

SPECIAL EQUIPMENT: kitchen string; six 1 1/2-cup ovenproof soup plates

MAKE THE CROUTONS: Heat 1/4 inch oil in a 10-inch heavy skillet over moderate heat until hot but not smoking. Add bread and cook, stirring frequently, until deep golden, about 1 minute. With a slotted spoon, transfer to paper towels to drain.

MAKE THE SOUP: Tie thyme, parsley, chives, and bay leaves together with kitchen string to make a bouquet garni. Combine lentils, chestnuts, water, bouquet garni, and salt in a 4-quart heavy saucepan and bring to a boil. Reduce heat and simmer, partially covered, until lentils are tender, 20 to 25 minutes.

MEANWHILE, MAKE THE CUSTARDS: Put racks in upper and lower thirds of oven and preheat oven to 325°F.

Combine foie gras, eggs, yolks, and kosher salt in a food processor and purée until very smooth. With motor running, add cream in a stream and blend until just combined; do not overprocess, or cream will curdle.

Put soup plates on two large baking sheets and divide custard among them. Bake until just set, 15 to 20 minutes (some custards may cook more quickly than others; check each one). Cool until warm.

FINISH AND SERVE THE SOUP: When lentils are tender, discard bouquet garni. Remove 2 cups cooking liquid from soup and reserve. Purée remaining soup in batches in a blender (use caution), then pour through a large medium-mesh sieve into a large bowl; discard solids. Whisk in enough reserved cooking liquid to reach a thin, creamy consistency, then season with salt and pepper. (Soup will continue to thicken as it stands; save reserved cooking liquid to thin it as needed.)

Reheat soup, stirring occasionally, until very hot. Beat cream in a bowl with an electric mixer until it just holds stiff peaks, then whisk vigorously into soup.

Pour soup over custards and sprinkle with croutons and almonds.

Minestrone

SERVES 6 TO 8 AS A MAIN COURSE (MAKES ABOUT 14 CUPS)
ACTIVE TIME: 1 HOUR ■ START TO FINISH: 2¾ HOURS PLUS SOAKING TIME FOR BEANS (AND ADDITIONAL TIME IF MAKING STOCK)

■ Real minestrone, with pancetta, Parmigiano-Reggiano, and kale, is one of the best vegetable soups on the planet. The secret is the kale, which grounds the soup and gives it a sturdy underpinning. If you omit it, you will have a perfectly nice vegetable soup, but it won't be minestrone. Note that there's no need to add pasta to stretch the soup.

We're particularly partial to the lacinato variety of kale (see Glossary). Be aware that lacinato has more aliases than a gangster on the lam. It can be called Tuscan kale, *cavolo nero* ("black cabbage"), black kale, or dinosaur kale. Its flavor is as deep as the color of its green-black leaves, with a sweetness reminiscent of artichokes. ■

Bouquet Garni

When you toss a bouquet garni into a soup (or into something like Coq au Vin, page 368), you are adding an essential building block of flavor, and you are adding nuance. This bundle of kitchen aromatics might include a bit of celery (wouldn't it be great if you could buy it a stalk at a time?), parsley, bay leaf, thyme, whole peppercorns or cloves, even garlic. Though some of these items can be bound together easily with a length of kitchen string and dropped into the pot, some of the other important components will get lost. One way to keep a bouquet garni together, no matter what its contents, is to wrap the ingredients in a two- or three-ply square of cheesecloth (6 inches is about right), tie it firmly, and let it drift through the broth while the soup cooks. When the soup is finished, so is the bouquet garni. The small, sodden cheesecloth parcel can be easily removed, wrung of remaining liquid (which goes back into the pot) when slightly cooled, and discarded.

- ½ pound (1¼ cups) dried white beans, such as great northern, picked over and rinsed
- ½ teaspoon salt
- ½ pound boiling potatoes
- ⅓ cup olive oil
- ¼ pound pancetta or lean bacon (4 slices), chopped
- 1 large onion, chopped
- 1 large carrot, cut into ½-inch cubes
- 1 celery rib, cut into ½-inch cubes
- 3 garlic cloves, finely chopped
- 2 zucchini (1 pound total), cut into ½-inch cubes
- ¼ pound green beans, cut into ½-inch pieces
- 4 cups shredded green cabbage, preferably savoy (¾ pound)
- ½ pound kale, stems and tough center ribs discarded and leaves chopped (6 cups)
- 1 (28- to 32-ounce) can whole tomatoes in juice, drained well and coarsely chopped
- 4½ cups (36 ounces) chicken stock or store-bought low-sodium broth
- Freshly ground black pepper

ACCOMPANIMENT: 1 cup finely grated Parmigiano-Reggiano (about 2 ounces)

Soak beans in cold water to cover by 2 inches, refrigerated, for at least 8 hours (or see page 267 for quick-soaking procedure); drain.

Transfer beans to a 3-quart heavy saucepan, add cold water to cover by 2 inches, and bring to a boil. Reduce heat and simmer, uncovered, adding more water if necessary to keep beans barely covered, until tender, about 50 minutes. Add salt and simmer for 5 minutes more. Remove from heat and let beans stand, uncovered.

Peel potatoes and cut into ¾-inch dice; put in a bowl of cold water.

Heat oil in a 6- to 8-quart heavy pot over moderate heat. Add pancetta and cook, stirring, until crisp and pale golden, 4 to 5 minutes. Add onion and cook, stirring, until softened, 4 to 5 minutes. Add carrot, celery, and garlic and cook, stirring, for 4 minutes. Drain potatoes well, add to pot, along with zucchini and green beans, and cook, stirring, for 4 minutes. Add cabbage and kale and cook, stirring, until cabbage is wilted, about 5 minutes. Add tomatoes and stock and bring to a simmer. Cover, reduce heat, and simmer for 1 hour.

Drain beans, reserving liquid. Purée half of beans with 1 cup reserved liquid in a blender or food processor (use caution). Stir into soup, along with remaining drained beans and reserved liquid. Simmer soup, uncovered, for 15 minutes. Season with salt and pepper.

Serve soup with cheese.

COOK'S NOTE

- The soup can be made up to 3 days ahead. Cool completely, uncovered, then refrigerate, covered. Thin with water, if desired, when reheating.

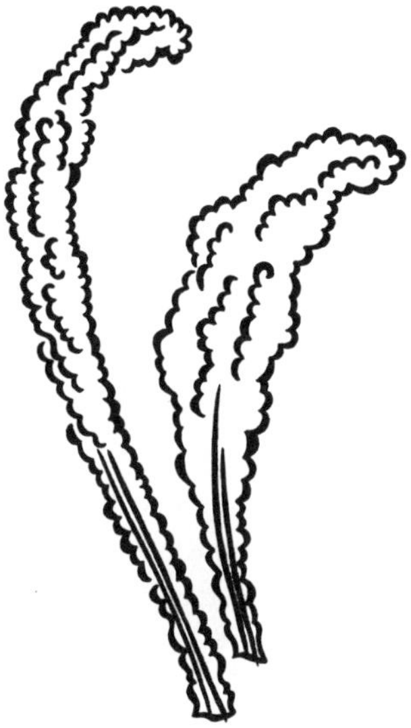

LACINATO KALE

Richard Olney's Soupe au Pistou

SERVES 6 (MAKES ABOUT 12 CUPS)
ACTIVE TIME: 35 MINUTES ■ START TO FINISH: 1¼ HOURS

■ Richard Olney, a native Iowan, spent nearly forty years in the French countryside living a life most Americans just dream about. From his rustic perch on a hillside near Toulon, he wrote and edited more than thirty-five books on food and wine. His most influential book, *Simple French Food,* was published in 1974 and caused an entire generation of American chefs to reconsider the way they cooked. This recipe from that book, for vegetable soup with *pistou*—a condiment that is essentially the French version of Italy's pesto (without nuts)—helps explain what all the fuss was about.

This soup is thoughtful, unpretentious, and highly adaptable to seasonal produce or the contents of your larder. ■

FOR SOUP

- 1 celery rib
- 3 fresh parsley sprigs
- 2 fresh thyme sprigs
- 1 Turkish bay leaf or ½ California bay leaf
- 10 cups water
- ¾ pound potatoes
- 2 medium leeks (white and pale green parts only), thinly sliced
- 1 medium onion, thinly sliced
- 2 medium carrots, halved lengthwise and thinly sliced
- ¾ pound butternut or other winter squash, peeled, seeded, and cut into ½-inch pieces
- 1 pound fresh white beans in the pod, shelled, or 1½ cups drained cooked white beans, rinsed if canned
- 6 ounces green beans, cut into ½-inch pieces
- 2 small zucchini (½ pound total), cut into ¼-inch-thick slices
- 1 cup elbow macaroni

FOR *PISTOU*

- 4 large garlic cloves, peeled
- ½ cup fresh basil leaves (not packed), preferably with blossoms
- ¼ teaspoon salt
- Freshly ground black pepper
- 1 cup finely grated Parmigiano-Reggiano (about 2 ounces)
- 1 firm but ripe medium tomato, peeled (see Tips, page 940), seeded, and cut into chunks
- 1–1¼ cups olive oil

SPECIAL EQUIPMENT: kitchen string

MAKE THE SOUP: Tie together celery, parsley, thyme, and bay leaf with kitchen string to make a bouquet garni.

Bring water to a boil in a 5-quart pot. Meanwhile, peel potatoes and quarter lengthwise, then cut crosswise into thin slices. Wash leeks well in a bowl of cold water; lift out and drain.

Add potatoes, leeks, onion, carrots, squash, fresh white beans, if using, and bouquet garni to pot and simmer until beans and squash are tender but still hold their shape, about 30 minutes.

Add green beans, zucchini, macaroni, and cooked white beans, if using, and simmer until macaroni is just tender, about 15 minutes. Discard bouquet garni.

WHILE THE SOUP COOKS, MAKE THE *PISTOU*: Mash garlic, basil, salt, and pepper to taste in a mortar with a pestle, alternating between pounding and turning with a grinding motion, until mixture forms a paste (or finely chop basil and garlic, then mash in a bowl with salt and pepper, using back of a spoon). Work in enough cheese to make a very stiff paste, then add about one third of tomato, pounding and grinding (or mashing) it into the paste. Gradually work in remaining cheese and tomato, along with enough olive oil to make a barely fluid paste. Then gradually work enough additional oil for *pistou* to become a sauce.

Serve soup with mortar (or bowl) of *pistou* on the side, to be added to taste by each person.

COOK'S NOTE

■ The oil in the *pistou* mixture will separate, so you will need to stir it each time before spooning it out.

Kale and White Bean Soup

SERVES 6 AS A MAIN COURSE (MAKES ABOUT 16 CUPS)
ACTIVE TIME: 1 HOUR ■ START TO FINISH: 2¼ HOURS PLUS SOAKING TIME FOR BEANS (AND ADDITIONAL TIME IF MAKING STOCK)

■ If you've been resisting the call for more beans and greens in your diet, stop right here. A heel of Parmesan works magic in a bean soup; it oozes little strands through the broth, making it rich and flavorful. Lacinato kale adds great depth, almost a meatiness, to the soup. ■

- 1 pound dried white beans, such as great northern, cannellini, or navy, picked over and rinsed
- 2 tablespoons olive oil
- 2 medium onions, coarsely chopped
- 4 garlic cloves, finely chopped

5 cups (40 ounces) chicken stock or store-bought low-sodium broth
8 cups water
1 (3-by-2-inch) piece Parmigiano-Reggiano rind
1 teaspoon finely chopped fresh rosemary
1 Turkish bay leaf or ½ California bay leaf
½ teaspoon freshly ground black pepper
1 pound smoked sausage, such as kielbasa, sliced ¼ inch thick (optional)
8 carrots, halved lengthwise and cut crosswise into ½-inch-thick slices
1 pound kale (preferably lacinato; see Glossary), stems and tough center ribs discarded, leaves coarsely chopped
2 teaspoons salt

Soak beans in water to cover by 2 inches, refrigerated, for at least 8 hours (or see page 267 for quick-soaking procedure); drain.

Heat oil in an 8-quart heavy pot over moderately low heat. Add onions and cook, stirring occasionally, until softened, 4 to 5 minutes. Add garlic and cook, stirring, for 1 minute. Add beans, stock, 4 cups water, cheese rind, rosemary, bay leaf, and pepper and bring to a boil. Reduce heat and simmer, uncovered, until beans are just tender, about 50 minutes.

Meanwhile, brown sausage, if using, in batches in a heavy skillet over moderate heat, stirring often. Transfer to paper towels to drain.

Stir carrots into soup and simmer for 5 minutes. Stir in kale, sausage, if using, remaining 4 cups water, and salt, bring to a simmer, and simmer, stirring occasionally, until kale is tender, 12 to 15 minutes. Season soup with additional salt, if necessary, and pepper. Discard bay leaf.

COOK'S NOTE

■ This soup is best if made 1 to 2 days ahead. Cool completely, uncovered, then refrigerate, covered. Thin with water if necessary when reheating.

Portuguese Kale Soup with Chorizo

Caldo Verde

SERVES 6 (MAKES ABOUT 12 CUPS)
ACTIVE TIME: 40 MINUTES ■ START TO FINISH: 1 HOUR

■ In Portugal, the potato-thickened green soup *caldo verde*—essentially the national dish—is made with Galician cabbage and the Portuguese sausage called *chouriço*, but kale and Spanish chorizo are great (and easily obtainable) substitutes. ■

3 tablespoons olive oil
1 large onion, finely chopped
1½ pounds large boiling potatoes
8 cups water
Salt
½ pound hot Spanish chorizo (spicy cured pork sausage), cut into ½-inch pieces
¾ pound lacinato kale (see Glossary) or regular kale, stems and tough center ribs discarded, leaves cut crosswise into thin slices

Heat oil in a 5-quart heavy pot over moderate heat. Add onion and cook, stirring occasionally, until pale golden, about 5 minutes. Meanwhile, peel potatoes and cut into thin slices.

Add potatoes to pot and cook, stirring occasionally, for 4 minutes. Add water and salt to taste and bring to a boil. Reduce heat and simmer, uncovered, until potatoes are very tender, about 15 minutes.

Meanwhile, cook chorizo in a large nonstick skillet over moderately high heat, stirring occasionally, until browned, about 5 minutes. Transfer to paper towels to drain.

Coarsely mash potatoes in pot (do not drain) with a potato masher. Stir in chorizo and simmer, uncovered, for 5 minutes. Stir in kale and simmer, uncovered, until just tender, 3 to 5 minutes. Season with salt and serve.

Black Bean Soup with Rum

SERVES 6 TO 8 (MAKES ABOUT 8½ CUPS)
ACTIVE TIME: 45 MINUTES ■ START TO FINISH: 4 HOURS PLUS SOAKING TIME FOR BEANS (AND ADDITIONAL TIME IF MAKING STOCK)

■ There are lots of black bean soups in the world, and many of them are sludgy and stodgy. You'll find this one a welcome change. It's brothier, and it gets an exotic little shimmy from dark rum. (It's very good without the rum as well.) The recipe is from the cookbook author and longtime *Gourmet* contributor Elisabeth Lambert Ortiz. You can serve it as a first course or a main dish. ■

- 2 cups dried black beans, picked over and rinsed
- 3 tablespoons unsalted butter
- 2 cups chopped onions
- 1 cup chopped celery
- 6 fresh flat-leaf parsley sprigs
- 2 fresh thyme sprigs
- 1 Turkish bay leaf or ½ California bay leaf
- 1 large ham hock (about 1¼ pounds)
- 6 cups (48 ounces) beef stock or store-bought broth
- 4 cups water
- Freshly ground black pepper
- ⅓ cup dark rum
- 1 tablespoon fresh lemon juice, or to taste
- Salt

OPTIONAL GARNISH: lemon slices, chopped hard-boiled eggs, and chopped fresh flat-leaf parsley

SPECIAL EQUIPMENT: a food mill fitted with a medium disk

Soak beans in cold water to cover by 2 inches, refrigerated, for at least 8 hours (or see page 267 for quick-soaking procedure); drain.

Melt butter in a 6- to 8-quart heavy pot over moderately low heat. Add onions, celery, parsley, thyme, and bay leaf and cook, stirring occasionally, until vegetables are softened, about 10 minutes. Add ham hock, beans, stock, water, and pepper to taste and bring to a boil. Reduce heat and simmer, uncovered, adding more water if necessary to keep beans covered, until beans are very tender, about 3 hours.

Discard ham hock and bay leaf. Force soup through food mill into a large bowl, then return to cleaned pot.

Stir in rum, lemon juice, and salt and pepper to taste. Reheat soup if necessary and thin to desired consistency with hot water. Ladle soup into six to eight bowls. If desired, top each bowl with a lemon slice and sprinkle with chopped egg and parsley.

Red Bean and Bacon Soup

SERVES 6 (MAKES ABOUT 12 CUPS)
ACTIVE TIME: 1 HOUR ■ START TO FINISH: 3 HOURS PLUS TIME FOR SOAKING BEANS (AND ADDITIONAL TIME IF MAKING STOCK)

■ Here's a perfect Sunday night supper. Just add cheese toasts and a green salad. ■

- 1 pound dried red beans, such as kidney or pinto, picked over and rinsed
- ½ pound lean bacon (8 slices), cut into ½-inch-wide pieces
- 1½ cups finely chopped onions
- 2 large garlic cloves, finely chopped
- 1 Turkish bay leaf or ½ California bay leaf
- 1 tablespoon chili powder
- 1½ teaspoons ground cumin
- ¼ teaspoon cayenne, or to taste
- 1½ cups chopped celery
- 1½ cups chopped carrots
- 4 cups (32 ounces) chicken stock or store-bought low-sodium broth
- 2 cups water
- 1 (28- to 32-ounce) can whole tomatoes in juice, drained (juice reserved) and chopped
- ½ cup medium-dry sherry, or to taste
- Salt and freshly ground black pepper

ACCOMPANIMENT: sour cream and chopped scallion greens

SPECIAL EQUIPMENT: a food mill fitted with a medium disk

Soak beans in cold water to cover by 2 inches, refrigerated, for at least 8 hours (or see page 267 for quick-soaking procedure); drain.

Cook bacon in a 6- to 7-quart heavy pot over moderately low heat, stirring occasionally, until crisp. With a slotted spoon, transfer to paper towels to drain. Pour off all but 1/4 cup fat from pot.

Add onions, garlic, bay leaf, chili powder, cumin, and cayenne to pot and cook, stirring, until onions are softened, 2 to 3 minutes. Add celery, carrots, beans, stock, and water and bring to a boil. Reduce heat and simmer, covered, until beans are tender, 1 to 1½ hours.

Add tomatoes with reserved juice and simmer, covered, for 20 minutes.

Discard bay leaf. Force soup in batches through food mill into a large saucepan. Stir in sherry and salt and pepper to taste. If necessary, thin soup to desired consistency with water. Simmer, stirring once or twice, for 5 minutes.

Serve soup sprinkled with bacon and with bowls of sour cream and scallion greens for topping, as desired.

Ham and Black-Eyed Pea Soup with Collard Greens

SERVES 4 (MAKES ABOUT 8 CUPS)
ACTIVE TIME: 20 MINUTES ■ START TO FINISH: 45 MINUTES PLUS ADDITIONAL TIME IF MAKING STOCK

■ Hoppin' John (see page 274) is the traditional good-luck dish of "peas" (botanically speaking, they're beans) and rice that is eaten on New Year's Day in much of the American South. It's usually served with collards (to bring lots of "folding green" money in the year ahead) that have been properly cooked—that is, with a ham bone. This quick one-pot twist on tradition is ideal for homesick transplanted southerners. ■

- 1/4 cup olive oil
- 2 medium onions, finely chopped
- 2 garlic cloves, finely chopped
- 1/2 pound cooked ham, cut into 1/4-inch dice
- 1 pound collard greens, stems and center ribs discarded, leaves finely chopped
- 6 cups water
- 2 cups (16 ounces) chicken stock or store-bought low-sodium broth
- 2 (16-ounce) cans black-eyed peas (3 cups), drained and rinsed
- 3/4 teaspoon salt
- 1/4 teaspoon freshly ground black pepper
- 2 teaspoons cider vinegar

Heat oil in a 4- to 6-quart heavy pot over moderate heat. Add onions, garlic, and ham and cook, stirring occasionally, until onions are soft, about 14 minutes.

Add collards, water, and stock and bring to a boil. Reduce heat and simmer, uncovered, until collards are tender, about 20 minutes.

Mash half of black-eyed peas with a fork in a bowl. Stir mashed and whole peas into soup and simmer, uncovered, for 5 minutes. Stir in salt, pepper, and vinegar.

Yellow Split Pea Soup

SERVES 8 (MAKES ABOUT 12 CUPS)
ACTIVE TIME: 30 MINUTES ■ START TO FINISH: 4½ HOURS

■ Basic ingredients simply prepared make this forthright soup a keeper. It's perfect for a wintry day. ■

- 8 cups water
- 1 pound yellow split peas, picked over and rinsed
- 1/2 pound meaty salt pork (rinsed if crusted with salt), cut into 1/2-inch cubes, or a meaty ham bone or ham hock
- 2 pounds onions (5 medium), finely chopped
- 1 medium leek (white and pale green parts only), chopped
- 2 tablespoons unsalted butter
- 1 teaspoon chopped fresh chives
- 1/2 teaspoon dried savory, crumbled
- 2 teaspoons salt
- 1/2 teaspoon freshly ground black pepper

Combine water, peas, salt pork, and half of onions in a 6- to 8-quart heavy pot and bring to a boil, skimming off froth. Reduce heat and simmer, partially covered, until split peas are tender but not falling apart, 1 to 1½ hours.

Meanwhile, wash leek well in a bowl of cold water;

lift out and drain well. Melt butter in a 12-inch heavy skillet over moderate heat. Add leek and remaining onions and cook, stirring, until softened, about 10 minutes. Remove from heat.

When split peas are tender, add leek mixture to soup, along with chives, savory, salt, and pepper. Continue to simmer, partially covered, until peas are falling apart and soup is thickened, 1 to 1½ hours.

If using ham bone or ham hock, remove from soup, remove and shred meat, and return meat to soup.

Curried Lentil Soup with Tomato and Spinach

SERVES 4 (MAKES ABOUT 6 CUPS)
ACTIVE TIME: 15 MINUTES ■ START TO FINISH: 45 MINUTES
PLUS ADDITIONAL TIME IF MAKING STOCK

■ The beauty of lentils is that they cook quickly. Curry, lentils, spinach, and tomatoes come together in a lively, flavorful, visually appealing soup that makes a great weeknight supper. ■

- ¼ cup vegetable oil
- ⅔ cup finely chopped onion
- 2 garlic cloves, minced
- 2 teaspoons finely grated peeled fresh ginger
- 1 tablespoon curry powder
- 1 teaspoon ground cumin
- 1 cup lentils, picked over and rinsed
- 2½ cups (20 ounces) chicken stock or store-bought low-sodium broth
- 2½ cups water
- ⅔ cup chopped drained canned tomatoes
- 2 cups coarsely chopped spinach
- Fresh lemon juice to taste
- Salt and freshly ground black pepper

Heat oil in a 4-quart heavy saucepan over moderate heat. Add onion and cook, stirring occasionally, until lightly browned, 6 to 8 minutes. Add garlic and ginger and cook, stirring, for 1 minute. Add curry powder and cumin and cook, stirring, for 30 seconds. Add lentils, stock, and water and bring to a boil. Reduce heat and simmer, covered, until lentils are tender, 20 to 25 minutes.

Stir in tomatoes and spinach and simmer, uncovered, stirring occasionally, until spinach is wilted, about 2 minutes. Add lemon juice and salt and pepper to taste.

Chickpea, Lentil, and Rice Soup

Harira

SERVES 8 (MAKES ABOUT 14 CUPS)
ACTIVE TIME: 40 MINUTES ■ START TO FINISH: 1¾ HOURS
PLUS SOAKING TIME IF USING DRIED CHICKPEAS

■ *Harira,* one of our very favorite soups, is commonly served during Ramadan, when fasting is practiced daily from dawn to sunset. Thick and substantial with chickpeas, lentils, rice, and lamb, it is the perfect restorative. We have the Palais Jamaï hotel in Fez to thank for this version. If you want to be authentic, precede the soup with a Moroccan-style orange salad, sprinkling the orange slices with the tiniest bit of cinnamon and orange blossom water. ■

- 1½ cups (8 ounces) dried chickpeas, picked over and rinsed, or 3 cups canned chickpeas, drained and rinsed
- ¼ pound boneless lamb shoulder, cut into ½-inch pieces
- 2 medium onions, finely chopped
- ¼ teaspoon crumbled saffron threads
- ¾ teaspoon freshly ground black pepper
- 8 cups water
- 1 cup lentils, picked over and rinsed
- ½ cup long-grain white rice
- 1 tablespoon tomato paste
- 1 cup finely chopped fresh flat-leaf parsley
- 1 cup finely chopped fresh cilantro
- 5 medium tomatoes (1¾ pounds), peeled (see Tips, page 940), seeded, and puréed in a food processor
- 2 teaspoons salt

If using dried chickpeas, soak in water to cover by 2 inches, refrigerated, for at least 8 hours (or see page 267 for quick-soaking procedure); drain.

Transfer soaked chickpeas to a large saucepan and add cold water to cover by 3 inches. Bring to a boil, then reduce heat and simmer chickpeas, covered, until just tender, about 1 hour; drain.

Combine chickpeas (freshly cooked or canned), lamb, onions, saffron, pepper, and water in a 6- to 8-quart heavy pot. Bring to a boil, then reduce heat and simmer, covered, for 45 minutes.

Stir in lentils, rice, tomato paste, parsley, cilantro, and tomato purée and bring to a boil. Reduce heat and simmer, covered, until lentils are tender, about 30 minutes. Stir in salt.

Mushroom Barley Soup

SERVES 10 TO 12 (MAKES ABOUT 17 CUPS)
ACTIVE TIME: 45 MINUTES ■ START TO FINISH: 1¾ HOURS

■ Dried mushrooms added to the classic combination of fresh white mushrooms and barley bring a deeper, foresty dimension to this soup. Once relegated to specialty foods shops, small packages of dried mushrooms are now available in most well-stocked supermarkets. Asian markets are also a good source for dried shiitakes (sometimes labeled as Chinese black mushrooms). ■

- 1 ounce dried shiitake or other mushrooms, such as porcini, morels, or chanterelles
- 1 cup boiling water
- ¼ cup olive oil
- 6 garlic cloves, finely chopped
- 3 medium onions, finely chopped (1½ cups)
- 2 pounds white mushrooms, trimmed and thinly sliced
- 1 tablespoon soy sauce
- ½ cup medium-dry sherry
- 5 cups (40 ounces) chicken stock or store-bought low-sodium broth
- 5 cups water
- 1 cup pearl barley
- 8 carrots, cut diagonally into ½-inch-thick slices
- ½ teaspoon dried thyme, crumbled
- ½ teaspoon dried rosemary, crumbled
- Salt and freshly ground black pepper
- ⅓ cup minced fresh flat-leaf parsley

Soak dried mushrooms in boiling water in a small bowl for 20 minutes.

Lift mushrooms from soaking liquid and transfer to a cutting board; reserve liquid. If using shiitakes, discard stems. Thinly slice mushrooms. Pour reserved liquid through a sieve lined with a dampened paper towel into another small bowl.

Heat oil in a 5- to 6-quart heavy pot over moderate heat. Add garlic and cook, stirring, until golden, about 1 minute. Add onions and cook, stirring occasionally, until pale golden, 8 to 10 minutes. Add white mushrooms, dried mushrooms, and soy sauce and cook over moderately high heat, stirring, until most of liquid mushrooms give off has evaporated, about 10 minutes. Add sherry and boil until evaporated, about 5 minutes.

Add stock, water, strained mushroom soaking liquid, barley, carrots, and dried herbs to pot and bring to a boil. Reduce heat and simmer, covered, for 1 hour. Season soup with salt and pepper and stir in parsley.

COOK'S NOTE

■ The soup can be made, without the parsley, up to 4 days ahead. Cool completely, uncovered, then refrigerate, covered. Thin with water to the desired consistency when reheating.

Garlic Soup with Poached Eggs

SERVES 4
ACTIVE TIME: 30 MINUTES ■ START TO FINISH: 30 MINUTES PLUS ADDITIONAL TIME IF MAKING STOCK

■ Garlic cooked in oil on the stovetop turns golden in flavor—there's no other way to describe it. This soup segues into a bowl of heady broth and poached eggs on toast before your very eyes. An especially satisfying soup, it's a staple in coffee shops throughout Mexico. ■

3 tablespoons olive oil
1 medium head garlic (2 inches in diameter), separated into cloves, peeled, and thinly sliced
8 (½-inch-thick) baguette slices
4 cups (32 ounces) chicken stock or store-bought low-sodium broth
½ teaspoon red pepper flakes
4 large eggs
Salt

GARNISH: ½ cup loosely packed small fresh cilantro sprigs
ACCOMPANIMENT: 4 lime wedges

Heat oil in a deep 10-inch heavy skillet over low heat. Add garlic and cook, stirring occasionally, until tender and pale golden, 8 to 10 minutes. With a slotted spoon, transfer garlic to a small bowl. Increase heat to moderate, add bread to skillet, and cook, turning once, until browned, about 4 minutes total. Divide toasts among four large soup bowls.

Add stock, red pepper flakes, and garlic to skillet and bring to a simmer. Break 1 egg into a cup and slide egg into simmering stock. Repeat with remaining eggs, spacing them evenly in pan. Poach eggs at a bare simmer until whites are firm but yolks are still runny, 3 to 4 minutes.

With slotted spoon, transfer eggs to toasts and season with salt. Ladle soup over eggs and garnish with cilantro. Serve with lime wedges.

COOK'S NOTE

- The poached eggs are not fully cooked. If this is a concern, see page 629.

Onion Soup Gratinée

SERVES 4 (MAKES ABOUT 6 CUPS)
ACTIVE TIME: 1½ HOURS ■ START TO FINISH: 2 HOURS PLUS ADDITIONAL TIME IF MAKING STOCK

■ Paris in the fifties and sixties found people eating onion soup in Les Halles at midnight—the most romantic thing imaginable. These days, good onion soup is hard to find in Paris, or anywhere else, for that matter. It most often suffers from what's been done to pizza—too much cheese. The key to its excellence is homemade beef stock as well as sensible proportions of soup, bread, and cheese. You'll be much happier making this French classic in your own kitchen than trying to find it elsewhere. The beauty of this recipe is that you don't need to fool with gratinéeing the tops of individual soup bowls. We cover the whole pot with a raft of cheese-topped bread, bake it until it bubbles, and then run it under the broiler for a final browning. (If you have an old-fashioned broiler underneath the oven, skip that last step.) ■

FOR SOUP
12 fresh parsley stems
½ teaspoon dried thyme, crumbled
8 black peppercorns
1 Turkish bay leaf or ½ California bay leaf
2 tablespoons unsalted butter
1 tablespoon olive oil
1½ pounds onions, thinly sliced crosswise
¾ teaspoon salt
¼ teaspoon freshly ground black pepper
Pinch of sugar
2 tablespoons all-purpose flour
6 cups beef stock or store-bought broth
⅓ cup dry vermouth
2 tablespoons Cognac or other brandy
2 teaspoons Worcestershire sauce, or to taste

FOR TOPPING
12–14 (1-inch-thick) baguette slices
½ stick (4 tablespoons) unsalted butter, melted
1 garlic clove, halved crosswise
1 cup grated Gruyère (about 4 ounces)
½ cup finely grated Parmigiano-Reggiano (1 ounce)

SPECIAL EQUIPMENT: cheesecloth; kitchen string

MAKE THE SOUP: Tie parsley stems, thyme, peppercorns, and bay leaf in a small square of cheesecloth with string to make a bouquet garni.

Melt butter with oil in a 3- to 4-quart ovenproof heavy saucepan over moderately low heat. Add onions, salt, and pepper and cook, covered, stirring occasionally, until onions are soft, about 18 minutes. Add sugar, increase heat to moderate, and cook, uncovered, stirring occasionally, until onions are golden brown, 15 to 18 minutes.

Add flour and cook, stirring, for 3 minutes. Stir in stock, vermouth, bouquet garni, and salt and pepper to taste and bring to a boil, stirring. Reduce heat, partially cover, and simmer, skimming off froth occasionally, for 30 minutes. Discard bouquet garni. Stir in Cognac and Worcestershire sauce.

MEANWHILE, MAKE THE TOASTS: Put a rack in middle of oven and preheat oven to 350°F.

Arrange bread on a baking sheet and brush both sides with some of melted butter. Bake, turning once, until golden, about 15 minutes total. Remove from oven and rub toasts with cut sides of garlic clove. (Leave oven on.)

GRATINÉE THE SOUP: Cover top of soup completely with toasted bread. Sprinkle evenly with cheeses and drizzle remaining melted butter on top. Bake until soup comes to a simmer, 15 to 20 minutes. Remove from oven.

Preheat broiler. Broil soup 4 to 6 inches from heat until cheese is golden, about 1 minute.

Broccoli, Red Pepper, and Cheddar Chowder

SERVES 4 (MAKES ABOUT 6 CUPS)
ACTIVE TIME: 45 MINUTES ■ START TO FINISH: 45 MINUTES

■ Almost everyone has a hunk of Cheddar in the fridge. Here we take the idea of broccoli with cheese sauce and turn it inside out. Nuggets of potato give the chowder heft, and red bell pepper adds color and sweetness. ■

- 1 small bunch broccoli (½ pound)
- 1 large boiling potato (½ pound)
- 2 tablespoons unsalted butter
- 1 large onion, chopped
- 1 red bell pepper, cored, seeded, and cut into ½-inch pieces
- 1 large garlic clove, finely chopped
- 1 teaspoon ground cumin
- ½ teaspoon dry mustard
- 1 teaspoon salt
- ¼ teaspoon freshly ground black pepper
- 2 tablespoons all-purpose flour
- ¾ cup heavy cream
- 1½ cups coarsely grated sharp Cheddar (about 6 ounces)

Cut off broccoli stems and discard tough lower third of stems. Peel stems and finely chop. Cut remaining broccoli into 1-inch florets.

Cook florets in a large pot of boiling salted water (1 tablespoon salt per every 4 quarts water) until just tender, 2 to 3 minutes. With a slotted spoon, transfer to a bowl of ice and cold water to stop the cooking, then drain. Reserve 3 cups cooking water.

Peel potato and cut into ½-inch cubes. Melt butter in a 3- to 4-quart heavy saucepan over moderate heat. Add potato, onion, bell pepper, broccoli stems, and garlic and cook, stirring occasionally, until onion is softened, 8 to 10 minutes. Add cumin, mustard, salt, and pepper and cook, stirring, for 1 minute. Add flour and cook, stirring, for 2 minutes. Add reserved cooking water, stirring, partially cover, and simmer, stirring occasionally, until potatoes are tender, about 10 minutes.

Add cream, then add cheese and cook, stirring, until cheese is melted. Season with salt and pepper.

Purée about 2 cups chowder in a blender until smooth (use caution) and return to pot. Add broccoli florets and cook over moderate heat, stirring occasionally, until heated through, about 2 minutes.

Ecuadorean Lenten Chowder

Fanesca

SERVES 8 (MAKES ABOUT 16 CUPS)
ACTIVE TIME: 1 HOUR ■ START TO FINISH: 2 HOURS
PLUS 1 TO 3 DAYS FOR SOAKING COD

■ The astonishing cod and vegetable chowder called *fanesca* is made in Ecuador only during Holy Week. The flavors are harmonious, and the textures are a field day for the mouth, even though the recipe includes everything but the proverbial kitchen sink.

Maricel Presilla, a food historian and the chef-owner of Zafra, in Hoboken, New Jersey, first offered her *fanesca,* a more elaborate rendition of the streamlined dish here, only during Holy Week, but it's now one of the restaurant's most popular weekend specials year-round. Presilla suggests using a combination of beans, such as chickpeas, small white beans, cranberry or small kidney beans, and pinto or canary beans. She also prefers to remove the salt cod from the chowder in one piece, but it is just as delicious if the fish flakes apart right in the broth.

The large tan or greenish pumpkin called *calabaza* is usually sold by the slice in Latino groceries; butternut squash is an able stand-in. *Queso fresco,* sometimes called *queso blanco,* is a Mexican fresh white cheese that is very creamy (mild, soft French feta is a good substitution). ■

- 1 pound choice-grade, center-cut, skinless, boneless salt cod (see page 19), rinsed well
- 1 tablespoon achiote (annatto) seeds (see Glossary)
- 1/4 cup vegetable oil
- 4 large garlic cloves, minced
- 4 scallions, finely chopped
- 1 teaspoon ground cumin
- 8 cups water
- 1 1/4 pounds *queso fresco* (see Glossary) or French feta, cut into 3/4-inch cubes
- 1/4 cup lentils, picked over and rinsed
- 1 pound carrots, cut into 1/2-inch-thick slices
- 4 ears corn, shucked
- 1 pound zucchini, cut into 1/2-inch-thick slices
- 1 (1-pound) piece *calabaza* or butternut squash, peeled and cut into 1-inch pieces
- 1 (1-pound) piece green cabbage, coarsely chopped
- 1 (10-ounce) package frozen baby lima beans
- 1 (10-ounce) package frozen baby peas
- 1/2 pound snow peas or green beans, cut into 1/2-inch-thick slices
- 5 cups whole milk, heated until hot
- 2 tablespoons unsalted butter
- 2 1/2 cups mixed canned beans (see headnote), drained and rinsed
- 1/2 cup rinsed canned hominy
- 1 (4-inch) piece canned heart of palm, sliced 1/4 inch thick

ACCOMPANIMENT: quartered hard-boiled eggs and avocado slices

Soak cod in a large bowl of water to cover by 2 inches, refrigerated, for 1 to 3 days, changing water three times a day to remove excess salt. Drain well and refrigerate until ready to use.

Combine achiote seeds and oil in a small saucepan and heat over moderate heat until oil begins to bubble, about 2 minutes; remove from heat. Cool seeds in oil, then pour oil through a sieve into an 8-quart heavy pot; discard seeds.

Heat achiote oil over moderately high heat until hot but not smoking. Add garlic and cook, stirring, for 30 seconds. Add scallions and cumin and cook, stirring occasionally, for 2 minutes. Add water and bring to a boil. Add two thirds of cheese and stir until incorporated. Stir in lentils and carrots, reduce heat, and simmer, uncovered, until lentils are tender, about 20 minutes.

Meanwhile, cut 2 ears corn crosswise into 1-inch-thick pieces. Cut corn kernels from remaining 2 ears, then scrape ears over a bowl to catch corn "milk." Discard cobs.

Stir all corn, including corn milk, into soup, along with zucchini, *calabaza,* cabbage, limas, baby peas, snow peas, hot milk, and butter, and simmer, uncovered, for 10 minutes. Stir in canned beans, hominy, and heart of palm and simmer, uncovered, for 5 minutes.

Add cod (in one piece) and cook for 2 minutes.

Remove cod from chowder and stir in remaining cheese. Cut cod into 8 pieces. Ladle chowder into eight bowls and top each serving with a piece of fish.

Serve topped with quartered eggs and avocado slices.

Fish Soup with Bread and Rouille

SERVES 6

ACTIVE TIME: 1 3/4 HOURS ■ START TO FINISH: 3 1/2 HOURS (INCLUDES MAKING ROUILLE) PLUS ADDITIONAL TIME IF MAKING STOCK

■ This is one of the best fish soups we've ever had. It's not at all aggressive; rather, it's light and brothy, and it takes a faintly smoky turn from the grilled bread used to make its croûtes. The secret to the croûtes, by the way, is a simple one. After the bread is grilled (use a good sourdough or *pain au levain,* which is French sourdough), tear it into rough pieces, leaving them craggy, like a coastline. When you bake them, the edges get beautifully crisp, and they are absolutely delicious in the soup. The rusty red sauce called rouille, which is both stirred into the soup and served as a condiment, makes the soup come alive. This recipe is from Melissa Kelly, the chef-owner of Primo, in Rockland, Maine. ■

- 1 large leek, green part coarsely chopped, white part cut into 1/4-inch pieces
- 5 tablespoons olive oil

- 1 medium onion, coarsely chopped
- 2 celery ribs, coarsely chopped
- 2 carrots, coarsely chopped
- 3 garlic cloves, smashed
- 1/4 teaspoon crumbled saffron threads
- 2 Turkish bay leaves or 1 California bay leaf
- 1 teaspoon red pepper flakes
- 1 1/4 pounds plum tomatoes, coarsely chopped
- 3 tablespoons canned tomato purée
- 2 cups dry white wine
- 6 cups Fish Stock (page 930) or store-bought broth
- 1 (8- to 9-inch) unsliced round or oval sourdough loaf (1 pound)
- 2 tablespoons unsalted butter
- 1 pound skinned white fish fillets, such as halibut, snapper, and/or bass, cut into 1-inch cubes
- 1 teaspoon salt
- Rouille (recipe follows)

GARNISH: 1 tablespoon chopped fresh oregano; 1 tablespoon chopped fresh flat-leaf parsley

MAKE THE BROTH: Wash green and white parts of leek separately in a bowl of cold water; lift out and drain well. Heat 3 tablespoons oil in a 6-quart heavy pot over moderate heat until hot but not smoking. Add leek greens, onion, celery, and carrots and cook, stirring, until beginning to soften, about 5 minutes. Add garlic and cook, stirring, for 3 minutes. Add saffron, bay leaves, and red pepper flakes and cook, stirring, for 2 minutes. Add plum tomatoes and tomato purée and cook, stirring, for 4 minutes. Add wine and simmer, uncovered, until liquid is reduced by about half, about 30 minutes.

Stir in stock and bring to a boil. Reduce heat and simmer, uncovered, for 30 minutes.

MEANWHILE, PREPARE THE CROÛTES: Put a rack in middle of oven and preheat oven to 300°F.

Heat a well-seasoned ridged grill pan over moderately high heat until hot. Remove crust from bread and brush bread with remaining 2 tablespoons oil. Grill, turning, until grill marks appear on all sides. Tear bread into rough 3-inch pieces and spread on a baking sheet. Bake until crisp outside but still soft inside, about 10 minutes. Cool croûtes.

FINISH THE SOUP: Pour broth through a fine-mesh sieve into a bowl; discard solids. Heat butter in a 4-quart heavy saucepan over moderate heat until foam subsides. Add white part of leek and cook, stirring, until beginning to soften, about 2 minutes. Add fish, hot broth, and salt and bring to a simmer (fish will be cooked through at this point). Remove from heat and stir in 1/2 cup rouille.

Put croûtes in six soup plates and ladle soup over. Sprinkle with oregano and parsley and serve remaining rouille on the side.

COOK'S NOTE

- The broth can be made up to 2 days ahead. Cool, uncovered, then refrigerate, covered. Reheat before proceeding.

Rouille

MAKES ABOUT 2 CUPS

ACTIVE TIME: 20 MINUTES ■ START TO FINISH: 40 MINUTES

■ Rouille (the French word for "rust," pronounced "roo-*ee*") is a spicy-hot sauce made from garlic, chiles, fresh bread crumbs, and olive oil. Testament to the magic of garlic, it is used as a condiment for bouillabaisse and other fish stews and soups. The bread crumbs thicken the sauce. Chef Melissa Kelly prefers brioche or challah, but firm white sandwich bread will do in a pinch. ■

- 2 red bell peppers
- 6 garlic cloves, peeled
- 1 teaspoon salt
- 1 jalapeño chile, seeded and chopped
- 1/2 cup fine fresh bread crumbs, preferably brioche or challah
- 3/4 cup extra-virgin olive oil
- 2 tablespoons fresh lemon juice
- 1/2 teaspoon freshly ground black pepper

Lay bell peppers on grates of two gas burners and turn flames on high. Roast, turning with tongs, until skins are blackened, 8 to 12 minutes. (Or broil on rack of a broiler pan about 2 inches from heat, turning, until skins are blackened, 8 to 12 minutes.) Transfer peppers to a bowl, cover, and let steam for 20 minutes.

Peel peppers and remove and discard stems and seeds. Tear peppers into large pieces.

Using a mortar and pestle, mash garlic to a paste

with salt (or mince garlic and mash with salt using a large knife).

Purée bell peppers with garlic paste, jalapeño, and bread crumbs in a food processor. With motor running, slowly add oil, then add lemon juice and pepper, blending until very smooth (rouille will look like an orange-pink mayonnaise).

COOK'S NOTE

- Rouille can be made up to 3 days ahead and refrigerated, covered. Bring to room temperature before using.

New England Clam Chowder

SERVES 4 (MAKES ABOUT 5 CUPS)
ACTIVE TIME: 35 MINUTES ■ START TO FINISH: 45 MINUTES

■ Behold the dowager of chowders. This is a far cry from other (read "gluey") versions out there. Because it derives its minimal thickening from the residual starch the potatoes leave behind rather than from flour, it isn't heavy or overly thick. Many classic recipes call for salt pork (and feel free to substitute it), but it can sometimes be hard to find, and we like the touch of smokiness that bacon provides. ■

- 36 small hard-shelled clams (less than 2 inches wide), such as littlenecks, scrubbed well
- 1½ cups cold water
- 2 medium boiling potatoes
- 2 tablespoons unsalted butter
- 2 bacon slices, chopped
- 1 small onion, chopped
- 1 cup half-and-half
- Freshly ground black pepper
- 2 tablespoons chopped fresh flat-leaf parsley

Put clams and cold water in a 4-quart saucepan and bring to a boil over moderately high heat. Cover and steam until clams open, 5 to 8 minutes, checking frequently after 5 minutes and transferring them to a bowl as they open. Discard any clams that have not opened. Reserve cooking liquid.

When clams are cool enough to handle, remove from shells and coarsely chop. Carefully pour cooking liquid through a fine-mesh sieve into a small bowl, leaving any grit in pan.

Peel potatoes and cut into ¼-inch dice.

Melt butter in a large saucepan over moderate heat. Add bacon and cook, stirring occasionally, until golden, 4 to 5 minutes. Add onion and cook, stirring, until softened, about 5 minutes. Stir in potatoes and reserved cooking liquid and simmer, covered, until potatoes are tender, 5 to 7 minutes.

Stir in clams, half-and-half, and pepper to taste and cook until heated through, about 1 minute; do not let boil. Stir in parsley.

Manhattan Clam Chowder

SERVES 6 AS A FIRST COURSE OR 8 TO 10 AS A MAIN COURSE (MAKES ABOUT 10 CUPS)
ACTIVE TIME: 40 MINUTES ■ START TO FINISH: 1 HOUR

■ If the only Manhattan clam chowder you've ever had has been the watery, dispiriting stuff too often served at coffee shops and diners, you are in for a treat. Our homemade version is both lighter and brighter. Because of the tomato broth, rather than the rich cream base of a New England–style chowder, it has a sharper, cleaner clam flavor. Manhattan clam chowder works well as a first course or a main. ■

- 3 tablespoons unsalted butter
- 2 large onions, finely chopped (2 cups)
- 2 celery ribs, cut into ½-inch pieces (1 cup)
- ¾ pound boiling potatoes
- 1 (28- to 32-ounce) can whole tomatoes in juice, drained (juice reserved) and chopped
- 2 garlic cloves, minced, or to taste
- 48 small hard-shelled clams (less than 2 inches wide), such as littlenecks, shucked (see page 51; liquor reserved) and coarsely chopped
- 3 (8-ounce) bottles clam juice, stirred together with 3 cups water
- 1 tablespoon chopped fresh basil or 1 teaspoon dried basil, crumbled
- ½ teaspoon dried thyme, crumbled

1 Turkish bay leaf or ½ California bay leaf
Freshly ground black pepper
⅔ cup minced fresh flat-leaf parsley
Salt

Melt butter in a 4- to 6-quart heavy pot over moderate heat. Add onions and celery and cook, stirring occasionally, until softened, about 8 minutes.

Meanwhile, peel potatoes and cut into ½-inch cubes.

Add potatoes, tomatoes, and garlic to onions and cook, stirring, for 2 minutes. Strain reserved clam liquor through a fine-mesh sieve and add to pot, along with reserved tomato juice and clam juice mixture. Add basil, thyme, bay leaf, and pepper to taste and bring to a boil. Reduce heat and simmer, uncovered, skimming off froth occasionally, until potatoes are tender, 15 to 20 minutes.

Stir in clams and parsley and cook over moderate heat, stirring, just until clams are firm, 1 to 2 minutes. Discard bay leaf and season with salt to taste.

Mussel Chowder

SERVES 8
ACTIVE TIME: 1 HOUR ■ START TO FINISH: 1¼ HOURS

■ Mussels were once dismissed as "poor man's oysters," but they can hold their own with oysters any day—and they are sweeter and tenderer than clams. It's now easy to find excellent cultivated mussels almost anywhere in the United States. Bring them to your table in this rich mussel-bound chowder, which rivals any clam-based version. ■

1 cup dry white wine
½ cup water
4½ pounds mussels, preferably cultivated, scrubbed well and beards removed
2 medium leeks (white and pale green parts only), finely chopped
½ stick (4 tablespoons) unsalted butter
2 tablespoons olive oil
2 medium carrots, finely chopped
2 large red, orange, or yellow bell peppers, cored, seeded, and finely chopped
1 large shallot, finely chopped
½ teaspoon salt
¼ teaspoon freshly ground black pepper
2 large garlic cloves, minced
¼ cup heavy cream

Bring ½ cup wine and water to a boil in a 5- to 6-quart heavy pot. Add mussels, cover, and steam, stirring occasionally, until mussels open, 3 to 6 minutes; check frequently after 3 minutes and transfer them to a bowl as they open. Discard any mussels that have not opened. Pour mussel cooking liquid through a fine-mesh sieve lined with a dampened paper towel into a bowl.

Set aside 24 mussels in their shells. Remove remainder from their shells, discarding shells, and halve crosswise.

Wash leeks in a bowl of cold water; lift out and drain well.

Melt butter with oil in cleaned pot over moderate heat. Add leeks, carrots, bell peppers, and shallot, season with salt and pepper, cover, and cook, stirring occasionally, until tender, about 7 minutes. Add garlic and cook, stirring, for 1 minute. Add strained mussel cooking liquid and remaining ½ cup wine and simmer, uncovered, for 10 minutes.

Stir in halved mussels and cream and simmer, stirring, for 5 minutes. Add mussels in shells and simmer until just heated through, about 1 minute. Season with salt and pepper.

Oyster Pan Roast

SERVES 4
ACTIVE TIME: 15 MINUTES ■ START TO FINISH: 15 MINUTES

■ An oyster pan roast sees neither oven nor fire. It's steamed in a double boiler, much like an oyster stew, except that there's less liquid. This meal might be one of the richest—and one of the quickest—you can make, so think of those who deserve it as much as you do, and you are in for an unforgettable treat. (It makes a lovely

Christmas Eve dinner.) The chili sauce is an important component of the overall flavor; ketchup is not a recommended substitution. We've adapted the recipe from one at the Oyster Bar & Restaurant in New York's Grand Central Station. ■

- 3/4 cup shucked small oysters (about 32 oysters), drained, liquor reserved
- Up to 2/3 cup bottled clam juice, if necessary
- 1/4 cup bottled ketchup-style chili sauce
- 1/4 cup dry white wine
- 4 teaspoons Worcestershire sauce
- 1/2 teaspoon celery salt
- 1 stick (8 tablespoons) unsalted butter, softened
- 1 cup heavy cream
- 4 slices crusty bread, toasted
- Pinch of paprika, or to taste

If oysters did not yield 1 cup liquor, add enough clam juice to measure 1 cup (if there is more than 1 cup liquor, discard excess).

Stir together oysters, liquor, chili sauce, wine, Worcestershire sauce, celery salt, and 2 tablespoons butter in a metal bowl or top of a double boiler. Set over simmering water and simmer, stirring occasionally, just until edges of oysters begin to curl, about 5 minutes. Add cream and bring to a bare simmer; do not let boil.

Top toast with remaining 6 tablespoons butter and put in four bowls. Ladle hot soup over toast and sprinkle with paprika.

Shrimp, Crab, and Oyster Gumbo

SERVES 10 TO 12 (MAKES ABOUT 16 CUPS)
ACTIVE TIME: 1 1/2 HOURS ■ START TO FINISH: 2 1/4 HOURS

■ A true melting-pot dish, gumbo embraces southern Louisiana's rich French, Acadian, Native American, and African heritage. The robust stewlike soup, with its heady perfume and deep flavors, is made with all sorts of meats, seafood, and vegetables in all sorts of combinations. It often contains the Cajun "holy trinity" of onion, green bell pepper, and celery, and it's always served over white rice. Gumbos are usually thickened with okra (the term *gombo* is French patois, derived from the Bantu word for okra, *quingombu*) or filé powder (ground dried sassafras leaves, originally used by Native Americans). In this case, though, we use a brown roux, a Louisiana variation of the classic French flour paste, prepared with vegetable oil instead of butter. Although roux often acts as a thickener, when cooked slowly until it turns a dark chestnut brown it transcends that purpose, lending a nutty essence and concentrating and extending the other flavors. We throw Alaskan king crab legs into the mix to give the stock added richness. Any self-respecting Louisiana cook would use heads-on shrimp to do the trick, but they can be hard to find in many parts of the country. The meat from the king crab legs is removed once they are cooked and added to the soup with the sweeter, more delicate lump crabmeat at the last minute. ■

- 1 1/2 pounds small shrimp in shells (36–40 per pound), peeled, shells reserved
- 2 pounds frozen Alaskan king crab legs (4 legs), rinsed and broken apart at joints into large pieces
- 1 medium onion, halved, plus 2 large onions, chopped (2 cups)
- 1 medium carrot, halved
- 2 fresh flat-leaf parsley sprigs
- 1 teaspoon black peppercorns
- 1 Turkish bay leaf or 1/2 California bay leaf
- 2 teaspoons salt
- 3 1/2 quarts water
- 1/3 cup vegetable oil
- 1/2 cup all-purpose flour
- 1 green bell pepper, cored, seeded, and chopped
- 2 celery ribs, chopped
- 1/2 pound lump crabmeat, picked over for shells and cartilage
- 1/2 cup shucked small oysters (about 24 oysters), with their liquor
- 1 cup thinly sliced scallion greens (from about 1 bunch)
- Pinch of cayenne, or to taste

ACCOMPANIMENT: cooked white rice

MAKE THE SHELLFISH STOCK: Combine shrimp shells (refrigerate shrimp, covered), crab legs, halved onion, carrot, parsley, peppercorns, bay leaf, 1 1/2 teaspoons salt, and water in a 9 1/2- to 10-quart pot and bring to a boil. Reduce heat and simmer, uncovered, for 30 minutes.

With tongs, transfer crab legs to a platter. Simmer

stock for 15 minutes more. Pour stock through a large fine-mesh sieve into a large bowl; discard solids. Return stock to pot and set aside, uncovered.

When crab legs are cool enough to handle, cut open shells with kitchen shears and remove meat; discard shells and cartilage. Cut meat into bite-sized pieces and transfer to a small bowl. Refrigerate, covered.

MAKE THE GUMBO: Combine oil and flour in a 12-inch heavy skillet, preferably cast-iron, and cook over moderately low heat, stirring constantly with a flat-edged metal or wooden spatula, until roux is dark reddish brown, 35 to 45 minutes.

Add chopped onions, bell pepper, and celery and cook, stirring occasionally, until softened, about 20 minutes. Remove from heat.

Meanwhile, reheat stock until hot. Add roux mixture by large spoonfuls to hot stock, stirring well after each addition, then bring to a boil, stirring. Reduce heat and simmer, uncovered, stirring occasionally, for 15 minutes. Add shrimp and simmer, stirring, for 2 minutes. Stir in king crabmeat, lump crabmeat, and oysters, with their liquor, and simmer, stirring occasionally, until edges of oysters begin to curl, about 2 minutes. Stir in scallions, cayenne, and remaining 1/2 teaspoon salt.

Serve gumbo ladled over rice in large soup plates.

COOK'S NOTES

- The roux can be made up to 1 week ahead. Cool completely, then refrigerate, covered, in a glass or stainless steel bowl. Reheat in the skillet over moderately low heat, stirring, before proceeding.
- The gumbo can be made up to 1 day ahead. Cool completely, uncovered, then refrigerate, covered.

Hot-and-Sour Shrimp Soup with Noodles and Thai Herbs

SERVES 4 AS A MAIN COURSE (MAKES ABOUT 12 CUPS)
ACTIVE TIME: 1 HOUR ■ START TO FINISH: 2 1/4 HOURS PLUS ADDITIONAL TIME IF MAKING STOCK

■ This aromatic soup, which captures the essence of Southeast Asia, is satisfaction in a bowl. A Big Bowl, that is—one of a group of restaurants started in Chicago by the Asian cooking authority Bruce Cost. We could eat this almost every day. ■

- 1 1/4 pounds medium shrimp in shells (31–35 per pound), peeled (shells reserved) and deveined
- 2 teaspoons salt, or to taste
- 1/2 teaspoon Asian sesame oil
- 1 small bunch spinach (1/2 pound), coarse stems removed
- 3 stalks lemongrass, ends trimmed and tough outer leaves removed
- 3 quarts (96 ounces) chicken stock or store-bought low-sodium broth
- 1 (1 1/2-inch piece) fresh galangal (see Glossary) or fresh ginger, peeled and thinly sliced
- 9 garlic cloves, smashed
- 1 cup chopped shallots (4 large)
- 3–4 fresh green Thai chiles or small serrano chiles (to taste), cut lengthwise into thin strips
- 1/3 cup Asian fish sauce, preferably *naam pla*
- 1 1/2 teaspoons sugar
- 1/2 pound 1/2-inch-wide dried flat rice noodles
- 1/3 cup chopped fresh cilantro
- 1/3 cup chopped fresh basil, preferably Thai basil
- 1/2 cup fresh lemon juice
- 1 teaspoon freshly ground black pepper

Toss shrimp with 1/2 teaspoon salt and sesame oil in a bowl. Refrigerate, covered.

Stack spinach leaves, a few at a time, and cut crosswise into very thin strips. Thinly slice lower third of lemongrass stalks diagonally; discard remainder.

Combine stock, lemongrass, galangal, and garlic in a 4-quart heavy saucepan and bring to a boil. Reduce heat and simmer gently, uncovered, for 35 minutes.

Add reserved shrimp shells to broth and simmer, uncovered, for 15 to 20 minutes, skimming off froth as necessary.

Pour broth through a sieve into a large bowl; discard solids.

Return broth to pan, add shallots and chiles, and bring to a boil. Reduce heat and simmer gently, uncovered, for 15 minutes. Add fish sauce, sugar, and remaining 1 1/2 teaspoons salt and simmer for 5 minutes more.

Meanwhile, cook noodles in a large pot of boiling (unsalted) water until tender, 6 to 8 minutes. Drain well and divide among four heated large (6-cup) bowls. Divide spinach among bowls.

Add shrimp, cilantro, basil, and lemon juice to

soup and let stand, off heat, uncovered, for 1 minute to just cook shrimp (shrimp will continue to cook as you serve soup).

Divide soup among bowls and sprinkle with pepper.

Congee

Chinese Chicken and Rice Porridge

SERVES 4

ACTIVE TIME: 40 MINUTES ■ START TO FINISH: 5¼ HOURS

■ In many Chinese households, the thick, hot rice porridge called *congee* (also known as *jook*) is enjoyed morning, noon, and night. It can be flavored with all sorts of different things; this one is made hearty with chicken. *Congee* is a great "get well" alternative to chicken soup. ■

- 1 (3½- to 4-pound) chicken, cut into 8 serving pieces
- 10 cups water
- 3 tablespoons Chinese rice wine or medium-dry sherry
- 3 (¼-inch-thick) slices fresh ginger
- 3 scallions, halved crosswise and smashed
- ½ teaspoon salt
- 1 cup long-grain rice

ACCOMPANIMENTS: fine slivers of fresh ginger, thinly sliced scallion, and Asian sesame oil

Combine chicken and water in a 5-quart heavy pot and bring to a boil, skimming froth. Add wine, ginger, scallions, and salt and cook at a bare simmer, uncovered, until breast meat is just cooked through, about 20 minutes.

Transfer one breast half to a bowl. Continue to cook stock at a bare simmer, skimming froth as necessary, for about 2 hours and 40 minutes.

Meanwhile, when chicken breast has cooled enough to handle, remove skin and remove meat from bones. Return skin and bones to stock.

When breast meat has cooled completely, tear into shreds. Refrigerate, covered.

Pour stock through a large medium-mesh sieve into a large bowl; discard solids (including remaining chicken). You should have about 8 cups stock: if less, add water to make 8 cups; if more, cook longer as necessary after adding rice.

Return stock to cleaned pot. Add rice, bring to a boil, and stir. Reduce heat to low, cover, and simmer, stirring frequently during last 30 minutes of cooking, until *congee* is the consistency of oatmeal, about 1¾ hours.

Meanwhile, bring shredded chicken to room temperature.

Season *congee* with salt and serve topped with chicken, ginger, and scallion. Drizzle with sesame oil.

COOK'S NOTE

■ The stock can be made up to 1 day ahead. Cool, uncovered, then refrigerate, covered. Remove and discard solidified fat before reheating.

Chicken and Rice Soup

SERVES 8 (MAKES ABOUT 16 CUPS)

ACTIVE TIME: 30 MINUTES ■ START TO FINISH: 1½ HOURS

■ This is probably the simplest soup ever made from scratch: you just throw everything into the pot at once and walk away. The rice cooks in the pot along with the chicken long enough to give its starches over for extra body. Everything you dislike about brown rice—its starchiness and heaviness—works to advantage here. It turns soft and almost falls apart but still has texture. Don't substitute white rice, because it would get mushy. This soup may not be beautiful, but it sure is good. ■

- 1 large onion, coarsely chopped
- 3 large celery ribs, cut into ¼-inch-thick slices
- 3 medium carrots, cut into ¼-inch-thick slices
- 1 (3½- to 4-pound) chicken
- 1 cup long-grain brown rice
- ⅓ cup packed fresh flat-leaf parsley leaves
- 1 tablespoon salt
- 3 quarts water
- Freshly ground black pepper

Combine onion, celery, carrots, chicken, rice, parsley, and 1 teaspoon salt in a 6-quart pot. Add water and bring to a boil, then reduce heat, cover, and simmer, skimming off fat as needed, for 1 hour.

Transfer chicken to a colander. When cool enough to handle, remove meat; discard skin and bones. Coarsely shred chicken and return to soup. Add remaining 2 teaspoons salt and pepper to taste and reheat if necessary.

Italian Chicken Soup with Egg Strands and Parmesan

Stracciatella

SERVES 4 AS A FIRST COURSE (MAKES ABOUT 4 CUPS)
ACTIVE TIME: 10 MINUTES ■ START TO FINISH: 10 MINUTES PLUS ADDITIONAL TIME IF MAKING STOCK

■ What better reason to have chicken stock on hand? Simple, quick, and enriched with strands of Parmesan-flavored egg—you can scrape this together at the end of a long day, and even if you resort to canned broth, you will be nourished. ■

- 2 large eggs
- 3 tablespoons finely grated Parmigiano-Reggiano, plus additional for sprinkling
- 1 tablespoon finely chopped fresh flat-leaf parsley
- 1 tablespoon minced scallion (white and pale green parts only)
- 4 cups (32 ounces) chicken stock or store-bought low-sodium broth
- Salt and freshly ground black pepper

Whisk together eggs, cheese, parsley, and scallion in a small bowl.

Bring stock to a boil in a medium saucepan. Add egg mixture in a stream, whisking constantly. Reduce heat and simmer for 2 minutes. Stir in salt and pepper to taste.

Serve soup sprinkled with additional cheese.

Chicken Soup with Almond Matzo Balls

SERVES 6
ACTIVE TIME: 40 MINUTES ■ START TO FINISH: 3¼ HOURS (INCLUDES CHILLING) PLUS ADDITIONAL TIME IF MAKING STOCK

■ Matzo balls swimming in bowls of golden chicken soup are a Passover tradition. This recipe, which tops the competition, deserves to be eaten all year round and certainly has crossover appeal. These matzo balls—small, firm, flavored with fresh dill and a little cinnamon, and crunchy with almonds—are refined cousins of those huge airy pillows you usually get in Jewish delicatessens. We have Muriel Reisman, a longtime reader from Fair Lawn, New Jersey, to thank for the recipe. ■

- 2 large eggs
- 2 tablespoons vegetable oil
- ½ cup matzo meal
- ½ cup (2 ounces) whole almonds with skins, coarsely chopped
- 2 tablespoons chopped fresh dill
- ¼ teaspoon ground cinnamon
- ¾ teaspoon salt
- ¼ teaspoon freshly ground black pepper
- 6⅓ cups chicken stock or store-bought low-sodium broth

OPTIONAL GARNISH: fresh dill sprigs

MAKE THE MATZO BALLS: Lightly beat eggs with oil in a medium bowl. Add matzo meal, almonds, dill, cinnamon, salt, pepper, and ⅓ cup stock and stir until well combined. Cover mixture with plastic wrap placed directly on surface and chill for at least 2 hours.

SHAPE AND COOK THE MATZO BALLS: Bring a 6-quart pot of salted water (1 tablespoon salt per every 4 quarts water) to a simmer. Meanwhile, with dampened hands, roll matzo mixture into 1-inch balls (you will have about 25) and place on an oiled plate.

Cook matzo balls in simmering water, covered, until cooked through, about 40 minutes. To test for doneness, halve a matzo ball. It should have a moist, uniform texture throughout; if it's not quite ready, it will have a dry, yellowish center.

Just before matzo balls are cooked, bring remaining 6 cups stock to a simmer in a 4- to 6-quart pot and season with salt and pepper.

With a slotted spoon, transfer matzo balls to broth and simmer, uncovered, for 5 minutes. Serve soup garnished with dill sprigs, if desired.

COOK'S NOTE

- The uncooked matzo mixture can be refrigerated, covered, for up to 1 day.

Turkey Soup

SERVES 6 TO 8 (MAKES ABOUT 10 CUPS)
ACTIVE TIME: 1¼ HOURS ■ START TO FINISH: 12¼ HOURS (INCLUDES CHILLING)

■ Turkey soup is Thanksgiving's most impressive curtain call. Flavorful broth is the key to success, and the way to make it is with fresh turkey. (If you insist on holding on to your turkey carcass until it looks like a bleached, desiccated Georgia O'Keeffe prop, you can try painting it, but don't bother making soup.) Before putting away the Thanksgiving leftovers, break up the carcass as directed below, keeping the wings intact and removing most of the rest of the meat in large pieces. Be sure to leave a generous fringe of meat on the frame, and save all the skin. It will add incomparable flavor and color to the broth, and we promise that you'll be able to discard every speck of fat later. So that the carcass will take up less room in the fridge (and in the pot), separate the rib section from the back (with your hands) and wrap them with the wings and all other reserved bones and skin until you are ready to make soup, ideally the next day. The three to four hours it takes to make the broth might seem like an eternity, but this step shouldn't be rushed, or the broth won't develop properly. Your goal is a rich blond broth with intoxicating aroma and flavor.

What we do next is a little unusual, but it makes a difference. We let the residue steep in the broth as it cools and chill it, covered, overnight. (Never cover a hot soup, or it will turn sour.) All the fat will solidify on the surface, making it easy to lift off in pieces. We then reheat the broth to a liquid state, season it, and strain it. ■

- 1 meaty turkey carcass (from a 12- to 14-pound turkey)
- Salt and freshly ground black pepper
- 2 tablespoons olive oil
- 2 medium onions, sliced (2 cups)
- 2 large carrots, sliced (1 cup)
- 2 celery ribs, sliced (1½ cups)
- ¼ cup raw long-grain white rice or ½ cup dried noodles or mashed potatoes
- 2 tablespoons chopped fresh flat-leaf parsley

Break up turkey carcass, keeping wings intact; reserve all skin. Leaving a generous fringe of meat on frame, remove rest of meat in large pieces and chop enough to measure 2 cups (reserve remainder for sandwiches or another use). Refrigerate, covered. Separate rib portion of carcass from back with your hands.

Put turkey wings, skin, and bones in a 5- to 6-quart pot and add enough cold water to cover by 3 inches. Bring to a boil, skimming off any froth. Reduce heat and simmer gently, uncovered, for 3 to 4 hours. Remove from heat and cool completely, uncovered. Refrigerate, covered, for at least 8 hours.

Remove congealed fat from broth and discard. Reheat broth over moderate heat until liquid, about 15 minutes. Season with salt and pepper. Pour broth through a colander into a large bowl; discard solids.

Heat oil in a 3- to 4-quart heavy saucepan over moderately high heat until hot but not smoking. Add onions, carrots, and celery and cook, stirring occasionally, just until golden, about 15 minutes. Add broth, bring to a simmer, and simmer until vegetables are tender, 15 to 17 minutes.

Stir in rice (or noodles or potatoes) and simmer, uncovered, until rice or noodles are tender or potatoes have thickened soup, about 15 minutes. Just before serving, stir in chopped turkey and parsley and heat through.

COOK'S NOTES

- The strained broth can be made up to 3 days ahead. Cool, uncovered, then refrigerate, covered. Or freeze for up to 1 month.
- The soup can be made up to 5 days ahead. Cool, uncovered, then refrigerate, covered.

Chinese Beef Noodle Soup

SERVES 4 TO 6 (MAKES ABOUT 10 CUPS)
ACTIVE TIME: 30 MINUTES ■ START TO FINISH: 3 HOURS

■ Half the pleasure of this soup is enjoying its complex aroma while it's sitting on a back burner. Star anise, cinnamon, and soy are among the flavors of the Shanghai specialty called red cooking, in which meats are gently simmered until incredibly succulent. Here, those flavors creep into rich short ribs and peppery turnips. In a traditional Chinese kitchen, noodles destined for soup are prepared separately and added at the last minute so their starch doesn't cloud the broth. Because we are aiming for a hearty dish, we cook the noodles right in the broth, allowing their starch to thicken the soup slightly. ■

- 2½ pounds beef short ribs, cut between bones into pieces
- 7 cups water
- ⅓ cup soy sauce
- ¼ cup Chinese rice wine or Scotch or medium-dry sherry
- 1 tablespoon sugar
- 6 (¼-inch-thick) diagonal slices fresh ginger
- 8 scallions, trimmed, 5 smashed with side of large heavy knife
- 3 large garlic cloves, chopped
- 1 (3-inch) cinnamon stick
- 1 star anise
- 1 teaspoon salt
- ¼ teaspoon red pepper flakes
- ½ pound turnips, peeled and cut into ¾-inch cubes
- ¼ pound dried egg noodles
- 1 teaspoon Asian sesame oil (optional)

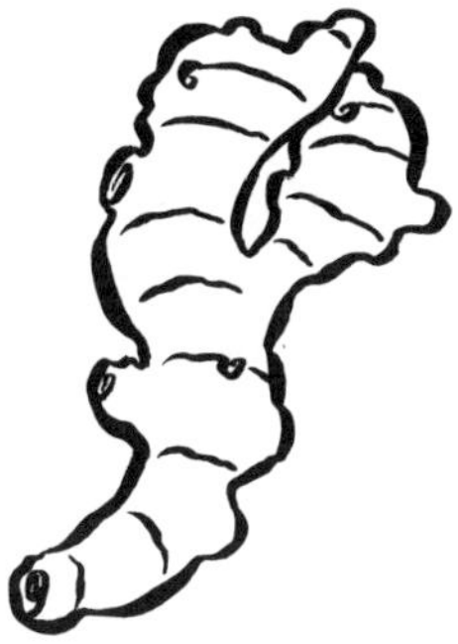

Combine short ribs, water, soy sauce, rice wine, and sugar in a 5- to 6-quart heavy pot and bring to a boil. Reduce heat to a simmer and skim off froth. Add ginger, smashed scallions, garlic, cinnamon, star anise, salt, and pepper flakes. Simmer, covered, until rib meat is tender, about 2 hours. Let ribs cool in broth, uncovered, for 30 minutes.

Transfer ribs to a cutting board. Remove meat, discarding fat and bones, and chop.

Pour broth through a large fine-mesh sieve into a large saucepan; discard solids. Skim off and discard fat. Add chopped meat and turnips, bring to a simmer, and simmer, covered, for 10 minutes. Add noodles, cover, and simmer, stirring occasionally, until tender, about 7 minutes.

Just before serving, thinly slice remaining 3 scallions. Stir into soup, with sesame oil, if using, and salt to taste.

COOK'S NOTE

■ The soup can be made, without the sliced scallions and sesame oil, up to 2 days ahead. Cool, uncovered, then refrigerate, covered.

Pho

Vietnamese-Style Beef Noodle Soup

SERVES 4
ACTIVE TIME: 35 MINUTES ■ START TO FINISH: 35 MINUTES PLUS ADDITIONAL TIME IF MAKING STOCK

■ If you are used to stopping into a Vietnamese restaurant for a quick, filling bowl of *pho* (pronounced "fuh"), the beef noodle soup that comes with a plate of leafy basil sprigs, lime wedges, bean sprouts, and hot chiles to be added according to your own taste, you might not be aware that the soup is very time-consuming to make. A lot goes into the stock, and it is slowly cooked for a long time. So we've cobbled together a quick version—a faux *pho*—using canned beef broth. We also take advantage of thinly sliced rare roast beef from the deli counter. The real thing comes with beef every which way, from shreds of steak to meatballs and even tendon. Our version is true to tradition in one respect, however: the broth has all the essence of beef but is not loaded with meat. ■

- 6 ounces rice stick noodles (rice vermicelli)
- 1/4 pound snow peas, cut diagonally into 1/4-inch-wide strips
- 1 tablespoon vegetable oil
- 1 cup sliced shallots (3 large)
- 3 (1/8-inch-thick) slices fresh ginger, smashed
- 1 teaspoon minced serrano chile (including seeds), or to taste
- 3 1/2 cups (28 ounces) beef stock or store-bought broth
- 1 3/4 cups water
- 1/2 pound very thinly sliced rare roast beef, torn into pieces
- 6 ounces fresh bean sprouts, rinsed
- 1/4 cup loosely packed fresh cilantro leaves
- 1/4 cup loosely packed fresh basil leaves, torn if large
- 1/4 cup loosely packed fresh mint leaves
- 3 tablespoons Asian fish sauce, or to taste
- 3 tablespoons fresh lime juice
- Salt

ACCOMPANIMENT: lime wedges

Cook noodles in a 4-quart saucepan of boiling (unsalted) water for 4 minutes. Add snow peas and boil for 1 minute. Drain in a colander and rinse under cold running water to stop the cooking. Drain well.

Divide noodles and snow peas among four large soup bowls.

Dry saucepan, add oil, and heat over moderate heat. Add shallots, ginger, and chile and cook, stirring occasionally, until shallots are browned, 7 to 8 minutes. Add stock and water, bring to a simmer, and simmer, uncovered, for 10 minutes.

Meanwhile, divide beef, bean sprouts, and herbs among soup bowls.

Remove ginger from broth and discard, then stir in fish sauce, lime juice, and salt to taste. Ladle broth into bowls and serve immediately with lime wedges.

Hearty Goulash Soup

SERVES 12 (MAKES ABOUT 20 CUPS)
ACTIVE TIME: 50 MINUTES ■ START TO FINISH: 2 1/4 HOURS PLUS ADDITIONAL TIME IF MAKING STOCK

■ When we discovered that warming bowls of this hearty beef and vegetable soup are served along the autobahn in Austria, we felt pangs of envy. Why can't we get road food this good, this sustaining, at a rest stop on one of America's highways? We'd drive miles for a bowl. This one is brothier than a classic Hungarian goulash. It serves a crowd, but the recipe can easily be cut in half. ■

- 5 bacon slices, chopped
- 3 pounds boneless beef chuck, trimmed and cut into 1/2-inch cubes
- 2 tablespoons vegetable oil
- 1 1/2 pounds onions (4 medium), finely chopped
- 3 garlic cloves, minced
- 3 tablespoons paprika, preferably Hungarian sweet
- 1 1/2 teaspoons caraway seeds
- 1/3 cup all-purpose flour
- 1/4 cup red wine vinegar
- 1/4 cup tomato paste
- 5 cups (40 ounces) beef stock or store-bought broth
- 5 cups water
- 1/2 teaspoon salt
- 2 red bell peppers, cored, seeded, and finely chopped
- 2 1/2 pounds russet (baking) potatoes (4 large)
- Freshly ground black pepper

Cook bacon in an 8-quart heavy pot over moderate heat, stirring, until crisp, about 5 minutes. With a slotted spoon, transfer to a large bowl. Brown beef in small batches in fat remaining in pot over high heat and transfer with slotted spoon to bowl.

Reduce heat to moderate and add oil. Add onions and garlic and cook, stirring occasionally, until golden, 7 to 8 minutes. Stir in paprika, caraway seeds, and flour and cook, stirring, for 2 minutes. Whisk in vinegar and tomato paste and cook, whisking, for 1 minute (mixture will be very thick).

Stir in stock, water, salt, bell peppers, beef, and bacon and bring to a boil over high heat, stirring occasionally. Reduce heat, cover, and simmer, stirring occasionally, for 45 minutes.

Peel potatoes and cut into ½-inch cubes. Add potatoes to soup, cover, and simmer, stirring occasionally, until tender, about 20 minutes. Season with salt and pepper.

COOK'S NOTE

- The soup can be made up to 3 days ahead. Cool, uncovered, then refrigerate, covered. Thin with water, if desired, when reheating.

SALADS

Salad as we know it is a peculiarly American institution. Reading through this chapter gives you a strong sense of how it got that way.

The story begins sedately, with a pristine *salade verte* from our earliest years. It moves on in a surprising direction, to the outrageously delicious (and now nearly forgotten) butter-dressed Bibb lettuce that was once a staple of elegant tables.

In its European incarnation, salad was a side dish, but sometime during the beginning of the twentieth century, our forefathers discovered that it could be a satisfying and sophisticated way to make much out of a minuscule amount of protein. Consider, for example, the Caesar salad. Invented for a Hollywood clientele in the twenties, it became an instant classic that has remained wildly popular ever since. It was a remarkably simple idea: add a bit of egg, some croutons, and a handful of grated cheese to a green salad and *voilà,* it is magically transformed into a meal.

It was not, however, meal enough for those later in the century. As salads took up a position as the mainstay of the menu, they began gathering more ingredients, growing bigger and fatter. The chef's salad came along, and the Cobb salad, both kitchen-sink concoctions laden with meat, eggs, and an entire garden's worth of vegetables. By the eighties, this sort of salad had replaced the casserole as the catchall American meal; the prime example must be the taco salad, with its crunch, its gusto, its swaggering flavors. We're proud of our version, a nod to history that comes straight from the supermarket.

The success of salad meant that as new ethnic ingredients came into the culture, they were immediately tossed into the bowl. Before long we were reveling in pasta salads, inventing tandoori shrimp salads, and adapting the cool, crisp, spicy salads native to Southeast Asia.

But what really fueled the salad revolution was the increasing availability of fresh, interesting vegetables. Farmers markets moved into American cities, bringing mesclun and arugula, mâche and tatsoi; fresh herbs became supermarket staples, and heirloom tomatoes came along to remind us how summer is supposed to taste. Suddenly salad became the most exciting part of the American menu. It is no accident that these greens and vegetables were soon joined by an abundance of fine, previously unavailable olive and nut oils, or that a growing variety of vinegars began strutting across our grocers' shelves.

The salads you'll find here run the gamut from French standards like frisée with lardons to an archetypal Viennese cucumber salad and a handful of classic American potato salads. We've brought back some old favorites (is there anything more refreshing than iceberg with blue cheese dressing?), included our best-loved new discoveries (raw asparagus with pistachios and mâche), and thrown in a few innovations you won't want to miss. Watermelon with tomatoes and feta may sound exotic, but it tastes so right that it is sure to become a standard in the American salad repertoire.

One more historical note: if you've been wondering about the pedigree of your favorite salad dressings, we've done the research. Here you'll find out who the Green Goddess really was and where to find the ranch where the first batch of the buttermilk dressing that is now a salad-bar staple was mixed.

Salade Verte

SERVES 8

ACTIVE TIME: 45 MINUTES ■ START TO FINISH: 45 MINUTES

■ This is a very refined green salad. The tough center ribs are removed from the greens, and a whisper of garlic seasons the salad without overwhelming the other components. (The trick is the heel of bread generously rubbed with a garlic clove, tossed with the greens and then discarded.) Our inspiration for this recipe is the professional chef and cookbook author Louis P. De Gouy, one of the founders of *Gourmet*. In an article on green salads, he quotes Fred Allen as saying, "A salad should be dressed like Dorothy Lamour—adequately but lightly." ■

FOR DRESSING

- 1½ tablespoons tarragon white-wine vinegar
- ⅛ teaspoon anisette or other anise-flavored liqueur (optional)
- ¼ teaspoon Dijon mustard
- 2 teaspoons finely chopped fresh flat-leaf parsley
- 2 teaspoons finely chopped fresh tarragon
- 2 teaspoons finely chopped fresh chervil
- ½ teaspoon salt
- ⅛ teaspoon freshly ground black pepper
- ⅓ cup vegetable oil or olive oil

FOR SALAD

- 1 head romaine (1 pound), leaves separated and tough center ribs discarded
- ½ head escarole (½ pound), pale green leaves only, ribs discarded
- ¼ head iceberg lettuce (¼ pound), leaves separated
- ½ head Boston lettuce (2 ounces), leaves separated
- 1 Belgian endive, leaves separated and torn crosswise in half
- 1 (3-inch-long) heel from a day-old baguette
- 1 garlic clove, halved crosswise

MAKE THE DRESSING: Whisk together all ingredients except oil in a small bowl. Add oil in a slow stream, whisking until well blended.

MAKE THE SALAD: Tear romaine, escarole, iceberg, and Boston lettuce into bite-sized pieces. Toss with endive in a large salad bowl (preferably wooden). Rub bread liberally all over with garlic and toss with greens (discard garlic). Add dressing and toss well, then discard bread.

Bibb Lettuce with Butter Dressing

SERVES 4

ACTIVE TIME: 20 MINUTES ■ START TO FINISH: 20 MINUTES

■ Although this old-fashioned butter dressing is rich in flavor, it has a surprisingly light and silky texture, which keeps it from weighing down the delicate Bibb lettuce (coincidentally also known as butterhead lettuce). As with many simple things, success hinges on getting the details right. The greens must be at room temperature—if they are cold, the warmed butter will solidify on the leaves. When all the elements come together in the right way, this salad is a revelation. ■

- 4 heads Bibb lettuce or 1 head Boston lettuce, at room temperature, leaves separated and torn into bite-sized pieces
- ½ stick (4 tablespoons) unsalted butter
- 1 garlic clove, halved lengthwise
- 4 teaspoons fresh lemon juice
- Scant ½ teaspoon salt
- Freshly ground black pepper

Put lettuce in a large bowl. Melt butter in a small heavy skillet over moderate heat. Add garlic and cook, stirring occasionally, until garlic is golden and butter has a slight nutty aroma, about 3 minutes. Remove skillet from heat, discard garlic, and add lemon juice, salt, and pepper to taste, swirling skillet to incorporate; butter will foam.

Pour warm dressing over lettuce and toss to coat. Serve immediately.

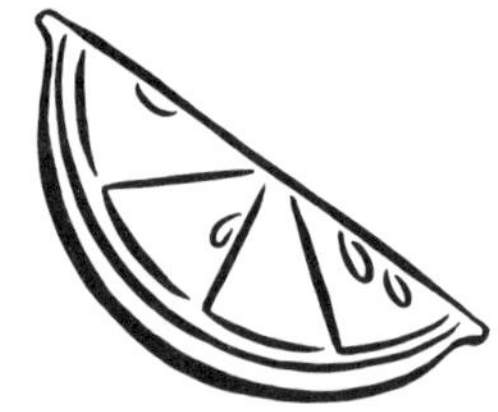

Milanese Mixed Salad

SERVES 4
ACTIVE TIME: 20 MINUTES ■ START TO FINISH: 20 MINUTES

■ The first thing you notice about this salad is how beautiful it is, with the contrasting strong, saturated colors of radicchio, arugula, and carrot. The flavors are intense too—the pleasantly bitter radicchio and peppery arugula are balanced by the carrots' sweetness. On a trip to Milan, we ate this salad all around town. ■

- 2½ tablespoons white wine vinegar
- 6 tablespoons extra-virgin olive oil
- ¾ teaspoon salt
- ⅛ teaspoon freshly ground black pepper
- 1 medium head radicchio, halved lengthwise and thinly sliced crosswise (2 cups)
- 2 bunches arugula, coarse stems discarded and leaves thinly sliced crosswise (3 cups)
- 3 carrots, coarsely shredded

Whisk together vinegar, oil, salt, and pepper in a large bowl. Add radicchio, arugula, and carrots and toss to combine. If necessary, season again with salt and pepper.

Baby Greens with Warm Goat Cheese

SERVES 4 AS A FIRST COURSE
ACTIVE TIME: 15 MINUTES ■ START TO FINISH: 30 MINUTES

■ Although goat cheese is common in many parts of the world, it didn't become popular in the United States until a few decades ago. Once perceived as a precious conceit of restaurant chefs, it is now available in supermarkets across the land. This salad alone is reason to be grateful. When little rounds of the mild cheese are dredged in dry bread crumbs and then sautéed, they soften rather than melt. There's a wonderful contrast between the warm, creamy cheese, the satisfyingly crisp crust, and the tender, flavorful baby salad greens. As far as the bread crumbs are concerned, we are very fond of panko, the ultracrisp ones from Japan (for more information, see page 48). ■

- 2 large egg whites
- 2 teaspoons water
- ⅔ cup plain dry bread crumbs, preferably panko (see above)
- 8 (⅓-inch-thick) rounds soft mild goat cheese (cut from a chilled 8-ounce log)
- 4 teaspoons cider vinegar
- ¼ teaspoon salt
- ⅛ teaspoon sugar
- ½ teaspoon Dijon mustard
- Freshly ground black pepper
- 7 tablespoons extra-virgin olive oil
- ¼ pound mesclun (mixed baby salad greens; 8 cups)

Whisk together egg whites and water in a shallow bowl. Spread bread crumbs on a plate. Dip cheese rounds in egg, letting excess drip off, then dredge in bread crumbs, pressing lightly so they adhere, and put on a plate. Refrigerate for 15 minutes.

Whisk together vinegar, salt, sugar, mustard, and a pinch of pepper in a large bowl. Add 4 tablespoons (¼ cup) oil in a slow stream, whisking until well blended.

Heat remaining 3 tablespoons oil in a 12-inch nonstick skillet over moderately high heat until hot but not smoking. Add cheese rounds and cook, turning once, until golden, about 1 minute total. Remove skillet from heat.

Add greens to dressing and toss gently to coat. Arrange salad on four plates and top with warm cheese.

COOK'S NOTE

■ The easiest way to cut goat cheese is with a piece of dental floss.

Salad Greens Primer

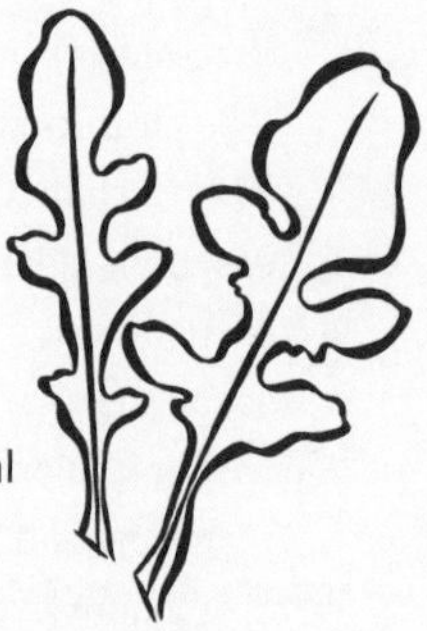

ARUGULA: The American name *arugula* is most likely derived from the Italian name for the plant, *rucola;* it's generally called rocket in Britain and on the West Coast. It was first grown in American gardens in Colonial times, not so much for the kitchen as for medicinal use. One taste of its peppery, pungent leaves and you won't be surprised to discover that it's related to the radish. In the South of France, *roquette,* as the green is known there, adds verve to the salad mix called *mesclun* (which means "mixture" in the local dialect).

BELGIAN ENDIVE: Belgian endive (botanically not a true endive, like chicory and escarole) appeared on the culinary scene in Brussels in the 1850s, and it's been enjoyed in Europe in both raw and cooked forms ever since. Its crisp, satiny white leaves tipped with yellow or red have helped fuel Americans' passion for bitter greens. It doesn't matter how you pronounce it, "*en*-dive" or "*ahn*-deev"; both are correct.

CHICORY: Chicory is a kind of endive—it is often called curly endive or curly chicory—and it resembles another member of the endive family, frisée. Its leaves can be too bitter and tough if you don't strip off the stems and center ribs. Once you've done that, you'll have spiky green curls that are tender and mild. The stems can be chopped and cooked in a soup, where they will turn sweet. Chicory also mellows beautifully when wilted in a hot dressing.

DANDELION: There are three great things about dandelions: a clean sharpness on the palate, an affinity for warm bacon dressings, and their gloriously evocative French name, *pissenlit,* which reflects their diuretic qualities. When we go shopping for them, we come back with a different variety each time. It turns out that some greens grown and sold as dandelions are actually chicories that have been bred to look and taste like dandelions—the Catalogna, also called Italian dandelion, for instance. Occasionally you'll find true dandelions at farmers markets in early spring.

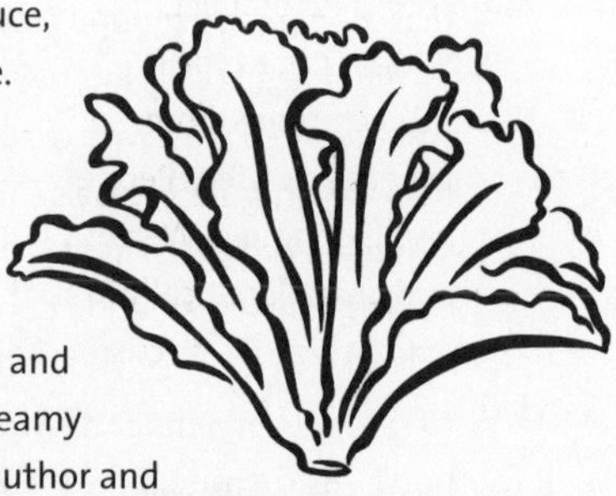

ESCAROLE: Escarole might look like a head of lettuce, but it's really an endive. In France, just before harvest, the heads of escarole often wear little white plastic hats that block the sun and blanch the centers a creamy white. (The cookbook author and teacher Georgeanne Brennan poetically describes this phenomenon as "rolling fields of white breasts.") Escarole's pleasant bitterness, like that of the closely related chicories, is a dead giveaway that it is an endive. We use the cream-colored and pale green inner leaves raw in the salad on page 137. The thick green outer leaves are wonderful cooked in bean soups or cut into very thin strips and sautéed with garlic and red pepper flakes.

FRISÉE: Sometimes called French or Italian curly chicory, this splayed-open little knot of springy pale yellow and green leaves is the diva of any salad. It is tender, sweet-bitter in flavor, and, because it is expensive to produce, relatively costly.

LETTUCES: Twenty years ago, our vegetable crispers were full of iceberg and romaine, and that was about it. Soporific fare, as every reader of *Peter Rabbit* will remember. What Beatrix Potter probably knew full well is that lettuce was once truly sleep-inducing; its milky sap contained a mild narcotic that made the plant a valuable crop in ancient Egypt (some of the oldest images in wall paintings and tomb reliefs date to 2680 B.C.). William Woys Weaver, in his classic *Heirloom Vegetable Gardening,* points out that lettuce assumed even greater medical, religious, and cultural import in the ancient Greek world. For instance, Aphrodite hid Adonis in a bed of lettuce, where he was killed by a wild boar — and salad became a metaphor for male impotence. By the first century A.D. (when bitterness, and thus the narcotic, was being bred out of lettuce varieties), the Roman elite was enjoying a lettuce salad, with a hot oil-and-vinegar dressing, as an appetizer to a rich, voluptuous meal.

For culinary purposes today, there are four categories of lettuces.

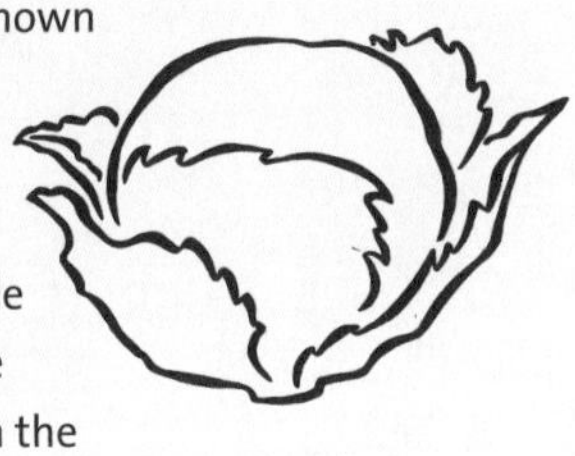

Crisphead: The most widely known example of this compact, cabbagelike lettuce type is iceberg, which stems from an old American variety. People either love it or hate it. We are firmly and unapologetically in the former camp; we love its crisp, crunchy succulence.

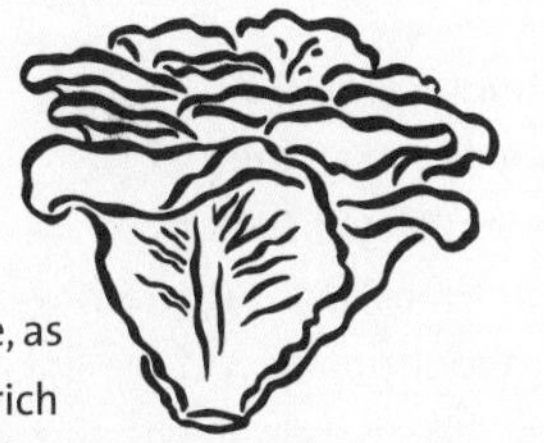

Butterhead: These lettuces have flat, thick, soft leaves that form a loose head. They may be large, like Boston, or small, like Bibb (also called limestone lettuce, as it was first bred in the limestone-rich soil of Kentucky by Major John Bibb in the mid-nineteenth century).

Loose-leaved: These are also called cutting lettuces, because you can cut the young roseate leaves from the growing plants as needed. The best-known variety today is oak-leaf.

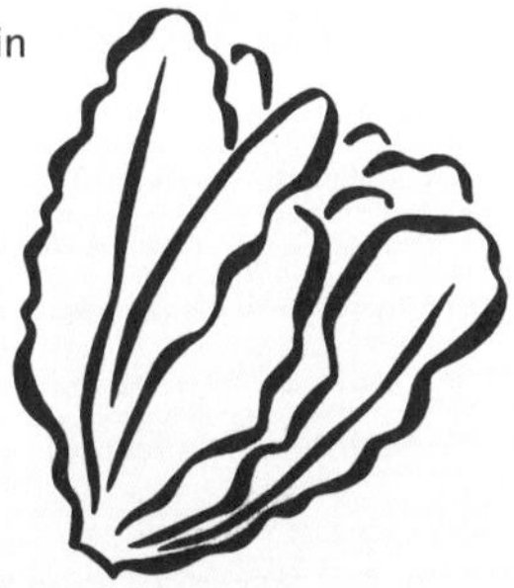

Long-leaved: Tall, upright leaves in a loose, cylindrical head were first grown in the papal gardens in Rome, so the French called the variety *romaine*. This type is often referred to as cos because, Weaver explains, some of the earliest seeds came to Europe from Cos, a Greek island that was a center of lettuce growing.

MÂCHE: The tender, succulent little leaves called mâche generally go by their French name, because their English ones — corn salad and lamb's lettuce — inspire endless confusion. The name corn salad refers to the fact that as early as the eighteenth century, the green was gathered from wheat fields (in England, wheat was known as corn). This green is not related to lamb's-quarters, a green something like spinach, or to lettuces. Mild and fresh-tasting, mâche makes a very pretty salad.

MESCLUN: The Provençal salad blend called mesclun was originally composed of the tender early shoots and leaves of wild plants. Today it is so popular that the greens are grown from seed specifically for mesclun. An authentic mix might include baby arugula, dandelion, mâche, purslane, chicory, and chervil. Unfortunately, commercial mesclun often turns up as a bag of bland, soft lettuces, or it's overloaded with spicy mustard greens and other mature leaves too tough to eat raw. Look for a balanced assortment of flavors and textures; once you can recognize a real mesclun, you are on your way to becoming a master chef *and* a naturalist. We recommend that you wash even the mesclun labeled "prewashed."

RADICCHIO: A decade or so ago, few Americans had even heard of radicchio (the *cch* is pronounced as in Pinocchio), but a farmer named Lucio Gomiero, in Salinas, California, thought that this country might just be ready for radicchio's sophisticated yet wild bitterness. Spurred on by the growth of the prepackaged-salad industry (which began using radicchio for its color), he helped bring the common Chioggia variety, with its tight head and white-veined maroon leaves, and the rarer loose-leafed, tapered Treviso variety to the American table.

TATSOI: In America, Elizabeth Schneider tells us in her landmark *Vegetables from Amaranth to Zucchini,* tatsoi is "the glossy lollipop leaf in mesclun mixes." Botanically, it's a bok choy, and even though it's commonly referred to by its Japanese name, in Chinatown markets it can be labeled *wu ta cai* or *tai koo choi.* The leaves are succulent, crisp, and somewhat like cabbage in flavor. They are delicious raw in salads; try the bigger leaves in a stir-fry or put them in soup.

WATERCRESS: It would be fair to say that watercress is the original hydroponic vegetable. Its natural habitat includes cold mountain springs and burbling brooks, and in Berks County, Pennsylvania, you can still find late-eighteenth-century farms with old ponds and waterways once used for watercress culture. Peppery, spicy, and intense, watercress stands up well to creamy dressings. It also makes a delicious bed for grilled steak; the meat juices cause it to wilt appealingly. Discard the tough stems if you are going to eat watercress raw. Asians use the whole sprigs, though, in soups and stir-fries, where the stems give a satisfying crunch.

Washing and Storing Greens

You can toss a head of iceberg lettuce into the vegetable bin and forget about it, but other salad greens require careful handling to keep them at their best. When you get home, examine the greens and discard any bruised, wilted, or broken leaves — they are a breeding ground for decay. It's a good idea to wash greens, even if they're organic or labeled "prewashed."

Technically, we suppose, greens should remain unwashed until you are ready to use them, but usually time is of the essence when getting dinner on the table, and if those greens aren't already clean, it's too easy to mutter, "Maybe tomorrow night." So we tend to wash our greens all at once in a just-cleaned sink of cold water. Gently agitate the leaves underwater, and any sand or little bugs will drift to the bottom of the sink. Let the debris settle, then lift the greens out of the water into a colander. Sandy greens, such as spinach and watercress, will benefit from a second bath.

Dry the greens in batches in a salad spinner, then transfer them to bags. Some people swear by muslin storage bags or a clean cotton pillowcase; others spread the greens out into a thin layer, loosely roll them up in a tea towel or between sheets of paper towel, and then put the roll in a plastic bag. The goal is to get rid of excess water on the greens (to prevent rotting) while retaining their natural moisture and giving them circulating air within a closed space. Greens will keep for two to four days this way, depending on their type; heartier greens will last longer than tender arugula and pale green lettuces. Watercress keeps best with its stems in a bowl of water, covered loosely with a plastic bag.

Mâche with Raw Asparagus, Pistachios, and Parmigiano-Reggiano

SERVES 6 AS A FIRST COURSE
ACTIVE TIME: 20 MINUTES ■ START TO FINISH: 20 MINUTES

■ Spring is really here when you find mâche (lamb's lettuce) and the first local asparagus in the markets. Search out large, meaty asparagus stalks, not the thin ones, for this salad. (The large ones aren't more mature than thin ones, as you might think, but a different variety.) This recipe comes from Judy Rodgers, the chef-owner of San Francisco's Zuni Café; she loves to use purple asparagus raw, so it holds its color (the stalks turn green when cooked). You may be surprised to learn that asparagus stems are sweeter than their tips, especially when raw, so trim away the tips and save them for pasta, risotto, or soup. This salad is great by itself, but try it piled on a small mound of prosciutto for a nice change. ■

- 2 tablespoons shelled unsalted natural pistachios (not dyed red)
- 1/4 cup extra-virgin olive oil
- 1 tablespoon Champagne vinegar or white wine vinegar
- Salt
- 6 jumbo asparagus spears (9 ounces), trimmed
- 6 ounces mâche, trimmed (6 cups)
- Freshly ground black pepper
- 1/3 cup shaved Parmigiano-Reggiano (use a vegetable peeler to shave cheese)

Position a rack in middle of oven and preheat oven to 350°F.

Heat pistachios on a small baking sheet in oven until just warm, 2 to 3 minutes. Coarsely chop.

Whisk together oil, vinegar, and salt to taste in a small bowl.

Cut tips from asparagus and reserve for another use. Starting at tip end, cut asparagus spears on a long diagonal into 1/8-inch-thick slices.

Gently toss mâche, asparagus, and pistachios in a large bowl with just enough vinaigrette to coat. Season with salt and pepper. Arrange salad on plates. Top with cheese shavings.

COOK'S NOTE

■ Mâche is worth seeking out for this salad, but if you can't find it, you can substitute Boston lettuce leaves torn into bite-sized pieces.

Fava Bean, Asparagus, and Arugula Salad with Shaved Pecorino

SERVES 4 AS A FIRST COURSE OR LUNCH MAIN COURSE
ACTIVE TIME: 1½ HOURS ■ START TO FINISH: 1½ HOURS

■ *La primavera* on a plate. Springtime in Rome means that the first pristine fava beans are eaten raw with sharp, salty pecorino Romano. This salad takes things a step further: the saltiness of the cheese sets off the peppery arugula and the crisp brightness of asparagus stalks, which are thinly sliced and served raw. We call for supermarket balsamic here, but if you happen to have an aged balsamic in a kitchen cupboard, by all means use it. ■

- 1/2 pound medium asparagus, trimmed
- 2 cups shelled fava beans (2½ pounds in pods) or shelled fresh edamame (soybeans)
- 2 tablespoons extra-virgin olive oil
- Salt and freshly ground black pepper
- 1/4 pound arugula, coarse stems discarded
- 1 (6- to 8-ounce) piece pecorino Romano or Parmigiano-Reggiano, for shaving (you will not use all the cheese)
- 2 teaspoons balsamic vinegar

Cut asparagus stalks on a long diagonal into 1/8-inch-thick slices, leaving tips 1 inch long; reserve tips separately.

Blanch asparagus tips (not sliced stalks) in a 4-quart saucepan of boiling well-salted water for 2 minutes, then immediately transfer with a slotted spoon to a bowl of ice and cold water to stop the cooking. Return water to a boil and blanch beans for 1 minute, then drain and immediately transfer to ice water to stop the cooking. Drain asparagus tips and beans. Gently peel skins from favas (it's not necessary to peel edamame).

Toss beans, asparagus tips, and raw sliced stalks in a bowl with 1 tablespoon oil and salt and pepper to taste. Divide among four plates. Toss arugula with remaining 1 tablespoon oil and salt and pepper to taste and mound on top of vegetables. Shave thin slices of cheese over salad with a vegetable peeler, then drizzle with vinegar.

COOK'S NOTE

- The beans can be blanched and peeled up to 1 day ahead. Refrigerate in a sealable plastic bag.

Chopped Salad

SERVES 4

ACTIVE TIME: 30 MINUTES ■ START TO FINISH: 30 MINUTES

■ A chopped salad can be whatever you want it to be. It's one way to make a large assortment of vegetables and greens easy to eat—a real gift to your guests. Don't forget to sharpen your knife well before getting down to work. ■

- 2 tablespoons fresh lemon juice
- 1 small garlic clove, minced
- 1½ teaspoons sugar
- ½ teaspoon salt
- ¼ teaspoon freshly ground black pepper
- ⅓ cup olive oil
- 1 medium head romaine, chopped
- 1 seedless cucumber (usually plastic wrapped), cut into ½-inch dice
- 2 medium tomatoes, cut into ½-inch dice
- 1 yellow bell pepper, cored, seeded, and cut into ½-inch dice
- 1 small red onion, finely chopped
- 1 cup loosely packed fresh flat-leaf parsley leaves
- ½ cup brine-cured black olives, pitted and quartered

Whisk together lemon juice, garlic, sugar, salt, and pepper in a large bowl. Add oil in a steady stream, whisking until well combined.

Add remaining ingredients to dressing and toss until well combined.

Iceberg and Watercress Salad with Blue Cheese Dressing

SERVES 4

ACTIVE TIME: 15 MINUTES ■ START TO FINISH: 15 MINUTES

■ Spicy, peppery watercress is a perfect match for the cool crispness of iceberg lettuce, which in turn has a great affinity for rich, creamy blue cheese dressing. Crunchy celery stalks dipped in blue cheese dressing are the traditional accompaniment for Buffalo Chicken Wings (page 54), which taste wonderful on a bed of this salad. ■

- ¼ cup mayonnaise
- ¼ cup sour cream
- 1 cup crumbled Roquefort or other blue cheese (about 4 ounces)
- 1 tablespoon fresh lemon juice
- 1 tablespoon finely chopped fresh chives
- ¼ teaspoon salt
- ¼ teaspoon freshly ground black pepper
- 1–2 tablespoons milk or water
- ½ head iceberg lettuce, thinly sliced crosswise
- 2 bunches watercress, coarse stems discarded (6 cups)
- 3 celery ribs, thinly sliced diagonally

Whisk together mayonnaise, sour cream, cheese, lemon juice, chives, salt, and pepper in a small bowl. Thin to desired consistency with milk.

Toss together iceberg, watercress, and celery in a large bowl. Serve drizzled with dressing.

Caesar Salad

SERVES 6 TO 8

ACTIVE TIME: 30 MINUTES ■ START TO FINISH: 40 MINUTES

■ Did the Tijuana restaurateur Caesar Cardini, who first coated crunchy romaine lettuce with his strongly flavored, creamy dressing back in 1924, have any idea that he'd created an instant classic? Our version breaks from tradition in that the dressing doesn't contain a one-minute coddled whole egg but two raw egg yolks (we think egg whites make things too watery). We understand if you want to skip the uncooked eggs for health reasons, but don't leave out the minced anchovy. It adds depth to the dressing without tasting at all fishy. ■

- 3 garlic cloves
- 1 teaspoon salt
- 9 tablespoons olive oil
- 5 slices firm white sandwich bread, crusts discarded and cut into ½-inch squares (2½ cups)
- 2 large egg yolks
- 1 tablespoon fresh lemon juice
- 1 tablespoon white wine vinegar
- 1 teaspoon Worcestershire sauce
- ¾ teaspoon minced flat anchovy fillet
- 2 large heads romaine, torn into bite-sized pieces (16 cups)
- ½ cup finely grated Parmigiano-Reggiano, or to taste
- Freshly ground black pepper

To make the croutons, put a rack in middle of oven and preheat oven to 350°F.

Mash garlic to a paste with ¼ teaspoon salt in a mortar with a pestle, then stir in 4 tablespoons (¼ cup) oil (or mince and mash to a paste with a large heavy knife, transfer to a bowl, and stir in oil). Force mixture through a medium-mesh sieve into a bowl.

Spread bread on a baking sheet and bake for 10 minutes. Add to garlic mixture and toss until well coated, then return croutons to baking sheet and bake until golden, about 7 minutes. Cool in pan on a rack.

Whisk together remaining 5 tablespoons oil, egg yolks, lemon juice, vinegar, Worcestershire, remaining ¾ teaspoon salt, and anchovy in a large bowl. Add lettuce and toss, then sprinkle with cheese, croutons, and salt and pepper to taste and toss until well combined.

COOK'S NOTE

■ The eggs in this recipe are not cooked. If this is a concern, see page 629.

Dandelion Salad with Warm Pecan Vinaigrette

SERVES 6

ACTIVE TIME: 25 MINUTES ■ START TO FINISH: 25 MINUTES

■ A hot dressing doesn't necessarily wilt the dandelion greens, but it mellows them and takes the edge off their rawness. Pecans add rich, suave sweetness. (For more about dandelion greens, see page 132.) ■

- 2 pounds dandelion greens (2 large bunches), tough stems discarded
- 3 tablespoons extra-virgin olive oil
- 3 garlic cloves, finely chopped
- ¼ cup pecans, coarsely chopped
- 1½ tablespoons balsamic vinegar
- 1 teaspoon salt
- ¼ teaspoon freshly ground black pepper

Cut top 5 inches from greens and transfer to a large heatproof serving bowl. Cut remaining greens into ¾-inch slices and add to bowl.

Heat oil in a small heavy skillet over moderate heat. Add garlic and nuts and cook, stirring, until garlic is golden. Stir in vinegar, salt, and pepper. Pour hot vinaigrette over greens and toss to combine.

Escarole Salad with Hazelnuts and Currants

SERVES 4

ACTIVE TIME: 15 MINUTES ■ START TO FINISH: 30 MINUTES

■ The creamy or pale yellow inside leaves of escarole (a tenderer bitter green than radicchio) make a gorgeous winter salad when wilted in an understated sweet-tart dressing. Save the tougher green outside leaves for soup. (For more about escarole, see page 132.) ■

2 tablespoons extra-virgin olive oil
1 teaspoon minced garlic
3 tablespoons dried currants
1 tablespoon cider vinegar
1/4 teaspoon salt
1/8 teaspoon freshly ground black pepper
2 heads escarole, dark outer leaves removed, pale green and yellow inner leaves torn into bite-sized pieces (16 cups)
1/4 cup loosely packed fresh flat-leaf parsley leaves
1/3 cup hazelnuts, toasted (see Tips, page 938) and chopped

Heat oil in an 8-inch nonstick skillet over moderate heat. Add garlic and cook, stirring, until fragrant, about 30 seconds. Add currants and cook, stirring, for 20 seconds. Whisk in vinegar, salt, and pepper and remove from heat.

Toss escarole, parsley, and nuts with warm dressing in a large bowl. Serve immediately.

Chicory Salad with Oranges and Red Onion

SERVES 8

ACTIVE TIME: 20 MINUTES ■ START TO FINISH: 25 MINUTES

■ A tangle of spiky chicory, bright orange slices, and rings of marinated red onion makes a remarkable salad that cuts the richness of winter's more substantial dishes. Many people associate chicory with overwhelming bitterness, but we discovered that most of the bitter taste is in the stems. Simply stripping the curly green leaves off the stems, something commonly done in Europe, definitely widens the field for chicory use. (For more about chicory, including what to do with those stems, see page 132.) ■

1/3 cup red wine vinegar
1 tablespoon sugar
1 1/2 teaspoons salt
1 medium red onion, sliced crosswise 1/8 inch thick and separated into rings
2 medium navel oranges
2 teaspoons whole-grain mustard
1 tablespoon chicken broth or water
1/4 teaspoon freshly ground black pepper
2 tablespoons olive oil
1/2 pound chicory (curly endive), stems and center ribs discarded, leaves torn into bite-sized pieces (10 cups)

Combine vinegar, sugar, and 1 teaspoon salt in a small saucepan and bring to a boil, stirring frequently until sugar is dissolved. Remove from heat.

Cook onion in a 4-quart saucepan of boiling well-salted water until crisp-tender, about 4 minutes. Drain in a colander, rinse under cold water to stop the cooking, and drain again. Stir onion into vinegar mixture and marinate for 10 minutes.

Meanwhile, cut peel and white pith from oranges with a sharp knife, then cut oranges crosswise into 1/4-inch-thick slices.

Drain onion in a sieve set over a salad bowl; set onion aside. Whisk mustard, broth, remaining 1/2 teaspoon salt, pepper, and oil into marinade. Add chicory, onion, and oranges and toss well.

Watercress and Apple Salad with Peanut Dressing

SERVES 8

ACTIVE TIME: 30 MINUTES ■ START TO FINISH: 30 MINUTES

■ If your idea of a treat is a smear of peanut butter on a slice of apple, you're going to love this. The slightly creamy dressing clings to the apple matchsticks and the snappy watercress leaves. Use your favorite apple here—one that is firm and crisp. This is a very pretty salad and delicious in cool weather. ■

3/4 pound apples
1 tablespoon fresh lime juice
1/4 cup plain yogurt
2 tablespoons smooth peanut butter
1 tablespoon water
1/4 teaspoon salt
8 cups watercress sprigs (2–3 bunches), coarse stems discarded

Core apples and cut into ⅛-inch-thick matchsticks (about 2 inches long), then toss with 1 teaspoon lime juice in a large bowl.

Whisk together yogurt, peanut butter, water, salt, and remaining 2 teaspoons lime juice in a small bowl. Add watercress to apples, then add dressing and toss well.

Spinach Salad with Gorgonzola Croutons and Bacon Twists

SERVES 4 AS A MAIN COURSE
ACTIVE TIME: 45 MINUTES ■ START TO FINISH: 45 MINUTES

■ Our take on the classic spinach salad with blue cheese and bacon is a satisfying yet light main course. Gorgonzola is spread on slices of bread that are cut into croutons and baked so that the flavor seeps in, and the bacon slices are twisted into spirals. ■

- 8 bacon slices (½ pound)
- ¼ cup crumbled Gorgonzola
- 1 tablespoon unsalted butter, softened
- 4 large (½-inch-thick) slices country bread, preferably sourdough
- 1 garlic clove
- ½ teaspoon salt
- ¼ cup mayonnaise
- 2 tablespoons olive oil
- 2 tablespoons red wine vinegar
- 2 teaspoons honey
- 1 pound spinach, coarse stems discarded
- 1 small red onion, very thinly sliced crosswise and separated into rings
- 2 hard-boiled large eggs, quartered

Put racks in upper and lower thirds of oven and preheat oven to 375°F.

Twist each bacon slice into a tight spiral and arrange twists on rack of a broiler pan, pressing ends onto pan (twists will unravel somewhat as they bake). Bake in upper third of oven until crisp, about 30 minutes. Transfer to paper towels to drain.

Meanwhile, mash together Gorgonzola and butter in a shallow bowl with a fork. Spread generously on bread slices. Cut slices into 1-inch squares and arrange on a baking sheet.

After bacon has cooked for 15 minutes, put croutons in lower third of oven. Bake until golden and crisp, about 15 minutes.

While croutons bake, using a large heavy knife, mince and mash garlic to a paste with salt. Combine mayonnaise, oil, vinegar, honey, and garlic paste in a blender and blend until smooth.

Toss together spinach, warm croutons, and onion in a serving bowl and toss with dressing. Top with bacon twists and eggs.

Frisée Salad with Lardons and Poached Eggs

SERVES 4 AS A FIRST COURSE OR LIGHT MAIN COURSE
ACTIVE TIME: 20 MINUTES ■ START TO FINISH: 20 MINUTES

■ The French bistro classic *salade lyonnaise* is among the world's most famous culinary combinations. You'll gain new appreciation for the power of poached eggs: the molten yolks coat the refreshingly bitter, almost wild-tasting greens and temper the vinegar in the dressing. Use very fresh eggs for the best results in poaching (see page 636) and slab or thick-cut bacon for the smoky, rich (and irresistible) little sticks called lardons. (If the bacon is particularly lean, add a tablespoon of vegetable oil to the skillet while cooking it.) In France, this salad is often served as a first course; it also makes a great lunch or Sunday night supper. ■

- ½ pound frisée, torn into bite-sized pieces
- 6 ounces slab bacon or thick-cut bacon
- 2 tablespoons distilled white vinegar
- 4 large eggs
- 2 tablespoons finely chopped shallots
- 3 tablespoons red wine vinegar
- ¾ teaspoon salt
- ¼ teaspoon freshly ground black pepper

Put frisée in a large bowl.

If using slab bacon, cut off rind, then cut bacon

lengthwise into 1/4-inch-thick slices. Cut bacon slices (either type) crosswise into 1/4-inch-wide sticks. Cook bacon in a 10- to 12-inch heavy skillet over moderate heat, stirring occasionally, until golden, about 7 minutes. Remove skillet from heat and set aside.

Fill an 8- to 9-inch skillet with 1 inch warm water. Half fill a 4-quart wide saucepan with water, stir in white vinegar, and bring to a bare simmer. Break 1 egg into a cup and slide egg into simmering liquid. Repeat with remaining eggs, spacing them evenly in pan. Poach eggs at a bare simmer until whites are firm but yolks are still runny, 3 to 4 minutes. With a slotted spoon, transfer poached eggs to skillet of warm water.

Reheat bacon in skillet over moderate heat. Add shallots and cook, stirring, for 1 minute. Add red wine vinegar and boil for 5 seconds, then immediately pour hot dressing over frisée. Sprinkle with salt and pepper and toss well.

Divide salad among four plates. With slotted spoon, transfer each egg to paper towels to drain briefly, then place on a salad. Season eggs with salt and pepper and serve immediately.

COOK'S NOTE

- The egg yolks in this recipe may not be fully cooked. If this is a concern, see page 629.

Shaved Raw Artichoke Salad

SERVES 4 AS A FIRST COURSE
ACTIVE TIME: 30 MINUTES ■ START TO FINISH: 30 MINUTES

■ Sliced very, very thin, raw artichokes have a nutty flavor and a distinctive dense crispness, like celery root or carrot. We first tasted this salad years ago in Italy, where the artichokes were layered with oak mushrooms, but we use the more common cremini or white mushrooms. It's surprising that something so bland-looking could have so much subtle, bosky flavor. In Italy, this salad is presented without color accents, but we love the splash of emerald green provided by chopped flat-leaf parsley. Make sure that the artichokes you buy are fresh—tightly closed and without any brown edges. And serve the salad right away, so it stays pale and pristine. ■

- 2 large artichokes (3/4 pound each)
- 2 lemons, halved
- 2 large (2-inch-diameter) very fresh cremini or white mushrooms
- 1 tablespoon mild extra-virgin olive oil, plus additional for drizzling
- 2 teaspoons chopped fresh flat-leaf parsley
- 1/2 teaspoon kosher salt
- 1/4 teaspoon freshly ground black pepper
- 1 (6- to 8-ounce) piece Parmigiano-Reggiano, for shaving (you will not use all the cheese)

SPECIAL EQUIPMENT: a mandoline or other adjustable-blade slicer, such as a Japanese Benriner

Cut off and discard stem of 1 artichoke. Cut off top inch of artichoke with a serrated knife. Bend back outer layer of leaves until they snap off close to base, then remove several more layers of leaves in same manner, discarding leaves, until you reach pale yellow leaves with pale green tips. With serrated knife, cut off tops of leaves flush with artichoke bottom, then pull out purple-tipped leaves and scoop out fuzzy choke with melon ball cutter or a sharp spoon (see page 518). Rub cut surfaces with a lemon half. Trim dark green fibrous parts from base and sides of artichoke with a sharp paring knife, then rub cut surfaces with same lemon half. Repeat with remaining artichoke and another lemon half.

Trim mushroom stems flush with caps, then rub mushrooms with another lemon half. Squeeze 1 teaspoon juice from remaining lemon half into a bowl. Shave artichokes and then mushrooms as thin as possible with slicer and toss immediately with lemon juice. Add oil, parsley, salt, and pepper and toss well.

Divide salad among four plates. Shave a few curls of cheese on top of each salad with slicer or a vegetable peeler and drizzle with olive oil.

Creamy Slaw

SERVES 4 TO 6
ACTIVE TIME: 15 MINUTES ■ START TO FINISH: 45 MINUTES

■ People have probably been making slaw for as long as they've been growing cabbage, and that is a very long time. This is a straightforward example; sour cream lightens the mayonnaise and adds a different sort of tang to the dressing. It's important to let the slaw sit after putting it together so the cabbage has a chance to wilt slightly, exuding its juices. Carrot and green bell pepper, both time-honored additions, contribute sweetness and zip, respectively. ■

- 1/3 cup mayonnaise
- 3 tablespoons sour cream
- 2 tablespoons cider vinegar
- 1/2 teaspoon salt
- 1/8 teaspoon freshly ground black pepper
- 1 1/2 pounds green cabbage, cored and thinly sliced (6 cups)
- 1 carrot, shredded
- 1/4 cup finely chopped green bell pepper
- 1/4 cup finely chopped onion

Whisk together mayonnaise and sour cream in a large bowl until smooth. Whisk in vinegar, salt, and pepper. Add remaining ingredients and toss well. Let stand, uncovered, at room temperature, tossing occasionally, until vegetables are wilted, about 30 minutes.

Coleslaw with Hot Caraway Vinaigrette

SERVES 10

ACTIVE TIME: 25 MINUTES ■ START TO FINISH: 25 MINUTES

■ Refreshing and full of robust flavor, this is just the ticket for those who don't like mayonnaisey dressings. It's a natural with grilled sausages. The name coleslaw, by the way, hasn't strayed far from its etymological roots: *cole*, from the Latin *caulis* and Greek *kaulos*, is the old English word for "cabbage"; *slaw*, meaning "salad," descends through either German or English. ■

- 2 small red onions, halved lengthwise and thinly sliced crosswise
- 6 cups thinly sliced green cabbage (about 1 1/2 pounds)
- 6 cups thinly sliced red cabbage (about 1 1/2 pounds)
- 5 carrots, coarsely shredded
- 5 tablespoons white wine vinegar
- 5 tablespoons olive oil
- 2 tablespoons caraway seeds
- 1 tablespoon mustard seeds
- 1 teaspoon salt
- 1/2 teaspoon freshly ground black pepper

Soak onions in a bowl of ice and cold water for 15 minutes. Drain well.

Toss green and red cabbage, onions, and carrots with vinegar in a large heatproof bowl.

Heat oil in a 9-inch skillet over moderate heat until hot but not smoking. Add caraway and mustard seeds, cover, and cook, stirring occasionally, until mustard seeds stop popping, 1 to 3 minutes. Immediately drizzle hot oil mixture over cabbage mixture, add salt and pepper, and toss well.

Chilled Celery Root in Mustard Sauce

SERVES 4

ACTIVE TIME: 20 MINUTES ■ START TO FINISH: 2 1/2 HOURS (INCLUDES MARINATING AND CHILLING)

■ Walk into virtually any bistro in France and you'll find *céleri rémoulade,* mild, nutty celery root dressed in a tangy mustard sauce. Celery root (sometimes called celeriac and closely related to bunch celery) used to be hard to find in the United States, but it has recently become more widely available, a happy result of the blossoming love affair between Americans and root vegetables. A small sharp knife trims the thick, knobbly skin from the root more easily than a peeler. ■

FOR CELERY ROOT

- 1 1/2 pounds celery root (celeriac), peeled with a sharp knife and cut into matchsticks
- 1/2 teaspoon salt
- 2 tablespoons fresh lemon juice

FOR SAUCE

- 1 tablespoon Dijon mustard
- 1 1/2 teaspoons fresh lemon juice
- 1 1/2 teaspoons white wine vinegar
- Pinch of sugar
- Salt and freshly ground black pepper
- 3 tablespoons olive oil or vegetable oil

GARNISH: 2 tablespoons finely chopped fresh chives or minced fresh flat-leaf parsley

MARINATE THE CELERY ROOT: Toss celery root with salt and lemon juice in a bowl. Marinate, covered and refrigerated, for 30 minutes to 1 hour.

MAKE THE SAUCE: Whisk together mustard, lemon juice, vinegar, sugar, and salt and pepper to taste in a bowl. Add oil in a slow stream, whisking until well blended.

ASSEMBLE THE SALAD: Drain celery root and return it to bowl. Pour dressing over celery root and toss. Refrigerate, covered, for at least 1 hour.

Sprinkle salad with chives before serving.

COOK'S NOTE

- The salad can be refrigerated for up to 3 hours.

Viennese Cucumber Salad

SERVES 6
ACTIVE TIME: 15 MINUTES ■ START TO FINISH: 2¼ HOURS (INCLUDES MARINATING AND CHILLING)

■ The cucumbers are wilted yet retain their crispness and are infused with flavor. This salad, inspired by one from our Austrian correspondent, the late Lillian Langseth Christensen, is a wonderful accompaniment to chilled poached salmon (or almost any fish, for that matter) in summer or to beef stew in winter. ■

- 2 large seedless cucumbers (usually plastic wrapped)
- 1 tablespoon salt
- ⅓ cup white wine vinegar
- ¼ cup water
- 2 teaspoons sugar
- 1 garlic clove, minced
- 1 teaspoon dill seeds

SPECIAL EQUIPMENT: a mandoline or other adjustable-blade slicer, such as a Japanese Benriner

Score cucumbers lengthwise with fork. Cut into 1/16-inch-thick slices with slicer. Toss with salt in a large bowl and let stand at room temperature for 1 hour.

Combine vinegar, water, sugar, garlic, and dill seeds in a small saucepan and bring to a boil, stirring until sugar is dissolved. Let cool.

Drain cucumbers in a colander and rinse under cold water, then drain well again, squeezing out excess liquid. Combine cucumbers with dressing in a bowl, tossing to coat. Cover and marinate, refrigerated, for at least 1 hour.

COOK'S NOTE

- The cucumbers can marinate for up to 6 hours. After about 2 hours, the skin will discolor, but there will be no effect on flavor.

SEEDLESS CUCUMBERS

In general, we're not impressed with cookie-cutter uniformity in produce, but for consistent flavor and crunch, it's hard to beat the long, narrow cucumbers grown in greenhouses and usually sold wrapped in plastic to protect their thin, delicate, blessedly unwaxed skin. They are often marketed as European, English, hothouse, or seedless cucumbers. Although they do contain tiny seeds, for horticultural purposes they are seedless — they have to be propagated from cuttings. We put them in all kinds of salads, and they make for a mighty fine sandwich too.

Asian Cucumber Ribbon Salad

SERVES 4
ACTIVE TIME: 15 MINUTES ■ START TO FINISH: 25 MINUTES

■ The dressing for this loose skein of long, paper-thin, juicy cucumber slices is Asian in flavoring but not assertively so, allowing this light salad to fit in anywhere. It makes a great side to grilled chicken breasts or steak. ■

- ¼ cup seasoned rice vinegar
- ½ teaspoon sugar

1 teaspoon soy sauce
½ teaspoon Asian sesame oil
1½ seedless cucumbers (usually plastic wrapped)

SPECIAL EQUIPMENT: a mandoline or other adjustable-blade slicer, such as a Japanese Benriner

Combine vinegar and sugar in a very small saucepan and bring to a simmer, stirring until sugar is dissolved. Cool to room temperature, then stir in soy sauce and sesame oil.

Cut whole cucumber crosswise in half. With mandoline, cut cucumbers lengthwise into ⅛-inch-thick ribbons. Toss cucumbers with dressing in a bowl and let stand for 5 minutes before serving.

COOK'S NOTE

- Do not let the dressed salad stand for more than 20 minutes before serving, or it will become soggy.

Greek Salad

Horiatiki Salata

SERVES 6

ACTIVE TIME: 20 MINUTES ■ START TO FINISH: 20 MINUTES

■ Many Greek salads are lettuce-based, but this one relies on fresh vegetables full of height-of-the-season flavor, which are simply drizzled with olive oil. Note that the only acid is from the tomatoes; moist, crumbly feta adds a salty sharpness. Most Greek feta, by the way, is actually made in Sardinia and sent to Greece, where it is shipped around the globe. If you find yourself in Greece, though, look for artisanal barrel-aged feta; its producers are a vanishing breed. ■

5 tomatoes (2 pounds total), quartered
1 small green bell pepper, cored, seeded, and cut into thin strips
½ seedless cucumber (usually plastic wrapped), halved lengthwise and cut into ¼-inch-thick slices
1 small red onion, thinly sliced crosswise and separated into rings
½ cup Kalamata olives, pitted
2 teaspoons dried oregano, preferably Greek, crumbled
¼ teaspoon kosher salt
¼ pound feta, preferably Greek, broken into chunks
¼ cup extra-virgin olive oil
Freshly ground black pepper

Gently toss together tomatoes, bell pepper, cucumber, onion, olives, oregano, and salt in a large bowl. Add feta. Drizzle salad with oil, then season with pepper to taste.

Green Bean Salad with Pumpkin Seed Dressing

SERVES 4

ACTIVE TIME: 25 MINUTES ■ START TO FINISH: 30 MINUTES

■ Green beans and tomatoes are enlivened by a thickened dressing that's almost like a Mexican pesto. Its body and creaminess come from ground toasted pumpkin seeds, or you can use pine nuts. ■

½ cup (about 2 ounces) green (hulled) pumpkin seeds or pine nuts
¼ cup extra-virgin olive oil
¼ cup water
1½ tablespoons fresh lemon juice
1 small garlic clove, minced
½ teaspoon ground cumin
½ teaspoon salt
2 tablespoons finely chopped fresh cilantro
¾ pound *haricots verts* or slender green beans
2 small tomatoes (½ pound total), halved lengthwise, seeded, and cut lengthwise into ¼-inch-wide strips

Toast pumpkin seeds in a dry small heavy skillet over moderately low heat, stirring frequently, until puffed but not browned, about 6 minutes. (If using pine nuts, toast until pale golden, about 7 minutes.) Transfer to a plate to cool.

Reserve 1 tablespoon seeds. Purée remaining seeds in a blender with oil, water, lemon juice, garlic, cumin, salt, and 1 tablespoon cilantro until smooth.

Cook beans in a 4-quart saucepan of boiling well-salted water, uncovered, until just tender, 4 to 6 minutes. Drain, then plunge into a bowl of ice and cold water to stop the cooking. Drain beans again and pat dry.

Arrange beans on a platter and drizzle with two thirds of pumpkin seed dressing. Top with tomatoes and remaining dressing and sprinkle with remaining 1 tablespoon cilantro and reserved pumpkin seeds.

Panzanella

Bread and Tomato Salad

SERVE 4 TO 6

ACTIVE TIME: 20 MINUTES ■ START TO FINISH: 40 MINUTES

■ This Italian salad, which evolved as a way for thrifty cooks to use up stale bread, is incredibly delicious and very easy to make. All you need are truly ripe, luscious tomatoes and a slightly stale loaf of chewy, substantial bread that will absorb the tomato juices without losing its texture. Bread that's a day old is best; if too fresh, it will turn gummy and fall to bits. This is a late-summer staple. ■

- 1/2 pound day-old crusty sourdough bread, cut into 3/4-inch cubes (6 cups)
- 4 large tomatoes (1 1/4 pounds total), cut into 3/4-inch pieces
- 3/4 seedless cucumber (usually plastic wrapped), cut into 1/2-inch pieces
- 1/2 cup sliced red onion
- 1/2 cup extra-virgin olive oil
- 2 tablespoons red wine vinegar
- 1 teaspoon minced garlic
- 1 teaspoon salt
- 1/4 teaspoon freshly ground black pepper
- 2/3 cup thinly sliced fresh basil leaves

Stir together bread, tomatoes, cucumber, and onion in a serving bowl.

Whisk together oil, vinegar, garlic, salt, and pepper in a small bowl. Add to bread mixture, along with basil, and toss to combine. Let stand at room temperature, stirring occasionally, for at least 20 minutes before serving.

COOK'S NOTE

■ The salad can be made up to 1 hour ahead.

Heirloom Tomatoes with Bacon, Blue Cheese, and Basil

SERVES 6

ACTIVE TIME: 40 MINUTES ■ START TO FINISH: 40 MINUTES

■ What exactly are heirloom tomatoes, anyway? Flavor aside, their most important characteristic is that they grow true year after year, unlike hybrids, which must be artificially crossed. Many heirlooms have been handed down through generations and have well-documented histories. Heirloom tomatoes, in fact, can be reason alone to frequent your local farmers market.

We had a little architectural fun here, layering slices of juicy tomatoes with bacon, blue cheese, and basil, but that really isn't necessary; you can arrange the tomato slices on a platter and take it from there. The sherry vinegar might seem like a precious touch, but it's a hearty vinegar and stands up well to the Maytag Blue. ■

- 1/4 pound bacon (4 slices)
- 6 slices firm white sandwich bread
- 6 tablespoons olive oil
- Salt and freshly ground black pepper
- 1/4 cup finely chopped shallots
- 3 tablespoons sherry vinegar
- 4 medium heirloom tomatoes in assorted colors (2 pounds total), cut into 1/4- to 1/3-inch-thick slices
- 30 small fresh basil leaves
- 1 1/2 ounces blue cheese, preferably Maytag Blue, crumbled, at room temperature

OPTIONAL GARNISH: very small heirloom cherry or currant tomatoes

SPECIAL EQUIPMENT: a 3-inch round cookie cutter

Cook bacon in a 10-inch heavy skillet over moderate heat until crisp. Transfer to paper towels to drain. Pour off bacon fat from skillet and reserve (do not clean skillet).

Meanwhile, cut 1 round from each bread slice with cookie cutter.

Heat 1 1/2 tablespoons oil in same skillet over moderate heat until hot but not smoking. Add 3 bread rounds and cook, turning once, until golden brown, about 3 minutes total. Transfer to a rack to cool and season with salt and pepper. Cook remaining 3 bread rounds in $1\frac{1}{2}$ tablespoons more oil in same manner.

Heat 2 tablespoons reserved bacon fat and remaining 3 tablespoons oil in a small heavy saucepan over moderate heat. Add shallots and cook, stirring, until softened, about 2 minutes. Add vinegar and simmer, whisking, until thoroughly incorporated, about 1 minute. Remove dressing from heat, season with salt and pepper, and cover to keep warm.

Crumble bacon. Arrange toasts on six plates and divide tomato slices among them, stacking tomatoes and sprinkling some basil and bacon between each slice. Sprinkle cheese and remaining basil and bacon over and around tomatoes. Spoon warm dressing over and around tomatoes and season with salt and pepper.

COOK'S NOTES

- The toasts can be made up to 3 hours ahead and kept in an airtight container at room temperature.
- The dressing can be made up to 1 hour ahead and refrigerated, covered. Reheat before using.

Watermelon, Tomato, and Feta Salad

SERVES 4

ACTIVE TIME: 25 MINUTES ■ START TO FINISH: 25 MINUTES

■ Watermelon and tomatoes have a curious but genuine affinity for each other—a quality, come to think of it, that's present in many a successful marriage. Crumbly, piquant feta adds something you'd miss if it weren't there. This makes an appealing side dish, but on a hot night in August, you might end up eating a large bowl as supper. ■

- 1 (3-pound) piece watermelon, rind removed, fruit cut into 3/4-inch chunks and seeded
- 2 large tomatoes, cut into 3/4-inch chunks
- 1 cup crumbled feta (about 4 ounces)
- 2/3 cup packed fresh cilantro sprigs, chopped
- 2 tablespoons extra-virgin olive oil
- 1 tablespoon white balsamic vinegar (see page 170)
- Salt and freshly ground black pepper

Stir together watermelon, tomatoes, feta, cilantro, oil, and vinegar in a large bowl. Season with salt and pepper.

STORING TOMATOES

Nothing will ruin good garden tomatoes faster than refrigeration. Why? They are tropical berries, says William Woys Weaver, the author of *Heirloom Vegetable Gardening,* who grows about 223 varieties of tomatoes on a rotating basis. Tomatoes are meant to be eaten when the sun is high and the weather is hot. They are very sensitive to cold, even cold rain. Refrigerating them causes them to lose flavor—rather like putting a good red wine on ice—and become mealy. Even if you rewarm them, they have an odd, gelatinous quality and lack the "ping" flavor and rich texture of really ripe ones. A sunny windowsill isn't the best place for tomatoes either; they do best at normal room temperature and in indirect light. They like to be stored stem side up so their shoulders don't get bruised. Under these conditions, gloriously ripe tomatoes will keep for a day or so, while underripe ones may take up to a week to reach their peak. If you find yourself with too many ripe tomatoes on hand, make a quick marinara sauce for the freezer—you'll be happy you did, come winter.

Endive, Pear, and Stilton Salad

SERVES 4 AS A FIRST COURSE
ACTIVE TIME: 35 MINUTES ■ START TO FINISH: 35 MINUTES

■ Crisp endive, golden sautéed pears, and rich blue-veined Stilton make a classic, elegant composed salad, in which the various ingredients are arranged artfully rather than tossed together. The presence of anise seeds in the dressing might seem odd, but anise does great things for endive. In this case, it heightens the salad's flavors and ties the whole thing together. This recipe is adapted from one served at Le Gavroche restaurant in Vancouver. For a more casual presentation, simply toss the sliced endive with the other ingredients. ■

FOR DRESSING
- 2 teaspoons anise seeds
- 3 tablespoons chopped shallots
- 1/3 cup vegetable oil
- 3 tablespoons white wine vinegar
- 1/4 teaspoon salt
- 1/8 teaspoon freshly ground black pepper

FOR SALAD
- 2 firm but ripe pears, preferably Bosc
- 2 tablespoons unsalted butter
- Salt and freshly ground black pepper
- 5 Belgian endives, trimmed and cut crosswise into 1/2-inch-thick slices
- 1 cup crumbled Stilton (about 5 ounces)

GARNISH: 2 tablespoons chopped fresh flat-leaf parsley

MAKE THE DRESSING: Toast anise seeds in a dry small heavy skillet over moderate heat, stirring, until fragrant, about 1 minute. Let cool.

Combine anise seeds, shallots, oil, vinegar, salt, and pepper in a blender and blend until very smooth; thin with a little water, if desired.

MAKE THE SALAD: Halve pears and core, preferably with a melon ball cutter. Cut into 1/4-inch-thick wedges. Heat butter in a 12-inch heavy skillet over moderately high heat until foam subsides. Add half of pears and cook, turning occasionally, until golden, about 3 minutes total. Transfer pears with a slotted spoon to a plate and season with salt and pepper. Cook remaining pears in same manner.

Toss endive with just enough dressing to coat and arrange half on a platter. Top with half of pears and half of Stilton. Make another layer with remaining endive, pears, and Stilton, then drizzle with some of remaining dressing and sprinkle with parsley.

Avocado, Orange, and Jicama Salad

SERVES 4
ACTIVE TIME: 20 MINUTES ■ START TO FINISH: 20 MINUTES

■ This cool, pretty, lightly curried salad is a study in contrasts, in the mouth as well as on the plate. Creamy, pale green avocado meets crisp, ivory-colored jicama and juicy, bright oranges. ■

- 3 navel oranges
- 1/2 teaspoon curry powder
- 1/2 teaspoon salt
- 1/4 teaspoon ground cumin
- 1/4 teaspoon sugar
- 2 tablespoons white wine vinegar
- 2 tablespoons extra-virgin olive oil
- 1 medium jicama (3/4 pound), peeled and cut into 1/4-inch-thick matchsticks
- 2 firm but ripe California avocados

Cut peel and pith from oranges with a sharp paring knife. Working over a bowl, cut segments free from membranes, letting them drop into bowl; squeeze enough juice from membranes into a large bowl to measure 1/4 cup. Whisk curry powder, salt, cumin, sugar, and vinegar into orange juice. Add oil in a slow stream, whisking until well blended. Add jicama, tossing to coat.

Halve, pit, and peel avocados. Thinly slice crosswise.

Lift jicama from vinaigrette and arrange on four plates, along with orange segments and avocado. Pour remaining vinaigrette over and around salads.

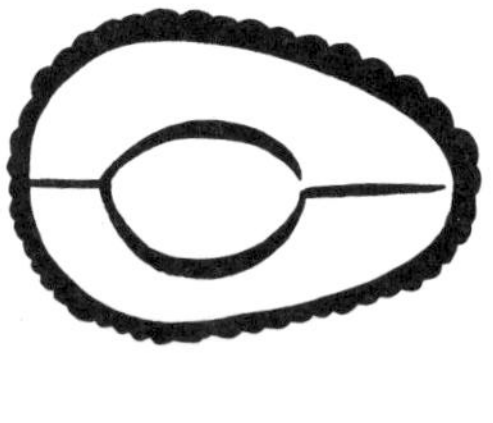

Parsley, Fennel, and Celery Root Salad

SERVES 10

ACTIVE TIME: 45 MINUTES ■ START TO FINISH: 45 MINUTES

■ People don't often think of parsley as a salad green, but tempered by dressing, it can be the star of the show. Curly and flat-leaf parsley taste pretty much the same: each has a fresh, delicate bitterness that hits the palate a little differently because of the distinctive shape of the leaves. The two combine to make this salad a particularly refreshing respite during a Thanksgiving feast or any other extensive, rich meal. We include celery root and fennel (look for a bulb with fronds attached, since you'll need them) for their crunch factor. ■

- 1 large fennel bulb with fronds (1¼ pounds), stalks cut off and discarded, fronds reserved
- 4½ cups loosely packed small fresh flat-leaf parsley sprigs (from 3 large bunches)
- 1½ cups loosely packed small curly parsley sprigs (from 2 large bunches)
- 1 medium celery root (celeriac; 1 pound), peeled with a sharp knife and cut into ⅛-inch-thick matchsticks
- 2½–3 tablespoons fresh lemon juice (to taste)
- 2 tablespoons minced shallots
- ¾ teaspoon sugar
- ½ teaspoon salt
- ¼ teaspoon freshly ground black pepper
- ⅓ cup olive oil

SPECIAL EQUIPMENT: a mandoline or other adjustable-blade slicer, such as a Japanese Benriner

Tear enough fennel fronds into small sprigs to measure 1½ cups; discard remainder. Quarter bulb lengthwise, then cut lengthwise into paper-thin slices with slicer. Toss together sliced fennel, fronds, parsley, and celery root in a large bowl.

Whisk together lemon juice, shallots, sugar, salt, pepper, and oil in a small bowl. Toss salad with dressing.

Roasted Beet Salad

SERVES 4 AS A FIRST COURSE

ACTIVE TIME: 25 MINUTES ■ START TO FINISH: 2¼ HOURS

■ Roasting beets concentrates their earthy sweetness and turns them satiny tender, making them a wonderful foil for toasted almonds and crisp, juicy sticks of Asian pear. This salad is also visually striking: the magenta juices of the beets bleed into the slices of white pear, marbleizing them, and dark green mâche or arugula is scattered over all. ■

- 1 bunch beets (1¼ pounds with greens, or ¾ pound without), trimmed
- ¼ cup sliced almonds
- 3 tablespoons olive oil
- Salt
- 1 tablespoon minced shallot
- 1 tablespoon fresh lemon juice
- 1½ tablespoons red wine vinegar
- ¼ teaspoon sugar
- 1 large Asian pear (see page 810)
- 3 ounces mâche or baby arugula (3 cups)

Put a rack in middle of oven and preheat oven to 400°F.

Tightly wrap beets in double layers of foil, making two packages. Roast on a baking sheet until tender, 1¼ to 1½ hours. Cool until warm in foil packages (the steam makes beets easier to peel), about 30 minutes.

Meanwhile, cook almonds in oil in a small skillet over moderate heat, stirring occasionally, until pale golden. Cool almonds in oil (nuts will darken as they cool). With a slotted spoon, transfer almonds to a small bowl, and season with salt.

Stir together shallot, lemon juice, vinegar, sugar, ½ teaspoon salt, and oil from almonds in a large bowl.

Slip skins from beets and halve large beets. Cut beets into ¼-inch-thick slices. Add to dressing, tossing to coat.

Quarter and core pear. Cut crosswise into matchsticks. Arrange beets on a platter and drizzle with any dressing remaining in bowl. Top with mâche and pear, then sprinkle with almonds.

COOK'S NOTE

■ The beets can be tossed with the dressing up to 1 day ahead and refrigerated, covered. Bring to room temperature before serving. (Store the toasted almonds, covered, at room temperature.)

Old-Fashioned Potato Salad

SERVES 6

ACTIVE TIME: 15 MINUTES ■ START TO FINISH: 45 MINUTES

■ The key to a great potato salad is to start with the right spuds. Round Maine potatoes, long whites, and yellow-fleshed varieties like Yukon Golds all work, but drier russet, or baking, potatoes are higher in starch and turn to mush. We simmer potatoes whole in their jackets, which makes for good flavor and texture, because they don't get waterlogged. It's helpful to buy potatoes that are all the same size so they cook evenly. Start potatoes in cold, not boiling, water, or the outsides will be done before the insides. And keep the water at a steady simmer. (This is a point to remember when cooking all sorts of vegetables: a rolling boil will jostle them, causing them to collide and break apart.) After draining, peel the potatoes (the skins are often bitter) and toss them in vinegar while they are still hot. The tart acidity will rapidly penetrate deep inside them, giving the finished salad a general liveliness. We experimented with several vinegars in this recipe, and the consensus was that the salad is much fresher-tasting with cider vinegar, an unfashionable but terrific staple that belongs in every kitchen cupboard. ■

2 pounds boiling potatoes
3 tablespoons cider vinegar
1 teaspoon salt
3/4 cup chopped celery
1/2 cup chopped white onion
3 hard-boiled large eggs, chopped
1 cup mayonnaise
Freshly ground black pepper

Combine potatoes with well-salted cold water to cover by 2 inches in a 3-quart saucepan and bring to a boil. Reduce heat and simmer, uncovered, until potatoes are just tender, 15 to 25 minutes, depending on size. Drain and cool slightly.

Meanwhile, whisk together vinegar and salt in a large bowl until salt is dissolved.

When potatoes are just cool enough to handle, peel and cut into 1-inch pieces, adding to vinegar mixture as you cut them, tossing gently with a rubber spatula to coat. Cool to room temperature.

Add celery, onion, eggs, mayonnaise, and salt and pepper to taste to potatoes and stir gently to combine. Serve at room temperature or chilled.

Potato and Thyme Salad

SERVES 6

ACTIVE TIME: 10 MINUTES ■ START TO FINISH: 25 MINUTES

■ When you find beautiful, small, truly new (freshly dug) potatoes at the farmers market, this is what you want to do with them. No suburban backyard potato salad here: there is no mayonnaise, hard-boiled egg, or celery to distract from the earthy flavor of potatoes heightened with good olive oil and fresh thyme. Simple and elegant, the salad is perfectly at home at a dinner party, but the absence of mayo or eggs means it is perfect at a summer picnic as well. The recipe is from the peerless Darina Allen, of Ballymaloe Cooking School, in County Cork, Ireland. ■

1 3/4 pounds small (1 1/2- to 2-inch-diameter) red boiling potatoes
1–2 tablespoons fresh thyme leaves and blossoms (to taste)
1/3 cup extra-virgin olive oil
Salt and freshly ground black pepper

Combine potatoes with well-salted cold water to cover by 2 inches in a 3-quart saucepan and bring to a boil. Reduce heat and simmer, uncovered, until potatoes are just tender, 15 to 20 minutes. Drain and cool for about 10 minutes.

When potatoes are just cool enough to handle, quarter and put in a large bowl. Sprinkle with thyme, oil, and salt and pepper to taste, tossing to coat well. Serve at room temperature.

Warm German Potato Salad

SERVES 6

ACTIVE TIME: 20 MINUTES ■ START TO FINISH: 40 MINUTES

■ This isn't a refined potato salad, but a bold one that makes a great side dish year-round. It's as good with a pork roast in the dead of winter as it is with grilled bratwursts on an afternoon in June. ■

- 3 pounds small (2-inch-diameter) red boiling potatoes, peeled if desired
- 10 bacon slices (½ pound), cut into ¼-inch-wide strips
- 1 large onion, chopped
- ½ teaspoon sugar
- 3 tablespoons cider vinegar
- ¾ cup beef stock or store-bought broth
- 2 tablespoons chopped fresh flat-leaf parsley
- ½ teaspoon salt, or to taste
- ⅛ teaspoon freshly ground black pepper, or to taste

OPTIONAL GARNISH: chopped fresh flat-leaf parsley

Combine potatoes with cold salted water (1 tablespoon salt per every 4 quarts water) to cover by 1 inch in a 6-quart pot, bring to a simmer, and simmer until just tender, about 20 minutes.

Meanwhile, cook bacon in a large heavy skillet over moderate heat, stirring, until browned and crisp, about 10 minutes. With a slotted spoon, transfer to paper towels to drain. Set skillet aside.

Drain potatoes. When just cool enough to handle, cut crosswise into ¼-inch-thick slices. Transfer to a large bowl, add bacon, and cover to keep warm.

Pour off all but 3 tablespoons fat from skillet. Add onion and cook over moderately high heat, stirring, until softened, about 3 minutes. Add sugar, 2 tablespoons vinegar, and stock, bring to a simmer, and simmer until slightly reduced, about 3 minutes.

Add onion mixture to potatoes, along with parsley, remaining 1 tablespoon vinegar, salt, and pepper, and toss gently.

Serve potato salad warm or at room temperature, sprinkled with additional parsley, if desired.

Gingered Noodle Salad with Mango and Cucumber

SERVES 6

ACTIVE TIME: 15 MINUTES ■ START TO FINISH: 30 MINUTES

■ This salad is wonderful with grilled chicken, pork tenderloin, even steak. It's inspired by Southeast Asian flavors, but the ingredients, including the bean thread noodles, can be found at the supermarket (look in the ethnic foods aisle). Dried semitransparent filaments made from mung bean starch, bean thread noodles must be soaked in cold water to soften them before cooking. Briefly boiled, they become slippery and translucent. Although practically flavorless, they readily take on the flavors of other ingredients. ■

FOR VINAIGRETTE

- 6 tablespoons seasoned rice vinegar
- 1½ tablespoons vegetable oil
- 1½ teaspoons chopped peeled fresh ginger
- 1 teaspoon minced jalapeño or serrano chile (including seeds), or to taste
- 1 garlic clove, chopped

FOR SALAD

- ½ pound bean thread (cellophane) noodles
- 1 seedless cucumber (usually plastic wrapped), halved lengthwise and thinly sliced diagonally
- 1 bunch scallions, thinly sliced diagonally (1 cup)
- 1 firm but ripe mango, peeled, pitted, and thinly sliced
- 2 thin carrots, very thinly sliced diagonally
- 1 cup loosely packed fresh cilantro sprigs

MAKE THE VINAIGRETTE: Combine all ingredients in a blender and blend until smooth.

MAKE THE SALAD: Soak noodles in cold water to cover until pliable, about 15 minutes. Drain noodles and cut in half with scissors.

Cook noodles in a 4-quart saucepan of boiling (unsalted) water, stirring occasionally, until just tender, about 2 minutes. Drain in a colander and rinse under cold water to stop the cooking. Drain noodles again well, then spread out on paper towels and blot excess liquid.

Toss noodles with dressing in a large bowl. Add cucumber, scallions, mango, and carrots and gently toss until just combined. Top with cilantro sprigs.

Warm Pasta Salad with Roasted Corn and Poblanos

SERVES 6 AS A MAIN COURSE
ACTIVE TIME: 50 MINUTES ■ START TO FINISH: 1 HOUR

■ Pasta in the summertime can be boring. But adjust your flavors slightly—tomatoes, garlic, and olive oil, yes, but also toasted corn and pumpkin seeds, smoky green chiles and fragrant cumin, fresh oregano instead of basil, and crumbles of fresh white cheese instead of Parmesan—and you've not only switched continents, you have a new (albeit slightly more involved) way to serve pasta. Dry-roasting or toasting is a technique used in Mexican cuisine to bring up the flavors of many ingredients. We created this salad as a main course, but you can also serve it as a side dish. ■

- 4 poblano chiles (1 pound total; see Glossary)
- 1 jalapeño chile
- 8 medium tomatoes (2 pounds total), coarsely chopped
- 3 tablespoons chopped fresh oregano
- 2 tablespoons chopped fresh cilantro
- 1/3 cup green (hulled) pumpkin seeds
- 4 ears corn, shucked and kernels cut off
- 1 large white onion, cut into 1/2-inch-thick rounds
- 1/4 cup olive oil
- 3 garlic cloves, minced
- 1 teaspoon ground cumin
- Salt and freshly ground black pepper
- 3/4 pound short pasta, such as gemelli or rotini
- 1 1/2 cups crumbled *queso fresco* (Mexican fresh white cheese) or ricotta salata (see Glossary)

OPTIONAL GARNISH: fresh cilantro leaves

Roast chiles on grates of gas burners over moderately high heat, turning occasionally with tongs, until skins are blackened, 5 to 8 minutes. (Or broil chiles on rack of a broiler pan about 2 inches from heat, turning occasionally.) Transfer chiles to a bowl, cover, and let steam for 10 minutes.

When cool enough to handle, peel poblanos, discard seeds and ribs, and coarsely chop. Peel jalapeño and chop (discard seeds before chopping if you want a less spicy salad). Transfer chiles to a large serving bowl and stir in tomatoes, oregano, and cilantro.

Toast pumpkin seeds in a dry 9- to 10-inch cast-iron skillet over moderate heat, stirring frequently, until puffed and lightly browned, 2 to 3 minutes (seeds will pop as they puff). Transfer to a small bowl.

Add half of corn to skillet and dry-roast over moderate heat, stirring frequently, until browned in spots, 4 to 5 minutes. Transfer to tomato mixture. Cook remaining corn in same manner and add to tomato mixture.

Add onion to skillet and dry-roast, turning frequently, until browned but still slightly crisp. Transfer to a cutting board to cool slightly.

Add oil to skillet and heat over moderate heat. Add garlic and cumin and cook, stirring, until fragrant, about 30 seconds. Stir into corn mixture. Coarsely chop onion and stir into corn mixture. Season vegetables with salt and pepper.

Cook pasta in a large pot of boiling salted water (1 tablespoon salt per every 4 quarts water) until al dente; drain.

Add pasta to corn mixture and toss. Season with salt. Sprinkle with pumpkin seeds and cheese and serve warm or at room temperature.

COOK'S NOTES

- The chiles can be roasted and the corn and onion dry-roasted up to 2 hours ahead. Mix with the tomatoes and keep, covered, at room temperature.
- The pumpkin seeds can be toasted up to 2 days ahead and kept in an airtight container at room temperature.

Crunchy Vegetable and Brown Rice Salad

SERVES 4 AS A MAIN COURSE
ACTIVE TIME: 20 MINUTES ■ START TO FINISH: 35 MINUTES

■ We found that if we boiled brown rice in lots of water, like pasta, rather than steaming it in the usual way, it works better for a salad: less starch, and a wonderful chew. The chicken stock adds flavor, but you can use vegetable broth if you want to make this a strictly vegetarian dish. ■

- 1/2 cup short-grain brown rice
- 1 medium zucchini, cut into 1/4-inch dice
- 2 celery ribs, cut into 1/4-inch dice
- 1 carrot, cut into 1/4-inch dice
- 1 yellow bell pepper, cored, seeded, and cut into 1/4-inch dice
- 1/4 cup chicken stock or store-bought low-sodium broth
- 2 tablespoons fresh lemon juice
- 1 tablespoon coarse-grain mustard
- 1 tablespoon olive oil
- 1/2 teaspoon salt
- 1/4 teaspoon freshly ground black pepper
- 1/2 bunch arugula (4 ounces), coarse stems discarded and leaves chopped
- 4 scallions, chopped

Fill a 2-quart saucepan three-quarters full with well-salted water and bring to a boil. Add rice and boil, uncovered, stirring occasionally, until al dente, about 25 minutes. Drain in a colander and rinse under cold running water until cool. Drain well.

Meanwhile, blanch zucchini, celery, carrot, and bell pepper in a large saucepan of boiling salted water (1 tablespoon salt per every 4 quarts water) for 1 minute. Drain in a sieve and transfer to a bowl of ice and cold water to stop the cooking, then drain well.

Whisk together stock, lemon juice, mustard, oil, salt, and pepper in a large bowl. Add rice, blanched vegetables, arugula, and scallions, tossing to combine well. Season with salt and pepper. Serve at room temperature.

Sushi-Roll Rice Salad

SERVES 4 AS A MAIN COURSE
ACTIVE TIME: 40 MINUTES ■ START TO FINISH: 1 1/2 HOURS

■ This deconstructed sushi roll—rice, avocado, cucumber, pickled ginger, shredded nori, and wasabi—looks like an intricate work of art, but it's surprisingly simple to prepare. Serve the salad as part of a buffet or with grilled meats. It can also double as a first course or a side dish. Most of the Japanese ingredients are available in larger supermarkets as well as in Asian markets, or see Sources. ■

- 1 1/2 cups sushi rice (Japanese medium-grain rice)
- 1 tablespoon sesame seeds
- 1 3/4 cups plus 1 1/2 tablespoons water
- 1/4 cup seasoned rice vinegar
- 1 tablespoon sugar
- 1 teaspoon salt
- 1 medium carrot
- 1 1/4 teaspoons wasabi paste (see Glossary)
- 1 1/2 tablespoons vegetable oil
- 1/2 large seedless cucumber (usually plastic wrapped), peeled, halved lengthwise, seeded, and chopped
- 3 scallions, thinly sliced diagonally
- 3 tablespoons drained sliced Japanese pickled ginger, coarsely chopped
- 1 firm but ripe California avocado
- 8 fresh *shiso* leaves (optional; see Glossary)
- 1 (6-inch) square toasted nori (dried laver; see Glossary), cut into very thin strips with scissors

Rinse rice in several changes of cold water in a bowl until water is almost clear. Drain in a colander for 30 minutes.

Meanwhile, toast seeds in a dry small heavy skillet over moderate heat, stirring, until fragrant and a shade or two darker. Transfer to a small bowl to cool.

Combine rice and 1 3/4 cups water in a 3- to 4-quart heavy saucepan and bring to a boil, then reduce heat and simmer, covered, for 2 minutes. Remove from heat and let rice stand, covered, for 10 minutes (do not lift lid).

Meanwhile, combine vinegar, sugar, and salt in a very small saucepan and bring just to a boil, stirring constantly until sugar is dissolved. Remove from heat and cool for 2 minutes.

Spread rice in a large shallow baking pan. Sprinkle with vinegar mixture and toss with a wooden spoon.

With a vegetable peeler, shave lengthwise slices from carrot, then cut slices diagonally into 1/4-inch-wide strips.

Whisk together wasabi, remaining 1 1/2 tablespoons water, and oil in a large bowl. Add rice, carrot, cucumber, scallions, pickled ginger, and sesame seeds and toss gently.

Halve, pit, and peel avocado. Cut crosswise into 1/4-inch-thick slices. Arrange 2 *shiso* leaves, if using, on each of four plates. Top with avocado and rice salad and sprinkle with nori strips.

Tabbouleh

SERVES 4 TO 6
ACTIVE TIME: 40 MINUTES ■ START TO FINISH: 40 MINUTES

■ This tabbouleh, gently seasoned and made refreshingly tart with lemon juice, highlights parsley, one of the world's more versatile herbs. The bulgur is merely a useful (and delicious) vehicle for it. Serve this Middle Eastern salad with pitas or other flatbread. ■

- 1/2 cup fine bulgur
- 3 tablespoons olive oil
- 2 cups finely chopped fresh flat-leaf parsley
- 1/2 cup finely chopped fresh mint
- 2 medium tomatoes, cut into 1/4-inch dice
- 1/2 seedless cucumber (usually plastic wrapped), peeled, halved lengthwise, seeded, and cut into 1/4-inch pieces
- 3 tablespoons fresh lemon juice
- 3/4 teaspoon salt
- 1/4 teaspoon freshly ground black pepper

Stir together bulgur and 1 tablespoon oil in a heatproof bowl. Pour 1 cup boiling water over bulgur, then cover bowl tightly with plastic wrap and let stand for 15 minutes.

Drain bulgur in a sieve, pressing on it to remove excess liquid. Transfer bulgur to a bowl and toss with remaining 2 tablespoons oil and remaining ingredients until well combined.

Bulgur and Lentil Salad with Tarragon and Walnuts

SERVES 4 AS A MAIN COURSE, 6 AS A SIDE DISH
ACTIVE TIME: 30 MINUTES ■ START TO FINISH: 50 MINUTES

■ This salad may be brown, but it is anything but a relic from your Mother Earth days. It's elegant, and the tarragon and walnuts give it finesse. ■

- 1/3 cup finely chopped shallots
- 3 tablespoons tarragon white-wine vinegar
- 1/2 cup brown or green lentils, preferably *lentilles du Puy* (French green lentils; see Glossary)
- Salt and freshly ground black pepper
- 1 cup bulgur, preferably fine
- 1 1/2 cups water
- 1/2 cup finely chopped celery
- 1/2 cup finely shredded carrot
- 3 tablespoons finely chopped fresh tarragon
- 3 tablespoons extra-virgin olive oil
- 1/2 cup walnuts, lightly toasted (see Tips, page 938) and finely chopped

Combine shallots and 1 tablespoon vinegar in a small bowl; set aside.

Combine lentils with water to cover by 2 inches in a small saucepan, bring to a simmer, and simmer, uncovered, until just tender but not falling apart, 15 to 20 minutes. Drain well and add hot lentils to shallots. Season with salt and pepper and cool, stirring occasionally.

Meanwhile, combine bulgur, 1 teaspoon salt, and 1 1/2 cups water in a small heavy saucepan, bring to a simmer, and simmer, covered, until water is absorbed, 12 to 15 minutes. Transfer bulgur to a large bowl and cool completely, stirring occasionally.

Add lentil and shallot mixture to bulgur, along with celery, carrot, tarragon, remaining 2 tablespoons vinegar, oil, walnuts, salt to taste, and 1/8 teaspoon pepper, and toss well.

COOK'S NOTE

■ The salad can be made up to 1 day ahead and refrigerated, covered. Bring to room temperature before serving.

Wheat Berry and Barley Salad with Smoked Mozzarella

SERVES 6 AS A MAIN COURSE, 8 TO 10 AS A SIDE DISH
ACTIVE TIME: 25 MINUTES ■ START TO FINISH: 1 1/2 HOURS

■ If you haven't cooked with whole grains, this is a good place to start. This salad possesses a wonderful texture and a satisfyingly substantial chew, and it's pretty, with the cream-colored barley and golden wheat berries. The wheat berries aren't remotely exotic—they're what's milled into flour. Look for them in natural foods stores. ■

- 1 cup wheat berries
- 1 cup pearl barley
- 2 garlic cloves
- Salt
- 1 small red onion, finely chopped
- ¼ cup balsamic vinegar
- ¼ cup olive oil, preferably extra-virgin
- 1½ cups corn (from 2–3 large ears), cooked
- ½ pound smoked mozzarella, finely diced
- 1 pint cherry tomatoes, halved
- 6 scallions, finely chopped
- ½ cup chopped fresh chives
- ½ teaspoon freshly ground black pepper

Add wheat berries to a large pot of boiling salted water (1 tablespoon salt per every 4 quarts water), stir, reduce heat, and simmer for 30 minutes.

Stir barley into pot and simmer for 40 minutes.

Meanwhile, with a sharp heavy knife, mince and mash garlic to a paste with ½ teaspoon salt. Stir together garlic paste, onion, vinegar, and oil in a large bowl.

Drain grains well, add to onion mixture, and toss well. Cool completely.

Add corn, mozzarella, cherry tomatoes, scallions, chives, 2 teaspoons salt, and pepper to grains and toss well.

COOK'S NOTE

■ The salad can be made up to 1 day ahead and refrigerated, covered. Bring to room temperature before serving.

Melon, Arugula, and Serrano Ham with Smoked Paprika Dressing

SERVES 6 AS A FIRST COURSE, 4 AS A LIGHT MAIN COURSE
ACTIVE TIME: 30 MINUTES ■ START TO FINISH: 30 MINUTES

■ This is a full meal for when it's too hot to eat anything heavy. The melons are intoxicating and sweet, and the tangy, rosy Serrano, a Spanish cured ham that has a heftier texture than prosciutto, adds its salt to the arugula's pepper. Smoked paprika gives the dressing adobe flecks. ■

FOR DRESSING

- 1½ tablespoons fresh lime juice
- ½ teaspoon Spanish smoked paprika (mild or hot; see Glossary)
- ¼ teaspoon salt
- ⅛ teaspoon freshly ground black pepper
- 5 tablespoons mild extra-virgin olive oil

FOR SALAD

- 4 cups 1-inch pieces cantaloupe (from 2½- to 3-pound melon)
- 4 cups 1-inch pieces honeydew (from 2½- to 3-pound melon)
- 1½ pounds arugula (4 large bunches), coarse stems discarded
- ½ pound sliced (1/16-inch-thick) Serrano ham (see Sources), cut crosswise into ¾-inch-wide strips
- Salt and freshly ground black pepper

MAKE THE DRESSING: Whisk together lime juice, paprika, salt, and pepper in a small bowl. Add oil in a slow stream, whisking until well blended.

MAKE THE SALAD: Toss cantaloupe and honeydew with half of dressing in a medium bowl. Toss arugula and ham with remaining dressing in a large bowl. Add melon and salt and pepper to taste, tossing gently. Serve immediately.

Shellfish Watermelon Ceviche

SERVES 6 AS A FIRST COURSE
ACTIVE TIME: 45 MINUTES ■ START TO FINISH: 1¾ HOURS (INCLUDES CHILLING)

■ Traditionally, ceviche begins with raw or barely cooked seafood that is marinated in a spicy lemon or lime juice mixture. The citrus acid turns translucent seafood white and nearly opaque; although it looks cooked, it isn't. Briefly poaching the shellfish eliminates any food-safety concerns, and tossing it with ginger, chiles, onion, and watermelon makes for a bright, beautiful salad. ■

- 1 navel orange
- ½ cup plus 2 tablespoons fresh orange juice
- ¼ cup fresh lime juice
- ½ cup diced (¼-inch) seeded watermelon
- ½ teaspoon finely grated peeled fresh ginger
- 1½ tablespoons finely diced red onion
- 2–3 teaspoons finely chopped jalapeño or serrano chile (to taste), including seeds
- ½ teaspoon salt
- ¼ pound sea scallops, tough side muscle removed from each if necessary, scallops cut into ½-inch pieces
- ¼ pound large shrimp in shells (21–25 per pound), peeled, deveined, and cut into ½-inch pieces
- ¼ pound cooked lobster, cut into ½-inch pieces
- 1½ tablespoons chopped fresh mint
- 3 small heads Bibb lettuce, leaves separated (optional)

Cut peel and white pith from orange with a sharp paring knife, then cut segments free from membranes. Chop enough segments to measure ¼ cup; discard remainder or reserve for another use. Combine chopped orange, orange juice, lime juice, watermelon, ginger, onion, jalapeño, and salt in a large bowl and stir until combined.

Bring a 1-quart saucepan of well-salted water to a boil, then add scallops and poach at a bare simmer until just cooked through, about 1 minute. With a slotted spoon, transfer to a bowl of ice and cold water to stop the cooking. Return water to a boil, add shrimp, and poach at a bare simmer until just cooked through, about 1 minute. Drain and transfer to bowl of ice water.

Drain scallops and shrimp well and pat dry.

Add scallops, shrimp, lobster, and mint to watermelon mixture and toss to combine, then season with salt. Refrigerate, covered, for at least 1 hour.

Serve ceviche with lettuce leaves on the side, if desired (use a slotted spoon for transferring ceviche to leaves).

COOK'S NOTE

■ The ceviche can be refrigerated for up to 3 hours.

Salade Niçoise

SERVES 6 AS A MAIN COURSE
ACTIVE TIME: 40 MINUTES ■ START TO FINISH: 40 MINUTES

■ For this composed salad, you will want to use good canned tuna packed in olive oil. The closest thing to Niçoise tuna is Ortiz's Bonito del Norte brand, but it can be tough to find. Of the supermarket brands, we like Progresso light tuna. We're also fond of Genova and La Giara (this last is *very* expensive—about $10—but it is available at many specialty foods shops). If you've been saving that fancy bottle of French olive oil for a special occasion, now is the time to use it. Our recipe, which includes the unusual addition of green bell pepper, is based on one we sampled in the village of Biot, outside Nice. ■

FOR DRESSING

- 3 tablespoons chopped shallots
- 1½ tablespoons fresh lemon juice
- 2 teaspoons Dijon mustard
- ½ teaspoon salt
- ⅛ teaspoon freshly ground black pepper
- 5 tablespoons extra-virgin olive oil
- 2 tablespoons coarsely chopped fresh flat-leaf parsley

FOR SALAD

- 1 pound fingerling potatoes or small boiling potatoes
- ½ pound green beans, trimmed
- Salt
- 1 green bell pepper, cored, seeded, and cut into thin strips

2 heads Boston lettuce (12 ounces total), torn into bite-sized pieces
3 hard-boiled large eggs, quartered
3 medium tomatoes, cut into 8 wedges each
2 (6-ounce) cans tuna in oil, drained and broken into chunks
1/4 cup Niçoise olives
1 tablespoon drained capers
2 tablespoons chopped fresh flat-leaf parsley

MAKE THE DRESSING: Blend shallots with lemon juice, mustard, salt, and pepper in a blender. With motor running, add oil in a slow stream, scraping down sides of blender as necessary, and blend until well combined. Add parsley and blend until finely chopped.

MAKE THE SALAD: Combine potatoes and cold well-salted water to cover by 2 inches in a 4-quart heavy saucepan and bring to a simmer. Simmer, uncovered, until just tender, 15 to 20 minutes. Drain.

Meanwhile, cook beans in a 2-quart saucepan of boiling well-salted water, uncovered, until crisp-tender, about 5 minutes. Drain in a colander, rinse under cold water to stop the cooking, and drain again; pat dry.

When cool enough to handle, peel potatoes and halve lengthwise. Toss with 2 tablespoons dressing and salt to taste in a large bowl. Add beans and bell pepper and toss.

Toss lettuce with just enough dressing to coat in another large bowl, then spread on a large platter. Scatter potatoes, beans, and bell pepper over lettuce and top with eggs, tomatoes, and tuna chunks. Drizzle more dressing over salad and top with olives, capers, and parsley.

The Perfect Hard-Boiled Egg

There are almost as many ways to hard-boil eggs as there are cookbooks. This procedure produces bright yellow velvety yolks (with no gray ring) every time; it's the one that the food scientist Shirley Corriher uses in her book *CookWise*. You'll find eggs easier to peel if you use ones that are at least a week old (not a concern if you buy them at the supermarket rather than a farmers market). Ease of peeling is related to pH level, and the older an egg is, the more alkaline it is (that's why you shouldn't add vinegar to the water). Put the eggs into a large heavy pot and cover them with 1 1/2 inches of cold tap water. Partially cover the pot and bring the water to a rolling boil. Reduce the heat to low, cover the pot completely, and cook the eggs for 30 seconds. Remove from the heat and let the eggs stand in the hot water, still covered, for 15 minutes. Then run the eggs under cold water for about 5 minutes—this stops the cooking and prevents yolk discoloration.

Chilled Seafood Salad with Herbed Olive Oil

SERVES 12 AS A FIRST COURSE
ACTIVE TIME: 40 MINUTES ■ START TO FINISH: 1 3/4 HOURS (INCLUDES CHILLING)

■ Sophisticated, elegant, and clean-tasting, this salad is perfect for the holidays. The key to its success is cooking the scallops, shrimp, and squid separately in the same pot of boiling water. That way, the flavor of each is preserved and sparkles on its own. The herbed oil drizzled over all adds a splash of jade green and fresh flavor, and a light crumble of sea salt reminds us that we are eating food from the sea. This recipe can be halved to serve six, but do not halve the herbed oil—a smaller amount will not blend well in the blender. ■

FOR HERBED OIL

- 3/4 cup extra-virgin olive oil
- 3/4 cup coarsely chopped fresh flat-leaf parsley
- 1/2 cup chopped fresh chives
- 1 tablespoon chopped fresh rosemary
- 1/2 teaspoon salt

FOR SALAD

- 1 pound cleaned squid
- 1 pound medium shrimp in shells (31–35 per pound), peeled, tail and first shell segment left intact, and deveined
- 1 pound small sea scallops, tough side muscle removed from each if necessary
- 2 lemons, thinly sliced
- 1 tablespoon fresh lemon juice, or to taste
- 1/4 teaspoon coarse sea salt, or to taste, plus additional for serving

MAKE THE HERBED OIL: Blend together all ingredients in a blender on high speed for 1 minute. Pour oil through a fine-mesh sieve into a bowl, pressing hard on solids; discard solids. Cover and refrigerate.

MAKE THE SALAD: Rinse squid under cold running water and pat dry. If squid are large, halve rings of tentacles, then cut longer tentacles crosswise into 2-inch-long pieces. Pull off flaps from squid bodies and cut into 1/4-inch-thick slices. Cut bodies into 1/4-inch-thick rings.

Cook shrimp in a 4-quart saucepan of boiling well-salted water until just cooked through, about 1 minute. With a slotted spoon, transfer to a large bowl of ice and cold water to stop the cooking. Add scallops to boiling water and cook at a bare simmer until just cooked through, about 2 minutes. With slotted spoon, transfer scallops to bowl of ice water. Add squid to boiling water and cook until just opaque, 20 to 30 seconds. Drain and transfer to bowl of ice water.

Drain all seafood well and transfer to a large bowl. Refrigerate, covered, until chilled, at least 1 hour.

An hour before serving, toss seafood with lemon slices and lemon juice and return to refrigerator. Return herbed oil to room temperature.

Divide seafood among twelve bowls and drizzle with herbed oil. Sprinkle salads with sea salt and serve additional sea salt on the side.

COOK'S NOTES

- The herbed oil can be made up to 2 days ahead and refrigerated, covered. (Bring to room temperature before using.)
- The cooked seafood (without the lemon) can be refrigerated for up to 1 day.
- If your sea salt is very coarse, crush it lightly in a mortar with a pestle or with the bottom of a heavy skillet.

Crab Louis

SERVES 4 AS A MAIN COURSE
ACTIVE TIME: 20 MINUTES ■ START TO FINISH: 30 MINUTES

■ The Gilded Age was all about gilding the lily. At least two San Francisco establishments from that period, Solari's restaurant and the St. Francis Hotel, have laid claim to this classic, a plate of crabmeat draped with a spicy mayonnaise and garnished with capers, wedges of tomato, and hard-boiled egg. Both places reportedly started serving crab Louis around 1915. You can use lump crabmeat for this recipe, but big, meaty Dungeness crabs (named for the small fishing village in Washington State where they were first harvested in the nineteenth century) are even better. Live Dungeness crabs are available all along the West Coast and in high-quality fish stores in the rest of the country. Avoid lightweight, soft-shelled ones—they were harvested too early, after a seasonal molt, and will contain little meat. A great mail-order source for frozen cooked Dungeness crabs (as well as live fresh crabs) is the Pacific Seafood Company (see Sources). ■

- 1 cup mayonnaise
- 1/4 cup ketchup-style chili sauce
- 1/4 cup minced scallions
- 2 tablespoons minced green olives
- 2 teaspoons fresh lemon juice
- 1 teaspoon Worcestershire sauce
- 1 teaspoon bottled horseradish
- Salt and freshly ground black pepper
- Shredded iceberg lettuce for serving
- 1 1/2 pounds jumbo lump crabmeat, picked over for shells and cartilage

GARNISH: capers, tomato wedges, hard-boiled eggs, and lemon wedges

Whisk together mayonnaise, chili sauce, scallions, olives, lemon juice, Worcestershire sauce, horseradish, and salt and pepper to taste in a small bowl.

Line four plates with shredded lettuce. Divide crabmeat among plates and sprinkle crabmeat with capers. Arrange tomatoes, hard-boiled eggs, and lemon wedges around the crabmeat. Serve with dressing.

Tarragon Lobster Salad

SERVES 4 TO 6 AS A MAIN COURSE
ACTIVE TIME: 1 HOUR ■ START TO FINISH: 2 HOURS

■ This salad is succulent, with chunks of lobster highlighted with a touch of tarragon. Mounded into a tomato (or just on its own), it makes a delightful lunch; piled into a warm, buttery hot dog bun, it's a terrific version of a New England clam shack classic. ■

- 3 tablespoons fine sea salt
- 4 (1½-pound) live lobsters
- ¼ cup finely chopped shallots
- 3 tablespoons fresh lemon juice
- ½ teaspoon salt
- ⅓ cup mayonnaise
- 2 tablespoons finely chopped fresh tarragon
- ¼ teaspoon freshly ground black pepper

ACCOMPANIMENT: lettuce leaves or hot dog buns (preferably top-split), buttered and grilled or toasted

Bring 6 quarts water and sea salt to a boil in an 8- to 10-quart pot. Plunge 2 lobsters headfirst into water and cook, covered, over high heat for 7 minutes from time lobsters enter water. Transfer with tongs to sink to drain, then transfer to a cutting board. Return water to a boil and cook remaining 2 lobsters in same manner.

While lobsters are cooking, stir together shallots, lemon juice, and salt in a large bowl. Let stand at room temperature for 30 minutes.

When lobsters are cool, crack shells and remove meat from claws, joints, and tails (see page 341). Discard tomalley, any roe, and shells. Cut meat into ½-inch pieces.

Whisk mayonnaise, tarragon, and pepper into shallot mixture. Add lobster meat and toss gently. Serve salad on lettuce leaves or mound in grilled hot dog buns.

COOK'S NOTE

■ The salad can be made up to 1 day ahead and refrigerated, covered.

Grilled Mussel and Potato Salad

SERVES 4 TO 6
ACTIVE TIME: 1 HOUR ■ START TO FINISH: 1¼ HOURS

■ Hold the mayo: grilling infuses this salad with a lightly smoky flavor, even though the mussels and blanched potatoes aren't on the fire for very long. You might not want to heat up the grill just for this recipe, but it makes a good first course (or side dish) with something else that is grilled—steaks, for example, so you can get a little surf-and-turf action going. ■

- 1 pound small (1½-inch-diameter) red boiling potatoes
- 6 tablespoons extra-virgin olive oil
- Salt and freshly ground black pepper
- 4 tablespoons fresh lemon juice
- 2 pounds mussels, preferably cultivated, scrubbed well and beards removed
- 1 fennel bulb (1 pound), stalks discarded, bulb halved lengthwise and very thinly sliced
- ½ cup finely chopped fresh flat-leaf parsley
- ⅓ cup brine-cured black olives, pitted and chopped
- 1 tablespoon drained capers

SPECIAL EQUIPMENT: a disposable aluminum baking pan (at least 1 inch deep)

Combine potatoes and well-salted water to cover by 1 inch in a 4-quart saucepan and bring to a simmer. Simmer, uncovered, until just tender, about 15 minutes. Drain in a colander and rinse under cold water to stop the cooking. Cool potatoes.

Prepare a charcoal or gas grill. If using a charcoal grill, open vents in bottom of grill and in lid, then light charcoal. If using a gas grill, preheat on high, covered, for 10 minutes, then reduce heat to moderately high.

Cut potatoes crosswise into thirds and arrange in one layer on a tray. Brush both sides of potatoes with oil (2 tablespoons total) and season with salt and pepper.

When fire is medium-hot (you can hold your hand 5 inches above rack for just 3 to 4 seconds), lightly oil grill rack. Grill potatoes, uncovered, turning once, until grill marks appear, about 2 minutes total. Transfer to a large bowl and toss with 2 tablespoons lemon juice.

Put mussels in aluminum pan, set on grill, cover with lid, and cook, stirring occasionally, just until they open wide, 5 to 6 minutes. With a slotted spoon, transfer mussels to a bowl. Discard any that haven't opened, then shuck remainder.

Add mussels to potatoes, along with fennel, parsley, olives, capers, and remaining 2 tablespoons lemon juice, and toss to combine. Let stand at room temperature, tossing occasionally, for 10 minutes.

Toss salad with remaining 4 tablespoons (1/4 cup) oil and salt and pepper to taste.

Tatsoi and Warm Scallop Salad with Spicy Pecan Praline

SERVES 6 AS A FIRST COURSE
ACTIVE TIME: 35 MINUTES ■ START TO FINISH: 45 MINUTES

■ This very *au courant* salad features tatsoi, a succulent Asian green that's a relatively new culinary pleasure in the United States (for more information, see page 134). The pecan praline, which has a spicy, savory edge from cayenne, plays up the sweetness of the scallops and adds a little crunch. Intended as a first course, this salad can, in larger portions, become a main course. ■

FOR PRALINE

- 1/3 cup pecans, finely chopped
- 1/2 teaspoon salt
- 1/8 teaspoon cayenne, or to taste
- 3 tablespoons sugar

FOR SALAD

- 1 tablespoon all-purpose flour
- 3/4 teaspoon salt
- 3/4 teaspoon ground cumin
- 1/8 teaspoon cayenne
- 3/4 pound sea scallops, tough side muscle removed from each if necessary
- 1/2 tablespoon unsalted butter
- 4 tablespoons extra-virgin olive oil
- 3 tablespoons fresh lemon juice
- 3/4 teaspoon Dijon mustard
- 1/4 teaspoon salt
- Freshly ground black pepper
- 1 large, firm, but ripe California avocado
- 7 cups tatsoi or baby spinach leaves

MAKE THE PRALINE: Stir together pecans, salt, and cayenne in a bowl. Cook sugar in a dry small heavy skillet over moderate heat, stirring with a fork, until melted, then cook without stirring, swirling skillet, until it becomes a golden caramel. Add pecans and stir to coat with caramel. Spoon praline onto a sheet of foil to cool.

Transfer cooled praline to a cutting board and finely chop.

MAKE THE SALAD: Combine flour, salt, cumin, and cayenne on a sheet of wax paper. Dip top and bottom of each scallop into mixture to coat, knocking off excess.

Heat butter and 1 tablespoon olive oil in a 12-inch heavy skillet over moderately high heat until foam subsides. Add scallops flat sides down and cook, turning once, until golden and just cooked through, 2 to 4 minutes total. Remove skillet from heat.

Whisk together lemon juice, mustard, salt, and pepper to taste in a large bowl. Add remaining 3 tablespoons olive oil in a stream, whisking until well blended.

Halve, pit, and peel avocado. Cut into 1/2-inch-thick wedges, cut wedges crosswise in half, and add to dressing. Add scallops, with any liquid remaining in skillet, tatsoi, and praline and gently toss to coat.

COOK'S NOTE

■ The praline can be made up to 3 days ahead and kept in an airtight container at room temperature.

Tandoori Shrimp and Mango Salad

SERVES 6 AS A MAIN COURSE
ACTIVE TIME: 1 HOUR ■ START TO FINISH: 1¼ HOURS

■ India's warm colors and flavors are very cooling on a hot summer night. Here the shrimp is in a spiced yogurt "tandoori" marinade (it's cooked on top of the stove instead of in a blistering-hot clay tandoor oven), and the dressing is based on chutney. This is a very pretty salad, with the orangey red mango, the pink shrimp, and the emerald green watercress. ■

FOR DRESSING

- ½ cup Major Grey chutney
- ⅔ cup fresh lime juice
- ½ cup vegetable oil
- 1 teaspoon cayenne
- ½ teaspoon salt

FOR MARINADE AND SHRIMP

- 1 tablespoon paprika
- 2 teaspoons ground cumin
- 2 teaspoons ground coriander
- 4 garlic cloves, crushed
- 1 (1-inch) piece fresh ginger, peeled and chopped
- 2 serrano chiles, seeded and chopped
- ¾ cup plain yogurt
- 1 teaspoon finely grated lime zest
- ½ teaspoon salt
- Freshly ground black pepper to taste
- 2 pounds large shrimp in shells (21–25 per pound), peeled and deveined

FOR COOKING SHRIMP AND MAKING SALAD

- ¼ cup vegetable oil
- 6 cups packed tender watercress sprigs (3 bunches)
- 1 cup loosely packed fresh cilantro sprigs
- 3 red bell peppers, cored, seeded, and cut into matchsticks
- 2 firm but ripe mangoes, peeled, pitted, and cut into matchsticks

MAKE THE DRESSING: Force chutney through a medium-mesh sieve into a small bowl. Whisk in lime juice, oil, cayenne, and salt.

MARINATE THE SHRIMP: Toast paprika, cumin, and coriander in a dry small heavy skillet over moderate heat, stirring occasionally, until fragrant and several shades darker, about 2 minutes (watch carefully, as spices burn easily). Transfer to a medium bowl to cool, then stir in remaining marinade ingredients. Pat shrimp dry and add to marinade, stirring to coat well. Marinate at room temperature for 15 minutes, or refrigerate, covered, for 1 hour.

COOK THE SHRIMP AND MAKE THE SALAD: Heat oil in a 12-inch nonstick skillet over moderately high heat until hot but not smoking. Drain shrimp; discard marinade. Cook shrimp in batches, without crowding, turning once, until golden and cooked through, 3 to 4 minutes. Transfer shrimp to paper towels to drain and cool slightly. Gently toss shrimp, watercress, cilantro sprigs, bell peppers, and mangoes with dressing in a large bowl.

COOK'S NOTE

■ The dressing can be made up to 1 day ahead and refrigerated, covered. Bring to room temperature before using.

Juicing Lemons and Limes

When a recipe calls for lots of fresh lemon or lime juice, start your prep at the grocery store. Look for thin-skinned fruits that yield to gentle pressure and are heavy for their size. Also, better safe than sorry—lemons' and limes' juiciness varies, so buy one or two extra. Before juicing, roll each lemon or lime back and forth on a work surface, applying pressure with the palm of your hand, to break down the fibrous membranes inside the fruit and let the juices run more freely. There are lots of gizmos for squeezing juice, including the simple handheld wooden reamer and the classic juicer that rests in its own shallow bowl (for the weak-wristed, electric versions of the classic juicer are also available). Sleekly designed, fun-to-use lemon and lime presses based on a traditional Mexican lime press can be had from Williams-Sonoma (see Sources).

Thai-Style Tomato and Shrimp Salad

SERVES 4 TO 6 AS A FIRST COURSE
ACTIVE TIME: 45 MINUTES ■ START TO FINISH: 45 MINUTES

■ Tomatoes and cukes are the perfect vehicle for this glorious herbal explosion. The fact that we call for two different Thai basils shouldn't stop you from making this salad—your garden-variety Italian basil will work fine. But if you can get your hands on any Asian basils, use them; they're a little sharper, a little more anisey, than Western varieties. ■

- 1 pound large shrimp in shells (21–25 per pound), peeled and deveined
- 2 limes
- 3 stalks lemongrass, root ends trimmed and tough outer leaves discarded
- 2 tablespoons fresh lime juice
- ¼ cup finely chopped red bell pepper
- 3 scallions, sliced ¼ inch thick
- 2 (3-inch-long) fresh green chiles, such as Thai (see Glossary) or serrano, minced (including seeds)
- 3–4 teaspoons Asian fish sauce (to taste)
- 1 tablespoon sugar
- ½ teaspoon salt
- 2 pounds beefsteak tomatoes, cut into 1-inch-thick wedges
- ¾ pound cucumbers (about 2), peeled, quartered lengthwise, and cut into 1-inch pieces
- ½ cup loosely packed fresh anise basil leaves
- ½ cup loosely packed fresh lemon basil leaves
- ½ cup loosely packed fresh cilantro leaves

Cook shrimp in a 4-quart saucepan of boiling well-salted water until just cooked through, 1 to 2 minutes. Drain and cool.

Cut peel and white pith from limes with a sharp knife. Cut lime segments free from membranes, then finely chop enough segments to measure ¼ cup; discard remainder or reserve for another use. Mince enough lemongrass from bottom 6 inches of stalks to measure 2 tablespoons; discard remainder.

Stir together chopped lime, minced lemongrass, lime juice, bell pepper, scallions, chiles, fish sauce, sugar, and salt in a large serving bowl until sugar is dissolved. Add shrimp, tomatoes, and cucumbers and toss well. Top with herbs.

Lemongrass

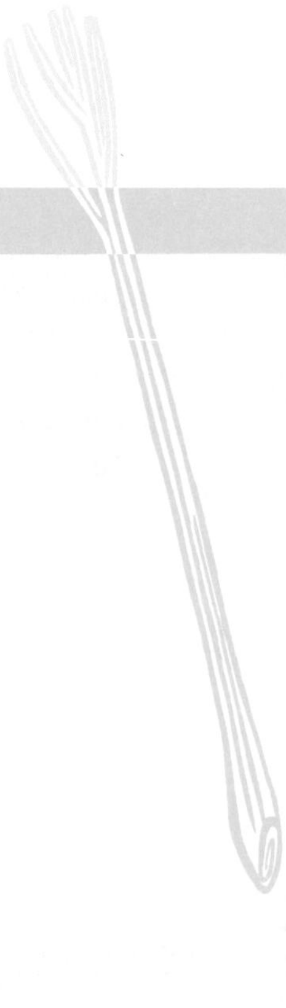

Lemongrass imparts a subtle lemony aroma and flavor to Southeast Asian dishes. Once found only in Asian markets, this dramatic, bladelike grass has become available in supermarkets across the country, thanks to America's passion for Asian food. Unfortunately, though, the quality of lemongrass is often poor, with dry, woody stems and papery skin. Fresh lemongrass is fat and firm (the thicker the stalks, the better), but it does dry out quickly. Whenever possible, buy lemongrass that is wrapped in plastic; if it hasn't been, wrap it up when you get home. It will keep nicely that way for up to two weeks in the refrigerator. It also freezes well; when you find fresh, healthy stalks, it's not a bad idea to stock up.

When using lemongrass, peel off the tough outer layers and cut off the top part. Starting from the root end of the stalk, cut paper-thin slices from the lower six inches or so of the stalk. The tough, fibrous remainder is perfect for tea or stock (include the above-mentioned layers and top part), or make a brush for basting by bashing one cut end until it splits and fans out.

Curried Chicken Salad

SERVES 4 TO 6 AS A MAIN COURSE
ACTIVE TIME: 30 MINUTES ■ START TO FINISH: 45 MINUTES

■ Although its ingredients are not particularly decadent, this salad has a voluptuous flavor. The mango adds its own natural richness, as do the cashews and yogurt. The curry, vibrant without being harsh or overwhelming, makes this a real crowd-pleaser. ■

FOR SALAD

- 4 skinless, boneless chicken breast halves (1½ pounds total)
- 2 tablespoons kosher salt
- 1 medium red onion, chopped
- 1 firm but ripe mango, peeled, pitted, and cut into ½-inch pieces
- 1 cup red seedless grapes, halved
- ½ cup salted roasted cashews, coarsely chopped

FOR DRESSING

- ½ cup mayonnaise
- ⅓ cup plain yogurt
- 5 teaspoons curry powder
- 1 tablespoon fresh lime juice
- 1 teaspoon honey
- ½ teaspoon ground ginger
- ½ teaspoon salt
- ¼ teaspoon freshly ground black pepper

POACH THE CHICKEN: Coat chicken with kosher salt in a bowl. Let stand at room temperature, turning once or twice, for 15 minutes.

Rinse salt from chicken. Poach chicken in a 3- to 4-quart saucepan of barely simmering well-salted water, uncovered, for 6 minutes. Remove from heat and let chicken stand in cooking liquid, covered, until just cooked through, 10 to 12 minutes. Transfer chicken to a plate and cool for 10 minutes.

MEANWHILE, MAKE THE DRESSING: Whisk together mayonnaise, yogurt, curry powder, lime juice, honey, ginger, salt, and pepper in a large bowl.

ASSEMBLE THE SALAD: Cut chicken into ½-inch pieces and add to dressing. Add onion, mango, grapes, and cashews and stir gently to combine.

Tarragon Chicken Salad with Walnuts

SERVES 6 TO 8 AS A MAIN COURSE
ACTIVE TIME: 35 MINUTES ■ START TO FINISH: 1 HOUR

■ This "company" chicken salad with tarragon and lightly toasted walnuts (toasting brings out the best in any nut) is one for the ages. Served on a bed of soft-leaf lettuce, it will be the centerpiece of any summer meal. ■

- 8 skinless, boneless chicken breast halves (3 pounds total)
- ¼ cup kosher salt
- 1½ tablespoons tarragon white-wine vinegar, or to taste
- 1 cup finely chopped celery
- ⅓ cup mayonnaise
- ⅓ cup sour cream
- 1 tablespoon chopped fresh tarragon or 1¼ teaspoons dried tarragon, crumbled, or to taste
- ½ teaspoon salt
- ¼ teaspoon freshly ground black pepper
- 1 cup (4 ounces) walnuts, lightly toasted (see Tips, page 938) and chopped

Coat chicken with kosher salt in a bowl. Let stand at room temperature, turning once or twice, for 15 minutes. Rinse salt from chicken. Poach chicken in a 5- to 6-quart pot of barely simmering salted water (1 tablespoon salt per every 4 quarts water), uncovered, for 6 minutes. Remove from heat and let chicken stand in cooking liquid, covered, until just cooked through, 10 to 12 minutes. Transfer chicken to a plate and cool for 10 minutes, then cut into ¾-inch pieces.

Toss chicken with vinegar and celery in a large bowl. Whisk together mayonnaise, sour cream, and tarragon in a small bowl. Add dressing to chicken, along with salt and pepper, and stir until well combined.

Serve at room temperature or chilled. Just before serving, stir in walnuts.

COOK'S NOTE

■ The salad can be made (without the walnuts) up to 1 day ahead and refrigerated, covered. Add the walnuts just before serving.

Layered Cobb Salad

SERVES 4 TO 6 AS A MAIN COURSE
ACTIVE TIME: 1¼ HOURS ■ START TO FINISH: 1½ HOURS

■ This casserole of the salad world was made famous by Robert Cobb's Brown Derby Restaurant, in Hollywood. Its essential elements include chicken, avocado, lettuce, bacon, tomatoes, Roquefort, watercress, and hard-boiled eggs. We like to layer the ingredients in a glass bowl to show off the bright colors and textures. Dress and toss the salad at the table for added drama. ■

FOR DRESSING

- 3 tablespoons red wine vinegar
- 1 tablespoon fresh lemon juice
- 2 teaspoons Dijon mustard
- 1 small garlic clove, minced
- ½ teaspoon salt
- ½ teaspoon sugar
- ¼ teaspoon freshly ground black pepper
- ½ cup extra-virgin olive oil

FOR SALAD

- 3 skinless, boneless chicken breast halves (1¼ pounds total)
- 2 tablespoons kosher salt
- 2 firm but ripe California avocados
- 1 head romaine, cut crosswise into ½-inch-wide slices (8 cups)
- 6 bacon slices, cooked until crisp, drained, and finely chopped
- 3 medium tomatoes, seeded and cut into ½-inch pieces
- ½–¾ cup crumbled Roquefort
- 2 bunches watercress, coarse stems discarded
- 2 hard-boiled large eggs, halved and forced through a coarse-mesh sieve
- ¼ cup finely chopped fresh chives

AVOCADOS

FUERTE

HASS

We prefer California avocados. Their texture is creamy, and we find their nutty flavor superior to that of avocados grown in Florida. The most widely available California variety, the oval-shaped Hass, is in season year-round, although it actually comes from California only from January to September or October. It's imported from Chile and Mexico for those few remaining months. It has dark, leathery skin that peels easily. The pear-shaped Fuerte has a smooth, thin green skin and is in season from late fall to early spring. However, it is pretty much unavailable except in local markets in California.

Florida avocados, native to the tropics, have a higher water content and a lower fat content than the California varieties. Because they are sweeter, milder, and lighter, they are used more like a fruit — in drinks, for instance, and in ice creams. They are larger as well — so large, in fact, that they cannot be substituted in equal numbers for California avocados in our recipes (we either specify California avocados or give a weight).

The best way to test an avocado's ripeness is to press it *very* gently: if it yields to pressure, it's ripe. Avocados are a delicate fruit and bruise easily, which can result in pockets of rot under the skin. Your best bet is to plan several days in advance, buying hard avocados and ripening them at home at room temperature. Their flesh oxidizes quickly after exposure to air, and contrary to popular opinion, leaving the pit inside doesn't make a bit of difference. Once you have cut an avocado open, brush the exposed surface with lemon or lime juice to minimize browning in the unused portion, wrap it tightly in plastic wrap, and refrigerate. Any flesh that darkens can be trimmed away.

MAKE THE DRESSING: Whisk together all ingredients except oil in a bowl. Add oil in a slow stream, whisking until well blended. Set aside.

MAKE THE SALAD: Coat chicken with kosher salt in a bowl. Let stand at room temperature, turning once or twice, for 15 minutes.

Rinse salt from chicken. Poach chicken in a 3- to 4-quart saucepan of barely simmering well-salted water, uncovered, for 6 minutes. Remove from heat and let chicken stand in cooking liquid, covered, until just cooked through, 10 to 12 minutes. Transfer chicken to a cutting board and cool completely, then cut into ½-inch cubes.

Halve, pit, and peel avocados, then cut into ½-inch cubes.

Spread romaine over bottom of a 6- to 8-quart glass bowl and top evenly with chicken. Sprinkle bacon over chicken, then continue layering with tomatoes, cheese, avocados, watercress, eggs, and chives.

At the table, pour dressing over salad and toss.

COOK'S NOTE

- The dressing can be made and the salad assembled up to 1 hour ahead and refrigerated separately, covered.

Duck and Wild Rice Salad

SERVES 6 TO 8 AS A MAIN COURSE
ACTIVE TIME: 1 HOUR ■ START TO FINISH: 2½ HOURS

■ Duck and wild rice are great companions—they come from the same habitat, after all. This recipe calls for *magrets*, which are the breasts of fatted Moulard ducks, a foundation of culinary tradition in Gascony. Because they taste like red meat, they should be cooked similarly for the best flavor and succulence—medium-rare, as here, or rare. *Magrets* are available at specialty butchers, or see Sources. ■

FOR DRESSING

Finely grated zest of 1 orange
⅔ cup fresh orange juice
⅓ cup extra-virgin olive oil
⅓ cup finely chopped shallots
1 teaspoon mild honey
1 teaspoon salt
½ teaspoon freshly ground black pepper

FOR SALAD

2 cups (10 ounces) wild rice
3 tablespoons unsalted butter
1 large onion, finely chopped
3 cups chicken stock or store-bought low-sodium broth
10 ounces sugar snap peas, trimmed and halved diagonally
2 (14-ounce) boneless *magrets* (duck breast halves) with skin
Salt and freshly ground black pepper
6 scallions, thinly sliced diagonally
1 cup (5 ounces) soft dried apricots, preferably California, cut into ¼-inch-wide strips
1½ cups (4½ ounces) pecans, toasted (see Tips, page 938) and chopped

SPECIAL EQUIPMENT: an instant-read thermometer

MAKE THE DRESSING: Whisk together all ingredients in a large bowl. Let stand at room temperature while you prepare rice.

COOK THE RICE: Rinse rice well in a large medium-mesh sieve under cold water; drain well. Heat butter in a 4- to 5-quart heavy pot over moderate heat until foam subsides. Add onion and cook, stirring occasionally, until golden, about 5 minutes. Add rice and cook, stirring, until fragrant, about 3 minutes. Stir in 4 cups water and stock and bring to a boil, then reduce heat and simmer, covered, until rice is tender, 1 to 1¼ hours (grains will split open, but not all liquid will be absorbed). Drain well in a colander and cool to warm (spread rice out in a shallow baking pan to cool it faster), then add to dressing.

MEANWHILE, COOK THE SUGAR SNAPS AND DUCK: Put a rack in middle of oven and preheat oven to 375°F. Lightly oil a baking sheet with sides.

Cook sugar snaps in a 4-quart pot of boiling well-salted water until crisp-tender, about 2 minutes. Drain in sieve and rinse under cold water to stop the cooking; drain well again.

Pat duck dry and season with salt and pepper. Score skin in a crosshatch pattern (do not cut into meat), and put skin sides up on oiled baking sheet. Roast until thermometer inserted horizontally into center registers 120°F (for medium-rare), about 25 minutes. Transfer duck to a cutting board. (Leave oven on.) Pour off fat from baking sheet and set pan aside.

When duck is just cool enough to handle, remove skin. Keep duck warm, loosely covered with foil. Thinly slice skin (scored sides down), put skin on baking sheet, and bake until very crisp, 15 to 20 minutes. With a slotted spoon, transfer skin to paper towels to drain.

ASSEMBLE THE SALAD: Cut duck breast halves horizontally in half, then cut across the grain into thin slices. Add duck and any juices to rice, along with sugar snaps, scallions, apricots, pecans, and 1 teaspoon salt, and toss gently to combine.

Just before serving, scatter crisp duck skin over top of salad.

Taco Salad with Salsa Vinaigrette

SERVES 6 AS A MAIN COURSE
ACTIVE TIME: 45 MINUTES ■ START TO FINISH: 45 MINUTES

■ What makes a great taco salad? The right proportions of juicy cumin- and tomato-spiked beef (think sloppy joes), crunchy tortilla chips, tangy Cheddar, and salad greens that are not an afterthought. It should be satisfying yet relatively light. And, as befits an example of classic melting-pot Americana, it must be made with supermarket ingredients. We go all out by making our own tortilla chips, but store-bought ones are perfectly fine. A salsa vinaigrette unites all the ingredients. ■

FOR SALAD

- 1½ tablespoons vegetable oil, plus about 4 cups for frying tortillas
- ¾ cup finely chopped onion
- 1 large garlic clove, minced
- 2 teaspoons ground cumin
- 2 teaspoons chili powder
- 1 pound ground beef chuck
- 2 tablespoons tomato paste
- ¾ teaspoon salt
- ¼ teaspoon freshly ground black pepper
- 6 (7-inch) corn tortillas, cut into 1-inch wedges
- 2 heads romaine, thinly sliced crosswise (8 cups)
- 3 tomatoes, cut into ½-inch wedges
- 1½ cups coarsely grated extra-sharp Cheddar (about 6 ounces)
- ⅓ cup thinly sliced scallions

FOR VINAIGRETTE

- 1 large garlic clove, chopped
- 3 tablespoons red wine vinegar
- 3 tablespoons fresh lemon juice
- ½ teaspoon ground cumin, or to taste
- ½ teaspoon salt
- ⅛ teaspoon freshly ground black pepper
- ½ cup plus 2 tablespoons olive oil
- 1 cup chopped seeded tomatoes
- 1 large jalapeño or serrano chile, seeded if desired and chopped
- ½ cup loosely packed fresh cilantro leaves

SPECIAL EQUIPMENT: a deep-fat thermometer

MAKE THE SALAD: Heat 1½ tablespoons oil in a 12-inch heavy skillet over moderately low heat. Add onion, garlic, cumin, and chili powder and cook, stirring, until onion is softened, about 8 minutes. Add beef and cook over moderate heat, stirring and breaking up any lumps, until no longer pink, about 5 minutes. Add tomato paste, salt, and pepper and cook, stirring, until meat is cooked through, about 4 minutes. Transfer mixture to a bowl to cool.

Heat ¾ inch oil in cleaned skillet until it registers 375°F on thermometer. Fry tortilla wedges in batches until golden, 30 seconds to 1 minute per batch. With a slotted spoon, transfer to paper towels to drain, then sprinkle with salt to taste. (Return oil to 375°F between batches.)

Spread romaine on a large deep platter or in a large shallow bowl and top with beef mixture. Arrange tortillas and tomatoes decoratively over beef and scatter Cheddar and scallions over top.

MAKE THE VINAIGRETTE: Blend garlic, vinegar, lemon juice, cumin, salt, and pepper in a blender until smooth. With motor running, add oil in a slow stream and blend until well combined. Add tomatoes, jalapeño, and cilantro and blend until smooth. Serve salad with vinaigrette on the side, or drizzle over salad and toss well.

COOK'S NOTE

■ The tortillas can be fried up to 1 day ahead and kept in an airtight container at room temperature.

Grilled Lemongrass Beef and Noodle Salad

SERVES 4 AS A MAIN COURSE
ACTIVE TIME: 50 MINUTES ■ START TO FINISH: 6 HOURS (INCLUDES MARINATING)

■ There is more to steak on the grill than . . . steak on the grill. We've adapted a Vietnamese favorite by using skirt or flank steak, which is marinated, grilled, and then sliced, instead of bottom round. Southeast Asian ingredients are increasingly available in the ethnic foods aisle of the supermarket. Two very authentic touches here are the *nuoc cham* and toasted rice powder. ■

FOR MARINADE

- 2 stalks lemongrass, root ends trimmed and tough outer layers discarded
- 6 garlic cloves, minced
- 2 tablespoons Asian fish sauce, preferably *nuoc mam*
- 1 tablespoon soy sauce
- 4 teaspoons sugar
- 2 tablespoons vegetable oil
- 1/2 teaspoon Asian sesame oil

FOR SALAD

- 1–1 1/4 pounds skirt steak or flank steak
- 1/2 pound rice stick noodles (rice vermicelli)
- 1/2 cup loosely packed fresh basil leaves, preferably Thai basil
- 1/2 cup loosely packed fresh mint leaves
- 1/2 cup loosely packed fresh cilantro leaves
- 1 cup Nuoc Cham (recipe follows)
- 1 seedless cucumber (usually plastic wrapped), halved lengthwise and cut diagonally into 1/4-inch-thick slices
- About 2 tablespoons Toasted Rice Powder (recipe follows)
- 2–4 (1- to 2-inch-long) thin fresh red or green Asian chiles or serrano chiles (to taste), seeded and very thinly sliced

OPTIONAL GARNISH: fresh basil, mint, or cilantro sprigs

MAKE THE MARINADE: Thinly slice lower 6 inches of lemongrass; discard remainder. Finely grind lemongrass and garlic in a food processor or blender. Add remaining ingredients and blend until well combined.

MARINATE THE STEAK: Combine marinade and steak in a sealable plastic bag and seal bag, pressing out excess air. Marinate steak, refrigerated, turning bag once or twice, for at least 4 hours.

MAKE THE SALAD: Prepare a charcoal or gas grill. If using a charcoal grill, open vents in bottom of grill, then light charcoal. If using a gas grill, preheat on high, covered, for 10 minutes, then reduce heat to moderately high.

While grill preheats, soak noodles in hot water to cover in a large bowl until softened and pliable, about 15 minutes.

Transfer steak to a platter; discard marinade. When fire is medium-hot (you can hold your hand 5 inches above rack for just 3 to 4 seconds), lightly oil grill rack. Grill steak, uncovered, turning once, for 4 to 6 minutes for skirt steak or 6 to 10 minutes for flank, for medium-rare. Transfer steak to a cutting board and let stand for 5 minutes.

Meanwhile, drain noodles. Cook in a 4-quart saucepan of boiling (unsalted) water until just tender, 30 seconds to 1 minute. Drain noodles in a colander and rinse under cold water to stop the cooking, then drain well again.

Toss noodles with herbs and half of *nuoc cham* in a large bowl. Divide cucumber among four bowls and top with noodles. Sprinkle each serving with 1 to 1 1/2 teaspoons rice powder. Holding knife at a 45-degree angle, thinly slice steak on the diagonal. Divide among noodles, mounding it on top. Sprinkle chiles over salad and garnish with herb sprigs, if desired. Serve remaining *nuoc cham* on the side.

COOK'S NOTE

■ The steak can also be broiled in a broiler pan about 3 inches from the heat, turning once, for 3 to 5 minutes.

Nuoc Cham

Vietnamese Lime Sauce

MAKES ABOUT 1 CUP
ACTIVE TIME: 10 MINUTES ■ START TO FINISH: 10 MINUTES

■ The thin dark sauce called *nuoc cham* is on every table in Vietnam, but it differs from one region to another. This one, with lime juice, sugar, and garlic, is from the south. As with Southeast Asian food in general, a balancing act is going on between salty, sweet, sour, and spicy, so don't let the fish sauce put you off. It's potent stuff, but along with the sugar, it smoothes out the lime juice. ■

- 6 tablespoons fresh lime juice
- 3 tablespoons Asian fish sauce, preferably *nuoc mam*
- 3 tablespoons sugar
- 3 tablespoons warm water
- 1 garlic clove, minced
- 2 (1- to 2-inch-long) thin fresh red or green Asian chiles or serrano chiles, seeded if desired and finely chopped

Stir together all ingredients in a small bowl until sugar is dissolved.

Cutting Up Chiles and Bell Peppers

Who knows where we picked up this trick, but it's worth sharing. Rather than cutting a chile or bell pepper in half, then carving out the seeds and ribs (the seeds always seem to scatter all over the kitchen), simply lop off the sides. If you're prepping chiles, you've just minimized your contact with the hot capsaicin in both seeds and ribs. And if you want flat pieces of bell pepper for grilling, this technique is a natural. You can also "fillet" a tomato, mango, or pineapple in the same way.

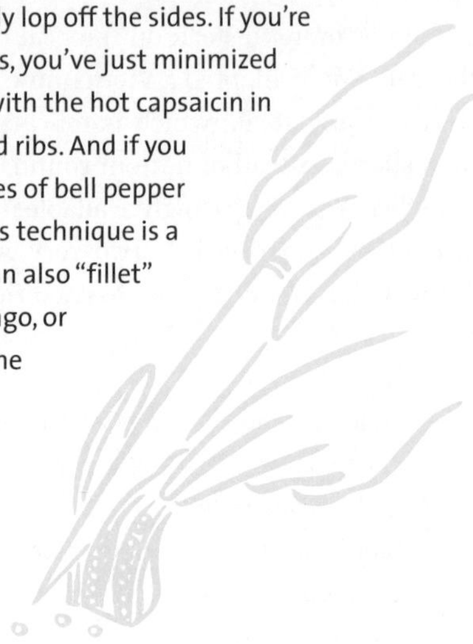

Toasted Rice Powder

MAKES ABOUT 2 TABLESPOONS
ACTIVE TIME: 10 MINUTES ■ START TO FINISH: 30 MINUTES

■ Raw white rice, toasted and finely ground, gives texture and a roasted flavor to many Southeast Asian salads. Don't rush the toasting—the rice should be a deep gold and fragrant. Make sure it's cool before you grind it. ■

- 2 tablespoons raw white rice

SPECIAL EQUIPMENT: an electric coffee/spice grinder (optional)

Toast rice in a dry small heavy skillet (not nonstick) over moderate heat, stirring, until deep gold, 5 to 8 minutes. Transfer to a bowl to cool.

Grind rice to a powder in coffee/spice grinder or in a blender. Sift through a fine-mesh sieve into a bowl; discard solids.

COOK'S NOTE

■ The powder keeps in a tightly sealed jar for up to 1 month.

Green Apple Salad with Grilled Beef

SERVES 4 AS A MAIN COURSE
ACTIVE TIME: 1 HOUR ■ START TO FINISH: 1½ HOURS

■ Cuisines, like languages, are always evolving; otherwise, they disappear. This salad is a great example. Mai Pham, a chef and cookbook author who came to the United States from Vietnam, often uses Granny Smith apple instead of green mango, an ingredient common in Southeast Asia but still elusive in this country. Drier than most other apples, the Granny Smith holds together when cut into matchsticks. This recipe is adapted from Pham's *Pleasures of the Vietnamese Table.* We increased the amount of beef to make it a more substantial—that is, a more typically American—main course. ■

FOR BEEF AND MARINADE

- 1 pound flank steak (about ½ inch thick)
- 3 stalks lemongrass, root ends trimmed and tough outer leaves discarded

1 tablespoon minced shallot
4 teaspoons Asian fish sauce, preferably *nuoc mam*
2 teaspoons soy sauce
2 teaspoons sugar

FOR CHILE LIME DRESSING

3 tablespoons fresh lime juice
¼ lime, peel and pith cut away with a sharp knife
3 tablespoons water
3 tablespoons sugar
3 tablespoons Asian fish sauce, preferably *nuoc mam*
1 large garlic clove, chopped
½–1 teaspoon chopped fresh red or green Asian chile or serrano chile (to taste), including seeds

FOR SALAD

4 Granny Smith apples
½ cup loosely packed small fresh basil leaves
¼ cup loosely packed fresh cilantro leaves
¼ cup chopped salted roasted peanuts

SPECIAL EQUIPMENT: bamboo skewers if necessary, soaked in water for 30 minutes; a mandoline or other adjustable-blade slicer, such as a Japanese Benriner (optional)

Prepare a charcoal or gas grill. If using a charcoal grill, open vents in bottom of grill, then light charcoal. If using a gas grill, preheat on high, covered, for 10 minutes, then reduce heat to moderately high.

MARINATE THE BEEF: Pat steak dry and cut across the grain into ¼-inch-thick slices. Mince enough lemongrass from lower 6 inches of stalks to measure ¼ cup; discard remainder. Stir together beef, lemongrass, and remaining ingredients in a bowl. Marinate, covered, at room temperature, stirring occasionally, for 20 minutes.

MEANWHILE, MAKE THE DRESSING: Combine all ingredients in a blender and purée until smooth.

GRILL THE BEEF: Thread any small pieces of meat on bamboo skewers to prevent them from falling through grill rack. When fire is hot (you can hold your hand 5 inches above rack for just 1 to 2 seconds), lightly oil grill rack. Grill beef slices, in batches if necessary, uncovered, turning once, until lightly charred, about 2 minutes per batch. Transfer to a plate.

MAKE THE SALAD: Cut (unpeeled) apples into thin matchsticks, about ⅛ inch thick, using a mandoline (work your way around cores) or a knife (cut thin slices from apples, stack, and cut into matchsticks). Gently toss apples with basil, cilantro, peanuts, and dressing to taste in a bowl.

Mound salad on four large plates and top with beef. Drizzle some of remaining dressing over beef.

COOK'S NOTES

- The beef can also be cooked, in batches, in a hot, lightly oiled, well-seasoned ridged grill pan over high heat.
- The dressing can be made up to 1 day ahead and refrigerated, covered.

Summer Fruit Salad with Mint Sugar

SERVES 6

ACTIVE TIME: 20 MINUTES ■ START TO FINISH: 20 MINUTES

■ Simplicity is the key to a successful fruit salad, so don't yield to the impulse to include every fruit you see on your cruise through the produce section. Think color, and a play of textures as well. Cherries (you can substitute berries), peaches, and grapes are among our favorite juicy, soft fruits; there's a subtle difference in texture between them. The mint sugar works with any combination, so feel free to vary the fruit according to what looks good. ■

¼ cup loosely packed fresh mint leaves
3 tablespoons sugar
1½ pounds sweet cherries, pitted and halved
3 firm but ripe medium peaches or nectarines, halved, pitted, and cut into ⅓-inch-thick wedges
½ pound seedless green grapes (1½ cups), halved

Pulse mint and sugar in a food processor until mint is finely ground. Sprinkle mint sugar over fruit in a large bowl and toss gently to combine. Let stand for 5 minutes before serving.

Basic French Vinaigrette

MAKES ABOUT ½ CUP
ACTIVE TIME: 5 MINUTES ■ START TO FINISH: 5 MINUTES

■ Here's the gold standard: all the elements come together in perfect harmony. Dijon mustard adds piquancy and body, minced shallots contribute a light sweetness, and salt, one of the most crucial ingredients in a salad dressing, counters the acid (a vinaigrette can taste sharp and raw without it). This is not the place for a richly flavored olive oil; use a mild olive oil or cut a stronger one with a more neutral oil, such as grapeseed. ■

- 2 tablespoons white wine vinegar or fresh lemon juice
- ½ teaspoon Dijon mustard
- 2 tablespoons minced shallots
- ¼ teaspoon salt
- ⅛ teaspoon freshly ground black pepper
- ⅓ cup olive oil

Whisk together vinegar, mustard, shallots, salt, and pepper in a bowl. Add oil in a slow stream, whisking until well blended.

VARIATION

■ Increase the vinegar to 3 tablespoons and stir in 2 teaspoons minced fresh flat-leaf parsley and ½ hard-boiled large egg, forced through a coarse-mesh sieve. The egg thickens the dressing and makes it a nice topping; try it with vegetables such as cauliflower and green beans.

Garlicky French Vinaigrette

MAKES ABOUT ½ CUP
ACTIVE TIME: 5 MINUTES ■ START TO FINISH: 20 MINUTES

■ The garlic's presence is mild and refined—we cook it in boiling water first to temper its lustiness. Cream, which takes the place of much of the usual oil, smoothes all the flavors out. This is a lovely light dressing. ■

- 2 garlic cloves, peeled
- 5 tablespoons heavy cream
- ½ teaspoon Dijon mustard
- 2 tablespoons fresh lemon juice
- ¼ teaspoon salt, or to taste
- Pinch of freshly ground black pepper
- 1 tablespoon olive oil

Cook garlic in a small saucepan of boiling water until tender, about 15 minutes; drain.

With a fork, mash garlic to a paste in a bowl. Add cream, mustard, lemon juice, salt, and pepper, whisking until slightly thickened. Add oil drop by drop, whisking, and whisk until well blended.

Creamy Vinaigrette

MAKES ABOUT 1 CUP
ACTIVE TIME: 5 MINUTES ■ START TO FINISH: 5 MINUTES

■ An egg yolk makes this dressing creamy and satiny, not thick like a mayonnaise. Using mild white pepper in light-colored foods, where specks of black pepper would stand out, is very traditional, very French. ■

- 1 large egg yolk
- ¼ cup tarragon white-wine vinegar or red wine vinegar
- 1 tablespoon Dijon mustard
- 1 tablespoon minced shallot
- ½ teaspoon salt, or to taste
- ⅛ teaspoon white pepper
- ¾ cup olive oil, or to taste

Combine yolk, vinegar, mustard, shallot, salt, and white pepper in a blender or food processor and blend until well combined. With motor running, add oil in a slow stream, blending until combined.

COOK'S NOTE

■ The egg yolk in this recipe is not cooked. If this is a concern, see page 629.

Oils and Vinegars

We keep our kitchen cabinets stocked with an assortment of oils and vinegars, because we use them for more than dressing salads. Inexpensive ones are for cooking, and the fancier, more distinctive ones are treated as condiments. When storing olive and nut oils, remember that heat, light, and age are all detrimental, so keep them in a dark, cool place and use within a year. Nut oils (and Asian sesame oil), which are especially perishable, are sometimes already rancid when you buy them; open the bottle when you get home and take a sniff—the oil should smell *good.* Store these fragile oils in the refrigerator and bring them to room temperature before using.

Oils from Our Pantry

ASIAN SESAME OIL: Make sure you buy dark brown, toasty-flavored Asian sesame oil, not the light-colored, plain sesame oil that's used for cooking. The Asian oil is stirred in at the end of cooking as a condiment, giving depth of flavor.

EXTRA-VIRGIN OLIVE OIL: The term *extra-virgin* signifies a grade of olive oil that contains less than 1 percent acidity and has not been treated with heat or chemicals. Like virgin olive oil (which can have up to 2 percent acidity and is not commonly found in stores), it is freshly squeezed by a process known as "first press" or "cold press." Extra-virgin oils from Italy, Spain, Greece, France, Morocco, Tunisia, and California encompass a wide range of prices and flavors (from mild to rustic and from fruity to the classic peppery Tuscans).

OLIVE OIL: Plain olive oil, often labeled "pure," is refined with steam and chemicals and then mixed with a better olive oil for a little flavor and aroma. It's what many people use for sautéing, although we usually prefer an inexpensive extra-virgin with a clean, light flavor—it's less processed.

NUT OILS: Rich walnut and hazelnut oils, often tempered with a more neutral oil, make lovely vinaigrettes for heartier greens or asparagus.

VEGETABLE OILS: Our current favorite "vegetable" oil is grapeseed, which is wonderfully neutral. We also use safflower and canola oils. For deep-frying, use any flavorless vegetable oil.

Vinegars from Our Pantry

BALSAMIC VINEGAR: The real thing carries the label *"aceto balsamico tradizionale,"* which means the vinegar has been aged in barrels of various woods for a minimum of twelve years under the watchful eye of the balsamic consortiums of Modena or Reggio, the two regions of Italy where true balsamic vinegar is produced. In Italy, a (very expensive) twenty-five-year-old balsamic is sipped as a liqueur or drizzled over fresh fruit or savory dishes; only rarely is it sprinkled on salad greens. When we call for balsamic vinegar in a recipe, we're generally referring to inexpensive commercial brands of consistent quality (such as Monari Federzoni), which are perfectly adequate for a salad dressing or a sauce reduction. Mid-range balsamics (available at specialty foods stores) make a stab at mimicking the quality of a true *balsamico.* The production of these vinegars, however, is not tightly regulated, so let taste, not the price or purported age of the vinegar, be your guide.

White balsamic vinegars, which are manufactured by filtering color from commercial balsamics or by blending aged white wine vinegar and concentrated grape must (the just-pressed juice of grapes, before fermentation occurs), have gradually won grudging acceptance in Italy. Authentic or not, they work nicely in marinades and where the absence of color is desirable. We like the round, mellow flavor of Colavita the best.

CIDER VINEGAR: We don't know what we'd do without this fresh-tasting, well-balanced vinegar. The unfiltered brands available in natural foods stores tend to be rounder in flavor than supermarket brands. Tossing hot, just-boiled potatoes with a little cider vinegar before adding the dressing really makes a potato salad.

RASPBERRY VINEGAR: Used sparingly, this vinegar isn't intrusive, especially when blended with a nut oil and tossed with a hearty salad green like spinach. It's also a nice thing to use when deglazing a pan to give a sauce a hint of a fruity tang.

RICE VINEGAR: Many Asian-inspired recipes require rice vinegar, but it's no longer necessary to travel to Chinatown to find it. Its low acidity, which has contributed to its popularity, makes for a gentle vinaigrette. Rice vinegar is available plain or seasoned with salt and sugar.

WINE VINEGARS: Every pantry needs a couple of representatives from the family of wine vinegars—red, white, Champagne, and sherry. Look for those on the low end of the acidity scale, 4 to 5 percent (the percentage will be printed on the bottle); a wine vinegar in the 7 percent range will be harshly acidic. Bad wine does not a good vinegar make, so you are safe in presuming that those with ridiculously low price tags might be less than wonderful and the expensive ones might be worth it.

Dress for Success

Salad dressings are something to relax and have fun with. Here are some tips for making them delicious.

- Buy good oil and vinegar; they can be among life's most inexpensive luxuries.
- A classic vinaigrette is a beautiful balancing act, one in which no one ingredient outweighs the others. The proportions are generally two or three parts oil to one part acid. You'll need less oil if you are using a low-acid vinegar, more oil if using a high-acid vinegar. (Information about the acidity is given on the bottle.) If the dressing is on the sweet side, the proportions can drop as low as a one-to-one ratio, a bonus for low-fat salads. Deep-flavored greens can stand a more acidic dressing, which might overwhelm tender lettuces.
- If a dressing is too acidic for your taste, you can always add a little more oil to adjust the balance, or more salt, which counteracts the acid. Adding minced shallots, the way the French do, will give sweetness, counteracting the acid as well.
- To give a dressing more body, whisk in a teaspoon or two of Dijon mustard. Or stir in a mashed hard-boiled egg yolk or two, or a couple of tablespoons of grated cheese such as Parmigiano-Reggiano or aged Asiago.
- Lemon juice brightens both vinegars and strong oils. It will also stand up to fragrant herbs. Lime juice enlivens sweet, salty, or pungent flavors.
- Stocks, broths, and pan juices give depth to dressings, while water will cut a vinaigrette that is too oily.
- A last word: any salad dressing will wilt greens in no time flat, so dress salads just before serving. This is especially important for young, tender spring lettuces—all they really need is a drizzle of good, mild olive oil and a sprinkle of *fleur de sel* (see Glossary) and freshly ground pepper.

Sherry–Walnut Oil Vinaigrette

MAKES ABOUT 1/2 CUP
ACTIVE TIME: 5 MINUTES ■ START TO FINISH: 5 MINUTES

■ This elegant, deep-flavored vinaigrette will lift a salad from the ordinary to the special; try it with slightly bitter greens. Walnut oil enhances the mild nuttiness of the sherry vinegar; like hazelnut oil (which could be substituted), it goes rancid quickly, so keep it in the refrigerator. ■

- 1 1/2 tablespoons sherry vinegar
- 1 teaspoon Dijon mustard
- 1/4 teaspoon salt, or to taste
- 1/8 teaspoon freshly ground black pepper
- 6 tablespoons walnut oil

Whisk together vinegar, mustard, salt, and pepper in a small bowl. Add walnut oil in a slow stream, whisking until well blended.

Carrot Ginger Dressing

MAKES ABOUT 1 3/4 CUPS
ACTIVE TIME: 10 MINUTES ■ START TO FINISH: 15 MINUTES

■ We were inspired here by the typical salad dressing we love in Japanese restaurants. It may sound ridiculous to call for two appliances—the dressing is made in the food processor, then given a whirl in the blender for added smoothness—but using both really does result in the best texture. This dressing is delicious over crisp iceberg or romaine. ■

- 1/2 pound carrots (3 medium), cut into 1/2-inch pieces
- 1/4 cup chopped peeled fresh ginger
- 1/4 cup chopped shallots
- 1/4 cup seasoned rice vinegar
- 1 tablespoon soy sauce
- 1 tablespoon Asian sesame oil
- 1/2 cup peanut oil or vegetable oil
- 1/4 cup water

Pulse carrots in a food processor until finely ground; they should be almost puréed. Add ginger, shallots, vinegar, soy sauce, and sesame oil and pulse until ginger and shallots are minced. With motor running, add peanut oil in a slow stream.

Transfer dressing to a blender, add water, and blend until smooth, 2 to 3 minutes.

Lime Molasses Vinaigrette

MAKES ABOUT 1/2 CUP
ACTIVE TIME: 15 MINUTES ■ START TO FINISH: 15 MINUTES

■ Molasses gives a complex, suave, almost caramel-like tang to this dressing. Toss it with mixed greens or spoon it over grilled chicken or quail. ■

- 2 tablespoons fresh lime juice
- 4 teaspoons molasses
- 1/4 teaspoon Tabasco
- 1/2 teaspoon salt
- 3 tablespoons olive oil
- 1 scallion, finely chopped
- 1/4 teaspoon ground cumin
- Pinch of ground allspice

Whisk together lime juice, molasses, Tabasco, and salt in a bowl.

Combine oil, scallion, cumin, and allspice in a small skillet and heat over moderate heat, stirring, until sizzling. Add to lime mixture in a slow stream, whisking until well blended. Serve warm or at room temperature.

Orange Cumin Vinaigrette

MAKES ABOUT 1 CUP
ACTIVE TIME: 10 MINUTES ■ START TO FINISH: 10 MINUTES

■ Point, counterpoint: earthy cumin meets sweet oranges. This strong, gutsy dressing is delicious with winter greens. ■

1 garlic clove
½ teaspoon salt
⅓ cup fresh orange juice
3 tablespoons fresh lime juice
1 tablespoon minced shallot
2 teaspoons honey
1 teaspoon cumin seeds, toasted (see Tips, page 939)
¼ teaspoon freshly ground black pepper
½ cup vegetable oil

Using a large heavy knife, mince and mash garlic to a paste with ¼ teaspoon salt. Whisk garlic paste together with orange and lime juices, shallot, honey, cumin, remaining ¼ teaspoon salt, and pepper in a bowl. Add oil in a slow stream, whisking until well blended.

Hot Garlic Dressing

MAKES ABOUT ½ CUP
ACTIVE TIME: 15 MINUTES ■ START TO FINISH: 15 MINUTES

■ Robust and richly flavored, this dressing is great with tender but hearty greens (about 1½ pounds) such as beet, mizuna, or mustard, or simply with mesclun. The recipe is from Chris Schlesinger, the cookbook author and chef-founder of four restaurants in New England. ■

⅓ cup olive oil
4 garlic cloves, minced
¼ cup cider vinegar
¼ teaspoon salt
Pinch of freshly ground black pepper

Heat oil and garlic in a small saucepan over moderate heat until fragrant, about 1 minute. Stir in vinegar and immediately pour over greens. Season with salt and pepper and toss well.

Parmesan Balsamic Vinaigrette

MAKES ABOUT ⅔ CUP
ACTIVE TIME: 10 MINUTES ■ START TO FINISH: 10 MINUTES

■ Combined, Parmigiano-Reggiano and rich, dark balsamic vinegar make a particularly appealing dressing for heartier salad greens during the dark days of winter. Once you taste it, though, it might become a year-round favorite. ■

1 garlic clove
½ teaspoon salt
2 tablespoons balsamic vinegar
1 teaspoon fresh lemon juice
3 tablespoons minced fresh basil
¼ cup finely grated Parmigiano-Reggiano
¼ teaspoon freshly ground black pepper
½ cup olive oil

Using a large heavy knife, mince and mash garlic to a paste with ¼ teaspoon salt. Whisk garlic paste together with vinegar, lemon juice, basil, cheese, remaining ¼ teaspoon salt, and pepper in a bowl. Add oil in a slow stream, whisking until well blended.

Tahini Dressing

MAKES ABOUT 1 CUP
ACTIVE TIME: 5 MINUTES ■ START TO FINISH: 5 MINUTES

■ This beautifully creamy dressing, made with tahini (Middle Eastern sesame seed paste), is very sumptuous. Since tahini, like any seed, can turn rancid over time, be sure to buy it from a place with a high turnover, such as a Middle Eastern market or natural foods store. If you must rely on the supermarket, hedge your bets and purchase two different brands if possible. ■

⅓ cup well-stirred tahini
⅓ cup water
4–5 tablespoons fresh lemon juice (to taste)

2 garlic cloves, chopped
3/4 teaspoon salt
1/4 teaspoon sugar (optional)

Combine all ingredients in a blender and blend until smooth.

Herbed Buttermilk Dressing

MAKES ABOUT 1 3/4 CUPS
ACTIVE TIME: 10 MINUTES ■ START TO FINISH: 10 MINUTES

■ Ranch dressing is wildly popular at salad bars and backyard barbecues throughout the land. It was developed by a real rancher, Steve Henson, at his Hidden Valley Guest Ranch, near Santa Barbara, California, in the late 1950s. Weekend guests started taking glass jars of the buttermilk-based dressing back home with them, and the rest, as they say, is history. This is our version: because the buttermilk lends a nice, creamy tang, you don't need many herbs or much garlic to achieve greatness. ■

1 cup well-shaken buttermilk
1/2 cup mayonnaise
2 tablespoons olive oil
1 tablespoon fresh lemon juice
1 garlic clove, minced
2 tablespoons chopped fresh chives
1 tablespoon chopped fresh flat-leaf parsley
1/4 teaspoon salt
1/8 teaspoon freshly ground black pepper

Combine all ingredients in a blender and blend until smooth.

COOK'S NOTE

■ The dressing keeps, covered and refrigerated, for up to 1 week.

Green Goddess Dressing

MAKES ABOUT 1 1/4 CUPS
ACTIVE TIME: 10 MINUTES ■ START TO FINISH: 10 MINUTES

■ Three English travelers whose plane has crashed in the mountains of the fictional Asian kingdom of Rukh are taken hostage by the rajah. His subjects believe that the Green Goddess has sent these unlucky three to take the place of his three brothers, who are about to be executed in India by the British. Will the hostages be rescued? Will the beautiful Englishwoman spurn the rajah's advances? Will the butler save the day or be hurled to his death? *The Green Goddess,* a melodrama written by the Scottish drama critic and playwright William Archer in 1920, starred George Arliss as the rajah. During the play's run in San Francisco, Arliss stayed at the Palace Hotel, and the chef there created this creamy, green-hued dressing in honor of the English actor. It's delicious over slices of California avocado. ■

1 cup mayonnaise
3 flat anchovy fillets, minced
1 scallion, chopped
2 tablespoons chopped fresh flat-leaf parsley
2 tablespoons chopped fresh chives
1 teaspoon chopped fresh tarragon
1 tablespoon tarragon vinegar
Salt and freshly ground black pepper

Combine all ingredients except salt and pepper in a food processor and purée until smooth. Season with salt and pepper.

COOK'S NOTE

■ The dressing keeps, covered and refrigerated, for up to 4 days.

Thousand Island Dressing

MAKES ABOUT 1 1/2 CUPS
ACTIVE TIME: 10 MINUTES ■ START TO FINISH: 10 MINUTES

■ This dressing, which dates back to the early twentieth century, was created in the small resort town of

Clayton, New York, by Sophia LaLonde, the wife of a fishing guide to the Thousand Islands area in the St. Lawrence River, between Canada and New York State. It was popularized first at Clayton's Herald Hotel and then at the Waldorf-Astoria in New York City (the Waldorf's owner summered in the Thousand Islands). The mayonnaise-based dressing gets its pale color from chili sauce, and it is wonderful with crisp iceberg lettuce (which, coincidentally, was developed at about the same time), romaine, chicken, or turkey. ■

- ⅔ cup mayonnaise
- 4 teaspoons ketchup-style chili sauce
- 2 tablespoons chopped shallots
- 1 tablespoon white wine vinegar
- 2 teaspoons Dijon mustard
- ¼ teaspoon salt
- ⅛ teaspoon freshly ground black pepper
- ½ cup vegetable oil

Combine all ingredients except oil in a blender and blend until smooth. With motor running, add oil in a slow stream and blend until well blended.

COOK'S NOTE

■ The dressing keeps, covered and refrigerated, for up to 1 week.

Hard-Boiled Egg Dressing with Tarragon and Cornichons

MAKES ABOUT ¾ CUP
ACTIVE TIME: 15 MINUTES ■ START TO FINISH: 15 MINUTES

■ The style and substance of this dressing, modeled on a classic French *sauce gribiche*, can overwhelm a plate of innocent young salad greens. Save it for leftover chicken or pot roast, or spoon it over green beans or cauliflower. ■

- 2 hard-boiled large eggs
- 1 tablespoon Dijon mustard
- 2 tablespoons tarragon vinegar
- ½ cup olive oil
- 2 tablespoons chopped drained cornichons (tiny French gherkins)
- 2 tablespoons minced fresh tarragon
- Salt and freshly ground black pepper

Discard white from 1 hard-boiled egg and mash whole egg and yolk together in a bowl. Whisk in mustard and vinegar, then add oil in a slow stream, whisking until well blended. Stir in cornichons, tarragon, and salt and pepper to taste.

COOK'S NOTE

■ The dressing keeps, covered and refrigerated, for up to 3 days.

Hot Bacon Dressing

MAKES ABOUT ¾ CUP
ACTIVE TIME: 15 MINUTES ■ START TO FINISH: 15 MINUTES

■ Rich and savory, this dressing is terrific spooned over shredded Napa cabbage or tossed with sliced just-boiled potatoes, steamed cauliflower, or even grilled fish. ■

- ½ pound bacon (8 slices)
- ¼ cup water
- ¼ cup cider vinegar
- Salt
- ¼ teaspoon freshly ground black pepper

Cook bacon in a large skillet over moderate heat until crisp. With a slotted spoon, transfer to paper towels to drain.

Pour off all but 2 tablespoons fat from skillet. Add water and vinegar to skillet and simmer, whisking constantly, for 1 minute. Add salt to taste and pepper. Crumble bacon into dressing just before using.

Poppy Seed Dressing

MAKES ABOUT 1¾ CUPS
ACTIVE TIME: 10 MINUTES ■ START TO FINISH: 3¼ HOURS (INCLUDES CHILLING)

■ If you like sweet dressings, you'll love this. It's good on iceberg or romaine, and it can take fruit—melon, for instance—in a savory direction if you want to serve it as a side to grilled pork tenderloin. ■

- ½ cup white wine vinegar
- ⅓ cup water
- ¼ cup sugar
- 1 teaspoon dry mustard
- ½ teaspoon minced garlic
- 1 tablespoon poppy seeds
- 1 tablespoon celery seeds
- 2 teaspoons salt
- Freshly ground black pepper
- 1 cup olive oil

Combine vinegar, water, sugar, mustard, garlic, poppy seeds, celery seeds, salt, and pepper to taste in a bowl, whisking until sugar is dissolved. Add oil in a slow stream, whisking until well blended.

Refrigerate dressing, covered, for 3 hours. Whisk well before using.

SANDWICHES AND PIZZAS

Europeans perfected the fork. The Chinese invented the chopstick. But no culture has ever done a better job at figuring out how—and what—to eat with fingers than our own. America is the perfect sandwich society.

As much as we respect the sandwich, we wouldn't dream of offering you recipes for anything ordinary. Although we firmly believe that the peanut butter and jelly sandwich (preferably with butter) is among the world's most underrated foods, you don't need our advice to make one. And you are entirely capable of whipping up a fine ham and cheese without any help from us. But over the years we have perfected the out-of-the-ordinary sandwich, and those are the ones we have included in this book.

On a sultry afternoon there is nothing more refreshing than a small, crisp cucumber sandwich, and the recipes include elegant little tea sandwiches along with open-faced Danish smørrebrød as lovely as jewels. Afternoon tea may be a thing of the past, but these little tidbits slide gracefully into a late brunch or early cocktail menu. Our historical selection includes the muffuletta, which was invented in New Orleans at the beginning of the twentieth century, and the croque-monsieur, which first saw the light of day in Paris at pretty much the same time. We know the exact date of the po'boy's first appearance: it was during the New Orleans streetcar workers' strike of 1929. Some ten years later, James Beard bestowed his wonderful onion sandwiches upon a grateful world. By this time the club sandwich was well established and at the height of its popularity. We have the latest trends in sandwich fashion in our repertoire as well. The newest is the wrap, which appeared about ten years ago and offered us a whole new way to eat without silverware.

To a sandwich, the wrapper is everything, for this is an art that must rigorously respect the bread. The right slice can make an ordinary sandwich sing, the wrong one sink an otherwise superb specimen. That is one of the reasons that American sandwiches have undergone their recent renaissance. As locally made breads have become increasingly available, our sandwiches have become increasingly delicious.

Because we think of pizza as a hot open-faced sandwich, we have included it in this chapter. Italians may eat their pizza with forks, but as a nation we delight in eating pizza by the slice and with our fingers. For that reason, the crust is truly important. The one we offer here is the best we've ever found. Crisp, chewy, and filled with flavor, it is easily made in your home oven. Having tasted this perfect little pie, you'll never again allow an ordinary pizza to cross your path. In fact, if you let them, all these recipes could have a profound impact on the midday meal at your house.

Sandwiches

Cucumber Tea Sandwiches

MAKES 24 TEA SANDWICHES
ACTIVE TIME: 40 MINUTES ■ START TO FINISH: 40 MINUTES

■ The beauty of this sandwich is in the texture: thin, crisp wafers of cucumber and white bread with just enough body (but not too much). Don't even think about getting out the mayonnaise jar. These must be made with good, sweet butter; we've added a touch of chives. ■

FOR CHIVE BUTTER

- 3/4 stick (6 tablespoons) unsalted butter, softened
- 2 teaspoons fresh lemon juice
- 1/4 teaspoon salt
- 2 tablespoons finely chopped fresh chives

FOR ASSEMBLING SANDWICHES

- 12 very thin slices firm white sandwich bread, crusts discarded
- 1 seedless cucumber (usually plastic wrapped), peeled and sliced paper-thin
- 1/2 teaspoon salt
- Freshly ground black pepper

MAKE THE CHIVE BUTTER: Stir together butter, lemon juice, and salt in a bowl until well combined, then stir in chives.

MAKE THE SANDWICHES: Spread chive butter on bread. Arrange 2 layers of cucumber on 6 slices and sprinkle with salt and pepper to taste. Top with remaining bread, pressing down gently. Cut each sandwich diagonally into quarters and arrange on a serving platter.

COOK'S NOTE

■ The sandwiches can be made up to 2 hours ahead and refrigerated, covered with plastic wrap.

Herbed Vidalia Onion Tea Sandwiches

MAKES 24 TEA SANDWICHES
ACTIVE TIME: 50 MINUTES ■ START TO FINISH: 50 MINUTES

■ Leave it to the late James Beard, the guru of American food (and a *Gourmet* contributor), to come up with these innovative and extremely popular sandwiches. Serving raw onion sandwiches at a cocktail party might be considered a gutsy move, but Beard made them part of his catering repertoire as early as the 1940s. He gives the recipe, called "onion rings," in his autobiography, *Delights and Prejudices*. In our rendition of this classic, we use sweet Vidalia onions, which are now available almost all year round. (Other sweet onions, such as Walla Wallas and those from Maui, will also do the trick.) Like Beard, we cut the bread into rounds and roll the edges of the sandwiches first in mayonnaise and then in parsley, which, Beard says, "should make a fairly heavy wreath." The trick to doing this easily is to use squares of wax paper for both the mayo and the parsley; you get an even coating that way, and cleanup is a snap. ■

- 2/3 cup mayonnaise
- 1 cup minced fresh curly parsley
- 2 tablespoons minced fresh tarragon (optional)
- 1 teaspoon fresh lemon juice, or to taste
- 1/4 teaspoon salt
- 1/8 teaspoon freshly ground black pepper
- 1/8 teaspoon Tabasco, or to taste
- 12 very thin slices firm white sandwich bread
- 2 Vidalia or other sweet onions (1 pound total), cut into 1/8-inch-thick rounds

SPECIAL EQUIPMENT: a 1 5/8-inch round cookie cutter

Stir together 1/3 cup mayonnaise, 1/4 cup parsley, tarragon, if using, lemon juice, salt, pepper, and Tabasco in a bowl.

Cut 4 rounds from each slice of bread with cookie cutter and arrange in one layer on a tray. Spread rounds evenly with herbed mayonnaise. Cut out 2 or 3 rounds from each onion slice with cutter. Top half of bread rounds with onion rounds, transferring onion rounds carefully with a spatula so rings don't separate. Invert remaining bread rounds on top of onions. (Reserve scraps of bread and onions for another use.)

Lay two 12-inch squares of wax paper on a work surface. Spread remaining 1/3 cup mayonnaise in a very thin layer over one square, and spread remaining 3/4 cup parsley evenly over other square.

Carefully roll edges of each sandwich first in mayonnaise to coat lightly, then in parsley, and arrange sandwiches on a serving platter.

COOK'S NOTE

- The sandwiches can be made up to 2 hours ahead and refrigerated, covered with plastic wrap.

Chicken Salad Tea Sandwiches with Smoked Almonds

MAKES 24 TEA SANDWICHES
ACTIVE TIME: 20 MINUTES ■ START TO FINISH: 45 MINUTES

■ News flash: smoked almonds are more than a cocktail nibble—they make a great ingredient. Here we've finely chopped the nuts and rolled the edges of little sandwiches in them. Their bold flavor and crispness infuse chicken salad, and the concept of tea sandwiches, with a modicum of oomph. These sandwiches are assembled and then cut into rounds, but cut them into squares or triangles if you prefer. ■

- 3 cups chicken stock or store-bought low-sodium broth or water
- 4 skinless, boneless chicken breast halves (1 1/2 pounds total)
- 1 cup mayonnaise
- 1/3 cup minced shallots
- 1 teaspoon minced fresh tarragon
- Fresh lemon juice to taste
- Salt and freshly ground black pepper
- 24 very thin slices firm white sandwich bread
- 1/2 cup (2 ounces) finely chopped smoked almonds

SPECIAL EQUIPMENT: a 2-inch round cookie cutter

Bring stock to a boil in a deep 12-inch skillet. Add chicken breasts in one layer, reduce heat, and poach chicken at a bare simmer, turning once, for 7 minutes. Remove skillet from heat and cool chicken in cooking liquid for 15 to 20 minutes.

When chicken is cool enough to handle, drain (reserve broth for another use, if desired) and finely shred chicken.

Stir together chicken, 1/2 cup mayonnaise, shallots, tarragon, lemon juice, and salt and pepper to taste in a bowl. Make sandwiches with chicken salad and bread, pressing together gently. With cookie cutter, cut 2 rounds from each sandwich.

Put almonds on a small plate. Spread remaining 1/2 cup mayonnaise on edges of sandwich rounds, then roll edges in almonds and arrange sandwiches on a serving platter.

COOK'S NOTE

- The sandwiches can be made up to 2 hours ahead and refrigerated, loosely covered with plastic wrap.

Smoked Salmon Smørrebrød

MAKES 8 OPEN-FACED SANDWICHES;
SERVES 4 AS A LIGHT MAIN COURSE
ACTIVE TIME: 30 MINUTES ■ START TO FINISH: 35 MINUTES

■ Smørrebrød, Denmark's famous open-faced sandwich on buttered dark rye, which is eaten with knife and fork, might look dainty, but think of it as a light yet satisfying meal (and a beautiful, artistic one). This one, with smoked salmon and creamy scrambled eggs, is perfect for brunch, Sunday night supper, or a late-night snack. Stock up on beer—Carlsberg or Tuborg, for instance—and you have an ideal holiday party. ■

FOR SCRAMBLED EGGS

- 10 large eggs
- 2 ounces cream cheese, cut into pieces and softened
- Salt and white pepper
- 3 tablespoons unsalted butter

FOR ASSEMBLING SANDWICHES

- ½ stick (4 tablespoons) unsalted butter, softened
- 8 slices rye bread
- 2 cups thinly sliced seedless cucumber (usually plastic wrapped)
- ¾ cup finely chopped red bell pepper
- 1 pound thinly sliced smoked salmon
- 8 thin lemon slices

ACCOMPANIMENT: lemon wedges

MAKE THE SCRAMBLED EGGS: Whisk together eggs, cream cheese, and salt and white pepper to taste in a bowl until cream cheese breaks up into very small pieces. Heat butter in a 10-inch nonstick skillet over moderate heat until foam subsides. Add eggs and cook, stirring constantly, until just cooked through. Transfer to a plate and cool.

MAKE THE SANDWICHES: Spread butter on bread and arrange cucumber slices, overlapping slightly, on top. Spoon eggs over cucumber and top with bell pepper, salmon, and lemon slices. Serve with lemon wedges for squeezing over salmon.

Shrimp Smørrebrød

MAKES 8 OPEN-FACED SANDWICHES; SERVES 4 AS A LIGHT MAIN COURSE

ACTIVE TIME: 45 MINUTES ■ START TO FINISH: 45 MINUTES

■ Anyone who loves shrimp cocktail will love this. The beauty of smørrebrød is that the dense texture of the bread and the layer of good sweet butter prevent the open-faced sandwiches from getting soggy. ■

- 1¼ pounds medium shrimp in shells (31–35 per pound)
- ¼ cup heavy cream
- ¼ cup sour cream
- 2 tablespoons drained bottled horseradish
- Salt and freshly ground black pepper
- 2 firm but ripe California avocados
- 1 tablespoon fresh lemon juice
- ½ stick (4 tablespoons) unsalted butter, softened
- 8 slices rye bread
- 8 Boston lettuce leaves
- ½ small red onion, thinly sliced
- 1½ tablespoons drained capers

Cook shrimp in a 4-quart saucepan of boiling well-salted water until just cooked through, 1 to 2 minutes. Drain in a colander and rinse under cold water to stop the cooking. Peel shrimp.

Whisk heavy cream in a bowl until it holds soft peaks, then whisk in sour cream, horseradish, and salt and pepper to taste. Halve, pit, and peel avocados, then slice crosswise. Drizzle slices with lemon juice.

Spread butter on bread and top each slice with a lettuce leaf. Arrange avocado slices, onion, and shrimp on lettuce. Spoon dollops of horseradish sauce on sandwiches and sprinkle with capers.

All About Capers

Capers have a unique salty, tangy, pungent flavor that adds a piquant note to a number of Mediterranean dishes as well as to the cuisines of Eastern Europe and Scandinavia. They are the green flower buds of caper bushes, native to the Mediterranean. The buds are never eaten fresh but harvested, sun-dried, and packed in a vinegar brine or salt. (If untouched, caper buds become pink-and-white blossoms.) The buds grow fast, so once the time is right, they must be harvested every day. The most prized capers are the smallest, called *nonpareils* in France; as their size increases, their value decreases. Caper berries, the beautiful, mature fruit of the same shrub, are larger and somewhat starchier than capers. You can chop them and use them in place of capers, but we prefer them as a garnish.

Grilled Portobello Sandwiches with Sweet Peppers and Onion Relish

MAKES 6 SANDWICHES
ACTIVE TIME: 1¼ HOURS ■ START TO FINISH: 2¼ HOURS (INCLUDES MARINATING)

■ Portobellos, often called portabellas, are the meat of the matter here. They're really nothing more than mature cremini mushrooms. But whatever they are called, they make a robust sandwich. This recipe is from the Four Seasons Hotel in Boston. ■

- 1 large onion, halved lengthwise and thinly sliced crosswise
- ¾ cup balsamic vinegar
- 1 tablespoon sugar
- 4 bell peppers of assorted colors (red, yellow, and/or orange)
- 5 garlic cloves, minced
- 2 teaspoons olive oil
- 2 teaspoons chopped fresh basil
- 2 teaspoons chopped fresh flat-leaf parsley
- Salt and freshly ground black pepper
- 6 portobello mushroom caps (about 4 inches in diameter)
- 6 kaiser rolls, split in half
- 3 cups loosely packed arugula, coarse stems discarded

Combine onion, ¼ cup vinegar, and sugar in a 2-quart heavy saucepan and cook over low heat, stirring occasionally, until most of liquid has evaporated and mixture is thick, about 30 minutes. Remove from heat.

Quarter bell peppers lengthwise and remove stems, seeds, and ribs.

Whisk together garlic, oil, remaining ½ cup vinegar, 1 teaspoon basil, 1 teaspoon parsley, and salt and pepper to taste in a large bowl. Transfer one third of vinaigrette to a small bowl and add bell peppers, tossing to coat. Add mushrooms to remaining vinaigrette, tossing to coat. Marinate peppers and mushrooms, loosely covered, at room temperature, stirring occasionally, for 1 hour.

Prepare a charcoal or gas grill. If using a charcoal grill, open vents in bottom of grill, then light charcoal. Fire is hot when you can hold your hand 5 inches above rack for just 1 to 2 seconds. If using a gas grill, preheat on high, covered, for 10 minutes, then reduce heat to moderately high.

Remove vegetables from vinaigrette; discard vinaigrette. Lightly oil grill rack. Grill mushrooms, uncovered, turning once, until tender, about 6 minutes total. Transfer to a platter. Grill peppers, turning once, until lightly charred and tender, about 8 minutes total. Transfer to platter. Grill rolls, cut sides down, until lightly toasted, about 1 minute.

Thinly slice mushrooms and toss together with remaining 1 teaspoon each basil and parsley. Divide mushrooms, peppers, onion relish, and arugula among bottom halves of rolls. Season with salt and pepper to taste and add top halves of rolls.

COOK'S NOTE

■ The onion relish can be made up to 1 week ahead and refrigerated, covered.

Mozzarella in Carrozza

SERVES 6
ACTIVE TIME: 20 MINUTES ■ START TO FINISH: 20 MINUTES

■ We ate "mozzarella in a carriage," a cross between a grilled cheese sandwich and savory French toast, all over Sicily. It is usually served there either with a layer of capers inside the sandwich, as we do in this recipe, or with a caper-anchovy sauce on the side. We like the way the astringency of the capers cuts the richness of the cheese. ■

- ¼ cup drained capers, chopped
- 12 slices firm white sandwich bread
- 6 ounces fresh mozzarella, cut into ¼-inch-thick slices, at room temperature
- Freshly ground black pepper
- ¼ cup all-purpose flour
- 2 large eggs
- 2 tablespoons whole milk
- Salt
- 1 tablespoon unsalted butter
- 2 tablespoons olive oil

Divide capers among bread slices, spreading them evenly. Divide mozzarella among 6 slices and season with pepper. Make into 6 sandwiches, then trim off crusts to form 3-inch squares; discard crusts.

Put flour on a plate and coat sandwiches with flour, knocking off excess. Beat together eggs, milk, and a pinch each of salt and pepper in a small shallow bowl.

Heat 1/2 tablespoon butter with 1 tablespoon oil in a 10-inch heavy skillet over moderate heat until foam subsides. Coat 3 sandwiches, one at a time, with egg mixture, letting excess drip off, and add to skillet. Fry, turning once, until golden brown, about 5 minutes total, then drain on paper towels. Coat remaining 3 sandwiches and fry in remaining oil and butter in same manner.

Cut sandwiches into quarters and serve immediately.

Grilled Eggplant Sandwiches with Lemon Aïoli, Feta, and Mint

MAKES 4 SANDWICHES

ACTIVE TIME: 20 MINUTES ■ START TO FINISH: 20 MINUTES

■ Grilling brings out the best in eggplant, imparting a smoky flavor and a soft, almost custardy texture. Pile on tangy feta, spread with aïoli for a lemony wallop, top with a little sprightly mint to lighten the intensity, and you've got a winner. ■

- 1 medium eggplant (1 pound), cut into 1/4-inch-thick slices
- 3 tablespoons olive oil
- Salt and freshly ground black pepper
- 2 tablespoons mayonnaise
- 1/4 teaspoon minced garlic, or to taste
- 1 teaspoon fresh lemon juice
- 1 (16-inch-long) baguette
- 3/4 cup crumbled feta
- 1/4 cup loosely packed fresh mint leaves

Prepare a charcoal or gas grill. If using a charcoal grill, open vents in bottom of grill, then light charcoal. Fire is hot when you can hold your hand 5 inches above rack for just 1 to 2 seconds. If using a gas grill, preheat on high, covered, for 10 minutes, then reduce heat to moderately high.

Brush eggplant with oil and season with salt and pepper. Lightly oil grill rack. Grill eggplant in batches, uncovered, turning once, until tender, about 3 minutes per batch. Transfer to a baking sheet to cool.

To make aïoli, whisk together mayonnaise, garlic, and lemon juice in a small bowl.

Cut bread into 4 pieces, then split each piece open. Divide eggplant, aïoli, feta, and mint among bread.

COOK'S NOTE

■ The eggplant can also be broiled. Arrange in one layer (cook in batches if necessary) on a lightly oiled broiler pan and broil 5 to 7 inches from the heat, turning once, until tender, about 3 minutes total (per batch).

Falafel Pitas

MAKES 6 SANDWICHES

ACTIVE TIME: 30 MINUTES ■ START TO FINISH: 25 HOURS (INCLUDES SOAKING CHICKPEAS)

■ For this Middle Eastern specialty, falafel—small, deep-fried balls or patties made from a spiced coarse chickpea paste—is stuffed into a pita with chopped vegetables and a tangy sauce and eaten like a sandwich. It makes a substantial meal. If you've never had homemade falafel, you are in for a treat. ■

- 1/2 pound dried chickpeas
- 1/2 cup minced scallions
- 1/4 cup minced fresh flat-leaf parsley
- 2 garlic cloves, minced
- 1 1/2 teaspoons salt
- 1/4 teaspoon baking powder
- 1 teaspoon ground cumin
- 3/4 teaspoon ground coriander
- 1/8 teaspoon cayenne
- 3 (6-inch) pita breads (with pockets)
- About 8 cups vegetable oil for deep-frying

ACCOMPANIMENT: Chopped Vegetable Salad (recipe follows) and Tahini Sauce (page 891)

SPECIAL EQUIPMENT: a deep-fat thermometer

Soak chickpeas in cold water to cover by 2 inches, refrigerated, for 24 hours. Drain well.

Finely grind chickpeas in a food processor. Add scallions, parsley, garlic, salt, baking powder, cumin, coriander, and cayenne and blend until as smooth as possible (mixture will remain grainy). Transfer to a bowl and let stand, covered, for 30 minutes.

Put a rack in middle of oven and preheat oven to 350°F.

Halve pitas crosswise, then stack pockets and wrap in foil. Heat in oven for 10 minutes.

Meanwhile, form falafel into eighteen 1½-inch-wide patties and arrange in one layer on a sheet of wax paper.

Heat 2½ inches vegetable oil in a heavy 4-quart saucepan until it registers 375°F on thermometer. Fry falafel in batches, turning once, until golden brown, 1 to 2 minutes per batch. Transfer to paper towels to drain. (Return oil to 375°F between batches.)

Fill each pita pocket with 3 falafel patties and top with a heaping spoonful of vegetable salad. Serve with tahini sauce.

Chopped Vegetable Salad

MAKES ABOUT 4 CUPS; SERVES 6

ACTIVE TIME: 45 MINUTES ■ START TO FINISH: 45 MINUTES

■ This refreshing salad sparkles with mint and lemon juice and is easy to eat in a sandwich. The traditional topping for a falafel sandwich, it's delicious on anything else in a pita. ■

- 1½ pounds tomatoes, peeled (see Tips, page 940), seeded, and chopped
- 1 small green bell pepper, cored, seeded, and chopped
- 1 small cucumber, peeled, halved lengthwise, seeded, and chopped
- 4 radishes, finely chopped
- 3 scallions, thinly sliced
- 2 tablespoons finely chopped fresh flat-leaf parsley
- 2 tablespoons finely chopped fresh mint
- 1 small garlic clove
- ½ teaspoon salt
- 3 tablespoons fresh lemon juice
- ¼ teaspoon freshly ground black pepper
- 3 tablespoons olive oil

Combine tomatoes, bell pepper, cucumber, radishes, scallions, parsley, and mint in a large bowl.

Using a large heavy knife, mince garlic and mash to a paste with salt. Whisk together garlic paste, lemon juice, and pepper in a small bowl. Add oil in a slow stream, whisking until well blended. Add dressing to salad and toss well.

Tomato and Cucumber Salad in Pita Bread with Za'atar

MAKES 6 SANDWICHES

ACTIVE TIME: 20 MINUTES ■ START TO FINISH: 20 MINUTES

■ You'll find that in sultry weather, you can practically live on this salad in a pocket, much as people in the Middle East do. A typical Israeli breakfast, for instance, might include it along with fresh mild goat cheese or feta. On a blazing August day, it's perfectly fine to eat it for breakfast and have more of the same for lunch. It's seasoned with *za'atar*, a blend of sesame, thyme, and sumac. ■

- 6 (6-inch) pita breads (with pockets)
- 3 medium tomatoes, coarsely chopped
- 1 large cucumber, peeled and chopped
- 4 scallions, thinly sliced
- ¼ cup chopped fresh flat-leaf parsley
- Salt and freshly ground black pepper
- 2 tablespoons fresh lemon juice
- ¼ cup extra-virgin olive oil

ACCOMPANIMENTS: olive oil and Sesame Thyme Seasoning (*za'atar;* recipe follows)

Put a rack in middle of oven and preheat oven to 350°F.

Stack pitas and wrap in foil. Heat in oven until warm, about 10 minutes.

Meanwhile, stir together tomatoes, cucumber, scallions, parsley, and salt and pepper to taste in a bowl. Drizzle lemon juice over salad and stir, then drizzle oil over and stir.

Cut warm pitas in half, then stuff each half with salad and sprinkle with olive oil and *za'atar*.

Sesame Thyme Seasoning
Za'atar

MAKES ABOUT 1/4 CUP
ACTIVE TIME: 15 MINUTES ■ START TO FINISH: 15 MINUTES

■ A popular seasoning throughout the Middle East, *za'atar* (Arabic for "wild thyme") is a delicious blend of that herb, ground sumac, toasted sesame seeds, and salt. Try baking some on a pita brushed with a little olive oil or sprinkling a bit on fried eggs, both traditional breakfast preparations in the Middle East. It's best to make your own. The kind sold in Middle Eastern markets and specialty foods shops can be as dry (and as tasteless) as dust. The only ingredient that can be hard to find is sumac, the funky-tart berries of the Sicilian, or elm-leafed, variety of the sumac tree, dried and ground to a purplish red powder. Look for it in Middle Eastern and other specialty markets, or see Sources. ■

- 2 tablespoons sesame seeds, toasted (see Tips, page 939)
- 2 teaspoons ground sumac (see above)
- 1½–2 tablespoons minced fresh thyme (to taste)
- ½ teaspoon salt

Stir together all ingredients in a small bowl.

COOK'S NOTE

■ *Za'atar* can be kept in an airtight container, refrigerated, for up to 1 week.

Moroccan Carrot and Goat Cheese Sandwiches with Green Olive Tapenade

MAKES 6 SANDWICHES
ACTIVE TIME: 30 MINUTES ■ START TO FINISH: 4½ HOURS (INCLUDES MARINATING)

■ Okay, this may sound a little weird, but it's one of our favorites. The carrots are sliced very thin, blanched, and then marinated. When finished, their texture resembles that of cold cuts. In fact, this sandwich, Moroccan in seasoning and complex in flavor, is as satisfying as a deli sandwich, but not as heavy. The tanginess of the goat cheese offsets the sweetness of the carrots, and tapenade (whether homemade, as here, or store-bought) adds a juicy savoriness. The inspiration for this recipe came from the Manhattan restaurant Alice's Tea Cup. These sandwiches are perfect for a picnic. ■

FOR CARROTS
- 2 tablespoons sugar
- 1 tablespoon fresh lemon juice
- 2 teaspoons sweet paprika, preferably Hungarian
- 1 teaspoon ground cumin
- ½ teaspoon ground cinnamon
- ¼ teaspoon cayenne
- 1 teaspoon salt
- ¼ cup olive oil
- 1½ pounds medium carrots (about 8)

FOR TAPENADE
- 1¼ cups green olives (6–7 ounces), such as Cerignola or Picholine, pitted
- 3 tablespoons drained capers, rinsed
- ¼ cup chopped fresh flat-leaf parsley
- 1 flat anchovy fillet, chopped
- 1 teaspoon finely grated lemon zest
- 1½ tablespoons fresh lemon juice
- ½ teaspoon freshly ground black pepper
- ¼ cup olive oil

FOR ASSEMBLING SANDWICHES
- 12 slices good pumpernickel bread
- ¾ cup (6 ounces) soft mild goat cheese, at room temperature

SPECIAL EQUIPMENT: a mandoline or other adjustable-blade slicer, such as a Japanese Benriner

PREPARE THE CARROTS: Whisk together sugar, lemon juice, spices, salt, and oil in a large bowl until sugar is dissolved.

Halve carrots on a long diagonal. Starting from cut ends, cut into 1/16-inch-thick slices with slicer.

Cook carrots in a 4- to 5-quart pot of boiling well-salted water until crisp-tender, about 45 seconds. Drain well and immediately toss with marinade. Cool to room temperature, stirring occasionally.

Marinate carrots, covered and refrigerated, for at least 4 hours, stirring occasionally. Season with salt if necessary.

MAKE THE TAPENADE: Pulse olives with capers, parsley, anchovy, lemon zest, juice, and pepper in a food processor until coarsely chopped. Scrape down sides of bowl with a rubber spatula. Pulsing motor, add oil in a slow stream, and continue to pulse just until mixture is finely chopped; do not pulse to a paste.

ASSEMBLE THE SANDWICHES: Spread tapenade on 6 bread slices and goat cheese on remaining 6 slices. Divide carrots among bread slices with tapenade and top with slices spread with goat cheese.

COOK'S NOTES

- The carrots can marinate for up to 2 days.
- The tapenade can be made up to 1 week ahead and refrigerated, covered.

Grilled Gorgonzola, Pear, and Watercress Sandwiches

MAKES 4 OPEN-FACED SANDWICHES
ACTIVE TIME: 20 MINUTES ■ START TO FINISH: 20 MINUTES

■ There's no law that says dinner has to end with dessert. Sometimes what's needed is an excuse to open another bottle of wine and keep the conversation rolling, which is where savories come in: a tidbit of something rich, piquant, and salty that nineteenth-century gentlemen could enjoy with brandy and an after-dinner cigar around fashionable tables or in their clubs. Thank goodness times have changed and men don't get to keep savories all to themselves anymore. Here, peppery watercress works beautifully with salty Gorgonzola and sweet pear; this would also make a wonderful supper dish in lieu of heavier food.

The concept of savories is English in origin, so we based this one on the Lockets Savoury found in the classic *English Food* by the late Jane Grigson, one of the world's most influential (and companionable) culinary writers. The author's own inspiration came from a London restaurant called Locket's. ■

1 firm but ripe pear, such as Bartlett or Anjou
4 slices whole-grain bread
1 cup watercress sprigs (1/2 bunch), coarse stems discarded
1/4 pound chilled Gorgonzola, thinly sliced

SPECIAL EQUIPMENT: a melon ball cutter

Preheat broiler. Halve pear lengthwise and core with melon ball cutter, then thinly slice crosswise.

Toast bread on a small baking sheet about 3 inches from heat, turning once, until golden, 2 to 4 minutes total. Divide watercress among toasts and cover with overlapping pear slices. Arrange cheese over pear slices, then broil sandwiches until cheese is melted, about 1 minute.

Tarragon-Shallot Egg Salad Sandwiches

MAKES 6 SANDWICHES
ACTIVE TIME: 25 MINUTES ■ START TO FINISH: 45 MINUTES

■ Shallots and tarragon take your basic lunch-box egg salad on a spin down the Champs-Élysées. This sandwich is sophisticated without being stuffy. ■

FOR EGG SALAD
8 large eggs
1/2 cup mayonnaise
3 tablespoons finely chopped shallots
1 1/2 tablespoons finely chopped fresh tarragon, or to taste
2 teaspoons tarragon white-wine vinegar or white wine vinegar
1/4 teaspoon salt, or to taste
1/4 teaspoon freshly ground black pepper, or to taste

FOR ASSEMBLING SANDWICHES
Mayonnaise (optional)
12 slices seedless rye bread or 6 kaiser rolls, split in half
3 cups tender pea shoots (see page 556) or shredded soft-leaf lettuce, such as Boston lettuce

MAKE THE EGG SALAD: Combine eggs and cold water to cover by 1 1/2 inches in a 2-quart heavy saucepan and bring to a rolling boil, partially covered. Reduce heat to low, cover pan completely, and cook eggs for 30 seconds. Remove pan from heat and let eggs stand in hot water, covered, for 15 minutes.

Drain eggs in a colander and run cold water over them for about 5 minutes to stop the cooking. Peel eggs and finely chop.

Stir together eggs and remaining salad ingredients in a bowl with a fork.

MAKE THE SANDWICHES: Spread mayonnaise, if using, on bread (or cut sides of rolls). Make sandwiches with egg salad and pea shoots.

COOK'S NOTE

- The egg salad can be made up to 1 day ahead and refrigerated, covered.

Tuna Niçoise Sandwiches

Pan Bagnat

MAKES 2 SANDWICHES

ACTIVE TIME: 40 MINUTES ■ START TO FINISH: 40 MINUTES

■ This overstuffed tuna sandwich on a roll is a specialty of Nice. It doesn't often appear outside its place of origin, much to the dismay of the writer Calvin Trillin. When his favorite *pan bagnat* maker from the market in Nice, Susy Achor, of Chez Theresa, visited New York, we made sure to get the recipe, and we invited Trillin to vet the result. "Sure," he said. "If I have the same sort of olive oil stains on my shirt, I'll know it's authentic." Trillin nailed it: this sandwich is all about olive oil (*pan bagnat* translates literally as "bathed bread"). Use French oil if you can find it (one of our favorites is Alziari; see Sources); otherwise, any mild olive oil will do—save that fancy Tuscan for something else.

The tuna and the bread are certainly important too. Forget about tuna packed in water. You want the kind packed in olive (not vegetable) oil. Imported tuna is best, but it can be expensive and hard to find. Of the supermarket brands available in the United States, we prefer Progresso light tuna. We experimented with rolls as well. Ciabatta didn't pass the test (too elastic), nor did a Portuguese roll. Anything whole wheat was all wrong. What worked best was a humble kaiser roll—it soaked up the oil in just the right way.

Don't rush the first step of mixing the onions with oil, vinegar, and seasonings. The onions need time to release their juices and mellow. (At home in Nice, Achor lets her onion mixture sit all night.) Part of the appeal of a *pan bagnat* is its appearance, so take care in the composition: let the lettuce leaves, tomatoes (if you can't get really good ones, leave them out), eggs, and olives peek out of the sandwich enticingly. Now you are ready to pack up a picnic and head for the beach. Or sit at the kitchen table and dream of the cobalt-blue Mediterranean and hot sunshine. ■

- 1/4 medium white onion, thinly sliced
- 1/8 small red onion, thinly sliced
- 2 tablespoons mild extra-virgin olive oil, preferably French, plus additional for drizzling
- 1 tablespoon red wine vinegar, or more to taste
- 1/4 teaspoon salt
- Freshly ground black pepper
- 1 (6-ounce) can tuna in olive oil (not drained)
- Fresh lemon juice to taste
- 2–4 green leaf or Boston lettuce leaves
- 8 tomato slices
- 2 plain kaiser rolls, split in half
- 1 hard-boiled large egg, sliced
- 4 flat anchovy fillets
- 8 Niçoise olives, pitted
- 2 tablespoons chopped scallion greens
- 2 tablespoons sliced radishes

Combine onions, olive oil, 1 tablespoon vinegar, salt, and pepper to taste in a bowl and mix and squeeze with your hands until onions release their juices (they will mellow in flavor), about 5 minutes. Work in tuna, with its oil, and season with lemon juice and vinegar, salt, and/or pepper to taste.

Put 1 or 2 lettuce leaves and 4 tomato slices on bottom half of each roll, then top each with half of tuna and 3 or 4 slices hard-boiled egg. Crisscross anchovy fillets on top and strew with olives, scallion greens, and radishes. Drizzle generously with additional olive oil and top with remaining roll halves, pressing down gently but firmly.

Tuna and Artichoke Panini

MAKES 4 SANDWICHES
ACTIVE TIME: 30 MINUTES ■ START TO FINISH: 30 MINUTES

■ A typical *panino* is spare and elegant—no Dagwood here. This one is an Italian spin on tuna salad, similar to something we had in Rome: tuna (the type packed in flavorful olive oil), jarred artichokes, black olives, and capers on a crusty roll. Something was missing, though, so we added some thoroughly American mayonnaise, and we really like the way it mellows the artichokes and olives. A hefty amount of flat-leaf parsley takes the place of lettuce. ■

- ½ cup brine-cured black olives, rinsed, drained, and pitted
- 2 teaspoons drained capers
- 1 small garlic clove, chopped
- ½ teaspoon finely grated lemon zest
- 2 (6½-ounce) jars marinated artichokes, drained (3 tablespoons marinade reserved) and chopped
- ½ cup mayonnaise
- 2 (6-ounce) cans tuna in olive oil, drained and any large chunks broken into smaller pieces
- 4 (7-inch-long) ciabatta rolls or other crusty rolls with soft, chewy crumb
- Freshly ground black pepper
- ¾ cup fresh flat-leaf parsley leaves

Combine olives, capers, garlic, zest, and reserved 3 tablespoons artichoke marinade in a blender and blend, scraping down sides frequently, until as smooth as possible, 1 to 2 minutes. Transfer to a bowl and stir in mayonnaise. Stir together artichokes and tuna in another bowl.

Split each roll open and hollow out top half, leaving a ½-inch-thick shell. Spread olive mayonnaise on both cut sides of rolls. Divide tuna and artichokes among bottom halves of rolls. Season with pepper and top with parsley and tops of rolls.

Oyster Po'Boys

MAKES 2 SANDWICHES
ACTIVE TIME: 30 MINUTES ■ START TO FINISH: 30 MINUTES

■ Most true New Orleanians will tell you that this sandwich was born in 1929, when the local streetcar workers' union, Division 194, went on strike. Two brothers, Benny and Clovis Martin, former streetcar conductors and proprietors of a sandwich shop, decided to show their support the best way they could: by feeding the striking workers, greeting each one with "Here comes another poor boy."

Sandwiches (and New Orleans) being fickle, there are no real rules as to what makes a good sandwich great, which is why we decided to take some liberties

How to Pit Olives

Some olives are easier to pit than others. If you're lucky, the pits will slide out under pressure from your thumb and forefinger. If they require persuasion, line a few up on a cutting board and press them with the side of a large heavy knife; the pits should slide right out. Or, for perfect halves, make a lengthwise incision around the olive with a small sharp knife. At this point, an opposing twist of each olive half between the fingers may free the pit. If not, pressure from the side of a large knife will do the trick. With green olives, which are less ripe and therefore firmer, you may have to cut the olive off the pit.

here. Once upon a time, the heat you got in Louisiana (culinarily speaking, that is) was from Tabasco. But we thought that the smoky smolder of chipotles in adobo mixed with mayonnaise might do something nice for fried oysters, and we were right.

This sandwich needs to be stuffed into a bread that is light in texture, mild in flavor, and substantial enough to hold its shape when the sweet oyster juices flow. We find that a soft-crusted French, Italian, Portuguese, or Cuban loaf works well. ■

FOR CHIPOTLE MAYONNAISE

- 1/2 cup mayonnaise
- 1 1/4 teaspoons minced canned chipotle chiles in adobo (see Glossary)
- 1/2 teaspoon fresh lemon juice

FOR FRIED OYSTERS

- 6 cups vegetable oil for deep-frying
- 1 large egg
- 1/4 cup whole milk
- 2 1/2 teaspoons salt
- 1 1/2 cups cornmeal
- 1/4 teaspoon freshly ground black pepper
- 1 pint shucked oysters (about 36), drained

FOR ASSEMBLING SANDWICHES

- 1 (12- to 14-inch-long) loaf soft-crusted bread (see above)
- 3 cups shredded iceberg lettuce

ACCOMPANIMENT: lemon wedges

SPECIAL EQUIPMENT: a deep-fat thermometer

MAKE THE CHIPOTLE MAYONNAISE: Whisk together mayonnaise, chipotles, and lemon juice in a small bowl. Refrigerate, covered.

FRY THE OYSTERS: Heat oil in a deep heavy pot, preferably cast-iron, over high heat until it registers 375°F on thermometer. Meanwhile, whisk together egg, milk, and 1 teaspoon salt in a bowl. Shake together cornmeal, remaining 1 1/2 teaspoons salt, and pepper in a plastic or paper bag until well combined.

Add one quarter of oysters to egg mixture, then lift out, letting excess drip off, and transfer to cornmeal mixture in bag, shaking to coat well. Carefully transfer oysters to oil, knocking off excess coating, and fry, turning occasionally, until golden and just cooked through, 1 to 2 minutes. With a slotted spoon, transfer to paper towels to drain. Coat and fry remaining oysters in three batches. (Return oil to 375°F between batches.)

ASSEMBLE THE SANDWICHES: Cut loaf crosswise in half, then split each half open. Spread bottom halves with chipotle mayonnaise. Top with oysters and lettuce, then top halves of bread, pressing down gently.

Serve with lemon wedges.

COOK'S NOTE

■ Transfer the remainder of the chiles and their tomatoey sauce to a glass jar; they'll keep almost forever in the fridge.

Chicken Club Sandwiches

MAKES 2 SANDWICHES
ACTIVE TIME: 45 MINUTES ■ START TO FINISH: 1 HOUR

■ Prevailing theories put the origin of the club sandwich in a private club setting or in the club car of a train en route from New York to Chicago. The problem with the modern incarnation is that all the components are usually made ahead of time: the bread is toasted and the bacon fried hours before; the tomatoes are presliced and dry out. Try this one and you'll find that a freshly made club is a whole new ball game. Our version returns this American classic to its former status, with poached chicken (you could also use poached turkey breast; see page 386), soft-leaf lettuce, and avocado. Sour cream adds a tangy note to the spread, but the sandwich is just as good without it. ■

- 2 (8-ounce) skinless, boneless chicken breast halves
- 1/2 teaspoon salt
- 1/4 cup mayonnaise
- 2 tablespoons sour cream (optional)
- 3 tablespoons chopped fresh flat-leaf parsley or basil
- 1 tablespoon finely grated lemon zest (from 2 lemons)
- 1 teaspoon fresh lemon juice
- 1/4 teaspoon cracked black pepper
- 6 bacon slices, cut crosswise in half
- 6 slices firm white sandwich bread, toasted
- 4 Boston lettuce leaves

4 (¼-inch-thick) large tomato slices
½ firm but ripe California avocado, peeled, pitted, and sliced crosswise (optional)

Combine chicken and water to cover in a 10-inch skillet and bring to a simmer. Reduce heat and simmer, turning once, for 5 minutes. Remove from heat, cover, and let stand until cooked through, 10 to 12 minutes.

Transfer chicken to a plate to cool and sprinkle with ¼ teaspoon salt. When cool enough to handle, thinly slice on the diagonal.

Stir together mayonnaise, sour cream, parsley, lemon zest, juice, remaining ¼ teaspoon salt, and cracked pepper in a small bowl until combined.

Cook bacon in a 12-inch heavy skillet over moderate heat, turning once, until browned, about 6 minutes total. Transfer to paper towels to drain.

Spread each slice of toast generously with mayonnaise mixture. Divide lettuce, tomato, bacon, and avocado, if using, between 2 slices. Top each with another piece of toast, mayonnaise side up, then top with chicken and remaining toast, mayonnaise side down. Cut each sandwich into quarters and secure with wooden picks.

Turkey Wraps with Chipotle Mayonnaise

MAKES 4 SANDWICHES
ACTIVE TIME: 30 MINUTES ■ START TO FINISH: 2½ HOURS (INCLUDES CHILLING)

■ For many of us, these turkey sandwiches are a post-Thanksgiving ritual. Spicy chipotle mayonnaise and Mexican pickled onion are the key players: both condiments are extremely easy to prepare and take virtually no time at all. As the onion cools in its brine, it turns the color of a pink piñata and becomes crisp. It will keep for weeks in a glass jar in the fridge. The mayo is made with canned chipotles in adobo sauce, one of our favorite pantry staples. Children might prefer *salsa rosada*—a combination of mayo and ketchup. The sandwiches are also delicious made with leftover pot roast, roast pork, roast chicken, you name it. ■

FOR PICKLED ONION

1 red onion (6 ounces), sliced crosswise ¼ inch thick
½ cup cider vinegar
¾ cup water
½ teaspoon salt

FOR CHIPOTLE MAYONNAISE

1½ teaspoons chopped canned chipotle chiles in adobo (see Glossary), including some adobo sauce
¼ cup mayonnaise

FOR ASSEMBLING WRAPS

4 (8-inch) flour tortillas, preferably whole wheat
¼ pound sliced or shredded roast turkey or chicken
¾ cup tender pea shoots (see page 556) or shredded lettuce leaves
Salt and freshly ground black pepper

MAKE THE PICKLED ONION: Blanch onion in a 1½-quart saucepan of boiling water for 1 minute; drain. Return onion to pan, add vinegar, water, and salt, and bring to a boil. Reduce heat and simmer, stirring occasionally, for 1 minute. Transfer mixture to a heatproof bowl. Cool, uncovered, then refrigerate until cold, covered, about 2 hours.

MAKE THE CHIPOTLE MAYONNAISE: Blend chipotle and mayonnaise in a blender or food processor until smooth.

MAKE THE WRAPS: Toast tortillas directly on (gas or electric) burners over moderate heat, turning over and rotating until slightly puffed and browned in spots, 40 to 60 seconds.

Spread 1 tablespoon chipotle mayonnaise on each tortilla. Arrange one quarter of turkey and pea shoots across middle of each tortilla and top with some drained pickled onion. Season with salt and pepper and roll up wraps.

COOK'S NOTE

■ Transfer the remaining chipotle chiles and adobo sauce to a glass jar and refrigerate; they'll keep almost indefinitely.

Croque-Monsieur

MAKES 4 SANDWICHES
ACTIVE TIME: 25 MINUTES ■ START TO FINISH: 25 MINUTES

■ What makes this French grilled ham and cheese sandwich sublime is the Mornay sauce (béchamel with cheese). It's the whole *point,* really, which is why the sandwich requires the use of a knife and fork. The first croque-monsieur was served in a Parisian café (but of course) in 1910, and the sandwich is still going strong in cafés and bistros the world over. Embellished with a fried egg on top, croque-monsieur becomes croque-madame. ■

- 5 tablespoons unsalted butter, softened
- 2 tablespoons all-purpose flour
- 1 cup whole milk
- 6 ounces thinly sliced Gruyère
- 1 teaspoon Dijon mustard
- Salt and freshly ground black pepper
- Pinch of freshly grated nutmeg, or to taste
- 8 slices firm white sandwich bread, crusts discarded
- ¼ pound thinly sliced ham

MAKE THE SAUCE: Melt 2 tablespoons butter in a small heavy saucepan over moderately low heat. Stir in flour and cook, stirring, for 2 minutes to make a roux. Whisk in milk and bring to a boil, whisking constantly. Reduce heat and simmer, whisking occasionally, for 5 minutes.

Meanwhile, chop enough cheese to measure ½ cup. Whisk chopped cheese and mustard into sauce, then whisk until cheese is melted. Remove from heat. Season with salt and pepper and sprinkle with nutmeg. Cover with wax paper placed directly on surface and keep warm.

MAKE THE SANDWICHES: Lay 4 slices bread on work surface. Divide ham and remaining cheese slices among them. Spread 1 tablespoon Mornay sauce evenly on each of remaining bread slices and invert over ham and cheese. Spread half of remaining butter evenly on top of sandwiches and transfer, buttered sides down, to an ovenproof 12-inch skillet. Spread remaining butter on top of sandwiches. Cook over low heat, turning once, until both sides are golden, 6 to 8 minutes total.

Preheat broiler. Leaving sandwiches in skillet, spread tops of sandwiches evenly with remaining Mornay sauce. Broil 5 to 6 inches from heat until sauce is bubbling and golden in patches, about 2 minutes. Transfer sandwiches to plates.

COOK'S NOTE

■ The cooled Mornay sauce can be refrigerated, the surface covered with wax paper or plastic wrap, for up to 3 days. Reheat over low heat.

Muffuletta

SERVES 6
ACTIVE TIME: 40 MINUTES ■ START TO FINISH: 5¼ HOURS (INCLUDES CHILLING)

■ Central Grocery on Decatur Street in New Orleans is where it all began. Around 1906, the grocery's founder, a recent Sicilian immigrant named Salvatore Lupo, started making the sandwich (named for a seeded round loaf of bread common back home) for fellow immigrants who stopped by his store every day to buy ingredients for their unvarying meal: meat, cheese, bread, and olive salad. The rest, as they say, is history. What makes this carved-out and overstuffed loaf so delicious is the garlicky olive salad; it acts as a seasoning and also adds crunch. True aficionados may quibble, but we've made this a little easier to eat by chopping the vegetables fine so they don't go flying at the first bite. ■

- ½ cup finely chopped celery
- ⅓ cup Kalamata olives (2 ounces), pitted and finely chopped
- ⅓ cup Italian green olives (2 ounces), pitted and finely chopped
- ¼ cup finely chopped fresh flat-leaf parsley
- 1 small garlic clove, finely chopped
- ½ cup finely chopped tomatoes
- 6 tablespoons extra-virgin olive oil
- 2 teaspoons red wine vinegar
- ¼ teaspoon freshly ground black pepper
- 1 round soft country loaf (about 10 inches; 1 pound)
- ⅓ pound thinly sliced provolone
- ⅓ pound thinly sliced Genoa salami
- ⅓ pound thinly sliced ham

Stir together celery, olives, parsley, garlic, tomatoes, 4 tablespoons (1/4 cup) oil, vinegar, and pepper in a bowl.

Cut bread horizontally in half with a serrated knife. Remove soft centers of both halves to make room for filling, leaving a 1/2-inch-thick shell. Drizzle both halves with remaining 2 tablespoons oil. Spread half of olive mixture in each half of bread, gently pressing down to help adhere. Layer cheese, salami, and ham on bottom half of bread. Cover with top half of bread. Wrap sandwich well in plastic wrap, then foil. Refrigerate for at least 4 hours.

Let sandwich stand at room temperature for 30 minutes before cutting into wedges.

COOK'S NOTE

- The muffuletta can be refrigerated for up to 24 hours.

Roast Beef Sandwiches with Roquefort and Caramelized Shallots

MAKES 4 SANDWICHES

ACTIVE TIME: 15 MINUTES ■ START TO FINISH: 40 MINUTES

■ Here we take a nice leftover and turn it into an event: our answer to the Philly cheese steak. In fact, this sandwich is so rich with caramelized shallots and melted Roquefort that you might want to roast beef specifically *for* the leftovers. A loaf of tangy sourdough cuts the sandwich's overall richness. ■

- 3 tablespoons unsalted butter
- 3/4 pound shallots, thinly sliced (1 1/2 cups)
- Salt and freshly ground black pepper
- 8 slices sourdough bread
- 1 pound thinly sliced medium-rare roast beef
- 3 ounces chilled Roquefort, crumbled (2/3 cup), or to taste

Put a rack in middle of oven and preheat oven to 375°F.

Melt butter in a heavy skillet over moderate heat. Add shallots, season with salt and pepper, and cook, stirring occasionally, until golden brown, about 10 minutes.

Lay 4 slices bread on work surface. Divide roast beef, Roquefort, and shallots among them and top with remaining bread. Put on a baking sheet and bake until cheese is melted and sandwiches are hot, 7 to 10 minutes.

Bacon, Arugula, Tomato, and Egg Sandwiches

MAKES 4 SANDWICHES

ACTIVE TIME: 40 MINUTES ■ START TO FINISH: 40 MINUTES

■ This is a BLT with a little sunshine added. Scrambled eggs make the sandwich more of a meal, and the piquant tomato chutney cuts the richness. But thin slices of a good, meaty beefsteak tomato will do the trick too. ■

- 1 pound thick-cut bacon
- 1 round sourdough loaf (10 inches), cut into 8 (1/3-inch-thick) slices and toasted
- 1/2 cup bottled tomato chutney, or to taste
- 7 large eggs
- 1/4 cup heavy cream
- Salt and freshly ground black pepper
- 2 tablespoons unsalted butter
- 12 arugula leaves or watercress sprigs, coarse stems discarded

Cook bacon in a 12-inch nonstick skillet until crisp. Transfer to paper towels to drain, then cover with foil to keep warm.

Spread each toast with 1 tablespoon chutney, or to taste. Whisk together eggs and cream in a bowl and season with salt and pepper. Heat butter in a 10-inch skillet over moderate heat until foam subsides. Add egg mixture and cook, stirring slowly but constantly, until just cooked through. Make sandwiches with toast, scrambled eggs, bacon, and arugula.

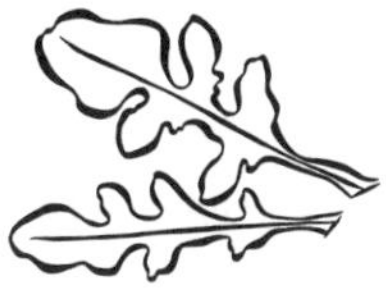

Cuban Sandwiches

MAKES 4 SANDWICHES
ACTIVE TIME: 40 MINUTES ■ START TO FINISH: 8 HOURS (INCLUDES MARINATING, ROASTING, AND CHILLING PORK)

■ The quintessential Cuban sandwich is heaven for pork lovers: bread stuffed with ham, roast pork, Swiss cheese, and pickles and cooked in a sandwich press. The filling warms in its own steam, and the bread toasts to a buttery crunch. You don't want these sandwiches too hefty; they are best when they are about an inch thick after pressing. If you don't have a sandwich press, all is not lost: two cast-iron skillets will do the trick nicely, or you can use a waffle iron, preferably one with flat plates. There is also always a trip to Miami, where you can order a Cuban sandwich and a tropical shake made with mamey, a fruit related to the mangosteen. Celestial. ■

- 8 teaspoons mayonnaise
- 4 Portuguese rolls (5–6 inches long), split, or 2 hero rolls (11–12 inches long), halved crosswise and split
- 4 teaspoons yellow ballpark mustard
- ¼ pound thinly sliced ham, preferably Virginia or Black Forest
- ½ pound cold Roast Pork Loin (page 468), thinly sliced
- 12 thin lengthwise slices dill pickles (about 2 pickles)
- 6 ounces thinly sliced Swiss cheese
- 3 tablespoons unsalted butter, melted

SPECIAL EQUIPMENT: a sandwich press

Spread 2 teaspoons mayonnaise on top half of each roll. Spread 1 teaspoon mustard on bottom half of each roll, then layer ham, roast pork, pickles, and cheese over mustard, dividing them evenly. Place top halves of rolls on top and press down firmly to flatten sandwiches.

Brush outside of 2 sandwiches, top and bottom, with half of melted butter and put in sandwich press. Cook until golden and crusty and cheese is melted, 4 to 6 minutes. Repeat with remaining sandwiches and melted butter.

Halve sandwiches diagonally and serve warm.

COOK'S NOTES

- The sandwiches can be assembled up to 3 hours ahead. Refrigerate, wrapped in foil, without buttering outsides of bread; brush with butter before cooking.
- If you don't have a sandwich press, you can cook the sandwiches in a dry heavy cast-iron skillet over moderately low heat. Place a second skillet on top, pressing down slightly. Turn the sandwiches halfway through cooking.

SANDWICH PRESSES

Electric sandwich presses are countertop grills that compress and cook sandwiches into sleek, toasty envelopes. Having become popular along with Cuban sandwiches and toasted *panini,* both of which require a good pressing to ensure their basic character, sandwich presses are now getting raves for their transforming effect on American classics like ham and cheese. There are a number of models to choose from, but the general design is two ridged rectangular cooking plates (typically nonstick) hinged together like a waffle iron. The heavy upper plate presses the sandwich into shape, and the whole apparatus heats up enough to toast the bread on both sides and melt any cheese within. Upscale models may feature floating hinges to accommodate sandwiches of varying thicknesses, and some models offer thermostat control.

Shredded Pork and Lemon Coleslaw Sandwiches

MAKES 4 SANDWICHES
ACTIVE TIME: 1½ HOURS ■ START TO FINISH: 3½ HOURS (INCLUDES MAKING AND CHILLING COLESLAW)

■ This is a lightened-up twist on a pulled-pork barbecue sandwich: we've used lean pork tenderloin instead of pork shoulder and combined it with a flavorful sauce. Lemon coleslaw adds coolness and snap. ■

- 1 tablespoon olive oil
- 1 medium onion, chopped

- 1 garlic clove, minced
- 2 tablespoons cider vinegar
- 1/4 cup ketchup
- 2 tablespoons ketchup-style chili sauce
- 2 teaspoons Worcestershire sauce
- 1 teaspoon Tabasco
- 3/4 cup water
- 1/2 teaspoon salt
- 1/4 teaspoon freshly ground black pepper
- 1 (3/4-pound) pork tenderloin, halved crosswise
- 4 hamburger buns, split
- Lemon Coleslaw (recipe follows)

Heat oil in a 3- to 4-quart heavy saucepan over moderate heat. Add onion and garlic and cook, stirring, until golden, about 8 minutes. Stir in remaining ingredients except pork, buns, and coleslaw, bring to a simmer, and simmer, covered, for 10 minutes.

Add pork, cover, and simmer, turning occasionally, until tender, about 45 minutes.

Transfer pork to a cutting board. Purée cooking liquid in a blender until smooth (use caution) and return to pan. When pork is cool enough to handle, shred with your fingers or two forks and add to sauce. Simmer, stirring, just until pork is heated through.

Divide pork and sauce among bottoms of buns and top with some coleslaw and tops of buns.

COOK'S NOTE

- The shredded pork in sauce can be made up to 1 day ahead and refrigerated, covered. Reheat before serving.

Lemon Coleslaw

MAKES ABOUT 3 CUPS; SERVES 4
ACTIVE TIME: 40 MINUTES ■ START TO FINISH: 1 3/4 HOURS (INCLUDES CHILLING)

■ Adding a little salt and sugar to sliced cabbage and grated carrots encourages their juices to flow, so you can get away with just a jot of mayonnaise. The result? A very clean-tasting slaw, and one that's not too sweet. Scallions bring a little zestiness to the party. ■

- 2 tablespoons sour cream
- 2 teaspoons mayonnaise
- 1/2 teaspoon finely grated lemon zest
- 4 teaspoons fresh lemon juice
- 3 tablespoons water
- 1 teaspoon sugar
- 1/4 teaspoon salt
- 1/8 teaspoon freshly ground black pepper
- 4 cups thinly sliced green cabbage (about 1 pound)
- 2 carrots, coarsely grated
- 1 cup thinly sliced scallions (1 bunch)
- 1/2 cup chopped fresh flat-leaf parsley

Whisk together sour cream, mayonnaise, zest, juice, water, sugar, salt, and pepper in a large bowl until sugar is dissolved. Add cabbage, carrots, scallions, and parsley and toss well. Refrigerate, covered, for 1 hour to allow flavors to develop.

Season coleslaw with salt and pepper.

Pizza Dough and Equipment

Great pizza is within the reach of every home cook. Here are a few tips from Chris Bianco, the chef in Phoenix who makes the best pizza we know (see the dough recipe on page 199). His pies are casual and rustic, with the toppings distributed with a light hand and fresh herbs put on after the pizza comes out of the oven. The heat makes their aroma bloom, but the greens don't blacken. Casual, yes, but never careless.

"YEAST IS INCREDIBLY FORGIVING." At Pizzeria Bianco the chef relies on fresh yeast, but in our test kitchens we used active dry yeast—easier for home cooks to come by and less intimidating all around.

"WET DOUGH EQUALS CRISP CRUST." If the dough seems wetter than you are used to, it's probably just right. And work the dough by hand—it's impossible to overknead that way.

"YOU DON'T WANT TO PRESS EVERYTHING THAT'S GOOD OUT OF THE DOUGH." After the dough has risen, resist the urge to punch it down—you want to keep in some of the air. If you press too hard, you will not get a crust that's properly bubbly and blistered. And at this point, handling it gently will give you a tenderer result. You'll notice how soft and pliable this dough is; it couldn't be easier to work with. The goal is to stretch the dough gradually without compressing it, so don't even think about using a rolling pin. Flour your hands lightly yet thoroughly; they should look as if you pulled on a pair of sheer white gloves.

"LET THE WEIGHT OF THE DOUGH DO THE WORK." Begin to form a round, holding the dough mass by the edge and letting it hang perpendicular to the work surface. Turn the dough almost as if you were turning a steering wheel, just grazing the work surface as you go. If your dough is resistant to stretching wide, don't fight it. Simply leave the round smaller and pull the edges out as much as you can after topping the pie.

Two tools we highly recommend investing in are a baker's peel for getting your pie in and out of the oven and a pizza stone. (Both are available from cookware shops and by mail from the Baker's Catalogue; see Sources.) Bianco doesn't sprinkle his peel with cornmeal. Instead, he rubs flour into the grain of the wood and shakes off the excess. He never washes that patina off his peel, preferring simply to scrape it clean and keep it dry. A floured peel slips easily under a pizza with a smooth, fluid thrust-and-release (use the same motion for getting the pizza off the peel and onto the stone.) A hot stone will produce deliciously chewy, blistered edges and a bottom crust that's crisp all the way across. If you have an electric stove, put the stone on the bottom rack; if you have a gas stove, put it on the floor of your oven. Turn on the oven an hour before baking pizza, as it will take that long to heat the stone. To care for your stone, season it before using it for the first time in a warm oven (most pizza stones come with manufacturer's instructions). Don't clean your pizza stone with soap—soap will be absorbed by the clay and in turn by the pizza.

Pizzas

Pizza Margherita

MAKES ONE 14-INCH PIZZA
ACTIVE TIME: 50 MINUTES ■ START TO FINISH: 2¾ HOURS (INCLUDES MAKING DOUGH)

■ This is pizza at its purest perfection, as it is encountered in Italy or on the French Riviera. It's not overloaded with toppings but is the model of restraint and balance. In the height of tomato season, use chopped uncooked tomatoes, just drizzled with olive oil and sprinkled with salt. Otherwise, as we've done here, make the simplest possible tomato sauce with either fresh or canned tomatoes. The pizza is commonly thought to have been created in honor of the Italian queen Margherita's visit to Naples in the late nineteenth century. The red tomato, white mozzarella, and green basil are said to be emblematic of the then new Italian flag. ■

- 1 pound plum tomatoes, peeled (see Tips, page 940), seeded, and chopped, or 1 (28- to 32-ounce) can whole tomatoes in juice, drained, seeded, and chopped
- ¼ teaspoon salt
- 3 tablespoons extra-virgin olive oil
- 1½ cups coarsely grated mozzarella (about 6 ounces)
- Basic Pizza Dough (page 199), shaped into a ball and allowed to rise
- 1–2 tablespoons cornmeal, for sprinkling baker's peel
- 6–8 medium fresh basil leaves, torn

SPECIAL EQUIPMENT: a pizza stone and a baker's peel rubbed with flour, both at least 14 inches in diameter (see Sources)

Put pizza stone on oven floor if using a gas oven, on lowest rack if using electric (remove other racks in either case), and preheat oven to highest setting (500°–550°F). Allow about 1 hour to preheat stone.

MEANWHILE, PREPARE THE TOPPING: Combine tomatoes, salt, and 2 tablespoons oil in a 10-inch heavy skillet and bring to a simmer over moderate heat. Simmer, stirring occasionally, until thickened and reduced to about 1 cup, 10 to 15 minutes. Transfer to a bowl to cool.

Toss together mozzarella and remaining 1 tablespoon oil.

SHAPE THE DOUGH: Shape dough into a 14-inch round according to directions in Basic Pizza Dough recipe, on page 200.

ASSEMBLE AND BAKE THE PIZZA: Sprinkle baker's peel with 1 tablespoon cornmeal. Carefully slide dough onto peel, then jerk peel once or twice: if dough sticks, lift it and sprinkle a little more cornmeal underneath. Spread tomato sauce evenly over dough, leaving a ½-inch border, and top sauce with mozzarella.

Line up far edge of peel with far edge of stone and tilt peel, jerking it gently to start pizza moving. When edge of pizza touches stone, quickly pull back peel to transfer pizza to stone (do not pull pizza back). Bake until crust is golden brown and cheese is melted and bubbling, about 8 minutes. Slide peel under pizza to remove from oven, then scatter basil leaves on top.

Grilled Pizza Margherita

MAKES TWO 9-INCH PIZZAS

■ Something almost indescribable happens to the crust of a grilled pizza: it's richly blistered and profoundly chewy around the edges, and there are delicious little smoky, scorched patches on the bottom. It's not perfect but tastes of reckless abandon. According to George Germon and Johanne Killeen, the chef-owners of Al Forno restaurant, in Providence, Rhode Island, who pioneered the technique in the early 1980s, grilled pizza tastes so good because it comes into direct contact with the fire. The dough, Killeen poetically tells us, "is licked by flame and caressed by smoke." By contrast, in a wood-burning pizza oven, the heat and smoke rise so it is untouched by either fire or smoke. ■

Prepare Basic Pizza Dough, divide it and shape into 2 balls, and allow to rise as directed on page 199.

Shape risen dough into two 9-inch rounds for grilling according to directions on page 200. While dough stands, prepare topping as in baked Pizza Margherita.

TO GRILL THE PIZZAS USING A CHARCOAL GRILL: Open vents in bottom of grill and in lid. Light a heaping chimneyful of charcoal, then pour it evenly over two opposite sides of bottom of grill (you will have a double or triple layer of charcoal), leaving middle clear.

Remove plastic wrap from dough and lightly brush dough with olive oil.

When fire is medium-hot (you can hold your hand 5 inches above rack for just 3 to 4 seconds), lightly oil grill rack. Carefully transfer rounds, oiled sides down, to grill rack with your hands, arranging in center of rack, with no coals underneath, then brush tops with oil. Grill crusts, uncovered, until undersides are golden brown, 4 to 6 minutes (rotate them if one side of grill is hotter than the other). Flip crusts over with two metal spatulas and spread each crust evenly with half of tomato sauce, leaving a ½-inch border. Top sauce with mozzarella. Grill pizzas, covered with lid, until undersides are golden brown and cheese is melted, about 5 minutes more.

TO GRILL THE PIZZAS USING A GAS GRILL: Preheat on high, covered, for 10 minutes, then reduce heat to moderately high.

Remove plastic wrap from dough and lightly brush dough with olive oil.

Lightly oil grill rack. Carefully transfer rounds, oiled sides down, to grill rack with your hands and brush tops with oil. Grill crusts, uncovered, until undersides are golden brown, about 2 minutes (rotate them if one side of grill is hotter than the other). Flip crusts over with two metal spatulas and spread each crust evenly with half of tomato sauce, leaving a ½-inch border. Top sauce with mozzarella. Grill pizzas, covered with lid, until undersides are golden brown and cheese is melted, about 3 minutes more.

Scatter basil leaves onto pizzas.

Robiola Pizza

MAKES ONE 14-INCH PIZZA
ACTIVE TIME: 1 HOUR ■ START TO FINISH: 2¾ HOURS (INCLUDES MAKING DOUGH)

■ Visually, this pizza calls little attention to itself, but its star ingredient, Robiola cheese, has a velvety, custardy richness that is worth searching out. Creamy Robiola is a fresh, rindless cheese from Italy's Piedmont region (not to be confused with Lombardy's semisoft cheese of the same name). At Maloney & Porcelli restaurant, in New York City, it's slathered over an exemplary thin crust and topped with zucchini, portobello mushrooms, and a final aromatic benediction of white truffle oil. (In the interests of full disclosure, it is perfectly delicious without the extravagant olfactory allure of the truffle oil, but the addition does send this pie right over the top.) ■

- Basic Pizza Dough (page 199), shaped into a ball and allowed to rise
- 1–2 tablespoons cornmeal, for sprinkling baker's peel
- 1¼ pounds portobello mushroom caps, gills scraped out and discarded, caps cut into ¼-inch dice (1 cup)
- ½ pound zucchini, quartered lengthwise, seeded, and cut into ¼-inch dice (1 cup)
- 3 tablespoons chopped fresh chives
- ½ teaspoon salt
- ¼ teaspoon freshly ground black pepper
- ½ pound creamy Robiola cheese, at room temperature
- 1 tablespoon truffle oil or extra-virgin olive oil

SPECIAL EQUIPMENT: a pizza stone and a baker's peel rubbed with flour, both at least 14 inches in diameter (see Sources)

Put pizza stone on oven floor if using a gas oven, on lowest rack if using electric (remove other racks in either case), and preheat oven to highest setting (500° to 550°F). Allow about 1 hour to preheat stone.

Shape dough into a 14-inch round according to directions on page 200.

Sprinkle baker's peel with 1 tablespoon cornmeal. Carefully slide dough onto peel, then jerk peel once or twice: if dough sticks, lift it and sprinkle a little more cornmeal underneath.

Stir together mushrooms, zucchini, chives, salt, and pepper in a bowl. Spread (or, if necessary, crumble) cheese evenly over pizza, leaving a 1-inch border, then sprinkle with vegetables.

Line up far edge of peel with far edge of stone and tilt peel, jerking it gently to start pizza moving. When edge of pizza touches stone, quickly pull back peel to transfer pizza to stone (do not pull pizza back). Bake until crust is golden brown, 10 to 12 minutes. Slide peel under pizza to remove from oven, then drizzle it with truffle oil.

Eggplant Pizza

MAKES ONE 14-INCH PIZZA
ACTIVE TIME: 1 HOUR ■ START TO FINISH: 2 3/4 HOURS
(INCLUDES MAKING DOUGH)

■ There is no tomato sauce here. Save this pizza, lush with bronze broiled eggplant and a generous amount of garlic, for grown-ups. It's from Geoffrey Selling, a Philadelphia reader. ■

- 1 large eggplant, cut into 1/3-inch-thick slices
- 5 tablespoons extra-virgin olive oil
- 1/2 teaspoon salt
- Basic Pizza Dough (page 199), shaped into a ball and allowed to rise
- 1–2 tablespoons cornmeal, for sprinkling baker's peel
- 3/4 cup coarsely grated whole-milk mozzarella
- 1/3 cup freshly grated Asiago or Parmigiano-Reggiano
- 2 tablespoons minced garlic
- 1/2 teaspoon red pepper flakes

SPECIAL EQUIPMENT: a pizza stone and a baker's peel rubbed with flour, both at least 14 inches in diameter (see Sources)

Preheat broiler. Arrange eggplant slices in one layer on a foil-lined large baking sheet. Lightly brush both sides of slices with oil (3 tablespoons total) and sprinkle with salt. Broil eggplant 2 to 3 inches from heat, turning once, until golden brown and tender, 6 to 16 minutes total. Set aside.

Put pizza stone on oven floor if using a gas oven, on lowest rack if using electric (remove other racks in

SPEEDY CHEESE PIZZA

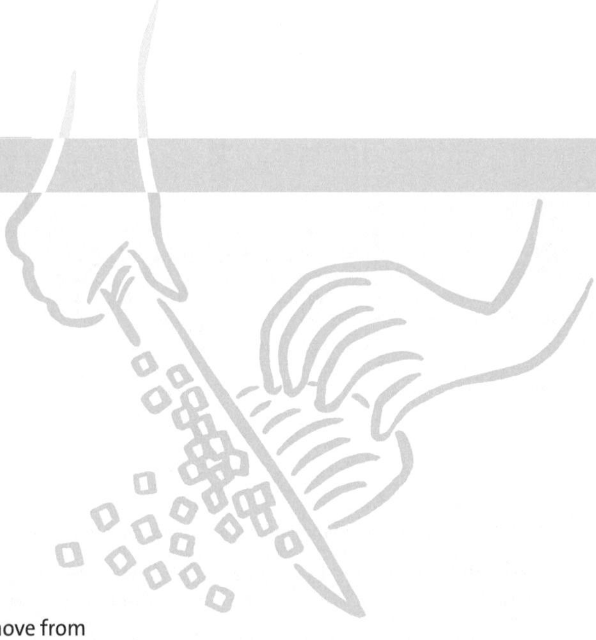

Yes, you can put pizzas on the table in less than half an hour without ordering takeout. This recipe for four individual pizzas uses flour tortillas — not a particularly new idea, but one with a new trick. The secret is to toast the tortillas first, which gets rid of the raw flavor and damp texture of supermarket tortillas.

One of our favorite toppings is onion and roasted red peppers. Cook 1 large onion, coarsely chopped, in a tablespoon of oil in a large heavy skillet over moderate heat, stirring, until softened. Add a 12-ounce jar of roasted red peppers, drained and coarsely chopped, season with salt and freshly ground black pepper, and remove from the heat. Then toast four 7-inch flour tortillas directly on the stove's burners (gas or electric) over moderately low heat, turning them once with tongs, until puffed slightly and browned in spots. (This will take just a minute.)

Arrange the tortillas on a large baking sheet and top each one with one quarter of the onions and peppers, leaving a narrow border around the edges of each pizza. Sprinkle the pizzas with a mixture of coarsely grated whole-milk mozzarella and pepper Jack (about 1/2 cup total) and bake them in the middle of a preheated 475°F oven until the cheese is melted and the edges of the tortillas are browned, about 5 minutes. If you like, take things a step further and put a handful of arugula or fresh basil leaves on top of the pizzas as soon as they come out of the oven.

You can personalize these little pizzas any way you like — with prosciutto, say, for a little ham and cheese action, or leftover roasted vegetables, or whatever your heart desires.

either case), and preheat oven to highest setting (500° to 550°F). Allow about 1 hour to preheat stone.

Shape dough into a 14-inch round according to directions on page 200.

Sprinkle baker's peel with 1 tablespoon cornmeal. Carefully slide dough onto peel, then jerk peel once or twice: if dough sticks, lift it and sprinkle a little more cornmeal underneath.

Stir together mozzarella and Asiago and sprinkle one quarter over dough, leaving a ½-inch border. Cover cheese with eggplant, overlapping slices, and sprinkle with remaining cheese. Heat remaining 2 tablespoons oil in a small skillet over moderate heat until hot but not smoking. Cook garlic and red pepper flakes, stirring, until just fragrant, 30 to 40 seconds. Spoon over eggplant.

Line up far edge of peel with far edge of stone and tilt peel, jerking it gently to start pizza moving. When edge of pizza touches stone, quickly pull back peel to transfer pizza to stone (do not pull pizza back). Bake until crust is golden brown, 12 to 15 minutes. Slide peel under pizza to remove from oven.

Potato Pizza with Bacon and Rosemary

MAKES ONE 14-INCH PIZZA
ACTIVE TIME: 1¼ HOURS ■ START TO FINISH: 3 HOURS (INCLUDES MAKING DOUGH)

■ It might seem odd to put a starch (potatoes) on top of another starch (pizza crust), but the potatoes add moisture to this no-tomato pie. Roman in inspiration, this pizza is simple, elegant, and unadorned. The potatoes are thinly sliced and overlap each other in a sweeping circle; the bacon and rosemary are our embellishments. ■

- ¼ pound lean bacon (4 slices), chopped
- Basic Pizza Dough (page 199), shaped into a ball and allowed to rise
- 1–2 tablespoons cornmeal, for sprinkling baker's peel
- ¾ pound red potatoes
- 1 tablespoon fresh rosemary leaves or 1 teaspoon dried rosemary, crumbled
- ¼ cup freshly grated Parmigiano-Reggiano
- 3 tablespoons extra-virgin olive oil

SPECIAL EQUIPMENT: a pizza stone and a baker's peel rubbed with flour, both at least 14 inches in diameter (see Sources); a mandoline or other adjustable-blade slicer, such as a Japanese Benriner

Put pizza stone on oven floor if using a gas oven, on lowest rack if using electric (remove other racks in either case), and preheat oven to highest setting (500° to 550°F). Allow about 1 hour to preheat stone.

Cook bacon in a heavy skillet over moderate heat, stirring occasionally, until fat is rendered but bacon is still pliable, 3 to 5 minutes. With a slotted spoon, transfer to paper towels to drain.

Shape dough into a 14-inch round according to directions on page 200.

Sprinkle baker's peel with 1 tablespoon cornmeal. Carefully slide dough onto peel, then jerk peel once or twice: if dough sticks, lift it and sprinkle a little more cornmeal underneath.

Cut potatoes into paper-thin slices with slicer. Arrange slices, overlapping, on dough, leaving a ½-inch border. Sprinkle bacon, rosemary, and cheese over potatoes, then drizzle with 2 tablespoons oil.

Line up far edge of peel with far edge of stone and tilt peel, jerking it gently to start pizza moving. When edge of pizza touches stone, quickly pull back peel to transfer pizza to stone (do not pull pizza back). Bake until crust is golden brown and potatoes are tender, 10 to 15 minutes. Slide peel under pizza to remove from oven, then drizzle with remaining 1 tablespoon oil.

New Haven–Style Clam Pizza

MAKES ONE 14-INCH PIZZA
ACTIVE TIME: 1 HOUR ■ START TO FINISH: 2¾ HOURS (INCLUDES MAKING DOUGH)

■ It's a mystery to us why the clam pizza, famous in New Haven and environs, isn't franchised from coast to coast. Maybe to the uninitiated it looks spartan, not gooey with cheese and other toppings. But looks can be deceiving. Taste the thin golden crust dotted with fresh, tender East Coast littlenecks (with just enough of their briny liquor to impart a wonderful oceanic tang) and generously seasoned with olive oil, garlic, a scattering of oregano, and sharp pecorino, and you'll want to keep eating long after you are full. ■

Basic Pizza Dough (this page), shaped into a ball and allowed to rise
- 1–2 tablespoons cornmeal, for sprinkling baker's peel
- 3 large garlic cloves, minced
- ¼ cup olive oil
- 12 small (less than 2 inches wide) hard-shelled clams, such as littlenecks, shucked (see page 51; reserve liquor) and cut in half if desired
- 1 teaspoon dried oregano, crumbled
- 2 tablespoons finely grated pecorino Romano or Parmigiano-Reggiano

SPECIAL EQUIPMENT: a pizza stone and a baker's peel rubbed with flour, both at least 14 inches in diameter (see Sources)

Put pizza stone on oven floor if using a gas oven, on lowest rack if using electric (remove other racks in either case), and preheat oven to highest setting (500° to 550°F). Allow about 1 hour to preheat stone.

Shape dough into a 14-inch round according to directions on page 200.

Sprinkle baker's peel with 1 tablespoon cornmeal. Carefully slide dough onto peel, then jerk peel once or twice: if dough sticks, lift it and sprinkle a little more cornmeal underneath.

Stir together garlic and oil in a small bowl, then brush evenly over dough, leaving a ½-inch border. Arrange clams evenly over oil, then sprinkle with oregano, cheese, and some of reserved clam liquor.

Line up far edge of peel with far edge of stone and tilt peel, jerking it gently to start pizza moving. When edge of pizza touches stone, quickly pull back peel to transfer pizza completely to stone (do not pull pizza back). Bake until crust is golden brown, 12 to 15 minutes. Slide peel under pizza to remove from oven.

Basic Pizza Dough

MAKES ENOUGH DOUGH FOR ONE 14-INCH PIZZA OR TWO 9-INCH PIZZAS

ACTIVE TIME: 30 MINUTES ■ START TO FINISH: 1¾ HOURS (INCLUDES RISING)

■ Pizza crust is not simply a vehicle for cheese. Think of it as bread—really, really good bread. When it is properly done, the toppings exist to enhance the crust. Of all the reliable pizza dough recipes we put through trials in our test kitchens, none approached that of the Phoenix chef Chris Bianco. Bianco likes to leave as much air in his risen dough as possible, so he handles it carefully when forming the pizza round (see page 200). The result is a thin, blistered crust that is crisp all across the bottom and chewy on the edges. Below is an adaptation of his crust that's ideal for most of the baked pizzas in this section. And, we discovered, it's great for grilled pizzas too. ■

- 1 (¼-ounce) package (2¼ teaspoons) active dry yeast
- About 1¾ cups unbleached all-purpose flour, plus additional for kneading and dredging
- ¾ cup warm water (105°–115°F)
- 1½ teaspoons salt
- 1½ teaspoons olive oil

MAKE THE DOUGH AND LET IT RISE: Stir together yeast, 1 tablespoon flour, and ¼ cup warm water in a measuring cup and let stand until surface appears creamy, about 5 minutes. (If mixture doesn't appear creamy, discard and start over with new yeast.)

Stir together 1¼ cups flour and salt in a large bowl. Add yeast mixture, oil, and remaining ½ cup warm water and stir until smooth. Stir in enough of remaining flour (about ½ cup) so dough comes away from sides of bowl. (The dough will be wetter than other pizza doughs you may have made.)

Knead dough on a dry surface with lightly floured hands (reflour hands when dough becomes too sticky) until smooth, soft, and elastic, about 8 minutes. Form into 1 ball if baking pizza or 2 balls if grilling, put on a lightly floured surface, and generously dust with flour. Loosely cover with plastic wrap and let rise in a warm draft-free place until doubled in bulk, about 1¼ hours.

TO SHAPE THE DOUGH FOR BAKING: Do not punch down dough. Carefully dredge dough in a bowl of flour to coat and transfer to dry work surface. Holding one edge of dough in the air with both hands and letting bottom touch work surface, carefully move hands around edge of dough (like turning a steering wheel), allowing weight of dough to stretch round to roughly 10 inches.

Lay dough flat on lightly floured work surface and continue to work edges with fingers, stretching it into a 14-inch round.

TO SHAPE THE DOUGH FOR GRILLING: Do not punch down dough. Carefully dredge 1 ball of dough in a bowl of flour to coat and transfer to dry work surface. Holding one edge of dough in the air with both hands and letting bottom touch work surface, carefully move hands around edge of dough (like turning a steering wheel), allowing weight of dough to stretch round to roughly 7 inches. Lay dough flat on lightly floured work surface and continue to work edges with fingers, stretching it into a 9-inch round. Transfer to a floured tray. Repeat procedure with remaining ball of dough. Lightly dust a piece of plastic wrap with flour and invert loosely over pizza rounds. Let stand for 10 to 20 minutes before grilling, to puff slightly.

Top and bake pizza(s) according to selected recipe.

COOK'S NOTES

- The dough can be allowed to rise, covered and refrigerated in a bowl (two bowls if making the grilled pizzas), for up to 1 day. Bring to room temperature before shaping.
- The dough can be frozen for up to 1 month. Thaw and bring to room temperature before shaping.

Deep-Dish Sausage and Tomato Pizza

MAKES ONE 10½-INCH DEEP-DISH PIZZA
ACTIVE TIME: 45 MINUTES ■ START TO FINISH: 2¼ HOURS (INCLUDES RISING TIME)

■ Rich and gooey, Chicago-style is the hearty casserole of pizzas, solidly traditional yet not heavy-handed. ■

FOR DOUGH

- ¼ teaspoon sugar
- ½ cup warm water (105°–115°F)
- 1 (¼-ounce) package (2½ teaspoons) active dry yeast
- 1½ cups unbleached all-purpose flour, plus additional for dusting
- ¼ cup yellow cornmeal
- ½ teaspoon salt
- 1 tablespoon olive oil

FOR TOPPING

- ½ pound fresh sweet or hot Italian sausage, casings discarded
- 1 (14- to 16-ounce) can whole tomatoes in juice, drained and chopped
- 1 teaspoon dried oregano, crumbled
- ¼ teaspoon salt
- ¼ teaspoon freshly ground black pepper
- 2 cups coarsely grated whole-milk mozzarella (about 8 ounces)

SPECIAL EQUIPMENT: a 10½-inch cast-iron skillet

MAKE THE DOUGH: Stir together sugar, warm water, and yeast in a large bowl and let stand until surface appears creamy, about 5 minutes. (If mixture doesn't appear creamy, discard and start over with new yeast.) Add flour, cornmeal, salt, and oil and stir until a dough forms. Knead dough on a floured surface, dusting with additional flour as necessary to prevent sticking, until smooth and elastic, about 5 minutes.

Alternatively, dough can be made in a food processor. Proof yeast in same manner as above. Process yeast mixture with flour, cornmeal, salt, and oil in processor until mixture forms a ball, adding more water 1 teaspoon at a time if dough is too dry or additional flour 1 tablespoon at a time if it is too wet. Process dough for 15 seconds more to knead.

Put dough in a deep oiled bowl and turn to coat with oil. Let rise, covered with plastic wrap, in a warm draft-free place until doubled in bulk, about 1 hour.

While dough is rising, cook sausage in a large heavy skillet over moderately high heat, stirring and breaking up lumps, until no longer pink, about 3 minutes. Stir in tomatoes, oregano, salt, and pepper, then transfer mixture to paper towels to drain and cool.

Preheat oven to 500°F. Grease cast-iron skillet.

Punch down dough and knead 4 times. Press dough into oiled skillet with oiled fingers until it comes 2 inches up sides and is an even thickness on bottom. Let dough rise, covered loosely with plastic wrap, in a warm place for 15 minutes.

Sprinkle dough with half of mozzarella, then top with sausage mixture and remaining mozzarella. Put skillet on floor of gas oven or in lower third of electric oven and bake for 12 minutes. Reduce oven temperature to 400°F and bake until edges of crust are golden, about 8 minutes more.

PASTA, NOODLES, AND DUMPLINGS

Of all the food revolutions of the past century—and they are legion—none has had a greater impact on our daily meal than the wild American love affair with pasta. Wander through any supermarket and you'll see aisles filled with pasta twisted into every conceivable shape standing next to bottled sauces whose sheer variety boggles the imagination.

This all seems so recent that when we embarked on this chapter, we expected it to be a journey that did not venture into the distant past. Imagine our surprise, therefore, when we discovered that *Gourmet*'s first spaghetti recipe was published in the magazine's first year and was followed by dozens more in the ensuing decade. That very first one, in fact, began, "There are scores of recipes for spaghetti sauce." We'll skip right over the strange second sentence ("If you'd like a shortcut, use canned spaghetti") and go straight to the heart of the matter, found at the end of the introductory note: "This dish will delight even an Italian."

The truth is that while pasta recipes may have abounded in the early days of *Gourmet,* they were considered foreign fare. The exception seems to be the many variations on "macaroni supreme," a casserole creation of the forties that inevitably included a bizarre combination of ingredients (one memorable iteration included lamb, parsley, anchovies, nutmeg, liverwurst, Swiss cheese, and blanched almonds). Spaghetti, gnocchi, lasagne, and the like were special treats and far too exotic to be the stuff of weekday dinners. It was not until the eighties, when we began flirting with fresh homemade pasta, that the revolution kicked into high gear.

Fresh became such a mania that for a while we seemed to get out the pasta maker every time we had an urge to eat Italian. That, thank goodness, was a fleeting phase, for many sauces go better with dried pasta than with fresh; linguine with clams comes immediately to mind, as does pasta with capers, garlic, and bread crumbs. But learning to roll out fresh sheets of dough was important, because it taught us that the pasta can be as critical as the sauce. In many classic dishes, like the superb pasta with Bolognese sauce you'll find in this chapter, or the sprightly spaghettini with garlic and lemon, or the rich, elegant fettuccine Alfredo, the sauce is meant to cling to the pasta rather than overwhelm it.

Having embraced Italian pasta, Americans went on to explore the pasta of the rest of the world. In this chapter you'll find fabulous couscous, Greek pastitsio (which, along with the many lasagnes you'll find here, is a truly great party dish), German spaetzle (perhaps the easiest kind of fresh pasta), and an entire universe of Asian noodles, from Chinese *chow fun* to the dried rice sticks that go into pad Thai to Japanese noodles like udon.

Although carbohydrates are currently considered the bad guys of the food chain, we remain committed pasta lovers, convinced that this is just an awkward phase in our culinary development. Pasta in its many delicious forms is such an important part of life at *Gourmet* that it took enormous restraint to pare the number of recipes down to the essentials that you find here. Of the thousands we've published over the years, these are, quite simply, the ones we couldn't live without.

Spaghettini with Garlic and Lemon

SERVES 6 TO 8 AS A FIRST COURSE, 4 AS A MAIN COURSE
ACTIVE TIME: 15 MINUTES ■ START TO FINISH: 25 MINUTES

■ This is a quick, efficient supper on a hot night when you want pasta but not anything too heavily sauced. In fact, the hot spaghettini soaks up the sauce so that what you have is simply flavorful pasta. Serve this with a platter of sliced ripe tomatoes scattered with a few basil leaves and you'll end the day thinking that life is good. ■

1 pound spaghettini or capellini
1/2 cup extra-virgin olive oil
4 large garlic cloves, minced
1/2–3/4 teaspoon red pepper flakes (to taste)
Finely grated zest of 2 lemons
3 tablespoons fresh lemon juice
1 1/2 teaspoons salt
1/2 teaspoon freshly ground black pepper
1/2 cup chopped fresh flat-leaf parsley

Cook pasta in a 6- to 8-quart pot of boiling salted water (1 tablespoon salt per every 4 quarts water) until al dente. Reserve 1 cup cooking water and drain pasta.

Meanwhile, heat oil in a 12-inch heavy skillet over moderately low heat. Add garlic and red pepper flakes and cook, stirring, until garlic is golden, about 3 minutes.

Stir lemon zest into skillet, then stir in juice, salt, pepper, and 1/2 cup reserved cooking water and bring to a simmer.

Toss pasta in sauce with parsley. Add more cooking water if pasta seems dry.

Spaghetti with Handfuls of Herbs

SERVES 4 AS A FIRST COURSE, 2 AS A MAIN COURSE
ACTIVE TIME: 40 MINUTES ■ START TO FINISH: 1 HOUR

■ You can eat this pasta all summer long, and it will never be the same twice if you vary the herbs according to your fancy (or what is running riot in the garden). Cheese would weigh this down, but crisp golden bread crumbs provide both color and texture. This recipe is from Deborah Madison's *The Savory Way.* ■

1 tablespoon olive oil
1/2 cup coarse fresh bread crumbs
1 cup chopped or shredded assorted fresh herb leaves, such as parsley, basil, mint, chives, cilantro, thyme, tarragon, sorrel, lovage, marjoram, and/or summer savory
2 small shallots, finely chopped
2 tablespoons extra-virgin olive oil
2 tablespoons unsalted butter, cut into bits
1/2 pound spaghetti
1/2 teaspoon salt
1/4 teaspoon freshly ground black pepper

Heat oil in a 12-inch skillet over moderate heat. Add bread crumbs and cook, stirring, until golden and crisp, about 3 minutes. Transfer crumbs to a small bowl.

Stir together herbs, shallots, extra-virgin olive oil, and butter in a serving bowl.

Cook spaghetti in a 6-quart pot of boiling salted water (1 tablespoon salt per every 4 quarts water) until al dente; drain.

Add spaghetti to herb mixture and toss until well coated. Sprinkle with salt, pepper, and bread crumbs.

Pasta with Capers, Garlic, and Bread Crumbs

SERVES 6 AS A FIRST COURSE, 4 AS A MAIN COURSE
ACTIVE TIME: 20 MINUTES ■ START TO FINISH: 20 MINUTES

■ This rustic dish is pungent with garlic and capers, and the bread crumbs give it texture and substance. We call for ruffly *campanelle* ("little bells," sometimes called *gigli,* or "lilies"), but a spiral-shaped pasta will work too. ■

1 (6-inch) piece stale baguette
3/4 pound *campanelle* or short spiral pasta
1/2 cup extra-virgin olive oil
4 garlic cloves, finely chopped

6 tablespoons drained capers, finely chopped
1/4 cup chopped fresh flat-leaf parsley
Finely grated Parmigiano-Reggiano (optional)

Using large holes of a box or hand grater, grate enough bread to measure 2/3 cup.

Cook pasta in a 6- to 8-quart pot of boiling salted water (1 tablespoon salt per every 4 quarts water) until al dente.

Meanwhile, heat oil in a large heavy skillet over moderately low heat. Add garlic and cook, stirring, just until pale golden, about 2 minutes. Stir in capers, parsley, and bread crumbs and cook, stirring, until bread crumbs and garlic are golden, 1 to 2 minutes.

Drain pasta and transfer to a large bowl. Pour sauce over pasta and toss to combine. Sprinkle with cheese, if desired.

Pasta with Asparagus Lemon Sauce

SERVES 8 AS A FIRST COURSE, 4 AS A MAIN COURSE
ACTIVE TIME: 35 MINUTES ■ START TO FINISH: 45 MINUTES

■ Happy Spring to asparagus lovers everywhere. No part of the vegetable is wasted here: the stalks are turned into a velvety sauce, in which the pasta and the asparagus tips are then finished. This can be assembled in a flash if you have everything ready to go. The recipe is from Faith Heller Willinger's classic *Red, White, and Greens: The Italian Way with Vegetables.* ■

How to Cook Pasta

A few simple steps will help ensure that your pasta has that genuine Italian texture and taste. Whether fresh or dried, pasta should be cooked in a large pot of water—a 6- to 8-quart pot for one pound of pasta. The pasta can swim freely that way instead of sticking together. Cover the pot and bring the water to a rolling boil. Then add plenty of salt (about 1 tablespoon per every 4 quarts of water), cover the pot again, and allow the water to return to a rapid boil. The amount of salt might seem like a lot, but don't worry—most of it will be drained away, and unsalted or insufficiently salted water will result in bland pasta.

Add the pasta all at once so it cooks evenly. Rather than breaking long pasta in half, let it soften and bend it with a wooden spoon, forcing the strands underwater. Immediately stir the pasta well to prevent sticking and cover the pot until the water returns to a boil. Then uncover the pot and cook the pasta at a rapid boil, stirring once or twice, until it is al dente. (Do not add oil to the water, or the wonderful sauce you are making will not cling to the pasta.) *Al dente* means "firm to the bite"—just tender, yet with some resistance to the tooth. Reserve a little cooking water before you drain the pasta, in case you want to thin the sauce.

Drain the pasta in a colander (never rinse it, except for cold pasta dishes), giving the colander a few vigorous shakes. Then, using tongs, immediately toss it with the sauce. Sometimes we toss the pasta with the sauce over heat to finish the cooking. Serve at once.

1 pound asparagus, trimmed
1 teaspoon finely grated lemon zest
1/4 cup extra-virgin olive oil
1 pound penne or other short pasta
1/2 cup finely grated Parmigiano-Reggiano
Salt and freshly ground black pepper

Cut asparagus into 1-inch pieces, keeping tips separate. Cook asparagus stems in a 6- to 8-quart pot of boiling salted water (1 tablespoon salt per every 4 quarts water) until very tender, 6 to 8 minutes. With a slotted spoon, transfer to a colander (keep water at a boil) and rinse under cold water. Drain asparagus well and transfer to a food processor or blender.

Cook asparagus tips in same boiling water until just tender, 3 to 5 minutes. With slotted spoon, transfer to colander (keep water at a boil) and rinse under cold water; drain.

Add zest, oil, and 1/2 cup asparagus cooking water to asparagus stems and purée. Transfer to a 4-quart saucepan.

Cook pasta in same boiling water just until it still offers considerable resistance to the tooth (about three quarters of the recommended cooking time). Reserve 2 cups cooking water and drain pasta.

Add pasta, asparagus tips, and 1/2 cup reserved cooking water to asparagus sauce and cook over high heat, stirring, for 3 to 5 minutes, or until pasta is almost al dente and sauce coats pasta. Add more cooking water 1/4 cup at a time until sauce coats pasta but is a little loose (the cheese will thicken it slightly).

Stir in cheese and salt and pepper to taste and cook, stirring, until cheese is melted. Serve immediately.

Penne with Broccoli Rabe

SERVES 8 AS A FIRST COURSE, 4 AS A MAIN COURSE
ACTIVE TIME: 30 MINUTES ■ START TO FINISH: 45 MINUTES

■ Pasta is a neutral foil for dark, intensely flavored greens such as broccoli rabe (pronounced "rahb"; another common alias is *rapini*). This Italian vegetable, which is more closely related to turnips than to conventional broccoli, is composed of juicy, slender, verdant stalks crowned with clusters of tiny buds and is packed with vitamins and minerals. It was once considered an "ethnic green," enjoyed primarily by Italians and Chinese, but no longer: American growers supply it to supermarkets almost all year round. Like other dark bitter greens, broccoli rabe has a strong affinity for garlic and red pepper flakes. This classic preparation makes a weeknight supper anything but bland. ■

2 pounds broccoli rabe
1 pound penne
1/3 cup extra-virgin olive oil
4 garlic cloves, sliced
1/2 teaspoon red pepper flakes, or to taste
Salt

ACCOMPANIMENT: finely grated Parmigiano-Reggiano

Trim and discard any yellow or coarse leaves and tough stem ends from broccoli rabe. Cut off florets and reserve. Cut stems and leaves crosswise into 1-inch-wide pieces. Wash stems, leaves, and florets and drain in a colander.

Cook broccoli rabe in a 6-quart pot of boiling salted water (1 tablespoon salt per every 4 quarts water) until stems are tender, about 5 minutes; drain.

Cook pasta in a large pot of boiling salted water until al dente.

Meanwhile, heat oil in a 12-inch heavy skillet over moderately low heat. Add garlic and red pepper flakes and cook, stirring, until garlic is golden, about 1 minute. Add broccoli rabe and salt to taste, increase heat to moderately high, and cook, stirring occasionally, for 3 to 5 minutes.

Drain pasta and toss with broccoli rabe until well combined. Transfer to a bowl and serve with cheese.

Pasta with Tomato and Basil

SERVES 6 AS A FIRST COURSE, 4 AS A MAIN COURSE
ACTIVE TIME: 35 MINUTES ■ START TO FINISH: 45 MINUTES

■ Save this recipe for summer, when tomatoes are in season, and then enjoy it all the time, as we do. It's adapted from a dish served at Antica Fattoria del Colle, a rural *pensione* in Deruta, Italy, where it's often part of a generous and relaxed evening meal that's eaten outside at long tables. It's delicious made with good dried egg fettuccine. We particularly like the very thin fettuccine packaged in nests by De Cecco and sold in many supermarkets. Another favorite is Cipriani tagliarelle (a similar ribbon pasta), which is available at some specialty foods shops and by mail from Dean & DeLuca (see Sources). ■

¼ cup extra-virgin olive oil
4 garlic cloves, thinly sliced
2½ pounds ripe tomatoes (5 medium), peeled (see Tips, page 938) and coarsely chopped
2 large basil branches, plus 1⅓ cups packed fresh basil leaves, coarsely chopped
½ teaspoon salt
Freshly ground black pepper
¾ pound good dried egg fettuccine or other long pasta

ACCOMPANIMENT: finely grated Parmigiano-Reggiano

Heat oil in a 6-quart pot over moderate heat until hot but not smoking. Add garlic and cook, stirring, until golden, about 1 minute. Stir in tomatoes, basil branches, salt, and pepper to taste, bring to a simmer, and simmer, stirring occasionally, for 20 minutes.

Meanwhile, cook fettuccine in a 6-quart pot of boiling salted water (1 tablespoon salt per every 4 quarts water) until al dente; drain.

Remove basil branches from sauce and stir in chopped basil. Toss fettuccine with sauce in a bowl. Serve with grated cheese.

Tomato Sauce

MAKES ABOUT 6 CUPS, OR ENOUGH FOR 2 POUNDS PASTA
ACTIVE TIME: 20 MINUTES ■ START TO FINISH: 1 HOUR

■ Remember the fable about the ant and the grasshopper? Well, we can't all be ants, industriously putting up tomato sauce in the height of the season. This is a great save for the grasshoppers—and they are us. It's superior to any sauce out of a jar. ■

3 tablespoons olive oil
1 medium onion, finely chopped
3 garlic cloves, minced
½ teaspoon dried oregano, crumbled
2 (28-ounce) cans whole tomatoes in juice, drained (juice reserved) and chopped
1 Turkish bay leaf or ½ California bay leaf
1¼ teaspoons salt
⅓ cup chopped fresh flat-leaf parsley (optional)

Heat oil in a 5- to 6-quart pot over moderately high heat until hot but not smoking. Add onion and cook, stirring, until golden, about 6 minutes. Add garlic and oregano and cook, stirring, for 1 minute. Add tomatoes, with their juice, bay leaf, and salt, bring to a simmer, and simmer, uncovered, stirring occasionally, until thickened, 30 to 35 minutes.

Discard bay leaf and stir in parsley, if using.

COOK'S NOTE

■ The sauce can be made up to 1 week ahead and refrigerated in an airtight container. It can also be frozen for up to 2 months.

Fresh Tomato Sauce

MAKES ABOUT 5 CUPS, OR ENOUGH FOR ABOUT 2 POUNDS PASTA
ACTIVE TIME: 30 MINUTES ■ START TO FINISH: 1½ HOURS

■ Terrific when summer is in full force and you've gotten your hands on a sackful of ripe, juicy, luscious tomatoes. No jarred sauce on earth can duplicate the taste of homemade. ■

6 pounds ripe tomatoes, such as beefsteak or plum, peeled (see Tips, page 940)
¼ cup extra-virgin olive oil
5 garlic cloves, thinly sliced
1 teaspoon sugar
1 teaspoon salt
¼ cup chopped fresh basil or flat-leaf parsley

Core tomatoes and halve crosswise. Working over a sieve set over a bowl, squeeze tomatoes gently to remove seeds. Discard seeds and reserve juice. Coarsely chop tomatoes.

Heat oil in a 6- to 7-quart pot over moderately high heat until hot but not smoking. Add garlic and cook, stirring, until just golden, about 1 minute. Add tomatoes, reserved juice, sugar, and salt, bring to a simmer, and simmer, uncovered, stirring occasionally, until thickened, 45 minutes to 1 hour.

Stir in basil and salt to taste.

COOK'S NOTE

- The sauce can be made up to 4 days ahead and refrigerated in an airtight container.

Arrabbiata Sauce

MAKES ABOUT 6 CUPS, OR ENOUGH FOR 2 POUNDS PASTA
ACTIVE TIME: 20 MINUTES ■ START TO FINISH: 1 HOUR

■ This mellow and rich-tasting *arrabbiata* ("angry" in Italian) has just the right amount of heat. It's traditional to add some fresh calamari or shrimp to the cooked sauce and simmer just until the seafood is tender, then serve it over linguine or spaghetti. Americans tend to sprinkle cheese indiscriminately over every plate of pasta with tomato sauce, but this doesn't need it, even if you don't serve it with the seafood. ■

- 3 tablespoons olive oil
- 4 garlic cloves, minced
- 1–1¼ teaspoons red pepper flakes
- 2 (28-ounce) cans whole tomatoes in juice, drained (juice reserved) and chopped
- 1¼ teaspoons salt
- ⅓ cup chopped fresh basil or flat-leaf parsley

Heat oil in a 5- to 6-quart pot over moderately high heat. Add garlic and red pepper flakes and cook, stirring, until garlic is golden, about 1 minute. Stir in tomatoes, with their juice, and salt, bring to a simmer, and simmer, uncovered, stirring occasionally, until thickened, 35 to 40 minutes.

Stir in basil.

COOK'S NOTE

- The sauce can be made up to 1 week ahead and refrigerated in an airtight container. It can also be frozen for up to 2 months.

CANNED TOMATOES OR FRESH?

What would we do without canned tomatoes? They are a great product — consistent, readily available, and inexpensive. A pasta sauce made with canned tomatoes tends to be heartier than one made with fresh tomatoes, and it can be a bit more acidic, depending on what brand you buy. For our recipes, if we call for canned tomatoes in juice, don't substitute canned tomatoes in purée — you won't get the same flavor, texture, or body.

Plum tomatoes (often called Romas) are a popular sauce tomato because they are so fleshy, but if you are making a fresh tomato sauce, any good ripe tomatoes will work well.

Fettuccine with Butter, Parmigiano-Reggiano, and Sage

SERVES 8 AS A FIRST COURSE, 4 AS A MAIN COURSE
ACTIVE TIME: 1 HOUR ■ START TO FINISH: 2½ HOURS
(INCLUDES MAKING PASTA)

■ Sage isn't just for Thanksgiving stuffing. Try this simple dish in early autumn, when you are craving fresh, heady herbs but summer's basil is no more. ■

- 1½ sticks (12 tablespoons) unsalted butter, softened
- 2 cups finely grated Parmigiano-Reggiano (about 4 ounces), plus additional for sprinkling
- ¼ cup minced fresh sage
- Salt and freshly ground black pepper
- 1 pound Fresh Fettuccine (page 210) or good dried egg fettuccine

Stir together butter, cheese, sage, and salt and pepper to taste in a large bowl.

Cook fettuccine in a 6- to 8-quart pot of boiling salted water (1 tablespoon salt per every 4 quarts water) until al dente. Drain well.

Toss pasta with butter mixture until well coated. Sprinkle with additional cheese.

COOK'S NOTE

- De Cecco's dried egg fettuccine, sold in coils in flat boxes, is an excellent brand.

Pasta Dough

MAKES ABOUT 1 POUND
ACTIVE TIME: 40 MINUTES ■ START TO FINISH: 1½ HOURS

■ Good homemade pasta and good dried pasta are not necessarily interchangeable in a recipe. Fresh pasta is softer and less chewy than dried, and it takes less time to cook. ■

3 cups unbleached all-purpose flour
4 large eggs, lightly beaten
2–3 tablespoons water
1 teaspoon salt

Combine flour, eggs, 2 tablespoons water, and salt in a food processor and blend until mixture just begins to form a ball, adding more water drop by drop if dough is too dry; dough should be firm and not sticky. Process dough for 15 seconds more to knead it. Transfer to a floured work surface and let stand, covered with an inverted bowl, for 1 hour to let the gluten relax and make rolling easier.

Alternatively, mound flour on a work surface, preferably wooden, and make a well in center. Add eggs, 2 tablespoons water, and salt to well. With a fork, gently beat eggs and water until combined. Gradually stir in enough flour to form a paste, pulling in flour closest to egg mixture and being careful not to make an opening in outer wall of well. Knead remaining flour into mixture with your hands to form a dough, adding more water drop by drop if dough is too dry; dough should be firm and not sticky. Knead dough until smooth and elastic, 8 to 10 minutes. Cover with an inverted bowl and let stand for 1 hour.

COOK'S NOTE

- The dough can be made up to 4 hours ahead and refrigerated, tightly wrapped in plastic wrap.

MAKING FRESH PASTA

Making fresh pasta is a roll-up-your-sleeves project, but is it ever worth it. After you have fed the pasta through your pasta machine one last time, drape it over the backs of your hands and marvel at its thinness: you'll be able to see your knuckles through the dough.

We often make fresh pasta in the food processor, but sometimes we fall back on the well method, which is how it's traditionally done in Italy. The trick to making pasta this way is that there is essentially no trick.

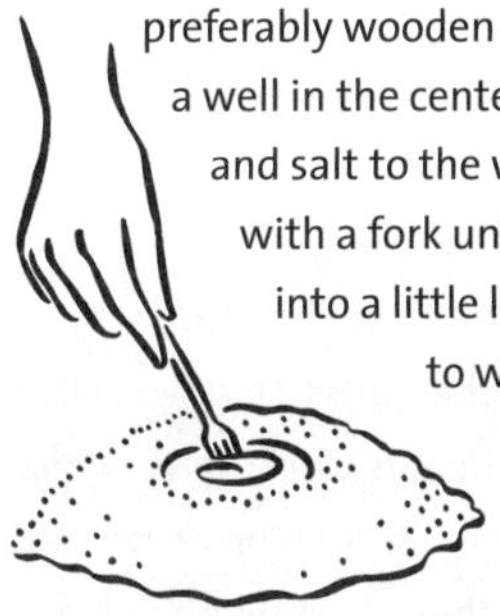

Mound the flour on a work surface, preferably wooden (not marble), and form a well in the center. Add the eggs, water, and salt to the well and gently beat with a fork until the mixture turns into a little lake, then gradually start to work away at the inside of the flour wall, incorporating it bit by bit into the lake. When the mixture becomes too cumbersome to stir with a fork, use your hands to work in the remaining flour, a little at a time, until the dough forms a ball. Knead the dough until it's smooth and elastic, five to ten minutes.

In Italy pasta is often made with a soft-wheat flour (low in protein and thus low in gluten) known as "00," which makes a dough that's easy to roll out and produces a tender finished pasta. The most common counterpart in the United States is unbleached all-purpose flour. It's made from a harder wheat (meaning that the protein/gluten content is higher), so we sometimes add cake flour (which is softer)—particularly when the dough will be used for filled pastas. Even though they have a double thickness at the edges, they will remain tender because of the softer flour.

Rolling Out Fresh Pasta

When kneading and rolling out pasta dough, you will frequently need to add a little flour, but be stingy with it. Pasta makers from the old school insist that hand-rolled pasta tastes noticeably better than machine-rolled, but that is debatable. A pasta machine produces excellent results, even for novices, and takes a fraction of the time. Hand-cranked pasta machines aren't expensive and don't take up much room in the kitchen cupboard. Don't buy one with nonstick rollers, though, because they will make the pasta too slick and the sauce won't cling the way it should. When you first use a new machine, you'll need to sacrifice a piece of dough to get the oil off the rollers. Never wash a pasta machine; simply clean it with a stiff dry brush such as a toothbrush.

It's a good idea to work on the largest surface available, since the strips of dough will get longer each time you put them through the rollers. Once you start rolling each strip, crank continuously until it has gone completely through the rollers. (Don't stop in midstream, so to speak.) Before you put the strip through again, run your hand along it to check for sticky spots that could get stuck in the machine. Dust any tacky bits with flour and brush off excess flour.

Two other pieces of equipment are helpful: a large wooden surface for mixing (unlike pastry dough, pasta dough shouldn't stay cool, or it won't be elastic) and a sharp metal scraper, known as a bench knife, for cleaning the work surface.

Ideally, fresh pasta should be cooked as soon as it is made, but if you want to prepare it ahead, it can be refrigerated for up to 12 hours *if* you dry the cut pasta for 30 minutes beforehand. The noodles should then be coiled into nests and stored in plastic bags so they won't tangle. About 2 hours before you're ready to cook the pasta, remove it from the bags and let it sit at room temperature to dry out any moisture that has accumulated in the refrigerator.

Fresh Fettuccine

Pasta is fun to make, but the directions can seem daunting if you've never made it before. Don't be deterred: we've included lots of tips. Long, ribbon-type fettuccine is one of the most popular kinds of pasta to make at home.

Pasta Dough (page 209)

SPECIAL EQUIPMENT: a pasta machine

ROLL OUT THE DOUGH: Divide dough into 8 pieces, then flatten each piece into a rough rectangle and cover rectangles with an inverted large bowl. Set rollers of pasta machine on widest setting.

Lightly dust 1 rectangle with flour and feed through rollers. Fold rectangle in half and feed it, folded end first, through rollers 7 or 8 more times, folding it in half each time and feeding a shorter end through, dusting with flour if necessary to prevent sticking. Turn dial to next (narrower) setting and feed dough through rollers without folding. Continue to feed dough through rollers without folding, once at each setting until you reach narrowest setting. Dough will be a smooth sheet about 36 inches long and 4 inches wide. Cut sheet crosswise in half. Lay sheets of dough on lightly floured baking sheets to dry until leathery but still pliable, about 15 minutes. (Alternatively, lightly dust pasta sheets with flour and hang over the backs of straight-backed chairs to dry.) Roll out remaining pieces of dough in same manner.

CUT THE PASTA INTO FETTUCCINE: If necessary, attach fettuccine blades (to cut 1/4-inch-wide strips) to pasta machine. Feed one end of driest pasta sheet (the first one you rolled out) into cutters, holding other end straight up, then catch strips from underneath machine before sheet goes completely through rollers and gently lay across floured baking sheets. (Alternatively, lightly flour strips and hang over backs of straight-backed chairs.) Repeat with remaining sheets of pasta. Let pasta dry for at least 5 minutes before cooking.

COOK'S NOTE

- The fettuccine can be dried until leathery but still pliable, about 30 minutes, then transferred to plastic bags and refrigerated for up to 12 hours.

Fettuccine Alfredo

SERVES 6 AS A FIRST COURSE, 4 AS A MAIN COURSE
ACTIVE TIME: 35 MINUTES ■ START TO FINISH: 40 MINUTES

■ We can't claim this is the definitive version of the creamy classic, but it is unbeatable. We call for dried pasta to make it work for a quick meal, but don't let us stop you from making fresh fettuccine if so inclined—it was meant for this kind of sauce. ■

- 3/4 pound good dried egg fettuccine or Fresh Fettuccine (opposite page)
- 1 stick (8 tablespoons) plus 1 tablespoon unsalted butter
- 1/2 cup finely grated Parmigiano-Reggiano, plus additional for sprinkling
- 2/3 cup heavy cream
- 1/4 teaspoon salt
- 1/4 teaspoon freshly ground black pepper

Cook fettuccine in a 6- to 8-quart pot of boiling salted water (1 tablespoon salt per every 4 quarts water) until al dente. Reserve 1/4 cup cooking water and drain pasta.

Meanwhile, thinly slice 3 tablespoons butter; set aside.

When pasta is cooked, melt remaining 3/4 stick (6 tablespoons) butter in a 2- to 3-quart flameproof gratin dish (see Cook's Note) over low heat. Add pasta and toss to coat, lifting strands. Add cheese, reserved cooking water, cream, reserved butter, salt, and pepper and toss to combine well. Sprinkle with additional cheese and serve immediately.

COOK'S NOTES

- You can use a large deep skillet to sauce the pasta. Serve the pasta on plates and sprinkle with additional cheese.
- De Cecco's dried egg fettuccine, sold in coils in boxes, is an excellent brand.

Pasta Primavera

SERVES 10 AS A FIRST COURSE, 6 AS A MAIN COURSE
ACTIVE TIME: 1 HOUR ■ START TO FINISH: 1½ HOURS

■ First introduced at the starry Le Cirque in New York City in the 1970s, pasta primavera rapidly became one of the most popular pasta dishes in America. Don't let the long list of ingredients faze you; once you've done the prep work, it's easy to throw together. One of the nice things about this version is that it calls for dried morels, frozen peas (more consistently sweet and tender than "fresh" peas), and asparagus (for better or worse, practically seasonless these days), so you don't have to wait until spring to make it. ■

- 1 ounce dried morel mushrooms
- 1½ cups warm water
- ½ pound asparagus, trimmed and cut into 1-inch pieces
- ¼ pound green beans, preferably *haricots verts*, cut into 1-inch pieces
- ¾ cup frozen baby peas, thawed
- 4 tablespoons extra-virgin olive oil
- 2 teaspoons minced garlic
- Rounded ½ teaspoon red pepper flakes
- Salt and freshly ground black pepper
- 1½ pints grape tomatoes
- 1 tablespoon balsamic vinegar
- 3 tablespoons water
- 1 pound spaghettini
- ½ stick (4 tablespoons) unsalted butter
- ⅔ cup heavy cream
- 1 teaspoon finely grated lemon zest
- 1 cup finely grated Parmigiano-Reggiano (about 2 ounces)
- ¼ cup finely chopped fresh flat-leaf parsley
- ¼ cup finely chopped fresh basil
- ⅓ cup (1½ ounces) pine nuts, lightly toasted (see Tips, page 938)

OPTIONAL GARNISH: Parmigiano-Reggiano shavings

PREPARE THE VEGETABLES: Soak morels in warm water in a small bowl for 30 minutes.

Lift mushrooms out of water and squeeze excess liquid back into bowl. Pour soaking liquid through a sieve lined with a dampened paper towel into a small bowl; reserve. Rinse morels thoroughly to remove grit, then squeeze dry. Cut off and discard any tough stems. Halve small morels lengthwise and quarter large ones.

Add asparagus and beans to a 6- to 8-quart pot of boiling salted water (1 tablespoon salt per every 4 quarts water) and cook, uncovered, for 3 minutes. Add peas and cook until beans and asparagus are just tender, 1 to 2 minutes more. Immediately transfer vegetables with a large slotted spoon to a bowl of ice and cold water to stop the cooking; reserve pot of water for cooking pasta. Drain cooled vegetables.

Heat 2 tablespoons oil in a 10- to 12-inch heavy skillet over moderately low heat. Add 1 teaspoon garlic and rounded ¼ teaspoon red pepper flakes and cook, stirring, just until garlic is fragrant, about 1 minute. Add drained vegetables and salt and pepper to taste and cook, stirring, for 2 minutes. Transfer to a bowl; set skillet aside.

COOK THE TOMATOES: Cut half of tomatoes into quarters and halve remainder lengthwise, keeping quarters and halves separate. Heat remaining 2 tablespoons oil in same skillet over moderately low heat. Add remaining 1 teaspoon garlic and remaining rounded ¼ teaspoon red pepper flakes and cook, stirring, just until garlic is fragrant, about 1 minute. Add quartered tomatoes, with salt and pepper to taste, and simmer, stirring occasionally, until tomatoes are softened, about 3 minutes. Add halved tomatoes, vinegar, and water and simmer, stirring occasionally, until sauce is thickened and halved tomatoes are softened, 3 to 4 minutes. Remove from heat and keep warm, covered.

COOK THE SPAGHETTINI: Return pot of water to a boil and cook spaghettini until al dente; drain in a colander.

Immediately add butter, cream, zest, and morels to (empty) pasta pot, bring to a simmer, and simmer gently, uncovered, for 2 minutes. Stir in cheese, then add pasta, tossing to coat and adding as much of reserved morel soaking liquid as necessary (½ to ⅔ cup) to keep pasta well coated. Add green vegetables, parsley, basil, pine nuts, and salt and pepper to taste and toss gently to combine.

Serve pasta topped with tomatoes and, if desired, Parmigiano-Reggiano shavings.

Sicilian Pasta with Eggplant

Pasta alla Norma

SERVES 8 AS A FIRST COURSE, 4 TO 6 AS A MAIN COURSE
ACTIVE TIME: 20 MINUTES ■ START TO FINISH: 45 MINUTES

■ *Pasta alla norma,* one of Sicily's most beloved dishes, is widely believed to have been named after the heroine of the opera of the same name by Vincenzo Bellini, a native Sicilian. But some insist that it derives from the Italian word *normale,* a reference to the fact that the dish has long been a staple of the islanders' daily diet. Whoever or whatever *norma* may have been, the perfectly calibrated mix of eggplant, ricotta salata, tomatoes, and pasta provides a great introduction to Sicily's vibrant cuisine. ■

- 2 pounds Italian (preferably small) or Asian eggplants
- 2 (28-ounce) cans whole tomatoes in juice
- 1 cup olive oil
- Salt and freshly ground black pepper
- 3 garlic cloves, minced
- 1 teaspoon sugar
- 1 pound ridged ziti or rigatoni
- 1 cup finely grated ricotta salata (about 3 ounces; see Glossary)

OPTIONAL GARNISH: fresh basil leaves

Trim ends of eggplants. Halve eggplants lengthwise and cut crosswise into ½-inch-thick slices. Drain tomatoes in a large sieve, then transfer to a bowl and squeeze to break into smaller pieces.

Heat oil in a 4- to 5-quart heavy pot over moderately high heat until hot but not smoking. Fry eggplant in 4 batches, turning once, until golden brown on both sides, about 3 minutes total per batch. With a slotted spoon, transfer eggplant to paper towels to drain, arranging it in one layer. Season with salt and pepper.

Pour off all but ¼ cup oil from pot. Add garlic and cook over low heat, stirring, until golden, about 1 minute. Stir in sugar and tomatoes, with any accumulated juices, and simmer, stirring frequently, until slightly thickened, about 15 minutes. Season with salt and pepper.

Meanwhile, cook pasta in a 6- to 8-quart pot of boiling salted water (1 tablespoon salt per every 4 quarts water) until al dente. Reserve 1 cup pasta cooking water and drain pasta.

Transfer half of tomato sauce to a large bowl and add half of ricotta salata. Add pasta and half of eggplant and toss, adding some reserved pasta cooking water if sauce becomes too thick. Transfer pasta to a serving bowl and top with remaining sauce and eggplant. Sprinkle with some of remaining cheese and garnish with basil leaves, if desired. Serve remaining cheese on the side.

COOK'S NOTE

- Small eggplants are preferable here because they yield slices that are similar in size to the pasta.

Orecchiette with Cauliflower and Lacinato Kale

SERVES 8 AS A FIRST COURSE, 4 AS A MAIN COURSE
ACTIVE TIME: 1¼ HOURS ■ START TO FINISH: 1½ HOURS

■ This gutsy country dish makes a great meatless main course. Its depth of flavor comes from rich, sweet lacinato kale, sometimes called *cavolo nero* ("black cabbage"), and anchovies, which provide a gentle background note. Cooks in Italy use red pepper flakes instead of fresh chiles in a recipe like this. But this version is from the chef Karen Martini, of the Melbourne Wine Room, and in Australia, which has longstanding and numerous Asian influences, fresh Thai chiles are used all the time. Serrano chiles have a similar heat and are more commonly available in this country. ■

- 1½ cups coarse fresh bread crumbs from a rustic Italian or French loaf (crust discarded)
- ½ head cauliflower (1 pound), cut into ½-inch pieces
- 1 pound lacinato kale (see Glossary) or regular kale, stems and ribs discarded, leaves coarsely chopped
- ⅓ cup plus 2 tablespoons extra-virgin olive oil
- 8–10 flat anchovy fillets, patted dry
- 2 large garlic cloves, thinly sliced
- 2 small serrano chiles or fresh Thai chiles, finely chopped (including seeds)
- 1 cup chopped fresh flat-leaf parsley
- Salt and freshly ground black pepper
- 1 pound orecchiette
- 1⅓ cups finely grated Parmigiano-Reggiano (about 3 ounces)

Put a rack in middle of oven and preheat oven to 350°F.

Spread bread crumbs in a shallow baking pan and bake, stirring occasionally, until golden, 8 to 12 minutes. Set aside.

Meanwhile, cook cauliflower in a 6- to 8-quart pot of boiling salted water (1 tablespoon salt per every 4 quarts water) until very tender, about 8 minutes. With a slotted spoon, transfer cauliflower to a bowl. Remove and reserve 1 cup cooking water. Cook kale in remaining boiling water until tender, about 8 minutes. Drain in a colander, pressing on kale to remove excess water.

Heat ⅓ cup oil in a deep 12- to 13-inch heavy skillet over moderate heat. Add anchovies, garlic, and chiles and cook, stirring, until anchovies break up but garlic is not browned, about 1 minute. Add cauliflower and coarsely mash with back of spoon or a potato masher. Stir in kale, ½ cup parsley, and ⅔ cup reserved cooking water. Bring to a boil and season with salt and pepper. Remove skillet from heat.

Cook pasta in a 6- to 8-quart pot of boiling salted water (1 tablespoon salt per every 4 quarts water) until al dente; drain.

Add pasta to sauce and heat over moderate heat, stirring. Stir in cheese and remaining ½ cup parsley. If pasta seems too dry, stir in a little more cooking water. Serve pasta drizzled with remaining 2 tablespoons oil and sprinkled with bread crumbs.

Steamed Couscous

MAKES ABOUT 9 CUPS; SERVES 12
ACTIVE TIME: 20 MINUTES ■ START TO FINISH: 1¼ HOURS

■ Packaged couscous, which is a granular form of pasta, has found its way into supermarkets across the country. Because it's precooked, it takes only about five minutes to prepare, making it one of the quickest side dishes going. In this recipe, however, we use a traditional North African technique, steaming the couscous in the top part of the special perforated pot called a *couscoussière* (should you be lacking one, a colander set over a large pot will work). This method takes longer, but it's very soothing, especially if you like to play with your food, and the finished dish is a revelation: plumper, fluffier, tenderer, and more satisfying than ordinary couscous. It's superb with Lamb Tagine with Prunes, Apricots, and Vegetables (page 510). ■

- 4 cups (1½ pounds) couscous
- Flour for dusting
- 1 teaspoon salt
- 1 cup water
- Vegetable oil

SPECIAL EQUIPMENT: a *couscoussière* (optional; see Sources); cheesecloth

Stir together couscous and 3 quarts water in a large bowl, then drain in a large fine-mesh sieve. Transfer couscous to a large shallow pan, spread it into an even layer, and let stand for 10 minutes.

Set top of *couscoussière* over bottom filled with water; top should not touch water (see Cook's Note). Cut a strip of cheesecloth 2 inches longer than circumference of rim of bottom of *couscoussière* and rinse in water. Wring out cloth and dust with flour, then wrap around seam between top and bottom of *couscousière* to seal. Bring water to a simmer (no steam should escape seal).

Break up any lumps in couscous by lifting and raking it with your fingers. Sprinkle one quarter of couscous in an even layer into top of *couscoussière* and steam, uncovered, over moderately high heat for 5 minutes. Sprinkle remaining couscous into *couscoussière*, forming a mound. Steam, uncovered, until steam begins to rise through mound, then reduce heat to moderate and steam, uncovered, for 20 minutes. Remove *couscoussière* from heat and transfer couscous to a large shallow pan, spreading it into an even layer. Set pot aside.

Sprinkle couscous with salt and water. When it is cool enough to handle, break up any lumps by lifting and raking it with your fingers. Lightly oil your hands and lift and rake couscous again, then smooth into an even layer and let dry for 10 minutes.

Set top of *couscoussière* over bottom again (adding water if necessary) and reseal seam with cheesecloth. Return couscous to steamer and steam, uncovered, over moderate heat for 20 minutes.

COOK'S NOTES

- The couscous can also be steamed in a large steamer basket or small-holed colander set over a 6- to 8-quart pot of simmering water (make sure the bottom of the steamer or colander does not touch the water).
- The couscous can be steamed the first time up to 4 hours ahead and left at room temperature, covered with a damp kitchen towel. Break up any lumps by lifting and raking the couscous with your fingers before the final steaming.

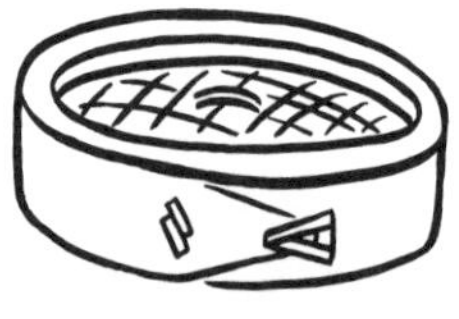

Israeli Couscous with Roasted Butternut Squash and Preserved Lemon

SERVES 6 AS A SIDE DISH
ACTIVE TIME: 45 MINUTES ■ START TO FINISH: 1 HOUR

■ This dish—a pretty accompaniment to lamb or any other grilled or roasted meat—is an argument for having a jar of preserved lemons in the refrigerator; their perfume and flavor make it special. Israeli couscous, also called pearl pasta, is larger and rounder than the usual kind, and it's more substantial. If you can't find it, the dish can also be made with *acini di pepe* (tiny peppercorn-shaped pasta). ■

- 8 wedges Moroccan-Style Preserved Lemon (page 908)
- 1½ pounds butternut squash, peeled, seeded, and cut into ¼-inch dice
- 3 tablespoons olive oil
- Salt
- 1 large onion, chopped
- 1¾ cups Israeli couscous
- 1 (3-inch) cinnamon stick
- 1 cup chopped fresh flat-leaf parsley
- ½ cup pine nuts, toasted (see Tips, page 938)
- ½ cup golden raisins
- ¼ teaspoon ground cinnamon

Put a rack in upper third of oven and preheat oven to 475°F.

Scoop lemon flesh out of peel; reserve both flesh and peel. Cut enough peel into ¼-inch dice to measure ¼ cup (reserve remaining peel for another use). Put lemon flesh in a sieve set over a bowl and press with back of a spoon to extract juice; discard solids. Set diced peel and juice aside.

Toss squash with 1 tablespoon oil and salt to taste in a large shallow baking pan, then spread in one layer. Roast until squash is just tender, about 15 minutes. Transfer to a large bowl.

Heat 1 tablespoon oil in a 10-inch heavy skillet over moderately high heat. Add onion and cook, stirring occasionally, until just beginning to turn golden. Add to squash.

Cook couscous with cinnamon stick in a 4-quart saucepan of boiling well-salted water until just tender, about 10 minutes; drain, and discard cinnamon stick. Add couscous to vegetables, along with remaining 1 tablespoon oil, and toss to coat.

Add lemon peel and juice, parsley, nuts, raisins, ground cinnamon, and salt to taste and toss until well combined.

Linguine with Clam Sauce

SERVES 8 AS A FIRST COURSE, 4 AS A MAIN COURSE
ACTIVE TIME: 20 MINUTES ■ START TO FINISH: 20 MINUTES

■ Sweet, tender, small fresh clams make all the difference in this Italian restaurant classic. As a matter of fact, we got this recipe from David Pasternack, the chef of Esca, an Italian seafood restaurant in New York City. There's a great balance between the clams, wine, pancetta, and hot chiles. Pasternack strongly recommends using a sturdy dried semolina pasta instead of fresh or dried egg linguine, and the smallest clams you can find. ■

- 8 tablespoons extra-virgin olive oil
- 6 ounces thinly sliced pancetta, cut into thin strips
- 1 garlic clove, thinly sliced
- 2 pounds mahogany clams or New Zealand cockles, scrubbed
- 1 cup bottled clam juice
- ⅓ cup dry white wine
- 4 (1-inch-long) dried hot chiles or 1 teaspoon red pepper flakes
- 14 ounces dried thin linguine *(linguine fini)*
- ¼ cup chopped fresh flat-leaf parsley

Heat 3 tablespoons oil in a deep 12-inch heavy skillet over moderately high heat until hot but not smoking. Add pancetta and cook, stirring occasionally, until golden, about 6 minutes. Add garlic and cook, stirring, until golden, about 30 seconds. Stir in clams (or cockles), clam juice, wine, and chiles, bring to a boil, and boil, covered, until clams open, 4 to 5 minutes; discard any clams that do not open. If using whole chiles, remove and discard.

Meanwhile, cook pasta in a 6- to 8-quart pot of boiling salted water (1 tablespoon salt per every 4 quarts water) until al dente; drain.

Add pasta to sauce and simmer, stirring, for 30 seconds. Toss with parsley and drizzle with remaining 5 tablespoons oil.

Pasta with Mussels and Chorizo

SERVES 6 AS A MAIN COURSE
ACTIVE TIME: 1 HOUR ■ START TO FINISH: 1¼ HOURS

■ Our taking-off point here was the marvelous clam and sausage combination seen throughout Portugal and in the Portuguese fishing communities of New England. Tossing mussels and chorizo with pasta makes it a great main course. (For more about mussels, see page 332.) ■

- ½ cup extra-virgin olive oil
- 2 (4-ounce) links Spanish chorizo (spicy cured pork sausage; see Glossary), finely chopped
- 2 shallots, finely chopped
- 1 tablespoon minced garlic
- ½ cup dry white wine (plus more for cooking mussels, if desired)
- 4 pounds mussels, preferably cultivated, well scrubbed and beards removed
- 1 pound dried pasta, such as *campanelle* ("little bells") or short spiral pasta
- ½ cup finely chopped fresh cilantro
- ¼ cup finely chopped fresh flat-leaf parsley
- 2 tablespoons fresh lemon juice, or to taste
- Salt and freshly ground black pepper

Heat oil in a 12-inch heavy skillet over moderately high heat until hot but not smoking. Add chorizo and shallots and cook, stirring, until chorizo is golden brown on edges, about 4 minutes. Add garlic and cook, stirring, for 1 minute. Add wine, bring to a simmer, and simmer until liquid is reduced by half, about 5 minutes. Remove from heat and cover to keep warm.

Bring 1 cup water (or a mix of water and white wine) to a boil in a 4- to 6-quart pot. Add mussels, cover, reduce heat to moderate, and cook, stirring occasionally, until mussels open wide, 3 to 6 minutes (check frequently after 3 minutes). With a slotted spoon, scoop out mussels (discard any that are unopened) and transfer to a bowl.

Cook pasta in a 6- to 8-quart pot of boiling salted water (1 tablespoon salt per every 4 quarts water) until al dente. Reserve 1 cup pasta cooking water and drain pasta.

Return pasta to pot and add sauce, mussels, cilantro, parsley, and ½ cup pasta cooking water. Cook over low heat, stirring, until mussels are heated through; add more cooking water if pasta seems dry.

Toss with lemon juice and salt and pepper to taste.

Sicilian-Style Pasta with Sardines

SERVES 4 AS A MAIN COURSE
ACTIVE TIME: 30 MINUTES ■ START TO FINISH: 45 MINUTES

■ *Pasta con le sarde* is a Sicilian staple, marrying the sea to the island's hillsides, where wild fennel grows in profusion. We've adapted this to an American kitchen, using canned sardines instead of fresh and the fennel commonly found in our supermarkets. ■

- 1 slice firm white sandwich bread
- ½ cup plus 2 tablespoons extra-virgin olive oil
- Salt
- 1 large fennel bulb
- ⅛ teaspoon crumbled saffron threads
- ½ cup raisins
- ½ cup dry white wine
- 1 medium onion, finely chopped
- 1 tablespoon fennel seeds, crushed
- 2 (3¾- to 4⅜-ounce) cans sardines in oil, drained
- 1 pound *perciatelli* (see page 219) or spaghetti
- ½ cup (2 ounces) pine nuts, toasted (see Tips, page 938)
- Freshly ground black pepper

Put a rack in middle of oven and preheat oven to 250°F.

Tear bread into 1-inch pieces, then pulse in a food processor until finely chopped. Spread crumbs on a baking sheet and bake, stirring once, until dry and very pale golden, about 10 minutes. Measure ⅓ cup crumbs (reserve remainder for another use) and toss with 2 tablespoons oil and salt to taste. Set aside.

Remove fennel fronds, chop, and reserve. Trim fennel stalks flush with bulb and discard. Cut any brown spots from outer layers and quarter bulb lengthwise. Cut out core and finely chop bulb. Combine saffron, raisins, and wine in a small bowl.

Heat remaining 1/2 cup oil in a 12-inch heavy skillet over moderate heat. Add onion, fennel bulb, fennel seeds, and salt to taste and cook, stirring, until fennel is tender, about 15 minutes. Add wine mixture and half of sardines, breaking up sardines with a fork, and simmer for 1 minute.

Meanwhile, cook pasta in a 6- to 8-quart pot of boiling salted water (1 tablespoon salt per every 4 quarts water) until al dente; drain.

Toss pasta in a bowl with fennel sauce, remaining sardines, fennel fronds, pine nuts, and salt and pepper to taste. Add bread crumbs and toss again.

Penne with Arugula and Prosciutto

SERVES 6 TO 8 AS A FIRST COURSE, 4 AS A MAIN COURSE
ACTIVE TIME: 15 MINUTES ■ START TO FINISH: 20 MINUTES

■ Keep this in mind when you need to get something on the table fast. Think of it as the Armani of pasta dishes: simple and clean, but with a smooth, suave quality. Arugula adds pepper, prosciutto adds salt, and lemon zest gives the fat quills of pasta a flavorful lift. When buying prosciutto for a recipe like this one, where it is chopped up and used as an ingredient (rather than being draped over a piece of melon, for example), have the butcher slice it thin but not paper-thin, or it will practically disappear. ■

- 1 pound penne, preferably ridged
- 1/4 pound thinly sliced prosciutto (see above), chopped
- 1 pound arugula (4 bunches), coarse stems discarded and leaves coarsely chopped
- 2/3 cup finely grated Parmigiano-Reggiano
- 3/4 teaspoon finely grated lemon zest
- Salt and freshly ground black pepper
- 1/4 cup extra-virgin olive oil

Cook pasta in a 6- to 8-quart pot of boiling salted water (1 tablespoon salt per every 4 quarts water) until al dente. Reserve 1 cup cooking water and drain pasta.

Return pasta to pot and toss with prosciutto, arugula, cheese, zest, and salt and pepper to taste. Drizzle oil over pasta and toss to combine, adding some of reserved cooking water if pasta seems dry.

Penne alla Vodka

SERVES 8 AS A FIRST COURSE, 4 TO 6 AS A MAIN COURSE
ACTIVE TIME: 25 MINUTES ■ START TO FINISH: 40 MINUTES

■ Although this dish, now listed on countless Italian restaurant menus, has a certain novelty, it takes just one bite to discover how successful the unusual combination is. This version comes from Le Sirenuse, in Positano, Italy. ■

- 1/2 stick (4 tablespoons) unsalted butter
- 1 medium onion, finely chopped
- 2/3 cup vodka
- 3/4 cup canned tomato purée
- 1 cup heavy cream
- 1/4 pound cooked ham, finely chopped
- 2 drops Tabasco, or to taste
- 1/2 teaspoon salt
- 1/4 teaspoon freshly ground black pepper
- 1 pound penne
- 3/4 cup finely grated Parmigiano-Reggiano

Melt butter in a deep 12-inch heavy skillet over moderately low heat. Add onion and cook, stirring occasionally, until it begins to soften, about 5 minutes. Stir in vodka, bring to a simmer, and simmer for 4 minutes. Add tomato purée and cream and simmer, stirring occasionally, until onion is soft, about 5 minutes. Stir in ham, Tabasco, salt, and pepper. Keep sauce warm over very low heat.

Cook pasta in a 6- to 8-quart pot of boiling salted water (1 tablespoon salt per every 4 quarts water) until al dente. Reserve 1/2 cup cooking water and drain pasta.

Add pasta to sauce and toss with sauce and cheese, adding some of reserved cooking water if pasta seems dry.

Pasta Shapes

Although Italians made pasta famous, its origins are fiercely debated. Some people claim that Marco Polo returned to Italy from the Far East with noodles, but that theory has been debunked; as far back as the first century B.C., Cicero mentioned *lágani,* which were thin sheets of dough — probably the prototype of modern lasagne. Most scholars feel that the Romans learned about pasta from their Arab neighbors. According to Guiliano Hazan, the author of *The Classic Pasta Cookbook,* when the first Italian immigrants arrived in America in the late nineteenth century, ships from Italy with cargoes of pasta soon followed. "By 1913," Hazan writes, "almost 700,000 tons were being exported to the New World."

There are two types of pasta: *pasta fresca,* fresh pasta (see page 209), which is homemade, and *pasta secca,* dried pasta, which is commercially produced. Fresh pasta is primarily associated with northern Italy, especially Emilia-Romagna. A supple dough made with flour, water, and usually egg is rolled out and cut into strips of smooth, flat noodles, such as fettuccine, or filled and formed into stuffed pasta, such as ravioli. Dried pasta originated in southern Italy, where the hearty semolina flour needed to produce it is plentiful. This sturdy dough — semolina, salt, and water — is used to create an impressive array of pasta shapes.

Here are a few of our favorites.

CAMPANELLE: These ruffly little cones ("little bells") are also known as *gigli* ("lilies"). Their nooks and crannies do a great job of catching sauces.

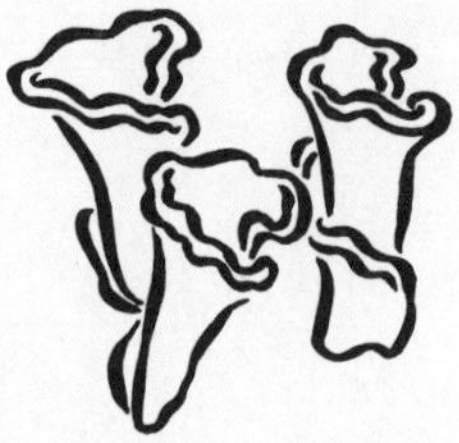

FARFALLE: The whimsical name means "butterflies," but this shape is known as bow-tie pasta in America. Bite-sized farfalle are good with vegetable or meat sauces.

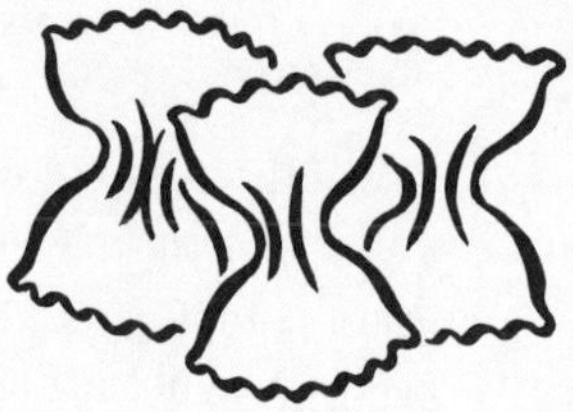

ACINI DI PEPE: This small roundish pasta, whose name means "peppercorns," is one of the shapes known as *pastina,* or "little pasta," which are often used in broths or soups. They are also a great substitute for Israeli couscous, sometimes called pearl pasta.

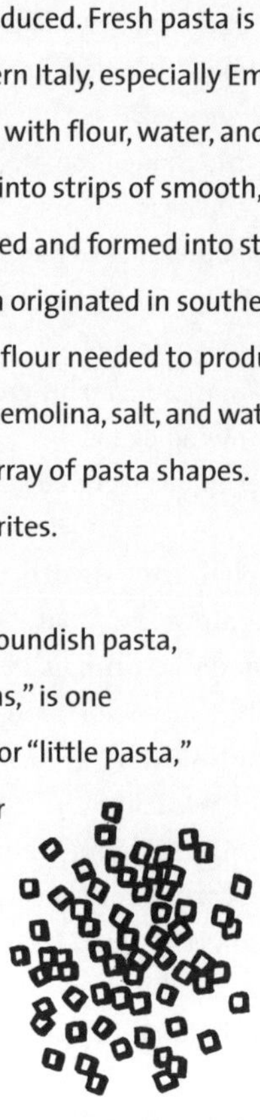

FETTUCCINE: This egg pasta, sometimes called *trenette,* is commonly made fresh but is available in dried form as well. Delicate, flat, and almost imperceptibly textured, it has a great affinity for butter and cream sauces.

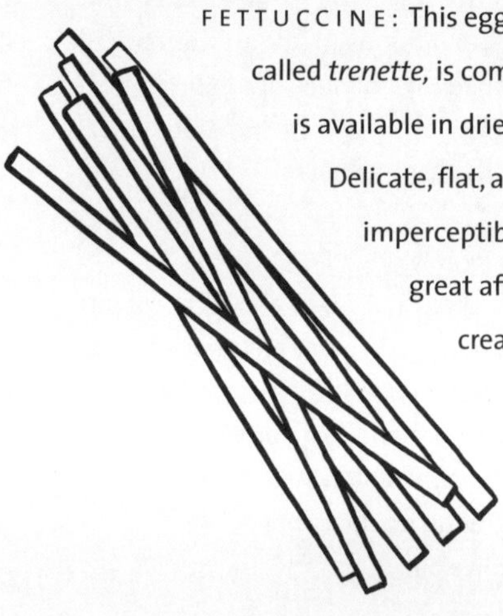

FUSILLI: Sometimes labeled "rotini," this tight, short spiral shape is extremely versatile, lending itself to all kinds of sauces. Its full name is *fusilli corti,* which means "short springs"; *fusilli lunghi,* or "long springs," is a longer spiral pasta, usually available only at Italian markets or specialty foods shops.

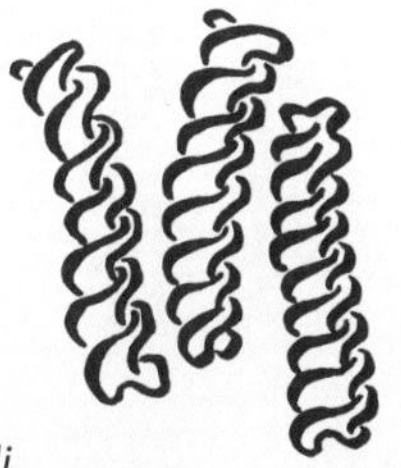

LASAGNE: These long, wide sheets of pasta are layered with a meat, seafood, or vegetable filling. If a recipe calls for dried lasagne noodles, we tend to prefer oven-ready lasagne noodles (sometimes labeled "no-boil") instead of the regular dried ones, which often have curly edges and are too thick.

LINGUINE: This flat, slithery pasta gets its name from the Italian word for tongues. It's more popular in America than in Italy.

ORECCHIETTE: These curved, firm little disks ("little ears") are a specialty of the Apulia region, in southeastern Italy. Rougher and more rustic in texture than farfalle, they are particularly suited to chunky, hearty sauces.

ORZO: In Italian, the word *orzo* means "barley," but orzo is really a small rice-shaped pasta. It's delicious in soups or served like rice.

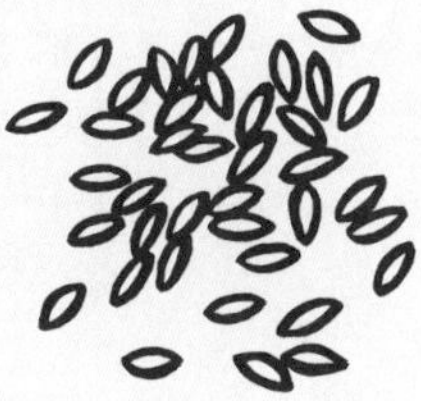

PENNE: The most common dried tube-shaped pasta, penne is available both smooth and ridged (*rigate*) and is incredibly versatile. It is satisfyingly chewy yet tender, and the cavities in the tubes are great for trapping sauces.

PERCIATELLI: Also called *bucatini,* this is essentially fat spaghetti with a hole, like a drinking straw (children are highly amused by this). *Perciatelli* takes beautifully to hearty sauces.

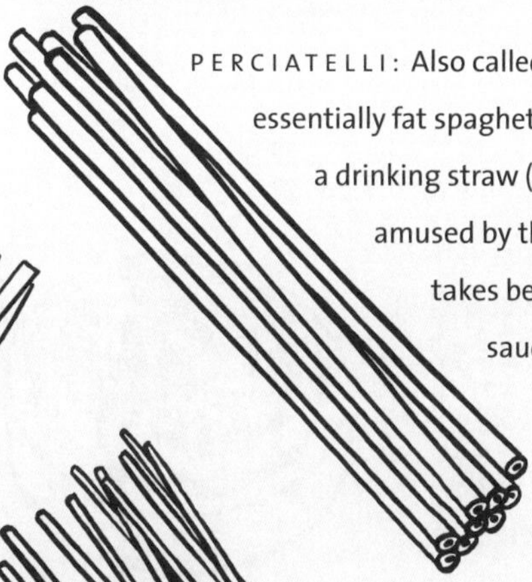

SPAGHETTI, SPAGHETTINI: Spaghetti, the best-known dried pasta, is a great vehicle for all sorts of sauces. Spaghettini, or thin spaghetti, is a little more delicate.

TAGLIATELLE: Invented in Bologna, these pasta ribbons, slightly broader than fettuccine, are classically served with Bolognese sauce.

Favorite Meats for Pasta Dishes

Depth of flavor in many pasta dishes comes from the Italian genius with pork. Here are three of our mainstays.

PANCETTA: Every time we use this Italian bacon from the pork belly, which has been salt-cured but not smoked, we are reminded again of how its flavor resonates through a dish. Pancetta is at its most voluptuous in something like spaghetti alla carbonara, but you can use it any time you want a hammy but not smoky flavor — in a minestrone, say, or with winter greens. Look for pancetta at Italian markets and specialty foods shops; the person behind the counter will slice it for you. Pancetta keeps, tightly wrapped, in the refrigerator for about a week or in the freezer for about three months.

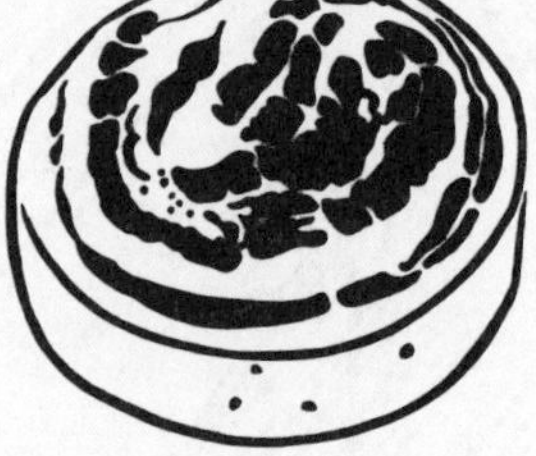

GUANCIALE: Similar in flavor to pancetta, *guanciale* ("gwan-*cha*-leh") is cured but not smoked pork jowl, or, to put it more politely, pig cheek. It has a higher proportion of fat than pancetta, enriching whatever it is cooked with. American producers include New York City's Salumeria Biellese and Niman Ranch, both of whom will ship (see Sources).

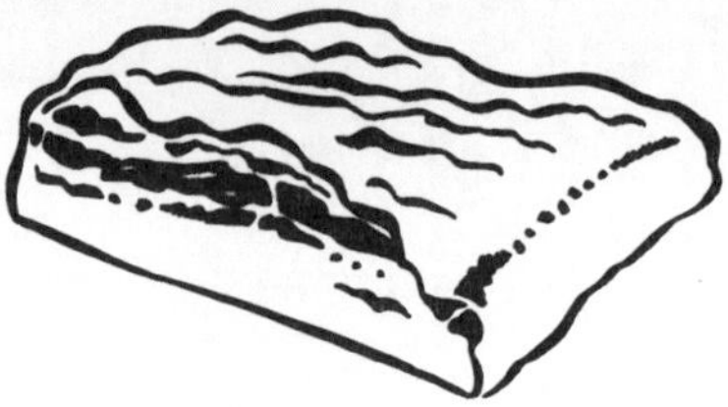

PROSCIUTTO: This is ham that has been salted and air-cured; like pancetta, it is never smoked, but it is leaner — it comes from the leg rather than the belly. The finest prosciutto, which comes from Parma, has a beautiful balance of saltiness and sweetness, and its flavor is more delicate and complex than that of pancetta. It is available at Italian markets and specialty foods shops, like pancetta, and can be kept in the same way.

Spaghetti alla Carbonara

SERVES 8 AS A FIRST COURSE, 4 AS A MAIN COURSE
ACTIVE TIME: 40 MINUTES ■ START TO FINISH: 40 MINUTES

■ This classic illustrates the Italian way of making something sublime out of something everyday—eggs, bacon, and cheese. It also underscores the Italian reliance on simple, stellar ingredients. If you want to do as the Romans do, use *guanciale* ("gwan-*cha*-leh"), which is similar in flavor to pancetta, an alternative that is easier to come by. You can also make this dish with regular bacon; it will taste different but still be delicious. ■

- 5 ounces *guanciale* (unsmoked cured hog jowl) or pancetta, cut into 1/3-inch dice
- 1 medium onion, finely chopped
- 1/4 cup dry white wine
- 1 pound spaghetti
- 3 large eggs
- 3/4 cup finely grated Parmigiano-Reggiano
- 1/3 cup finely grated pecorino Romano
- 1/4 teaspoon salt
- 1 teaspoon coarsely ground black pepper

Cook *guanciale* in a deep 12-inch heavy skillet over moderate heat, stirring, until it begins to render its fat, 1 to 2 minutes. Add onion and cook, stirring occasionally, until golden, about 10 minutes. Add wine and boil until reduced by about half.

Meanwhile, cook spaghetti in a 6- to 8-quart pot of boiling salted water (1 tablespoon salt per every 4 quarts water) until al dente.

Whisk together eggs, cheeses, salt, and pepper in a small bowl.

Drain spaghetti, add to onion mixture, and toss over moderate heat until coated. Remove from heat and add egg mixture, tossing to combine. Serve immediately.

COOK'S NOTE

- The eggs in this recipe are not fully cooked. If this is a concern, see page 629.

Pasta with Bolognese Sauce

SERVES 4 AS A MAIN COURSE
ACTIVE TIME: 30 MINUTES ■ START TO FINISH: 2 HOURS

■ Stirring a pot of Bolognese on the stove makes you realize how important good ingredients are to Italian cooking. Everything adds up: the kind of meat you use (pork, beef, veal), aromatics, oil, spices. A specialty of northern Italy's Emilia-Romagna and named for the region's capital, Bolognese is a meat sauce, but not a deep, dark, tomatoey one. Classically paired with tagliatelle (see page 219), it also works well with a variety of other pasta shapes that trap the savory sauce. When tossing the pasta with what may seem a relatively small amount of sauce, don't worry: that's how it's done in Italy, and you'll discover that the sauce is so flavorful, there's no need to drown the pasta. ■

- 2 tablespoons olive oil
- 2 tablespoons unsalted butter
- 1 large onion, finely chopped
- 2 garlic cloves, finely chopped
- 2 carrots, finely chopped
- 2 celery ribs, finely chopped
- 2 tablespoons tomato paste
- 1 pound meat loaf mix (equal parts ground beef, pork, and veal)
- 1 cup whole milk
- 1/2 teaspoon salt
- 1/4 teaspoon freshly ground black pepper
- 1/8 teaspoon freshly grated nutmeg
- 1 cup dry white wine
- 1 (28-ounce) can whole tomatoes in juice
- 1 pound dried pasta, such as penne, rigatoni, fusilli, or orecchiette

ACCOMPANIMENT: finely grated Parmigiano-Reggiano

Heat oil and butter in a 6- to 8-quart heavy pot over moderately high heat until foam subsides. Add onion, garlic, carrots, and celery and cook, stirring, for 2 minutes. Stir in tomato paste and cook for 1 minute. Add meat loaf mix and cook, stirring, until meat is no longer pink, about 4 minutes. Add milk, salt, pepper, and nutmeg and cook, stirring, until most of milk has evaporated, about 8 minutes. Add wine and cook, stirring occasionally, until all liquid has evaporated, about 8 minutes.

Coarsely purée tomatoes, with their juice, in a blender or food processor. Stir tomatoes into pot. Cook sauce at a bare simmer, uncovered, stirring occasionally, for about 1¼ hours (sauce will thicken). Season with salt and pepper.

When sauce is almost done, cook pasta in a 6- to 8-quart pot of boiling salted water (1 tablespoon salt per every 4 quarts water) until al dente; drain.

Immediately toss pasta with sauce in a large bowl. Serve with cheese.

COOK'S NOTE

■ The sauce keeps, covered and refrigerated, for up to 2 days. It can also be frozen for up to 1 month.

Perciatelli with Sausage Ragù and Meatballs

SERVES 8 TO 10 AS A MAIN COURSE
ACTIVE TIME: 2¼ HOURS ■ START TO FINISH: 4 HOURS (INCLUDES MAKING MEATBALLS)

■ The perfect meal for an informal Saturday night with friends. Just add good crusty bread and bottles of Chianti. You can have it simmering away that afternoon, and the aroma alone will make people wild with hunger. In Sicily, this is a part of Carnival celebrations on Shrove Tuesday, just before Lent begins. The pasta with ragù is served as a first course and the sausages and meatballs as the main course. We decided to break with tradition and pile everything on top of the pasta. ■

- 1–2 tablespoons extra-virgin olive oil
- Sicilian Meatballs (recipe follows)
- 12 sweet Italian sausages (2 pounds total)
- 1 large onion, finely chopped
- 1 large garlic clove, smashed with side of a heavy knife
- 2 cups dry red wine
- 2 tablespoons tomato paste
- 1 (28-ounce) can crushed tomatoes in purée
- 1 Turkish bay leaf or ½ California bay leaf
- 1½ pounds *perciatelli* (see page 219) or ridged penne
- 1 cup frozen peas, thawed
- Salt and freshly ground black pepper

Heat 1 tablespoon oil in an 8- to 9-quart wide heavy pot over moderately high heat until hot but not smoking. Brown meatballs in batches, turning occasionally, about 4 minutes per batch. Transfer to a plate. Prick sausages all over with a fork and brown in same pot, turning occasionally and adding remaining 1 tablespoon oil if necessary, about 5 minutes. Transfer to another plate.

Reduce heat to moderate and cook onion in fat remaining in pot, stirring occasionally, until softened, about 4 minutes. Add garlic and cook, stirring, for 2 minutes. Stir in wine, tomato paste, tomatoes in purée, and bay leaf. Arrange meatballs and sausages, with any juices, in middle of pot. Cover and simmer ragù for 1¼ hours.

Meanwhile, cook pasta in a 6- to 8-quart pot of boiling salted water (1 tablespoon salt per 4 every quarts water) until al dente. Drain well and return to pot.

Add peas to ragù and simmer, covered, for 5 minutes more. With tongs and a slotted spoon, transfer meatballs and sausages to a serving dish and cover to keep warm. Skim fat from sauce, if desired.

Toss pasta with some sauce and salt and pepper to taste. Serve topped with meatballs and sausage.

COOK'S NOTE

■ The ragù can be made, without the peas, up to 1 day ahead. Reduce the simmering time to 50 minutes and cool the ragù completely, uncovered, then refrigerate, covered. To serve, simmer the ragù until the meats are heated through, 15 to 25 minutes, then add the peas and simmer for 5 minutes.

Sicilian Meatballs

MAKES ABOUT 36 MEATBALLS
ACTIVE TIME: 45 MINUTES ■ START TO FINISH: 45 MINUTES

■ Cinnamon, currants, pine nuts: the slightly exotic flavor of these meatballs is typical of many Sicilian dishes. Strategically situated off the coast of Africa on the shipping routes to Europe, Sicily was ruled by the Arabs for four hundred years. Mixtures of spices, nuts, bread crumbs, and currants or golden raisins are a culinary vestige of that influence. ■

- ¾ cup fine fresh bread crumbs from Italian bread (crusts discarded)

- 1/4 cup whole milk
- 1/2 cup (2 3/4 ounces) whole almonds with skin, toasted (see Tips, page 938)
- 1 1/2 teaspoons sugar
- 1 pound ground beef chuck
- 1/2 cup finely grated pecorino Romano or Parmigiano-Reggiano
- 1/4 cup dried currants
- 1/4 cup pine nuts, lightly toasted (see Tips, page 938)
- 2 teaspoons salt
- 1/4 teaspoon ground cinnamon
- 1 large egg

Stir together bread crumbs and milk in a medium bowl.

Pulse almonds with sugar in a food processor until finely ground. Add to bread crumb mixture, along with remaining ingredients, and mix with your hands until just combined.

Roll mixture into 1-inch meatballs and transfer to a plate. Refrigerate if not cooking immediately.

COOK'S NOTE

- The meatballs can be made up to 1 day ahead and refrigerated, covered.

Macaroni and Cheese

SERVES 8 AS A MAIN COURSE, 12 TO 14 AS A SIDE DISH
ACTIVE TIME: 30 MINUTES ■ START TO FINISH: 1 HOUR

■ This is arguably the best mac and cheese on the planet. One secret is a dollop of Dijon mustard, which tempers the richness, in effect saving the dish from itself. Another secret is the fluffy, crisp Japanese bread crumbs called panko used in the topping. For those who prefer a greater ratio of crunchy topping to creamy center, we suggest splitting the macaroni and cheese between two three-quart shallow baking dishes and doubling the topping recipe, dividing it between the two. ■

FOR TOPPING

- 1/4 stick (2 tablespoons) unsalted butter, melted
- 2 cups panko (Japanese bread crumbs) or coarse dry bread crumbs
- 1 cup coarsely grated extra-sharp Cheddar (about 4 ounces)

FOR CHEESE SAUCE AND MACARONI

- 3 tablespoons unsalted butter
- 3 tablespoons all-purpose flour
- 1/2 teaspoon red pepper flakes
- 2 3/4 cups whole milk
- 3/4 cup heavy cream
- 4 cups coarsely grated extra-sharp Cheddar (about 1 pound)
- 2 teaspoons Dijon mustard
- 1 1/2 teaspoons salt
- 1/4 teaspoon freshly ground black pepper
- 3/4 pound elbow macaroni

Put a rack in middle of oven and preheat oven to 400°F. Butter a 3-quart shallow baking dish.

MAKE THE TOPPING: Stir together butter, panko, and cheese in a bowl until well combined.

MAKE THE SAUCE: Melt butter in a 5-quart heavy pot over moderately low heat. Whisk in flour and red pepper flakes and cook, whisking, for 3 minutes to make a roux. Whisk in milk in a slow stream, then bring sauce to a boil, whisking constantly. Simmer, whisking occasionally, for 3 minutes. Stir in cream, Cheddar, mustard, salt, and pepper. Remove pot from heat and cover surface of sauce with wax paper to prevent a skin from forming.

COOK THE MACARONI AND ASSEMBLE THE DISH: Cook macaroni in a 6-quart pot of boiling salted water (1 tablespoon salt per every 4 quarts water) until al dente. Reserve 1 cup pasta cooking water and drain macaroni.

Stir together macaroni, reserved cooking water, and sauce in a large bowl, then transfer to baking dish (mixture will be loose).

Sprinkle topping evenly over macaroni. Bake until top is golden and bubbling, 25 to 35 minutes.

COOK'S NOTE

- The topping can be made up to 1 day ahead and refrigerated, covered.

Baked Four-Cheese Farfalle

SERVES 6 AS A MAIN COURSE
ACTIVE TIME: 30 MINUTES ■ START TO FINISH: 1¼ HOURS

■ We use four different Italian cheeses here: mozzarella, Fontina, pecorino Romano, and Gorgonzola. The combination creates almost a new cheese, one that has some mystery to it. Farfalle (usually called bow-tie pasta in America) makes a lighter baked pasta than the more traditional macaroni. This is perfect for Super Bowl Sunday. Just add a green salad and a loaf of crusty bread . . . and a few of your favorite sports fans. ■

- ½ stick (4 tablespoons) unsalted butter
- 2 tablespoons all-purpose flour
- 1½ cups whole milk
- 1 (28- to 32-ounce) can whole Italian tomatoes in juice, drained (1¼ cups juice reserved) and finely chopped
- ½ teaspoon salt
- ¼ teaspoon freshly ground black pepper
- 1 pound farfalle
- 1½ cups coarsely grated mozzarella (about 6 ounces)
- ½ cup crumbled Gorgonzola
- ½ cup diced Italian Fontina
- 1⅓ cups finely grated pecorino Romano (about 3 ounces)
- ½ cup finely chopped fresh flat-leaf parsley

Put a rack in middle of oven and preheat oven to 375°F. Butter a 3- to 4-quart gratin dish or other shallow baking dish.

Melt butter in a 4-quart heavy saucepan over moderately low heat. Add flour and cook, whisking, for 3 minutes to make a roux. Add milk and reserved tomato juice in a slow stream, whisking, then bring to a boil, whisking constantly. Stir in tomatoes, salt, and pepper and simmer until thickened, about 3 minutes. Remove from heat.

Cook pasta in a 6- to 8-quart pot of boiling salted water (1 tablespoon salt per every 4 quarts water) until just al dente; drain.

Stir together pasta, sauce, mozzarella, Gorgonzola, Fontina, 1 cup Romano, and parsley in a large bowl. Transfer to gratin dish and sprinkle with remaining ⅓ cup Romano.

Bake until golden and bubbling, 25 to 30 minutes. Let stand for 10 minutes before serving.

Baked Orzo with Shrimp, Tomato Sauce, and Feta

SERVES 6
ACTIVE TIME: 25 MINUTES ■ START TO FINISH: 45 MINUTES

■ Shrimp matched with tomatoes and tangy feta is a Greek tradition in and of itself. We added the small rice-shaped pasta called orzo to make this a heartier main course. ■

- 2 tablespoons olive oil
- 1 medium onion, finely chopped
- 3 garlic cloves, minced
- ½ teaspoon dried oregano, crumbled
- ¼ teaspoon red pepper flakes
- ½ cup dry white wine
- 1 (28-ounce) can crushed tomatoes in purée
- 1 teaspoon salt
- 1½ pounds large shrimp in shells (21–25 per pound), peeled and deveined
- 1 pound orzo
- ½ cup Kalamata or other brine-cured black olives, pitted and chopped
- Freshly ground black pepper
- 1 pound feta, patted dry and crumbled (about 3 cups)

Put a rack in middle of oven and preheat oven to 425°F. Oil a 13-by-9-inch baking dish.

Heat 1 tablespoon oil in a 4-quart heavy saucepan over moderately high heat. Add onion, garlic, oregano, and red pepper flakes and cook, stirring, until onion is softened, about 3 minutes. Add wine, bring to a boil, and boil until reduced by half, about 3 minutes. Stir in tomatoes and salt, reduce heat, and simmer briskly, stirring frequently, until sauce is slightly thickened, about 8 minutes.

Stir shrimp into sauce and simmer, stirring occasionally, until shrimp are just cooked through, about 3 minutes.

Meanwhile, cook orzo in a 6- to 8-quart pot of boiling salted water (1 tablespoon salt per every 4 quarts water) until al dente. Reserve ½ cup cooking water and drain orzo in a sieve. Return orzo to pot and toss with remaining 1 tablespoon oil.

Stir sauce and reserved cooking water into orzo, then add olives and salt and pepper to taste. Spoon half of pasta into oiled baking dish and sprinkle with half of feta. Top with remaining pasta and feta.

Bake, uncovered, until cheese is slightly melted and orzo is heated through, 10 to 15 minutes.

Baked Pasta with Tomatoes, Shiitake Mushrooms, and Prosciutto

SERVES 6 TO 8

ACTIVE TIME: 1 HOUR ■ START TO FINISH: 2 HOURS

■ A good casserole can be a lifesaver when entertaining, because most of the work is done before your guests arrive. This one is easy and elegant. Although it is Italian in spirit, we use an Asian mushroom in place of a more traditional one and a blend of three cheeses rather than the usual mozzarella. ■

- 2 tablespoons olive oil
- 2 cups finely chopped onions
- 2 large garlic cloves, minced
- 1/4 teaspoon red pepper flakes, or to taste
- 1 teaspoon dried basil, crumbled
- 1 teaspoon dried oregano, crumbled
- 1 pound shiitake mushrooms, stems discarded and caps sliced
- 1/2 stick (4 tablespoons) unsalted butter
- 3 tablespoons all-purpose flour
- 2 cups whole milk
- 2 (28-ounce) cans Italian tomatoes in juice, drained well and chopped
- 1/4 pound thinly sliced prosciutto, cut into strips
- 1 cup finely grated Italian Fontina (about 4 ounces)
- 1 cup crumbled Gorgonzola (about 4 ounces)
- 1 1/2 cups finely grated Parmigiano-Reggiano (about 3 ounces)
- 2/3 cup minced fresh flat-leaf parsley
- 1 pound farfalle or penne
- Salt and freshly ground black pepper

Put a rack in middle of oven and preheat oven to 450°F. Butter a 3- to 4-quart shallow baking dish.

Heat oil in a large skillet over moderately low heat. Add onions, garlic, red pepper flakes, basil, and oregano and cook, stirring, until onions are softened, about 6 minutes. Add mushrooms, increase heat to

Grating Hard Cheeses

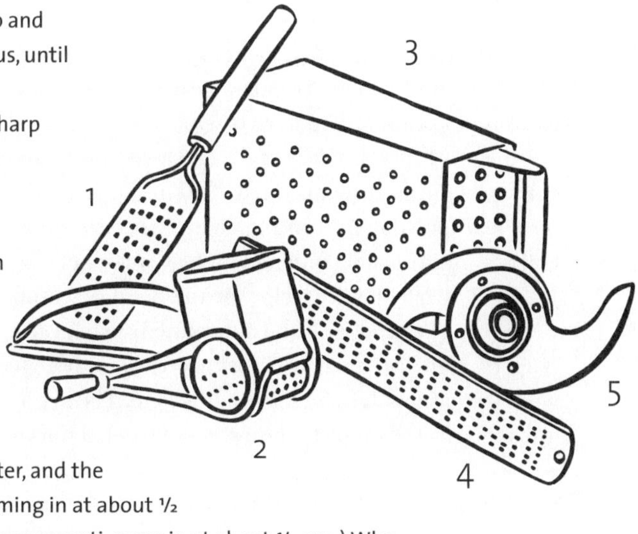

Exactly how to grate hard cheeses such as Parmigiano-Reggiano and pecorino Romano may seem a trivial matter—at least it did to us, until the Microplane rasp (available at cookware stores) came along. Suddenly we were getting far more volume from its tiny razor-sharp blades than we were from the small teardrop-shaped holes of a hand or box grater, making our cup and weight measures inconsistent. So we wondered just how different the volume produced by the various tools of the trade might be. Our kitchen drawers revealed a hand grater (1), a rotary grater (2), a box grater (3), and the rasp (4). We set them next to a food processor (5), then subjected an ounce of cheese to each. The results ranged from a scant 1/3 cup of finely ground nuggets (food processor) to about 1 1/4 cups of tissue-thin wisps (rasp). The fine shreds created by the hand grater, the rotary grater, and the box grater (our standard method) varied in volume the least, coming in at about 1/2 cup. (One ounce of powdery pregrated cheese, snubbed by the cognoscenti, came in at about 1/3 cup.) Who knew that there would be such discrepancies? For these recipes, we grated the cheese with a box or other hand-held grater or a rotary grater.

moderate, and cook, stirring, until mushrooms are tender, about 10 minutes. Transfer to a large bowl.

Melt 3 tablespoons butter in same skillet over moderately low heat. Whisk in flour and cook, whisking, for 3 minutes to make a roux. Add milk in a slow stream, whisking, and simmer, whisking constantly, until thickened, about 2 minutes. Pour sauce over mushroom mixture. Stir in tomatoes, prosciutto, Fontina, Gorgonzola, 1¼ cups Parmesan, and parsley.

Cook pasta in a 6- to 8-quart pot of boiling salted water (1 tablespoon salt per every 4 quarts water) for 5 minutes (pasta will not be tender). Drain well.

Add pasta and salt and pepper to taste to mushroom mixture and toss until well combined. Transfer to buttered baking dish, sprinkle with remaining ¼ cup Parmesan, and dot with remaining 1 tablespoon butter. Bake until top is golden and pasta is tender, 25 to 30 minutes.

COOK'S NOTE

■ The casserole can be assembled up to 1 day ahead and refrigerated, covered. Bring to room temperature, then sprinkle with cheese and dot with butter before baking.

Chicken Tetrazzini

SERVES 4

ACTIVE TIME: 35 MINUTES ■ START TO FINISH: 4 HOURS

■ This dish was named in honor of Luisa Tetrazzini, an Italian soprano who was popular in America during the early 1900s. Famously plump (she once said, "I must not diet. If I diet, my face sag"), she loved pasta and chicken with mushrooms. Fred Plotkin, an authority on opera and Italian food, speculates that the pasta creation was probably invented for her by a hotel chef. It's an especially handy recipe for the holiday season, when leftover turkey can be substituted for chicken. Forget about listening to Christmas carols, though; what you need is *La Traviata* or *Rigoletto.* The sherry gives this dish a bouquet reminiscent of toasted nuts. ■

- 1 (4-pound) chicken, cut into 8 serving pieces
- 4 quarts water
- 2½ teaspoons salt
- 5 tablespoons unsalted butter
- ¾ pound mushrooms, trimmed and thinly sliced
- ½ pound spaghetti
- 2 tablespoons all-purpose flour
- 1 cup heavy cream
- 3–4 tablespoons medium-dry sherry (to taste)
- ¾ cup finely grated Parmigiano-Reggiano
- ⅛ teaspoon freshly grated nutmeg
- 1 teaspoon freshly ground black pepper

Combine chicken, water, and 1 teaspoon salt in a 6- to 8-quart pot and bring to a boil, then reduce heat and simmer, uncovered, until chicken is tender, about 25 minutes. Cool chicken in broth until it can be handled, about 1½ hours (chicken will continue to cook as it stands).

Remove chicken from broth and separate meat from skin and bones. Return skin and bones to broth and coarsely shred meat. Refrigerate meat, covered. Bring broth to a simmer and simmer until reduced by about half, about 1 hour.

Pour broth through a fine-mesh sieve into a large bowl; discard solids. Skim fat from broth, return to pot, and bring to a boil. Boil until reduced to about 2 cups, about 1¼ hours.

While broth is reducing, melt 2 tablespoons butter in a 4-quart heavy saucepan over moderate heat. Add mushrooms and cook, stirring, until liquid they give off has evaporated and mushrooms are softened, about 8 minutes. Remove from heat and set aside.

Cook spaghetti in a 6-quart pot of boiling salted water (1 tablespoon salt per every 4 quarts water) until al dente; drain well.

Put a rack in middle of oven and preheat oven to 350°F. Generously butter a 2½-quart baking dish.

Melt remaining 3 tablespoons butter in a 1½-quart heavy saucepan over moderately low heat. Add flour and cook, whisking, for 3 minutes to make a roux. Gradually whisk in reduced broth, cream, and sherry and bring sauce to a boil, whisking constantly. Simmer, whisking occasionally, for 5 minutes. Stir in ¼ cup Parmesan, nutmeg, remaining 1½ teaspoons salt, and pepper.

Stir spaghetti and half of sauce into mushrooms. Transfer to buttered baking dish and make a well in center of spaghetti. Stir chicken into remaining sauce and spoon into well. Sprinkle with remaining ½ cup Parmesan.

Bake until pale golden, 25 to 30 minutes.

COOK'S NOTES

- The chicken can be cooked and shredded up to 1 day ahead and refrigerated, covered.
- The broth can be reduced up to 1 day ahead and refrigerated, covered.

Lamb and Eggplant Pastitsio

SERVES 6 TO 8

ACTIVE TIME: 35 MINUTES ■ START TO FINISH: 2½ HOURS

■ Our light, juicy version of this Greek classic has become one of our favorite casseroles. The Greek cooking authority Diane Kochilas tells us that the custom of baking pasta with meats originally came to Greece from the Near East. ■

FOR LAMB SAUCE

- 1 tablespoon olive oil
- 1 large onion, chopped
- 1 pound lean ground lamb
- 1 garlic clove, minced
- 1 teaspoon dried oregano, crumbled
- ½ teaspoon ground cinnamon
- ¼ teaspoon sugar
- 1½ teaspoons salt
- ¼ teaspoon freshly ground black pepper
- 1 pound eggplant, peeled and cut into ½-inch cubes
- 1 (28-ounce) can crushed tomatoes in purée

FOR CHEESE SAUCE

- 2 tablespoons unsalted butter
- 2 tablespoons all-purpose flour
- 2 cups whole milk
- 1 garlic clove
- 1 whole clove
- ½ pound feta, crumbled (about 1½ cups)
- ½ teaspoon salt
- ¼ teaspoon freshly ground black pepper
- 2 large eggs

FOR PASTA

- 10 ounces (3 cups) penne

MAKE THE LAMB SAUCE: Heat oil in a 4-quart heavy saucepan over moderately low heat. Add onion and cook, stirring, until softened, 3 to 5 minutes. Add lamb, increase heat to moderately high, and cook, stirring and breaking up lumps, until no longer pink, about 5 minutes.

Add garlic, oregano, cinnamon, sugar, salt, and pepper and cook, stirring, for 2 minutes. Stir in eggplant and tomatoes, cover, and simmer gently, stirring occasionally, until eggplant is just tender, about 40 minutes.

Remove lid and simmer, stirring occasionally, until sauce is thickened, about 15 minutes more. Season with salt and pepper. Remove from heat.

Put a rack in middle of oven and preheat oven to 425°F.

MEANWHILE, MAKE THE CHEESE SAUCE AND COOK THE PASTA: Melt butter in a 2-quart heavy saucepan over moderate heat. Whisk in flour and cook, whisking, for 3 minutes to make a roux. Whisk in milk and bring to a boil, whisking constantly. Add garlic and clove, reduce heat, and simmer, whisking occasionally, for 5 minutes. Add feta, salt, and pepper and cook, whisking vigorously, until cheese is well incorporated. Remove from heat and discard garlic and clove.

Beat eggs in a 6-quart bowl. Gradually add sauce to eggs, whisking constantly.

Cook pasta in a 6-quart pot of boiling salted water (1 tablespoon salt per every 4 quarts water) until just al dente; drain.

Toss half of pasta with lamb sauce and half with cheese sauce.

ASSEMBLE THE PASTITSIO: Pour pasta with lamb sauce into a shallow 3-quart baking dish, spreading it evenly. Spoon pasta with cheese sauce on top, spreading it evenly.

Bake pastitsio, uncovered, until bubbling and top is golden, 25 to 30 minutes. Let stand for 5 minutes before serving.

COOK'S NOTE

- The lamb sauce and cheese sauce can be made up to 1 day ahead, cooled completely, uncovered, and refrigerated, covered.

Spinach and Cheese Cannelloni

SERVES 8 AS A FIRST COURSE, 4 AS A MAIN COURSE
ACTIVE TIME: 2 HOURS ■ START TO FINISH: 4 HOURS (INCLUDES MAKING PASTA)

■ You're restlessly casting about for a rainy-day project, and fresh pasta comes to mind. This cannelloni filling—spinach, cheese, and a white sauce—is easy to put together. We love what a little prosciutto does, but you can omit it to make this a vegetarian main course. Because the dish is so straightforward, buy the best cheese you can find. (For more about Italian cheeses, see page 232.) ■

FOR SAUCE
- 1½ tablespoons unsalted butter
- 1½ tablespoons all-purpose flour
- 2 cups whole milk
- ¼ teaspoon salt
- ¼ teaspoon freshly ground black pepper
- Pinch of freshly grated nutmeg
- ⅓ cup finely grated pecorino Romano or Parmigiano-Reggiano

FOR CANNELLONI
- 3 tablespoons extra-virgin olive oil
- 1 small onion, chopped
- 2 garlic cloves, finely chopped
- 10 ounces baby spinach
- 1¾ cups ricotta (12 ounces fresh or 15 ounces supermarket-style)
- 1 large egg, lightly beaten
- ½ cup chopped fresh flat-leaf parsley
- 3 ounces thinly sliced prosciutto, chopped (optional)
- ¼ teaspoon salt
- ¼ teaspoon freshly ground black pepper
- ½ cup finely grated pecorino Romano or Parmigiano-Reggiano
- 8 Fresh Pasta Rectangles (page 230) or oven-ready (no-boil) lasagne noodles (each about 6 by 3 inches)

SPECIAL EQUIPMENT: a flameproof rectangular 3-quart baking dish (about 13 by 9 inches; not glass)

MAKE THE SAUCE: Melt butter in a 1½- to 2-quart heavy saucepan over moderately low heat. Whisk in flour and cook, whisking, for 3 minutes to make a roux. Add milk in a slow stream, whisking, and bring to a boil over high heat, whisking constantly. Reduce heat and simmer, whisking occasionally, for 2 minutes. Whisk in salt, pepper, and nutmeg. Remove from heat and whisk in cheese, then cover pan to keep warm.

MAKE THE FILLING: Heat oil in a 5- to 6-quart heavy pot over moderately high heat until hot but not smoking. Add onion and garlic and cook, stirring occasionally, until lightly browned, about 5 minutes. Add spinach and cook, stirring, until just wilted, about 3 minutes. Remove from heat and cool completely.

Stir together ricotta, egg, parsley, prosciutto (if using), salt, pepper, and ⅓ cup cheese in a bowl. Stir in spinach mixture.

Boil noodles a few at a time in a 6- to 8-quart pot of boiling salted water (1 tablespoon salt per every 4 quarts water), stirring to separate, until al dente, about 2 minutes for fresh pasta or about 6 minutes for dried noodles. Gently transfer with tongs and a slotted spatula to a large bowl of cold water to stop the cooking, then lift out, shaking off water, and lay flat on kitchen towels (not terry cloth). Pat dry with paper towels.

Put a rack in middle of oven and preheat oven to 425°F. Butter baking dish.

Spread ⅔ cup sauce in baking dish. Spread about ⅓ cup ricotta filling in a line along one short side of one pasta rectangle, then roll up to enclose filling and transfer, seam side down, to baking dish. Make 7 more cannelloni in same manner, arranging them in one snug layer. Spread ½ cup more sauce over cannelloni and sprinkle with remaining cheese.

Cover with foil and bake until sauce is bubbling, about 20 minutes. Remove from oven and turn on broiler.

Remove foil and broil cannelloni about 4 inches from heat until lightly browned, 2 to 4 minutes. Let stand for 5 minutes before serving.

Meanwhile, reheat remaining sauce. Serve with cannelloni.

COOK'S NOTE

■ The cannelloni can be assembled up to 1 day ahead and refrigerated, covered with plastic wrap. Let stand at room temperature for 20 minutes before baking. Thin the extra sauce as necessary with milk when reheating.

Seafood Cannelloni

SERVES 6
ACTIVE TIME: 1¾ HOURS ■ START TO FINISH: 3½ HOURS (INCLUDES MAKING PASTA)

■ This is an elegant party dish. It requires more work than a spaghetti supper or a basic lasagne—you'll need to make a seafood mousse as well as assemble the cannelloni—but all of that can be done ahead of time. ■

- 5 tablespoons unsalted butter, softened
- ⅓ cup finely chopped shallots
- 2 tablespoons finely chopped carrot
- 2 tablespoons finely chopped celery
- 1 pound medium shrimp in shells (31–35 per pound), peeled, shells reserved, and deveined
- 1 pound sea scallops, tough muscle removed from side of each if necessary and reserved
- 1 teaspoon tomato paste
- 1 cup dry white wine
- 3 cups water
- 1 tablespoon seafood glaze (optional; see Sources)
- 2 fresh flat-leaf parsley sprigs
- 3 tablespoons all-purpose flour
- 1 cup heavy cream
- ½ teaspoon fresh lemon juice, or to taste
- 1½ teaspoons salt
- ½ teaspoon freshly ground black pepper
- 2 tablespoons Cognac or other brandy
- ½ cup finely chopped fresh chives
- 14 Fresh Pasta Rectangles (page 230) or oven-ready (no-boil) lasagne noodles (each about 6 by 3 inches)

SPECIAL EQUIPMENT: a flameproof rectangular 3-quart baking dish (about 13 by 9 inches; not glass)

MAKE THE SAUCE: Melt 3 tablespoons butter in a 2- to 3-quart heavy saucepan over moderately low heat. Add shallots, carrot, celery, reserved shrimp shells, and reserved scallop muscles (if you have them) and cook, uncovered, stirring occasionally, until vegetables are softened and pale golden, about 5 minutes. Add tomato paste and cook, stirring, for 1 minute. Add wine, bring to a boil, and boil, stirring occasionally, until reduced to about ¼ cup, 6 to 8 minutes.

Add water, seafood glaze (if using), and parsley sprigs, bring to a simmer, and simmer, covered, for 30 minutes.

Discard parsley. Purée stock, including shrimp shells, in 2 batches in a blender (use caution). Pour through a fine-mesh sieve into a bowl, pressing on solids; discard solids.

Melt remaining 2 tablespoons butter in cleaned saucepan over moderately low heat. Add flour and cook, whisking, for 3 minutes to make a roux. Add warm seafood stock all at once, whisking, and bring to a boil, whisking. Add ½ cup cream and gently simmer sauce, whisking occasionally, for 10 minutes. Stir in lemon juice, ½ teaspoon salt, and ¼ teaspoon pepper.

Transfer ½ cup sauce to a bowl set in a larger bowl of ice and cold water to cool for filling. Set remaining sauce aside.

MAKE THE SEAFOOD FILLING: Cut one third of shrimp and one third of scallops into ¼-inch pieces and toss with ¼ teaspoon salt. Combine remaining shrimp and scallops with Cognac, cooled ½ cup sauce, remaining ¾ teaspoon salt, and remaining ¼ teaspoon pepper in a food processor and purée. Add remaining ½ cup cream and pulse just until combined. Transfer mousse to a large bowl and stir in chopped shrimp and scallops and chives.

Put a rack in middle of oven and preheat oven to 350°F.

COOK THE PASTA AND ASSEMBLE THE CANNELLONI: Boil noodles a few at a time in a 6- to 8-quart pot of boiling salted water (1 tablespoon salt per every 4 quarts water), stirring to separate, until al dente, about 2 minutes for fresh noodles or about 6 minutes for dried noodles. Gently transfer noodles with tongs and a slotted spatula to a large bowl of cold water to stop the cooking, then lift out, shaking off water, and lay flat on kitchen towels (not terry cloth). Pat dry with paper towels.

Spread about ½ cup sauce in bottom of baking dish. Spread ⅓ cup mousse over each noodle, leaving a ½-inch border on both short ends. Starting with a short end, loosely roll up each noodle and arrange cannelloni seam sides down in one snug layer on sauce. Pour remaining sauce over cannelloni.

Cover with foil and bake until sauce is bubbling and filling is just cooked through, 25 to 30 minutes. To test filling for doneness, insert a metal skewer into a cannelloni and hold it there for 5 seconds. Remove skewer and press it against your bottom lip: if metal is warm, casserole is hot all the way through and filling is cooked. Remove from oven and preheat broiler.

Remove foil and broil cannelloni about 3 inches from heat until brown spots appear on top, 3 to 5 minutes. Let stand for 10 minutes before serving.

COOK'S NOTE

- The casserole can be assembled up to 4 hours ahead and refrigerated, covered with plastic wrap. Let stand at room temperature for 20 minutes before baking.

Fresh Pasta Rectangles or Squares

MAKES 8 PASTA RECTANGLES FOR CANNELLONI OR ABOUT 24 SQUARES FOR *PANSOTI*
ACTIVE TIME: 1 HOUR ■ START TO FINISH: 2 HOURS

■ This will give you a tender pasta that's perfect for cannelloni or *pansoti* (see page 237). The pasta dries out quickly, however, so you will need to form the *pansoti* as soon as you have cut it, or it will become difficult to seal. ■

- 1 cup cake flour (not self-rising)
- 1/4 cup all-purpose flour, plus additional for kneading
- 1/2 teaspoon salt
- 2 large egg yolks
- 1 1/2 tablespoons extra-virgin olive oil
- 1/4 cup water

SPECIAL EQUIPMENT: a pasta machine

MAKE THE DOUGH: Combine all ingredients in a food processor and process until mixture begins to form a ball. Turn dough out onto a lightly floured surface and knead, incorporating only as much additional flour as necessary to keep dough from sticking, until smooth and elastic, 6 to 8 minutes. Wrap dough in plastic wrap and let stand at room temperature for 1 hour.

ROLL OUT THE DOUGH: Set rollers of pasta machine on widest setting. Cut dough into 4 pieces. Work with one piece at a time, keeping remaining pieces covered with plastic wrap. Flatten dough into a rectangle and lightly dust with flour. Feed through rollers. Fold rectangle in half and feed, folded side first, through rollers again. Feed dough through rollers 7 more times, folding it in half each time and dusting with flour if necessary to prevent sticking.

Turn dial to next (narrower) setting and feed dough through without folding. Catch pasta sheet with your hand as it comes through rollers instead of letting it crumple at base of machine, and continue to feed through rollers without folding, once at each setting, dusting dough with flour if it begins to stick, until you reach second-narrowest setting. Lay sheet on a lightly floured surface.

TO CUT THE PASTA FOR CANNELLONI: Cut pasta sheet into two 6-by-4-inch rectangles. Roll out and cut remaining 3 pieces of dough in same manner, to make a total of 8 pasta rectangles.

TO CUT THE PASTA FOR *PANSOTI*: Cut pasta sheet into 3 1/2-inch squares. Gather trimmings into a ball and wrap in plastic wrap. Transfer squares to a wax paper–lined baking sheet and cover with plastic wrap. Roll out and cut remaining dough in same manner, then roll out and cut trimmings.

COOK'S NOTES

- Though it's best used immediately, the dough can be made up to 1 day ahead and refrigerated, wrapped in plastic wrap. Bring to room temperature before rolling out.
- The trimmings from cannelloni can be cut into odd-shaped pieces and used in soup. In Italian they are called *maltagliati,* which means "badly cut."

Mushroom, Radicchio, and Smoked Mozzarella Lasagne

SERVES 6 AS A MAIN COURSE, 12 AS A SIDE DISH
ACTIVE TIME: 40 MINUTES ■ START TO FINISH: 1½ HOURS

■ Radicchio and mushrooms make this lasagne very dark in color, and deep in flavor as well. It's a true Italian-style lasagne, meaning that it's not overstuffed, like the ones commonly made in America. Despite its thinner layers, though, it is substantial. The radicchio mellows when cooked, and the smoked cheese brings out its sweet meatiness. Serve this with a beautiful green salad or present it as a vegetarian option at Thanksgiving. ■

- 4 tablespoons vegetable oil
- 1½ pounds radicchio, chopped
- 2¼ pounds mushrooms, trimmed, half quartered, half thinly sliced
- Salt and freshly ground black pepper
- ½ stick (4 tablespoons) unsalted butter
- ¼ cup all-purpose flour
- 2½ cups whole milk
- 2 garlic cloves, minced
- 1 cup fresh flat-leaf parsley leaves, finely chopped
- 2 teaspoons fresh lemon juice, or to taste
- 2 cups grated smoked mozzarella (about 8 ounces)
- 1 cup grated mozzarella (about 4 ounces)
- 9 oven-ready (no-boil) lasagne noodles

Heat 2 tablespoons oil in a 12- to 14-inch nonstick skillet over moderately high heat until hot but not smoking. Add radicchio and cook, stirring, until wilted and golden, about 5 minutes. Meanwhile, pulse quartered mushrooms in a food processor until finely chopped.

Add chopped mushrooms to radicchio, with salt and pepper to taste, and cook, stirring, until liquid mushrooms give off has evaporated, about 5 minutes. Remove from heat.

Melt butter in a 4-quart heavy saucepan over moderately low heat. Whisk in flour and cook, whisking, for 3 minutes to make a roux. Add milk in a slow stream, whisking constantly, and season with salt and pepper. Bring to a simmer, whisking, and simmer, whisking occasionally, until thick, about 5 minutes. Stir mushroom mixture into sauce. Remove from heat.

Heat remaining 2 tablespoons oil in cleaned skillet over moderately low heat. Add garlic and cook, stirring, until softened, about 2 minutes. Add sliced mushrooms, increase heat to moderately high, and cook, stirring, until mushrooms are golden and liquid they give off has evaporated, about 10 minutes. Stir in parsley and salt and pepper to taste. Remove from heat and let cool, then stir in lemon juice.

Put a rack in middle of oven and preheat oven to 375°F.

Reserve ½ cup smoked mozzarella. Combine remaining smoked mozzarella with regular mozzarella in a bowl.

Pour 1 cup mushroom sauce into a 13-by-9-inch baking dish (sauce will not cover bottom completely). Cover with 3 lasagne noodles, leaving space between noodles (pasta will expand). Spread about 1 cup sauce over pasta. Top with one third of sliced mushroom mixture and half of mixed cheeses. Make one more layer in same manner, beginning with sauce and ending with cheese, and top with remaining 3 pasta noodles. Spread remaining sauce evenly over pasta, making sure it is completely covered. Spread remaining sliced mushroom mixture evenly over sauce and sprinkle with reserved smoked mozzarella.

Cover dish tightly with buttered foil, tenting it slightly to prevent foil from touching top of lasagne. Bake for 30 minutes. Remove foil and bake lasagne until top is bubbling and golden, about 10 minutes more.

COOK'S NOTE

■ The mushroom sauce can be made up to 3 days ahead and refrigerated in an airtight container, its surface covered with wax paper.

Italian Cheeses

MOZZARELLA: This cow's milk cheese should be absolutely fresh and moist, and it is best eaten within two or three days of purchase. Imported mozzarella (or American artisanal mozzarella, made by hand in small batches) is worth seeking out: it is tender and sweet, with a lovely elastic texture. (Supermarket mozzarella is a pale imitation of the real thing. If you must, use it in fillings and as a topping for pizza, but never in salad.) Traditionally mozzarella was made from the milk of the Indian water buffalo that were taken to Italy from Asia in the sixteenth century. *Mozzarella di bufala* is still made in Campania and Apulia and plays a major role in Neapolitan cooking. It has more depth of flavor than cow's milk mozzarella. Smoked mozzarella looks almost roasted and has a wonderful sweet, woodsy flavor that is more assertive.

RICOTTA: Made from whey that is heated twice, this moist dairy product is technically not a cheese but a by-product of cheesemaking. (*Ricotta* means "recooked.") Traditional ricotta is made from sheep's milk, but today it's often made from cow's or goat's milk. The fresh cheese has a smoother, more satiny texture and a sweeter flavor than the commercial supermarket variety. As fresh ricotta ages, it becomes dry, so it should be eaten soon after purchase.

RICOTTA SALATA: This firm, crumbly white cheese is made from sheep's milk, but it's milder and nuttier than many other sheep's milk cheeses. Ricotta salata keeps very well — up to three weeks in the refrigerator.

FONTINA: There is only one true Fontina, and it comes from the Valley of Aosta, near the Swiss border. A semisoft cow's milk cheese, it has a thin brownish rind and a pale yellow interior with tiny round holes. It is buttery and nutty in taste and a great melting cheese. Danish Fontina has none of the complexity of flavor of Italian Fontina. Unlike other firm cheeses, Fontina can get too strong once cut, so buy only what you'll consume within a week.

GORGONZOLA: Named for a town outside Milan, this blue-veined, cream-colored cow's milk cheese has been made in Lombardy since the ninth century. The cheese is sold in two varieties: *dolce,* or sweet, the most familiar type, is milder and less veined than *naturale* (or *piccante,* as it is sometimes called), which is aged and more assertive. Both *dolce* and *naturale* are creamier than Roquefort or Stilton, soft but not runny. The veins should be a vivid blue-green. As the cheese ages, it gets cakey and dry; it's best if eaten within a week to ten days.

PARMIGIANO-REGGIANO: This hard cow's milk cheese is arguably the king of cheeses, but it's important to buy the genuine article. Production is closely regulated, so look for the words *Parmigiano-Reggiano;* they should be clearly stamped all over the smooth, oily, golden rind of the cheese. If they are not, you're probably looking at an Italian Grana Padano, which should cost half as much as Parmigiano, or an American-made *grana*. Parmigiano-Reggiano is best when it is *stravecchio* ("very old"), aged for more than two years. Its interior should be straw-colored, moist, and somewhat shardlike in texture. Slightly salty, nutty, and sharp, this cheese is usually used for grating, but it is often eaten as a table cheese in Italy. It should always be grated fresh, since it quickly loses its flavor after grating. A hunk keeps for months, wrapped in foil, in the bottom of the refrigerator. Be sure to save the rind to flavor soups.

GRANA PADANO: Like Parmigiano-Reggiano, this cow's milk cheese is generically classified as a *grana* cheese, a reference to its fine grain. Made throughout the Emilia-Romagna region, it is much less expensive than Parmigiano-Reggiano, and its flavor is not nearly as distinctive. In contrast to Parmigiano, it's not aged for a very long time, the milk with which it is made can come from anywhere, and it can be made year-round, not just during a specific season. If you can't find true Parmigiano, however, Grana Padano is an acceptable substitute.

PECORINO ROMANO: This hard grating cheese made from sheep's milk is probably one of Italy's oldest cheeses. True pecorino Romanos come from the area around Rome, but nowadays many come from Sardinia and Tuscany. Pecorino is sharper than Parmigiano-Reggiano, paler in color, and sometimes too salty. Using a combination of the two cheeses can give greater complexity to a dish. Most of the pecorino available at supermarkets, especially the pregrated stuff (often simply labeled "Romano"), is vile; one whiff is enough to turn anyone off. If that's the only pecorino you can find, stick to Parmigiano. Like Parmigiano, a wedge of pecorino Romano will keep for months, wrapped in foil, in the bottom of the refrigerator.

Butternut Squash and Hazelnut Lasagne

SERVES 6 AS A MAIN COURSE, 10 AS A SIDE DISH
ACTIVE TIME: 1½ HOURS ■ START TO FINISH: 2½ HOURS

■ In Italy, pasta and pumpkin or winter squash are often paired in ravioli or tortellini. We think a lasagne works beautifully too, especially with the addition of hazelnuts. They add texture and a toasty flavor to the delicate pasta and squash, and they make the dish heartier as well. This is a perfect vegetarian dish for fall or winter. ■

FOR FILLING

- 3 tablespoons unsalted butter
- 1 large onion, chopped
- 3 pounds butternut squash, peeled, seeded, and cut into ½-inch pieces
- 1 teaspoon minced garlic
- 1 teaspoon salt
- ¼ teaspoon white pepper
- 2 tablespoons chopped fresh flat-leaf parsley
- 4 teaspoons chopped fresh sage
- 1 cup (about 4 ounces) hazelnuts, toasted (see Tips, page 938), loose skins rubbed off with a kitchen towel, and coarsely chopped

FOR SAUCE

- 3 tablespoons unsalted butter
- 1 teaspoon minced garlic
- 5 tablespoons all-purpose flour
- 5 cups whole milk
- 1 Turkish bay leaf or ½ California bay leaf
- 1 teaspoon salt
- ⅛ teaspoon white pepper

FOR ASSEMBLING

- 2 cups coarsely grated fresh mozzarella (about 8 ounces)
- 1 cup finely grated Parmigiano-Reggiano (about 2 ounces)
- 12 oven-ready (no-boil) lasagne noodles

MAKE THE FILLING: Melt butter in a deep 12-inch heavy skillet over moderate heat. Add onion and cook, stirring occasionally, until golden, about 10 minutes. Add squash, garlic, salt, and white pepper and cook, stirring occasionally, until squash is just tender, about 15 minutes. Remove from heat and stir in parsley, sage, and nuts. Let cool.

MEANWHILE, MAKE THE SAUCE: Melt butter in a 3-quart heavy saucepan over moderately low heat. Add garlic and cook, stirring, for 1 minute. Whisk in flour and cook, whisking, for 3 minutes to make a roux. Add milk in a slow stream, whisking constantly. Add bay leaf and bring to a boil, whisking constantly, then reduce heat and simmer, whisking occasionally, for 10 minutes. Whisk in salt and white pepper and remove from heat. Discard bay leaf. (Cover surface of sauce with wax paper if not using immediately.)

Put a rack in middle of oven and preheat oven to 425°F. Butter a 13-by-9-inch baking dish.

ASSEMBLE THE LASAGNE: Toss cheeses together. Spread ½ cup sauce in buttered baking dish and cover with 3 lasagne noodles, leaving space between noodles (pasta will expand). Spread with ⅔ cup sauce and one third of filling, then sprinkle with a heaping ½ cup cheese. Top with 3 more noodles and another ⅔ cup sauce, one third filling, and heaping ½ cup cheese. Repeat layering one more time, beginning with sauce and ending with cheese, then top with remaining 3 lasagne noodles, remaining sauce, and remaining cheese.

Tightly cover baking dish with buttered foil and bake lasagne for 30 minutes. Remove foil and bake until golden and bubbling, 10 to 15 minutes more. Let lasagne stand for 15 to 20 minutes before serving.

COOK'S NOTE

■ The filling and sauce can be made up to 1 day ahead and refrigerated, covered. Bring to room temperature before assembling the lasagne.

Beef and Sausage Lasagne

SERVES 10 AS A MAIN COURSE
ACTIVE TIME: 45 MINUTES ■ START TO FINISH: 2 HOURS

■ The flavor of beef, the binding qualities of veal, and the succulence of pork sausage combine to make this meaty lasagne light and juicy. Don't be tempted to cut a caloric corner by substituting lean ground beef. The amount of fat in the beef affects the moisture as well as the texture of the cooked dish. ■

FOR SAUCE

- 2 tablespoons olive oil
- 1 medium onion, finely chopped
- 2 garlic cloves, minced
- 1/2 pound sweet Italian sausage, casings discarded
- 1/2 pound ground beef chuck
- 1/2 pound ground veal
- 2 (28-ounce) cans whole tomatoes in juice, drained (juice reserved) and chopped
- 1 teaspoon salt
- 1/4 teaspoon freshly ground black pepper

FOR FILLING

- 1 pound fresh ricotta or supermarket-style ricotta
- 1 large egg, lightly beaten
- 1/2 cup finely grated Parmigiano-Reggiano
- 1/4 cup finely chopped fresh flat-leaf parsley
- 1/4 teaspoon salt
- 1/4 teaspoon freshly ground black pepper
- Pinch of freshly grated nutmeg

FOR ASSEMBLING

- 16 oven-ready (no-boil) lasagne noodles (two 9-ounce packages)
- 1/4 cup finely grated Parmigiano-Reggiano
- 1/2 pound fresh mozzarella, coarsely grated

MAKE THE SAUCE: Heat oil in a 5- to 6-quart heavy pot over moderately high heat until hot but not smoking. Add onion and cook, stirring, until golden, about 6 minutes. Add garlic and cook, stirring, for 1 minute. Stir in sausage, beef, and veal and cook, stirring and breaking up larger pieces, until no longer pink, about 5 minutes. Add tomatoes, with their juice, salt, and pepper, bring to a simmer, and simmer, stirring occasionally, until sauce is thickened, about 30 minutes. Remove from heat.

MAKE THE FILLING: Stir together ricotta, egg, Parmesan, parsley, salt, pepper, and nutmeg in a bowl until combined.

Put a rack in middle of oven and preheat oven to 375°F. Oil a 13-by-9-inch baking dish.

ASSEMBLE THE LASAGNA: Spread 1 1/4 cups sauce in baking dish. Arrange 4 lasagne noodles, slightly overlapping, over sauce, then spread one third of ricotta mixture over noodles. Sprinkle 2 tablespoons Parmesan over ricotta, then spread 1 1/4 cups sauce over Parmesan. Top with 4 more noodles and spread with another one third of ricotta mixture and 2 tablespoons Parmesan. Top with 4 more noodles, remaining ricotta mixture, and 1 1/4 cups sauce. Top with remaining 4 noodles, then spread with remaining sauce and sprinkle with mozzarella.

Cover lasagne with buttered foil and bake for 40 minutes. Remove foil and bake until top is bubbling and lightly browned, 10 to 15 minutes more. Let stand for 15 minutes before serving.

Jumbo Ravioli

MAKES ABOUT 24 RAVIOLI; SERVES 8
ACTIVE TIME: 1 1/4 HOURS ■ START TO FINISH: 2 3/4 HOURS
(INCLUDES MAKING PASTA)

■ This is southern Italian home-style cooking at its most inviting. Large ravioli are less time-consuming to put together than small ones and make a hearty and satisfying meal. ■

- 1 1/2 pounds ricotta, preferably fresh, at room temperature
- 2 large eggs, lightly beaten
- 1 cup finely grated Parmigiano-Reggiano (about 2 ounces)
- 1/4 cup finely chopped fresh flat-leaf parsley
- 1 1/4 teaspoons salt
- 1/4 teaspoon freshly ground black pepper
- 1/8 teaspoon freshly grated nutmeg
- Pasta Dough (page 209)
- 1 large egg white lightly beaten with 2 teaspoons water, for egg wash

ACCOMPANIMENT: Tomato Sauce (page 207)
SPECIAL EQUIPMENT: a pasta machine

MAKE THE FILLING: Stir together ricotta, eggs, Parmesan, parsley, salt, pepper, and nutmeg in a bowl until well combined.

ROLL, CUT, AND FILL THE RAVIOLI: Set rollers of pasta machine at widest setting. Cut pasta dough into 6 pieces, then flatten each piece into a rectangle and cover with a kitchen towel.

Lightly dust one rectangle with flour and feed through rollers. Fold rectangle in half and feed through rollers again, a shorter end first. Feed dough through rollers 7 more times, folding it in half each time and feeding a shorter end through first, dusting with flour as necessary to prevent sticking. Turn dial to next (narrower) setting and feed dough through without folding. Continue to feed dough through without folding, once at each setting until you reach narrowest setting. (Sheet of dough will be about 36 inches long and 4 inches wide.) Cut sheet crosswise in half, lay on a floured surface, and cover with a clean kitchen towel. Roll out and cut remaining pieces of dough in same manner.

Put one dough strip on a floured work surface. Drop four 2-tablespoon mounds of ricotta filling 1½ inches apart in a row down center of strip. Brush egg wash around each mound, place a second dough strip on top, and press down firmly around each mound, forcing out air. (Air pockets increase the chance that ravioli will break during cooking.) With a fluted pastry cutter or sharp knife, cut pasta (between mounds) into 3-inch squares, trimming edges if necessary. Repeat with remaining dough strips and filling.

Let ravioli dry on floured baking sheets, covered with kitchen towels, for at least 30 minutes and up to 1 hour.

COOK THE RAVIOLI: Bring a 6- to 8-quart pot of salted water (1 tablespoon salt per every 4 quarts water) to a boil; reduce heat to a gentle boil. Cook ravioli in 2 batches, gently stirring to separate, until pasta is tender and cooked through, 6 to 8 minutes. With a slotted spoon, transfer ravioli to a large serving bowl, and spoon sauce over them.

Butternut Squash, Sage, and Goat Cheese Ravioli with Hazelnut–Brown Butter Sauce

SERVES 6 GENEROUSLY AS A MAIN COURSE
ACTIVE TIME: 1 HOUR ■ START TO FINISH: 2 HOURS

■ Goat cheese adds richness, creaminess, and tang to a winning combination, and a nutty brown butter sauce makes it magical. Wonton wrappers, available at specialty markets and many supermarkets, serve as tender and convenient stand-ins for fresh pasta. ■

FOR FILLING

- 1 (2-pound) butternut squash, halved lengthwise and seeded
- 1 tablespoon unsalted butter
- 1 medium onion, chopped
- 1½ teaspoons ground sage
- Salt and freshly ground black pepper
- 1 garlic clove, minced
- 3 ounces aged goat cheese, such as Coach Farm, grated

FOR RAVIOLI AND SAUCE

- 60 wonton wrappers (from 2 packages), thawed if frozen
- 1 stick (8 tablespoons) unsalted butter
- ⅓ cup hazelnuts, lightly toasted (see Tips, page 938), loose skins rubbed off with a kitchen towel, and coarsely chopped
- Salt and freshly ground black pepper

Put a rack in middle of oven and preheat oven to 425°F. Lightly grease a baking sheet.

MAKE THE FILLING: Put squash cut sides down on baking sheet and roast until flesh is very tender, 30 to 35 minutes. Set aside to cool. When squash is cool enough to handle, scoop out flesh into a medium bowl and discard skin. Mash squash with a fork until smooth.

Meanwhile, melt butter in a 10-inch skillet over moderate heat. Add onion, sage, and salt and pepper to taste and cook, stirring, until onion is golden brown, 5 to 8 minutes. Stir in garlic and cook, stirring, for 1 minute.

Cool onion mixture slightly, then add to squash in bowl. Add goat cheese and stir until well combined.

MAKE THE RAVIOLI AND SAUCE: Put 1 wonton wrapper on a lightly floured surface (keep remaining wrappers in plastic wrap) and mound 1 tablespoon filling in center. Lightly brush edges of wrapper with water, put a second wrapper over it, and press around filling to force out air and seal edges well. (Air pockets increase the chance that ravioli will break during cooking.) If desired, trim excess dough with a cookie cutter or a sharp knife. Transfer ravioli to a kitchen towel (not terry cloth). Make more ravioli with remaining wrappers and filling in same manner. Turn formed ravioli occasionally to dry slightly on both sides.

Preheat oven to 200°F.

Cook butter with hazelnuts in 10-inch skillet over

moderate heat until butter begins to brown, about 3 minutes. Immediately remove from heat (nuts will continue to cook). Season hazelnut butter with salt and pepper and cover to keep warm.

COOK THE RAVIOLI: Add one third of ravioli to a 6-quart pot of gently boiling salted water (1 tablespoon salt per every 4 quarts water) and cook until they rise to surface and are tender, about 6 minutes (do not let water boil vigorously after ravioli have been added). With a slotted spoon, transfer ravioli (letting excess cooking liquid drip off) to a buttered baking sheet with sides and keep warm, covered with foil, in oven. Cook remaining ravioli in 2 batches in same manner.

Divide ravioli among six plates and top with sauce.

Walnut and Pancetta Pansoti with Asparagus in Parmesan Broth

SERVES 8 AS A FIRST COURSE, 4 AS A MAIN COURSE
ACTIVE TIME: 1¾ HOURS ■ START TO FINISH: 2¾ HOURS (INCLUDES MAKING PASTA)

■ The plump ravioli called *pansoti* ("little bellies"), which are a Ligurian specialty, are often dressed with a walnut sauce. We stray from tradition a bit and tuck the walnuts into the filling instead. Be sure to buy pancetta that is well marbled; if it's too lean, it won't render enough fat to flavor the filling. And be sure to brown the onion well—the caramelization lends a depth and a lushness that are essential to the dish. ■

FOR *PANSOTI* AND BROTH

- 1 (3-ounce) piece pancetta (not lean), finely chopped (⅔ cup)
- 1 tablespoon olive oil
- 1 large onion, finely chopped
- ¾ teaspoon dried marjoram, crumbled
- ½ cup (2 ounces) walnuts, finely chopped
- 2 tablespoons finely chopped fresh flat-leaf parsley
- ¼ teaspoon salt
- ¼ teaspoon freshly ground black pepper
- 2 cups water
- ⅛ teaspoon red pepper flakes
- 1 (3-by-2-inch) rind from a wedge of Parmigiano-Reggiano
- 24 Fresh Pasta Squares (page 230)

FOR ASPARAGUS

- 1½ cups asparagus tips (from 2 pounds asparagus), halved lengthwise (see Cook's Note)
- 1 teaspoon extra-virgin olive oil

ACCOMPANIMENT: finely grated Parmigiano-Reggiano

MAKE THE FILLING: Cook pancetta in oil in a 12-inch heavy skillet over moderately low heat, stirring frequently, until it is golden and fat is rendered, 10 to 12 minutes. Add onion and marjoram and cook, stirring occasionally, until onion is well browned, 10 to 15 minutes. Transfer half of mixture to a 2-quart saucepan and remaining half to a bowl. Stir walnuts, parsley, ⅛ teaspoon salt, and pepper into mixture in bowl. Let filling cool.

MAKE THE BROTH: Add water, red pepper flakes, and cheese rind to pancetta mixture in saucepan, bring to a simmer, and simmer briskly, uncovered, until reduced to about 1 cup, about 12 minutes. Pour through a fine-mesh sieve into a bowl; discard solids. Stir remaining ⅛ teaspoon salt into broth. Set aside.

FORM THE *PANSOTI*: Place 1 level teaspoon filling in center of one pasta square (keep remaining squares covered tightly with plastic wrap). Moisten edges of pasta square with water and fold in half to form a triangle, pressing around filling to force out air (air pockets increase the chance that *pansoti* will break during cooking) and then pressing edges to seal. Transfer to a kitchen towel (not terry cloth). Using remaining squares and filling, make more *pansoti* in same manner.

COOK THE ASPARAGUS AND *PANSOTI*: Cook asparagus tips in a small saucepan of boiling well-salted water until crisp-tender, about 2 minutes. Drain in a sieve and plunge into a bowl of ice and cold water to stop the cooking. Drain and pat dry.

Bring a 6-quart pot of salted water (1 tablespoon salt per 4 quarts water) to a boil. Add *pansoti*, reduce heat slightly, and cook at a strong simmer, gently stirring once or twice, until tender, 3 to 5 minutes.

Meanwhile, cook asparagus tips in oil in a small skillet over low heat until heated through, 1 to 2 minutes.

Heat broth in a 12-inch skillet over moderate heat until hot. With a slotted spoon, transfer *pansoti* to broth and heat, stirring gently, for 1 minute. Transfer *pansoti* to plates, then top with broth and scatter asparagus tips over top. Serve with cheese.

COOK'S NOTES

- If you don't have time to make fresh pasta, you can use wonton wrappers.
- The *pansoti* can be formed up to 1 day ahead. Arrange in one layer on a kitchen towel–lined baking sheet with sides, cover tightly with plastic wrap, and refrigerate.
- The broth can be made up to 1 day ahead. Cool, uncovered, then refrigerate, covered.
- The asparagus tips can be boiled up to 1 day ahead. Refrigerate in a sealed plastic bag, along with a paper towel to absorb excess moisture. The asparagus stalks can be used for a puréed soup.

Gnocchetti all'Amatriciana

Tiny Potato Dumplings with Tomato, Onion, and Pancetta Sauce

SERVES 10 AS A FIRST COURSE
ACTIVE TIME: 1½ HOURS ■ START TO FINISH: 2 HOURS

■ Our gnocchetti are lighter than most because they don't contain egg. They are delicate yet not insubstantial. The richness comes from the tomato-pancetta sauce. Making gnocchetti requires patience—creating the typical little ridges on one side of the dumplings is definitely a skill, but don't agonize over it. The point is that each dumpling should have a little roughness, a little character, to give the sauce something to adhere to. (For more about making gnocchi of any size, see page 240.) ■

FOR SAUCE

1 tablespoon olive oil
5 ounces sliced pancetta, finely chopped (½ cup)
1 large red onion, finely chopped (1¼ cups)
1 small garlic clove, minced
1 (28-ounce) can plum tomatoes, drained (juice reserved) and finely chopped
½ cup water
1 teaspoon sugar
½ teaspoon salt

FOR GNOCCHETTI

1½ pounds yellow-fleshed potatoes, such as Yukon Gold
1½ cups all-purpose flour, plus additional for dusting
1¼ teaspoons salt

ACCOMPANIMENT: finely grated pecorino Romano
SPECIAL EQUIPMENT: a potato ricer or food mill

MAKE THE SAUCE: Heat oil in a 5- to 6-quart heavy pot over moderately high heat until hot but not smoking. Add pancetta and onion and cook, stirring, until onion is golden, about 6 minutes. Add garlic and cook, stirring, until golden, about 1 minute. Add tomatoes, with their juice, water, sugar, and salt, bring to a simmer, and simmer, uncovered, stirring occasionally, until thickened, about 30 minutes. Remove from heat.

MEANWHILE, COOK THE POTATOES: Combine potatoes with salted water (1 tablespoon salt per every 4 quarts water) to cover by 2 inches in a large pot, bring to a simmer, and simmer, uncovered, until very tender, about 25 minutes. Drain in a colander and let cool slightly.

MAKE THE GNOCCHETTI: As soon as potatoes are cool enough to handle, peel. Force warm potatoes through ricer or food mill into a large bowl. Add flour and salt and stir with a wooden spoon until mixture begins to come together. Gently form dough into a ball and cut in half.

Knead each half on a lightly floured surface until smooth, about 1 minute (if dough is sticking, dust lightly with additional flour). Cut each half into 10 equal pieces.

Keeping remaining pieces covered with a kitchen towel, roll 1 piece of dough into a 14-inch-long rope (½ inch thick). Cut rope into ¼-inch pieces and toss lightly with flour on work surface. One at a time, press a piece of dough against tines of a floured fork and push with a floured thumb in a forward rolling motion toward end of tines, letting dough fall onto a well-floured baking sheet with sides. Make more gnocchetti in same manner.

Reheat sauce over low heat. Keep warm.

COOK THE GNOCCHETTI: Cook gnocchetti in 4 batches. Just before cooking, shake each batch in a large medium-mesh sieve to knock off excess flour. Add gnocchetti to a 5- to 6-quart pot of boiling salted water (1 tablespoon salt per every 4 quarts water) and cook until they float, about 1 minute. With a slotted spoon, transfer to a large shallow bowl, and spoon some sauce on top. Serve with cheese.

COOK'S NOTES

- The sauce can be made up to 2 days ahead and refrigerated, covered.
- The gnocchetti can be formed up to 1 week ahead. Freeze them in a single layer on a floured baking sheet, covered, until firm, about 3 hours, then transfer to a sealable plastic bag and freeze. Do not thaw before cooking, and do not shake off excess flour. Boil gnocchetti for about 2 minutes.

Spinach Gnocchi Gratin

SERVES 8 AS A FIRST COURSE, 4 TO 6 AS A MAIN COURSE
ACTIVE TIME: 40 MINUTES ■ START TO FINISH: 1 HOUR

■ These gnocchi are made in the Parisian style, meaning that they're made from a *pâte à choux*, or cream puff pastry, instead of the more traditional potato or semolina dough. We love this method because it is a relatively easy way to make gnocchi. ■

- 3/4 pound spinach (1 bunch), coarse stems discarded
- 1/2 cup whole milk
- 1/2 cup water
- 1/2 stick (4 tablespoons) unsalted butter, cut into pieces
- 1 cup all-purpose flour
- 4 large eggs
- 3/4 teaspoon salt
- 1/2 teaspoon freshly ground black pepper
- 1/4 teaspoon freshly grated nutmeg, or to taste
- 1/3 cup heavy cream
- 1/2 cup finely grated Parmigiano-Reggiano

Rinse spinach and drain. Cook spinach in water clinging to leaves in a 4-quart heavy saucepan, covered, over moderate heat, stirring once or twice, until wilted, 3 to 4 minutes. Transfer to a colander and rinse under cold water, then squeeze dry by the handful and finely chop.

Meanwhile, put a rack in middle of oven and preheat oven to 425°F. Bring a 6- to 8-quart pot of salted water (1 tablespoon salt per every 4 quarts water) to a boil. Butter a 1½- to 2-quart gratin dish or flameproof shallow baking dish (not glass).

Combine milk, water, and butter in a 3-quart heavy saucepan and bring just to a boil, stirring until butter is melted. Add flour all at once and stir vigorously with a wooden spoon until mixture pulls away from sides of pan and forms a ball. Cook over moderate heat, stirring, for 1 minute, then transfer dough to a bowl. With an electric mixer at medium speed, beat in eggs one at a time, beating well after each addition. Beat in salt, pepper, nutmeg, and spinach.

Working in batches of 10 gnocchi, drop walnut-sized spoonfuls of dough into pot of boiling water and simmer, uncovered, until they rise to the surface and are cooked through, about 5 minutes per batch. With a slotted spoon, transfer gnocchi to a large colander, and drain well.

Arrange gnocchi in one layer in buttered gratin dish. Drizzle with cream and sprinkle with cheese. Season with salt and pepper.

Bake gnocchi for 10 minutes. Remove from oven and turn on broiler. Broil gnocchi about 4 inches from heat until lightly browned, 2 to 3 minutes.

Know Your Gnocchi

Nobody ever said that making the fluffy little potato dumplings called gnocchi ("*nyo*-kee") was easy, exactly, but it's amazing what a light touch and a little practice will do. (If you have a knack with biscuits, you'll be good at this.) The procedure for creating the characteristic little ridges on one side of the dumplings is kind of like tap dancing: once you develop the technique, you can't think about it — you just have to let your body do it.

1. Roll each portion of gnocchi dough very gently into a log. If the dough is overhandled, the gnocchi will be tough and heavy.

2. If your knife begins to stick while you're cutting each log into pieces, dip the blade in flour.

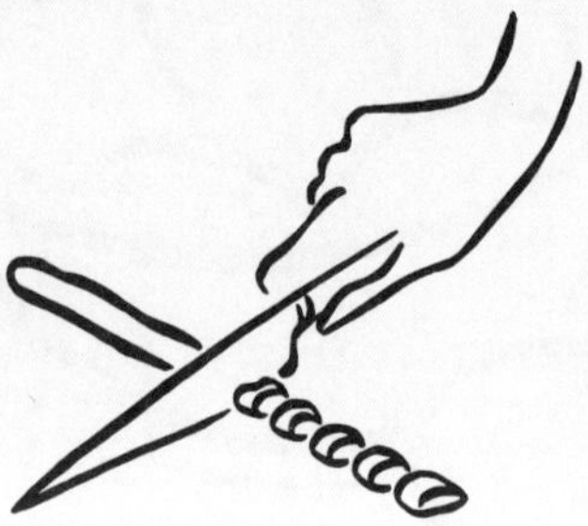

3. To form the gnocchi, push with a floured thumb as you simultaneously roll a piece of dough against the curve of the fork tines.

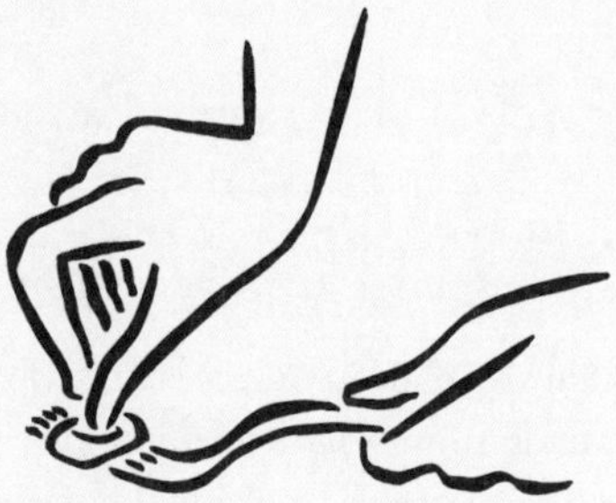

4. You want to flick, not drag, the gnocchi off the fork.

Herbed Spaetzle

SERVES 4 AS A SIDE DISH
ACTIVE TIME: 30 MINUTES ■ START TO FINISH: 30 MINUTES

■ The tiny drop-style German dumplings called spaetzle are judged by their lightness, and these practically take flight. They are actually easier to make than you might think. We simply press the batter through a colander into simmering water, but if you get hooked and want to make spaetzle often, do yourself a favor and buy a spaetzle maker. A couple of different ones are available: one is a rotary contraption that sits over the pot of water and works like a food mill; the other has a little hopper set on a perforated track that you slide back and forth like a trolley over the pot, cutting off the spaetzle with each pass. Some authorities say the word *spaetzle* derives from the fact that the rounded little dumplings are reminiscent of plump little sparrows (*Spatzen* in south German dialect); others maintain that it comes from the Italian *spezzare*, "to cut into pieces." ■

- 1½ cups all-purpose flour
- 1 teaspoon salt
- 2 large eggs, lightly beaten
- ½ cup whole milk
- ½ stick (4 tablespoons) unsalted butter, cut into tablespoons
- ¼ teaspoon freshly ground black pepper
- ¼ cup finely chopped fresh chives
- ¼ cup finely chopped fresh flat-leaf parsley
- ¼ cup finely chopped fresh dill

Bring a 6-quart pot of salted water (1 tablespoon salt per every 4 quarts water) to a simmer.

Meanwhile, stir together flour and ¾ teaspoon salt in a large bowl. Whisk together eggs and milk in a bowl, then whisk into flour until batter is smooth.

With a rubber spatula, press dough through a colander (not a sieve) into simmering water (or use a spaetzle maker set over pot). Cook spaetzle until firm, 2 to 3 minutes.

Drain spaetzle well in cleaned colander and toss with butter, remaining ¼ teaspoon salt, pepper, and herbs in a bowl.

Noodle Pudding

Lukshen Kugel

SERVES 6 AS A SIDE DISH
ACTIVE TIME: 20 MINUTES ■ START TO FINISH: 1¼ HOURS

■ There's no need to wait until Rosh Hashanah, the Jewish New Year, to enjoy this rich, savory kugel. With its generous amounts of cottage cheese, butter, and sour cream, the recipe might be considered old-fashioned—it came from the author Mildred Grosberg Bellin in 1958—but we call it timeless. We particularly like it alongside another humble favorite, pot roast. ■

- 2 cups medium egg noodles
- 3 tablespoons unsalted butter, softened
- 2 large eggs
- 1 cup cottage cheese (not low-fat)
- ½ cup sour cream
- ½ teaspoon salt
- ¼ teaspoon white pepper

ACCOMPANIMENT: sour cream

Put a rack in middle of oven and preheat oven to 350°F. Butter a deep 1-quart baking dish.

Cook noodles in a large saucepan of boiling salted water (1 tablespoon salt per every 4 quarts water) until tender. Drain well and toss with butter in a bowl.

Whisk together eggs, cottage cheese, sour cream, salt, and white pepper in a large bowl. Stir in noodles. Transfer to buttered baking dish.

Bake until set, 45 minutes to 1 hour. Serve with sour cream.

Wild Mushroom Pierogi

SERVES 12 AS A FIRST COURSE, 6 AS A MAIN COURSE
ACTIVE TIME: 1¼ HOURS ■ START TO FINISH: 2 HOURS

■ Pierogi, the savory stuffed half-moon dumplings that are Polish in origin, can be stuffed with potatoes, cheese, sauerkraut, or wild mushrooms. In this version, dried porcini and cremini mushrooms combine to bring a woodsy depth to the filling. Served with sour cream and flecks of golden sautéed onion, these dumplings are sophisticated little comfort creatures. ■

FOR PIEROGI

- 1 cup boiling water
- 2/3 ounce (about 1/2 cup) dried porcini mushrooms
- 1 medium onion, quartered
- 2 garlic cloves, crushed
- 6 ounces cremini mushrooms, trimmed and quartered
- 1 1/2 tablespoons unsalted butter
- 1 tablespoon finely chopped fresh flat-leaf parsley
- Salt and freshly ground black pepper
- Pierogi Dough (recipe follows)

FOR ONION TOPPING

- 1/2 stick (4 tablespoons) unsalted butter
- 1 pound onions, chopped
- Salt and freshly ground black pepper

ACCOMPANIMENT: sour cream

SPECIAL EQUIPMENT: a 2 1/2-inch round cookie cutter

MAKE THE PIEROGI FILLING: Pour boiling water over porcini in a small bowl and let soak until softened, 10 to 20 minutes.

Lift porcini out of water, squeeze excess liquid back into bowl, and rinse porcini well to remove any grit. Pour soaking liquid through a sieve lined with a dampened paper towel into a bowl and reserve.

Finely chop onion and garlic in a food processor. Add cremini and porcini and pulse until very finely chopped.

Heat butter in a 12-inch heavy skillet over moderate heat until foam subsides. Add mushroom mixture and cook, stirring frequently, until mushrooms are dry and one shade darker, about 8 minutes. Add reserved soaking liquid, bring to a simmer, and simmer, stirring frequently, until mixture is thick, dry, and beginning to brown, about 15 minutes. Stir in parsley and salt and pepper to taste. (You will have about 1 cup filling.) Cool completely.

ASSEMBLE THE PIEROGI: Halve dough. Roll out one half on a lightly floured surface into a 15-inch round (keep remaining dough wrapped). Cut out rounds (about 24) with floured cutter; discard trimmings. Put 1 teaspoon filling in center of each round. One at a time, moisten edges with water, fold in half to form a half-moon, and press down around filling to force out air. (Air pockets increase the chance that pierogi will break during cooking.) Pinch edges together to seal. Transfer to a flour-dusted kitchen towel (not terry cloth). Make more pierogi in same manner with remaining dough and filling.

COOK THE ONIONS AND PIEROGI: Melt butter in a large heavy skillet over moderately low heat. Add onions and cook, stirring frequently, until golden brown, about 30 minutes. Season with salt and pepper, remove from heat, and cover to keep warm.

Meanwhile, cook pierogi in a 6- to 8-quart pot of boiling salted water (1 tablespoon salt per every 4 quarts water) until tender, 12 to 15 minutes. With a slotted spoon, transfer to skillet with onions. Toss gently to coat and serve immediately, with sour cream.

COOK'S NOTES

- The filling can be made up to 2 days ahead and refrigerated, covered.
- The filled pierogi can be frozen for up to 1 month. Freeze on a tray until firm, about 2 hours, then transfer to sealable plastic bags and freeze. Spread out in one layer on a tray to thaw before cooking.

Pierogi and Vareniki Dough

MAKES ENOUGH FOR ABOUT 48 PIEROGI OR 32 *VARENIKIS*; SERVES 6 AS A MAIN COURSE

ACTIVE TIME: 20 MINUTES ■ START TO FINISH: 50 MINUTES

■ Every country or culture has a dumpling to call its own. Here's a dough for pierogi that also works for the Ukrainian dessert dumplings called *varenikis* (see page 818). ■

- 1 cup all-purpose flour, plus additional for kneading
- 3/4 cup cake flour (not self-rising)
- 2 large eggs
- 1/8 teaspoon salt
- 1/4 cup water

Stir together flours in a bowl. Make a well in flour. Add eggs, salt, and water to well and stir together with a fork. Continue stirring, gradually incorporating flour into well, until a soft dough forms.

Transfer dough to a lightly floured work surface and knead, adding only as much additional flour as necessary to keep dough from sticking, until smooth and elastic, about 8 minutes. (Dough will be soft.) Cover with plastic wrap and let rest at room temperature for 30 minutes.

COOK'S NOTE

- The dough can be made up to 2 hours ahead and refrigerated, wrapped well in plastic wrap. Bring to room temperature before using.

Peanut Sesame Noodles

SERVES 6 AS A SIDE DISH, 4 AS A MAIN COURSE
ACTIVE TIME: 30 MINUTES ■ START TO FINISH: 30 MINUTES

■ The trick to this bold Sichuan dish—street food–style noodles that took this country by storm in the 1980s and became an all-American favorite—is not to let the noodles sit in the sauce for very long. Toss them together a few seconds before serving. You can find recipes that are more authentic than this one (we've stuck to supermarket ingredients), but we doubt they'll be better. If you want to dress up the noodles for a party, spread them on a roomy platter and garnish them with all sorts of interesting things. Make concentric rings of bright bell pepper slices, sliced scallions, shredded carrots, shredded chicken, and cilantro, for instance, or arrange the garnishes in lines, as on a traditional Cobb salad. Gorgeous. ■

FOR DRESSING

- 1/2 cup smooth peanut butter
- 1/4 cup soy sauce
- 1/3 cup warm water
- 2 tablespoons chopped peeled fresh ginger
- 1 medium garlic clove, chopped
- 2 tablespoons red wine vinegar
- 1 1/2 tablespoons Asian sesame oil
- 2 teaspoons honey
- 1 teaspoon red pepper flakes

FOR NOODLES

- 3/4 pound dried thin linguine (*linguine fini*) or spaghetti
- 4 scallions, thinly sliced
- 1 red bell pepper, cored, seeded, and cut into 1/8-inch-wide strips
- 1 yellow bell pepper, cored, seeded, and cut into 1/8-inch-wide strips
- 3 tablespoons sesame seeds, toasted (see Tips, page 939)

MAKE THE DRESSING: Combine all ingredients in a blender and blend until smooth, about 2 minutes. Transfer to a large bowl.

MAKE THE NOODLES: Cook pasta in a 6- to 8-quart pot of boiling salted water (1 tablespoon salt per every 4 quarts water) until tender. Drain in a colander, then rinse well under cold water.

Add pasta, scallions, bell peppers, and sesame seeds to dressing, tossing to combine. Serve immediately.

Curried Noodles with Vegetables

SERVES 8 AS A SIDE DISH, 6 AS A MAIN COURSE
ACTIVE TIME: 20 MINUTES ■ START TO FINISH: 1 1/4 HOURS

■ In Hong Kong, stir-fried rice noodles lightly seasoned with curry powder and garnished with pork and shrimp are relished by visitors and locals alike. This version, from the Chinese cooking authority Nina Simonds, skips the meat and shellfish, and it can be made with whatever vegetables are in season. Don't let the long list of ingredients deter you: they add up to flavors that are beautifully balanced, and the cooking is practically instantaneous. This is equally good as a side dish with grilled meats or by itself as a light lunch or dinner. ■

- ½ pound very thin rice stick noodles (rice vermicelli)
- ¼ cup chicken stock or store-bought low-sodium broth
- 3 tablespoons soy sauce
- 1 teaspoon salt
- ½ teaspoon sugar
- ¼ teaspoon freshly ground black pepper
- 2 tablespoons vegetable oil
- 1½ tablespoons minced garlic
- 1 tablespoon minced peeled fresh ginger
- 1½ tablespoons curry powder
- 2 medium red onions, thinly sliced
- 2 red bell peppers, cored, seeded, and cut into very thin strips
- 3 medium carrots, finely shredded
- ½ medium head Napa cabbage, thinly sliced
- 2 tablespoons Chinese rice wine or sake
- 2 cups (about 6 ounces) bean sprouts, rinsed and dried

Soak noodles in boiling water to cover in a large bowl for 30 minutes. Drain.

Stir together chicken stock, soy sauce, salt, sugar, and pepper in a small bowl.

Heat oil in a wok or deep 12-inch skillet over high heat until it begins to smoke. Add garlic, ginger, and curry powder and stir-fry until fragrant, about 15 seconds. Add onions and stir-fry until slightly wilted, about 1 minute. Add bell peppers, carrots, cabbage, and wine and stir-fry until vegetables are tender, 5 to 7 minutes.

Add stock mixture, noodles, and bean sprouts and stir-fry until most of liquid is absorbed. Transfer to a platter.

Linguine with Shrimp and Scallops in Thai Green Curry Sauce

SERVES 4 AS A MAIN COURSE
ACTIVE TIME: 40 MINUTES ■ START TO FINISH: 40 MINUTES

■ Thai green curry paste packs an exciting explosion of flavor, and it's become practically a supermarket staple, although it's not hard to make your own (see page 934). The sauce gets its creaminess from coconut milk, and in a cross-cultural move, linguine takes the place of Asian rice noodles. ■

- 2½ tablespoons vegetable oil
- 1 (4-inch-long) hot red chile, such as cayenne, thinly sliced
- 3 scallions, thinly sliced, white and green parts reserved separately
- 1 pound sea scallops, tough muscle removed from side of each if necessary
- ¾ pound large shrimp in shells (21–25 per pound), peeled and deveined
- Salt
- 1 (14-ounce) can unsweetened coconut milk
- 1 tablespoon Thai green curry paste (see Glossary)
- ¼ cup chicken stock or store-bought low-sodium broth, or water
- 1 tablespoon packed light brown sugar
- 1½ tablespoons Asian fish sauce
- 1 tablespoon fresh lime juice
- ¾ pound dried thin linguine (*linguine fini*)
- ½ cup chopped fresh cilantro

Heat 1 tablespoon oil in a 12-inch nonstick skillet over moderately high heat until hot but not smoking. Add chile and white parts of scallions and cook, stirring occasionally, until lightly browned. With a slotted spoon, transfer to paper towels to drain. Set skillet aside.

Pat scallops and shrimp dry (separately) and season with salt. Heat remaining 1½ tablespoons oil in same skillet over moderately high heat until hot but not smoking. Add scallops and cook, turning once, until browned, 2 to 3 minutes on each flat side. Transfer to a bowl. Cook shrimp in skillet, stirring occasionally, until almost cooked through, about 3 minutes. Add shrimp to scallops.

Add coconut milk, curry paste, stock, brown sugar, fish sauce, and lime juice to skillet, bring to a simmer, stirring, and simmer, stirring occasionally, for 5 minutes.

Meanwhile, cook linguine in a 6-quart pot of boiling salted water (1 tablespoon salt per every 4 quarts water) until al dente; drain.

Stir scallops and shrimp, with any liquid in bowl, into sauce and bring to a boil. Reduce heat and simmer until scallops and shrimp are just cooked through, about 2 minutes. With slotted spoon, transfer seafood to a clean bowl. Add linguine and cilantro to sauce, tossing to coat.

Divide pasta and sauce among four bowls. Top with seafood and sprinkle with scallion greens and chile-scallion mixture.

Pad Thai

Stir-Fried Rice Noodles with Shrimp

SERVES 4 AS A MAIN COURSE
ACTIVE TIME: 1½ HOURS ■ START TO FINISH: 1½ HOURS

■ With its signature fettuccine-width rice noodles, this mainstay of Thailand is found there in innumerable variations. It's usually made one serving at a time by street vendors, who prepare the dish according to each customer's taste. This version is well balanced in flavor and not too sweet.

There are no American shortcuts here (although if you must, you can use a large skillet instead of a wok), but all the exotic ingredients are available in Asian markets and increasingly in supermarkets, or by mail (see Sources). ■

- 1 cup boiling water
- 2 tablespoons tamarind (from a pliable block)
- 3 tablespoons Asian fish sauce, preferably *naam pla*
- 3 tablespoons packed palm sugar or light brown sugar
- 1 tablespoon granulated sugar
- ¼ teaspoon salt
- 1 (7-ounce) package dried flat rice noodles (⅛ inch wide)
- 2 tablespoons vegetable oil
- 2 large eggs, lightly beaten
- 6 garlic cloves, finely chopped
- 3 small shallots, coarsely chopped
- ½ pound medium shrimp in shells (31–35 per pound), peeled, deveined, and cut into ½-inch pieces
- ½ pound plain baked tofu, rinsed, patted dry, and cut into ½-inch cubes
- 2½ cups (½ pound) bean sprouts, rinsed and dried
- 8 scallions, quartered lengthwise and cut crosswise into 1-inch pieces
- 4 tablespoons crushed unsalted roasted peanuts (use a rolling pin)
- 1½ teaspoons red pepper flakes

ACCOMPANIMENT: lime wedges

Pour boiling water into a bowl, add tamarind, and stir, mashing gently, for 3 minutes to soften. Pour mixture through a fine-mesh sieve into a bowl, pressing hard on solids; discard solids.

Combine fish sauce, tamarind mixture, palm sugar, granulated sugar, and salt in a small saucepan and heat over moderate heat, stirring, until sugar is dissolved, 1 to 2 minutes. Remove from heat.

Soak noodles in 10 cups boiling water in a large bowl until softened, 5 to 8 minutes. Drain well.

Heat 1 tablespoon oil in a wok (or a large deep skillet) over moderate heat until hot but not smoking. Add eggs and cook, stirring, until scrambled and just cooked through, about 1 minute. Transfer eggs to a bowl and tear into small pieces.

Heat remaining 1 tablespoon oil in wok (or skillet) over moderately high heat until just beginning to smoke. Add garlic and shallots and stir-fry until just beginning to brown, about 1 minute. Add shrimp and stir-fry for 1 minute, then add tofu and stir-fry until shrimp is just cooked through, 1 to 2 minutes. Transfer to bowl with eggs.

Heat wok over moderately high heat until hot. Add tamarind sauce and bring to a boil. Add noodles and stir-fry until tender and excess sauce is absorbed, 2 to 3 minutes. Add egg and shrimp mixture, 1½ cups bean sprouts, scallions, 2 tablespoons peanuts, and red pepper flakes and toss well.

Mound pad Thai on a platter, top with remaining 1 cup bean sprouts, and sprinkle with remaining 2 tablespoons peanuts. Serve with lime wedges.

COOK'S NOTES

- If using palm sugar, coarsely grate it, then pack it into the measuring spoon.
- If you can find only flavored baked tofu, rinse it, pat it dry, then cut it into cubes.
- The tamarind sauce can be made up to 1 day ahead. Cool completely, then refrigerate, covered.
- The noodles can be soaked and drained up to 1 hour ahead and kept in a bowl, tightly covered with plastic wrap, at room temperature. If they become sticky, rinse in a sieve and drain well before proceeding.

Asian Noodles

For the pasta lover who craves a change, Asian noodles offer a whole new reason to boil water. They can be found in the ethnic foods aisle of well-stocked supermarkets and in the Asian markets that are cropping up in more and more American cities. They can also be ordered by mail from Uwajimaya and Ethnicgrocer.com (see Sources).

Asian noodles differ from other pastas mainly in the greater range of flours and starches used — and in their length. In many parts of Asia, noodles are a symbol of long life and happiness, and so they are customarily manufactured in longer strands than western noodles are. Like pasta, though, there is a vast array of noodles to choose from. Here are the ones we use most often.

BEAN THREAD: These silvery dried filaments, which go by various aliases, including cellophane and glass noodles, are made from mung bean starch and (sometimes) tapioca starch mixed with water. They become almost clear after being heated. Usually the noodles are extruded as thin round strands, but sometimes you'll see a flat variety, like fettuccine, that is practically identical to rice noodles. Bean threads have a wonderfully chewy, gelatinous texture, and because they are almost flavorless, they absorb fragrant broths readily. Bean threads are usually softened in water before being used.

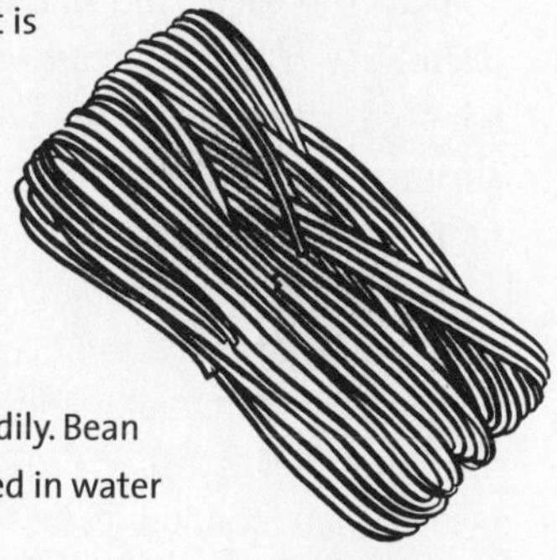

RICE STICK (also called rice vermicelli): These are the most widely available noodles made with rice flour. Thin and off-white, they are usually sold dried and turn a brighter white when cooked. Despite the name, they are not stick-straight but are generally gathered into wide, wiry skeins. Like bean threads, rice sticks should be softened in water before use.

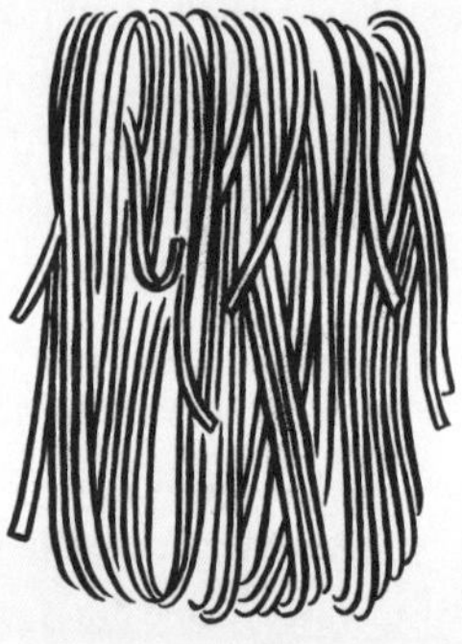

Another kind of dried rice noodle is flat and about the width of fettuccine but much longer. This shape is most often used in Thai and other Southeast Asian cuisines. These should also be softened in water.

FRESH RICE NOODLES: Noodle factories deliver fresh rice noodles daily to Chinatown markets, where they are sold precut or, more commonly, in loosely folded oiled sheets that can be cut into wide ribbons for *chow fun*, a dish that's made with panfried noodles. They may be labeled *he fun, ho fun,* or *ho fan.* The Vietnamese call them *banh uot* or *pho,* and the Thais call them *gueyteow.* Although they soak up flavors well, fresh rice noodles are really all about texture — they have a terrific chewiness. Use them as soon as possible or they'll lose their suppleness.

SOBA: These straight taupe-colored Japanese noodles, usually square in cross section, are made with protein-rich buckwheat flour or a combination of buckwheat and wheat flour. Nutty in flavor, soba noodles are eaten either in soup or cold and on their own with a dipping sauce. American-made brands are widely available at natural foods stores and many supermarkets; imported soba can be purchased at Japanese markets.

UDON: These Japanese wheat noodles are fat, white, shiny, and unbelievably satisfying. Available in fresh, fresh/frozen, and dried forms, they are traditionally eaten in soup, but you'll also see them served cold.

Udon Noodle Salad with Grilled Chicken and Asian Dressing

SERVES 4

ACTIVE TIME: 1 HOUR ■ START TO FINISH: 1½ HOURS

■ The thick white Japanese noodles called udon have a wonderful texture that's soft and slightly chewy; they are hearty, not heavy. Long a staple of the Japanese culinary world, udon have migrated into many supermarkets. Cilantro and parsley give the salad some color, and grilled chicken gives it heft. ■

- 4 skinless, boneless chicken breast halves (1½ pounds total)
- 3 tablespoons soy sauce
- 2 garlic cloves, minced
- 2 teaspoons finely grated peeled fresh ginger
- ⅓ cup plus 1 tablespoon seasoned rice vinegar
- ¾ pound dried udon (thick Japanese noodles)
- 1¾ cups chicken stock or store-bought low-sodium broth
- 2 cups loosely packed fresh cilantro sprigs, plus ¼ cup loosely packed leaves
- 1 cup loosely packed fresh flat-leaf parsley leaves
- 2 tablespoons vegetable oil
- 2 teaspoons Asian sesame oil
- 3 scallions, thinly sliced

SPECIAL EQUIPMENT: a well-seasoned large ridged grill pan

Combine chicken with 1 tablespoon soy sauce, garlic, ginger, and 1 tablespoon vinegar in a sealable plastic bag and seal bag. Marinate chicken, refrigerated, for 1 hour.

Heat grill pan over high heat until hot. Remove chicken from marinade (discard marinade) and pat dry. Reduce heat to moderate and grill chicken, turning once, until just cooked through, about 12 minutes total. Transfer to a cutting board and let cool slightly, about 10 minutes, then cut crosswise into ¼-inch-wide strips.

Bring 4 quarts (unsalted) water to a boil in a 6-quart pot. Cook noodles for 2 minutes. Stir in 1 cup cold water and bring to a boil again, then reduce heat and simmer noodles until just tender, about 5 minutes. Drain noodles in a colander, rinse under cold water, and drain again.

Combine stock, cilantro sprigs, parsley, vegetable oil, and remaining 2 tablespoons soy sauce in a 1-quart saucepan and bring to a simmer. Transfer to a blender and purée until almost smooth (use caution), about 1 minute. Transfer to a small bowl and stir in remaining ⅓ cup vinegar and sesame oil.

Toss noodles with dressing in a large bowl. Divide among four bowls and top with chicken, scallions, and cilantro leaves.

COOK'S NOTE

■ The chicken can also be grilled on a charcoal or gas grill, on a lightly oiled rack set 5 to 6 inches over glowing coals.

Chicken Long Rice

SERVES 12 AS A FIRST COURSE, 8 AS A MAIN COURSE

ACTIVE TIME: 25 MINUTES ■ START TO FINISH: 2 HOURS

■ Despite its name, this dish is not rice at all but noodles—and not even rice noodles, but shimmering, transparent bean threads, with lots of gingery chicken flavor. It's true comfort food; the cooked noodles are incredibly juicy because they stand off the heat for a half hour, gently absorbing the cooking broth. You'll always find a big pot of chicken long rice at a real Hawaiian luau, which is not the sort of tourist affair with leis, grass skirts, mai tais, and Samoan fire knife dancers but one of the world's ultimate expressions of community through food. This recipe is from the Honolulu chef Alan Wong. ■

- 2½ pounds whole chicken thighs
- 1½ tablespoons minced peeled fresh ginger
- 2 teaspoons salt
- 2½ quarts water
- 1 large onion, finely chopped
- 1½ extra-large (Knorr) or 2 regular chicken bouillon cubes
- 4 small dried shiitake mushrooms, stems discarded
- ½ pound bean thread (cellophane) noodles, cut into 3-inch lengths with kitchen scissors
- ½ cup chopped scallions
- 1 teaspoon freshly ground black pepper

Combine chicken, ginger, and salt in a 5-quart pot, add 2 quarts water, and bring to a simmer. Partially cover and simmer, skimming froth occasionally, until chicken is very tender, about 40 minutes. Transfer chicken to a bowl; set broth aside.

When chicken is cool, discard skin and bones and shred meat.

Pour broth through a fine-mesh sieve into a bowl; discard ginger. Return broth to cleaned pot, add remaining 2 cups water, onion, bouillon cubes, and mushrooms, cover, and bring to a boil. Add noodles, reduce heat to moderate, cover, and cook, stirring occasionally, for 5 minutes. Turn off heat and let noodles stand, covered, for 30 minutes.

Stir chicken into noodles and heat over moderate heat just until hot. Stir in scallions, salt to taste, and pepper.

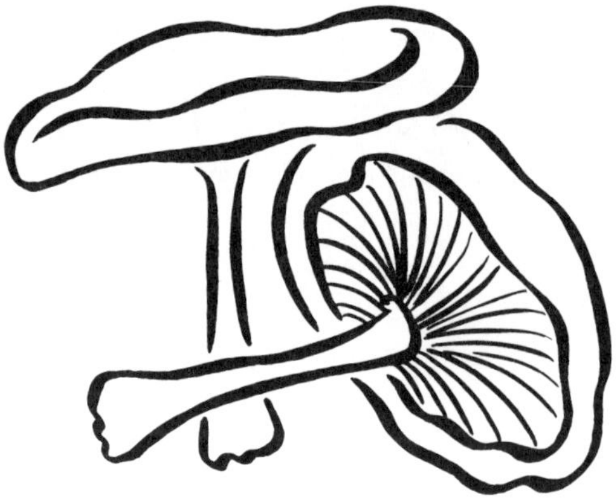

Spicy Pork with Bean Thread Noodles

Ants on a Tree

SERVES 4 TO 6
ACTIVE TIME: 20 MINUTES ■ START TO FINISH: 45 MINUTES

■ Chinese noodle dishes allow you to make something glorious out of inexpensive ingredients. In this classic preparation, for example, delicate bean thread noodles are dressed with a spicy sauce and enriched with little nubbins of ground pork that cling to the noodles—the "ants" of the dish's Kiplingesque name. ■

- ¾ pound ground pork
- 1 tablespoon plus 2 teaspoons rice vinegar (not seasoned)
- 1 tablespoon plus 2 teaspoons soy sauce
- 2 teaspoons Asian sesame oil
- 6½ ounces bean thread (cellophane) noodles
- 2 tablespoons vegetable oil
- 1 tablespoon minced garlic
- 1 tablespoon minced peeled fresh ginger
- ½ cup thinly sliced scallions
- 2 teaspoons Asian chili paste (see Glossary) or ½ teaspoon red pepper flakes
- 1½ cups chicken stock or store-bought low-sodium broth
- 3 tablespoons Chinese rice wine or sake
- 1 teaspoon sugar
- 3 tablespoons chopped fresh cilantro, or to taste (optional)

Gently combine pork with 2 teaspoons vinegar, 2 teaspoons soy sauce, and 1 teaspoon sesame oil in a bowl. Marinate at room temperature for 20 minutes.

Meanwhile, soak noodles in warm water to cover for 15 minutes. Drain noodles and, using scissors, cut into 3- to 4-inch lengths.

Heat vegetable oil in a wok or large heavy skillet over moderately high heat until it just begins to smoke. Add garlic, ginger, and ¼ cup scallions and stir-fry for 30 seconds. Add pork and chili paste and stir-fry, breaking up lumps, until meat is no longer pink. Add noodles, stock, rice wine, sugar, and remaining 1 tablespoon each soy sauce and vinegar, bring to a simmer, and simmer, stirring occasionally, until noodles have absorbed liquid, 3 to 5 minutes.

Transfer to a platter, drizzle with remaining 1 teaspoon sesame oil, and sprinkle with cilantro (if using) and remaining 1/4 cup scallions.

Chow Fun with Chinese Barbecued Pork and Snow Peas

SERVES 2 TO 4 AS A MAIN COURSE
ACTIVE TIME: 1¼ HOURS ■ START TO FINISH: 6 HOURS (INCLUDES MAKING CHAR SIU)

■ This recipe from the Asian food expert Bruce Cost incorporates two popular foods from the Toi San region of southern China: the boneless barbecued pork strips known as *char siu* and fresh rice noodles, which have a lovely, tender, chewy texture. Snow peas add color and crunch. The dish is a great excuse for a trip to Chinatown. Cooking in a wok imparts a special flavor, but if you don't have one, a large deep skillet will work. ■

- 14 ounces fresh rice noodles (see page 246), cut into ½-inch-wide strips if necessary
- ¼ cup plus 1 teaspoon peanut oil
- ¾ cup chicken stock or store-bought low-sodium broth
- 2 tablespoons oyster sauce
- 1 tablespoon light soy sauce
- 1 tablespoon Chinese rice wine or sake
- 2 teaspoons sugar
- ¼ pound snow peas, trimmed
- 4 scallions, cut into thin 2-inch-long strips
- 6 ounces Char Siu (page 478), thinly sliced
- 2 teaspoons finely chopped garlic
- 2 teaspoons finely chopped peeled fresh ginger
- ½ teaspoon cornstarch, stirred together with 2 teaspoons water
- ½ cup bean sprouts, rinsed and dried
- A few drops of Asian sesame oil
- Freshly ground black pepper

Separate noodles, then toss with 1 teaspoon peanut oil in a bowl.

Stir together 1/2 cup stock, oyster sauce, soy sauce, rice wine, and sugar in a small bowl.

Heat a wok (or a large deep skillet) over high heat until a bead of water dropped onto cooking surface evaporates immediately. Add remaining 1/4 cup peanut oil, swirl wok to coat evenly, and heat until it just begins to smoke. Add noodles and stir-fry, tossing frequently, until soft and translucent, 3 to 4 minutes (noodles will stick together). Add snow peas and scallions and stir-fry until snow peas are bright green and crisp-tender, about 1 minute. Add pork, garlic, and ginger and stir-fry for 1 minute.

Add stock mixture and bring to a boil, stirring, then add remaining 1/4 cup stock. When mixture boils, stir cornstarch mixture and add to wok, then boil, stirring, until sauce is thickened and noodles are well coated, about 30 seconds. Stir in bean sprouts and remove wok from heat. Season with sesame oil and pepper to taste.

GRAINS AND BEANS

Gourmet was born into a meat-and-potatoes world. In 1941, the word *tofu* would have drawn a blank stare from most Americans. *Risotto* and *polenta* would have been equally meaningless back then, and the only beans that most of our readers would have recognized were baked.

But our culinary world has expanded enormously, and nowhere do you get as clear a sense of this as in our use of grains, beans, and legumes. That is why, of all the chapters in this book, this one has the fewest recipes from the distant past. Rice now comes in a rainbow of colors and an assortment of sizes and shapes. You can easily find polenta, tabbouleh, and quinoa in both regular and instant forms, most supermarkets now carry both soft and firm tofu, and a simple stroll down the aisles reveals a vast variety of beans.

We owe much of this change to the food revolution of the sixties, a time when young Americans devoured books like *Diet for a Small Planet* and began to embrace meatless eating as a moral stance. It is no accident that you will find wonderful vegetarian entrées in this chapter, such as broiled polenta with tomato sauce and red lentil and tofu dal.

But our new love of grains and beans is also due to an ever-growing appreciation of all things Italian and Asian. This chapter is filled with all manner of risottos and polentas, along with fried rice, Thai sticky rice with coconut, and Persian rice with pistachios.

As we have become more comfortable with grains, we've left behind the notion that they are difficult to cook. And beans, once considered seriously slow food, have lost that reputation. We no longer believe that every bean must be soaked; many lentil dishes can be made in less than half an hour. Among the recipes you'll find here are a classically decadent French cassoulet (along with a remarkably easy American version) and decidedly smoky black beans from Brazil. We also have beans from North Africa, Asia, and Europe. Of course, we have also included a really spectacular version of good old-fashioned baked beans (the secret is maple syrup).

One note about beans: cooking times can vary widely, depending on their age. Older beans require longer cooking than newly harvested and dried ones. It is impossible to know how long your beans have languished in the store (or the warehouse), so you have to be flexible about cooking times. Your best bet is to buy beans from natural foods stores, where they are likely to have a fast turnover.

We may have come a long way, but we believe that our national love affair with legumes is just beginning. When the *Expanded Gourmet Cookbook* comes out twenty-five years from now, this chapter will undoubtedly be four times its current size.

A Rice Primer

Rice can be classified in several different ways: by the size of the grains, which range from long to short (they are measured not just by length but by the ratio of length to the width of the grain), by botanical varieties (such as Arborio and basmati), and by their degree of stickiness. This last characteristic depends on the proportion of the two starches that exist in all rices, amylose and amylopectin. Sticky rice (frequently labeled "glutinous rice") contains a higher proportion of amylopectin. Depending on what you are cooking, other characteristics that can affect a dish are the color and aroma of the rice.

AMERICAN LONG-GRAIN RICE: The grains of long-grain rice are more than three times as long as they are wide. In general, they are less starchy (and therefore less sticky) than the grains of short- and medium-grain rices. Long-grain rice from South Carolina's Low Country was once famous throughout America and Europe for its nutty yet delicate flavor and its texture—the grains become separate and dry when cooked. (Seeds from the original variety, imported from Madagascar in the late 1600s, were resurrected by Richard and Patricia Schulze, and their heirloom Carolina Gold is now available in limited quantities; see Sources.) The terms *long-grain* and *Carolina* are often used interchangeably; these days, *Carolina* is usually applied to any good long-grain rice grown in the United States. The name is also a trademark of Riviana brand rice (marketed as "extra long grain"). We prefer long-grain to converted rice (*converted* is actually a trademark of Uncle Ben's, identifying the company's parboiled rice). To our minds, converted rice is not fluffy and is almost too firm—it doesn't absorb a sauce the way regular long-grain rice does.

ARBORIO RICE: Arborio rice is ideal for making risotto. Turning creamy as it slowly absorbs stock, it nonetheless retains its shape and firm texture while taking on the flavors of any ingredients cooked with it. This medium-grain rice from northern Italy is readily available. Carnaroli and Vialone Nano (a variety especially appreciated in the area around Verona and Mantua), other fine medium-grain Italian rices, can be substituted. All Italian rices, by the way, are classified according to grain length, from longest to shortest: *superfino* (which includes Arborio and Carnaroli), *fino, semifino* (which includes Vialone Nano), and *commune* or *originario.*

BASMATI RICE: India is home to many rice varieties that differ in flavor and aroma, but the Indian rice best known in the United States is basmati, whose name means "queen of fragrance" in Hindi. More than twenty distinct varieties of basmati are grown in India, the most prized of which is cultivated in the foothills of the Himalayas. Categorized as a long-grain rice, basmati is often described as needle-shaped, because the grains taper to long, thin points. As they cook, they expand lengthwise instead of plumping, becoming even narrower. The grains also stay distinct and firm when completely cooked, and they have a subtle, buttery, nutty aroma. Basmati is at its best when aged for a few years before being milled and sold. Both white and brown basmati rices are available. We generally prefer white because the flavor and texture are more delicate. American hybrids such as Texmati and Jasmati are widely available in supermarkets, but their fragrance is less compelling, and the cooked grains aren't as long as those of true basmati.

BLACK RICE: There are more than two hundred varieties of black rice. The Chinese variety called Forbidden Rice, trademarked by Lotus Foods and available at specialty foods shops and by mail from Lotusfoods.com (see Sources), is a medium-grain rice that is not sticky like Thai black rice. Legend has it that it was once reserved solely for emperors. All black rices are unmilled; the outer coating, or bran layer, turns a beautiful purplish black when cooked. The darker the bran layer is, the richer the rice is in nutrients.

JAPANESE RICE (SUSHI RICE): When cooked, this medium-grain rice is slightly moist and sticky but with separate, firm grains. It's versatile, providing a marvelous backdrop for all kinds of fish and seafood. Although in Japan the term *sushi rice* simply means cooked rice that has been seasoned with vinegar, sugar, and salt, ready for use in a sushi preparation, in the United States it applies to the raw rice, which is usually labeled as such. True Japanese varieties are not imported into this country, but good Japanese-style rice is grown here. Look for Kokuho Rose, Calrose, or Nishiki brand, available at Japanese and other Asian markets and some supermarkets.

JASMINE RICE: Jasmine rice, often labeled "scented" or "fragrant" rice, is a long-grain white rice from Thailand. When cooked, the grains are soft, moist, and seductively aromatic, with a nutty flavor similar to that of Indian basmati. According to the Thai cookbook author Kasma Loha-Unchit, the name comes from *mali,* a very sweet jasmine flower. Thai jasmine rice is widely available in Asian markets in the United States; American-grown jasmine is found in many supermarkets.

STICKY RICE: Sticky rice is renowned for its texture (it sticks to itself, not to your fingers). The relatively high proportion of amylopectin gives cooked sticky rice its characteristic clingy, chewy quality; it forms clumps that can easily be picked up with fingers. If cooked like regular rice, sticky rice will become mushy, because it's so starchy. It needs to be soaked so that it can absorb some water, then drained and steamed until it's dry. Sticky rice, which tastes slightly sweet, comes in long-grain and short-grain varieties. The recipes in this book call for Thai sticky rice (available at Asian markets), which is long-grain; do not substitute Chinese (short-grain) sticky rice or Japanese sticky rice, also a short-grain. (In Japan, sticky rice, called *mochi-gome,* is used to make *omochi,* or rice taffy, and other confections; it is never used to make sushi.) Some long-grain hybrids with a delicate aroma are known as jasmine sticky rices.

WILD RICE: There is no substitute for the great texture, earthy flavor, and beautiful long grains of wild rice, which is higher in protein than common rice and rich in lysine, an amino acid lacking in most grains. In fact, wild rice isn't really rice, which is native to India, Indonesia, and Africa. Rather, it is the seed of a grass that grows in marshes and small lakes from Minnesota to Ontario. The Anishinabe (Ojibwa) still harvest it in the traditional way, slapping the ripe rice grains off into canoes, but most of the wild rice sold in supermarkets is commercially grown and mechanically harvested. Avoid packages that contain lots of broken pieces.

Foolproof Long-Grain Rice

MAKES ABOUT 4½ CUPS; SERVES 6
ACTIVE TIME: 5 MINUTES ■ START TO FINISH: 30 MINUTES

■ People who grow up eating rice tend to cook it successfully without thinking twice about it, but plenty of others claim that they cannot cook rice. This recipe is for them. ■

- 2¾ cups water
- 1½ cups long-grain white rice (not converted)
- 1¼ teaspoons salt

Stir together water, rice, and salt in a 2½- to 3-quart heavy saucepan, bring to a boil, and boil, uncovered, without stirring, until steam holes appear in rice and grains on surface look dry, about 8 minutes. Reduce heat to very low, cover pan with a tight-fitting lid, and simmer for 15 minutes. Remove pan from heat and let rice stand, covered, for 5 minutes.

Fluff rice with a fork before serving.

Curried Rice

SERVES 8
ACTIVE TIME: 15 MINUTES ■ START TO FINISH: 45 MINUTES

■ Although this rice is particularly terrific with Grilled Jerk Chicken (page 365), don't think of it as an accompaniment only to Indian and Caribbean dishes. We've used a light hand with the curry, and the flavorful result is delicious with just about anything from steak to black beans. Cooking it uncovered and then steaming it covered to finish it ensures perfectly cooked grains. ■

- 3 tablespoons olive oil
- 1 medium onion, finely chopped
- 3 garlic cloves, finely chopped
- 4 teaspoons curry powder
- 2 cups long-grain white rice
- 3¼ cups water
- 2 teaspoons salt

Heat oil in a 3- to 4-quart heavy saucepan over moderately low heat. Add onion and garlic and cook, stirring, until softened, 8 to 10 minutes. Add curry powder and rice and cook, stirring, for 1 minute. Add water and salt, bring to a boil, and boil, uncovered, without stirring, until steam holes appear in rice and grains on surface look dry, about 8 minutes.

Reduce heat to very low, cover pan with a tight-fitting lid, and cook for 15 minutes.

Remove pan from heat and let rice stand, covered, for 5 minutes, then fluff with a fork.

Jasmine Rice with Cilantro and Peanuts

SERVES 6
ACTIVE TIME: 10 MINUTES ■ START TO FINISH: 20 MINUTES

■ In Thailand, jasmine rice is traditionally steamed, but it can also simply be boiled in water, as it is here. We chose it for its aromatic qualities, but really any long-grain rice (except sticky rice) will work. We've jazzed up the jasmine with Southeast Asian flavors. This is great with steak, chicken, or fish. ■

- 1¾ cups (12 ounces) Thai jasmine rice (see Sources)
- ½ cup (about 2 ounces) salted peanuts, chopped
- ½ cup chopped fresh cilantro sprigs
- 4 scallions, sliced
- 1 tablespoon peanut oil
- 2 tablespoons seasoned rice vinegar, or to taste
- 1 tablespoon fresh lime juice, or to taste
- Salt and freshly ground black pepper to taste

Cook rice in a 4-quart saucepan of boiling well-salted water, stirring occasionally, until tender, 10 to 15 minutes; drain. Toss rice with remaining ingredients in a bowl.

"Paella" Fried Rice

SERVES 4 AS A MAIN COURSE
ACTIVE TIME: 35 MINUTES ■ START TO FINISH: 35 MINUTES

■ This takeoff on two classic dishes, fried rice and paella, might sound a little wacky, but it's one of our favorite last-minute dinners. Inspired by the fried rice recipes of the Chinese cooking authorities Nina Simonds and Bruce Cost, it looks like a colorful paella and is full of lusty flavors. The combination of cumin and chorizo, the spicy Spanish sausage, is especially wonderful. Be aware that you absolutely cannot make delicious fried rice using freshly cooked rice, because it is too soft and clumps together when fried. If you cook the rice yourself (a day to a week ahead), use long-grain rice and follow the package instructions for making drier rice. Or just ask for an extra-large carton of rice the next time you order Chinese takeout. ■

- ¼ cup extra-virgin olive oil
- 1 tablespoon cumin seeds
- ½ teaspoon red pepper flakes
- 1 large onion, chopped
- 1 large red bell pepper, cored, seeded, and chopped
- 2 (3- to 4- ounce) links mild Spanish chorizo (spicy cured pork sausage; see Glossary), quartered lengthwise and cut crosswise into ¼-inch-thick slices
- 4 cups cold cooked long-grain rice (1½ cups uncooked rice)
- 1½ teaspoons salt
- 1 (10-ounce) package frozen baby peas
- ⅓ cup green (hulled) pumpkin seeds, toasted (see Tips, page 939)
- 1 cup finely chopped fresh cilantro

Heat oil in a 12-inch nonstick skillet over moderate heat until hot but not smoking. Add cumin and red pepper flakes and cook, stirring, for 1 minute. Add onion and bell pepper and cook, stirring, until softened, about 5 minutes. Add chorizo, increase heat to moderately high, and cook, stirring, until sausage begins to brown, about 3 minutes.

Add rice, crumbling it to break up lumps, and salt. Cook, stirring, until some grains of rice begin to turn golden, about 3 minutes. Add peas and cook, stirring, just until heated through. Remove from heat and stir in pumpkin seeds and cilantro.

Risotto with Peas and Prosciutto

SERVES 6 TO 8 AS A FIRST COURSE, 4 AS A MAIN COURSE
ACTIVE TIME: 35 MINUTES ■ START TO FINISH: 35 MINUTES

■ The inspiration for this risotto is the soupy dish called *risi e bisi* ("rice and peas"), which is Venetian in origin and is traditionally eaten on St. Mark's Day, April 25, when the first local peas appear in the Rialto market. We call for frozen baby peas (unless fresh peas are *really* fresh, they can be too starchy), and we eat this year-round. We stir in some prosciutto for depth (pancetta will work well too) and a bit of lemon zest to perk things up. ■

- 5 cups chicken stock or store-bought low-sodium broth
- ½ stick (4 tablespoons) unsalted butter
- ½ cup finely chopped onion
- 1½ cups (about 10 ounces) Arborio rice
- ½ cup dry white wine
- 1 cup frozen baby peas, thawed
- 2 ounces thinly sliced prosciutto, cut crosswise into ¼-inch-wide strips
- ½ teaspoon finely grated lemon zest
- ⅔ cup finely grated Parmigiano-Reggiano, plus additional for serving
- 3 tablespoons finely chopped fresh flat-leaf parsley
- Salt and freshly ground black pepper

Bring stock to a simmer in a medium saucepan; reduce heat, cover, and keep at a bare simmer.

Melt 2 tablespoons butter in a 3- to 4-quart heavy saucepan over moderate heat. Add onion and cook, stirring occasionally, until softened, 3 to 4 minutes. Add rice and cook, stirring, for 1 minute. Add wine, bring to a simmer, and simmer, stirring, until it is absorbed.

Add 1 cup stock and cook at a strong simmer, stirring constantly, until it is absorbed. Continue adding stock, about ½ cup at a time, stirring constantly and letting each addition be absorbed before adding next, until rice is tender and creamy-looking but still al dente, 18 to 20 minutes (there will be leftover stock).

Stir in peas, prosciutto, lemon zest, cheese, parsley, remaining 2 tablespoons butter, and salt and pepper to taste. If necessary, thin risotto with some of remaining stock. Serve immediately, with additional cheese.

Risotto with Porcini

SERVES 8 AS A FIRST COURSE, 6 AS A MAIN COURSE
ACTIVE TIME: 30 MINUTES ■ START TO FINISH: 1 HOUR

■ Creamy risotto acquires woodsy, deep flavor and mystery with the addition of dried porcini mushrooms. Once each grain of rice is cooked to the properly tender but still al dente state and the cheese is added, your risotto might not be as moist as you like; if it isn't, add some of the remaining stock (fortified by the fragrant porcini soaking liquid) to make it, as the Italians say, *all'onda* ("wavy"). This recipe is from Elizabeth Schneider, the author of the classic *Vegetables: From Amaranth to Zucchini.* ■

- 1½ cups water
- 5½ cups chicken stock or store-bought low-sodium broth
- 1¼ ounces (about 1¾ cups) dried porcini mushrooms
- 2 tablespoons olive oil
- ½ stick (4 tablespoons) unsalted butter
- ¼ cup finely chopped onion
- 2 cups (about 14 ounces) Arborio rice
- 1 cup finely grated Parmigiano-Reggiano (about 2 ounces), plus additional for serving
- ½ teaspoon salt
- ¼ teaspoon freshly ground black pepper

Combine water and 1 cup stock in a small saucepan and heat until hot. Put mushrooms and 1 tablespoon oil in a bowl and pour hot liquid over them. Let soak for 30 minutes.

Lift porcini out of soaking liquid, squeeze excess liquid back into bowl, and rinse well to remove any grit. Coarsely chop porcini. Pour soaking liquid through a fine sieve lined with a dampened paper towel into a large saucepan. Add remaining 4½ cups stock and bring to a simmer. Reduce heat, cover, and keep at a bare simmer.

Melt 2 tablespoons butter with remaining 1 tablespoon oil in a 4-quart saucepan over moderate heat. Add onion and cook, stirring, until softened, about 3 minutes. Add rice and cook, stirring, for 2 minutes. Add ½ cup stock and cook at a strong simmer, stirring constantly, until stock is absorbed. Continue adding stock, about ½ cup at a time, stirring constantly and letting each addition be absorbed before adding next, until rice is tender and creamy-looking but still al dente, 18 to 20 minutes (there will be leftover stock).

Stir in mushrooms, remaining 2 tablespoons butter, cheese, salt, and pepper. If necessary, thin risotto with some of remaining stock. Serve immediately, with additional cheese.

Red Wine Risotto

SERVES 10 TO 12 AS A FIRST COURSE,
6 TO 8 AS A MAIN COURSE
ACTIVE TIME: 45 MINUTES ■ START TO FINISH: 45 MINUTES

■ The idea of wine-dark risotto might seem peculiar, but it's a staple of Italy's Piedmont. The region is known for the vast rice-producing Po River Valley as well as for wonderful red wines and food that can be described as simultaneously luxurious and simple. This dish is a perfect example. ■

- 3 cups water
- 2 cups chicken stock or store-bought low-sodium broth
- 6 ounces thinly sliced pancetta, chopped
- 2 tablespoons unsalted butter
- 1 cup finely chopped onion
- 1 tablespoon finely chopped fresh rosemary or 1 teaspoon dried rosemary, crumbled
- 1 tablespoon finely chopped fresh sage or 1 teaspoon dried sage, crumbled
- Salt and freshly ground black pepper
- 3 cups (about 1¼ pounds) Arborio rice
- 2 cups dry red wine, such as Rosso di Montalcino
- 3 tablespoons finely chopped fresh flat-leaf parsley
- 1 cup finely grated Parmigiano-Reggiano (about 2 ounces)

OPTIONAL GARNISH: Parmigiano-Reggiano shavings and fresh rosemary sprigs

Combine water and stock in a medium saucepan and bring to a simmer. Reduce heat, cover, and keep at a bare simmer.

Cook pancetta in a 5- to 6-quart heavy pot over moderate heat, stirring, until fat is rendered, about 5 minutes. Add butter, onion, rosemary, sage, and salt and pepper to taste and cook, stirring, until onion is softened, about 3 minutes. Add rice and cook, stirring, for 1 minute. Add 1 cup wine and cook, stirring constantly, until absorbed. Add remaining 1 cup wine and cook, stirring constantly, until absorbed. Add 1 cup stock and cook at a strong simmer, stirring constantly, until absorbed. Continue adding stock, about 1/2 cup at a time, stirring constantly and letting each addition be absorbed before adding next, until rice is tender and creamy-looking but still al dente, 20 to 25 minutes (there will be leftover stock).

Stir in parsley, cheese, and salt and pepper to taste. Serve immediately, garnished with Parmesan shavings and rosemary sprigs, if desired.

Risotto Milanese

SERVES 6 TO 8 AS A FIRST COURSE, 6 AS A SIDE DISH
ACTIVE TIME: 30 MINUTES ■ START TO FINISH: 30 MINUTES

■ We were curious about why saffron is essential to this Italian classic, traditionally served with osso buco. (It also makes a great accompaniment to fish or chicken.) Two Italian cooking authorities, Maureen Fant and Lynne Rossetto Kasper, weighed in with their thoughts.

One of Fant's sources recounts a most likely apocryphal but enchanting story set in 1574, during the construction of the Duomo of Milan. A master glassmaker relied on the help of a talented pupil nicknamed Zafferano (Saffron) because he used a pinch of saffron to make yellow glass. The master teased him: "One day you'll even put saffron in the risotto!" When the boss's daughter later got married, to the guests' amazement the risotto served at the banquet was yellow, like gold. Young Zafferano had conspired with the chef, and this was his wedding gift. The dish was a stunning success and by the next day was being copied all over Milan.

This story ties in with Kasper's theory that the pairing probably relates to several things: the Renaissance passion for all things golden; the Milanese court's close links with Spain (the Arabs were cultivating saffron in that country by A.D. 960); and the fact that saffron was considered beneficial to health (it "delights the heart, cools the brain, and stimulates desire," according to a fourteenth-century medical handbook). Saffron was (and still is) expensive, turning something quite ordinary into something flashy—just what every nobleman wanted on his banquet table. ■

- 4 cups chicken stock or store-bought low-sodium broth
- 2 cups water
- Scant 1/4 teaspoon crumbled saffron threads
- 3 tablespoons unsalted butter
- 1 small onion, finely chopped
- 1 1/2 cups (about 10 ounces) Arborio rice
- 1/4 cup finely grated Parmigiano-Reggiano
- Salt and freshly ground black pepper

Combine stock and water in a 2- to 3-quart saucepan and bring to a simmer. Transfer 1 cup stock to a measuring cup and stir in saffron until dissolved. Cover remaining stock, reduce heat, and keep at a bare simmer.

Melt 2 tablespoons butter in a 2 1/2- to 3-quart heavy saucepan over moderate heat. Add onion and cook, stirring occasionally, until softened, about 5 minutes. Add rice and cook, stirring, for 1 minute. Stir in 1/2 cup stock mixture (without saffron) and cook at a strong simmer, stirring frequently, until stock is absorbed. Continue adding stock 1/2 cup at a time, stirring frequently and letting each addition be absorbed before adding the next, for 10 minutes. Add half of saffron broth and simmer, stirring, until absorbed. Add remaining saffron broth and simmer, stirring, until absorbed. Continue to add stock mixture, 1/2 cup at a time, until rice is tender and creamy-looking but still al dente, 18 to 25 minutes total. (There may be stock left over.)

Stir in cheese, remaining 1 tablespoon butter, and salt and pepper to taste. Serve immediately.

Foolproof Basmati Rice

SERVES 4

ACTIVE TIME: 30 MINUTES ■ START TO FINISH: 30 MINUTES

■ As close-minded as it may seem, using the microwave doesn't feel like real cooking to us. But at some point we found ourselves browsing through Julie Sahni's *Moghul Microwave,* and one sentence jumped out: "I don't think I fully appreciated the microwave until I saw how it cooked basmati." Could it be? Sure enough, every grain of the delicate Indian long-grain rice comes out distinct yet fluffy. Here is our adaptation of Sahni's method. ■

2 cups (about 12 ounces) white basmati rice
3 cups water

Put rice and water in a 3-quart microwave-safe dish. Cook on high in microwave, uncovered, until steam holes appear in rice, about 15 minutes. Cover dish and cook on high for 5 minutes more.

Let rice stand, covered, for 5 minutes, then fluff with a fork.

Indian Baked Rice

SERVES 8

ACTIVE TIME: 35 MINUTES ■ START TO FINISH: 1½ HOURS

■ This dish, from the Indian cooking authority and actress Madhur Jaffrey, is a rice with distinction, at home next to grilled chicken, lamb chops, or pork roast. Rub any leftover garam masala onto skinless, boneless chicken breasts or stir it into ground beef for burgers. ■

3 cups (about 1¼ pounds) white basmati rice
4 cups chicken stock or store-bought low-sodium broth
5 tablespoons vegetable oil
¼ cup slivered almonds
1 large onion, halved lengthwise and thinly sliced crosswise
1 large garlic clove, minced
1 small jalapeño chile, seeded and thinly sliced crosswise
1 teaspoon Garam Masala (page 932)
1 teaspoon finely grated peeled fresh ginger
½ teaspoon salt

Wash rice in 6 or 7 changes of cold water in a large bowl until water is almost clear. Drain in a large sieve for 10 minutes.

Put a rack in middle of oven and preheat oven to 325°F.

Bring stock to a simmer in a saucepan; reduce heat, cover, and keep at a bare simmer.

Heat oil in a 4- to 5-quart heavy ovenproof pot over moderate heat until hot but not smoking. Add almonds and cook, stirring frequently, until golden, 3 to 4 minutes. With a slotted spoon, transfer to paper towels to drain. Add onion to pot, increase heat to moderately high, and cook, stirring frequently, until onion is pale golden, 6 to 8 minutes. Add garlic, jalapeño, garam masala, ginger, and salt and cook, stirring frequently, for 1 minute. Add rice, reduce heat to moderately low, and cook, stirring frequently, for 6 minutes.

Add stock and simmer briskly, uncovered, until top of rice appears dry, about 8 minutes.

Cover pot and bake until rice is tender and liquid has been absorbed, about 20 minutes. Remove from oven and let stand, covered, for 15 minutes.

Serve rice sprinkled with almonds.

COOK'S NOTE

■ Long-grain white rice (do not rinse) can be used instead of basmati, but the flavor will not be as nutty.

Persian Rice with Pistachios and Dill

SERVES 8 TO 10

ACTIVE TIME: 20 MINUTES ■ START TO FINISH: 1½ HOURS (INCLUDES OPTIONAL STANDING TIME)

■ Rice is the stuff of Persian legend; it was taken from northern India into what is now Iran by Turkic tribes around two thousand years ago. Generally speaking, it's not considered a common starch in Iran (except in the north by the Caspian Sea, where it's grown) but is reserved for special occasions and family gatherings. This very simple treatment may well be the best rice you've ever tasted. The rich, golden crust (*tah-dig*, or "bottom of the pot," in Farsi) is considered a delicacy and a sign of the cook's prowess. It's made by covering the bottom of the pot with melted butter before adding rice that's been briefly boiled. Then the rice is steamed until it is tender and the crust underneath is crisp. The *tah-dig* is served (if it makes it out of the kitchen, that is) on a separate plate or broken into pieces and placed on top of or around the rice. In this recipe, fresh dill brings out the natural sweetness of the pistachios.

For the best results, use basmati rice (the closest thing to true Persian varieties) rather than one of the North American basmati-type hybrid rices, such as Texmati. ■

- 3 cups (about 1¼ pounds) white basmati rice
- 3 tablespoons salt
- ¾ stick (6 tablespoons) unsalted butter
- ⅔ cup chopped fresh dill
- 1 cup (5 ounces) coarsely chopped shelled natural pistachios (not dyed red)

Wash rice in 6 or 7 changes of cold water in a large bowl until water is almost clear. Drain in a large sieve for 10 minutes.

Bring 4 quarts water and salt to a boil in a 6-quart heavy pot. Add rice and boil, uncovered, for 5 minutes. Drain in sieve.

Melt butter in cleaned pot over moderate heat. Spoon layers of rice over it, alternating with sprinklings of dill and pistachios and mounding it loosely, ending with rice. Make 5 or 6 holes in rice to bottom of pot with handle of a wooden spoon. Cover pot with a kitchen towel and a heavy lid and fold edges of towel up over lid (so towel won't burn). Cook over moderately low heat until rice is tender and a crust has formed on bottom, 30 to 35 minutes. Let stand off heat, tightly covered and undisturbed, for at least 30 minutes.

Spoon loose rice onto a platter. Dip bottom of pot in a large bowl of cold water for 30 seconds to loosen the *tah-dig* (crust), then remove *tah-dig* with a large spoon and serve over rice.

COOK'S NOTES

- The rice can be parboiled and drained up to 4 hours ahead; transfer to a bowl and keep covered with a dampened towel at room temperature.
- The rice can stand off the heat for up to 1 hour.
- If you're short on time, you can skip letting the rice stand after cooking. Simply spoon the loose rice onto a platter and then dip the bottom of the pot into a large bowl of cold water for 30 seconds to loosen the crust.

Jeweled Rice with Dried Fruits

SERVES 8 TO 10
ACTIVE TIME: 25 MINUTES ■ START TO FINISH: 1½ HOURS
(INCLUDES OPTIONAL STANDING TIME)

■ Golden rice studded with sparkling "gems"—dried fruits and nuts reminiscent of diamonds, rubies, topaz, and emeralds—is one of the glories of Persian cuisine and a favorite at wedding banquets in Iran. It's thought to bring good luck and sweetness to the happy couple. Despite its sumptuous, exotic appearance, jeweled rice contains simple ingredients and is not hard to make. ■

- 3 cups (about 1¼ pounds) white basmati rice
- 3 tablespoons salt
- ½ cup (3½ ounces) dried apricots, quartered
- ½ cup (3 ounces) golden raisins
- ½ cup (2 ounces) dried cherries or cranberries
- 1 stick (8 tablespoons) unsalted butter
- ½ teaspoon ground cardamom
- ½ teaspoon freshly ground black pepper
- ½ cup (2½ ounces) coarsely chopped shelled natural pistachios (not dyed red)

Wash rice in 6 or 7 changes of cold water in a large bowl until water is almost clear. Drain in a large sieve for 10 minutes.

Bring 4 quarts water and salt to a boil in a 6-quart heavy pot. Add rice and boil, uncovered, stirring occasionally, for 5 minutes. Drain in sieve.

Toss together dried fruit in a bowl. Melt 6 tablespoons butter with cardamom and pepper in cleaned (and dried) pot. Layer rice and dried fruit alternately in pot, beginning and ending with rice and mounding it loosely. Make 5 or 6 holes in rice to bottom of pot with handle of a wooden spoon. Cover pot with a kitchen towel and a heavy lid and fold edges of towel up over lid (so towel won't burn). Cook over moderately low heat until rice is tender and a crust has formed on bottom, 30 to 35 minutes. Let stand off heat, tightly covered and undisturbed, for at least 30 minutes.

Melt remaining 2 tablespoons butter in a small skillet over moderate heat. Add pistachios and cook, stirring, until toasted, 2 to 3 minutes. Remove from heat.

Spoon loose rice onto a platter. Dip bottom of pot in a large bowl of cold water for 30 seconds to loosen the crust. Remove crust with a large spoon and serve over rice. Sprinkle with pistachios.

COOK'S NOTES

- The rice can be parboiled and drained up to 4 hours ahead; transfer to a bowl and keep covered with a dampened towel, at room temperature.
- The rice can stand off the heat for up to 1 hour.
- If you're short on time, you can skip letting the rice stand after cooking. Simply spoon the loose rice onto a platter and then dip the bottom of the pot into a large bowl of cold water for 30 seconds to loosen the crust.

Sesame Black Rice

SERVES 4

ACTIVE TIME: 5 MINUTES ■ START TO FINISH: 45 MINUTES

■ Chinese black rice is an exotic and alluring whole grain that is becoming more widely available. Its nutty taste and distinctive texture are particularly wonderful with scallops. ■

3/4 cup Forbidden Rice (black rice; see page 253)
1 1/2 cups water
2 teaspoons Asian sesame oil
Salt and freshly ground black pepper

Combine rice and water in a 1 1/2- to 2-quart heavy saucepan and bring to a boil over moderately high heat. Cover pan, reduce heat to low, and cook until rice is tender and most of water has evaporated, about 30 minutes. Remove pan from heat and let stand, covered, for 10 minutes.

Fluff rice with a fork, then stir in sesame oil and salt and pepper to taste.

Foolproof Thai Sticky Rice

SERVES 4

ACTIVE TIME: 10 MINUTES ■ START TO FINISH: 3 1/2 HOURS (INCLUDES SOAKING RICE)

■ Aptly named, sticky rice—a staple in Thailand, Laos, and parts of China and Vietnam—is slightly sweet, rather sticky, and fun to eat; children love it. The traditional way is to gently gather a little clump of it into a ball and dip it into a spicy, pungent sauce or use it to nab a sliver of meat (in Asia, meat is a condiment to rice, not the other way around). ■

2 cups (about 13 ounces) Thai (long-grain) sticky rice (see Cook's Note)

SPECIAL EQUIPMENT: cheesecloth

Rinse rice in 2 or 3 changes of cold water until water is clear. Soak rice in fresh water to cover for at least 3 hours.

Drain rice and put in a cheesecloth-lined sieve or colander. Set over 1 inch of boiling water in a large pot; do not let rice touch boiling water. Cover pot and steam rice, checking water level occasionally and adding more boiling water if necessary, until shiny and tender, about 20 minutes. Remove from heat and let stand, covered, for 5 minutes before serving.

COOK'S NOTES

- The rice can be soaked, covered and refrigerated, for up to 8 hours.
- When shopping for sticky rice, which is available at Asian markets and by mail (see Sources), make sure you buy the long-grain rice from Thailand, not the short-grain sticky rice from China.

Thai Sticky Rice with Toasted Coconut and Fried Shallots

SERVES 4

ACTIVE TIME: 20 MINUTES ■ START TO FINISH: $3\frac{3}{4}$ HOURS (INCLUDES SOAKING RICE)

■ You don't have to reserve this dish for an Asian main course. Embellished with coconut milk and cilantro, it's just as delicious with grilled chicken or pork. ■

- 1 cup (about 6 ounces) Thai (long-grain) sticky rice (see Cook's Note)
- $\frac{1}{3}$ cup well-stirred canned unsweetened coconut milk
- $\frac{1}{4}$ cup vegetable oil
- 2 large shallots, cut crosswise into thin rings ($\frac{1}{2}$ cup)
- $\frac{1}{3}$ cup sweetened flaked coconut, toasted (see Tips, page 939)
- Salt
- 2 tablespoons chopped fresh cilantro

SPECIAL EQUIPMENT: cheesecloth

Rinse rice in 2 or 3 changes of cold water in a bowl until water is clear. Soak rice in fresh water to cover for at least 3 hours.

Drain rice and transfer to a cheesecloth-lined sieve or colander. Set in a large pot filled with 1 inch of boiling water; do not let rice touch boiling water. Cover pot and steam rice, checking water level occasionally and adding more boiling water if necessary, for 20 minutes.

Fluff rice with a fork and gradually pour coconut milk over it. Steam rice, covered, until just tender, about 10 minutes more.

While rice is steaming, heat oil in a 7-inch heavy skillet over moderate heat. Add shallots and cook, stirring occasionally, until golden, 7 to 8 minutes. Transfer to paper towels to drain.

Transfer rice to a bowl and stir in coconut and salt to taste. Sprinkle with shallots and cilantro and serve immediately.

COOK'S NOTES

- The rice can be soaked, covered and refrigerated, for up to 8 hours.
- When shopping for sticky rice, available at Asian markets and by mail (see Sources), make sure you buy the long-grain sticky rice from Thailand, not the short-grain sticky rice from China.

Cooking Sticky Rice

Distinct, separate grains are the last thing you want when you cook sticky rice. To achieve the proper, addictively chewy texture, Thai cooks steam the rice in a large conical basket set over a lightweight pot. You can find both the basket and the pot at Southeast Asian markets, but we were successful using a large sieve or footed colander set over a deep pot or one of those pasta pots that come with a deep basket or steamer insert (because the sieve, colander, and steamer insert all have large holes, line them with cheesecloth).

Wild Rice and Toasted Almond Pilaf

SERVES 6

ACTIVE TIME: 10 MINUTES ■ START TO FINISH: 1½ HOURS

■ Wild rice and lightly toasted almonds are a classic pairing. It's a crime to undercook or overcook wild rice: you want to simmer it until the grains just start to splay open. Depending on the variety and how old it is, wild rice varies greatly in the amount of water it absorbs, so this can take from an hour to an hour and fifteen minutes. ■

- 2 cups (about 12 ounces) wild rice
- 2 tablespoons olive oil
- 1 medium onion, finely chopped
- 3 cups chicken stock or store-bought low-sodium broth
- 4 cups water
- 2 teaspoons unsalted butter
- 1 cup (3½ ounces) sliced almonds
- 1 teaspoon salt
- ¼ teaspoon freshly ground black pepper

Rinse rice in a large sieve under cold water; drain. Heat oil in a 5-quart heavy pot over moderate heat until hot but not smoking. Add onion and cook, stirring occasionally, until golden, about 5 minutes.

Add rice and cook, stirring, until fragrant, about 3 minutes. Stir in stock and water and bring to a boil. Reduce heat to low and simmer, covered, until rice is tender (grains will split open), 1 to 1¼ hours. Drain well in sieve and transfer to a bowl.

Meanwhile, heat butter in a 10-inch skillet over moderate heat until foam subsides. Add almonds and cook, stirring, until golden, about 3 minutes. Remove from heat.

Add almonds, salt, and pepper to rice and stir gently to combine.

Herbed Bulgur

SERVES 4

ACTIVE TIME: 10 MINUTES ■ START TO FINISH: 35 MINUTES

■ Like couscous, this is a summer starch that doesn't have to be served warm. Toss the bulgur with vegetables (either fresh or leftover cooked) to make a main-course salad. You can also play around with the herbs to suit whatever dish this will accompany. ■

- ¾ cup bulgur
- 1 cup boiling water
- ¼ cup chopped fresh dill
- 2 tablespoons chopped fresh tarragon
- 2 tablespoons finely chopped fresh chives
- 1 tablespoon olive oil
- Salt and freshly ground black pepper

Combine bulgur and boiling water in a large bowl and let stand for 20 minutes.

Fluff bulgur with a fork and stir in herbs, oil, and salt and pepper to taste.

Bulgur Pilaf with Pine Nuts, Raisins, and Orange Zest

SERVES 4

ACTIVE TIME: 20 MINUTES ■ START TO FINISH: 45 MINUTES

■ People generally think of the Middle Eastern salad called tabbouleh when they think of bulgur—wheat that's been steamed, dried, and cracked. But bulgur is also a great alternative to rice, and a nice way to get another whole grain into your diet. ■

2 tablespoons unsalted butter
3/4 cup finely chopped onion
1 cup bulgur
1 teaspoon finely grated orange zest
1/4 cup raisins
1 3/4 cups chicken stock or store-bought low-sodium broth
Salt and freshly ground black pepper
6 tablespoons pine nuts, lightly toasted (see Tips, page 938)
1/4 cup minced fresh flat-leaf parsley
1/4 cup thinly sliced scallion greens

Melt butter in a 2- to 3-quart heavy saucepan over moderately low heat. Add onion and cook, stirring, until softened, about 3 minutes. Stir in bulgur and zest and cook, stirring, for 1 minute. Add raisins, stock, and salt and pepper to taste and bring to a boil. Reduce heat to low and cook, covered, until liquid is absorbed, about 10 minutes.

Fluff pilaf with a fork and cool for 15 minutes.

Fluff pilaf again and stir in pine nuts, parsley, and scallion greens.

COOK'S NOTE

- The pilaf, without the nuts, parsley, and scallions, can be made up to 6 hours ahead, cooled completely, and refrigerated, covered. Bring to room temperature and fluff with a fork before adding nuts, parsley, and scallions.

Herbed Quinoa

SERVES 6

ACTIVE TIME: 35 MINUTES ▪ START TO FINISH: 35 MINUTES

▪ Quinoa (pronounced "*keen*-wah") is the ancient "mother grain" of the Incas. It's loaded with essential amino acids as well as with lots of minerals and vitamins. And it cooks quickly. We parboil it in a generous amount of water, then steam it so it becomes dry and fluffy. Quinoa has a far more interesting texture than couscous and a nutty flavor. It makes a great side dish. ▪

1 1/2 cups (8 ounces) quinoa
2 1/2 tablespoons extra-virgin olive oil
Salt and freshly ground black pepper
1/2 cup thinly sliced scallion greens
1 teaspoon fresh thyme leaves

Rinse quinoa in 5 changes of water in a bowl, rubbing grains and letting them settle each time before pouring off water (if quinoa does not settle, drain in a large fine-mesh sieve after each rinse).

Cook quinoa in a 3- to 4-quart saucepan of boiling well-salted water for 10 minutes. Drain in sieve and rinse under cold water.

Bring about 1 1/2 inches water to a boil in same saucepan. Set sieve with quinoa over saucepan (or transfer quinoa to a cheesecloth-lined colander and set over pan); quinoa should not touch water. Cover with a kitchen towel and lid and fold edges of towel up over lid (so towel won't burn). Steam quinoa until fluffy and dry, 10 to 12 minutes; check water level occasionally and add boiling water if necessary.

Toss quinoa with oil and salt and pepper to taste in a large bowl. Cool, then toss with scallion greens and thyme.

COOK'S NOTE

- The quinoa, without the scallion greens and thyme, can be made up to 1 day ahead, cooled completely, and refrigerated, covered. Bring to room temperature and toss with the scallion greens and thyme before serving.

Barley "Risotto" with Vegetables

SERVES 6 AS A FIRST COURSE, 8 AS A SIDE DISH

ACTIVE TIME: 1 HOUR ▪ START TO FINISH: 7 HOURS (INCLUDES SOAKING BARLEY)

▪ Gradually adding stock to barley gives it a creamy consistency; this is the same method used for risotto. The recipe was brought to us by the Italian cooking authority Faith Heller Willinger. It's from one of her favorite restaurants, Gostilna Devetak, outside the city of Gradisca d'Isonzo, in the Friuli region. Chef Michela Devetak, whose family has been in the restaurant business for more than a hundred years, changes the vegetables in this dish with the season, using those included here in autumn. ■

- 1 cup pearl barley
- 8 cups Vegetable Stock (page 930)
- ½ stick (4 tablespoons) unsalted butter
- 1 medium onion, finely chopped
- 2 medium zucchini, cut into ¼-inch dice
- 1 large carrot, cut into ¼-inch dice
- ½ cup finely grated Parmigiano-Reggiano
- 2 teaspoons minced fresh flat-leaf parsley
- Freshly ground black pepper

Put barley in a bowl, add water to cover by 2 inches, and let soak for at least 6 hours. Drain.

Bring stock to a simmer in a large saucepan. Reduce heat and keep at a bare simmer.

Melt 2 tablespoons butter in a 5-quart heavy pot over moderately low heat. Add onion and cook, stirring occasionally, until softened, about 5 minutes. Add barley and 2 cups stock and cook at a slow boil, stirring frequently, until some stock is absorbed, 6 to 10 minutes. Continue to add stock, 1 cup at a time, stirring frequently and letting each addition be partially absorbed before adding next, until about half of stock has been added, about 20 minutes. Stir in zucchini and carrot and continue to cook, adding stock ½ cup at a time, until barley is tender, about 20 minutes more. (Mixture will be soupy; you may have leftover stock.)

Stir in cheese, remaining 2 tablespoons butter, parsley, and pepper to taste. Remove from heat and let stand for 5 minutes before serving.

COOK'S NOTE

■ The barley can soak in the refrigerator, covered, for up to 1 day.

Wheat Berries with Pecans

SERVES 6

ACTIVE TIME: 15 MINUTES ■ START TO FINISH: 1¼ HOURS

■ Wheat berries, which are what's milled into flour, have a nutlike sweetness and gratifying chewiness. They are often labeled "hard" or "soft" wheat in natural foods stores, but if they are unlabeled, you can presume that they're hard wheat, especially if they are dark red. For this recipe we prefer the hard-wheat (high-protein) kind to the soft-wheat (low-protein) kind. If you can find only soft-wheat berries, subtract ten minutes from the cooking time. Like all grains, wheat berries can turn musty with age, so buy them from a source with a high turnover. Toasted pecans make this dish a little more sophisticated; it would be a terrific addition to the Thanksgiving table. ■

- 2 cups (12 ounces) hard-wheat berries
- 2 tablespoons unsalted butter
- 1½ teaspoons vegetable oil
- 1 medium onion, chopped
- 1 large garlic clove, finely chopped
- 1 teaspoon salt, or to taste
- ¼ teaspoon freshly ground black pepper
- 1 cup (about 4 ounces) pecans, toasted (see Tips, page 938) and chopped

Cook wheat berries in a 4-quart saucepan of boiling (unsalted) water, uncovered, until tender, about 1 hour. Drain in a large sieve.

Meanwhile, after wheat berries have cooked for about 45 minutes, melt butter with oil in a 12-inch heavy skillet over moderate heat. Add onion and cook, stirring, until softened, about 6 minutes. Add garlic and cook, stirring, until fragrant, about 1 minute.

Stir in wheat berries, salt, pepper, and pecans.

COOK'S NOTE

■ The wheat berries can be cooked up to 1 day ahead, cooled completely, and refrigerated, covered. Reheat in a baking dish, covered, in a 350°F oven for about 30 minutes, then stir in the pecans, salt, and pepper.

Basic Polenta

MAKES ABOUT 10 CUPS; SERVES 8 TO 10

ACTIVE TIME: 15 MINUTES ■ START TO FINISH: 1 HOUR

■ Polenta has been a staple in Italy since the early days of Rome. The porridge was originally made with millet, which was superseded by corn in the mid-sixteenth century, when it arrived from the New World. Now the word *polenta* has come to mean both the dish—basically, cornmeal mush—and the cornmeal itself. The secret to getting the right consistency is long, slow cooking, so that it cooks all the way through. The "no stirring" method in this recipe is based on one from Paula Wolfert, the Mediterranean cooking authority. You do stir the polenta, but not constantly, as you do in strictly traditional recipes. ■

- 8 cups water
- 2 teaspoons salt
- 2 cups (10 ounces) polenta (not quick-cooking) or yellow cornmeal (not stone-ground)

Bring water and salt to a boil in a 4-quart heavy saucepan. Add polenta in a thin stream, whisking constantly. Cook over moderate heat, whisking, for 2 minutes. Reduce heat to low, cover, and simmer, stirring for 1 minute after every 10 minutes of cooking, until very thick, about 45 minutes total. Serve warm.

COOK'S NOTE

■ The polenta can be kept, covered, at room temperature for 20 minutes after cooking; do not let it stand longer, or it will solidify.

Creamy Parmesan Polenta

MAKES ABOUT 4 CUPS; SERVES 4
ACTIVE TIME: 15 MINUTES ■ START TO FINISH: 1 HOUR

■ This soft, creamy polenta, a wonderfully warming addition to many meals, is enriched with lots of flavorful, salty Parmigiano-Reggiano. ■

- 3 cups water
- ½ teaspoon salt
- ¾ cup polenta (not quick-cooking) or yellow cornmeal (not stone-ground)
- 1 cup finely grated Parmigiano-Reggiano (about 2 ounces), or to taste
- 1 tablespoon unsalted butter
- Salt and freshly ground black pepper

Bring water and salt to a boil in a 2-quart heavy nonstick saucepan. Add polenta in a thin stream, whisking constantly. Cook over moderate heat, whisking, for 2 minutes. Reduce heat to low, cover, and simmer, stirring for 1 minute after every 10 minutes of cooking, until very thick, about 45 minutes total.

Remove polenta from heat and stir in cheese, butter, and salt and pepper to taste. Serve immediately.

Baked Polenta with Parmesan

SERVES 4 TO 6
ACTIVE TIME: 20 MINUTES ■ START TO FINISH: 2½ HOURS (INCLUDES CHILLING)

■ The consistency of polenta varies according to how it is cooked. It may be spooned up directly from the pot, like grits, or allowed to cool and become firm and then be broiled, sautéed, or baked, as it is here. After baking, simply pop it under the broiler to give it a cheese crust. ■

- 4 cups water
- 1 teaspoon salt
- 1 cup polenta (not quick-cooking) or yellow cornmeal (not stone-ground)
- ½ stick (4 tablespoons) unsalted butter
- Freshly ground black pepper
- 6 tablespoons finely grated Parmigiano-Reggiano

Bring water and salt to a boil in a 2- to 3-quart heavy saucepan. Add polenta in a thin stream, whisking constantly. Reduce heat to moderately low and cook, stirring constantly, until polenta is very thick, about 15 minutes.

Remove polenta from heat and stir in butter and pepper to taste. Spoon polenta into a well-buttered 8-inch square flameproof shallow baking dish (not glass) and smooth top. Sprinkle with Parmesan and refrigerate, covered, for at least 1 hour.

Put a rack in middle of oven and preheat oven to 400°F.

Bake polenta for 25 minutes, or until heated through. Remove from oven. Set broiler rack about 4 inches from heat and turn oven to broil.

Broil polenta until lightly browned, about 3 minutes. Cut into squares and serve immediately.

COOK'S NOTE

- The cooked polenta, with the Parmesan, can be refrigerated for up to 1 day. Bake and broil just before serving.

Broiled Polenta with Tomato Sauce

SERVES 4 AS A MAIN COURSE
ACTIVE TIME: 40 MINUTES ■ START TO FINISH: 2¼ HOURS (INCLUDES MAKING POLENTA)

■ If you're tired of pasta with tomato sauce, try polenta instead—the combination is an Italian standby. Broiling is an easy alternative to sautéing individual slices of firm polenta. ■

½ recipe (5 cups) Basic Polenta (page 264), still warm
1 cup finely grated Fontina, preferably Italian (about 4 ounces)
2 tablespoons olive oil, plus additional for brushing
1½ cups diced (¼-inch) onions
Salt
1 garlic clove, finely chopped
1 (28- to 32-ounce) can whole tomatoes in juice
1 tablespoon chopped fresh flat-leaf parsley
ACCOMPANIMENT: finely grated Parmigiano-Reggiano

Stir together warm polenta and Fontina in a bowl until smooth. Pour into a lightly oiled shallow 1½-quart metal or glass bowl and cool completely, about 1 hour (polenta will firm as it cools).

Meanwhile, heat oil in a 12-inch skillet over moderately high heat until hot but not smoking. Add onions, season with salt, and cook, stirring, until golden and tender, about 10 minutes. Add garlic and cook, stirring, for 1 minute. Add tomatoes, with their juice, stirring to break up tomatoes, and bring to a simmer. Reduce heat, cover, and simmer for 30 minutes. Stir in parsley and keep sauce warm over very low heat.

Set broiler rack about 3 inches from heat and preheat broiler. Lightly oil a baking sheet with sides.

Unmold polenta onto a cutting board and cut into ¾-inch-thick slices. Arrange slices in one layer on baking sheet and brush with oil.

Broil polenta until edges are golden, about 3 minutes. Turn slices over and broil until edges are golden, about 3 minutes more. Arrange polenta on a platter and spoon sauce over it. Serve with cheese.

COOK'S NOTE

- The polenta can be cooked (but not broiled) up to 2 days ahead and refrigerated, covered, in the bowl.

Drunken Beans

SERVES 4 TO 6
ACTIVE TIME: 20 MINUTES ■ START TO FINISH: 45 MINUTES PLUS SOAKING TIME FOR BEANS

■ This smoky, salty, spicy interplay of beans, bacon, onion, chiles, and beer is an excellent side to almost any Mexican meal—a *taquiza,* or taco party, for instance—as well as anything from the grill. The cooked beans are whole, perfectly tender, and swimming in a generous amount of broth. ■

2 cups (1 pound) dried pinto beans, picked over and rinsed
½ pound bacon (8 slices), chopped
1 large white onion, chopped
1 garlic clove, finely chopped
1 tablespoon dried oregano, preferably Mexican (see Sources), crumbled
6 cups water
½ cup sliced pickled jalapeño chiles
1 (12-ounce) bottle dark Mexican beer, such as Negra Modelo or Dos Equis
2 teaspoons salt, or to taste

Soak beans in cold water to cover by 2 inches, refrigerated, for at least 8 hours (or see opposite page for quick-soaking procedure). Drain.

Put a rack in middle of oven and preheat oven to 300°F.

Cook bacon, onion, garlic, and oregano in a 6- to 7-quart ovenproof pot over moderately high heat, stirring and scraping up any brown bits, until onion is lightly browned. Add beans, water, jalapeños, and beer and bring to a boil.

Cover pot, transfer to oven, and bake beans until soft, 1½ to 2 hours. (Add additional water if beans begin to dry out; mixture should be soupy and beans very soft but not falling apart.)

Stir in salt and bake beans, covered, for 10 minutes more. Check seasoning and add more salt if necessary.

COOK'S NOTE

- The beans can be cooked up to 2 days ahead. Cool, uncovered, then refrigerate, covered. Reheat, covered, over low heat.

Smoky Black Beans

SERVES 4

ACTIVE TIME: 20 MINUTES ■ START TO FINISH: 40 MINUTES

■ Using canned beans makes this recipe relatively quick. The chipotle in adobo sauce gives the dish a little smoky kick, and the sweetness of the orange juice balances the heat of the chile. The beans are delicious on their own, but combined with rice, cheese, and fresh vegetables, they make a terrific filling for burritos. This recipe is from one of our readers, William Lee, of New York City. ■

- 1 canned chipotle chile in adobo (see Glossary), minced, or 1 dried chipotle chile
- 1 small onion, minced
- 2 teaspoons olive oil
- 2 (15- to 16-ounce) cans black beans, drained and rinsed
- 1 cup water
- ½ cup fresh orange juice (from about 2 juice oranges)
- ½ teaspoon salt

If using dried chipotle, soak in boiling water to cover in a bowl for 5 minutes. Drain and mince.

Cook onion in oil in a 2- to 3-quart heavy saucepan over moderately low heat, stirring, until softened, 4 to 5 minutes. Add chipotle and cook, stirring, for 2 minutes. Add beans, water, and orange juice, bring to a simmer, and simmer, mashing beans about 8 times with a potato masher, until slightly thickened, about 20 minutes. Stir in salt.

QUICK-SOAKING DRIED BEANS

Soaking beans overnight in preparation for cooking them the next day is something that really organized people do. Bully for them. More often than not, we find ourselves fast-tracking a meal, and we use the quick-soak method. It still takes an hour, but by the time the beans are done, you'll have chopped up the rest of your ingredients or assembled the other dinner components.

Put the beans in a saucepan and cover with cold water by 2 inches. Bring to a boil and boil for 2 minutes, then remove from the heat and let the beans soak, covered, for 1 hour. Drain.

Cuban Black Beans

SERVES 6 TO 8

ACTIVE TIME: 15 MINUTES ■ START TO FINISH: 29 HOURS (INCLUDES SOAKING BEANS AND OVERNIGHT CHILLING)

■ For tender beans in a creamy liquid, simmer them very slowly over low heat. Making them a day ahead allows the flavors to develop fully. This recipe is from the *Gourmet* contributor Elizabeth Perez. She learned it from her mother, Bettina Perez, who, notwithstanding her New York Italian and Polish parentage, became the best Cuban cook in the family. ■

- 1 pound (about 2 cups) dried black beans, picked over and rinsed
- 3–4 bacon slices
- 1 large onion, finely chopped
- 1 large green bell pepper, cored, seeded, and finely chopped
- 2 tablespoons cider vinegar
- 2 Turkish bay leaves or 1 California bay leaf
- 1¼ teaspoons salt, or to taste

Put beans in a 4-quart heavy saucepan, add hot water to cover by 2 inches, and soak for 1 hour.

Bring beans to a boil in soaking water, adding more water if necessary to keep beans covered by 1½ inches and skimming foam. Reduce heat and simmer gently, partially covered, until beans are just tender, about 1 hour.

Meanwhile, cook bacon in a large heavy skillet over moderate heat until golden and crisp. Transfer to paper towels to drain and add 1 tablespoon bacon fat to beans (reserve bacon and remaining fat, if desired, for another use).

Stir remaining ingredients into beans and simmer gently, partially covered, until beans are tender and liquid is thickened, 2 to 3 hours more. Discard bay leaves.

Cool beans, uncovered, then refrigerate, covered, for at least 1 day. To serve, reheat, covered, over low heat.

COOK'S NOTE

- The beans can be refrigerated for up to 5 days.

Black Bean Chili

SERVES 4 AS A MAIN COURSE
ACTIVE TIME: 30 MINUTES ■ START TO FINISH: 3 HOURS PLUS SOAKING TIME FOR BEANS

■ There are lots of meatless chilis in the world, but this one has far more finesse than most. It's from the renowned vegetarian restaurant Greens, in San Francisco, and is perfect for a blustery day—or anytime the fog rolls in. ■

- 1 pound (about 2 cups) dried black beans, picked over and rinsed
- 1 tablespoon cumin seeds
- 2 teaspoons paprika
- ½ teaspoon cayenne
- 1 teaspoon dried oregano, crumbled
- 1 small dried pasilla chile (see Glossary), stem and seeds discarded, chile coarsely chopped
- 3 tablespoons vegetable or peanut oil
- 1 medium onion, finely chopped
- 1 green bell pepper, cored, seeded, and finely chopped
- 4 garlic cloves, minced
- 1 tablespoon chopped canned chipotle chiles in adobo (see Glossary)
- 1 Turkish bay leaf or ½ California bay leaf
- 6 cups water
- 1 (14-ounce) can whole tomatoes in juice, drained (juice reserved) and chopped
- Salt
- ½ cup chopped fresh cilantro

ACCOMPANIMENT: sour cream
SPECIAL EQUIPMENT: an electric coffee/spice grinder

Soak beans in water to cover by 2 inches, refrigerated, for at least 8 hours (or see page 267 for quick-soaking procedure). Drain.

Toast cumin, paprika, cayenne, and oregano in a dry small heavy skillet over moderate heat, stirring constantly, until fragrant and a shade or two darker, about 2 minutes (watch carefully, as spices burn easily). Transfer to a small bowl.

Finely grind pasilla in coffee/spice grinder, then stir into spices.

Heat oil in a 5- to 6-quart wide heavy pot over moderately high heat until hot but not smoking. Add onion and bell pepper and cook, stirring occasionally, until onion is golden, 6 to 8 minutes. Add garlic, chipotles, and spice mixture, reduce heat to moderate, and cook, stirring occasionally, for 5 minutes. Add beans, bay leaf, and water, bring to a simmer, and simmer, covered, until beans are tender, 1 to 1½ hours.

Add tomatoes, with their juice, and salt to taste and simmer, uncovered, for 15 minutes, or until chili is slightly thickened. Discard bay leaf. Just before serving, stir in cilantro. Serve with sour cream.

COOK'S NOTE

- You can use 4 large ripe tomatoes, peeled (see Tips, page 940), seeded, and chopped, in place of the canned.

Brazilian-Style Black Bean Stew

SERVES 8 AS A MAIN COURSE
ACTIVE TIME: 40 MINUTES ■ START TO FINISH: 3 HOURS PLUS SOAKING TIME FOR BEANS

■ This robust dish is our homage to a Brazilian *feijoada* ("fay-*zhwa*-duh"), a bean stew packed with a staggering array of fresh and preserved meats. Our faux *feijoada*, assembled with supermarket ingredients for the practically inclined, makes a big impression. Serve it with white rice and an orange and bitter-green salad. A flan for dessert adds a little more Latino flair. ■

- 2 pounds (about 4 cups) dried black beans, picked over and rinsed
- 2½ quarts water
- 6 lean bacon slices, finely chopped
- 1 pound lean boneless beef chuck, cut into 2-inch pieces
- 1 pound Spanish chorizo (spicy cured pork sausage; see Glossary), cut into 1-inch-long pieces
- ½ pound Canadian bacon or boneless smoked pork butt, cut into 1-inch pieces
- ¼ cup olive oil
- 1½ cups finely chopped onions
- 1 tablespoon finely chopped garlic
- 1 (28-ounce) can whole tomatoes in juice, drained and chopped
- 2 tablespoons minced seeded fresh or pickled jalapeño chile, or to taste
- Tabasco to taste
- Salt and freshly ground black pepper
- ½ pound kale, coarse stems discarded and leaves finely chopped
- ½ cup long-grain white rice
- ½ cup finely chopped fresh cilantro
- ⅓ cup fresh orange juice

ACCOMPANIMENT: warm flour tortillas

Soak beans in cold water to cover by 2 inches, refrigerated, for at least 8 hours (or see page 267 for quick-soaking procedure). Drain well.

Bring water to a boil in a 6- to 8-quart heavy pot. Stir in beans and chopped bacon and bring to a boil, skimming froth. Reduce heat and simmer, covered, for 45 minutes.

Stir in beef, cover, and simmer, stirring occasionally and skimming fat, for 45 minutes.

Stir in chorizo and Canadian bacon and simmer, covered, until beans are tender, about 30 minutes. Skim fat from surface and remove from heat.

Heat oil in a deep 12-inch skillet over moderately low heat. Add onions and garlic and cook, stirring occasionally, until onions are softened, about 8 minutes. Stir in tomatoes, jalapeño, Tabasco, and salt and pepper to taste and simmer, stirring occasionally, for 5 minutes.

With a slotted spoon, transfer 2 cups beans to skillet and, with back of a wooden spoon, mash them thoroughly into onion mixture, gradually adding 2 cups bean cooking liquid. Simmer, stirring occasionally, until thickened, about 15 minutes.

Add onion mixture to beans remaining in pot. Stir in kale and rice and simmer, stirring occasionally, until rice is tender, about 20 minutes.

Stir in cilantro, orange juice, and salt and pepper to taste. Serve with warm tortillas.

Maple Baked Beans

SERVES 8
ACTIVE TIME: 15 MINUTES ■ START TO FINISH: 3½ HOURS PLUS SOAKING TIME FOR BEANS

■ The months of March and April are sugaring season up north, when the sap is running from still-bare sugar maple trees. In one of Quebec's *cabanes à sucre,* or sugar shacks, you'll find treats like baked beans flavored with pure maple syrup instead of the more usual molasses. A far cry from store-bought baked beans, these aren't hard to prepare (and the heat from the oven keeps the kitchen warm). Serve them as part of a buffet or for Sunday night supper. ■

- 2 cups (about 14 ounces) dried navy beans, picked over and rinsed
- 7 ounces salt pork (rinsed if crusted with salt) or thick-sliced bacon, cut into ¼-inch dice
- 1 cup chopped onions
- 2 teaspoons salt
- ½ teaspoon freshly ground black pepper
- ⅔ cup pure maple syrup
- 1 teaspoon dry mustard
- 4 cups water

Soak beans in cold water to cover by 2 inches, refrigerated, for at least 8 hours (or see page 267 for quick-soaking procedure). Drain.

Put a rack in middle of oven and preheat oven to 300°F.

Put beans in an ovenproof 3-quart wide shallow pot or flameproof baking dish. Add remaining ingredients and stir to combine. Bring to a boil, then cover tightly, transfer to oven, and bake until beans are just tender, about 2 hours.

Uncover pot and bake until most of liquid is absorbed and top is slightly crusty, 1 to 1½ hours more.

Slow-Cooked Tuscan Beans

SERVES 6

ACTIVE TIME: 15 MINUTES ■ START TO FINISH: 3¾ HOURS (IF MADE IN A TERRA-COTTA POT)

■ If you take real care with beans, treating them gently and simply, you have something sublime. In this recipe from the Italian cooking authority Faith Heller Willinger, they're infused with lovely, subtle flavors. We tried cooking the beans two ways: in a traditional Italian terra-cotta bean pot (called a *fagioliera*), as Willinger does, and in a regular heavy pot. We prefer the bean pot (see Sources), because it cooks the beans more gently, allowing them to retain their shape and texture; they seem more flavorful too. The slow, easy cooking of this method makes it unnecessary to presoak the beans.

In Italy, each serving is dressed with good olive oil at the table, and any leftover beans (which aren't dressed) are used in the next day's soup or reheated with more garlic and sage. ■

- 1 pound (2½ cups) dried white beans, such as great northern or navy, picked over and rinsed
- 10 cups water
- 2 fresh sage sprigs
- 1 Turkish bay leaf or ½ California bay leaf
- 1 head garlic
- 1 tablespoon coarse sea salt
- Freshly ground black pepper

ACCOMPANIMENT: fine extra-virgin olive oil, preferably Tuscan

If using a terra-cotta pot for the first time, soak it in water to cover for at least 6 hours; drain.

Put beans, water, sage, bay leaf, and whole head of garlic in bean pot or a 5-quart heavy pot. Cover and slowly bring to a simmer over low heat (this can take 2¾ hours in bean pot or 1 hour in regular pot). Simmer beans until tender but not mushy, about 45 minutes in bean pot or 35 to 40 minutes in metal pot. Remove from heat and cool, covered, for 15 minutes.

Stir in sea salt. Drain almost all cooking liquid from beans (reserve for another use, if desired). Discard sage sprigs, bay leaf, and garlic, and season beans with sea salt and pepper to taste.

Dress beans with oil at the table.

COOK'S NOTE

■ The beans can be cooked up to 1 day ahead. Cool completely, uncovered, then refrigerate, covered. Reheat, covered, over low heat.

Escarole, Sausage, and White Bean Stew

SERVES 4 TO 6 AS A MAIN COURSE

ACTIVE TIME: 40 MINUTES ■ START TO FINISH: 40 MINUTES

■ This is a good way to turn canned beans into a hearty main dish in under an hour. White beans are wonderful cooked with sausage and pleasantly bitter escarole, a green that looks like a head of lettuce but is in fact an endive. The recipe is from *American Brasserie*, by the Chicago chefs Rick Tramonto and Gale Gand, and it sums up their great affection for often unsung and unpretentious ingredients. ■

- 1 teaspoon olive oil
- 1 pound bulk Italian sausage (sweet and/or hot), broken into 1-inch pieces
- 5 large garlic cloves, minced
- ½ teaspoon red pepper flakes, or to taste
- 1 head escarole, trimmed and cut into 2-inch pieces
- 3 cups cooked or canned white beans, such as great northern or navy, drained and rinsed if canned
- 3 cups chicken stock or store-bought low-sodium broth
- ½ stick (4 tablespoons) unsalted butter
- ½ cup finely grated Parmigiano-Reggiano or a combination of Parmigiano and pecorino Romano
- 2 plum tomatoes, diced
- 2 tablespoons chopped fresh flat-leaf parsley
- Kosher salt and freshly ground black pepper

ACCOMPANIMENT: extra-virgin olive oil for drizzling and shaved or grated Parmigiano-Reggiano

Heat oil in a deep 12-inch skillet over moderately high heat until hot but not smoking. Brown sausage, stirring, for 7 to 10 minutes. Add garlic and red pepper flakes and cook, stirring, until garlic is softened, about 2 minutes. Add escarole and cook, stirring, until wilted, about 2 minutes. Add beans and cook, stirring, for 1 minute.

Add stock and bring to a gentle boil. Stir in butter, cheese, tomatoes, and half of parsley and cook, stirring, until butter is melted and stew is heated through. Season with salt and pepper.

Ladle stew into bowls and sprinkle with remaining parsley. Serve with extra-virgin olive oil and Parmesan.

White Bean Gratin

SERVES 6 TO 8
ACTIVE TIME: 35 MINUTES ■ START TO FINISH: 2 HOURS PLUS SOAKING TIME FOR BEANS

■ If you are bored with rice and potatoes, try this. It makes a satisfying side dish (think leg of lamb), especially in cold weather. ■

- 1 pound (2½ cups) dried white beans, such as great northern or navy, picked over and rinsed
- 1½ pounds onions, chopped (4 cups)
- ¼ cup peeled garlic cloves, plus 1 garlic clove, minced
- 1 carrot, halved
- 1 celery rib, halved
- 3 fresh thyme sprigs
- 2½ quarts water
- 6 tablespoons olive oil
- 2 teaspoons white wine vinegar
- Salt and freshly ground black pepper
- ½ cup fine dry bread crumbs
- 1 cup coarsely grated Gruyère (about 4 ounces)
- ½ cup finely grated Parmigiano-Reggiano

Soak beans in cold water to cover by 2 inches, refrigerated, for at least 8 hours (or see page 267 for quick-soaking procedure). Drain.

Transfer beans to a 6- to 8-quart pot and stir in onions, whole garlic cloves, carrot, celery, thyme, and water. Bring to a simmer and simmer until beans are tender, 35 to 45 minutes.

Drain beans in a colander set over a large bowl. Discard garlic cloves, carrot, celery, and thyme. Transfer beans to a 3-quart gratin dish or other shallow baking dish. Return cooking liquid to pot and boil until reduced to about 1½ cups, 5 to 10 minutes.

Put a rack in middle of oven and preheat oven to 425°F.

Combine 1 cup beans, reduced cooking liquid, 3 tablespoons oil, vinegar, and salt to taste in a blender and purée. Stir purée into whole beans and season with salt and pepper.

Toss together bread crumbs, Gruyère, Parmesan, and minced garlic in a bowl, then sprinkle over gratin. Drizzle with remaining 3 tablespoons oil. Bake gratin until bubbling and golden, about 20 minutes.

COOK'S NOTE

■ The gratin can be prepared, without the bread crumbs, up to 2 days ahead and refrigerated, covered. Bring to room temperature before proceeding.

Easy Cassoulet

SERVES 6 TO 8 AS A MAIN COURSE
ACTIVE TIME: 1¼ HOURS ■ START TO FINISH: 4 HOURS
PLUS SOAKING TIME FOR BEANS

■ This cassoulet has all the flavor of labor-intensive traditional versions, yet it doesn't take days to make. A lifesaver during the holiday season, it can be assembled a day ahead, so all you have to do is slip it into the oven when guests arrive. You can mix drinks and share conversation as its wonderful aroma fills your house. When the perfume reaches its peak, simply carry the cassoulet to the table and announce that dinner is ready. ■

- 1 pound (2½ cups) dried white beans, such as great northern or navy, picked over and rinsed
- 8 cups cold water
- 2 cups beef stock or store-bought broth
- 1 tablespoon tomato paste
- 2 cups chopped onions (about ¾ pound)
- 3 tablespoons finely chopped garlic
- 1 (3-inch) piece celery, cut into thirds
- 3 fresh thyme sprigs
- 1 Turkish bay leaf or ½ California bay leaf
- 3 whole cloves
- 3 fresh flat-leaf parsley sprigs, plus ½ cup chopped leaves
- ¼ teaspoon black peppercorns
- 1 (14-ounce) can stewed tomatoes, puréed or finely chopped (with juice)
- 1¾ pounds confit duck legs (see Sources)
- 1–2 tablespoons olive oil (if necessary)
- 1 pound cooked garlic pork sausage (see Sources) or smoked pork kielbasa, cut into ⅓-inch-thick slices
- 2 cups coarse fresh bread crumbs, preferably from a baguette
- 1½ teaspoons salt
- ½ teaspoon freshly ground black pepper

SPECIAL EQUIPMENT: cheesecloth; kitchen string; a 4½- to 5-quart casserole dish (3–4 inches deep)

SOAK AND COOK THE BEANS: Soak beans in cold water to cover by 2 inches, refrigerated, for at least 8 hours (or see page 267 for quick-soaking procedure). Drain.

Transfer beans to a 6- to 8-quart pot, add cold water, stock, tomato paste, onions, and 2 tablespoons garlic, and bring to a boil. Wrap celery, thyme, bay leaf, cloves, parsley sprigs, and peppercorns in a square of cheesecloth and tie with string to make a bouquet garni. Add to beans, reduce heat, and simmer, uncovered, until beans are almost tender, 45 minutes to 1 hour.

Stir in tomatoes, with their juice, and simmer until beans are just tender, about 15 minutes more.

MEANWHILE, PREPARE THE DUCK AND SAUSAGE: Remove all skin and fat from duck legs and cut skin and fat into ½-inch pieces. Separate duck meat from bones, leaving it in large pieces, and transfer to a bowl. Add bones to simmering beans.

Combine duck skin and fat with ¼ cup cold water in a 10-inch heavy skillet and cook, stirring, over moderate heat until water has evaporated and fat is rendered, about 5 minutes. Continue to cook, stirring frequently, until skin is crisp, 3 to 6 minutes more.

With a slotted spoon, transfer cracklings to paper towels to drain, leaving fat in skillet. You should have about ¼ cup fat; if not, add olive oil as necessary.

Brown sausage in batches in fat in skillet over moderate heat. Transfer to bowl with duck meat and set skillet aside.

Put a rack in bottom third of oven and preheat oven to 350°F.

MAKE THE BREAD CRUMB TOPPING: Add remaining 1 tablespoon garlic to fat in skillet and cook over moderate heat, stirring, for 1 minute. Stir in bread crumbs and cook, stirring, until pale golden, about 2 minutes. Remove from heat and stir in chopped parsley, ½ teaspoon salt, ¼ teaspoon pepper, and cracklings. Set aside.

ASSEMBLE THE CASSEROLE: Remove bouquet garni and duck bones from beans and discard. Stir in sausage, duck meat, remaining 1 teaspoon salt, and remaining ¼ teaspoon pepper.

Ladle cassoulet into casserole dish, distributing meat and beans evenly. (Meat and beans should be level with liquid; if they are submerged, ladle excess liquid back into pot and boil until reduced slightly, then pour back into casserole dish.) Spread bread crumb topping evenly over cassoulet.

Bake, uncovered, until cassoulet is bubbling and crust is golden, about 1 hour.

COOK'S NOTE

- The cassoulet can be assembled up to 1 day ahead. Let cool before adding topping, then top and refrigerate, covered. Let stand at room temperature for 30 minutes before baking.

Cassoulet de Canard

SERVES 10 AS A MAIN COURSE
ACTIVE TIME: 2 HOURS ■ START TO FINISH: 2 DAYS

■ Never forget that the simple white bean is the star of the show here. The Paris-based writer Michael Lewis adapted this recipe from one in Julia Child's *Mastering the Art of French Cooking,* changing the meats (a lot) and the seasonings (a bit). He also tinkered with cooking times and the sequence of events. As you can see, this cassoulet is a two-day adventure but well worth the time and energy: it is absolutely delicious and will leave dinner guests half crazed with equal parts envy and awe. ■

- 2½ pounds (about 6¼ cups) dried white beans, such as great northern or navy, picked over and rinsed
- ½ pound fresh pork rind
- 2½ pounds confit duck legs (see Sources)
- 6 fresh parsley stems (without leaves)
- 4 fresh thyme sprigs
- 5 whole cloves
- 12 garlic cloves
- 1 (1-pound) piece slab bacon, halved crosswise
- 3 cups chopped onions (about 1 pound)
- 1 teaspoon salt
- 1 cup goose fat (see Sources)
- 1 pound meaty mutton or lamb bones, cracked by the butcher
- 5 Turkish bay leaves or 2½ California bay leaves
- 4 cups Beef Stock (page 928; not canned broth)
- 6 large tomatoes (3 pounds total), peeled (see Tips, page 938), halved, seeded, and chopped
- 1 (750-milliliter) bottle dry white wine
- 2 teaspoons freshly ground black pepper
- 2½ pounds fresh garlic pork sausages (not sweet or very spicy), such as *saucisson à l'ail au vin rouge* or *saucisse de canard à l'Armagnac* (see Sources), or a mixture of the two
- 1½ cups coarse dry bread crumbs
- 1 cup chopped fresh flat-leaf parsley

SPECIAL EQUIPMENT: cheesecloth; kitchen string; a well-seasoned large ridged grill pan; a wide 10-quart enameled cast-iron pot

ON DAY 1: Bring 5 quarts of water to a boil in an 8-quart heavy pot. Add beans and boil, uncovered, for 1½ minutes. Remove from heat and let soak for 50 minutes.

Meanwhile, put pork rind in a 3-quart saucepan of cold water and bring to a boil. Boil for 1 minute. Drain and rinse under cold running water, then repeat. Cut the pork rind into 2-inch pieces.

Remove skin from duck legs; discard. Scrape off and discard fat from duck legs. Shred meat (discard bones); set aside.

Wrap parsley stems, thyme, cloves, and 8 garlic cloves in a square of cheesecloth and tie with string to make a bouquet garni.

Add pork rind pieces, slab bacon, 1 cup onions, bouquet garni, and salt to beans and bring to a simmer. Simmer, covered, for 1¼ hours, skimming regularly. Remove from heat and cool, uncovered, then cover pot and refrigerate.

Meanwhile, heat goose fat in enameled cast-iron pot over moderate heat until it smokes. Add mutton bones and cook, stirring occasionally, until browned, about 5 minutes. Remove bones and set aside on a plate. When cooled, remove any meat from bones and reserve. Add remaining 2 cups onions to pot and cook, stirring, until browned, about 15 minutes.

Add browned bones, shredded duck, and any mutton to pot of onions. Add bay leaves, stock, tomatoes, remaining 4 garlic cloves, white wine, and pepper and bring to a simmer. Reduce heat, cover, and simmer for 1½ hours. Remove from heat and cool to room temperature, uncovered, then cover pot and refrigerate overnight.

ON DAY 2: Prick sausages with a fork. Cook slowly in grill pan over moderately low heat for 20 minutes to render fat. (Sausages should still be slightly undercooked inside.) Transfer to a cutting board and cool slightly, then slice into ¼-inch-thick rounds.

Remove and discard bones and bay leaves from onion pot. With a slotted spoon, transfer duck and any mutton to a plate. Reserve cooking liquid in pot.

Remove bacon from beans and cut into tiny fat-free pieces. Discard bacon fat. Remove pork rind and bouquet garni from beans and discard.

Pour reserved meat cooking liquid into beans. Bring to a simmer over moderately high heat, stirring occasionally, and simmer for 5 minutes, skimming any foam. Remove from heat and let sit for 5 minutes.

Put a rack in middle of oven and preheat oven to 375°F.

Spread one layer of beans in bottom of enameled cast-iron pot. Layer half of sausages and bacon on top, then top with another layer of beans, half of duck (and any mutton), and another layer of beans. Repeat layering, ending with a layer of beans. Add enough remaining liquid from bean pot to cover beans. Sprinkle with bread crumbs and chopped parsley.

Bring to a simmer, uncovered, over moderately low heat. Transfer to oven and bake for 20 minutes. Break through bread crumbs in several places with a spoon, allowing the liquid to spread, then reduce heat to 350°F and bake for 40 minutes more. Serve hot.

Chesapeake Bay Baked Lima Beans

SERVES 8 TO 12
ACTIVE TIME: 20 MINUTES ■ START TO FINISH: 3½ HOURS PLUS SOAKING TIME FOR BEANS

■ This dish is made with dried limas, not fresh ones. (They turn from pale green to creamy white when dried.) They're baked in a tomatoey, barbecue-style sauce that gets a mild smokiness from thick-sliced bacon. The recipe is from the late Eve Norton, of New York City's Greenwich Village, a reader of many years. On "gardening day" in her neighborhood community garden, she simmered a ham on top of the stove and made these beans with the resulting "ham liquor" (simmering liquid) instead of chicken broth. If you have some on hand, you'll want to do that too. ■

- 1½ pounds (about 3 cups) dried lima beans, preferably giant, picked over and rinsed
- 1 (28-ounce) can crushed tomatoes in purée
- ⅓ cup molasses (not robust or blackstrap)
- 2 teaspoons dry mustard
- 2 cups chicken stock or store-bought low-sodium broth
- Salt and freshly ground black pepper
- 1–2 large Spanish (yellow) onions, cut into ¼-inch-thick rounds
- ¾ pound thick-sliced bacon (9–10 slices)

Soak lima beans in cold water to cover by 2 inches, refrigerated, for at least 8 hours (or see page 267 for quick-soaking procedure). Drain.

Transfer beans to a 6-quart pot, add cold water to cover by 2 inches, and bring to a simmer, skimming off any foam. Simmer beans, partially covered, until just tender, about 40 minutes. Drain.

Put a rack in middle of oven and preheat oven to 350°F. Grease a 4- to 5-quart shallow baking dish or two 2-quart dishes.

Stir together tomatoes, molasses, mustard, stock, and salt and pepper to taste in a large bowl and toss with beans. Transfer to greased baking dish. Cover bean mixture completely with onion rounds and top onions with bacon. Press down on top of mixture with a spatula to moisten onions.

Bake until beans have soaked up half of liquid (there should be 1 inch of liquid remaining) and bacon strips are well browned, about 2½ hours. Pat top with paper towels to absorb excess fat.

Hoppin' John

Black-Eyed Peas and Rice

SERVES 8 TO 10
ACTIVE TIME: 25 MINUTES ■ START TO FINISH: 3½ HOURS (INCLUDES MAKING RICE) PLUS SOAKING TIME FOR PEAS

■ On New Year's Day, hoppin' John is eaten all over the American South, particularly in the Low Country of South Carolina and Georgia, for good luck. It's a plain dish, lightly seasoned and best served with corn bread and a platter of braised greens (they symbolize "folding green" money) and their "pot likker." Collards are traditional, but lacinato kale, with its deep meaty savor, is delicious too. Because black-eyed peas can cook surprisingly fast, we first make a ham-hock broth to cook the peas in, giving them maximum smoky flavor. Traditionally the raw rice is added to the pot of peas, but we like to cook it separately.

This combination was probably brought to America

by slaves shipped from the rice plantations of the French West Indies to those in South Carolina. One theory suggests that the name hoppin' John is a corruption of *pois à pigeon* ("pwah-zah-pee-*jon*"), French for pigeon peas, an African crop that flourished in the Caribbean but was replaced by cowpeas and black-eyed peas in the United States. However, the food historian Karen Hess, who devotes an entire chapter to hoppin' John in her extraordinary *Carolina Rice Kitchen*, argues that the etymology is more ancient and complex, with Hindi and Malay roots. Rice and beans, after all, have sustained rich and poor alike in Asia and the Middle East for thousands of years. ■

- 1 pound (2½ cups) dried black-eyed peas, picked over and rinsed
- 2 meaty ham hocks (1¾ pounds total)
- 9 cups water
- 2 tablespoons vegetable oil
- 2 medium onions, chopped
- ¼ teaspoon salt
- 1 small (1½- to 2-inch-long) dried hot chile or ¼ teaspoon red pepper flakes
- Freshly ground black pepper

ACCOMPANIMENT: Foolproof Long-Grain Rice (page 254) and (optional) Tabasco

Soak peas in cold water to cover by 2 inches, refrigerated, for at least 8 hours (or see page 267 for quick-soaking procedure). Drain in a colander and rinse well.

Combine ham hocks and water in a deep 3½- to 4-quart saucepan, bring to a simmer, and simmer, uncovered, until meat is tender, 1½ to 2 hours. Transfer hocks to a cutting board and measure broth. If you have more than 6 cups, boil until reduced to 6 cups; if less, add enough water to total 6 cups.

When hocks are cool enough to handle, remove meat, discarding skin and bones, and chop.

Heat oil in a 5- to 6-quart heavy pot over moderately low heat. Add onions and salt and cook, covered, stirring occasionally, until softened, 10 to 12 minutes. Add chile, drained peas, ham-hock broth, and ham and simmer, partially covered, until peas are tender but not falling apart, 20 to 40 minutes. Season with salt and pepper and discard chile.

Serve spooned over rice, with Tabasco, if desired.

COOK'S NOTE

■ The peas can be made up to 3 days ahead. Cool completely, uncovered, then refrigerate, covered. Reheat over low heat, thinning with a little water if necessary.

Pickled Black-Eyed Peas

SERVES 4

ACTIVE TIME: 15 MINUTES ■ START TO FINISH: 4½ HOURS (INCLUDES CHILLING) PLUS SOAKING TIME FOR PEAS

■ The black-eyed pea, a little black-dotted legume indigenous to Africa and brought to America on slave ships, is one of our favorite dried beans. We like its texture (creamier and less starchy than that of many other dried beans), its readiness to absorb the flavors of other ingredients, and its affinity for pickling. Enthusiasts in the American West call these pickled peas "Texas caviar." Serve them on toasts or with grilled or roasted meats. ■

- 1 cup dried black-eyed peas, picked over and rinsed
- 1 yellow bell pepper, cored, seeded, and cut into ¼-inch dice
- ½ red bell pepper, cored, seeded, and cut into ¼-inch dice
- ½ jalapeño chile, seeded and minced
- ¼ cup extra-virgin olive oil
- ¼ cup white wine vinegar
- ¼ cup minced fresh chives
- 2 tablespoons minced red onion
- 1 teaspoon minced garlic
- Salt and freshly ground black pepper to taste

Soak peas in cold water to cover by 2 inches, refrigerated, for at least 8 hours (or see page 267 for quick-soaking procedure). Drain.

Transfer peas to a 3-quart saucepan, add water to cover, and bring to a simmer. Simmer until tender, about 20 minutes. Drain.

Stir peas together with remaining ingredients in a bowl. Refrigerate, covered, for at least 4 hours.

Serve peas chilled or at room temperature.

COOK'S NOTE

- The pickled peas can be refrigerated for up to 2 days.

Moroccan Chickpea Tomato Stew

SERVES 8 AS A MAIN COURSE
ACTIVE TIME: 40 MINUTES ■ START TO FINISH: 3½ HOURS PLUS SOAKING TIME FOR BEANS

■ Preserved lemons lift this dish out of the "nice but stodgy vegetarian meal" category up into the "absolutely delicious" realm. The downside is that you need to have preserved lemons on hand. But you'll be happy in the long run, because preserved lemons, which keep for months in the fridge, are an amazingly useful condiment for any savory dish to which you would add salt or lemon juice. And once you add the pulp to bloody Marys, you'll never look back. ■

- 1 pound (2⅓ cups) dried chickpeas, picked over and rinsed
- 2 (3-inch) cinnamon sticks, broken in half
- 1 teaspoon cumin seeds
- ¼ cup olive oil
- 3 large onions, thinly sliced (7 cups)
- ¾ teaspoon ground cumin
- ½ teaspoon ground coriander
- 2 (28- to 32-ounce) cans whole tomatoes in juice, drained (juice reserved) and chopped
- 1 cup raisins
- ⅓ cup chopped peel from Moroccan-Style Preserved Lemons (page 908)
- 1½ pounds spinach, coarse stems discarded (10 cups packed leaves)
- Salt and freshly ground black pepper

ACCOMPANIMENT: couscous and crusty bread

Soak chickpeas in water to cover by 2 inches, refrigerated, for at least 8 hours (or see page 267 for quick-soaking procedure). Drain.

Combine chickpeas, cinnamon, and cumin seeds in a 3-quart saucepan, add water to cover by 2 inches, and bring to a simmer. Simmer, partially covered, adding more water if necessary, until chickpeas are just tender, 1 to 1¼ hours. Discard cinnamon. Set pan aside.

Heat oil in a 6- to 8-quart heavy pot over moderate heat until hot but not smoking. Add onions and cook, stirring occasionally, until deep golden brown, about 15 minutes. Add ground cumin and coriander and cook, stirring, until fragrant, 2 to 3 minutes. Stir in chickpeas, with their cooking liquid, tomatoes, with their juice, raisins, and preserved lemon peel, bring to a simmer, and simmer, uncovered, until chickpeas are tender and liquid is slightly thickened, about 45 minutes.

Stir in spinach a heaping handful at a time and cook until wilted and just tender. Season with salt and pepper. Serve stew over couscous with crusty bread.

COOK'S NOTE

- The chickpeas can be precooked with the cinnamon and cumin up to 1 day ahead. Cool completely, then refrigerate in cooking liquid, covered.

Lentil and Brown Rice Stew

SERVES 6 TO 8 AS A MAIN COURSE
ACTIVE TIME: 25 MINUTES ■ START TO FINISH: 1¼ HOURS

■ In cold weather, when we ponder what dish will provide comfort all weekend long, we decide with remarkable frequency to make this stew. The beauty of using brown rice is that it keeps its texture during the long cooking time (white rice becomes too soft). Adding about a pound of smoked sausage makes a great dish even better. For a vegetarian meal, use vegetable stock in place of the chicken stock. ■

- 1 (28- to 32-ounce) can whole tomatoes in juice
- 5 cups chicken stock or store-bought low-sodium broth, plus additional to thin stew if desired
- 3 cups water
- 1½ cups lentils, picked over and rinsed
- 1 cup brown rice
- 3 carrots, halved lengthwise and cut crosswise into ¼-inch-wide pieces
- 1 onion, chopped
- 1 celery rib, chopped
- 3 garlic cloves, minced
- 1 teaspoon chopped fresh thyme
- 1 Turkish bay leaf or ½ California bay leaf
- ⅓–½ cup minced fresh cilantro or flat-leaf parsley (to taste)
- 2 tablespoons cider vinegar, or to taste
- 1½ teaspoons salt, or to taste
- ½ teaspoon freshly ground black pepper

Combine tomatoes, with their juice, stock, water, lentils, rice, carrots, onion, celery, garlic, thyme, and bay leaf in a 6-quart heavy pot and bring to a boil. Reduce heat, cover, and simmer, stirring occasionally, until lentils and rice are tender, 45 to 55 minutes.

Stir in cilantro, vinegar, salt, and pepper and discard bay leaf. Stew will be thick, and it will continue to thicken as it stands; if desired, thin with additional hot chicken broth or water before serving.

Lentils and Curried Rice with Fried Onions

SERVES 6

ACTIVE TIME: 45 MINUTES ■ START TO FINISH: 1 HOUR

■ You could say that lentils are the ultimate oldie-but-goody of the legume world. They were there In the Beginning—Genesis 25: 34, to be precise—as the tempting soup for which Esau gave up his birthright. They also fueled the builders of Egypt's great pyramids and sustained the Roman legions on their quest for empire. Today their popularity continues unabated because of their versatility—they're as good in a cold salad as they are in a hot soup—and the fact that they require no soaking but plump up nicely with a fifteen- to thirty-minute simmer.

This hearty dish, based on an Indian rice and lentil combination called *khichri,* is wonderful with lamb or chicken. The curried rice adds color and flavor, and the fried onions—another idea we borrowed from India—are much more than a garnish; they add a meaty savoriness. ■

- About 2 cups vegetable oil for shallow-frying, plus 2 tablespoons
- 1 pound onions, thinly sliced
- Salt
- 1 cup lentils, picked over and rinsed
- 1 cup long-grain white rice
- 1 tablespoon curry powder
- ⅛ teaspoon cayenne
- 2 cups water
- ½ cup loosely packed fresh flat-leaf parsley leaves

Heat ¼ inch oil in a 12-inch skillet over moderately high heat until hot but not smoking. Add one third of onions and fry, stirring occasionally, until golden brown, about 12 minutes. Transfer with a slotted spoon to a plate and season with salt. Fry remaining onions in 2 batches.

Combine lentils with cold well-salted water to cover by 2 inches in a 3- to 4-quart saucepan and bring to a boil. Reduce heat and cook lentils at a bare simmer until just tender, about 15 minutes. Drain in a sieve and gently rinse under cold water.

Meanwhile, heat remaining 2 tablespoons oil in a 1½- to 2-quart saucepan over high heat. Add rice and cook, stirring, for 1 minute. Add curry and cayenne and cook, stirring, for 1 minute. Add 1 teaspoon salt

and 2 cups water, bring to a boil, and boil, uncovered, stirring occasionally, until surface of rice is covered with steam holes and grains on top appear dry, about 12 minutes.

Reduce heat to low, cover pan with a tight-fitting lid, and cook for 15 minutes more. Remove rice from heat and let stand, covered, for 5 minutes.

Transfer rice to a bowl and fluff with a fork. Add lentils and parsley and toss well. Serve warm or at room temperature, topped with onions.

COOK'S NOTE

- The lentils and curried rice (but not the parsley or the fried onions) can be made and combined up to 1 day ahead and refrigerated, covered. Bring to room temperature before adding parsley and topping with the onions.

Red Lentil and Tofu Dal

SERVES 2 AS A MAIN COURSE
ACTIVE TIME: 15 MINUTES ■ START TO FINISH: 30 MINUTES

■ You won't miss meat in this dish—it's full of flavor and has a terrific texture, thanks in large part to the red lentils (their color is actually closer to coral). As they cook, they turn yellow and fall apart into a creamy purée. You can use brown lentils, but the result will be different because they hold their shape (and take a little longer to cook). In India, lentils, along with other dried legumes such as peas and beans, are called dals, and the word also refers to the dishes made from them. The creamy consistency is enhanced by the addition of tender cubes of tofu, which are remarkably similar in texture and color to *paneer,* a mild, fresh Indian cheese that's often added to dals. ■

2 tablespoons vegetable oil
1 small onion, thinly sliced
1 garlic clove, minced
1 teaspoon finely chopped peeled fresh ginger
½ cup red lentils, picked over and rinsed
3½ cups water
½ pound firm tofu
½ teaspoon cumin seeds
½ teaspoon Garam Masala (page 932) or curry powder
½ teaspoon salt
Generous pinch of cayenne
3 tablespoons chopped fresh cilantro

ACCOMPANIMENT: cooked rice

Heat 1 tablespoon oil in a 2-quart heavy saucepan over moderate heat. Add onion and garlic and cook, stirring, until golden. Add ginger and cook, stirring, for 1 minute. Add lentils and water, bring just to a boil, and gently boil, uncovered, until lentils fall apart, about 20 minutes. Remove from heat and keep warm, covered.

Meanwhile, rinse tofu and trim ends. Cut tofu into ½-inch cubes and gently press between paper towels to remove excess moisture.

When lentils are cooked, heat remaining 1 tablespoon oil in a small heavy skillet over moderate heat until hot but not smoking. Add cumin seeds and cook, stirring, until a shade darker, about 1 minute. Add garam masala, salt, and cayenne and cook, stirring, until fragrant, 15 to 30 seconds.

Stir hot spice oil into lentils, then gently stir in tofu cubes. Let curry stand, covered, for 5 minutes to allow flavors to develop, then stir in cilantro and salt to taste. Serve with rice.

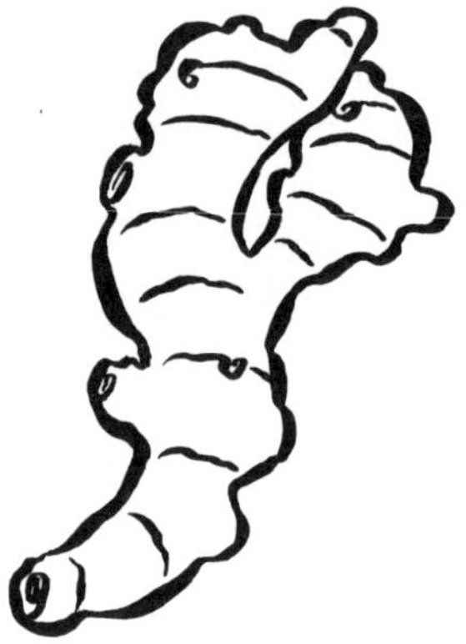

Silken Tofu and Carrot with Soy Ginger Sauce

SERVES 2 AS A FIRST COURSE
ACTIVE TIME: 10 MINUTES ■ START TO FINISH: 10 MINUTES

■ We've all found ourselves staring meditatively at the snowy blocks of tofu, or soybean curd, in the store. There's nothing to dislike about it, but then again, it isn't particularly alluring. You need to look at its innocuousness, though, as opportunity, for it soaks up the flavor of a sauce or marinade like a sponge. Here we've used silken tofu, which has the consistency of baked custard. This dish is a perfect choice in hot weather, because it isn't cooked; it's cooling and refreshing. You could easily double the recipe and serve it as a main course with rice, a rice salad, or room-temperature steamed broccoli. ■

- 1½ tablespoons soy sauce
- 1 tablespoon seasoned rice vinegar
- ¾ teaspoon finely grated peeled fresh ginger
- ¾ teaspoon sugar
- ½ pound silken or soft tofu, drained and halved
- 1 small carrot, finely grated
- 1 tablespoon thinly sliced scallion greens

Stir together soy sauce, vinegar, ginger, and sugar in a small bowl until sugar is dissolved. Put tofu on two plates, spoon sauce over it, and sprinkle with carrot and scallion greens.

Panfried Tofu on Sesame Watercress with Soy Orange Dressing

SERVES 2 AS A MAIN COURSE
ACTIVE TIME: 15 MINUTES ■ START TO FINISH: 25 MINUTES

■ Here are Asian flavors without lots of ingredients or prep time. This dish is quick, light, and just right. Tofu can be fragile, depending on the texture; we chose the extra-firm kind for this recipe because it stands up to panfrying better than the soft or silken types do. ■

- 1 tablespoon sesame seeds
- ¾ pound extra-firm tofu, rinsed, drained, and cut into ½-inch-thick slices
- 1½ tablespoons vegetable oil
- 1½ bunches watercress, tough stems discarded
- 2 teaspoons grated peeled fresh ginger
- 1 large garlic clove, minced
- ¼ cup fresh orange juice
- 2 tablespoons soy sauce
- 2 teaspoons Asian sesame oil

Toast sesame seeds in a dry heavy skillet over moderate heat, stirring, until fragrant and a shade or two darker. Transfer to a bowl.

Pat tofu dry. Heat 1 tablespoon vegetable oil in a 12-inch nonstick skillet over moderately high heat until hot but not smoking. Add tofu and cook, turning once, until golden brown, 6 to 8 minutes total. Transfer to a plate. Heat remaining 1½ teaspoons vegetable oil in skillet over moderate heat until hot but not smoking. Add watercress and cook, turning with tongs, until just wilted. Stir in sesame seeds. Transfer watercress to a platter (reserve skillet) and arrange tofu on top.

Combine ginger, garlic, orange juice, soy sauce, and sesame oil in skillet and bring to a simmer. Simmer for 1 minute and drizzle sauce over tofu.

Panfried Tofu with Chinese Black Bean Sauce

SERVES 3 OR 4 AS A MAIN COURSE
ACTIVE TIME: 20 MINUTES ■ START TO FINISH: 20 MINUTES

■ Meaty, satisfying—this will change people's minds about tofu. There's a great contrast between the crisp golden outside, the tender white inside, and the pungent sauce, which is made from Chinese fermented black beans. Not the turtle beans you see in black bean soup or burritos, these are black soybeans that have been steamed, then fermented with salt and spices. Although the ingredients list for the sauce, as for many Chinese dishes, may look a bit long, the actual time in putting the dish together is not. Our version of this sauce has evolved over the years, reflecting the ingredients we have on hand. Maple syrup certainly isn't Chinese, but it doesn't have to be dissolved, like sugar, and it adds a multidimensional sweetness. Cider vinegar is a staple in our cupboard, but we have substituted balsamic vinegar in a pinch. Serve this with rice and broccoli (pouring the sauce over all) and you've got a great Sunday night supper. ■

- 1 (14-ounce) block extra-firm tofu, rinsed, drained, and cut crosswise into 6 slices
- 4 garlic cloves
- 1 (1-inch) piece peeled fresh ginger, quartered
- 2 tablespoons Chinese fermented black beans (see Glossary)
- 1½ cups water
- ¼ cup soy sauce
- 3 tablespoons sherry
- 1 tablespoon pure maple syrup
- 2 teaspoons cider vinegar
- 1½ tablespoons cornstarch
- 3 tablespoons vegetable oil

ACCOMPANIMENTS: cooked rice and steamed broccoli

Put tofu slices between several layers of paper towels to drain while you make sauce. (You will need to replace paper towels at least once.)

Mince garlic and ginger in a food processor. Rinse beans in a small sieve until water runs clear, then add to processor and pulse until coarsely chopped. Transfer to a bowl.

Stir together water, soy sauce, sherry, maple syrup, cider vinegar, and cornstarch in a small bowl until cornstarch is dissolved.

Heat 2 tablespoons oil in a 2-quart heavy saucepan over moderately high heat until hot but not smoking. Add bean mixture and stir-fry until fragrant, about 30 seconds. Stir cornstarch mixture, add to pan, and bring sauce to a boil, whisking occasionally. Reduce heat and simmer for 1 minute. Remove from heat.

Heat remaining 1 tablespoon oil in a 12-inch nonstick skillet over high heat until hot but not smoking. Blot any excess moisture remaining on tofu with paper towels, then lay tofu in skillet. Fry slices on all sides (forgo short ends), turning occasionally, until golden and crisp, 8 to 10 minutes total. (You may need to lower heat as frying progresses.) Transfer tofu to paper towels to drain.

Reheat sauce and serve tofu with sauce, rice, and broccoli.

Ma-Po Tofu

SERVES 3 OR 4 AS A MAIN COURSE
ACTIVE TIME: 45 MINUTES ■ START TO FINISH: 45 MINUTES

■ This fiery Sichuan classic is named for the pockmarked (*ma*) old woman (*po*) who supposedly invented it at her husband's restaurant. The late Chinese authority Barbara Tropp had made a version of it for years, but when attending culinary school in Chengdu, the capital of the Sichuan province, she picked up the technique of poaching the tofu before stir-frying to freshen and tenderize it. ■

FOR SAUCE

- ¾ cup chicken stock or store-bought low-sodium broth
- 2 tablespoons Chinese hot bean sauce (see Glossary)
- 2 tablespoons soy sauce
- Kosher salt to taste

FOR TOFU

- 1 pound regular or soft (not silken) tofu, drained and cut into ½-inch cubes
- 1½–2 tablespoons corn, peanut, or canola oil
- ½ pound ground pork shoulder (preferably 75% lean)
- 4 teaspoons finely minced garlic

- 4 teaspoons finely minced peeled fresh ginger
- 1 tablespoon cornstarch, dissolved in 2 tablespoons water
- 1½ teaspoons Japanese sesame oil
- ½–1 teaspoon Toasted Sichuan Peppercorn Powder (page 395), to taste, or ½ teaspoon *sansho* (Japanese pepper; see Glossary) plus ⅛–¼ teaspoon freshly ground black pepper
- 3 tablespoons thinly sliced scallions

ACCOMPANIMENT: cooked rice

MAKE THE SAUCE: Stir together stock, bean sauce, soy sauce, and salt in a small bowl.

POACH THE TOFU AND COOK THE PORK: Slide tofu into a saucepan of simmering water and keep at a bare simmer.

While tofu is simmering, heat a wok or large heavy skillet over high heat until hot. Add 1½ tablespoons corn oil, swirling to coat. Add pork and stir-fry, breaking up lumps and adding remaining 1½ teaspoons corn oil if meat sticks, until no longer pink. Add garlic and ginger, reduce heat to moderate, and stir-fry until very fragrant, about 2 minutes.

FINISH THE STIR-FRY: Stir sauce, then add to pork and bring to a simmer. Drain tofu in a large sieve and slide into pork mixture, stirring gently.

Stir cornstarch mixture and add to stir-fry. Bring to a boil, stirring gently, and cook until sauce is thickened and glossy, about 15 seconds. Turn off heat, sprinkle stir-fry with sesame oil, Sichuan peppercorn powder, and 2 tablespoons scallions, and stir once or twice. Sprinkle with remaining 1 tablespoon scallions and serve with rice.

FISH AND SHELLFISH

Of all the foods that Americans eat, none is more regional than fish. In spite of all the advances in transportation, in spite of refrigeration and overnight air freight, the seafood we eat still varies enormously from one side of the country to the other. On the West Coast, the crabs are large and Dungeness; on the East Coast, they are small and blue. While one coast is indulging in shad and its roe, the other is happily eating the sweet little sand dabs that swim in the Pacific, and the tiny bay scallops of the East rarely make their way west.

On top of that, supplies change radically with the times. This can be the natural result of shifting tides that sweep whole schools of fish onto a different course or of the normal variations in ocean temperature. Too often today, however, it is the result of human intervention: overfishing, the effects of pollution, or simply the misuse of the resources of the sea. Sturgeon were once so abundant that caviar was offered as a free bar snack all over New York City; cheap oyster saloons dotted the streets, but we ate too many too fast and depleted the beds. Lobsters were so inexpensive in the nineteenth century that prisoners rioted, demanding an end to lobster dinners; they'd be shocked to discover that lobsters are now luxury fare. And walleye pike, which were the pride of the Great Lakes, have become an occasional—and imported—treat. There is also the fear factor to contend with. Many cooks are afraid of fish, because the timing can be tricky (overcooked or undercooked seafood is hard to love). And many American diners are worried about bones, refusing any fish not in the form of a fillet.

For the serious cook, all of this makes serving seafood that much more appealing; who can resist the challenge of introducing new foods into our national conversation? Besides, there is almost nothing as impressive as a great bouillabaisse served at home, or as comforting as rich little ramekins of coquilles St. Jacques. Fish can be marvelously simple: our skate with black butter takes all of ten minutes to prepare. And it can be inspiring: for sheer beauty, a whole poached salmon is hard to beat, and if your guests want to think that you spent hours slaving in the kitchen (when it's actually pretty easy), what's the harm?

Our goal has always been to help our readers tackle cooking obstacles, and we think this chapter does the job particularly well. We went through hundreds and hundreds of recipes, winnowing them down to this group of foolproof favorites. Although many recipes are written for a specific variety of fish, in most cases we have suggested substitutions of similar fish that may be easier to find (or less expensive) in your part of the country.

We argued long and hard over each recipe. The longest debate concerned the showstopping coulibiac of salmon; it is truly time-consuming, but so wonderful that when we tested it our kitchen was filled with moans of appreciation. Since then every one of us has served it at a party, and we figured that if we wanted it so much, you would too.

The dishes in this chapter range from a simply seared sea bass with fresh herbs and lemon to spicy blackened catfish and a stately salmon poached with truffles. We have a lovely romaine-wrapped halibut, a down-home and delicious Louisiana crawfish boil, and classic quenelles. Fish tacos and tuna burgers and crabmeat-stuffed sole also make an appearance. Here you will find, in fact, eighty-nine reasons to fall in love with fish.

Sole Meunière

Fillet of Sole Panfried in Butter

SERVES 2

ACTIVE TIME: 15 MINUTES ■ START TO FINISH: 15 MINUTES

■ In French, *meunière* means "miller's wife" and, in cooking, refers to anything dusted with flour. Sole meunière is one of the most perfect dishes in the French culinary repertoire. The fish are panfried whole in a special large oval pan and served with *beurre noisette*—butter browned to the color of a hazelnut—and lemon juice. We've used fillets and simplified the method for the home cook. Dover sole is worth seeking out for this recipe; it's the only true sole available here, but because it must be imported from the European Atlantic, it's not always easy to find and is very expensive. (For more about sole, see opposite page.) ■

- 1 cup all-purpose flour
- 2 (6-ounce) Dover, gray, or lemon sole fillets
- Salt
- $\frac{1}{2}$ stick (4 tablespoons) unsalted butter
- 1 tablespoon chopped fresh flat-leaf parsley
- 1 teaspoon fresh lemon juice

ACCOMPANIMENT: lemon wedges

Spread flour on a plate. Pat fillets dry and season with salt. Dredge fillets in flour, shake off excess, and transfer to another plate.

Heat 3 tablespoons butter in a 12-inch nonstick skillet over moderately high heat until golden brown and fragrant. Add parsley, shaking skillet to distribute it. Add fish, reduce heat to moderate, and cook for $1\frac{1}{2}$ to 2 minutes, or until undersides are golden. Turn fillets over, using two spatulas, and cook for $1\frac{1}{2}$ to 2 minutes more, or until fish is golden and almost cooked through (it should be slightly translucent in center; it will continue to cook when removed from heat). Transfer fillets to two plates.

Add lemon juice, $\frac{1}{4}$ teaspoon salt, and remaining 1 tablespoon butter to skillet and cook over moderately high heat until butter has melted and foam subsides. Immediately pour sauce over fish. Serve with lemon wedges.

Seared Sea Bass with Fresh Herbs and Lemon

SERVES 4

ACTIVE TIME: 25 MINUTES ■ START TO FINISH: 25 MINUTES

■ It doesn't get much simpler than this: beautifully crisp fillets with herbs, butter, lemon juice, and white wine. Cutting the fillets in half diagonally before cooking makes them particularly easy to turn over. You can substitute any firm-fleshed white fish with skin, such as red snapper. ■

- 4 (6-ounce) pieces sea bass fillet with skin (1 inch thick)
- Salt and freshly ground black pepper
- 1 tablespoon olive oil
- 3 tablespoons unsalted butter
- $\frac{1}{2}$ cup dry white wine
- 1 tablespoon fresh lemon juice, or to taste
- $\frac{2}{3}$ cup loosely packed mixed fresh herbs, such as parsley, dill, and chives, chopped

Using tweezers or needle-nose pliers, remove any bones from sea bass. Pat fillets dry. With a sharp knife, cut parallel slashes just through skin of each fillet in 4 places. Cut each fillet diagonally in half and season with salt and pepper.

Heat oil and 1 tablespoon butter in a 12-inch nonstick skillet over moderately high heat until foam subsides. Add fish skin side down and sear until skin is golden, about 3 minutes. Turn fish over and cook until just cooked through, about 2 minutes. Transfer to four plates.

Add wine to skillet and deglaze by boiling, stirring and scraping up brown bits with a wooden spoon, for 1 minute. Remove from heat and add lemon juice, herbs, remaining 2 tablespoons butter, and salt and pepper to taste, stirring until butter is incorporated. Spoon sauce over fish.

Scrod with Tomatoes, Bacon, and Sherry

SERVES 4

ACTIVE TIME: 25 MINUTES ■ START TO FINISH: 25 MINUTES

■ This recipe is quick and easy. We used scrod (young cod or haddock under 2½ pounds) and bacon for a little surf-and-turf action. ■

- ¼ pound bacon (4 slices)
- 1 medium onion, chopped
- 1 cup chopped drained canned tomatoes in juice
- 6 tablespoons medium-dry sherry
- 1½ tablespoons soy sauce
- ¼ teaspoon sugar
- 4 (6-ounce) pieces scrod, haddock, or hake fillet
- Salt and freshly ground black pepper

Cook bacon in a 12-inch heavy skillet over moderate heat, turning occasionally, until crisp. With a slotted spatula, transfer to paper towels to drain and cool, then crumble.

Pour off all but 1 tablespoon fat from skillet. Add onion and cook, stirring, until it begins to turn golden, 2 to 3 minutes. Add tomatoes, sherry, soy sauce, and sugar and simmer, stirring occasionally, until sauce thickens, about 5 minutes.

Add scrod to sauce and simmer, covered, for 4 minutes. Turn scrod over and simmer, covered, until just cooked through, about 3 minutes more. With a slotted

Sole Nomenclature

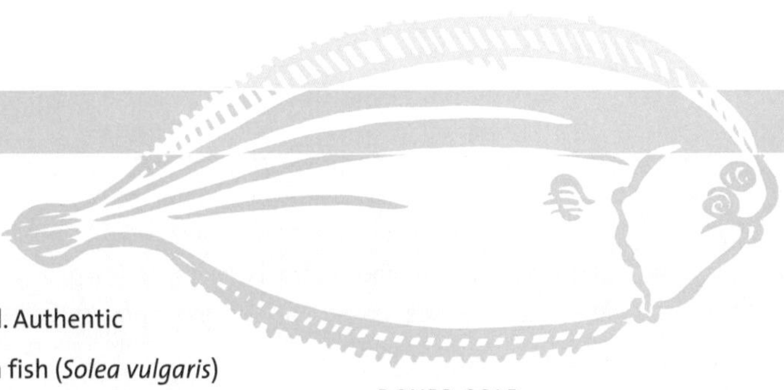

DOVER SOLE

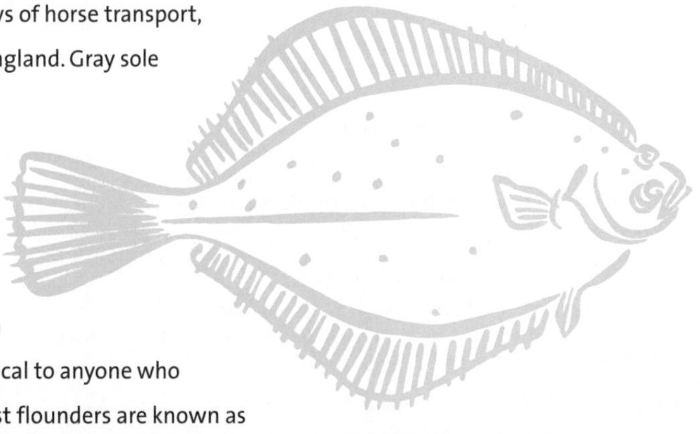

FLOUNDER

Numerous classic French fish preparations involve sole: its texture and delicate flavor are enhanced by sauces, herbs, and even other seafood without being overwhelmed. Authentic sole, which is rarely seen in the United States, is a European fish (*Solea vulgaris*) from the family Soleidae. Found from the Mediterranean to Denmark, it is often referred to as Dover sole, a name that dates back to the days of horse transport, when most of the catch was landed at the port of Dover, England. Gray sole and lemon sole, from North America, are from the family Pleuronectidae and are technically flounders.

Both sole and flounders are flatfish, as opposed to what are called round fish. They *are* relatively flat, but their oddest characteristic is that both eyes are on the top side, and they lie and travel on one side rather than belly down. Sole and many flounders look practically identical to anyone who isn't an ichthyologist, which is why in the marketplace most flounders are known as sole. Savvy marketers have gotten into the name game as well, realizing that, for example, "gray sole" sounds much more glamorous than "witch flounder." Lemon sole is the U.S. market name for a winter flounder that weighs more than three pounds (they're called blackbacks when they weigh less). And one Pacific flounder (*Microstomus pacificus*) looks so much like Dover sole that it is often sold as such, but avoid it: it is markedly inferior. (It is never sold whole, whereas the real thing usually is.)

spatula, transfer scrod to four plates and cover with a large piece of foil to keep warm.

Boil sauce to thicken slightly, uncovered, for 1 minute. Season with salt and pepper, spoon over scrod, and sprinkle with bacon.

Panfried Red Snapper with Chipotle Butter

SERVES 4

ACTIVE TIME: 15 MINUTES ■ START TO FINISH: 15 MINUTES

■ Chefs love red snapper for its inherent drama. The fillets are often served skin side up because the skin is so beautiful. The sweet, mild flavor of the fish contrasts with the smoky heat of canned chipotle chiles in a tomatoey adobo sauce. If you can't find red snapper, you can substitute grouper, yelloweye rockfish, or onaga (Hawaiian red snapper), as long as the fillets are the same size and thickness, preferably with skin on. ■

- ½ stick (4 tablespoons) unsalted butter, softened
- ½–1 tablespoon finely chopped canned chipotle chiles in adobo (to taste; see Glossary) plus 2 teaspoons sauce from can
- ½ teaspoon salt
- ⅓ cup all-purpose flour
- 4 (6-ounce) red snapper fillets with skin
- Freshly ground black pepper
- About 3 tablespoons vegetable oil

ACCOMPANIMENT: lime wedges

Mash together butter, chipotles, adobo sauce, and salt in a small bowl with a fork until blended.

Spread flour on a plate. Pat fish dry and cut each fillet crosswise in half. Season with salt and pepper. Dredge fish in flour and shake off excess.

Heat 1½ tablespoons oil in a 12-inch nonstick skillet over moderately high heat until hot but not smoking. Add 2 fillets, skin side up, and panfry, turning once, until browned and just cooked through, 4 to 6 minutes. With a slotted spatula, transfer to plates and loosely cover to keep warm. Add oil to skillet as needed, heat until very hot, and cook remaining 2 fillets in same manner. Top fish with dollops of chipotle butter and serve with lime wedges.

Skate with Black Butter

SERVES 2

ACTIVE TIME: 10 MINUTES ■ START TO FINISH: 10 MINUTES

■ Black butter, or *beurre noir,* is a great example of how you can cook an ingredient to change the nature of its flavor (and a great example of French cooking at its simplest). The butter is heated until the milk solids are caramelized and a toasty golden brown—not really black—and then flavored with an acid such as vinegar. It's absolutely delicious with eggs and fish. This recipe is from a slim 1930 masterpiece called *French Cooking in Ten Minutes,* by Édouard de Pomiane, a Pasteur Institute scientist who also lectured on nutrition, hosted a radio show, and wrote numerous cookbooks. When you go to the seafood store for the skate, ask your fishmonger to fillet it for you. ■

- ¾ pound skate or sole fillets
- Salt
- 3 tablespoons unsalted butter
- 1 tablespoon chopped fresh flat-leaf parsley
- 1 teaspoon red wine vinegar

Pat skate dry and season with salt. Heat butter in a 10-inch nonstick skillet over moderately high heat until foam subsides and butter is golden brown. Stir in parsley, then reduce heat to moderate, add skate, and cook, turning once, until just cooked through, about 4 minutes. Remove skillet from heat and, with a slotted spatula, transfer skate to plates. Stir vinegar and salt to taste into butter in skillet and pour sauce over skate.

Sautéed Halibut Fillets with Pecan Shallot Topping

SERVES 4

ACTIVE TIME: 20 MINUTES ■ START TO FINISH: 30 MINUTES

■ A topping of suave, buttery pecans and subtle shallots enhances the mild flavor of halibut without overpowering it. ■

- 4 (6-ounce) pieces halibut fillet (1¼ inches thick), skinned
- Salt and freshly ground black pepper
- 3 tablespoons olive oil
- 1 cup chopped shallots
- ½ cup (2 ounces) pecans, chopped
- ½ tablespoon unsalted butter
- ½ teaspoon finely grated lemon zest
- 2 tablespoons finely chopped fresh flat-leaf parsley

ACCOMPANIMENT: lemon wedges

Preheat oven to 200°F.

Pat halibut dry and season with salt and pepper. Heat 2 tablespoons oil in a 12-inch heavy skillet over moderately high heat until hot but not smoking. Add fish and cook, turning once, until golden and just cooked through, 4 to 6 minutes. Transfer to a platter and keep warm in oven, loosely covered with foil.

Add remaining 1 tablespoon oil to skillet, then add shallots and cook over moderate heat, stirring occasionally, until pale golden, 3 to 4 minutes. Add pecans, increase heat to moderately high, and cook, stirring, until pecans are fragrant and a shade darker, about 3 minutes. Add butter and stir until melted. Remove from heat and stir in zest, parsley, and salt and pepper to taste.

Spoon pecan topping over fish and serve with lemon wedges.

Grouper with Tomato and Basil

SERVES 2

ACTIVE TIME: 15 MINUTES ■ START TO FINISH: 25 MINUTES

■ Here is a simple, straightforward Provençal treatment for grouper, a fish native to Florida and the Caribbean. It has firm, lean, sweet flesh. ■

HOW TO REMOVE SKIN FROM FISH FILLETS

Many fish fillets — salmon and halibut, for instance — are usually sold with the skin on. The skin helps hold the fish together during cooking, especially if you are grilling or broiling. But there are times when you want the skin off, and if you don't have a fishmonger who will skin to order, fear not: it's easy enough to do yourself. We tend to pick up a large chef's knife for the task, but if you own a fillet knife, by all means use it. Put the fillet skin side down and, starting at one corner, separate the skin from the flesh by cutting a little flap of skin loose. Fish skin is tough stuff, and this is the hardest part of the whole process. Fish skin is also slippery, which is why a paper towel comes in handy. Holding the loose flap of skin firmly with the paper towel and keeping the skin taut, scrape the flesh off the skin. It helps if your knife is sharp, of course, and you'll need to experiment a little to find just the right angle; keep the blade edge against the skin and you'll get a clean and tidy separation.

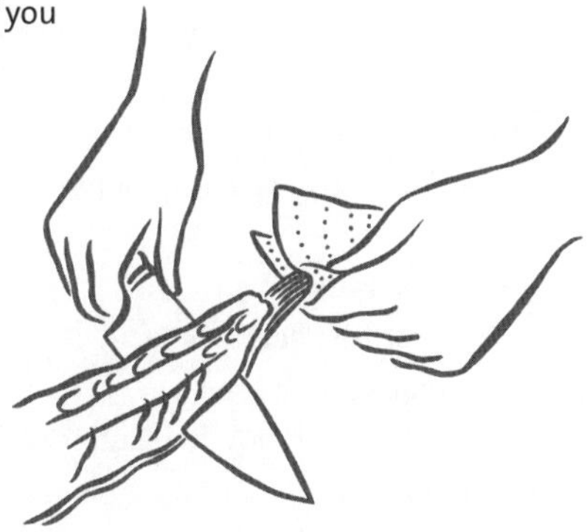

2 tablespoons extra-virgin olive oil
1 (1-pound) piece grouper or red snapper fillet (3/4 inch thick), skinned and halved crosswise
1/4 teaspoon salt
1/8 teaspoon freshly ground black pepper
1/2 cup coarsely chopped tomato
1 small garlic clove, minced (optional)
2 tablespoons thinly sliced fresh basil leaves

Put 1 tablespoon oil in a 10-inch nonstick skillet and add fish, turning to coat on both sides, then arrange skinned side down. Sprinkle with salt and pepper.

Toss together tomato, garlic (if using), basil, remaining 1 tablespoon oil, and salt and pepper to taste in a small bowl, then mound on top of fish. Cover skillet with a tight-fitting lid and cook over moderately high heat until fish is just cooked through, about 8 minutes.

Catfish Fillets with Pecan Butter Sauce

SERVES 6
ACTIVE TIME: 15 MINUTES ■ START TO FINISH: 40 MINUTES

■ Catfish and pecans both have roots in the American South, and the two ingredients have a beautiful affinity. If catfish isn't available, any of the following fish can be substituted, as long as the fillets are the same size and thickness: red snapper, grouper, rockfish, freshwater whitefish, tilefish, halibut, cod, haddock, lingcod, salmon, striped bass, sea bass, shark, tuna, or mahimahi. ■

1 cup all-purpose flour
Salt and freshly ground black pepper
1 large egg
3 tablespoons water
6 (6-ounce) catfish fillets, skinned
About 1/3 cup vegetable oil
3/4 stick (6 tablespoons) unsalted butter
1/4 cup minced onion
1 garlic clove, minced
1/2 cup (2 ounces) pecans, lightly toasted (see Tips, page 938) and finely chopped
1 tablespoon fresh lemon juice, or to taste
Tabasco

OPTIONAL ACCOMPANIMENT: lemon wedges

Line a baking sheet with wax paper. Put flour in a shallow dish and season with salt and pepper. Lightly beat egg with water in another shallow dish. Working with 1 fillet at a time, dredge fish in flour, shake off excess, dip into egg mixture, let excess drip off, and then dredge in flour again and shake off excess. Transfer to wax paper–lined baking sheet.

Heat 2 tablespoons oil in a 12-inch nonstick skillet over moderately high heat until hot but not smoking. Add fish in 2 batches and cook, turning once, until it just flakes, 6 to 8 minutes per batch; transfer to paper towels to drain and keep warm, loosely covered with foil. Add more oil to skillet as needed between batches.

Wipe out skillet and melt butter over moderately low heat. Add onion and garlic and cook, stirring, until softened, about 4 minutes. Add pecans, increase heat to moderately high, and cook, swirling skillet, until butter is browned and pecans are well toasted, about 2 minutes. Stir in lemon juice, Tabasco, and salt and pepper to taste.

Divide fish among six plates and top with butter sauce. Serve with lemon wedges, if desired.

Spicy Blackened Catfish

SERVES 4
ACTIVE TIME: 10 MINUTES ■ START TO FINISH: 20 MINUTES

■ The "blackened" technique of cooking fish, popularized by the New Orleans chef Paul Prudhomme, is too often a synonym for "burned" or "overspiced," but not here: this version is really delicious. If you do much cooking, you are likely to have all the spices necessary in your kitchen cupboard. ■

4 teaspoons sweet paprika
1 teaspoon dried oregano, crumbled
1 teaspoon dried thyme, crumbled
1/2 teaspoon cayenne, or to taste
1 teaspoon sugar
1 teaspoon salt
1/4 teaspoon freshly ground black pepper
4 (8-ounce) catfish, tilapia, or mahimahi fillets, skinned
2 tablespoons olive oil

2 large garlic cloves, thinly sliced
2 tablespoons unsalted butter
ACCOMPANIMENT: lemon wedges

Stir together paprika, oregano, thyme, cayenne, sugar, salt, and black pepper in a small bowl. Pat catfish dry, then sprinkle spice mixture on both sides of fillets, coating well.

Heat oil in a 12-inch nonstick skillet over moderately high heat until hot but not smoking. Add garlic and cook, stirring, until golden brown, about 30 seconds. With a slotted spoon, remove garlic and discard. Add 1 tablespoon butter to skillet and heat until foam subsides. Add 2 catfish fillets and cook, turning once, until cooked through, about 8 minutes total. With a slotted spatula, transfer fillets to plates and keep warm, loosely covered with foil. Add remaining 1 tablespoon butter to pan and cook remaining 2 fillets in same manner. Serve with lemon wedges.

Catfish Fillets with Tahini Sauce

SERVES 4
ACTIVE TIME: 10 MINUTES ■ START TO FINISH: 20 MINUTES

■ The thick sesame seed paste called tahini is integral to Middle Eastern dishes such as hummus and baba ghanouj. It might seem an unlikely match for fish because it is so rich, but the combination is common in Egypt and absolutely wonderful, especially with the addition of coriander seeds. Tahini can be found in any well-stocked supermarket. ■

2 garlic cloves, coarsely chopped
1/2 cup well-stirred tahini (Middle Eastern sesame paste)
2/3 cup water
3 tablespoons fresh lemon juice
1/2 teaspoon ground cumin
1/2 teaspoon salt
4 (6-ounce) catfish or mahimahi fillets, skinned
Freshly ground black pepper
2 tablespoons olive oil
4 teaspoons coriander seeds, coarsely crushed with side of a large knife
GARNISH: 1/4 cup coarsely chopped fresh flat-leaf parsley

Combine garlic, tahini, water, lemon juice, cumin, and salt in a blender and purée until smooth.

Pat catfish dry and season with salt and pepper. Heat 1 tablespoon oil in a 12-inch nonstick skillet over moderately high heat until hot but not smoking. Add 2 fillets and sear until golden, about 3 minutes. Turn fish over and sprinkle half of crushed coriander around it, then sear until just cooked through, about 2 more minutes. Transfer fish to a platter and wipe out skillet. Heat remaining 1 tablespoon oil in skillet and cook remaining 2 fillets in same manner, adding remaining coriander when you turn fish.

Divide tahini sauce among four plates and top with fish. Spoon crushed coriander and oil from skillet over fish and sprinkle with parsley.

Salmon Cooked on Salt

SERVES 4
ACTIVE TIME: 10 MINUTES ■ START TO FINISH: 20 MINUTES

■ Salmon cooked this way—resting on a bed of salt, without being turned—is just perfection. The salt both insulates the salmon slightly from the direct heat of the stovetop, so it cooks gently, and absorbs the oily juices from the fish. Somewhat surprisingly, the salmon isn't overly salty, but the skin is; you'll need to slide a spatula between the flesh and the skin, which sticks to the salt. The recipe came from the novelist and *Gourmet* contributor Diane Johnson, who included it in her story on the cooking of Parisian housewives. In France, cooks use sea salt as a matter of course, but staying with the marine theme isn't cheap; kosher salt is a fine alternative. ■

2 cups coarse sea salt or kosher salt
1 (1 1/4-pound) center-cut piece salmon fillet with skin
Salt and freshly ground black pepper

Spread salt evenly in a dry 10-inch heavy skillet, preferably cast-iron, and heat over moderately high heat until salt is hot to the touch and just beginning to smoke, about 4 minutes.

Pat salmon dry and season flesh with salt and pepper. Put skin side down on salt, cover, and cook, without turning, until almost cooked through, 8 to 12 minutes. Remove from heat and let stand, covered, until salmon is just cooked through, 1 to 2 minutes.

Slide a spatula between salmon skin and flesh and transfer salmon to a platter.

Seared Salmon with Balsamic Glaze

SERVES 4
ACTIVE TIME: 10 MINUTES ■ START TO FINISH: 15 MINUTES

■ Along with tuna and swordfish, salmon is considered a "red meat" of the fish world, and it can stand up to strong flavors like balsamic vinegar. Here we reduce the vinegar to a glaze, tempering the sharpness of the acid. The tangy sauce that results brings out the sweetness of the crisp-crusted salmon. ■

- 1/4 cup balsamic vinegar
- 1/4 cup water
- 1 1/2 tablespoons fresh lemon juice
- 1 tablespoon plus 1 teaspoon packed light brown sugar
- 4 (6-ounce) center-cut pieces salmon fillet with skin
- Salt and freshly ground black pepper
- 2 teaspoons vegetable oil

Stir together vinegar, water, lemon juice, and brown sugar in a small bowl.

Pat salmon dry and season with salt and pepper. Heat oil in a 12-inch nonstick skillet over moderately high heat until hot but not smoking. Increase heat to high, add salmon skin side up, and sear until well browned, about 4 minutes. Turn fish over and sear until just cooked through, 3 to 4 minutes more.

Transfer salmon to plates and carefully add vinegar mixture to skillet (liquid will bubble vigorously and steam). Simmer, stirring, until thickened and reduced to about 1/3 cup, about 2 minutes. Spoon glaze over salmon.

Poached Salmon with Truffles and Shrimp in Cream Sauce

SERVES 4 AS A MAIN COURSE, 8 AS A FIRST COURSE
ACTIVE TIME: 1 1/2 HOURS ■ START TO FINISH: 1 3/4 HOURS

■ Wine, cream, truffles, Cognac, shrimp, butter: there is unadulterated pleasure to be savored in this luxurious Old World classic. ■

FOR SHRIMP AND SHRIMP BUTTER

- 10 ounces medium shrimp in shells (31–35 per pound)
- 1/4 teaspoon salt
- 3/4 stick (6 tablespoons) unsalted butter
- 2 tablespoons Cognac or other brandy
- 1 tablespoon water

FOR SALMON

- 8 (3/4-inch-wide) slices center-cut salmon fillet (1 1/2–2 pounds total), skinned
- 1 ounce (28 grams) fresh, jarred, or canned black winter truffles (see Sources)
- 1/4 teaspoon salt
- 1 cup dry white wine

FOR SAUCE

- 1 1/2 cups French Chablis or other dry white wine
- 1/3 cup finely chopped shallots
- 1 1/2 cups heavy cream
- 1 teaspoon arrowroot
- 2 teaspoons Cognac or other brandy
- 1/2 teaspoon salt
- 1/8 teaspoon freshly ground white or black pepper

SPECIAL EQUIPMENT: eight 18-inch-long pieces kitchen string

COOK THE SHRIMP AND MAKE THE SHRIMP BUTTER: Cut through each shrimp shell lengthwise down back with scissors, leaving last segment of shell intact, then devein shrimp, leaving shells in place. Rinse shrimp and pat dry, then sprinkle with salt.

Heat butter in a 10-inch nonstick skillet over moderately high heat until foam subsides. Add shrimp and cook, turning once or twice, until just cooked through, about 3 minutes. Transfer shrimp and butter to a sieve set over a bowl; set skillet aside.

When just cool enough to handle, shell shrimp, leaving shell on tail segment; reserve shells and butter. Refrigerate shrimp, covered, until ready to use.

Return shells and butter to skillet and reheat briefly to liquefy butter. Transfer to a food processor, add Cognac and water, and purée until as smooth as possible, about 2 minutes. Force mixture through a fine-mesh sieve into a small bowl; discard solids. Refrigerate shrimp butter, covered.

PREPARE THE SALMON: Curl each salmon slice into a circle, skinned side in, and tie with string so it holds its shape.

Cut forty-eight 3/4-by-1/16-inch-thick strips from truffles. Mince remaining truffles. Reserve liquid if using canned or jarred truffles.

Make 6 evenly spaced slits in top of each salmon slice with tip of a small knife and push a truffle strip into each slit. Sprinkle salmon with salt and place on a tray. Cover tightly with plastic wrap and refrigerate until ready to poach.

BEGIN THE SAUCE: Simmer Chablis with shallots in a 2-quart heavy saucepan until reduced to about 1/4 cup, about 15 minutes. Add cream and return to a simmer. Pour through fine-mesh sieve into another small heavy saucepan, pressing on shallots; discard shallots. Add minced truffles and any truffle juice and simmer sauce until reduced to about 1 1/4 cups, about 5 minutes.

Stir together arrowroot and Cognac until smooth and whisk into sauce. Simmer, whisking occasionally, until slightly thickened, about 2 minutes, then stir in salt and pepper. Remove from heat.

POACH THE SALMON: Butter bottom of a deep 12-inch heavy skillet and arrange salmon in it. Add wine and enough water to just cover fish, then top with a round of buttered parchment or wax paper, buttered side down. Bring to a simmer over moderately high heat, then reduce heat and poach at a bare simmer until salmon is just cooked through, 8 to 10 minutes total. With a slotted spatula, transfer salmon to plates and remove string.

MEANWHILE, FINISH THE SAUCE: Combine sauce and shrimp in a heavy skillet and bring to a simmer over moderate heat. Add shrimp butter and swirl skillet until butter is incorporated. Season sauce with salt and pepper.

Serve salmon with sauce.

COOK'S NOTES

- The shrimp butter can be made and the sauce begun up to 1 day ahead. Refrigerate separately, covered; reheat the sauce over low heat, stirring, before finishing.
- The salmon can be prepared (not cooked) up to 1 day ahead.

Salmon Burgers with Spinach and Ginger

SERVES 4

ACTIVE TIME: 40 MINUTES ■ START TO FINISH: 45 MINUTES

■ This preparation plays up the meaty aspect of salmon. Note that the salmon isn't ground, which would make it pasty; instead, it's cut into little dice and blended with baby spinach and ginger, always great with fish. You don't really need buns—the burgers are delicious on their own. These are also a good option when all that's left in the fish market are the ends of fillets; most people want center-cut pieces of fillet, and they go fast. ■

- 1 (1-pound) piece salmon fillet, skinned and cut into 1/4-inch dice
- 1/4 pound baby spinach, coarsely chopped (3 cups)
- 3 scallions, minced
- 1 tablespoon finely grated peeled fresh ginger
- 1/4 teaspoon salt
- 1/4 teaspoon freshly ground black pepper
- 1 large egg white
- 1 tablespoon soy sauce
- 1 tablespoon vegetable oil
- 2 tablespoons drained sliced Japanese pickled ginger

Stir together salmon, spinach, scallions, fresh ginger, salt, and pepper in a large bowl until well combined. Beat egg white with soy sauce in a small bowl and stir into salmon mixture. Form into four 1/2-inch-thick patties.

Heat oil in a 12-inch nonstick skillet over moderate heat until hot but not smoking. Add patties and cook, carefully turning once, until golden brown and cooked through, 6 to 7 minutes total.

Serve burgers topped with pickled ginger.

COOK'S NOTE

■ The patties can be formed up to 4 hours ahead and refrigerated on a wax paper–lined baking sheet, covered with plastic wrap.

Bluefish with Lemon Caper–Brown Butter Sauce

SERVES 4

ACTIVE TIME: 10 MINUTES ■ START TO FINISH: 15 MINUTES

■ Bluefish has a reputation for having a strong flavor, but when it's very fresh and properly handled, nothing can beat it. Butter, lemon juice, and capers are a classic combination with fish, but browning the butter first adds another, deeper dimension to the dish. ■

- 4 (6-ounce) pieces bluefish or mackerel fillet with skin
- Salt and freshly ground black pepper
- 2 tablespoons vegetable oil
- ½ stick (4 tablespoons) unsalted butter
- 2 tablespoons fresh lemon juice
- 4 teaspoons drained capers

Pat bluefish dry and season with salt and pepper. Heat oil in a 12-inch nonstick skillet over moderately high heat until hot but not smoking. Add bluefish skin side down and cook, turning once, until just cooked through, 6 to 8 minutes.

Meanwhile, cook butter in a small heavy saucepan over moderately high heat, swirling pan occasionally, until foam has subsided and butter is golden brown. Remove pan from heat and swirl in lemon juice and capers.

Transfer bluefish to four plates and spoon butter sauce over.

Monkfish Medallions with Tomato Lemon Coulis

SERVES 4

ACTIVE TIME: 15 MINUTES ■ START TO FINISH: 25 MINUTES

■ Monkfish is dense and substantial. We treat it like a pork or beef tenderloin by cutting it into medallions and sautéing them. Then you only need garlic, tomatoes, lemon juice, and parsley to make a quick coulis at the end. ■

- 4 small monkfish fillets (2 pounds total), any membrane and dark meat discarded, cut crosswise into 1-inch-thick medallions
- 1¼ teaspoons dried thyme, crumbled
- Salt and freshly ground black pepper
- 4½ tablespoons unsalted butter
- 2 teaspoons minced garlic
- 3 medium tomatoes, coarsely chopped
- 2 tablespoons fresh lemon juice, or to taste
- 2 tablespoons minced fresh flat-leaf parsley

Preheat oven to 200°F.

Pat monkfish dry and sprinkle with 1 teaspoon thyme and salt and pepper to taste. Heat 1½ tablespoons butter in a 12-inch heavy skillet over moderately high heat until foam subsides. Add half of monkfish and sear, turning once, until cooked through, about 10 minutes. Transfer to an ovenproof platter and keep warm in oven, loosely covered with foil. Cook remaining monkfish in 1 more tablespoon butter in same manner. Transfer to platter to keep warm in oven, loosely covered.

Melt remaining 2 tablespoons butter in skillet over moderately low heat. Add garlic and cook, stirring, until golden, about 30 seconds. Add tomatoes, lemon juice, and remaining ¼ teaspoon thyme and cook coulis, stirring, for 5 minutes. Stir in any juices accumulated on platter, add parsley and salt and pepper to taste, and spoon coulis over monkfish.

Sautéed Swordfish with Niçoise Vinaigrette

SERVES 4

ACTIVE TIME: 20 MINUTES ■ START TO FINISH: 30 MINUTES

■ Swordfish is a very special treat, but the fisheries, especially in the Atlantic, have been in peril and are only slowly making their way back, so we need to be careful about indulging. Dense, meaty, and substantial, swordfish can stand up well to bold Mediterranean flavors—black olives, capers, roasted red peppers, and anchovies, in this case. If swordfish is unavailable, mako, other shark, or halibut can be substituted, as long as the steaks are the same size and thickness. ■

- 4 (6-ounce) swordfish steaks (1¼ inches thick)
- 10 tablespoons olive oil
- 1 small garlic clove
- ½ teaspoon salt
- ½ cup finely chopped pitted Kalamata or other brine-cured black olives
- ½ cup finely chopped drained bottled roasted red peppers
- ⅓ cup finely chopped fresh flat-leaf parsley
- 2 tablespoons drained capers, finely chopped
- 2 flat anchovy fillets, minced
- ¼ cup minced scallions
- 3 tablespoons red wine vinegar
- Freshly ground black pepper

ACCOMPANIMENT: lemon wedges

Pat swordfish dry. Heat 3 tablespoons oil in a 12-inch skillet, preferably nonstick, over moderately high heat until hot but not smoking. Add swordfish and cook, turning once, until just cooked through, 8 to 10 minutes total.

Meanwhile, using a large knife, mince and mash garlic to a paste with salt. Combine garlic paste, olives, roasted red peppers, parsley, capers, anchovies, scallions, vinegar, and remaining 7 tablespoons oil in a bowl and stir to blend. Season with salt and pepper to taste.

Transfer swordfish to plates and spoon sauce over it. Serve with lemon wedges.

Crisp Red-Cooked Bass Fillets

SERVES 2

ACTIVE TIME: 30 MINUTES ■ START TO FINISH: 30 MINUTES

■ The Shanghai method of red cooking calls for the slow simmering of rich meats in a combination of Shaoxing rice wine, rock sugar (a semirefined sugar that helps make Chinese sauces and glazes translucent), and dark soy sauce. It is one of the most delectable things going, and it works well with fish. We love the contrast between crisp skin and moist, flavorful meat, so first we sear the fillets skin sides down, then we turn them over and poach them briefly in the red sauce. This taste of the exotic is only as far away as the supermarket: regular sugar stands in for rock sugar, and anise seeds take the place of traditional star anise. ■

FOR SAUCE

- 1½ tablespoons soy sauce
- 1 tablespoon Chinese rice wine, sake, or medium-dry sherry
- 1 teaspoon minced peeled fresh ginger
- ½ teaspoon sugar
- ½ teaspoon cornstarch
- ¼ teaspoon anise seeds, crushed with a rolling pin
- ⅛ teaspoon ground cinnamon
- ¾ cup water

FOR FISH

- 2 (8-ounce) black bass, snapper, or other white-fleshed fish fillets with skin (¾–1 inch thick)
- 2½ teaspoons cornstarch
- 1 tablespoon vegetable oil

GARNISH: 1 scallion, minced

MAKE THE SAUCE: Whisk together all ingredients in a small saucepan and bring to a boil, whisking. Reduce heat and simmer, covered, for 5 minutes. Remove from heat.

MEANWHILE, COOK THE FISH: Pat fillets dry and rub both sides with cornstarch; shake off excess. Heat oil in a 12-inch nonstick skillet over moderately high heat until it just begins to smoke. Add fillets skin sides down and sear, pressing with a spatula to flatten, until golden, about 4 minutes.

Turn fillets over and pour sauce through a fine-mesh sieve into skillet. Simmer until fish just flakes, about 3 minutes. With a slotted spatula, transfer fillets, skin sides up, to plates. Simmer sauce, stirring, until slightly thickened. Spoon sauce around fillets and garnish with scallion.

Sole Goujonettes with Paprika Salt

SERVES 4 AS A MAIN COURSE, 6 AS AN HORS D'OEUVRE
ACTIVE TIME: 25 MINUTES ■ START TO FINISH: 25 MINUTES

■ *Goujon* is French for "gudgeon," a slender little European fish, but the word *goujonettes* is used to refer to thin strips of larger fish fillets that are deep-fried. They are irresistible. *Goujonettes* are usually made from sole, but because a true European sole such as Dover sole can be hard to find in the United States (and is very expensive), we substituted lemon sole, which is actually a flounder, with great success. We serve *goujonettes* with smoked paprika salt rather than the more traditional flavored mayonnaise or spritz of lemon. ■

- 1 tablespoon plus 3/4 teaspoon salt
- 1/2 teaspoon sweet or hot Spanish smoked paprika (see Glossary) or 1 teaspoon sweet or hot regular paprika
- About 8 cups vegetable oil for deep-frying
- 2 pounds lemon sole, catfish, or Alaskan pollack fillets
- 3/4 cup all-purpose flour
- 1/4 teaspoon freshly ground black pepper
- 1 cup seltzer or club soda, chilled

SPECIAL EQUIPMENT: a deep-fat thermometer

Stir together 1 tablespoon salt and 1/4 teaspoon paprika in a small bowl; set aside. Heat 2 inches oil in a 4-quart wide heavy pot over moderate heat until it registers 375°F on thermometer.

Meanwhile, pat sole dry, then cut diagonally into 1/2-inch-wide strips. Whisk together flour, remaining 1/4 teaspoon paprika, remaining 3/4 teaspoon salt, and pepper in a medium bowl, then whisk in seltzer. Working in batches of 6, dip fish strips in batter to coat, shake off excess, and add to hot oil. Fry, turning occasionally, until golden brown and just cooked through (cut a piece open to test), 3 to 4 minutes. With a slotted spoon, transfer to paper towels to drain, then sprinkle with some paprika salt. (Skim any bits of fried batter from pot and return oil to 375°F between batches.)

Serve remaining paprika salt on the side for dipping.

Pike Quenelles with White Wine–Mushroom Cream Sauce

SERVES 2 AS A MAIN COURSE, 6 AS A FIRST COURSE
ACTIVE TIME: 1½ HOURS ■ START TO FINISH: 3½ HOURS (INCLUDES MAKING STOCK)

■ Quenelles—light, delicate fish mousse dumplings that are formed into an egg shape and gently poached—are classic French cooking at its most ethereal and sublime. They were once reserved for professional chefs, but the food processor makes them much easier: you purée the fish instead of pounding it until smooth. Although the procedure still involves some work, you will be thrilled by what you've created. ■

FOR QUENELLES

- 3/4 pound pike or other fish fillets, such as whiting, red snapper, or salmon, skinned and cut into 1-inch pieces
- 2½ teaspoons salt
- 1/8 teaspoon white pepper
- 1/8 teaspoon freshly grated nutmeg
- 1 large egg white
- 3/4 cup very cold heavy cream

FOR SAUCE

- 1½ cups dry white wine
- 1/4 cup finely chopped shallots
- 1½ cups Fish Stock (page 930)
- 1½ cups heavy cream
- 1/2 pound mushrooms, stems discarded, caps thinly sliced
- 1/2 teaspoon salt
- 1/4 teaspoon white pepper
- 1/8 teaspoon freshly grated nutmeg
- 1 tablespoon arrowroot
- 1 tablespoon Cognac or other brandy
- 2 tablespoons finely chopped fresh chives or dill

MAKE THE QUENELLE MIXTURE: Combine fish, 1/2 teaspoon salt, pepper, and nutmeg in a food processor and process until smooth. Add egg white and process until incorporated. Using a rubber spatula, force mixture through a large medium-mesh sieve into a metal bowl; discard any sinew that remains in sieve. Put bowl in a larger bowl filled with ice and add cream to fish a little at a time, working it in with rubber spatula. Refrigerate mousse, covered, until stiff, at least 2 hours.

MEANWHILE, MAKE THE SAUCE: Combine wine and shallots in a 2-quart heavy saucepan, bring to a boil, and boil until liquid is reduced to 1/4 cup, 10 to 15 minutes. Add stock and boil until reduced to about 1 cup, about 10 minutes.

Pour liquid though a fine-mesh sieve into a 3- to 4-quart wide heavy saucepan, pressing on solids; discard solids. Add cream, mushrooms, salt, white pepper, and nutmeg, bring to a simmer, and simmer until reduced to 3 cups, about 5 minutes.

Stir together arrowroot and Cognac in a small bowl until smooth, then whisk into sauce. Simmer, stirring occasionally, until sauce is slightly thickened, about 2 minutes. Stir in chives and season with salt and white pepper. Remove from heat.

FORM AND POACH THE QUENELLES: Bring 2 inches water to a simmer in a wide 3- to 4-quart pot and add remaining 2 teaspoons salt.

Using two large soupspoons dipped in cold water, scoop out 1/3 cup mousse and form into an oval, then gently place on oiled parchment or wax paper. Form 5 more quenelles in same manner. (If quenelles seem very delicate, chill again before poaching.) With a metal spatula, transfer quenelles to simmering water and poach at a bare simmer, turning occasionally, until just cooked through, about 8 minutes. With a slotted spoon, transfer quenelles to paper towels to drain, and cool for 10 minutes.

ASSEMBLE THE DISH: Transfer quenelles to warm sauce and gently heat over low heat until heated through, about 5 minutes. With a spoon, transfer quenelles to shallow soup plates and top with some sauce.

COOK'S NOTES

- The quenelle mixture can be refrigerated for up to 1 day.
- The quenelles can be poached up to 4 hours ahead. Cool, uncovered, then refrigerate, covered. Reheat in the sauce for about 10 minutes.
- The sauce can be made, without the chives, up to 1 day ahead. Cool, uncovered, then refrigerate, covered. Reheat gently, then stir in chives and season with salt and pepper before proceeding.
- You will have leftover sauce, which is excellent served over rice or tossed with pasta.

Fish in Crispy Tacos with Avocado and Tropical Fruit Salsa

SERVES 4 TO 6
ACTIVE TIME: 1 1/2 HOURS ■ START TO FINISH: 1 1/2 HOURS (INCLUDES MAKING SALSA)

■ These tacos are not the classic fried fish tacos of Baja California or San Diego (see page 296) but a much lighter version. The fish is sautéed (not coated in batter and fried), tossed with smoky chipotle chiles, spooned into crisp taco shells instead of soft tacos, and served with a fruity salsa instead of a tomatoey one. This recipe comes from Cibolo Creek, a dude ranch in Shafter, Texas.

If you can't find red snapper, any of the following fish will work, as long as the fillets are the same size and thickness: grouper, yelloweye rockfish, onaga (Hawaiian red snapper), catfish, shark, or mahimahi. ■

About 6 cups canola or vegetable oil for deep-frying taco shells, plus 6 tablespoons oil
12 taco shells
Salt
1 tablespoon fresh lime juice
Freshly ground black pepper
2 pounds red snapper fillets, skinned and cut into 1-inch pieces
6 scallions, chopped
2 canned chipotle chiles in adobo (see Glossary), finely chopped
3 cups arugula leaves or watercress sprigs, coarse stems discarded, leaves torn into bite-sized pieces

ACCOMPANIMENT: Avocado and Tropical Fruit Salsa (recipe follows)

SPECIAL EQUIPMENT: a deep-fat thermometer

Heat 2 inches oil in a 4-quart saucepan over moderately high heat until it registers 375°F on thermometer. Fry taco shells 2 at a time, turning occasionally, until a shade darker, about 1 minute. Transfer to paper towels to drain and sprinkle with salt.

To make dressing, whisk together juice, 3 tablespoons oil, and salt and pepper to taste in a medium bowl.

Pat fish dry and season with salt and pepper. Heat remaining 3 tablespoons oil in a large nonstick skillet over moderately high heat until hot but not smoking. Add scallions and cook, stirring, for 1 minute. Add fish and cook, stirring occasionally, until just cooked through, about 3 minutes. Remove skillet from heat, add chipotles, and gently toss with fish to combine.

Toss arugula with dressing and salt and pepper to taste. Fill taco shells with arugula and fish mixture and top with salsa.

Avocado and Tropical Fruit Salsa

MAKES ABOUT 3 CUPS
ACTIVE TIME: 20 MINUTES ■ START TO FINISH: 20 MINUTES

■ This salsa is great with other fish or even with pork. At Cibolo Creek, they make it both with and without avocado; we like it with. ■

2 cups finely diced tropical fruit, such as kiwi, pineapple, mango, and papaya
2 California avocados, pitted, peeled, and cut into 1/4-inch dice
1/4 cup chopped fresh cilantro
1/4 cup finely chopped red onion
1 serrano or jalapeño chile, seeded and finely chopped
2 tablespoons fresh lime juice, or to taste
Salt and freshly ground black pepper to taste

Gently toss together all ingredients in a bowl.

Classic Baja-Style Fish Tacos

SERVES 4 TO 6
ACTIVE TIME: 45 MINUTES ■ START TO FINISH: 1 3/4 HOURS

■ A dramatic contrast of textures—crisp fried fish against a tender corn tortilla—is the key to a great fish taco. This specialty of Baja, introduced to San Diego by the restaurateur Ralph Rubio in 1983, has become the city's most famous dish: fast food with an epicurean reputation. Our recipe is adapted from the tacos served at Rubio's Baja Grill. Frying the fish twice gives it a crisper crust. If cod isn't available, you can use Alaskan pollack, catfish, tilapia, shark, or mahimahi. ■

FOR BATTER
1 cup plus 2 tablespoons beer (not dark)
1 cup all-purpose flour
1 1/2 teaspoons salt
1 teaspoon garlic powder
1 teaspoon dry mustard
1 teaspoon dried oregano, preferably Mexican (see Sources), crumbled
1/2 teaspoon freshly ground black pepper

FOR SAUCE
2/3 cup mayonnaise
1/3 cup plain yogurt
1/2 teaspoon kosher salt

FOR FISH AND TACOS
About 8 cups vegetable oil for deep-frying
About 1 cup all-purpose flour
1 (1-pound) cod fillet, cut into 3-by-1/2-inch-wide strips
12 corn tortillas

ACCOMPANIMENTS: finely shredded cabbage, lime wedges, Guacamole (page 9), and salsa (such as Fresh Tomato Salsa, page 896)

SPECIAL EQUIPMENT: a deep-fat thermometer

MAKE THE BATTER: Combine beer, flour, salt, garlic powder, dry mustard, oregano, and pepper in a blender and blend until smooth, about 20 seconds. Transfer to a bowl and let stand, covered, for 1 hour.

MAKE THE SAUCE: Stir together mayonnaise, yogurt, and salt in a small bowl. Cover and refrigerate.

FRY THE FISH: Put a rack in middle of oven and preheat oven to 350°F.

Heat 2 inches oil in a 4-quart deep heavy saucepan until it registers 350°F on thermometer. Put flour in a pie plate or shallow dish. Dredge 10 cod strips in flour, shake off excess, then coat in batter, letting excess drip off, and add to hot oil. Fry, stirring, until pale golden, 2 to 3 minutes. With a slotted spoon, transfer to paper towels to drain. Repeat with remaining fish. (Return oil to 350°F between batches.) Set pan of oil aside.

HEAT THE TORTILLAS AND REFRY THE FISH: Wrap tortillas in stacks of 6 in foil and heat in oven until hot, 12 to 15 minutes. Unwrap tortillas and transfer to a cloth-lined basket, folding cloth over them to keep warm.

Meanwhile, reheat oil until it registers 375°F. Refry fish strips in batches of 10, stirring, until golden brown, 1 to 2 minutes. With a slotted spoon, transfer to paper towels to drain again.

Top tortillas with fish, cabbage, and sauce. Squeeze limes over tacos and serve with guacamole and salsa.

Fried Perch Fillets with Fresh Cucumber Relish

SERVES 8 TO 10

ACTIVE TIME: 1 HOUR ■ START TO FINISH: 1 HOUR

■ Double-dipping lake perch fillets in a crumb coating results in extra-crisp fish, and it helps the fillets hold up while you are frying subsequent batches. The herb and cheese coating has a wonderful flavor and works beautifully with the mild perch; the freshness of the relish cuts the richness of the fried fish. This recipe, from the Oyster Bar in Fort Wayne, Indiana, can be halved. ■

FOR RELISH

- 2 tablespoons fresh lemon juice
- 2 tablespoons rice vinegar (not seasoned)
- 1/3 cup olive oil
- 1/2 large cucumber, peeled, seeded, and finely chopped
- 1/2 small red bell pepper, cored, seeded, and finely chopped
- 1/4 cup finely chopped red onion
- 1/2 cup finely chopped celery
- 1/4 teaspoon salt

FOR FILLETS

- 2 large eggs
- 1 cup whole milk
- 3 cups fine fresh bread crumbs
- 3 cups all-purpose flour
- 3/4 cup finely grated Parmigiano-Reggiano
- 3 tablespoons minced fresh dill
- 1 1/2 tablespoons minced fresh thyme
- 2 teaspoons salt
- 1 1/2 teaspoons white pepper
- 1 1/2 pounds skinless lake perch fillets (about 30)
- About 6 cups peanut oil for deep-frying

SPECIAL EQUIPMENT: a deep-fat thermometer

MAKE THE RELISH: Whisk together lemon juice and vinegar in a bowl, then add oil in a slow stream, whisking until well blended. Stir in remaining ingredients and set aside.

FRY THE FISH: Whisk together eggs and milk in a shallow bowl. Stir together bread crumbs, flour, Parmesan, dill, thyme, salt, and pepper in another shallow bowl. Working in batches, dip fillets into egg mixture, letting excess drip off, then dredge in flour mixture. Coat fillets with egg and flour mixtures a second time, then transfer to a wax paper–lined tray.

Heat 1 inch oil in a deep 10-inch heavy skillet over moderately high heat until it registers 350°F on thermometer. Fry fillets in 4 or 5 batches, turning, until golden, 2 to 3 minutes per batch. (Return oil to 350°F between batches.) Transfer to paper towels to drain and season with salt.

Serve with cucumber relish.

Tuna Burgers with Chimichurri

SERVES 4
ACTIVE TIME: 30 MINUTES ■ START TO FINISH: 11 HOURS (INCLUDES CHILLING)

■ Chimichurri, a pungent herb sauce that's popular all over Argentina, is usually served with grilled meats. It makes a great condiment for a variety of other dishes too. Chef Norman Van Aken, of Norman's, in Coral Gables, Florida, puts this burger on Cuban bread (a firm white loaf traditionally used for pressed sandwiches), but we like it on a baguette as well. It's important to purchase the best tuna for this recipe, as the burgers are served medium-rare. ■

FOR CHIMICHURRI

- 1 teaspoon cumin seeds, toasted (see Tips, page 939)
- ½ cup minced fresh flat-leaf parsley
- ½ cup extra-virgin olive oil
- 2 tablespoons sherry vinegar
- 6 garlic cloves, minced
- 1 teaspoon black peppercorns, crushed with bottom of a heavy skillet
- 1 teaspoon cayenne
- ½ teaspoon kosher salt

FOR BURGERS

- 1¼ pounds highest-quality tuna, cut into 1-inch pieces
- 1 tablespoon olive oil

ACCOMPANIMENTS: grilled or sautéed onions and toasted split Cuban bread or baguette cut into 4 pieces

SPECIAL EQUIPMENT: an electric coffee/spice grinder

MAKE THE CHIMICHURRI: Grind cooled cumin seeds in coffee/spice grinder. Stir cumin together with remaining ingredients in a bowl, mixing well. Refrigerate, covered, for 8 hours to blend flavors.

MAKE THE BURGERS: Pulse tuna in a food processor until it just holds together in a mass, 3 or 4 times (be careful not to grind to a paste). Transfer to a bowl and stir in ⅓ cup chimichurri. Form into four 1-inch-thick burgers. Refrigerate, covered, for 2 hours.

Heat oil in a 10-inch cast-iron skillet over moderately high heat until hot but not smoking. Add burgers and cook until undersides are browned, about 4 minutes. Turn burgers over, reduce heat to moderate, and cook for 5 to 6 minutes more for medium-rare.

Serve with onions on Cuban bread or baguette.

COOK'S NOTE

■ The recipe will make more chimichurri than you need for the burgers, but the remainder can be refrigerated for up to 5 days. It goes very well with grilled or roasted chicken, meat, or other fish.

Sushi-Grade Fish

We've all walked into a fish store and seen specimens labeled "sushi-grade" or, more properly, "sashimi-grade" (sashimi refers to sliced raw fish, whereas sushi preparations involve rice). It must be the freshest, most pristine fish in the store, right? Not necessarily, according to the seafood expert Jon Rowley.

For the average American consumer, *sushi-grade* is a marketing term intended to convey the idea that the fish is of such high quality that a Japanese sushi chef would buy it. "Traditionally, a sushi chef undergoes a seven-year apprenticeship, and becoming an accomplished fish buyer is part of that training," Rowley says. "A good Japanese sushi chef would not consider much of the 'sashimi-grade' tuna offered by typical American distributors of high enough quality to serve as sushi or sashimi." So don't be lured into thinking that you are necessarily buying impeccably fresh fish when you pony up for something labeled "sushi-grade." Smart shoppers will buy from a fishmonger they know and trust, especially if they are serving something like tuna raw, rare, or medium-rare.

Shad Roe with Lemon Butter

SERVES 6

ACTIVE TIME: 15 MINUTES ■ START TO FINISH: 15 MINUTES

■ Shad roe is available in the spring, when the fish are spawning, and this eagerly awaited delicacy makes a wonderful, rich meal. Cooking it just right, so it's neither too mushy nor too firm, can be a bit tricky, so don't walk away or take a phone call when you're at the stove. Lobes of roe are usually sold in pairs, or "sets"; look for lobes that are rosy. ■

- 3 pairs shad roe (about $1\frac{1}{2}$ pounds total)
- $\frac{1}{3}$ cup all-purpose flour
- 1 teaspoon salt
- $\frac{1}{4}$ teaspoon freshly ground black pepper
- $\frac{3}{4}$ stick (6 tablespoons) unsalted butter
- 3 tablespoons fresh lemon juice
- 2 tablespoons finely chopped fresh flat-leaf parsley

Rinse roe and pat dry, handling it gently to prevent membranes from tearing. Stir together flour, salt, and pepper and spread on a sheet of wax paper.

Melt 2 tablespoons butter in a 12-inch heavy skillet over moderate heat. Dredge roe in flour, gently shake off excess, and add to skillet. Cook, turning once with a wide spatula, until roe just begins to feel firm to the touch at the thickest part, 4 to 9 minutes total. With spatula, transfer roe to a platter; set aside. Cut pairs apart with a sharp knife and cover loosely with foil to keep warm.

Cut remaining $\frac{1}{2}$ stick butter into tablespoons. Add lemon juice to skillet and bring to a boil, then swirl in butter until melted. Remove from heat, stir in parsley, and season with salt and pepper.

Serve roe topped with sauce.

Grilled Tuna with Warm White Bean Salad

SERVES 4

ACTIVE TIME: 15 MINUTES ■ START TO FINISH: $1\frac{1}{2}$ HOURS PLUS SOAKING TIME FOR BEANS

■ In Italy, good canned tuna is often tossed with white beans in summer and served as an antipasto. We've achieved the same sort of effect with grilled fresh tuna. This makes a hearty meal. ■

- $\frac{1}{2}$ pound ($1\frac{1}{4}$ cups) dried great northern beans, picked over and rinsed
- 2 garlic cloves
- 1 teaspoon salt
- 2 ounces arugula, coarse stems discarded (2 cups)
- 1 small red onion, thinly sliced
- 2 tablespoons chopped fresh flat-leaf parsley
- 3 tablespoons fresh lemon juice
- 3 tablespoons extra-virgin olive oil
- Freshly ground black pepper
- 4 (6-ounce) tuna steaks ($\frac{1}{2}$ inch thick)
- 1 teaspoon fennel seeds, crushed with bottom of a heavy skillet

COOK THE BEANS: Soak beans in cold water to cover by 2 inches for at least 8 hours (or see page 267 for quick-soaking procedure); drain. Smash 1 garlic clove with side of a large heavy knife. Combine beans, crushed garlic, 4 cups water, and $\frac{1}{2}$ teaspoon salt in a 3- to 4-quart saucepan, bring to a simmer, and simmer until beans are tender, about 1 hour. Reserve $\frac{1}{4}$ cup cooking liquid and drain beans.

PREPARE A CHARCOAL OR GAS GRILL: If using a charcoal grill, open vents in bottom of grill, then light charcoal. Fire is medium-hot when you can hold your hand 5 inches above rack for just 3 to 4 seconds. If using a gas grill, preheat on high, covered, for 10 minutes, then reduce heat to moderately high.

MEANWHILE, MAKE THE SALAD: Mash $\frac{1}{2}$ cup beans with a fork in a small bowl, then transfer to cleaned saucepan. Add whole beans and reserved liquid and stir well. Mince remaining garlic clove and mash to a paste with remaining $\frac{1}{2}$ teaspoon salt. Chop half of arugula and stir into beans, along with garlic paste, onion, parsley, 2 tablespoons lemon juice, 2 tablespoons oil, and salt and pepper to taste. Cover and keep warm over very low heat while you cook tuna.

GRILL TUNA: Put tuna steaks on a plate and drizzle with remaining 1 tablespoon each lemon juice and olive oil, turning to coat both sides. Sprinkle both sides with fennel seeds and salt and pepper to taste.

Lightly oil grill rack and grill fish, uncovered, turning once, until barely cooked through, about 6 minutes total. Arrange bean salad and remaining arugula on four plates and top with fish.

COOK'S NOTE

- The fish can be cooked in a well-seasoned ridged grill pan over moderately high heat in the same manner.

Broiled Bluefish Fillets with Fennel Mayonnaise

SERVES 4
ACTIVE TIME: 10 MINUTES ■ START TO FINISH: 20 MINUTES

■ Bluefish is at its freshest when it's in season, during the summer. Fennel is good with most fish, and mayonnaise is a wonderful way to carry its flavor. We spread the fennel mayonnaise over the bluefish before broiling, forming a protective coating that helps keep the fish moist and succulent. This is one of the easiest ways to cook fish, and it's a great spur to creativity—experiment with other flavorings for the mayonnaise and different kinds of fish. ■

- 2 teaspoons fennel seeds
- 2 large garlic cloves
- 1 teaspoon salt
- 1/4 cup mayonnaise
- 1 tablespoon fresh lemon juice
- Freshly ground black pepper
- 4 (8-ounce) pieces bluefish or mackerel fillet with skin

Preheat broiler. Oil a shallow baking pan large enough to hold fillets in one layer.

Toast fennel seeds in a dry small skillet over moderate heat, stirring, until fragrant, about 3 minutes; remove from heat. Using a large heavy knife, mince garlic and fennel seeds with salt. Stir fennel mixture together with mayonnaise, lemon juice, and pepper to taste in a small bowl.

Arrange fillets skin sides down in baking pan and spread fennel mayonnaise evenly over tops. Broil about 6 inches from heat, without turning, until just cooked through, 6 to 8 minutes.

Grilled Mackerel with Spicy Tomato Jam

SERVES 4
ACTIVE TIME: 1½ HOURS ■ START TO FINISH: 1½ HOURS

■ Grilling imparts a hearty flavor to fish. Mackerel not only flourishes over high heat but can stand up to robust accompaniments such as our spicy tomato jam. Like bluefish, it can be too strong if not pristinely fresh. If it smells at all fishy, choose a different kind of fish and make another recipe. ■

- 3 medium tomatoes (1 pound total), peeled (see Tips, page 940), halved, seeded, and chopped
- 1 small onion, chopped
- 1/3 cup apple jelly
- 3 tablespoons cider vinegar
- 2 tablespoons chopped fresh tarragon
- 1/2 teaspoon red pepper flakes
- 1/4 teaspoon salt
- 4 (6-ounce) pieces mackerel or bluefish fillet with skin
- Freshly ground black pepper

Combine tomatoes, onion, jelly, vinegar, tarragon, red pepper flakes, and salt in a 1-quart heavy saucepan and bring to a boil over moderately low heat, stirring occasionally. Cook, stirring occasionally, until thickened, 30 to 40 minutes. Cool jam to room temperature.

Prepare a charcoal or gas grill: If using a charcoal grill, open vents in bottom of grill, then light charcoal. Fire is medium-hot when you can hold your hand 5 inches above rack for just 3 to 4 seconds. If using a gas grill, preheat on high, covered, for 10 minutes, then reduce heat to moderately high.

Season mackerel fillets with salt and pepper. Lightly oil grill rack and grill mackerel, uncovered, skin side down, until just cooked through, 9 to 13 minutes (do not turn fish).

Serve each fillet topped with 2 tablespoons jam.

COOK'S NOTE

- The jam will keep, covered and refrigerated, for up to 1 month. Bring to room temperature before serving. Try it with grilled or roasted chicken or pork or scrambled eggs.

Baked Flounder Fillets in Lemon Soy Vinaigrette

SERVES 4

ACTIVE TIME: 15 MINUTES ■ START TO FINISH: 25 MINUTES

■ The fine texture and delicate flavor of flounder is enlivened with a little garlic, lemon juice, and soy sauce. This makes a good, quick weeknight supper served with rice. If flounder isn't available, any of the following can be substituted, as long as the fillets are the same size and thickness: red snapper, grouper, rockfish, tilefish, halibut, cod, haddock, lingcod, salmon, striped bass, white sea bass, or mahimahi. ■

4 (6-ounce) flounder fillets, skinned
2 garlic cloves, minced
1/4 cup fresh lemon juice
4 teaspoons soy sauce
1 teaspoon sugar
1/2 teaspoon salt
1/4 cup olive oil
GARNISH: thinly sliced scallions

Put a rack in middle of oven and preheat oven to 450°F. Oil a baking dish just large enough to hold fillets in one layer.

Arrange fish in baking dish. Stir together garlic, lemon juice, soy sauce, sugar, and salt in a small bowl. Whisk in oil until well blended, then pour vinaigrette over fish.

Bake fish until just cooked through, 5 to 7 minutes. Sprinkle with scallions.

Crispy Oven-Fried Cod

SERVES 4

ACTIVE TIME: 10 MINUTES ■ START TO FINISH: 25 MINUTES

■ If you like fish-and-chips but don't like deep-fat frying, this method is for you. The crumb-coated fish is first panfried in a heavy skillet on the stovetop, then finished in the oven; Roasted French Fries (page 568) complete the picture. We use traditional cod or scrod (young cod or haddock under 2 1/2 pounds). If cod isn't available, any of the following can be substituted, as long as the fillets are the same size and thickness: haddock, halibut, Alaskan pollack, cusk, or hake. ■

3/4 cup fine dry bread crumbs
3/4 cup yellow cornmeal
1 teaspoon salt
1/4 teaspoon cayenne
2 large eggs
4 (6-ounce) pieces center-cut cod or scrod fillet (3/4 inch thick)
Freshly ground black pepper
6 tablespoons vegetable oil
ACCOMPANIMENT: lemon wedges and Tartar Sauce (page 885)

Put a rack in upper third of oven and preheat oven to 500°F.

Combine bread crumbs, cornmeal, salt, and cayenne in a large sealable plastic bag, seal, and shake to mix. Lightly beat eggs in a shallow bowl.

Season fish with salt and pepper on both sides. Working with one piece at a time, put fish in bag and shake to coat well with crumbs, then dip fish in eggs, shake in crumbs again to coat, and transfer to a plate.

Heat 3 tablespoons oil in a 12-inch heavy ovenproof skillet, preferably cast-iron, over high heat until hot but not smoking. Add fish and fry until undersides are golden brown, about 1 minute. Turn fish over, add remaining 3 tablespoons oil, and cook until golden brown on second side, about 1 minute more.

Transfer skillet to oven and bake until fish is cooked through, about 5 minutes. Serve with lemon wedges and tartar sauce.

Cod Marinated in Sake Kasu

SERVES 6

ACTIVE TIME: 30 MINUTES ■ START TO FINISH: 2½ HOURS

■ In Japan, nothing is wasted, especially any by-product of rice, an almost sacred ingredient. So *sake kasu,* the lees (solids) that remain after sake is made from fermented rice mash, is prized as a heady flavoring agent (as well as a preservative). It is pressed into sheets that are the consistency of modeling clay; when using it, simply tear off what you need. In the Pacific Northwest, where Asians make up a large part of the population, chefs embellish *kasu* with other flavors. In this recipe from the Salish Lodge & Spa in Snoqualmie, Washington, an unpromising-looking gloppy brown mixture turns the outside of the fish into a deeply flavored, gorgeous mahogany coat that contrasts with the tender, snowy white flesh. Black cod is also known as sablefish, and it is often smoked. Despite its name, it is not related to regular cod, which won't do for this recipe—it doesn't have the appropriate lushness; if necessary, substitute salmon. Look for *sake kasu* and the other Asian ingredients at an Asian market, or see Sources. ■

- 6 (6-ounce) pieces black cod (1½ inches thick), skinned
- 1 (1-inch-thick) slice fresh ginger, peeled and chopped
- 1 cup mirin (Japanese sweet rice wine)
- ½ cup *sake kasu*
- ½ cup tamari or soy sauce
- ¼ cup white miso (fermented soybean paste)
- ¼ cup rice vinegar (not seasoned)
- 2 tablespoons packed brown sugar
- 1 tablespoon vegetable oil

MARINATE THE FISH: Arrange fish in a 2-inch-deep baking dish just large enough to hold it in one layer.

Combine remaining ingredients except oil in a blender or food processor and blend until smooth. Pour over fish and turn fish to coat well. Marinate, covered and refrigerated, for at least 2 hours.

COOK THE FISH: Put a rack in middle of oven and preheat oven to 400°F.

Remove fish from marinade, letting excess drip off, and transfer to a plate. Discard marinade.

Heat oil in a 12-inch nonstick ovenproof skillet over moderately high heat until hot but not smoking. Add fish (skillet will be crowded; use caution, as oil will splatter) and sear on one side only until golden brown, 3 to 4 minutes.

Gently turn fish over, transfer to oven, and roast until just cooked through, 5 to 6 minutes.

COOK'S NOTES

- The fish can marinate for up to 1 day.
- If substituting salmon, reduce the roasting time to 3 to 4 minutes.

Fish en Papillote with Tomatoes and Olives

SERVES 4

ACTIVE TIME: 25 MINUTES ■ START TO FINISH: 35 MINUTES

■ Cooking something *en papillote* means that you encase it in a wrapping of parchment paper (or foil) and essentially steam it in its own juices. In this recipe, red snapper is baked with a piquant combination of tomatoes, black olives, herbs, and orange zest. This recipe can be made with a wide number of fish, as long as the fillets are the same size and thickness; try tilefish, halibut, cod, haddock, salmon, striped bass, white sea bass, or mahimahi. ■

- 4 (6-ounce) red snapper fillets (1 inch thick), skinned
- Salt and freshly ground black pepper
- 12 (¼-inch-thick) tomato slices (from 3–4 medium tomatoes)
- 8 Kalamata or other brine-cured black olives, pitted and thinly sliced
- ½ teaspoon red pepper flakes
- 2 tablespoons unsalted butter, cut into bits
- Zest from ½ orange, removed in long wide strips with a vegetable peeler and cut crosswise into very thin strips
- 4 fresh herb sprigs, such as sage, thyme, or parsley

Put a rack in middle of oven and preheat oven to 500°F.

Cut four 12-by-15-inch sheets of parchment paper (or foil). Fold each sheet crosswise in half to crease, then unfold. Season fish with salt and pepper and put 1 fillet to right of crease on each sheet. Top each fillet with 3 tomato slices, one quarter of olives, ⅛ teaspoon red pepper flakes, one quarter each of butter and zest, and 1 herb sprig. Working with one package at a time, fold left half of parchment over fillet. Starting at one corner of crease, fold edge of parchment over in triangles (each fold should overlap previous one), following a semicircular path around fillet, smoothing out folds as you go and tucking last fold under to seal *papillote* completely.

Heat a large baking sheet in oven for 5 minutes.

Put *papillotes* on hot baking sheet and bake for 9 minutes.

To serve, transfer packets to four plates; with a knife, slit top of each packet and tear it to expose fish (use caution: steam will escape). Slide fish and sauce onto plates and discard paper.

Ocean Perch Fillets with Fennel and Tomato

SERVES 4
ACTIVE TIME: 20 MINUTES ■ START TO FINISH: 1 HOUR

■ Ocean perch is a lovely little fish with a wonderful texture and body. It takes well to a lusty Mediterranean combination of fennel, tomatoes, olives, and garlic. ■

- ⅓ cup plus ¼ cup olive oil
- 1 onion, finely chopped
- 1 medium fennel bulb (1¼ pounds), stalks discarded, bulb cored and finely chopped (2 cups)
- 3 garlic cloves, minced
- ¼ teaspoon fennel seeds, lightly crushed with bottom of a heavy skillet
- ⅓ cup thinly sliced fresh basil leaves
- 2 tablespoons finely chopped fresh flat-leaf parsley
- 3 plum tomatoes, finely chopped
- ¼ cup chopped pitted brine-cured black olives
- ⅛ teaspoon cayenne
- ½ teaspoon salt
- White pepper
- 4 (6-ounce) ocean perch or black sea bass fillets
- 1 tablespoon minced shallot
- ½ cup dry white wine
- 2 tablespoons fresh lemon juice

OPTIONAL GARNISH: thin lemon slices

Put a rack in middle of oven and preheat oven to 425°F.

Heat ⅓ cup oil in a large skillet over moderate heat until hot but not smoking. Add onion, fennel, and one third of garlic and cook, stirring occasionally, until vegetables are tender, 13 to 15 minutes. Add fennel seeds, basil, parsley, tomatoes, olives, cayenne, salt, and white pepper to taste and cook until just heated through. Remove from heat and keep warm, covered.

While vegetables are cooking, season fillets with salt and white pepper; set aside. Heat remaining ¼ cup oil in a 1½-quart saucepan over moderately low heat. Add shallot and remaining garlic and cook, stirring occasionally, for 1 minute. Add wine and lemon juice and bring to a boil, then boil until reduced by about half, about 5 minutes.

Pour shallot mixture into a baking pan large enough to hold fillets in one layer. Put fillets skin sides down in pan and bake until they just flake, about 12 minutes.

Divide vegetable mixture among four plates and put a fillet on each bed of vegetables. Garnish with lemon slices, if desired.

Romaine-Wrapped Halibut Fillets

SERVES 4
ACTIVE TIME: 25 MINUTES ■ START TO FINISH: 45 MINUTES

■ Most people don't think of cooking romaine, or any lettuce, for that matter. But in this dish, the romaine wrapping keeps the fish moist and tender, both by releasing its own moisture and by protecting the fillets from the direct heat of the oven. And the sweetness of the lettuce goes well with the mild flavor of halibut. ■

- 3 tablespoons unsalted butter, softened
- 1 lemon, halved
- 2 tablespoons finely chopped shallots
- Salt and freshly ground black pepper
- 10 unblemished large outer romaine leaves (from 2 heads)
- 4 (6-ounce) pieces halibut, cod, or other white-fleshed fish fillet (1¼–1½ inches thick)

Put a rack in middle of oven and preheat oven to 450°F. Grease a 13-by-9-inch baking or gratin dish with 1 tablespoon butter.

Cut 2 thin slices from each lemon half and squeeze juice from remaining lemon. Mash together remaining 2 tablespoons butter, 1 teaspoon lemon juice, shallots, and salt and pepper to taste in a small bowl. Sprinkle remaining juice into baking dish.

Cook lettuce in a 4-quart saucepan of boiling well-salted water for 1 minute; immediately transfer with tongs to a bowl of ice and cold water to cool. Drain lettuce, then cut out ribs, leaving top 1 inch of leaves intact.

Lay out 1 lettuce leaf lengthwise on a work surface. Put another leaf on top, overlapping leaves enough to cover slits where ribs were removed (use one of the 2 extra leaves if necessary). Season 1 piece of halibut with salt and pepper, lay across center of lettuce, and spread top of fish with one quarter of shallot butter. Wrap lettuce around fish to form a packet (don't worry if ends aren't covered by lettuce) and transfer to baking dish. Make 3 more packets in same manner, placing them close together in baking dish. Top each packet with a lemon slice.

Cover packets with a sheet of wax or parchment paper, then cover dish tightly with foil. Bake until centers of packets are just firm to the touch, 15 to 20 minutes (depending on thickness of fish). Serve with pan juices poured over packets.

Crabmeat-Stuffed Sole

SERVES 4
ACTIVE TIME: 25 MINUTES ■ START TO FINISH: 45 MINUTES

■ Stuffed seafood dishes aren't known for being low in fat, but, inspired by a classic butter-heavy recipe, we developed this light, modern, crabmeat-stuffed sole. Dispensing with the cream sauce into which the seafood is typically plunked, we rely instead on high-heat oven cooking and a covered pan to release the natural juices of the crab and sole. The result is a delicate, self-saucing dish—one component of a simple, summery dinner. We call for small fillets, but if you can only find larger ones, simply bump up the other ingredients accordingly. Of course, feel free to use full-fat (and full-flavored) mayonnaise. ■

FOR CRAB STUFFING AND FISH

- 1/4 pound (1 cup) jumbo lump crabmeat, picked over for shells and cartilage
- 1 1/2 tablespoons reduced-fat (not low-fat) mayonnaise
- 1/4 cup finely diced yellow bell pepper
- 1 tablespoon chopped fresh flat-leaf parsley
- Salt and freshly ground black pepper
- 4 (4-ounce) gray sole fillets

FOR GARLIC BREAD CRUMBS

- 1 small garlic clove, minced
- 2 teaspoons extra-virgin olive oil
- 1/4 cup fine fresh bread crumbs, preferably from a baguette
- 1 teaspoon finely grated lemon zest
- Salt and freshly ground black pepper

PREPARE THE STUFFING AND FISH: Put a rack in upper third of oven and preheat oven to 450°F. Lightly oil a 9-inch pie plate.

Stir together crab, mayonnaise, bell pepper, and parsley in a small bowl. Season with salt and pepper.

Lay sole fillets flat, darker sides up, and season with salt and pepper. Divide stuffing among fillets, mounding it on thicker half of each. Fold thinner half of fillet over stuffing and tuck end under to form a packet. Arrange fillets in oiled pie plate. Cover with a round of parchment or wax paper, then cover pie plate tightly with foil.

Bake until sole is just cooked through and stuffing is hot, about 20 minutes.

MEANWHILE, MAKE THE BREAD CRUMBS: Cook garlic in oil in a small skillet over moderate heat, stirring, until fragrant, about 30 seconds. Stir in bread crumbs and cook, stirring, until golden brown, 4 to 5 minutes. Remove from heat, stir in zest, and season with salt and pepper.

Transfer sole to four plates and pour pan juices through a fine-mesh sieve into a bowl. Spoon some of juices over fish and sprinkle with bread crumbs.

Roasted Striped Bass with Chive and Sour Cream Sauce

SERVES 6

ACTIVE TIME: 25 MINUTES ■ START TO FINISH: 30 MINUTES

■ The elegant celadon green sauce for this fish adds a little richness without making the dish heavy, and all you need are some simple sides—new potatoes and zucchini, for instance. If you're unable to find striped bass, any of the following can be substituted (as long as they are purchased with the skin on): freshwater whitefish, red snapper, grouper, halibut, cod, haddock, tilefish, tautog, white sea bass, or salmon. ■

FOR SAUCE

- 2/3 cup sour cream
- 2 tablespoons water
- 4 teaspoons fresh lemon juice
- 1/4 teaspoon salt
- 1/2 cup finely chopped fresh chives
- Freshly ground black pepper

FOR FISH

- 6 (5-ounce) pieces striped bass fillet with skin
- Salt and freshly ground black pepper
- 1 1/2 tablespoons vegetable oil
- 1 lemon, cut into 6 wedges

MAKE THE SAUCE: Combine sour cream, water, juice, salt, and chives in a blender and blend until mixture just turns pale green. Season with pepper. Set aside.

PREPARE THE FISH: Put a rack in middle of oven and preheat oven to 450°F. Oil a shallow baking pan.

Remove any pinbones from fish with tweezers or needle-nose pliers and pat fish dry with paper towels. With a thin sharp knife, score skin in several places to prevent fish from curling (do not cut through flesh). Season with salt and pepper.

Heat oil in a 12-inch nonstick skillet over high heat until hot but not smoking. Add fish skin side down, in 2 batches, and sear until skin is golden brown and crisp, 3 to 4 minutes per batch (fish will not be fully cooked). Transfer with a slotted spatula to oiled baking pan, turning fish skin side up.

Roast fish, uncovered, until just cooked through, 7 to 8 minutes.

Spoon 3 tablespoons sauce onto each of six plates and top with fish. Squeeze a lemon wedge over each fillet.

COOK'S NOTE

- The sauce can be made up to 1 day ahead and refrigerated, covered.

Sea Bass Chermoula with Braised Fennel

SERVES 6

ACTIVE TIME: 1 HOUR ■ START TO FINISH: 2 HOURS

■ If you are one of those people who tend to think fish is too bland, this will be right up your alley, because fish, like meats and poultry, takes beautifully to the vibrant, intense flavors and colors of *chermoula,* a fragrant North African blend of herbs and spices. As exotic and impressive as it is, the recipe can be made with supermarket ingredients. ■

FOR *CHERMOULA*

- ½ teaspoon ground cumin
- ½ teaspoon ground coriander
- 12 black peppercorns
- ¼ teaspoon red pepper flakes
- ½ teaspoon coarse sea salt or kosher salt
- 1 teaspoon paprika
- ¼ cup finely chopped fresh flat-leaf parsley
- ¼ cup finely chopped fresh cilantro
- 2 tablespoons olive oil
- 2 tablespoons fresh lemon juice
- 1 tablespoon minced garlic

FOR FISH AND FENNEL

- 6 (5- to 6-ounce) skinless firm white-fleshed fish fillets, such as sea bass or red snapper (1 inch thick)
- 1¼ teaspoons salt, or to taste
- ½ teaspoon freshly ground black pepper, or to taste
- 4 medium fennel bulbs (3 pounds total), stalks discarded, fronds reserved for garnish if desired
- ½ cup water
- 2 tablespoons unsalted butter

OPTIONAL GARNISH: finely chopped fresh flat-leaf parsley and reserved fennel fronds

SPECIAL EQUIPMENT: an electric coffee/spice grinder

MAKE THE *CHERMOULA*: Finely grind cumin, coriander, peppercorns, red pepper flakes, and coarse salt together in coffee/spice grinder. Transfer to a small bowl and stir in remaining ingredients.

MARINATE THE FISH: Butter a 13-by-9-inch baking dish. Pat fish dry and season with ¾ teaspoon salt and ¼ teaspoon pepper. Arrange fillets in one layer in buttered baking dish and top evenly with *chermoula*. Refrigerate, covered with plastic wrap, for 45 minutes, then let sit at room temperature for 15 minutes.

PREPARE THE FENNEL AND BAKE THE FISH: Put a rack in middle of oven and preheat oven to 350°F.

Halve each fennel bulb lengthwise and cut out cores. With a sharp knife, cut fennel lengthwise into ¼-inch-wide strips. Combine water and butter in a 12-inch heavy skillet and bring to a boil over moderately high heat. Add fennel, cover, and cook, stirring occasionally, for 10 minutes. Uncover fennel and cook, stirring occasionally, until tender, 5 to 10 minutes more. Season with remaining ½ teaspoon salt and ¼ teaspoon pepper.

Meanwhile, bake fish, uncovered, until just cooked through, 12 to 18 minutes.

Serve each fillet on a bed of fennel, garnished with parsley and fennel fronds, if desired.

Slow-Roasted Salmon with Mustard Parsley Glaze

SERVES 8

ACTIVE TIME: 10 MINUTES ■ START TO FINISH: 40 MINUTES

■ The technique of slow roasting gives a firm-bodied fish like salmon such a tender texture that it practically melts in your mouth. To test for doneness, look not for flakiness but for a change in appearance from translucent to opaque. Chef Sarah Stegner at the Ritz-Carlton in Chicago serves this with buttered asparagus. ■

- ¾ stick (6 tablespoons) unsalted butter, softened
- 3 tablespoons fine dry bread crumbs
- 2 tablespoons chopped fresh flat-leaf parsley
- 1 tablespoon mustard seeds
- 1 tablespoon fresh lime juice
- 2 teaspoons Dijon mustard
- 1 teaspoon honey
- 8 (5-ounce) pieces center-cut salmon fillet, skinned
- Salt to taste
- ½ teaspoon white pepper

Put a rack in middle of oven and preheat oven to 225°F. Butter a roasting pan large enough to hold salmon without crowding.

Stir together butter, bread crumbs, parsley, mustard seeds, lime juice, mustard, and honey in a small bowl until well combined.

Arrange salmon skinned side down in roasting pan and sprinkle with salt and white pepper. Spread mustard glaze evenly over salmon.

Roast until fish is just cooked through (it will turn opaque), 25 to 30 minutes.

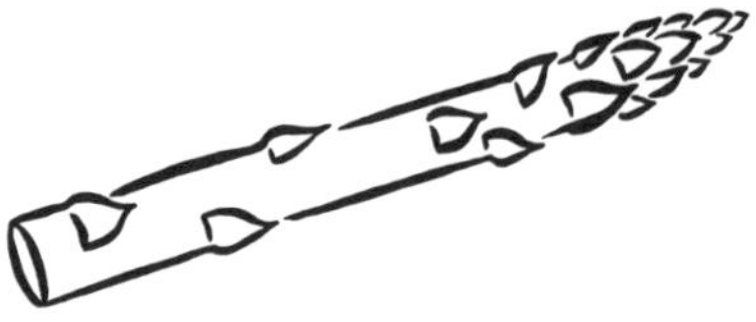

Salmon with Horseradish Crust, Cucumbers, and Salmon Caviar

SERVES 6

ACTIVE TIME: 1 HOUR ■ START TO FINISH: 3 HOURS (INCLUDES CHILLING)

■ This elegant company dish combines three forms of salmon in a fresh, innovative way. Smoked salmon is blended with horseradish, butter, and bread crumbs and spread on top of a salmon fillet. When broiled, the crust simultaneously holds its own flavor and seals in the flavor of the fish; it also provides a wonderfully crisp texture. To top it all off, the dish is served with salmon caviar and a creamy cucumber sauce. We adapted this from a recipe by the chef Terrance Brennan, of New York City's Picholine restaurant. ■

- ½ pound sliced firm white sandwich bread, crusts discarded and slices quartered
- 1 horseradish root or ½ cup (4 ounces) bottled horseradish
- ¼ pound sliced smoked salmon
- 1 stick (8 tablespoons) unsalted butter, cut into tablespoons, softened
- 1½ tablespoons Dijon mustard
- ¾ teaspoon cayenne
- Fine sea salt
- 2 seedless cucumbers (usually plastic wrapped), peeled, halved lengthwise, seeded, and cut diagonally into ¼-inch-thick slices
- 6 (6-ounce) pieces center-cut salmon fillet, skinned
- Freshly ground black pepper
- 1 tablespoon olive oil
- 1 cup crème fraîche
- 3 tablespoons chopped fresh flat-leaf parsley
- 2 tablespoons chopped fresh dill
- 2 tablespoons chopped fresh chives
- 1 tablespoon chopped celery leaves
- 6 tablespoons (3 ounces) salmon caviar (see Sources)

MAKE THE HORSERADISH PASTE: Pulse enough bread in a food processor to measure 2½ cups fine crumbs. Transfer to a bowl.

If using fresh horseradish, peel it and finely grate enough on small tear-shaped holes of a box grater to measure ½ cup. Combine horseradish (fresh or bottled) and smoked salmon in food processor and process to a smooth paste. Add butter, mustard, cayenne, and 2 cups bread crumbs and blend to a smooth paste. Season with sea salt. Refrigerate horseradish paste, covered, for at least 2 hours to allow flavors to blend. Let soften slightly at room temperature before using.

PREPARE THE CUCUMBERS: Toss cucumbers with 1 teaspoon sea salt in a sieve set over a bowl. Let cucumbers drain, refrigerated, for 2 hours.

COOK THE SALMON: Put a rack in middle of oven and preheat oven to 350°F.

Spread remaining ½ cup bread crumbs in a shallow baking pan and bake until dry but not colored, about 8 minutes.

Preheat broiler. Pat salmon dry and season with sea salt and pepper. Heat oil in a 12-inch nonstick skillet over moderately high heat until hot but not smoking. Add salmon fillets in 2 batches, skinned sides down, and sear until bottom ¼ to ½ inch of each is opaque, about 1 minute. With a slotted spatula, transfer fillets, sautéed sides down, to a large shallow baking pan. With a rubber spatula, spread ¼ cup horseradish paste in a thick, even layer on top of each fillet. Sprinkle toasted bread crumbs evenly over horseradish paste and press lightly so they adhere.

Broil salmon about 6 inches from heat until crust is golden brown and salmon is just cooked through, 6 to 8 minutes.

Meanwhile, combine crème fraîche and drained cucumbers in a saucepan and heat over low heat, stirring occasionally, until warmed through.

Divide cucumber mixture among six plates. Toss together herbs and celery leaves in a small bowl and sprinkle over cucumbers and around plates. Dot caviar around cucumbers and arrange salmon on top.

Pistachio-Crusted Arctic Char

SERVES 6

ACTIVE TIME: 30 MINUTES ■ START TO FINISH: 40 MINUTES

■ Arctic char, native to the northern parts of North America and Eurasia, is part of the salmonid family, which includes lake and brook trout. The flesh ranges in color from white to pink, and although it can look like salmon, it's generally milder, moister, and tenderer, with a smaller flake. Arctic char has converted many non–fish lovers into big fans. Here we've put an herb-pistachio coating on it. Cooking fish with a top coating like this is easy: it's not necessary to turn it over, so you don't run the risk of having it break apart. This recipe is adapted from one by the chef Greg Aitken, at the Inn at St. Peters on Prince Edward Island, in the Canadian Maritimes. ■

- 1 cup (4 ounces) shelled natural pistachios (not dyed red)
- 1/2 cup packed fresh basil leaves
- 2 tablespoons minced shallots
- 1/4 teaspoon salt
- 1/4 teaspoon freshly ground black pepper
- 3/4 stick (6 tablespoons) unsalted butter, softened, plus 1/2 tablespoon butter
- 6 (6-ounce) pieces Arctic char fillet with skin (1–1 1/4 inches thick)
- 1 1/2 teaspoons vegetable oil

Put a rack in middle of oven and preheat oven to 400°F. Lightly oil a shallow baking pan large enough to hold fish without crowding.

Finely chop pistachios in a food processor. Add basil, shallots, salt, pepper, and 3/4 stick butter and purée until a paste forms. Set aside.

Remove any bones from fish with tweezers or needle-nose pliers and pat fish dry. Heat oil and remaining 1/2 tablespoon butter in a 12-inch nonstick skillet over moderately high heat until foam subsides. Cook fish, skin side down, in 2 batches, until skin is brown and crisp, 3 to 4 minutes per batch (do not turn over). With a slotted spatula, transfer fish, skin side down, to oiled baking pan.

Divide pistachio paste among fillets and spread evenly over tops in a 1/8-inch-thick layer. Bake fillets until just cooked through, 9 to 11 minutes.

COOK'S NOTE

■ The pistachio paste can be made up to 4 hours ahead and refrigerated, covered. Bring to room temperature before using.

Coulibiac

Salmon with Rice and Mushrooms in Pastry

SERVES 6

ACTIVE TIME: 3 1/2 HOURS ■ START TO FINISH: 4 HOURS

■ This ultimate one-dish meal, a fabulous mosaic of salmon, rice, and minced mushrooms, is the pinnacle of Russian cuisine, perhaps best described by the court secretary in Chekhov's "The Siren": "The *kulebyaka* should be appetizing, shameless in its nakedness, a temptation to sin." Even in this simplified version, it is a project for weekend hobbyists. But is it ever worth it. ■

FOR SALMON

- 3 cups water
- 2 1/2 cups dry white wine
- 1 teaspoon salt
- 4 (8-ounce) salmon steaks (1 inch thick)

FOR DOUGH

- 1/2 cup whole milk
- 1 tablespoon sugar
- 1 (1/4-ounce) package active dry yeast (2 1/4 teaspoons)
- 3/4 stick (6 tablespoons) unsalted butter
- 2 large eggs
- 1/4 cup sour cream
- 3–3 1/4 cups all-purpose flour
- 1 teaspoon salt

FOR FILLING

- 3/4 cup long-grain white rice
- 4 tablespoons vegetable oil
- 2 tablespoons unsalted butter
- 2 medium onions, finely chopped
- 1 pound mushrooms, trimmed and finely chopped
- 1/4 cup finely chopped fresh dill

$\frac{1}{4}$ cup finely chopped fresh flat-leaf parsley
$\frac{2}{3}$ cup sour cream
3 tablespoons fresh lemon juice
Salt and freshly ground black pepper
$\frac{1}{4}$ cup fine dry bread crumbs
4 hard-boiled large eggs, chopped
1 large egg lightly beaten with 1 teaspoon water, for egg wash

ACCOMPANIMENT: melted butter

SPECIAL EQUIPMENT: an instant-read thermometer; parchment paper

POACH THE SALMON: Combine water, wine, and salt in a deep 12-inch heavy skillet and bring to a boil. Add salmon (it should be just covered by liquid; add more water if necessary), reduce heat, cover, and poach at a bare simmer until surface of fish just flakes but interior is still rare, 5 to 6 minutes.

With a slotted spatula, transfer salmon to a platter and let cool until it can be handled, about 15 minutes. Reserve 1$\frac{1}{4}$ cups poaching liquid, covered and refrigerated.

Gently separate each salmon steak into 2 pieces, discarding skin and bones. Discard any dark flesh. Refrigerate salmon, covered.

MAKE THE DOUGH: Heat $\frac{1}{4}$ cup milk in a small saucepan until it reaches 105°–115°F on thermometer. Pour into a large bowl, stir in sugar and yeast, and let stand until foamy, about 5 minutes. (If mixture does not foam, discard and start over with new yeast.)

Melt butter in cleaned saucepan over moderately low heat. Stir in remaining $\frac{1}{4}$ cup milk and remove from heat. Whisk together eggs and sour cream in a small bowl. Add egg mixture, butter mixture, 2$\frac{3}{4}$ cups flour, and salt to yeast mixture and stir until a sticky dough forms.

Turn dough out onto a lightly floured surface and knead, adding enough of remaining $\frac{1}{4}$ to $\frac{1}{2}$ cup flour as needed to keep dough from sticking, until smooth and elastic, 6 to 8 minutes. Form into a ball and transfer to a buttered large bowl. Cover bowl with plastic wrap and let dough rise in a warm draft-free place until doubled in bulk, 50 minutes to 1 hour.

MEANWHILE, MAKE THE FILLING: Bring reserved salmon poaching liquid to a boil in a 2-quart heavy saucepan. Stir in rice, cover tightly, and cook over low heat, undisturbed, for 20 minutes. Remove pan from heat and let rice stand for 5 minutes. Fluff with a fork and cover to keep warm.

Heat 2 tablespoons oil and 1 tablespoon butter in cleaned 12-inch skillet over moderate heat. Add onions and cook, stirring occasionally, until golden, 8 to 10 minutes. Transfer to a large bowl. Heat remaining 2 tablespoons oil and remaining 1 tablespoon butter in skillet over moderately high heat. Add mushrooms and cook, stirring occasionally, until liquid they give off has evaporated and mushrooms are golden, about 8 minutes. Add mushrooms to onions, along with rice, dill, parsley, sour cream, lemon juice, and salt and pepper to taste, and stir until well combined.

ASSEMBLE THE COULIBIAC: Put a rack in middle of oven and preheat oven to 425°F. Line a large baking sheet with parchment paper.

Divide dough into 2 pieces, one slightly larger than the other. Form both pieces into logs and cover larger piece with plastic wrap. On a lightly floured surface, roll out and stretch smaller piece of dough into a 16-by-8-inch rectangle. Transfer, without stretching dough, to parchment-lined baking sheet and turn sheet if necessary so a long side of rectangle is nearest you.

Sprinkle dough with bread crumbs, leaving a 2-inch border on all sides. Spread half of rice mixture over bread crumbs, patting it down to help rice stick together, then arrange salmon in one layer over rice, piecing it together where necessary. Top salmon evenly with hard-boiled eggs and spread remaining rice mixture evenly over eggs, patting it into a loaf shape.

Roll out and stretch larger piece of dough into an 18-by-10-inch rectangle. Drape it over filling and press edges of dough together to seal. Trim edges of dough with a sharp knife, leaving a 1-inch border all around base of filling; reserve trimmings. Turn $\frac{1}{2}$ inch of border under and crimp edges. Make eight $\frac{1}{4}$-inch-long steam vents in top crust with knife.

Roll out dough trimmings on lightly floured surface and cut out decorative shapes (such as leaves) with knife or a cookie cutter. Brush entire surface of dough with some egg wash. Arrange decorations on dough, pressing firmly to adhere, and brush shapes with egg wash.

Bake coulibiac for 10 minutes, then reduce heat to 350°F and bake until deep golden, 20 to 25 minutes more (check after 15 minutes; if coulibiac is browning too quickly, tent with foil).

Slide coulibiac, on parchment, onto a rack and let cool for 10 minutes. Cut into 1½-inch-thick slices and serve drizzled with melted butter.

COOK'S NOTES

- The salmon can be poached up to 1 day ahead and refrigerated, covered. Let stand at room temperature for 45 minutes before proceeding.
- The filling can be made up to 1 day ahead.
- The dough can be made up to 1 day ahead. Punch it down after it rises and refrigerate in bowl, covered. Bring to room temperature before proceeding.

Roasted Monkfish with Chanterelles, Leeks, and Ginger

SERVES 4

ACTIVE TIME: 30 MINUTES ■ START TO FINISH: 1¼ HOURS

■ Monkfish, which is not as inexpensive as it once was but is still economical, has often been referred to as "poor man's lobster" because it has a similar texture. Since it's so firm and meaty, it takes well to roasting. Ginger, which is absolutely wonderful with fish, lightens everything up. ■

- 4 medium leeks (1 pound total; white and pale green parts only), cut into ¼-inch-thick slices
- 3 small boiling potatoes (¾ pound total)
- 1 large garlic clove
- 1 (1-inch) piece fresh ginger, peeled
- 1 (1¾-pound) monkfish fillet, halved crosswise, or 2 smaller fillets (1¾ pounds total), any membrane and dark meat discarded
- ½ pound chanterelle mushrooms, trimmed, halved lengthwise if large
- ½ teaspoon salt
- ¼ teaspoon freshly ground black pepper
- 4 tablespoons warm Clarified Butter (page 935)
- White pepper
- 2 tablespoons tawny port
- 1 tablespoon soy sauce

OPTIONAL GARNISH: fresh chives, cut into 1-inch pieces

SPECIAL EQUIPMENT: a 13-by-9-by-2-inch roasting pan

Put a rack in middle of oven and preheat oven to 475°F.

Wash leeks in a bowl of cold water; lift out and drain well.

Peel potatoes and cut crosswise into ¼-inch-thick slices. Blanch potatoes in a 1½-quart saucepan of boiling well-salted water for 5 minutes; drain.

Cut half of garlic clove into 8 slivers and finely chop remaining half. Cut half of ginger into 8 slivers and finely chop remaining half. Make 8 shallow slits in monkfish with a sharp paring knife and insert a sliver of garlic and of ginger into each one.

Heat roasting pan in oven for 10 minutes. Toss together leeks, potatoes, mushrooms, chopped garlic and ginger, salt, black pepper, and 3 tablespoons clarified butter in pan and roast vegetables for 15 minutes.

Pat fish dry and season with white pepper and salt. Heat remaining 1 tablespoon clarified butter in a 12-inch nonstick skillet over moderately high heat until hot but not smoking. Add fish and cook, turning once, until golden brown, about 4 minutes total. With a slotted spatula, transfer fish to a plate.

Add port and soy sauce to skillet and deglaze by boiling, stirring and scraping up any brown bits, for 30 seconds. Pour sauce over roasted vegetables, toss to coat, and place fish on top. Roast until fish is just cooked through, 12 to 15 minutes (fish will be firm, not flaky).

Cut fish crosswise into slices and serve with vegetables. Garnish with chives, if desired.

Halibut with Grapefruit Beurre Blanc

SERVES 4

ACTIVE TIME: 1¼ HOURS ■ START TO FINISH: 1¼ HOURS

■ Halibut is not a strongly flavored fish and can benefit from intrigue. Grapefruit (which deserves to make a leap from the breakfast table), with its sweet-sour complexity mellowed in a *beurre blanc* (white butter sauce), is a good match for endive, whose bitter edge is smoothed out by brief cooking. We love the combination with the delicate fish. ■

FOR *BEURRE BLANC*

- 3 grapefruit, preferably 2 white and 1 pink or red
- 1/4 cup dry white wine
- 2 tablespoons white wine vinegar
- 1 shallot, minced
- 1 1/4 sticks (10 tablespoons) unsalted butter, cut into tablespoons
- Salt and freshly ground black pepper

FOR FISH AND VEGETABLES

- 4 (8-ounce) halibut steaks with skin (1/2 inch thick)
- Salt and freshly ground black pepper
- 3 tablespoons vegetable oil
- 1 pound shiitake mushrooms, stems discarded and caps thinly sliced
- 2 Belgian endives, trimmed and cut crosswise into 1-inch-wide slices

MAKE THE *BEURRE BLANC*: Finely grate 1 teaspoon zest from 1 white grapefruit, then halve it and squeeze 1/2 cup juice. With a sharp paring knife, cut peel and all white pith from remaining 2 grapefruit and cut segments free from membranes; discard seeds. Chop enough grapefruit segments (both colors) to measure 1/2 cup. Reserve 1 cup of remaining whole segments.

Combine grapefruit juice, wine, vinegar, and shallot in a 1-quart heavy saucepan, bring to a boil, and boil until reduced to about 1 tablespoon. Reduce heat to low and whisk in butter one piece at a time, adding each new piece before previous one has completely melted and lifting pan from heat occasionally to cool sauce (sauce should not get too hot, or it will separate). Stir in chopped grapefruit and season with salt and pepper. Transfer *beurre blanc* to a metal bowl and set it over a saucepan of hot water to keep warm.

COOK THE FISH AND VEGETABLES: Put a rack in middle of oven and preheat oven to 250°F.

Pat halibut dry and season with salt and pepper. Heat 1 1/2 tablespoons oil in a large nonstick skillet over moderately high heat until hot but not smoking. Cook fish, in 2 batches if necessary, turning once, until golden brown and just cooked through, about 5 minutes total (per batch). With a slotted spatula, transfer fish to a shallow baking pan and keep warm in oven.

Wipe skillet clean and heat remaining 1 1/2 tablespoons oil over moderately high heat until hot but not smoking. Add mushrooms, season with salt and pepper, and cook, stirring, until golden brown, 5 to 7 minutes. Add endive and cook, stirring, until leaves are slightly wilted, about 1 minute. Stir in reserved grapefruit segments and remove from heat.

Serve fish over mushrooms, drizzled with *beurre blanc* and sprinkled with reserved zest.

Pan-Roasted Mahimahi with Butter and Lime

SERVES 4

ACTIVE TIME: 10 MINUTES ■ START TO FINISH: 30 MINUTES

■ Reference books list this fish as dolphin, but almost everyone uses its Hawaiian name to distinguish it from the marine mammal. The meat—lean, firm, and fine-textured—is delicious when briefly sautéed, then roasted. This recipe, from *Great Fish, Quick* by Leslie Revsin, a veteran chef who once presided at Restaurant Leslie and One Fifth Avenue in New York City, couldn't be less intimidating. We love the lime here; it has a little more perfume and complexity than lemon. ■

- 1/4 cup all-purpose flour
- 4 (7-ounce) pieces mahimahi fillet (1 inch thick)
- Salt and freshly ground black pepper
- 3 tablespoons unsalted butter
- 2 tablespoons fresh lime juice

OPTIONAL GARNISH: 1 teaspoon chopped fresh flat-leaf parsley

Put a rack in middle of oven and preheat oven to 350°F.

Put flour on a plate. Season fillets on both sides with salt and pepper. Lightly dredge in flour and shake off any excess. Melt 2 tablespoons butter in a 12-inch ovenproof skillet over moderately high heat. Add fillets and cook just until very pale golden (lower heat if necessary to keep butter from browning) on the first side, 2 to 3 minutes. Turn fillets over, transfer skillet to oven, and roast until butter is golden brown and fillets are just cooked through, 6 to 8 minutes.

Transfer fillets to four plates and cover loosely with foil to keep warm. Immediately add lime juice and remaining 1 tablespoon butter to hot skillet and deglaze by boiling, stirring and scraping up any brown bits. Season sauce with salt and pepper.

Spoon sauce over fillets and sprinkle with parsley, if desired.

Halibut with Spicy Asian Vinaigrette and Wasabi Cream

SERVES 4

ACTIVE TIME: 15 MINUTES ■ START TO FINISH: 20 MINUTES

■ This is a terrific example of pan-Asian cooking. It's from Highland's Garden Café, in Denver, and presents halibut with two simple sauces: one with the flavors of Southeast Asia, the other with those of Japan. Not only is there an interesting play between two distinct flavors, there is the contrast between a creamy sauce and a vinaigrette, as well as two different kinds of heat. The *sambal* vinaigrette has the clear heat of chiles, which hits you right away. The wasabi cream, made with pungent Japanese horseradish, sneaks up on you. This is a great example of how to layer flavors. The halibut would be perfectly fine with one sauce; with two, it is magnificent. ■

FOR *SAMBAL* VINAIGRETTE

1½ tablespoons rice vinegar (not seasoned)
2 teaspoons *sambal oelek* (Southeast Asian chile sauce; see Glossary)
1½ teaspoons Dijon mustard
⅓ cup vegetable oil
Salt

FOR WASABI CREAM

2 teaspoons wasabi powder (see Glossary)
3 tablespoons water
¼ cup sour cream
Salt

FOR HALIBUT

1 (2-pound) halibut steak (1½ inches thick), skinned, boned, and cut into 4 pieces
Salt and freshly ground black pepper
¼ cup finely chopped fresh flat-leaf parsley
1½ teaspoons vegetable oil

ACCOMPANIMENT: drained sliced Japanese pickled ginger

Put a rack in middle of oven and preheat oven to 400°F.

MAKE THE VINAIGRETTE: Combine vinegar, *sambal oelek*, mustard, and oil in a blender and blend until smooth. Season with salt.

MAKE THE WASABI CREAM: Whisk together wasabi powder and water in a small bowl until smooth. Whisk in sour cream. Season with salt.

COOK THE HALIBUT: Pat fish dry and season with salt and pepper. Sprinkle one side of each piece with parsley. Heat a large well-seasoned cast-iron skillet or other heavy ovenproof skillet over high heat until hot. Add oil, then add fish, parsley side up, and sear until undersides are brown, about 1 minute.

Turn fish over, put skillet in oven, and roast fish until just cooked through, 4 to 5 minutes.

Serve fish parsley side up, with a spoonful each of vinaigrette and cream and some pickled ginger.

Oven-Poached Halibut in Olive Oil

SERVES 4 TO 6

ACTIVE TIME: 15 MINUTES ■ START TO FINISH: 1½ HOURS

■ Poaching fish in oil may seem like an unusual cooking method, but it's actually a little like confit, the traditional preparation in which meat is cooked in its own fat. We got the idea from Mario Batali, the chef of New York City's Babbo, and adapted the technique for home use. The fillets stay extremely moist, but without any taste of oil, and the layers of lemon slices, which lose their tartness when heated with the oil and salt, infuse the dish with wonderful citrus notes. Another bonus: the oil doesn't pick up any fish flavor—it tastes lemony and slightly salty—and only a small amount is served with the dish, so the rest can be used again in a vinaigrette, added to mashed potatoes, or saved for cooking. Some greens and boiled potatoes round out the dish beautifully. ■

- 2½ pounds halibut fillets (1 inch thick)
- 1½ teaspoons salt
- ½ teaspoon freshly ground black pepper
- ¼ cup capers (preferably packed in salt), rinsed
- 1½ large lemons, thinly sliced
- 3 tablespoons loosely packed fresh flat-leaf parsley leaves
- 2 cups extra-virgin olive oil

GARNISH: 1 tablespoon loosely packed fresh flat-leaf parsley leaves

Put a rack in middle of oven and preheat oven to 250°F.

Pat fish dry, then sprinkle with salt and pepper. Let stand for 10 minutes. Chop half of capers.

Arrange half of lemon slices in one layer in an 8-inch square glass baking dish. Arrange fish in one layer over lemons. Top with all of capers, remaining lemon slices, and 3 tablespoons parsley, then pour oil over fish.

Bake, covered, until fish just flakes and is cooked through, 1 to 1¼ hours.

Serve fish with some of lemon slices, capers, and oil spooned over. Sprinkle with parsley leaves.

COOK'S NOTE

■ To reuse the leftover olive oil, strain through a paper towel–lined sieve and let cool to room temperature. It will keep, covered and refrigerated, for up to 1 week.

Garlic-Roasted Whole Striped Bass

SERVES 4

ACTIVE TIME: 15 MINUTES ■ START TO FINISH: 35 MINUTES

■ A whole striped bass in all its glory makes for a great presentation, and this method couldn't be simpler. ■

- 2 (1¼-pound) whole striped bass or red snappers, cleaned, heads and tails left intact, rinsed, and patted dry
- 3 tablespoons olive oil
- 4 garlic cloves
- 1 lemon, halved
- Salt and freshly ground black pepper

Put a rack in middle of oven and preheat oven to 500°F. Put a baking sheet with sides on rack.

Cut 3 deep crosswise slits (down to the bone) in each side of fish and put fish on a tray. Rub inside and out with 2 tablespoons oil. Cut 1 garlic clove in half and rub all over skin of fish. Thinly slice all garlic cloves and insert into slits and cavities of fish. Squeeze lemon juice over both sides of fish and season with salt and pepper.

Quickly brush hot baking sheet with remaining 1 tablespoon oil and transfer fish to sheet (they will sizzle). Roast fish until just cooked through, 18 to 20 minutes.

Remove top fillet from each fish by cutting through skin along top edge of back and along belly, then carefully sliding a large metal spatula between backbone and fillet, and invert fillet onto a platter. Pull out backbone, starting from tail end, and discard. Transfer bottom fillets to platter.

Bass Nomenclature

Striped bass, black sea bass, Chilean sea bass—which are the true bass? It's hard to say. Technically, bass have notched dorsal fins and are members of the Acropomatidae, Serranidae, or Moronidae family—more than a hundred species all told. And there are even more pretenders. We have limited this list to common varieties.

BLACK SEA BASS, *Centropristis striata,* aka blackfish (although that name is more commonly used for the tautog, a different fish altogether), sea bass

Size: 1 to 3 pounds

Location: Eastern seaboard

Bass? Yes, and quite a tasty one

BLUE BASS, *Sebastes mystinus,* aka blue rockfish, rock cod, black rockfish, priestfish

Size: 1 pound or less

Location: Pacific coast

Bass? No, a rockfish—and not always blue

CHANNEL BASS, *Sciaenops ocellata,* aka red drum, redfish, red bass

Size: 1 to 2 pounds or larger

Location: Now mostly farmed in Texas and Ecuador; originally found in the Gulf of Mexico and up the East Coast, though almost fished out after being popularized by Paul Prudhomme's blackened redfish

Bass? No, a member of the croaker (or drum) family

CHILEAN SEA BASS, *Dissostichus eleginoides,* aka Patagonian toothfish

Size: About 20 pounds

Location: The southernmost oceans around New Zealand, South Africa, Chile, and Argentina

Bass? No, a hideously ugly fish unrelated to bass that tastes little like any real bass (it has a fuller flavor and texture). Named "Chilean sea bass" on the (accurate) presumption that few people would order Patagonian toothfish in a restaurant. *Note:* Along with environmentally conscious chefs, we have stopped using Chilean sea bass, because increased demand has led to its being overfished almost to the point of extinction. At this writing, the illegal catch is estimated to be five times the legal catch.

EUROPEAN BASS, *Dicentrarchus labrax,* aka bass, sea bass, *bar, loup de mer,* branzino

Size: 1½ to 3 pounds

Location: Eastern Atlantic, Mediterranean; farmed in Norway

Bass? Yes

SEA BASS, *Epinephelus quernus,* aka *Hapu'upu'u,* Hawaiian grouper

Size: 5 to 30 pounds

Location: Hawaii

Bass? Yes, actually a grouper, a subclass of the bass family

SPOTTED SEA BASS, *Dicentrarchus punctatus*

Size: 3 pounds or more

Location: Eastern Atlantic, south of Bay of Biscay

Bass? Yes

STONE BASS, *Polyprion americanus,* aka wreckfish

Size: 6 to 10 pounds

Location: Atlantic, Mediterranean, and southwest Pacific

Bass? Yes, a type of grouper, a subclass of the bass family

STRIPED BASS, *Morone saxatilis* (farmed version is a cross between *M. saxatilis* and *M. chrysops,* the freshwater white bass), aka striper, rockfish, California bass

Size: 3 pounds or more in the wild

Location: East Coast, waters north of Monterey, California

Bass? Yes

WHITE SEA BASS, *Atractoscion nobilis,* aka white weakfish, California white sea bass, king croaker, sea trout

Size: 10 to 15 pounds standard, but may be up to 80 pounds

Location: Pacific coast, from Baja California to Alaska

Bass? No, another croaker

Salt-Baked Branzino

SERVES 2

ACTIVE TIME: 15 MINUTES ■ START TO FINISH: 30 MINUTES

■ *Branzino* is the Italian name for the European bass (in France, it's called *loup de mer*). When you can get this mild, flaky fish really fresh, give it the star turn it deserves. Baking it in a salt crust, which protects the fish so it cooks in nothing but its own juices, is a time-honored method in the Mediterranean. Contrary to what you might think, the fish is not overly salty but perfectly seasoned. It's also really fun to put this together, especially if you loved making mud pies when you were a child. For this recipe, David Pasternack, of New York City's Esca restaurant, uses unrefined sea salt, which has no additives that prevent caking, so it tends to be moist. However, sea salt is not cheap, and you need lots of it. Alternatively, you can coat the fish with the same amount of an additive-free kosher salt, which works nicely but requires more egg whites—five to six, in fact. ■

- 3 cups (1¾ pounds) fine sea salt, preferably unrefined
- 2–4 large egg whites
- 2 (1-pound) whole branzino (European sea bass) or other small sea bass, cleaned, heads and tails left intact
- 6 fresh parsley sprigs
- 4 fresh rosemary sprigs
- 2 garlic cloves, sliced
- 4 lemon slices, halved

SPECIAL EQUIPMENT: parchment paper

Put a rack in middle of oven and preheat oven to 400°F. Line a large baking sheet with parchment paper.

Put salt in a bowl and add egg whites one at a time, stirring, until mixture looks like wet sand (the number of egg whites needed will vary). Rinse fish and pat dry. Place fish on parchment-lined baking sheet and divide herbs, garlic, and lemon slices between cavities of fish.

Firmly pat half of salt mixture evenly over each fish to cover fish completely. Bake fish until salt crust just begins to turn golden at edges, 15 to 18 minutes (see Cook's Notes).

Crack salt crust away from fish and discard. Remove top fillet from each fish by cutting through skin along top edge of back and along belly, then carefully sliding a large metal spatula between backbone and fillet, and invert fillet onto a platter. Pull out backbones, starting from tail end, and discard. Transfer bottom fillets to platter.

COOK'S NOTES

- If your fish weigh slightly less or more than 1 pound, adjust the cooking time accordingly.
- The salt crust may turn golden at the edges before the fish is done; if it is not cooked through when you remove the crust, return it briefly to the oven.

Oven-Steamed Whole Snapper with Black Bean Sauce

SERVES 4

ACTIVE TIME: 35 MINUTES ■ START TO FINISH: 1¼ HOURS

■ Serving whole fish makes an outstanding impression, often much greater than the sum of its parts. Shiitake mushrooms and fermented black beans (Chinese preserved small soybeans, not the black beans popular in Mexico and Latin America) can now be found in many supermarkets as well as in Asian markets. ■

- 2 (1½-pound) whole red snappers, cleaned, heads and tails left intact, rinsed, and patted dry
- 1 tablespoon minced peeled fresh ginger
- 2 garlic cloves, minced
- ½ teaspoon salt
- 4 tablespoons Chinese rice wine, sake, or medium-dry sherry
- 3 tablespoons soy sauce
- ½ pound shiitake mushrooms, stems discarded and caps thinly sliced
- 4 medium carrots, cut into matchsticks
- 6 scallions, cut into thin strips
- 2 tablespoons Chinese fermented black beans (see Glossary), lightly rinsed
- 2 tablespoons water
- 2 teaspoons cornstarch

ACCOMPANIMENT: cooked rice

Put a rack in middle of oven and preheat oven to 450°F.

Cut 3 parallel slashes about ½ inch deep in each side of each fish and rub ginger, garlic, and salt into slashes. Drizzle 2 tablespoons rice wine and 1½ tablespoons soy sauce into a 13-by-9-inch baking dish and place fish in dish. Drizzle with remaining 2 tablespoons rice wine and 1½ tablespoons soy sauce and scatter mushrooms, carrots, scallions, and black beans over fish. Cover dish tightly with foil.

Bake fish until just cooked through, 30 to 35 minutes. Gently push black bean mixture off fish and, with two large metal spatulas, transfer fish to a platter. Cover to keep warm.

Transfer black bean mixture and pan juices to a 2- to 3-quart heavy saucepan and bring to a boil. Stir together water and cornstarch in a small bowl until smooth and stir into black bean mixture. Simmer sauce until thickened slightly, about 1 minute. Remove the top fillet of each fish by cutting through skin along top edge of back and along belly, then carefully sliding a large metal spatula between backbone and fillet, and invert fillet into a platter or plate. Pull out backbone, starting from tail end, and discard it. Transfer bottom fillet to platter. Pour sauce over fish. Serve with rice.

Whole Red Snapper Veracruz

SERVES 4 TO 6

ACTIVE TIME: 1 HOUR ■ START TO FINISH: 2 HOURS

■ It's common to find this dish made with fillets, but the extra flavor that results from slowly braising the whole fish in the sauce really makes it sing. We call for dried Mexican oregano, a variety that is mintier than dried regular oregano, which can taste musty; it has become more widely available in supermarkets. This recipe is adapted from *The Cuisines of Mexico,* by the Mexican food authority Diana Kennedy. ■

FOR FISH

- 2 (2½-pound) whole red snappers, cleaned, heads and tails left intact, rinsed, and patted dry
- 1½ teaspoons sea salt
- 2 tablespoons fresh lime juice

FOR SAUCE

- 4 tablespoons olive oil
- 1 large onion, halved lengthwise and thinly sliced crosswise
- 4 garlic cloves, minced
- 1 teaspoon dried Mexican oregano (see Sources), crumbled
- ½ teaspoon salt
- 3 pounds tomatoes, peeled (see Tips, page 940), halved, seeded, and chopped
- ¼ cup (2 ounces) green olives, pitted and quartered lengthwise
- 2 tablespoons drained capers, rinsed
- 2 tablespoons chopped pickled jalapeño chiles
- Freshly ground black pepper

OPTIONAL GARNISH: chopped fresh flat-leaf parsley

PREPARE THE FISH: Cut 3 parallel slashes about ½ inch deep in each side of each fish and rub fish inside and out, including slashes, with salt and lime juice.

Arrange fish side by side and head to tail in an oiled 2-inch-deep baking dish (preferably oval) or roasting pan just large enough to hold them. Cover and refrigerate for 30 minutes.

Put a rack in middle of oven and preheat oven to 350°F.

PREPARE THE SAUCE: Heat 3 tablespoons oil in a 12-inch heavy skillet over moderately low heat. Add onion and garlic and cook, stirring, until softened, about 5 minutes. Add oregano and salt and cook, stirring, for 2 minutes. Add tomatoes, olives, capers, and chiles and simmer, uncovered, stirring occasionally, until sauce is thickened, about 10 minutes. Season with salt and pepper. Remove from heat.

BAKE THE FISH: Lift up fish and spoon about one quarter of sauce under it. Spoon remainder on top, spreading it evenly. Drizzle with remaining 1 tablespoon olive oil. Bake until fish is just cooked through, 35 to 45 minutes.

Gently push sauce off fish. Remove top fillet from each fish by cutting through skin along top edge of back and along belly, then carefully sliding a large metal spatula between backbone and fillet, and invert fillet into a platter or plate. Pull out backbone, starting from tail end, and discard it. Transfer bottom fillet to platter and serve with sauce spooned on top. Garnish with parsley, if desired.

COOK'S NOTE

- The sauce can be made up to 1 day ahead. Cool, uncovered, then refrigerate, covered. Reheat before cooking fish.

Bacon-Wrapped Trout with Rosemary

SERVES 2

ACTIVE TIME: 10 MINUTES ■ START TO FINISH: 20 MINUTES

■ These flavors of the Great Outdoors translate beautifully to the Great Indoors. Be sure to wrap the bacon around the trout in a spiral so it will baste the fish evenly. ■

- 2 (10- to 12-ounce) whole trout, cleaned, heads and tails left intact, rinsed, and patted dry
- Salt and freshly ground black pepper
- 4 (4- to 5-inch) fresh rosemary sprigs
- 6 bacon slices
- 6 (1/8-inch-thick) lemon slices

Preheat broiler. Put fish on a small baking sheet with sides or in a large heavy ovenproof skillet. Season cavities with salt and pepper. Put 2 rosemary sprigs inside each cavity and season skin of fish with salt and pepper. Wrap bacon slices around fish.

Broil fish 5 to 7 inches from heat until skin and bacon are crisp, about 5 minutes. Gently turn fish over with a spatula and broil for 2 minutes more. Arrange lemon slices in one layer in sheet alongside fish and continue to broil until fish is just cooked through and bacon is crisp all over, 2 1/2 to 3 minutes more.

Transfer trout to plates and serve, accompanied by broiled lemons.

Hazelnut-Crusted Trout

SERVES 2

ACTIVE TIME: 25 MINUTES ■ START TO FINISH: 25 MINUTES

■ A nice hazelnut crust is wonderful on trout. For a simple dinner, serve this with roasted potatoes and a green salad tossed with pears and crumbled blue cheese. ■

- 1/2 cup hazelnuts
- 1 large egg
- 2 (10- to 12-ounce) whole trout, cleaned, heads and tails left intact, rinsed, and patted dry
- Salt
- 2 tablespoons vegetable oil
- 1 tablespoon unsalted butter
- 1 teaspoon fresh lemon juice
- Freshly ground black pepper

GARNISH: 1 tablespoon chopped fresh flat-leaf parsley

Pulse nuts in a food processor until finely ground (do not grind to a paste). Spread on a plate. Lightly beat egg in a pie plate.

Season trout inside and out with salt. Dip both sides of trout first in egg and then in nuts to coat. Heat oil in a 12-inch heavy skillet over moderate heat until hot but not smoking. Add trout and cook, shaking skillet occasionally to prevent sticking and turning once with a metal spatula, until browned on both sides and just cooked through, about 12 minutes total.

Meanwhile, melt butter in a small saucepan and stir in lemon juice, then season with salt and pepper.

Transfer trout to plates. Pour lemon butter over trout and sprinkle with parsley.

Poached Salmon in Aspic

SERVES 8
ACTIVE TIME: 1¾ HOURS ■ START TO FINISH: 12 HOURS (INCLUDES CHILLING)

■ This is the perfect centerpiece for a cold buffet; people love it because it is absolutely beautiful and tastes delicious. The ingredients list may look somewhat daunting, and the recipe does take some effort, especially the flavorful aspic that helps keep the cooked salmon moist. But everything, including making the accompanying green mayonnaise, can be done ahead. Before you start the recipe, make sure there's room in your refrigerator for a 24-inch fish poacher and a 25-inch platter. ■

FOR SALMON

- 1 (6-pound) whole salmon, cleaned and backbone removed (have the fishmonger do this), head and tail left intact, rinsed, and patted dry
- 1 teaspoon salt
- 6 quarts cold water, or as necessary
- ½ cup fresh lemon juice
- 1 large onion, coarsely chopped
- 2 carrots, coarsely chopped
- 2 celery ribs with leaves, cut into 4-inch pieces
- 2 Turkish bay leaves or 1 California bay leaf
- 6 fresh parsley stems (without leaves)
- 2 fresh thyme sprigs
- ¼ teaspoon black peppercorns

FOR ASPIC

- 1 cup dry white wine
- 2 tablespoons Sercial (dry) Madeira
- 1 fresh thyme sprig
- 1 teaspoon salt
- 1 large leek, 2 dark green outer leaves reserved for garnish, white and pale green parts chopped
- 1 carrot, coarsely chopped
- 1 celery rib, coarsely chopped
- 3 large egg whites, lightly beaten; shells reserved and crushed
- 1 tablespoon unflavored gelatin (from two ¼-ounce packages)
- ¼ cup cold water

ACCOMPANIMENT: Green Mayonnaise (page 887)

SPECIAL EQUIPMENT: two 35-inch-long pieces of cheesecloth; kitchen string; a 24-inch-long fish poacher (see Sources); an instant-read thermometer; a 25-inch-long platter

POACH THE SALMON: Sprinkle inside of salmon with salt. Lay 1 piece of cheesecloth on top of the other, wrap fish snugly in it, and tie ends (close to fish) with kitchen string. Place on rack in poacher and set poacher across two burners. Add cold water (it should cover fish by 1 inch), lemon juice, onion, carrots, celery, bay leaves, parsley stems, thyme sprigs, and peppercorns. Bring to a boil, partially covered, over high heat (this will take about 25 minutes; fish should register 145°F on thermometer inserted into thickest part). Transfer poacher to a wire rack and cool fish, uncovered, in broth, for 30 minutes.

Refrigerate fish in broth in poacher, uncovered, for at least 8 hours.

REDUCE THE BROTH FOR THE ASPIC: Lift fish on poacher rack out of broth and drain well (reserve broth), then transfer to a large baking sheet with sides and refrigerate. Pour broth through a medium-mesh sieve into a large bowl (discard solids). Transfer 8 cups broth to a 4-quart heavy saucepan; reserve remainder for another use. Add white wine, Madeira, thyme sprig, and salt to broth, bring to a boil, and boil until reduced to about 5 cups, 30 to 40 minutes. Let cool for 20 minutes.

MEANWHILE, PREPARE THE SALMON FOR GLAZING: Wash reserved leek leaves and chopped leek in a bowl of cold water; lift out and drain well. Cut leaves into decorative strips and blanch in a saucepan of boiling water for 1 minute, then transfer to a bowl of ice and cold water to cool. Drain and pat dry.

Untie cheesecloth and open cloth but don't remove salmon. Remove fatty strip and small bones (they look like a comb) from spine of fish, from head to tail. Trim any fat from edges of belly. Carefully remove bony section under gills, then remove skin and dark flesh from top side of fish by gently scraping with a small sharp knife. Using the cheesecloth, roll fish over onto platter. Remove bony section under gills on this side, then remove skin and dark flesh. Wipe platter clean, cover fish with dampened paper towels, and refrigerate until aspic is ready.

CLARIFY THE BROTH AND MAKE THE ASPIC: Whisk together reduced broth, chopped leek, carrot, celery, egg whites, and shells in a 4- to 6-quart heavy pot. Bring to a boil, whisking constantly, then reduce heat to low and cook, undisturbed, at a bare simmer for 30 minutes.

Ladle broth through sieve lined with a double thickness of dampened paper towels into a 1-quart glass measure, pressing on solids; discard solids.

Sprinkle gelatin over cold water in a 1-quart saucepan and let soften for 1 minute. Add 3 cups broth (reserve any remaining broth for another use, if desired), bring to a simmer, and simmer, stirring, until gelatin is dissolved, about 2 minutes. Remove aspic from heat.

GLAZE THE SALMON: Ladle ⅔ cup aspic into a metal bowl set in a larger bowl of ice and cold water and let stand, stirring occasionally, just until aspic is the consistency of raw egg whites. Remove bowl from ice water and spoon a thin layer of aspic evenly over fish, then refrigerate until aspic is set, about 10 minutes. Arrange leek garnish on fish and spoon another layer of aspic over fish. Refrigerate fish, uncovered, until ready to serve.

Meanwhile, pour remaining aspic into a 13-by-9-inch baking dish and refrigerate until set, about 1 hour. Cut into ½-inch cubes.

To serve, arrange aspic cubes around salmon on platter. Serve with green mayonnaise.

COOK'S NOTES

- The salmon can be poached and chilled in broth up to 2 days ahead.
- The salmon can be glazed up to 1 day ahead. Refrigerate remaining aspic in baking dish, covered.

Scallops Provençale

SERVES 4

ACTIVE TIME: 30 MINUTES ■ START TO FINISH: 30 MINUTES

■ Scallops are a great weeknight supper because they cook so quickly. Here is a simple sauté with the flavors of Mediterranean France. ■

- 2 pounds large sea scallops, tough muscle removed from side of each if necessary
- 1 teaspoon salt
- ½ teaspoon freshly ground black pepper
- 5 tablespoons olive oil
- 4 garlic cloves, thinly sliced
- 2 large tomatoes (1 pound total), halved, seeded, and diced (2½ cups)
- 1 teaspoon chopped fresh thyme
- ½ cup shredded fresh basil leaves

Preheat oven to 200°F.

Pat scallops dry and season with ¾ teaspoon salt and ¼ teaspoon pepper.

Heat 2 teaspoons oil in a 12-inch nonstick skillet over high heat until hot but not smoking. Sear one third of scallops, turning once, until golden brown and just cooked through, 2 to 4 minutes total. With a slotted spoon, transfer scallops to a small platter and keep warm in oven, loosely covered with foil. Sear remaining scallops in 2 batches, using 2 more teaspoons oil for each batch, and transfer to platter.

Add remaining 3 tablespoons oil to skillet, add garlic, and cook over moderate heat, stirring, until pale golden, 1 to 2 minutes. Add tomatoes and thyme and cook over high heat, stirring, for 2 minutes. Season with remaining ¼ teaspoon salt and ¼ teaspoon pepper.

Spoon tomato mixture over and around scallops and sprinkle with basil.

Baked Bay Scallops

SERVES 2 AS A MAIN COURSE, 4 AS A FIRST COURSE
ACTIVE TIME: 35 MINUTES ■ START TO FINISH: 1½ HOURS

■ Any bay scallops will do for this dish, but if you can find ones from Nantucket, snap them up. They are unusually delicate, perhaps because of the unique currents in the bays where they reside, and people go to great lengths to get them. This recipe comes from *Gourmet*'s former executive food editor Sally Darr, who served it at La Tulipe, her restaurant in Greenwich Village. ■

- ¾ pound bay scallops, preferably Nantucket, tough muscle removed from side of each if necessary
- ½ cup whole milk
- ¼ teaspoon kosher salt plus more for lining baking sheet
- ½ stick (4 tablespoons) unsalted butter, cut into bits, softened
- ¼ cup minced scallions or shallots
- ⅛ teaspoon freshly ground black pepper
- ¼ cup fine fresh bread crumbs
- ½ teaspoon chopped fresh thyme

ACCOMPANIMENT: lemon wedges
SPECIAL EQUIPMENT: 4 large scallop shells (see Sources)

Soak scallops in milk in a small bowl, covered and refrigerated, for 15 minutes to 1 hour.

Put a rack in middle of oven and preheat oven to 450°F.

Drain scallops and pat dry. Spread a layer of kosher salt in a baking sheet with sides, to keep scallop shells level. Rub scallop shells with some butter and arrange in pan. Divide scallops among shells. Dot scallops with remaining butter and sprinkle with scallions, salt, and pepper. Bake scallops until opaque and just cooked through, 4 to 5 minutes. Remove from oven.

Set broiler rack about 3 inches from heat and preheat broiler. Toss together bread crumbs and thyme in a small bowl and sprinkle over scallops. Spoon some of melted butter in shells on top of crumbs.

Broil scallops until crumbs are lightly browned, about 1 minute.

Serve immediately, with lemon wedges.

Coquilles St. Jacques

Scallops with Mushrooms in White Wine Sauce

SERVES 4 AS A MAIN COURSE, 8 AS A FIRST COURSE
ACTIVE TIME: 30 MINUTES ■ START TO FINISH: 1 HOUR

■ Who needs Venus on the half shell when you can have coquilles St. Jacques? This French classic is traditionally served in scallop shells, but you can use ramekins or little individual casserole dishes. It is very simple, very rich, and very sure of itself. And it is a beautiful study in texture: tender scallops, crisp, buttery bread crumbs, and a lovely sauce that enhances the seafood. ■

- ¼ cup coarse fresh bread crumbs from a baguette
- ¼ cup finely grated Parmigiano-Reggiano
- 1¼ cups dry white wine
- 1 cup water
- ½ small onion, sliced
- ½ Turkish bay leaf or ¼ California bay leaf
- ½ teaspoon salt
- ¼ teaspoon freshly ground black pepper
- 1 pound sea scallops, tough muscle removed from side of each if necessary, scallops cut into ¾-inch pieces
- ¾ stick (6 tablespoons) unsalted butter
- ½ pound small mushrooms, trimmed, halved lengthwise, and thinly sliced lengthwise
- ½ cup heavy cream
- 1 large egg yolk
- 1 tablespoon all-purpose flour
- Kosher salt for lining baking sheet if using scallop shells
- 1½ tablespoons minced fresh flat-leaf parsley

SPECIAL EQUIPMENT: 4 or 8 large scallop shells (see Sources) or four or eight 2-ounce ramekins

Put a rack in middle of oven and preheat oven to 350°F.

Toast bread crumbs on a baking sheet with sides in oven until pale golden, 6 to 8 minutes. Transfer to a bowl and toss with cheese.

Combine wine, water, onion, bay leaf, salt, and pepper in a 2½- to 3-quart heavy saucepan, bring to a simmer, and simmer, uncovered, for 5 minutes. Add scallops and simmer, stirring occasionally, until just cooked through, 2 to 3 minutes. With a slotted spoon, transfer scallops to a large plate to cool; return any onions to pan. Boil cooking liquid until reduced to about 1 cup, 8 to 10 minutes. Pour liquid through a sieve into a bowl; discard solids.

Melt 2 tablespoons butter in a 10- to 12-inch heavy skillet over moderate heat. Add mushrooms and cook, stirring occasionally, until most of liquid mushrooms give off has evaporated, about 5 minutes. Season with salt and pepper and remove from heat.

Whisk together cream and egg yolk in a heatproof medium bowl. Melt 2 tablespoons butter in 2½- to 3-quart saucepan over moderately low heat. Add flour and cook, whisking, for 2 minutes to make a roux. Remove pan from heat and add reduced cooking liquid, whisking constantly. Return pan to heat and simmer, whisking, for 1 minute. Pour sauce in a slow stream into cream mixture, whisking constantly. Pour sauce back into pan and simmer, whisking, for 1 minute. Remove from heat and season with salt and pepper.

Set broiler rack about 4 inches from heat and preheat broiler. Stir scallops and mushrooms into sauce, then divide among scallop shells or ramekins. Sprinkle with bread crumb mixture. If using shells, spread an even layer of kosher salt in a large baking sheet with sides, then nestle shells in salt; or place ramekins on a baking sheet. Dot scallops with remaining 2 tablespoons butter.

Broil until golden, about 2 minutes. Sprinkle with parsley.

COOK'S NOTE

- The scallop mixture can be made up to 1 day ahead and refrigerated, covered. Reheat briefly in a heavy saucepan over moderate heat, stirring constantly, before spooning into shells or ramekins.

Soy Citrus Scallops with Soba Salad

SERVES 6

ACTIVE TIME: 15 MINUTES ■ START TO FINISH: 25 MINUTES

■ Marinating scallops briefly before sautéing them adds tremendous flavor, and sesame seeds, toasted to heighten their nutty flavor, give an appealing crunch. You don't have to make the accompanying soba noodle salad, but the sauce is lovely with it. ■

- ⅔ cup soy sauce
- ¼ cup fresh lemon juice
- ¼ cup fresh lime juice
- 3 tablespoons plus 1 teaspoon sugar
- 2 teaspoons finely grated peeled fresh ginger
- 2 teaspoons Asian sesame oil
- 2 pounds large sea scallops, tough muscle removed from side of each if necessary
- About 2½ teaspoons vegetable oil

OPTIONAL GARNISH: 2 teaspoons sesame seeds, preferably black, toasted (see Tips, page 939)

ACCOMPANIMENT: Soba Salad (recipe follows)

Whisk together soy sauce, lemon and lime juices, sugar, ginger, and sesame oil in a wide shallow bowl. Add scallops in a single layer and marinate, covered, at room temperature for 5 minutes. Turn scallops over and marinate for 5 minutes more (do not marinate any longer, or scallops will become mushy when cooked). Transfer scallops to a plate, reserving marinade.

Preheat oven to 200°F.

Heat ½ teaspoon vegetable oil in a 12-inch nonstick skillet over moderately high heat until hot but not smoking. Cook scallops in batches, 6 to 8 at a time, turning once, until golden brown and just cooked through, 4 to 6 minutes per batch. Transfer cooked scallops to a platter and keep warm in oven, loosely covered. Wipe out skillet and add ½ teaspoon oil between batches, heating oil before adding scallops.

Wipe out skillet, add reserved marinade, and boil until reduced to about ⅓ cup, about 2 minutes. Serve scallops on soba salad and drizzle with sauce, then sprinkle with sesame seeds, if desired.

COOK'S NOTE

- Sesame seeds become rancid quickly because of their high oil content, so be sure to smell them before using.

Soba Salad

SERVES 6
ACTIVE TIME: 45 MINUTES ■ START TO FINISH: 55 MINUTES

■ Taupe-colored Japanese soba noodles look beautiful with scallops. Hearty in flavor, they're a good match for mizuna, a feathery salad green with a refreshing bite. ■

- 6 ounces soba (Japanese buckwheat noodles; see page 246)
- 1 teaspoon Asian sesame oil
- 1 medium red bell pepper, cored, seeded, and cut lengthwise into thin strips
- ½ seedless cucumber (usually plastic wrapped), halved lengthwise, seeded, and cut into ⅛-inch-thick matchsticks
- ½ medium jicama, peeled and cut into ⅛-inch-thick matchsticks
- 2 ounces (2 cups) mizuna or chopped trimmed baby mustard greens
- 4 scallions, cut into very thin 3-inch-long strips
- 1 tablespoon seasoned rice vinegar
- ¼ teaspoon salt

Bring 4 quarts water to a rolling boil in a 5- to 6-quart pot over moderately high heat. Stir in noodles and ½ cup cold water. When water returns to a boil, add another ½ cup cold water and bring to a boil again; repeat procedure once more. Test noodles for doneness: they should be just tender but still firm and chewy throughout. Drain noodles in a colander and rinse well under cold water, then drain thoroughly. Toss with sesame oil in a large bowl.

Toss together remaining ingredients in a medium bowl, add to noodles, and toss again to combine.

Shrimp and Corn with Basil

SERVES 2
ACTIVE TIME: 15 MINUTES ■ START TO FINISH: 15 MINUTES

■ One of the quickest and most satisfying one-dish meals you could hope for, this summery recipe is all about restraint: shrimp, corn, basil, a smattering of scallions. Don't be tempted to gussy it up with anything else. Well, you could serve a platter of sliced tomatoes and a loaf of crusty bread on the side. . . . ■

- 2 tablespoons unsalted butter
- 1½ cups corn kernels (from 2 ears)
- ½ pound large shrimp in shells (21–25 per pound), peeled and deveined
- 4 scallions, chopped
- ¼ cup fresh basil leaves, thinly sliced
- Salt and freshly ground black pepper

Melt butter in a 12-inch nonstick skillet over moderately high heat. Add corn and shrimp and cook, stirring, until shrimp are cooked through, 3 to 5 minutes. Stir in scallions and basil and season with salt and pepper.

Shrimp in Adobo Sauce

SERVES 4 TO 6
ACTIVE TIME: 45 MINUTES ■ START TO FINISH: 1¼ HOURS

■ An *adobo* (meaning "preparation" or "sauce" in Spanish) can be a dry mix, used as a rub, or a liquid, used as a marinade or sauce. In this intriguing dish, shrimp are simmered in a piquant adobo. The ancho chiles—sweeter and often milder than other dried chiles—are tempered by the acidity of the white wine and vinegar and offset with a buttery avocado garnish. The recipe is from Elisabeth Lambert Ortiz, who was married to a Mexican diplomat posted to the United Nations. She fell in love with his native food and became one of its most fluent interpreters for English-speaking cooks. ■

- 4 large dried ancho chiles (2 ounces)
- 1 medium onion, chopped
- 2 garlic cloves, chopped
- ¼ teaspoon dried oregano, preferably Mexican (see Sources), crumbled
- 3–4 tablespoons warm water
- ¼ cup olive oil
- ½ cup dry white wine
- ¼ cup distilled white vinegar
- 1½ teaspoons sugar, or to taste (optional)
- ½ teaspoon salt

1½ pounds large shrimp in shells (21–25 per pound), peeled and deveined

OPTIONAL GARNISH: diced avocados and chopped fresh cilantro

ACCOMPANIMENT: cooked rice

Heat a dry griddle or heavy skillet, preferably cast-iron, over moderate heat until hot. Toast chiles 1 or 2 at a time for a few seconds on each side, pressing down with tongs, until more pliable and a shade darker.

Remove and discard stems, seeds, and veins and tear chiles into small pieces. Soak chiles in warm water to cover for 30 minutes; drain.

Combine chiles, onion, garlic, and oregano in a blender or food processor and blend with enough warm water to form a thick purée.

Heat oil in a 12-inch heavy skillet over moderate heat until hot but not smoking. Stir in purée and cook, stirring constantly, for 5 minutes. Add wine, vinegar, sugar (if using), and salt and simmer, stirring, for 5 minutes; sauce should be very thick.

Add shrimp, stirring to coat, and simmer, covered, until shrimp are just cooked through, 4 to 6 minutes. Season with salt and serve over rice, garnished with avocados and cilantro, if desired.

Shrimp in Coconut Milk

SERVES 4 TO 6

ACTIVE TIME: 1 HOUR ■ START TO FINISH: 1¼ HOURS

■ Coconut milk, lime juice, cilantro—at first glance, the ingredients seem Southeast Asian. But think of them as equatorial instead; this rich, flavorful dish was actually inspired by a trip to Brazil. ■

- 1½ pounds large shrimp in shells (21–25 per pound), peeled, shells reserved, and deveined
- 4 cups water
- ½ teaspoon salt
- 2 tablespoons fresh lime juice
- 3 tablespoons vegetable oil
- 2 garlic cloves, chopped
- 1 red bell pepper, cored, seeded, and thinly sliced
- 2 medium onions, thinly sliced
- 3 tablespoons all-purpose flour
- 2 (14- to 16-ounce) cans whole tomatoes in juice, drained, seeded, and chopped
- 2 cups well-stirred unsweetened coconut milk (from two 14-ounce cans)
- Freshly ground black pepper
- ½ cup sliced scallion greens (from 2 large scallions)
- ½ cup coarsely chopped fresh cilantro sprigs

ACCOMPANIMENT: cooked rice

Combine shrimp shells, water, and salt in a 3-quart saucepan, bring to a simmer, and simmer until reduced to about 2 cups, 15 to 20 minutes. Pour shrimp broth through a sieve into a large glass measuring cup; discard shells.

Meanwhile, combine shrimp, lime juice, and salt to taste in a bowl and refrigerate, covered.

Heat oil in a 4-quart heavy saucepan over moderate heat. Add garlic, bell pepper, and onions and cook, stirring occasionally, until softened, about 5 minutes. Add flour and cook, stirring, for 1 minute. Stir in tomatoes, coconut milk, and shrimp broth and simmer, stirring occasionally, until vegetables are soft, 15 to 20 minutes.

Drain shrimp, add to saucepan, and simmer, stirring occasionally, until just cooked through, 2 to 3 minutes. Season with salt and pepper and sprinkle with scallions and cilantro. Serve with rice.

Chinese-Style Steamed Shrimp with Garlic and Scallions

SERVES 2

ACTIVE TIME: 20 MINUTES ■ START TO FINISH: 45 MINUTES

■ This delicate dish, soothing and reviving all at once, shows how subtle Chinese food can be. Soak the bamboo steamer while you prep the ingredients and marinate the shrimp. ■

3 scallions, white parts minced, green parts thinly sliced
1½ tablespoons soy sauce
1 tablespoon rice vinegar (not seasoned)
1 tablespoon minced garlic
2 teaspoons finely grated peeled fresh ginger
1 teaspoon sugar
½ teaspoon red pepper flakes
¼ teaspoon salt
1–2 teaspoons Asian sesame oil
1 pound large shrimp in shells (21–25 per pound), peeled, tail and first shell segment left intact, and deveined

ACCOMPANIMENT: cooked rice

SPECIAL EQUIPMENT: a bamboo steamer and a wok large enough for steamer to sit in

To prevent scorching of steamer rim, soak bamboo steamer in enough water to come up to lattice tray for 30 minutes.

Stir together minced scallions, soy sauce, vinegar, garlic, ginger, sugar, red pepper flakes, salt, and 1 teaspoon oil in a large bowl. Add shrimp and toss to coat. Marinate at room temperature, stirring occasionally, for 15 minutes.

Set steamer in wok, add enough water so that bottom rim sits in water but lattice tray sits above it, and bring to a boil.

Spread shrimp evenly in a glass pie plate or wide heatproof dish large enough to fit inside bamboo steamer with at least ¾ inch all around; discard any remaining marinade. Wearing oven mitts, put dish on steamer rack, cover, and steam shrimp until just firm to the touch, 4 to 8 minutes.

Wearing oven mitts, remove steamer from wok. Sprinkle shrimp with scallion greens and drizzle with remaining 1 teaspoon oil, if desired. Serve with rice.

Grilled Shrimp Rémoulade

SERVES 8

ACTIVE TIME: 1¼ HOURS ■ START TO FINISH: 1½ HOURS

■ A Louisiana-style rémoulade is essentially a jazzed-up mustard vinaigrette; this one is chunky with dill pickle. We grill the shrimp in their shells (deveining them but leaving the shells on to protect them during cooking) and toss them in the rémoulade while still hot. The sauce works its way into the shrimp, and the diners peel their own. This is gloriously messy finger food and couldn't be more scrumptious. ■

FOR RÉMOULADE

¼ cup Creole mustard (see Sources) or other coarse-grain mustard
¼ cup white wine vinegar
⅔ cup vegetable oil
3 tablespoons minced fresh flat-leaf parsley
2½ tablespoons drained bottled horseradish
2½ tablespoons minced dill pickle
2 tablespoons minced scallion greens
2 teaspoons sweet paprika
1½ teaspoons cayenne
1¼ teaspoons salt
½ teaspoon freshly ground black pepper

FOR SHRIMP

3 pounds large shrimp in shells (21–25 per pound)
¼ cup vegetable oil
1 teaspoon salt
½ teaspoon freshly ground black pepper

SPECIAL EQUIPMENT: fourteen 12-inch wooden skewers, soaked in water for 30 minutes

MAKE THE RÉMOULADE: Whisk together mustard and vinegar in a large bowl until well combined, then whisk in oil, parsley, horseradish, pickle, scallions, paprika, cayenne, salt, and black pepper.

PREPARE THE SHRIMP: With scissors, snip through shells of shrimp down middle of back, exposing vein and leaving tail and first segment of shell intact. Devein shrimp, leaving shells in place. Toss shrimp with oil, salt, and pepper, then thread about 6 shrimp onto each skewer.

PREPARE A CHARCOAL OR GAS GRILL: If using a charcoal grill, open vents in bottom of grill, then light charcoal. Fire is medium-hot when you can hold your hand 5 inches above rack for just 3 to 4 seconds. If using a gas grill, preheat on high, covered, for 10 minutes, then reduce heat to moderately high.

GRILL THE SHRIMP: Lightly oil grill rack and grill shrimp (covered only if using gas grill), turning once, until just cooked through, 3 to 4 minutes total. Transfer to a plate.

When shrimp are just cool enough to handle, push off skewers into bowl of rémoulade sauce, then toss to combine well. Cool for at least 15 minutes and serve warm or at room temperature.

COOK'S NOTES

- The rémoulade can be made up to 6 hours ahead and refrigerated, covered.
- The shrimp can be threaded onto skewers 2 hours ahead and refrigerated on a large tray, covered.
- The shrimp can also be broiled in 2 batches about 6 inches from the heat, turning over once, about 6 minutes per batch.

Emeril's Barbecued Shrimp with Mini Buttermilk Biscuits

SERVES 4

ACTIVE TIME: 1½ HOURS ■ START TO FINISH: 1½ HOURS

■ We couldn't stop eating this modern rendition of a local dish that's been around New Orleans forever. It's rich and spicy, and the miniature biscuits are an inspired touch. You'll want them to mop up every vestige of sauce, but they don't dwarf the shrimp. Their creator, the chef Emeril Lagasse, came up with this dish with his sous-chef at his first venture, Emeril's Restaurant. ■

FOR SHRIMP

- 2 pounds medium shrimp in shells (31–35 per pound), peeled, tail and first shell segment left intact and shells reserved for sauce, and deveined
- 1 tablespoon Creole Seasoning (recipe follows)
- Scant 1/8 teaspoon freshly ground black pepper, or to taste
- 3 tablespoons olive oil

FOR SAUCE

- 1 tablespoon olive oil
- 1/4 cup chopped onion
- 2 tablespoons minced garlic
- 1 tablespoon Creole Seasoning (recipe follows)
- 3 Turkish bay leaves or 1½ California bay leaves
- 3 lemons, peel and pith cut away with a sharp knife, lemons halved
- 2 cups water
- 1/2 cup Worcestershire sauce
- 1/4 cup dry white wine
- 1/4 teaspoon salt
- Scant 1/8 teaspoon freshly ground black pepper, or to taste
- 2 cups heavy cream
- 2 tablespoons unsalted butter, cut into bits

FOR BISCUITS

- 1 cup all-purpose flour
- 1 teaspoon baking powder
- 1/8 teaspoon baking soda
- 1/4 teaspoon salt
- 2 tablespoons cold unsalted butter, cut into bits
- 1/4 cup plus 2 teaspoons well-shaken buttermilk

OPTIONAL GARNISH: fresh chives

SPECIAL EQUIPMENT: 1-inch round cutter (or a shot glass)

PREPARE THE SHRIMP: Sprinkle shrimp with Creole seasoning and pepper, then rub seasoning over them to coat well. Arrange shrimp in one layer on a baking sheet and refrigerate, uncovered.

BEGIN THE SAUCE: Heat oil in a 4-quart saucepan over moderately high heat until hot but not smoking. Add onion and garlic and cook, stirring, for 1 minute. Add reserved shrimp shells, Creole seasoning, bay leaves, lemons, water, Worcestershire sauce, wine, salt, and pepper and bring to a boil, stirring. Reduce heat and simmer for 30 minutes.

Pour sauce through a fine-mesh sieve into a small saucepan; discard solids. Boil until reduced to about 1/4 cup, 12 to 15 minutes. Remove from heat.

MEANWHILE, MAKE THE BISCUITS: Put a rack in middle of oven and preheat oven to 375°F. Line a baking sheet with parchment or wax paper.

Sift together flour, baking powder, baking soda, and salt into a medium bowl. Blend in butter with your fingertips or a pastry blender until mixture resembles coarse meal. Stir in buttermilk with a fork just until a dough forms. Gather dough into a ball and gently knead 4 times on a lightly floured surface.

Pat dough out into a 6-inch round. Cut out 16 biscuits with floured 1-inch cutter (or shot glass) and transfer biscuits to baking sheet, arranging them 1½ inches apart. Bake until biscuits are golden, 14 to 16 minutes. Remove from oven and leave on baking sheet to keep warm.

COOK THE SHRIMP: Heat 1 tablespoon oil in a large heavy skillet over moderately high heat until hot but not smoking. Add one third of shrimp and sear, shaking skillet occasionally and turning once, for 2 minutes total. Transfer shrimp to a bowl. Sear remaining shrimp in 2 batches in same manner, adding 1 tablespoon oil to skillet per batch.

FINISH THE DISH: Add cream and sauce to skillet, stir, and bring to a simmer. Simmer, stirring occasionally, until reduced to about 2 cups, 8 to 10 minutes. Stir in shrimp and simmer until cooked through, about 1 minute. Stir in butter until it melts.

Spoon shrimp and sauce onto four plates and garnish with chives, if desired, then top with biscuits.

Creole Seasoning

MAKES ⅔ CUP
ACTIVE TIME: 5 MINUTES ■ START TO FINISH: 5 MINUTES

■ Intense and flavorful, this seasoning blend is New Orleans in a bowl. It really is worth making yourself; no packaged stuff can compare with a freshly mixed blend. We use this on just about anything, whether seafood, chicken, beef, or pork. ■

2½ tablespoons sweet paprika
2 tablespoons garlic powder
2 tablespoons salt
1 tablespoon freshly ground black pepper
1 tablespoon onion powder
1 tablespoon cayenne
1 tablespoon dried oregano, crumbled
1 tablespoon dried thyme, crumbled

Stir together all ingredients in a small bowl.

COOK'S NOTE

■ Keep leftover seasoning in an airtight container away from heat and light.

Shrimp de Jonghe

SERVES 2 AS A MAIN COURSE, 4 AS A FIRST COURSE
ACTIVE TIME: 45 MINUTES ■ START TO FINISH: 1 HOUR

■ Buttery, garlicky bread crumbs are layered with shrimp, insulating them as they bake. Sherry and almonds combine with the browned bread crumbs to impart a nuttiness to the dish. Created at de Jonghe's Restaurant in Chicago, this recipe is a testament to the days when we were afraid of garlic but not of butter. The amount of garlic—originally one clove—was considered outrageously racy when we first published it. ■

1¼ pounds large shrimp in shells (21–25 per pound), peeled and deveined
2 medium garlic cloves
Salt
1 stick (8 tablespoons) unsalted butter, softened
2 tablespoons medium-dry sherry
½ cup fine dry bread crumbs
¼ cup finely chopped fresh flat-leaf parsley
Freshly ground black pepper
¼ cup sliced almonds, lightly toasted (see Tips, page 938)

ACCOMPANIMENT: lemon wedges

Put a rack in middle of oven and preheat oven to 400°F. Butter a 1-quart gratin dish or other shallow baking dish.

Blanch shrimp in a 2½- to 3-quart saucepan of boiling water for 30 seconds, then drain in a colander and rinse under cold water until cool. Pat shrimp dry and arrange in one layer in buttered baking dish.

Mince and mash garlic to a paste with a pinch of salt, then stir together with butter and sherry in a medium bowl until blended. Stir in bread crumbs, parsley, and salt and pepper to taste. Dot shrimp with crumb mixture and sprinkle with almonds.

Bake until shrimp are just cooked through and topping is lightly browned, about 15 minutes. Serve with lemon wedges.

Steamers in Beer

SERVES 4
ACTIVE TIME: 10 MINUTES ■ START TO FINISH: 20 MINUTES

■ Steaming clams in beer is a traditional practice, and for a very good reason: the malty flavor and aroma of the beer enriches the steaming liquid as well as the shellfish. An inexpensive American pilsner works best here; a highly hopped beer tends to make the broth too bitter. The Atlantic steamer is a soft-shelled clam.

When it is cooked, the outer membrane that stretches over the shell and covers the foot often splits; if it doesn't, pull the membrane apart to get at the rich, velvety, almost mousselike meat. ■

- 1 stick (8 tablespoons) unsalted butter, cut into tablespoons
- 2 shallots, finely chopped
- 2 cups beer (not dark)
- 4 pounds steamers (less than 2 inches wide), well scrubbed
- 2 tablespoons finely chopped fresh flat-leaf parsley
- ½ teaspoon salt

Melt 1 tablespoon butter in a large saucepan over moderate heat. Add shallots and cook, stirring, until softened, about 2 minutes. Add beer and clams, cover, and bring to a boil, stirring occasionally, until clams open, 4 to 5 minutes. With a slotted spoon, transfer clams as they open to a bowl; cover to keep warm. Discard any clams that have not opened.

Pour cooking liquid through a paper towel–lined sieve into a 1½-quart saucepan. Heat over moderate heat until hot, then whisk in remaining 7 tablespoons butter. Remove from heat and stir in parsley and salt.

Serve clams with broth for dipping.

Clams Oreganata

SERVES 4 AS A MAIN COURSE, 8 AS A FIRST COURSE
ACTIVE TIME: 50 MINUTES ■ START TO FINISH: 1¼ HOURS

■ This simple, rustic dish featuring bowls of tiny clams in their pan juices topped with toasted bread crumbs is equally at home at an Italian Christmas Eve celebration or a casual supper at the kitchen table. Unlike the overbreaded clams found all too often in restaurants, these have a succulent flavor that comes shining through. People on the West Coast should use tiny Manila clams; easterners may find cockles more readily available. ■

- 3 cups fine fresh bread crumbs from a baguette or sourdough loaf
- ½ cup extra-virgin olive oil
- Fine sea salt
- 2 garlic cloves, minced
- 4 canned plum tomatoes, drained, seeded, and coarsely chopped
- 2 tablespoons minced fresh oregano
- Freshly ground black pepper
- 3 pounds very small hard-shelled clams (about 1 inch wide), such as Manila, or cockles, well scrubbed
- 1 teaspoon finely grated lemon zest

Put a rack in middle of oven and preheat oven to 350°F.

Spread bread crumbs in a baking sheet with sides and bake, stirring occasionally, until golden, 10 to 15 minutes. Transfer crumbs to a bowl. Drizzle with ¼ cup oil, season with sea salt, and stir until crumbs are coated.

Heat remaining ¼ cup oil in a 4- to 6-quart deep heavy pot over moderately low heat. Add garlic and cook, stirring, until fragrant, about 1 minute. Stir in tomatoes and 1 tablespoon oregano and cook, stirring occasionally, until tomatoes break down, 4 to 5 minutes. Season with pepper. Add clams, stirring well to coat, then cover pot tightly and increase heat to moderately high. Cook, stirring once, until clams open, 5 to 7 minutes. Discard any clams that have not opened.

Meanwhile, toss together bread crumbs, zest, and remaining 1 tablespoon oregano.

Divide clams and pan juices among four shallow bowls and sprinkle with bread crumbs. Serve immediately.

COOK'S NOTES

- ■ Larger hard-shelled clams (2 to 2½ inches wide) can be used; increase the cooking time to 8 to 10 minutes.
- ■ The crumbs can be made up to 1 day ahead and kept, covered, at room temperature.

Portuguese Clams

SERVES 4

ACTIVE TIME: 30 MINUTES ■ START TO FINISH: 45 MINUTES

■ There is something about clams that allows them to handle assertive seasonings with aplomb. Take pork, for instance: clams have an affinity for it. The spicy cured sausage called *chouriço* (chorizo, the Spanish version, is more widely available) is a popular addition to clam dishes in Portugal and in the Portuguese fishing communities of the United States. This light stew, made hearty by the addition of potatoes, is from the Toronto chef Albino Silva. At his restaurant, Chiado, he serves it in the classic copper pan called a *cataplana,* but a heavy-bottomed skillet will do nicely. *Cataplana,* incidentally, is the name of both the container and the dish, from the Algarve, Portugal's southernmost province. Make sure you buy either *chouriço* or Spanish chorizo. Mexican chorizo is sold fresh rather than cured and is too spicy and crumbly to work here. ■

- 3 bell peppers (preferably 1 each red, green, and yellow), halved lengthwise, cored, and seeds and ribs removed
- 2 medium boiling potatoes, peeled
- 2 pounds small to medium hard-shelled clams (less than 2 inches wide), well scrubbed
- 2 medium red onions, halved lengthwise and thinly sliced crosswise
- ¼ cup olive oil
- 8 garlic cloves, minced
- Salt and freshly ground black pepper
- 1 Turkish bay leaf or ½ California bay leaf
- 2 medium tomatoes, thinly sliced
- 8 fresh flat-leaf parsley sprigs
- ½ cup dry white wine
- 1 cup tomato sauce
- ½ pound Portuguese *chouriço* or hot Spanish chorizo (spicy cured pork sausage; see Glossary), cut into ¼-inch-thick slices

Preheat broiler. Put peppers skin sides up on rack of a broiler pan and broil 2 inches from heat until blistered and charred, 8 to 12 minutes. Transfer to a bowl, cover tightly, and let stand for 20 minutes. Peel peppers and cut into thin strips.

Cut potatoes crosswise into thin slices. Arrange clams and half of onions evenly in bottom of a deep 12-inch heavy skillet and drizzle with oil. Sprinkle with half of garlic and salt and pepper to taste, then add bay leaf. Add remaining onions, tomatoes, and roasted peppers in layers. Top with remaining garlic and parsley. Pour wine over and top with potatoes. Pour tomato sauce over potatoes, then top with *chouriço.* Sprinkle with salt and pepper to taste.

Cover skillet tightly with lid or foil and bring to a boil over moderately high heat. Cook until potatoes are just tender and clams are open, about 12 minutes. Discard any unopened clams. Transfer to a platter, arranging clams on top. Discard bay leaf.

Clam, Potato, and Bacon Potpie

SERVES 6 TO 8

ACTIVE TIME: 1¼ HOURS ■ START TO FINISH: 2¼ HOURS

■ Clam chowder in a crust, and really terrific. This is a good use for larger hard-shelled clams—cherrystones, for example—because they will be chopped. Make the dough first and prepare the filling while it is chilling. ■

- 1½ pounds boiling potatoes
- 6 lean bacon slices
- 2 tablespoons unsalted butter
- 1 medium onion, finely chopped
- 3 tablespoons all-purpose flour
- 1 cup heavy cream
- 1 cup whole milk
- 1 pint shucked hard-shelled clams (about 3 pounds in the shell), drained (¼ cup liquor reserved) and coarsely chopped
- ¼ teaspoon Worcestershire sauce
- 2 tablespoons finely chopped fresh flat-leaf parsley
- 1 teaspoon chopped fresh thyme or ¼ teaspoon dried thyme, crumbled
- 1 teaspoon fresh lemon juice
- ½ teaspoon salt, or to taste
- ¼ teaspoon freshly ground black pepper, or to taste
- Basic Pastry Dough for a double-crust pie (page 790)

1 large egg lightly beaten with 1 teaspoon water, for egg wash

SPECIAL EQUIPMENT: a 10-inch pie plate

Peel potatoes and cut into ½-inch cubes. Combine potatoes with well-salted water to cover by 1 inch in a 3-quart saucepan, bring to a simmer, and simmer, uncovered, until tender, about 5 minutes. Drain.

Meanwhile, cook bacon in a 4- to 5-quart heavy pot over moderate heat until crisp, 8 to 10 minutes. Transfer to paper towels to drain; crumble when cool.

Pour off all but 2 tablespoons fat from pot. Add butter and melt it, then add onion and cook, stirring occasionally, until softened and pale golden, 3 to 5 minutes. Add flour and cook over low heat, whisking, for 3 minutes to make a roux. Whisk in cream, milk, reserved clam liquor, and Worcestershire sauce, bring to a simmer, whisking, and simmer, whisking occasionally, for 5 minutes. Remove from heat and stir in potatoes, clams, parsley, thyme, lemon juice, bacon, salt, and pepper until well combined. Cool to room temperature.

Put a rack in lower third of oven and preheat oven to 400°F.

On a lightly floured surface, roll out 1 disk of dough into a 13-inch round. Fit into pie plate and trim, leaving a ½-inch overhang. Pour cooled filling into shell. Roll out remaining disk of dough into a 12-inch round and place over filling. Crimp edges together decoratively. Brush top crust with egg wash and make a few slits in it with tip of a paring knife for steam to escape.

Bake until crust is golden, 35 to 45 minutes.

Fried Oysters Rémoulade

SERVES 2 AS A MAIN COURSE, 4 AS A FIRST COURSE
ACTIVE TIME: 25 MINUTES ■ START TO FINISH: 1½ HOURS

■ We've melded two recipes here: the fried oysters are from our kitchens, and the rémoulade is from the New England seafood authority and chef Jasper White. The sauce is beautifully balanced and worth making all year long. It's delicious with any cold shellfish or with cold or grilled fish. ■

FOR RÉMOULADE

- ½ cup mayonnaise
- 1½ teaspoons coarse-grain mustard
- 1 teaspoon tomato paste
- ½ teaspoon minced shallot
- 2 tablespoons minced dill pickle
- 1½ teaspoons minced scallion
- ⅛ teaspoon Worcestershire sauce
- ¼ teaspoon Old Bay seasoning
- 1½ teaspoons minced fresh flat-leaf parsley
- ¼ teaspoon sugar
- ¼ teaspoon red wine vinegar
- Pinch of cayenne

FOR OYSTERS

- 12 oysters, shucked (see page 53), bottom shells reserved, thoroughly scrubbed, and dried
- ½ cup whole milk
- 1 large egg
- ½ teaspoon salt
- ½ teaspoon freshly ground black pepper
- 30 saltines, coarsely ground
- About 6 cups vegetable oil for deep-frying

SPECIAL EQUIPMENT: a deep-fat thermometer

MAKE THE RÉMOULADE: Stir together all ingredients in a small bowl. Chill, covered, for 1 hour.

MEANWHILE, MAKE THE OYSTERS: Put oysters in a colander to drain. Set a rack in a baking sheet with sides lined with paper towels.

Whisk together milk, egg, ¼ teaspoon salt, and ¼ teaspoon pepper in a small bowl. Stir together saltine crumbs and remaining ¼ teaspoon each salt and pepper in a shallow baking pan.

Heat 1¾ inches oil in a 4-quart heavy saucepan over moderately high heat until it registers 375°F on thermometer. Meanwhile, dip half of oysters in egg mixture, then dredge in cracker crumbs, knock off excess, and transfer to a large plate. Dip and dredge remaining oysters in same manner and transfer to another plate.

Fry first batch of oysters, stirring gently, until golden, 1½ to 2 minutes, then transfer to rack in baking sheet to drain. Return oil to 375°F and fry remaining oysters in same manner.

Serve oysters in shells, topped with rémoulade.

Oysters

What makes oysters so endlessly fascinating is that they take on the flavor characteristics—sweet, briny, metallic, buttery—of the water where they grow. This explains why each "variety" is named after the place it is harvested. Other factors also come into play, of course, including freshness, weather (heavy rainfall, for instance, can dilute flavor), and seasonality. But while there are hundreds of specifically named oysters, from Apalachicola to Yaquina Bay, on the half-shell market today, they all come from just five species that are grown commercially in the United States and Canada: Eastern, Olympia, Pacific (Japanese), Kumamoto, and European flat.

EASTERN (*Crassostrea virginica*): This species, indigenous to the East and Gulf coasts of North America, is now cultivated on the West Coast as well. The oysters' flavor is not especially complex but has a wonderful oceanic tang. Preshucked oysters for cooking are generally *virginica* oysters from southern waters, since they tend to be larger than those from the North.

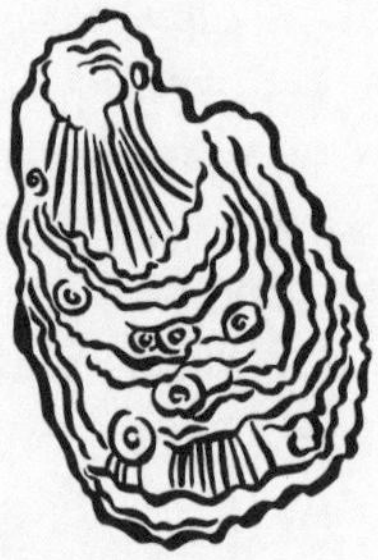

OLYMPIA (*Ostrea lurida*): The only oyster native to the West Coast, this species was so popular back in Gold Rush–era California restaurants that it was harvested to the point of extinction. Oystermen fought to bring the Olympia back, only to have it nearly wiped out again by pollution in the 1920s and '30s. Today supplies remain limited. The tiny size of this oyster belies its robust, coppery flavor.

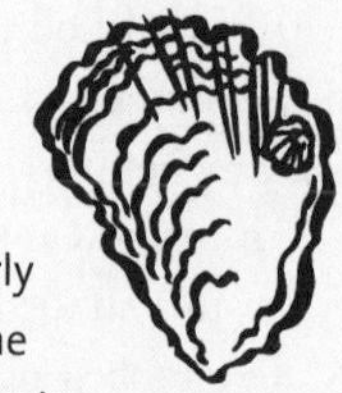

PACIFIC (*Crassostrea gigas*): In the 1920s, the Pacific oyster was brought from Japan to Washington to replace the Olympia, which was almost extinct at the time. It's now the most common oyster on the West Coast and in Europe. Because Pacifics vary enormously from inlet to inlet, it's hard to describe their flavor, but they are generally plump and creamy, often with a faint cucumber or melon taste.

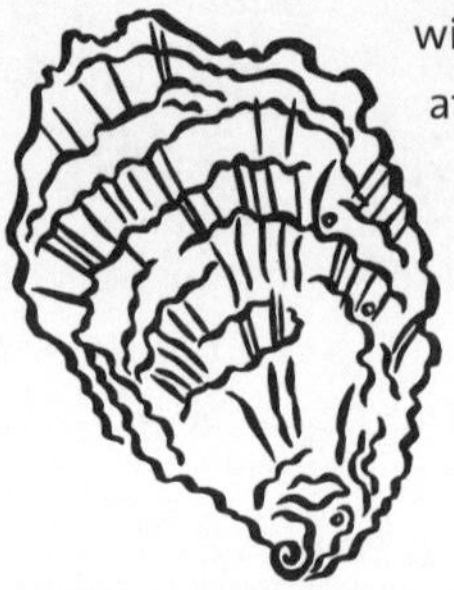

KUMAMOTO (*Crassostrea sikamea*): This small, deep-cupped oyster is native to the Kumamoto prefecture in Japan, where today it is thought to be extinct. Sweet, buttery, and moderately briny, the Kumamoto is a raw-bar favorite.

EUROPEAN FLAT (*Ostrea edulis*): As the name suggests, these round, flat-shelled oysters are indigenous to Europe, where they are known by such legendary names as Belon, Marennes, and Colchester, after their growing locations. Today they are cultivated on both coasts of North America, where their names usually derive from their growing area plus the word *flat*, such as Westcott Flat and Hog Island Flat. European flats are meaty, with a complex, sweet, minerally flavor and a metallic aftertaste that you either love or hate.

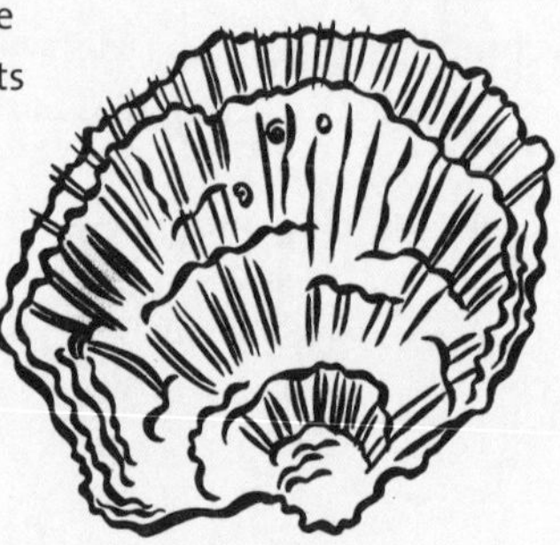

The seafood authority Jon Rowley tells us that some companies are becoming so caught up in all the excitement and romance of oysters that they are naming them after growing beds that have nothing to do with their actual locations. Saddle Rocks, for example, are named for a place close to Manhattan where oysters haven't been harvested for a few hundred years. And genuine Blue Points, from Long Island's Great South Bay, are essentially gone, although the generic term *bluepoints* has come to mean any Eastern oyster. Below is a list of names, by no means conclusive, that have a genuine ring when you see them on a half-shell menu. That old saying about eating oysters only in the *r* months has its basis in fact, by the way; oysters spawn in the spring and summer, and the texture isn't as firm and succulent then as it could be.

Pacific Oysters

Chef's Creek (British Columbia)

Dabob Bay (Washington)

Fanny Bay (British Columbia)

Hama Hama (Washington)

Hog Island (California)

Judd Cove (Washington)

Pearl Point (Oregon)

Penn Cove (Washington)

Samish Bay (Washington)

Snow Creek (Washington)

Steller Bay (British Columbia)

Totten Inlet (Washington)

Westcott Bay (Washington)

Yaquina Bay (Oregon)

Eastern Oysters

Apalachicola (Florida)

Bras d'Or (Nova Scotia)

Bristol (Maine and Rhode Island)

Caraquet (New Brunswick)

Chatham (Massachusetts)

Cotuit (Massachusetts)

Fishers Island (New York)

Malpeque (Prince Edward Island)

Martha's Vineyard (Massachusetts)

Nantucket (Massachusetts)

Narragansett Bay (Rhode Island)

Pine Island (New York)

Rappahannock River (Virginia)

Wellfleet (Massachusetts)

The Cultivated Mussel

Most mussels sold today in North America are cultivated, meaning that they're farmed on suspended ropes or in beds on the ocean floor and closely monitored. After harvest, they're carefully cleaned and graded. The mussels we find most often on the East Coast are cultivated blue ones from Prince Edward Island, and we love their consistently high quality. Blue mussels (*Mytilus edulis*) from P.E.I. are also common in West Coast markets, although in Washington and Oregon, native West Coast mussels (*M. trossulus*) from Penn Cove Shellfish seem to be featured more prominently in restaurants. According to the seafood authority Jon Rowley, more Mediterranean mussels (*M. galloprovincialis*) are being grown in California and Washington each year. Blue and Penn Cove mussels are best during the cooler months, but "Meds," which spawn at a different time, have an opposite seasonality: they are best during July, August, and September. Like the flavor of other shellfish, that of mussels reflects the waters in which they are grown. In general, a mussel at its best will be plump and have a rich saline taste.

The key to great mussels is freshness—you want them alive. And ask for the harvest date at the market; it's best if they're no more than four days old. Proper handling is also crucial: they should be stored in or on ice. Select those with closed shells and take a sniff; they should smell pleasantly briny. Once home, drain off any liquid before refrigerating them in a bowl, covered with a wet towel. Don't worry if some open while in the fridge; most likely they are catching their breath. When ready to cook them—the same day is best—tap those with open shells, and discard any that don't close by themselves.

TO CLEAN AND STEAM MUSSELS

Clean mussels by scrubbing them with a brush under cold water and scraping off any barnacles with a knife. Discard any mussels with cracked or broken shells. If the beard (byssus) is still attached (most cultivated mussels have been trimmed mechanically), remove it by (1) pulling it from tip to hinge or (2) pulling and cutting it off with a knife. Do this just before cooking, since mussels die shortly after their beards are removed.

1

2

To steam 1½ to 4½ pounds of mussels, put 1 cup of liquid—water or a mix of water and white wine or beer (not dark)—into a 4- to 6-quart pot. Bring the liquid to a boil over high heat, then dump in the mussels and cover the pot. Reduce the heat to moderate and cook the mussels, stirring occasionally, until they open wide. This will take 3 to 6 minutes, but check frequently after 3 minutes, and scoop out the mussels as they open with a slotted spoon. Discard any that remain closed, and save the flavor-packed cooking liquid, if desired.

Mussels with Garlic and White Wine

SERVES 2 AS A MAIN COURSE, 4 AS A FIRST COURSE
ACTIVE TIME: 10 MINUTES ■ START TO FINISH: 15 MINUTES

■ Feel like a quick trip to Paris or the fishing villages of Brittany? Then sit down to a bowl of these classic *moules à la marinière* and be transported. The natural sweetness of the mussels is enhanced nicely by white wine, shallots, and parsley. Don't forget a crusty baguette and good butter. ■

- 3 tablespoons unsalted butter
- 2 small shallots, finely chopped
- 1 garlic clove, minced
- 1 pound mussels, preferably cultivated, scrubbed well and beards removed
- ½ cup dry white wine
- 2 tablespoons chopped fresh flat-leaf parsley
- Salt

ACCOMPANIMENT: crusty French bread

Heat 2 tablespoons butter in a 5- to 6-quart heavy pot over moderately high heat until foam subsides. Add shallots and garlic and cook, stirring, until golden, about 4 minutes.

Add mussels and wine, cover, and cook, stirring occasionally, until mussels open wide. This will take 4 to 6 minutes, but check frequently after 4 minutes and transfer them to a bowl as they open. Discard any unopened mussels. Remove pot from heat and stir in remaining 1 tablespoon butter, parsley, and salt to taste. Serve sauce over mussels, with crusty bread.

Spicy Thai Steamed Mussels

SERVES 4 AS A MAIN COURSE, 6 AS A FIRST COURSE
ACTIVE TIME: 20 MINUTES ■ START TO FINISH: 30 MINUTES

■ With the proliferation of Thai ingredients on supermarket shelves, this exotic-sounding dish is practically a pantry recipe. The coconut milk adds a creamy note to the broth, and the red curry paste gives it a kick. The recipe, from the Silver Thatch Inn, in Charlottesville, Virginia, is quick and very doable for a group. ■

- 1 (14-ounce) can unsweetened coconut milk
- ⅓ cup fresh lime juice
- ⅓ cup dry white wine
- 1½ tablespoons Thai red curry paste (see Glossary)
- 1½ tablespoons minced garlic
- 1 tablespoon Asian fish sauce
- 1 tablespoon sugar
- 5 pounds mussels, preferably cultivated, scrubbed well and beards removed
- 2 cups chopped fresh cilantro sprigs

ACCOMPANIMENT: lime wedges

Combine coconut milk, lime juice, wine, curry paste, garlic, fish sauce, and sugar in a 6- to 8-quart wide pot and bring to a boil over high heat. Cover and boil, stirring occasionally, for 2 minutes. Add mussels and toss to combine. Cover pot and cook, stirring occasionally, until mussels just open wide, about 6 minutes. Discard any unopened mussels.

Just before serving, toss mussels with cilantro. Serve with lime wedges.

Baked Mussels with Parsley Garlic Butter

SERVES 2 AS A MAIN COURSE, 4 AS A FIRST COURSE
ACTIVE TIME: 20 MINUTES ■ START TO FINISH: 35 MINUTES

■ Here's an unusual, hassle-free treatment for mussels. Simply slather them, unopened, with garlic-parsley butter (it's very similar to a classic French snail butter) and bake them. As they open, their juices mingle with the butter. ■

- 2 pounds mussels, preferably cultivated, scrubbed well and beards removed
- 3 garlic cloves, coarsely chopped
- 1 cup fresh flat-leaf parsley leaves
- ½ stick (4 tablespoons) unsalted butter, cut into pieces
- ¼ teaspoon salt
- ¼ teaspoon freshly ground black pepper

ACCOMPANIMENT: crusty bread

Put a rack in middle of oven and preheat oven to 450°F.

Spread mussels in a 13-by-9-inch baking dish. Combine garlic, parsley, butter, salt, and pepper in a food processor and blend until smooth. Spoon butter over mussels. Cover baking dish tightly with foil and bake until mussels open wide, 12 to 15 minutes. Discard any unopened mussels. Serve with pan juices and crusty bread.

Mussels Gratin

SERVES 6

ACTIVE TIME: 1 HOUR ■ START TO FINISH: 1¼ HOURS

■ Steamed mussels meet tomatoes, cheese, and garlic in an easy one-dish meal; this is fork food, not finger food. ■

- 4 pounds mussels, preferably cultivated, scrubbed well and beards removed
- 2 pounds plum tomatoes, halved lengthwise, seeded, and each half cut into sixths
- ½ cup chopped fresh basil
- ½ cup crème fraîche
- ½ cup finely grated Parmigiano-Reggiano
- 2 large garlic cloves, 1 minced, 1 halved
- ½ teaspoon salt
- ¼ teaspoon freshly ground black pepper
- 15 (⅓-inch-thick) baguette slices
- 2 tablespoons extra-virgin olive oil

Put a rack in middle of oven and preheat oven to 450°F. Oil a 13-by-9-inch or other shallow 3-quart baking dish.

Bring 1 cup water to a boil in a 4- to 6-quart pot. Add mussels, cover, and cook over moderately high heat until they just open wide, checking frequently after 3 minutes and transferring them to a large bowl. Discard any mussels that remain closed after 6 minutes. Shuck mussels, discarding shells.

Toss together mussels, tomatoes, basil, crème fraîche, cheese, minced garlic, salt, and pepper in bowl, then transfer to baking dish.

Rub one side of each slice of bread with halved garlic and arrange bread, garlic side up, over mussels; discard garlic. Brush bread with oil.

Bake until bread is golden brown, about 15 minutes. Serve mussels spooned over garlic toasts.

Roasted Mussels with Almonds and Garlic

SERVES 4

ACTIVE TIME: 15 MINUTES ■ START TO FINISH: 45 MINUTES

■ Mussels with almonds? An unusual combination, but it works: the nuts complement the texture of the mussels, and you have three different kinds of sweet meatiness going on—mussels, almonds, and garlic. ■

- 5 pounds mussels, preferably cultivated, scrubbed well and beards removed
- 8 garlic cloves, minced
- 1 cup packed fresh flat-leaf parsley leaves, chopped
- 1½ cups dry white wine
- ¾ stick (6 tablespoons) unsalted butter, cut into pieces
- ¼ teaspoon salt
- ¼ teaspoon freshly ground black pepper
- ½ cup (3 ounces) whole almonds with skins, toasted (see Tips, page 936) and finely chopped

Put a rack in middle of oven and preheat oven to 425°F.

Combine mussels, garlic, parsley, wine, butter, salt, and pepper in a 6- to 8-quart heavy ovenproof pot. Roast, uncovered, stirring once halfway through roasting, until mussels have opened wide, 15 to 20 minutes. Discard any unopened mussels. Add almonds and toss to combine.

COOK'S NOTE

■ It is very important for the oven to maintain its high heat so the mussels roast properly. Do not open the oven door until halfway through roasting, when the mussels are ready for a quick stir, and don't take the time to remove any mussels that may be open at this point.

Crab Cakes

SERVES 2 (GENEROUSLY) AS A MAIN COURSE,
4 AS A FIRST COURSE
ACTIVE TIME: 15 MINUTES ■ START TO FINISH: 40 MINUTES

■ Crab cakes are often more about the filler than about the crabmeat, but not these, which are nothing but beautiful nuggets of pure crab gently held together with mayonnaise and a whisper of egg. Because they are so light and delicate, they're baked, not sautéed. The recipe comes from the chef Jimmy Sneed, at the Frog and the Redneck, in Richmond, Virginia, who gets his stellar blue crabs from the Chesapeake Bay. ■

- ½ cup mayonnaise
- 1½ tablespoons lightly beaten egg
- 1 tablespoon whole-grain mustard
- 1 pound jumbo lump crabmeat, picked over for shells and cartilage

ACCOMPANIMENT: lemon wedges

Put a rack in middle of oven and preheat oven to 400°F. Oil a small baking sheet.

Whisk together mayonnaise, egg, and mustard in a medium bowl. Fold in crabmeat until just combined. Gently form mixture into four 1-inch-thick cakes and transfer to baking sheet.

Bake crab cakes until golden, 15 to 20 minutes. Let stand on baking sheet for 5 minutes before serving with lemon wedges.

Deviled Crab with Sherry Sauce

SERVES 6
ACTIVE TIME: 20 MINUTES ■ START TO FINISH: 25 MINUTES

■ Because crabmeat is so delicate, it benefits from the subtle heat of dry mustard and cayenne rather than the brash heat of chiles or red pepper flakes. The nuttiness of sherry plays up the deviled crab nicely, and the egg yolks enrich the sauce, giving it a silkiness you would miss if it weren't there. ■

- 2 pounds cooked king crab legs in the shell, thawed if frozen, shells split lengthwise, or 1 pound jumbo lump crabmeat, picked over for shells and cartilage
- ½ stick (4 tablespoons) unsalted butter
- 2 tablespoons all-purpose flour
- 1 cup whole milk
- 1 large garlic clove, lightly crushed
- 2 large egg yolks
- ⅓ cup medium-dry sherry
- ½ teaspoon dry mustard
- ⅛ teaspoon freshly grated nutmeg
- ⅛ teaspoon cayenne
- ½ teaspoon salt
- 2 tablespoons finely chopped fresh flat-leaf parsley
- ¼ cup fine dry bread crumbs
- ¼ cup finely grated Parmigiano-Reggiano

SPECIAL EQUIPMENT: an instant-read thermometer; six 4-ounce ramekins

Put a rack in upper third of oven and preheat oven to 450°F.

If using king crab, remove crabmeat from shells and remove any cartilage. Cut meat into ½-inch pieces.

Melt 2 tablespoons butter in a 1½-quart heavy saucepan over moderately low heat. Add flour and cook, whisking, for 2 minutes to make a roux. Add milk in a slow stream, whisking constantly, then add garlic and bring to a boil, whisking. Reduce heat and simmer, whisking, for 3 minutes. Remove sauce from heat and discard garlic.

Whisk together egg yolks, sherry, mustard, nutmeg, cayenne, and salt in a medium bowl, then add sauce in a slow stream, whisking. Pour mixture back into saucepan and cook over very low heat, whisking constantly, until thermometer registers 160°F, about 2 minutes. Remove from heat and gently stir in crabmeat and parsley. Divide mixture among ramekins.

Melt remaining 2 tablespoons butter and cool slightly. Stir together melted butter, bread crumbs, and cheese in a small bowl with a fork, then sprinkle over crab. Put ramekins in a baking sheet with sides and bake until crab mixture is bubbling and crumbs are golden brown, about 5 minutes.

COOK'S NOTE

■ The deviled crab mixture can be prepared up to 4 hours ahead and refrigerated, covered. Bring to room temperature before baking.

CLEANING SOFT-SHELLED CRABS

No doubt about it, dressing—that is, cleaning—soft-shelled crabs can be a gruesome task. Who relishes cutting a creature while it's still alive? If you are going to cook softshells, though, it's essential to start with live ones. The quality of these crabs deteriorates by the minute after they die. Marine scientists assure us that crabs are low on the evolutionary ladder and don't have a sophisticated central nervous system. Still squeamish? Ask your fishmonger to clean them. In any case, cook them the day you buy them.

1. With kitchen scissors, swiftly cut off the eyes and mouth from each crab. (When doing this, you are also cutting out what little central nervous system there is.)

2. Whether you press out the sand sac (stomach) and what watermen call the mustard is up to you. The sand sac rarely contains grit. The mustard is adored by some, but others find it bitter.

3. Lift up the points on opposite sides of the crab and cut away the spongy gills.

4. Turn the crab over, then lift up the "apron" (abdomen) and cut it off.

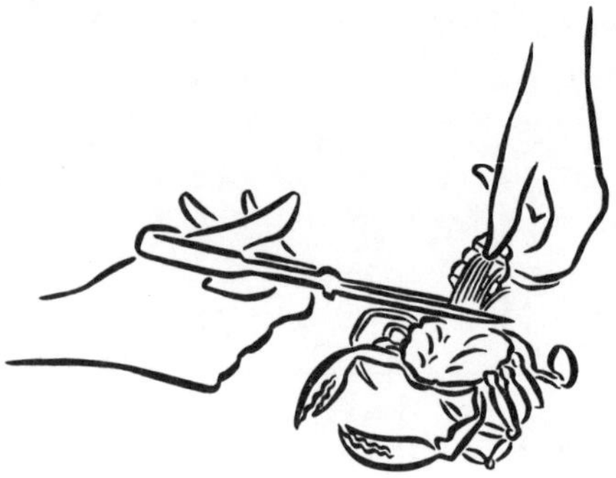

Soft-Shelled Crabs Meunière

SERVES 2

ACTIVE TIME: 1 HOUR ■ START TO FINISH: 1¾ HOURS

■ The Atlantic blue crab is a crustacean whose taxonomic name, *Callinectes sapidus*, translates as "savory beautiful swimmer," providing a hint of its culinary seductiveness. It's never more desirable than in the spring, when the first softshells—crabs that have shed their old shell to make way for a new one—come into season. Sautéed in butter, they are a Chesapeake Bay classic. ■

- 1 cup whole milk
- 1 teaspoon kosher salt
- ¼ teaspoon freshly ground black pepper
- 4 small live soft-shelled crabs (4 inches wide), cleaned (see opposite page)
- 1 cup Wondra or all-purpose flour
- ¼ cup Clarified Butter (page 935)
- 1½ tablespoons unsalted butter, cut into 3 pieces
- 1 tablespoon fresh lemon juice
- 2 tablespoons chopped fresh flat-leaf parsley

Combine milk, salt, and pepper in a shallow dish. Add crabs and soak for 5 minutes.

Put flour in a shallow bowl. Lift one crab out of milk, letting excess drip off, and dredge in flour, then knock off excess flour and transfer to a tray. Repeat with remaining crabs, arranging them in one layer.

Heat clarified butter in a 12-inch nonstick skillet over moderately high heat until hot but not smoking. Add crabs, upside down, and cook until golden brown, about 2 minutes. Turn over and cook until golden brown on second side, 2 to 3 minutes more. Transfer crabs to a serving dish.

Add unsalted butter to skillet and cook until it is golden brown with a nutty aroma. Add lemon juice and parsley and remove from heat.

Season pan sauce with salt and pepper and drizzle over crabs.

COOK'S NOTE

■ If the crabs you get are larger and won't all fit in the skillet, cook them in batches or in two skillets, using more clarified butter.

Boiled Lobsters with Tarragon Vermouth Sauce

SERVES 4

ACTIVE TIME: 30 MINUTES ■ START TO FINISH: 1 HOUR

■ Vermouth adds a light, aromatic, herbal note to the béarnaise-style sauce here, playing up the flavor of the lobster. With a main course this rich, you'll want to have simple sides—parsleyed new potatoes, perhaps, and a tomato and corn salad. ■

FOR LOBSTERS

- 3 tablespoons fine sea salt
- 4 (1¼- to 2-pound) live lobsters

FOR SAUCE

- 1 stick (8 tablespoons) unsalted butter
- 3 tablespoons dry vermouth
- 1 tablespoon tarragon white-wine vinegar
- 3 large egg yolks
- ¼ teaspoon salt
- ¼ teaspoon freshly ground black pepper
- ½ teaspoon fresh lemon juice
- 1½ teaspoons chopped fresh tarragon

SPECIAL EQUIPMENT: an instant-read thermometer

COOK THE LOBSTERS: Bring 6 quarts water and sea salt to a boil in an 8- to 10-quart pot over high heat. Plunge 2 lobsters headfirst into water and cook, covered, for 6 minutes for 1¼-pound lobsters, 7 minutes for 1½-pound lobsters, or 13 minutes for 2-pound lobsters, from time lobsters enter water. Transfer with tongs to sink to drain. Return water to a boil and cook remaining 2 lobsters in same manner.

MEANWHILE, MAKE THE SAUCE: Melt butter and cool until just warm. Whisk together vermouth, vinegar, and egg yolks in a small metal bowl. Set bowl over a small saucepan of boiling water and heat mixture, whisking constantly, until warm. Add melted butter in a slow stream, whisking, then whisk in salt and pepper. Cook, whisking, until sauce thickens and registers 160°F on thermometer, about 5 minutes. Remove pan from heat, keeping bowl over saucepan. Just before serving, stir in lemon juice and tarragon.

Working from belly side, halve each lobster lengthwise with a sharp heavy knife or kitchen shears. Serve with sauce.

Grilled Lobster with Orange Chipotle Vinaigrette

SERVES 8

ACTIVE TIME: 25 MINUTES ■ START TO FINISH: 45 MINUTES

■ Spicy, smoky chipotle chiles aren't an obvious flavoring when you're considering the oceanic tang of lobster, but this recipe falls into the category of making a good thing even better. The chiles, tempered by orange juice and zest, are used so judiciously that they become a savory echo of the sweetness and smokiness of lobster on the grill. And the vinaigrette is a lighter embellishment than the usual melted butter or mayonnaise. ■

- 3/4 teaspoon finely grated orange zest
- 1 cup fresh orange juice
- 1/4 cup white wine vinegar
- 1 1/2 tablespoons chopped canned chipotle chiles in adobo (see Glossary), or to taste
- 3 tablespoons plus 2 1/2 teaspoons fine sea salt
- 1 teaspoon packed brown sugar
- 1 cup olive oil
- 8 (1 1/2-pound) live lobsters
- 2 tablespoons chopped fresh basil

OPTIONAL GARNISH: fresh basil sprigs

Combine zest, juice, vinegar, chipotles, 2 1/2 teaspoons salt, and sugar in a blender and blend until chipotles are finely chopped. With motor running, add oil in a slow stream and process until well blended.

Bring 6 quarts water and remaining 3 tablespoons salt to a boil in an 8- to 10-quart pot over high heat. Plunge 2 lobsters headfirst into water and cook, covered, for 3 minutes from time they enter water (they will be only partially cooked). Transfer with tongs to sink to drain. Return water to a boil if necessary and cook remaining 6 lobsters in 3 more batches.

When lobsters are cool enough to handle, twist off tails and break off claws at body; discard bodies. With kitchen shears, halve tails lengthwise through shell. Do not remove meat from tail or claw shells.

Prepare a charcoal or gas grill: If using a charcoal grill, open vents in bottom of grill, then light charcoal. Fire is medium-hot when you can hold your hand 5 inches above rack for just 3 to 4 seconds. If using a gas grill, preheat on high, covered, for 10 minutes, then reduce heat to moderately high.

Lightly oil grill rack and grill claws, uncovered (in batches if necessary), turning occasionally, until liquid bubbles at open ends, 5 to 7 minutes. Transfer to a platter.

Stir basil into chipotle vinaigrette and transfer 1 1/4 cups to a small pitcher. Brush meat in lobster tails with some of remaining vinaigrette and grill tails, meat side down (in batches if necessary), for 3 minutes. Turn tails meat side up, brush with more vinaigrette, and grill until juices are bubbling and meat is opaque, 3 to 5 minutes. Transfer tails to platter.

Serve lobster warm or chilled, with pitcher of vinaigrette. Garnish with basil sprigs, if desired.

COOK'S NOTES

- The vinaigrette, without the basil, can be made up to 3 days ahead and refrigerated, covered. Bring to room temperature and stir in the basil before using.
- The lobsters can be parboiled and the tails and claws removed up to 1 day ahead. Refrigerate, covered.
- The lobsters can be grilled up to 2 hours ahead. Cool, uncovered, then refrigerate, covered. Serve chilled.

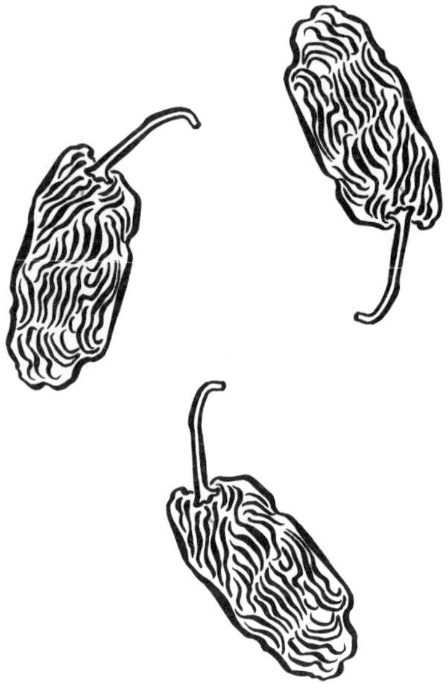

Lobster Deconstructed

Sweet and intensely oceanic, lobster is a great American treasure. The very best place to buy it, of course, is straight off a lobsterman's boat, but we can't all be so lucky. The North Atlantic coast is dotted with hundreds of companies that sell primarily to seafood markets and restaurants, but many of them have a retail market, many also ship, and many conveniently sell lobsters ready-boiled. If you are buying from a regular fish market, make sure that it's a busy one with a brisk turnover and that the lobsters are kept in aerated saltwater tanks, not on shoals of ice. Buy the most energetic ones you can see, and remember that they are strong and fierce, so handle them with care when you get them home. If you can't ferry them straight to the stovetop, refrigerate them as soon as possible. They will keep, wrapped in damp — not wet — newspaper (don't let it dry out), for a day or so. If they start looking feeble, drop everything and cook them immediately (then eat, or refrigerate until ready to serve).

The most common way to cook lobsters is to plunge them headfirst into a large deep pot of boiling water. Generously salt the water to retain the natural brininess of the lobsters, and use enough water, or the lobsters will bring down its temperature, making it tough to gauge the cooking time. Keep time from the moment you put the lobsters in the pot, *not* from when the water resumes a rolling boil. One fun fact we stumbled across: the reason a lobster's shell turns scarlet when cooked is that most of the other colors in the shell — brown, green, sometimes blue — are masked during the process, but the red pigment is a very stable one.

Lobsters, like other crustaceans, outgrow their shells as they mature. They are called "shedders" or "new shells" during the molting period and while they harden their new, paper-thin larger shell. The meat isn't quite as firm then as it could be (although it is usually very sweet and tender), and because the lobsters haven't had time to grow into their shells, water collects inside the carapace. A Maine lobsterman we know describes shedders this way: "When you pick 'em up, there's nobody home." If you are ordering lobsters to be shipped by air, realize that shedders are fragile and expensive, given how much of their weight is water. Lobsters are at their best in winter; try to avoid ordering them in summer, when shedders are prevalent.

The only inedible parts of a lobster are the ganglia, the small bits of nerve tissue between the eyes that function as the brain; the grain, or head, sac (essentially the stomach, which is filled with grit); and the spongy-looking gills, just aft of the small walking legs. You might want to discard the green stuff — the soft, liverlike tomalley — which is where contaminants accumulate; health issues have recently been raised about this. Still, some people prize tomalley: it's fabulous spread on toast or whisked into a pan sauce. The red stuff — the coral, or roe, of the female lobster — is also edible; it adds fullness, depth, and luster to a stock or sauce. (Both coral and tomalley are highly perishable; cooked, they keep only one day in the fridge.) All of these parts are in the lobster carcass, or what every self-respecting New Englander calls "the body."

Rich is one word that always seems to come to mind when we think about lobster, so we were surprised to learn that it is actually low in fat. The meat is also low in cholesterol, about 95 grams per 3½ ounces — comparable to skinless chicken. That's about the amount of meat in a one-pounder, which brings us to another point. Lobster, like filet mignon, is not cheap. But you can eat *all* the filet. With lobster, you are paying in large part for the shell, so you might want to consider making lobster stock and oil (see page 342) to get the most bang for your buck.

Lobster Newburg

SERVES 4
ACTIVE TIME: 50 MINUTES ■ START TO FINISH: 1 HOUR

■ The histories of lobster Newburg and lobster Thermidor are closely entertwined—so closely, in fact, that the *Gourmet* chef Louis P. DeGouy got these two extravagantly rich creations of the Gilded Age confused and published this recipe in the 1940s as a Thermidor (made with a flour-thickened béchamel sauce) instead of a Newburg (made with cream, egg yolks, and sherry). More than half a century later, we stand corrected, and the recipe, somewhat to our surprise, stands the test of time. It is not remotely stodgy or heavy; rather, the eggs and cream give the dish a sleek, silky quality, and the richness is tempered by the nutlike flavor of the sherry. This is absolutely outstanding. ■

- 3 tablespoons plus 3/4 teaspoon fine sea salt
- 2 (1 1/2-pound) live lobsters
- 1 cup heavy cream
- 1/2 stick (4 tablespoons) unsalted butter
- 1/4 pound mushrooms, trimmed and thinly sliced

TO REMOVE MEAT FROM LOBSTERS

1. Twist off the tails. Break off the claws (the big one is the crusher, the smaller one is the pincer) at the body.

2. With a pair of kitchen shears, remove the thin, hard membrane from the underside of the tail by cutting just inside the outer edge of the shell on both sides.

3. Firmly grasp the chunk of lobster meat and pull it from the shell.

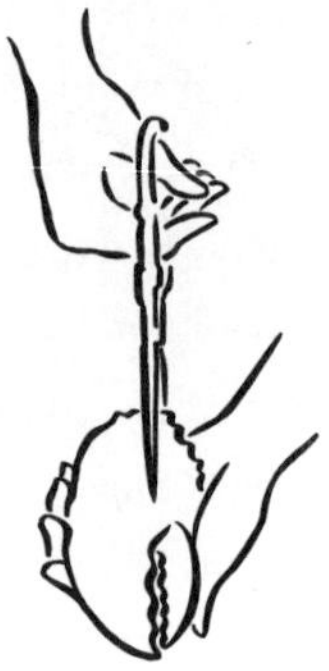

4. Instead of cracking the claws and picking out the tender, juicy meat, simply cut them open with the kitchen shears and pull the shell away.

½ teaspoon paprika
¼ teaspoon freshly ground black pepper
2 tablespoons medium-dry sherry
2 large egg yolks

SPECIAL EQUIPMENT: an instant-read thermometer

Bring 6 quarts water and 3 tablespoons salt to a boil in an 8- to 10-quart pot over high heat. Plunge lobsters headfirst into water and cook, covered, for 7 minutes from time they enter water. Transfer with tongs to sink to drain.

When lobsters are cool enough to handle, twist off claws (leaving body and tail intact) and crack them. With kitchen shears, halve lobsters lengthwise, beginning from tail end. Remove meat from tails, claws, and joints, reserving shells. Cut all meat into ¼-inch pieces. Remove and discard any remaining lobster innards and rinse and dry shells.

Bring cream just to a simmer in a small saucepan over moderate heat; remove from heat. Keep warm, covered.

Heat butter in a 2-quart heavy saucepan over moderate heat until foam subsides. Add mushrooms and cook, stirring, until liquid they give off evaporates and they begin to brown, about 5 minutes. Add lobster meat, paprika, remaining ¾ teaspoon salt, and pepper, reduce heat to low, and cook, shaking pan gently, for 1 minute. Add 1 tablespoon sherry and ½ cup hot cream and simmer for 5 minutes.

Meanwhile, whisk together yolks and remaining 1 tablespoon sherry in a small bowl. Slowly pour in remaining ½ cup hot cream, whisking constantly, then transfer to a small heavy saucepan. Cook custard sauce over very low heat, whisking constantly, until it is slightly thickened and registers 160°F on thermometer.

Add custard sauce to lobster mixture, stirring gently. Remove from heat and keep warm, partially covered.

Set broiler rack about 6 inches from heat and preheat broiler. Arrange shells of lobster bodies cut side up in a shallow baking pan and spoon lobster with some of sauce into shells. Broil until golden brown, 4 to 5 minutes.

Serve lobsters with remaining sauce on the side.

Calcutta Lobster in Spinach and Yogurt Sauce

SERVES 4
ACTIVE TIME: 20 MINUTES ■ START TO FINISH: 40 MINUTES

■ Here is a great winter recipe for lobster, the time when, contrary to popular opinion, it is at its best (and cheapest). Although lobster most often brings New England to mind, the crustacean is enjoyed in other parts of the world as well. In this easy seafood curry from the writer Laxmi Hiremath, spinach, yogurt, and seasonings unite to make the dish complex and interesting; it tastes (and looks) like the best creamed spinach you've ever had. ■

½ teaspoon brown or black mustard seeds (see Glossary)
3 tablespoons plus 1 teaspoon fine sea salt
2 (1½-pound) live lobsters
1 bunch spinach, coarse stems discarded
2 tablespoons vegetable oil
1 medium onion, chopped
4 large garlic cloves, minced
1 small serrano chile, minced
1 (1-inch) piece fresh ginger, peeled and minced
2 teaspoons ground coriander
1 cup plain yogurt

ACCOMPANIMENT: cooked white or brown basmati rice
SPECIAL EQUIPMENT: an electric coffee/spice grinder

Coarsely grind mustard seeds in coffee/spice grinder; set aside.

Bring 6 quarts water and 3 tablespoons salt to a boil in an 8- to 10-quart pot over high heat. Plunge lobsters headfirst into water and cook, covered, for 7 minutes from time they enter water. Transfer with tongs to sink to drain.

When lobsters are cool enough to handle, remove meat from claws, joints, and tails (see opposite page). Discard tomalley, any roe, and shells (or save for another use). Cut meat into bite-sized pieces.

Chop enough spinach to measure 2 cups (reserve remainder, if any, for another use). Heat oil in a 10- to 12-inch heavy skillet over moderate heat until hot but not smoking. Add onion, garlic, chile, ginger, and mustard seeds and cook, stirring, until onion begins to brown, about 5 minutes. Add coriander and cook, stirring, for 1 minute. Stir in spinach and cook until it begins to wilt, about 30 seconds. Gradually add yogurt, stirring until well combined. Stir in lobster and remaining 1 teaspoon salt. Simmer gently until just heated through. Serve with rice.

Louisiana Crawfish Boil

SERVES 4

ACTIVE TIME: 1 HOUR ■ START TO FINISH: $1\frac{3}{4}$ HOURS

■ Sweeter and tenderer than lobster, crawfish is the quintessential Cajun food. It is rare in bayou country to have a crawfish boil with less than a forty-pound sack of the crustaceans; in fact, many families make a day of going to a fish-your-own pond and then returning home to cook their catch on an outdoor gas cooker. We adapted this tradition for those who can find live crawfish in their markets (the high season for Louisiana crawfish is March through May, and they may be available in other months, depending on the weather) but who don't have the outdoor space to handle cooking such large quantities.

It's best to add one batch of crawfish at a time to the boiling water, so a large sieve and a lightweight pot come in handy for transferring them from the sink to the cooking pot. Because crawfish are the main event, the accompanying vegetables are kept to a minimum. It's customary to dip the cooked peeled crawfish, boiled potatoes, and saltines into horseradish cocktail sauce and to have plenty of cold beer on hand to wash

Lobster Stock and Lobster Oil

You can use lobster stock for soups, chowders, or sauces and lobster oil in vinaigrettes or mayonnaise (it makes a really elegant potato salad). We also love the oil drizzled over poached or grilled fish or mashed potatoes.

TO MAKE LOBSTER STOCK: Split 2 lobster bodies down the middle and remove the grain sacs. Heat 2 tablespoons olive oil in a 6- to 8-quart pot over moderate heat. Add 1 chopped carrot, 1 chopped celery rib, 1 chopped onion, 5 minced garlic cloves, a bay leaf, and a fresh thyme sprig and cook until vegetables are softened. Stir in broken-up lobster bodies, add 4 quarts water, and bring to a boil. Lower heat and simmer until reduced to about 6 cups, about $1\frac{1}{2}$ hours.

Strain stock through a cheesecloth-lined fine-mesh sieve. Cool stock and refrigerate for up to 4 days or freeze for up to 3 months.

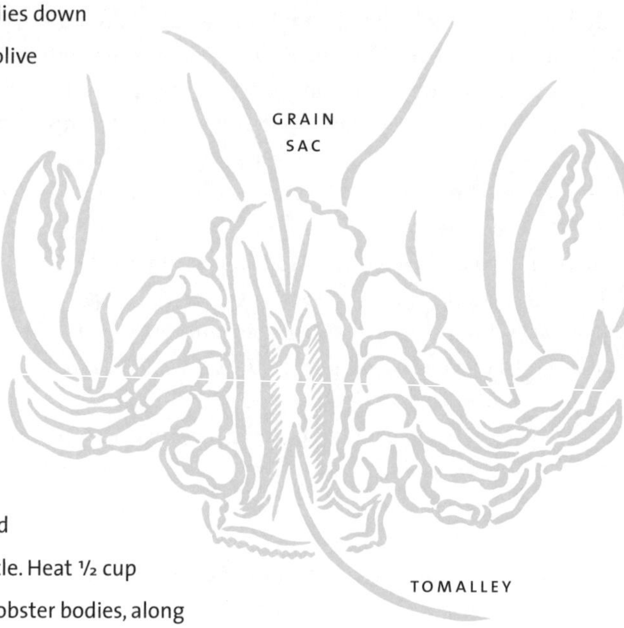

TO MAKE LOBSTER OIL: Remove grain sacs and coarsely crush 2 lobster bodies in a large mortar with a pestle. Heat $\frac{1}{2}$ cup canola oil in a 3-quart pot over moderately high heat. Add lobster bodies, along with a fresh tarragon sprig and a 4-inch strip of orange zest, and cook, stirring, until very bright, about 5 minutes. Add $3\frac{1}{2}$ more cups canola oil and bring to a simmer. Simmer over low heat for 40 minutes.

Strain oil through a cheesecloth-lined fine-mesh sieve. Cool and refrigerate for up to 2 weeks or freeze for up to 1 month. Bring to room temperature before using.

it all down. It's also customary to suck on the crawfish heads to draw out the soft, liverlike "fat"—what lobster lovers would call tomalley. ■

3½–4 quarts water (depending on size of stockpot)
1 (3-ounce) bag Cajun seafood-boil spices, such as Zatarain's (see Sources)
¾ cup salt
5 tablespoons cayenne
1 large onion, halved
1 lemon, halved
1 head garlic (left whole)
8 pounds live crawfish (see Sources)
4 medium red boiling potatoes (1 pound total)
4 ears corn, shucked

ACCOMPANIMENT: Horseradish Cocktail Sauce (recipe follows) and saltines

SPECIAL EQUIPMENT: a 12- to 14-quart stockpot with a lid; a lightweight 8-quart pot; newspaper

Combine water, seafood-boil spices, salt, cayenne, onion, lemon, and garlic in stockpot, cover, and bring to a boil.

Meanwhile, put crawfish in sink; discard any crushed or dead ones. Wash crawfish under cold water for 3 minutes. (Crawfish can also be rinsed in a large colander or a large perforated steamer insert.)

Add potatoes to boiling seasoned water and boil, uncovered, until tender, 15 to 20 minutes. Transfer to a large bowl using a slotted spoon and cover with foil to keep warm. Add corn to water and boil until just tender, about 5 minutes. Transfer to bowl of potatoes to keep warm.

Bring water to a rolling boil. With a large sieve, transfer half of crawfish to lightweight pot, then turn out into boiling water, pushing them down with a large spoon to immerse. Partially cover pot, return water to a boil, and boil for 2 minutes. Turn off heat and let crawfish stand in water, covered, for 10 minutes to absorb seasoning.

With sieve, transfer crawfish to a large platter and keep warm, covered with several layers of newspaper, while you cook remaining crawfish. Return water to a rolling boil before adding them.

Serve crawfish with potatoes and corn, cocktail sauce, and saltines. To eat crawfish, twist off head, then peel tail to get at meat.

COOK'S NOTE

- To make cleanup easier, serve the whole boil on layers of newspaper. Then just roll up the mess when finished and discard.

Horseradish Cocktail Sauce

MAKES ABOUT 1½ CUPS
ACTIVE TIME: 5 MINUTES ■ START TO FINISH: 5 MINUTES

■ We think this mayonnaise-based, coral-colored cocktail sauce is more urbane than a bright red tomatoey version. ■

¾ cup ketchup
⅔ cup mayonnaise
2 tablespoons drained bottled horseradish
1 tablespoon fresh lemon juice
Salt to taste

Whisk together all ingredients in a bowl.

COOK'S NOTE

- The sauce can be made up to 1 day ahead and refrigerated, covered.

Stuffed Squid

SERVES 2 AS A MAIN COURSE, 4 AS A FIRST COURSE
ACTIVE TIME: 45 MINUTES ■ START TO FINISH: 1¼ HOURS

■ This dish is beloved in the Aeolian Islands, the rugged archipelago north of Sicily. There it's made with *totani*, or flying squid. Stuffed with bread crumbs, a little grated cheese, and chopped tentacles and simmered in a light tomato sauce until tender, the squid is a tribute to the subtle flavors of just a few understated ingredients. This is adapted from a recipe by Maria and Gaetana Biviano, two sisters who were born and raised in the house where they still live, on the island of Salina, and appears in Susan Lord and Danilo Baroncini's *Pani Caliatu: Recipes and Food Lore from Aeolian Kitchens as Told by the Islanders.* ■

- 8 (5- to 6-inch-long) cleaned squid with tentacles (1½ pounds total), rinsed
- 6 tablespoons extra-virgin olive oil
- 1 (14-ounce) can stewed tomatoes, puréed in a blender or food processor
- 15 fresh basil leaves
- Rounded ¼ teaspoon fine sea salt
- ½ teaspoon freshly ground black pepper
- ½ cup finely grated aged pecorino
- ½ cup fine fresh bread crumbs, preferably from an Italian loaf
- ¼ cup chopped fresh flat-leaf parsley
- 4 garlic cloves, minced
- 2 large eggs, lightly beaten

SPECIAL EQUIPMENT: 8 wooden picks

Finely chop squid tentacles. Heat 4 tablespoons (¼ cup) oil in a 5- to 6-quart wide heavy pot over moderately high heat until hot but not smoking. Add tentacles and cook, stirring, until just cooked through, about 1 minute. With a slotted spoon, transfer to a bowl and let cool.

Stir puréed tomatoes into oil remaining in pot, along with basil, sea salt, and ¼ teaspoon pepper, and simmer, uncovered, stirring occasionally, for 10 minutes.

Meanwhile, stir together cheese, bread crumbs, parsley, garlic, eggs, sautéed tentacles, and remaining ¼ teaspoon pepper in a bowl. Gently stuff each squid body with a slightly rounded tablespoon of bread-crumb mixture and pat outside of squid to distribute filling evenly. Weave a wooden pick horizontally across wide opening of each squid to close. (During cooking, stuffing will expand and squid will shrink, forming a rounded, well-stuffed squid.)

Heat remaining 2 tablespoons oil in a 12-inch heavy skillet over moderately high heat until hot but not smoking. Add squid and cook, turning once, until browned and any liquid squid gives off has evaporated, about 6 minutes total.

Transfer squid to tomato sauce, cover, and simmer, turning occasionally, until squid are tender, 25 to 30 minutes. Discard picks and serve squid with sauce.

Grilled Calamari with Arugula

SERVES 4 AS A LIGHT MAIN COURSE, 6 AS A FIRST COURSE
ACTIVE TIME: 40 MINUTES ■ START TO FINISH: 1½ HOURS

■ This is a perfect dish when you are going to be cooking outside. Squid's soft flesh won't fall apart on the grill. The most important thing to remember is to cook it quickly—just until it turns opaque—or it will have the consistency of a rubber band. Squid can vary quite a bit in size. If you get lots of little ones (under 2 inches each, not including tentacles), they'll need less preparation. Larger squid have to be scored to stay tender. ■

- 1½ pounds cleaned squid
- ¼ cup fresh lemon juice
- ½ cup extra-virgin olive oil
- 1 large garlic clove, minced
- ½ teaspoon salt
- ⅛ teaspoon freshly ground black pepper
- ½ pound arugula, coarse stems discarded

ACCOMPANIMENT: lemon wedges

SPECIAL EQUIPMENT: 15 to 20 wooden skewers, soaked in cold water for 30 minutes

Prepare a charcoal or gas grill: If using a charcoal grill, open vents in bottom of grill, then light charcoal. Fire is hot when you can hold your hand 5 inches above rack for just 1 to 2 seconds. If using a gas grill, preheat on high, covered, for 10 minutes.

While grill heats, rinse squid under cold running water and pat dry with paper towels. If tentacles are large, halve lengthwise and cut longer ones crosswise into 2-inch pieces. Pull off flaps from squid bodies, if attached, and reserve. Slice open each body lengthwise along "seam" and open flat. Score large squid and flaps lengthwise with a sharp knife, making cuts about ⅛ inch apart (like ridges of rigatoni), being careful not to cut all the way through, then halve bodies crosswise.

Whisk together lemon juice, oil, garlic, salt, and pepper in a small bowl until well combined. Transfer ¼ cup dressing to a large shallow bowl, add squid, tossing to coat, and marinate at room temperature, turning once, for 10 minutes. Set remaining dressing aside.

Thread 2 skewers through each squid body, parallel and close to opposite sides of body, to keep squid flat during grilling. Thread all flaps onto 1 or 2 skewers. Thread tentacles crosswise (through thickest part), without crowding, onto skewers, letting tentacles dangle. Discard marinade.

Lightly oil grill rack and grill squid, uncovered, turning once, until it just turns opaque, 1 to 1½ minutes total. Transfer to a cutting board and remove skewers. Cut squid bodies lengthwise into 1½-inch-wide strips; halve strips crosswise again if using larger squid, if desired.

Toss squid with 3 tablespoons reserved dressing and salt and pepper to taste in a clean bowl. Toss arugula in another bowl with just enough of remaining dressing to coat, then season with salt and pepper.

Divide arugula among plates and top with squid. Serve with lemon wedges.

COOK'S NOTE

- The squid can also be grilled in a lightly oiled, well-seasoned large ridged grill pan over high heat.

Grilled Octopus with Oregano

SERVES 6 TO 8
ACTIVE TIME: 30 MINUTES ■ START TO FINISH: 25 HOURS (INCLUDES MARINATING)

■ Octopus has to be cooked really carefully so it does not become rubbery and tough. This preparation is very straightforward, and the flavors are fabulous; it reminds us of being in Greece. ■

- 3 (2-pound) frozen cleaned octopuses (see Sources), thawed and rinsed
- 1 lemon, cut into ¼-inch-thick slices
- 3½ teaspoons fine sea salt
- 1 teaspoon black peppercorns
- 1½ cups extra-virgin olive oil
- ¼ cup red wine vinegar
- 1 tablespoon dried oregano, crumbled
- ½ teaspoon freshly ground black pepper

Cut octopus pouches (heads) from tentacles, leaving enough of head to keep tentacles together in one piece. Combine octopus heads and tentacles, lemon, 2 teaspoons salt, peppercorns, and water to cover by 2 inches in an 8-quart heavy pot. Bring to a simmer and simmer gently, covered, until octopus is just tender, 20 to 30 minutes. Drain octopus (discard lemon and peppercorns) and cool slightly.

When octopus is cool enough to handle, rub off purplish skin from heads and tentacles with your fingers (skin around suction cups may not come off completely).

Whisk together oil, vinegar, oregano, remaining 1½ teaspoons salt, and pepper in a large bowl and add octopus, turning to coat. Cover and refrigerate, turning occasionally, for 24 hours.

Transfer octopus to paper towels to drain; reserve marinade.

Prepare a charcoal or gas grill: If using a charcoal grill, open vents in bottom of grill, then light charcoal. Fire is medium-hot when you can hold your hand 5 inches above rack for just 3 to 4 seconds. If using a gas grill, preheat on high, covered, for 10 minutes, then reduce heat to moderately high.

Lightly oil grill rack and grill octopus (covered only if using gas grill), turning occasionally, until browned, 8 to 10 minutes. Cut octopus into bite-sized pieces and toss while still hot with reserved marinade.

Provençal Braised Octopus

SERVES 4 TO 6
ACTIVE TIME: 45 MINUTES ■ START TO FINISH: 2¼ HOURS

■ The interplay of tomatoes, wine, onions, and herbs makes this braise richly satisfying but not at all heavy. The octopus turns sweet and succulent, like lobster, and in fact has a similar texture; the brininess of the olives, fittingly enough, reminds us of the sea. The chiles might seem unusual, but Provençal cooks are not averse to using a touch of them to add brightness to a dish. ■

2 (2-pound) frozen cleaned octopuses (see Sources), thawed and rinsed
3 medium onions, 1 quartered, 2 finely chopped
6 garlic cloves, peeled, 2 left whole, 4 finely chopped
4 fresh thyme sprigs, plus 1 teaspoon finely chopped thyme
4 fresh flat-leaf parsley sprigs
1 Turkish bay leaf or 1/2 California bay leaf
10 black peppercorns
1 1/4 teaspoons salt
1/4 cup olive oil
1 1/2 cups dry white wine
3 cups peeled, seeded, and finely chopped tomatoes (about 3 pounds total; see Tips, page 938), with their juice, or 2 (14- to 16-ounce) cans whole tomatoes in juice, chopped, juice reserved
1/2 cup brine-cured black olives, pitted and quartered lengthwise
1/4 teaspoon cracked black pepper
1–2 small (1- to 2-inch-long) dried hot chiles, such as peperoncini, árbol, or Thai (see Glossary)

OPTIONAL GARNISH: chopped fresh flat-leaf parsley
ACCOMPANIMENT: cooked rice

Put octopus in a 6-quart pot and add enough water to cover by 2 inches. Add quartered onion, whole garlic cloves, thyme sprigs, parsley sprigs, bay leaf, and peppercorns and bring to a simmer. Reduce heat and simmer gently, partially covered, until octopus is tender when pierced with a fork and purple outer coating rubs off easily, about 1 1/4 hours.

Drain octopus (discard solids), then transfer to a bowl of cold water to cool slightly. Rub off purple outer coating, skin, and fatty layer from octopus, leaving suckers intact, if desired. Cut tentacles from octopus head just below eyes and discard heads. Cut tentacles into 1 1/4-inch pieces and toss with 1/4 teaspoon salt.

Heat oil in a 4- to 5-quart wide heavy pot over moderate heat until hot but not smoking. Add chopped onion and garlic and cook, stirring, until softened, about 3 minutes. Add wine, tomatoes, with their juice, octopus, olives, chopped thyme, remaining 1 teaspoon salt, cracked pepper, and chiles (to taste), partially cover, and gently simmer, stirring occasionally, until octopus is very tender and sauce is slightly thickened, about 45 minutes.

Serve octopus with rice, sprinkled with parsley, if desired.

COOK'S NOTE

- The octopus can be made up to 1 day ahead. Cool, uncovered, then refrigerate, covered. Reheat over low heat, stirring, for about 15 minutes before serving.

Bouillabaisse

SERVES 6 TO 8
ACTIVE TIME: 1 1/4 HOURS ■ START TO FINISH: 2 1/4 HOURS (INCLUDES MAKING STOCK)

■ This celebrated fish stew commands the deepest loyalty of any citizen of Marseille, where it originated. In fact, a charter signed by eleven restaurants (seven in Marseille) in 1980 dictates what kinds of fish form the basis of an authentic bouillabaisse. These are generally unavailable in the United States, so we suggest using the freshest nonoily fish you can find, preferably three to five different kinds. As long as we were taking liberties, we added lobster, and we use fennel fronds rather than pastis, the anise-flavored liqueur. The broth and croutons are usually served separately from the fish itself in Marseille, but we enjoy everything together. ■

FOR CROUTONS
12–16 (1/2-inch-thick) baguette slices
3 tablespoons extra-virgin olive oil
1 garlic clove, halved

FOR SOUP
1 (1- to 1 1/4-pound) live lobster
1/2 cup extra-virgin olive oil
2 large tomatoes, peeled (see Tips, page 940), halved, seeded, and coarsely chopped
1 large onion, chopped
4 garlic cloves, chopped
1 pound boiling potatoes
1/3 cup finely chopped fennel fronds
1 Turkish bay leaf or 1/2 California bay leaf
1/4 teaspoon crumbled saffron threads
1 1/2 tablespoons coarse sea salt
1/2 teaspoon freshly ground black pepper
9 cups Fish Stock (page 930)
3 pounds mixed skinned white-fleshed fish fillets (such as monkfish, turbot, red snapper, striped bass, porgy, grouper, and/or cod), cut into 2-inch pieces
Rouille (recipe follows)

MAKE THE CROUTONS: Put a rack in middle of oven and preheat oven to 250°F.

Arrange bread in one layer on a baking sheet and brush both sides with oil. Bake until crisp, about 30 minutes. Rub one side of each toast with cut sides of garlic halves; discard garlic. Set toasts aside.

MAKE THE SOUP: Plunge lobster headfirst into a 6- to 8-quart pot of boiling water, cover, and cook for 2 minutes from time lobster enters water. With tongs, transfer lobster to sink to drain (discard cooking water). When it is cool enough to handle, put lobster in a shallow baking pan and twist off claws, with joints. Crack claws with a mallet or rolling pin and separate claws from joints. Halve lobster lengthwise through shell with kitchen shears and discard grain sac (see page 342), then cut crosswise through shell into 2-inch pieces. Reserve lobster juices that accumulate in pan.

Heat oil in cleaned 6- to 8-quart pot over moderate heat. Add tomatoes, onion, and garlic and cook, stirring occasionally, until onion is softened, 5 to 7 minutes.

Meanwhile, peel potatoes and cut into ½-inch cubes. Stir potatoes into tomatoes, along with fennel fronds, bay leaf, saffron, sea salt, and pepper. Add stock and bring to a boil, then reduce heat, cover, and simmer until potatoes are almost tender, 8 to 10 minutes.

Add thicker pieces of fish to soup and simmer, uncovered, for 2 minutes. Stir in all lobster (in shells), including reserved juices, and remaining fish and simmer, uncovered, until just cooked through, 3 to 5 minutes.

Meanwhile, in a small bowl, stir 3 tablespoons broth from soup into rouille until blended.

Arrange 2 croutons in each of 6 to 8 deep soup bowls. With a slotted spoon, carefully transfer fish and lobster from soup to bowls, then ladle some broth with vegetables over seafood. Top each serving with 1 teaspoon rouille and serve remainder on the side.

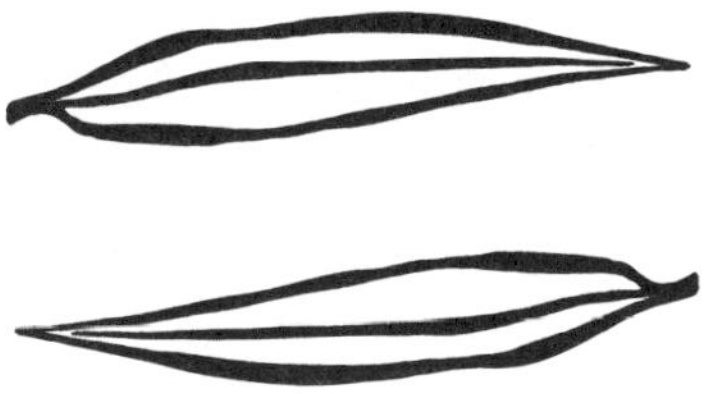

Rouille

MAKES ABOUT ½ CUP
ACTIVE TIME: 15 MINUTES ■ START TO FINISH: 15 MINUTES

■ The garlicky, spicy sauce called *rouille* (pronounced "roo-*ee*," it means "rust" in French) is used as a condiment for bouillabasse and other fish stews and soups; it also enlivens lentil soup and tomato-based soups. ■

- 3 tablespoons water
- ¾ cup coarse fresh bread crumbs, preferably from a baguette (crust removed)
- 3 garlic cloves, peeled
- ½ teaspoon coarse sea salt
- ½ teaspoon cayenne
- 3 tablespoons extra-virgin olive oil

Pour water over bread crumbs in a small bowl.

Using a mortar and pestle (see Cook's Note), mash garlic to a paste with sea salt and cayenne. Mash moistened bread crumbs into garlic paste. Add oil in a slow stream, mashing and stirring vigorously until well combined.

COOK'S NOTE

■ If you don't have a mortar and pestle, use a large heavy knife to mince and mash the garlic with the salt and cayenne on a cutting board. Transfer paste to a bowl and vigorously stir in bread with a fork. Gradually add the oil, stirring with the fork.

Cioppino

San Francisco–Style Seafood Stew

SERVES 6

ACTIVE TIME: 45 MINUTES ■ START TO FINISH: 1½ HOURS

■ The name *cioppino* may stem from a real Italian word, but legend has it that the term evolved from the expression "chip in." Created by San Francisco's Italian and Portuguese fishermen, who chipped in the odds and ends from their daily catch to make a communal stew, cioppino has always been exceptionally versatile. Use whatever seafood looks best at the market—the success of your cioppino will depend on the freshness of your selection. Serve with our focaccia and you've got a delicious meal that's easy to share. ■

- ¼ cup olive oil
- 2 medium onions, finely chopped
- 4 large garlic cloves, minced
- 1 Turkish bay leaf or ½ California bay leaf
- 1 teaspoon dried oregano, crumbled
- 1 teaspoon red pepper flakes
- 1½ teaspoons salt
- ½ teaspoon freshly ground black pepper

DUNGENESS CRABS

Dungeness crabs, named for the small fishing village in Washington State where they were first harvested in the nineteenth century, are in season from December 1 until mid-August. They are prized for their mild, sweet flavor and abundant succulent meat. They are plentiful on the West Coast, where they're harvested from Alaska's Pribilof Islands down to Santa Barbara; elsewhere in the country, you'll need to locate a good fish store. If you are lucky enough to get your hands on some live ones, it's helpful to know how to handle them. When you are buying them, avoid lightweight or soft-shelled specimens—they were harvested too early and will contain little meat.

To cook the crabs, lower them upside down into rapidly simmering salted water, submerging them completely. (Having the thicker top shell lying closest to the heat will help insulate the delicate meat; the salt preserves the natural brininess of the crabs.) Cook for 10 minutes from the time the crabs are submerged (not 10 minutes after the water resumes boiling), then remove the crabs with tongs and set them right side up on a tray to cool.

To excavate the meat, pull up and remove the tablike apron folded under the body of each crab. The apron of a male crab is thin and pointed; a female crab's apron is triangular or rounded. The top shell comes off easily. Discard the long, feathery gills. Save the butter or "mustard" (the fat and edible organs) for those who love the "gunk." Then break the body in two with your hands. Using a needle-nose cracker, crack the claws. (A mallet, hammer, or rolling pin will also work.) The main source of crabmeat is at the intersection of the legs and body.

1 green bell pepper, cored, seeded, and cut into ¼-inch dice
2 tablespoons tomato paste
1½ cups dry red wine
1 (28-ounce) can whole plum tomatoes, drained (juice reserved) and chopped
1 cup bottled clam juice
1 cup chicken stock or store-bought low-sodium broth
1 (1-pound) king crab leg, thawed if frozen
1½ pounds small hard-shelled clams (2 inches wide), such as littlenecks, well scrubbed
1 pound skinless red snapper or halibut fillets, cut into 1½-inch pieces
1 pound large shrimp in shells (21–25 per pound), peeled, tail and first shell segment left intact, and deveined
¾ pound sea scallops, tough muscle removed from side of each if necessary
¼ cup finely chopped fresh flat-leaf parsley
3 tablespoons finely chopped fresh basil

OPTIONAL GARNISH: shredded fresh basil leaves plus small whole leaves

ACCOMPANIMENT: Rosemary Focaccia (page 606) or sourdough bread

Heat oil in an 8-quart heavy pot over moderate heat. Add onions, garlic, bay leaf, oregano, red pepper flakes, salt, and pepper and cook, stirring, until onions are softened, about 5 minutes. Add bell pepper and tomato paste and cook, stirring, for 1 minute. Add wine and boil until reduced by about half, 5 to 6 minutes. Add tomatoes, with their juice, clam juice, and stock and simmer, covered, for 30 minutes. Season with salt and pepper.

Meanwhile, with a large heavy knife, hack crab leg into 2- to 3-inch pieces. Add crab pieces (in shell) and clams to stew and simmer, covered, until clams just open, 5 to 10 minutes, transferring clams as they open to a bowl with tongs or a slotted spoon; discard any unopened clams. Lightly season fish fillets, shrimp, and scallops with salt, add to stew, and simmer, covered, until just cooked through, about 5 minutes. Discard bay leaf.

Return clams to pot and gently stir in parsley and chopped basil. Serve cioppino in large soup bowls, garnished with basil, if desired, and accompanied by focaccia or bread.

COOK'S NOTES

- The stew, without the seafood, can be made up to 1 day ahead. Cool, uncovered, then refrigerate, covered. Bring to a simmer before adding the seafood.
- If you are in San Francisco and the Pacific Northwest and want to use Dungeness crab in place of the king crab, remove the top shell from a whole cooked crab, working over a bowl to catch any juices, then remove and discard the spongy gills and translucent cartilage. Cut the crab into 6 pieces and add it, along with the strained juices, to the stew with the clams.

Seafood Paella

SERVES 8

ACTIVE TIME: 3 HOURS ■ START TO FINISH: 3¾ HOURS (INCLUDES MAKING STOCK)

True, this may be a somewhat daunting project, but you are making a feast. And when you've finished, you get to sit down with your guests—there is no hopping up and down and darting into the kitchen for any last-minute preparations. If you follow paella with an already-made salad and a dessert, you are set for the evening.

This recipe does require a 17-inch paella pan, available at some cookware shops and by mail (see Sources). To ensure even heating, place the pan over two burners and frequently give it a quarter turn while moving it back and forth over the burners. The ingredients are added to the pan in rapid succession, so it's important to have them all ready before beginning to cook; you'll need several large platters and bowls. All the ingredients except the tomatoes can be prepared up to six hours ahead and refrigerated, covered.

We learned from the Spanish food authority Penelope Casas that the crucial step in making a paella comes right at the end. Most people presume that the rice should be cooked completely, but the secret to having separate, fluffy grains of rice is to undercook it slightly, then steam it, out of the oven, to finish the cooking and give it the proper texture. So even though those good smells will tempt you to put the paella on the table immediately, *don't:* cover it tightly with foil and let it sit for ten minutes, and every grain of rice will be perfectly done. ■

- 2 (1½-pound) live lobsters, halved lengthwise (see Cook's Note)
- 1 pound extra-large shrimp in shells (16–20 per pound), peeled, shells reserved, and deveined
- 2 teaspoons fine sea salt
- 1 pound cleaned small squid, cut crosswise into ½-inch-wide rings
- 1 teaspoon Spanish smoked paprika (see Glossary) or Hungarian paprika
- 3 medium tomatoes (1 pound total), coarsely chopped
- 8 garlic cloves, peeled
- 5½ cups Fish Stock (page 930)
- ¼ teaspoon crumbled saffron threads
- 6 tablespoons dry white wine
- 2 tablespoons fresh lemon juice
- 8 tablespoons olive oil
- 1 red bell pepper, cored, seeded, and cut into 1-by-¼-inch strips
- 1 green bell pepper, cored, seeded, and cut into 1-by-¼-inch strips
- 3 cups (1¼ pounds) Spanish short-grain rice, such as SOS or Calasparra (see Sources), or Arborio rice
- 2 tablespoons finely chopped fresh flat-leaf parsley
- ½ Turkish bay leaf or ¼ California bay leaf
- 3 scallions, cut into ¼-inch-thick slices
- ½ cup fresh or thawed frozen peas
- ½ teaspoon freshly ground black pepper
- ½ pound small mussels, preferably cultivated, scrubbed well and beards removed

OPTIONAL GARNISH: chopped fresh flat-leaf parsley

ACCOMPANIMENT: lemon wedges and Alioli de Limón (recipe follows)

SPECIAL EQUIPMENT: a 17-inch paella pan

Twist off lobster tails and claws with joints. Discard bodies. Cut split tails crosswise in half with kitchen shears (for a total of 8 pieces). Slightly crush shells of lobster claws with back of a heavy knife to make it easy to remove meat later. Transfer tails and claws to a platter. Sprinkle shrimp with ¼ teaspoon sea salt, then sprinkle squid with ¼ teaspoon salt.

Put a rack in middle of oven and preheat oven to 400°F if using a gas oven, 450°F if using an electric one.

Sprinkle paprika over tomatoes in a small bowl. Mince and mash garlic with 1 teaspoon sea salt to make a paste. Bring stock to a simmer in a 3-quart saucepan; cover and keep at a bare simmer. Stir together saffron, wine, and lemon juice in a cup.

Heat 6 tablespoons oil in paella pan set over two burners at moderately high heat until hot but not smoking. Using tongs, add lobster pieces (oil will spatter) and stir-fry, rotating pan frequently and moving it back and forth over burners as necessary for even heating, for 2 minutes. Transfer lobster to a clean platter (it will not be cooked through). Stir-fry shrimp in same manner in oil remaining in pan for 2 minutes, then transfer with a slotted spoon to another platter. Add 1 tablespoon oil to pan and stir-fry squid for 2 minutes, then transfer to platter with shrimp. Add remaining 1 tablespoon oil to pan and stir-fry peppers for 2 minutes. Stir in garlic paste and stir-fry for 1 minute. Add tomatoes and stir-fry for 1 minute. Add rice and stir to coat.

Measure hot stock and add water if necessary to make 5½ cups. Stir stock, wine mixture, parsley, and bay leaf into rice. Bring to a boil over high heat and cook, stirring constantly but gently and frequently rotating pan, until liquid bubbles, thickens, and is reduced enough so that most of rice appears on surface, about 6 minutes (spoon should leave a path exposing bottom of pan when pulled through center of rice).

Remove pan from heat and quickly stir in shrimp, squid, scallions, peas, black pepper, and remaining ½ teaspoon sea salt. Gently push lobster and mussels decoratively into rice and drizzle with any juices accumulated on platters. Bake, uncovered, until a crust forms around edges of pan, almost all liquid is absorbed, and rice has slightly more bite than desired, 10 to 12 minutes in a gas oven, 15 to 20 minutes in an electric one. If rice is too hard and paella seems dry, sprinkle with 2 tablespoons water and bake for a few minutes longer; if rice is cooked but too much liquid remains, cook paella on top of stove over moderately high heat, without stirring, frequently rotating pan, until liquid is absorbed. Transfer pan to a rack, cover tightly with foil, and let paella stand for 10 minutes (rice will continue to cook).

Discard bay leaf and sprinkle paella with parsley, if desired. Serve paella directly from pan, with lemon wedges and *alioli* on the side.

COOK'S NOTE

- Ask your fishmonger to split the lobsters and clean the squid for you.

Alioli de Limón

Garlic Mayonnaise with Lemon

MAKES ABOUT 1 CUP
ACTIVE TIME: 5 MINUTES ■ START TO FINISH: 5 MINUTES

- 1 teaspoon finely grated lemon zest
- 3 tablespoons fresh lemon juice
- 2 teaspoons minced garlic
- 1 cup mayonnaise
- ½ teaspoon salt
- ¼ teaspoon freshly ground black pepper

Stir together all ingredients in a small bowl.

COOK'S NOTE

- The *alioli* can be made up to 2 days ahead and refrigerated, covered. Season with salt and pepper if necessary before serving.

POULTRY

Whenever we get to feeling sad about the state of America's food supply, we turn our thoughts to birds. It is a very happy story. Yes, yes, we know all the tales of tasteless chickens and turkeys bred to be nothing but breast. And it's certainly true that in an effort to keep prices low and plunk a chicken into every pot, supermarkets went through a lackluster period when poultry lost its soul and most of its flavor.

But things are definitely looking up. These days almost everyone has access to free-range chickens and turkeys. And wild turkeys, once an endangered species, have made such a remarkable comeback that the great proud birds now roam happily throughout the Northeast. More varieties of ducks are available all the time; the Long Island duckling once reigned supreme, but today farmers are experimenting with tasty lean birds like Rouen Clairs. Meanwhile, other fowl—geese, quail, pheasant, and squabs—are returning to the butcher counter.

Choosing the recipes for this chapter was particularly difficult because of the sheer numbers we began with. After all, we've done more than sixty variations on the Thanksgiving turkey theme, and there wasn't one we didn't like. How to choose the best? And when you start out with hundreds of recipes for fried chicken, how do you decide which one to include? Cook-offs were the answer.

Along the way we encountered a few very pleasant surprises. One

was a recipe for poached turkey breast that we first published almost twenty years ago. It is not only a perfect party dish but also a remarkable way to turn the dreariest turkey into something soft, tender, and delicious.

Poultry is so versatile that we've included a whole world of dishes, from rowdy Malaysian curries to crisp and savory Chinese ducks. You'll find tandoori-spiced chicken thighs and Mexican chicken in a gentle pumpkin seed sauce. We've got homey chicken with biscuits, exotic *b'stilla* (the sweet, flaky, festive chicken pie of Morocco), and a plain roast chicken that is the very soul of comfort cuisine. We've brought back some too-good-to-be-forgotten classics, like a *salmi* of squab in which the bird is roasted and served in a rich sauce made of its own bones, and fine country dishes like panfried quail with creamed corn and bacon.

There are birds glazed with berries, birds pressed under weights, birds stuffed with oysters, and poached birds served with pine nuts. We even have a turkey-based meat loaf appealing enough to rival—and surpass—traditional versions.

Some people believe that birds are a bore. We are not among them, and once you've cooked the dishes in this chapter, you won't be either.

Roast Chicken with Pan Gravy

SERVES 4

ACTIVE TIME: 20 MINUTES ■ START TO FINISH: 1¾ HOURS

■ To find the most succulent and simplest roast chicken, one with moist, tender meat and crisp skin, we roasted a lot of birds. We wanted the final word on whether brining, basting, and turning the chicken are worth the effort. Fresh kosher birds tasted great, but the skin didn't seem to brown well or become as crisp as we like. The winner was an organic chicken, salted, peppered, and brushed with butter, then turned from side to side during roasting, basted twice, and finished breast up. ■

FOR CHICKEN

- 1 teaspoon salt
- ½ teaspoon freshly ground black pepper
- 1 (3- to 3½-pound) chicken, rinsed and patted dry
- 3 tablespoons unsalted butter, melted

FOR PAN GRAVY

- ¾ cup chicken stock or store-bought low-sodium broth
- ¾ cup water
- 1 tablespoon cornstarch, stirred together with 1 tablespoon water
- Lemon juice
- Salt and freshly ground black pepper

SPECIAL EQUIPMENT: an instant-read thermometer

ROAST THE CHICKEN: Put a rack in middle of oven and preheat oven to 400°F.

Stir together salt and pepper in a small cup and rub all over chicken, inside and out. Put chicken on a rack in a small flameproof roasting pan and pour butter over it, then turn it onto one side.

Roast chicken for 25 minutes. Baste with pan juices, then turn it over onto opposite side and roast for 25 minutes more.

Turn chicken breast side up, baste with pan juices, and continue to roast until thermometer inserted into thickest part of a thigh (without touching bone) registers 170°F, about 20 minutes. Tilt chicken to drain juices from cavity into roasting pan, then transfer it to a platter and let stand for 15 minutes.

MEANWHILE, MAKE THE GRAVY: Transfer pan juices to a 1½-quart saucepan and skim off fat. Put roasting pan on a burner, add stock and water, and deglaze pan by boiling over moderately high heat, stirring and scraping up brown bits, for 1 minute. Add stock mixture to pan juices and bring to a boil. Stir cornstarch mixture and whisk into pan juices, then boil, whisking, until slightly thickened, about 1 minute. Remove from heat and stir in lemon juice and salt and pepper to taste.

Cut chicken into serving pieces and serve with gravy.

Chicken with Forty Cloves of Garlic

SERVES 4

ACTIVE TIME: 15 MINUTES ■ START TO FINISH: 1 HOUR

■ Garlic is one of the most provocative of foods. In this family-style dish, long, slow cooking transforms its pungency into a sweet, mellow mash, perfect for smearing on a piece of crusty bread. Follow that with greedy forkfuls of the bird, and use a remnant of bread to sop up the luxurious juices. ■

- 1 (4-pound) chicken, rinsed and patted dry
- ½ teaspoon salt
- ¼ teaspoon freshly ground black pepper
- 1 scant cup olive oil
- 2 fresh flat-leaf parsley sprigs
- 1 fresh rosemary sprig
- 1 fresh thyme sprig
- 1 fresh sage sprig
- 1 Turkish bay leaf or ½ California bay leaf
- 1 celery rib
- 40 garlic cloves, peeled (from 3–4 heads)

ACCOMPANIMENT: toasted baguette slices

SPECIAL EQUIPMENT: kitchen string; an instant-read thermometer

Put a rack in middle of oven and preheat oven to 350°F.

Sprinkle chicken inside and out with salt and pepper. Tie legs together with kitchen string and fold wings under chicken. Heat oil in a 6- to 8-quart wide heavy ovenproof pot over moderately high heat until hot but not smoking. Add chicken and sear, turning it carefully, until golden brown all over, about 10 minutes. Transfer chicken to a plate.

Tie herbs and celery together with string to make a bouquet garni and add to pot. Scatter garlic over bottom of pot and put chicken breast side up on top of garlic. Cover tightly, transfer to oven, and bake, basting twice, until thermometer inserted into thickest part of a thigh (without touching bone) registers 170°F, 30 to 40 minutes. Transfer chicken to a cutting board and let stand for 10 minutes; reserve pan juices.

Spread roasted garlic on toasts and cut chicken into serving pieces. Serve chicken drizzled with some of pan juices.

Hunan-Style Tea-Smoked Chicken

SERVES 6

ACTIVE TIME: 20 MINUTES ■ START TO FINISH: 2½ HOURS (INCLUDES MARINATING)

■ Most of the smoked foods we are familiar with are smoked *before* cooking—bacon, for example. But the Chinese use smoking as a means for quickly flavoring foods after they are cooked. Chicken is excellent treated this way, as this moist and distinctly Hunan dish proves. First the bird is steamed until it's thoroughly cooked, then it's briefly smoked over tea leaves and brown sugar, which gives it an exotic nuance of flavor and beautifully burnished skin. A last-minute brushing of sesame oil reinforces the toasty smokiness. The beauty of the method is that an outdoor grill or smoker is not required—all you need is a (well-ventilated) kitchen and a wok with a lid and you're in business. This recipe is from the Chinese cooking authority Nina Simonds, a longtime contributor to our pages. ■

2 tablespoons Chinese rice wine or sake
2 teaspoons salt
1½ teaspoons Sichuan peppercorns (optional; see Glossary), crushed
3 scallions, cut into 2-inch-long pieces and smashed
2 (¼-inch-thick) slices peeled fresh ginger, smashed
1 (3-pound) chicken, rinsed and patted dry
½ cup Chinese black tea leaves
2 tablespoons packed dark brown sugar
Asian sesame oil for brushing chicken

SPECIAL EQUIPMENT: a wok with a lid; an instant-read thermometer

Stir together rice wine, salt, peppercorns, scallions, and ginger in a large bowl. Add chicken and rub well all over with marinade. Marinate, covered and refrigerated, for at least 1 hour.

Put scallions and ginger in cavity of chicken and discard marinade. Put chicken on a steamer rack set over 2 inches of simmering water in wok, cover, and steam until thermometer inserted into a thigh (without touching bone) registers 170°F, 20 to 25 minutes. Transfer chicken to a plate.

Clean and dry wok and line bottom and lid with heavy-duty foil. Stir together tea leaves and brown sugar in a small cup and sprinkle mixture in bottom of wok. Set a rack 2 inches above bottom and place chicken breast side up on rack. Cover wok and heat over moderately high heat until smoke begins to appear, 3 to 5 minutes, then smoke chicken for 6 minutes longer. Turn chicken over and smoke, covered, for 6 minutes. Remove wok from heat and let chicken stand, covered, for 15 minutes.

Transfer chicken to a cutting board and brush with sesame oil, then cut it into serving pieces.

COOK'S NOTE

■ The chicken can marinate for up to 8 hours.

Garlic Lime Chicken Breasts

SERVES 4

ACTIVE TIME: 15 MINUTES ■ START TO FINISH: 2¾ HOURS (INCLUDES MARINATING)

■ Garlic and citrus is a great flavor combination that's used all over the world. It doesn't taste particularly exotic, it just tastes *good.* Lime has a slightly more complex flavor than lemon, and it's more aromatic. This recipe is from Bella Jarrett, of New York City, who was inspired by a box of limes she received from Florida. ■

- 1/4 cup fresh lime juice
- 1/4 cup olive oil
- 1 tablespoon minced garlic
- 1/2 teaspoon salt
- 1/4 teaspoon freshly ground black pepper
- 4 chicken breast halves (2 pounds total), rinsed and patted dry

ACCOMPANIMENT: lime wedges

Whisk together lime juice, oil, garlic, salt, and pepper in a large bowl. Add chicken, turning to coat. Marinate chicken, covered and refrigerated, turning once or twice, for at least 2 hours.

Put a rack in upper third of oven and preheat oven to 400°F.

Remove chicken from marinade (discard marinade) and arrange skin side up, without crowding, in a shallow baking pan. Season with salt and pepper. Roast until just cooked through, 25 to 30 minutes.

Turn oven to broil. Broil chicken about 2 inches from heat until skin is crisp, about 2 minutes. Serve with lime wedges.

COOK'S NOTE

- The chicken can marinate for up to 8 hours.

Parmesan Chicken

SERVES 6

ACTIVE TIME: 15 MINUTES ■ START TO FINISH: 40 MINUTES

■ One of the things that can be dispiriting about skinless, boneless chicken breasts is that they lack the luscious contrast between crisp golden skin and moist, tender meat. Not here. We use English muffin crumbs and Parmesan to make a coating for the chicken. This is classic comfort food without too much fat. ■

- 3 tablespoons Dijon mustard
- 1 teaspoon white wine vinegar
- 1/2 teaspoon salt
- 1/2 teaspoon freshly ground black pepper
- 6 small skinless, boneless chicken breast halves (scant 2 pounds total), rinsed and patted dry
- 1 1/2 English muffins
- 3/4 cup finely grated Parmigiano-Reggiano
- 1 tablespoon unsalted butter, melted

SPECIAL EQUIPMENT: parchment paper

Put a rack in middle of oven and preheat oven to 450°F. Line a baking sheet with parchment.

Whisk together mustard, vinegar, salt, and 1/4 teaspoon pepper in a large bowl. Add chicken, tossing to coat well.

Pulse English muffins in a food processor until finely ground. Add cheese, butter, and remaining 1/4 teaspoon pepper and pulse until well combined. Transfer to a shallow dish or pie plate.

Dredge chicken one piece at a time in crumbs, coating completely and pressing gently so crumbs adhere, then transfer to baking sheet. Bake until golden brown and cooked through, 15 to 20 minutes.

COOK'S NOTE

- The chicken can marinate in the mustard mixture, covered and refrigerated, for up to 2 hours.

Chicken Piccata with Niçoise Olives

SERVES 4

ACTIVE TIME: 30 MINUTES ■ START TO FINISH: 30 MINUTES

■ This Italian menu staple is usually made with veal, pounded thin, sautéed in butter, and served with a sauce of the pan drippings, lemon juice, and more butter. We've chosen to use chicken and incorporate slivers of briny Niçoise olives. They give another dimension to the dish and provide an attractive contrast to the golden chicken, pale sauce, and scattering of bright green parsley. ■

- 4 small skinless, boneless chicken breast halves (1 1/2 pounds total), rinsed and patted dry
- Salt and freshly ground black pepper
- 2 tablespoons olive oil
- 3/4 stick (6 tablespoons) unsalted butter, cut into tablespoons
- 1/4 cup dry white wine
- 1 tablespoon fresh lemon juice

¼ cup Niçoise olives, rinsed, pitted, and cut into slivers
2 tablespoons finely chopped fresh flat-leaf parsley

Butterfly each chicken breast half by cutting horizontally through meat with a sharp knife, keeping one long side intact, and opening it up like a book. Gently pound chicken between sheets of plastic wrap with a flat meat pounder or a rolling pin until ⅛ inch thick. Pat dry and season with salt and pepper.

Heat oil and 2 tablespoons butter in a 12-inch heavy skillet over moderately high heat until foam subsides. Add 1 piece of chicken and cook, turning once, until golden and just cooked through, about 2 minutes total. Transfer to a platter and keep warm, loosely covered with foil. Cook remaining chicken in same manner, adding 2 more tablespoons butter to skillet as needed.

Pour off any fat from skillet. Off heat, add wine to skillet, then return to heat and boil to deglaze skillet, stirring and scraping up brown bits, for about 30 seconds. Stir in lemon juice and remaining 2 tablespoons butter and heat, swirling skillet, until butter is just incorporated. Remove from heat and stir in olives and salt and pepper to taste, then sprinkle in parsley.

Spoon sauce over chicken.

Cold Poached Chicken with Ginger Scallion Oil

SERVES 4
ACTIVE TIME: 15 MINUTES ■ START TO FINISH: 45 MINUTES

■ This is a good reminder that Chinese food isn't all about stir-frying. Quick and easy, it's inspired by the flavor-packed ginger scallion oil served with chicken and duck at New York Noodle Town, in Manhattan. ■

FOR POACHED CHICKEN
½ cup Chinese rice wine, sake, or medium-dry sherry
8 (¼-inch-thick) slices fresh ginger
1 teaspoon salt
4 small skinless, boneless chicken breast halves (1½ pounds total), rinsed and patted dry

FOR GINGER SCALLION OIL
¼ cup vegetable oil
4 teaspoons finely grated peeled fresh ginger
4 teaspoons minced scallion
2 teaspoons Asian sesame oil

POACH THE CHICKEN: Combine 4 cups water, rice wine, ginger, and salt in a 3-quart saucepan and bring to a boil. Add chicken and cook at a bare simmer, uncovered, for 6 minutes. Remove pan from heat and let stand, covered, until chicken is just cooked through, about 15 minutes.

Transfer chicken to a bowl and refrigerate for 20 minutes; discard poaching liquid.

MEANWHILE, MAKE THE GINGER SCALLION OIL: Stir together all ingredients in a small bowl.

Cut chicken across grain into thin slices and arrange on a platter. Stir oil and spoon over chicken.

Chicken Kiev

SERVES 4
ACTIVE TIME: 45 MINUTES ■ START TO FINISH: 2¾ HOURS

■ With its thin crust of crisp bread crumbs, succulent white meat, and heart of herbed butter, chicken Kiev is a show-stopping entrée, a dish that needs little embellishment. The romanticized classic (it doesn't seem to have had a prerevolutionary history in Russia) was at its height of popularity in America in the 1950s and '60s; we're all for bringing back a little grandeur. One of the first lessons we learned while making this delicately fried ode to buttery excess is that pounding a chicken breast is distinct from bludgeoning it, which produces holes. Fortunately, though, chicken is easily patched; simply overlap any torn pieces and gently pound them together. Other tricks are to beat in a circular pattern for evenness and to make the edges thinner than the middle, since they are doubled over on themselves when the chicken is rolled. The object of coating the rolled-up chicken with flour, egg, and bread crumbs is to seal all the seams and other potential routes for the butter to escape before you want it to. ■

- 1 large garlic clove
- 1/2 teaspoon salt
- 1 stick (8 tablespoons) unsalted butter, softened
- 1 tablespoon minced fresh flat-leaf parsley
- 1 tablespoon minced fresh chives
- 1/4 teaspoon finely grated lemon zest
- 1 teaspoon fresh lemon juice
- 4 small skinless, boneless chicken breast halves with tenders (1 1/2 pounds total), rinsed and patted dry
- Freshly ground black pepper
- 2 large eggs
- 1 tablespoon vegetable oil, plus about 7 cups oil for deep-frying
- 1 cup all-purpose flour
- 1 1/2 cups fine dry bread crumbs

OPTIONAL GARNISH: fresh chives

SPECIAL EQUIPMENT: a deep-fat thermometer

With a heavy knife, mince and mash garlic with salt to a paste.

Stir together butter, garlic paste, parsley, chives, zest, lemon juice, and salt to taste in a small bowl. Spread into a 3-inch square on a sheet of wax paper. Wrap butter and refrigerate until hard, about 1 hour.

Cut butter square into 4 equal sticks, wrap in wax paper, and refrigerate.

Score thicker areas of breast pieces with a knife for easier flattening. Gently pound breasts and tenders between two sheets of plastic wrap with a flat meat pounder or rolling pin until 1/4 inch thick, then pound tenders and outer edges of breasts (about 1 inch all around) slightly thinner.

Season breasts with salt and pepper. Put 1 herb butter stick in center of each breast and place flattened tenders over butter sticks. Working with one breast at a time, fold a long side of breast over butter, then fold over ends and remaining side to enclose butter and gently press on seam to seal.

Whisk together eggs and 1 tablespoon oil in a shallow dish. Put flour and bread crumbs into two other shallow dishes. Working with one piece at a time, dust chicken with flour and coat with egg, letting excess drip off, then roll in bread crumbs, coating thoroughly, and place in a shallow baking pan. Refrigerate chicken, uncovered, for 1 hour.

Heat 5 inches oil in a 4- to 5-quart deep heavy pot until it registers 360°F on thermometer. Fry chicken until golden, about 6 minutes, then transfer to several layers of paper towels to drain. Serve garnished with chives, if desired.

Chicken Divan

SERVES 6

ACTIVE TIME: 40 MINUTES ■ START TO FINISH: 1 1/4 HOURS

■ There's a reason that fancy casseroles have always been so popular: they are perfect for entertaining. Revisiting this classic was like seeing an old friend. It was created at New York's Divan Parisien restaurant in the 1950s and soon became standard dinner-party fare. Our version is sensational. ■

- 1 1/4 pounds skinless, boneless chicken breast halves, rinsed and patted dry
- Salt and freshly ground black pepper
- 1 tablespoon olive oil
- 1 large bunch broccoli (1 1/2 pounds), trimmed and cut into 4-inch-long florets
- 1/2 stick (4 tablespoons) unsalted butter, cut into pieces
- 5 tablespoons all-purpose flour
- 2 cups chicken stock or store-bought low-sodium broth
- 1/2 cup heavy cream
- 1/4 cup medium-dry sherry, or to taste
- 2 teaspoons fresh lemon juice
- 1 cup finely grated Parmigiano-Reggiano (2 ounces)

Season chicken with salt and pepper. Heat oil in a 12-inch heavy skillet over moderately high heat until hot but not smoking. Add chicken and cook, turning once, until cooked through, 8 to 12 minutes total. Let stand for 5 minutes, then cut into thin slices.

Meanwhile, cook broccoli in a 4- to 5-quart pot of boiling well-salted water until just tender, 6 to 8 minutes; drain.

Put a rack in middle of oven and preheat oven to 375°F.

Melt butter in a heavy saucepan over moderately low heat. Add flour and cook, whisking, for 3 minutes to make a roux. Add stock in a slow stream, whisking constantly, and bring to a boil, whisking. Reduce heat and simmer, whisking occasionally, for 10 minutes. Reduce heat to moderately low and cook, whisking occasionally, for 10 minutes more. Remove from heat.

Beat cream with an electric mixer until it holds stiff peaks. Fold cream into sauce, along with sherry and lemon juice. Stir in 1/4 teaspoon salt and 1/8 teaspoon pepper.

Arrange broccoli evenly in bottom of a 2-quart gratin or other flameproof shallow baking dish. Pour half of sauce over broccoli. Stir 1/2 cup Parmesan into remaining sauce. Arrange chicken over broccoli and pour remaining sauce over chicken. Sprinkle with remaining 1/2 cup Parmesan.

Bake until just hot, about 15 minutes. Turn oven to broil and broil about 5 inches from heat until sauce is golden and bubbling, about 1 minute.

COOK'S NOTE

- The casserole can be assembled up to 1 day ahead. Refrigerate, covered, and bring to room temperature before baking.

Malaysian-Style Chicken Curry

SERVES 6

ACTIVE TIME: 30 MINUTES ■ START TO FINISH: 1 1/4 HOURS

■ The food of Malaysia is an astonishing kaleidoscope of indigenous, Chinese, Nonya (Malay-Chinese), Indian, and Eurasian cuisines and yet can be surprisingly accessible to westerners. This curry—rich with coconut milk, pungent with shallots, garlic, and ginger, and fragrant with clove, cinnamon, and star anise—is a perfect case in point. We prefer to use whole boneless chicken breasts with the skin on (it adds flavor), but skinless, boneless breasts will work too (they'll take less time to cook). ■

- 6 large shallots, coarsely chopped (1 1/4 cups)
- 4 large garlic cloves, coarsely chopped
- 1 (1-inch) piece fresh ginger, peeled and coarsely chopped
- 3 tablespoons water
- 3 whole boneless chicken breasts with skin (2 1/2 pounds total), halved, rinsed, and patted dry
- Salt
- 2 tablespoons vegetable oil
- 2 tablespoons curry powder
- 1 (14-ounce) can unsweetened coconut milk
- 1 1/2 cups chicken stock or store-bought low-sodium broth
- 1 jalapeño chile, slit lengthwise in 4 places
- 1 (3-inch) cinnamon stick
- 1 whole clove
- 1 star anise

GARNISH: 1/3 cup coarsely chopped fresh cilantro

ACCOMPANIMENT: cooked rice

Finely chop shallots, garlic, and ginger in a food processor, scraping down sides frequently. Add water and purée to a paste.

Season chicken with salt. Heat oil in a 5-quart wide pot over moderately high heat until hot but not smoking. Brown chicken in 3 batches, turning occasionally, about 5 minutes per batch. Transfer to a large plate.

Reduce heat to moderately low, add shallot paste, and cook, stirring constantly, for 1 minute. Add curry powder and cook, stirring, for 1 minute. Add chicken, with any juices accumulated on plate, and remaining ingredients, cover, and simmer, turning chicken once, until just cooked through, 15 to 20 minutes.

Transfer chicken to a plate. Simmer sauce, whisking occasionally, until slightly thickened, about 10 minutes. Discard jalapeño, cinnamon stick, clove, and star anise.

Add chicken and heat through. Sprinkle with cilantro and serve with rice.

Moroccan Chicken with Preserved Lemons and Green Olives

SERVES 4

ACTIVE TIME: 40 MINUTES ■ START TO FINISH: 40 MINUTES

■ Preserved lemons can turn boneless chicken breasts into something special. The lemons are a common ingredient in Moroccan dishes; we also love them in all kinds of soups, stews, and salads. Usually only the rind is used; you can save the pulp for bloody Marys or anything else that can be enlivened by a little lemon juice and salt. If you happen across Meyer lemons in the store, snap them up and preserve them. Their complex, floral, sweet-tart taste and scent are wonderful here. ■

- 4 small skinless, boneless chicken breast halves (about 1½ pounds total), rinsed and patted dry
- Salt and freshly ground black pepper
- 2 tablespoons olive oil
- 2 medium onions, sliced ¼ inch thick
- 2 garlic cloves, thinly sliced
- ½ teaspoon turmeric
- 8 pieces Moroccan-Style Preserved Lemon (page 908)
- ½ cup chicken stock or store-bought low-sodium broth
- ¼ cup dry white wine
- 16 green olives, pitted and halved

GARNISH: 2 tablespoons coarsely chopped fresh cilantro

Season chicken with salt and pepper. Heat 1 tablespoon oil in a 12-inch nonstick skillet over moderately high heat until hot but not smoking. Brown chicken, turning once, about 6 minutes total. Transfer chicken to a plate and keep warm, covered.

Add remaining 1 tablespoon oil to skillet, reduce heat to moderate, and add onions and garlic. Cook, stirring frequently, until softened but not browned, 8 to 10 minutes. Add turmeric and ½ teaspoon pepper and cook, stirring, for 1 minute.

Meanwhile, scrape pulp from preserved lemon (reserve for another use, if desired). Cut rind into thin strips.

Add preserved lemon rind to onions, along with stock, wine, and olives. Return chicken, with any juices accumulated on plate, to skillet. Simmer, covered, until chicken is cooked through, about 12 minutes. Serve sprinkled with cilantro.

Chicken in Pumpkin Seed Sauce

Pollo en Pipián Verde

SERVES 8

ACTIVE TIME: 1¼ HOURS ■ START TO FINISH: 1½ HOURS

■ The Mexican states of Puebla and Veracruz are known for the nutty, herbaceous, almost creamy pumpkin seed sauce called *pipián*. Seasoned with spices and green chiles, it is intriguing in flavor, gentle in heat, and very easy to make. Hulled green pumpkin seeds, or *pepitas*, are the whole point here, so select them with care (see opposite page). Serve the chicken and sauce with rice; it also makes a great taco filling (see Cook's Note). ■

FOR CHICKEN

- 8 chicken quarters (4 pounds total), rinsed and patted dry
- 1 head garlic, halved horizontally
- ½ large white onion
- 6 large fresh cilantro sprigs
- ½ teaspoon salt
- 6 black peppercorns
- 3 allspice berries

FOR PUMPKIN SEED SAUCE

- 1½ cups (7½ ounces) green (hulled) pumpkin seeds
- 2 tablespoons sesame seeds
- ½ teaspoon cumin seeds
- 4 allspice berries
- 3 whole cloves
- 6 black peppercorns
- 1 pound fresh tomatillos or 1 (28-ounce) can tomatillos (see Glossary)
- 6 serrano chiles, stemmed
- ½ large white onion, quartered
- 4 garlic cloves, smashed
- ½ cup packed coarsely chopped fresh cilantro
- 2 teaspoons salt
- ¼ cup lard or vegetable oil
- 1 poblano chile, roasted (see Tips, page 941), peeled, and seeded

OPTIONAL GARNISH: chopped toasted green (hulled) pumpkin seeds and chopped fresh cilantro

SPECIAL EQUIPMENT: an electric coffee/spice grinder

COOK THE CHICKEN: Combine chicken, garlic, onion, cilantro, salt, peppercorns, and allspice with water to cover in a 6-quart heavy pot and bring to a simmer. Simmer, covered, until chicken is just tender, about 50 minutes. Transfer chicken to 13-by-9-inch baking pan. Let stock cool.

Pour stock through a fine-mesh sieve into a bowl, pressing garlic pulp through sieve; discard solids. Measure 3½ cups stock for sauce and reserve remainder for another use.

MAKE THE SAUCE: Heat a dry 10-inch heavy skillet over moderate heat until hot, then toast pumpkin seeds, stirring constantly, until puffed and beginning to pop, 3 to 5 minutes. Transfer to a plate to cool. Add sesame and cumin seeds, allspice, cloves, and peppercorns to skillet and heat, stirring, until fragrant, about 1 minute; transfer to plate. When seeds and spices are cool, grind to a powder, in 4 batches, in coffee/spice grinder.

If using fresh tomatillos, remove husks and rinse with warm water to remove stickiness. Combine fresh tomatillos, serranos, and salted water to cover in a 5-quart heavy pot, bring to a simmer, and simmer for 10 minutes. Using a slotted spoon, transfer tomatillos and serranos to a blender. Or, if using canned tomatillos, drain them and transfer to blender, along with uncooked serranos. Add onion, garlic, ¼ cup cilantro, and salt to blender and purée until completely smooth (use caution).

Put a rack in middle of oven and preheat oven to 350°F.

Heat lard (or oil) in a 5-quart heavy pot. Add tomatillo purée and simmer, stirring frequently, for 10 minutes. Add 3 cups reserved stock and stir in ground pumpkin seed mixture. Simmer over moderate heat, stirring frequently, until some greenish oil is visible on surface, 15 to 20 minutes.

Meanwhile, purée poblano with remaining ½ cup stock and ¼ cup cilantro in blender until completely smooth.

Stir poblano purée into sauce and pour over chicken. Bake just until chicken is heated through, about 20 minutes. Garnish with pumpkin seeds and cilantro, if desired.

COOK'S NOTES

- The chicken and stock can be made up to 1 day ahead. Cool completely, uncovered, then refrigerate separately, covered. The extra stock can be frozen for up to 1 month.
- The sauce can be made, without the poblano purée, up to 1 day ahead. Cool completely, uncovered, then refrigerate, covered. Reheat over moderate heat before proceeding.
- You can use this as a taco filling by shredding the chicken (discarding bones and skin) and stirring it into the sauce with the poblano purée before baking. Serve with warm tortillas.

PUMPKIN SEEDS

Green (hulled) pumpkin seeds, or *pepitas,* are an essential part of Chicken in Pumpkin Seed Sauce. They're a terrific cocktail nibble as well: toast them in a hot cast-iron skillet until they puff up (stir constantly so they don't get too dark), then drizzle them with a little olive oil and sprinkle them with sea salt. Because the seeds go rancid quickly, buy them at a place with a high turnover. We've had the best luck at natural foods stores. Store them in the freezer.

Gratinéed Chicken and Vegetables in Cream Sauce

Poulet à la Fermière

SERVES 4

ACTIVE TIME: 35 MINUTES ■ START TO FINISH: 1 HOUR

■ As the name suggests, *poulet à la fermière* contains a farmwife's bounty: chicken, cheese, vegetables, and herbs. To taste a dish like this is to transport yourself back to the heady time when Julia Child's cookbooks held sway and classic French cuisine was the culinary ideal to which we all aspired. The chicken isn't drizzled or dotted or dipped—it's lusciously *sauced*, in white wine and crème fraîche, sprinkled with Gruyère, and broiled. You'll definitely want to have a nice hunk of bread for sopping. ■

- 2 pounds chicken thighs and drumsticks, rinsed and patted dry
- Salt and freshly ground black pepper
- 1 tablespoon unsalted butter
- 6 fresh flat-leaf parsley sprigs
- 2 fresh thyme sprigs
- 1 Turkish bay leaf or ½ California bay leaf
- 4 carrots, cut diagonally into 1-inch-thick pieces
- 2 cups frozen small onions, thawed and patted dry
- ½ cup dry white wine
- ⅓ cup chicken stock or store-bought low-sodium broth
- 1 pound small (1½-inch) boiling potatoes, peeled and halved
- ⅔ cup crème fraîche
- 1 cup frozen baby peas, thawed
- 1 cup coarsely grated Gruyère (about 4 ounces)

SPECIAL EQUIPMENT: cheesecloth; kitchen string

Season chicken with salt and pepper. Heat butter in a 12-inch ovenproof deep heavy skillet over moderately high heat until foam subsides. Brown chicken, in batches if necessary, 8 to 10 minutes per batch. Transfer to a plate and cover loosely with foil. Pour off all but 1 tablespoon fat from pan.

Wrap parsley, thyme, and bay leaf in a square of cheesecloth and tie with string to make a bouquet garni. Add to skillet, along with carrots and onions, and stir to coat vegetables with fat. Add wine and deglaze by boiling over high heat, stirring and scraping up brown bits, for 1 minute, then boil until liquid is reduced by half, about 2 minutes more. Add stock and chicken, skin side up, with any juices accumulated on plate, bring to a simmer, and simmer, covered, for 10 minutes. Add potatoes and salt and pepper to taste and simmer, covered, until chicken is cooked through and potatoes are tender, about 15 minutes. Remove from heat and discard bouquet garni.

Preheat broiler. Stir crème fraîche and peas into sauce, add salt and pepper to taste, and turn chicken in sauce to coat. Sprinkle all over with Gruyère and broil 4 to 5 inches from heat until cheese is browned and sauce is bubbling, 3 to 4 minutes.

Philippine-Style Chicken Adobo

SERVES 4
ACTIVE TIME: 15 MINUTES ■ START TO FINISH: 3½ HOURS (INCLUDES MARINATING)

■ The Philippines are one of the world's great melting pots of cuisines, with Malay, Spanish, Chinese, Indian, Arab, and indigenous influences. Here, an *adobo* (Spanish for "preparation" or "sauce"), which carries a wash of flavor in various incarnations throughout the Spanish-speaking world, gets a boost from soy sauce. The beauty of this recipe is that it is so simple: you both marinate and bake the chicken in the clean, tangy adobo, then you reduce the marinade to a sauce while crisping the chicken under the broiler. Because there are so few ingredients, do splurge on the best chicken you can find. In just fifteen minutes of active time, you've got a weekend supper. ■

- ½ cup cider vinegar
- ¼ cup soy sauce
- 1 tablespoon minced garlic
- 2 Turkish bay leaves or 1 California bay leaf
- ½ teaspoon freshly ground black pepper
- 4 whole chicken legs (2½ pounds total), rinsed, patted dry, and cut into drumsticks and thighs

ACCOMPANIMENT: cooked rice

Stir together vinegar, soy sauce, garlic, bay leaves, and pepper in a bowl, then pour marinade into a sealable plastic bag. Add chicken, seal bag, pressing out air, and turn to coat chicken thoroughly. Put bag in a baking pan and refrigerate, turning occasionally, for 2 hours.

Let chicken stand at room temperature for 45 minutes before baking.

Put a rack in middle of oven and preheat oven to 425°F.

Arrange chicken skin side up in one layer in a 13-by-9-inch baking pan and pour marinade over it. Bake until cooked through, 30 to 35 minutes. Transfer chicken, skin side up, to a broiler pan. Pour pan juices into a small saucepan.

Turn oven to broil. Broil chicken about 4 inches from heat until skin is golden and crisp, 2 to 3 minutes.

While chicken broils, skim fat from pan juices and bring to a boil. Remove from heat and discard bay leaves.

Serve chicken and sauce with rice.

Tandoori-Spiced Chicken Thighs

SERVES 6

ACTIVE TIME: 20 MINUTES ■ START TO FINISH: 8½ HOURS (INCLUDES MARINATING)

■ The tastes of India, in the form of a judicious combination of supermarket spices, infuse this yogurt marinade. Don't let the lengthy list of ingredients deter you: this recipe is very easy and very good. Broiling the chicken is the next best thing to cooking it in the traditional blistering-hot clay tandoor oven. ■

- 1 small onion, quartered
- 2 garlic cloves, smashed
- 1 (2-inch) piece fresh ginger, peeled and grated
- ½ cup plain yogurt
- 1 tablespoon fresh lemon juice
- 2 teaspoons salt
- ½ teaspoon turmeric
- ½ teaspoon ground cumin
- ½ teaspoon freshly ground black pepper
- ¼ teaspoon cayenne
- ¼ teaspoon freshly grated nutmeg
- ¼ teaspoon ground cinnamon
- ¼ teaspoon ground coriander
- 8 skinless, boneless chicken thighs (3½ pounds total), rinsed and patted dry

OPTIONAL GARNISH: lime wedges and fresh cilantro leaves

Combine onion, garlic, ginger, yogurt, lemon juice, salt, and spices in a food processor or blender and pulse until smooth.

Make 3 diagonal cuts about ¼ inch deep in each chicken thigh. Put chicken and yogurt marinade in a large sealable plastic bag, seal bag, and turn to coat chicken. Refrigerate, turning bag occasionally, for at least 8 hours.

Line a broiler pan with foil and oil broiler rack. Preheat broiler. Remove chicken from marinade (discard marinade) and arrange on broiler rack. Broil 5 to 6 inches from heat, turning once, until just cooked through, 12 to 17 minutes total. Serve garnished with lime wedges and cilantro, if desired.

COOK'S NOTE

■ The chicken can marinate for up to 12 hours.

Foolproof Grilled Chicken

SERVES 6

ACTIVE TIME: 1 HOUR ■ START TO FINISH: 10 HOURS (INCLUDES BRINING)

■ The secret to juicy, flavorful grilled chicken is to brine it first, then toss it in a robust vinaigrette while it's still hot from the grill. We've given the vinaigrette an Asian cast; see the variation for one that's Mediterranean. The fish sauce won't make the chicken taste the least bit fishy, but it adds depth and richness to the vinaigrette. ■

- ¼ cup sugar
- ½ cup plus 1 teaspoon kosher salt
- 6 pounds chicken parts, rinsed and patted dry
- ¼ cup fresh lime juice
- 2 tablespoons Asian fish sauce
- 1 large garlic clove, minced
- ¼ cup finely chopped fresh cilantro
- 3 tablespoons finely chopped fresh mint
- 1 teaspoon red pepper flakes
- ½ cup vegetable oil
- 4 limes, halved

OPTIONAL GARNISH: fresh mint and cilantro leaves

BRINE THE CHICKEN: Combine 4 quarts water, sugar, and ½ cup salt in an 8-quart pot and bring to a boil. Reduce heat and simmer, uncovered, for 15 minutes. Let cool completely.

Add chicken to brine, cover, and refrigerate for 6 hours.

MAKE THE VINAIGRETTE: Whisk together lime juice, fish sauce, garlic, cilantro, mint, red pepper flakes, and remaining 1 teaspoon salt in a large bowl. Add oil in a slow stream, whisking until combined.

Remove chicken from brine and pat dry.

TO COOK THE CHICKEN USING A CHARCOAL GRILL: Open vents in bottom of grill and in lid. Light 80 to 100 briquettes, then mound lighted charcoal on one side of bottom of grill (you should have a double or triple layer of charcoal), leaving other side empty. Fire is medium-hot when you can hold your hand 5 inches above rack for just 3 to 4 seconds.

For legs, thighs, and wings: Lightly oil grill rack and sear chicken, in 2 batches, directly over coals, turning once, until well browned, 6 to 8 minutes per batch; transfer to a tray. Then put all seared chicken on side of grill with no coals underneath, cover with lid, and cook, switching position of pieces as necessary to prevent flare-ups and turning occasionally, until just cooked through (meat will no longer be pink when cut near joint), 12 to 20 minutes, depending on size of pieces. Transfer cooked chicken to vinaigrette and turn to coat, then transfer to a serving platter and keep warm, loosely covered with foil.

For chicken breasts: Add 15 new briquettes to fire, arranging them on top of coals, and wait until they just light, about 5 minutes. (They won't be grayish white yet but will give off enough heat with other briquettes to maintain correct cooking temperature.) Place chicken breasts skin sides down on rack directly over coals, in batches if necessary, and sear, turning once, until well browned, 6 to 8 minutes total. Move chicken breasts to side of grill with no coals underneath, cover with lid, and cook, switching position of pieces as necessary to prevent flare-ups and turning occasionally, until just cooked through (meat next to the tender, when cut open slightly, will be moist but no longer pink), 12 to 15 minutes. Transfer to vinaigrette and turn to coat, then transfer to platter.

TO COOK THE CHICKEN USING A GAS GRILL: Preheat all burners on high, covered, for 10 minutes, then reduce heat to moderately high.

For legs, thighs, and wings: Lightly oil grill rack and sear chicken, in 2 batches, covered with lid, turning once, until well browned, 6 to 8 minutes total; transfer to a tray. Turn off one burner (the middle burner if there are three) and arrange all seared chicken on rack above shut-off burner. Cover with lid and cook, switching position of pieces as necessary to prevent flare-ups and turning occasionally, until just cooked through (meat will no longer be pink when cut near joint), 12 to 20 minutes, depending on size of pieces. Transfer cooked chicken to vinaigrette and turn to coat, then transfer to a serving platter and keep warm, loosely covered with foil.

For chicken breasts: Turn burner back on. Place chicken, in 2 batches if necessary to avoid crowding, skin sides down on rack, cover with lid, and sear, turning, until well browned, 8 to 10 minutes total. Turn off one burner (the middle burner if there are three) and arrange all breasts on rack over shut-off burner. Cover with lid and cook, switching position of pieces to prevent flare-ups and turning occasionally, until just cooked through (meat next to the tender, when cut open slightly, will be moist but no longer pink), 18 to 20 minutes more. Transfer chicken to vinaigrette and turn to coat, then transfer to platter.

TO GRILL LIMES (BY EITHER METHOD): When chicken is done, grill lime halves, cut sides down, uncovered, over hot fire until grill marks appear, about 3 minutes. Transfer to platter with chicken.

Garnish chicken with mint and cilantro leaves, if desired, and serve with limes and with vinaigrette on the side.

COOK'S NOTES

- The chicken can be brined up to 1 day ahead. Remove from the brine after 6 hours and pat dry, then refrigerate, covered.
- If possible, use hardwood charcoal.
- The chicken can also be roasted. Arrange it skin side up in two lightly oiled shallow baking pans and place in the upper and lower thirds of a preheated 500°F oven. Roast, switching the position of the pans and turning the chicken over halfway through roasting, until the skin is crisp and the chicken is cooked through, 30 to 40 minutes total. The limes can be grilled in a well-seasoned ridged grill pan over high heat.

VARIATION

- MEDITERRANEAN VINAIGRETTE: Whisk together 1/4 cup fresh lemon juice, 1 minced garlic clove, 1 tablespoon chopped fresh rosemary, 1 teaspoon red pepper flakes, and 1 teaspoon kosher salt in a bowl. Add 1/3 cup olive oil in a slow stream, whisking until well blended.

Grilled Jerk Chicken

SERVES 8
ACTIVE TIME: 45 MINUTES ■ START TO FINISH: 14½ HOURS (INCLUDES MARINATING)

■ True jerk seasoning is a spicy wet paste usually made with Scotch bonnet chiles, allspice, thyme, garlic, black pepper, onions, nutmeg, and cinnamon, but recipes vary widely. It originated in Jamaica, where it's traditionally used on pork and chicken, and it has happily spread all over the Caribbean and the United States. If we were in Jamaica, we'd cook our jerk over a fire of allspice wood (called *pimento* there, not to be confused with pimiento, the pepper), but plebeian charcoal works well too. Because the jerk marinade can burn easily, the chicken requires slow cooking on the grill, which helps keep the meat moist. If you want more of a calypso kick, ratchet up the chiles. ■

4 chicken breast halves (with skin and bones; 3 pounds total), rinsed, patted dry, and halved crosswise
2½–3 pounds chicken thighs and drumsticks, rinsed and patted dry
Jerk Marinade (page 933)
ACCOMPANIMENT: Papaya Pineapple Salsa (page 897)

Divide chicken pieces between two sealable plastic bags and pour half of marinade into each one. Seal bags, pressing out excess air, and turn bags several times to distribute marinade. Put bags in a shallow pan and refrigerate for at least 12 hours, turning once or twice.

Let chicken stand at room temperature for 1 hour before cooking.

TO COOK THE CHICKEN USING A CHARCOAL GRILL: Open vents in bottom of grill and in lid. Light about 100 briquettes, then mound lighted charcoal on one side of bottom of grill (you should have a double or triple layer of charcoal). Fire is medium-hot when you can hold your hand 5 inches above rack for just 3 to 4 seconds.

Lightly oil grill rack. Sear chicken in batches over coals, turning occasionally, until well browned on all sides, 15 to 20 minutes. As chicken is seared, move to

side of grill with no coals underneath. When all chicken is seared, cover with lid and grill until cooked through, 25 to 30 minutes more.

TO COOK THE CHICKEN USING A GAS GRILL: Preheat burners on high, then reduce heat to moderate. Sear chicken in batches, uncovered, turning occasionally, until well browned on all sides, 15 to 20 minutes. Reduce heat to low, return all chicken to grill, cover with lid, and grill until chicken is cooked through, about 25 minutes more.

Serve chicken with salsa.

COOK'S NOTES

- The chicken can marinate for up to 24 hours.
- You can also roast the chicken. Arrange it skin sides up on two large baking sheets with sides. Place in the upper and lower thirds of a 400°F oven and roast, switching the position of the sheets halfway through roasting, until cooked through, 40 to 45 minutes.

Chicken Scarpariello

SERVES 4
ACTIVE TIME: 45 MINUTES ■ START TO FINISH: 45 MINUTES

■ *Scarpa* means "shoe" in Italian, and *scarpariello*, in the "shoemaker's style." According to the restaurateur and cookbook author Lidia Bastianich, there doesn't seem to be an Italian antecedent for the dish—it is strictly an Italian-American creation. Stories abound about how it got its name. One theory is that it's made from ingredients that can easily be cobbled together.

Another is that the small chicken bones resemble the nails of a shoemaker's trade. You can save some prep time by asking the butcher to cut the chicken thighs in half (or into thirds if large) through the bone for you. Hot cherry peppers give this *scarpariello* a pleasant sizzle; it's particularly good served over orzo. ■

- 2½ pounds chicken thighs, rinsed and patted dry
- Salt and freshly ground black pepper
- 3 tablespoons olive oil
- 1 large onion, chopped
- 2 red bell peppers, cored, seeded, and cut into ¾-inch pieces
- 2–4 jarred hot cherry peppers in vinegar (to taste), drained and finely chopped
- 5 garlic cloves, thinly sliced
- ⅓ cup dry white wine
- ⅓ cup chicken stock or store-bought low-sodium broth
- ⅓ cup chopped fresh flat-leaf parsley

Hack each thigh in half (or into thirds if large) through the bone with a cleaver or a sharp heavy knife. Season with salt and pepper.

Heat 1 tablespoon oil in a 12-inch heavy skillet over moderately high heat until hot but not smoking. Add half of chicken, skin side down, and cook, turning occasionally and adjusting heat if necessary to prevent burning, until cooked through and well browned on all sides, 10 to 12 minutes. Transfer to a plate and keep warm, covered loosely with foil. Add another 1 tablespoon oil to skillet and cook remaining chicken in same manner.

Pour off all but 1 tablespoon fat from skillet. Add remaining 1 tablespoon oil, then add onion, bell peppers, and cherry peppers, reduce heat to moderate, cover, and cook, stirring occasionally, until softened, about 7 minutes. Add garlic and cook, stirring, until golden, about 2 minutes. Add wine and stock, increase heat, and boil, uncovered, until most of liquid has evaporated, about 4 minutes. Add chicken, with any juices accumulated on plate, and parsley and cook over moderate heat, stirring, until heated through, about 5 minutes. Season with salt.

COOK'S NOTE

■ If you can't find cherry peppers, substitute ¼ teaspoon red pepper flakes, adding it along with the garlic.

Paprika Chicken

SERVES 4

ACTIVE TIME: 20 MINUTES ■ START TO FINISH: 45 MINUTES

■ Chicken seasoned with paprika is an enduring gift from Hungary. If you're craving a comforting, old-fashioned chicken dish, this is it. Fat rendered from the chicken skin helps give the sauce its rich flavor. ■

- 8 small chicken thighs (2¼ pounds total), rinsed and patted dry
- 1 tablespoon olive oil
- 2 medium onions, finely chopped
- ¼ teaspoon salt
- 2 tablespoons sweet Hungarian paprika
- 1 (14-ounce) can whole tomatoes in juice, drained
- ½ cup chicken stock, store-bought low-sodium broth, or water
- 1½ teaspoons all-purpose flour, stirred together with 1 tablespoon water
- 2 tablespoons sour cream

OPTIONAL GARNISH: 2 tablespoons chopped fresh flat-leaf parsley

ACCOMPANIMENT: sour cream and (optional) egg noodles or rice

Remove chicken skin and reserve. Heat oil in a 5-quart heavy pot over moderate heat until hot. Add skin and cook until it renders about ¼ cup fat. Remove skin with a slotted spoon and discard.

Add onions and salt to pot, increase heat to moderately high, cover, and cook, stirring occasionally and reducing heat if necessary, until onions are very tender but not browned, about 5 minutes.

Add paprika and cook, stirring, for 1 minute. Add tomatoes and stock, stirring vigorously to break up tomatoes. Add chicken, cover, and simmer, stirring occasionally, for 10 minutes. Uncover and simmer, stirring occasionally, until chicken is just cooked through, 5 to 10 minutes more.

Stir flour mixture and stir into sauce. Simmer, stirring, until sauce is slightly thickened, about 2 minutes. Remove from heat, season with salt, and stir in sour cream.

Sprinkle with parsley, if using, and serve over noodles or rice, if desired, with additional sour cream on the side.

COOK'S NOTE

- The chicken can be made, without the sour cream, up to 2 days ahead. Cool, uncovered, then refrigerate, covered. Reheat gently, then season and stir in sour cream.

Coriander and Mustard Seed Chicken

SERVES 4

ACTIVE TIME: 20 MINUTES ■ START TO FINISH: 40 MINUTES

■ The secret ingredient here is a dab of red currant or apple jelly; its tart sweetness balances the other flavors in a pan sauce that's spooned over chicken thighs and drumsticks. ■

4 whole chicken legs (2 pounds total), rinsed and patted dry
Salt and freshly ground black pepper
1 tablespoon olive oil
2 shallots, finely chopped
1 tablespoon mustard seeds
1 teaspoon coriander seeds
¼ cup dry white wine
¼ cup water
1 teaspoon red currant or apple jelly
1 tablespoon chopped fresh cilantro

Season chicken with salt and pepper. Heat oil in a 12-inch heavy skillet over high heat until hot but not smoking. Add chicken and brown well, turning once, about 8 minutes total. Transfer to a plate.

Add shallots to skillet, reduce heat to moderate, and cook, stirring, until golden, about 2 minutes. Stir in mustard and coriander seeds, wine, and water and bring to a boil. Return chicken, skin side up, to skillet, reduce heat, and simmer, covered, until cooked

PAPRIKA

Like cayenne, brick-red paprika is made from the finely ground pods of various kinds of *Capsicum,* or pepper, plants — an enormous, unwieldy genus that ranges from fiery Scotch bonnet chiles to sweet bell peppers. Major producers of paprika are California, Spain, and of course Hungary. Hungarian farmers cultivate more than forty kinds of paprika chiles with varying degrees of heat. The spice — integral to such traditional Eastern European dishes as goulash, Paprika Chicken (opposite page), and Liptauer Cheese (page 8), a wonderful old-fashioned spread for crackers — can be either mild or hot, depending on the type of chiles used.

Paprika is graded according to quality and pungency. Scan your supermarket shelves for cheery bright-red cans of Hungarian paprika, full of flavor. (Hungarian paprika — sweet and "half-sharp," which is hot — is also available from Penzeys Spices; see Sources.)

Spanish smoked paprika is slowly becoming more available. In the remote, austere region of west-central Spain called Extremadura, the deep-flavored chiles (brought from the New World by Christopher Columbus) aren't dried in the sun, as they are in Hungary, but roasted over smoldering oak fires before being ground to a velvety powder. Smoked paprika comes in three strengths: sweet, bittersweet, and hot. It is too strong for our Paprika Chicken, but try sprinkling a small amount on plain roast chicken; it's also terrific in black bean soup. La Chinata brand is available at some specialty foods shops and by mail; see Sources.

through, 20 to 25 minutes. Transfer chicken to a platter.

Add jelly and cilantro to sauce and stir until jelly is melted. Season sauce with salt and pepper and spoon over chicken.

Claritha's Fried Chicken

SERVES 4
ACTIVE TIME: 1½ HOURS ■ START TO FINISH: 10½ HOURS (INCLUDES MARINATING)

■ After years of searching, we found this incredible recipe for fried chicken. It first appeared in *Tender at the Bone,* a tasty memoir by our editor in chief, Ruth Reichl. She originally wrested the recipe, with some guile, from a woman named Claritha whom she met in a bar in Ann Arbor, Michigan, during the 1960s. Our adaptation pieces together almost all the methods we've ever used for frying chicken, but it adds one more technique that we find intriguing: coating the chicken with kosher salt. The salt not only acts as a brine, which has a salubrious effect on lean meats, but it draws excess moisture out of the chicken, resulting in far less spattering than usual. Amazingly, the meat remains moist and tender. If you have a cast-iron skillet, by all means use it to fry chicken. Since these skillets don't always have lids, you can jury-rig one using a baking sheet or large stockpot lid. ■

- 1 (2½- to 3-pound) chicken, rinsed, patted dry, cut into 8 serving pieces, and, if necessary, large pieces halved
- ½ cup plus 1½ teaspoons kosher salt
- 3 cups well-shaken buttermilk
- 2 onions, thinly sliced
- 1 cup all-purpose flour
- ½ teaspoon cayenne
- 1 teaspoon cracked black pepper
- 2 cups vegetable shortening
- 1 stick (8 tablespoons) unsalted butter

Put chicken in a bowl and sprinkle evenly with ½ cup kosher salt. Cover with plastic wrap and refrigerate for 1 hour.

Combine buttermilk and onions in a large bowl. Rinse chicken well and add to buttermilk. Marinate, covered and refrigerated, for at least 8 hours.

Put flour, cayenne, cracked pepper, and remaining 1½ teaspoons salt in a paper or plastic bag and shake to combine well. Remove 1 piece of chicken from buttermilk, shake off excess liquid, put in bag, and shake to coat well. Transfer to a sheet of wax paper. Coat remaining chicken 1 piece at a time in same manner. Let chicken air-dry for 30 minutes.

Preheat oven to 200°F.

Heat shortening and butter in a 12-inch heavy skillet, preferably cast-iron, over moderately high heat until hot but not smoking. Add one third of chicken pieces, cover, reduce heat to low, and cook for 10 minutes. Turn chicken over and cook, covered, until juices run clear when meat is pierced with a sharp knife, about 8 minutes for breasts or 12 minutes for legs and thighs. Transfer chicken to a paper towel–lined platter to drain and keep warm in oven. Cook remaining chicken pieces in 2 batches in same manner.

COOK'S NOTE

■ The chicken can marinate in the buttermilk for up to 1 day.

Coq au Vin

SERVES 4
ACTIVE TIME: 45 MINUTES ■ START TO FINISH: 2 HOURS

■ Braising is a tried-and-true technique for wringing flavor and tenderness out of a tough old chicken—not that you ever see those in a supermarket anymore. It's also a great excuse for a cold-weather dinner party. *Coq au vin rouge* is probably more familiar to Americans, but *coq au vin blanc* is just as traditional in France, and we think white wine makes for a more visually appealing dish. Classic accompaniments are parsleyed potatoes and green peas. ■

- 10 ounces (2 cups) pearl onions
- 10 ounces slab bacon, cut into 1-by-¼-inch strips
- 1 (4-inch) piece celery rib
- 6 fresh flat-leaf parsley sprigs
- 1 fresh thyme sprig
- 1 Turkish bay leaf or ½ California bay leaf

- 1 (3½-pound) chicken, rinsed, patted dry, and cut into 8 serving pieces
- ¾ teaspoon salt
- ¼ teaspoon freshly ground black pepper
- 1½ cups dry white or red wine, preferably Burgundy
- ¾ cup chicken stock or store-bought low-sodium broth
- 1 pound small mushrooms, trimmed and halved
- ¼ cup Cognac or other brandy
- 3 tablespoons all-purpose flour
- 1½ tablespoons unsalted butter, softened

GARNISH: 1½ tablespoons chopped fresh flat-leaf parsley

SPECIAL EQUIPMENT: cheesecloth; kitchen string

Blanch onions in a 3-quart saucepan of boiling water for 1 minute, then, with a slotted spoon, transfer to a bowl of cold water to stop the cooking. Add bacon to boiling water and boil for 4 minutes, then drain and transfer to another bowl of cold water.

Drain onions and peel. Drain bacon and pat dry with paper towels.

Cook bacon in a 12-inch heavy skillet over moderate heat, stirring occasionally, until it is browned but not crisp and most of fat has been rendered, about 8 minutes. With slotted spoon, transfer bacon to paper towels to drain. Pour off and reserve all but 2 tablespoons fat from skillet; set skillet aside.

Wrap celery, parsley sprigs, thyme sprig, and bay leaf in cheesecloth and tie with kitchen string to make a bouquet garni.

Sprinkle chicken with salt and pepper. Heat fat remaining in skillet over moderately high heat until hot but not smoking. Brown chicken in 2 batches, turning occasionally, 6 to 10 minutes per batch. Transfer to a plate.

Add onions to skillet and cook, shaking pan frequently, until browned, about 10 minutes. Transfer onions to a 5-quart heavy pot (set skillet aside), add bacon, and stir in wine and stock. Add bouquet garni, bring to a simmer, and simmer, covered, for 10 minutes. Add chicken and simmer, covered, for 15 minutes.

Meanwhile, heat fat in skillet over moderately high heat until hot but not smoking. Add mushrooms and cook, stirring frequently, until they release their liquid, 5 to 8 minutes. Add Cognac and cook until liquid is reduced to ¼ cup, about 3 minutes.

Add mushroom mixture to chicken and simmer, covered, until chicken is tender, about 10 minutes more.

With slotted spoon, transfer chicken, bacon, and vegetables to a platter, and keep warm, covered with foil. Discard bouquet garni.

Make a *beurre manié* by mashing flour and butter into a paste with a fork in a small bowl. Bring braising liquid to a simmer and whisk in *beurre manié* a little at a time. Simmer, whisking constantly, until sauce is smooth and slightly thickened, about 2 minutes.

Season sauce with salt and pepper and spoon over chicken, then sprinkle with parsley.

Chicken and Sausage Jambalaya

SERVES 6 TO 8

ACTIVE TIME: 1½ HOURS ■ START TO FINISH: 2½ HOURS

■ There are two general techniques for making jambalaya, perhaps the most versatile dish to come out of Louisiana cooking. The first involves stirring together the rice, chicken or meat, and vegetables just before serving. The second uses cooking liquid from the meat and vegetables for the rice, infusing it with those flavors. We chose the latter—it takes a bit more effort, but you get the full impact of all the ingredients. Departing from tradition, we leave the stovetop and bake the rice in the oven to ensure even cooking. ■

5½ pounds chicken parts (drumsticks, thighs, and breast halves)
Salt
4 tablespoons vegetable oil
1½ pounds andouille (see Sources) or other spicy smoked pork sausage, cut into ¼-inch slices
3 medium onions, chopped
2 celery ribs, chopped
1 green bell pepper, cored, seeded, and chopped
4 large garlic cloves, finely chopped
2 cups chicken stock or store-bought low-sodium broth
1½ cups water
1 (14- to 16-ounce) can whole tomatoes in juice, drained and chopped
¼ teaspoon cayenne (optional)
2½ cups long-grain white rice, rinsed and drained well
1 cup thinly sliced scallion greens

Pat chicken dry and season with salt. Heat 2 tablespoons oil in a 10- to 12-inch heavy skillet over moderately high heat until hot but not smoking. Brown chicken in batches, without crowding, turning once, 6 to 8 minutes per batch. Transfer to a bowl and add remaining 2 tablespoons oil as needed between batches.

Reduce heat to moderate and brown sausage in 4 batches in fat remaining in skillet, turning occasionally, 3 to 4 minutes per batch. Transfer to a paper towel–lined bowl.

Pour off all but about 1 tablespoon fat from skillet. Add onions, celery, and bell pepper and cook over moderate heat, stirring occasionally, until onions are golden brown and softened, about 8 minutes. Add garlic and cook, stirring, for 1 minute. Add 1 cup stock and cook, stirring, for 1 minute. Transfer mixture to a wide 8-quart heavy ovenproof pot.

Add chicken, water, tomatoes, cayenne (if using), and remaining 1 cup stock. Bring to a simmer and simmer, partially covered, until chicken is tender, about 30 minutes.

Meanwhile, put a rack in middle of oven and preheat oven to 325°F.

Transfer chicken to a clean bowl. Measure cooking liquid with vegetables and add additional water if necessary to measure 7 cups; return to pot. If you have more than 7 cups, boil to reduce. Stir rice into cooking liquid. Arrange chicken over rice (do not stir) and bring to a boil over high heat, uncovered, without stirring.

Cover, transfer to oven, and bake until rice is tender and most of liquid is absorbed, about 30 minutes. Let jambalaya stand, covered, for 10 minutes.

Gently stir in scallion greens, sausage, and salt to taste.

Colombian Chicken, Corn, and Potato Stew

Ajiaco

SERVES 6

ACTIVE TIME: 45 MINUTES ■ START TO FINISH: 1½ HOURS

■ *Ajiaco* (pronounced "ah-hee-*ah*-ko") is practically Colombia's national dish. It's served everywhere from casual restaurants to formal family celebrations. The hearty stew makes good use of the mountainous country's potato bounty: grated russets thicken the broth, while yellow-fleshed varieties lend a golden color and contrasting texture. Traditionally the accompaniments are served on the side so guests can add cubes of buttery avocado, a touch of cream, a briny dash of capers, and a sprinkle of aromatic cilantro to suit their own taste. ■

1 (3½- to 4-pound) chicken, rinsed, patted dry, and cut into 8 serving pieces
1¾ teaspoons salt
1½ teaspoons freshly ground black pepper
3 tablespoons unsalted butter
1 large white onion, finely chopped
2 teaspoons dried oregano, crumbled
1½ pounds russet (baking) potatoes
6 cups chicken stock or store-bought low-sodium broth
1 cup water
2 pounds yellow-fleshed potatoes, such as Yukon Gold, peeled, cut into ½-inch cubes, and covered with water in a bowl
3 ears corn, shucked and cut crosswise into 1-inch pieces

ACCOMPANIMENTS: ½ cup chopped fresh cilantro; 1 cup heavy cream; 3 tablespoons drained capers; 3 California avocados, quartered, pitted, peeled, and cut into ½-inch cubes

Sprinkle chicken with ¾ teaspoon salt and ½ teaspoon pepper. Heat butter in a 7- to 8-quart wide heavy pot over moderately high heat until foam subsides. Add chicken in 2 batches, skin side down, and brown, turning occasionally, about 10 minutes per batch. Transfer to a plate.

Add onion to pot, along with oregano and remaining 1 teaspoon each salt and pepper, and cook, stirring, until light golden, about 5 minutes. Meanwhile, peel and coarsely grate russet potatoes.

Add grated potatoes to pot, along with chicken, stock, and water. Bring to a simmer, cover, reduce heat, and simmer, stirring occasionally, until chicken is cooked through, about 25 minutes. Transfer chicken to a cutting board to cool.

Drain cubed yellow potatoes and add to pot. Cover and simmer, stirring occasionally, until yellow potatoes are almost tender, about 20 minutes.

Add corn and simmer, covered, until tender, 5 to 10 minutes more.

While corn is cooking, remove skin and bones from chicken and coarsely shred meat. Add meat to pot and simmer until heated through.

Serve stew with accompaniments in small bowls.

EIGHT EASY PIECES

Once you've become adept at cutting a whole chicken into eight serving pieces — pairs of breasts, wings (with a nugget of breast meat or not), drumsticks, and thighs — you'll never buy chicken parts again. The technique couldn't be simpler, and the result is a beautiful thing: inexpensive chicken parts that are in proportion (because they come from the same bird), each covered with enough skin to help protect the meat while browning. There are many different ways to approach the task, but here's how we most often handle it.

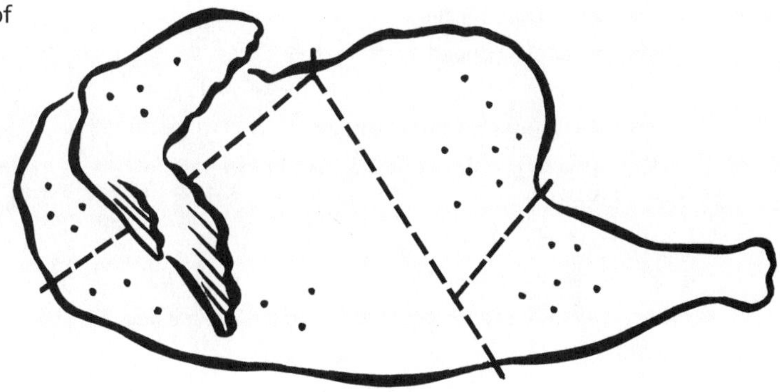

First, remove the backbone: Beginning at the back end, or the "pope's nose," maneuver around the thigh joint on each side. (If you have a boning knife, it comes in handy for this first step; otherwise, use a large sharp knife or poultry shears.) As you work, keep your knife always touching the bone; that way, you leave most of the "oyster" — the morsel of meat on either side of the backbone — attached to the thigh. (Save the backbone, along with the giblets, for stock.) Next, separate the legs from the breast section (which includes the wings) by pulling each drumstick toward you so that when you cut off the thigh, the breast stays covered with skin. Cut the drumstick from each thigh at the joint. When disjointing any bird, try to stay loose-wristed; you shouldn't have to exert a huge amount of force, because it's actually easy to cut through a joint. If necessary, stop and take a look to reorient yourself. Halve the breast section by putting it skin side down on a work surface and cutting straight down through the breastbone (if you've been using a boning knife, put it down now and pick up a large sharp knife or shears). Some of us prefer to remove the cartilage separating the two halves of the breast; others simply cut through it. Either cut each breast half diagonally so that a generous nugget of breast meat is left on the wing section or just cut off the wing at the joint. Finally, cut off the wing tips so the wings will brown more evenly.

Chicken Fricassee

SERVES 4

ACTIVE TIME: 30 MINUTES ■ START TO FINISH: 1 HOUR

■ This is a hearty stew that will be much appreciated in cooler weather. The chicken is first browned, then braised in a full-bodied sauce. After it is cooked, heavy cream and egg yolk enrich the sauce and make it beautifully silky. Egg noodles are a good accompaniment for this dish. ■

- 1 (3½-pound) chicken, rinsed, patted dry, and cut into 8 serving pieces
- 1 teaspoon salt
- ¼ teaspoon freshly ground black pepper
- 2 tablespoons vegetable oil
- 1 medium onion, chopped
- 1 celery rib, chopped
- 1 garlic clove, minced
- ½ teaspoon chopped fresh thyme
- 10 ounces mushrooms, trimmed and sliced (3 cups)
- 2 tablespoons all-purpose flour
- 1¾ cups chicken stock or store-bought low-sodium broth
- ½ cup heavy cream
- 1 large egg yolk

GARNISH: 1 tablespoon chopped fresh flat-leaf parsley

Sprinkle chicken with salt and pepper. Heat oil in a 12-inch heavy skillet over moderately high heat until hot but not smoking. Add chicken, skin side down, in 2 batches, and cook, turning occasionally, until browned on all sides, 6 to 10 minutes per batch. Transfer to a plate.

Add onion, celery, garlic, and thyme to skillet and cook, stirring occasionally, until vegetables are softened, 3 to 4 minutes. Add mushrooms and cook, stirring frequently, until they release their liquid, 5 to 6 minutes. Sprinkle flour over vegetables and cook, stirring, for 2 minutes. Add stock and bring to a boil. Add chicken, skin side up, along with any juices accumulated on plate, reduce heat, and simmer, covered, until chicken is just cooked through, 20 to 25 minutes. Transfer chicken to a platter and keep warm, loosely covered with foil.

Whisk together cream and yolk in a small bowl until blended, then add ½ cup sauce in a slow stream, whisking constantly. Whisk cream mixture into sauce in skillet and gently simmer over low heat (do not boil), whisking, just until sauce is slightly thickened, about 1 minute.

Spoon sauce over chicken and sprinkle with parsley.

Persian-Style Chicken with Walnut, Onion, and Pomegranate Sauce

Fesenjan

SERVES 4

ACTIVE TIME: 1 HOUR ■ START TO FINISH: 1¼ HOURS

■ The pairing of walnuts, once reserved for Persian kings, and pomegranates, which originated in northern Persia, goes back to ancient times in the Middle East. This dish, traditionally made with duck, is elegant, aristocratic, and rich. The walnuts are ground before they are added to the sauce, helping to thicken it. This is a type of *khoresh*, or delicate stew, and it should be served with rice. ■

- 1 large pomegranate
- 1 (2½- to 3-pound) chicken, rinsed, patted dry, and cut into 8 serving pieces
- Salt and freshly ground black pepper
- ½ stick (4 tablespoons) unsalted butter
- 2 onions, thinly sliced
- 1 teaspoon ground cinnamon
- 2 cups (about 6 ounces) walnuts, toasted (see Tips, page 938), cooled, and coarsely ground in a food processor
- ½ cup tomato sauce
- 1½ cups chicken stock or store-bought low-sodium broth
- 4 teaspoons fresh lemon juice
- 1 tablespoon molasses (not robust or blackstrap)

Halve pomegranate. Remove and reserve ⅓ cup seeds; squeeze ⅔ cup juice from pomegranate halves.

Season chicken with salt and pepper. Heat butter in a 12-inch heavy skillet over moderately high heat until foam subsides. Add chicken and cook in 2 batches, turning once, until well browned, about 15 minutes per batch. Transfer to a plate.

Cook onions in fat remaining in skillet over moderately low heat, stirring and scraping up brown bits, until softened and golden, about 10 minutes. Add cinnamon and cook, stirring, for 1 minute. Add walnuts and cook, stirring, for 1 minute. Stir in pomegranate seeds and juice, tomato sauce, stock, lemon juice, molasses, ¼ teaspoon salt, and ¼ teaspoon pepper and bring to a boil. Reduce heat and simmer sauce, stirring occasionally, for 3 minutes.

Add chicken, along with any juices accumulated on plate, and simmer, covered, until just cooked through, 15 to 20 minutes.

Chicken with Cornmeal Dumplings

SERVES 4

ACTIVE TIME: 40 MINUTES ■ START TO FINISH: 1¾ HOURS

■ The down-home classic—big pieces of chicken and cornmeal dumplings simmered in creamy gravy—needs no improvement. We like the finesse given by shallots and white wine. ■

FOR CHICKEN

- 1 (3- to 3½-pound) chicken, rinsed, patted dry, and cut into 8 serving pieces
- Salt and freshly ground black pepper
- 1 tablespoon unsalted butter
- 1 tablespoon vegetable oil
- 1 cup chopped shallots
- ½ cup dry white wine

FOR DUMPLINGS

- ¾ cup all-purpose flour
- ¼ cup yellow cornmeal
- 1 teaspoon baking powder
- ¼ teaspoon baking soda
- ¼ teaspoon salt
- ⅛ teaspoon freshly ground black pepper
- 2 tablespoons cold unsalted butter, cut into bits
- 2 tablespoons finely chopped fresh chives
- 1 tablespoon finely chopped fresh flat-leaf parsley
- ⅔ cup well-shaken buttermilk

FOR GRAVY

- 3 cups chicken stock or store-bought low-sodium broth
- ¼ cup heavy cream
- 2½ tablespoons all-purpose flour
- Salt and freshly ground black pepper

GARNISH: finely chopped fresh chives and parsley

COOK THE CHICKEN: Season chicken with salt and pepper. Heat butter and oil in a deep 12-inch heavy skillet over moderately high heat until foam subsides. Add chicken in 2 batches and brown well on all sides, turning occasionally, about 8 minutes per batch. Arrange all chicken pieces skin sides up in skillet and sprinkle with shallots. Add wine and bring to a boil. Reduce heat and simmer, covered, until chicken is just cooked through, 20 to 25 minutes.

Meanwhile, preheat oven to 200°F.

With tongs, transfer chicken to an ovenproof platter, leaving juices in skillet. Cover chicken with foil and keep warm in oven.

MAKE THE DUMPLINGS: Sift together flour, cornmeal, baking powder, baking soda, salt, and pepper into a bowl. Blend in butter with a pastry blender or your fingertips until mixture resembles coarse meal. Stir in chives and parsley, then add buttermilk, stirring just until dough is moistened; do not overmix.

MAKE THE GRAVY AND COOK THE DUMPLINGS: Skim fat from juices in skillet. Add 2¾ cups stock and bring to a boil. Whisk together cream, flour, and remaining ¼ cup stock in a small bowl until smooth, then whisk into boiling stock and season with salt and pepper.

Drop 8 heaping tablespoons of dough into simmering gravy, spacing them about 2 inches apart to allow dumplings to expand. Reduce heat and simmer gently, covered, until tops of dumplings are dry to the touch, 15 to 20 minutes.

Spoon dumplings and gravy over chicken and sprinkle with chives and parsley.

Chicken Pie with Biscuit Crust

SERVES 4

ACTIVE TIME: 45 MINUTES ■ START TO FINISH: 1½ HOURS

■ This is the ultimate winter comfort dish, to prepare as well as to eat. The recipe calls for cubes of cooked chicken (you can use turkey), making it a good way to use leftovers. Biscuits are much less intimidating to make than a pastry crust. ■

FOR FILLING

- 4 cups chicken stock or store-bought low-sodium broth
- 3 carrots, peeled and cut into ¼-inch-thick slices
- ¾ pound red potatoes, quartered lengthwise and cut crosswise into ½-inch-thick slices
- 2 large celery ribs, cut into ½-inch-thick slices
- 2½ cups cubed cooked chicken (about 1 pound)
- ¾ stick (6 tablespoons) unsalted butter
- 1 medium onion, chopped
- 6 tablespoons all-purpose flour
- ¼ teaspoon freshly grated nutmeg, or to taste
- ½ cup minced fresh flat-leaf parsley
- 1 teaspoon chopped fresh thyme
- Salt and freshly ground black pepper

FOR BISCUIT CRUST

- 1⅓ cups all-purpose flour
- 1½ teaspoons baking powder
- ½ teaspoon baking soda
- ½ teaspoon salt
- 2 tablespoons cold unsalted butter, cut into bits
- 2 tablespoons vegetable shortening, chilled and cut into bits
- ⅓ cup grated sharp Cheddar
- 1 large egg
- About ⅓ cup well-shaken buttermilk
- 1 large egg yolk lightly beaten with 1 tablespoon milk, for egg wash

SPECIAL EQUIPMENT: a 2-inch fluted round cutter

MAKE THE FILLING: Bring stock to a boil in a 3½- to 4-quart heavy saucepan. Add carrots, potatoes, and celery and simmer, uncovered, until tender, 10 to 15 minutes. With a slotted spoon, transfer vegetables to a large bowl. Reserve 3 cups broth for sauce and save remainder for another use. Add chicken to vegetables.

Melt butter in 2- to 3-quart heavy saucepan over moderately low heat. Add onion and cook, stirring, until softened, about 6 minutes. Add flour and cook, stirring, for 3 minutes to make a roux. Add reserved 3 cups broth in a slow stream, whisking constantly, and bring to a boil, whisking. Reduce heat and simmer, whisking, for 3 minutes. Stir in nutmeg, parsley, thyme, and salt and pepper to taste.

Pour sauce over chicken and vegetables, stirring gently until just combined. Transfer to a 2-quart shallow baking dish or divide among four 2-cup shallow baking dishes.

MAKE THE BISCUIT CRUST: Put a rack in middle of oven and preheat oven to 450°F.

Sift together flour, baking powder, baking soda, and salt into a bowl. Blend in butter and shortening with your fingertips or a pastry blender until mixture resembles coarse meal. Stir in cheese.

Break egg into a liquid measuring cup, add enough buttermilk to total ½ cup, and beat with a fork. Add to flour mixture, stirring just until a dough forms. Gather dough into a ball.

On a lightly floured surface, roll out dough ½ inch thick. Cut out as many rounds as possible with lightly floured cutter. Gather scraps, reroll dough, and cut out more rounds in same manner.

Arrange rounds on top of filling, then brush tops of rounds with egg wash and prick all over with a fork. Bake until biscuits are puffed and golden and filling is bubbling, 15 to 25 minutes.

COOK'S NOTE

■ The filling can be made up to 1 day ahead. Cool, uncovered, then refrigerate, covered. Bring to room temperature before proceeding.

Individual B'stillas

Moroccan Chicken and Almond Pies

SERVES 6 TO 8 (MAKES 9 *B'STILLAS*)

ACTIVE TIME: 1 HOUR ■ START TO FINISH: 3 HOURS

■ The traditional *b'stilla* is an enormous pigeon or chicken pie wrapped in paper-thin golden pastry leaves.

The idea of meat blended with spices and encased in pastry was taken to Morocco by Arabs from the Middle East; the delicate pastry sheets, it is thought, came from Persia. We love the combination of a moist, sweet-savory chicken filling surrounded by shatteringly crisp, buttery shards of pastry. There's no substitute for *ras el hanout,* a fragrant Moroccan spice blend, but it's easy to make. Rather than one big *b'stilla,* we make small individual ones wrapped in store-bought phyllo dough. They are much less cumbersome to assemble and look very pretty on the plate. ■

FOR FILLING

- 1/4 teaspoon crumbled saffron threads
- 2 tablespoons boiling water
- 3 tablespoons unsalted butter
- 1 medium onion, chopped
- 2 garlic cloves, thinly sliced, then cut into thin strips
- 3/4 teaspoon ground ginger
- 2 teaspoons Ras el Hanout (page 933)
- 1/2 teaspoon freshly ground black pepper
- 2 pounds chicken parts (1 whole breast, 2 thighs, and 2 legs), rinsed and patted dry
- 1 3/4 cups chicken stock or store-bought low-sodium broth
- 3 large eggs, lightly beaten
- 6 tablespoons chopped fresh flat-leaf parsley
- 3 tablespoons chopped fresh cilantro
- 1 1/2 tablespoons fresh lemon juice, or to taste
- Salt

FOR *B'STILLAS*

- 1/2 cup (about 3 ounces) whole almonds with skin, toasted (see Tips, page 938)
- 3 tablespoons granulated sugar
- 1 teaspoon ground cinnamon
- 9 tablespoons unsalted butter
- 18 (17-by-12-inch) phyllo sheets (from 1 1/2 packages), thawed if frozen

GARNISH: cinnamon and confectioners' sugar

MAKE THE FILLING: Stir together saffron and boiling water in a small bowl and let stand for 10 minutes.

Heat butter in a 4-quart saucepan over moderately high heat until foam subsides. Add onion and garlic and cook, stirring occasionally, until onion is golden, about 4 minutes. Reduce heat to moderate, add ginger, *ras el hanout,* and pepper, and cook, stirring, for 3 minutes. Add chicken, stock, and saffron mixture and bring to a simmer. Cover and simmer, turning chicken once, until chicken is cooked through and very tender, 25 to 35 minutes.

Let chicken stand in cooking liquid off heat for 30 minutes.

Transfer chicken to a plate; reserve cooking liquid in pan. When chicken is cool enough to handle, shred, discarding skin and bones. Reserved cooking liquid should measure 1 3/4 cups; if there is more, boil until reduced to 1 3/4 cups.

Bring cooking liquid to a boil, then reduce heat to moderate. Add eggs in a slow stream, whisking constantly, and cook, stirring, until eggs are set, about 3 minutes. Pour mixture into a large sieve set over a bowl and let drain, undisturbed, for 10 minutes.

Transfer egg mixture to a large bowl (discard drained liquid) and stir in chicken, parsley, cilantro, lemon juice, and salt and pepper to taste.

ASSEMBLE THE *B'STILLAS:* Put a rack in middle of oven and preheat oven to 425°F. Butter a large baking sheet with sides.

Finely grind almonds with sugar and cinnamon in a food processor. Melt butter and keep warm (not hot).

Cut phyllo sheets lengthwise in half and stack them, then cover with plastic wrap and a dampened kitchen towel. Take one sheet of phyllo from stack, place on a work surface with a short end facing you, and brush with melted butter. Top with 3 more sheets, brushing each with butter.

Sprinkle 1 scant tablespoon almond sugar at end of buttered stack nearest you to cover an area roughly 2 1/2 by 4 inches, leaving a 1-inch border on both sides and along bottom. Spread 1/3 cup chicken filling evenly over almond sugar. Sprinkle chicken with another scant tablespoon almond sugar, then roll up filling in phyllo, folding in sides after first roll. Transfer *b'stilla* seam side down to buttered baking sheet and brush with melted butter, then immediately refrigerate. Make 8 more *b'stillas* in same manner.

BAKE THE *B'STILLAS:* Bake until tops and ends are puffed and browned, 15 to 20 minutes. With a spatula, transfer to rack to cool for 5 minutes.

Sprinkle with cinnamon and confectioners' sugar before serving.

COOK'S NOTES

- The filling can be made up to 1 day ahead and refrigerated, covered.

- The almond sugar can be made up to 1 day ahead and kept in an airtight container at room temperature.
- The *b'stillas* can be assembled up to 4 hours ahead. Cover them lightly with plastic wrap once they are cold.

Asian Chicken and Water Chestnut Patties

SERVES 6

ACTIVE TIME: 20 MINUTES ■ START TO FINISH: 20 MINUTES

■ The Chinese use ground water chestnuts to lend body to all sorts of things—filled dumplings, for instance. Here they prevent coarsely chopped chicken from becoming pasty and give a marvelous texture to the patties. Minced jalapeño provides a tiny hit of heat. You could serve these on a bed of plain rice or even bean thread (cellophane) noodles tossed with the Vietnamese dipping sauce Nuoc Cham (page 165). Note that the patties are delicate and very lean, so it's crucial not to overcook them. We thread them on skewers to facilitate turning. ■

- 1½ pounds skinless, boneless chicken breasts, rinsed, patted dry, and cut into 1½-inch pieces
- 1 (8-ounce) can whole water chestnuts, rinsed and drained
- 1 bunch scallions, chopped (1 cup)
- 1 teaspoon minced jalapeño chile (including seeds)
- 2 tablespoons chopped fresh cilantro
- 1¼ teaspoons salt
- 2 teaspoons vegetable oil

SPECIAL EQUIPMENT: six 8-inch wooden skewers, soaked in water for 30 minutes

Pulse chicken in a food processor until coarsely chopped. Transfer to a large bowl. Add water chestnuts, scallions, and jalapeño to processor and pulse until finely chopped, then add to chicken, along with cilantro and salt. Mix together with your hands until just combined.

Form mixture into eighteen 2-inch-wide patties and place them on a baking sheet. Thread 3 patties horizontally (through their sides) onto each skewer.

Heat 1 teaspoon oil in a 12-inch nonstick skillet over moderate heat until hot but not smoking. Using a large metal spatula, transfer 3 skewers of patties to skillet and cook, turning once, until golden and just cooked through, about 6 minutes total. Transfer to a platter and keep warm, covered with foil. Add remaining 1 teaspoon oil to skillet and cook remaining patties in same manner.

Roast Turkey with Herbed Bread Stuffing and Giblet Gravy

SERVES 8

ACTIVE TIME: 1½ HOURS ■ START TO FINISH: 5¾ HOURS (INCLUDES MAKING STOCK)

■ An American icon. We call for a kosher turkey here because it tends to surpass both supermarket brands and free-range birds in flavor as well as moistness. Be aware, though, that you'll need to allow time to "groom" a kosher turkey, removing remaining feathers and quills. (This is a happy sign that the bird has been minimally processed, and you can do it the day before cooking.) ■

- 1 (12- to 14-pound) kosher turkey, any feathers and quills removed with tweezers or needle-nose pliers, neck and giblets (except liver) reserved for stock
- Salt and freshly ground black pepper
- Herbed Bread Stuffing (page 378)
- ¾ stick (6 tablespoons) unsalted butter
- ¼ cup chicken stock or store-bought low-sodium broth
- ¼ cup water
- 4 cups Turkey Giblet Stock (recipe follows)
- ¼ cup all-purpose flour

OPTIONAL GARNISH: fresh sage, rosemary, and thyme sprigs

SPECIAL EQUIPMENT: small wooden or metal skewers; kitchen string; an instant-read thermometer

ROAST THE TURKEY: Put a rack in middle of oven and preheat oven to 425°F. Butter a 3-quart shallow baking dish.

Rinse turkey inside and out and pat dry. Season inside and out with salt and pepper. Loosely fill neck cavity with stuffing, then fold neck skin under body and fasten with a skewer. Loosely fill body cavity with stuffing. Tie drumsticks together with kitchen string and, if desired, secure wings with skewers for a nicer appearance. Transfer remaining stuffing to baking dish and refrigerate, covered.

Put turkey on a rack set in a roasting pan. Roast for 30 minutes.

Melt 4 tablespoons butter. Reduce oven temperature to 325°F and pour melted butter over turkey. Roast turkey, basting with pan juices every 20 minutes, until thermometer inserted in center of stuffing in body cavity registers 165°F (thigh will be about 180°F), 3 to $3\frac{1}{2}$ hours more. Transfer turkey to a heated platter, leaving juices in pan; set pan aside. Remove skewers and string. Transfer stuffing from turkey cavities to a serving dish and keep warm, covered. Let turkey stand for at least 30 minutes and up to 45 minutes.

Increase oven temperature to 375°F. Stir together chicken stock and water and drizzle over reserved stuffing in baking dish. Dot stuffing with remaining butter and bake for 40 minutes: for moist stuffing, bake covered entire time; for less moist stuffing with a slightly crisp top, uncover after 10 minutes.

ABOUT 15 MINUTES BEFORE SERVING, MAKE THE GRAVY: Bring turkey stock to a simmer in a medium saucepan. Skim fat from pan juices and reserve $\frac{1}{4}$ cup fat. Set roasting pan over two burners, add 1 cup stock, and deglaze pan by boiling over moderately high heat, stirring and scraping up brown bits, for 1 minute. Add pan juices to remaining 3 cups stock and bring to a simmer.

Meanwhile, whisk together reserved fat and flour in a large heavy saucepan and cook over moderately low heat, whisking, for 3 minutes to make a roux. Add hot stock to roux in a fast stream, whisking constantly to prevent lumps, and simmer, whisking occasionally, until thickened, about 10 minutes. Stir in any juices accumulated on turkey platter and season gravy with salt and pepper.

Garnish platter with herb sprigs, if desired. Carve turkey and serve with stuffing and gravy.

COOK'S NOTE

- If you choose not to cook any of the stuffing inside the bird, your turkey will take less time to roast, only 2 to 3 hours (the thigh should register 170°F).

An Upside-Down Turkey

If tender, succulent breast meat is more important to you than getting the skin that covers it golden and crisp, cook your bird upside down. The turkey looks pallid when flipped, breast side up, onto the platter, but there is plenty of crackly brown skin on the bottom for snacking. This unorthodox approach also eliminates the need for basting, because gravity works its magic: when the bird roasts upside down, the juices stay right where they're supposed to. If this is the way you want to go, follow the recipe on this page but put the bird breast side down on the rack. Secure the stuffing inside the bird with a heel of bread lodged in the opening.

Turkey Giblet Stock

MAKES ABOUT 4 CUPS

ACTIVE TIME: 10 MINUTES ■ START TO FINISH: 1 HOUR

■ There's no great mystery to giblets. They're simply the edible internal organs of poultry—heart, liver, kidneys, and gizzard—often collected in a tidy plastic packet and tucked inside the fowl. Minus the liver (which would result in bitterness), they add depth and richness to stock or, minced, to gravy. ■

1 tablespoon vegetable oil
Neck and giblets (except liver) from a 12- to 14-pound turkey
1 celery rib, coarsely chopped
1 carrot, coarsely chopped
1 onion, quartered
4 cups water
1 3/4 cups chicken stock or store-bought low-sodium broth
1 Turkish bay leaf or 1/2 California bay leaf
1 teaspoon black peppercorns
1 teaspoon dried thyme, crumbled

Heat oil in a 2-quart saucepan over moderately high heat until hot but not smoking. Brown neck and giblets, turning occasionally, about 5 minutes. Add remaining ingredients, bring to a simmer, and simmer until liquid is reduced to about 4 cups, 40 to 45 minutes.

Pour stock through a fine-mesh sieve into a bowl. Skim off and discard any fat.

COOK'S NOTE

- The stock can be made up to 1 day ahead. Cool completely, uncovered, then refrigerate, covered.

Herbed Bread Stuffing

MAKES ABOUT 12 CUPS
ACTIVE TIME: 35 MINUTES ■ START TO FINISH: 1 HOUR

■ Store-bought packaged stuffing mix is an honorable Thanksgiving shortcut, but two of the nice things about homemade stuffing are that you have more control over the seasonings and you get bigger pieces of bread, which translates to more texture and greater eye appeal. The easiest way to vary a basic bread stuffing is to change the type of bread. Be aware, though, that the heavier the bread, the heavier the stuffing. Oysters or precooked sausage or bacon adds richness and more complex flavors. Lightly sautéed celery or fennel and/or lightly toasted nuts contribute some crunch. (See the recipes that follow this one.)

Any frozen turkey destined for stuffing must be completely thawed. (Check the body cavity for ice crystals; if you see any, submerge the turkey in cold water, changing the water every 30 minutes, until the turkey is thoroughly thawed.) Let the stuffing cool completely or, if you've made it ahead and refrigerated it, bring it to room temperature before spooning it into the bird. And don't pack it in too tightly; stuffing expands as it cooks. Always stuff the turkey immediately before roasting, never earlier; this is meant not to sabotage your schedule but to prevent food poisoning. ■

BRINING TURKEY

Brining turkey is the best way we know to guarantee moist, tender meat. The basic point is to soak the bird in a mixture of salt and water; the electrically charged ions of the salt plump up the muscle fibers, allowing them to absorb water. This changes the structure of the proteins, preventing the water from escaping during cooking. In addition to keeping the meat moist, the salt intensifies the flavor.

For a basic brine, stir together 8 quarts water and 2 cups kosher salt in a clean 5-gallon bucket or container with a cover. If you like, you can add a bit of sugar to the brine, along with whatever spices strike your fancy. Add the raw turkey, cover, and chill for 10 hours. If you want to soak the bird for 24 hours, reduce the amount of salt to 1 cup.

12 (1-inch-thick) slices crusty country-style bread (1 pound), cut into 1-inch cubes (10 cups)
1 stick (8 tablespoons) unsalted butter
3 medium onions, chopped
3 celery ribs, thinly sliced
1 teaspoon dried thyme, crumbled
½ teaspoon dried sage, crumbled
½ teaspoon dried rosemary, crumbled
1½ cups chicken stock or store-bought low-sodium broth
½ cup water
Salt and freshly ground black pepper

Put a rack in middle of oven and preheat oven to 325°F.

Spread bread on a baking sheet with sides and bake until just dry, 25 to 30 minutes. Let bread cool on sheet on a rack.

Melt butter in a 12-inch heavy skillet over moderately low heat. Add onions, celery, and herbs and cook, stirring occasionally, until celery is softened, about 10 minutes. Transfer to a large bowl.

Add bread, stock, water, and salt and pepper to taste to vegetable mixture and stir to mix well. Let cool completely, uncovered.

COOK'S NOTE

- The stuffing can be made up to 1 day ahead and refrigerated, covered. Bring to room temperature before using.

Oyster Stuffing

SERVES 8 TO 10 (MAKES ABOUT 10 CUPS)
ACTIVE TIME: 1 HOUR ■ START TO FINISH: 2 HOURS

■ Chopped oysters add a flavorful background note to stuffing, imparting richness without making it taste even remotely fishy. They give a certain depth that you would miss if they weren't there. ■

2 loaves Italian or French bread (1 pound total), cut into ¾-inch cubes (12 cups)
½ pound bacon (8 slices), cut into ½-inch pieces
2–3 tablespoons olive oil (if needed)
2 medium onions, finely chopped
1½ cups chopped celery
1 tablespoon minced garlic
3 tablespoons chopped fresh thyme or 1 tablespoon dried thyme, crumbled
1 tablespoon finely chopped fresh sage or 2 teaspoons dried sage, crumbled
½ teaspoon salt
¼ teaspoon freshly ground black pepper
⅔ cup finely chopped fresh flat-leaf parsley
1 stick (8 tablespoons) unsalted butter, melted
18 oysters, shucked (see page 53), drained, and chopped (¾ cup)
2¼ cups Turkey Giblet Stock (page 377), chicken stock, or store-bought low-sodium chicken broth

Put racks in upper and lower thirds of oven and preheat oven to 325°F. Butter a 3- to 3½-quart shallow baking dish.

Spread bread cubes on two baking sheets with sides. Bake, switching position of sheets halfway through baking, until golden, 25 to 30 minutes. Let bread cool on sheets on racks, then transfer to a large bowl. (Leave oven on and reposition one rack in middle of oven.)

Meanwhile, cook bacon in a 12-inch heavy skillet over moderate heat, stirring occasionally, until crisp, about 10 minutes. Transfer to paper towels to drain, reserving fat in skillet.

If bacon rendered less than ¼ cup fat, add enough oil to skillet to measure ¼ cup. Add onions, celery, garlic, thyme, sage, salt, and pepper to skillet and cook over moderate heat, stirring occasionally, until vegetables are softened, 8 to 10 minutes. Transfer to bowl of bread cubes, then stir in bacon, parsley, butter, and oysters. Drizzle with stock, season with salt and pepper, and toss well.

Transfer stuffing to baking dish. Bake, covered, for 30 minutes. Uncover and bake until browned on top, about 30 minutes more.

COOK'S NOTES

- The stuffing can be assembled, without the oysters, up to 2 days ahead and refrigerated, covered. Bring to room temperature and stir in the oysters before baking.
- We often prefer to bake the stuffing in a dish as we do here, but if you want to bake it inside the bird, this

recipe is enough for a 12- to 14-pound turkey, with some left over for baking separately. See Roast Turkey with Herbed Bread Stuffing (page 376) for directions on stuffing a turkey.

Sausage Fennel Stuffing

SERVES 8 TO 10 (MAKES ABOUT 10 CUPS)
ACTIVE TIME: 1 HOUR ■ START TO FINISH: 3¾ HOURS (INCLUDES MAKING CORN BREAD)

■ Sausage and corn bread is a great combination. Because we use sweet Italian sausage seasoned with fennel, adding fennel seeds and lightly cooked fennel instead of the traditional celery is the natural thing to do. ■

- 7 cups coarsely crumbled Buttermilk Corn Bread (recipe follows)
- 1 pound sweet Italian sausage, casings discarded
- 1 stick (8 tablespoons) unsalted butter
- 2 medium onions, finely chopped
- 2 medium fennel bulbs (1½ pounds total), stalks discarded, bulbs cored and coarsely chopped
- ½ teaspoon salt
- ¼ teaspoon freshly ground black pepper
- 2 teaspoons fennel seeds
- 2 teaspoons dried thyme, crumbled
- 2 teaspoons dried tarragon, crumbled
- 1 cup Turkey Giblet Stock (page 377), chicken stock, or store-bought low-sodium chicken broth

SPECIAL EQUIPMENT: an electric coffee/spice grinder

Put racks in upper and lower thirds of oven and preheat oven to 325°F. Butter a 3- to 3½-quart shallow baking dish.

Spread bread crumbs on two baking sheets with sides and bake until golden and dry, about 15 minutes. Let crumbs cool in pans on racks, then transfer to a large bowl. (Leave oven on and reposition one rack in middle of oven.)

Cook sausage in a dry 12-inch nonstick skillet over moderate heat, stirring and breaking it up with a fork, until browned and cooked through, 6 to 8 minutes. With a slotted spoon, transfer to bowl with crumbs.

Melt 6 tablespoons butter in skillet, then add onions, chopped fennel, salt, and pepper and cook, stirring frequently, until vegetables are softened, 10 to 15 minutes.

Meanwhile, finely grind fennel seeds in coffee/spice grinder. Add ground fennel to vegetables, along with thyme and tarragon, and cook, stirring, for 1 minute. Transfer vegetables to bowl of bread crumbs and sausage and toss gently but thoroughly.

Spoon stuffing into baking dish. Drizzle with stock and dot with remaining 2 tablespoons butter. Bake, covered, for 30 minutes, then uncover and bake until browned on top, about 30 minutes more.

COOK'S NOTES

- The stuffing can be assembled up to 2 days ahead and refrigerated, covered. Bring to room temperature before baking.
- We often prefer to bake the stuffing in a dish, but if you want to bake it inside the bird, this recipe is enough for a 12- to 14-pound turkey with some left over for baking separately. See Roast Turkey with Herbed Bread Stuffing (page 376) for directions on stuffing a turkey.

Buttermilk Corn Bread

MAKES ABOUT 7 CUPS COARSELY CRUMBLED
ACTIVE TIME: 10 MINUTES ■ START TO FINISH: 1 HOUR (INCLUDES COOLING)

■ This corn bread was developed to be used for stuffing, so it's drier than some other versions. It's still good for eating, however, especially when spread lavishly with butter. ■

- 1 cup all-purpose flour
- ¾ cup yellow cornmeal
- 1½ teaspoons baking powder
- ½ teaspoon baking soda
- ½ teaspoon salt
- 1 cup well-shaken buttermilk
- 2 large eggs
- ½ stick (4 tablespoons) unsalted butter, melted and cooled
- ½ teaspoon finely chopped fresh sage (optional)

Put a rack in middle of oven and preheat oven to 425°F. Butter an 8-inch square baking pan.

Whisk together flour, cornmeal, baking powder, baking soda, and salt in a large bowl. Whisk together buttermilk, eggs, butter, and sage, if using, in another bowl. Add to flour mixture and stir until just combined.

Spread batter evenly in buttered baking pan and bake until golden, about 25 minutes. Let cool in pan on a rack.

COOK'S NOTE

- The corn bread can be made — and crumbled for stuffing — up to 3 days ahead and kept in a sealed plastic bag at room temperature.

Chestnut Stuffing

SERVES 8 TO 10 (MAKES ABOUT 10 CUPS)
ACTIVE TIME: 45 MINUTES ■ START TO FINISH: 1¼ HOURS

■ Stuffing of some sort has been around since the Middle Ages, but chestnut stuffing, like oyster stuffing, was an eighteenth-century English innovation. Roasting and shelling the nuts to get at the sweet, rich meat no longer has to be a labor of love (or martyrdom), though: bottled peeled cooked chestnuts, a late-twentieth-century innovation, are as close as your supermarket (or see Sources). ■

6 (½-inch-thick) slices country-style bread, cut into ½-inch cubes (6 cups)
1 stick (8 tablespoons) unsalted butter
2 onions, chopped
4 celery ribs, chopped
3 tablespoons minced fresh sage or 1 tablespoon dried sage, crumbled
2 tablespoons minced fresh thyme or 2 teaspoons dried thyme, crumbled
1 tablespoon minced fresh rosemary or 1½ teaspoons dried rosemary, crumbled
1 tablespoon minced fresh savory or 1 teaspoon dried savory, crumbled
2 cups (14 ounces) bottled cooked (peeled) whole chestnuts, coarsely chopped
1 cup Turkey Giblet Stock (page 377), chicken stock, or store-bought low-sodium chicken broth
½ cup finely chopped fresh flat-leaf parsley
Salt and freshly ground black pepper

Put a rack in middle of oven and preheat oven to 325°F. Butter a 2½- to 3-quart shallow baking dish.

Spread bread cubes on a baking sheet with sides and toast in oven, stirring occasionally, until golden, 10 to 15 minutes. Transfer to a large bowl. (Leave oven on.)

Melt butter in a 12-inch skillet over moderately low heat. Add onions, celery, and herbs and cook, stirring, until vegetables are softened, 10 to 12 minutes. Add chestnuts and cook, stirring, for 1 minute. Transfer to bowl of bread cubes and add stock, parsley, and salt and pepper to taste. Toss until well combined.

Transfer stuffing to baking dish. Cover with foil and bake for 20 minutes. Uncover and bake until golden on top, about 10 minutes more.

COOK'S NOTES

- The stuffing can be assembled up to 1 day ahead. Cool completely, then refrigerate, covered. Bring to room temperature before baking.
- If you want to bake the stuffing inside the bird, this recipe is enough for a 12- to 14-pound turkey with some left over for baking separately. See Roast Turkey with Herbed Bread Stuffing (page 376) for directions on stuffing a turkey.

Grilled Turkey with Cranberry Gravy

SERVES 8
ACTIVE TIME: 45 MINUTES ■ START TO FINISH: 4¼ HOURS (INCLUDES MAKING STOCK)

■ Cooking your Thanksgiving turkey on the grill (in a roasting pan over indirect heat) results in a juicy bird with crisp skin, and, not incidentally, it frees up precious oven space for all those side dishes. We like the way lemon halves and herbs enhance the flavor of the turkey and the pan juices. We don't recommend stuffing a turkey that's to be grilled, because it's difficult to maintain the steady temperature necessary to cook the stuffing.

If possible, use hardwood charcoal for this recipe. But if you're planning on using a gas grill, make sure your grill is up to the task before you begin. You need one with three burners and a thermometer for gauging the temperature inside the grill; it also needs to accommodate the turkey in its roasting pan. If your grill doesn't have a smoker-box attachment, however, don't worry—we've spelled out how to improvise. ■

FOR TURKEY

- 1 (12- to 14-pound) turkey, preferably kosher, any feathers and quills removed with tweezers or needle-nose pliers, neck and giblets (except liver) reserved for stock if desired
- Salt and freshly ground black pepper
- 2–3 lemons, halved
- A handful of fresh herb sprigs, such as sage, parsley, and thyme
- 1 stick (8 tablespoons) unsalted butter, softened
- 1 cup water

FOR GRAVY

- 1 (12-ounce) bag fresh or unthawed frozen cranberries
- 3/4 cup sugar
- 3 tablespoons all-purpose flour
- 4 cups Turkey Giblet Stock (page 377), chicken stock, or store-bought low-sodium chicken broth
- Salt and freshly ground black pepper

OPTIONAL GARNISH: lemon slices and fresh thyme or flat-leaf parsley sprigs

SPECIAL EQUIPMENT: small metal skewers; kitchen string; 2 cups apple, cherry, or hickory wood chips (optional; see Sources); an instant-read thermometer; if using a gas grill, two 8-by-3 3/4-by-2 1/2-inch disposable loaf pans

PREPARE THE TURKEY: Rinse turkey inside and out and pat dry. Season inside and out with salt and pepper and loosely pack neck cavity with 1 or 2 lemon halves and some herb sprigs. Fold neck skin under body and fasten with a skewer. Loosely fill body cavity with remaining lemon halves and herb sprigs. Tie drumsticks together with kitchen string and, if desired, secure wings with skewers for a nicer appearance.

Rub turkey with butter and put on an oiled rack set in a large flameproof roasting pan. Pour 1 cup water into pan.

TO GRILL THE TURKEY USING A CHARCOAL GRILL: If using wood chips, wrap them tightly in heavy-duty foil and poke several holes in foil.

Prepare grill: Open vents in bottom of grill and in lid. Pour half of charcoal (50 briquettes total) onto each of two opposite sides of grill, leaving middle clear, and light. When charcoal turns grayish white and you can hold your hand above top rack for just 3 to 4 seconds, put foil package of wood chips over coals on one side.

Place turkey in roasting pan on center of grill rack, with no coals underneath, cover with lid, and cook for 1 hour. (Do not remove lid during cooking.)

Remove lid and add 10 more briquettes to each side of grill. Rotate roasting pan 180 degrees, cover with lid, and grill for 1 hour more.

Remove lid and add 10 more briquettes to each side of grill. Continue to grill turkey, covered with lid, until thermometer inserted into fleshy part of a thigh (without touching bone) registers 180°F, about 1 hour more (3 hours total). If turkey is not done after 1 additional hour, add 10 more briquettes to each side of grill and continue to grill, covered, testing for doneness every 15 minutes.

Transfer turkey to a platter, reserving juices in pan, and let stand, loosely covered with foil, for 30 minutes.

TO GRILL THE TURKEY USING A GAS GRILL: Soak wood chips, if using, in water to cover for 30 minutes, then drain well.

While wood chips soak, prepare grill: Preheat all burners on high, covered, for 10 minutes. Turn off middle burner and reduce heat of other burners to medium (350°–375°F).

With a skewer, punch holes in bottom of one disposable loaf pan at 1-inch intervals and put drained wood chips in loaf pan. Pour 3 cups water into second loaf pan. Put pans side by side on burner tents of (turned-off) middle burner (under grill rack).

Place turkey in roasting pan in center of grill rack over loaf pans (roasting pan will extend over lit burners), cover with lid, and grill, adjusting heat as necessary to maintain temperature, for 1 hour (do not raise lid during cooking).

Check level of water in loaf pan under grill rack: add more if less than 1 inch remains in pan. (Continue to check water level at 1-hour intervals from this point on, adding water as needed.) Continue to grill turkey, covered with lid, until thermometer inserted into fleshy part of thigh (without touching bone) registers 180°F, 2 to 2 1/2 hours. If turkey is not done after 2 1/2 hours, continue to grill, covered, testing for doneness every 15 minutes.

Transfer turkey to a platter, reserving juices in pan, and let stand, loosely covered with foil, for 30 minutes.

MEANWHILE, MAKE THE CRANBERRY PURÉE FOR THE GRAVY: Combine cranberries and sugar in a heavy saucepan and cook over moderately low heat, stirring frequently, until sugar is dissolved and cranberries have burst, about 10 minutes. Purée mixture in batches in a blender (use caution) until smooth; transfer to a bowl.

WHILE THE TURKEY STANDS, MAKE THE GRAVY: Skim fat from pan juices, reserving 3 tablespoons fat. Set roasting pan over two burners, add water, and deglaze pan by boiling, stirring and scraping up brown bits, for 1 minute. Remove from heat.

Whisk together reserved fat and flour in a large heavy saucepan and cook over moderate heat, whisking, for 3 minutes to make a roux. Add pan juices and stock in a slow stream, whisking constantly, then whisk in cranberry purée. Boil, whisking occasionally, until reduced to about 5 cups, 15 to 20 minutes.

Pour gravy through a sieve into a bowl; stir in any turkey juices accumulated on platter and season with salt and pepper.

Remove lemon halves and herb sprigs from turkey cavities and discard.

Garnish platter with lemon slices and thyme or parsley sprigs, if desired. Carve turkey and serve with gravy.

COOK'S NOTE

- The cranberry purée can be made up to 1 day ahead and refrigerated, covered. Bring to room temperature before using.

Lemon-Marinated Turkey with Golden Raisins, Capers, and Pine Nuts

SERVES 8 TO 10
ACTIVE TIME: 1 HOUR ■ START TO FINISH: 7 HOURS (INCLUDES POACHING TURKEY BREAST)

■ Turkey is commonly thought of as the quintessential American bird, but in fact it has been enthusiastically consumed on festive occasions in Italy since the sixteenth century. This dish is light and extremely sophisticated. The raisin, pine nut, and caper combination exemplifies the Italian culinary concept of *agrodolce*, sweet and sour, and poaching the turkey breast results in fine-textured white meat. This is a splendid dish for entertaining. ■

- 2/3 cup golden raisins
- 2 large lemons
- Poached Whole Turkey Breast (page 386), meat removed in 2 large pieces, skin and bones discarded
- 1 tablespoon balsamic vinegar
- 1/2 teaspoon salt
- 1/4 teaspoon freshly ground black pepper
- 1 cup olive oil
- 1/4 cup drained capers
- 2 tablespoons finely chopped fresh flat-leaf parsley
- 2 tablespoons finely chopped fresh mint
- 6 tablespoons (2 1/4 ounces) pine nuts, toasted (see Tips, page 938)

Soak raisins in boiling water to cover for 5 minutes; drain well.

Meanwhile, remove zest from lemons in long thin strips with a vegetable peeler or citrus zester. Halve lemons and squeeze 6 tablespoons juice.

Put turkey in a shallow bowl just large enough to hold it. Whisk together lemon juice, vinegar, salt, and pepper in a small bowl, then add oil in a slow stream, whisking until well blended. Stir in zest, raisins, and capers and pour marinade over turkey. Marinate turkey, covered and refrigerated, turning once, for at least 4 hours.

Let turkey stand in marinade at room temperature for 20 minutes. Transfer to a cutting board, reserving marinade. Cut turkey diagonally into 1/4-inch-thick slices and transfer to a platter.

Pour marinade through a sieve into a bowl and sprinkle zest, raisins, and capers over turkey. Whisk parsley, mint, and salt and pepper to taste into strained marinade, then spoon over turkey. Sprinkle with pine nuts.

COOK'S NOTE

- The turkey can marinate for up to 12 hours.

BONING A TURKEY BREAST AND PREPARING IT FOR STUFFING

A turkey breast is one of the simplest and most straightforward meats to bone. Unlike a leg of lamb, for instance, where the bones are hidden inside, you can see every bone in a turkey breast, with the exception of the little wishbone, which is easily removed.

That said, this is not a particularly quick process. Unless you are exceptionally handy with a knife, it will probably take you about 45 minutes to convert a bone-in breast into an evenly thick, boneless whole breast (sometimes called a double breast) that is ready to be stuffed and cooked. In spite of the time involved, though, there is much to be said for doing this work yourself, as there is for many other such culinary processes. If you have the time, it will teach you something about turkey anatomy, and it will end up giving you more pride of ownership in the final dish. To make it a bit more practical, you can bone the breast up to a day before you plan to cook it, then cover and refrigerate it until you're ready to stuff it.

Here's how to do it: Begin by removing the wishbone, using your fingers and a sharp knife. Now place the turkey breast skin side down on a work surface and, starting at the severed backbone and working toward the ridge of the breastbone, cut the meat of half of the breast away from the carcass, keeping the blade of the knife angled against the bones and gently pulling the meat away from them as you cut.

Turn the breast around so the other side of the severed backbone is nearest you, then cut the meat away from the bones on this side in the same manner.

Keeping the knife angled against the breastbone and being careful not to cut the skin, sever the meat completely from the bones. Reserve the bones for Turkey Breast Stock (page 386).

With the breast skin side down, remove the tenders. Trim away any tendons or sinews, which you can reserve to use in the *ballottine* stuffing (see opposite page).

You now have a boneless breast, but in order to stuff it, you need to make it evenly thick and relatively flat. To achieve a uniform thickness of about one inch, slice horizontally into the thicker sections and lay the slices open like a book. Use some of the trimmings to patch any thin areas or gaps as necessary; reserve the remaining trimmings. Finally, cover the breast with plastic wrap and pound the meat with a mallet or rolling pin to flatten it slightly. (This will have the beneficial effect of spreading out the breast meat, giving you a larger surface area on which to place the filling.)

Pistachio Turkey Ballottine with Madeira Sauce

SERVES 20
ACTIVE TIME: 2½ HOURS ■ START TO FINISH: 6¾ HOURS
(INCLUDES BONING TURKEY BREASTS AND MAKING STOCK)

■ A *ballottine* is poultry, meat, or fish that is boned, stuffed, rolled, and tied into a bundle, then braised or roasted and usually served hot. Making two of them for a crowd sounds like a fair amount of work, and it is, but they are a great buffet party dish because they are easy to serve, easy to eat, and very elegant—perfect for an engagement party or rehearsal dinner, say. (You can also halve this recipe to serve ten.) With the green pistachios and the pink ham, this is especially good-looking when sliced. The Madeira sauce that bathes the slices of *ballottine* is sweet, nutty, and elegant as well. ■

FOR *BALLOTTINES*

- 2 (8-pound) turkey breasts, rinsed, patted dry, and boned (see opposite page), tenders and trimmings reserved for stuffing and bones reserved, if desired, for Turkey Breast Stock
- 3 tablespoons dry vermouth
- Salt and freshly ground black pepper
- ½ teaspoon dried thyme, crumbled
- 1⅓ cups (6 ounces) shelled natural pistachios (not dyed red)
- ½ pound bacon (8 slices), chopped
- 6 large eggs
- 2 cups heavy cream
- ½ teaspoon freshly grated nutmeg
- 1 pound baked ham, coarsely ground in a food processor
- 1 pound lean ground pork
- 1⅓ cups minced scallions (3 bunches)
- ½ cup vegetable oil

FOR MADEIRA SAUCE

- 1 cup dry white wine
- 4 cups Turkey Breast Stock (page 386), chicken stock, or store-bought low-sodium chicken broth
- ½ cup Sercial (dry) Madeira
- 2 tablespoons arrowroot
- Salt and freshly ground black pepper

SPECIAL EQUIPMENT: a kitchen scale; cheesecloth; kitchen string; 2 flameproof roasting pans; an instant-read thermometer

PREPARE THE *BALLOTTINES:* Weigh reserved turkey breast trimmings, and if necessary trim enough additional meat from edges of breasts to make 1 pound. Grind trimmings in a meat grinder or food processor. Cut reserved tenders lengthwise into ½-inch-wide strips and toss with vermouth and salt and pepper to taste in a medium bowl.

Put each turkey breast skin side down on a large piece of doubled cheesecloth (about 3 inches longer at each end than breast). Sprinkle with thyme and season with salt. Set aside.

Blanch pistachios in a saucepan of boiling water for 2 minutes; drain. Rub skins off in a kitchen towel.

Combine bacon with ground trimmings in a food processor and purée. Add eggs one at a time, blending well after each addition. With motor running, add cream in a steady stream, then add 1½ teaspoons salt, 1 teaspoon pepper, and nutmeg and blend until just smooth. Transfer to a large bowl, add ham, pork, pistachios, and scallions, and mix with your hands until well combined. Refrigerate, covered, until firm, about 30 minutes.

Drain tender strips and pat dry. Divide filling into 4 equal portions. Spread one portion filling over a turkey breast, leaving a 1-inch border all around edges. Arrange half of tender strips lengthwise in one layer over filling, pressing down gently so they adhere, then top with another portion of filling, spreading it evenly. Turn turkey breast if necessary so a long side is nearest you and, using cheesecloth, bring two long sides of breast together to form a roll, enclosing stuffing. Tightly roll edges of cheesecloth together along length of turkey, then tie roll together at 1-inch intervals with kitchen string. Firmly twist ends of cheesecloth together and tie each with kitchen string. (Don't worry if filling squeezes out a bit at ends and along seam of roll; cheesecloth will contain it.) Stuff remaining turkey breast with remaining filling and tender strips in same manner.

ROAST THE *BALLOTTINES:* Put racks in upper and lower thirds of oven and preheat oven to 325°F.

Pat *ballottines* dry. Heat ¼ cup oil in each of two flameproof roasting pans over moderately high heat until hot but not smoking. Add *ballottines* (in cheesecloth) and cook, turning occasionally, until well browned, about 20 minutes total.

Turn *ballottines* seam side down in pans. Roast, switching position of pans and basting *ballottines* with pan juices every 30 minutes, until thermometer inserted 2 inches into center (through cheesecloth) registers 160°F, 2 to 2½ hours. Transfer *ballottines* to a cutting board (set roasting pans aside) and remove strings. Carefully peel off cheesecloth. Let *ballottines* stand for 20 minutes.

MEANWHILE, MAKE THE SAUCE: Skim fat from pan juices. Put each roasting pan on a burner, add ½ cup wine to each, and deglaze pans by boiling over high heat, stirring and scraping up brown bits, for 1 minute. Then continue boiling until liquid in each pan is reduced by about half, about 5 minutes.

Pour liquid from both pans into a large saucepan. Add stock and ¼ cup Madeira and boil for 5 minutes. Stir together arrowroot and remaining ¼ cup Madeira in a small bowl until arrowroot is dissolved, then add to sauce, whisking constantly. Boil, whisking, until thickened, about 2 minutes. Season with salt and pepper, then pour through a sieve into a sauceboat or serving bowl.

Cut *ballottines* into ¼- to ⅓-inch-thick slices and serve with sauce.

COOK'S NOTE

- The *ballottines* can be assembled, but not cooked, up to 1 day ahead and refrigerated, covered.

Turkey Breast Stock

MAKES ABOUT 8 CUPS
ACTIVE TIME: 15 MINUTES ■ START TO FINISH: 2 HOURS

If you've just boned turkey breasts for *ballottines*, it's time to make stock. You won't be sorry you did; this turkey stock is rich and full-flavored.

- 2 onions
- 3 whole cloves
- Bones from 2 turkey breasts, chopped with a cleaver
- 2 carrots, coarsely chopped
- 1 celery rib, coarsely chopped
- 4 quarts water
- 1 teaspoon black peppercorns
- ½ teaspoon dried thyme, crumbled
- 1 Turkish bay leaf or ½ California bay leaf
- 12 fresh parsley stems (without leaves)

Quarter onions and stick 3 quarters with 1 clove each. Combine turkey bones, carrots, celery, and onions in a large pot, add water, and bring to a boil, skimming froth. Add remaining ingredients, reduce heat, and simmer stock, uncovered, until liquid is reduced to about 8 cups, about 1½ hours.

Pour stock through a large fine-mesh sieve into a large bowl and discard solids. Skim off and discard any fat.

COOK'S NOTE

- The stock can be made up to 2 days ahead. Cool completely, uncovered, then refrigerate, covered, or freeze for up to 3 months. Discard the solidified fat before reheating.

Poached Whole Turkey Breast

SERVES 8
ACTIVE TIME: 20 MINUTES ■ START TO FINISH: 2½ HOURS

This is a fabulous cooking method in the summer, when it's too hot to turn on the oven. Poached turkey is great for sandwiches and turkey salad as well as for the Lemon-Marinated Turkey on page 383.

- 1 (5½- to 6-pound) whole turkey breast, rinsed and patted dry
- 1 large onion, chopped
- 3 carrots, chopped
- 2 Turkish bay leaves or 1 California bay leaf
- 2 tablespoons salt
- 1 teaspoon black peppercorns
- 6 tablespoons distilled white vinegar

Put turkey breast in a deep 8- to 10-quart pot and add enough cold water to cover by 1 inch, then remove turkey. Add onion, carrots, bay leaves, salt, peppercorns, and vinegar to pot and bring to a boil. Carefully lower turkey breast into pot, reduce heat to a bare simmer, and poach turkey, covered, for 1¼ hours.

Remove from heat and let turkey cool in liquid, uncovered, for 30 minutes.

Drain turkey and discard solids. Let cool slightly, then remove meat from bones in 2 large pieces, discarding skin and bones.

COOK'S NOTE

- The turkey can be poached and the meat removed from the bones up to 1 day ahead. Refrigerate, covered.

Parmesan-Coated Turkey Cutlets

SERVES 4

ACTIVE TIME: 20 MINUTES ■ START TO FINISH: 20 MINUTES

■ A flourless Parmesan batter makes a lighter, thinner coating than bread crumbs and adds flavor to these cutlets. ■

- 1¼ pounds turkey breast cutlets, rinsed, patted dry, and halved crosswise if large
- 2 large eggs
- 1 tablespoon water
- ¼ teaspoon salt
- ¼ teaspoon freshly ground black pepper
- ¾ cup finely grated Parmigiano-Reggiano
- 2 tablespoons chopped fresh flat-leaf parsley or basil
- 2 tablespoons unsalted butter
- 2 tablespoons olive oil

ACCOMPANIMENT: lemon wedges

With a flat meat pounder or a rolling pin, gently pound turkey cutlets between sheets of plastic wrap until ¼ inch thick.

Whisk together eggs, water, salt, pepper, cheese, and parsley in a shallow bowl (batter will be thick).

Heat 1 tablespoon butter and 1 tablespoon oil in a 12-inch nonstick skillet over moderately high heat until foam subsides. Working quickly, dip 1 cutlet in batter, let excess drip off, and add to skillet. Repeat with about 3 more cutlets (do not crowd) and cook, turning once, until golden and just cooked through, about 4 minutes total. Transfer to a platter and keep warm, loosely covered with foil. Repeat with remaining butter, oil, and cutlets.

Serve turkey with lemon wedges.

Turkey Meat Loaf

SERVES 6

ACTIVE TIME: 45 MINUTES ■ START TO FINISH: 1¾ HOURS

■ You won't miss the beef in this meat loaf. It's important to use a mix of light and dark turkey here. Packages aren't usually labeled as such in the supermarket, but avoid those that say "all white meat." The dark meat adds moistness and flavor, and the mushrooms reinforce both qualities. If you are looking at this as a low-fat alternative to conventional meat loaf, you can use one-percent milk. ■

- 1 teaspoon olive oil
- 1½ cups finely chopped onion (1 large)
- 1 tablespoon minced garlic
- 1 medium carrot, cut into ⅛-inch-dice
- ¾ pound cremini mushrooms, trimmed and very finely chopped in a food processor
- 1 teaspoon salt
- ½ teaspoon freshly ground black pepper
- 1½ teaspoons Worcestershire sauce
- ⅓ cup finely chopped fresh flat-leaf parsley
- 5 tablespoons ketchup
- 1 cup fine fresh bread crumbs
- ⅓ cup whole milk
- 1 large egg, lightly beaten
- 1 large egg white, lightly beaten
- 1¼ pounds ground turkey (mix of dark and light meat)

ACCOMPANIMENT: Roasted Red Pepper–Tomato Sauce (recipe follows) or ketchup

SPECIAL EQUIPMENT: an instant-read thermometer

Put a rack in middle of oven and preheat oven to 400°F. Lightly oil a 13-by-9-inch baking pan.

Heat oil in a 12-inch nonstick skillet over moderate heat. Add onion and garlic and cook, stirring, until onion is softened, about 2 minutes. Add carrot and cook, stirring, until softened, about 3 minutes. Add mushrooms, 1/2 teaspoon salt, and 1/4 teaspoon pepper and cook, stirring occasionally, until liquid mushrooms give off has evaporated and mushrooms are very tender, 10 to 15 minutes.

Stir in Worcestershire sauce, parsley, and 3 tablespoons ketchup, then transfer vegetables to a large bowl and let cool.

Stir together bread crumbs and milk in a small bowl and let stand for 5 minutes. Stir in egg and egg white, then add to vegetables, along with turkey, remaining 1/2 teaspoon salt, and remaining 1/4 teaspoon pepper, and mix well with your hands (mixture will be very moist).

Form into a 9-by-5-inch oval loaf in oiled baking pan. Brush meat loaf evenly with remaining 2 tablespoons ketchup. Bake until thermometer inserted in center registers 170°F, 50 to 55 minutes.

Let meat loaf stand for 5 minutes before serving, with sauce or ketchup.

Roasted Red Pepper–Tomato Sauce

MAKES ABOUT 3/4 CUP
ACTIVE TIME: 10 MINUTES ■ START TO FINISH: 1 1/2 HOURS

■ With the roasted sweetness of red pepper, this sauce is great with turkey meat loaf, but it's also delicious on just about anything—grilled chicken or steak, fish, even burgers. ■

- 1 small head garlic (2 inches in diameter)
- 1/2 pound plum tomatoes, halved lengthwise
- Salt
- 1 large red bell pepper
- 1 teaspoon olive oil
- 1 1/2 teaspoons fresh lemon juice
- 1/2 teaspoon balsamic vinegar, or to taste
- Freshly ground black pepper

Put a rack in middle of oven and preheat oven to 375°F.

Cut off and discard top quarter of garlic head. Wrap garlic in foil. Arrange tomatoes cut sides up in a foil-lined 13-by-9-inch baking pan and season lightly with salt. Add bell pepper and garlic (in foil) to pan and roast for 1 hour, turning occasionally.

Transfer bell pepper to a small bowl, cover bowl with plastic wrap, and let stand for 20 minutes.

When it is cool enough to handle, peel pepper and discard stem and seeds. Transfer to a food processor or blender and add tomatoes. Unwrap garlic and squeeze roasted cloves into food processor; discard skins. Add oil, lemon juice, vinegar, and salt and pepper to taste and purée sauce until smooth.

COOK'S NOTE

■ The sauce can be made up to 1 day ahead and refrigerated, covered.

Turkey Chipotle Chili

SERVES 6 TO 8 (MAKES ABOUT 14 CUPS)
ACTIVE TIME: 30 MINUTES ■ START TO FINISH: 2 HOURS

■ This chili, flavored with the lovely, smoky heat of chipotle chiles, is a staff favorite. It doesn't produce the familiar-looking beefy red chili (it's more green than red), and it's not as heavy, but trust us, it's just as satisfying. ■

- 2 canned chipotle chiles in adobo (see Glossary), or 2 dried chipotle chiles, stemmed and seeded
- 1 cup water (boiling if using dried chiles)
- 2 pounds fresh tomatillos, husked and rinsed well, or 3 (18-ounce) cans whole tomatillos (see Glossary), drained
- 3 tablespoons vegetable oil
- 2 large onions, chopped
- 4 tablespoons minced garlic
- 2 tablespoons ground cumin
- 4 pounds ground turkey (not lean)
- 2 cups chicken stock or store-bought low-sodium broth
- 1 Turkish bay leaf or 1/2 California bay leaf
- 1 1/2 teaspoons dried oregano, crumbled
- 2 teaspoons salt, or to taste
- 1 green bell pepper, cored, seeded, and chopped

2 (4-ounce) cans mild green chiles, drained and chopped
1 tablespoon cornmeal
1 (19-ounce) can white beans, rinsed and drained
½ cup chopped fresh cilantro
GARNISH: chopped fresh cilantro
ACCOMPANIMENT: sour cream

If using canned chipotle chiles, purée them with 1 cup water in a blender and transfer to a bowl. If using dried chiles, soak in boiling water in a small bowl for 20 minutes, then purée with water in blender and transfer to a bowl.

If using fresh tomatillos, blanch them in a large saucepan of boiling water for 5 minutes; drain. Purée fresh or canned tomatillos in blender.

Heat oil in an 8- to 10-quart heavy pot over moderate heat. Add onions and 2 tablespoons garlic and cook, stirring, until onions are softened, about 10 minutes. Add cumin and cook, stirring, for 30 seconds. Add turkey and cook, stirring and breaking up lumps, until no longer pink, about 8 minutes.

Add chipotle purée, tomatillo purée, stock, bay leaf, oregano, and salt and simmer, uncovered, adding more water if necessary to keep turkey barely covered, for 1 hour.

Add bell pepper, green chiles, and cornmeal and simmer, stirring occasionally, for 30 minutes.

Stir in white beans, remaining 2 tablespoons garlic, and salt to taste and simmer until beans are heated through, 3 to 5 minutes. Discard bay leaf and stir in cilantro.

Garnish chili with cilantro and serve with sour cream.

COOK'S NOTE

- The chili, without the cilantro, can be made up to 3 days ahead. Cool, uncovered, then refrigerate, covered. Reheat, and stir in cilantro just before serving.

Bacon-Wrapped Cornish Hens with Raspberry Balsamic Glaze

SERVES 8
ACTIVE TIME: 25 MINUTES ■ START TO FINISH: 1 HOUR

■ This is an elegant but easy party dish to add to your culinary repertoire. A playful balance goes on: the balsamic vinegar is tart, but with an underlying sweetness, while the raspberry jam is sweet, but with an underlying tartness. And the bacon takes it all home. ■

⅔ cup seedless raspberry jam
½ cup balsamic vinegar
16 bacon slices (about 1 pound)
4 (1½- to 1¾-pound) Cornish hens, rinsed and patted dry
Salt and freshly ground black pepper

Combine jam and vinegar in a small saucepan and simmer briskly, uncovered, stirring occasionally, until reduced to about ½ cup, about 8 minutes. Let cool to room temperature; glaze will thicken slightly as it cools.

Put a rack in middle of oven and preheat oven to 450°F.

Cook bacon in batches in a large heavy skillet over moderate heat, turning occasionally, until it has rendered some of its fat but is still translucent and pliable, 5 to 7 minutes per batch. Transfer to paper towels to drain.

With kitchen shears, cut out and discard backbone from each hen, then halve each hen lengthwise. Season hens with salt and pepper. Arrange skin sides up in a large roasting pan. Brush hens liberally with some glaze and wrap 2 slices of bacon around each half, tucking ends under.

Roast, brushing with pan juices and glaze after 10 minutes and then again after 20, until juices run clear when thigh is pierced, 30 to 35 minutes total. Discard any unused glaze.

Assorted Fowl

CAPON: Capons are young male chickens that have been neutered. Because they lack certain hormones, their muscles stay soft as they grow and are marbled with fat, like those of a steer (which is also a young neutered male). Their breast meat is very white and tender. They are fed a rich diet of grain and milk and slaughtered when they are four months old, when they weigh eight to ten pounds. Capons are traditionally served at Christmas in France and Italy. In the United States, they are often served at Easter.

CHICKEN: Descendants of wild jungle fowl in India and Southeast Asia, chickens were domesticated as early as the second millennium B.C. A standard supermarket broiler (sometimes labeled "broiler/fryer") usually weighs three to four pounds or more. Most supermarkets carry an array of choices that reflect how the chickens are raised—*kosher, free-range,* and *certified organic* are just a few of the terms used. All of these cost more than mass-market chickens but usually offer a big payoff in flavor and texture.

CORNISH HEN: These miniature "game" birds are actually a cross between the White Plymouth Rock and Cornish breeds, two big, meaty chickens that form the basic gene pool for most of the broilers you see in the supermarket. What sets them apart from ordinary chickens is that they are slaughtered at four to five weeks, when they weigh between one and two pounds.

DUCK: The whole ducks sold frozen in supermarkets are Pekin (also known as Long Island) ducks, not to be confused with "Peking," a Chinese style of cooking them. Originally from China and once a specialty of Long Island, New York, the birds are now raised on farms throughout the country. These commercially marketed ducks generally weigh four and a half to five pounds, but because they are heavier-boned than chickens and have more fat (which is rendered during cooking), you won't get as much meat as you think you might. The duck bred for foie gras is the Moulard, the sterile offspring of a female Pekin and a male Muscovy (also known as Barbary). *Magrets* are the breasts of either Moulard or Muscovy ducks; they are available from specialty butchers and by mail (see Sources). Large, meaty, and dark, they should be cooked like red meat.

GOOSE: In Europe, goose is often the holiday bird of choice. The meat is rich, juicy, dark, and deep-flavored. The rendered fat can be used to cook what are arguably the best potatoes you've ever had. We generally call for geese in the twelve-pound range, since they can be cooked more successfully than larger ones.

GUINEA HEN: Guinea hens, originally from West Africa, have been known in Europe since classical times. They are similar to chickens in size. The meat, a little darker than chicken, is leaner and more flavorful, but don't count on getting much off the legs.

PHEASANT: This prized bird, originally from Asia, has been the centerpiece of banquets for centuries. A whole pheasant weighs about two and a half pounds and serves two people. They are very lean, so take care not to overcook them.

POUSSIN: These tender baby chickens, slaughtered at three to four weeks, when they weigh about one pound, are popular with chefs because they neatly serve one person. They are a little harder to find than Cornish hens.

QUAIL: Plump, succulent, tiny quail have dark meat and a deep flavor that belies their size. They are the most forgiving of the game birds to cook.

SQUAB: Squabs (young pigeons), which are not technically game birds because they're harvested before they can fly, have a rich flavor. They taste and look like red meat, which is why they are usually cooked only until medium-rare.

TURKEY: Native to North America, turkeys are now raised around the world. We tend to stick with birds in the twelve- to fourteen-pound range because they can be cooked more successfully than larger ones. The bigger the bird, the greater chance you have of overcooking the breast meat while waiting until the dark meat is done. Fresh, frozen, and kosher are the three mainstream choices facing consumers today, but certified organic, free-range, and heritage breeds (old-fashioned breeds that were once common on American farms) are rising in popularity.

Note: Farm-raised game — duck, quail, and squab, for instance — bears little resemblance to true wild game, which is much leaner. Our recipes were tested with farm-raised birds sold at supermarkets, butcher shops, and by mail (see Sources).

Moroccan-Style Roast Cornish Hens with Vegetables

SERVES 8

ACTIVE TIME: 45 MINUTES ■ START TO FINISH: 2¼ HOURS

■ If you haven't had Moroccan food, this is a great place to start. The Arabs took spices such as cinnamon, cumin, and ginger to Morocco, along with the Persian concept of sweet-and-sour cookery. Cornish hens roast up perfectly (split each one to serve two people) with all those alluring spices and some juicy vegetables right in the same pan. This simple dish is delicious over couscous, a vehicle for the flavorful broth. ■

- 1 teaspoon caraway seeds
- 1½ tablespoons salt
- 4 garlic cloves
- ¼ cup mild honey
- ¼ cup fresh lemon juice
- 2 tablespoons olive oil
- 2 tablespoons paprika
- 4 teaspoons ground cumin
- 2 teaspoons ground ginger
- 1½ teaspoons ground cinnamon
- ½ teaspoon cayenne
- 1 teaspoon freshly ground black pepper
- 4 (1¼- to 1½-pound) Cornish hens, rinsed and patted dry
- 2 large zucchini (1¼ pounds total), halved lengthwise and cut into 1½-inch pieces
- 2 medium turnips (½ pound total), peeled, halved lengthwise, and cut into 1-inch-thick pieces
- 2 red bell peppers, cored, seeded, and cut into 1½-inch pieces
- 1½ pounds butternut squash, peeled, seeded, and cut into 1½-inch chunks
- 2 medium onions, cut into 1-inch-thick wedges
- 1 (28-ounce) can whole tomatoes in juice, drained and chopped
- ½ cup chicken stock or store-bought low-sodium broth

GARNISH: 6 tablespoons chopped mixed fresh flat-leaf parsley, cilantro, and mint

ACCOMPANIMENT: cooked couscous

Put a rack in middle of oven and preheat oven to 425°F. Oil a large roasting pan.

Coarsely grind caraway seeds with salt in an electric coffee/spice grinder, or crush with a rolling pin. Mince garlic, then mash to a paste with caraway mixture, using side of a large heavy knife. Transfer paste to a large bowl and whisk in honey, lemon juice, oil, and spices.

With kitchen shears, cut out and discard backbone from each hen, then halve each hen lengthwise.

Put zucchini, turnips, bell peppers, butternut squash, and onions in oiled roasting pan, add half of spice mixture, and toss until well coated. Add tomatoes and stock and stir well, then spread vegetables out in pan. Add hens to remaining spice mixture and toss to coat, then arrange hens breast sides up over vegetables in pan.

Cover pan tightly with foil and roast for 1 hour.

Uncover and roast until hens are browned and vegetables are tender, 20 to 30 minutes more. Skim fat from cooking liquid. Serve hens and vegetables over couscous, sprinkling herbs on top and spooning some cooking liquid over hens.

Grilled Cornish Hens with Basil Butter

SERVES 4

ACTIVE TIME: 30 MINUTES ■ START TO FINISH: 1 HOUR

■ Getting into the habit of making a simple compound butter like the one here—softened butter blended with basil, garlic, salt, and pepper—could change your life. And learning how to open out and flatten a bird (technically, it's called spatchcocking; see opposite page) maximizes the acreage, so to speak, so the chicken cooks more evenly. It's a technique that will stand you in good stead for years to come. ■

- ¾ stick (6 tablespoons) unsalted butter, softened
- ¼ cup chopped fresh basil
- 3 garlic cloves, minced
- 1 teaspoon salt
- ½ teaspoon freshly ground black pepper
- 2 (1¼- to 1½-pound) Cornish hens, rinsed and patted dry

Stir together butter, basil, garlic, 1/2 teaspoon salt, and 1/4 teaspoon pepper in a small bowl.

Prepare a charcoal or gas grill: If using a charcoal grill, open vents in bottom of grill and in cover. Spread charcoal evenly on one side of grill (about 60 briquettes) and light. Fire is medium-hot when you can hold your hand 5 inches above rack for just 3 to 4 seconds. If using a gas grill, preheat on high, covered, for 10 minutes, then reduce heat to moderate.

Meanwhile, flatten hens (see below). With kitchen shears, cut out backbones. Pat hens dry again, then spread flat, skin side up, on a cutting board. Cut a 1/2-inch slit in each side of each hen in center triangle of skin between thigh and breast (near drumstick). Then tuck bottom knob of drumstick through slit. Tuck wing tips under breasts. Work your fingers between skin and flesh of breasts and legs and loosen skin without detaching it entirely, being careful not to tear it. Spread butter under and over skin. Sprinkle hens with remaining 1/2 teaspoon salt and 1/4 teaspoon pepper.

Lightly oil grill rack and grill hens (covered only if using gas), turning once, until browned, about 10 minutes. Transfer hens to side of charcoal grill with no coals, or, if using gas, move hens to one side and shut off burner below them. Cover with lid and grill until cooked through, 20 to 25 minutes more.

COOK'S NOTE

- The hens can be prepared for cooking and rubbed with butter up to 2 hours ahead; refrigerate, covered.

FLATTENING A BIRD

We first learned about spatchcocking — splitting and flattening a bird so that it is uniformly thick and therefore cooks more quickly and evenly — in one of Richard Olney's cookbooks years ago. (According to Alan Davidson's *Oxford Companion to Food,* it's an old term, probably Irish, and probably derived from the phrase "dispatch cock," meaning "to kill" as well as "to dispose of a task quickly and efficiently.") This useful technique comes in handy for two of our recipes — Grilled Cornish Hens with Basil Butter (above) and Panfried Pressed Poussins (page 402). First you remove the backbone by snipping down each side of it with kitchen shears (save the backbone for stock), working your way around the thigh joint, across the ribs, and out through the shoulder joint (1). Cut little slits in the triangles of skin between breast and thigh and gently push in each drumstick (2); that prevents them from splaying. Finally, tuck the wing tips under so they won't burn (3). For our panfried poussin recipe, based on one from the Republic of Georgia, you weight the birds to flatten them even more. For a crowd, do a couple of chickens this way and rub them with Jerk Marinade (page 933). They cook quickly in a hot oven or on the grill — in about 45 minutes — and stay juicy.

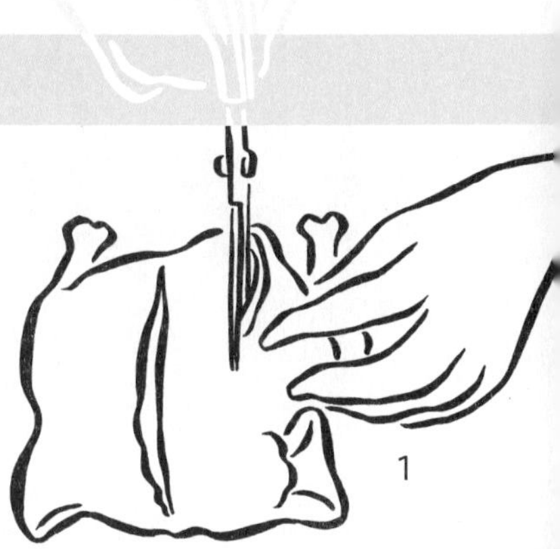
1

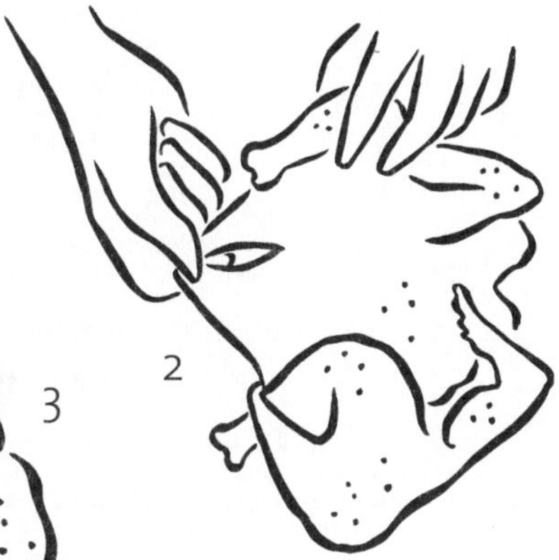
2

3

Fragrant Crispy Duck

SERVES 4

ACTIVE TIME: 1¼ HOURS ■ START TO FINISH: 13¼ HOURS (INCLUDES MARINATING AND AIR-DRYING)

■ Here is a perfect illustration of the Chinese way with duck, in which contrasting textures are as important as flavor. The juicy, succulent meat and crackling skin come from first marinating and steaming the bird, then air-drying and deep-frying it. Although there are quite a few steps, they are all easy, and they transform the duck into a wonder of subtle spiciness. This is a big-deal dish but not for a fancy dinner party; rather, it's a kitchen table feast for you and your three best friends. The recipe is from the late Barbara Tropp, a Chinese cooking authority in the United States, who discovered the dish on a spectacular eating tour of China (for cooking tips, see below). ■

- 1 (4½- to 5½-pound) Pekin (Long Island) duck
- 6 tablespoons Toasted Sichuan Peppercorn Salt (recipe follows)
- 1 tablespoon Chinese five-spice powder
- 2 tablespoons Chinese rice wine or dry sherry
- 6 (⅛-inch-thick) slices fresh ginger, smashed with side of a large heavy knife
- 4 scallions, cut into 2-inch pieces and smashed
- About 3 quarts corn, peanut, or canola oil for frying
- 2 tablespoons dark (black or mushroom) soy sauce (see Sources)
- ⅓ cup all-purpose flour

SPECIAL EQUIPMENT: a 10-inch glass pie plate or shallow heatproof bowl; a 16- to 18-inch wok with a lid and a 9½- to 10-inch round metal rack, or a 14-inch wok and same rack plus a large pot (at least 12 inches wide and 5 inches deep); long oven mitts; a bulb baster; an electric fan; a deep-fat thermometer; 2 large Chinese mesh skimmers or large slotted spoons

Make Room for Duck

Chopstick-tender meat and crackling skin result from first steaming, then deep-frying the duck. The one-two punch is a perfect example of Chinese ingenuity in the kitchen, but this amazing recipe is not to be entered into lightly. It is a serious project, so be prepared. If you have a glass-top range, check with the manufacturer as to whether a special wok ring is required. (We didn't inquire, and our stovetop shattered!) Good exhaust ventilation will keep the rest of your home from reminding you of the duck long after it's consumed. If you want to steam and deep-fry in the same wok, as we did, you'll need a 16- to 18-inch one. The duck can be steamed in a smaller (14-inch) wok, a more commonly available size, but don't try to deep-fry in it; it's not large enough. Instead, choose a wide (12-inch) pot at least 5 inches deep, to prevent the hot oil from bubbling over. And although a Chinese metal or bamboo steamer may be strictly authentic, it isn't necessary; a 9½- to 10-inch round metal cake rack is all you need to support the duck in a pie plate. If you are the proud owner of a Chinese steamer and want to use it, make sure it is at least 13 inches in diameter, and if it's bamboo, make sure the bottom rim rests in the water so it doesn't scorch. If you are wokless, you can improvise a steamer: choose a pot that's at least 1 inch wider than the pie plate to allow the steam to work its magic. Later, plunk down your fried wonder on the table and let everyone go at it with their chopsticks—that's how it's done in China.

MARINATE THE DUCK: Cut off wing tips with poultry shears or a sharp knife. Remove and discard excess fat from body cavity and neck, then rinse inside and out. Pat dry inside and out. Press hard on breastbone to break it and flatten duck slightly.

Heat peppercorn salt and five-spice powder in a small dry skillet over moderate heat, stirring, until hot. Remove from heat. Measure out 3 tablespoons and rub 1 tablespoon in body cavity and 2 tablespoons all over outside of duck, including under wings and legs. Reserve remaining spiced salt for serving with duck.

Put duck in a bowl and marinate, covered and refrigerated, for at least 8 hours.

STEAM THE DUCK: Drain any liquid from cavity and put duck in glass pie plate. Rub rice wine over it. Put one third each of ginger and scallions in cavity and scatter remainder over duck.

Fill wok with water to come 1/2 inch below rack and bring to a rolling boil. Wearing oven mitts, put pie plate with duck on rack and cover wok with lid. Reduce heat to moderate and steam duck for 2 hours, checking every 30 minutes to siphon off fat and juices from around it and from cavity with bulb baster and replenishing boiling water as necessary. Wearing oven mitts, remove pie plate from steamer. Remove and discard all ginger and scallions (including those from cavity). Drain duck and cool in pie plate for 15 minutes.

AIR-DRY THE DUCK: Slide duck onto a rack set over a baking sheet with sides (to catch juices) and pat dry with paper towels. Position duck in front of fan, making sure air blows directly onto it, and air-dry for 2 hours.

FRY THE DUCK: Heat 2 1/2 inches oil in large wok or large pot until it registers 375°F on thermometer. Meanwhile, brush outside of duck with soy sauce, then dust with flour and gently knock off excess. Dip mesh skimmers in hot oil (to keep duck from sticking), then use to lower duck gently into hot oil. Fry duck, spooning hot oil over top, for 2 minutes. Carefully turn it over and fry for 1 minute more. With extreme care, remove duck from oil with mesh skimmers, drain cavity, and transfer to paper towels to drain.

Heat oil to 400°F and fry duck again in same manner until dark brown and crisp, 30 seconds to 1 minute on each side. Again with extreme care, remove it from oil, drain cavity, and transfer to paper towels to drain briefly.

Carve duck and serve with small dishes of reserved spiced salt for dipping.

COOK'S NOTE

- The duck can marinate for up to 24 hours.

Toasted Sichuan Peppercorn Powder or Salt

MAKES ABOUT 1/4 CUP PEPPERCORN POWDER, ABOUT 1/2 CUP PEPPERCORN SALT

ACTIVE TIME: 20 MINUTES ■ START TO FINISH: 20 MINUTES

■ Sichuan peppercorns—the aromatic, tongue-tingling spice from south-central China that seasons Fragrant Crispy Duck—are a staple of Sichuan and Hunan cooking.

Barbara Tropp typically toasted 1/4 cup peppercorns at a time (it's hard to grind much less) and used any extra powder to season rubs, flatbreads, and stir-fries. Once ground, however, this spice quickly loses its pungency. Keep leftover powder or salt in an airtight container away from heat and light, and discard it when it is no longer vibrantly aromatic. ■

1/4 cup Sichuan peppercorns (see Glossary), or
2 tablespoons *sansho* (Japanese pepper) plus
1 1/2–2 teaspoons freshly ground black pepper
1/2 cup kosher salt (if making peppercorn salt)

SPECIAL EQUIPMENT: an electric coffee/spice grinder

FOR PEPPERCORN POWDER: Shake peppercorns in a sieve to get rid of dust, then spread in small batches on a white plate and discard any twigs, leaves, thorns, or black seeds.

Toast peppercorns in a small dry heavy skillet over moderate heat, stirring, until very fragrant and smoking, 3 to 5 minutes; be careful not to let them burn.

While still hot, grind to a powder in coffee/spice grinder, then sift through a fine sieve, discarding hulls.

FOR PEPPERCORN SALT: Follow the procedure for peppercorn powder but toast salt with peppercorns in skillet before grinding.

Duck Breasts with Orange–Ancho Chile Sauce

SERVES 6

ACTIVE TIME: 40 MINUTES ■ START TO FINISH: 1¼ HOURS

■ Body is probably not a characteristic that comes to mind when you're looking at an ancho chile (a dried poblano), but soaked and puréed, it gives richness and roundness to a sauce such as the one here. The heat is present, but it's balanced by the sweetness of the orange juice. What you end up with is a beautiful, deep red, earthy sauce, a New World treatment of an Old World pairing. ■

- 3 dried ancho chiles (1¼ ounces; see Glossary), stemmed and seeded
- 2 cups boiling water
- 1 garlic clove, minced
- ½ cup sugar
- ½ cup fresh orange juice
- ¼ cup fresh lime juice
- 6 (½-pound) Muscovy duck breast halves (also called *magrets;* see Sources), rinsed and patted dry
- 1½ teaspoons salt
- ¼ teaspoon freshly ground black pepper
- 1 tablespoon unsalted butter

SPECIAL EQUIPMENT: an instant-read thermometer

Toast chiles in a small dry heavy skillet over moderate heat until slightly darker, turning once with tongs, about 40 seconds total. Transfer to a small heatproof bowl, add boiling water, and soak until softened, about 20 minutes.

With a slotted spoon, transfer chiles to a blender. Add 1 cup soaking liquid and garlic and blend until smooth.

Cook sugar in a dry 1½-quart heavy saucepan over moderate heat, undisturbed, until it begins to melt. Continue to cook, stirring occasionally with a fork, until sugar has melted to a deep golden caramel, about 8 minutes. Carefully add orange and lime juices (caramel will steam vigorously and harden). Cook over moderately low heat, stirring, until hardened caramel is dissolved, about 5 minutes. Remove from heat.

With a sharp paring knife, score skin, through fat, on each duck breast in a crosshatch pattern, making score marks about 1 inch apart. Pat dry and sprinkle with salt and pepper.

Put 3 breast halves skin side down in a 12-inch heavy skillet and turn heat to moderate. Cook until skin is well browned, about 10 minutes. Pour off and discard rendered fat, turn breasts over with tongs, and cook until meat is browned, about 3 minutes. Transfer to a plate and brown remaining duck in same manner.

Return all breast halves to skillet (set plate aside), cover, and cook over moderate heat until thermometer inserted horizontally into center of a breast registers 135°F for medium-rare, about 6 minutes. Transfer duck to a carving board and let stand, uncovered, while you make sauce. (Duck will continue to cook as it stands.)

Pour off all but 2 tablespoons fat from skillet, add chile purée and any duck juices from plate, and cook over moderately high heat, stirring and scraping up any brown bits, until thickened, about 6 minutes. Add caramel and any juices accumulated on carving board and simmer for 5 minutes more. Whisk in butter until incorporated, then whisk in salt to taste.

Slice duck breasts and serve with sauce.

COOK'S NOTE

■ The USDA recommends cooking duck breasts to an internal temperature of 170°F to ensure that any harmful bacteria are killed, but since we prefer the meat medium-rare, we cook it to only 135°F. To our taste, that yields the perfect degree of doneness.

Glazed Duck with Clementine Sauce

SERVES 8

ACTIVE TIME: 1½ HOURS ■ START TO FINISH: 7½ HOURS (INCLUDES CHILLING)

■ This play on duck *à l'orange* fuses two of the world's most venerable cuisines. We love the Chinese "twice-cooked" method, so we braise the duck first for tender meat, then roast it in a hot oven to crisp the skin. Clementines take the place of oranges in this delightful twist on a French classic.

When using citrus zest or rind, it's best to use unsprayed or certified organic fruit. In any event, wash it with soap and water and rinse thoroughly. ■

- 2 (6- to 7-pound) Pekin (Long Island) ducks, excess fat from body cavity and neck discarded
- 2 tablespoons kosher salt
- 2 onions, quartered
- 1 large celery rib, cut into 4 pieces
- ½ cup plus 2 tablespoons sugar
- 3 pounds clementines
- ½ cup red wine vinegar
- ⅓ cup finely chopped shallots
- 3 tablespoons Mandarin Napoleon liqueur or Cointreau
- 1½ tablespoons arrowroot
- Salt and freshly ground black pepper

BRAISE THE DUCKS: Put a rack in middle of oven and preheat oven to 350°F.

Working from large cavity end, separate duck skin (with fat) from breast meat as much as possible by working your fingers between skin and meat, being careful not to tear skin. Prick skin all over with a fork. Put ducks breast sides up, side by side, in a large deep flameproof roasting pan. Rub each duck inside and out with 1 tablespoon kosher salt. Divide onions and celery between cavities and sprinkle ½ cup sugar around ducks. Pour enough boiling water over ducks (this will help tighten skin) to reach halfway up them; don't fill roasting pan to more than 1 inch from rim. Cover pan tightly with heavy-duty foil, carefully transfer to oven, and braise for 1 hour.

Remove pan from oven and remove foil (do not discard). Carefully turn ducks over, using one large wooden spoon to turn each duck and another inside cavity to hold it. Cover with foil again, carefully return to oven, and braise until meat is very tender but not falling off the bone, about 1 hour more.

CHILL THE DUCKS: Remove pan from oven and, with wooden spoons, transfer ducks to two large plates. Drain any juices inside ducks back into pan, then transfer cooking liquid to a large bowl. Return ducks to roasting pan, breast sides up. Cool ducks and cooking liquid (separately), uncovered. Refrigerate, uncovered, for at least 4 hours to firm up duck before roasting and to solidify fat on cooking liquid.

PREPARE THE GLAZE AND START THE SAUCE: Remove all fat from chilled cooking liquid and discard. Set liquid aside.

Remove zest from 2 large or 4 small clementines with a vegetable peeler. Trim any white pith from zest with a sharp paring knife and cut zest into very fine strips. Blanch strips in a small saucepan of boiling water for 5 minutes; drain. Squeeze enough juice from remaining clementines to measure 2 cups. Pour through a fine-mesh sieve into a 3-quart heavy saucepan. Add vinegar and remaining 2 tablespoons sugar, bring to a boil, and boil until reduced to about ⅓ cup (glaze will bubble up and darken), about 15 minutes. Transfer 1 tablespoon glaze to a cup and reserve for brushing on ducks. Stir zest strips and 1 cup cooking liquid into glaze remaining in pan and reserve for sauce. Set remaining cooking liquid aside.

ROAST THE DUCKS AND FINISH THE SAUCE: Put a rack in middle of oven and preheat oven to 500°F.

Roast ducks, uncovered, until skin is crisp, 25 to 35 minutes. Brush reserved 1 tablespoon glaze over ducks, then transfer ducks to a platter and let stand while you finish sauce.

Pour off all but 1 tablespoon fat from roasting pan. Set pan over two burners. Add shallots and cook over moderately low heat, stirring, until softened and pale golden, 3 to 5 minutes. Add 2 cups reserved cooking liquid (discard any remaining liquid) and deglaze pan by boiling, scraping up brown bits, for 2 minutes. Pour through a fine-mesh sieve into glaze and zest mixture and bring to a boil.

Stir together liqueur and arrowroot in a small cup until smooth and whisk into sauce. Simmer, whisking occasionally, until thickened, 3 to 5 minutes. Season with salt and pepper.

Serve ducks, presenting them whole or carved into serving pieces, with sauce.

COOK'S NOTES

- The ducks can be braised and refrigerated up to 1 day ahead.
- The glaze can be made and the sauce started up to 6 hours ahead. Cool separately, uncovered, then refrigerate, covered. Reheat the glaze and stir before using.

Duck Legs and Carrots

SERVES 6

ACTIVE TIME: 40 MINUTES ■ START TO FINISH: 2½ HOURS

■ The beauty of this recipe, adapted from one by Fergus Henderson, at London's St. John restaurant, is that you are braising and roasting at the same time: you add just enough stock to the pan so most of each leg is submerged but the skin is not. The result is unctuous meat with crisp skin on top. And the carrots become infused with lots of flavor. Truly a revelation. ■

- 2 medium leeks (white and pale green parts only), chopped (1½ cups)
- 6 duck legs (6 pounds total; see Sources)
- 1 teaspoon fine sea salt
- ½ teaspoon freshly ground black pepper
- 1 medium white onion, halved lengthwise and thinly sliced lengthwise
- 8 garlic cloves, peeled
- 14 medium carrots, cut into ½-inch-thick slices
- 3 fresh flat-leaf parsley sprigs
- 1 (4-inch) fresh rosemary sprig
- 2 Turkish bay leaves or 1 California bay leaf
- 1 (3- to 4-inch-long) jalapeño chile
- About 6 cups Chicken Stock (page 928)

SPECIAL EQUIPMENT: kitchen string

Put a rack in middle of oven and preheat oven to 400°F.

Wash leeks in a large bowl of cold water; lift out and drain well.

Rinse duck and trim visible fat, reserving it. Chop fat and transfer to a 12-inch heavy skillet. Pat duck legs dry and sprinkle with sea salt and pepper. Cook fat over moderately low heat, stirring, until melted, then pour off all but 1½ tablespoons from skillet (save for another use).

Increase heat to moderately high and heat fat until hot but not smoking. Add 3 duck legs, skin side down, and cook until skin is browned, 4 to 5 minutes. Turn legs over and cook until undersides are browned, about 3 minutes more. Transfer to a plate and brown remaining 3 duck legs in same manner.

Discard all but 2 tablespoons fat from skillet. Add leeks, onion, and garlic and cook, stirring frequently, until softened, 3 to 4 minutes. Add carrots and cook, stirring frequently, for 3 minutes. Season with sea salt and pepper and spread vegetables in a large roasting pan.

Tie parsley, rosemary, and bay leaves into a bundle with kitchen string to make a bouquet garni and add to vegetables, along with jalapeño. Nestle duck legs skin side up in vegetables and add just enough stock to submerge most of each leg but not skin.

Bake, uncovered, until meat is tender and skin is crisp, 1½ to 1¾ hours. Transfer vegetables and duck to a platter. Discard bouquet garni. Skim fat from pan juices and serve juices on the side.

Spiced Roast Goose with Dried Fruit

SERVES 8

ACTIVE TIME: 1 HOUR ■ START TO FINISH: 4 HOURS

■ A savory-sweet combination is a hallmark of classic Scandinavian cuisine. Here goose is paired with roasted dried figs, apricots, and prunes. The dried fruits absorb some of the juices from the goose, making them succulent little nuggets. The crisp skin is seasoned with spicy peppercorns and mellow allspice, providing a perfect counterpoint to the moist, rich meat. A traditional accompaniment is potatoes roasted in fat rendered from the bird. ■

- ½ pound (1⅓ cups) dried figs, preferably Calimyrna, stems discarded
- ½ pound (1¼ cups) dried apricots
- ½ pound (1¼ cups) pitted prunes
- 1 tablespoon allspice berries
- 1 tablespoon mixed peppercorns (black, white, green, and pink)
- ½ stick (4 tablespoons) unsalted butter, melted
- 1 (12-pound) goose, rinsed, patted dry, and wing tips removed
- Salt
- 2 medium onions, quartered
- ⅓ cup finely chopped shallots
- ⅔ cup Armagnac
- 2 cups veal demi-glace (see Sources)
- 2 tablespoons apricot jam or preserves

SPECIAL EQUIPMENT: five 8-inch metal or wooden skewers; pliers (if necessary); kitchen string; an adjustable V-rack; a large flameproof roasting pan at least 2 inches deep (not nonstick); a metal (not plastic) bulb baster; an instant-read thermometer

PREPARE THE DRIED FRUIT: Combine figs, apricots, and prunes in a 3-quart saucepan, add water to cover, and bring to a simmer. Simmer, covered, for 20 minutes; drain. Reserve 2 cups fruit and thread remainder onto 4 skewers.

PREPARE THE GOOSE: Put a rack in middle of oven and preheat oven to 425°F.

Crack allspice and peppercorns in a mortar with a pestle (or spread spices on a kitchen towel and crack with bottom of a heavy skillet). Stir spices into melted butter.

Discard neck and giblets and remove any loose fat from goose. Using pliers, pull out any remaining quills. Prick skin all over (especially thighs and breast) with remaining skewer, holding skewer nearly parallel to skin to avoid puncturing meat. Fold neck skin under body and fasten with skewer. Season goose well inside and out with salt. Put onions and reserved 2 cups fruit in cavity and tie legs together loosely with string. Rub skin all over with spiced butter.

ROAST THE GOOSE: Put goose on V-rack in roasting pan and roast for 30 minutes.

Reduce oven temperature to 325°F and continue to roast, basting goose with pan juices and removing excess fat (reserve fat for another use, if desired) with bulb baster every 30 minutes, for 1 hour more.

Arrange skewers of fruit on rack around goose (if rack is too small to hold all skewers, tuck some into wings). Continue to roast goose, basting and removing fat in same manner, until thermometer inserted into fleshy part of a thigh (without touching bone) registers 170°F and several fruits from bottom of cavity, speared on thermometer, register 160°–165°F, about 1 hour more (2½ hours total; juices will be slightly pink when thigh is pierced, and temperature will rise to 175°F as goose stands).

Remove fruit from skewers and transfer to a bowl. Keep warm, covered. With two large spatulas, transfer goose to a cutting board and let stand, loosely covered with foil, for 30 minutes.

WHILE THE GOOSE STANDS, MAKE THE PAN SAUCE: Pour off fat from roasting pan. Set pan over two burners, add shallots, and cook over moderately high heat, stirring, until golden, about 3 minutes. Add Armagnac and deglaze pan by boiling over moderately high heat, stirring and scraping up brown bits, for 1 minute. Add demi-glace and jam and simmer briskly, whisking, until jam is incorporated and sauce is slightly thickened, about 3 minutes. Pour sauce through sieve, if desired, and keep warm, covered.

Remove onions from cavity of goose and discard; add fruit to other fruit in bowl and cover again.

Carve goose, cutting breast into ¼-inch-thick slices. Serve fruit and sauce on the side.

Roast Capon with Chile Cilantro Rub and Roasted Carrots

SERVES 6

ACTIVE TIME: 45 MINUTES ■ START TO FINISH: 3½ HOURS

■ The meat of capons has a finer texture than that of chickens and turkeys. An eight- or nine-pound bird isn't much bigger than a typical supermarket roaster, but it's somewhat meatier. Capons are available fresh or frozen at most supermarkets or your local butcher shop, but you can substitute a large roasting chicken here if necessary. This recipe is from Deborah Madison, the chef and cookbook author. ■

- 1 (8-pound) capon, rinsed and patted dry
- Kosher salt
- 4 large garlic cloves, coarsely chopped
- ½ cup finely chopped fresh cilantro
- 1 tablespoon pure mild red chile powder, such as ground ancho
- 2 teaspoons ground cumin
- 3 tablespoons unsalted butter, softened
- 2 pounds medium carrots, halved lengthwise and cut crosswise into thirds
- Freshly ground black pepper
- ½ cup water

ACCOMPANIMENT: Red Chile Sauce (recipe follows)

SPECIAL EQUIPMENT: kitchen string; an instant-read thermometer

Snip away any excess fat from cavity of capon using kitchen shears. Season inside and out with salt. Let stand at room temperature for 30 minutes.

Put a rack in middle of oven and preheat oven to 375°F. Butter a roasting pan.

Mash garlic to a paste with 2 teaspoons kosher salt in a mortar with a pestle (or mince and mash with a large heavy knife). Add cilantro, chile powder, cumin, and butter and mash to a paste.

Turn capon breast side up, so neck is toward you. Gently work your fingers between skin and flesh of breast, working your way down to thighs and being careful not to tear skin. Push one third of chile butter under skin and massage skin to spread butter evenly over breast. Rub another third of butter in cavity of bird. Tie legs together with kitchen string.

Put capon in buttered roasting pan. Scatter carrots around it, season carrots with salt and pepper, and pour water over them. Roast for 45 minutes.

Remove pan from oven and brush top and sides of bird with remaining chile butter. Roast, basting capon and carrots with pan juices every 20 minutes (tent capon with foil if it gets too brown), until thermometer inserted 2 inches into fleshy part of a thigh (without touching bone) registers 170°F, about 2 hours more.

Transfer carrots, with some of pan juices, to a serving dish and keep warm, covered. Let capon stand for 20 minutes before carving. Serve with chile sauce.

Red Chile Sauce

Chile Colorado

MAKES ABOUT 2½ CUPS
ACTIVE TIME: 1 HOUR ■ START TO FINISH: 1 HOUR

■ The word *colorado* means that this sauce is red. It uses one of our all-time favorite sources of pizzazz, dried New Mexico chiles. They're joined by guajillos ("gwa-*hee*-yos"), one of the most commonly used dried chiles in Mexico and a source of deep heat and sweetness. Deborah Madison partners this sauce with roast capon, but it is also wonderful with grilled meats and vegetables. ■

- 2 ounces (about 6) dried New Mexico chiles (see Glossary)
- 1 ounce (about 6) dried guajillo chiles (see Glossary)
- 4 cups boiling water
- 2 tablespoons vegetable oil
- 3 tablespoons finely chopped white onion
- 3 garlic cloves, minced
- 1½ teaspoons ground cumin
- ¾ teaspoon dried oregano, crumbled
- 1 tablespoon all-purpose flour
- 1 tablespoon kosher salt, or to taste
- 2 teaspoons sherry vinegar, or to taste
- 1 teaspoon sugar, or to taste

Rinse chiles and split open; discard stems, seeds, and ribs.

Heat a medium well-seasoned cast-iron skillet over moderate heat until hot. Toast chiles skin sides up, in batches, until slightly darker, about 30 seconds per batch (be careful not to burn them, or sauce will be bitter). Transfer chiles to a heatproof bowl and pour boiling water over them. Cover bowl and let them soak, stirring occasionally, until softened, about 15 minutes.

Transfer chiles to a blender and add three quarters of soaking liquid (reserve remainder). Purée until smooth (use caution). Pour purée through a medium-mesh sieve into a bowl, pressing on solids; discard solids. Whisk in reserved soaking liquid.

Heat oil in a large heavy saucepan over moderately low heat. Add onion, garlic, cumin, and oregano and cook, stirring, for 2 minutes. Add flour and cook, stirring, for 2 minutes. Whisk in chile purée, partially cover, and simmer, whisking occasionally, until reduced to about 2½ cups, about 30 minutes. Stir in salt, vinegar, and sugar.

COOK'S NOTE

■ The sauce can be made up to 1 week ahead. Cool completely, uncovered, then refrigerate, covered.

Roasted Poussins with Cumin and Lemon

SERVES 2
ACTIVE TIME: 20 MINUTES ■ START TO FINISH: 1 HOUR

■ Poussins, or baby chickens, are a little harder to find than Cornish hens (look for them at butcher shops and high-end supermarkets, or see Sources), but they are worth the effort. We rub a seasoned butter under the skin to flavor the chicken from the inside out and keep the meat moist. We use a vaguely Latino combination of cilantro, lemon zest, and cumin, but you can try any of the compound butters on pages 894–95. ■

- 3 tablespoons unsalted butter, softened
- 3 tablespoons chopped fresh cilantro
- 1/2 teaspoon finely grated lemon zest
- 1/4 teaspoon ground cumin
- 1/4 teaspoon salt
- 1/8 teaspoon freshly ground black pepper
- 2 (1-pound) poussins or 2 (1 1/4-pound) Cornish hens, rinsed and patted dry
- 1 tablespoon unsalted butter, melted
- 1/3 cup dry white wine

SPECIAL EQUIPMENT: kitchen string; small metal skewers or wooden picks; an instant-read thermometer

Put a rack in upper third of oven and preheat oven to 425°F.

Stir together softened butter, cilantro, zest, cumin, salt, and pepper in a small bowl.

If necessary, trim necks of poussins flush with bodies. Working from cavity end of each bird, work your fingers between skin and flesh of breasts and legs to loosen skin, being careful not to tear it. Using a teaspoon, push butter under skin and massage skin to spread butter evenly over breasts and legs. Tie legs of each bird together with kitchen string and secure wings to sides with skewers.

Arrange birds in a roasting pan just large enough to hold them. Brush melted butter onto birds. Season with salt. Roast until thermometer inserted in meatiest part of an inner thigh (without touching bone) registers 170°F, about 45 minutes. Transfer birds to a platter and remove string and skewers. Cover loosely with foil to keep warm.

Add wine to roasting pan and deglaze by boiling over moderately high heat, stirring and scraping up brown bits, for 1 minute. Remove from heat and skim fat from sauce, if desired.

Serve birds with sauce.

Grilled Lemon Herb Poussins

SERVES 6

ACTIVE TIME: 30 MINUTES ■ START TO FINISH: 1 1/2 HOURS

■ Whole poussins, which weigh about one pound each, cook perfectly on the grill. Garnish these with whatever garden herbs you have and serve with summer vegetables. ■

- 3/4 stick (6 tablespoons) unsalted butter, softened
- 1 tablespoon finely grated lemon zest
- 2 teaspoons chopped fresh thyme, plus 6 large sprigs
- 1 teaspoon chopped fresh rosemary
- 1/2 teaspoon salt
- 1/2 teaspoon freshly ground black pepper
- 6 (3/4- to 1-pound) poussins (see Sources) or Cornish hens, rinsed and patted dry
- 2 lemons, each cut into 6 wedges
- 2 tablespoons unsalted butter, melted

SPECIAL EQUIPMENT: kitchen string; small metal skewers or wooden picks; an instant-read thermometer

Prepare a charcoal or gas grill: If using a charcoal grill, open vents in bottom of grill and in lid, then light charcoal. Fire is medium-hot when you can hold your hand 5 inches above rack for just 3 to 4 seconds. If using a gas grill, preheat on high, covered, for 10 minutes, then reduce heat to moderate.

Meanwhile, stir together softened butter, zest, chopped thyme, rosemary, salt, and pepper in a small bowl.

Season cavities of poussins with salt and pepper. Working from cavity end of each bird, work your fingers between skin and flesh of breasts and legs to loosen skin, being careful not to tear it. Push lemon butter under skin and massage skin to spread butter evenly over breasts and legs. Insert a thyme sprig and 2 lemon wedges into cavity of each poussin, then tie legs together with kitchen string and secure wings to sides with skewers. Brush birds with melted butter and season with salt and pepper.

Lightly oil grill rack. Place poussins breast sides up on grill, cover with lid, and grill, turning every 15 minutes, until thermometer inserted in fleshy part of a thigh (without touching bone) registers 170°F, 45 to 55 minutes.

Transfer birds to a platter and remove string and skewers. Let stand for 10 minutes.

COOK'S NOTE

- The poussins can also be roasted in a 450°F oven. Use a shallow baking pan large enough to hold them without crowding and roast in the upper third of the oven for 30 to 40 minutes.

Panfried Pressed Poussins

SERVES 4
ACTIVE TIME: 15 MINUTES ■ START TO FINISH: 50 MINUTES

■ The Republic of Georgia is at the crossroads of East and West; here, Jason sought the Golden Fleece and discovered the sorceress Medea instead. We discovered a terrific dish called *tabaka:* small chickens are flattened and then weighted while they are in the skillet so they cook evenly and quickly. They stay incredibly juicy too. We call for poussins or Cornish hens, but the same technique works well with a frying chicken. (See page 393 for more about how to flatten a bird for panfrying or grilling.) ■

2 (1¼-pound) poussins (see Sources) or Cornish hens, rinsed and patted dry
1 teaspoon fine sea salt
½ teaspoon freshly ground black pepper
3 tablespoons unsalted butter
¾ cup chicken stock or store-bought low-sodium broth
SPECIAL EQUIPMENT: two 10-inch heavy skillets (one preferably well-seasoned cast-iron or nonstick); parchment paper; 5–6 pounds of weights, such as three 28-ounce cans of tomatoes

With kitchen shears, cut out and discard backbones from birds. Pat birds dry again, then spread flat, skin sides up, on a cutting board. Cut a ½-inch slit in each side of each bird in center of triangle of skin between thighs and breasts (near drumstick), then tuck bottom knob of drumstick through slit. Tuck wing tips under breasts. Sprinkle birds on both sides with sea salt and pepper.

Heat butter in cast-iron or heavy nonstick skillet over moderate heat until foam subsides. Add birds skin sides down and cover with a 10-inch parchment round and second skillet. Top with weights and cook birds until skin is browned, about 15 minutes. Turn birds over, cover with parchment round, skillet, and weights again, and cook until just cooked through, 10 to 15 minutes more. Transfer birds to a platter and cover loosely with foil.

Add stock to skillet and deglaze by boiling over high heat, stirring and scraping up brown bits, for 1 minute, then boil until reduced to about ½ cup, about 5 minutes. Skim fat from surface.

Cut birds lengthwise in half and serve drizzled with pan juices.

Spice-Rubbed Quail

SERVES 4
ACTIVE TIME: 20 MINUTES ■ START TO FINISH: 1½ HOURS

■ The molasses in this dish gives depth to the sauce, so that it stands up to the meatiness of the birds. What we've done with the molasses and lime juice, in essence, is make a contemporary version of the classic French *gastrique,* a reduction of refined sugar and red wine vinegar. Quail can be found at most butcher shops and some supermarkets, or see Sources for our favorite mail-order supplier. The term *semiboneless* means that the backbone, rib cage, and thigh bones have been removed by the butcher, leaving just the wing bones and drumsticks intact. ■

1 teaspoon salt
¾ teaspoon freshly ground black pepper
Scant ½ teaspoon cayenne
Scant ½ teaspoon ground allspice
8 (4- to 5-ounce) semiboneless quail, rinsed and patted dry
½ cup chicken stock or store-bought low-sodium broth
¼ cup fresh lime juice
3 tablespoons mild molasses

2 tablespoons finely chopped scallions
1 tablespoon unsalted butter
3 tablespoons olive oil

Stir together salt, black pepper, cayenne, and allspice and rub all over quail. Arrange quail in one layer in a baking pan. Cover and refrigerate for at least 1 hour.

Combine stock, lime juice, molasses, and scallions in a small heavy saucepan, bring to a simmer, and simmer, uncovered, stirring occasionally, until slightly thickened, 8 to 10 minutes. Remove from heat and whisk in butter until incorporated. Season sauce with salt and pepper and keep warm, covered.

Preheat broiler. Lightly oil rack of a broiler pan and heat under broiler until hot. Brush quail with olive oil on both sides, place on hot rack, and broil 2 inches from heat, turning once, until just cooked through, 6 to 10 minutes total.

Serve quail drizzled with sauce.

COOK'S NOTE

- The quail can marinate for up to 1 day.

Panfried Quail with Creamed Corn and Bacon

SERVES 4

ACTIVE TIME: 1½ HOURS ■ START TO FINISH: 1½ HOURS

■ The mild yet rich flavor of quail adapts well to all sorts of seasonings. Panfried quail is paired with a transcendental version of that American classic creamed corn in this recipe from the New York City chef David Shack and the cookbook editor and author Judith Sutton. Quail can be found at most butcher shops and some supermarkets, or see Sources. ■

FOR CREAMED CORN

6 ears corn, shucked (see Cook's Note)
6 ounces thick-sliced bacon (4–5 slices), cut crosswise into ⅛-inch-wide strips
1 large bunch scallions
⅔ cup heavy cream
¼ cup water
1 teaspoon fresh lemon juice
1 tablespoon unsalted butter
Salt and freshly ground black pepper

FOR QUAIL

6 whole (6- to 8-ounce) jumbo quail, rinsed and patted dry
1 cup all-purpose flour
1½ tablespoons salt
2 teaspoons freshly ground black pepper
1 teaspoon cayenne (optional)
½ cup whole milk
About 2½ cups corn or canola oil for frying

ACCOMPANIMENT: lemon wedges

MAKE THE CREAMED CORN: Bring a 6- to 8-quart pot of water to a boil. Add corn and simmer for 4 minutes. With tongs, transfer corn to a large bowl of ice and cold water to stop the cooking. When cool enough to handle, drain and cut kernels from cobs.

Cook bacon in a 10-inch heavy skillet over moderate heat, stirring occasionally, until browned, 5 to 8 minutes. Transfer to paper towels to drain.

Thinly slice enough scallions to measure 1 cup.

Combine cream, water, lemon juice, bacon, sliced scallions, and butter in a 3-quart heavy saucepan, bring to a simmer, and simmer, stirring, for 1 minute. Add corn and salt and pepper to taste and cook until liquid is slightly thickened, about 5 minutes. Remove from heat and cover to keep warm.

COOK THE QUAIL: With poultry shears or a sharp knife, cut off necks and first 2 wing joints of each quail and discard. Cut out and discard backbones. Halve each quail lengthwise through breast and cut off legs.

Stir together flour, salt, pepper, and cayenne (if using) in a shallow bowl. Pour milk into another shallow bowl.

Heat ½ inch oil in a 12-inch heavy skillet over moderate heat until hot but not smoking. Meanwhile, working with one piece at a time, dip quail in milk, letting excess drip off, then dredge in flour mixture, shake off excess, and place on a tray. Using tongs, put half of pieces, skin sides down, into hot oil. Fry quail, turning several times, until golden brown and just cooked through, about 6 minutes total. Transfer to paper towels to drain and keep warm, covered. Reheat oil and fry remaining quail in same manner. Reheat corn over low heat if necessary.

Serve quail with creamed corn and lemon wedges.

COOK'S NOTE

- You can use 3 cups frozen corn kernels (from a 1-pound package) in place of the fresh corn. Cook in 1 cup water until tender, about 5 minutes, then drain.

Roasted Guinea Hens with Whole-Grain Mustard and Herbs

SERVES 6

ACTIVE TIME: 1¾ HOURS ■ START TO FINISH: 2½ HOURS

■ This dish is typical of the homey cooking that the New York City chef Daniel Boulud grew up with on a farm near Lyon, the gastronomic capital of France. He adapted this recipe from one of his grandmother's. ■

- 8 garlic cloves, halved lengthwise
- 1 pound fingerling potatoes or small boiling potatoes
- 1 Turkish bay leaf or ½ California bay leaf
- Salt
- ¾ stick (6 tablespoons) unsalted butter, softened
- 2½ tablespoons whole-grain mustard
- 1 tablespoon chopped fresh chives
- Freshly ground black pepper
- 2 (2½-pound) guinea hens (see Sources), rinsed and patted dry
- 4 large fresh thyme sprigs, leaves removed and stems reserved
- 4 fresh tarragon sprigs, leaves removed and stems reserved
- 4 fresh flat-leaf parsley sprigs, leaves removed and stems reserved
- 2 tablespoons extra-virgin olive oil
- 6 medium to large shallots (½ pound)
- ½ cup chicken stock or store-bought low-sodium broth

SPECIAL EQUIPMENT: a 17-by-11-inch flameproof roasting pan; kitchen string; 2 or 4 wooden picks; an instant-read thermometer

COOK THE GARLIC AND POTATOES: Fill a 3-quart saucepan with water and bring to a boil. Add garlic, reduce heat, and simmer for 5 minutes. Remove garlic with a slotted spoon and reserve. Add potatoes to water, along with bay leaf and salt to taste, and simmer, covered, for 10 minutes (potatoes will not be fully cooked). Let potatoes cool in water, uncovered, then drain and peel. Discard bay leaf.

MEANWHILE, MAKE MUSTARD BUTTER AND PREPARE THE HENS: Put roasting pan on middle oven rack and preheat oven to 425°F.

Melt 1 tablespoon butter; set aside. Mash together remaining 5 tablespoons butter, mustard, chives, and salt and pepper to taste. Reserve 1 tablespoon mustard butter for sauce.

Remove excess fat from cavities and necks of hens. Working from cavity end of each bird, work your fingers between skin and flesh of breasts and legs of each hen to loosen skin (outsides of thighs are easier to reach from neck end), being careful not to tear it. Push remaining mustard butter under skin and massage skin to spread butter evenly over breasts and legs. Season hens inside and out with salt and pepper and put half of herb stems in cavity of each bird. Tie legs together with kitchen string and close cavities with wooden picks. Brush melted butter over hens.

ROAST THE HENS: Remove hot roasting pan from oven and add oil, carefully tilting to coat. Put hens in pan, breast sides up, and scatter potatoes and shallots around them. Roast hens, basting every 10 minutes with pan juices and turning vegetables, for 30 minutes.

Scatter garlic and thyme leaves around hens and roast, basting frequently and turning vegetables, until thermometer inserted in thickest part of a thigh (without touching bone) registers 170°F and vegetables are tender, 20 to 30 minutes more.

Remove string and toothpicks from hens and transfer hens to a platter (set pan aside). Surround with vegetables and keep warm, loosely covered, while you make sauce.

MAKE THE SAUCE: Skim fat from pan juices and add stock. Set roasting pan over two burners and deglaze by boiling, stirring and scraping up brown bits, for 1 minute. Then boil until liquid is reduced to about ½ cup. Meanwhile, chop tarragon and parsley leaves.

Pour sauce through a fine-mesh sieve into a sauceboat and stir in reserved mustard butter and salt and pepper to taste.

Scatter chopped herbs over hens and vegetables. Serve with sauce.

COOK'S NOTES

- The garlic and potatoes can be cooked up to 1 day ahead and refrigerated, covered (peel the potatoes before refrigerating).
- The mustard butter can be made up to 1 day ahead and refrigerated, covered. Bring to room temperature before using.

Braised Pheasant with Red Cabbage and Wild Rice

SERVES 2

ACTIVE TIME: 1 HOUR ■ START TO FINISH: 3½ HOURS

■ The fine texture and subtle yet distinct flavor of this luxurious bird is highlighted in this dish. Wild rice makes a great accompaniment for the lean, light meat. Farm-raised pheasant is now widely available. ■

FOR WILD RICE

- ½ cup wild rice
- 1½ cups chicken stock or store-bought low-sodium broth
- 1 tablespoon olive oil
- Salt and freshly ground black pepper
- ¼ pound bacon (4 slices)
- 1 small onion, thinly sliced
- 2 cups thinly sliced red cabbage
- 2 teaspoons red wine vinegar

FOR PHEASANT AND SAUCE

- 1 (2-pound) pheasant (see Sources), rinsed and patted dry
- 1½ cups water
- 1 Turkish bay leaf or ½ California bay leaf
- ½ teaspoon salt
- ¼ teaspoon freshly ground black pepper
- ¼ teaspoon ground allspice
- 1½ tablespoons olive oil
- ⅓ cup golden raisins
- ¼ cup minced shallots
- ¼ cup gin
- ½ cup dry white wine
- 1 teaspoon tomato paste
- 1 (3-inch) fresh rosemary sprig, plus ½ teaspoon minced leaves
- ½ cup halved red and/or green seedless grapes

MAKE THE WILD RICE: Put a rack in middle of oven and preheat oven to 350°F.

Rinse rice well in a fine-mesh sieve and drain. Bring stock to a simmer in a small saucepan.

Heat oil in a 2- to 3-quart heavy ovenproof saucepan over moderately high heat until hot but not smoking. Add rice and cook, stirring to coat, for 1 minute. Stir in hot stock and salt and pepper to taste. Bring to a boil, then cover, transfer pan to oven, and bake until liquid is absorbed and rice is tender, about 1¼ hours. Remove from oven and keep warm. (Leave oven on.)

Meanwhile, cook bacon in a 10-inch skillet over moderate heat until crisp. Transfer to paper towels to drain and cool.

Transfer all but 1 tablespoon fat from skillet to a small bowl and reserve. Heat fat remaining in skillet over moderately high heat until hot but not smoking. Add onion and cabbage and cook, stirring, until softened, about 15 minutes. Add vinegar and salt and pepper to taste and cook, stirring, for 1 minute. Remove from heat and keep warm, covered. Chop bacon.

WHILE RICE IS BAKING, PREPARE THE PHEASANT AND THE SAUCE: With poultry shears or a sharp knife, cut off feet, neck, and wing tips from pheasant and transfer to a small saucepan. Cut out backbone and add to pan. Cut pheasant into 4 serving pieces and set aside. Add water and bay leaf to saucepan, bring to a simmer, and simmer, uncovered, until liquid is reduced to about ¾ cup, about 30 minutes. Pour stock through a fine-mesh sieve into a heatproof bowl.

Stir together salt, pepper, and allspice in a small bowl. Pat pheasant dry again and sprinkle evenly with allspice mixture. Heat oil with 1 tablespoon reserved bacon fat in a 12-inch heavy ovenproof skillet over moderately high heat until hot but not smoking. Add pheasant and sear, turning once, until golden, about 10 minutes total. Transfer to a plate.

Cook raisins and shallots in fat remaining in skillet over moderate heat, stirring, until shallots are softened, about 3 minutes. Stir in gin and boil until almost all of it has evaporated, about 2 minutes. Stir in wine and boil until reduced by about half, about 4 minutes. Stir in stock, tomato paste, rosemary sprig, and salt and pepper to taste and bring sauce to a boil.

Add pheasant, skin side down, to sauce, tightly cover, and braise in oven until breast meat is cooked through and tender, 15 to 20 minutes. Transfer breasts to a clean plate and keep warm, covered. Continue to braise legs and thighs, tightly covered, until cooked through and tender, 15 to 20 minutes more. Transfer to plate and keep warm, covered.

Stir minced rosemary and grapes into sauce and boil over moderately high heat until slightly thickened, about 1 minute.

Just before serving, stir cabbage mixture and bacon into wild rice.

Arrange pheasant on two dinner plates. Spoon sauce over it and serve with wild rice.

Roasted Squab

SERVES 4

ACTIVE TIME: 40 MINUTES ■ START TO FINISH: 1½ HOURS

■ Shallots, thyme, butter, lemon: rich, classic, correct. Squab benefits from being cooked medium-rare; longer cooking accentuates the gaminess of the meat, and it becomes livery in taste. Squab is an exquisite bird to accompany red wine, so splurge on a gorgeous Bordeaux. ■

- 2 sticks (½ pound) unsalted butter, softened
- ¼ cup minced shallots
- 2 tablespoons chopped fresh thyme
- 2 teaspoons finely grated lemon zest
- 1 teaspoon salt
- ½ teaspoon freshly ground black pepper
- 4 (12- to 14-ounce) squabs (see Sources), rinsed and patted dry
- ½ cup olive oil

SPECIAL EQUIPMENT: kitchen string; an instant-read thermometer

Stir together 1 stick butter, shallots, thyme, lemon zest, ½ teaspoon salt, and ¼ teaspoon pepper in a small bowl.

Working from cavity end of each bird, work your fingers between skin and flesh of breasts and legs to loosen skin, being careful not to tear it. Push shallot butter under skin and massage skin to spread butter evenly over breasts and legs. Tie legs together with kitchen string. Sprinkle remaining ½ teaspoon salt and ¼ teaspoon pepper onto squabs.

Put a rack in middle of oven and preheat oven to 450°F.

Heat remaining stick of butter with oil in a 10-inch heavy skillet over moderately high heat until foam subsides. Fry squabs one at a time, turning, until golden brown on all sides. Transfer to a large baking pan.

Roast squabs until thermometer inserted into a breast (without touching bone) registers 140°F, 15 to 20 minutes. Remove from oven and let stand for 5 minutes (temperature will rise to 145°F) before serving.

COOK'S NOTES

- The USDA recommends cooking whole game birds such as squabs to an internal temperature of 180°F to ensure that any harmful bacteria are killed, but since we prefer the meat medium-rare, we cook it to only 140°F. To our taste, that yields the perfect degree of doneness.
- The squabs can be rubbed with butter up to 2 hours ahead and refrigerated, covered.

Squab Salmi

SERVES 6

ACTIVE TIME: 1¼ HOURS ■ START TO FINISH: 3 HOURS

■ The word *salmi* is an abbreviation of *salmagondis*, the name of an old French dish that, according to the eighteenth-century *Dictionnaire de Trévoux*, was essentially a game stew. A *salmi* differs from many poultry recipes in that it is not about the contrast between crisp skin and tender, moist flesh. Instead, partially roasted rich, dark meat cooks further in a splendid sauce. A *salmi* may be unprepossessing to look at, but looks can be deceiving: it is delicious. Here no part of the squab is wasted; the liver is cooked and mashed with Cognac and butter, then spread on warm toasts, and the *salmi* is served on top. ■

4 (14- to 16-ounce) squabs (see Sources), rinsed and patted dry, giblets (including livers) reserved

FOR STOCK

- 2 tablespoons unsalted butter
- ½ carrot, quartered
- ½ celery rib, quartered
- ½ onion, unpeeled
- 6 cups cold water

FOR ROASTED SQUABS AND SAUCE

- 1 teaspoon salt
- ½ teaspoon freshly ground black pepper
- 1 teaspoon chopped fresh thyme
- ¾ stick (6 tablespoons) plus ½ tablespoon unsalted butter
- 1 medium carrot, finely chopped
- 1 celery rib, finely chopped
- 1 small onion, finely chopped
- 2 tablespoons all-purpose flour
- 1 pound small (1-inch) mushrooms, trimmed and halved (4 cups)

FOR TOASTS

- 6 (½-inch-thick) slices brioche
- ½ stick (4 tablespoons) unsalted butter, softened
- ¼ teaspoon Cognac or other brandy
- Salt and freshly ground black pepper

SPECIAL EQUIPMENT: a 3- to 4-inch round cookie cutter

Using kitchen shears, cut off necks and wing tips from squabs and cut into 2-inch pieces. Cut out backbones and cut into 2-inch pieces. Cut 1 squab into 2-inch pieces. Refrigerate remaining 3 squabs, loosely covered, while you make stock.

MAKE THE STOCK: Reserve livers, refrigerated, for toasts. Pat squab pieces and remaining giblets dry. Heat butter in a 6-quart heavy pot over moderately high heat until foam subsides. Add squab pieces and giblets, carrot, celery, and onion and cook, stirring occasionally, until well browned, about 15 minutes.

Add water and bring to a boil, stirring and scraping up browned bits. Reduce heat and simmer, uncovered, until stock is reduced by about half, 1 to 1¼ hours.

Pour stock through a fine-mesh sieve lined with a paper towel into a bowl, pressing on solids; discard solids.

ROAST THE SQUABS AND MAKE THE SAUCE: Bring squabs to room temperature. Put a rack in middle of oven and preheat oven to 425°F.

Pat squabs dry and sprinkle with salt, pepper, and ½ teaspoon thyme. Arrange in a small roasting pan. Melt 2 tablespoons butter and pour over squabs.

Roast squabs for 30 minutes (they will not be fully cooked).

While squabs roast, melt 3 tablespoons butter in a 12-inch heavy skillet over moderate heat. Add carrot, celery, onion, and remaining ½ teaspoon thyme and cook, stirring occasionally, until onion is softened, 5 to 7 minutes. Sprinkle vegetables with flour and cook, stirring, for 2 minutes. Add stock and simmer, stirring frequently, until vegetables are tender and sauce is slightly thickened, 10 to 15 minutes. Remove from heat.

Meanwhile, heat remaining 1½ tablespoons butter in a 10-inch skillet over moderately high heat until foam subsides. Add mushrooms and cook, stirring frequently, until they have released their liquid, 5 to 8 minutes. Continue to cook, stirring occasionally, until liquid has evaporated and mushrooms are browned, about 6 minutes. Remove from heat.

Purée thickened sauce in 2 batches in a blender until smooth (use caution). Transfer to a 3-quart heatproof bowl and add mushrooms.

Halve squabs lengthwise and add to sauce. Set bowl over a 6-quart pot half filled with simmering water (water should not touch bowl) and cook squabs in sauce, uncovered, turning occasionally, until tender, about 25 minutes (flesh will be rosy).

MEANWHILE, MAKE THE TOASTS: Cut rounds from brioche slices with cookie cutter; discard crusts.

Heat 1 tablespoon butter in a small skillet over moderate heat. Add squab livers and cook, turning once or twice, just until browned but still pink inside, about 2 minutes. Transfer livers to a small bowl, add Cognac and 1 tablespoon butter, and mash with a fork until almost smooth. Season with salt and pepper.

Melt remaining 2 tablespoons butter in 12-inch skillet over moderately low heat, add brioche rounds, and toast, turning once, until golden, 3 to 4 minutes. Spread liver purée on toasts.

Serve squabs on warm toasts and spoon sauce over.

COOK'S NOTES

- The stock can be made up to 1 day ahead. Cool, uncovered, then refrigerate, covered.
- The toasts, without the liver, can be made up to 2 hours ahead. Reheat in a 350°F oven for 5 minutes before assembling.

Minced Squab and Pork with Rice Stick Noodles

SERVES 6

ACTIVE TIME: 1 HOUR ■ START TO FINISH: 1 3/4 HOURS

■ Squab is common in Cantonese cooking, and this classic dish, called "squab in jade," in which the meat is minced, stir-fried, and served in cups of lettuce, is an example of the brilliance of Chinese cuisine. The pungency of the ginger, fresh crispness of the lettuce, and crunchiness of the fried noodles blend in a marriage of superb flavors and textures. This recipe is from Nina Simonds, the Chinese cooking authority. Dark-meat chicken can be substituted for the squab if desired. ■

FOR SQUAB AND PORK

- 1/2 ounce (1/4 cup) dried shiitake mushrooms
- 3 tablespoons soy sauce
- 1 tablespoon Chinese rice wine or sake
- 2 1/2 teaspoons Asian sesame oil
- 1 (1 1/4- to 1 1/2-pound) squab (see Sources), rinsed, patted dry, skinned, boned, and meat minced, or 1 cup minced raw chicken thighs
- 1/2 pound boneless pork tenderloin, trimmed and minced
- 1/4 cup water
- 3/4 teaspoon sugar
- 1/2 teaspoon salt
- 1 teaspoon cornstarch
- 1/4 cup peanut oil
- 2 tablespoons minced scallions
- 1 (2-inch) piece fresh ginger, peeled and minced
- 3/4 cup canned whole water chestnuts, rinsed, drained, and minced

FOR NOODLES

- 4 cups peanut oil
- 2 ounces dried rice stick noodles (rice vermicelli)

ACCOMPANIMENT: Boston lettuce leaves

SPECIAL EQUIPMENT: a deep-fat thermometer

PREPARE THE MEAT MIXTURE: Soak mushrooms in 1 cup warm water until softened, about 20 minutes. Lift mushrooms out of soaking liquid and remove and discard stems. Mince caps.

Stir together 1 tablespoon soy sauce, rice wine, and 1 1/2 teaspoons sesame oil in a medium bowl. Stir in squab and pork and marinate for 20 minutes; drain.

MEANWHILE, COOK THE NOODLES: Heat 4 cups peanut oil in a wok or a 4-quart heavy saucepan over moderate heat until it registers 375°F on thermometer. Fry half of noodles (noodles will expand), turning once with a slotted spoon, until pale golden, about 1 minute. With slotted spoon, transfer to paper towels to drain. Cook and drain remaining noodles in same manner. Transfer noodles to a platter.

STIR-FRY THE MEAT MIXTURE: Stir together water, remaining 2 tablespoons soy sauce, remaining 1 teaspoon sesame oil, sugar, salt, and cornstarch in a small bowl until sugar is dissolved.

Heat 1/4 cup peanut oil in cleaned wok or a 12-inch heavy skillet over moderately high heat until hot but not smoking. Add squab mixture and stir-fry until no longer pink, about 3 minutes. Add mushrooms, scallions, and ginger and stir-fry for 1 minute. Add water chestnuts and stir-fry for 30 seconds. Add soy sauce mixture and cook, stirring, until slightly thickened, about 1 minute.

Top noodles with meat and serve with lettuce leaves for wrapping.

Rabbit with Mustard Sauce

SERVES 4

ACTIVE TIME: 1 HOUR ■ START TO FINISH: 1 3/4 HOURS

■ People liken the taste of rabbit, with its smooth white meat, to that of chicken, but it has more flavor and succulence without being at all gamy. As this French bistro classic clearly demonstrates, rabbit and mustard have a definite affinity for each other. We lightened the dish a bit by leaving out the heavy cream and added some complexity by using both Dijon and whole-grain mustard. Rabbit is available at butcher shops and by mail from D'Artagnan (see Sources). ■

- 1 (3-pound) rabbit, cut into 8 serving pieces
- 1/2 teaspoon salt
- 1/2 teaspoon freshly ground black pepper
- 2 tablespoons vegetable oil
- 2 1/2 tablespoons unsalted butter
- 2/3 cup finely chopped shallots
- 1 1/4 cups dry white wine

- $1\frac{3}{4}$ cups chicken stock or store-bought low-sodium broth
- 2 tablespoons Dijon mustard
- 2 tablespoons whole-grain mustard
- 1 teaspoon cornstarch
- 1 tablespoon cold water
- 2 tablespoons chopped fresh flat-leaf parsley

Pat rabbit pieces dry and sprinkle with salt and pepper. Heat oil in a 12-inch heavy skillet over moderate heat until hot but not smoking. Add rabbit in 2 batches and cook, turning occasionally, until well browned on all sides, about 6 minutes per batch. Transfer to a large bowl. Pour off fat from skillet.

Melt 1 tablespoon butter in skillet over moderately low heat, add shallots, and cook, stirring and scraping up brown bits, until softened, about 3 minutes. Add wine, bring to a boil, and boil until reduced by about half, about 6 minutes. Return rabbit to skillet, add stock, and bring to a simmer. Simmer rabbit, covered, until tender, 40 to 45 minutes.

Transfer rabbit to a clean large bowl and boil sauce until reduced to about 2 cups, about 6 minutes. Whisk together $\frac{1}{4}$ cup sauce and mustards in a small bowl, then whisk into sauce in skillet. Stir together cornstarch and cold water in another small bowl until cornstarch is dissolved, then whisk into sauce and simmer, whisking, until thickened, about 3 minutes. Whisk in remaining $1\frac{1}{2}$ tablespoons butter, parsley, and salt and pepper to taste. Return rabbit to skillet, reduce heat to moderately low, and cook, turning rabbit to coat with sauce, until heated through.

BEEF, VEAL, PORK, AND LAMB

"The only thing we want for Christmas this year is a boar's head," began one memorable article that appeared in *Gourmet*'s first year. (If you're interested, the editors wanted that pickled, roasted, and served on a solid gold platter, with the tusks gilded and an apple in its mouth.) Another early article praised the muskrat, "which faintly and pleasantly resembles wild duck." In the ensuing years, we proudly ran recipes for creamed woodchuck, roasted possum, beaver tails, and alligator.

You will probably be relieved to learn that none of those recipes are included in this book. As time progressed, *Gourmet*'s recipes for hunters were replaced with recipes for travelers. Readers went to Italy and came back with tales of a fabulous milk-braised shoulder of pork, and they went to Germany, where they tasted sauerbraten for the very first time. In Morocco tourists discovered the wonders of lamb tagines enriched with prunes, apricots, and exotic spices. They wanted recipes, and we complied. Readers returning from Provence were eager to relive the vacation by cooking leg of lamb glinting with garlic and tomatoes, and people who would not normally dig the marrow out of bones wrote with requests for the spectacular osso buco they had tasted in Milan.

While we were doing all this traveling, something else rather wonderful occurred: in the early eighties, America took a look at itself and fell in love. Suddenly the magazine was filled with regional recipes like Lillie's North Carolina chopped

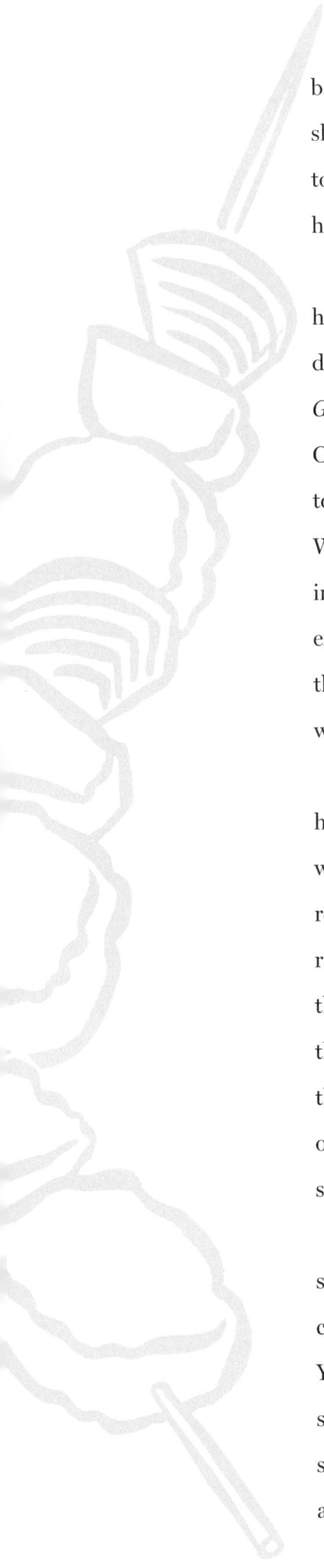

barbecue and deviled beef ribs. The new interest in southwestern flavors brought us skirt steak fajitas, and as our love affair with American food continued, it inspired us to perfect what many people consider our country's greatest culinary inspiration: the hamburger.

Reading through this chapter gives you a fascinating tour of the changes that have taken place in the American kitchen over the past sixty years. The recipes that did not make it into this part of the book tell a similar story. In its early incarnation, *Gourmet* was fat with ways to prepare brains, kidneys, tripe, sweetbreads, and liver. Our growing prosperity changed that; as Americans became richer, we began literally to eat higher on the hog, and the recipes for variety meats slowly began to dwindle. We have printed thousands of recipes for offal over the years, but only a handful are included here. These are the best of a wonderful lot, and if you have never experienced the soft sweetness of Venetian calf's liver with plenty of golden onions or the amazingly tender succulence of tongue served with mustard horseradish sauce, we urge you to give them a try.

The most dramatic change that time has wrought in America's meat-eating history, though, is in the meat itself. When we retested old recipes, we found that we were dealing with entirely new animals; our meat is changing so rapidly that any recipe more than five years old needed to be adjusted. The meat of the lean factory-raised pigs now sold in the supermarket bears very little resemblance to the meat of the fattened pigs of the past; if you can find free-range pork, you will be astounded by the difference in taste. And beef, which is now leaner and significantly less flavorful than it once was, is so different from its predecessor that many of us prefer the flavor of buffalo that have been allowed to roam free. To see if you agree, try the deeply satisfying buffalo prime rib with orange balsamic glaze.

That dish, like many you will find here, was designed as the centerpiece of a special-occasion meal. Other splendidly festive recipes include beef roasted in a salt crust, crown roast of pork with apple stuffing, and hibiscus-marinated leg of lamb. You will also find everyday fare, like a comforting pot-au-feu, a soothing posole, and a sturdy Irish stew. Robust and filling, these are not dishes that could ever be happy on solid gold platters, but on nights when the family is gathered around the table, they are very hard to beat.

Beef

Herbed Rib Roast

SERVES 8

ACTIVE TIME: 30 MINUTES ■ START TO FINISH: 11½ HOURS (INCLUDES MARINATING)

■ For most Americans, a standing rib roast (also known as prime rib) is the ne plus ultra of beef, the cut that you order in a fancy restaurant or serve to guests when you are really putting on the dog. And with good reason: this beautifully marbled piece of meat combines luxurious tenderness with full-bodied flavor. Since it's a roast, it's also very easy to cook. Ask your butcher for the section of ribs near the smaller end of the rib cage. It's closer to the extra-tender loin area, so it will be a little more succulent than the section from the larger end of the rib cage, which is adjacent to the shoulder. ■

FOR ROAST

- 1 (7- to 8-pound) standing rib roast (bone-in rib-eye roast; 3 or 4 ribs), trimmed
- 1 tablespoon black peppercorns

CUTS OF BEEF AND VEAL

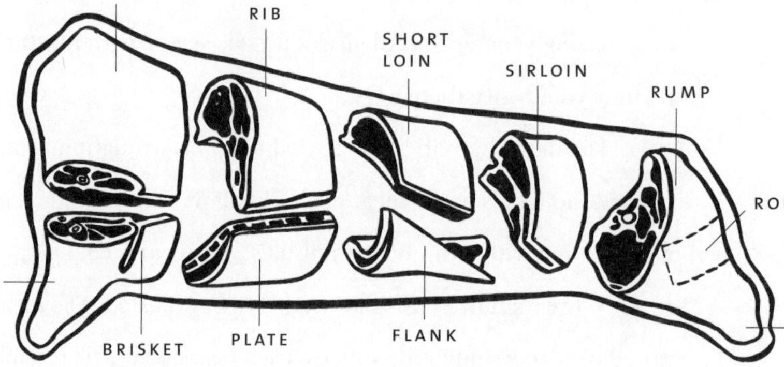

CHUCK
Blade roast
Chuck roast
Chuck steak
Chuck blade steak
Chuck eye roast
Chuck shoulder steak
Short ribs
Top blade steak
Veal shoulder roast

RIB
Rib-eye steak
Standing rib roast
Veal rib chops

SHORT LOIN
Beef tenderloin roast
Top loin steak
Center-cut beef tenderloin
Filet mignon
Porterhouse steak
T-bone steak
Tenderloin steak
Veal loin roast

SIRLOIN
Sirloin steak
Ground sirloin

RUMP
Rump roast
Veal cutlets

ROUND
Eye of round roast
Top round

HINDSHANK
Veal shank

FLANK
Flank steak
Skirt steak

PLATE
Hanger steak
Veal breast

BRISKET
Brisket

2 Turkish bay leaves or 1 California bay leaf
1 tablespoon kosher salt
3 garlic cloves
1 teaspoon chopped fresh thyme
1 teaspoon chopped fresh rosemary
1 tablespoon olive oil

FOR *JUS*

2 cups beef stock or store-bought broth
1 small fresh rosemary sprig
1 small fresh thyme sprig
1 garlic clove, smashed
Salt and freshly ground black pepper

SPECIAL EQUIPMENT: an electric coffee/spice grinder; an instant-read thermometer

PREPARE THE ROAST: Trim all but a thin layer of fat from roast. Combine peppercorns, bay leaves, and salt and grind to a powder in coffee/spice grinder. Transfer to a mortar, add garlic, thyme, and rosemary, and pound to a smooth paste with pestle (or mince and mash on a cutting board with a large heavy knife, then transfer to a small bowl). Stir in oil. Rub paste all over roast. Transfer roast to a rack set in a small roasting pan, cover, and marinate, refrigerated, for at least 8 hours.

COOK THE ROAST: Let roast stand at room temperature for 1 hour. Put a rack in middle of oven and preheat oven to 450°F.

Roast beef for 20 minutes. Reduce oven temperature to 350°F and roast until thermometer inserted 2 inches into center of meat (without touching bone) registers 110°F, 1½ to 1¾ hours more. Transfer beef to a large platter and let stand, loosely covered with foil, for 25 minutes. (It will continue to cook, reaching 130°F for medium-rare.)

WHILE THE BEEF STANDS, MAKE THE *JUS*: Skim fat from pan juices. Add stock, rosemary, thyme, and garlic and deglaze pan on top of stove by boiling over moderately high heat, stirring and scraping up brown bits, for 1 minute. Transfer to a small saucepan, add any juices that have accumulated on platter, and bring just to a simmer. Simmer gently for 10 minutes. Skim fat and season *jus* with salt and pepper.

Carve roast and serve with *jus*.

COOK'S NOTE

- The roast can marinate for up to 24 hours.

Beef Roasted in a Salt Crust

SERVES 8
ACTIVE TIME: 15 MINUTES ■ START TO FINISH: 3 HOURS

■ Roasting meat, poultry, or fish in a salt crust is a time-honored way of keeping it tender and moist. In this ultimately simple recipe, we apply that technique to the aristocrat of beef, a standing rib roast. Surprisingly, the meat is not particularly salty after you remove the crust—but it is very, very tasty. ■

4 cups kosher salt
1 cup water
1 (7- to 8-pound) standing rib roast (bone-in rib-eye roast; 3 or 4 ribs), trimmed

SPECIAL EQUIPMENT: an instant-read thermometer

Put a rack in middle of oven and preheat oven to 325°F.

Stir together salt and water in a bowl until mixture forms a slightly stiff paste.

Put roast fat side up in a roasting pan. Coat completely with salt mixture (it will be about ¼ inch thick).

Roast beef until thermometer inserted 2 inches into center of meat (without touching bone) registers 120°F, 2½ to 3 hours.

Transfer beef to a cutting board and let stand, loosely covered with foil, for 15 minutes. (It will continue to cook, reaching 130°F for medium-rare.) Remove and discard salt crust, then carve roast.

Testing for Doneness

Part of developing the self-confidence it takes to be a good cook is recognizing when something is done. There are lots of variables to juggle, including the kind of heat used (oven or grill, for example), the size of what you are cooking, and the sort of pan you are using. Depending on the meat you are preparing, you can choose among several different methods for testing doneness.

For roasts you'll need a thermometer, and you'll want a good one. We tend to prefer instant-read dial thermometers, because they are more reliable and longer-lasting than other types. They also give a faster reading and can be recalibrated at home (directions are on the package). If you cook roasts often, you might want to try what's usually called a thermometer/timer, which sits outside the oven and is connected to a probe by a long wire. To use it, you push the probe into the roast, put the roast into the oven, and set the thermometer/timer to the internal temperature you want the meat to cook to. When the roast comes to that temperature, the timer goes off. Brilliant. When checking the internal temperature of a roast — everything from prime rib to the Thanksgiving turkey — remember to check in several places: sometimes it's useful to be able to take an average.

More direct methods are in order for testing the doneness of steaks and chops. If you cook lots of meat, you might already be familiar with the "hand method" used by professional chefs. This involves prodding the meat with a finger and comparing certain levels of doneness to the texture of various parts of your hand. The firmer the meat (or poultry or fish) is, the more done it is. A rare steak feels fleshy to the touch, like the area midway between your thumb and index finger; well-done meat is firm to the touch, like the ball of your thumb. We don't usually use the hand method to describe doneness, because it's cumbersome to express in words; we tend to go by timing as well as the "nick and peek" method: make a small slit in the meat and look inside. Don't worry that the juices will run out; the tiny amount you lose is a small price to pay for a perfectly cooked piece of meat. And keep in mind that the meat will continue to cook as it stands (see page 417), so compensate for that as well. If you want a steak medium-rare, say, pull it off the fire when it is still on the rare side.

When assessing the readiness of braised or stewed meat, internal temperature isn't the point. The meat reaches the maximum temperature long before it is done — in this case, meaning that it becomes fork-tender. Testing for doneness is equally easy with small cuts such as short ribs and oxtails. Simply turn a fork on its side and see if you can cut the meat that way. For a larger cut — a veal breast, for instance — slide a kitchen fork in and out of the meat; it should encounter no resistance at all. You will have to slice the meat with a knife for serving, but the slices themselves should be tender enough to cut with a fork.

Deviled Beef Ribs

SERVES 2

ACTIVE TIME: 15 MINUTES ■ START TO FINISH: 15 MINUTES

■ Wait—don't give those leftover bones to your dog. People love them too, particularly when they are coated with mustard, Parmesan cheese, and parsley, then doused in butter. This is a primal, satisfying eating experience for any true carnivore. ■

- 6 tablespoons heavy cream
- 2 tablespoons dry mustard
- 1/4 cup finely grated Parmigiano-Reggiano
- 2/3 cup fine dry bread crumbs
- 2 tablespoons chopped fresh flat-leaf parsley
- 1/2 teaspoon salt
- 1/4 teaspoon freshly ground black pepper
- 4 cooked meaty bones from a standing rib roast, cut apart if still attached
- 1/2 stick (4 tablespoons) unsalted butter, melted

Preheat broiler. Stir together cream, mustard, and Parmesan in a small bowl. Stir together bread crumbs, parsley, salt, and pepper on a sheet of wax paper. Spread mustard paste all over bones, then dredge bones in bread crumbs.

Transfer ribs to a baking sheet with sides and drizzle with butter. Broil ribs about 2 inches from heat, turning frequently, until bread crumbs are golden, about 5 minutes.

Buffalo Prime Rib with Orange Balsamic Glaze

SERVES 8

ACTIVE TIME: 40 MINUTES ■ START TO FINISH: 4 1/4 HOURS (3 3/4 HOURS IF USING BEEF)

■ Buffalo meat can be very red, even when cooked to medium-rare. This color is not a problem; it has to do with the animal's diet and how little fat is marbled through the muscle. It does mean, though, that you need to rely on your meat thermometer rather than your eye to tell you when this roast is done. Before you put the meat in the oven, roughly calculate the total roasting time. Plan on about sixteen minutes per pound once the oven temperature is reduced to 350°F, but start checking the meat thirty minutes before you think it will be done. ■

- 1 (7- to 8-pound) bone-in buffalo standing rib roast (see Sources) or beef standing rib roast (bone-in rib-eye roast; 3 or 4 ribs), at room temperature (allow 1 hour)
- Salt and freshly ground black pepper
- Orange Balsamic Glaze (recipe follows)

FOR *JUS*

- 2/3 cup dry red wine
- 1/4 cup Sercial (dry) Madeira
- 1 1/2 cups beef stock or store-bought broth
- Salt

SPECIAL EQUIPMENT: a V-rack for roasting; an instant-read thermometer

COOK THE ROAST: Put a rack in middle of oven and preheat oven to 450°F.

If using beef, trim all but a thin layer of fat from roast. Generously season buffalo or beef with salt and pepper. Put buffalo fat side up on V-rack in a 17-by-12-inch flameproof roasting pan, or put beef (which will be taller and narrower than buffalo) in a 13-by-9-inch pan. Roast for 15 minutes.

Reduce oven temperature to 350°F, add 1/2 cup water to roasting pan, and roast meat for 30 minutes more. Brush meat with some glaze, add another 1/2 cup water to pan, and continue to roast, brushing with glaze and adding 1/2 cup water to pan every 15 minutes, until thermometer inserted 2 inches into center of meat (without touching bone) registers 125°F for buffalo, 2 to 2 1/4 hours more, or 115°F for beef, 1 3/4 to 2 hours more. Transfer meat to a large platter and let stand, loosely covered with foil, for 25 minutes. (It will continue to cook, reaching about 135°F for medium-rare buffalo or 130°F for medium-rare beef.)

WHILE THE MEAT STANDS, MAKE THE *JUS*: If using buffalo, set roasting pan over two burners, add red wine and Madeira, and deglaze pan by boiling over moderately high heat, stirring and scraping up brown bits, for 2 minutes. Add stock and boil until reduced to about 1 1/2 cups, about 3 minutes.

If using beef, first pour pan juices into a 1-quart fat separator or glass measure, skim off fat if using a glass measure, and then pour defatted juices back into pan. Set roasting pan over two burners and deglaze pan by boiling juices over moderately high heat, stirring and scraping up brown bits, for 2 minutes. Then boil until reduced to about 2/3 cup, about 6 minutes. Add red wine and Madeira and boil until reduced to about 2/3 cup, 3 to 4 minutes. Add stock and boil until reduced to about 2 cups, about 6 minutes.

Stir in any buffalo or beef juices accumulated on platter and season *jus* with salt if necessary. Pour *jus* through a fine-mesh sieve into a gravy boat and cover to keep warm.

Carve roast and serve with *jus*.

Orange Balsamic Glaze

MAKES ABOUT 2 1/4 CUPS
ACTIVE TIME: 20 MINUTES ■ START TO FINISH: 45 MINUTES

■ This sweet-tart glaze is excellent for any roasted red meat. ■

- 1 1/2 tablespoons unsalted butter
- 1 cup finely chopped shallots
- 1 cup (8 ounces) thawed frozen orange juice concentrate
- 1/2 cup water
- 1/2 cup sweet orange preserves
- 1/2 cup balsamic vinegar
- 1 tablespoon salt
- 1 1/2 teaspoons cracked black peppercorns
- 1 1/2 teaspoons finely grated orange zest

Heat butter in a 3-quart heavy saucepan over moderate heat until foam subsides. Add shallots and cook, stirring, until golden brown, about 5 minutes. Stir in remaining ingredients and simmer briskly, uncovered, stirring occasionally, until glaze is thickened and reduced to about 2 1/4 cups, about 25 minutes.

COOK'S NOTE

■ The glaze can be made up to 3 days ahead and refrigerated, covered. Bring to room temperature before using.

Beef Tenderloin with Cornichon Tarragon Sauce

SERVES 18
ACTIVE TIME: 35 MINUTES ■ START TO FINISH: 1 HOUR

■ If tenderness is your holy grail, this is for you. A fillet of beef is cut from the tenderloin muscle, which sits on top of the steer's back and does none of the work of moving the animal around. As a result, it has little of the connective tissues and sinews that make meat tough. (It is also surrounded by fat, which contributes to its butter-soft texture.) Accompanied by a wine and cream sauce sparked with fresh tarragon and petite cornichons, it makes a very lavish roast, a great dish for any special occasion when you have a crowd on hand. ■

- 3 (3- to 3 1/2-pound) trimmed and tied center-cut beef tenderloin roasts, at room temperature
- 1 1/2 teaspoons salt
- 3/4 teaspoon freshly ground black pepper
- 3 tablespoons vegetable oil
- 1 1/4 cups minced shallots
- 5 cups dry white wine
- 1/2 cup minced fresh tarragon
- 2 sticks (1/2 pound) unsalted butter, softened
- 2/3 cup Dijon mustard
- 1/3 cup heavy cream
- 40 cornichons (tiny French gherkins), cut into thin strips (1 cup)

SPECIAL EQUIPMENT: an instant-read thermometer

Put a rack in middle of oven and preheat oven to 350°F.

Pat beef dry and sprinkle each piece with 1/2 teaspoon salt and 1/4 teaspoon pepper. Heat oil in a large flameproof roasting pan over moderately high heat. Brown beef well on all sides, about 10 minutes total.

Transfer pan to oven and roast until a thermometer inserted diagonally 2 inches into center of one piece registers 120°F, 25 to 30 minutes. Transfer beef to a cutting board and let stand, loosely covered with foil, for 15 minutes. (It will continue to cook, reaching 130°F for medium-rare.)

While beef stands, combine shallots, wine, and tarragon in a 3-quart saucepan, bring to a simmer over moderately high heat, and simmer until liquid is reduced to about 1 cup, about 15 minutes. Meanwhile, beat together butter and mustard in a medium bowl with an electric mixer.

Add cream and cornichons to sauce in pan, then reduce heat to low and whisk in mustard butter a little at a time and then any meat juices accumulated on platter. Season sauce with salt and pepper and keep warm over very low heat (do not let boil).

Remove string from beef and discard. Slice fillets and serve with sauce.

COOK'S NOTE

- The mustard butter and the reduced shallot mixture, without the cream and cornichons, can be made up to 1 day ahead. Refrigerate separately, covered. Reheat shallot mixture and bring the butter to room temperature before proceeding.

Beef Tenderloin with Bordelaise Sauce

SERVES 8
ACTIVE TIME: 3 HOURS ■ START TO FINISH: 25 HOURS (INCLUDES SOAKING MARROW)

■ Beef tenderloin is the cut filets mignons come from, but roasting a tenderloin is much easier than cooking individual steaks. Not only is the presentation more impressive, the meat stays moister. The bordelaise sauce, a French classic that begins with a red wine reduction, is fantastic even without the marrow rounds, but they do add a noticeable depth of flavor—and a taste of sybaritic luxury. ■

LETTING MEAT STAND

You've just pulled that magnificent prime rib out of the oven or those porterhouses off the grill. Dinner's ready, right? Well, actually, not yet. Letting the meat stand for a while—even though it may go against your inclination to serve everything piping hot—is the last part of the cooking process and shouldn't be skipped. The meat has to have time to collect itself, so to speak. It will continue to cook as it stands (which is why we always take it off the heat a little early), and then, after it comes to temperature, it will begin to cool down. As it cools, the flavorful juices are reabsorbed by the protein molecules (which exude liquid during cooking) and redistributed throughout the meat. As a result, the meat will slice beautifully (it both loses its juices and shreds unbecomingly if sliced hot), its color will darken to a deep pink, and it will be juicy and tender on the plate. There's no hard-and-fast rule about how long to let a piece of meat stand; it depends on how large it is. The wait is a gift to the cook in any event: use the time to make a pan sauce, reheat side dishes and adjust the seasoning, or pour yourself a glass of wine.

3 pounds (3- to 4-inch-long) beef marrow bones (about 6 bones), with marrow exposed at both ends

FOR SAUCE

- 2 cups dry red wine, preferably Bordeaux
- ⅓ cup finely chopped shallots
- ½ cup chopped mushrooms
- 1 small carrot, finely chopped
- 2 large fresh thyme sprigs
- 1 Turkish bay leaf or ½ California bay leaf
- 10 black peppercorns, cracked
- 2 cups Veal Stock (page 929) or store-bought broth
- 4 teaspoons arrowroot
- 1 tablespoon Sercial (dry) Madeira
- ¼ teaspoon salt
- Freshly ground black pepper to taste

FOR BEEF

- 1 (2¾- to 3-pound) trimmed and tied center-cut beef tenderloin roast
- ½ teaspoon salt
- ¼ teaspoon freshly ground black pepper
- 1 tablespoon vegetable oil
- 1 tablespoon unsalted butter

FOR POACHING MARROW

- 1 cup beef stock or store-bought broth
- 1 cup water
- ½ teaspoon salt

OPTIONAL GARNISH: watercress sprigs

SPECIAL EQUIPMENT: an instant-read thermometer

PREPARE THE MARROW: Rinse marrow bones, then soak in warm water to cover for 10 minutes.

Press on marrow at small opening at end of one bone with your thumb and push marrow out other end. Discard bone and repeat with remaining bones. Cut marrow into ⅛-inch-thick rounds. Cover with cold water in a bowl and refrigerate, changing water twice, for 24 hours.

MAKE THE SAUCE: Combine wine, shallots, mushrooms, carrot, thyme, bay leaf, and peppercorns in a 3-quart heavy saucepan, bring to a boil, and boil until reduced to about ½ cup, about 15 minutes.

Add veal stock and return to a boil. Pour broth through a fine-mesh sieve into a 2-quart heavy saucepan, pressing on solids; discard solids.

Return sauce to heat and bring to a boil. Stir together arrowroot and Madeira in a small cup until smooth and whisk into sauce. Simmer, whisking occasionally, until slightly thickened, about 2 minutes. Stir in salt and pepper. Remove from heat.

ROAST THE BEEF: Put a rack in middle of oven and preheat oven to 350°F.

Pat beef dry and sprinkle with salt and pepper. Heat oil and butter in a small flameproof roasting pan over moderately high heat until foam subsides. Brown beef well on all sides, about 10 minutes total.

Transfer roasting pan to oven and roast until thermometer inserted diagonally 2 inches into center of meat registers 120°F, 25 to 30 minutes. Transfer beef to a cutting board and let stand, loosely covered with foil, for 15 minutes. (It will continue to cook, reaching 130°F for medium-rare.)

WHILE THE BEEF STANDS, POACH THE MARROW: Combine stock, water, and salt in a 1½-quart saucepan and bring to a simmer. Drain marrow, transfer to saucepan, and poach at a bare simmer for 8 minutes.

Bring sauce to a simmer. With a slotted spoon, transfer marrow to sauce.

Remove string from beef and discard. Cut beef into ½-inch-thick slices. Pour some sauce over beef and serve remainder on side. If desired, arrange marrow rounds between beef slices, using slotted spoon, and garnish with watercress.

COOK'S NOTES

- Many butcher shops will have marrow bones on hand, but it's a good idea to call ahead.
- The sauce, before the marrow is added, can be made up to 1 day ahead. Cool, uncovered, then refrigerate, covered.

Twenty-First-Century Beef Wellington

SERVES 12

ACTIVE TIME: 1½ HOURS ■ START TO FINISH: 5½ HOURS (INCLUDES MAKING DOUGH AND FILLING)

■ When a truly grand occasion comes along, it's nice to serve something equally splendid to celebrate it. This showy dish certainly fills that bill. The traditional version consists of a fillet of beef covered with pâté de foie gras and mushrooms, encased in pastry, and baked. For our updated version, we've kept the pastry but replaced the pâté with a cilantro and walnut filling that is not only lighter but also brighter in flavor. Tenderloin roasts vary in shape, size, and weight. For this recipe it's important to have one of uniform shape. If you can't find a whole tenderloin, two center-cut pieces will work. (Don't halve them crosswise after patting them dry as directed below.) ■

- 1 (4½- to 5-pound) center-cut beef tenderloin roast (16 inches long and 3 inches in diameter), trimmed and tied
- 1 teaspoon salt
- ½ teaspoon freshly ground black pepper
- 1 tablespoon vegetable oil
- Sour Cream Pastry Dough (recipe follows)
- Cilantro Walnut Filling (recipe follows)
- 1 large egg lightly beaten with 1 tablespoon water, for egg wash

SPECIAL EQUIPMENT: an instant-read thermometer

Pat tenderloin dry. Halve crosswise and sprinkle with salt and pepper. Heat oil in a 12-inch heavy skillet over moderately high heat until just smoking. Add beef and sear, turning with tongs, until well browned on all sides, about 5 minutes total. Transfer to a platter. If necessary, remove any string.

Roll out dough on a lightly floured surface with a floured rolling pin into a 19-by-15-inch rectangle slightly less than ¼ inch thick. Cut a 1-inch strip of dough from a shorter end, place on a small baking sheet, and refrigerate. Place dough rectangle lengthwise on a large baking sheet or tray (about 17½ by 12½ inches), letting excess hang over sides. Spread one third of filling lengthwise down middle of rectangle, forming a 16-by-2-inch strip. Arrange beef pieces end to end on filling and spread remaining filling all over beef. Brush edges of dough with egg wash, then fold up long sides of dough to enclose beef completely and press seam to seal. Fold short ends of dough over beef and seal edges. Invert a large baking sheet over beef and invert beef onto sheet so that pastry is seam side down. Brush dough evenly with egg wash. Cut out decorative shapes from reserved pastry strip with a sharp paring knife and arrange on dough, pressing gently so they adhere. Brush decorations with egg wash. Make small steam vents every 3 inches in top of dough with paring knife. Refrigerate beef, loosely covered, for at least 1 hour.

Put a rack in middle of oven and preheat oven to 400°F.

Bake beef Wellington until pastry is golden brown and thermometer inserted diagonally 2 inches into center of meat registers 115°F, 45 to 55 minutes. Let beef stand on sheet on a rack, uncovered, for 25 minutes before slicing. (It will continue to cook, reaching 125°–130°F for medium-rare.)

COOK'S NOTE

■ The uncooked beef Wellington can be refrigerated for up to 6 hours.

Sour Cream Pastry Dough

MAKES ENOUGH DOUGH TO WRAP A 5-POUND BEEF TENDERLOIN ROAST

ACTIVE TIME: 15 MINUTES ■ START TO FINISH: 2¼ HOURS (INCLUDES CHILLING)

■ This dough is exceptionally tender but still strong enough to hold together when enclosing beef Wellington; sour cream adds moisture and a little extra fat. And it's easy to work with—it rolls out well and is very supple. ■

- 3¼ cups all-purpose flour
- 2½ sticks (½ pound plus 4 tablespoons) cold unsalted butter, cut into ½-inch cubes
- 1 teaspoon salt
- 1¼ cups very cold sour cream
- 4–6 tablespoons ice water

Combine flour, butter, and salt in a bowl and blend together with your fingertips or a pastry blender (or pulse in a food processor) until mixture resembles coarse meal with some pea-sized lumps of butter. Add sour cream and stir with a fork (or pulse) just until incorporated. Drizzle evenly with 4 tablespoons (¼ cup) ice water and gently stir (or pulse) until incorporated. Squeeze a small handful of dough: if it doesn't hold together, add more ice water 1 tablespoon at a time, stirring (or pulsing) until just incorporated. Do not overwork dough, or pastry will be tough.

Turn dough out onto a lightly floured surface and divide into 4 portions. With heel of your hand, smear each portion once or twice in a forward motion across work surface to help distribute fat. Gather dough together (using a pastry scraper if you have one), then flatten into a 5-by-4-inch rectangle. Dust dough all over with flour and refrigerate, wrapped in plastic wrap, until firm, at least 2 hours.

COOK'S NOTE

- The dough can be refrigerated for up to 1 day.

Cilantro Walnut Filling

MAKES ABOUT 3½ CUPS
ACTIVE TIME: 45 MINUTES ■ START TO FINISH: 45 MINUTES

■ This filling is like a pesto but more substantial. Spinach and parsley add flavor and color; fresh cilantro and coriander seeds give a lemony and ever so slightly floral boost. ■

- 2 (12-ounce) bunches spinach, coarse stems discarded
- 3 cups packed fresh cilantro sprigs (1½ large bunches)
- 2 cups packed fresh flat-leaf parsley sprigs (1 large bunch)
- 2 cups (about 7 ounces) walnut pieces, toasted (see Tips, page 938) and cooled
- 4 garlic cloves, minced
- 1 cup fine fresh bread crumbs
- ¼ cup honey
- 2 large egg whites
- 1½ teaspoons salt
- 1 teaspoon ground cumin
- 1 teaspoon ground coriander
- ¼ teaspoon freshly ground black pepper

Blanch spinach in a 3-quart saucepan of well-salted water for 30 seconds. Add cilantro and parsley and blanch for 10 seconds more. Drain spinach and herbs in a colander and transfer to a bowl of ice and cold water to stop the cooking. Drain spinach and herbs again and squeeze them a small handful at a time until as dry as possible.

Pulse walnuts in a food processor just until finely ground. Add garlic, spinach mixture, and remaining ingredients and pulse just until smooth.

COOK'S NOTE

- The filling can be made up to 2 days ahead and refrigerated, covered.

Cold Roast Beef Tenderloin with Jellied Horseradish Cream

SERVES 8 TO 12
ACTIVE TIME: 30 MINUTES ■ START TO FINISH: 3 HOURS

■ Jellied horseradish cream is an unusual savory accompaniment for beef tenderloin. Cold squares of this cream, which look a bit like slices of mozzarella, alternate with slices of the super-tender, room-temperature meat. This is an excellent dish for a summer buffet party.

If you wish, you can easily turn it into an hors d'oeuvre by putting the beef and its cool, creamy topping on little toasts. ■

- 4¾ teaspoons unflavored gelatin (from two ¼-ounce envelopes)
- ¼ cup cold water
- 4½ cups sour cream
- 6 tablespoons drained bottled horseradish
- 6 tablespoons minced fresh flat-leaf parsley
- 2 teaspoons salt
- 1 (3½-pound) trimmed and tied center-cut beef tenderloin roast, at room temperature
- ⅓ cup coarsely ground black pepper
- 2 tablespoons vegetable oil

OPTIONAL GARNISH: watercress sprigs
SPECIAL EQUIPMENT: an instant-read thermometer

Sprinkle gelatin over cold water in a small saucepan and let soften for 1 minute.

Stir together sour cream, horseradish, parsley, and 1½ teaspoons salt in a large bowl. Add 1 cup sour cream mixture to gelatin mixture and heat over moderately low heat, stirring, until gelatin is melted; do not let boil. Add gelatin mixture to remaining sour cream mixture and stir well. Spoon horseradish cream into a 13-by-9-inch baking pan and refrigerate, covered, until firm, about 2 hours.

Put a rack in middle of oven and preheat oven to 350°F.

Pat tenderloin dry, then coat on all sides (not ends) with pepper and remaining 1/2 teaspoon salt. Heat oil in a flameproof roasting pan over high heat. Brown tenderloin on all sides (not ends), about 10 minutes total.

Transfer pan to oven and roast tenderloin until thermometer inserted diagonally 2 inches into center of meat registers 120°F, 25 to 30 minutes. Transfer beef to a cutting board and let cool to room temperature. (It will continue to cook, reaching 130°F for medium-rare.)

Remove string and discard. Cut tenderloin into 1/3-inch-thick slices. Cut horseradish cream into 2 1/2-by-1 1/2-inch rectangles. Arrange tenderloin on a platter, alternating slices of meat with rectangles of horseradish cream (you will have leftover horseradish cream). Garnish with watercress, if desired.

COOK'S NOTES

- The horseradish cream can be refrigerated for up to 1 day.
- The tenderloin can be roasted up to 1 day ahead and refrigerated, wrapped well in plastic wrap. Bring to room temperature before serving.

Oven-Braised Beef with Tomato Sauce and Garlic

SERVES 6
ACTIVE TIME: 15 MINUTES ■ START TO FINISH: 4 1/4 HOURS

■ Here's a good demonstration of why the most expensive meat is not always the best. A fancy cut would be too lean for this dish, and it would dry out during the long, slow cooking; you're better off using an economical chuck roast from the supermarket. Given its short preparation time, this dish is ideal to put together while you're making another meal—just slide it into the oven and let it cook. When you serve the beef, you can either squeeze the garlic pulp out of the skins beforehand or let your guests do it themselves. ■

1 (28-ounce) can whole tomatoes in juice
1 (3- to 3 1/2-pound) boneless beef chuck roast, rolled and tied
1 head garlic, separated into cloves but left unpeeled
Salt and freshly ground black pepper

ACCOMPANIMENT: cooked orzo

Put a rack in middle of oven and preheat oven to 300°F.

Coarsely chop tomatoes, with their juice, in a food processor. Put roast in an ovenproof 4- to 5-quart heavy pot or a casserole dish with a lid, pour tomatoes over it, and scatter garlic around it. Season with salt and pepper.

Cover and braise in oven until very tender, 3 to 4 hours.

Remove string and discard. Cut roast into 1/4-inch-thick slices and serve with sauce, orzo, and garlic.

COOK'S NOTE

- The braised beef will improve in flavor if made 24 hours ahead. Cool completely, then refrigerate, covered. Skim off excess fat before reheating.

Sauerbraten

SERVES 6
ACTIVE TIME: 1 1/2 HOURS ■ START TO FINISH: 4 1/2 HOURS PLUS AT LEAST 2 DAYS FOR MARINATING BEEF

■ You might not think that a dish called "sour roast"—the literal translation of the name of this German specialty—would be sensational, but you would be mistaken. This recipe, a Bavarian version made by the grandmother of a New York reader, Katherine Soper, is mouthwatering: rich beef chuck roast bathed for days in a tart red wine and vinegar marinade sparked with juniper berries, cloves, and peppercorns, then braised for hours to falling-apart tenderness. To finish it off, we make a sauce from the marinade with plumped raisins and a couple of crushed gingersnaps for a touch of sweetness. ■

FOR BEEF

- 3 cups dry red wine
- 1 cup water
- ½ cup red wine vinegar
- 1 carrot, sliced
- 3 garlic cloves, chopped
- 2 Turkish bay leaves or 1 California bay leaf
- 10 black peppercorns
- 3 whole cloves
- 2 juniper berries (optional; see Glossary)
- ½ teaspoon dried thyme, crumbled
- 2½ teaspoons salt
- 3 medium onions, halved lengthwise and thinly sliced
- 1 (3- to 3¼-pound) boneless lean beef chuck roast, rolled and tied
- ½ teaspoon freshly ground black pepper
- 2 tablespoons vegetable oil

FOR SAUCE

- ⅓ cup raisins
- 2 tablespoons unsalted butter
- 2 tablespoons all-purpose flour
- 2 tablespoons sugar
- 1½ teaspoons red wine vinegar, or to taste
- 2 gingersnaps, coarsely crushed
- Salt and freshly ground black pepper

MARINATE THE BEEF: Combine wine, water, vinegar, carrot, garlic, bay leaves, peppercorns, cloves, juniper berries (if using), thyme, 1 teaspoon salt, and one third of onions in a 3- to 4-quart stainless steel or enameled saucepan and bring to a boil, then reduce heat and simmer, covered, for 15 minutes. Remove from heat and cool completely.

Put beef in a large sealable plastic bag and pour marinade over it, adding more water if necessary to barely cover beef. Seal bag and marinate beef, refrigerated, for at least 2 days.

BRAISE THE BEEF: Put a rack in middle of oven and preheat oven to 300°F.

Remove beef from marinade, reserving marinade. Pat meat dry and sprinkle with remaining 1½ teaspoons salt and pepper. Pour marinade through a fine-mesh sieve into a bowl and reserve solids and liquid separately.

Heat oil in a wide 6- to 7-quart heavy stainless steel or enamel ovenproof pot over moderately high heat. Brown beef on all sides, about 20 minutes total. Transfer beef to a plate. Reduce heat to moderate, add remaining onions to pot, and cook, stirring, until softened, about 6 minutes. Add reserved marinade solids and cook, stirring, for 2 minutes.

Return beef to pot, along with any juices accumulated on plate, add enough reserved marinade to reach halfway up sides of beef, and bring to a boil (discard remaining marinade). Cover pot and transfer to oven. Braise beef until it is very tender when pierced with a fork, about 2¾ hours.

Transfer beef to a platter and cover loosely with foil to keep warm.

MAKE THE SAUCE: Pour braising liquid through fine-mesh sieve into a bowl (discard solids) and skim fat. Soak raisins in ⅓ cup strained braising liquid in a small bowl for 15 minutes.

Melt butter in cleaned pot over moderately low heat. Add flour and sugar, whisking constantly, and cook, whisking, until golden brown, about 3 minutes. Add 3 cups strained braising liquid in a steady stream, whisking constantly. Add raisin mixture, increase heat to moderate, and bring to a boil, whisking constantly. Add vinegar, increase heat to high, and boil until liquid is reduced to about 2 cups, about 5 minutes.

Add gingersnaps, reduce heat, and simmer until sauce is glossy and slightly thickened, about 2 minutes. Season with salt and pepper.

Remove string from beef and discard. Thinly slice beef and arrange on a platter. Nap slices with some sauce and serve remainder on the side.

COOK'S NOTES

- The beef can marinate for up to 4 days.
- The beef can be braised up to 1 day ahead. Cool completely in the braising liquid, uncovered, then cover and refrigerate. To reheat, bring to a boil, covered, on the stovetop, then reduce heat and simmer until the meat is heated through, about 45 minutes. Transfer the beef to a platter, cover loosely, and proceed as directed.

Brisket à la Carbonnade

SERVES 8

ACTIVE TIME: 25 MINUTES ■ START TO FINISH: 4½ HOURS

■ Brisket, a large, flat, fatty cut of meat from the front of the steer, was long a favorite of peasant cooks because it was considered rather undesirable and was therefore inexpensive. Over the centuries, a panoply of excellent brisket dishes developed, all based on the simple fact that long, slow cooking renders this cut superlatively tender. This recipe, in which brisket is braised in beer with plenty of onions, is one of the national dishes of Belgium.

Two brisket cuts are available in most supermarkets. If you prefer a more marbled piece of beef, look for the thicker end, known as the point, which may be labeled as "front," "thick second," or "nose" cut. The thinner, leaner end of the brisket is the flat, sometimes called the first, or thin, cut. Either will work well in this recipe, so buy the one you like best. ■

- 1 (3½- to 4-pound) beef brisket, trimmed of excess fat
- ¾ teaspoon salt
- ½ teaspoon freshly ground black pepper
- 2 tablespoons olive oil
- 2 pounds onions, halved lengthwise and thinly sliced lengthwise (6 cups)
- 1 Turkish bay leaf or ½ California bay leaf
- 1 (12-ounce) bottle beer (not dark)
- 1 dried-porcini bouillon cube (less than ½ ounce; see Sources) or beef bouillon cube, crumbled
- 1 tablespoon balsamic vinegar

Put a rack in middle of oven and preheat oven to 350°F.

Pat brisket dry and sprinkle with salt and pepper. Heat oil in a 6- to 8-quart wide heavy ovenproof pot over moderately high heat until hot but not smoking. Brown meat well on all sides, about 10 minutes total. Transfer to a platter.

Add onions and bay leaf to fat remaining in pot and cook over moderate heat, stirring occasionally, until onions are golden, 10 to 12 minutes. Remove from heat and transfer half of onions to a bowl. Set brisket over onions in pot, then top with remaining onions. Add beer, bouillon cube, and vinegar (liquid should come about halfway up sides of meat; add water if necessary) and bring to a boil.

Cover pot, transfer to oven, and braise until meat is very tender, 3 to 3½ hours. Let meat cool in sauce, uncovered, for 30 minutes.

Transfer brisket to a cutting board. Skim off any fat from sauce, discard bay leaf, and season sauce with salt and pepper. Slice meat across the grain and serve with sauce.

COOK'S NOTE

■ The brisket actually improves in flavor if braised 2 days ahead. Cool the meat in the sauce, uncovered. Cover it with parchment paper or wax paper, then the lid, and refrigerate. Remove any solidified fat before reheating. To reheat, slice the cold meat across the grain and arrange in a shallow baking pan. Spoon the sauce over the meat and reheat in a 325°F oven for 45 minutes.

Pot-au-Feu

SERVES 12

ACTIVE TIME: 2 HOURS ■ START TO FINISH: 4½ HOURS

■ This dish evokes a French farmhouse kitchen where something fragrant is always simmering on the back of the stove. The strained broth is traditionally served first, with the toasts and the marrow bones. The meat and vegetables, accompanied by pungent horseradish and mustard sauces and cornichons, follow as the main course. If you choose to serve the meat and vegetables in the broth, don't make the sauces; instead, put out horseradish and Dijon mustard for guests to stir into their broth. ■

FOR MEAT AND VEGETABLES

- 5 quarts water
- 1 cup dry white wine
- 1 (3-pound) boneless beef chuck roast, tied
- 3 pounds beef short ribs (1 inch thick)
- Salt
- 1 celery rib, cut into 4-inch lengths
- 6 long sprigs fresh thyme or ½ teaspoon dried thyme, crumbled
- 6 long sprigs fresh flat-leaf parsley
- 2 Turkish bay leaves or 1 California bay leaf
- ½ teaspoon black peppercorns
- 5 cloves
- 1 medium onion
- 12 small or 6 medium leeks (1¾ pounds total), trimmed to about 7 inches, root ends left intact
- 2 pounds large carrots, peeled and cut diagonally into 1-inch-thick pieces
- 1 pound parsnips, peeled and cut diagonally into 1-inch-thick pieces
- 1 pound turnips, peeled and cut into 1-inch-wide wedges
- Freshly ground black pepper

FOR TOASTS (OPTIONAL)

- 1 baguette, cut into ½-inch-thick slices
- 3 tablespoons unsalted butter, softened
- Salt and freshly ground black pepper
- 2 garlic cloves, halved

FOR MARROW BONES (OPTIONAL)

- 8 cups water
- 1½ tablespoons salt
- 12 (1½-inch-thick) pieces cross-cut beef marrow bones (2–3 pounds)

FOR HORSERADISH SAUCE

- ½ cup finely grated peeled fresh horseradish (6 ounces) or 2 (6-ounce) jars horseradish, drained
- 1 (16-ounce) container sour cream
- 1 teaspoon salt

FOR MUSTARD SAUCE

- ½ cup Dijon mustard
- ¼ cup minced shallots
- ¼ cup vegetable oil
- Salt and freshly ground black pepper

ACCOMPANIMENTS: cornichons (tiny French gherkins) and coarse sea salt

SPECIAL EQUIPMENT: a 12-quart heavy-bottomed stockpot; cheesecloth; kitchen string

COOK THE MEAT AND VEGETABLES: Combine water, wine, chuck, short ribs, and 2 tablespoons salt in stockpot (add more water if meat is not covered) and bring to a simmer, skimming froth. Reduce heat to low and cook at a bare simmer, uncovered, skimming froth, for 30 minutes.

Wrap celery, thyme, parsley, bay leaves, and peppercorns in a square of cheesecloth, then tie into a bundle with string to make a bouquet garni. Stick cloves into onion. Add to pot, along with bouquet garni, and continue to cook at a bare simmer, uncovered, until meat is almost tender, about 1½ hours more.

Slit leeks lengthwise to within 1½ inches of root ends and wash well. Tie leeks in 2 or 3 bundles with string. Add to pot, along with carrots, and simmer for 20 minutes. Add parsnips and turnips and continue to simmer, uncovered, until vegetables and meat are tender, 30 to 40 minutes more.

MEANWHILE, PREPARE THE TOASTS AND MARROW BONES (if using): Put a rack in middle of oven and preheat oven to 350°F.

Arrange slices of bread in one layer on a baking sheet. Spread tops with butter and season with salt and pepper to taste. Toast in oven until golden, 10 to 15 minutes.

Rub toasts with cut sides of garlic and set aside. Reduce oven temperature to 275°F.

Bring water, with salt, to a simmer in a 4- to 6-quart wide pot. Using tongs, stand marrow bones upright in pot; add more hot water if necessary to just cover bones. Bring to a simmer and simmer, covered, until marrow is tender, about 20 minutes. Remove from heat and keep bones warm in pot, partially covered.

PREPARE THE MEAT AND VEGETABLE PLATTER AND STRAIN THE BROTH: Remove and discard onion and bouquet garni from broth. Transfer chuck to a cutting board, cover with foil, and let stand for 20 minutes.

Transfer short ribs to a large ovenproof platter, discarding any loose bones, and surround with vegetables (leave room for sliced chuck). Keep warm, covered with foil, in oven.

Pour broth through a large sieve into a large bowl; discard solids. Line cleaned sieve with a dampened paper towel and pour broth through sieve again (to obtain a clear broth) into a 5-quart pot. Reheat broth and season with salt and pepper. Keep warm over low heat.

MAKE THE HORSERADISH SAUCE: Stir together horseradish, sour cream, and salt in a medium bowl.

MAKE THE MUSTARD SAUCE: Whisk together mustard and shallots in a small bowl, then add oil in a slow stream, whisking until well blended. Whisk in 1/4 cup strained broth and salt and pepper to taste.

TO SERVE THE SOUP: Reserve 2 cups hot broth for moistening meat. With tongs, transfer a marrow bone (if using) to each of twelve soup bowls, then ladle remaining broth into bowls. If using bones, serve with toasts and coarse sea salt for eating marrow.

TO SERVE THE MEAT AND VEGETABLES: Remove string from chuck and cut into 1/2-inch-thick slices. Arrange slices on platter with short ribs and drizzle reserved broth over meat. Serve with sauces and cornichons.

COOK'S NOTES

- Many butcher shops will have marrow bones on hand, but it is a good idea to call ahead.
- The pot-au-feu (but not the marrow bones) can be made up to 1 day ahead. Arrange the sliced meat and vegetables in a roasting pan and add enough strained broth to cover. Cool, uncovered, then refrigerate, covered. Cool the remaining broth, uncovered, and refrigerate separately, covered. To serve, reheat the meat and vegetables, still covered with broth, in a 350°F oven until hot, about 30 minutes. Remove from the oven and reduce the oven temperature to 275°F. Transfer the meat and vegetables to an ovenproof platter and moisten with some of the broth. Keep warm, covered with foil, in the oven. Pour the broth remaining in the roasting pan through a paper towel–lined sieve into a 4-quart saucepan. Add the refrigerated reserved broth and reheat for the soup while you poach the marrow.
- The toasts can be made up to 1 day ahead and kept in an airtight container at room temperature.
- The sauces can be made up to 1 day ahead and refrigerated, covered. Bring to room temperature before serving.

Rib-Eye Steak with Wild Mushrooms

SERVES 4

ACTIVE TIME: 1 HOUR ■ START TO FINISH: 1 HOUR

■ You can also use the flavorful spice mixture that we rub on this thick rib eye when sautéing thinner individual steaks (which won't require finishing in the oven), although you may need to double the amount if cooking four steaks. The mushrooms, enlivened with just a touch of maple syrup and lime juice, can be served as a side dish on their own. This hearty, spice-rubbed steak was inspired by a version that Robert del Grande serves at Café Annie, in Houston. ■

FOR STEAK

- 1 teaspoon kosher salt
- 1 teaspoon freshly ground black pepper
- 1 teaspoon minced garlic
- 1 teaspoon chili powder
- 2 tablespoons olive oil
- 1 (2-inch-thick) rib-eye steak (1 1/2–2 pounds)

FOR MUSHROOMS

- 2 tablespoons extra-virgin olive oil
- 4 bacon slices, finely chopped
- 1 medium onion, finely chopped
- 3/4 pound shiitake mushrooms, stems discarded and caps quartered
- 2 dried guajillo chiles (see Glossary), seeded and chopped, or 1/4 teaspoon red pepper flakes
- 1 1/2 cups chicken stock or store-bought low-sodium broth
- 4 large garlic cloves (or to taste), chopped
- 1/4 cup chopped fresh flat-leaf parsley
- 2 tablespoons pure maple syrup
- 2 tablespoons fresh lime juice
- Salt

SPECIAL EQUIPMENT: an instant-read thermometer

Put racks in upper and lower thirds of oven and preheat oven to 350°F.

PREPARE THE STEAK: Stir together salt, pepper, garlic, chili powder, and 1 tablespoon oil in a small bowl. Rub on both sides of steak. Heat remaining 1 tablespoon oil in a 10-inch heavy ovenproof skillet over moderately high heat. Sear steak, turning once, for 4 to 6 minutes total. Transfer to a rack set in a small roasting pan.

PREPARE THE MUSHROOMS: Heat oil in cleaned skillet over moderately high heat. Add bacon and onion and cook until bacon begins to sizzle. Stir in mushrooms and chiles. Put pan with steak in upper third of oven and skillet of mushrooms in lower third and cook until thermometer inserted in thickest part of steak registers 125°F for medium-rare or 135°F for medium, 15 to 25 minutes. Transfer steak to a cutting board (set pan aside) and let stand, loosely covered with foil, for 10 minutes.

While steak stands, remove skillet from oven and add stock to mushrooms. Bring to a boil on stovetop and boil until stock is reduced by about half, about 8 minutes. Add garlic, parsley, maple syrup, lime juice, and any meat juices in roasting pan and simmer, stirring, until sauce is slightly thickened, about 2 minutes. Season with salt.

Serve steak with sauce.

Steak au Poivre

SERVES 4

ACTIVE TIME: 30 MINUTES ■ START TO FINISH: 1½ HOURS

■ If you want to fancy up a steak, there are few better options than this bistro standby. It's quick and easy, but it has a very sophisticated flavor, thanks to the Cognac and shallots in the sauce. It's important to crush the peppercorns rather than grind them in a pepper mill, because the intense bursts of flavor caused by biting into the little chunks of pepper are a hallmark of the dish. ■

- 3 tablespoons black peppercorns
- 4 (¾-inch-thick) boneless top loin steaks (about 8 ounces each)
- Salt
- 1 tablespoon vegetable oil
- 3 tablespoons unsalted butter
- ¼ cup minced shallots
- ½ cup Cognac
- ⅔ cup heavy cream

OPTIONAL GARNISH: watercress sprigs

Coarsely crush peppercorns in a sealed plastic bag, or between two sheets of wax paper, with the bottom of a heavy skillet.

Pat steaks dry. Press pepper onto both sides of steaks and let stand at room temperature, loosely covered with wax paper, for 1 hour.

Preheat oven to 200°F.

Season steaks with salt. Heat oil and 1 tablespoon butter in a 10- to 11-inch heavy skillet over moderately high heat until foam subsides. Add steaks in 2 batches and cook, turning once, until meat is just springy to the touch, 4 to 5 minutes per batch for medium-rare. With a slotted spatula, transfer steaks to a baking sheet with sides and keep warm in oven.

Pour off fat in skillet, then add shallots and remaining 2 tablespoons butter and cook over moderate heat, stirring, until shallots are softened, 1 to 2 minutes. Add Cognac, bring to a boil, and boil until reduced to a glaze, about 2 minutes. Add cream and any meat juices accumulated on baking sheet, bring to a boil, and boil, stirring occasionally, until sauce is slightly thickened and reduced to about ¾ cup, about 3 minutes. Season with salt.

Serve steaks with sauce, garnished with watercress, if desired.

Meat and Greet

"Boneless beef top loin steak" doesn't sound nearly as dashing as "New York strip" (or "Kansas City," "ambassador," or "shell" steak), but that's the correct technical term in the *Uniform Retail Meat Identity Standards,* the meat industry's bible. Getting a handle on those aliases can save you from meat-counter meltdown. The cut is one of our favorites — it's well marbled, though not as fatty as a rib eye, and the texture is tender but still meaty.

the line of gristle that runs down the center. To our minds, cutting that out is a small price to pay for rich texture and deep flavor. ■

Salt-Fried Rib-Eye Steak

SERVES 4

ACTIVE TIME: 15 MINUTES ■ START TO FINISH: 20 MINUTES

■ Rib eyes, which are basically slices of prime rib roast, are nicely marbled with fat, the way other steaks used to be. And the truth is, fat equals flavor. So if you're going to eat extravagantly, make it something special. No oil is needed to sauté the rib eyes; the juices from the meat mix with the salt to form a crusty coating that not only prevents the steaks from sticking to the pan but adds a great caramelized flavor. ■

2 (1¼-inch-thick) rib-eye steaks (1¾ pounds total)
4 teaspoons kosher salt

SPECIAL EQUIPMENT: a well-seasoned 10-inch cast-iron skillet

Pat steaks dry. Sprinkle salt evenly in skillet. Heat skillet over moderately high heat until faint wisps of smoke are visible. Add steaks and cook, shaking skillet after 1 or 2 minutes to loosen them from bottom, for 6 minutes. Turn steaks over and cook for 5 minutes more for medium-rare. Transfer to a cutting board and let stand, loosely covered with foil, for 5 minutes before slicing.

COOK'S NOTE

■ This same method can be used to cook four 6-ounce hamburgers (1¼ inch thick), using only 2 teaspoons salt.

Chuck Blade Steak with Herb Wine Sauce

SERVES 4

ACTIVE TIME: 20 MINUTES ■ START TO FINISH: 25 MINUTES

■ The chuck blade steak is our candidate for most underappreciated cut of beef. It is the second most tender part on the entire steer, after the ultra-tender (and ultra-expensive) tenderloin, and because it is from the chuck, it has plenty of flavor. Despite these qualities, it is much cheaper than most other steaks. The reason is

4 (½-inch-thick) boneless chuck top blade steaks (1¼ pounds total)
1 teaspoon salt
½ teaspoon freshly ground black pepper
3 tablespoons unsalted butter
1 tablespoon olive oil
1 large shallot, finely chopped
½ cup dry white wine
3 tablespoons finely chopped fresh chives
2 tablespoons finely chopped fresh flat-leaf parsley

Pat steaks dry and sprinkle both sides with salt and pepper.

Heat 1 tablespoon butter and oil in a 12-inch heavy skillet over moderately high heat. Add steaks and cook, turning once, for 5 to 6 minutes total for medium-rare. Transfer steaks to a plate and keep warm, loosely covered with foil.

Add remaining 2 tablespoons butter to skillet. Add shallot, reduce heat to moderate, and cook, stirring, until softened, about 2 minutes. Remove from heat and carefully add wine and any meat juices accumulated on plate with steaks. Return to heat and simmer until liquid is reduced by half, about 3 minutes. Remove from heat and stir in chives, parsley, and salt and pepper to taste.

Serve steaks with sauce poured over.

Steak Diane

Steak with Cognac Shallot Sauce

SERVES 4

ACTIVE TIME: 25 MINUTES ■ START TO FINISH: 25 MINUTES

■ Traditionally this dish was served tableside in grand French restaurants by a captain, who would add the brandy to the sauce at the last minute and light it up. Very dramatic. We've simplified it for the home cook, and even though you lose a little of the grandeur, all the taste is there. Pounding the meat achieves two key goals: you get a dish that cooks quickly, and the meat is tenderized, so you can use relatively inexpensive (and more flavorful) sirloin in place of the classic tenderloin. All in all, few dishes are as impressive as this one, which you can get on the table in twenty-five minutes, start to finish. ■

- 2/3 cup beef stock or store-bought broth
- 4 teaspoons Worcestershire sauce
- 2 teaspoons fresh lemon juice
- 2 teaspoons Dijon mustard
- 1 tablespoon Cognac
- 1 tablespoon medium-dry sherry
- 4 (6-ounce) boneless sirloin steaks
- 1/2 teaspoon salt
- 1/4 teaspoon freshly ground black pepper
- 1 tablespoon olive oil
- 3 tablespoons unsalted butter
- 1 cup thinly sliced shallots
- 1 tablespoon minced fresh flat-leaf parsley

Preheat oven to 200°F.

Stir together stock, Worcestershire sauce, lemon juice, mustard, Cognac, and sherry in a small bowl.

With a mallet or the flat side of a cleaver, pound meat between sheets of plastic wrap to a 1/4-inch thickness. Pat meat dry and season with salt and pepper. Heat oil and 1 tablespoon butter in a 10-inch heavy skillet over moderately high heat until foam subsides. Add steaks in 2 batches and cook, turning once, about 1 1/2 minutes total per batch for medium-rare. Transfer to a heatproof plate and keep warm in oven.

Cook shallots in fat remaining in skillet over moderately low heat, stirring, until golden, about 5 minutes. Stir in stock mixture and any meat juices accumulated on plate. Bring to a boil and boil sauce, stirring, until reduced by about half, about 3 minutes. Add parsley and remaining 2 tablespoons butter and cook, swirling skillet until butter is incorporated, 1 minute.

Spoon sauce over steaks.

Pan-Seared Filet Mignon with Merlot Sauce

SERVES 6

ACTIVE TIME: 40 MINUTES ■ START TO FINISH: 1 1/4 HOURS

■ Beef with red wine sauce: what could be more classic? But this isn't just any beef, nor just any wine sauce. The beef is filet mignon, a steak that is justly legendary for its incredible tenderness, and the wine sauce, enriched with veal stock, is a buttery complement. This truly is a match made in heaven—or at least in a great kitchen. ■

FOR SAUCE

- 1/4 cup water
- 1/4 cup sugar
- 3 tablespoons red wine vinegar
- 3 tablespoons unsalted butter
- 1 medium onion, finely chopped
- 2 cups Merlot or other dry red wine
- 2 cups Veal Stock (page 929), or 1 cup veal demi-glace (see Sources) plus 1 cup water
- 1/2 teaspoon salt, or to taste
- 1/4 teaspoon freshly ground black pepper, or to taste

FOR STEAKS

- 6 (1 1/4-inch-thick) filets mignons (2 1/4 pounds total)
- 1 teaspoon salt
- 1/2 teaspoon freshly ground black pepper
- 2 tablespoons vegetable oil

MAKE THE SAUCE: Combine water and sugar in a 1-quart heavy saucepan and bring to a boil, stirring until sugar is dissolved. Boil syrup, without stirring, until it is a golden caramel. Remove pan from heat and carefully add vinegar, pouring it down side of pan (caramel will steam vigorously and harden). Cook caramel over moderate heat, stirring, until dissolved, about 2 minutes. Remove from heat.

Melt butter in a 2-quart heavy saucepan over moderate heat. Add onion and cook, stirring, until golden, about 5 minutes. Add wine, bring to a boil, and boil until reduced to about 1 cup, about 15 minutes. Add stock, bring to a boil, and boil until sauce is reduced to about 2 cups, about 10 minutes. Stir in salt and pepper.

Pour sauce through a sieve into pan of caramel,

pressing on solids; discard solids. Bring to a simmer, then remove from heat and season with salt and pepper. Cover to keep warm.

COOK THE STEAKS: Put a rack in middle of oven and preheat oven to 425°F.

Pat steaks dry and sprinkle with salt and pepper. Heat oil in a 12-inch heavy skillet over moderately high heat until hot but not smoking. Add steaks and sear, turning once, until well browned, about 5 minutes total. Arrange steaks on a baking sheet with sides and roast for 10 minutes for medium-rare. Transfer to a plate and let stand, loosely covered with foil, for 5 minutes.

Transfer steaks to six plates and drizzle with some sauce. Serve remaining sauce on the side.

COOK'S NOTE

- The sauce can be made up to 2 days ahead. Cool completely, then refrigerate, covered. Reheat before serving.

Flank Steak with Chimichurri

SERVES 4 TO 6

ACTIVE TIME: 10 MINUTES ■ START TO FINISH: 30 MINUTES

■ Flank steak is a long, relatively thin steak with a distinctive longitudinal grain. When improperly prepared, it can be quite tough, but if cooked quickly to rare or medium-rare and sliced very thin on the bias, against the grain, it is perfectly tender. We serve this full-flavored steak with chimichurri, a thick herb sauce that typically accompanies steak in Argentina. ■

FOR STEAK

- 1½ pounds trimmed flank steak
- 1 teaspoon kosher salt
- ½ teaspoon ground cumin
- ½ teaspoon ground coriander
- ¼ teaspoon freshly ground black pepper

FOR CHIMICHURRI SAUCE

- 1 large garlic clove
- 1½ cups loosely packed fresh cilantro leaves
- 1½ cups loosely packed fresh flat-leaf parsley leaves
- ¼ cup distilled white vinegar
- ⅓ cup olive oil
- ¼ teaspoon cayenne
- ½ teaspoon kosher salt

BROIL THE STEAK: Put broiler pan under broiler and preheat broiler. Pat steak dry. Stir together salt, cumin, coriander, and pepper in a small bowl and rub onto both sides of steak.

Broil steak on hot broiler pan about 4 inches from heat, turning once, for 12 minutes total for medium-rare. Transfer to a cutting board and let stand, loosely covered with foil, for 5 minutes.

MEANWHILE, MAKE THE SAUCE: With motor running, add garlic to a food processor and finely chop. Add cilantro, parsley, vinegar, oil, cayenne, and salt and pulse until herbs are finely chopped.

Holding a knife at a 45-degree angle, thinly slice steak against grain. Serve with sauce.

Pan-Seared Ancho Skirt Steak

SERVES 4

ACTIVE TIME: 20 MINUTES ■ START TO FINISH: 20 MINUTES

■ You can never have enough easy dishes up your sleeve for hectic weeknights or lazy days at the shore. Skirt steak, which is very quick to cook, is perfect for those occasions. We slather it with a Mexican-inspired sauce of ancho chiles, orange juice, and garlic before tossing it into the skillet. Be sure to slice it on an angle across the grain. ■

- 2 large or 4 small dried ancho or New Mexico chiles (1 ounce total; see Glossary)
- ⅔ cup fresh orange juice
- 2 garlic cloves
- 1 tablespoon olive oil
- Salt
- 1½ pounds skirt steak, cut into 4 pieces
- 2 tablespoons vegetable oil

ACCOMPANIMENT: avocado slices

Heat a small heavy skillet, preferably well-seasoned cast-iron, over moderate heat. Toast chiles, pressing down with tongs, until slightly darker, 5 to 10 seconds on each side. Remove and discard stems and seeds.

Soak chiles in hot water to cover for 5 minutes. Drain and tear into pieces.

Combine chiles, orange juice, garlic, olive oil, and salt to taste in a blender and purée until smooth, about 2 minutes. Transfer half of sauce to a small serving bowl.

Season steak with salt and coat generously with remaining sauce.

Heat two 12-inch heavy skillets (or cook steak in 2 batches) over high heat until hot but not smoking. Add 1 tablespoon vegetable oil to each, swirling to coat bottom of skillets. Add steak and cook, turning once, 4 to 6 minutes total for medium-rare. Transfer steak to a platter and let stand, loosely covered with foil, for 5 minutes.

Slice steak on an angle across the grain and serve with avocado slices and reserved sauce.

Skirt Steak Fajitas with Lime and Black Pepper

SERVES 6

ACTIVE TIME: 40 MINUTES ■ START TO FINISH: 40 MINUTES

■ This is the dish that took skirt steak from an inexpensive and rather obscure cut of beef to a highly popular supermarket item. Fajitas, which originated among Hispanic ranch workers in south Texas in the 1930s, take their name from the Spanish *faja,* which means belt. It's an apt word to describe the long, ropy skirt steak, a then undesirable cut that ranchers often gave to workers as part of their pay. After tenderizing the meat in lime juice, the workers would grill it over mesquite and wrap it in tortillas along with some grilled onions: *tacos de fajitas.* Over the years, the dish caught on with home cooks and restaurateurs in the American Southwest and then rolled across the country like tumbleweed. ■

- 2 large onions, peeled and cut lengthwise into 6 wedges, root ends left intact
- 2½ tablespoons olive oil
- Salt and freshly ground black pepper
- ¼ cup fresh lime juice
- 2 pounds skirt steak, cut into 2 pieces
- 2½ teaspoons balsamic vinegar
- 18 (8-inch) flour tortillas
- 1 cup loosely packed fresh cilantro leaves

ACCOMPANIMENT: tomatillo or tomato salsa; lime wedges

SPECIAL EQUIPMENT: metal skewers or a grill basket

Prepare a charcoal or gas grill: If using a charcoal grill, open vents in bottom of grill, then light charcoal. Fire is medium-hot when you can hold your hand 5 inches above rack for just 3 to 4 seconds. If using a gas grill, preheat on high, covered, for 10 minutes, then reduce heat to moderately high.

Thread onions onto skewers, brush with 1½ teaspoons oil, and season with salt and pepper. Or brush with oil, season, and put in grill basket. Grill onions, turning occasionally, until tender, 16 to 20 minutes. Transfer to a cutting board to cool slightly.

Meanwhile, stir together lime juice, 1 teaspoon salt, and remaining 2 tablespoons oil in a shallow dish. Add steak, turn to coat, and marinate at room temperature, turning once, for 10 minutes.

When onions are just cool enough to handle, cut into 1-inch pieces and toss with vinegar and ½ teaspoon salt.

Pat steak dry and rub with 2½ teaspoons pepper. Lightly oil grill rack. Grill steak, turning once, for 6 to 10 minutes total for medium-rare. Transfer to a cutting board and let stand, loosely covered with foil, for 5 minutes.

While steak is standing, toast tortillas on grill rack, turning once, until slightly puffed and browned in spots, about 1 minute total.

Cut steak diagonally across grain into thin slices. Serve steak, onions, and cilantro wrapped in tortillas, with salsa and lime wedges, or let your guests assemble their own.

COOK'S NOTE

■ The onions (no need to skewer) and steak can also be cooked in a lightly oiled, well-seasoned, ridged grill pan over moderately high heat. Cut the steak into pieces to fit in the grill pan and grill in batches, without crowding. The tortillas can be toasted over a gas burner — hold them with tongs — or directly on electric burners.

Flank, Hanger, and Skirt Steak

FLANK, HANGER, AND SKIRT STEAK

Generally speaking, steaks are cut from thick muscles, primarily from the short loin and sirloin. The exceptions to this rule are the three thinner flat steaks: flank steak, skirt steak, and hanger steak. All of them are cut from the chest and side of the animal, and all are long, relatively thin, quite tough, and coarse-grained. Because of these qualities, they used to be considered low-class. But they also share another characteristic: rich, deep, beefy flavor. As American cooks have become more aware of this, all three steaks have become very popular.

Fortunately, FLANK STEAK is easy to find in any butcher shop or supermarket. Recognizable by its longitudinal grain, flank has terrific flavor and is quite tender if cooked to rare or medium-rare and sliced thin against the grain. Unfortunately, largely because of the popularity of fajitas and London broil (the name popularly given to marinated flank steak), this cut has become relatively expensive.

FLANK STEAK

HANGER STEAK, a thick muscle attached to the diaphragm, derives its name from the fact that when the steer is butchered, the steak hangs down into the center of the carcass. Because hanger steak is a classic French bistro dish, the cut is highly prized by restaurants and therefore difficult to find even in butcher shops.

HANGER STEAK

SKIRT STEAK, the cut originally used in fajitas, used to be hard to locate but is now often available in supermarkets—a good thing, because it is a wonderful piece of meat. It has more fat than the hanger or flank, which makes it juicier and richer; at the same time, it has a deep, full flavor that outdoes both the hanger and the flank.

SKIRT STEAK

Grilling Tips and Techniques

There is no question that gas is the most convenient fuel for grilling, but it lacks the high heat provided by wood, charcoal briquettes, and hardwood charcoal. If your top priority is convenience, gas is for you; otherwise, go with live fire.

CHOOSING YOUR FUEL: In the United States, pillow-shaped charcoal briquettes are the default fuel for live-fire cooking, and they work very well. But they have one fundamental problem: they are not entirely charcoal. Invented early in the twentieth century by Henry Ford to use scrap wood left over from forms made for building cars, briquettes are composed of low-quality powdered charcoal mixed with extraneous binders so they can be compressed into those little pillows. The next best thing to wood itself (which is too inconsistent and hard to manage for most home grillers) is hardwood charcoal. Made by the traditional process of burning hardwood in a closed container with very little oxygen, this kind of charcoal is almost pure carbon. As a result, it lights more readily than briquettes, burns cleaner and slightly hotter, and is more responsive to changes in the oxygen level, which means you can regulate it more easily.

STARTING THE FIRE: Treat yourself to a chimney starter, a tool that is simple, inexpensive, and virtually foolproof. It's nothing more than a sheet-metal cylinder open at both ends, with ventilation holes around the bottom, an inside grate several inches from the bottom, and a handle. To use it, fill the bottom section with a few sheets of crumpled newspaper, set it in the middle of the grill, and fill it with charcoal. Light the newspaper; the flames will sweep up through the chimney, igniting the charcoal. When the charcoal is red-hot, which should take about five minutes, dump it out and put any additional charcoal you want on top of or around it. That's all there is to it, and it works every time.

An electric coil starter—a thick, oval electrical coil with a plastic handle—is another option. Put it right on the fire grate, mound charcoal over it, and plug it into a grounded outlet. The coil will soon become red-hot, igniting the charcoal it's touching. Unplug the coil and remove it; the hot coals will ignite the others. Set the coil aside on a fireproof surface, making very sure it is out of reach of children and pets.

LAYING THE FIRE: This is probably the single most important tip we can give you. When you build your fire, always leave about one quarter of the bottom of the grill free of charcoal and bank the charcoal in the remaining three quarters, so the coals are about three times as high on one side as on the other. This way, if your food begins to burn on the outside before it's done on the inside or if it flares up, you can move it to the cooler portion of the fire or even to the area where there is no fire at all. This arrangement also provides varying levels of heat in the same fire, which is handy if you want to grill a steak over a very hot fire and asparagus over a medium fire at the same time.

CHECKING THE TEMPERATURE OF THE FIRE: Always check the temperature before you begin to cook. First allow the flames to build up and subside. Then, when the coals are uniformly gray, put your hand about five inches above the grill rack, palm side down. If you can hold it there for one to two seconds, you have a hot fire; three to four seconds is within the medium range; five to six seconds means you have a low fire.

COVERING THE FIRE: Of course you'll cover the grill when you are cooking by indirect heat. But don't use the cover when the food is directly over the coals; it gives the food an off flavor, which we believe comes from the fat that drips directly onto the coals, vaporizes, and is trapped inside the cover. Also, many sources advise you to use the cover to douse a flare-up: don't. Instead, if you have laid a fire as described, simply move the food away from the coals until the flare-up has died down.

SALTING PROPERLY: This principle doesn't have anything to do with the fire itself, but it does affect how your food will taste. Please forget the old rule that you shouldn't salt food before cooking because it draws out moisture. Salt interacts with the food to amplify its flavor, which more than compensates for the small amount of moisture it draws to the surface. It also intensifies the browning process, which creates more flavor. And consider using a bit more salt than you are used to. Of course, this is all a matter of taste, and you know what you like; we're simply suggesting that you try a slightly bolder approach and see what you think. (If you're worried about the health effects of using more salt, remember that more than 75 percent of the sodium consumed by the average American comes from processed food — so cut down on hot dogs, luncheon meats, chips, and frozen meals instead.)

Grilled Porterhouse Steak

SERVES 6

ACTIVE TIME: 20 MINUTES ■ START TO FINISH: 1 HOUR

■ Considered the king of grilled steaks, the porterhouse, which comes from the short loin section of the steer, has a large bone running down the middle and is actually two steaks in one. It includes a section of the ultratender tenderloin on one side of the bone and a section of the flavorful top loin on the other side. It shares this admirable characteristic with the T-bone, but the porterhouse comes from the rear section of the short loin, where the tenderloin muscle is thicker, so it has a higher overall tenderness quotient. To add even more robust flavor, we rub the steak with crushed mixed peppercorns, available in bottles in many supermarkets. ■

- 3 (1½- to 1¾-pound) porterhouse steaks (1½ inches thick), trimmed
- 3 tablespoons mixed peppercorns
- 1½ teaspoons kosher salt

SPECIAL EQUIPMENT: a large chimney starter (if using a charcoal grill); an instant-read thermometer

Let steaks stand at room temperature for 30 minutes.

Prepare a charcoal or gas grill: If using a charcoal grill, open vents in bottom of grill and in lid. Light a heaping chimneyful of charcoal, then pour lit charcoal onto opposite sides of bottom of grill, leaving middle clear. Fire is medium-hot when you can hold your hand 5 inches above rack with coals underneath for just 3 to 4 seconds. If using a gas grill, preheat on high, covered, for 10 minutes.

Coarsely crush peppercorns in a sealed plastic bag, or between sheets of wax paper, with the bottom of a heavy skillet. Stir together with salt in a small bowl. Pat steaks dry and rub seasoning onto both sides, pressing so it adheres.

Lightly oil grill rack. Sear steaks over coals (covered only if using gas), turning once, until grill marks appear on both sides, about 2 minutes total. Move steaks to area with no coals underneath, or turn off burner under steaks if using gas and reduce remaining burners to moderate heat, and grill, covered, turning occasionally, until thermometer inserted horizontally 2 inches into meat (without touching bone) registers 120°F, 15 to 18 minutes.

Transfer to a plate and let stand, loosely covered with foil, for 10 minutes (steak will continue to cook, reaching medium-rare).

COOK'S NOTE

■ The steaks can be broiled on the oiled rack of a broiler pan about 4 inches from the heat, turned once, for about 20 minutes total. Let stand as above.

Grilled Rib-Eye Steak with Béarnaise Butter

SERVES 4

ACTIVE TIME: 30 MINUTES ■ START TO FINISH: 1½ HOURS

■ A rib eye has a near-ideal combination of tenderness and deep, beefy taste, making it a perfect choice for a luxe steak dinner. When you serve this flame-charred cut with a little pat of béarnaise butter melting gently over the top, it's virtually irresistible. ■

FOR BÉARNAISE BUTTER

- 3 tablespoons unsalted butter, softened
- 2 teaspoons finely chopped fresh tarragon
- 2 teaspoons minced shallot
- ½ teaspoon fresh lemon juice, or to taste
- ⅛ teaspoon salt

FOR STEAK

- 4 (1-inch-thick) rib-eye steaks (4 pounds total)
- 1½ tablespoons vegetable oil
- 1½ teaspoons salt
- ½ teaspoon freshly ground black pepper

MAKE THE BÉARNAISE BUTTER: Blend together all ingredients on a small plate with a fork. Transfer to a sheet of wax paper and, using wax paper as an aid, shape butter into a 3-inch-long log; wrap in wax paper. Refrigerate until firm, at least 1 hour.

GRILL THE STEAKS: Prepare a charcoal or gas grill: If using a charcoal grill, open vents in bottom of grill, then light charcoal. Fire is hot when you can hold your hand 5 inches above rack for just 1 to 2 seconds. If using a gas grill, preheat on high, covered, for 10 minutes, then reduce heat to moderately high.

Pat steaks dry. Rub with oil and sprinkle with salt and pepper. Grill steaks, uncovered, turning once, for 8 to 10 minutes total for medium-rare. Transfer steaks to a platter and let stand, loosely covered with foil, for 5 minutes.

Serve steaks topped with thin slices of béarnaise butter.

COOK'S NOTES

- The béarnaise butter can be refrigerated for up to 5 days.
- The steaks can also be cooked in a hot, well-seasoned, ridged grill pan over moderately high heat.

Grilled Korean-Style Steak with Spicy Cilantro Sauce

SERVES 6

ACTIVE TIME: 30 MINUTES ■ START TO FINISH: 1½ HOURS

■ We liven up one of our favorite cuts of meat with cilantro, lime, and sesame oil, along with chiles (when we want to ratchet up the spice factor). Use cilantro with stems and roots: unlike those of most other herbs, the stems are tender and flavorful, and the roots, often used in Southeast Asian cooking, have an intensity that is tempered by sweetness. (For more about boneless beef top loin steaks, see page 426.) ■

- ¾ cup plus 3 tablespoons soy sauce
- ¼ cup medium-dry sherry
- 3 tablespoons sugar
- 2 tablespoons minced garlic
- 1 tablespoon plus ½ teaspoon Asian sesame oil
- 1 teaspoon red pepper flakes
- 6 (1-inch-thick) boneless beef top loin steaks (about 4½ pounds total)
- ¾ cup chopped fresh cilantro (including roots if attached and stems)
- ⅓ cup vegetable oil
- 1 tablespoon fresh lime juice
- ½ teaspoon minced seeded habanero or serrano chile (optional)
- 1 (4-inch-long) fresh hot red chile, chopped (optional)

Stir together ¾ cup soy sauce, sherry, sugar, 1½ tablespoons garlic, 1 tablespoon sesame oil, and red pepper flakes in a 13-by-9-inch baking dish until sugar is dissolved. Add steaks and turn to coat. Cover and marinate steaks at room temperature, turning once, for 1 hour.

Prepare a charcoal or gas grill for cooking: If using a charcoal grill, open vents in bottom of grill, then light charcoal. Fire is medium-hot when you can hold your hand 5 inches above rack for just 3 to 4 seconds. If using a gas grill, preheat on high, covered, for 10 minutes, then reduce heat to moderately high.

Stir together cilantro, vegetable oil, lime juice, remaining 3 tablespoons soy sauce, remaining 1½ teaspoons garlic, remaining ½ teaspoon sesame oil, and chiles (if using) in a small bowl.

Lightly oil grill rack. Lift steaks from marinade, letting excess drip off (discard marinade). Grill steaks, turning once, for 6 to 8 minutes total for medium-rare. Transfer to a cutting board and let stand, loosely covered with foil, for 5 minutes.

Cut steaks into ¾-inch-thick slices. Top with some sauce and serve remaining sauce on the side.

Grilled Beer-Marinated Chuck Steak and Onions

SERVES 6 TO 8

ACTIVE TIME: 20 MINUTES ■ START TO FINISH: 13 HOURS (INCLUDES MARINATING)

■ The great thing about beef chuck is that it has so much rich taste; the drawback is that it is often quite tough. But by piercing chuck steaks all over with a fork, then marinating them overnight in a flavorful beer-based marinade with plenty of onions, we make them tender and enrich them at the same time. ■

- 2 medium yellow or red onions
- 1 (12-ounce) bottle beer (not dark)
- 2/3 cup vegetable oil
- 2 tablespoons cider vinegar
- 1 tablespoon Worcestershire sauce
- 1½ teaspoons salt
- 1 teaspoon freshly ground black pepper
- 3 (1-inch-thick) boneless chuck steaks (3½ pounds total), trimmed and pierced all over (on both sides) with a fork

SPECIAL EQUIPMENT: an instant-read thermometer

Cut six ½-inch-thick crosswise slices from onions, then grate enough from remaining onion to measure 1 tablespoon. Secure each onion slice horizontally with a wooden pick.

Stir together beer, oil, vinegar, Worcestershire sauce, salt, pepper, and grated onion in a large shallow baking dish or a large sealable plastic bag. Add steaks and onion slices and turn to coat well. Cover or seal bag and marinate, refrigerated, turning occasionally, for at least 12 hours.

Let steaks stand at room temperature for 30 minutes.

While steaks stand, prepare a charcoal or gas grill: If using a charcoal grill, open vents in bottom of grill and light charcoal. Fire is medium-hot when you can hold your hand 5 inches above rack for just 3 to 4 seconds. If using a gas grill, preheat on high, covered, for 10 minutes, then reduce heat to moderate.

Lightly oil grill rack. Lift steaks from marinade, letting excess drip off, and grill (covered only if using gas), turning once, until thermometer inserted horizontally 2 inches into meat registers 120°F, 6 to 8 minutes total. Transfer to a plate and let stand, loosely covered with foil, for 10 minutes. (Steaks will continue to cook, reaching medium-rare.)

While steaks stand, grill onions (covered only if using gas), turning occasionally, until tender, 6 to 8 minutes. Remove and discard wooden picks. Discard marinade.

Holding knife at a 45-degree angle, cut steaks across the grain into thin slices. Serve with onions.

COOK'S NOTE

- The steaks can marinate for up to 24 hours.

Grilled Stuffed Flank Steak

Matambre

SERVES 6

ACTIVE TIME: 2½ HOURS ■ START TO FINISH: 3 HOURS

■ *Matambre* (literally, "kill the hunger") is a classic dish of Argentina and Uruguay, where beef is king. Every family has its own favorite filling—some use vegetables, eggs, and nuts; others use ground pork, calves' brains, and spinach. We keep it simple and roll the flank steak up around a well-seasoned mixture of spinach and carrots. With the richness of the steak and bacon, the freshness of the herbs, and the sweetness of the vegetables, this dish provides a terrific combination of flavors. Although it is traditionally poached, we grill ours, adding yet another layer of flavor. It's great served hot, but it's also quite delicious at room temperature, which makes it an excellent choice for a buffet. ■

- 4 medium carrots, peeled if desired and cut into thirds
- 6 bacon slices, cut into ½-inch-wide pieces
- 1 cup fine fresh bread crumbs
- ¼ cup finely chopped fresh flat-leaf parsley
- 2 garlic cloves, minced
- 1 teaspoon finely chopped fresh oregano
- 2 teaspoons kosher salt
- ½ teaspoon freshly ground black pepper
- ⅛ teaspoon ground cloves
- ⅛ teaspoon freshly grated nutmeg
- 1 (2½-pound) flank steak, trimmed
- ½ pound spinach, stems discarded

SPECIAL EQUIPMENT: kitchen string; a large chimney starter (if using a charcoal grill); an instant-read thermometer

Cook carrots in a 1½-quart saucepan of boiling well-salted water until barely tender, 6 to 8 minutes; drain. When cool, cut each section lengthwise into 3 pieces.

Cook bacon in a 10-inch skillet over moderate heat, stirring, until crisp. With a slotted spoon, transfer to paper towels to drain; reserve fat.

Stir together bacon, bread crumbs, parsley, garlic, oregano, salt, pepper, cloves, nutmeg, and 2 tablespoons bacon fat in a small bowl until well combined; discard remaining fat.

BUTTERFLY THE STEAK: Put steak on two overlapping sheets of plastic wrap (each about 2 feet long) with a short end of steak nearest you. Anchor meat with one hand; hold a sharp knife in other hand parallel to work surface. On long side, begin to cut through meat horizontally (1). Lift top layer and continue to cut meat almost in half, stopping about 1/2 inch from edge; do not cut all the way through (2). Open meat like a book.

Turn steak so a long side is nearest you. Arrange spinach evenly over steak, leaving a 1-inch border along edge farthest from you. Top spinach with carrot pieces, arranging them parallel to long sides and spacing them evenly. Sprinkle evenly with bread crumb mixture.

Beginning with side nearest you and using plastic wrap as an aid, roll up steak, gently pressing on filling (do not roll too tightly, or filling will slip out from ends). Tie steak crosswise with string at 3/4-inch intervals. Season with salt and pepper.

TO COOK THE STEAK USING A CHARCOAL GRILL: Open vents in bottom of grill and in lid. Light a heaping chimneyful of charcoal and pour it evenly over one side of bottom of grill (you should have a double or triple layer of charcoal). Fire is medium-hot when you can hold your hand 5 inches above rack with coals underneath for just 3 to 4 seconds.

Lightly oil grill rack. Sear steak on all sides over coals until well browned, 8 to 10 minutes.

Move steak to side of grill with no coals, cover with lid, and cook, turning once, until thermometer inserted diagonally 2 inches into thickest part of steak registers 125°F, 25 to 30 minutes total.

TO COOK THE STEAK USING A GAS GRILL: Preheat grill on high, covered, for 10 minutes, then reduce heat to moderately high. Lightly oil grill rack and sear steak on all sides until well browned, 8 to 10 minutes. Turn off burner below steak, cover with lid, and cook, turning once, until thermometer inserted diagonally 2 inches into thickest part of steak registers 125°F, 25 to 30 minutes total.

Transfer steak to a cutting board and let stand, covered loosely with foil, for 20 minutes. (It will continue to cook, reaching 130°F for medium-rare.)

Remove and discard string, being careful not to unroll steak. Cut steak into 1/2-inch-thick slices with a sharp knife.

HOW TO BUTTERFLY A FLANK STEAK

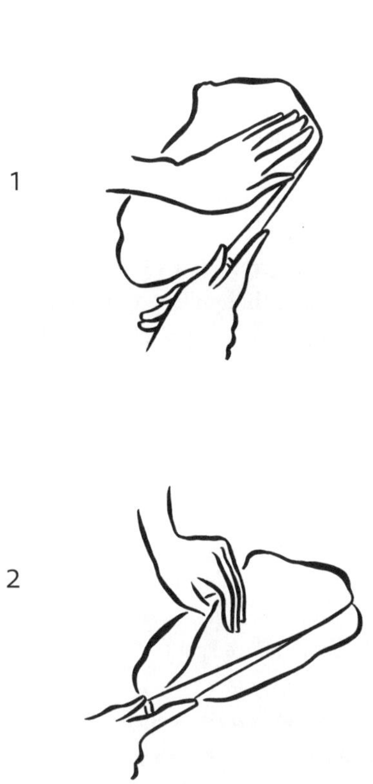

COOK'S NOTES

- The steak can be rolled and tied up to 1 day ahead. Refrigerate, wrapped in plastic wrap. Bring to room temperature before grilling.
- The steak can also be seared in a 12-inch heavy skillet (the ends of the roll will come up the sides). Heat the remaining bacon fat or 1 tablespoon olive oil over moderately high heat. Sear the steak on all sides, 8 to 10 minutes total. Transfer to a roasting pan and roast in the middle of a 350°F oven for 20 to 25 minutes. Let stand as above.

London Broil with Ravigote Sauce

SERVES 6
ACTIVE TIME: 30 MINUTES ■ START TO FINISH: 12½ HOURS (INCLUDES MARINATING)

■ The term *London broil* originally designated a flank steak that was first marinated, then broiled or grilled and cut across the grain at a 45-degree angle into thin slices. These days, though, the term is commonly applied to two boneless cuts of beef, top round (which comes from the upper rear leg) and chuck shoulder steak, which are cooked and served in the same way. We call for top round because it's more widely available and easier to carve. But chuck shoulder steak, which has a little gristle but more flavor, is also a fine choice. To complement the flavorful steak, we serve a traditional French sauce made with herbs and capers. ■

- 2 tablespoons minced garlic
- 2 tablespoons soy sauce
- 2 tablespoons red wine vinegar
- 1 tablespoon vegetable oil
- ½ teaspoon red pepper flakes
- ½ teaspoon sugar
- ½ teaspoon salt
- 1 (1½-pound) London broil (from top round; 1¼ inches thick)
- Ravigote Sauce (recipe follows)

SPECIAL EQUIPMENT: a large chimney starter (if using a charcoal grill); an instant-read thermometer

MARINATE THE STEAK: Combine garlic, soy sauce, vinegar, oil, red pepper flakes, sugar, and salt in a blender and blend until pepper flakes are finely chopped. Put steak in a large sealable plastic bag, add marinade, and seal bag, forcing out excess air. Refrigerate steak, turning occasionally, for 12 hours.

Let steak stand at room temperature for 30 minutes. Meanwhile, prepare a charcoal or gas grill.

TO COOK THE STEAK USING A CHARCOAL GRILL: Open vents in bottom of grill. Light a heaping chimneyful of charcoal, then pour lit charcoal into bottom of grill, leaving about one quarter of bottom free of charcoal and banking remaining coals across rest of bottom so that coals are about three times higher on side opposite charcoal-free area. Fire is medium-hot when you can hold your hand 5 inches above rack with thickest layer of coals underneath for just 3 to 4 seconds.

Lightly oil grill rack. Lift steak from marinade, letting excess drip off. Sear steak over thickest layer of coals, uncovered, turning once, until grill marks appear on both sides, about 2 minutes total. Move steak to area over fewer coals and grill, uncovered, turning occasionally and moving to coolest area of grill if flare-ups occur, until thermometer inserted horizontally 2 inches into meat registers 120°F, 8 to 10 minutes. Transfer to a plate and let stand, loosely covered with foil, for 10 minutes. (Steak will continue to cook, reaching medium-rare.)

TO COOK THE STEAK USING A GAS GRILL: Preheat grill on high, covered, for 10 minutes. Lightly oil grill rack. Lift steak from marinade, letting excess drip off. Sear steak, covered, turning once, until grill marks appear on both sides, about 2 minutes total. Reduce heat to moderate and grill steak, covered, turning occasionally, until thermometer inserted horizontally 2 inches into meat registers 120°F, 8 to 10 minutes. Transfer to a plate and let stand, loosely covered with foil, for 10 minutes. (Steak will continue to cook, reaching medium-rare.)

Thinly slice steak with a knife held at a 45-degree angle and serve with sauce.

COOK'S NOTE

■ The steak can also be cooked in a well-seasoned, ridged grill pan over moderately high heat, turning once, about 16 minutes total.

Ravigote Sauce

MAKES ABOUT 1½ CUPS
ACTIVE TIME: 20 MINUTES ■ START TO FINISH: 20 MINUTES

■ There are two versions of this classic French sauce. We prefer this one—basically a vinaigrette flavored with onion, shallots, capers, and herbs—to a richer velouté, a white sauce made with broth. You can serve it cold with seafood and vegetables or, as here, at room temperature with meat. ■

- $^2/_3$ cup finely chopped onion
- 2 tablespoons Dijon mustard
- 4 teaspoons white wine vinegar
- $^2/_3$ cup olive oil
- $^1/_4$ cup drained capers, chopped
- $^1/_4$ cup minced fresh flat-leaf parsley
- 2 tablespoons minced shallots
- 2 tablespoons finely chopped fresh chives or scallion greens
- $1^1/_2$ teaspoons finely chopped fresh tarragon or $^1/_2$ teaspoon dried tarragon, crumbled
- Salt and freshly ground black pepper

Soak onion in a bowl of water for 3 minutes. Drain and squeeze dry in a kitchen towel.

Whisk together mustard and vinegar in a medium bowl. Add oil in a slow stream, whisking until well blended. Stir in onion, capers, parsley, shallots, chives, tarragon, and salt and pepper to taste.

COOK'S NOTE

- The sauce, without the herbs, can be made up to 1 day ahead and refrigerated, covered. Bring to room temperature and stir in the parsley, tarragon, and chives before serving.

Beef Stroganoff

SERVES 6

ACTIVE TIME: 35 MINUTES ■ START TO FINISH: 35 MINUTES

■ Stroganoff is one of those dishes whose once stellar reputation has been besmirched by generations of ersatz renditions. But this one is the real deal: tender beef chunks are briefly sautéed, then swirled together with a creamy sauce flavored with a perfectly balanced combination of shallots, mushrooms, mustard, and fresh dill. Once you make it, you (and your guests) will understand just why this dish, created in Russia well over a hundred years ago, is still an international favorite. ■

- $3^1/_2$ tablespoons unsalted butter
- 1 tablespoon all-purpose flour
- 1 cup beef stock or store-bought broth
- 1 (1-pound) piece beef tenderloin, trimmed, sliced $^1/_4$ inch thick, and cut into 1-inch pieces, or 1 pound filet mignon, cut into 1-inch pieces
- Salt and freshly ground black pepper
- 2 tablespoons olive oil
- $^1/_2$ cup thinly sliced shallots
- $^3/_4$ pound cremini mushrooms, trimmed and halved, or quartered if large
- 3 tablespoons sour cream, at room temperature
- 1 teaspoon Dijon mustard
- 2 tablespoons chopped fresh dill

ACCOMPANIMENT: buttered wide egg noodles

Melt $1^1/_2$ tablespoons butter in a 1-quart heavy saucepan over moderate heat. Whisk in flour and cook, whisking constantly, for 2 minutes to make a roux. Add stock in a slow stream, whisking constantly, and bring to a boil. Reduce heat and simmer, whisking occasionally, for 3 minutes. Remove from heat and cover to keep warm.

Pat beef dry and season well with salt and pepper. Heat 1 tablespoon butter and 1 tablespoon oil in a 12-inch heavy skillet over moderately high heat until foam subsides. Add beef in 2 batches and cook, turning once, until browned on both sides but still pink inside, about 1 minute per batch. With a slotted spoon, transfer to a plate.

Add remaining 1 tablespoon each butter and oil to skillet and heat until hot but not smoking. Add shallots and cook, stirring occasionally, until golden brown, about 3 minutes. Add mushrooms and cook, stirring occasionally, until liquid mushrooms give off has evaporated and mushrooms are browned, 8 to 10 minutes.

Return meat, with its juices, to skillet and stir to combine, then transfer to a platter.

Reheat sauce over low heat, then whisk in sour cream, mustard, dill, $^1/_2$ teaspoon salt, and $^1/_4$ teaspoon pepper (do not let boil). Pour sauce over beef and serve over noodles.

Beef Bourguignon

SERVES 8
ACTIVE TIME: 1¼ HOURS ■ START TO FINISH: 5 HOURS

■ Some dishes are simply famous. This version of beef bourguignon, adapted from Suzanne Rodriguez-Hunter's *Found Meals of the Lost Generation,* is a case in point. Be sure that you brown the beef very well. The high-heat reaction between the proteins and sugars on the surface of the meat, known as the Maillard reaction, creates a layer of intense flavor, which gets distributed throughout during braising. Peeled boiled potatoes tossed with butter and parsley are the ideal accompaniment. ■

- ¼ pound thick-sliced bacon (3 slices), cut into 1-inch-wide pieces
- 3 pounds boneless beef chuck, cut into 2-inch chunks
- Salt and freshly ground black pepper
- ⅓ cup all-purpose flour
- 2 tablespoons vegetable oil
- 4½ tablespoons unsalted butter
- ½ cup brandy
- 1 (4-inch) piece celery rib
- 4 fresh parsley stems (without leaves)
- 4 fresh thyme sprigs
- 2 Turkish bay leaves or 1 California bay leaf
- 2 whole cloves
- 2 onions, finely chopped
- 3 large garlic cloves, finely chopped
- 2 carrots, peeled if desired and cut into ¼-inch-thick slices
- 1 tablespoon tomato paste
- 1 (750-milliliter) bottle dry red wine, preferably Burgundy or Côtes du Rhône
- 1 pound small (1½-inch-wide) boiling onions or pearl onions
- 1 pound mushrooms, trimmed, quartered if large

SPECIAL EQUIPMENT: kitchen string

Cook bacon in a 3-quart saucepan of boiling water for 3 minutes, then drain.

Pat beef dry and season with salt and pepper. Divide flour between two large sealable plastic bags. Divide beef between bags, seal bags, and shake to coat meat.

Heat 1½ tablespoons oil and 1½ tablespoons butter in a 6- to 8-quart wide heavy pot over moderately high heat until hot but not smoking. Brown beef well in 2 or 3 batches, without crowding, adding remaining ½ tablespoon oil as needed. Transfer to a bowl.

Pour off any excess oil from pot, then add brandy and deglaze pot by boiling over high heat, stirring and scraping up brown bits, for 1 minute. Pour over beef.

Tie celery, parsley, thyme, bay leaves, and cloves together with kitchen string to make a bouquet garni (stick cloves into celery so they don't fall out). Heat 1 tablespoon butter in cleaned pot over moderately high heat until foam subsides, then cook bacon, stirring, for 2 minutes. Add chopped onions, garlic, and carrots and cook, stirring occasionally, until pale golden, about 5 minutes. Add tomato paste and cook, stirring, for 1 minute. Add wine, meat with its juices, and bouquet garni, bring to a simmer, and simmer gently, partially covered, until meat is tender, 3½ to 4 hours.

Choosing Meat for Stewing

When buying meat for a stew, you generally have two options: you can pick up packaged stew meat or you can buy a larger cut and cube it yourself. The first option is certainly more convenient, but we don't recommend it, because you don't know what part of the animal the meat came from. Certain cuts, mostly from the shoulder — like beef chuck and veal shank — are best for stewing. They have lots of connective tissue and fat to provide plenty of flavor and moistness during lengthy cooking. Packaged meat includes some of those cuts, but it may also include trimmings from others, such as round or sirloin, that turn dry when cooked slowly for a long time. Buying a larger piece of the right cut and dealing with it yourself gives you the chance to cut it into the size specified in the recipe. The same philosophy, by the way, holds true for buying meat for stir-frying.

Meanwhile, blanch boiling onions in a 4-quart saucepan of boiling well-salted water for 1 minute; drain (blanching onions makes peeling easier). Rinse under cold running water, then peel.

Heat 1 tablespoon butter in a 3-quart heavy saucepan over moderately high heat until foam subsides. Add boiling onions and cook, stirring occasionally, until browned in patches. Season with salt and pepper. Add 2 cups water (1½ cups if using pearl onions), bring to a simmer, and simmer, partially covered, until onions are tender, 15 to 20 minutes. Increase heat and boil, uncovered, stirring occasionally, until liquid is reduced to a glaze, 5 to 10 minutes. Remove from heat.

Heat remaining 1 tablespoon butter in a 12-inch nonstick skillet over moderately high heat until foam subsides. Add mushrooms and cook, stirring, until golden brown and any liquid mushrooms give off has evaporated, about 8 minutes. Season with salt and pepper. Remove from heat.

When meat is tender, stir onions and mushrooms into stew and simmer for 10 minutes. Remove and discard bouquet garni and skim any fat from surface of stew. Season with salt and pepper.

COOK'S NOTE

- The beef bourguignon can be made up to 1 day ahead, and in fact it tastes even better made ahead, because this gives the flavors time to develop. Cool, uncovered, then refrigerate, covered. Chilling also makes it easy to remove the fat from the surface.

Braised Beef, Peppers, and Onions

Ropa Vieja

SERVES 8

ACTIVE TIME: 1½ HOURS ■ START TO FINISH: 3½ HOURS

■ Skirt or flank steak, first simmered to tenderness, then shredded and stewed with bell peppers, onions, and tomatoes, is a staple of Cuban cuisine. It gets its name—"old clothes"—from the shreds of meat, peppers, and onions, which are said to resemble a mess of colorful rags. Don't let its name distract you, though; this hearty, flavorful stew is not to be missed. ■

- 3 pounds skirt or flank steak, trimmed and, if necessary, cut into 6- to 8-inch sections to fit in pot
- 8 cups water
- 2 carrots, coarsely chopped
- 1 large onion, coarsely chopped
- 2 celery ribs, coarsely chopped
- 1 Turkish bay leaf or ½ California bay leaf
- 6 garlic cloves, 3 lightly crushed, 3 minced
- 1¼ teaspoons dried oregano, crumbled
- 2 teaspoons ground cumin
- 2 teaspoons salt
- ¼ teaspoon black peppercorns
- 4 tablespoons olive oil
- 2 green bell peppers, cored, seeded, and cut into ¼-inch-wide strips
- 1 red onion, halved lengthwise and sliced lengthwise into ¼-inch-wide strips
- 1 (14- to 16-ounce) can whole tomatoes in juice, drained (juice reserved) and chopped
- 3 tablespoons tomato paste
- ½ teaspoon freshly ground black pepper, or to taste
- 2 red bell peppers, cored, seeded, and cut into ¼-inch-wide strips
- 2 yellow bell peppers, cored, seeded, and cut into ¼-inch-wide strips
- 1 cup frozen peas (not thawed)
- ½ cup pimiento-stuffed green olives, drained and halved

ACCOMPANIMENT: cooked rice

Combine beef, water, carrots, chopped onion, celery, bay leaf, crushed garlic, 1 teaspoon oregano, 1 teaspoon cumin, 1 teaspoon salt, and peppercorns in a 5-quart heavy pot and bring to a simmer. Simmer, uncovered, skimming froth as needed, until beef is tender, about 1½ hours. Remove from heat and let meat cool in cooking liquid for 30 minutes.

With a slotted spoon, transfer meat to a large plate. Pour liquid through a large sieve into a bowl, pressing on solids; discard solids and skim fat. Return liquid to pot, bring to a boil, and boil until reduced to about 3 cups, about 30 minutes. Pour reduced cooking liquid into a bowl. Wipe out pot.

While liquid reduces, with your fingers, pull meat into roughly 3-by-½-inch shreds; set aside.

Heat 2 tablespoons oil in cleaned pot over moderate heat. Add green bell peppers and red onion and cook, stirring, until softened, about 10 minutes. Add shredded meat, 2 cups cooking liquid, tomatoes, with their juice, tomato paste, minced garlic, remaining 1/4 teaspoon oregano, 1 teaspoon cumin, and 1 teaspoon salt, and ground pepper. Bring to a simmer and simmer, covered, for 20 minutes.

Meanwhile, heat remaining 2 tablespoons oil in a 12-inch heavy skillet over moderate heat. Add red and yellow bell peppers and cook, stirring occasionally, until softened, about 15 minutes.

Stir peppers into stew, along with enough of remaining cooking liquid to thin to desired consistency. Simmer, uncovered, for 5 minutes. Stir in peas and olives and simmer, uncovered, for 5 minutes.

Serve with rice.

COOK'S NOTE

- The beef can be simmered and the cooking liquid reduced up to 1 day ahead. Cool completely, uncovered, then refrigerate separately, covered.

Spicy Stir-Fried Beef with Tangerine and Cinnamon

SERVES 4

ACTIVE TIME: 1¼ HOURS ■ START TO FINISH: 10 HOURS (INCLUDES MARINATING) PLUS 3 DAYS FOR DRYING TANGERINE PEEL, IF PREPARING

■ Since ancient times the Chinese have found the pungent flavor of cinnamon to be a fine partner for beef, and this dish from Nina Simonds is a testament to the wisdom of that idea. If you don't feel like making your own dried tangerine peel, you can buy it in Asian markets. It's often labeled "dried citrus peel"; the pieces are dark orange-brown and very thin. Check, though, to make sure the bag does not also include thicker pieces of peel from oranges or grapefruit. ■

- 1½ pounds boneless beef chuck, trimmed
- 6 tablespoons Chinese rice wine or sake
- 2 (¼-inch-thick) slices fresh ginger, smashed with side of a large heavy knife
- ¾ teaspoon salt
- 2 pieces dried tangerine peel
- 1¼ cups water
- 3 tablespoons sugar
- 1½ tablespoons soy sauce
- 2 cups peanut oil or corn oil
- 4 tablespoons Asian sesame oil
- 4 (3-inch-long) dried red chiles, stemmed, seeded, and cut diagonally into ¼-inch pieces
- ⅛ teaspoon Sichuan peppercorns (optional; see Glossary)
- 1 teaspoon star anise pieces
- 1 (4-inch) cinnamon stick
- 1 teaspoon rice vinegar (not seasoned)

ACCOMPANIMENT: cooked rice

SPECIAL EQUIPMENT: a wok; a deep-fat thermometer

Cut beef lengthwise into 1-by-1½-inch-wide strips, then cut across the grain into ¼-inch-wide slices. Toss with 3 tablespoons rice wine, ginger, and salt in a medium bowl. Marinate, covered and refrigerated, for at least 8 hours.

Meanwhile, soak tangerine peel in hot water to cover in a small bowl for 1 hour. Drain and cut into very thin strips.

Stir together water, sugar, soy sauce, and remaining 3 tablespoons rice wine in another small bowl until sugar is dissolved.

Heat peanut oil in a wok over high heat until it reg-

Drying Tangerine Peel

Homemade dried tangerine peel is easy to make and has more flavor and fragrance than store-bought.

Scrub peels of tangerines or clementines, then remove in large pieces with your fingers. Arrange peels in one layer on a tray or large plate. Dry peel, uncovered, in a dry place, turning occasionally, for 3 to 4 days. The dried peel keeps for up to 6 months in an airtight container or a sealed plastic bag at room temperature.

isters 400°F on thermometer. Add beef in 4 batches and fry, stirring, until golden brown and slightly crisp, 3 to 4 minutes per batch. With a skimmer or slotted spoon, transfer to paper towels to drain. (Return oil to 400°F between batches.)

Pour off oil and wipe wok clean with paper towels. Heat wok over high heat until very hot. Add 2 tablespoons sesame oil and heat until very hot. Add chiles and stir-fry until they turn black, about 2 minutes. Transfer to a plate. Add 1 tablespoon sesame oil to wok and heat until very hot. Add peppercorns (if using) and star anise and stir-fry until fragrant, about 15 seconds. Add beef, soy sauce mixture, tangerine peel, and cinnamon stick and bring to a boil. Reduce heat, partially cover, and simmer until liquid is reduced to about 3/4 cup, about 40 minutes.

Increase heat to high and boil, stirring constantly, until sauce is reduced to a syrupy glaze (about 2 tablespoons), about 5 minutes. Add chiles, rice vinegar, and remaining 1 tablespoon sesame oil and toss until well combined.

Remove and discard cinnamon stick and star anise, if desired, and transfer beef to a platter. Serve with rice.

COOK'S NOTE

- The beef can marinate for up to 12 hours.

Stir-Fried Pepper Beef

SERVES 6

ACTIVE TIME: 45 MINUTES ■ START TO FINISH: 1 HOUR

■ Beef and bell peppers are a classic combination in Mexican as well as Chinese restaurants. The *Gourmet* correspondent Nina Simonds, who developed this recipe, told us that her family calls it "Chinese fajitas." Although rice would be a suitable accompaniment, Simonds prefers to play up the cross-cultural similarity by serving the stir-fry with flour tortillas, in the form of mock Mandarin pancakes. ■

- 1 pound flank steak, trimmed
- 4 1/2 tablespoons soy sauce
- 2 1/2 tablespoons Chinese rice wine or sake
- 1 teaspoon Asian sesame oil
- 2 1/2 teaspoons cornstarch
- 1/2 cup chicken stock, store-bought low-sodium broth, or water
- 1 teaspoon sugar
- 4 1/2 tablespoons vegetable oil
- 2 tablespoons Chinese fermented black beans (see Glossary), rinsed, drained, and chopped
- 1 1/2 tablespoons minced garlic
- 1 1/2 tablespoons minced peeled fresh ginger
- 1/2 teaspoon red pepper flakes
- 2 small red onions, halved lengthwise and thinly sliced lengthwise
- 2 red bell peppers, cored, seeded, and cut into 1/8-inch-wide strips
- 1 yellow bell pepper, cored, seeded, and cut into 1/8-inch-wide strips
- 1 orange bell pepper, cored, seeded, and cut into 1/8-inch-wide strips
- 3 tablespoons chopped fresh cilantro
- Salt and freshly ground black pepper

ACCOMPANIMENT: Mock Mandarin Pancakes (page 490) or cooked rice

Cut beef lengthwise into 2- to 3-inch-wide strips, then cut strips across the grain into 1/8-inch-thick slices. Toss beef with 2 1/2 tablespoons soy sauce, 1 1/2 tablespoons rice wine, sesame oil, and 1 1/2 teaspoons cornstarch in a bowl. Cover and marinate at room temperature for 30 minutes.

To make sauce, stir remaining 1 teaspoon cornstarch into stock in a small bowl until dissolved. Whisk in remaining 2 tablespoons soy sauce, remaining 1 tablespoon rice wine, and sugar.

Heat a wok or deep 12-inch skillet over high heat until hot. Add 3 tablespoons vegetable oil and heat until just smoking. Add beef (discard marinade) and stir-fry until it is no longer pink and slices separate, about 3 minutes. Transfer to a large sieve set over a bowl and drain (discard liquid).

Wipe out wok with paper towels. Heat wok over high heat until hot, then add remaining 1 1/2 tablespoons vegetable oil and heat until just smoking. Add black beans, garlic, ginger, and red pepper flakes and stir-fry until it is fragrant, about 15 seconds. Add onions and bell peppers and stir-fry until softened, 2 to 3 minutes. Stir sauce, then add to vegetables and stir-fry until slightly thickened, about 3 minutes.

Add beef and stir-fry until heated through. Stir in cilantro and salt and pepper to taste. Serve wrapped in pancakes or with rice.

Spanish-Style Oxtails Braised with Chorizo

SERVES 6 TO 8

ACTIVE TIME: 40 MINUTES ■ START TO FINISH: 4½ HOURS

■ Oxtails sometimes actually are the tails of oxen, but more often these days they are the tails of standard beef cattle. When cooked properly, they have superb flavor. Spicy chorizo and earthy smoked paprika give them a Spanish cast. You can use standard paprika, of course, but the subtle note added by *pimentón de la Vera* or any other excellent smoked paprika from Spain lifts the dish from very good to truly great. ■

- 6 pounds meaty oxtails from naturally raised cattle (2- to 3-inch pieces)
- 1½ teaspoons salt
- 1 teaspoon freshly ground black pepper
- 1½ tablespoons extra-virgin olive oil
- ¼ pound mild Spanish chorizo (spicy cured pork sausage; see Sources), casings discarded
- 1 (28- to 32-ounce) can whole tomatoes in purée
- 1 large onion, coarsely chopped
- 4 medium carrots, peeled if desired and coarsely chopped
- 4 garlic cloves, chopped
- 1 Turkish bay leaf or ½ California bay leaf
- ½ teaspoon sweet or hot Spanish smoked paprika (see Glossary)
- 1 cup dry white wine
- 2 tablespoons chopped fresh flat-leaf parsley
- 2 tablespoons chopped fresh cilantro
- 1 tablespoon sherry vinegar or red wine vinegar

Put a rack in lower third of oven and preheat oven to 350°F.

Pat oxtails dry and sprinkle with salt and pepper. Heat oil in an 8- to 9-quart heavy ovenproof pot (see Cook's Note) over moderately high heat until hot but not smoking. Brown oxtails in batches, without crowding, turning occasionally, about 5 minutes per batch. Transfer to a bowl. Pour off all but 1 tablespoon fat from pot. Set pot aside.

Finely chop chorizo in a food processor; transfer to a small bowl. Add tomatoes, with their purée, to processor and coarsely chop.

Cook chorizo, onion, carrots, garlic, and bay leaf in fat remaining in pot over moderate heat, stirring occasionally, until onion is softened, 6 to 7 minutes. Add paprika and cook, stirring, for 1 minute. Add wine and deglaze pot by bringing to a boil, stirring and scraping up any brown bits. Add oxtails, with any juices accumulated in bowl, and tomatoes (liquid should come about halfway up sides of meat; if necessary, add water) and bring to a boil.

Cover pot, transfer to oven, and braise oxtails, turning once or twice, until very tender, 3 to 3½ hours.

Skim fat from sauce. Discard bay leaf and stir in parsley, cilantro, vinegar, and salt and pepper to taste.

COOK'S NOTES

- The oxtails improve in flavor if braised 2 days ahead. Cool in the pot, uncovered, then cover the surface with parchment or wax paper, cover the pot with the lid, and refrigerate. Remove any solidified fat before reheating. Add the parsley, cilantro, and vinegar just before serving.
- If you don't have a large ovenproof pot, you can braise the oxtails in a flameproof roasting pan. Brown them in batches in a 12-inch heavy skillet, then transfer them to a roasting pan just large enough to hold them in one layer. Cook the chorizo and vegetables with the bay leaf in the skillet, then add paprika and wine, as above. Add to the roasting pan, along with tomatoes, bring to a boil on the stovetop, and then cover tightly with a lid or foil and braise in the oven.

Braised Beef Short Ribs with Horseradish Cream

SERVES 4

ACTIVE TIME: 2¼ HOURS ■ START TO FINISH: 21½ HOURS (INCLUDES MAKING STOCK)

■ Horseradish cream provides just the right jolt of flavor to accent the rich, hearty taste of these long-braised ribs, which are prepared with classic European aromatics. We adapted this recipe from one served at the restaurant Alison by the Beach, in eastern Long Island. The butcher can cut the short ribs to whatever length you like, but we found two inches to be ideal here. ■

- 1 tablespoon black peppercorns
- 1 teaspoon dried thyme, crumbled
- 1 Turkish bay leaf or ½ California bay leaf
- 5 pounds short ribs (2 inches long)
- ½ teaspoon plus ⅛ teaspoon salt
- ¼ teaspoon freshly ground black pepper
- 2 tablespoons vegetable oil
- 2 medium onions, chopped
- 2 carrots, chopped
- 3 celery ribs, chopped, plus 1 tablespoon chopped celery leaves
- 3 garlic cloves
- 1 (750-milliliter) bottle dry red wine, preferably Burgundy or Côtes du Rhône
- 4 cups Veal Stock (page 929)
- ¼ cup crème fraîche
- 1 tablespoon finely grated peeled fresh horseradish or drained bottled horseradish

SPECIAL EQUIPMENT: cheesecloth; kitchen string

Wrap peppercorns, thyme, and bay leaf in a square of cheesecloth and tie into a bundle with kitchen string to make a bouquet garni.

Pat ribs dry and sprinkle with ½ teaspoon salt and pepper. Heat oil in a 12-inch heavy skillet over moderately high heat until just smoking. Add ribs and sear, turning with tongs, until well browned on all sides, about 8 minutes total. Transfer ribs bone sides up to a roasting pan large enough to hold them in one layer. Set aside.

Put a rack in middle of oven and preheat oven to 375°F.

Add onions, carrots, celery ribs, garlic, bouquet garni, and wine to skillet, bring to a boil, and boil until liquid is reduced to about ⅓ cup, 15 to 20 minutes.

Stir stock into vegetables and bring to a boil. Pour stock mixture over ribs and cover pan tightly with foil. Transfer to oven and braise until meat is tender and falling off the bone, about 2½ hours. Let cool slightly.

When ribs are cool enough to handle, remove any excess fat and discard bones. (Set pan aside.) Transfer beef to a bowl and cover to keep warm.

Pour cooking liquid through a fine-mesh sieve into a small saucepan, pressing on solids; discard solids and skim fat. Bring to a boil and boil sauce until reduced to about 1 cup, about 10 minutes.

Meanwhile, stir together crème fraîche, horseradish, celery leaves, and remaining ⅛ teaspoon salt in a small saucepan and heat over moderate heat, stirring, just until hot.

Serve beef topped with sauce and horseradish cream.

COOK'S NOTE

■ The ribs can be braised up to 2 days ahead. Let cool completely in the braising liquid, uncovered, then refrigerate, covered. Remove any solidified fat before reheating in a 325°F oven.

Korean Short Ribs

SERVES 4

ACTIVE TIME: 1 HOUR ■ START TO FINISH: 7 HOURS (INCLUDES MARINATING)

■ These ribs, known as *kalbi,* are a great example of the way a handful of ingredients can create a complex flavor profile. The dish also features the use of sugar in a savory preparation, an approach typical of Vietnamese as well as Korean cooking. We like the deep caramel color you get from sprinkling the ribs with sugar and allowing them to sit for several hours so the sugar liquefies and seeps into the meat, but in a pinch you can skip this step and simply mix the sugar in with the remaining ingredients. *Kalbi* is typically grilled, and you can certainly do that, but because grilling is not always an option, we have adapted the traditional recipe for the broiler. ■

4½ pounds meaty beef short ribs (3 large), cut crosswise into 2½-inch pieces by the butcher
3 tablespoons sugar
½ cup soy sauce
2 tablespoons Asian sesame oil
¼ cup chopped scallions
1 tablespoon sesame seeds
1 tablespoon minced garlic
1½ teaspoons finely grated peeled fresh ginger
½ teaspoon freshly ground black pepper

Score the meaty side of each short rib: make two ½-inch-long lengthwise cuts through meat, then make 2 crosswise cuts in same manner, forming 9 squares. Put ribs in a 13-by-9-inch baking dish and sprinkle on all sides with sugar. Refrigerate ribs, covered, for at least 4 hours.

Stir together soy sauce, sesame oil, scallions, sesame seeds, garlic, ginger, and pepper in a small bowl. Spoon marinade over ribs, spreading it with your fingers to coat them evenly. Refrigerate, covered, turning ribs once, for 2 hours.

Preheat broiler. Let ribs stand at room temperature for 15 minutes.

Broil ribs on rack of broiler pan about 6 inches from heat, turning once and rotating pan once or twice, until ribs are dark caramel-brown but still slightly pink inside, about 15 minutes total. (If ribs begin to turn black, move pan farther away from heat and continue cooking.) Let ribs stand for 5 minutes before serving.

COOK'S NOTE

- Sprinkled with sugar, the ribs can be refrigerated for up to 8 hours.

Horseradish Steak Tartare with Watercress

SERVES 2 AS A LIGHT MAIN COURSE OR FIRST COURSE
ACTIVE TIME: 30 MINUTES ■ START TO FINISH: 30 MINUTES

■ Steak tartare takes its name from the French word for the Tatars, a fierce Turco-Mongol tribe from Central Asia that invaded Europe in the thirteenth century. The story is that the Tatars put lean raw meat under their saddles to tenderize as they rode during the day, then at dinnertime chopped the meat and ate it raw with spices. Attributing the Tatars' prowess in battle to this practice, Europeans began to imitate them, and this famous dish was born. For our version, we add a bit of horseradish for tang and serve the meat with watercress and radishes, both excellent foils for the richness. Don't be tempted to shortcut the process and use a food processor: you'll wind up with mushy meat rather than the tiny, separate chunks you are looking for. ■

1 (¾-pound) boneless sirloin steak, chilled
1 teaspoon Dijon mustard
1½ teaspoons Worcestershire sauce, or to taste
2 teaspoons vegetable oil
1 tablespoon drained bottled horseradish, or to taste
1 teaspoon fresh lemon juice
2 teaspoons chopped drained capers
2 tablespoons minced scallion greens
½ teaspoon salt, or to taste
¼ teaspoon freshly ground black pepper, or to taste
2 cups loosely packed watercress sprigs
2 small radishes, halved lengthwise and thinly sliced crosswise

Trim all fat from steak, then finely chop meat.

Whisk together mustard, Worcestershire sauce, oil, horseradish, and lemon juice in a medium bowl. Add meat, capers, scallion, salt, and pepper and mix well with your hands.

Mound steak tartare on two plates and arrange watercress and radishes around it.

Hamburgers

SERVES 6

ACTIVE TIME: 40 MINUTES ■ START TO FINISH: 40 MINUTES PLUS 1 DAY FOR CURING BEEF

■ Sometimes if you want the very best, you have to do it yourself. When it comes to making the ideal burger, that means grinding the meat at home rather than buying it already ground at the supermarket. Not only is it fresher, but you'll also get a coarser grind—plus you'll know exactly what cut it is. Burgers are best when made with fatty chuck that is well marbled, with a strip of fat running through the middle. Higher-end meat, such as sirloin, is often leaner and trimmed of excess fat, which makes for a dry burger. The step of chilling the salted meat for twenty-four hours before grinding it is one we learned from the San Francisco chef Judy Rodgers. In her *Zuni Café Cookbook*, she explains that a brief curing enhances the texture and helps the meat retain its moisture. Chilling it ensures that the fat doesn't soften during grinding and mixing. (If you don't want to salt the meat, simply chill it for two hours or so before grinding.) ■

- 2½ pounds boneless chuck steak
- 2 teaspoons salt
- ⅛ teaspoon freshly ground black pepper

SPECIAL EQUIPMENT: a meat grinder with a ⅜- or ¼-inch die

ACCOMPANIMENT: grilled or toasted Hamburger Buns (page 614) or kaiser rolls

Sprinkle steak with 1½ teaspoons salt. Transfer to a sealable plastic bag and refrigerate for 24 hours.

Prepare a charcoal or gas grill: If using a charcoal grill, open vents in bottom of grill, then light charcoal. Fire is medium-hot when you can hold your hand 5 inches above rack for just 3 to 4 seconds. If using a gas grill, preheat on high, covered, for 10 minutes, then reduce heat to moderately high.

Rinse steak under cold water, then pat dry and cut into 1-inch cubes. Feed cubes through meat grinder into a chilled bowl. Lightly mix meat with your hands to distribute fat evenly, then divide into 6 balls. Flatten balls into patties about ¾ inch thick and 4 inches wide and refrigerate until ready to grill.

Sprinkle burgers with remaining ½ teaspoon salt and pepper. Lightly oil grill rack. Grill burgers (covered only if using gas grill), turning once, for about 5 minutes total for rare or about 6 minutes for medium-rare. (Burgers will continue to cook slightly off the grill.)

Serve burgers on buns.

COOK'S NOTE

■ The burgers can also be cooked on a well-seasoned cast-iron griddle over moderately high heat, turning once, for about 6 minutes for rare, 7 minutes for medium-rare.

Blue Cheese Hamburgers with Caramelized Onion

SERVES 4

ACTIVE TIME: 15 MINUTES ■ START TO FINISH: 15 MINUTES

■ Here we prefer ground sirloin to our usual chuck because the lean beef offsets the richness of the cheese inside the burgers. Gild the lily with caramelized onion. ■

- 1½ pounds ground beef sirloin
- 3 ounces mild blue cheese, such as Saga Blue, crumbled (about ½ cup)
- 2 tablespoons olive oil
- 1 large onion, thinly sliced
- Salt and freshly ground black pepper

ACCOMPANIMENT: toasted Hamburger Buns (page 614) or kaiser rolls

Quarter beef and form into 4 balls. Make a large indentation in center of each ball with your thumb. Form cheese into 4 balls and put one into each indentation. Shape beef over cheese to enclose, and flatten each burger so it is ¾ inch thick and about 4 inches wide.

Heat oil in a 12-inch heavy skillet over moderate heat until hot but not smoking. Add onion and cook, stirring frequently, until softened and golden, 10 to 12 minutes. Transfer to a bowl and season with salt and pepper.

Season burgers with salt and pepper. Heat cleaned skillet over high heat until hot but not smoking. Reduce heat to moderate, add burgers, and cook, turning once, about 5 minutes on each side for medium-rare.

Serve burgers topped with onions on buns.

Meatballs in Tomato Sauce

SERVES 4

ACTIVE TIME: 40 MINUTES ■ START TO FINISH: 45 MINUTES

■ We've used just a small amount of red pepper flakes here, but if you like hot food, feel free to add more. Serve these hearty meatballs over noodles or with mashed potatoes. ■

- 1 (28- to 32-ounce) can whole tomatoes in juice
- 2 garlic cloves, chopped
- 1 teaspoon dried oregano, crumbled
- 1½ teaspoons salt
- ½ cup fine fresh bread crumbs
- ½ cup whole milk
- 1½ pounds meat loaf mix (equal parts ground beef, pork, and veal)
- 1 medium onion, coarsely grated
- 5 tablespoons chopped fresh flat-leaf parsley
- ¼ teaspoon red pepper flakes
- 1½ tablespoons vegetable oil

ACCOMPANIMENT: egg noodles

Pulse tomatoes, with their juice, in a food processor until chopped. Transfer to a 3-quart heavy saucepan, add garlic, oregano, and ½ teaspoon salt, and bring to a simmer. Simmer, uncovered, stirring occasionally, until sauce is thickened, about 20 minutes.

Meanwhile, stir together bread crumbs and milk in a large bowl and let stand for 5 minutes. Add meat, onion, 3 tablespoons parsley, red pepper flakes, and remaining 1 teaspoon salt and blend with your hands until just combined; do not overmix. Form 2-tablespoon amounts of mixture into meatballs (you will have about 20).

Heat oil in a 12-inch heavy skillet over high heat until hot but not smoking. Cook meatballs in 2 batches, turning occasionally, until well browned, about 5 minutes per batch. With a slotted spoon, transfer to tomato sauce.

Cover and simmer, stirring occasionally, until meatballs are cooked through, about 5 minutes. Serve over noodles, sprinkled with remaining 2 tablespoons parsley.

Old-Fashioned Meat Loaf

SERVES 4 TO 6

ACTIVE TIME: 40 MINUTES ■ START TO FINISH: 2 HOURS

■ This meat loaf has the best texture when you make it with coarsely ground meat. Unfortunately, the kind available at the supermarket meat counter is often ground twice, and it is therefore quite fine. We recommend buying boneless beef chuck and pork tenderloin and asking your butcher to grind the meat once for you. ■

- 2 tablespoons unsalted butter
- 2 medium onions, finely chopped (2 cups)
- 1 tablespoon minced garlic
- 1 medium celery rib, finely chopped
- 1 medium carrot, peeled if desired, finely chopped
- 3 scallions, finely chopped (½ cup)
- 2 teaspoons salt
- 1½ teaspoons freshly ground black pepper
- 2 teaspoons Worcestershire sauce
- ⅔ cup ketchup
- 1½ pounds ground beef chuck
- ¾ pound ground pork
- 1 cup fine fresh bread crumbs
- 2 large eggs, lightly beaten
- ⅓ cup minced fresh flat-leaf parsley

SPECIAL EQUIPMENT: an instant-read thermometer

Put a rack in middle of oven and preheat oven to 350°F.

Melt butter in a 12-inch heavy skillet over moderate heat. Add onions, garlic, celery, carrot, and scallions and cook, stirring, for 5 minutes. Cover skillet, reduce heat to low, and cook, stirring occasionally, until carrot is tender, about 5 minutes. Add salt, pepper, Worcestershire sauce, and ⅓ cup ketchup and cook, stirring, for 1 minute.

Transfer to a large bowl. Add meats, bread crumbs,

eggs, and parsley and blend with your hands; do not overmix.

Form mixture into a 10-by-5-inch oval loaf in a 13-by-9-inch baking pan. Spread top with remaining ⅓ cup ketchup.

Bake until thermometer inserted into center of meat loaf registers 155°F, 1 to 1¼ hours. Let meat loaf stand, loosely covered with foil, for 5 minutes before serving.

Beef and Veal Loaf

Polpettone

SERVES 8

ACTIVE TIME: 45 MINUTES ■ START TO FINISH: 1½ HOURS

■ As much as we love good old American meat loaf, we can't resist this Italianate version. A combination of veal and beef is jazzed up with pancetta, Parmigiano-Reggiano, and lemon zest, nicely browned in a skillet, and baked in a little white wine. It emerges from the oven gloriously delicious, a stellar take on an old standard. ■

- 4–6 slices Italian bread (4 ounces), crusts discarded, bread cut into 1½-inch pieces (4 cups)
- 1 cup whole milk
- 1 pound ground beef, preferably 20% fat chuck
- 1 pound ground veal
- 2 large eggs, lightly beaten
- 3 ounces thinly sliced pancetta, finely chopped (½ cup)
- ¾ cup finely grated Parmigiano-Reggiano
- ⅓ cup chopped fresh flat-leaf parsley
- 1½ teaspoons finely grated lemon zest
- 1½ teaspoons salt
- ½ teaspoon freshly ground black pepper
- 2 tablespoons olive oil
- 1 cup dry white wine

SPECIAL EQUIPMENT: an instant-read thermometer

Put a rack in middle of oven and preheat oven to 375°F.

Soak bread in milk in a small bowl for 10 minutes.

Combine beef, veal, eggs, pancetta, Parmesan, parsley, zest, salt, and pepper in a large bowl. Squeeze bread a handful at a time to remove excess milk, then finely chop and add to meat. Mix meat mixture with your hands until well combined; do not overmix. Turn out onto a cutting board and shape into a 10-by-4-inch cylinder.

Heat oil in a 12-inch nonstick ovenproof skillet over moderately high heat until hot but not smoking. Carefully transfer *polpettone* to skillet with two large spatulas and brown on all sides, gently turning with spatulas, 8 to 12 minutes total. Transfer to a plate.

Spoon off fat from skillet, add wine, and deglaze by boiling, stirring and scraping up any brown bits, for 1 minute. Return *polpettone* to skillet, along with any juices accumulated on plate, then transfer skillet to oven. Bake, basting *polpettone* occasionally with pan juices, until thermometer inserted 2 inches into center registers 150°F, about 45 minutes.

Transfer *polpettone* to a cutting board or a platter and let stand, loosely covered with foil, for 10 minutes.

Pour pan juices through a fine-mesh sieve into a small bowl and skim fat.

Cut *polpettone* into ½-inch-thick slices and serve with pan juices.

Buffalo Meat Loaf

SERVES 6

ACTIVE TIME: 40 MINUTES ■ START TO FINISH: 2 HOURS

■ If you are trying to cut back on animal fat in your diet but still crave red meat, buffalo may be what you're looking for. It has roughly 25 percent less fat than beef (and half the calories), and despite what you may have heard, it is not at all gamy—in fact, it tastes sweeter and cleaner than beef. That makes it a terrific substitute in dishes like meat loaf, the ultimate American comfort food. ■

- 1 tablespoon vegetable oil
- 1 cup chopped onion
- 2 celery ribs, cut into ¼-inch dice
- 1 carrot, cut into ¼-inch dice
- 1 tablespoon chopped garlic
- ¾ cup fine fresh bread crumbs
- ½ cup chopped fresh flat-leaf parsley
- 1 large egg, lightly beaten
- 2 tablespoons ketchup
- 1 tablespoon Worcestershire sauce
- 2 teaspoons salt
- ¼ teaspoon freshly ground black pepper
- 1¾ pounds ground buffalo (see Sources)
- 6 shallots, cut into ⅓-inch-thick wedges
- 6 plum tomatoes, each cut into 6 wedges
- ⅓ cup water

SPECIAL EQUIPMENT: an instant-read thermometer

Put a rack in middle of oven and preheat oven to 375°F.

Heat 2 teaspoons oil in a 12-inch nonstick skillet over moderate heat. Add onion, celery, carrot, and garlic and cook, stirring, until onion is softened. Transfer to a large bowl.

Stir bread crumbs, parsley, egg, ketchup, Worcestershire sauce, salt, and pepper into vegetables. Mix in buffalo using your hands; do not overmix. Form mixture into a 10-by-4-inch oval loaf on a large baking sheet with sides.

Toss shallots and tomatoes with remaining 1 teaspoon oil and salt and pepper to taste, then scatter around meat loaf.

Bake until thermometer inserted 2 inches into center of meat loaf registers 160°F, about 1 hour and 10 minutes. Transfer meat loaf and vegetables to a platter and let stand for 10 minutes.

Meanwhile, add water to baking sheet and deglaze by boiling on stovetop over moderately high heat, stirring and scraping up brown bits, for 1 minute. Pour sauce through a fine-mesh sieve into a bowl.

Serve meat loaf with shallots, tomatoes, and sauce.

Spicy Beef and Red Bean Chili

SERVES 8

ACTIVE TIME: 1 HOUR ■ START TO FINISH: 3½ HOURS

■ We particularly like this chili because of its complex flavors: it gets richness from the bacon and beef, heat from the jalapeño, chili powder, and cayenne, and a pleasant edge of bitterness from the coffee and chocolate. For this recipe, we recommend using standard chili powder, which includes other spices in addition to ground dried chiles; pure chile powder would be too strong. Serve the accompaniments in small bowls so your guests can add them as they like. ■

- ½ pound bacon (8 slices)
- 4 pounds boneless beef chuck, cut into 1-inch cubes
- Salt and freshly ground black pepper
- 2 tablespoons vegetable oil
- 1 large white onion, chopped
- 1–2 jalapeño chiles (to taste), chopped (including seeds)
- 4 large garlic cloves, minced
- 2 teaspoons dried oregano, crumbled
- ¼ cup chili powder
- 1 tablespoon ground cumin
- ¼ teaspoon cayenne
- 1 (14½-ounce) can beef broth
- 1 cup brewed coffee
- 1 cup water
- 1 (28-ounce) can crushed tomatoes in purée
- 1 ounce good bittersweet chocolate (not unsweetened), chopped
- 2 (19-ounce) cans small red beans or kidney beans, drained and rinsed

ACCOMPANIMENT: toasted salted pumpkin seeds, chopped red onion, torn fresh cilantro sprigs, diced avocado, lime wedges, sour cream, and warmed corn chips

Cook bacon in a 6- to 8-quart wide heavy pot over moderate heat, turning occasionally, until crisp, about 12 minutes. Transfer to paper towels to drain, then crumble when cool. Pour off all but 2 tablespoons fat from pot.

Pat beef dry and season with salt and pepper. Add oil to pot and heat over moderately high heat until hot but not smoking. Working in 4 to 6 batches, brown beef, without crowding, about 5 minutes per batch. Transfer with a slotted spoon to a plate. Add onion and jalapeños to pot, reduce heat to moderate, and cook, stirring and scraping up brown bits, until softened, about 5 minutes. Add garlic, oregano, chili powder, cumin, and cayenne and cook, stirring, for 1 minute. Return beef to pot, with any juices accumulated on plate, and add broth, coffee, water, and tomatoes, with their purée. Bring to a simmer and simmer, uncovered, stirring occasionally, for 1 hour.

Partially cover pot and continue to simmer until beef is very tender, 1½ to 2 hours more.

Stir in chocolate and beans and cook, stirring, until chocolate is melted and beans are heated through.

Ladle chili into eight bowls and top with crumbled bacon. Serve accompaniments separately.

COOK'S NOTE

- The chili can be made up to 2 days ahead. Cool completely, uncovered, then refrigerate the chili and bacon separately, covered.

Veal

Vitello Tonnato

Veal in Tuna Sauce

SERVES 6
ACTIVE TIME: 30 MINUTES ■ START TO FINISH: 11 HOURS (INCLUDES CHILLING)

■ Though veal and tuna might seem an unlikely pair, they actually marry perfectly, a fact that Italian cooks discovered long ago. In this well-known dish, a silky, sensual, rather pungent tuna-anchovy sauce makes a fine match for the refined taste of gently poached veal loin. The dish is usually served in summer, and it is ideal for those of us who hate last-minute preparation, because it is served cold or at room temperature and can be made up to a day ahead. ■

FOR VEAL

- 1 (2- to 2½-pound) boneless veal loin roast, tied
- 4 cups chicken stock or store-bought low-sodium broth
- 1 cup dry white wine
- 1 medium carrot, cut into 2-inch pieces
- 1 celery rib, cut into 2-inch pieces
- 1 medium onion, halved
- 3 large sprigs fresh flat-leaf parsley
- 1 Turkish bay leaf or ½ California bay leaf
- 1 teaspoon salt

FOR TUNA SAUCE

- 1 (6-ounce) can light tuna packed in olive oil, preferably Italian, drained
- 4 large flat anchovy fillets
- 1 cup mayonnaise
- ½ cup extra-virgin olive oil
- 3 tablespoons drained capers
- 2–3 tablespoons fresh lemon juice (to taste)

OPTIONAL GARNISH: capers, lemon slices, and chopped fresh flat-leaf parsley

SPECIAL EQUIPMENT: an instant-read thermometer

POACH THE VEAL: Put veal in a 6- to 8-quart heavy pot and add stock, wine, carrot, celery, onion, parsley, bay leaf, salt, and enough water to cover veal by 1 inch. Remove veal from pot and bring liquid to a boil. Return veal to pot, reduce heat, and poach at a bare simmer, uncovered, skimming froth, until thermometer inserted diagonally 2 inches into thickest part of loin registers 150°F, 1 to 1¼ hours.

Let veal cool in broth, uncovered, about 1 hour (its temperature will rise to 165°F while it stands).

MAKE THE SAUCE: Combine tuna, anchovies, mayonnaise, oil, capers, and lemon juice in a blender and purée until very smooth.

ASSEMBLE THE DISH: Transfer veal to a cutting board, discard string, and cut meat into thin slices. Spread a thin layer of sauce on a platter and arrange veal slices, slightly overlapping, on top. Spoon remaining sauce over veal. Refrigerate, covered with plastic wrap, for at least 8 hours so flavors can mingle.

Serve veal cold or at room temperature, garnished, if desired, with capers, lemon slices, and parsley.

COOK'S NOTE

- The dish can be assembled up to 24 hours ahead and refrigerated, covered.

Matzo-Stuffed Breast of Veal

SERVES 6
ACTIVE TIME: 45 MINUTES ■ START TO FINISH: 4¼ HOURS

■ The breast is perhaps the tastiest cut of veal, and its shape lends itself very nicely to stuffing. The wheaty, toasty flavor of matzo provides a surprising but just-right base for the stuffing. Like all braises, this hearty dish has a delightful roundness that is perfect for a cold winter night. Since it tastes best after it has had a chance to sit and mellow, it is a sensational dish to make ahead. ■

FOR STUFFING

- ¼ cup vegetable oil
- 2 medium onions, chopped
- 3 carrots, cut into ¼-inch dice
- 2 celery ribs, cut into ¼-inch dice
- 3 (6-inch-square) matzos, broken into ½-inch pieces
- 2 tablespoons chopped fresh flat-leaf parsley leaves
- 1 large egg, lightly beaten
- ¾ teaspoon salt
- ¼ teaspoon freshly ground black pepper

FOR VEAL

- 1 (3½- to 4-pound) boneless veal breast (1½ inches thick)
- 1 small onion, quartered
- 2 garlic cloves, smashed with side of a large heavy knife
- 1 tablespoon vegetable oil
- 2 teaspoons paprika, preferably sweet Hungarian
- 1½ teaspoons salt
- 1 teaspoon freshly ground black pepper
- 2 fresh thyme sprigs
- 1½ cups water

SPECIAL EQUIPMENT: a carpet, darning, or upholstery needle (see Sources); kitchen string

MAKE THE STUFFING: Heat oil in a 3½- to 5-quart wide heavy pot over moderate heat. Add onions, carrots, and celery and cook, stirring occasionally, until vegetables begin to brown, 8 to 10 minutes.

Meanwhile, put matzo in a colander and run under hot water until softened.

Remove pot from heat and transfer half of vegetables to a medium bowl; set pot aside. Cool vegetables in bowl for 5 minutes, then stir in matzo, parsley, egg, salt, and pepper. Let cool.

PREPARE THE VEAL: Put a rack in middle of oven and preheat oven to 350°F.

Put veal on a cutting board. Trim as much excess fat as possible from it. Cut a large pocket in veal breast (see opposite page).

Combine onion, garlic, oil, paprika, salt, and pepper in a food processor or blender and purée. Rub inside of pocket in veal with 2 tablespoons purée. Fill pocket loosely with matzo stuffing, leaving a 1-inch border on cut side. Sew pocket closed.

Pat veal dry and rub both sides with remaining purée. Put thyme sprigs, then veal, on vegetables remaining in pot. Add water and bring to a boil.

Cover pot, transfer to oven, and braise until meat is very tender, 3 to 3½ hours.

With a wide metal spatula, transfer veal to a clean cutting board and let stand, loosely covered with foil, for 30 minutes. Discard thyme sprigs and skim any fat from sauce, then keep sauce warm over very low heat, covered.

Remove and discard string, then cut veal across the grain into 1-inch-thick slices. Serve with sauce.

COOK'S NOTE

■ The veal improves in flavor if braised 2 days ahead. Cool in the sauce, uncovered, then cover the surface with parchment or wax paper, cover the pot with the lid, and refrigerate. To serve, remove any solidified fat and slice the cold meat across the grain. Arrange veal in a shallow baking pan, top with sauce, cover, and reheat in a 325°F oven for about 45 minutes.

STUFFING A VEAL BREAST

Boneless breast of veal can be found at butcher shops and in most supermarkets. It's usually sold cut in half. The thicker part of the breast (often called the first, or brisket, cut) is preferable for stuffing because there's more meat, which makes cutting a pocket for the stuffing easier. The thinner part requires more sewing, but it's just as delicious. Trim off all excess fat before stuffing and sewing up the meat. No matter what piece of veal breast you start with, it will be somewhat irregular in shape, but it's important to make it as neat and shapely as possible. That way it will cook evenly and be easy to slice.

You'll need kitchen string and a large needle with an eye big enough for the string to pass through for sewing up the breast. A carpet, darning, or upholstery needle fits the bill nicely. Use a blanket stitch to secure the pocket.

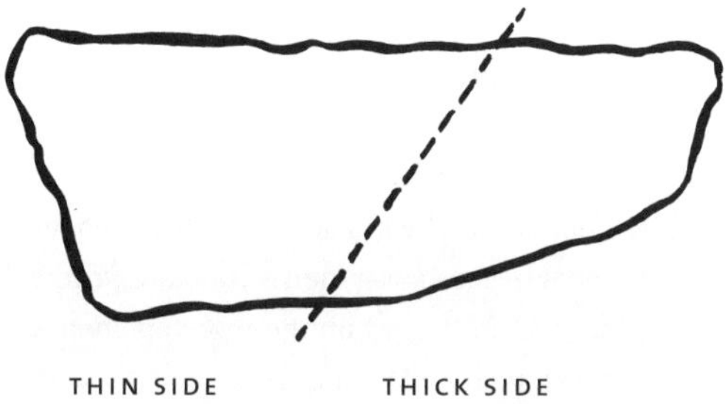

FOR A THICK PIECE OF VEAL BREAST: Cut a pocket in the meat: insert a sharp large knife horizontally into the center of the thickest side and then cut into the center as evenly as possible, leaving a 1-inch border on the three remaining sides. Fill the pocket loosely with stuffing.

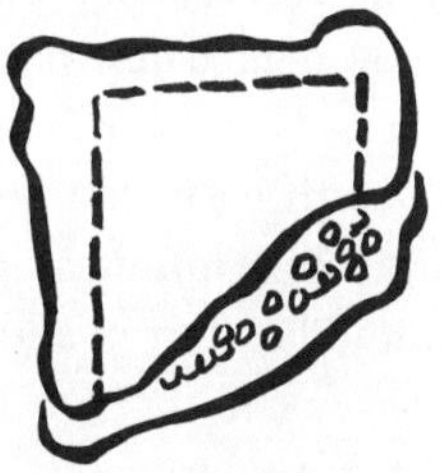

FOR A THIN PIECE OF VEAL BREAST: Put the stuffing on one long half. Fold the other half over. Fold in the small flap on the end to make a seam, enclosing the stuffing. Sew up the opening of the thin breast.

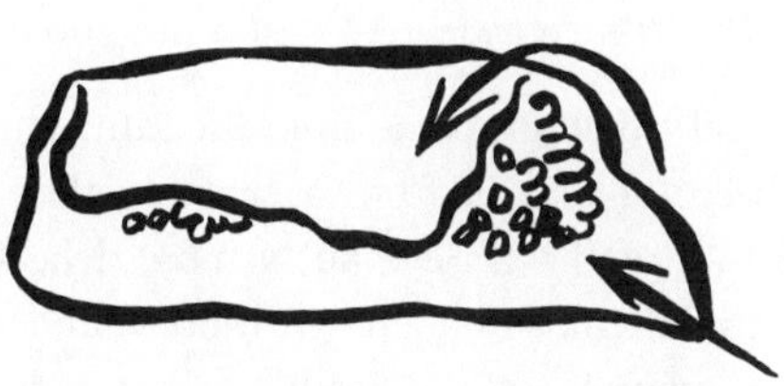

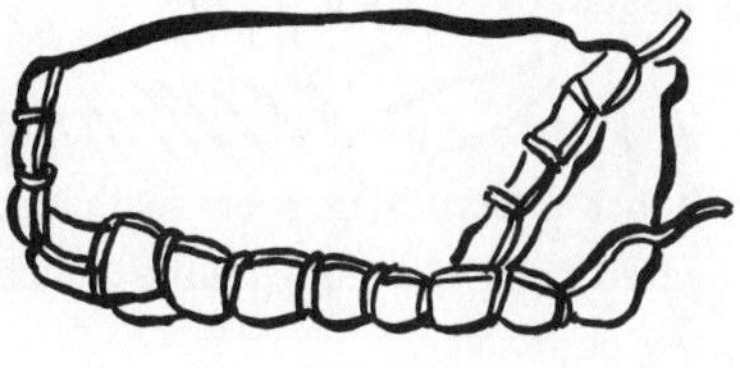

Sew up the opening of the thick breast.

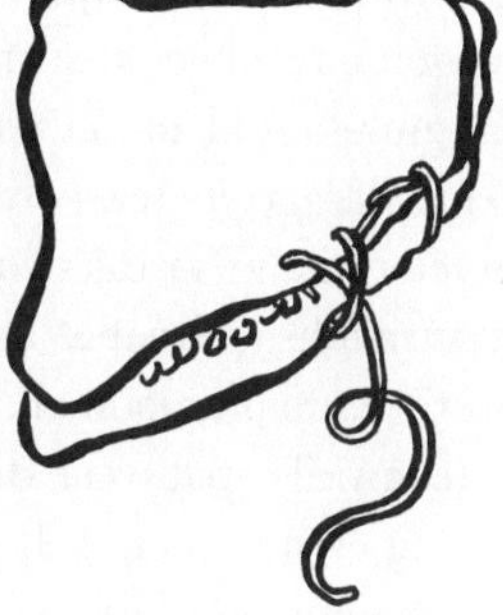

Veal Braised in Tomato Sauce

SERVES 4 TO 6
ACTIVE TIME: 1 HOUR ■ START TO FINISH: 3½ HOURS

■ If you think veal is a pale, tasteless imitation of beef, the veal shoulder roast is the perfect cut to dispel this notion. The collagen-rich, flavorful meat takes perfectly to braising, as in this recipe from contributor John Golden. The braising liquid can be served as is or, if you like a sauce with a bit more body, reduced by boiling it down a little, which concentrates it. ■

- 2 (28- to 32-ounce) cans whole tomatoes in juice, drained and chopped
- 1 teaspoon chopped fresh basil or ½ teaspoon dried basil, crumbled
- 1 tablespoon unsalted butter
- 5 tablespoons olive oil
- 2 medium onions, chopped (2 cups)
- 2 garlic cloves, minced
- 2 teaspoons dried oregano, crumbled
- 1 teaspoon salt
- ½ teaspoon freshly ground black pepper
- 1 (3-pound) boneless veal shoulder roast, rolled and tied
- ½ cup dry red wine
- 1 Turkish bay leaf or ½ California bay leaf

OPTIONAL GARNISH: minced fresh flat-leaf parsley

Toss tomatoes with basil in a bowl. Let stand at room temperature for 30 minutes.

Put a rack in middle of oven and preheat oven to 300°F.

Heat butter and 3 tablespoons oil in a 6- to 8-quart wide heavy ovenproof pot over moderate heat. Add onions and cook, stirring, until softened, about 10 minutes. Add tomatoes, garlic, oregano, ½ teaspoon salt, and ¼ teaspoon pepper and simmer, uncovered, stirring occasionally, until sauce begins to thicken slightly, about 15 minutes. Remove from heat and stir in 1 tablespoon oil.

Meanwhile, pat veal dry and sprinkle with remaining ½ teaspoon salt and ¼ teaspoon pepper. Heat remaining 1 tablespoon oil in a 12-inch heavy skillet over moderately high heat until just smoking. Add veal and cook, turning with tongs, until well browned on all sides, about 12 minutes total.

Transfer veal to pot with sauce. Add wine to skillet and deglaze by boiling over high heat, stirring and scraping up brown bits, for 1 minute. Add wine and bay leaf to pot and simmer, uncovered, for 5 minutes.

Cover pot and transfer to oven. Braise veal, turning two or three times, until very tender when pierced with a two-prong fork, 1½ to 2 hours. Transfer veal to a platter and let stand, loosely covered with foil, for 15 minutes.

Skim fat from sauce and discard bay leaf. If sauce is too thin, boil over high heat, stirring, until slightly thickened, 5 to 10 minutes. Season with salt and pepper.

Remove string from meat and cut meat across the grain into ⅓-inch-thick slices. Garnish with parsley, if desired, and serve with sauce.

COOK'S NOTE

■ The veal can be braised up to 2 days ahead. Cool the meat in the sauce, then refrigerate, covered. Bring to a simmer in the pot on the stovetop, then transfer to a 350°F oven and heat until the meat is warmed through before proceeding.

Veal Chop "Schnitzel" with Arugula Salad

SERVES 4
ACTIVE TIME: 45 MINUTES ■ START TO FINISH: 45 MINUTES

■ Veal rib chops come from the same part of a calf as rib-eye steaks do from a steer, so they have all the virtues of the rib eye but a more delicate flavor. We pound them thin, then lightly bread and sauté them in the manner of schnitzel and serve them with an arugula salad to cut their richness. ■

FOR VEAL CHOPS

- 4 (1-inch-thick) veal rib chops (with rib bones), frenched if desired (have the butcher do this)
- ¾ teaspoon salt
- ¼ teaspoon freshly ground black pepper
- 1½ cups fine fresh bread crumbs

2 large eggs
2/3 cup all-purpose flour
1/2 cup vegetable oil
2 tablespoons unsalted butter
2 large garlic cloves, quartered

FOR SALAD

1 tablespoon white wine vinegar
1 teaspoon Dijon mustard
1/8 teaspoon dried thyme, crumbled
1/8 teaspoon salt
Pinch of freshly ground black pepper
2 tablespoons olive oil
1 pound arugula or watercress, coarse stems discarded (4 cups)
8 cherry or grape tomatoes, quartered
2 tablespoons shredded carrot

ACCOMPANIMENT: lemon wedges

COOK THE VEAL CHOPS: Preheat oven to 200°F.

With a mallet or rolling pin, pound meat of chops between sheets of plastic wrap to 1/2 inch thick, being careful not to separate meat from bones. Pat dry and sprinkle with 1/2 teaspoon salt and pepper.

Stir remaining 1/4 teaspoon salt into bread crumbs in a shallow bowl. Lightly beat eggs in another shallow bowl. Spread flour on a plate. Dredge chops in flour and shake off excess, dip in egg, letting excess drip off, then coat with bread crumbs, shake off excess, and transfer to a plate.

Heat 1/4 cup oil and 1 tablespoon butter in a 12-inch heavy skillet over moderately high heat until hot but not smoking. Add half of garlic and cook, stirring, until golden, about 2 minutes. Discard garlic. Add 2 chops and cook, turning once, until just cooked through, 4 to 6 minutes total (meat will still be slightly pink inside). Transfer to paper towels to drain, then transfer to a clean plate, cover loosely, and keep warm in oven. Wipe out skillet with paper towels and repeat with remaining oil, butter, garlic, and chops. Put on same plate in oven.

MAKE THE SALAD: Whisk together vinegar, mustard, thyme, salt, and pepper in a large bowl. Add oil in a slow stream, whisking until well blended. Add arugula, tomatoes, and carrot and toss until well coated.

Serve chops with salad and lemon wedges.

Roasted Double Veal Chops

SERVES 6

ACTIVE TIME: 20 MINUTES ■ START TO FINISH: 1½ HOURS

■ If anything can take the already superb taste of a veal chop to new heights, it's pancetta, the lightly spiced, salt-cured Italian version of bacon. We sauté some pancetta, brown the chops in its fat before putting them in the oven, and then use the pancetta to punch up a white wine and herb pan sauce to drizzle over the sliced veal. You'll need to order this cut of veal, a two-rib chop—really a mini-roast—from your butcher. When you carve the meat, the first one or two slices may contain a bit of gristle, but after that the veal will be beautifully tender. ■

1½ ounces sliced pancetta, cut into 1/4-inch-wide strips
1–2 tablespoons olive oil
2 (2-rib) veal chops (4 pounds total)
Salt and freshly ground black pepper
1 garlic clove, minced
1/2 cup dry white wine
1 cup Veal Stock (page 929), chicken stock, or store-bought low-sodium chicken broth
2 teaspoons unsalted butter
1 tablespoon finely chopped fresh flat-leaf parsley
1 teaspoon finely chopped fresh thyme

SPECIAL EQUIPMENT: an instant-read thermometer

COOK THE PANCETTA AND CHOPS: Put a rack in middle of oven and preheat oven to 400°F.

Cook pancetta in 1 tablespoon oil in a large heavy skillet over moderately low heat, stirring occasionally, until pancetta is browned and fat is rendered. Transfer to paper towels to drain, leaving fat in skillet.

Pat chops dry and season with salt and pepper. Heat fat in skillet over moderately high heat until hot but not smoking. Brown chops on all sides, about 10 to 15 minutes total, adding more oil if necessary. Transfer to a small roasting pan, bone sides down, and set skillet aside.

Roast chops until thermometer inserted 2 inches into center of meat (without touching bone) registers 135°F for medium, about 1 hour. Transfer chops to a cutting board and let stand, loosely covered with foil, for 15 minutes. (Their internal temperature will rise to about 140°F as they stand.) Set roasting pan aside.

WHILE THE CHOPS ROAST, BEGIN THE SAUCE: Discard all but 1 tablespoon fat from skillet. Heat remaining fat in skillet over moderate heat until hot but not smoking. Add garlic and cook, stirring, until fragrant, about 30 seconds. Add wine and deglaze skillet by boiling over high heat, stirring and scraping up brown bits, for 1 minute. Add stock, bring to a boil, and boil until mixture is reduced to about 3/4 cup, about 5 minutes. Remove from heat.

FINISH THE SAUCE WHILE THE CHOPS STAND: Set roasting pan over a burner. Add wine mixture and deglaze pan by boiling over high heat, stirring and scraping up brown bits, for 1 minute. Transfer sauce to a small saucepan and skim off any fat. Reheat and stir in butter, parsley, thyme, any juices accumulated on cutting board, pancetta, and pepper to taste.

With chops on their sides, cut parallel to bones into thin slices. Serve with sauce.

Saltimbocca

Veal Cutlets with Prosciutto and Sage

SERVES 4

ACTIVE TIME: 30 MINUTES ■ START TO FINISH: 30 MINUTES

■ Saltimbocca is among the best known of Italian veal dishes. Its name translates as "jump in the mouth," and its flavors, round and mellow but still intense, do exactly that. Although restaurant chefs usually make this with thin slices from a boneless veal loin, a better option for home cooks is veal cutlets, which are less expensive and more widely available. If the cutlets you buy are thicker than specified, use the smooth side of a mallet to pound them between sheets of plastic wrap to less than 1/8 inch thick. ■

- 8 thin (less than 1/8-inch-thick) veal cutlets (also called scaloppine; 1 1/4 pounds total)
- 1/8 teaspoon freshly ground black pepper
- 3 garlic cloves
- 1/4 teaspoon salt
- 16–24 large (2 1/2- to 3-inch-long) fresh sage leaves
- 8 thin slices prosciutto (about 1/4 pound total)
- 1/4 cup olive oil
- 1/3 cup dry white wine
- 1/3 cup chicken stock or store-bought low-sodium broth
- 2 tablespoons unsalted butter

Pat veal cutlets dry and sprinkle with pepper. Using a large heavy knife, mince garlic and mash to a paste with salt. Spread about 1/4 teaspoon garlic paste on one side of 1 veal cutlet and arrange 2 or 3 sage leaves on top in one layer. Cover cutlet with 1 slice of prosciutto and secure prosciutto and sage with wooden picks threaded through sage leaves and meat (like a straight pin). Transfer cutlet, prosciutto side down, to a tray and make 7 more saltimbocca in same manner.

Heat oil in a 12-inch heavy skillet over high heat until it just begins to smoke. Add 2 veal cutlets, prosciutto sides down, and cook for 30 to 45 seconds. Turn cutlets over and cook until just cooked through (meat will still be slightly pink inside), about 15 seconds more. Transfer to a platter and keep warm, loosely covered with foil. Cook remaining cutlets 2 at a time in same manner.

Pour off oil from skillet, then add wine and deglaze skillet by boiling over high heat, stirring and scraping up brown bits, for 1 minute. Continue boiling until wine is reduced to about 3 tablespoons, about 3 minutes more. Add stock and boil until reduced to about 1/3 cup, about 5 minutes. Add butter and swirl skillet until incorporated.

Remove and discard picks and serve veal with sauce drizzled over.

Veal Scallops with Lemon and Capers

SERVES 4

ACTIVE TIME: 30 MINUTES ■ START TO FINISH: 30 MINUTES

■ In today's world, cooks are always looking for dishes that provide a big flavor reward for little time and effort. Some of the recipes that deliver this combination are new creations; others are time-honored classics like this one, in which veal cutlets are pounded thin (so they cook quickly), sautéed in butter and oil (for the best combination of flavor and browning), and served with a white wine pan sauce featuring the traditional Italian combination of tart lemon and salty capers. It's a dish you could be very happy to cook (and eat) once a week for the rest of your life. ■

- 1½ pounds veal cutlets (also called scaloppine; preferably ⅛ inch thick)
- ½ teaspoon salt
- ¼ teaspoon freshly ground black pepper
- 4 tablespoons olive oil
- 5 tablespoons unsalted butter
- ½ cup all-purpose flour
- ½ cup dry white wine
- ¼ cup chicken stock or store-bought low-sodium broth
- 6 (⅛-inch-thick) lemon slices, halved
- 2 teaspoons drained capers, rinsed
- 2 teaspoons minced fresh flat-leaf parsley

If necessary, using a mallet or a rolling pin, pound veal cutlets between two sheets of plastic wrap to ⅛ inch thick.

Pat veal dry and sprinkle both sides with salt and pepper. Heat 1 tablespoon oil and ½ tablespoon butter in a 12-inch heavy skillet over moderately high heat until foam subsides. Meanwhile, quickly dredge 2 or 3 cutlets in flour, shaking off excess. Add veal to skillet, without crowding, and cook for 30 to 45 seconds. Turn veal over and cook until just cooked through (meat will still be slightly pink inside), about 15 seconds more. Transfer to a platter and keep warm, loosely covered with foil. Pour off fat from skillet and cook remaining cutlets in 3 more batches, using remaining 3 tablespoons oil and 1½ tablespoons more butter.

Add wine, stock, and any meat juices accumulated on platter to skillet and deglaze by boiling over high heat, stirring and scraping up brown bits, for 1 minute. Continue to boil until reduced to about ⅓ cup, about 3 minutes. Stir in remaining 3 tablespoons butter, lemon slices, capers, parsley, and salt and pepper to taste.

Serve veal topped with sauce.

Veal Marsala

SERVES 4

ACTIVE TIME: 45 MINUTES ■ START TO FINISH: 45 MINUTES

■ Sweet Marsala and subtle veal are one of those matches so right that you fall in love with them. Ernie's restaurant in San Francisco was justly famed for its version of this beloved standard. We've updated its recipe, substituting a store-bought beef or veal demi-glace for the rather complicated brown sauce that took three hours to make, but the spirit and the taste remain true to the original. Serve over egg noodles tossed with butter. ■

- 3 tablespoons unsalted butter
- 1 pound mushrooms, trimmed and quartered
- 1 large garlic clove, minced
- 2 tablespoons chopped fresh flat-leaf parsley
- 1½ pounds veal cutlets (also called scaloppine; ¼ inch thick)
- ½ teaspoon salt
- ¼ teaspoon freshly ground black pepper
- ¼ teaspoon dried thyme, crumbled
- ¼ teaspoon dried oregano, crumbled
- 1½ tablespoons olive oil
- ½ cup all-purpose flour
- ⅔ cup sweet Marsala wine
- 1 cup veal demi-glace (see Sources)

ACCOMPANIMENT: buttered noodles

Heat 2 tablespoons butter in a 12-inch heavy skillet over high heat until foam subsides. Add mushrooms and cook, stirring frequently, until liquid mushrooms give off has evaporated and mushrooms begin to brown, about 10 minutes. Add garlic and parsley and cook, stirring, for 1 minute. Transfer to a bowl and wipe skillet clean.

Pat veal dry and sprinkle with salt, pepper, thyme, and oregano.

Heat 1½ teaspoons oil with 1 teaspoon butter in same skillet over moderately high heat until hot but not smoking. Meanwhile, quickly dredge 2 or 3 pieces of veal in flour, shaking off excess. Add veal to skillet, without crowding, and cook, turning once, until just cooked through, 2 to 3 minutes total (meat will still be slightly pink inside). Transfer to a platter and keep warm, loosely covered with foil. Cook remaining veal in 2 more batches, using remaining 1 tablespoon oil and 2 teaspoons butter.

Add Marsala to skillet and deglaze by boiling, stirring and scraping up brown bits, for 1 minute. Continue to boil until reduced by half. Stir in demi-glace and simmer, stirring occasionally, for 2 minutes. Stir in mushroom mixture and any veal juices accumulated on platter and season with salt and pepper if necessary. Simmer for 2 minutes more and spoon over veal. Serve with noodles.

Veal Birds Paprika

SERVES 6

ACTIVE TIME: 1 HOUR ■ START TO FINISH: 1¼ HOURS

■ Long ago, some unknown poet of the kitchen looked at these little veal rolls arranged on a platter and decided that they looked like a flock of headless birds. And *oiseaux sans têtes* they remain to this day in the cuisines of countries as diverse as Belgium, Italy, and France. Whatever you call them, they are delicious—tender, thin slices of veal wrapped around a filling rich with mushrooms, butter, and basil, draped with a tomato–sour cream sauce. This recipe uses a fair amount of paprika, so be sure that yours is fresh, with a bright, sweetish taste and no hint of mustiness. ■

- 9 tablespoons unsalted butter
- 1½ cups finely chopped onions (1¼ pounds)
- 1 pound mushrooms, trimmed and finely chopped
- ¼ cup fine dry bread crumbs
- 2 tablespoons chopped fresh basil
- Salt and freshly ground black pepper
- 6 veal cutlets (also called scaloppine; ¼ inch thick)
- 1 cup Veal Stock (page 929), chicken stock, or store-bought low-sodium chicken broth
- ½ cup water
- ½ cup canned tomato purée
- 2 tablespoons paprika
- 1 cup sour cream

ACCOMPANIMENT: buttered noodles

SPECIAL EQUIPMENT: kitchen string

Melt 6 tablespoons butter in a 12-inch heavy skillet over moderate heat. Add ½ cup onions and mushrooms and cook, stirring occasionally, until onions are golden, about 6 minutes. Stir in bread crumbs, basil, and salt and pepper to taste, remove from heat, and let cool.

With a mallet or rolling pin, pound veal cutlets between two sheets of plastic wrap to ⅛ inch thick. Divide mushroom filling among cutlets. Working with one cutlet at a time, fold over about ½ inch of long sides, then, starting with a short side, roll up cutlet. Tie rolls at each end with kitchen string.

Pat veal rolls dry and sprinkle with ¼ teaspoon salt and ⅛ teaspoon pepper. Heat 2 tablespoons butter in a cleaned skillet over moderately high heat until foam subsides. Brown veal, turning occasionally, about 8 minutes total. Transfer to a plate.

Add remaining 1 tablespoon butter to skillet and reduce heat to moderate. Add remaining 1 cup onions and cook, stirring, until golden, about 6 minutes. Stir in stock, water, tomato purée, and paprika, then add veal, with any juices accumulated on plate. Bring to a simmer, cover, and simmer until veal is tender, 30 to 35 minutes. Transfer to a platter and remove string.

Whisk sour cream, ¼ teaspoon salt, and ⅛ teaspoon pepper into sauce in skillet and cook over low heat, stirring occasionally, until hot, about 2 minutes; do not let boil.

Serve veal and noodles with sauce on the side.

Osso Buco

SERVES 8

ACTIVE TIME: 2 HOURS ■ START TO FINISH: 4¾ HOURS

■ Few American cooks were familiar with veal shanks until this dish (literally, "pierced bone") swept to popularity. Shanks have since become a fairly standard supermarket item. That's a very good thing, because they possess an almost magical quality. Veal contains a lot of collagen—much more than beef—and the shanks have more than most other cuts. As they cook slowly in liquid, their collagen melts into gelatin and the cooking liquid takes on a silky quality. When the shanks emerge from the oven, they are surrounded by a sauce as smooth as any butter sauce you could make. ■

FOR OSSO BUCO

- 8 (12- to 14-ounce) meaty cross-cut veal shanks (osso buco; 6–6½ pounds total), tied
- 2¼ teaspoons salt
- 1⅛ teaspoons freshly ground black pepper
- ¾ cup all-purpose flour
- ½ stick (4 tablespoons) unsalted butter
- 2 tablespoons olive oil
- 1½ cups dry white wine
- 1 Turkish bay leaf or ½ California bay leaf
- 6 fresh flat-leaf parsley sprigs
- 4 fresh thyme sprigs
- 1 medium onion, finely chopped
- 2 medium carrots, finely chopped
- 2 celery ribs, finely chopped
- 1 large garlic clove, minced
- 4 plum tomatoes (1 pound total), seeded and chopped, or 1½ cups drained canned plum tomatoes (from a 20-ounce can), chopped
- 2–3 cups chicken or beef stock or store-bought low-sodium chicken broth or beef broth

FOR GREMOLATA

- ¼ cup minced fresh flat-leaf parsley
- 1 tablespoon finely grated lemon zest
- 1½ teaspoons minced garlic

SPECIAL EQUIPMENT: cheesecloth; kitchen string

MAKE THE OSSO BUCO: Put a rack in middle of oven and preheat oven to 325°F.

Pat veal shanks dry and sprinkle with 2 teaspoons salt and 1 teaspoon pepper. Dredge shanks in flour and shake off excess. Heat 1 tablespoon butter and 1 tablespoon oil in a 7- to 9-quart heavy ovenproof pot wide enough to hold shanks in one layer (see Cook's Note) over moderately high heat until foam subsides. Add 4 shanks and cook, turning once, until well browned, 12 to 15 minutes total. Transfer to a plate. Wipe pot clean with paper towels and brown remaining 4 shanks in another 1 tablespoon butter and remaining 1 tablespoon oil in same manner; transfer to plate.

Pour off fat from pot, then add wine, bring to a boil, and boil over high heat, stirring and scraping up brown bits, until reduced to about ½ cup, about 10 minutes. Transfer wine to a small bowl. Wipe out pot.

Wrap bay leaf, parsley, and thyme sprigs in cheesecloth and tie into a bundle with kitchen string to make a bouquet garni. Melt remaining 2 tablespoons butter in same pot over moderately low heat. Add onion, carrots, celery, and garlic and cook, stirring occasionally, until softened, about 8 minutes. Stir in tomatoes, bouquet garni, remaining ¼ teaspoon salt, and remaining ⅛ teaspoon pepper. Add shanks, along with any juices accumulated on plate, wine, and enough stock to reach three quarters of the way up sides of shanks, and bring to a simmer.

Cover pot, transfer to oven, and braise shanks until very tender, 2 to 2½ hours.

With a slotted spoon, transfer shanks to a roasting pan (leave oven on) and remove string. Keep them warm, loosely covered with foil. Pour braising liquid through a large fine-mesh sieve into a heavy saucepan, pressing on solids; discard solids and skim fat from sauce. Bring to a boil and boil, uncovered, stirring occasionally, until reduced to about 3 cups, about 15 minutes. Stir in salt and pepper to taste and remove from heat.

Baste shanks with some sauce, then bake, uncovered, basting 3 or 4 more times with sauce, until glazed, about 15 minutes.

MEANWHILE, MAKE THE GREMOLATA: Stir together parsley, zest, and garlic in a small bowl.

Sprinkle shanks with gremolata and pour some sauce around them. Serve with remaining sauce on the side.

COOK'S NOTES

- The veal shanks can be braised (but not glazed) up to 2 days ahead. Cool completely in the pot, uncovered, then refrigerate, covered. Bring to a simmer on top of the stove and simmer until heated through, then proceed with the recipe.
- If you don't have a 7- to 9-quart ovenproof pot, you can braise the shanks in a roasting pan. Brown the shanks in a 12-inch heavy skillet and transfer to a 17-by-12-inch roasting pan. Reduce the wine in the skillet as in the recipe and transfer to the roasting pan. Cook the vegetables in the skillet, then stir in the tomatoes, bouquet garni, stock, salt, and pepper. Bring to a simmer and transfer to the roasting pan; cover pan with foil and braise as directed.

Veal Stew with Lemon and Crème Fraîche

SERVES 4 TO 6
ACTIVE TIME: 1½ HOURS ■ START TO FINISH: 3 HOURS

■ The particulars of this recipe came to us from the novelist Diane Johnson, who wrote a piece for the magazine on how Parisian housewives cook. Although this is indeed a stew, it is not prepared as most stews are, with meat and liquid and vegetables all sharing the same pot. Instead, the veal is first cooked to tenderness, then kept warm while the vegetables are simmered briefly in the strained stock. The vegetables join the veal, the stock is set on a back burner to reduce, and the mushrooms are cooked in butter and added to the veal. Finally the stock is transformed into an exquisite sauce that is poured over the other ingredients. It's much less complicated than it sounds, and the result is the cleanest, freshest stew you have ever tasted. ■

FOR MEAT AND VEGETABLES

- 2¾ pounds bone-in veal breast (see Cook's Note)
- 1 pound boneless veal shoulder, trimmed and cut into 2-inch pieces
- 2½ quarts water
- 6 fresh flat-leaf parsley sprigs
- 2 fresh thyme sprigs
- 1 Turkish bay leaf or ½ California bay leaf
- 4 black peppercorns
- 2 onions, halved
- 1 leek (white and pale green parts only), halved lengthwise and cut crosswise into ½-inch pieces
- 4 carrots, peeled if desired and quartered
- 2 tablespoons unsalted butter
- ½ pound mushrooms, trimmed and quartered
- Salt and freshly ground black pepper

FOR SAUCE

- 3 tablespoons unsalted butter
- 3 tablespoons all-purpose flour
- 2 large egg yolks
- 2 tablespoons crème fraîche
- 1½ tablespoons fresh lemon juice
- Salt and freshly ground black pepper

SPECIAL EQUIPMENT: cheesecloth; kitchen string; an instant-read thermometer

STEW THE MEAT AND VEGETABLES: Cut meat away from veal breastbone, reserving bone. Cut meat into 2-inch pieces. Combine veal breast and shoulder pieces, bone, and water in a 7- to 8-quart heavy pot and bring to a boil over moderate heat, skimming froth. Meanwhile, wrap parsley, thyme, bay leaf, and peppercorns in a small square of cheesecloth and tie into a bundle with string to make a bouquet garni.

Add bouquet garni and onions to pot, reduce heat, and simmer, uncovered, until veal is tender, 1¼ to 1½ hours.

Preheat oven to 300°F.

Wash leek in a bowl of cold water; lift out and drain well.

When veal is tender, transfer with a slotted spoon to a heatproof serving dish. Keep warm in oven, covered with foil.

Discard veal bone, onions, and bouquet garni and pour stock through a fine-mesh sieve into a large bowl. Return stock to cleaned pot, add carrots and leek, bring to a simmer, and simmer until vegetables are tender, 10 to 12 minutes. Transfer vegetables to serving dish with slotted spoon, cover, and keep warm in oven. Boil stock until reduced to about 2½ cups, about 10 minutes. Remove from heat.

While stock is reducing, heat butter in a 10-inch heavy skillet over moderate heat until foam subsides. Add mushrooms and cook, stirring, until just tender, 6 to 8 minutes. Transfer to serving dish and season veal and vegetables with salt and pepper. Cover and keep warm in oven.

MAKE THE SAUCE: Melt butter in a 2- to 3-quart heavy saucepan over moderately low heat. Stir in flour and cook, stirring, for 3 minutes to make a roux (do not let brown). Whisk in reduced stock, bring to a simmer, and simmer, uncovered, whisking occasionally, for 15 minutes.

Whisk together yolks and crème fraîche in a small bowl, then whisk in 1 cup sauce. Whisk yolk mixture into remaining sauce, whisk in lemon juice, and cook over moderately low heat (do not let boil), stirring constantly, until sauce registers 160°F on thermometer and coats back of a wooden spoon.

Season sauce with salt and pepper and pour over veal and vegetables.

COOK'S NOTE

- Veal breast is available at butcher shops and some supermarkets; in either case, you will have to order this, a portion of a whole breast, ahead.

Sliced Calf's Liver with Golden Onions

SERVES 4

ACTIVE TIME: 45 MINUTES ■ START TO FINISH: 45 MINUTES

■ This simple liver recipe is a staple in the city of Venice. The twin keys to success here are to slice the liver and onions very thin and to work rapidly to avoid overcooking the liver. Polenta is a perfect accompaniment. ■

- 1 (1-pound) piece calf's liver
- ½ stick (4 tablespoons) unsalted butter or 4 tablespoons extra-virgin olive oil (or a combination)
- ¾ pound onions, sliced paper-thin
- Salt and freshly ground black pepper
- ⅓ cup water
- 1 tablespoon chopped fresh flat-leaf parsley

ACCOMPANIMENT: Basic Polenta (page 264)

Rinse liver to remove any traces of blood. Remove and discard membrane and any tough veins. Cut crosswise into ⅛-inch-thick slices.

Melt 2 tablespoons butter (or heat 2 tablespoons oil) in a 12-inch heavy skillet over moderate heat. Add onions and cook, stirring, for 1 minute. Cover skillet and cook, stirring occasionally, until onions are softened and golden brown, about 10 minutes. Transfer to a bowl and cover to keep warm.

Pat half of liver slices dry and season with salt and pepper to taste. Heat 1 tablespoon butter (or oil) in skillet over moderately high heat until foam subsides. Add seasoned liver and cook, shaking skillet and turning liver occasionally, until browned on both sides but still pink inside, about 2 minutes total. Put cooked liver on top of onions and cover again.

Add water to skillet and deglaze by boiling over high heat, stirring and scraping up brown bits, for 1 minute. Continue to boil until liquid is slightly reduced, 1 to 2 minutes. Pour sauce over cooked liver and wipe skillet clean.

Cook remaining liver in remaining 1 tablespoon butter (or oil) as above, then add to onions, along with parsley, and toss to combine.

Tongue with Mustard Horseradish Sauce

SERVES 6

ACTIVE TIME: 30 MINUTES ■ START TO FINISH: 3½ HOURS

■ Dense and meaty, tongue acquires a delightfully tender, silken texture after long, slow cooking in liquid. It's a very good way to get rich beefy flavor for little money. The rather pungent mustard horseradish sauce is the perfect complement. If you have a good deli near you, it may sell tongue; otherwise, ask your butcher. ■

FOR TONGUE

- 1 (3½-pound) fresh beef tongue
- 1 large onion, sliced
- 6 garlic cloves, smashed
- 1 Turkish bay leaf or ½ California bay leaf
- 1 star anise
- 2 tablespoons salt
- ½ teaspoon black peppercorns

FOR SAUCE

- 2 tablespoons unsalted butter
- ¼ cup chopped shallots
- 1½ tablespoons all-purpose flour
- ¼ cup heavy cream
- 2 tablespoons whole-grain mustard
- 1 tablespoon drained bottled horseradish
- 1 tablespoon chopped fresh flat-leaf parsley
- 1 tablespoon chopped fresh dill
- ¼ teaspoon fresh lemon juice
- Salt and freshly ground black pepper

COOK THE TONGUE: Rinse tongue well under cold water and put in a 6- to 8-quart deep heavy pot. Add onion, garlic, bay leaf, star anise, salt, peppercorns, and cold water to cover by 3 inches. Bring to a boil, covered, then reduce heat and simmer, partially covered, until tongue is fork-tender, 2½ to 3 hours.

Transfer tongue to a cutting board; reserve 1½ cups cooking liquid. When tongue is cool enough to handle, peel off skin and trim any fat or gristle. Keep tongue warm, covered with foil. Skim off fat from cooking liquid and pour liquid through a paper towel–lined sieve into a large bowl; discard solids.

MAKE THE SAUCE: Melt butter in a 2-quart heavy saucepan over moderate heat. Add shallots and cook, stirring frequently, until softened. Add flour and cook, whisking, for 1 minute to make a roux. Gradually add reserved cooking liquid and cream, whisking constantly, then bring to a boil, whisking. Reduce heat and simmer, whisking constantly, until sauce is slightly thickened, 2 to 3 minutes. Whisk in mustard, horseradish, parsley, dill, lemon juice, and salt and pepper to taste.

Slice tongue very thin and serve with sauce.

Crispy Sweetbreads with Parsnip Potato Purée, Braised Endives, and Port Sauce

SERVES 4

ACTIVE TIME: 2¼ HOURS ■ START TO FINISH: 14 HOURS (INCLUDES SOAKING AND WEIGHTING SWEETBREADS)

■ Give yourself a treat and try this recipe. Sweetbreads have a creamy texture and a lovely delicate flavor that we enhance by sautéing them in butter. (In order to make them easier to slice, we first soak them in cold water, then blanch and weight them to give them a firmer texture.) We serve them with three blandishments, each of which brings out a different aspect of their appeal: the parsnip potato purée accents their sweetness, the braised endives tease out a trace of bitterness, and the port sauce emphasizes their richness. ■

FOR SWEETBREADS

- 1½ pounds veal sweetbreads, rinsed
- 1 tablespoon plus ½ teaspoon salt
- 1 stick (8 tablespoons) unsalted butter, cut into tablespoons
- ¼ teaspoon freshly ground black pepper
- 1 cup all-purpose flour

FOR PARSNIP POTATO PURÉE

- 1 pound parsnips
- 1 pound boiling potatoes
- 2 cups water
- 2 tablespoons unsalted butter
- 1 teaspoon salt
- ¼ teaspoon freshly ground black pepper

FOR BRAISED ENDIVES

- 1½ tablespoons unsalted butter
- 1⅓ pounds Belgian endives (4–6), halved lengthwise and cut lengthwise into ½-inch-wide strips
- ¼ teaspoon salt, or to taste

FOR SAUCE

- 2 tablespoons minced shallots
- 1 cup Veal Stock (page 929), boiled until reduced to ½ cup, or ½ cup veal demi-glace (see Sources)
- 2 tablespoons tawny port
- 1 tablespoon unsalted butter
- Salt and freshly ground black pepper

SPECIAL EQUIPMENT: 2 pounds weights, such as large cans of soup or vegetables; a potato ricer

PREPARE THE SWEETBREADS: Soak sweetbreads in a large bowl of ice and cold water to cover in refrigerator, changing water once or twice, for at least 8 hours.

Drain sweetbreads and transfer to a 3-quart saucepan. Add water to cover by 1 inch, then add 1 tablespoon salt. Bring to a boil, then reduce heat and simmer, uncovered, for 3 minutes. Drain sweetbreads and transfer to a large bowl of ice and cold water to stop the cooking; drain again.

With a sharp paring knife, cut away any fat and as much membrane and connective tissue as possible without breaking up sweetbreads. Arrange sweetbreads in one layer in a baking dish, cover with plastic wrap, and top with another baking dish or plate. Set weights on top and refrigerate for at least 4 hours.

Holding a knife at a 30-degree angle, cut sweetbreads diagonally into ½-inch-thick slices. Set aside.

CLARIFY THE BUTTER FOR SAUTÉING THE SWEETBREADS: Melt butter in a 1-quart heavy saucepan over low heat. Remove from heat and let stand for 3 minutes. Skim froth, then slowly pour butter into a measuring cup, leaving milky solids in bottom of pan (discard solids). Set aside.

MAKE THE PURÉE: Peel parsnips and potatoes and cut into ½-inch cubes. Transfer to a 3-quart heavy saucepan and add water, butter, salt, and pepper. Bring to a boil, covered, then reduce heat and simmer, covered, until vegetables are very tender, 20 to 25 minutes.

Put a rack in middle of oven and preheat oven to 200°F.

When vegetables are tender, using a slotted spoon, transfer them to ricer and force through ricer into a heatproof bowl. Stir in as much cooking liquid as necessary to make a stiff purée. Cover with foil and keep warm in oven.

COOK THE ENDIVES: Melt butter in a 10-inch heavy skillet over moderate heat. Stir in endives and salt, cover, and cook, stirring occasionally, until endives are wilted, 3 to 5 minutes. Continue to cook, uncovered, stirring occasionally, until endives are tender and edges are golden, about 5 minutes more. Remove from heat and cover to keep warm.

SAUTÉ THE SWEETBREADS: Pat sweetbreads dry and sprinkle with remaining ½ teaspoon salt and pepper. Dredge sweetbreads in flour, shake off excess, and transfer to a wax paper–lined tray.

Heat clarified butter in a 10- to 12-inch heavy skillet over moderately high heat until hot but not smoking. Add sweetbreads in 2 or 3 batches, without crowding, and cook, turning once, until golden brown, about 6 minutes per batch. Transfer to a baking sheet with sides, in one layer, and keep warm, uncovered, in oven. (Do not clean skillet.)

MAKE THE SAUCE: Pour off all but 1 tablespoon fat from skillet. Add shallots and cook over moderately low heat, stirring, until softened, 1 to 2 minutes. Stir in reduced stock and port, bring to a boil, and boil until slightly thickened, about 2 minutes. Remove from heat and swirl in butter. Pour sauce through a fine-mesh sieve into a bowl, pressing on solids; discard solids. Season with salt and pepper.

Divide purée among four dinner plates, top with endives and sweetbreads, and spoon sauce over all.

COOK'S NOTES

- The sweetbreads can be soaked in cold water for up to 12 hours. The weighted sweetbreads can be refrigerated for up to 12 hours.
- The purée can be made up to 1 day ahead. Cool, uncovered, then refrigerate, covered. Reheat, covered, over low heat, stirring occasionally.
- The endives can be cooked up to 1 day ahead. Cool, uncovered, then refrigerate, covered. Reheat, covered, over moderately low heat, stirring occasionally.
- The clarified butter can be made up to 1 week ahead and refrigerated, covered.

SWEETBREADS

Sweetbreads are the thymus gland of calves or occasionally lambs. They come in two parts: a thin, long lobe, called the throat sweetbread, and a thicker, more bulbous lobe, called the heart sweetbread. Although they taste the same, the thicker lobe is considered more aesthetically pleasing. Sweetbreads are light and delicate in flavor—much milder than kidneys or liver—and firmer in texture than brains. Like most offal, they are highly perishable and should be cooked within a day or so of purchase. They must be soaked in several changes of water to give them their characteristic white color inside and out and then blanched to firm up their texture. They are often weighted to flatten them for slicing and make the texture a little denser.

Tripe Roman Style

SERVES 4

ACTIVE TIME: 45 MINUTES ■ START TO FINISH: 7 HOURS

■ In Rome, where innards of all kinds have long been in favor, you'll find this dish on menus of restaurants from homey to fancy. The sauce is a little sweet and very rich, and the tripe has a terrific texture, with just a bit of chewiness left. This dish is also great as a sauce served over pasta. ■

- 3 pounds beef honeycomb tripe
- 1/3 cup extra-virgin olive oil
- 1 large onion, chopped
- 2 carrots, chopped
- 2 celery ribs, chopped
- 2 garlic cloves, chopped
- 1/2 teaspoon salt
- 1/4 teaspoon freshly ground black pepper
- 2/3 cup dry white wine
- 1 (28- to 32-ounce) can whole tomatoes in juice
- 2 cups cold water
- 1/4 cup chopped fresh mint

GARNISH: finely grated pecorino Romano and chopped fresh mint

Trim any fat from tripe, then rinse under cold water. Soak in a large bowl of cold water for 1 hour, then rinse again.

Put tripe in an 8-quart pot of cold water and bring to a boil; drain and rinse. Fill pot with fresh cold water, add tripe, and bring to a boil again. Reduce heat and simmer, uncovered, turning tripe occasionally and adding more hot water to pot if necessary to keep it covered, until very tender, about 4 hours (tripe will have a pungent aroma while simmering). Drain and cool completely.

After tripe has cooked for about 3½ hours, heat oil in a 6- to 8-quart heavy pot over moderate heat until hot but not smoking. Add onion, carrots, celery, and garlic and cook, stirring frequently, until softened, about 8 minutes. Add salt, pepper, and wine, bring to a boil, and boil, stirring, for 1 minute. Pour juice from tomatoes into sauce, then chop tomatoes. Add tomatoes, water, and mint to sauce and simmer, uncovered, for 30 minutes.

Trim any remaining fat from tripe and cut tripe into 2-by-½-inch strips. Add to sauce and simmer, uncovered, stirring occasionally, until tripe is a bit tenderer but still slightly chewy, 45 minutes to 1 hour. Season with salt and pepper.

Serve tripe sprinkled with cheese and mint.

COOK'S NOTE

■ The tripe can be cooked in the sauce up to 2 days ahead. Cool, uncovered, then refrigerate, covered. Reheat before serving.

Tripe Talk

A bathing cap? An Elizabethan ruff? A piece of coral? Though it looks a bit like all of these, it's honeycomb tripe, the lining from the second chamber of a ruminant's stomach, most commonly a steer's. Grayish in color, it's usually bleached to a more appealing snowy white. You can find other kinds of tripe, but honeycomb is by far the tenderest and most flavorful. Many supermarkets carry it, although (as with most offal) a butcher shop is likely to have the freshest. This cast-off part of the animal, an economical staple to people in many parts of the world, isn't to everyone's taste, but we think it's delicious, and we like the concept of "waste not, want not."

Pork

Arista

Tuscan-Style Roast Pork

SERVES 6

ACTIVE TIME: 20 MINUTES ■ START TO FINISH: 2½ HOURS

■ In 1430, the clergy of the Greek Orthodox and Roman Catholic churches came together over a banquet to try to settle their differences. The convocation was a great success. The most impressive part of the banquet, the story goes, was a whole roast of pork with beautiful bronzed skin and succulent meat. Upon tasting the roast, the Greek prelate threw up his hands in delight and declared the pork "*arista!*"—"the best!" Although the churches were at peace with each other only temporarily, Italians have been calling roast pork *arista* ever since.

You will have to order this roast from your butcher; reassembling the roast with the bones means that the meat gets extra flavor while cooking. When you're ready to serve the meal, it's easy to remove the bone and slice the meat.

This recipe comes to us from the Italian cooking authority Faith Heller Willinger. In her kitchen in Florence, she uses a mechanical meat spit (called a *giarrosto*, or *spiedo*) in her fireplace; the drippings from the glistening pork are caught in a terra-cotta dish underneath on the hearth. We found the meat is also very delicious cooked in the oven. ■

CUTS OF PORK

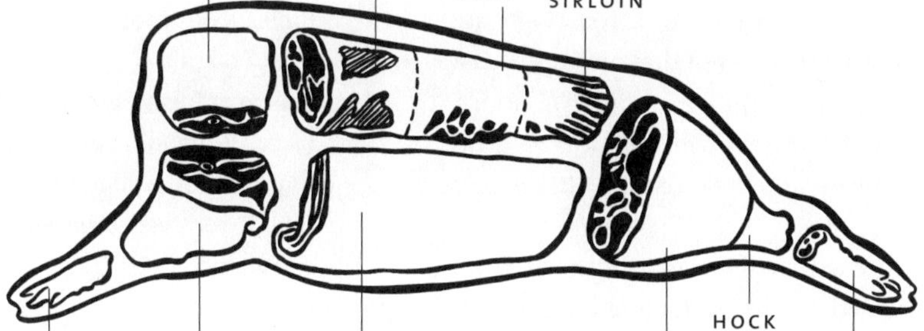

SHOULDER	CENTER LOIN	SIRLOIN	PICNIC SHOULDER
Pork shoulder	Center-cut pork loin	Pork loin roast	Arm picnic roast
Pork butt (Boston butt)	Crown roast		Arm roast
	Loin chop (center-cut)	LEG	Arm steak
BLADE END	Rib chop	Cured ham	Smoked pork shoulder (picnic ham)
Baby back ribs		Fresh ham	Picnic shoulder
Canadian bacon			
Country-style ribs		SIDE AND BELLY	
Tenderloin		Bacon	
		Spareribs	

6 garlic cloves
¼ cup fresh rosemary leaves
2 teaspoons fine sea salt
¼ teaspoon freshly ground black pepper
1 (4½- to 5-pound) rib section center-cut pork loin roast, boned, roast reassembled (with bones), and tied by the butcher

SPECIAL EQUIPMENT: an instant-read thermometer

Mince together garlic and rosemary. Stir together with salt in a small bowl and season with pepper. Make a slit that runs lengthwise through pork loin: Insert a sharp long thin knife into middle of one end of roast toward center of loin, then repeat at opposite end of loin to make an incision that runs lengthwise through roast. Open up incision with your fingers, working from both ends, to create a ¾-inch-wide opening, then pack with 1½ tablespoons garlic mixture, pushing it through with the handle of a long wooden spoon. Rub remaining garlic mixture all over pork. Let marinate at room temperature for 30 minutes.

Put a rack in middle of oven and preheat oven to 350°F.

Put loin fat side up on a rack in a roasting pan. Roast until thermometer inserted diagonally at least 2 inches into meat registers 145°F, about 1½ hours. Let pork stand, loosely covered with foil, for 20 minutes. (Its internal temperature will rise 5 to 10 degrees as it stands.)

Remove and discard string. Separate meat from bones and cut crosswise into ¾-inch-thick slices. If desired, serve bones cut into ribs.

COOK'S NOTE

- The roast can be stuffed and rubbed with the garlic mixture up to 1 day ahead and refrigerated, covered. Bring to room temperature before roasting.

Roast Pork with Apricot and Shallot Stuffing

SERVES 8
ACTIVE TIME: 45 MINUTES ■ START TO FINISH: 2 HOURS

■ Of all the cuts of meat, the center-cut pork loin may be the most versatile. Relatively lean, with a tender, fine-grained texture, it tastes wonderful on its own but also takes on other flavors readily. Here, sweet apricots and shallots give the stuffing a gentle, savory bite. Making an incision through the center of the roast and pushing the stuffing into it creates a beautiful mosaic in every slice. ■

3 slices firm white sandwich bread, crusts discarded
½ pound firm but ripe apricots (3 large), pitted and cut into ⅓-inch pieces, or 6 ounces dried apricots (20–25)
2 tablespoons unsalted butter
½ cup chopped shallots
2 tablespoons chopped fresh flat-leaf parsley
½ teaspoon salt
¼ teaspoon freshly ground black pepper
1 (3- to 3½-pound) boneless center-cut pork loin roast (3½ inches in diameter)
2 tablespoons vegetable oil
½ cup water

SPECIAL EQUIPMENT: an instant-read thermometer

Put a rack in middle of oven and preheat oven to 375°F.

MAKE THE STUFFING: Cut enough bread into ⅓-inch pieces to measure 1 cup. Spread evenly in a shallow baking pan and toast in oven, stirring occasionally, until golden, about 10 minutes. Transfer to a bowl. (Leave oven on.)

If using dried apricots, bring 3 cups water to a simmer in a medium saucepan. Add dried apricots and simmer for 5 minutes to plump. Drain well, then cut into ⅓-inch pieces.

Melt butter in a 12-inch nonstick skillet over moderately low heat. Add shallots and cook, stirring occasionally, until softened, about 10 minutes. Add apricots and cook, stirring, for 3 minutes (fresh apricots will soften slightly). Remove from heat and stir in bread, parsley, salt, and pepper.

STUFF AND ROAST THE PORK: If pork loin has been tied, remove and discard string. Make a hole that runs lengthwise through pork loin for stuffing: Insert a sharp long thin knife into middle of one end toward center of loin, then repeat at opposite end to make an incision that runs lengthwise through roast. Open up incision with your fingers, working from both ends, to create a 1½-inch-wide opening. Pack all of stuffing into pork, pushing from both ends toward center. Pat pork dry and season well with salt and pepper.

Heat oil in a 12-inch heavy skillet over high heat until just smoking. Brown pork on all sides, about 8 minutes total.

Transfer pork to a roasting pan and roast until thermometer inserted diagonally 2 inches into meat (avoid stuffing) registers 150°F, 40 to 50 minutes. Transfer pork to a cutting board, cover loosely with foil, and let stand for 20 minutes. (Its internal temperature will rise 5 to 10 degrees as it stands.)

Meanwhile, set roasting pan over two burners. Add water and deglaze pan by boiling over moderate heat, scraping up brown bits, for 1 minute.

Slice meat and serve with sauce.

Not Your Grandmother's Pork

Today's pork has about 50 percent less fat than pork did back in the early 1960s; cuts from the loin have almost 70 percent less. This might be good news for the dieters among us, but not for our taste buds: when the fat was bred out of pigs, the flavor went too. The lean meat is easy to overcook, making it tough and dry.

There are several ways of upping the flavor profile of pork. To begin with, don't overcook it because you're worried about trichinosis. Cooking a roast to medium — the final internal temperature should be 150°–155°F — is enough to kill the *Trichinella* parasite (which today infects only 1 percent or less of American hogs). At this point the roast will still be slightly pink, not gray, and will retain its succulence. When cooking chops, start checking for doneness early to make sure you don't overcook them.

You can also add flavor to pork by brining (see page 473) or marinating it. And if a recipe calls for searing a large cut, don't rush the process; wait for the dark brown color that tells you the outside of the meat has gained a whole new layer of flavor.

Last but by no means least, when possible, put your money where your mouth is. More and more farms are humanely raising heirloom breeds of pigs that pay off in exceptional taste and texture. They eat natural feed, without added steroids, hormones, or antibiotics, and they carry plenty of fat, insulation against cold and heat, thus allowing them to live outdoors rather than in factories. You can buy free-range pork at many butcher shops, specialty foods stores, and supermarkets.

Cuban Roast Pork Loin

SERVES 4 TO 6
ACTIVE TIME: 20 MINUTES ■ START TO FINISH: 3½ HOURS (INCLUDES MARINATING)

■ The combination of orange and lime juices mimics the tang in a marinade of bitter oranges, which would traditionally be used. Serve with rice and beans, or use the meat in our Cuban Sandwich (page 192). ■

- 4 large garlic cloves
- 1 teaspoon dried oregano, crumbled
- 1 teaspoon salt
- ¼ teaspoon freshly ground black pepper
- 1 (2-pound) boneless center-cut pork loin roast with a thin layer of fat, tied
- ½ cup fresh orange juice
- ¼ cup fresh lime juice
- 2 tablespoons olive oil
- 1 tablespoon unsalted butter

SPECIAL EQUIPMENT: a 3- to 4-quart heavy ovenproof oval or round pot with a lid; an instant-read thermometer

MARINATE THE PORK: Using a large heavy knife, mince and mash garlic to a paste with oregano, salt, and pepper. Rub mixture all over pork. Put pork in a sealable plastic bag. Stir together juices and 1 tablespoon olive oil and pour over pork. Seal bag, pressing out as much air as possible so marinade coats pork. Marinate pork, refrigerated, turning occasionally, for at least 2 hours.

ROAST THE PORK: Put a rack in middle of oven and preheat oven to 325°F.

Lift pork from marinade, reserving marinade, and pat dry. Heat butter and remaining 1 tablespoon oil in pot over moderate heat until foam subsides. Brown pork on all sides, about 8 minutes total. Remove pot from heat and pour reserved marinade around pork.

Cover pot and roast until thermometer inserted diagonally at least 2 inches into center of pork registers 145°F, about 45 minutes. Transfer pork to a plate and let stand, loosely covered with foil, for 10 minutes. (Its internal temperature will rise 5 to 10 degrees as it stands).

Bring cooking juices to a boil and boil until reduced by half, 5 to 10 minutes. Slice pork and serve with sauce.

COOK'S NOTE

■ The pork can marinate for up to 24 hours.

Roast Pork with Sweet-and-Sour Chile Cilantro Sauce

SERVES 8
ACTIVE TIME: 1 HOUR ■ START TO FINISH: 2 HOURS

■ The bright flavors of Mexico and the American Southwest—earthy coriander, fiery chiles, tart lime juice, aromatic cilantro—combine with honey to give this roast complexity with little effort. You can ask your butcher to butterfly the pork loin, or you can do it yourself. ■

FOR PORK

- ⅓ cup coriander seeds
- 1½ cups fine dry bread crumbs
- ½ cup extra-virgin olive oil
- ¾ teaspoon salt
- 1 teaspoon cracked black pepper
- 1 (3-pound) boneless center-cut pork loin roast, trimmed and butterflied
- Freshly ground black pepper

FOR SAUCE

- 1 red bell pepper, cored, seeded, and cut into ½-inch pieces
- ½ cup crushed dried New Mexico chiles or mild guajillo chiles (see Glossary and Cook's Note)
- 1 cup honey
- ½ cup fresh lime juice
- 1 teaspoon salt
- ¼ cup chopped fresh cilantro

SPECIAL EQUIPMENT: a mortar and pestle or an electric coffee/spice grinder; kitchen string; an instant-read thermometer

PREPARE THE PORK LOIN: Put a rack in middle of oven and preheat oven to 400°F.

Coarsely crush coriander seeds in mortar with pestle or in grinder. Stir together with bread crumbs, oil, salt, and cracked pepper in a small bowl.

Position pork fat side down with a long side nearest you. Season with salt and ground pepper. Pat one third of seasoned crumbs onto pork, leaving a 2-inch border along top edge. Starting with side nearest you, roll meat into a cylinder and tie securely with kitchen string. Coat pork with remaining crumbs.

Put pork on a rack in a roasting pan and roast for 15 minutes. Reduce oven temperature to 325°F and roast until thermometer inserted diagonally at least 2 inches into meat registers 150°F, 1 to 1¼ hours more. Let pork stand, loosely covered with foil, for 10 minutes. (Its internal temperature will rise 5 to 10 degrees as it stands.)

MEANWHILE, MAKE THE SAUCE: Combine bell pepper, chiles, honey, lime juice, and salt in a 1-quart heavy saucepan, bring to a simmer, and simmer, stirring occasionally, until sauce is slightly thickened, about 30 minutes. Let sauce cool to warm or room temperature. Just before serving, stir cilantro into sauce. Slice pork and serve with sauce.

BUTTERFLYING PORK LOIN

This technique for butterflying a boneless pork loin, called the spiral-cut method, results in a beautifully uniform piece of meat that holds stuffing evenly and rolls up like a dream.

1. You'll see that a flap is already beginning at one side of the loin, where the bone was removed. Using a boning knife or a very sharp small knife, make one long cut lengthwise down that side to within 1 inch of the bottom: you are starting the spiral.

2. Turn the knife parallel to the bottom of the loin and begin to cut your way inward, parallel to the cutting board. Use your other hand to gently lift off and pull the top section of meat away from your knife.

3. Here you are close to the end of the spiral.

4. Don't be tempted to leave the last 2 to 3 inches uncut—you want the result to be as flat as possible.

COOK'S NOTES

- If using whole dried chiles, you will need 2 ounces: remove and discard the stems, tear the chiles into pieces, and pulse in a food processor until coarsely chopped (the seeds will remain whole).
- The sauce, without the cilantro, can be made up to 2 days ahead and refrigerated, covered. Heat over low heat until warm and stir in the cilantro.

Mortadella- and Truffle-Stuffed Pork Loin with Rosemary Roast Potatoes

SERVES 8

ACTIVE TIME: 45 MINUTES ■ START TO FINISH: 2 HOURS

■ In this recipe, the mortadella sausage and truffle butter infuse the pork, giving it richness and a new level of texture. The dish was inspired by a truffled mortadella we tasted at La Bottega del Vino, in Rome. Good mortadella can be found at butcher shops and Italian markets and in the deli section of many supermarkets. ■

FOR PORK AND POTATOES

- 2 tablespoons black peppercorns
- 3½ teaspoons kosher salt
- 5 garlic cloves
- 2 tablespoons unsalted butter, softened
- 1 (3- to 3½-pound) boneless center-cut pork loin roast (4–5 inches in diameter), trimmed, leaving a ¼-inch layer of fat, and butterflied (see page 469)
- 3 tablespoons black truffle butter (see Sources), softened
- ½ pound thinly sliced mortadella
- 4 pounds small (2-inch-wide) boiling potatoes, preferably yellow-fleshed, peeled and halved
- 3 tablespoons extra-virgin olive oil
- 1 tablespoon chopped fresh rosemary
- ¼ teaspoon freshly ground black pepper

FOR SAUCE

- ¾ cup chicken stock or store-bought low-sodium broth
- ¼ cup water
- 1½ teaspoons cornstarch
- 1 tablespoon black truffle butter

SPECIAL EQUIPMENT: a mortar and pestle; kitchen string; an instant-read thermometer

PREPARE THE PORK: Put a rack in middle of oven and preheat oven to 450°F.

Coarsely crush peppercorns and 2 teaspoons salt in mortar with pestle, then add garlic and mash until a paste forms. Stir in unsalted butter; set aside.

Put pork fat side down on a cutting board lined with plastic wrap. Cover with another sheet of plastic wrap and pound to ½ inch thick with a smooth meat pounder or rolling pin. Remove plastic wrap and spread 1 tablespoon truffle butter over pork. Top with half of mortadella, slightly overlapping slices. Spread 1 tablespoon truffle butter over mortadella, then top with remaining mortadella and spread with remaining 1 tablespoon truffle butter. Beginning with a long side, roll up loin tightly and turn seam side down on cutting board. Make very close crosswise cuts in fat layer (about ⅛ inch apart; do not cut through to meat), then tie with kitchen string at 1-inch intervals. Rub roast all over with peppercorn butter, covering fat layer well.

Oil a rack, preferably a V-rack. Put pork fat side up on rack in a roasting pan. Roast for 20 minutes.

MEANWHILE, PREPARE THE POTATOES: Parboil potatoes in a 5- to 6-quart pot of boiling salted water (1 tablespoon salt per every 4 quarts water) for 5 minutes. Drain in a colander and let stand for 5 minutes, then toss potatoes with oil, rosemary, remaining 1½ teaspoons salt, and pepper in a large bowl.

Remove pork from oven and reduce oven temperature to 325°F. Add potatoes to roasting pan, turning them in pan juices to coat. Roast potatoes with pork until thermometer inserted diagonally 2 inches into meat registers 150°F, 45 to 55 minutes. Transfer pork to a platter and let stand, loosely covered with foil, while potatoes finish roasting. (Its internal temperature will rise 5 to 10 degrees as it stands.)

Increase oven temperature to 450°F. Remove rack from roasting pan and spread potatoes out in pan. Roast, stirring every 5 minutes, until potatoes are golden brown, about 20 minutes more. Transfer to a serving bowl and cover loosely to keep warm.

MAKE THE SAUCE: Skim as much fat as possible from pan juices. Set roasting pan over two burners, add stock, and deglaze pan by boiling over high heat, stirring and scraping up brown bits, for 1 minute. Stir together water and cornstarch in a small bowl, add to stock mixture, and boil, whisking, for 1 minute. Remove from heat and whisk in truffle butter.

Slice pork and serve with sauce and potatoes.

COOK'S NOTE

- The pork can be butterflied and stuffed up to 1 day ahead and refrigerated, covered. Bring to room temperature before roasting.

Garlic- and Soy-Marinated Pork Roast with Shiitake Mushroom Gravy

SERVES 6 TO 8

ACTIVE TIME: 45 MINUTES ■ START TO FINISH: 10 HOURS (INCLUDES MARINATING)

■ A long marination before cooking and a shiitake-spiked gravy make this Asian-inspired pork roast particularly flavorful. ■

FOR PORK

- 2/3 cup soy sauce
- 1/3 cup medium-dry sherry
- 1/4 cup packed brown sugar
- 3 garlic cloves, minced
- 1 teaspoon freshly ground black pepper
- 1 (4 1/2- to 5-pound) bone-in center-cut pork loin roast (4 inches in diameter; may include a few ribs), chine removed (have the butcher do this)
- 1 teaspoon salt
- 3 medium onions, coarsely chopped (1 1/2 cups)
- 1 tablespoon olive oil
- 1 cup water

FOR GRAVY

- 1 1/2 tablespoons olive oil
- 1/2 pound shiitake mushrooms, stems discarded and caps thinly sliced
- 1/4 teaspoon salt
- 1/8 teaspoon freshly ground black pepper
- 1 cup dry white wine
- 2 cups chicken stock or store-bought low-sodium broth
- 3 tablespoons unsalted butter, softened
- 3 tablespoons all-purpose flour

SPECIAL EQUIPMENT: an instant-read thermometer

MARINATE THE PORK: Whisk together soy sauce, sherry, brown sugar, garlic, and 1/2 teaspoon pepper in a small bowl until sugar is dissolved. Fit one heavy-duty sealable 1-gallon plastic bag inside another one to create a double layer, then pour in marinade. Add pork roast and seal bags, pressing out excess air. Turn pork to coat with marinade, then put in a baking pan and refrigerate, turning bag occasionally, for at least 8 hours.

ROAST THE PORK: Put a rack in middle of oven and preheat oven to 350°F.

Transfer pork to a work surface; discard marinade. Pat roast dry and season with salt and remaining 1/2 teaspoon pepper. Toss onions with oil in a large flameproof roasting pan. Add pork and pour 2/3 cup water over onions.

Roast pork, stirring onions occasionally and adding remaining 1/3 cup water to pan as needed to prevent them from burning, until thermometer inserted 2 inches into center of roast (without touching bone) registers 145°F, about 1 hour and 25 minutes. Transfer pork to a cutting board and let stand, loosely covered with foil, for 25 minutes. (Its internal temperature will rise 5 to 10 degrees as it stands.) Set roasting pan aside.

WHILE THE PORK STANDS, MAKE THE GRAVY: Heat oil in a 12-inch heavy skillet over moderate heat. Add mushrooms, salt, and pepper and cook, stirring, until mushrooms are tender, about 5 minutes. Remove from heat.

Set roasting pan over two burners, add wine, and deglaze pan by boiling over moderately high heat, stirring and scraping up brown bits, for 1 minute. Continue to boil until liquid is reduced to about 2 tablespoons, about 7 minutes. Stir in stock, then pour through a fine-mesh sieve into a 2-quart heavy saucepan, pressing hard on solids; discard solids.

Make a *beurre manié* by mashing together butter and flour with a fork in a small bowl. Bring liquid in saucepan to a boil, then add *beurre manié* a little at a time, whisking until smooth after each addition. Add mushrooms and simmer for 2 minutes. Stir in any meat juices accumulated on cutting board, along with salt and pepper to taste.

Slice pork and serve with gravy.

COOK'S NOTE

- The pork can marinate for up to 24 hours.

Roast Loin of Pork with Red Cabbage and Port Wine Sauce

SERVES 6

ACTIVE TIME: 1 HOUR ■ START TO FINISH: 4½ HOURS (INCLUDES MAKING SAUCE) PLUS AT LEAST 2 DAYS FOR BRINING

■ One way to make pork moister and amplify its taste is to brine it (see opposite page). For a little extra oomph, add herbs and spices to the brine, as we do in this recipe from the chefs Nancy Silverton and Mark Peel, of Campanile, in Los Angeles. ■

FOR PORK

- 4 allspice berries
- 2 tablespoons plus 1 teaspoon black peppercorns
- 8 cups water
- ⅓ cup kosher salt
- 3 tablespoons sugar
- 1 tablespoon dried thyme, crumbled
- 4 whole cloves
- 1 Turkish bay leaf or ½ California bay leaf
- 1 (6-rib) center-cut pork loin roast (3½ pounds), chine removed and bottom of ribs cracked (have the butcher do this)
- 1 large onion
- 2 tablespoons vegetable oil

FOR CABBAGE

- 1 pound red cabbage (½ medium head), quartered, cored, and cut into ¼-inch-wide slices
- 1 tablespoon vegetable oil
- 1 teaspoon finely chopped garlic
- ¼ cup balsamic vinegar
- 2½ teaspoons finely chopped fresh sage
- 1 tablespoon drained capers
- ½ teaspoon salt
- ¼ teaspoon freshly ground black pepper

ACCOMPANIMENT: Port Wine Sauce (recipe follows)

SPECIAL EQUIPMENT: an instant-read thermometer

BRINE THE PORK: Crack allspice and 2 tablespoons peppercorns in a mortar with a pestle (or wrap loosely in a kitchen towel or put in a heavy-duty sealable plastic bag and crack with bottom of a heavy skillet).

Combine water, cracked allspice and peppercorns, salt, sugar, thyme, cloves, and bay leaf in a 4-quart saucepan and bring to a boil, then reduce heat and simmer, uncovered, for 15 minutes. Pour brine into a deep 5-quart bowl or pot and cool, then refrigerate, covered, until cold, about 2 hours.

Add pork to brine, making sure it is completely covered. Marinate, covered and refrigerated, for at least 2 days.

ROAST THE PORK: Put a rack in middle of oven and preheat oven to 400°F.

Cut onion crosswise into ½-inch-thick rounds (do not separate into rings). Crack remaining 1 teaspoon peppercorns.

Drain pork, discarding brine, and pat dry; do not remove any spices still adhering to it. Sprinkle pork with cracked peppercorns. Heat oil in a 10- to 12-inch heavy ovenproof skillet, preferably cast-iron, over moderately high heat until hot but not smoking. Brown pork on all sides, 10 to 15 minutes total. Transfer to a plate.

Arrange onion rounds in skillet and place pork fat side up on top. Transfer to oven and roast until thermometer inserted 2 inches into center of meat (without touching bone) registers 140°F, 45 minutes to 1 hour. Transfer pork to a cutting board and let stand, loosely covered with foil, for 20 minutes. (Its internal temperature will rise 10 to 15 degrees as it stands.) Set skillet with onions aside.

WHILE THE PORK ROASTS, BLANCH THE CABBAGE: Put cabbage in a large sieve, lower sieve into a 5-quart pot of boiling salted water (1 tablespoon salt per every 4 quarts water), and blanch for 30 seconds. Plunge cabbage, still in sieve, into a bowl of ice and cold water to stop the cooking. Drain and pat dry. Set aside.

WHILE THE PORK STANDS, COOK THE CABBAGE: Remove caramelized onion rounds from skillet and cut into quarters. Heat oil in cleaned skillet over moderately high heat until hot but not smoking. Add cabbage and garlic and cook, stirring, until cabbage is crisp-tender, 5 to 6 minutes. Add vinegar and caramelized onion and cook, stirring, until vinegar has evaporated, about 1 minute. Stir in sage, capers, salt, and pepper.

Cut pork into 6 slices and serve with cabbage and sauce.

COOK'S NOTES

- The pork can marinate for up to 3 days.
- The cabbage can be blanched (but not cooked) up to 1 day ahead and refrigerated in a sealable plastic bag.

Port Wine Sauce

MAKES ABOUT 1 CUP
ACTIVE TIME: 15 MINUTES ■ START TO FINISH: 45 MINUTES PLUS 1 DAY IF MAKING STOCK

■ This superb sauce, perfect for any kind of roast pork, is an argument for having veal stock, which is more robust than chicken stock, in the freezer. Veal demi-glace can be substituted; see Cook's Note. ■

- 1 tablespoon unsalted butter
- 2 tablespoons chopped shallots
- ¼ cup balsamic vinegar
- 1 cup ruby port
- 1 cup Veal Stock (page 929)

Heat butter in a 1½- to 2-quart heavy saucepan over moderate heat until foam subsides. Add shallots and cook, stirring, until golden, about 3 minutes. Add vinegar, bring to a simmer, and simmer until most of liquid has evaporated, 3 to 4 minutes. Add port and simmer, uncovered, until sauce is reduced to about ½ cup, 12 to 15 minutes.

Brining Pork

Brining pork—that is, soaking it in a mixture of salt and water that has been seasoned—makes it wonderfully juicy and flavorful. It also lessens the risk of overcooking, which can happen in a flash with a lean cut of meat. The salt is key: its electrically charged ions plump up the muscle fibers, letting them absorb more water. The structure of the proteins changes too, preventing water from escaping during cooking.

Brining is nothing new, but it wasn't until about fifteen years ago that restaurant chefs, including Santa Fe's Mark Miller, in his first cookbook, *Coyote Café,* popularized the technique. These days it should be in the repertoire of every savvy home cook who's after flavor, not fat. The downside to brining is that you do have to plan ahead. We get good results when we brine pork for a day and even better results when we brine it for two days.

Add stock and simmer until sauce is reduced to about 1 cup, about 15 minutes. Pour sauce through a fine-mesh sieve into a small bowl.

COOK'S NOTES

- The sauce can be made up to 1 day ahead. Cool, uncovered, then refrigerate, covered. Reheat before serving.
- You can substitute veal demi-glace for the veal stock. For this recipe we use More Than Gourmet Demiglace Gold (see Sources), which is extremely concentrated. Dilute 1 tablespoon with 1 cup water.

Crown Roast of Pork with Apple Stuffing

SERVES 8 TO 10
ACTIVE TIME: 1 HOUR ■ START TO FINISH: 3½ HOURS (INCLUDES MAKING GLAZED APPLES)

■ A little drama at the dinner table can be a good thing—at least when it's of the culinary variety—and a crown roast certainly provides it. Despite its star quality, though, this recipe is fairly uncomplicated, even with the addition of an apple stuffing and glazed apples. Don't expect to see a crown roast sitting in the supermarket meat case; you'll have to order it from a butcher. Make sure that you have the butcher french (clean) the rib ends for you (but there's no need to bother with those little white hats the ribs once had to wear when they appeared in polite society). ■

FOR STUFFING

- 6 slices firm white sandwich bread, cut into 1-inch squares
- ¾ stick (6 tablespoons) unsalted butter
- ½ cup finely chopped onion
- ½ cup finely chopped celery, including some leaves
- 1½ pounds tart apples, such as Granny Smith, peeled, cored, and cut into ¼-inch-thick wedges
- ⅓ cup sugar
- 1 teaspoon salt
- ½ teaspoon freshly ground black pepper
- 1 teaspoon chopped fresh sage or ¼ teaspoon dried sage, crumbled
- 1 teaspoon chopped fresh thyme or ¼ teaspoon dried thyme, crumbled
- ¼ teaspoon freshly grated nutmeg
- Pinch of ground cinnamon
- ¼ cup chopped fresh flat-leaf parsley
- 2 tablespoons chopped fresh chives

FOR PORK

- 1 (9- to 11-pound) crown roast of pork
- 1½ teaspoons salt
- ½ teaspoon freshly ground black pepper
- ⅓ pound bacon (about 4 slices)

FOR SAUCE

- 1½ cups water
- ¼ cup red currant jelly or apple jelly
- Salt and freshly ground black pepper

ACCOMPANIMENT: Glazed Apples (recipe follows)
SPECIAL EQUIPMENT: an instant-read thermometer

MAKE THE STUFFING: Put a rack in middle of oven and preheat oven to 350°F.

Spread bread squares in one layer on a baking sheet with sides and bake until dry and lightly toasted, about 15 minutes. Remove bread from oven. (Leave oven on.)

Melt butter in a 12-inch heavy skillet over moderate heat. Add onion and celery and cook, stirring occasionally, until softened, 4 to 5 minutes. Stir in apples, sugar, salt, pepper, sage, thyme, nutmeg, and cinnamon. Reduce heat to low, cover, and cook, stirring occasionally, until apples are tender, about 15 minutes. Stir in bread squares, parsley, and chives and remove from heat.

ROAST THE PORK: Transfer rack to lower third of oven. Sprinkle roast inside and out with salt and pepper and put in a large roasting pan. Mound stuffing in cavity. Wrap tips of rib bones with foil to prevent burning and wrap meat below bones with overlapping bacon strips, securing them with wooden picks.

Roast pork, covering stuffing loosely with foil after first 30 minutes, until thermometer registers 150°F when inserted 2 inches into center of meat (without touching bones), 2¼ to 2¾ hours total. Transfer roast to a carving board and let stand, loosely covered with foil, for 15 to 20 minutes. (Its internal temperature will rise 5 to 10 degrees as it stands.)

MEANWHILE, MAKE THE SAUCE: Skim fat from pan drippings. Set pan over two burners, add water, and deglaze pan by boiling over high heat, stirring and scraping up brown bits, for 1 minute. Pour through a fine-mesh sieve into a 1- to 2-quart saucepan; discard solids.

Add jelly and any juices accumulated on carving board to sauce and bring to a simmer. Simmer, whisking occasionally and skimming any fat, until jelly is melted. Season with salt and pepper.

Remove foil from rib bones and carve roast into chops by cutting between ribs. Serve with stuffing, sauce, and glazed apples.

Glazed Apples

SERVES 8 TO 10

ACTIVE TIME: 25 MINUTES ■ START TO FINISH: 45 MINUTES

■ These pretty apples have the sophistication to match up with our crown roast of pork. It's important to use an apple variety that will not fall apart when cooked. Sweet Golden Delicious fill this bill nicely, as do Galas, which have a pronounced sweet-tart balance. Cook and drain the apples while the roast finishes in the oven; broil them while the roast stands. ■

- 1 cup water
- ½ cup plus 1 tablespoon sugar
- 2 pounds Golden Delicious or Gala apples, peeled, cored, and each cut into 8 wedges

Bring water and ½ cup sugar to a boil in a 3-quart saucepan, stirring until sugar is dissolved. Reduce heat and simmer for 5 minutes. Add apples and simmer, stirring occasionally, until just tender, about 15 minutes.

With a slotted spoon, transfer apples to a rack set over a baking pan and drain for 10 minutes; reserve poaching syrup.

Preheat broiler. Arrange apple wedges in one layer in a flameproof shallow baking pan and sprinkle with remaining 1 tablespoon sugar. Broil about 6 inches from heat, rotating pan occasionally and basting twice with reserved poaching syrup, until apples are lightly browned on edges, 3 to 5 minutes.

Island Pork Tenderloin

SERVES 6

ACTIVE TIME: 20 MINUTES ■ START TO FINISH: 50 MINUTES

■ As its name suggests, the tenderloin is the tenderest cut of pork. It is also very low in fat, about the same per serving as a boneless, skinless chicken breast. Being relatively small (about one pound), it is versatile and quick to cook. This robustly spiced rendition is our spin on jerk pork, although it's not as fiery as traditional versions. It's great sliced and served over a salad of greens, red bell pepper, avocado, and oranges. ■

FOR PORK

- 2 teaspoons salt
- ½ teaspoon freshly ground black pepper
- 1 teaspoon ground cumin
- 1 teaspoon chili powder
- 1 teaspoon ground cinnamon
- 2 pork tenderloins (2¼–2½ pounds total), trimmed
- 2 tablespoons olive oil

FOR GLAZE

- 1 cup packed dark brown sugar
- 2 tablespoons finely chopped garlic
- 1 tablespoon Tabasco

SPECIAL EQUIPMENT: an instant-read thermometer

PREPARE THE PORK: Put a rack in middle of oven and preheat oven to 350°F.

Stir together salt, pepper, cumin, chili powder, and cinnamon in a small bowl. Coat pork with spice rub.

Heat oil in an ovenproof 12-inch heavy skillet over moderately high heat until just beginning to smoke. Brown pork, turning occasionally, about 4 minutes total. Remove from heat; leave pork in skillet.

MAKE THE GLAZE AND ROAST THE PORK: Stir together brown sugar, garlic, and Tabasco in a small bowl. Pat the mixture onto tops of tenderloins. Roast until thermometer inserted diagonally in center of each tenderloin registers 140°F, about 20 minutes. Let pork stand in skillet, loosely covered with foil, for 10 minutes. (Its internal temperature will rise 10 to 15 degrees as it stands.)

Cut pork at a 45-degree angle into ½-inch-thick slices and arrange on a platter. Pour any juices from skillet over pork.

Grilled Pork Tenderloin with Mojo Sauce

SERVES 4

ACTIVE TIME: 30 MINUTES ■ START TO FINISH: 35 MINUTES

■ Pork tenderloin is ideal for grilling. Here we match it up with the Latin orange-garlic-oregano combination known as *mojo* sauce. Be sure that the fire is hot when you put the tenderloins on the grill, so you can get a good sear on the outside without overcooking the inside. ■

- 4 garlic cloves, minced
- 1½ teaspoons salt
- 5 tablespoons fresh orange juice
- 3 tablespoons olive oil
- 1 teaspoon dried oregano, crumbled
- 2 pork tenderloins (1½ pounds total), trimmed
- ½ teaspoon freshly ground black pepper

SPECIAL EQUIPMENT: an instant-read thermometer

Prepare a charcoal or gas grill: If using a charcoal grill, open vents in bottom of grill and lid, then light charcoal. Fire is hot when you can hold your hand 5 inches above rack for just 1 to 2 seconds. If using a gas grill, preheat on high, covered, for 10 minutes, then reduce heat to moderately high.

Using a mortar and pestle, mash garlic to a paste with ½ teaspoon salt (or mince and mash with a large heavy knife). Whisk garlic paste together with orange juice, 2 tablespoons oil, and ½ teaspoon oregano in a small bowl. Set sauce aside.

Pat pork dry. Rub each tenderloin with 1½ teaspoons oil, ½ teaspoon salt, ¼ teaspoon oregano, and ¼ teaspoon pepper.

Lightly oil grill rack. Grill pork, covered, turning once, until thermometer inserted diagonally into center of each tenderloin registers 150°F, 10 to 14 minutes total. Transfer pork to a cutting board and let stand, loosely covered with foil, for 10 minutes. (Its internal temperature will rise 5 to 10 degrees as it stands.)

Slice pork and serve drizzled with *mojo* sauce.

Cider-Braised Pork Shoulder with Caramelized Onions

SERVES 4 TO 6

ACTIVE TIME: 30 MINUTES ■ START TO FINISH: 3 HOURS

■ Make this dish and forget about it: after just half an hour of prep time, you can slide it into the oven and not think about it again until you're ready to serve dinner. It takes advantage of fresh pork shoulder, a very inexpensive cut that's ideal for braising; skin-on shoulder works especially well. The meat becomes juicy and tender during the slow cooking process. Cider adds a touch of sweetness to balance the savoriness and gives the dish rich color. If you're really hungry, you can pull the tender meat right off the bone with your fingers. Or serve the pork with noodles and salad for a winter meal. Fresh pork picnic shoulder is available at many supermarkets and some ethnic markets. ■

- 1 (3- to 4-pound) bone-in fresh pork shoulder half (preferably arm picnic)
- 2 garlic cloves, cut into slivers
- Salt and freshly ground black pepper
- 2 tablespoons olive oil
- 1½ pounds onions (5–6 medium), halved lengthwise and cut lengthwise into ¼-inch-thick slices
- ¾ cup unfiltered apple cider

Put a rack in middle of oven and preheat oven to 325°F.

Score fat and any skin on pork in a crosshatch pattern. Make slits all over meat with a small sharp knife and insert a garlic sliver in each slit. Pat pork dry and season with salt and pepper.

Heat oil in a 4- to 5-quart heavy ovenproof pot over moderately high heat until hot but not smoking. Brown meat on all sides, turning occasionally with tongs and a carving fork, about 8 minutes total. Transfer pork to a plate.

Add onions to pot and cook, stirring occasionally, until softened and starting to turn golden, about 5 minutes. Add ¾ teaspoon salt and cook, stirring occasionally, until onions are golden and caramelized, 8 to 10 minutes more.

Stir in cider and return pork to pot. Cover pot

tightly, transfer to oven, and braise pork until very tender, 2½ to 3 hours.

With tongs and carving fork, transfer pork to a serving dish. Boil cooking liquid until reduced to about 2 cups, 2 to 3 minutes. Season with salt and pepper and serve with pork.

COOK'S NOTE

- The pork can be braised up to 1 day ahead. Cool, uncovered, in the cooking liquid, then refrigerate, covered. Reheat in the cooking liquid, covered, in a 325°F oven for about 1 hour before reducing cooking liquid.

Roast Pork Shoulder Cubano

Puerco Asado

SERVES 8

ACTIVE TIME: 45 MINUTES ■ START TO FINISH: 5 HOURS

■ This is one of those dishes that prove conclusively that fabulous food does not have to be complicated or difficult. Be sure to get a picnic shoulder with skin on (available at supermarkets and ethnic markets) for this recipe—the crackly skin is unbelievably delicious. (For more on picnic shoulder, see page 495.) The recipe is from *Gourmet*'s longtime staff photographer Romulo Yanes and his family, who celebrate Thanksgiving with a Cuban feast. It was developed by his mother, Caridad Yanes, and adapted for American ingredients by his sister, Cira Delia. ■

- 1 cup fresh lime juice (from about 6 limes)
- 8 garlic cloves, minced
- 3 tablespoons salt
- 1 tablespoon dried oregano, crumbled
- 1 tablespoon ground cumin
- 1 (8-pound) bone-in fresh pork arm picnic shoulder with skin
- 3 cups water
- 6 tablespoons distilled white or cider vinegar

Put a rack in middle of oven and preheat oven to 375°F.

Stir together 3 tablespoons lime juice, garlic, 2½ tablespoons salt, oregano, and cumin in a small bowl. Pat pork dry. With a small sharp knife, make 1-inch-long by ¾-inch-deep incisions 2 inches apart all over pork skin. Push about ½ teaspoon garlic mixture into each incision and rub remainder on meaty ends not covered by skin.

Transfer pork, skin side up, to a nonreactive roasting pan and pour remaining lime juice around it. Roast, uncovered, until most of juice has evaporated and brown bits are beginning to form on bottom of pan, about 30 minutes.

Stir together water and vinegar in a bowl and pour around pork. Cover pan tightly with foil and roast for 1 hour.

Using a small ladle, baste meat only, not skin, with pan juices. Cover and roast for 1 hour more.

With a sharp knife, gently loosen skin from meat without cutting through skin and leaving fat layer attached to skin, and, using a spoon or baster, baste meat under skin with pan juices. Sprinkle remaining 1½ teaspoons salt over skin. Roast pork, uncovered, basting meat, not skin, every 20 minutes, until skin is crisp, about 1½ hours more (about 4 hours total roasting time). Transfer pork to a cutting board and let stand, loosely covered with foil, for 20 minutes. Skim fat from pan juices.

Cut pork into ¼-inch-thick slices and serve with skin and pan juices.

COOK'S NOTE

- For a more intensely flavored sauce, boil the pan juices until reduced by about half (1½ cups), about 30 minutes.

Milk-Braised Pork

SERVES 4 TO 6

ACTIVE TIME: 15 MINUTES ■ START TO FINISH: 3¼ HOURS

■ In this simple recipe, an adaptation of the Bolognese-style pork loin braised in milk made by Marcella Hazan, the legendary Italian cooking authority, the meat acquires a delicate texture and the milk slowly evolves into a rich sauce. We substitute pork shoulder for loin because it has enough fat to stay moist through the long, slow cooking. Don't be put off by the homely appearance of this dish; the way it tastes makes up for it. ■

- 1 (2½-pound) fresh boneless pork shoulder roast (do not trim fat)
- Salt and freshly ground black pepper
- 2 tablespoons vegetable oil
- 2 cups whole milk

Pat pork dry and season with salt and pepper.

Heat oil in a 4-quart heavy saucepan over moderately high heat until hot but not smoking. Brown pork on all sides, about 5 minutes total. Remove saucepan from heat and carefully add milk (mixture will splatter). Bring just to a simmer, cover, and simmer gently for 2 hours.

Continue to simmer pork, partially covered, until very tender, about 1 hour more. Transfer pork to a cutting board and let stand, loosely covered with foil, for 5 minutes.

Season cooking liquid with salt and pepper if necessary and boil until slightly thickened, about 2 minutes.

Thinly slice pork and transfer to a platter. Skim fat from cooking liquid and spoon sauce over pork.

Char Siu

Chinese Barbecued Boneless Pork

SERVES 4

ACTIVE TIME: 30 MINUTES ■ START TO FINISH: 5½ HOURS (INCLUDES MARINATING)

■ *Char siu* is usually served as one of many dishes in a Chinese main course. The leftovers are much prized, because the glaze is so flavorful that just a small amount of pork can bring another recipe, such as a stir-fry or rice dish, to life. If you make *char siu* at home, you can avoid the red food coloring common to the Chinatown version (red is a most auspicious color in China, especially if paired with pork, the meat of choice there). Rest assured that happiness and good fortune will be yours if you have a stash of homemade *char siu* in the freezer. ■

- 1 (1-pound) piece boneless pork butt or shoulder
- ¼ cup hoisin sauce
- ¼ cup soy sauce
- ¼ cup Chinese rice wine or sake
- 2 tablespoons honey
- 1 tablespoon finely chopped peeled fresh ginger
- 1 teaspoon finely chopped garlic
- ½ teaspoon salt

Cut pork along the grain into long strips 1½ to 2 inches wide. Remove and discard any sinew but do not trim fat. Transfer pork to a large sealable plastic bag. Stir together remaining ingredients in a small bowl until well combined. Add to pork and turn pork to coat, then squeeze bag to eliminate as much air as possible and seal. Marinate pork, refrigerated, for at least 4 hours.

Put a rack in lower third of oven and preheat oven to 375°F. Fill a 13-by-9-inch roasting pan with ½ inch water and place a wire rack across top of pan.

Remove pork from marinade, reserving marinade, and position pork strips 1 inch apart on wire rack. Roast for 15 minutes.

Meanwhile, bring marinade to a boil in a 1-quart saucepan (marinade may look curdled). Remove from heat.

Brush some marinade over pork and roast for 10 minutes more. Generously baste meat with marinade, turn each piece over, and baste again. Roast pork for 20 minutes more, basting 2 or 3 more times with remaining marinade.

Increase oven temperature to 400°F and roast pork until mahogany-colored and caramelized on edges, 10 to 15 minutes more (about 1 hour total roasting time). Transfer to a cutting board and let stand, loosely covered with foil, for 10 minutes. (Its internal temperature will rise 10 to 15 degrees as it stands.)

To serve, cut pork across the grain into ½-inch-thick slices.

COOK'S NOTES

- If you can't find pork butt or shoulder, you can use pork tenderloin.
- The pork can marinate for up to 24 hours.
- The intensity of the flavor fades when the pork is sliced, so cut it as needed. Keep the remaining unsliced pork wrapped in foil and refrigerated for up to 3 days.
- Any leftover pork can be frozen, tightly wrapped in plastic wrap and placed in a sealable plastic bag, for up to 1 month.

Lillie's North Carolina Chopped Barbecue

SERVES 4 TO 6 (MAKES ABOUT 4 CUPS)
ACTIVE TIME: 40 MINUTES ■ START TO FINISH: 4¼ HOURS
(INCLUDES MAKING BARBECUE SAUCE)

■ The shoulder cut sometimes called pork butt is often overlooked by today's cooks. It is inexpensive and easy to prepare, and it has terrific flavor, but it's sometimes considered difficult to work with because it contains a lot of sinew and fat. If the cooking is long and slow, however, as here, it becomes extremely tender, and the fat helps keep it from drying out.

This recipe is from Lillie Charlton, who came to New York City from North Carolina in the late 1950s, when she was eighteen, and has lived here ever since. Missing the barbecue she grew up with, which is slowly pit-roasted over glowing hardwood coals and then chopped, she developed this indoor version and shared it with us, along with the tangy tomato sauce popular in her part of North Carolina. Although it may lack the special smokiness of the outdoor variety, we find it soulfully satisfying, particularly because we can make it at any time of the year. ■

- 1 (3-pound) boneless pork shoulder roast (often called pork butt or Boston butt), tied
- ¾ cup plus ⅓ cup cider vinegar
- 1 carrot, chopped
- 1 celery rib, chopped
- 1 medium onion, chopped
- 3 garlic cloves
- 8 black peppercorns
- Tomato Barbecue Sauce (recipe follows)

ACCOMPANIMENTS: split hard rolls and Creamy Slaw (page 140)

Combine pork, ¾ cup vinegar, carrot, celery, onion, garlic, and peppercorns in a 5- to 6-quart heavy pot and add enough water to just cover pork. Bring to a boil over moderately high heat, skimming froth. Reduce heat, partially cover, and simmer, skimming froth occasionally and adding more water as needed to keep pork submerged, until tender, about 2 hours.

Meanwhile, put a rack in middle of oven and preheat oven to 350°F.

With tongs, transfer pork to a rack set in a roasting pan; discard cooking liquid. Pour remaining ⅓ cup vinegar over pork. Roast, turning every 15 minutes, until it is golden on all sides and fat is crisp, about 1 hour. Transfer to a cutting board and let stand, loosely covered with foil, for 15 minutes. Reduce oven temperature to 325°F.

Remove and discard string from pork. Finely chop meat, then transfer it to a shallow 2-quart baking dish. Stir in barbecue sauce. Cover and bake until heated through, about 20 minutes.

Serve on rolls with coleslaw.

COOK'S NOTE

■ The barbecue can be chopped and sauced up to 1 day ahead and refrigerated, covered. Reheat in a 325°F oven for 30 minutes.

Tomato Barbecue Sauce

MAKES ABOUT 2¾ CUPS
ACTIVE TIME: 10 MINUTES ■ START TO FINISH: 20 MINUTES

■ Enjoy this sweet barbecue sauce with grilled chicken, short ribs, or other meat as well as pork. Because it has plenty of sugar, don't brush it on until just before you are ready to take the food off the grill, or it will burn. ■

- 1 cup plus 2 tablespoons tomato purée
- ¾ cup cider vinegar
- ⅓ cup Worcestershire sauce
- 3 tablespoons apple juice
- 3 tablespoons unsweetened pineapple juice
- 3 tablespoons packed brown sugar
- 1 tablespoon dry mustard
- 1½ teaspoons salt
- 1½ teaspoons chili powder
- 1½ teaspoons Tabasco
- ¾ teaspoon cayenne
- ¾ teaspoon ground celery seed
- ½ teaspoon ground cinnamon

Stir together all ingredients in a 2- to 3-quart heavy saucepan and bring to a boil, stirring. Reduce heat and simmer, partially covered, for 5 minutes.

COOK'S NOTE

■ The sauce can be made up to 1 day ahead and refrigerated, covered.

Pork Chops with Sautéed Apples and Cider Cream Sauce

SERVES 6

ACTIVE TIME: 45 MINUTES ■ START TO FINISH: 45 MINUTES

■ Nothing says fall like the classic combination of apples, cream, and pork, a specialty of Normandy. It's everything you want for dinner on those days when the leaves are spinning down from the trees and winter is peeking around the corner. Use thick bone-in chops for the full effect. Readily available Golden Delicious apples are fine in this recipe—they hold their shape and are sweet. The more complexly flavored Galas hold together well too. ■

- 3 tablespoons unsalted butter
- 1 large shallot, minced
- ½ cup apple cider
- ½ cup cider vinegar
- ½ teaspoon finely chopped fresh sage or ¼ teaspoon dried sage, crumbled
- 1¼ cups chicken stock or store-bought low-sodium broth
- ⅔ cup heavy cream
- 6 (¾-inch-thick) pork loin chops (2½ pounds total)
- ½ teaspoon salt
- ¼ teaspoon freshly ground black pepper
- 3 Golden Delicious or Gala apples, peeled, cored, and each cut into 8 wedges
- 2 tablespoons packed light brown sugar

Melt 1 tablespoon butter in a 2-quart heavy saucepan over moderately low heat. Add shallot and cook, stirring occasionally, until tender, about 5 minutes. Add apple cider, vinegar, and sage, bring to a boil, and boil until reduced to about ½ cup, about 8 minutes.

Add 1 cup stock and boil until reduced to about ¾ cup, about 12 minutes. Add cream and boil until reduced to about 1 cup, about 8 minutes.

Meanwhile, pat pork dry and sprinkle with salt and pepper. Heat 1 tablespoon butter in a 12-inch skillet over moderately high heat until foam subsides. Add chops in 2 batches and cook, turning once, until just cooked through, 6 to 8 minutes per batch. Transfer chops to a warm platter and cover loosely with foil to keep warm.

Pour off fat from skillet. Add remaining 1 tablespoon butter, then add apples and cook over moderate heat, turning occasionally, until golden and just tender, 4 to 5 minutes. Transfer to a bowl and gently toss with brown sugar.

Add remaining ¼ cup stock to skillet and deglaze by boiling over high heat, stirring and scraping up brown bits, for 1 minute. Stir deglazing liquid into sauce, along with any meat juices accumulated on platter and salt and pepper to taste. Transfer apples to platter with pork and pour sauce over top.

Pork Chops with Onion Marmalade

SERVES 4

ACTIVE TIME: 35 MINUTES ■ START TO FINISH: 1¼ HOURS

■ When we think of classic midwestern cooking, one of the first things that comes to mind is the pork chop, a favorite of farm cooks everywhere. There are excellent reasons for its popularity—it's satisfying, readily available, and very easy to cook. Although all pork chops come from the loin, there are differences between them. Loin chops, which we use here, are often simply labeled "center-cut chops." They come from the center and rear-center sections of the loin and are the tenderest of the various pork chops. The slightly sweet onion marmalade complements them well. ■

- 4 (1-inch-thick) boneless pork loin chops (1½ pounds total)
- 1 teaspoon dried rosemary, crumbled
- ¾ teaspoon salt, or to taste
- ½ teaspoon freshly ground black pepper, or to taste
- 2 tablespoons olive oil
- 2 large onions (1½ pounds total), halved lengthwise and thinly sliced crosswise
- ½ cup water
- ¼ cup balsamic vinegar
- ¼ cup red currant jelly

SPECIAL EQUIPMENT: an instant-read thermometer

Trim some but not all fat from chops. Pat chops dry and sprinkle evenly on both sides with rosemary, salt, and pepper. Heat oil in a 12-inch heavy skillet over moderately high heat until hot but not smoking. Brown chops, turning once, about 5 minutes total. Transfer to a plate.

Add onions to fat remaining in skillet and cook over moderately high heat, stirring, until browned, about 5 minutes. Add water, vinegar, and jelly and bring to a boil, stirring, until jelly melts, about 1 minute. Reduce heat, cover, and simmer until onions are very tender, about 25 minutes.

Return pork, with any juices accumulated on plate, to skillet. Cover and cook over moderate heat, turning once, until thermometer inserted horizontally into a chop registers 145°F and almost all of liquid has evaporated, about 12 minutes (if liquid evaporates before pork is cooked through, add 1 tablespoon water to skillet to keep onions from sticking). Let chops stand, loosely covered with foil, for 10 minutes. (Their internal temperature will rise 10 to 15 degrees as they stand.)

Serve chops with onions.

Pork Chops with Sour Cherry Sauce

SERVES 8

ACTIVE TIME: 1 HOUR ■ START TO FINISH: 1 HOUR

■ Sour cherries are plump, meaty, and bracingly tart. Unfortunately, this fruit is almost impossible for most of us to get our hands on, even during its short midsummer season. Frozen sour cherries are available in some stores, but we prefer the dried version. With these in your pantry, you can enjoy sour cherries at any time of year. ■

FOR SAUCE

- 3 tablespoons balsamic vinegar
- 3 tablespoons sugar
- 3/4 cup dry red wine
- 1/4 cup minced shallots
- 1 (3-inch) cinnamon stick
- 1 cup chicken stock or store-bought low-sodium broth
- 3/4 cup (about 4 ounces) dried sour cherries
- 1 tablespoon cornstarch stirred together with 1 tablespoon cold water
- 2 teaspoons fresh lime juice, or to taste
- 1/4 teaspoon salt
- 1/8 teaspoon freshly ground black pepper

FOR CHOPS

- 8 (3/4-inch-thick) boneless pork loin chops (2 pounds total)
- 1 teaspoon salt
- 1/2 teaspoon freshly ground black pepper
- 2 tablespoons vegetable oil

MAKE THE SAUCE: Combine vinegar and sugar in a 1- to 2-quart heavy saucepan, bring to a boil over moderate heat, stirring, and boil, stirring until reduced to a glaze, about 4 minutes (be careful not to burn glaze). Add wine, shallots, and cinnamon stick, bring to a boil, and boil until reduced to about 1/4 cup, about 10 minutes.

Add stock and cherries, bring to a simmer, and simmer, uncovered, until cherries plump, about 5 minutes. Stir cornstarch mixture, add to sauce, and simmer, uncovered, whisking occasionally, for 2 minutes. Discard cinnamon stick, then stir in lime juice, salt, and pepper. Remove from heat and keep sauce warm, covered.

COOK THE CHOPS: Pat chops dry and sprinkle with salt and pepper. Heat 1 tablespoon vegetable oil in a 10- to 12-inch heavy skillet, preferably well-seasoned cast-iron, over high heat until just smoking. Cook half the chops, turning once, until just cooked through, 6 to 8 minutes total. Transfer chops to a platter and loosely cover with foil to keep warm. Cook remaining chops in remaining 1 tablespoon oil in same manner.

Serve chops with sauce spooned over.

Pork Chops with Mustard Crumbs

SERVES 4

ACTIVE TIME: 25 MINUTES ■ START TO FINISH: 25 MINUTES

■ The rib chop comes from the part of the loin nearest the shoulder, which means it has a little more fat than the other center-cut chops. It can be distinguished by the small curved section of rib bone that runs along one side. It's our favorite among pork chops because of its extra fat. We brown the chops on top of the stove, cover them with mustard and rye bread crumbs flavored with garlic and sage, and finish them in the oven, which keeps them moister than panfrying would. ■

- 3 tablespoons olive oil
- 1⅓ cups coarse fresh rye bread crumbs
- 2 garlic cloves, minced
- 1 tablespoon finely chopped fresh sage or ½ teaspoon dried sage, crumbled
- ½ teaspoon salt
- ¼ teaspoon freshly ground black pepper
- 4 (¾- to 1-inch-thick) pork rib chops (about 2 pounds total)
- 2 tablespoons Dijon mustard

Put a rack in middle of oven and preheat oven to 425°F.

Heat 2 tablespoons oil in a 10-inch heavy skillet over moderately high heat until hot but not smoking. Add bread crumbs, garlic, sage, salt, and pepper and cook, stirring, until crumbs are golden brown, 3 to 5 minutes. Transfer to a bowl.

Pat pork dry. Heat remaining 1 tablespoon oil in cleaned skillet over moderately high heat until hot but not smoking. Brown chops in 2 batches, turning once, about 4 minutes per batch. Transfer to a baking sheet with sides.

Spread tops of chops with mustard and then scatter bread crumbs over them. Roast until meat is just cooked through, 5 to 7 minutes. Transfer chops to a platter and let stand, loosely covered with foil, for 5 minutes.

Brined Pork Chops

SERVES 6

ACTIVE TIME: 20 MINUTES ■ START TO FINISH: 1 HOUR PLUS AT LEAST 1 DAY FOR BRINING

■ Brining these pork chops for at least one day, or as long as two days, makes them tenderer, juicier, and tastier. The Riesling pan sauce, which adds a pleasant sweetness, takes just a few minutes to prepare while the chops are resting. ■

- 8 cups water
- ¼ cup kosher salt
- ¼ cup mustard seeds
- ¼ cup sugar
- 2 tablespoons pickling spices
- 6 garlic cloves, smashed with side of a large knife
- 6 (1½-inch-thick) pork rib chops
- 4–6 tablespoons olive oil
- ½ cup dry Riesling
- ½ cup chicken broth or store-bought low-sodium broth

SPECIAL EQUIPMENT: an instant-read thermometer

BRINE THE PORK CHOPS: Combine water, salt, mustard seeds, sugar, pickling spices, and garlic in a 4-quart saucepan and bring to a boil, then reduce heat and simmer for 15 minutes. Cool brine completely. Transfer to a very large bowl.

Add chops and refrigerate, covered, for at least 1 day.

ROAST THE CHOPS: Put a rack in middle of oven and preheat oven to 425°F.

Remove chops from brine and pat dry; discard brine. Heat 2 tablespoons oil in a 12-inch heavy skillet over moderately high heat until hot but not smoking. Brown chops in batches, without crowding, turning once, for 6 to 8 minutes per batch. Transfer to a roasting pan, arranging chops in a single layer. Add more oil, 1 to 2 tablespoons at a time, as needed between batches.

Roast chops until thermometer inserted 2 inches horizontally into center of meat (without touching bone) registers 145°F, 10 to 15 minutes.

Transfer chops to a platter and let stand, loosely covered with foil, for 10 minutes. (Their internal temperature will rise 10 to 15 degrees as they stand.)

Set roasting pan across two burners. Add wine and stock, along with any meat juices from platter, and deglaze by boiling over moderately high heat, stirring and scraping up brown bits, for 1 minute. Continue to boil until reduced to about 1/2 cup, about 3 minutes. Season sauce with salt and pepper and serve with chops.

Smoked Pork Chops with Pineapple Rosemary Sauce

SERVES 2

ACTIVE TIME: 35 MINUTES ■ START TO FINISH: 1 1/4 HOURS

■ We love smoked pork chops, and because they're already fully cooked, they just need to be heated through. This sauce takes advantage of the "extra-sweet" pineapples now available at supermarkets. We don't recommend doubling the sauce ingredients if you're cooking for more than two people, because the sauce will lose its intensity. Instead, make two batches.

Smoked pork chops are available at some supermarkets and butcher shops or by mail (see Sources). ■

- 1 pineapple (labeled "extra-sweet"), peeled (rind reserved), quartered, and cored
- 1/4 cup olive oil
- 1 (4-inch) fresh rosemary sprig
- 1 large garlic clove, smashed
- 2 teaspoons fresh lemon juice
- 1/8 teaspoon salt
- 2 (6- to 8-ounce) fully cooked smoked pork chops
- Rounded 1/4 teaspoon freshly ground black pepper

SPECIAL EQUIPMENT: cheesecloth

Refrigerate one quarter of pineapple for another use. Cut enough of remainder into 1/4-inch dice to measure 1/2 cup; set aside. Cut the rest into 1-inch chunks. With your hands, squeeze juice from reserved rind into a blender. Add pineapple chunks and purée at high speed until very smooth, about 1 minute. Pour purée through a sieve lined with dampened cheesecloth set over a bowl. Let drain (do not press on solids) until you have enough juice to measure 1 cup, about 30 minutes.

Discard solids in sieve. Pour juice into a small skillet and boil over moderately high heat until reduced to about 1/4 cup, 10 to 14 minutes.

Meanwhile, combine oil, rosemary sprig, and garlic in a small heavy saucepan and cook over moderately low heat, stirring, until garlic is golden, 2 to 3 minutes. Remove from heat, discard rosemary and garlic, and transfer 1 tablespoon oil to a 10-inch heavy skillet. Whisk remaining oil into reduced juice and stir in diced pineapple, lemon juice, and salt.

Pat chops dry and sprinkle with pepper. Heat garlic oil in skillet over moderately high heat until hot but not smoking. Add chops and sear, turning once, until browned and heated through, about 5 minutes. Transfer to a platter and cover loosely with foil to keep warm.

Discard fat from skillet, add pineapple sauce, and bring to a boil over moderate heat, stirring and scraping up any brown bits. Pour sauce over chops.

Grilled Pork Kebabs with Manchamantel Sauce

SERVES 6 TO 8

ACTIVE TIME: 2 HOURS ■ START TO FINISH: 8 HOURS (INCLUDES MARINATING)

■ In this Mexican take on pork kebabs, the tenderloin—which is somewhat bland because it has so little fat and no connective tissue—is transformed by the boldness of the marinade as well as the accompanying *manchamantel* sauce. The sauce, whose name translates as "tablecloth stainer," is a classic combination from central Mexico, in which the sweetness of the fruit counteracts the heat of the chiles. ■

1 dried ancho chile (see Glossary)
1 cup cold water
1 onion, chopped
4 garlic cloves, chopped
2 tablespoons chopped fresh thyme or 2 teaspoons dried thyme, crumbled
2 tablespoons chopped fresh oregano or 2 teaspoons dried oregano, crumbled
1½ tablespoons ground cumin
2½ teaspoons salt, or to taste
2 teaspoons black peppercorns, crushed
⅓ cup olive oil
⅓ cup fresh lemon juice
2¼ pounds pork tenderloin (2–3 tenderloins), trimmed and cut into 1½-inch cubes
24 (1-inch) fresh pineapple chunks (from a 4-pound pineapple)
24 (1-inch) red onion chunks (from 2 large onions)

ACCOMPANIMENT: Manchamantel Sauce (recipe follows)
SPECIAL EQUIPMENT: eight 12-inch bamboo skewers, soaked in water for 30 minutes

Heat a dry heavy skillet over moderately low heat until hot. Toast chile, turning once and pressing down with tongs, until slightly darker, 30 to 40 seconds total. Halve chile lengthwise and remove and discard seeds, stems, and ribs. Transfer chile to a bowl, pour enough boiling water over to cover, and let stand for 30 minutes.

Drain chile well and coarsely chop.

Combine chile, cold water, onion, garlic, thyme, oregano, cumin, salt, peppercorns, oil, and lemon juice in a blender and blend until smooth. Pour marinade into a large heavy-duty sealable plastic bag, add pork, press out excess air, and seal bag, turning to coat pork with marinade. Marinate, refrigerated, for at least 6 hours.

Prepare a charcoal or gas grill: If using a charcoal grill, open vents in bottom of grill, then light charcoal. Fire is medium-hot when you can hold your hand 5 inches above rack for just 3 to 4 seconds. If using a gas grill, preheat on high, covered, for 10 minutes, then reduce heat to moderate.

Drain pork and pat dry; discard marinade. Thread 3 pieces of pork, 3 pieces of pineapple, and 3 pieces of onion loosely on each skewer. Lightly oil grill rack. Grill kebabs (covered only if using gas), turning occasionally, until just cooked through, 14 to 15 minutes if using charcoal, 12 minutes if using gas. Transfer kebabs to a platter and let stand, loosely covered with foil, for 5 minutes.

Serve kebabs with sauce.

COOK'S NOTES

- The pork can marinate for up to 24 hours.
- The kebabs can also be broiled on the oiled rack of a broiler pan 2 inches from the heat.

Manchamantel Sauce

MAKES ABOUT 3½ CUPS
ACTIVE TIME: 50 MINUTES ■ START TO FINISH: 50 MINUTES

■ Since this sauce is fairly time-consuming to prepare, we recommend that you make it the day before. Serve it with the grilled pork kebabs or shrimp. ■

2 ounces (3–5) dried ancho chiles (see Glossary)
3½ tablespoons vegetable oil
1 cup finely chopped onion
1 tablespoon minced garlic
2¼ teaspoons salt
½ teaspoon plus ⅛ teaspoon freshly ground black pepper
1 tablespoon sugar
1½ tablespoons cider vinegar, or to taste
1 cup chicken stock or store-bought low-sodium broth
½ cup water
1 cup chopped fresh pineapple or 1 (20-ounce) can pineapple chunks in juice
1 small banana, sliced (¾ cup)
½ teaspoon ground cinnamon
Pinch of ground cloves

Heat a dry heavy skillet over moderately low heat until hot. Toast chiles one at a time, turning once and pressing down with tongs, until slightly darker, 30 to 40 seconds each. Halve chiles lengthwise and remove and discard seeds, stems, and ribs. Transfer chiles to a bowl, pour enough boiling water over to cover, and let stand for 30 minutes.

Drain chiles well and coarsely chop.

Heat 2 tablespoons oil in a 4-quart heavy saucepan over moderately low heat. Add onion, garlic, ¼ teaspoon salt, and 1/8 teaspoon pepper and cook, stirring occasionally, until onion is softened and pale golden, about 15 minutes.

Add sugar and 1 1/2 tablespoons vinegar and cook, stirring, for 1 minute. Transfer mixture to a blender and add chiles, stock, water, pineapple, banana, cinnamon, cloves, remaining 2 teaspoons salt, and remaining 1/2 teaspoon pepper. Blend until very smooth. Add additional vinegar, if desired.

Heat remaining 1 1/2 tablespoons oil in cleaned saucepan over moderately high heat until hot but not smoking. Add sauce (use caution, as sauce will spatter) and simmer, stirring, for 5 minutes.

COOK'S NOTE

- The sauce can be made up to 1 day ahead. Cool, uncovered, then refrigerate, covered. Reheat over low heat just before serving.

Clay Pot Pork

SERVES 4

ACTIVE TIME: 30 MINUTES ■ START TO FINISH: 2 HOURS

■ Cooking meat in caramel sauce is a popular technique in Vietnam; the sweet/bitter sauce makes a perfect foil for slow-braised pork. This is traditionally made in a clay pot, but a heavy saucepan or small Dutch oven also works well. The relatively large amount of fish sauce is important to the flavor of the dish. Serve the pork over white rice. ■

- 1/3 cup sugar
- 3/4 cup chicken stock or store-bought low-sodium broth or water
- 1/3 cup Asian fish sauce, preferably Vietnamese
- 3 shallots, thinly sliced
- 2 garlic cloves, thinly sliced
- 3 scallions, thinly sliced diagonally, white and green parts kept separate
- 1 pound trimmed boneless pork shoulder, cut into 1-inch cubes
- 1 teaspoon freshly ground black pepper

ACCOMPANIMENT: cooked rice

Cook sugar in a dry 3-quart heavy saucepan over moderate heat, without stirring, until it begins to melt. Continue to cook, stirring occasionally with a fork, until sugar has melted into a deep golden caramel. Carefully add stock and fish sauce (caramel will harden and steam vigorously) and cook, stirring, until caramel is dissolved. Add shallots, garlic, and white part of scallions and simmer, uncovered, stirring occasionally, for 4 minutes.

Toss pork with pepper in a bowl and stir into sauce. Bring to a simmer, then cover pan, reduce heat to low, and braise pork, stirring once or twice, until very tender, 1 1/4 to 1 1/2 hours.

Stir in scallion greens and serve with rice.

Georgian Pork Stew

SERVES 6

ACTIVE TIME: 30 MINUTES ■ START TO FINISH: 1 1/2 HOURS

■ The unusual cooking method in this recipe makes for a fragrant and unforgettable stew. The spices—fenugreek, coriander seeds, and earthy golden marigold or turmeric—are common to the Republic of Georgia, whose culinary traditions are heavily influenced by India. This recipe is from the food historian and cookbook author Darra Goldstein, who has traveled extensively in Georgia. She drew her inspiration from an old friend, Gulisa Lataria, who runs a guesthouse in Tbilisi. Traditionally, pomegranate seeds are sprinkled over the stew just before serving. ■

2 1/2 pounds trimmed boneless pork shoulder, cut into 3/4-inch pieces
1 1/4 teaspoons kosher salt
Freshly ground black pepper
3 large garlic cloves
1 teaspoon dried summer savory, crumbled
3/4 teaspoon coriander seeds
1/2 teaspoon fenugreek seeds
2 tablespoons olive oil
1 large red onion, finely chopped
1/2 teaspoon ground dried marigold (see Sources) or turmeric
1 cup water
1/2 cup chopped fresh cilantro
3 tablespoons Georgian Salsa (page 896), plus more for serving

ACCOMPANIMENT: Grits Pudding with Cheese (recipe follows), mashed potatoes, or noodles
SPECIAL EQUIPMENT: a mortar and pestle or an electric coffee/spice grinder

Put pork in a 4-quart heavy saucepan and sprinkle with 1/2 teaspoon salt and pepper to taste. Cover pot and steam meat in its own juices over high heat, stirring once, for 10 minutes. Remove lid and cook, stirring occasionally, until juices have evaporated, 8 to 10 minutes.

Meanwhile, mash garlic, savory, and remaining 3/4 teaspoon salt to a paste in mortar with pestle, then scrape paste into a small bowl. Coarsely grind coriander and fenugreek seeds in mortar. Alternatively, mash garlic, savory, and salt with the side of a large knife and grind spices in coffee/spice grinder.

Stir 1 tablespoon oil into pork and cook, stirring occasionally, until meat is browned, 6 to 8 minutes. Add garlic paste to pork, along with remaining 1 tablespoon oil, reduce heat to moderate, and cook, stirring, for 1 minute. Add onion, fenugreek mixture, and marigold and cook, stirring occasionally, until onion is softened, about 5 minutes.

Add water and bring to a boil. Reduce heat and cook, covered, at a bare simmer until meat is tender, about 1 hour.

Stir in cilantro, salsa, and pepper to taste. Serve with grits pudding, potatoes, or noodles, with more salsa on the side.

Grits Pudding with Cheese

SERVES 4 TO 6
ACTIVE TIME: 20 MINUTES ■ START TO FINISH: 30 MINUTES

■ This cheesy accompaniment to the pork stew is made with grits, which best capture the texture of the white cornmeal found in the Republic of Georgia. Ordinary supermarket mozzarella works better than fresh mozzarella as a substitute for the pliant fresh Georgian cheese called *sulguni*. ■

3 cups water
3/4 teaspoon salt
3/4 cup regular grits (not stone-ground or quick-cooking)
3/4 pound mozzarella, cut into 1/2-inch cubes

Combine water and salt in a 2 1/2- to 3-quart heavy saucepan and bring to a boil. Add grits in a thin stream, stirring constantly, and return to a boil. Reduce heat to low and simmer, stirring constantly, until grits are thick, porridgelike, and tender, about 18 minutes.

Increase heat to moderate and gradually add mozzarella, stirring until it is melted into grits. (Cheese will be stringy but molten.) Serve piping hot.

Posole

Pork and Hominy Stew

SERVES 6
ACTIVE TIME: 40 MINUTES ■ START TO FINISH: 2 1/4 HOURS

■ As with chili, there are many versions of posole, the thick, hearty stew that originated in the Mexican state of Jalisco. The one ingredient they all have in common is hominy, dried white or yellow corn kernels from which the hull has been removed. We are partial to this version, which was sent to us by J. Kent Chesnut, of Mérida, Mexico; it gets its enticing undertones and heat from the combination of two chiles. Like most stews, posole improves in flavor after a day or two. ■

2 dried pasilla chiles or New Mexico chiles (see Glossary)
2 dried guajillo chiles (see Glossary)
2 cups water

2 teaspoons dried oregano, preferably Mexican (see Sources), crumbled
1½ teaspoons salt
¼ teaspoon cumin seeds
¼ teaspoon freshly ground black pepper
1 large garlic clove, crushed
1 medium tomato, coarsely chopped
½ white onion, coarsely chopped (¾ cup)
2 pounds boneless pork shoulder or country-style pork ribs, trimmed of excess fat and cut into 1-inch cubes
3 (15-ounce) cans white hominy, rinsed and drained

ACCOMPANIMENTS: chopped radishes, white onion, fresh cilantro, iceberg lettuce, and/or seeded fresh chiles; lime wedges; and warm corn or flour tortillas or tortilla chips

Stem and seed chiles. Combine with 2 cups water in a small saucepan, bring to a simmer, and simmer until softened, about 15 minutes.

Transfer chiles, with cooking water, to a blender. Add remaining ingredients except pork and hominy and blend until smooth (use caution).

Transfer chile purée to a 4-quart heavy saucepan, stir in pork, and bring to a boil. Reduce heat, cover, and simmer, stirring occasionally, for 1 hour.

Add hominy and simmer, covered, until pork is tender, about 30 minutes more. Skim fat from sauce and season posole with salt to taste. Serve with any or all of the suggested accompaniments.

COOK'S NOTES

- Canned white hominy is available in Latino markets and most supermarkets.
- The posole can be made up to 3 days ahead. Cool, uncovered, then refrigerate, covered.

Spicy Stir-Fried Pork and Peppers

SERVES 4

ACTIVE TIME: 45 MINUTES ■ START TO FINISH: 1½ HOURS

■ In much of China, when you say *meat,* people assume that you mean pork. This dish takes full advantage of the natural affinity between pork and the other classic ingredients of the Chinese pantry. ■

1½ tablespoons plus ¾ teaspoon cornstarch
1 large egg white
1½ tablespoons Chinese rice wine or sake
1 tablespoon Asian sesame oil
1 tablespoon plus 1 teaspoon soy sauce
1 pound boneless pork loin, fat trimmed, cut crosswise into ⅛-inch-thick slices and then into ¼-inch-wide strips
3 tablespoons chicken stock or store-bought low-sodium broth
½ teaspoon rice vinegar (not seasoned)
½ teaspoon sugar
About 3 cups vegetable oil, preferably safflower or corn oil, for frying
1 red bell pepper, cored, seeded, and cut lengthwise into ⅛-inch-wide strips
1 (3-inch) green or red chile, seeded if desired and minced
2 tablespoons minced garlic
½ teaspoon Sichuan peppercorns (see Glossary), lightly crushed, or ½ teaspoon *sansho* (Japanese pepper) plus ⅛–¼ teaspoon freshly ground black pepper
1 tablespoon minced peeled fresh ginger
2 teaspoons Asian chili paste (see Glossary)
Salt

ACCOMPANIMENT: cooked rice

SPECIAL EQUIPMENT: a wok; a deep-fat thermometer

Stir together 1½ tablespoons cornstarch, egg white, 1 tablespoon rice wine, 2 teaspoons sesame oil, and 1 teaspoon soy sauce in a bowl. Add pork and stir until well coated. Refrigerate, covered, for at least 30 minutes.

Meanwhile, stir together stock and remaining ¾ teaspoon cornstarch in a small bowl until cornstarch is dissolved. Stir in rice vinegar, sugar, remaining 1½ teaspoons rice wine, remaining 1 teaspoon sesame oil, and remaining 1 tablespoon soy sauce. Set sauce aside.

Heat wok over high heat until hot. Add 1¼ inches vegetable oil and heat until it registers 400°F on thermometer. Fry pork in 2 batches, stirring, until strips separate and are just cooked through, 15 to 30 seconds per batch. With a slotted spoon, transfer to a large sieve set over a bowl. (Return oil to 400°F between batches.)

Pour off oil from wok (transfer it to a saucepan to cool, then discard). Add 3 tablespoons vegetable oil to wok and heat over high heat until hot but not smoking. Stir-fry bell pepper until crisp-tender, 10 to 20 seconds. With slotted spoon, transfer to a bowl. Pour off all but 1 tablespoon oil from wok, add chile pepper, garlic, Sichuan peppercorns, ginger, and chili paste, and stir-fry until fragrant, 5 to 15 seconds. Stir sauce, then add to wok and bring to a boil, stirring. Add pork and bell pepper and stir-fry, tossing constantly, until heated through, 30 seconds to 1 minute. Season with salt and serve with rice.

COOK'S NOTES

- The pork can marinate, refrigerated, for up to 8 hours.
- If you don't have a wok, use a large skillet.

Chop Suey

SERVES 6

ACTIVE TIME: 1¼ HOURS ■ START TO FINISH: 1¼ HOURS

■ As with most folk recipes, the origin of chop suey is shrouded in myth and legend. Until recently, the consistent thread in all the stories we had heard was that this dish was an American invention with no history in China. Now, however, E. N. Anderson has claimed that a very similar dish actually did exist in the province from which most early Chinese immigrants came to the United States. In the end, though, what really matters is not where chop suey came from but the fact that when properly made—which is to say, when the vegetables are not overcooked into mush—its widely assorted tastes and textures come together to make a lively and delicious whole. Plus, for anyone raised on Chinese takeout, this is real comfort food. ■

- 2 garlic cloves, minced
- 1 tablespoon plus 1 teaspoon oyster sauce
- 1½ teaspoons soy sauce
- 1 teaspoon salt
- 1½ teaspoons cornstarch
- 1 (1-pound) pork tenderloin, halved lengthwise and cut crosswise into ⅛-inch-thick slices
- ¼ cup vegetable oil
- 2 celery ribs, cut diagonally into ¼-inch-thick slices
- 6 ounces snow peas, trimmed and cut diagonally into ¼-inch-thick slices
- ¼ pound mushrooms, trimmed and cut into ¼-inch-thick slices
- 1 onion, halved lengthwise and cut into ¼-inch-wide strips
- 1 green bell pepper, cored, seeded, and cut lengthwise into ¼-inch-wide strips, strips halved crosswise
- 1 (5-ounce) can sliced water chestnuts, drained and rinsed
- 1 (5-ounce) can sliced bamboo shoots, drained and rinsed
- ¼ pound mung bean sprouts, rinsed and drained
- ½ pound bok choy, cut crosswise into ¼-inch-thick slices, leaves and ribs kept separate
- ¼ cup chicken stock or store-bought low-sodium broth

ACCOMPANIMENT: cooked rice

SPECIAL EQUIPMENT: a wok

Stir together garlic, 1 tablespoon oyster sauce, soy sauce, salt, and ½ teaspoon cornstarch in a large bowl. Add pork, stir to coat, and marinate at room temperature for 15 minutes.

Heat wok over high heat until a bead of water dropped onto cooking surface evaporates immediately. Drizzle 1 teaspoon oil around sides of wok, add celery with salt to taste, and stir-fry until crisp-tender, about 2 minutes. Transfer to a large bowl.

Cook remaining vegetables in batches: Reheat wok and stir-fry each vegetable separately in same manner, adding 1 teaspoon oil to wok before each batch and seasoning with salt. Allow only 1 minute for bean sprouts to cook, and when stir-frying bok choy, begin with ribs, then add leaves and 1 tablespoon water after 1 minute. Transfer vegetables to bowl with celery.

Stir together stock, remaining 1 teaspoon oyster sauce, and remaining 1 teaspoon cornstarch in a small bowl; set aside.

Reheat wok over high heat until a bead of water dropped onto cooking surface evaporates immediately. Drizzle remaining 1 tablespoon oil around sides of wok, then add pork and stir-fry until just cooked through, about 2 minutes.

Return all vegetables to wok and toss well. Make a well in center, stir stock mixture, and add to well. Bring sauce to a boil without stirring, then stir to combine with pork and vegetables. Serve with rice.

COOK'S NOTE

- If you don't have a wok, use a large skillet.

Mu Shu Vegetables with Barbecued Pork

SERVES 6

ACTIVE TIME: 1½ HOURS ■ START TO FINISH: 3½ HOURS

■ In this variation of the northern Chinese stir-fried meat and vegetable mixture known as mu shu pork, the cookbook author Nina Simonds barbecues the meat, eliminates the eggs, and adds more vegetables to make the dish lower in fat and, to our palates, even better than the original. She has also found a convenient substitute for the traditional Mandarin pancakes. ■

FOR BARBECUED PORK

- 2 tablespoons hoisin sauce
- 1 tablespoon soy sauce
- 1 tablespoon Chinese rice wine or sake
- 1 tablespoon ketchup
- 1½ teaspoons sugar
- 1½ teaspoons minced garlic
- 1 (1-pound) boneless center-cut pork loin roast

FOR SAUCE

- 2 teaspoons cornstarch
- ¼ cup chicken stock, store-bought low-sodium broth, or water
- ¼ cup soy sauce
- ¼ cup Chinese rice wine or sake
- 1 teaspoon sugar
- ½ teaspoon freshly ground black pepper

FOR STIR-FRIED VEGETABLES

- 4 medium leeks (white parts only), halved lengthwise and cut into thin 2- to 3-inch-long strips (2 cups)
- 2 tablespoons vegetable oil
- 1½ tablespoons minced garlic
- 1 (1-inch) piece fresh ginger, peeled and minced
- 1 teaspoon red pepper flakes
- ½ pound shiitake mushrooms, stems discarded and caps thinly sliced
- 4 cups thinly sliced Napa cabbage (14 ounces; about ½ head)
- 2 tablespoons Chinese rice wine or sake
- ½ pound snow peas, trimmed and sliced on a long diagonal

ACCOMPANIMENTS: hoisin sauce and Mock Mandarin Pancakes (recipe follows)

SPECIAL EQUIPMENT: an instant-read thermometer; a wok

MAKE THE BARBECUED PORK: Put a rack in middle of oven and preheat oven to 350°F.

Whisk together all ingredients except pork in a bowl. Add pork and turn to coat. Transfer pork and marinade to a shallow baking pan.

Bake until pork registers 150°F on thermometer, about 1 hour. Cool completely.

Thinly slice pork across the grain and cut slices into thin strips.

MAKE THE SAUCE: Stir together cornstarch and stock in a small bowl until cornstarch is dissolved, then stir in remaining ingredients.

STIR-FRY THE VEGETABLES AND FINISH THE DISH: Wash leeks well in a bowl of cold water; lift out and pat dry.

Heat a wok or a deep 12- to 14-inch skillet over high heat until hot. Add oil and heat until it just begins to smoke. Add leeks, garlic, ginger, red pepper flakes, and mushrooms and stir-fry until vegetables are softened, 1 to 2 minutes. Add cabbage and rice wine and stir-fry until cabbage is wilted, 1 to 2 minutes. Stir sauce, then add to vegetables, along with snow peas and pork. Stir-fry until sauce is thickened and snow peas are bright green, 1 to 2 minutes. Transfer to a platter.

Spread a dab of hoisin sauce on oiled side of each pancake. Spoon some of stir-fry into center and roll up.

COOK'S NOTE

■ The pork can be baked 1 day ahead, cooled, and refrigerated, covered. When you are ready to serve it, bring to room temperature, slice, and add to the vegetable mixture with the snow peas.

Mock Mandarin Pancakes

MAKES 12 PANCAKES
ACTIVE TIME: 5 MINUTES ■ START TO FINISH: 20 MINUTES

■ Nina Simonds borrowed the idea of using flour tortillas in place of mandarin pancakes from Chris Schlesinger, the owner of the East Coast Grill, in Cambridge, Massachusetts. The tortillas are brushed lightly with Asian sesame oil for enhanced flavor, arranged in pairs with the oiled sides together (as in a traditional Mandarin pancake recipe, to keep their inner surface soft and pliable), and heated before serving. ■

12 (6½-inch) flour tortillas
1 tablespoon Asian sesame oil

Put a rack in middle of oven and preheat oven to 350°F.

Working with 2 tortillas at a time, brush one side of each lightly with oil and sandwich oiled sides together. Stack tortillas, wrap tortilla stack loosely in foil, and heat in oven until warm, about 15 minutes.

Separate into individual tortillas before serving.

Barbecued Chile-Marinated Spareribs

SERVES 6
ACTIVE TIME: 25 MINUTES ■ START TO FINISH: 10½ HOURS (INCLUDES MARINATING)

■ Zanne Stewart, *Gourmet*'s executive food editor, is addicted to these ribs. Her grandmother cooked a version of them throughout her childhood, and when our editors sampled them, there were universal raves for the fall-apart-tender meat infused with spicy chile sauce and a nice edge of smokiness from the final cooking over flames. These ribs are delicious enough to impress even the most adamant barbecue fanatic. ■

2 racks pork spareribs (6 pounds total)
8 dried New Mexico chiles (about 2 ounces; see Glossary), stems discarded, chiles rinsed and torn into pieces (including seeds)
¾ cup boiling water
½ cup ketchup
2 garlic cloves
½ cup cider vinegar
3 tablespoons packed brown sugar
2 teaspoons salt, or to taste
3 tablespoons tequila
½ cup vegetable oil
½ teaspoon ground cumin
⅛ teaspoon ground allspice

SPECIAL EQUIPMENT: an 8- to 10-quart pot

Put spareribs in 8- to 10-quart pot, add 5 quarts water, and bring to a boil. Reduce heat and simmer, skimming froth, for 50 minutes. Drain ribs well and pat dry, then transfer to a shallow baking pan.

Combine remaining ingredients in a blender and purée until smooth, about 2 minutes. Coat spareribs all over with 1 cup chile sauce. Transfer ½ cup remaining sauce to a small bowl for basting, and transfer remaining 1 cup sauce to another bowl. Refrigerate both, covered, until ready to use. Cover ribs and marinate, refrigerated, for at least 8 hours.

Bring spareribs to room temperature, about 30 minutes.

Prepare a charcoal or gas grill: If using a charcoal grill, open vents in bottom of grill and lid, then light charcoal. Fire is low when you can hold your hand 5 inches above rack for 5 to 6 seconds. If using a gas grill, preheat on high, covered, for 10 minutes, then reduce heat to moderate.

Lightly oil grill rack. Grill ribs, covered, turning occasionally and basting frequently with reserved ½ cup chile sauce during last 15 minutes of cooking, until tender, about 35 minutes total. Transfer ribs to a platter and let stand, loosely covered with foil, for 5 minutes.

Meanwhile, reheat reserved 1 cup sauce in a small saucepan over low heat. Serve with spareribs.

COOK'S NOTES

- The ribs can marinate for up to 1 day.
- The ribs can be baked instead of grilled after marinating. Arrange in one layer on a baking sheet with sides and bake in the middle of a 350°F oven until tender, about 1¼ hours. Baste with the sauce every 20 minutes for the first 40 minutes of baking instead of at the end.

Paprika-Glazed Baby Back Ribs

SERVES 4
ACTIVE TIME: 30 MINUTES ■ START TO FINISH: 27 HOURS (INCLUDES MARINATING)

■ The paprika glaze we use here punches up the flavor of these baby back ribs. You can use sweet paprika or a combination of sweet and smoked; the smoked version gives more pizzazz. Whichever you use, be sure that it has not been sitting in your cupboard for more than a few months, or it will have lost its potency. ■

- 2 racks baby back pork ribs (4 pounds total), cut into individual ribs
- 6 garlic cloves, finely chopped
- 1½ cups dry red wine
- ½ cup water
- 2 tablespoons sweet paprika or 1 tablespoon each sweet paprika and Spanish smoked paprika (see Glossary)
- 3 tablespoons sherry vinegar
- 1½ tablespoons packed brown sugar
- 1 tablespoon salt
- 2 teaspoons freshly ground black pepper

Divide ribs between two large sealable plastic bags. Stir together remaining ingredients in a bowl and pour over ribs, dividing marinade evenly. Seal bags, pressing out excess air. Marinate ribs, refrigerated, turning bags occasionally, for 24 hours.

Put a rack in middle of oven and preheat oven to 375°F.

Transfer ribs and marinade to a roasting pan large enough to hold them in one layer. Roast ribs, turning every 30 minutes, until they are tender and well browned and marinade is slightly thickened and reduced to about 1½ cups, about 2 hours.

Let ribs stand, loosely covered with foil, for 5 minutes.

Skim fat from marinade and serve marinade with ribs.

COOK'S NOTE

■ These ribs are best served the day they are cooked, since the sauce would reduce too much during reheating if made ahead.

Chinese-Hawaiian "Barbecued" Ribs

SERVES 3 TO 4
ACTIVE TIME: 15 MINUTES ■ START TO FINISH: 5 HOURS (INCLUDES MARINATING)

■ Hawaiian food has often gotten a bad rap, no doubt owing to the mediocrity of the pupu platters thrust

Pork Ribs

Pork rib cuts can be confusing. Spareribs come from the belly of the beast, right next to the bacon cut, so it's not surprising that they are full of succulent flavor. They are sold in slabs, or racks, of about thirteen bones, and they vary in size depending on the weight of the hog. Smaller slabs are generally tenderer than larger ones.

Baby back ribs are smaller, tapered bones from the blade and center section of the pork loin (the back of the hog). They're somewhat less flavorful but more tender than spareribs and cook more quickly.

Country-style ribs are found near the baby backs but farther forward, right behind the shoulder. Sold as individual ribs, not in racks, they are the meatiest cut — more like narrow chops than ribs.

upon unsuspecting tourists. But these phenomenal ribs, which are easy to prepare and require nothing you can't find at your local supermarket, show that bad reputations are often undeserved. The secret of their preparation, incidentally, was divulged to us by none other than Donn Beach, the owner of the original Don the Beachcomber's Restaurant. ■

- 3/4 cup sugar
- 1/2 cup soy sauce
- 1/2 cup ketchup
- 1/4 cup medium-dry sherry
- 1 teaspoon salt
- 1 garlic clove, smashed
- 1 (1-inch) cube peeled fresh ginger, smashed
- 3 racks baby back pork ribs (3 pounds total; do not cut ribs apart)

Stir together sugar, soy sauce, ketchup, sherry, and salt in a small bowl until sugar is dissolved. Pour marinade into a roasting pan, then add garlic and ginger. Add ribs and turn to coat. Cover and refrigerate, turning occasionally, for at least 3 hours.

Put a rack in middle of oven and preheat oven to 325°F.

Line a broiler pan with foil. Arrange ribs, rounded sides up, on broiler rack; reserve marinade for basting (discard garlic and ginger). Roast, basting with marinade every 20 minutes (do not baste during last 10 minutes of cooking), until ribs are tender and glaze is well browned, about 1 3/4 hours; discard any unused marinade.

Let racks of ribs stand for 5 minutes, loosely covered with foil, then cut into individual ribs.

COOK'S NOTE

■ The ribs can marinate for up to 1 day.

Homemade Sausage Patties

MAKES ABOUT EIGHTEEN 3-INCH PATTIES
ACTIVE TIME: 50 MINUTES ■ START TO FINISH: 1 HOUR

■ These patties have all the flavor but little of the work of traditional sausage. Since they can be formed a day in advance, they are ideal for a spectacular breakfast. Try them with our Pecan Waffles (page 653). ■

- 2 tablespoons plus 1/2 teaspoon vegetable oil
- 1 medium onion, finely chopped
- 1/2 cup coarse fresh bread crumbs
- 2 tablespoons milk
- 2 pounds ground pork (not lean)
- 2 teaspoons salt
- 1 teaspoon white pepper
- 1/4 teaspoon freshly grated nutmeg
- 1/4 teaspoon ground cinnamon
- 1/4 teaspoon cayenne
- 1/8 teaspoon ground cloves
- 1 teaspoon finely chopped fresh thyme or 1/2 teaspoon dried thyme, crumbled
- 1 teaspoon chopped fresh sage or 1/2 teaspoon dried sage, crumbled
- 2 large egg yolks

Heat 2 tablespoons oil in a small heavy skillet over moderately low heat. Add onion and cook, stirring occasionally, until softened and beginning to brown, 8 to 10 minutes. Cool for 10 minutes.

Meanwhile, stir together bread crumbs and milk in a large bowl. Let stand until crumbs absorb milk.

Preheat oven to 250°F.

Add onion and remaining ingredients (except remaining oil) to crumb mixture and stir with a fork until well blended. With dampened hands, form sausage mixture into 3-inch patties (about 1/2 inch thick) and arrange on a wax paper–lined tray.

Heat remaining 1/2 teaspoon oil in a 12-inch heavy skillet over moderately high heat until hot but not smoking. Add patties in 3 batches and cook, turning once, until browned and just cooked through, 4 to 6 minutes per batch. Drain patties briefly on paper towels, then transfer to a shallow baking pan and keep warm in oven, covered with foil, while you cook remaining batches.

COOK'S NOTE

■ The sausage patties can be formed up to 1 day ahead and refrigerated, covered with plastic wrap.

Tourtière

French-Canadian Pork Pie

SERVES 6

ACTIVE TIME: 45 MINUTES ■ START TO FINISH: 1½ HOURS

■ In Quebec, the meat pies known as *tourtières* are popular all year round, although they are a particular favorite during the Christmas season. Various thickeners (flour, as in this recipe, crushed crackers, and even oats) can be used to bind the filling, which is enclosed in a tender biscuit crust. Set this out along with a dish of chutney and you've got a holiday lunch or supper. ■

FOR FILLING

- 1½ pounds ground pork
- 1 large onion, finely chopped (1 cup)
- 2 garlic cloves, minced
- ¾ teaspoon dried summer savory, crumbled
- 1 teaspoon salt
- ½ teaspoon ground allspice
- ½ teaspoon freshly ground black pepper
- 4½ tablespoons all-purpose flour

FOR PASTRY

- 1½ cups all-purpose flour
- 1½ teaspoons baking powder
- 1 teaspoon salt
- 3 tablespoons cold vegetable shortening
- 2 tablespoons cold unsalted butter, cut into ½-inch cubes
- ½ cup plus 1 tablespoon whole milk

MAKE THE FILLING: Combine pork, onion, garlic, savory, salt, allspice, and pepper in a 12- to 14-inch heavy skillet and cook over moderate heat, stirring frequently and breaking up lumps with a fork, until pork is no longer pink, 5 to 7 minutes. Sprinkle with flour and cook, stirring, until juices are thickened, 3 to 4 minutes. Cool completely.

WHILE THE FILLING COOLS, MAKE THE PASTRY: Put a rack in middle of oven and preheat oven to 425°F.

Whisk together flour, baking powder, and salt in a medium bowl. Blend in shortening and butter with a pastry blender or your fingertips until mixture resembles coarse meal. Add ½ cup milk and stir with a fork just until a dough forms. Turn dough out onto a lightly floured surface and gently knead 10 to 12 times.

Divide dough into 2 pieces, one slightly larger than the other. Roll out larger piece of dough on lightly floured surface with a floured rolling pin into a 13-inch round (⅛ inch thick), dusting with just enough additional flour to keep dough from sticking. Fit into a 9-inch pie plate.

ASSEMBLE AND BAKE THE PIE: Spoon cooled filling into shell. Roll out remaining piece of dough into an 11-inch round. Cover pie with pastry round and trim excess with kitchen shears, leaving a ½-inch overhang. Press edges together, then crimp decoratively. Cut 3 steam vents in top crust with a small sharp knife. Brush pastry with remaining 1 tablespoon milk.

Bake *tourtière* until crust is golden, about 30 minutes. Let stand for 10 minutes before slicing.

COOK'S NOTES

- The filling can be made and cooled up to 1 day ahead and refrigerated, covered. Bring to room temperature before proceeding.
- The pie can be baked up to 6 hours ahead. Cool, uncovered, then refrigerate, covered. Serve at room temperature or reheat in a 350°F oven until warm, about 15 minutes.

Herb-Braised Picnic Ham

SERVES 8

ACTIVE TIME: 1½ HOURS ■ START TO FINISH: 4½ HOURS

■ Technically speaking, the picnic is not a true ham, from the hind leg, but comes from the shoulder. Shoulder cuts are ideal for braising; here the herb-spiked braising liquid gets turned into a satiny sauce while the ham rests after cooking. When shopping for picnic ham, be aware that this smoked pork shoulder is available partially or fully cooked. Which one you choose will affect the braising time; a partially cooked ham takes about 1 hour longer. Blanching the ham before braising helps eliminate excessive saltiness in both the ham and the broth, and leaving the skin on adds body to the resulting sauce. (For more about picnic hams, see page 495.) ■

1 (11- to 13-pound) bone-in smoked pork shoulder (picnic ham)
2 medium leeks (white and pale green parts only), chopped
5 tablespoons unsalted butter, softened
1 large onion, chopped
3 medium carrots, cut into ½-inch dice
2 celery ribs, cut into ½-inch dice
2 garlic cloves, finely chopped
6 (5-inch) fresh thyme sprigs, plus 2 tablespoons finely chopped leaves
6 fresh flat-leaf parsley stems, plus ¼ cup finely chopped leaves
¼ nutmeg, smashed with side of a large heavy knife
1 teaspoon black peppercorns
4 whole cloves
2 cups dry white wine
4 cups water
⅓ cup all-purpose flour

SPECIAL EQUIPMENT: a 12- to 20-quart deep pot (such as a stockpot or canning pot); a 7-quart wide heavy ovenproof pot, if you have an 11-pound ham, or a 9- to 10-quart wide heavy ovenproof pot, if you have a 13-pound ham; a remote digital thermometer with a probe or an instant-read thermometer

Put ham in 12- to 20-quart pot and cover with cold water (don't worry if bone sticks out). Bring to a boil, then drain.

Put a rack in lower third of oven (remove other racks) and preheat oven to 350°F.

Wash leeks in a bowl of cold water; lift out and drain well. Melt 2 tablespoons butter in 7- to 10-quart wide pot over moderately high heat. Add leeks, onion, carrots, celery, garlic, thyme sprigs, parsley stems, nutmeg, peppercorns, and cloves and cook, stirring occasionally, until vegetables are softened and beginning to brown, about 10 minutes. Add wine and bring to a boil.

Add ham, skin side down, and water (liquid will not cover ham) and return to a boil. Cover pot tightly with lid or, if ham sticks up over top of pot, with heavy-duty foil. Transfer ham to oven and braise for 1 hour.

Turn ham skin side up and continue to braise, covered, until thermometer inserted into center of ham (without touching bone) registers 120°F if ham was labeled "fully cooked," about 1 hour, or 160°F if ham was labeled "partially cooked," about 2 hours.

Meanwhile, mash together flour and remaining 3 tablespoons butter with a fork in a small bowl to make a *beurre manié.*

Transfer ham to a platter and let stand, loosely covered with foil, for 45 minutes.

Meanwhile, pour braising liquid through a fine-mesh sieve into a 3-quart saucepan, pressing on solids; discard solids and skim off any fat. Bring braising liquid to a simmer and whisk in *beurre manié* ½ tablespoon at a time (sauce may become lumpy). Reduce heat and simmer, whisking, until sauce is smooth and slightly thickened, about 5 minutes. Remove from heat and stir in chopped thyme and parsley.

Remove skin from ham. Slice meat and serve with sauce.

COOK'S NOTE

- The ham can be braised up to 2 days ahead. Cool in the braising liquid, uncovered, then refrigerate, covered. Skim any fat before reheating the ham in the braising liquid on top of the stove.

Braised Ham with Maple Raisin Sauce

SERVES 8 TO 12
ACTIVE TIME: 20 MINUTES ■ START TO FINISH: 4 HOURS

■ We can't think of an easier way to get a big-deal meal on the table than to use a fully cooked ham. This version, braised in maple syrup, maple sugar, and apple juice, came to us from one of the restaurants that spring up during March and April when the sap is running in southern Quebec. Like the rest of the food served in these *cabanes à sucre,* or sugar shacks, it's hearty and homey. ■

1 (7- to 8-pound) fully cooked bone-in shank-end ham
6 cups water
¼ cup pure maple syrup
10 whole cloves or ¼ teaspoon ground cloves
1 cup granulated maple sugar (see Sources)
1 teaspoon dry mustard
¼ cup apple juice
2 cups (10 ounces) raisins

SPECIAL EQUIPMENT: a deep heavy 10-quart pot

Put ham cut side down in 10-quart pot and add water and syrup. Bring to a boil, then reduce heat to low and gently simmer ham, covered, until tender, 2 to 2 1/2 hours. Uncover and let cool slightly.

Put a rack in middle of oven and preheat oven to 350°F.

When ham is cool enough to handle, remove from pot, reserving cooking liquid. Cut off any rind and excess fat, leaving a thin layer. If using whole cloves, stick them into fat side of ham, distributing them evenly. Transfer ham to a roasting pan.

Whisk together maple sugar, mustard, apple juice, and ground cloves, if using, in a small bowl, then spoon over ham. Add raisins and 1 cup reserved cooking liquid to roasting pan. Bake, basting ham occasionally, until ham is glazed and sauce is bubbling, 30 to 40 minutes. Serve warm or at room temperature with sauce on the side.

COOK'S NOTE

- The ham can be simmered up to 1 day ahead. Cool completely in the cooking liquid, then refrigerate in the pot. Remove from the liquid and bring to room temperature before baking.

HAM, SHOULDER, BUTT, AND PICNIC: WHAT'S IT ALL ABOUT?

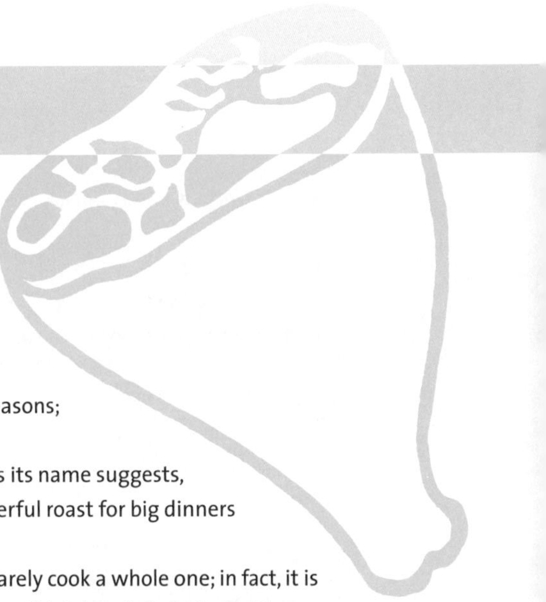

Technically speaking, the term *ham* refers to the cured whole hind leg of a pig. But, as is often the case with food, that's not the whole story. There is also such a thing as *fresh ham,* not to mention *picnic ham,* which isn't a true ham at all.

What comes to mind for most of us when we hear the word *ham* is the cured version. Curing simply means preserving, which may be done by salting, smoking, or a combination of the two. Originally ham was cured for practical reasons; today, it is cured primarily because we enjoy the flavor.

Recently, though, cooks have been rediscovering the joys of fresh ham. As its name suggests, this is an uncured bone-in leg of pork. Sweet and tender, a fresh ham is a wonderful roast for big dinners and has the added advantage of being less expensive than a pork loin roast.

As you can imagine, an entire ham is one serious hunk of meat, and we rarely cook a whole one; in fact, it is difficult to find a whole one at most markets. What you are thinking of when you think *ham* is in fact a half ham, which may be either the shank section or the rump section. The rump section, which is the top half of the leg, is bigger than the shank end, but it is also harder to carve, since it contains part of the femur as well as the aitchbone (part of the pelvic bone). The shank end has less connective tissue, less fat, and more uniform meat, so it cooks more evenly. It also makes for a handsomer presentation. All in all, we generally recommend a shank-end ham, whether cured or fresh.

When you see the term *picnic,* that's a sign that the meat isn't from the hind leg but from the lower shoulder. How the word became associated with pork shoulder is one of life's mysteries, but the meat is tasty and inexpensive. It requires longer and moister cooking than true hams do, but you will be rewarded with very tender meat. Picnic hams are always cured and/or smoked.

The cut called picnic shoulder is fresh rather than cured. Farther up on the shoulder is what's familiarly called pork butt. And where does that bit of nomenclature come from? The prevailing theory is that the meat was once commonly shipped in the large wooden casks called butts. In any event, pork butt is ideal for roasting, braising, and stewing; it's one of the most versatile parts of the pig. If you have a pork butt in your refrigerator, you will be eating high on the hog.

Fresh Ham with Cracklings and Pan Gravy

SERVES 8 TO 10

ACTIVE TIME: 1 HOUR ■ START TO FINISH: 5 HOURS

■ If you've never had fresh ham, you're in for a treat. Rubbed with herbs and roasted with a beer marinade, the meat is extraordinary, and the skin becomes one of our very favorite treats, cracklings. To round it all off, there's a mouth-pleasing pan gravy. You will probably have to order this cut at the supermarket; it's somewhat easier to find in ethnic markets. (For more about fresh ham, see page 495.) ■

FOR HAM

- 1 (8- to 10-pound) shank-end leg of pork with skin (fresh ham), not tied
- 2 tablespoons vegetable oil
- 1 tablespoon kosher salt
- ½ teaspoon dried thyme, crumbled
- ½ teaspoon dried sage, crumbled
- ½ teaspoon freshly ground black pepper
- 1 teaspoon dry mustard
- 1 (12-ounce) bottle pilsner beer (not dark)

FOR GRAVY

- 1 cup water
- 2 tablespoons all-purpose flour
- 1 cup beef stock or store-bought broth
- ½ teaspoon dry mustard
- ¼ teaspoon dried sage, crumbled
- ⅛ teaspoon dried thyme, crumbled
- ¼ teaspoon sugar
- 2 teaspoons cider vinegar
- Salt and freshly ground black pepper

SPECIAL EQUIPMENT: kitchen string; a large roasting pan with a V-rack; an instant-read thermometer

ROAST THE HAM: Put a rack in middle of oven and preheat oven to 500°F.

Prick skin of ham all over with a small sharp knife, then make 4 parallel ¼-inch-deep incisions through skin down entire length of ham. Rub ham lightly with oil. Stir together salt, thyme, sage, pepper, and mustard in a small bowl and rub over entire surface of ham. Tie large end of ham with string and put in V-rack set in roasting pan.

Put pan in oven, immediately reduce oven temperature to 325°F, and roast ham for 1 hour.

Pour half of beer over ham and roast for 30 minutes more.

Pour remaining beer over ham and roast until thermometer inserted into ham (without touching bone) reads an average of 155°F (test in several places, since different muscles cook at different speeds; temperature should range from 145° to 160°F), about 2½ hours more. Remove from oven and let stand in rack in pan for 15 minutes, loosely covered with foil. Increase oven temperature to 350°F.

Pull off crisp brown skin, leaving layer of fat on ham. Transfer ham to a platter, reserving drippings in roasting pan, and keep warm, loosely covered with foil. Cut skin into small pieces with kitchen shears. Spread cracklings in one layer in a baking sheet with sides and season with salt. Bake, stirring occasionally, until very crisp and browned, about 15 minutes. With a slotted spoon, transfer to paper towels to drain.

MEANWHILE, MAKE THE GRAVY: Skim fat from juices in roasting pan. Set pan over two burners, add water, and deglaze by boiling over moderate heat, stirring and scraping up brown bits, for 1 minute. Pour liquid through a sieve into a 1- to 2-quart heavy saucepan.

Whisk together flour and ¼ cup stock in a small bowl until smooth, then, off heat, whisk into liquid in saucepan. Whisk in remaining ¾ cup stock, mustard, sage, thyme, and sugar. Bring to a boil, whisking. Add vinegar and salt and pepper to taste, reduce heat, and simmer gravy, whisking, for 5 minutes.

Trim fat from ham. Slice meat and serve with cracklings and gravy.

Deviled Ham

MAKES ABOUT 4 CUPS

ACTIVE TIME: 15 MINUTES ■ START TO FINISH: 15 MINUTES

■ That old saw about eternity being the amount of time it takes two people to finish a ham is rendered absurd if you have a recipe for deviled ham in the house. Spooned onto crackers and spread on bread for sandwiches, the biggest ham is gone in no time. Like deviled eggs, it's a retro favorite. ■

3 cups cooked ham cut into ¾-inch pieces
½ stick (4 tablespoons) unsalted butter, softened
¼ cup Dijon mustard
¼ cup Major Grey chutney

Pulse ham in a food processor until finely chopped. Transfer to a bowl. Add butter, mustard, and chutney to processor and blend until smooth. Stir into ham.

COOK'S NOTE

■ The deviled ham can be made up to 2 days ahead and refrigerated, covered.

Choucroute Garni

SERVES 6 TO 8
ACTIVE TIME: 1¼ HOURS ■ START TO FINISH: 3¼ HOURS

■ This French dish is substantial, somewhat homely, and completely comforting. The name means "garnished sauerkraut," and if you consider braised pork chops, an assortment of sausages, and Yukon Gold potatoes to be garnish, it is definitely the dish for you. Try it on a cold winter night. ■

8 cups drained sauerkraut (from a 4-pound package; not canned)
½ pound thick-sliced bacon (about 6 slices), cut into ¼-inch-wide strips
6 smoked pork chops (2½ pounds total; see Sources)
2 medium onions, halved lengthwise and thinly sliced crosswise
2 large garlic cloves, thinly sliced
1 medium carrot, peeled if desired and cut into ¼-inch-thick slices
2 cups dry Riesling or other dry fruity white wine
2 cups chicken stock or store-bought low-sodium broth
10 juniper berries (see Sources), crushed with side of a large knife
1 Turkish bay leaf or ½ California bay leaf
1 teaspoon caraway seeds
½ teaspoon coarsely ground black pepper
2½ pounds assorted precooked sausages (about 12), such as knockwurst, bratwurst, weisswurst, French garlic, and kielbasa
6 medium Yukon Gold potatoes (1½ pounds total)

Soak sauerkraut in cold water to cover in a large bowl, changing water once halfway through soaking, for 20 minutes. Drain in a colander, squeezing out excess liquid with your hands.

While sauerkraut soaks, cook bacon in a 6- to 8-quart wide heavy pot over moderate heat, stirring occasionally, until golden, about 10 minutes. With a slotted spoon, transfer to paper towels to drain. Brown pork chops in 2 batches in fat remaining in pot, turning once, about 6 minutes per batch. Transfer to a plate. Pour off all but 2 tablespoons fat from pot and reserve. Do not clean pot.

Put a rack in middle of oven and preheat oven to 325°F.

Cook onions and garlic in fat remaining in pot over moderately low heat, stirring occasionally, until onions are softened, about 10 minutes. Stir in sauerkraut, bacon, carrot, wine, stock, juniper berries, bay leaf, caraway seeds, and pepper. Nestle pork chops in sauerkraut, then cover pot and bring to a simmer.

Transfer pot to oven and braise until pork chops are just tender, about 1½ hours.

Meanwhile, heat 1 tablespoon reserved fat in a 12-inch skillet over moderate heat. Brown sausages in 2 batches, turning, about 4 minutes per batch. Transfer to a plate.

Nestle sausages in braised sauerkraut and add any juices accumulated on plate. Cover pot and continue to braise, covered, for 30 minutes more.

Meanwhile, peel potatoes and cut in half. Combine potatoes with cold well-salted water to cover by 2 inches in a 4-quart saucepan and bring to a boil. Reduce heat and simmer, uncovered, until just tender, about 15 minutes. Drain and keep warm, covered.

Transfer sauerkraut to a heated platter, discard bay leaf, and arrange pork chops and sausages on top of sauerkraut. Serve potatoes and some of cooking liquid on the side.

COOK'S NOTE

■ The sauerkraut and pork chops can be braised up to 1 day ahead. Add the browned sausages and cool the *choucroute* completely, uncovered. Refrigerate, covered. To reheat, bring to a simmer on top of the stove, then cover and braise in the middle of a 325°F oven for 30 minutes.

Lamb

Mustard- and Herb-Crusted Rack of Lamb

SERVES 8
ACTIVE TIME: 25 MINUTES ■ START TO FINISH: 1¼ HOURS

■ A rack of lamb is seven or eight little loin rib chops still joined together as a roast. Because the racks are quite small compared to most other roasts, you can sear them on top of the stove in a skillet, which ensures that they get nicely browned. We then coat them with mustard, bread crumbs, and fresh herbs and put them in the oven to finish cooking. It's a relatively quick and simple way to prepare an elegant main course. ■

- 1½ cups fine fresh bread crumbs
- 3 tablespoons finely chopped fresh flat-leaf parsley
- 1 tablespoon finely chopped fresh mint
- 1½ tablespoons minced fresh rosemary
- ½ teaspoon salt
- ¼ teaspoon freshly ground black pepper
- 3½ tablespoons olive oil
- 3 (8-rib) racks of lamb (1½ pounds each), trimmed of all but a thin layer of fat at room temperature
- 2 tablespoons Dijon mustard

SPECIAL EQUIPMENT: an instant-read thermometer

Stir together bread crumbs, parsley, mint, rosemary, salt, and pepper in a small bowl, drizzle with 2½ tablespoons oil, and toss until well combined.

Put a rack in middle of oven and preheat oven to 400°F.

Season lamb with salt and pepper. Heat remaining 1 tablespoon oil in a large heavy skillet over moderately high heat until hot but not smoking. Brown lamb one rack at a time, turning once, about 4 minutes per rack. Transfer to a 13-by-9-inch baking pan, fatty sides up.

Spread fatty side of each rack with 2 teaspoons mustard. Divide bread crumb mixture into 3 portions and pat one portion over mustard coating on each rack, gently pressing so crumbs adhere.

CUTS OF LAMB

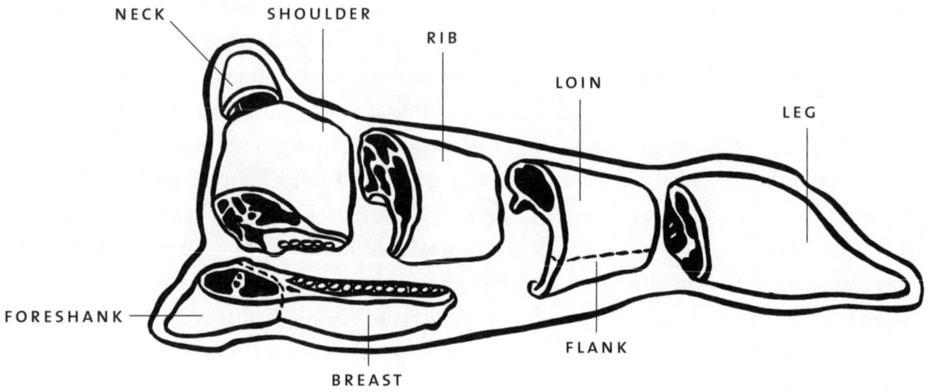

SHOULDER	RIB	LOIN	LEG
Shoulder roast	Crown roast	Loin chops	Lamb shank
Shoulder chops	Rack of lamb	Saddle	Leg of lamb
Stew meat	Rib chops		Sirloin
			Stew meat

Roast lamb until thermometer inserted 2 inches into center (without touching bone) registers 130°F for medium-rare, 20 to 25 minutes. Transfer to a cutting board and let stand for 10 minutes, loosely covered with foil, then cut into chops.

Crown Roast of Lamb

SERVES 6

ACTIVE TIME: 30 MINUTES ■ START TO FINISH: 6¼ HOURS (INCLUDES MAKING STOCK)

■ Crown roast is an impressive dish, so sophisticated and fancy that it has come to be virtually synonymous with luxurious eating. It is also remarkably delicious and easy, assuming that you have the butcher form the crown for you. (He will do this by cutting through the backbone and the chine, then forming the racks of ribs into a circle; ask him to save the trimmings for you, to make the stock.) It's best to keep the preparation simple so the delicate flavor of the lamb comes through. We just rub the roast with aromatic thyme and rosemary before it goes into the oven and, while it is resting afterward, make a pan gravy that gets a flavor boost from port. ■

- 3 garlic cloves, minced
- ¾ teaspoon dried thyme, crumbled
- ¾ teaspoon dried rosemary, crumbled
- 1 teaspoon salt
- ½ teaspoon freshly ground black pepper
- 1 (16-chop) crown roast of lamb, trimmings reserved
- 2½ cups Beef Stock (page 928), made with reserved lamb trimmings instead of veal shanks
- 2 tablespoons arrowroot
- ¼ cup heavy cream
- 2 tablespoons tawny port

OPTIONAL GARNISH: small watercress sprigs

SPECIAL EQUIPMENT: an instant-read thermometer

Put a rack in middle of oven and preheat oven to 425°F.

Combine garlic, ½ teaspoon thyme, ½ teaspoon rosemary, salt, and pepper in a small bowl and rub on lamb. Fit a ball of foil snugly in center of crown so it holds its shape while roasting, and cover bone ends of chops with foil. Oil a roasting pan just large enough to hold lamb and put roast in it.

Roast for 20 minutes. Reduce oven temperature to 350°F and roast until thermometer inserted into thickest part of lamb (without touching bone) registers 135°F for medium-rare, about 25 minutes more. Transfer lamb to a platter and let stand, covered loosely with foil, for 30 minutes.

Meanwhile, skim fat from pan drippings. Set roasting pan over two burners, add stock and remaining ¼ teaspoon each thyme and rosemary, and deglaze pan by boiling over moderately high heat, stirring and scraping up brown bits, for 1 minute. Transfer to a 2½- to 3-quart heavy saucepan.

Just before serving, stir together arrowroot, cream, and port in a small bowl until smooth. Bring stock to a boil over moderately high heat. Stir arrowroot mixture and add to stock in a slow stream, whisking constantly, then whisk until sauce is slightly thickened, about 1 minute. Add salt and pepper to taste and transfer sauce to a sauceboat.

Remove foil from lamb and garnish with watercress, if desired. Serve lamb with sauce.

Leg of Lamb with Tomatoes and Garlic

SERVES 8

ACTIVE TIME: 45 MINUTES ■ START TO FINISH: 2¾ HOURS

■ Rural French home cooks have a genius for creating wonderful food with a few good ingredients. This recipe comes from the kitchen of Nathalie Waag, who at one time ran a small cooking school in her Provençal farmhouse. The few fortunate guests got to spend several days shopping and cooking with her. The classic flavors of the Provence pantry—tomatoes, garlic, rosemary, olive oil—are supporting players for the lamb. As the dish cooks, the tomatoes melt down into a sauce flavored with the herbs and the meat's own juices, and the whole heads of garlic sweeten and mellow. Serve each guest a head of garlic, so he or she can squeeze the flesh out of the skin and spread it on the lamb or on bread. ■

- 2½ pounds plum tomatoes, cut into ¼-inch-thick slices
- 1 (6- to 8-pound) leg of lamb, aitchbone removed by the butcher and trimmed
- 8 heads garlic, papery outer skin discarded
- 3 fresh rosemary sprigs or 1 teaspoon dried rosemary, crumbled
- 2 teaspoons salt
- 1 teaspoon freshly ground black pepper
- 4 tablespoons extra-virgin olive oil, or as needed

SPECIAL EQUIPMENT: an instant-read thermometer

Put a rack in middle of oven and preheat oven to 450°F.

Arrange tomatoes in a 17½-by-12-inch roasting pan and place lamb on top. Arrange garlic around lamb. Lay rosemary sprigs on lamb (or sprinkle with dried rosemary), then sprinkle with salt and pepper. Drizzle with 2 tablespoons oil.

Roast lamb for 15 minutes. Reduce oven temperature to 350°F and continue roasting lamb, basting garlic with some of remaining 2 tablespoons oil every 20 minutes to keep it from drying out, until thermometer inserted into thickest part of lamb (without touching bone) registers 135°F for medium-rare, 1¼ to 1½ hours more.

Transfer lamb to a cutting board and let stand, loosely covered with foil, for 30 minutes. Stir tomato mixture and transfer to a sauceboat.

Carve lamb and serve with tomato sauce and roasted garlic.

COOK'S NOTE

- If tomatoes are not in season, use a 28- to 32-ounce can of whole plum tomatoes in juice. Coarsely chop the tomatoes and pour the juice over them in the roasting pan.

Hibiscus-Marinated Leg of Lamb

SERVES 8
ACTIVE TIME: 1 HOUR ■ START TO FINISH: 15 HOURS (INCLUDES MARINATING)

■ Sometimes an idea that seems a little odd turns out to be inspired. This is one such case. Hibiscus flowers are used to make tea in Mexico and are the basis for Red Zinger tea here in the United States. One of our

Leg of Lamb

Tender and tasty, a leg of lamb is a great company meal. Since lambs used for meat are relatively small, a whole leg usually weighs only 6 to 8 pounds. Because of that, we usually call for an entire leg. However, when you are cooking for fewer people, you can easily find a half leg in most stores. We prefer the sirloin half, from nearer the hip, because it is somewhat tenderer than the shank end.

When buying a leg of lamb, it's important to be sure that the butcher has removed the aitchbone, which is part of the pelvic bone; otherwise, you'll have trouble carving the meat. Also, look for meat that is pinkish red; the darker the color, the older the lamb. The meat should look moist and bright rather than sticky, and the fat should be waxy white rather than yellowish.

food editors, who lived and cooked for years in Mexico, thought that hibiscus tea, with its tart, flowery flavor, would make an interesting marinade for lamb. There were some doubters in the test kitchens—until they tasted the dish. The delicate tartness and aroma of the hibiscus turns out to be a perfect complement to the rich meat. In addition to being mouthwatering, the sauce made from the cooked-down hibiscus marinade is a strikingly beautiful garnet color. ■

FOR MARINADE

- 4 cups water
- 3 large garlic cloves, peeled and smashed with side of a large knife
- 10 black peppercorns, coarsely cracked
- 1 cup (1½ ounces) dried organic nontoxic hibiscus flowers (see Sources) or leaves from 20 bags Red Zinger tea (1 box)
- ¼ cup sugar

FOR LAMB

- 1 (6- to 8-pound) leg of lamb, aitchbone removed by the butcher, trimmed
- 2 tablespoons olive oil
- Salt and freshly ground black pepper
- 1 tablespoon red currant jelly
- 2 tablespoons cold unsalted butter, cut into pieces

SPECIAL EQUIPMENT: 2 extra-large (2-gallon) sealable plastic bags; an instant-read thermometer

MAKE THE MARINADE: Combine water, garlic, and peppercorns in a 2-quart saucepan and bring to a boil. Add hibiscus flowers, reduce heat, and simmer gently for 5 minutes. Remove from heat and let steep for 30 minutes.

Pour marinade through a fine-mesh sieve into a bowl, pressing on solids; discard solids. Add sugar, stirring until dissolved, and refrigerate until cold.

MARINATE THE LAMB: Remove most of fat from lamb. Put lamb in double layer of sealable plastic bags and add marinade. Seal bags and marinate lamb, refrigerated, turning once or twice, for at least 12 hours.

ROAST THE LAMB: Put a rack in upper third of oven and preheat oven to 450°F.

Remove lamb from bags, reserving marinade, and transfer to a flameproof roasting pan just large enough to hold it. Pat dry and rub with oil, then season generously with salt and pepper.

Put lamb in oven and reduce heat to 350°F. Roast until thermometer inserted in thickest part of leg (without touching bone) registers 125°F, 1 to 1½ hours. Transfer lamb to a platter, cover with foil, and let stand for 15 to 25 minutes. (Its internal temperature will rise to about 135°F as it stands.)

While lamb is standing, pour reserved marinade into roasting pan. Set pan over two burners, bring marinade to a boil, stirring and scraping up brown bits, and boil until reduced to about 1 cup. Add any meat juices that have accumulated on platter and whisk in jelly and salt and pepper to taste. Add butter and swirl or shake pan until incorporated.

Pour sauce through a fine-mesh sieve into a sauceboat and serve with lamb.

COOK'S NOTE

■ The lamb can marinate for up to 24 hours.

Slow-Roasted Leg of Lamb

Gosht Korma

SERVES 8

ACTIVE TIME: 1¼ HOURS ■ START TO FINISH: 10¾ HOURS (INCLUDES MARINATING)

■ This is one of the great dishes of Indian cooking. A leg of lamb is rubbed with a savory spice paste and allowed to sit for several hours, which imbues it with many levels of bold flavor. Then it is enhanced with a citrus-honey sauce and roasted, first covered and then uncovered, for almost five hours. When it comes out of the oven, it is so tender that it falls off the bone as soon as you touch it with your fork. As if it needed yet another virtue, it can be made two days ahead and reheated. Serve it with a spicy fruit chutney or sour lime pickle—or both. ■

FOR SPICE PASTE

- 1 (3- to 4-inch) cinnamon stick, halved
- 2 tablespoons cumin seeds
- 1 small onion, chopped
- 1/3 cup chopped peeled fresh ginger
- 3 tablespoons chopped garlic
- 2 tablespoons Garam Masala (page 932)
- 1/2 cup water
- 1 tablespoon paprika
- 2 teaspoons salt

FOR LAMB

- 1 (6- to 7-pound) leg of lamb, aitchbone removed by the butcher and trimmed
- Salt and freshly ground black pepper
- 2 tablespoons unsalted butter
- 2 tablespoons honey
- 2 tablespoons fresh lemon juice
- 2 tablespoons fresh lime juice

SPECIAL EQUIPMENT: an electric coffee/spice grinder

MAKE THE SPICE PASTE: Finely grind cinnamon and cumin seeds in coffee/spice grinder. Combine ground spices with remaining ingredients in a blender and purée, scraping down sides occasionally, until smooth, about 1 minute.

MARINATE THE LAMB: Lightly oil a roasting pan just large enough to hold lamb. Rinse lamb and pat dry. With a small sharp knife, make 6 deep (to the bone) 1-inch-long slits at about 1½-inch intervals on each of 3 sides of leg. Place lamb meaty side up in pan and season with salt and pepper. Rub spice paste into slits and all over lamb.

Cover with plastic wrap and marinate, refrigerated, for at least 4 hours.

Let lamb stand at room temperature for 1 hour before roasting.

ROAST THE LAMB: Put a rack in middle of oven and preheat oven to 325°F.

Discard plastic wrap and cover pan with several layers of foil, sealing it tightly. Roast lamb for 2 hours.

Melt butter with honey in a small saucepan and stir in lemon and lime juices. Uncover lamb and pour half of honey sauce over it.

Cover pan tightly and roast lamb for 1 hour more.

Uncover lamb, pour remaining honey sauce over it, and tightly cover pan again. Continue to roast, basting lamb twice with pan juices, for 1 hour. Uncover lamb and roast until meat is almost falling off bone, about 30 minutes more (4½ to 5 hours total). If surface of lamb begins to blacken, cover loosely with foil.

Transfer lamb to a platter and let stand, loosely covered with foil, until cool enough to handle. Skim fat from pan juices.

Serve lamb whole with pan juices on the side, or pull meat from bone and drizzle with juices.

COOK'S NOTE

- The lamb can be roasted up to 2 days ahead. Cool completely, uncovered, then refrigerate, covered; refrigerate the pan juices separately, covered. Bring the lamb to room temperature before reheating, covered, in a 350°F oven. Reheat the pan juices in a small saucepan.

Grilled Butterflied Leg of Lamb with Lemon, Herbs, and Garlic

SERVES 8

ACTIVE TIME: 1 HOUR ■ START TO FINISH: 2½ HOURS

■ Lamb lends itself particularly well to grilling; the smoky fragrance and crusty searing that the meat picks up over the fire work perfectly with its pronounced flavor. A boned and butterflied leg of lamb is easy to cook and carve. To help it cook more evenly, you can secure the loose flaps of meat by running two long metal skewers lengthwise and two skewers crosswise through the lamb, bunching the meat together. ■

FOR HERB RUB

- 8 garlic cloves, finely chopped
- 3 tablespoons chopped fresh thyme
- 2 tablespoons chopped fresh rosemary
- 2 tablespoons chopped fresh flat-leaf parsley
- 1/2 teaspoon freshly ground black pepper
- 1 tablespoon kosher salt
- 3 tablespoons olive oil

FOR LAMB

- 1 (7- to 8-pound) leg of lamb, trimmed, boned, and butterflied (have the butcher do this, or buy a 4- to 4¾-pound butterflied leg)
- 1 lemon, halved and seeded

SPECIAL EQUIPMENT: an instant-read thermometer

MAKE THE HERB RUB: Stir together all ingredients in a small bowl.

MARINATE THE LAMB: Put lamb in a large glass or ceramic dish and cut ½-inch-deep slits all over it with tip of a small sharp knife held at a 45-degree angle. Rub herb mixture into slits and all over lamb. Let lamb sit, covered, at room temperature for 1 hour.

GRILL THE LAMB: Prepare a charcoal or gas grill: If using a charcoal grill, open vents in bottom of grill, then light charcoal. Fire is medium-hot when you can hold your hand 5 inches above rack for just 3 to 4 seconds. If using a gas grill, preheat on high, covered, for 10 minutes, then reduce heat to moderate.

Lightly oil grill rack. Grill lamb (covered only if using gas grill), turning occasionally, until thermometer inserted into thickest piece of meat registers 130°F for medium-rare, 20 to 25 minutes. (Cover grill if flare-ups occur.) Transfer lamb to a cutting board, squeeze lemon juice over it, and let stand for 20 minutes, loosely covered with foil.

Cut lamb into slices and serve with any juices accumulated on cutting board.

COOK'S NOTE

- The lamb can also be roasted in the middle of a 425°F oven until the meat registers 130°F on an instant-read thermometer, about 25 minutes.

Long-Cooked Lamb Shoulder

SERVES 4 TO 6

ACTIVE TIME: 45 MINUTES ■ START TO FINISH: 6½ HOURS

■ Shoulder is the lamb equivalent of beef chuck. It's big-flavored, but because it also has a lot of connective tissue, it can be tough. If you cook it for a long time, however, the connective tissue is transformed into gelatin. Double cooking—roasting it, then braising it in white wine—results in incredibly moist, tender meat with all the earthiness and aromatic sweetness that good lamb has. An added boon, especially for people who hate to carve, is that it can be served with a spoon. Note that lamb shoulder is sometimes sold with the neck and some ribs attached, which will increase the weight to about eight pounds. No need to change the recipe, though—just follow it as written, and you'll be able to feed a few more guests. ■

- 6 medium onions (2½ pounds total), quartered
- 3 heads garlic, cloves separated and peeled
- 2 Turkish bay leaves or 1 California bay leaf
- 6 fresh thyme sprigs
- 1 (6-pound) bone-in lamb shoulder, trimmed
- Salt and freshly ground black pepper
- 2 (750-milliliter) bottles dry white wine, such as Chardonnay
- 6 large boiling potatoes (3 pounds total)
- 6 plum tomatoes (1 pound total), chopped

Put a rack in middle of oven and preheat oven to 425°F.

Distribute onions, garlic, bay leaves, and thyme evenly in bottom of a flameproof roasting pan large enough to hold lamb and potatoes. Put lamb rib side down on top. Roast, uncovered, for 30 minutes.

Generously season lamb with salt and pepper and roast for another 30 minutes.

Remove pan from oven (leave oven on) and slowly pour wine over lamb. Set pan over two burners and bring to a boil over high heat. Cover pan tightly with foil. Transfer to oven and braise until lamb is very tender and falling off the bone, about 4 hours.

Peel potatoes and cut into 1-inch-thick wedges. Scatter potatoes and tomatoes around lamb, cover pan tightly with foil, and continue to braise until potatoes are tender, 1 to 1½ hours more.

Season lamb and vegetables with salt, then transfer lamb to a platter. With a slotted spoon, transfer vegetables to platter. Skim fat from pan juices and serve juices on the side.

COOK'S NOTE

- The lamb can be braised, without the potatoes and tomatoes, up to 1 day ahead. Cool, uncovered, then refrigerate, covered. Reheat in a 425°F oven, covered, until hot before proceeding.

Lamb Chops with Mustard Sauce and Fried Capers

SERVES 4

ACTIVE TIME: 20 MINUTES ■ START TO FINISH: 30 MINUTES

■ Lamb loin chops are like baby T-bones, each one containing a small piece of the tenderloin muscle and a larger piece of the top loin muscle, divided by a T-shaped bone. The most expensive kind of lamb chops, they cook quickly and have a delicate flavor that is appreciated even by people who think they are not fond of lamb. We match them with a piquant mustard pan sauce and fried capers, which provide a salty bite. ■

- 4 (1¼-inch-thick) loin lamb chops (about 2 pounds total)
- Salt and freshly ground black pepper
- 5½ tablespoons vegetable oil
- 2 tablespoons unsalted butter
- 1 cup minced onion
- 1 cup heavy cream
- 2 tablespoons Dijon mustard
- 1 tablespoon fresh lemon juice
- ¼ cup drained capers, patted dry
- 2 tablespoons minced fresh flat-leaf parsley

Put a rack in middle of oven and preheat oven to 200°F.

Pat lamb chops dry and season with salt and pepper.

Heat 1½ tablespoons oil in a 12-inch heavy skillet over moderately high heat until hot but not smoking. Add lamb chops and cook, turning once, 8 to 10 minutes total for medium-rare. Transfer to an ovenproof platter and keep warm in oven.

Pour off fat from skillet and add butter, then add onion and cook over moderately low heat, stirring, until softened, about 3 minutes. Stir in cream and any juices accumulated on platter, bring to a boil, and boil until sauce begins to thicken, 1 to 2 minutes. Remove skillet from heat and stir in mustard, lemon juice, and salt and pepper to taste. Keep sauce warm over low heat.

Heat remaining 4 tablespoons (¼ cup) oil in a 6-inch heavy skillet over high heat until hot but not smoking. Add capers and fry until they are crisp and buds have opened, 1 to 2 minutes. Transfer to paper towels to drain.

Pour sauce through a fine-mesh sieve into a bowl, pressing gently on solids; discard solids. Spoon sauce around lamb chops and sprinkle chops with capers and parsley.

Lemon Garlic Lamb Chops with Yogurt Sauce

SERVES 4

ACTIVE TIME: 20 MINUTES ■ START TO FINISH: 45 MINUTES

■ In Turkey, lamb—the meat of choice—is very often served with this simple yogurt sauce, a Mediterranean classic (the key is fragrant mint). To give the yogurt a thicker texture, we drain it before mixing in the garlic and mint. We prefer to use shoulder chops for this recipe, since they have a more robust flavor than the leaner (and pricier) rib chops. Serve with boiled potatoes and sautéed greens for a quick weeknight dinner. ■

FOR YOGURT SAUCE

- 1 cup plain yogurt
- 1 garlic clove, minced
- 2 tablespoons chopped fresh mint
- Salt and freshly ground black pepper

FOR CHOPS

- ¼ cup fresh lemon juice
- 2 large garlic cloves, chopped
- ½ teaspoon dried oregano, crumbled
- 3 tablespoons olive oil
- 4 (½-inch-thick) shoulder lamb chops
- Salt and freshly ground black pepper
- 1 tablespoon water

SPECIAL EQUIPMENT: cheesecloth

MAKE THE YOGURT SAUCE: Set a sieve lined with a double thickness of cheesecloth over a bowl, add yogurt to sieve, and let drain at room temperature for 20 minutes. Transfer yogurt to a bowl and stir in garlic, mint, and salt and pepper to taste.

MEANWHILE, PREPARE THE CHOPS: Stir together lemon juice, garlic, oregano, and 2 tablespoons oil in a shallow baking dish. Add lamb chops, turn to coat, and marinate for 20 minutes.

Remove lamb from marinade (reserve marinade) and season with salt and pepper. Heat remaining 1 tablespoon oil in a 12-inch nonstick skillet over moderately high heat until hot but not smoking. Cook chops in 2 batches, turning once, about 4 minutes per batch for medium-rare. Transfer to plates and cover loosely with foil.

Add reserved marinade to skillet, along with water, and deglaze skillet by boiling, stirring and scraping up any brown bits, for 1 minute. Pour pan sauce over chops and serve with yogurt sauce.

COOK'S NOTE

- The yogurt sauce can be made up to 1 day ahead and refrigerated, covered. Bring to room temperature before serving.

Grilled Chermoula Lamb Chops

SERVES 6
ACTIVE TIME: 30 MINUTES ■ START TO FINISH: 2½ HOURS (INCLUDES MARINATING)

■ *Chermoula* is a delightful, spice-heavy marinade widely used in Moroccan cooking. It matches up particularly well with lamb, which has an underlying sweetness that echoes the sweet spices. If you have your butcher french (scrape the bones clean) your racks of lamb and cut them into chops, half your work will be done. The chops then require only a quick marinade and grill. ■

SHOPPING FOR LAMB CHOPS

We bought a number of loin chops and were amazed at how differently they were trimmed. High-end butcher shops sold us nice big, wide chops with the "tail" (more properly called the flank) included (1). Supermarkets tend to sell chops with the tail trimmed off (2), and some ruthlessly remove every scrap of fat, leaving a mingy chop (3). If that's all you can get, buy two per person.

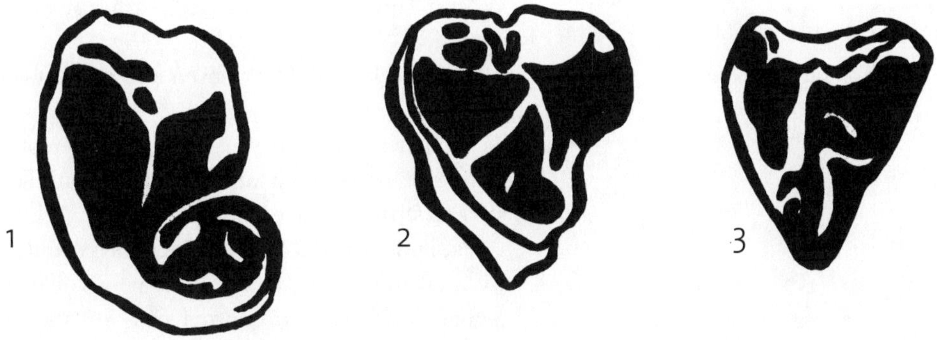

1 (3-inch) cinnamon stick, broken into 1-inch pieces
1 tablespoon coriander seeds
1 tablespoon cumin seeds
3 whole cloves
2 tablespoons sweet paprika
½ teaspoon cayenne
3 tablespoons olive oil
1 tablespoon finely chopped garlic
2 (8-rib) racks of lamb, frenched and cut into chops (2¾ pounds frenched)
Salt
2 cups finely chopped fresh cilantro (2 large bunches)

SPECIAL EQUIPMENT: an electric coffee/spice grinder

Finely grind cinnamon stick, coriander, cumin, and cloves in coffee/spice grinder. Stir together with paprika and cayenne in a small bowl.

Stir together oil and garlic in a large bowl. Add lamb and toss to coat. Season with salt and toss with spice mixture and cilantro. Transfer lamb with marinade to a large sealable plastic bag and marinate, refrigerated, for at least 2 hours.

Prepare a charcoal or gas grill: If using a charcoal grill, open vents in bottom of grill, then light charcoal. Fire is medium-hot when you can hold your hand 5 inches above rack for just 3 to 4 seconds. If using a gas grill, preheat on high, covered, for 10 minutes, then reduce heat to moderately high.

Remove lamb from bag and season with salt.

Lightly oil grill rack. Grill chops for about 4 minutes on one side, then 2 minutes on the other for medium-rare. Transfer chops to a platter, loosely cover with foil, and let stand for 5 minutes.

COOK'S NOTE

■ The lamb can marinate for up to 24 hours.

Lamb Stew with Spring Vegetables

SERVES 6

ACTIVE TIME: 1 HOUR ■ START TO FINISH: 2 HOURS

■ Although modern animal husbandry has made lamb available year-round, this French classic is the perfect dish for saying farewell to winter and hello to spring: it offers heartiness paired with the sweetness of young, tender vegetables. Be sure to use lamb shoulder, the proper cut for braising, not leg of lamb. Cut the shoulder into rather large chunks so you can brown them well at the beginning without cooking them all the way through. That way the meat develops a rich brown crust but does not dry out. Boiling the vegetables separately instead of braising them along with the meat produces an especially fresh and colorful stew. For a more substantial dish, serve with boiled small white potatoes. ■

6 fresh parsley sprigs
2 fresh thyme sprigs
2 fresh rosemary sprigs
2 Turkish bay leaves or 1 California bay leaf
6 black peppercorns
3 pounds boneless lamb shoulder, trimmed
Salt and freshly ground black pepper
3 tablespoons olive oil
1 large onion, finely chopped
4 garlic cloves, finely chopped
2½ cups beef stock or store-bought broth
1½ cups dry white wine
10 ounces pearl onions (not peeled)
½ pound baby turnips, trimmed, halved lengthwise if large
½ pound baby carrots, peeled, trimmed, and halved lengthwise if large
½ pound baby zucchini, trimmed and halved lengthwise
½ pound sugar snap peas, trimmed
2 tablespoons unsalted butter, softened
3 tablespoons all-purpose flour

SPECIAL EQUIPMENT: cheesecloth; kitchen string

Put a rack in middle of oven and preheat oven to 325°F.

Wrap herb sprigs, bay leaves, and peppercorns in a square of cheesecloth and tie into a bundle with kitchen string to make a bouquet garni.

Pat lamb dry. Cut into 1½-inch pieces and season with salt and pepper. Heat 2 tablespoons oil in a 6- to 7-quart wide heavy ovenproof pot over moderately high heat until hot but not smoking. Brown lamb in 3 batches, turning occasionally, about 4 minutes per batch. Transfer to a bowl.

Add remaining 1 tablespoon oil to pot, then add chopped onion and garlic and cook, stirring, until onion is golden, about 6 minutes. Add stock and wine and deglaze by boiling, stirring and scraping up brown bits, for 1 minute. Return lamb to pot, along with any juices that have accumulated in bowl, and add bouquet garni.

Cover pot, transfer to oven, and braise lamb until tender, about 1½ hours.

While lamb is braising, cook pearl onions in a 5- to 6-quart pot of boiling salted water (1 tablespoon salt per every 4 quarts water) until tender, about 10 minutes. With a slotted spoon, transfer to a large bowl of ice and cold water to stop the cooking (keep cooking water hot), then remove onions and peel.

Cook turnips, carrots, zucchini, and sugar snaps separately in reserved boiling water until just tender, about 5 minutes for turnips, 4 to 6 minutes for carrots, 2 minutes for zucchini, and 1½ minutes for sugar snaps. Transfer each batch of vegetables to ice water and, when all are cooked, drain in a colander.

Make a *beurre manié* by stirring together butter and flour in a small bowl to form a paste.

When lamb is tender, remove from oven and stir in 1 teaspoon salt and ¼ teaspoon pepper. Bring to a simmer on stovetop and whisk in enough *beurre manié*, bit by bit, to thicken to desired consistency, then simmer for about 2 minutes. Add vegetables and simmer, stirring occasionally, until heated through, about 2 minutes. Season with salt and pepper.

COOK'S NOTES

- The lamb can be braised up to 2 days ahead. Cool, uncovered, then refrigerate, covered. Reheat before adding the *beurre manié* and vegetables.
- The vegetables can be cooked up to 1 day ahead and refrigerated, wrapped in paper towels in a sealable plastic bag.

Ballymaloe Irish Stew

SERVES 4 TO 6

ACTIVE TIME: 30 MINUTES ■ START TO FINISH: 1¾ HOURS

■ When Darina Allen, of Ballymaloe Cooking School in County Cork, Ireland, prepares this recipe, which we adapted from her *Complete Book of Irish Country Cooking*, she uses only organic produce and locally raised lamb. But even when made with ordinary supermarket ingredients, this layered stew is something special. Allen's method of rendering the fat from the shoulder chops, then browning the meat, onions, and carrots in that fat, reinforces the flavor. ■

- 3 pounds (1- to 2-inch-thick) shoulder lamb chops
- Salt and freshly ground black pepper
- 1 pound small onions, peeled and root ends trimmed
- 1 pound carrots, cut into 2-inch pieces
- 2½ cups chicken stock or store-bought low-sodium chicken broth
- 1 fresh thyme sprig
- 2 pounds small boiling potatoes
- 1½ tablespoons unsalted butter
- 2 tablespoons all-purpose flour
- 2 tablespoons chopped fresh flat-leaf parsley
- 2 tablespoons chopped fresh chives

Put a rack in middle of oven and preheat oven to 350°F (unless simmering stew on the stovetop).

Cut chops lengthwise in half. Trim off and reserve excess fat. Cook fat in a 12-inch heavy skillet over low heat, stirring occasionally, until rendered, about 10 minutes; discard solid bits. Set skillet aside.

Pat chops dry and season with salt and pepper. Brown chops in 2 batches in fat in skillet over moderately high heat. Transfer to a dish. Add onions and carrots to skillet and toss well to coat with fat, about 1 minute. Remove from heat.

Arrange half of lamb in a 4-quart heavy ovenproof pot and season with salt and pepper. Top with onions and carrots, then with remaining lamb, seasoning each layer with salt and pepper.

Add stock to skillet and bring to a boil, scraping up brown bits. Pour stock into pot and add thyme. Peel potaotes and halve, if desired. Arrange potatoes on top, season with salt and pepper, and bring liquid to a simmer.

Cover pot, transfer to oven, and cook until meat is tender and vegetables are cooked through, 1 to 1¼ hours. (Alternatively, stew may be simmered gently on stovetop.)

Carefully tilt pot and ladle liquid from stew into a bowl. Let liquid stand for 5 minutes, then skim off fat.

Melt butter in a small heavy saucepan over moderate heat. Add flour and cook, stirring, for 2 minutes to make a roux. Whisk in hot liquid and simmer, whisking constantly, until slightly thickened, about 5 minutes. Stir in parsley and chives.

Pour sauce back into stew and reheat.

COOK'S NOTE

- The stew is best made at least 1 day ahead (do not add the herbs), and it can be made up to 2 days in advance. Cool completely, uncovered, then refrigerate, covered. Reheat and stir in the herbs just before serving.

Shepherd's Pie

SERVES 6

ACTIVE TIME: 1 HOUR ■ START TO FINISH: 2¾ HOURS

■ Shepherd's pie was originally created as a way to use up leftovers from a dinner of roast lamb and potatoes. Like many such dishes created by thrifty home cooks, though, it is worth making from scratch. Our version has culinary finesse, adding leeks, white wine, and fresh thyme to the more traditional onions, carrots, and turnips that accompany the lamb. You can even serve this on an occasion that calls for a somewhat formal presentation: simply divide the filling among individual flameproof serving dishes before topping it with the potatoes and putting it under the broiler. ■

FOR LAMB AND VEGETABLE FILLING

- 10 ounces pearl onions (not peeled)
- 4 medium leeks (white and pale green parts only), cut into ½-inch-thick slices
- 2 pounds boneless lamb shoulder, trimmed and cut into 1-inch cubes
- 2 teaspoons salt
- ½ teaspoon freshly ground black pepper
- 5 tablespoons all-purpose flour
- 3½ tablespoons unsalted butter, softened
- 2 tablespoons chopped garlic
- ½ cup dry white wine
- 1½ tablespoons tomato paste
- 1 cup beef stock or store-bought broth
- 1 cup water
- 2 teaspoons chopped fresh thyme
- 5 carrots, cut diagonally into ⅓-inch-thick slices
- 2 medium turnips, peeled and cut into ½-inch pieces

FOR MASHED POTATO TOPPING

- 2 pounds russet (baking) potatoes
- ½ cup heavy cream
- ½ cup milk
- 3 tablespoons unsalted butter
- 1 teaspoon salt
- ¼ teaspoon freshly ground black pepper

SPECIAL EQUIPMENT: a wide 3-quart enameled cast-iron pot (about 2 inches deep) or heavy flameproof skillet; a potato ricer or a food mill fitted with a medium disk

MAKE THE FILLING: Blanch onions in a 2- to 3-quart saucepan of boiling well-salted water for 1 minute, then transfer to a bowl of ice and cold water to stop the cooking (blanching makes peeling onions easier). Drain onions and peel, trimming root ends with a paring knife.

Wash leeks well in a bowl of cold water; lift out and drain.

Put a rack in middle of oven and preheat oven to 350°F.

Pat lamb dry and sprinkle with 1 teaspoon salt and ¼ teaspoon pepper. Put lamb and 3 tablespoons flour in a large sealable plastic bag, seal bag, and shake to coat lamb.

Melt 2 tablespoons butter in cast-iron pot or skillet over moderately high heat until foam subsides. Brown half of lamb, turning occasionally, about 6 minutes. Add 1 tablespoon garlic and cook, stirring, for 2 minutes. With a slotted spoon, transfer browned lamb and garlic to a plate. Repeat with remaining lamb and garlic (do not add more butter).

Add wine to pot and deglaze by boiling over high heat, stirring and scraping up brown bits, for 1 minute. Stir in tomato paste and boil, stirring, until liquid is reduced by half, about 5 minutes. Add stock, water, thyme, browned lamb, with any juices accumulated on plate, onions, leeks, carrots, turnips, remaining 1 teaspoon salt, and remaining ¼ teaspoon pepper and stir to combine. Bring to a simmer over moderately high heat, then remove from heat.

Cover pot with lid or foil, transfer to oven, and braise, stirring once or twice, until lamb is tender, 1½ to 2 hours. Season with salt and pepper and remove from oven.

MEANWHILE, MAKE THE TOPPING: Peel

and quarter potatoes. Combine potatoes with well-salted cold water to cover by 1 inch in a 4-quart heavy saucepan, bring to a simmer, and simmer, uncovered, until very tender, 20 to 25 minutes. Drain in a colander.

Add cream, milk, and butter to saucepan and bring to a simmer over moderate heat, stirring occasionally until butter is melted. Remove from heat and stir in salt and pepper. Force hot potatoes through ricer into hot cream mixture and stir gently to combine. Keep warm, covered.

ASSEMBLE THE PIE AND BROIL THE TOPPING: Preheat broiler. Make a *beurre manié* by stirring together remaining 1½ tablespoons butter and remaining 2 tablespoons flour in a small bowl to form a paste. Spoon 1 cup cooking liquid from pot into a 1-quart saucepan and bring to a boil. Whisk in *beurre manié* bit by bit, then simmer, whisking occasionally, until sauce is thickened, about 2 minutes. Gently stir sauce into lamb and vegetables.

Spoon potatoes over lamb and vegetables and spread evenly with a fork, making a pattern with tines. Broil about 3 inches from heat until top is golden, about 3 minutes.

COOK'S NOTE

- The filling can be made up to 1 day ahead. Cool, uncovered, then refrigerate, covered. Bring to a simmer over low heat before topping with warm potatoes and broiling.

Sultan's Delight

Braised Lamb over Silky Eggplant Purée

SERVES 4

ACTIVE TIME: 45 MINUTES ■ START TO FINISH: 3½ HOURS

■ Created in the kitchens of Topkapi Palace in Istanbul during the Ottoman Empire, this dish is said to have been prepared first for Sultan Murad IV in the early 1600s. The tender lamb, with its slight edge of gaminess, is a perfect match for the meaty smokiness of the eggplant. Soaking the eggplant in lemon water after grilling preserves its color and freshens its flavor. ■

FOR LAMB

- 2¼ pounds boneless lamb shoulder, trimmed and cut into 1-inch cubes
- Salt and freshly ground black pepper
- 1½ tablespoons unsalted butter
- 1 large tomato, peeled (see Tips, page 940), seeded, and finely chopped
- 1¼ cups water

FOR EGGPLANT PURÉE

- 1 large eggplant (1½ pounds)
- 3 tablespoons fresh lemon juice
- 3 tablespoons unsalted butter
- 3 tablespoons all-purpose flour
- 1 cup whole milk
- 3 tablespoons finely grated kasseri, pecorino fresco, or other semihard sheep's milk cheese
- 1¼ teaspoons kosher salt
- Freshly ground black pepper

BRAISE THE LAMB: Pat one third of lamb dry and season with salt and pepper. Heat about ½ tablespoon butter in a 4-quart heavy saucepan over moderately high heat until foam subsides. Brown seasoned lamb, turning occasionally, about 6 minutes. Transfer to a plate and brown remaining lamb in same manner in 2 batches, adding more butter as necessary. When third batch of lamb is browned, return rest of lamb, with any juices, to pan and add tomato, water, and 1 teaspoon salt. Cover and cook at a bare simmer, stirring occasionally, until meat is very tender, 2½ to 3 hours. Season with salt and pepper.

MEANWHILE, MAKE THE EGGPLANT PURÉE: Prepare a charcoal or gas grill: If using charcoal grill, open vents in bottom of grill, then light charcoal. Fire is medium-hot when you can hold your hand 5 inches above rack for just 3 to 4 seconds. If using a gas grill, preheat on high, covered, for 10 minutes, then reduce heat to moderately high.

Prick eggplant in several places with a skewer or wooden pick (to prevent bursting). Light oil grill rack and grill eggplant, turning occasionally, until charred all over and tender, about 15 minutes. Remove from heat and let cool slightly (eggplant will collapse).

Fill a large bowl with cold water and add lemon juice. Peel eggplant with a small sharp knife while still warm, leaving stem intact. (That makes the eggplant easier to handle; it may fall apart otherwise.)

Soak eggplant in lemon water for 15 minutes. Transfer to a colander. Discard stem and drain eggplant for 45 minutes.

While eggplant drains, preheat oven to 200°F. Melt butter in a 9- to 10-inch heavy skillet over moderate heat, add flour, and cook, stirring constantly, to make a roux, then continue cooking until it just begins to brown, 3 to 4 minutes. Add milk in a slow stream, whisking constantly, and bring sauce to a boil, whisking. Reduce heat and simmer, whisking occasionally, until thick, about 3 minutes.

Add drained eggplant to sauce and stir and mash with a fork until incorporated. Stir in cheese and salt and season with pepper. Keep warm, covered, in oven.

Serve eggplant topped with braised lamb.

COOK'S NOTE

- The eggplant can be broiled (instead of grilled) about 4 inches from the heat, turning occasionally, for about 10 minutes, but it will not have the distinctive smoky flavor.

Lamb Tagine with Prunes, Apricots, and Vegetables

SERVES 4

ACTIVE TIME: 45 MINUTES ■ START TO FINISH: 2¼ HOURS

■ Moroccan tagines are celebratory stews that get their name from the dish in which they are traditionally cooked and served. This version, adapted from Faye Levy's book *1,000 Jewish Recipes*, brings together the sweet tastes of the Ashkenazic traditions of Levy's childhood and the aromatic seasonings of the Moroccan-Jewish traditions of her husband's family. If you happen to have a tagine (see opposite page), by all means use it; if not, a shallow enameled cast-iron pot makes a fine stand-in. Serve with couscous or an Israeli salad of tomato, cucumber, and sweet onion. ■

- 2 pounds (1-inch-thick) shoulder lamb chops
- 1 tablespoon vegetable oil
- 1 large onion, chopped
- 1½ cups water
- Pinch of saffron threads, crumbled
- ¾ teaspoon salt
- ¼ teaspoon freshly ground black pepper
- 1½ large carrots, cut into ¼-inch-thick slices
- 1 small sweet potato, peeled and cut into ¾-inch pieces
- ¾ teaspoon ground ginger
- ⅛ teaspoon ground cinnamon
- ⅔ cup pitted prunes
- ½ cup dried apricots, preferably Turkish
- 1 medium yellow squash, cut into ¾-inch pieces
- 2 teaspoons honey (optional)
- Pinch of freshly grated nutmeg, or to taste

ACCOMPANIMENT: cooked couscous

SPECIAL EQUIPMENT: a 4- to 6-quart enameled cast-iron pot (at least 2¾ inches deep) or a large deep heavy ovenproof skillet

Cut lamb from bones, reserving bones. Cut meat into 1-inch pieces and pat dry.

Heat 1½ teaspoons oil in cast-iron pot or skillet over moderately high heat until hot but not smoking. Brown meat on all sides in 2 batches, about 5 minutes per batch. Transfer to a plate. Brown bones and transfer to plate.

Add remaining 1½ teaspoons oil to pot, then add onion and cook, stirring, until softened. Return meat and bones to pot. Stir in water, saffron, salt, and pepper and bring to a boil. Reduce heat, cover tightly, and simmer, stirring occasionally, until lamb is tender, about 1¼ hours.

With a slotted spoon, transfer lamb to a clean plate. Remove any meat from lamb bones and add to rest of meat; discard bones.

Add carrots and sweet potato to pot, cover, and simmer, stirring occasionally, until barely tender, about 10 minutes.

Add ginger, cinnamon, prunes, apricots, and squash, cover, and simmer, stirring occasionally, until vegetables and fruits are tender, about 5 minutes.

Return lamb to stew and add honey, if using. Season with salt and pepper and sprinkle with nutmeg. Simmer, uncovered, stirring occasionally, for 5 minutes. Serve with couscous.

Lamb Shank Stifado with Sautéed Potatoes

SERVES 4
ACTIVE TIME: 1 HOUR ■ START TO FINISH: 3½ HOURS

■ This hearty Greek stew can be made with any kind of meat suited to long, slow cooking; we use lamb shanks, which go very well with the cinnamon. No matter what the meat, though, the dish always includes copious quantities of small whole onions, since it's named for a variety of Greek onion called *stifado*. These are not available in the United States, so we have substituted the small white onions easily found in any supermarket. To accompany this unpretentious stew, we make simple but delectable sautéed potatoes. ■

- ¼ cup sugar
- ½ cup red wine vinegar
- 1 (28- to 32-ounce) can whole tomatoes in juice, drained (juice reserved) and chopped
- 1 cup dry red wine
- 2 teaspoons dried rosemary, crumbled
- 1 (3-inch) cinnamon stick
- 1 Turkish bay leaf or ½ California bay leaf
- 2 teaspoons salt
- 1 teaspoon freshly ground black pepper
- 6 (1-pound) lamb shanks
- 1 pound small (1¼-inch-wide) white onions (not peeled)
- 2 pounds small (2-inch-wide) red potatoes, scrubbed
- 1 tablespoon olive oil
- 3 large garlic cloves, thinly sliced

SPECIAL EQUIPMENT: a 9-quart heavy ovenproof pot with a lid

Put a rack in middle of oven and preheat oven to 350°F.

Cook sugar in pot over moderate heat, without stirring, until it begins to melt. Continue to cook, stirring with a wooden spoon, until sugar becomes a deep golden caramel, about 5 minutes. Carefully add vinegar (mixture will steam and bubble vigorously) and stir until caramel is dissolved. Stir in tomatoes, with their juice, wine, rosemary, cinnamon, bay leaf, salt, and pepper and bring to a boil.

Add lamb shanks, cover, and transfer to oven. Braise, turning shanks occasionally, until tender, 2 hours.

Meanwhile, cook onions in a 4-quart saucepan of

Cooking in a Clay Pot

Tagine ("tah-*jheen*") is the name for both a shallow North African casserole with a conical lid and the delicious stew cooked inside. You don't need this dish to cook the tagine on the opposite page; we used a wide, shallow, enameled cast-iron pot and were very happy with the results. But if you are as entranced as we are with the tagine's centuries-old design and just have to have one, be aware that not every tagine is really for cooking. That's a shame, because rarely does form follow function so neatly: the tall lid collects condensed steam and returns it to the stew below, keeping it moist; the knobby handle stays cool; and the dish is shallow enough so you can eat *à la marocaine,* with the first three fingers of the right hand. The cookbook author Paula Wolfert likes to cook in the ones offered by Tagines.com; just make sure they don't have a painted glaze. (If you're not sure about whether or not a tagine is safe for cooking, you can easily test it with a Lead Check test kit, available at hardware stores. See Sources for another place to find tagines.)

boiling water until just tender, 8 to 10 minutes; drain. Cool onions, then peel.

Quarter potatoes. Steam in a steamer rack set over simmering water, covered, until just tender, 8 to 10 minutes.

Heat oil in a 12-inch nonstick skillet over moderate heat. Add garlic and cook, stirring, until pale golden. Add potatoes with salt and pepper to taste, increase heat to moderately high, and cook, stirring occasionally, until potatoes are golden and tender, 5 to 7 minutes. Remove from heat and keep warm, covered.

With a large slotted spoon, transfer meat to a platter. Discard cinnamon stick and bay leaf. Add onions to pot and boil until sauce is slightly thickened, 3 to 5 minutes. Spoon sauce and onions over meat and surround with potatoes.

COOK'S NOTES

- The braised lamb shanks will improve in flavor if made 1 day ahead. Cool in the braising liquid, uncovered, then refrigerate, covered. Skim and discard the fat from the surface of the stew and reheat on top of the stove before proceeding.
- The onions can be boiled and peeled up to 1 day ahead. Refrigerate, covered.

Braised Lamb Shanks with White Beans

SERVES 4

ACTIVE TIME: 1 HOUR ■ START TO FINISH: 4 HOURS

■ Because they come from the leg, one of the hardest-working, most densely muscled parts of the animal, shanks are very tough. But when braised, they turn buttery, just the thing for a cold winter night when the body requires real sustenance. This recipe, which we adapted from one that was served at the New York restaurant Alison on Dominick Street, is a takeoff on the popular Italian dish osso buco, traditionally made with veal shanks (see page 458). Like osso buco, it is served with the garnish known as gremolata, which nicely cuts the richness of the lamb, and with white beans. If you love beans, feel free to add another cup of them. ■

FOR LAMB SHANKS

4 (1-pound) lamb shanks
Salt and freshly ground black pepper
2 tablespoons olive oil
1 medium onion, coarsely chopped
1 medium carrot, coarsely chopped
1 celery rib, coarsely chopped
8 garlic cloves, coarsely chopped
1 (750-milliliter) bottle full-bodied red wine, preferably Bordeaux
4 cups chicken stock or store-bought low-sodium broth
1 tablespoon tomato paste
2 fresh thyme sprigs

FOR GREMOLATA

3 tablespoons chopped fresh flat-leaf parsley
1 teaspoon finely grated lemon zest
3 garlic cloves, minced

FOR BEANS

2 tablespoons extra-virgin olive oil
2 small onions, finely chopped
2 small carrots, finely chopped
2 celery ribs, finely chopped
3 garlic cloves, minced
2 cups cooked white beans, preferably great northern or navy, rinsed if canned
2–2½ cups chicken stock or store-bought low-sodium broth
2 tablespoons unsalted butter
1 Turkish bay leaf or ½ California bay leaf
Salt and freshly ground black pepper

FOR FINISHING SAUCE

3 fresh tarragon sprigs
1 tablespoon unsalted butter

SPECIAL EQUIPMENT: an 8-quart heavy pot

MAKE THE LAMB SHANKS: Pat lamb shanks dry and season with salt and pepper. Heat oil in pot over moderately high heat until hot but not smoking. Brown shanks well all over, in batches, 5 to 8 minutes per batch, and transfer to a plate. Add onion, carrot, celery, and garlic and cook, stirring, until onion is softened, about 3 minutes. Add wine, bring to a brisk simmer, and simmer, stirring occasionally, until liquid is reduced to about 3 cups, 6 to 8 minutes.

Stir in stock, tomato paste, and thyme and return shanks to pot. Bring to a boil, then cover, reduce heat, and simmer, stirring and turning shanks occasionally, for 1½ hours.

Uncover pot and simmer, stirring occasionally, until lamb shanks are tender, about 1 hour more.

MEANWHILE, MAKE THE GREMOLATA: Stir together all ingredients in a small bowl. Cover and set aside.

MAKE THE BEANS: Heat oil in a 4-quart heavy saucepan over moderately high heat until hot but not smoking. Add onions, carrots, celery, and garlic and cook, stirring, until onions are softened, 2 to 3 minutes. Add beans, 2 cups stock, butter, and bay leaf and simmer, stirring occasionally and adding remaining stock as necessary to keep beans moist, until they have a creamy consistency, about 30 minutes. Discard bay leaf and stir in half of gremolata and salt and pepper to taste. Remove from heat and cover to keep warm.

When lamb shanks are tender, transfer to a plate and keep warm, covered with foil. Pour braising liquid through a sieve into a 3- to 4-quart saucepan; discard solids. Stir in tarragon and butter. Boil, stirring occasionally, until sauce is slightly thickened and reduced to about 2½ cups, 25 to 30 minutes. Pour sauce through sieve into a bowl and season with salt and pepper.

Meanwhile, just before serving, reheat beans over low heat, stirring occasionally. Sprinkle lamb shanks with remaining gremolata and serve with beans and sauce.

Lamb Kofte with Garlic Yogurt Sauce

SERVES 4 TO 6

ACTIVE TIME: 45 MINUTES ■ START TO FINISH: 1 HOUR

■ *Kofte,* cigar-shaped lamb meatballs, are popular throughout Turkey. This version calls for mildly hot and intensely flavorful Maras and Urfa dried red pepper flakes; red-black Urfa is earthy and slightly smoky, while deep red Maras has a bright berry taste. Together they make these *kofte* impossible to resist. (If you can't find them, you can use a good brand of paprika; they won't taste quite the same but will still be delicious.) *Baharat,* the classic Turkish spice blend that typically includes cinnamon, cloves, and allspice, along with red and black pepper, adds yet another layer of flavor.

Be sure to knead the bread and meat together thoroughly before you form the *kofte;* the kneading distributes the fat evenly and creates a lovely smooth texture. This recipe is from Valerie and Ihsan Gurdal, the owners of the renowned specialty foods shop Formaggio Kitchen, in Cambridge, Massachusetts.

The dried peppers and *baharat* are available from Formaggio (see Sources) and in Middle Eastern markets. ■

FOR SAUCE

- 1 cup plain yogurt, preferably whole-milk
- 1 teaspoon minced garlic
- Salt

FOR *KOFTE*

- 2 slices firm white sandwich bread, torn into pieces
- 1 pound ground lamb
- 1 small red onion, minced or grated
- ⅓ cup finely chopped fresh flat-leaf parsley
- 1 tablespoon *baharat* spice mix
- 1½ teaspoons Maras pepper flakes
- 1½ teaspoons Urfa pepper flakes
- 2 teaspoons salt

OPTIONAL ACCOMPANIMENT: 16 soft lettuce leaves for wrapping

SPECIAL EQUIPMENT: sixteen 10-inch-long wooden skewers, soaked in water for 30 minutes

MAKE THE SAUCE: Stir yogurt together with garlic and salt to taste in a small bowl.

MAKE THE *KOFTE:* Cover bread with water in a small bowl and let soak for 30 minutes.

Meanwhile, prepare a charcoal or gas grill: If using a charcoal grill, open vents in bottom of grill, then light charcoal. Fire is hot when you can hold your hand 5 inches above rack for just 1 to 2 seconds. If using a gas grill, preheat on high, covered, for 10 minutes, then reduce heat to moderately high.

Squeeze bread to remove as much moisture as possible. Put in a large bowl, add remaining ingredients, and mix with your hands until thoroughly blended. Divide lamb mixture into 16 portions and form each into a ball. Roll each ball into a 7- to 8-inch-long cigar, rolling it first between your hands and then on a work surface (be sure the *kofte* are uniformly thin for even cooking). Slide a skewer lengthwise through center of each *kofte.*

Oil grill rack and grill *kofte,* turning once, until golden and just cooked through, 4 to 6 minutes. Let stand for 5 minutes, loosely covered with foil, and serve warm with yogurt sauce, wrapping them in lettuce leaves, if using.

COOK'S NOTE

- The *kofte* can also be broiled on an oiled baking sheet 5 inches from the heat, turning once, for 4 to 6 minutes.

Lamb and Feta Patties with Pepper Relish

SERVES 4
ACTIVE TIME: 30 MINUTES ■ START TO FINISH: 45 MINUTES

■ Greek-inspired lamb patties, invigorated with tangy feta cheese and aromatic mint, are an excellent alternative to standard beef burgers. You can, of course, serve them without the accompanying relish, but it is easy and colorful and can be made in advance. ■

FOR RELISH
- 3/4 cup cider vinegar
- 1/4 cup sugar
- 2/3 cup water
- 2 orange or red bell peppers, cored, seeded, and cut into 1/2-inch pieces
- 1/3 cup golden raisins
- 1 Golden Delicious apple, peeled, cored, and cut into 1/2-inch cubes
- 1 teaspoon mustard seeds
- 1/8 teaspoon cayenne
- 1/2 teaspoon salt

FOR PATTIES
- 1 slice firm white sandwich bread, torn into pieces
- 1 scallion, coarsely chopped
- 1 garlic clove
- 1/3 cup coarsely chopped fresh mint
- 1 1/4 pounds ground lamb
- 1 large egg, lightly beaten
- 1/4 pound feta, crumbled (scant 1 cup)
- 3/4 teaspoon salt
- 1/4 teaspoon freshly ground black pepper

MAKE THE RELISH: Combine vinegar and sugar in a 2-quart heavy nonreactive saucepan and bring to a boil, stirring until sugar is dissolved. Boil, uncovered, for 1 minute. Add remaining ingredients and simmer briskly, uncovered, stirring occasionally, until peppers and apple are tender, about 25 minutes. Remove from heat.

MEANWHILE, MAKE THE PATTIES: Preheat broiler.

Pulse bread, scallion, garlic, and mint in a food processor until finely chopped. Transfer to a medium bowl and add lamb, egg, feta, salt, and pepper. Blend with your hands until just combined; do not overwork mixture, or patties will be tough. Form into four 4 1/2-inch-wide patties (about 1/2 inch thick).

Oil rack of a broiler pan and broil patties 5 inches from heat, turning once, until browned but still slightly pink in center, about 8 minutes total. Serve with relish.

COOK'S NOTE

- The relish can be made up to 3 days ahead, covered, and refrigerated. Serve at room temperature or reheat.

Moussaka

SERVES 8
ACTIVE TIME: 1 HOUR ■ START TO FINISH: 1 3/4 HOURS

■ Greek cuisine has not yet become as popular in the United States as it deserves to be, but virtually everyone knows about moussaka. This layered combination of lamb, eggplant, and cheese delicately seasoned with cinnamon and allspice is a good choice for a party, since it's an excellent make-ahead dish. ■

FOR LAMB AND EGGPLANT
- 9 tablespoons olive oil
- 1 large onion, finely chopped
- 3 garlic cloves, minced
- 1 1/4 pounds ground lamb
- Rounded 1/4 teaspoon ground cinnamon
- Rounded 1/4 teaspoon ground allspice
- 3 (14-ounce) cans Italian plum tomatoes, drained (1 1/2 cups juice reserved) and chopped
- 1 1/2 teaspoons dried mint
- Salt and freshly ground black pepper
- 3 1/2 pounds medium eggplants, cut into 1/3-inch-thick slices

FOR TOPPING

- 2½ tablespoons unsalted butter
- 3½ tablespoons all-purpose flour
- 1½ cups whole milk
- Freshly ground black pepper
- ¼ pound feta, crumbled (scant 1 cup)
- 1 large egg, lightly beaten with 1 large egg yolk
- ⅓ cup finely grated Parmigiano-Reggiano

MAKE THE LAMB AND EGGPLANT: Heat 3 tablespoons oil in a 4-quart heavy saucepan over moderately low heat. Add onion and cook, stirring, until softened, about 3 minutes. Add garlic and cook, stirring, for 1 minute. Add lamb, increase heat to moderate, and cook, stirring and breaking up lumps, until lamb is no longer pink, about 4 minutes. Stir in cinnamon and allspice. Add tomatoes, with reserved juice, mint, and salt and pepper to taste and bring to a boil. Reduce heat and cook at a brisk simmer, stirring occasionally, until slightly thickened, 20 to 25 minutes.

Meanwhile, preheat broiler. Oil two baking sheets. Arrange eggplant slices in one layer on baking sheets, then lightly brush with 3 tablespoons oil. Broil about 4 inches from heat until golden brown, 3 to 5 minutes. Turn eggplant slices over, lightly brush with remaining 3 tablespoons oil, and broil until golden brown and tender, 3 to 5 minutes more. Remove from broiler and reduce oven temperature to 400°F.

Oil a 13-by-9-inch baking dish. Arrange half of eggplant slices, slightly overlapping, in dish. Spread lamb mixture evenly over eggplant and cover with remaining eggplant slices, slightly overlapping.

MAKE THE TOPPING: Melt butter in a 2½- to 3-quart heavy saucepan over moderately low heat. Add flour and cook, whisking, for 3 minutes to make a roux. Add milk in a slow stream, whisking constantly, then bring to a boil, whisking. Reduce heat and simmer, whisking, for 3 minutes. Add feta and cook over low heat, whisking, until cheese is melted; do not let boil. Season sauce with pepper to taste and let cool, covered, for 5 minutes.

Add beaten egg mixture to sauce in a slow stream, whisking. Pour sauce evenly over eggplant and lamb mixture and sprinkle with Parmesan.

Bake moussaka in middle of oven until golden and bubbling, 30 to 35 minutes. Let stand for 10 minutes before serving.

COOK'S NOTE

- The moussaka, without the topping, can be assembled up to 1 day ahead. Cool completely, uncovered, then refrigerate, covered. Bring to room temperature, about 1 hour, before topping with sauce and cheese and baking.

VEGETABLES

If you had shown our original subscribers recipes for grilled radicchio, stir-fried pea shoots, or yuca fries, they would have looked at you in sheer astonishment. Those vegetables were unknown in America in the forties, and not one of them could have been found in stores. By the same token, early readers would have been stunned by the little red rocks that pass for tomatoes in much of modern America, and by the starchy corn that now sits in our supermarkets all year long. In the early forties, America was still a nation of farmers, and almost half the population grew their own vegetables. Even those who lived in big cities were accustomed to eating freshly picked greens from nearby farms. This meant that most Americans ate with the seasons, which was probably one reason that frozen vegetables were greeted with such joy. Peas all year round!

The introduction of frozen foods was an enormous change that revolutionized the American diet. In some cases it was an improvement; because sugar quickly converts to starch, we still recommend using frozen peas unless you have a few plants growing in your own garden. But mostly it was not, and before long much of the nation forgot what fresh young vegetables taste like. As frozen foods pushed the fresh ones from the shelves, it seemed for a time as if every American family existed on a handful of standard vegetables (carrots, green beans, spinach, and peas).

Fortunately, the green-market movement of the past two decades has changed all that. Between the arrival with immigrants of new vegetables like bok choy and chayote, the rediscovery of forgotten greens like purslane, and the introduction of new varieties like Yukon Gold potatoes, our vegetable landscape has undergone another dramatic transformation. These days *Gourmet*'s cooks spend a lot of time poking around farms and farm markets, asking farmers for recipes and trying to discover the best ways to use all the exciting new vegetables that keep turning up.

As we argued over which of the thousands of recipes we've published over the years to include in this chapter, we kept asking ourselves this question: if we could eat nothing but the vegetable dishes printed in this book for the rest of our lives, what would we want them to be? Each recipe had passionate defenders, and in many cases the cook-offs to decide between two versions of, say, corn pudding or creamed spinach were fierce.

We have tried to include a wide variety of vegetables and a number of different techniques. When you're contemplating a cauliflower, we want you to be able to decide whether to roast it with garlic, make a simple purée, splash it with cheese sauce, or spice it with ginger and mustard seeds. We can't tell which one you're likely to choose, but we can promise this: these recipes are so good that people who think they don't like certain vegetables have been known to take one bite and change their minds.

Artichoke Bottoms Braised in Olive Oil with Garlic and Mint

SERVES 6

ACTIVE TIME: 1 HOUR ■ START TO FINISH: 1½ HOURS

■ Artichoke bottoms *alla romana*—braised in olive oil with garlic and mint until they are meltingly tender—are reason enough to tackle what might be the world's least user-friendly vegetable. The garlic-mint paste flavors the braising liquid, which is then reduced to a sauce. ■

- 6 large artichokes (10–12 ounces each)
- 1 lemon, halved
- 1 tablespoon finely chopped garlic
- 2 teaspoons kosher salt
- 1 tablespoon finely chopped fresh mint
- 1 cup water
- ⅓ cup extra-virgin olive oil

OPTIONAL GARNISH: chopped fresh mint

Leave artichoke stems attached. Cut off top inch of 1 artichoke with a serrated knife (1). Bend back outer leaves until they snap off close to base; remove and discard several more layers of leaves in the same manner until you reach pale yellow leaves with pale green tips (2). Using a sharp knife, cut remaining leaves flush with top of artichoke bottom. Pull out purple leaves and scoop out fuzzy choke with a melon ball cutter or sharp spoon (3). Trim dark green fibrous parts from base and sides of artichoke with a sharp paring knife (4) and rub cut surfaces with 1 lemon half. Cut ¼ inch from end of stem and trim sides of stem down to pale inner core. Rub cut surfaces again with lemon half. Trim remaining artichokes in same manner.

Mince and mash garlic to a paste with 1 teaspoon salt, then mix in mint. Rub one sixth of garlic paste into cavity of each artichoke.

Combine water and oil in a 4-quart heavy saucepan. Stand artichokes upside down in pan and sprinkle remaining 1 teaspoon salt over them. Bring to a simmer and simmer, covered, over low heat until tender, 20 to 30 minutes.

HOW TO TRIM ARTICHOKES

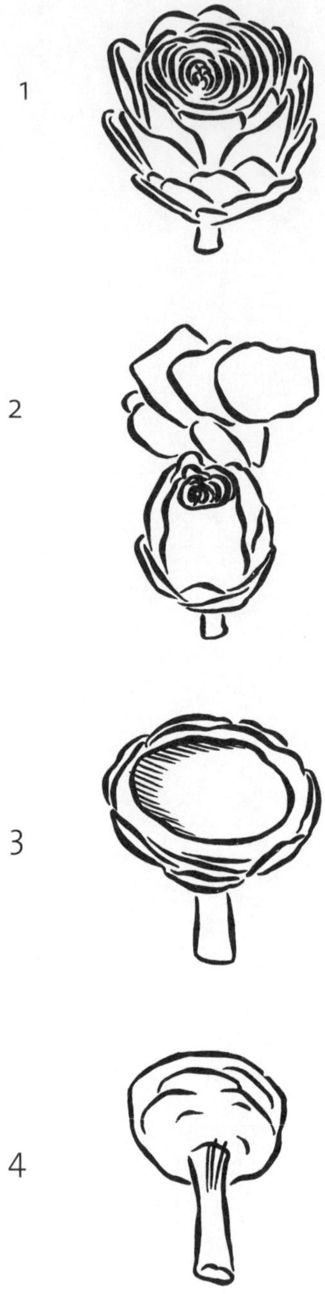

Transfer artichokes to a serving dish. Boil cooking liquid, whisking, until blended and reduced to about ⅓ cup. Pour sauce over artichokes and serve warm or at room temperature, garnished with mint, if desired.

COOK'S NOTE

- The artichokes can be cooked up to 2 days ahead and refrigerated, covered, in the reduced sauce.

Artichokes with Garlic Pimiento Vinaigrette

SERVES 6

ACTIVE TIME: 30 MINUTES ■ START TO FINISH: 1 HOUR

■ Whole artichokes are cooked and served with a vinaigrette spooned in and among the leaves. The piquant sweetness of pimientos in the garlicky vinaigrette accentuates the nutty flavor of the artichokes. ■

- 6 large artichokes (10–12 ounces each)
- 1/2 lemon
- 1/4 cup fresh lemon juice
- 2 large garlic cloves
- 1 teaspoon salt
- 6 tablespoons white wine vinegar
- 3/4 cup extra-virgin olive oil
- 6 tablespoons finely chopped drained pimientos
- 1/4 cup finely chopped fresh flat-leaf parsley
- 1/2 teaspoon freshly ground black pepper

Cut off artichoke stems and discard. Cut off top 1/2 inch of 1 artichoke with a serrated knife, then cut about 1/2 inch off remaining leaf tips with kitchen shears. Rub cut leaves with lemon half. Open out leaves slightly with your thumbs and pull out purple leaves from center and enough yellow leaves to expose fuzzy choke. Scoop out choke with a melon ball cutter or sharp spoon and squeeze some lemon juice into cavity. Trim remaining artichokes in same manner.

Add lemon juice to an 8-quart pot of boiling salted water (1 tablespoon salt per every 4 quarts water). Boil artichokes, uncovered, until bottoms are tender when pierced with a knife, 20 to 25 minutes. Transfer artichokes to a bowl of ice and cold water to stop the cooking, then drain well, upside down, in a colander, and transfer to paper towels.

Using a large heavy knife, mince and mash garlic to a paste with salt. Whisk together garlic paste and vinegar in a small bowl. Add oil in a slow stream, whisking until well blended. Whisk in pimientos, parsley, and pepper.

Slightly separate leaves of artichokes and place artichokes on six salad plates. Spoon dressing in and around them.

COOK'S NOTE

- The artichokes can be cooked (but not dressed) up to 1 day ahead and refrigerated, covered.

Fried Artichokes

SERVES 4 TO 6

ACTIVE TIME: 1 HOUR ■ START TO FINISH: 1 HOUR

■ These are inspired by the famous *carciofi alla giudia* of Rome, whole artichokes flattened into the shape of a chrysanthemum and then deep-fried (see page 69). Cutting the artichokes into wedges helps them cook more evenly, so they have crisper edges. It also makes them easier to eat. They are irresistible. ■

- 2 lemons, halved
- 4 large artichokes (10–12 ounces each)
- About 6 cups olive or vegetable oil for deep-frying
- Salt

SPECIAL EQUIPMENT: a deep-fat thermometer

Fill a large bowl with cold water. Squeeze juice from 2 lemon halves into bowl.

Leave artichoke stems attached. Cut off top inch of 1 artichoke with a serrated knife. Bend back outer leaves until they snap off close to base; remove and discard several more layers of leaves in same manner until you reach pale yellow leaves with pale green tips. Trim dark green fibrous parts from base and side of artichoke with a sharp paring knife, then rub cut surfaces with a lemon half. Trim 1/4 inch from end of stem and trim sides of stem down to pale inner core (don't worry if remaining stem is very thin). Cut off pale green top of artichoke and cut artichoke into 6 wedges. Cut out purple leaves and fuzzy choke. Rub all cut surfaces with lemon half and put in bowl of lemon water. Prepare remaining artichokes in same manner, using remaining lemon half when needed.

Transfer artichokes to paper towels and drain well, then pat dry. Heat 1¾ inches oil in a 4-quart deep heavy saucepan over moderate heat until thermometer registers 220°F. Add artichokes and simmer, occasionally stirring gently, until tender, about 15 minutes. Transfer to paper towels to drain.

Heat oil until thermometer registers 375°F. Fry artichokes in 4 batches, gently stirring, until leaves are curled, browned, and crisp, 30 to 40 seconds per batch, then drain well on paper towels and season with salt. (Return oil to 375°F between batches.)

COOK'S NOTE

- The artichokes can be simmered (in 220°F oil) up to 4 hours ahead. Keep, uncovered, at room temperature and fry just before serving.

Asparagus with Tarragon Sherry Vinaigrette

SERVES 4

ACTIVE TIME: 30 MINUTES ■ START TO FINISH: 30 MINUTES

■ Chilled poached asparagus is a classically French preparation that has appeared in *Gourmet* since the very beginning. In our favorite version, tarragon, which manages to be strong and subtle at the same time, gets a little extra finesse from sherry vinegar and shallot. The pretty sieved egg on top is said to resemble mimosa blossoms. For that reason, this dish was often called asparagus mimosa on the menus of grand hotels. ■

1½ pounds medium asparagus, trimmed
1 tablespoon sherry vinegar
2 teaspoons minced shallot
¼ teaspoon Dijon mustard
¼ teaspoon salt
⅛ teaspoon freshly ground black pepper
3 tablespoons extra-virgin olive oil
1½ teaspoons finely chopped fresh tarragon
1 hard-boiled large egg

Cook asparagus in a 4- to 5-quart wide pot of boiling well-salted water, uncovered, until just tender, 3 to 5 minutes, depending on thickness. With tongs, transfer to a bowl of ice and cold water to stop the cooking. Drain well and pat dry with paper towels.

Whisk together vinegar, shallot, mustard, salt, and pepper in a small bowl, then add oil in a slow stream, whisking until well blended. Whisk in tarragon.

Halve egg and force through a coarse-mesh sieve into a bowl. Toss asparagus with 1 tablespoon vinaigrette and divide among four plates. Spoon remaining vinaigrette over asparagus and top with egg.

VARIATIONS

- Another possible topping for boiled asparagus is Maître d'Hôtel Butter (page 894), with a sprinkling of chopped hazelnuts.
- One pound of *haricots verts* can be substituted for the asparagus. Boil until just tender, about 4 minutes.

Roasted Asparagus with Shallots and Sesame Seeds

SERVES 8

ACTIVE TIME: 25 MINUTES ■ START TO FINISH: 25 MINUTES

■ Roasting brings out a different aspect of asparagus—the sugars caramelize and a slight bitterness emerges, giving complexity to the pure flavor of the vegetable. Johanne Killeen and George Germon, of Al Forno restaurant, in Providence, Rhode Island, introduced us to this technique. ■

2½ pounds medium asparagus, trimmed
1½ tablespoons olive oil
2 tablespoons minced shallots
2 tablespoons sesame seeds, lightly toasted (see Tips, page 939)
¼ teaspoon salt
Fresh lemon juice to taste

Put a rack in middle of oven and preheat oven to 500°F.

Toss asparagus with oil on a large baking sheet with sides, then spread out in one layer. Roast, shaking pan every 2 minutes, until barely tender, 6 to 8 minutes.

Sprinkle asparagus with shallots and sesame seeds and roast until asparagus is crisp-tender, about 1 minute more. Sprinkle with salt and lemon juice.

Grilled Asparagus

SERVES 4

ACTIVE TIME: 15 MINUTES ■ START TO FINISH: 30 MINUTES

■ This is a revelation: the heat and smoke of the fire bring out the vegetable's sweet meatiness. Because the difference between perfectly done and overdone asparagus is a matter of seconds, we thread the spears onto skewers, which makes them easy to snatch from the grill at just the right moment. The skewers also make it impossible for the spears to roll through the rack into the coals. ■

- 1½ pounds medium asparagus, trimmed
- 2 tablespoons extra-virgin olive oil
- Kosher salt

SPECIAL EQUIPMENT: eight 6-inch wooden skewers, soaked in warm water for 10 minutes

Prepare a gas or charcoal grill: If using a charcoal grill, open vents in bottom of grill, then light charcoal. Fire is moderately hot when you can hold your hand 5 inches above rack for just 3 to 4 seconds. If using a gas grill, preheat all burners on high, covered, for 10 minutes.

Divide asparagus into 4 bunches. Lay spears in each bunch side by side, aligning bottoms, and thread 2 skewers crosswise through each bunch, about 2 inches apart. (Skewered asparagus will look like rafts; parallel skewers make it easier to turn asparagus.) Brush asparagus with oil and sprinkle with salt.

Lightly oil grill rack. Grill asparagus, uncovered, turning over once, until tender, 6 to 10 minutes total.

COOK'S NOTE

■ The asparagus can also be grilled in a well-seasoned ridged grill pan over moderately high heat.

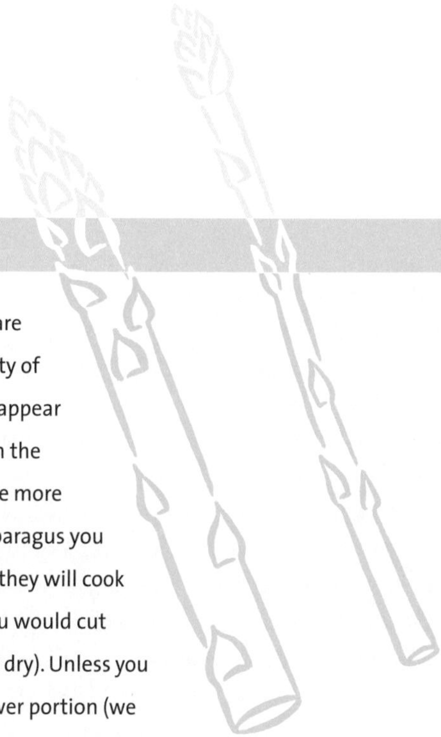

ASPARAGUS

True or false: slender spears of asparagus are better than thick ones, because they are younger and therefore tenderer. Believe it or not, the answer is "false." It's the variety of asparagus that determines the thickness. Fat spears are already plump when they appear above ground level, and thin ones won't get substantially thicker as they mature. In the United States, the thin ones seem to be more popular, but generally the fat ones are more succulent, almost meaty in texture. Whatever your preference, buy the freshest asparagus you can find and make sure that all the spears in the bunch are about the same size so they will cook evenly. If you need to store them in the refrigerator for a few days, keep them as you would cut flowers — upright in a couple of inches of water (trim the bottoms first if they look dry). Unless you get the pencil-thin Twiggys of the asparagus world, you might want to peel the lower portion (we often don't). We especially like medium to thick asparagus roasted or grilled. The bigger the spears, the longer they take to cook, of course — and the more grilled or roasted flavor they'll have.

Green Beans with Almonds

SERVES 4
ACTIVE TIME: 15 MINUTES ■ START TO FINISH: 15 MINUTES

■ This deceptively simple recipe yields the best green beans we've ever had. Unlike other versions, where the beans are tossed with sliced or slivered almonds, the almonds are whizzed in the food processor before being lightly toasted in garlic butter. They make a crunchy, even coating for the beans. ■

- 1 pound green beans, trimmed
- 2 tablespoons unsalted butter
- 1 garlic clove, minced
- 1/2 cup skinned whole almonds, finely ground in a food processor
- Salt and freshly ground black pepper

Cook beans in a 3-quart saucepan of boiling well-salted water until crisp-tender, about 4 minutes; drain.

Melt butter in a 12-inch nonstick skillet over moderate heat. Add garlic and cook, stirring, until it just begins to turn golden, about 1 minute. Add almonds and cook, stirring, until they begin to color slightly, about 2 minutes. Add beans and cook, stirring, until tender and heated through, about 2 minutes. Season with salt and pepper.

VARIATION

■ Toss the cooked beans in the garlic butter with 1/4 cup minced fresh flat-leaf parsley and 1 teaspoon minced anchovy fillet, patted dry.

Dry-Curried Green Beans

SERVES 6
ACTIVE TIME: 20 MINUTES ■ START TO FINISH: 20 MINUTES PLUS 1 HOUR SOAKING TIME IF USING PACKAGED COCONUT

■ This is an extraordinary, perfectly balanced example of the South Indian specialty called a dry curry, in which only a small amount of water is used to soften the vegetables. The flavors are delicious, but it's really the exquisite myriad textures—coconut, seeds, and dal (lentils)—that set this dish apart. There is no getting around the fact that you will have to visit an Indian market or order some of these ingredients by mail (see Sources). But the great thing about dabbling in Indian flavors is that many of the ingredients (coconut, mustard seeds, and asafetida powder, for instance) will last almost forever if you wrap them well and keep them in the freezer. Believe us, you will want to use them again. (For more about these ingredients, see Glossary.) ■

- 3/4 cup finely grated fresh coconut or 1/2 cup packaged finely shredded unsweetened coconut
- 2 teaspoons vegetable oil
- 1 1/2 teaspoons black mustard seeds
- 1 1/2 teaspoons cumin seeds
- 1 1/2 teaspoons (picked-over) split skinned *urad dal*
- 1 1/2 teaspoons (picked-over) split skinned *chana dal*
- 1/2 teaspoon asafetida powder
- 1 fresh hot red chile, such as serrano or Thai, halved lengthwise
- 4 fresh curry leaves
- 1 1/2 pounds green beans, trimmed and cut into 1/4-inch pieces
- 1/2 cup water
- Salt

If using packaged coconut, soak in warm water to cover for 1 hour, then drain well.

Heat oil in a 3-quart heavy saucepan over moderate heat until hot but not smoking. Add mustard seeds, cumin seeds, both dals, asafetida, chile, and curry leaves and cook, stirring occasionally, until mustard seeds begin to pop, about 45 seconds. Stir in green beans, water, and salt to taste, cover, and simmer until beans are just tender and most of water has evaporated, 6 to 8 minutes.

Remove chile, if desired, and stir in coconut.

COOK'S NOTE

■ The beans can be made up to 6 hours ahead and refrigerated, covered. Be sure to undercook the beans slightly so they retain their color when reheated.

Dry-Cooked String Beans

SERVES 6

ACTIVE TIME: 30 MINUTES ■ START TO FINISH: 30 MINUTES

■ Put these Chinese-style beans on a bowl of rice and you have a very satisfying supper. Despite the name, the beans are fried in oil before being stir-fried with the pork. Cooking them twice makes them brilliant green and intensely flavorful. We use regular green beans here, but if you have access to long beans (also called yard-long beans—for good reason—and available in Asian markets), use them. ■

- 1 teaspoon sugar
- ¼ teaspoon salt, or to taste
- 2 tablespoons soy sauce
- 1 tablespoon rice wine or sake
- 2 teaspoons Asian sesame oil
- About 6 cups vegetable oil for deep-frying
- 1½ pounds green beans, trimmed
- 1 tablespoon minced garlic
- 2 teaspoons red pepper flakes
- 1 tablespoon minced peeled fresh ginger
- ⅓ pound ground pork
- 3 tablespoons minced scallion greens

SPECIAL EQUIPMENT: a deep-fat thermometer

Stir together sugar, salt, soy sauce, rice wine, and sesame oil in a small bowl.

Heat 2 inches vegetable oil in a wok (see Cook's Note) until it registers 375°F on thermometer. Fry beans, a small handful at a time, for 30 seconds. With a skimmer or slotted spoon, transfer to paper towels to drain. (Return oil to 375°F between batches.)

Pour all but 3 tablespoons oil into a saucepan to cool before you dispose of it. Heat remaining oil over high heat until hot but not smoking. Add garlic, red pepper flakes, and ginger and stir-fry for 10 seconds. Add pork and stir-fry, breaking up any lumps, until lightly browned, about 2 minutes. Add beans and stir-fry for 30 seconds. Add soy sauce mixture and scallion greens and stir-fry until beans are heated through and well coated with sauce, about 30 seconds.

COOK'S NOTE

■ If you don't have a wok, you can use a 5-quart pot for deep-frying and a 12-inch skillet for the stir-fry.

Honey-Glazed Wax Beans

SERVES 6

ACTIVE TIME: 15 MINUTES ■ START TO FINISH: 25 MINUTES

■ Wax beans are so subtle in flavor that you don't want to do too much to them. A little honey adds sweetness, and some lemon zest reinforces the sunny look of late summer. ■

- 1¼ pounds wax (yellow) or green beans, trimmed
- 1 tablespoon mild honey
- ¾ teaspoon finely grated lemon zest
- ¼ teaspoon salt

Cook beans in a 4-quart saucepan of boiling well-salted water until just tender, 6 to 8 minutes. Drain, then immediately toss with honey, lemon zest, and salt in a large bowl.

Beets with Lime Butter

SERVES 4

ACTIVE TIME: 15 MINUTES ■ START TO FINISH: 15 MINUTES

■ There's no getting around the fact that sweet, juicy beets leave their mark in the form of lurid fuchsia stains on hands and quite possibly a favorite white T-shirt. (This is where protective gloves and an apron come in handy.) But the deep, saturated color also makes beets such a painterly vegetable that it's worth it (think of serving beets in a heavy white earthenware bowl). This might be the fastest beet recipe on record, because the beets are grated before cooking. It's also one of the best, with the earthiness of the root vegetables set off by the sprightly lime juice and zest. ■

3 tablespoons unsalted butter
1½ pounds beets, peeled and coarsely grated (3½ cups)
¼ teaspoon finely grated lime zest
1 tablespoon fresh lime juice, or to taste
¾ teaspoon salt
¼ teaspoon freshly ground black pepper
OPTIONAL GARNISH: finely chopped scallion greens

Melt 2 tablespoons butter in a 10- to 12-inch heavy skillet over moderately high heat. Add beets and lime zest and cook, stirring, until beets are crisp-tender, about 5 minutes. Remove skillet from heat and stir in remaining 1 tablespoon butter, lime juice, salt, and pepper. Serve garnished with scallion greens, if desired.

Bok Choy with Soy Sauce and Butter

SERVES 4
ACTIVE TIME: 10 MINUTES ■ START TO FINISH: 10 MINUTES

■ Bok choy, one of the first Asian vegetables to burst out of Chinatown, is now found alongside Napa cabbage and kale in supermarket produce aisles throughout the country. With its brilliant green leaves and snowy white stalks, the vegetable virtually sells itself. Small green-stemmed Shanghai bok choy and miniature varieties (often called baby bok choy) are becoming increasingly available as well. ■

2 tablespoons water
1 tablespoon soy sauce
1 tablespoon oyster sauce
2 tablespoons vegetable oil
2 heads bok choy (2 pounds total), trimmed and cut crosswise into ¼-inch-thick slices
½ teaspoon salt
2 tablespoons unsalted butter

Stir together water and soy and oyster sauces in a small bowl.

Heat oil in a 10- to 12-inch heavy skillet over moderately high heat until hot but not smoking. Add bok choy and salt and stir-fry for 2 minutes. Add soy mixture and butter and stir-fry until bok choy is crisp-tender, 1 to 2 minutes.

Steamed Broccoli with Caper Brown Butter

SERVES 4
ACTIVE TIME: 20 MINUTES ■ START TO FINISH: 20 MINUTES

■ The term *brown butter* refers to butter that has been cooked to a light hazelnut color; that's why it's called *beurre noisette* in French. It smells divine and is an easy way to dress up a vegetable for company. The capers become tiny bullets of brine—they're tangy and bright in contrast to the brown butter. ■

1½ pounds broccoli
¾ stick (6 tablespoons) unsalted butter
3 tablespoons drained capers, chopped
3 tablespoons chopped fresh flat-leaf parsley
¼ teaspoon salt
⅛ teaspoon freshly ground black pepper

Cut stalks from broccoli and peel with a paring knife, trimming any fibrous parts, then cut into ¼-inch-thick slices. Cut heads of broccoli into 1½-inch-wide florets.

Steam broccoli stalks and florets in a steamer rack set over boiling water, covered, until tender, about 6 minutes.

Meanwhile, melt butter in a small saucepan over moderate heat. Stir in capers and cook, stirring occasionally, until butter is golden brown, about 4 minutes. Stir in parsley, salt, and pepper.

Toss broccoli with caper butter in a bowl.

Broccoli with Mustard Seeds and Horseradish

SERVES 4
ACTIVE TIME: 20 MINUTES ■ START TO FINISH: 20 MINUTES

■ This steamed broccoli with a warm dressing is so satisfying that some of us have been known to make a meal out of it. The technique of toasting the mustard seeds until they pop is borrowed from Indian cooking; it brings out the seeds' nuttiness and eliminates their bitter edge. You'll come across several different kinds of mustard seeds in an Indian market, but in this case the ones found at the supermarket are perfectly fine. ■

- 1½ pounds broccoli
- ¾ stick (6 tablespoons) unsalted butter
- 3 tablespoons mustard seeds
- 2 tablespoons drained bottled horseradish
- 1 tablespoon fresh lemon juice
- ⅛ teaspoon salt
- ⅛ teaspoon freshly ground black pepper

Cut stalks from broccoli and peel with a paring knife, trimming any fibrous parts, then cut into ¼-inch-thick slices. Cut heads of broccoli into 1½-inch-wide florets.

Steam broccoli stalks and florets in a steamer rack set over boiling water, covered, until tender, about 6 minutes.

Meanwhile, melt butter in a small saucepan over moderate heat. Stir in mustard seeds and cook, partially covered, swirling pan occasionally, until seeds just begin to pop and turn one shade darker, about 3 minutes. Stir in horseradish, lemon juice, salt, and pepper.

Toss broccoli with butter mixture in a bowl.

Spicy Sautéed Broccoli Rabe with Garlic

SERVES 4

ACTIVE TIME: 30 MINUTES ■ START TO FINISH: 30 MINUTES

■ Broccoli rabe is particularly prized in Italy, where it goes by numerous aliases, among them *rapini, cime di rapa,* and *broccoletti di rape.* This bitter green (which, despite its name, is more closely related to turnips than to regular broccoli) packs quite a wallop. Its mustardy bite, which has a tonic effect, provides a welcome counterpoint to rich or fatty foods. It has an affinity for garlic and is wonderful with pasta. ■

- 2 pounds broccoli rabe, trimmed and any hollow stems discarded
- 4 teaspoons olive oil
- 3 garlic cloves, minced
- ½ teaspoon red pepper flakes
- ¼ cup chicken stock or store-bought low-sodium broth
- ½ teaspoon salt

Cook broccoli rabe in a 6- to 8-quart pot of boiling salted water (1 tablespoon salt per every 4 quarts water) until stems are crisp-tender, about 5 minutes. Drain, then plunge into a large bowl of ice and cold water to stop the cooking; drain well.

Heat 2 teaspoons oil in a 12-inch nonstick skillet over moderately high heat until hot but not smoking. Add half of garlic and ¼ teaspoon red pepper flakes and cook, stirring, until garlic is golden, about 1 minute. Add half of broccoli rabe and 2 tablespoons broth and cook, stirring, until heated through, about 2 minutes.

Transfer to a serving dish, then cook remaining broccoli rabe in same manner. Sprinkle with salt.

VARIATION

■ Substitute broccoli for the broccoli rabe. Cut the heads of broccoli into 2-inch-wide florets. Trim and peel the stalks and cut into ¼-inch-thick slices. Cook in the same manner.

Brussels Sprout Chiffonade

SERVES 4 TO 6

ACTIVE TIME: 25 MINUTES ■ START TO FINISH: 25 MINUTES

■ Bending over a cutting board slicing Brussels sprouts into shreds might seem silly, but the result is a quick-cooking, bright-looking, fluffy slaw. (The French term *chiffonade* means, literally, "made of rags.") The lime juice and cumin add lively notes, making this a terrific dish for very early spring, when steamed Brussels sprouts and other winter vegetables have lost their appeal and the tender young green things haven't yet arrived. ■

- 1 pound Brussels sprouts
- ½ stick (4 tablespoons) unsalted butter
- 1 teaspoon cumin seeds
- ½ teaspoon salt
- ¼ teaspoon freshly ground black pepper
- 1 tablespoon fresh lime juice

Trim Brussels sprouts and halve lengthwise, then cut lengthwise into very thin slices.

Heat 2 tablespoons butter in a 12-inch heavy skillet over moderately high heat until foam subsides. Add half of sprouts, ½ teaspoon cumin seeds, ¼ teaspoon salt, and ⅛ teaspoon pepper and cook, stirring occasionally, until sprouts are tender, 3 to 5 minutes. Transfer to a serving bowl. Cook remaining sprouts with remaining ingredients in same manner. Transfer to bowl and stir in lime juice and salt and pepper to taste.

Pan-Browned Brussels Sprouts

SERVES 2 OR 3
ACTIVE TIME: 20 MINUTES ■ START TO FINISH: 35 MINUTES

■ These golden-brown nuggets are so nutlike in flavor that you could almost serve them with drinks. The recipe is from John Dombek, of Santa Clara, Utah, who claims that a number of Brussels sprouts detractors were transformed by his recipe. We believe we've made a few converts as well. ■

- 1½ tablespoons unsalted butter
- 1 tablespoon olive oil
- 2 large garlic cloves, thinly sliced
- ½ pound Brussels sprouts, trimmed and halved lengthwise
- 2 tablespoons pine nuts
- Salt and freshly ground black pepper

Melt 1 tablespoon butter with oil in a 10-inch heavy skillet, preferably cast-iron, over moderate heat. Add garlic and cook, stirring, until pale golden, about 3 minutes. With a slotted spoon, transfer to a small bowl.

Reduce heat to low, arrange sprouts cut sides down in skillet in one layer, and sprinkle with pine nuts and salt to taste. Cook, uncovered, without turning, until sprouts are crisp-tender and undersides are golden brown, 10 to 15 minutes. With tongs, transfer sprouts, browned sides up, to a plate, leaving pine nuts in pan.

Add remaining ½ tablespoon butter to skillet and cook nuts over moderate heat, stirring, until evenly pale golden, about 1 minute. Stir in garlic, then spoon mixture over sprouts and season with pepper.

Winter Vegetables with Horseradish Dill Butter

SERVES 6 TO 8
ACTIVE TIME: 20 MINUTES ■ START TO FINISH: 40 MINUTES

■ Vinegar, horseradish, and butter do great things for winter vegetables, and this dish has zip and color. It's delicious with corned beef or pot roast. ■

- 1½ pounds small red potatoes
- 1 pound carrots, peeled and cut diagonally into 1-inch-long pieces
- 1 pound Brussels sprouts, trimmed and halved lengthwise
- ¾–1 pound parsnips, peeled and cut into 2-by-1-inch sticks
- ½ pound small turnips, peeled and cut into 1-inch-thick wedges
- ¾ stick (6 tablespoons) unsalted butter
- 2 tablespoons drained bottled horseradish
- 1½ tablespoons cider vinegar
- 2 tablespoons minced fresh dill
- 1¾ teaspoons salt
- Freshly ground black pepper

SPECIAL EQUIPMENT: 2 large steamer racks

Set steamer racks over boiling water in two 4-quart saucepans. Quarter potatoes. Steam potatoes and carrots in one rack, covered, and steam Brussels sprouts, parsnips, and turnips in other rack, covered, until just tender, 18 to 24 minutes.

Melt butter in a small saucepan over moderate heat, then stir in horseradish, vinegar, dill, salt, and pepper to taste. Toss steamed vegetables with butter mixture in a large bowl.

COOK'S NOTE

■ The vegetables can be kept warm on a large baking sheet with sides, loosely covered, in a 200°F oven until you are ready to serve.

Crisp Sautéed Cabbage with Caraway

SERVES 4

ACTIVE TIME: 20 MINUTES ■ START TO FINISH: 20 MINUTES

■ Slicing a vegetable like cabbage or Brussels sprouts into thin strips or shreds is one of our favorite culinary techniques. Treated this way, the vegetable cooks quickly yet retains texture. Short cooking also seems to cut down on the aggressive smell that gives cabbage a reputation for being difficult. Caraway—warm, sweet, and pungent—is characteristic of many German and Austrian dishes. ■

- 2 tablespoons unsalted butter
- 2 tablespoons vegetable oil
- 2 medium onions, coarsely chopped
- 1 tablespoon caraway seeds
- 1 small head green cabbage (2 pounds), cored and very thinly sliced
- 3/4 teaspoon salt
- 1/4 teaspoon freshly ground black pepper
- 2 teaspoons fresh lemon juice

HOW TO CHOP AN ONION

Choose a knife with a wide blade and nice balance — that way, its weight will do most of the work — and make sure it is sharp. (No, you really shouldn't use the food processor; you'll end up with a mixture of onion chunks and slush.)

Prep the onion: Beginning at the root end, cut the onion lengthwise in half (1). Then, starting at the blossom end (opposite the root end) of each half, peel off all the papery skin and the leathery outermost layer just under the papery skin, including the sheer, sticky membrane. That outer layer will never become tender, and the sheer one can cause your knife to slip. Put each half cut side down on a cutting board and cut off the tip of the blossom end; leave the root end intact.

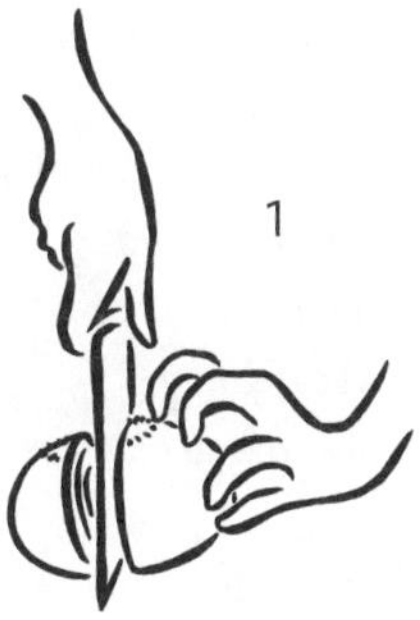
1

Chop the onion: Holding the knife parallel to the cutting board, make a series of even parallel cuts in the onion, stopping the knife short of the root end (2). The root keeps the onion layers together and provides a kind of button to grasp as you work. Again stopping short of the root end, make a series of lengthwise cuts in the onion (3). Next, slice across the cuts you just made, and watch perfectly diced onion fall from your blade (4). (Be sure to curl the fingers holding the onion under while you're slicing to protect them.) You can slice all the way to the root button, which you can now discard. Repeat with the second onion half.

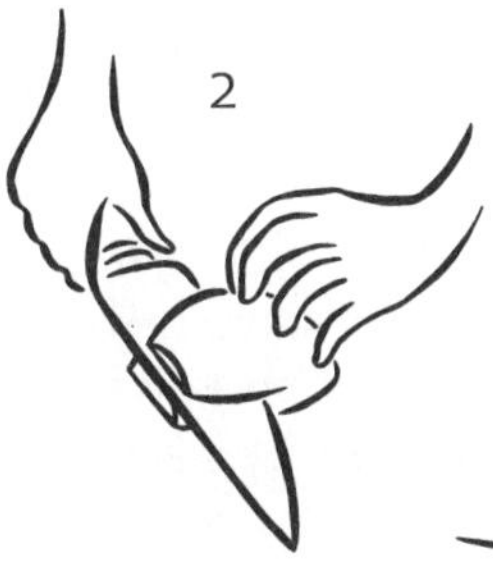
2

3

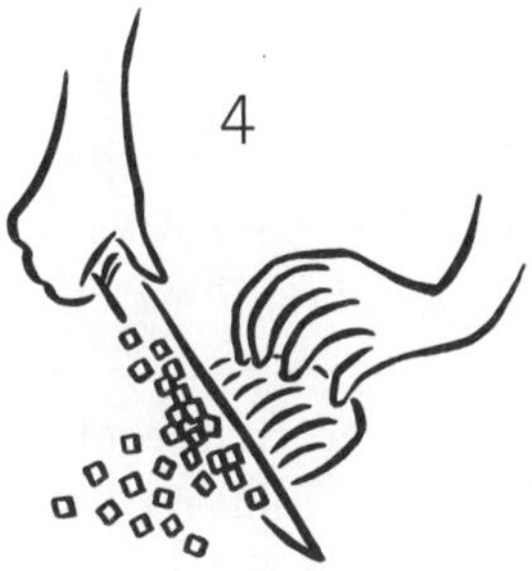
4

Why is uniformity so important? The more regular the pieces, the more evenly they will cook. Or if the pieces are to be left raw — destined for a salsa, for instance — they will look much prettier.

Melt butter with oil in a deep 12-inch heavy skillet over moderately low heat. Add onions and cook, stirring, until softened, 3 to 4 minutes. Add caraway, cabbage, salt, and pepper, increase heat to moderately high, and cook, stirring, until cabbage is crisp-tender, 5 to 7 minutes. Sprinkle with lemon juice.

Sautéed Cabbage with Bacon and Cream

SERVES 4

ACTIVE TIME: 15 MINUTES ■ START TO FINISH: 25 MINUTES

■ This dish is so rich that you'll want to serve it with something rather plain, such as roast pork or chicken, instead of something sumptuous and meaty, like rib eye. ■

- 1/4 pound bacon (4 slices), cut crosswise into 1/2-inch-wide pieces
- 1 small head green cabbage (2 pounds), cored and very thinly sliced
- 1 teaspoon salt
- 1/2 cup heavy cream
- Freshly ground black pepper

Cook bacon in a deep 12-inch heavy skillet over moderately high heat, stirring, until golden, 3 to 4 minutes. Add cabbage and salt and cook over moderate heat, stirring, until cabbage is wilted, about 3 minutes. Add cream, reduce heat to moderately low, cover, and cook, stirring occasionally, until cabbage is tender, 10 to 15 minutes more. Season with salt and pepper.

Braised Red Cabbage

SERVES 8

ACTIVE TIME: 30 MINUTES ■ START TO FINISH: 1 3/4 HOURS

■ Red cabbage recipes generally contain some sort of acid—vinegar, wine, or fruit—to brighten the vegetable's beautiful color. Cooked until meltingly tender, it is a classic side dish for roasts, especially goose and venison. ■

- 1 medium head red cabbage (3 1/2 pounds), quartered, cored, and thinly sliced crosswise
- 1/4 pound bacon (4 slices), chopped
- 1 tablespoon unsalted butter
- 2 large sweet onions, thinly sliced
- 1/2 cup white wine vinegar
- 3 tablespoons packed brown sugar
- 1 tablespoon salt
- 1 teaspoon freshly ground black pepper

Rinse cabbage under cold water, then drain; do not pat dry.

Cook bacon in a 6- to 8-quart heavy pot over moderately low heat, stirring, until crisp, about 3 minutes. With a slotted spoon, transfer bacon to paper towels to drain. Add butter to bacon fat, increase heat to moderate, and add onions. Cook, stirring, until golden brown, 12 to 15 minutes. Stir in cabbage, vinegar, brown sugar, salt, and pepper, cover, and simmer, stirring occasionally, until cabbage is tender, about 1 1/4 hours.

Sprinkle cabbage with bacon just before serving.

COOK'S NOTE

■ The cabbage can be cooked up to 1 day ahead. Cool, uncovered, then refrigerate, covered. Refrigerate bacon separately, covered. Bring bacon to room temperature before using and reheat cabbage over moderate heat, stirring occasionally.

Carrots Vichy

SERVES 4

ACTIVE TIME: 25 MINUTES ■ START TO FINISH: 25 MINUTES

■ This dish has a fancy name, but it couldn't be homier. It's simply thinly sliced carrots covered with a bit of water, butter, and sugar and cooked until the water has evaporated and the carrots are coated with a translucent glaze. Traditionally, the water would be Vichy brand mineral water, because its high sodium content is thought to bring out the vegetable's delicate flavor, but we found the carrots delicious with plain tap water. ■

- 1 1/2 pounds carrots, peeled if desired and cut diagonally into 1/8-inch-thick slices

2 tablespoons unsalted butter
¼ cup water
1 teaspoon sugar
¼ teaspoon salt, or to taste

Combine carrots, butter, water, and sugar in a 3-quart heavy saucepan, cover, and cook over moderately low heat, stirring occasionally, until most of liquid has evaporated and carrots are tender, about 15 minutes.

Remove lid, increase heat to moderately high, and cook, stirring occasionally, until carrots are glazed, 3 to 5 minutes more. Remove from heat and stir in salt.

Moroccan-Style Carrots

SERVES 4 TO 6
ACTIVE TIME: 20 MINUTES ■ START TO FINISH: 40 MINUTES (INCLUDES COOLING)

■ Only small amounts of seasonings are needed here to give an exotic impression, and you don't have to make a trip to a specialty market for the spices. With very little effort, you've made a side dish (ideal with grilled fish) that is much more satisfying than plain steamed carrots. ■

2 pounds carrots, peeled if desired and cut into 3-by-½-inch sticks
1 medium garlic clove, minced
2 tablespoons olive oil
½ teaspoon ground cumin
¼ teaspoon ground cinnamon
1 teaspoon honey or sugar
Pinch of cayenne
1½ teaspoons fresh lemon juice, or to taste
Salt and freshly ground black pepper

Steam carrots, covered, in a steamer rack set over boiling water until just tender, 6 to 8 minutes. Remove from heat.

Cook garlic in oil in a 12-inch heavy skillet over moderate heat, stirring, until fragrant, about 1 minute. Add cumin, cinnamon, honey, cayenne, and carrots and cook, stirring, until carrots are well coated, about 2 minutes. Stir in lemon juice and salt and pepper to taste, then transfer carrots to a bowl and cool to room temperature before serving.

Roasted Carrots and Parsnips with Herbs

SERVES 8
ACTIVE TIME: 15 MINUTES ■ START TO FINISH: 1¼ HOURS

■ Roasting does wonders for plebeian root vegetables, making them intensely flavorful but mellow. Parsnips, for example, caramelize on the outside, becoming ever so slightly bitter, while turning sweet and creamy inside. ■

2 pounds parsnips
2 pounds medium carrots, peeled if desired and cut diagonally into ¾-inch-long pieces
⅓ cup extra-virgin olive oil
2 teaspoons chopped fresh rosemary
2 teaspoons chopped fresh sage
2 teaspoons salt
2 teaspoons freshly ground black pepper
¼ cup water

Put a rack in lower third of oven and preheat oven to 350°F.

Peel parsnips. Halve each one crosswise at the point where it becomes narrow. Cut narrow portions diagonally into ¾-inch-long pieces. Quarter wider portions lengthwise, core, and cut diagonally into ¾-inch-long pieces.

Toss parsnips and carrots with oil, rosemary, sage, salt, and pepper in a large bowl. Spread on a large baking sheet with sides and add water. Roast vegetables, stirring occasionally, until tender, 50 to 55 minutes.

Carrot Purée

SERVES 4 TO 6
ACTIVE TIME: 25 MINUTES ■ START TO FINISH: 25 MINUTES

■ Everyone loves this simple purée: children devour it because it doesn't look virtuous, and grown-ups appreciate the way a small amount of cream turns a kitchen staple into something lush and elegant. We think this recipe alone justifies having a food processor. ■

- 2½ pounds carrots, peeled if desired and cut into ⅓-inch-thick slices
- 5 tablespoons heavy cream
- ¼ teaspoon salt
- ⅛ teaspoon freshly grated nutmeg, or to taste

Cook carrots in a 4-quart saucepan of boiling well-salted water to cover by 1 inch until very tender, about 15 minutes. Drain and transfer to a blender or food processor.

Purée carrots (use caution) with cream, salt, and nutmeg just until smooth.

Roasted Cauliflower with Garlic

SERVES 10

ACTIVE TIME: 15 MINUTES ■ START TO FINISH: 1 HOUR

■ This recipe is simple, straightforward, and just as delicious with prime rib or beef tenderloin as it is with the Thanksgiving turkey. If the sulfurous smell of cauliflower and other members of the cabbage family bothers you, relax; roasting the vegetable in the oven until it is rich and golden gives it a nutty aroma. ■

- 3 medium heads cauliflower (6 pounds total), cored and cut into 2-inch-wide florets
- ½ cup olive oil
- 4 garlic cloves, minced
- ½ teaspoon salt
- ¼ teaspoon freshly ground black pepper

Position racks in upper and lower thirds of oven and preheat oven to 425°F.

Toss cauliflower with oil, garlic, salt, and pepper in a large bowl. Spread evenly on two baking sheets with sides. Roast, stirring occasionally and switching position of sheets halfway through roasting, until cauliflower is golden and crisp-tender, 25 to 30 minutes.

Cauliflower with Cheddar Sauce and Rye Bread Crumbs

SERVES 8

ACTIVE TIME: 40 MINUTES ■ START TO FINISH: 1½ HOURS

■ "Cauliflower cheese" is generally thought of as stodgy comfort food best left in Barbara Pym novels, but toasted rye bread crumbs make all the difference. The dish is especially flavorful if you use rye bread with caraway seeds. ■

- 3 slices rye bread, finely ground in a food processor
- 3 cups whole milk
- ½ stick (4 tablespoons) unsalted butter
- 1 small onion, finely chopped
- 2 tablespoons all-purpose flour
- ½ teaspoon salt
- ¼ teaspoon freshly ground black pepper
- 2 cups coarsely grated sharp Cheddar (about 6 ounces)
- 1½ medium heads cauliflower (3 pounds total), cored and cut into 2-inch-wide florets

Put a rack in middle of oven and preheat oven to 350°F.

Toast bread crumbs on a baking sheet with sides until golden, about 5 minutes. Cool on sheet on a rack.

Bring milk just to a boil in a 1½-quart saucepan; remove from heat. Melt 2 tablespoons butter in a 2- to 3-quart heavy saucepan over moderately low heat, add onion, and cook, stirring, until softened, about 5 minutes. Reduce heat to low and stir in flour, salt, and pepper. Cook, stirring, for 3 minutes to make a roux. Add milk in a steady stream, whisking constantly, and whisk until sauce is smooth. Simmer, whisking occasionally, for 20 minutes.

Add Cheddar and cook, stirring, until just melted. Remove from heat, cover surface of sauce with wax paper (to prevent a skin from forming), and let cool.

Preheat oven to 400°F. Butter a 2½-quart baking dish.

Cook cauliflower in a 4- to 5-quart heavy pot of boiling well-salted water until tender, about 10 minutes. With a slotted spoon, transfer cauliflower to a bowl of ice and cold water to stop the cooking, then drain well and pat dry. Transfer to buttered baking dish.

Melt remaining 2 tablespoons butter and toss with bread crumbs in a small bowl. Pour Cheddar sauce over cauliflower and sprinkle with bread crumbs. Bake until sauce is bubbling, about 15 minutes.

COOK'S NOTES

- The bread crumbs can be made up to 1 week ahead and kept in an airtight container at room temperature.
- The Cheddar sauce can be made up to 2 days ahead and refrigerated, covered. Bring to room temperature before using.
- The cauliflower can be boiled up to 1 day ahead and refrigerated, covered. Bring to room temperature before using.

Cauliflower with Ginger and Mustard Seeds

SERVES 6

ACTIVE TIME: 15 MINUTES ■ START TO FINISH: 25 MINUTES

■ It's no surprise that cauliflower is a favored vegetable in India; its mild flavor takes beautifully to bold spices like mustard seeds and ginger. Mustard seeds, like any other seeds, contain oil and can turn rancid easily. If digging around in your cupboard produces a jar bought ages ago, take a whiff to make sure the seeds are still fresh before using. ■

- 3 tablespoons vegetable oil
- 2 teaspoons black mustard seeds (see Glossary) or yellow mustard seeds
- 2 teaspoons grated peeled fresh ginger
- ½ teaspoon turmeric
- 1 medium head cauliflower (2 pounds), cored and cut into 1-inch-wide florets
- ½ cup water
- 1½ teaspoons fresh lemon juice, or to taste
- ¼ teaspoon salt
- ¼ teaspoon freshly ground black pepper
- 3 tablespoons chopped fresh cilantro (optional)

Heat oil in a 12-inch heavy skillet over moderate heat until hot but not smoking. Add mustard seeds, cover, and cook, stirring occasionally, until they pop and popping subsides, about 1½ minutes. Add ginger and turmeric and cook, stirring, until fragrant, about 30 seconds. Add cauliflower, stirring to coat with oil. Add water, cover, and steam cauliflower, adding more water a few tablespoons at a time if it evaporates, until just tender, 6 to 10 minutes. Season with lemon juice, salt, and pepper, and stir in cilantro, if desired.

Cauliflower Purée

SERVES 4

ACTIVE TIME: 10 MINUTES ■ START TO FINISH: 20 MINUTES

■ The term *boiled* is too often a synonym for "carelessly cooked." That's not the case here. The cauliflower is simmered in chicken stock for just ten minutes before being turned into a silken purée. ■

- 1 medium head cauliflower (2 pounds), cored and chopped (about 11 cups)
- 3 garlic cloves, smashed
- 1⅓ cups chicken stock or store-bought low-sodium broth
- 1 teaspoon salt
- 5 tablespoons heavy cream
- 1 tablespoon unsalted butter

Combine cauliflower, garlic, stock, and salt in a 3- to 4-quart heavy saucepan, bring to a simmer, and simmer, covered, until cauliflower is very tender, about 10 minutes.

Purée mixture with cream and butter in a food processor until smooth (use caution), or, for a coarser purée, mash together with a potato masher or a fork. Season with salt.

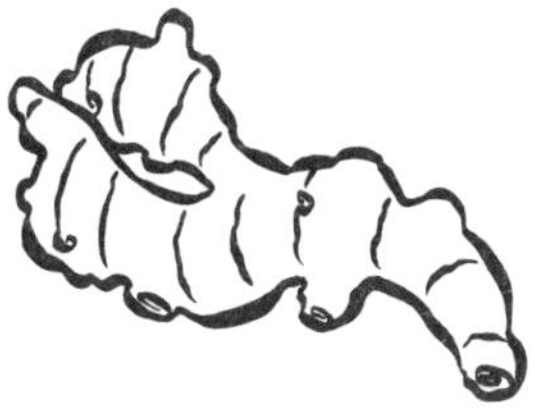

Celery Victor

SERVES 6
ACTIVE TIME: 15 MINUTES ■ START TO FINISH: 2½ HOURS (INCLUDES CHILLING)

■ This is our take on the suave San Francisco original created around 1916 at the Hotel St. Francis by the chef Victor Hirtzler. It's often served topped with anchovies, but we love the way it tastes without them. ■

- 3 celery hearts with leaves (1½ pounds total), ribs cut into 3-inch-long pieces, leaves reserved
- About 3 cups chicken stock or store-bought low-sodium broth
- 3 tablespoons Dijon mustard
- 1 teaspoon sugar
- 1½ tablespoons canola oil
- Salt and freshly ground black pepper
- 1 tablespoon finely chopped fresh chives

Arrange celery ribs in one layer in a 12-inch heavy skillet and add just enough stock to cover. Bring to a boil, then reduce heat, cover, and simmer gently until celery is tender, 8 to 10 minutes.

Transfer celery and broth to a bowl and refrigerate, uncovered, until cold, at least 2 hours.

Whisk together mustard, sugar, and 3 tablespoons celery cooking broth in a small bowl until sugar is dissolved. Add oil in a slow stream, whisking until well blended. Season with salt and pepper. Stir in chives.

With a slotted spoon, transfer celery to plates, drizzle with vinaigrette, and scatter celery leaves on top.

COOK'S NOTES

- The cooked celery can be refrigerated for up to 1 day. Cover celery after 2 hours.
- The vinaigrette can be made up to 1 day ahead and refrigerated, covered. Bring to room temperature before using.

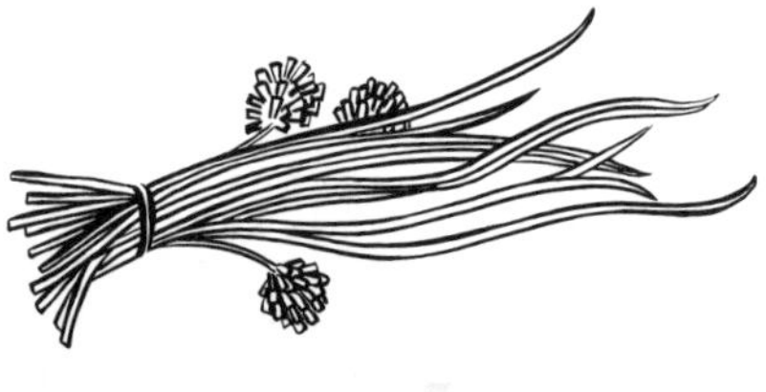

Celery and Fennel with Bacon

SERVES 8
ACTIVE TIME: 1 HOUR ■ START TO FINISH: 1 HOUR

■ Celery and fennel are assertive, aromatic vegetables that work well together. In this recipe, they're first blanched to tame their herbaceous character, then cooked in smoky bacon drippings until softened and unctuous. Fennel is sometimes (mis)labeled "anise" at supermarkets; the plants are related botanically but are not the same thing. Serve as a midwinter accompaniment to fish. ■

- 1 bunch celery, with leaves
- 2 large fennel bulbs, with stalks and fronds attached
- ¼ pound bacon (4 slices), cut into ½-inch-wide pieces
- 1 cup chopped shallots
- 1 cup chicken stock or store-bought low-sodium broth
- ¼ cup coarsely chopped fresh flat-leaf parsley
- Salt and freshly ground black pepper

Trim celery, reserving ½ cup leaves. Remove strings from celery with vegetable peeler, then cut into 3-by-¼-inch sticks.

Trim enough fronds from fennel to make ½ cup; reserve. Cut off fennel stalks. Cut any brown spots from outer layers of bulbs and quarter bulbs lengthwise. Cut out most of cores, leaving just enough to hold layers together. Cut bulbs lengthwise into ¼-inch-wide slices.

Cook celery in a 4-quart saucepan of boiling well-salted water for 2 minutes. With a slotted spoon, transfer to a bowl of ice and cold water to stop the cooking. Return water to a boil and cook fennel for 2 minutes, then transfer to another bowl of ice and cold water. When vegetables are cool, drain both in a colander.

Cook bacon in a 6- to 8-quart heavy pot over moderate heat until crisp. With slotted spoon, transfer to paper towels to drain. Add shallots to bacon fat and cook, stirring, until softened, 2 to 3 minutes. Add celery and fennel and cook, stirring, until vegetables begin to brown, about 10 minutes. Add stock and simmer, uncovered, stirring frequently, until vegetables are just tender, 12 to 15 minutes.

Meanwhile, coarsely chop reserved celery leaves

and fennel fronds. Remove pot from heat and stir in leaves and fronds, parsley, bacon, and salt and pepper to taste.

COOK'S NOTE

- The celery and fennel can be cut (but not cooked) up to 1 day ahead and refrigerated separately in large sealable plastic bags lined with paper towels.

Roasted Celery Root

SERVES 6

ACTIVE TIME: 10 MINUTES ■ START TO FINISH: 1¾ HOURS

■ Celery root is closely related to bunch celery, but its gnarled, spherical, rather intimidating shape belies the hauntingly mild celery flavor held within. Roasted, it becomes very tender in texture, not starchy, like many other root vegetables. ■

- 4 pounds celery root (celeriac), peeled with a sharp knife and cut into 1-inch cubes
- ⅓ cup vegetable oil
- 1 teaspoon salt

Put a rack in middle of oven and preheat oven to 425°F.

Toss celery root with oil and salt in a large roasting pan. Roast for 30 minutes.

Stir celery root, reduce temperature to 375°F, and roast, stirring after 30 minutes, until celery root is tender, about 1 hour more. Season with salt.

Creamed Chayote with Chives

SERVES 6

ACTIVE TIME: 25 MINUTES ■ START TO FINISH: 25 MINUTES

■ Chayote is typically served stuffed in New Orleans or the Caribbean, but its mild, subtle, crisp flesh becomes flavorful and soft when it's cooked with cream, as here. (For more about chayote, see page 534.) Serve this with grilled meats. ■

CELERY ROOT

Celery root, sometimes called celeriac, and regular stalk celery are different varieties of the same plant. Celery root is milder in flavor than stalk celery, with a dense, fine-grained sweetness when eaten raw (as in the classic rémoulade) and an incomparable velvety texture when cooked; it lends great body and finesse to soups. A gnarled sphere of celery root is usually sandy, so scrub it well and give it a solid footing on the cutting board by lopping off top and bottom. A sharp small knife is the best tool for peeling celery root: guide the knife blade in a single sweep from top to bottom, hugging the curves and removing one slice of peel at a time, working around the sphere. To cut celery root into matchsticks or julienne strips, slice a whole peeled one into even planks with a large knife. Stack the planks three or four at a time and cut into thin strips about the same thickness as the planks. The flesh of celery root will oxidize quickly; if you are peeling more than one, transfer them to a bowl of lemon water as you work to keep them from turning brown.

3 chayotes (2½ pounds total)
2 tablespoons vegetable oil
¾ cup heavy cream
3 tablespoons chopped fresh chives
Salt

Halve chayotes lengthwise and discard seeds, then cut crosswise into ¼-inch-thick slices.

Heat oil in a 12-inch heavy skillet over moderate heat until hot but not smoking. Add chayote and cook, stirring frequently, until crisp-tender, 5 to 8 minutes. Add cream and simmer, stirring occasionally, until chayote is tender and cream is slightly thickened, about 3 minutes. Add chives and season with salt.

Brown-Buttered Corn with Basil

SERVES 4

ACTIVE TIME: 15 MINUTES ■ START TO FINISH: 15 MINUTES

■ Everyone knows what corn on the cob with butter tastes like, and it's hard to beat. But browning the butter and then sautéing corn kernels in it ratchets up the flavor, while adding shreds of basil at the last minute keeps the dish fresh and tasting of summer. ■

2 tablespoons unsalted butter
3 cups corn kernels (from about 4 ears)
¼ teaspoon salt
⅛ teaspoon freshly ground black pepper
1 cup finely shredded fresh basil

Heat butter in a 12-inch heavy skillet over moderately high heat until foam subsides and most of butter is golden brown. Add corn, season with salt and pepper, and cook, stirring, until tender, about 4 minutes. Remove from heat and stir in basil.

Creamy Corn with Sugar Snap Peas and Scallions

SERVES 8

ACTIVE TIME: 30 MINUTES ■ START TO FINISH: 40 MINUTES

■ This is as far as you can possibly get from opening a can and heating what comes out. And it is absolutely worth the work. (We find that the easiest way to remove corn kernels from the cob is to lay the ear on the cutting board and cut the kernels off the side, turning the cob as you go.) Sugar snaps provide a verdant counterpoint to the sweet creamed fresh corn. ■

1½ pounds sugar snap peas, trimmed
6 ears corn, shucked
½ cup heavy cream
1 bunch scallions, thinly sliced
1½ teaspoons kosher salt
1½ teaspoons freshly ground black pepper

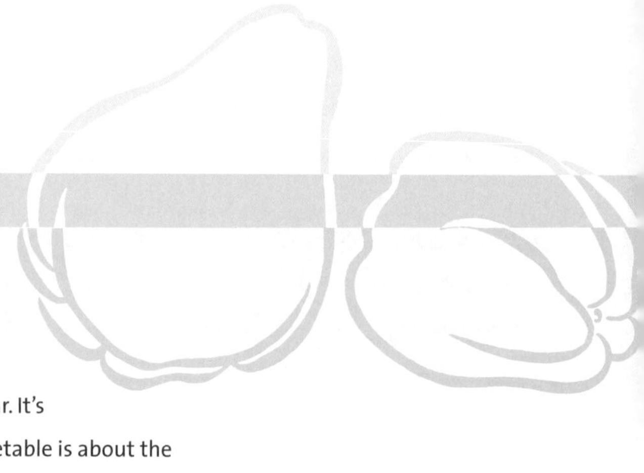

Chayote

Chayote (pronounced "chai-*oh*-teh"), a member of the enormous gourd family, is a culinary chameleon — its names include *mirliton* (Louisiana and the French Caribbean), *christophene* and *chocho* (English Caribbean), *cayote* (Spanish Caribbean), and vegetable pear. It's so beautiful that it practically compels you to cook with it: the vegetable is about the size of a pear but rounder, with furrowed sides, and most often apple green in color. Sauté or grill slices as you would zucchini. You can treat it as a bland foil for spicy foods or accentuate its creaminess with long, slow cooking. Young, tender chayote needs no peeling, but if you find some with prickly bits, trim them off with a vegetable peeler.

Cook sugar snap peas in 3 batches in a 4- to 5-quart pot of boiling well-salted water until crisp-tender, about 1 minute per batch (return water to a boil between batches). With a slotted spoon, transfer to a large bowl of ice and cold water to stop the cooking. Drain sugar snaps and pat dry with paper towels.

Cook corn in same pot of boiling water until just tender, about 3 minutes. With tongs, transfer to another bowl of ice and cold water. Drain corn, pat dry with paper towels, and cut off kernels.

Just before serving, combine cream and scallions in same pot, bring to a boil, and boil over high heat until slightly thickened, about 2 minutes. Add sugar snaps, corn, salt, and pepper and cook, tossing, until vegetables are coated and heated through, about 2 minutes.

COOK'S NOTE

- The sugar snaps and corn can be cooked up to 1 day ahead and refrigerated separately in sealed plastic bags lined with paper towels.

CORN: WHAT TO LOOK FOR

Frenzied shoppers stripping husks from ears of corn and tossing the rejected ears back on the heap are an all-too-common sight at farmers markets. But this corn carnage results in ruined ears: the husks preserve the fresh sweetness of the kernels, which begin to dry out as soon as they are exposed to air. You can tell if plump, even rows of kernels fill out the whole cob simply by feeling the top of the ear through the husk. Examine the ears carefully for freshness. The stems should look recently cut, not dried out; the husks should be vibrant green and slightly damp; and the brown silk exposed at the top should feel slightly sticky. The occasional harmless worm — a happy sign that the cornfield wasn't overloaded with chemical pesticides — is easily removed along with the silk. If you can't serve the corn right away, store it, unhusked, in a plastic bag in the coldest part of the fridge. The chill will slow down the conversion of sugar to starch, which begins soon after the ears are picked.

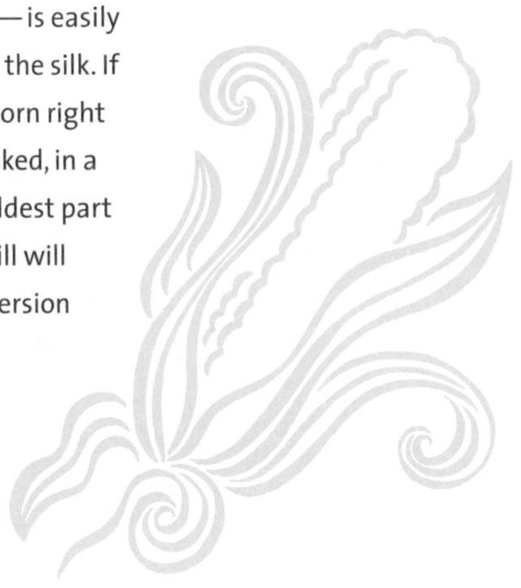

Creamless Creamy Corn with Chives

SERVES 4

ACTIVE TIME: 30 MINUTES ■ START TO FINISH: 30 MINUTES

■ The creaminess comes from the milky starch in the corn itself. This is the essence of fresh corn; the recipe serves four, but you might not want to share. ■

- 4 ears corn, shucked
- 1/4 teaspoon salt
- 3/4 teaspoon cornstarch
- Pinch of sugar (optional)
- 2 tablespoons unsalted butter
- 1/4 cup finely chopped onion
- 1/3 cup water
- Freshly ground black pepper
- 2 tablespoons finely chopped fresh chives

Working with 1 ear at a time, lay cob on its side on a cutting board and cut off kernels with a large knife, rotating cob as you go. Transfer kernels to a medium bowl, then hold cob upright in bowl and scrape with knife to extract "milk."

Transfer 2 cups corn kernels to a food processor and purée for 2 minutes, scraping down sides once or twice. Force purée through a fine-mesh sieve into a bowl; discard solids. Stir in salt, cornstarch, and sugar, if using.

Melt butter in a 2- to 3-quart saucepan over moderately low heat. Add onion and cook, stirring occasionally, until softened, about 3 minutes. Add remaining corn kernels, corn milk, and water, cover, and simmer briskly, stirring occasionally, until corn is crisp-tender, 4 to 5 minutes.

Stir corn purée, then stir into corn kernels. Bring to a boil, stirring, then reduce heat and simmer, stirring frequently, for 2 minutes. (If desired, thin with water.) Season with pepper and stir in chives.

Chive Corn Pudding

SERVES 8

ACTIVE TIME: 25 MINUTES ■ START TO FINISH: 1¾ HOURS

■ No, there isn't a mistake in the ingredients list below: it does include a vanilla bean. And no, this is not a dessert: the vanilla is almost undetectable but enhances the sweetness of the corn. You can make this savory pudding with frozen corn as well as farm-fresh ears and enjoy it whenever you are yearning for summer. It's as great a side dish for roast beef as it is for a steak on the grill. ■

- 4 cups fresh corn kernels (from 6 ears) or 2 (10-ounce) packages frozen corn kernels, thawed
- ¼ cup sugar
- 1¼ teaspoons salt
- ½ vanilla bean, halved lengthwise (optional)
- 2 cups whole milk
- 4 large eggs
- ½ stick (4 tablespoons) unsalted butter, melted and cooled
- 3 tablespoons all-purpose flour
- ¼ cup chopped fresh chives
- Pinch of freshly grated nutmeg

OPTIONAL GARNISH: chopped fresh chives

Put a rack in middle of oven and preheat oven to 350°F. Butter a 1½-quart quiche dish or 10-inch pie plate.

Pulse half of corn in a food processor until coarsely chopped. Transfer to a large bowl and stir in remaining corn kernels, sugar, and salt.

Scrape seeds from vanilla bean, if using, into a medium bowl. Add milk, eggs, butter, flour, and chives and whisk together. Add to corn and stir until well combined. Pour mixture into buttered dish and sprinkle with nutmeg.

Bake pudding on a baking sheet until center is just set, 50 minutes to 1 hour. Let stand for 15 minutes before serving.

Sprinkle pudding with chopped chives, if desired.

COOK'S NOTE

■ The pudding can be baked up to 1 day ahead. Cool, uncovered, then refrigerate, covered. Reheat in a 350°F oven for 15 minutes, or reheat in a microwave.

Corn on the Cob with Cheese and Lime

SERVES 4

ACTIVE TIME: 35 MINUTES ■ START TO FINISH: 45 MINUTES

■ Grilled ears of corn rolled in a spiced cream and then in grated cheese are a popular street snack in Mexico. They translate well as a first course at a backyard barbecue, although they're so irresistible that some guests might not want to move on to the main event. *Crema* is a thin cultured Mexican cream with an almost nutty flavor; it's available at Latino markets, but for this recipe, mayonnaise is an able substitute. We also call for *cotija*, a crumbly, salty aged cheese that ranges in consistency from soft to hard, depending on the producer. (We use Los Fortales, a hard variety available at cheese shops and some specialty foods shops.) Feel free to substitute feta, which is much more widely available. The *crema* and cheese, as well as a squeeze of fresh lime juice, have tangy notes that counter the sweetness of the corn. ■

- 4 ears corn in the husk
- ¼ cup *crema* (see above) or mayonnaise
- ⅛ teaspoon cayenne, or to taste
- 3 ounces *cotija* (see above) or feta

ACCOMPANIMENT: lime wedges

Prepare a charcoal or gas grill: If using a charcoal grill, open vents in bottom of grill, then light charcoal. Fire is medium-hot when you can hold your hand 5 inches above rack for just 3 to 4 seconds. If using a gas grill, preheat all burners on high, covered, for 10 minutes.

Pull husks back from corn, leaving them attached at base, and discard silks. Wrap husks back around ears and soak in water to cover for 10 minutes. Drain well.

Lightly oil grill rack. Grill corn (in husks), uncovered, turning occasionally to brown evenly, for 10 minutes. Carefully pull back husks and grill corn, turning occasionally, until kernels are browned and tender, about 5 minutes more.

Meanwhile, whisk together *crema* and cayenne in a small bowl. Grate *cotija* using the small teardrop-shaped holes on a box grater, or finely crumble feta.

Brush *crema* onto hot corn and sprinkle with cheese. Serve with lime wedges.

Corn on the Cob with Garlic Ancho Butter

SERVES 8

ACTIVE TIME: 20 MINUTES ■ START TO FINISH: 1 HOUR

■ Who would have thought that corn on the cob could be sophisticated? An ancho chile turns the butter a deep terra-cotta color, and it looks gorgeous on the corn. The chile also gives the butter a very adult, almost fruity, sweet heat, offsetting the corn's uncomplicated, sunny flavor. ■

- 1 dried ancho or guajillo chile (see page 562), stemmed, seeded, and torn into pieces
- 1/4 cup loosely packed fresh cilantro leaves
- 3 garlic cloves, peeled
- 1 tablespoon fresh lime juice
- 3/4 teaspoon salt
- Pinch of sugar
- 1 stick (8 tablespoons) unsalted butter, softened
- 8 ears corn, shucked

Soak chile in 1/2 cup boiling water in a 1-cup glass measure or small bowl until softened, 20 to 30 minutes; drain well.

Finely chop cilantro and garlic together in a food processor. Add chile, lime juice, salt, and sugar and process until chile is finely chopped. Add butter and blend until smooth. Spoon butter into a ramekin or small bowl.

Cook corn in a 6- to 8-quart pot of boiling (unsalted) water until crisp-tender, 4 to 5 minutes. Transfer with tongs to a platter and serve with butter.

COOK'S NOTE

■ The garlic ancho butter keeps, covered tightly and refrigerated, for up to 1 week.

Broiled Eggplant with Cilantro Vinaigrette

SERVES 6

ACTIVE TIME: 30 MINUTES ■ START TO FINISH: 30 MINUTES

■ So simple, so good. This makes a great first course or side dish with lamb. The eggplant, first broiled, then roasted until tender, will drink up the flavorful vinaigrette. ■

- 6 small eggplants (1/4 pound each)
- 8 tablespoons olive oil
- Salt
- 1/2 teaspoon cumin seeds, toasted (see Tips, page 939)
- 1/4 cup loosely packed fresh cilantro leaves
- 1/4 cup loosely packed fresh flat-leaf parsley leaves
- 1 garlic clove, chopped
- 1/8 teaspoon cayenne
- 3 tablespoons fresh lemon juice

Preheat broiler. Halve eggplants lengthwise. Brush cut sides with 2 tablespoons oil and season with salt. Put cut sides up on rack of a broiler pan and broil 2 to 3 inches from heat until browned, about 5 minutes.

Reduce oven temperature to 450°F and move broiler pan to middle of oven. Roast eggplant until fork-tender, about 12 minutes. Let cool to room temperature.

Combine remaining 6 tablespoons oil and remaining ingredients in a blender, add 1/4 teaspoon salt, and blend until thoroughly combined.

Serve eggplant drizzled with vinaigrette.

Caponata

SERVES 6 TO 8

ACTIVE TIME: 1½ HOURS ■ START TO FINISH: 11 HOURS (INCLUDES CHILLING)

■ The Spanish addition of cocoa powder takes this Sicilian eggplant dish to a mysterious place, rendering it richer in consistency and color. The recipe is from Mary Taylor Simeti's *Pomp and Sustenance*, a book that made us fall in love with Sicilian food. Caponata is thought to have been created as seagoing fare, since the vinegar acts as a preservative. It is often part of an antipasto platter or used as a relish with meats. ■

- 2 large eggplants (2½ pounds total), cut into ¾-inch cubes
- Kosher salt
- 6 celery ribs, cut into 1-inch pieces
- 1½ cups olive oil (not extra-virgin)
- 1 medium onion, thinly sliced
- 1 cup (4–5 ounces) green olives, pitted and coarsely chopped
- Scant ½ cup (3 ounces) drained capers
- 1½ cups Sicilian Tomato Sauce (recipe follows)
- ½ cup white wine vinegar, or to taste
- 2 tablespoons sugar
- 2 tablespoons unsweetened cocoa powder (optional)
- ¼ teaspoon freshly ground black pepper
- ¾ cup (3 ounces) slivered almonds, lightly toasted (see Tips, page 938)

Toss eggplant with 2 tablespoons kosher salt in a colander set over a bowl and let drain for 1 hour.

Meanwhile, blanch celery in a 1½-quart saucepan of boiling well-salted water for 1 minute; drain well.

Rinse eggplant well and pat dry with paper towels. Heat 1 cup oil in a deep 12-inch heavy skillet over moderately high heat until hot but not smoking. Fry eggplant in small batches, stirring and turning, until golden brown and tender, 3 to 4 minutes per batch. With a slotted spoon, transfer to paper towels to drain. Discard any oil remaining in skillet.

Add remaining ½ cup oil to skillet, then add onion and cook over moderate heat, stirring occasionally, until golden, about 10 minutes. Add celery and cook, stirring, for 1 minute. Stir in olives, capers, tomato sauce, vinegar, sugar, cocoa powder (if using), ½ teaspoon kosher salt, and pepper, bring to a simmer, and simmer, uncovered, for 5 minutes. Add eggplant and simmer, uncovered, stirring occasionally, for 10 minutes.

Transfer caponata to a wide shallow dish. Cool, uncovered, then refrigerate, covered, for at least 8 hours to allow flavors to develop.

Serve at room temperature, sprinkled with almonds.

COOK'S NOTE

■ The caponata (without the almonds) can be refrigerated for up to 4 days.

Sicilian Tomato Sauce

MAKES ABOUT 4 CUPS
ACTIVE TIME: 15 MINUTES ■ START TO FINISH: 45 MINUTES

■ This subtle sauce, integral to the caponata, should be made with juicy, vine-ripe tomatoes. It is also soothing on pasta; because it is so simply and gently flavored, it is particularly nice for children. After cooking the pasta, add it to the sauce and cook it a few moments more so that the sauce coats every strand. The technique of passing the cooked tomatoes through a food mill before seasoning ensures that you don't throw away any oil and seasonings with the skins, and it preserves the flavor of the fresh tomatoes. ■

- 4 pounds very ripe tomatoes, preferably plum, cored
- ½ cup water
- 2–3 garlic cloves (to taste), lightly smashed
- 2 fresh basil sprigs
- ½ cup olive oil
- 1 teaspoon salt
- Pinch of sugar (optional)

SPECIAL EQUIPMENT: a food mill fitted with a fine or medium disk

Combine tomatoes and water in a 5-quart nonreactive pot (water should just cover bottom of pot) and bring to a bare simmer over moderately low heat. Cover and cook tomatoes, stirring once, until just softened, 5 to 7 minutes; drain.

Force tomatoes through food mill into a 3-quart saucepan; discard seeds and skins. Add garlic, basil, and oil, bring to a simmer, and simmer sauce, stirring occasionally, until slightly thickened and reduced to about 4 cups, 20 to 25 minutes (sauce will look paler and slightly creamy). Remove and discard garlic and basil sprigs, then stir in salt. Add pinch of sugar if sauce tastes too acidic.

COOK'S NOTE

■ The sauce can be made up to 4 days ahead. Cool, uncovered, then refrigerate, covered.

Braised Belgian Endive Gratin

SERVES 8

ACTIVE TIME: 25 MINUTES ■ START TO FINISH: 1 HOUR

■ Belgian endive is one of the most elegant and self-possessed vegetables. Braising mellows and mutes its raw edginess, and it becomes a sponge for stock and lemon juice. Paired with roast beef or rack of lamb (instead of more predictable accompaniments like potatoes and peas), this gratin says that you've been around and know a thing or two. ■

- 8 Belgian endives (2 pounds total), trimmed, root ends left intact, and halved lengthwise
- 1½ tablespoons fresh lemon juice
- 3 tablespoons unsalted butter, cut into bits
- ½ teaspoon salt
- 2 teaspoons sugar
- ¾ cup chicken stock or store-bought low-sodium broth
- ⅔ cup finely grated Gruyère
- ½ cup plain dry bread crumbs

Arrange endives cut sides down in two layers in a 10- to 11-inch-wide heavy pot. Add lemon juice, butter, salt, sugar, and stock. Cover mixture with a buttered round of wax paper, buttered side down, then with a lid, and bring to a boil. Reduce heat and simmer, covered, until endives are very tender, 20 to 30 minutes.

Preheat broiler. Butter a flameproof 13-by-9-inch gratin dish or other large shallow baking dish (not glass).

With a slotted spoon, transfer endives to buttered dish, arranging them cut sides down in one layer. Stir together cheese and bread crumbs in a small bowl, then sprinkle evenly over endives. Broil about 4 inches from heat until topping is golden and cheese is melted, 3 to 4 minutes.

Baked Belgian Endive with Pecorino and Walnuts

SERVES 6 TO 8

ACTIVE TIME: 10 MINUTES ■ START TO FINISH: 1 HOUR

■ Crisp and pleasantly bitter when served raw, Belgian endive turns sweet and mellow when baked. It combines beautifully with the richness of walnuts and the sharpness of pecorino Romano. This also makes a good first course. ■

- 8 Belgian endives (2 pounds total)
- ¼ cup extra-virgin olive oil
- Salt and freshly ground black pepper
- ¼ cup walnuts, coarsely chopped
- ⅓ cup finely grated pecorino Romano

Put a rack in middle of oven and preheat oven to 350°F.

Trim endives, keeping bottoms intact, then quarter lengthwise. Toss with oil and salt and pepper to taste in a 13-by-9-inch baking dish, then arrange in one snug layer. Cover with foil and bake until tender, 30 to 40 minutes.

Sprinkle endives evenly with walnuts and cheese and bake, uncovered, until cheese is melted, about 10 minutes more.

Braised Fennel with Olives

SERVES 12

ACTIVE TIME: 1 HOUR ■ START TO FINISH: 1½ HOURS

■ In the wintertime, this combination will make you think of Provence. It's silky, festive, and substantial. The tomatoes and orange zest bring the sun in. (The recipe is easily halved; use a smaller pot.) ■

½ cup olive oil
2 large onions, coarsely chopped (5 cups)
4 garlic gloves, minced
2 (28- to 32-ounce) cans whole plum tomatoes in juice, drained (1 cup juice reserved) and chopped
1½ cups chicken stock or store-bought low-sodium broth
3 pounds small fennel bulbs, stalks discarded and each bulb trimmed and cut into 8 wedges
1½ cups pitted and sliced Kalamata olives (9 ounces)
2 teaspoons fennel seeds
1 teaspoon finely grated orange zest
¼ teaspoon salt
½ teaspoon freshly ground black pepper
1 tablespoon fresh lemon juice

Heat oil in a 7- to 8-quart wide heavy pot over moderate heat. Add onions and cook, stirring occasionally, until softened, about 10 minutes. Add garlic and cook, stirring, for 4 minutes. Add tomatoes, with reserved juice, stock, fennel, olives, fennel seeds, orange zest, salt, and pepper and bring to a boil, then reduce heat, cover, and simmer for 30 minutes.

Uncover and simmer, stirring occasionally, until fennel is very tender and liquid is reduced by half, about 30 minutes. Stir in lemon juice and salt and pepper to taste. Serve hot or at room temperature.

COOK'S NOTE

- The fennel can be made up to 2 days ahead and refrigerated, covered. Bring to room temperature or reheat before serving.

Collard Greens Miniera

SERVES 4

ACTIVE TIME: 25 MINUTES ■ START TO FINISH: 25 MINUTES

■ We learned this way of preparing greens in Brazil, where it's generally used with kale, and it was a real eye-opener. Unlike the long-simmered recipes common to the American South, here the greens are thinly shredded and cooked fast, so they stay bright green and crisp-tender, almost like a hot slaw. Because they cook so quickly, this is a great way to work collards and other hearty greens into your weeknight culinary repertoire.

Collards arrived in the United States with the English (the word is a corruption of *colewort,* a nonheading cabbage) and took the place of African greens in the slave diet. But their connection to the American South is not unique; they are used in many other parts of the world. This preparation is named after the Minas Gerais region of Brazil. An old folktale says a woman isn't ready for marriage until she knows how to shred the greens just right. The easiest way to deal with the flexible, floppy collards is to remove the stems and center ribs, then roll a few stacked leaves at a time into a cigar shape and slice the cigar crosswise into thin strips. ■

1¼ pounds collard greens, halved lengthwise, stems and center ribs discarded
3 bacon slices, finely chopped
Salt

FENNEL

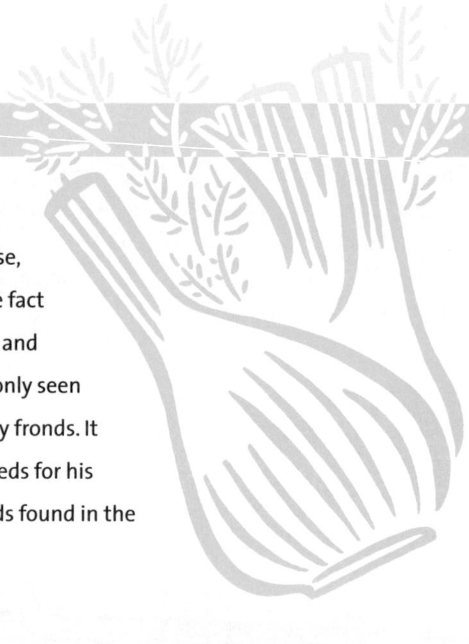

Fennel is often labeled "anise" in the supermarket, but the two are not the same thing. (And neither one is related to the Asian spice known as star anise, which is the seedpod of a Chinese evergreen.) The confusion stems from the fact that the two plants contain an essential oil of similar chemical composition and thus share a licorice-like flavor and aroma. Florence fennel, the most commonly seen variety in the United States, has a fat, compact bulb, long stalks, and feathery fronds. It was first grown here by Thomas Jefferson; in 1824 he received a packet of seeds for his garden at Monticello from the American consul in Florence. (The fennel seeds found in the spice section of supermarkets come from a different variety.)

Stack collard leaves a few at a time, roll into a cigar shape, and cut into very thin slices (no wider than 1/8 inch) with a sharp knife.

Cook bacon in a 12-inch nonstick skillet over moderate heat, stirring, until crisp. Add collards, tossing to coat, and cook until just bright green, about 1 minute. Season with salt.

Collard Greens with Red Onions and Bacon

SERVES 8

ACTIVE TIME: 1 HOUR ■ START TO FINISH: 2 HOURS

■ Many southerners get their year started off right with a plate of hoppin' John (rice and black-eyed peas; see page 274) for luck, along with sides of skillet corn bread and collards, which are said to bring folding green money in the year ahead. Why tempt fate? ■

- 1/2 pound bacon (8 slices), cut crosswise into quarters
- 3 medium red onions, coarsely chopped (4 cups)
- 1 1/4 cups chicken stock or store-bought low-sodium broth
- 1/4 cup cider vinegar
- 2 tablespoons firmly packed dark brown sugar, or to taste
- 1/2 teaspoon red pepper flakes, or to taste
- 1 teaspoon salt
- 4 pounds collard greens (preferably with small leaves), coarse stems and center ribs discarded, leaves and thin stems coarsely chopped

Cook bacon in 2 batches in a 6- to 8-quart heavy pot over moderate heat until crisp, about 10 minutes. Transfer to paper towels to drain. Pour off all but about 3 tablespoons fat from pot. Cook onions in fat, stirring occasionally, until softened, about 5 minutes. With a slotted spoon, transfer onions to a bowl.

Add stock, vinegar, brown sugar, red pepper flakes, salt, and half of bacon to pot and simmer, stirring, until sugar is dissolved, about 1 minute. Add half of collards, tossing until slightly wilted, then add remaining collards, tossing until wilted and combined. Simmer, covered, stirring occasionally, for 30 minutes.

Stir in onions and simmer, covered, until collards are very tender, about 30 minutes more. Serve topped with remaining bacon.

Sautéed Kale with Bacon and Vinegar

SERVES 4

ACTIVE TIME: 30 MINUTES ■ START TO FINISH: 30 MINUTES

■ One of the great culinary combinations in the world is greens and smoked meat. This recipe is particularly delicious with dark, rich lacinato kale (often called dinosaur or black kale; see Glossary). Fresh-tasting cider vinegar is added to so many recipes like this because it yanks things back from being too over-the-top smoky rich. ■

- 1 1/4 pounds kale (1 large bunch), stems and center ribs discarded, leaves coarsely torn
- 1/4 pound bacon (4 slices), chopped
- 1 tablespoon olive oil
- 1 tablespoon cider vinegar, or to taste
- 1/4 teaspoon salt
- 1/4 teaspoon freshly ground black pepper

Cook kale in a 6- to 8-quart heavy pot of boiling salted water (1 tablespoon salt per every 4 quarts water), uncovered, for 5 minutes; drain well.

Cook bacon in a 12-inch heavy skillet over moderate heat, stirring, until crisp, about 5 minutes. Pour off all but 1 tablespoon fat from skillet. Add oil and kale to bacon, increase heat to moderately high, and cook, stirring, until heated through, about 3 minutes. Toss kale with vinegar, salt, and pepper.

Sautéed Mustard Greens with Garlic

SERVES 6

ACTIVE TIME: 20 MINUTES ■ START TO FINISH: 20 MINUTES

■ Mustard greens, with a lighter, brighter color and flavor, are a zesty alternative to spinach. If you have a choice, buy young, small leaves—they're tenderer. ■

3 large garlic cloves
¼ teaspoon salt
¼ cup olive oil
1½ pounds mustard greens (2 bunches), stems and center ribs discarded, leaves halved
½ cup water

Using a large knife, mince and mash garlic to a paste with salt. Heat oil in a 5-quart heavy pot over moderately high heat until hot but not smoking. Add garlic paste and cook, stirring, until fragrant, 15 to 30 seconds. Add half of greens and toss with tongs to coat with oil, then add remaining greens as they wilt. Add water, cover, and cook, stirring occasionally, for 5 minutes. Continue to cook, uncovered, until greens are just tender and most of liquid has evaporated, about 2 minutes. Season with salt.

Swiss Chard with Olives and Raisins

SERVES 4
ACTIVE TIME: 40 MINUTES ■ START TO FINISH: 40 MINUTES

■ American chefs have popularized Swiss chard, a member of the beet family that has long been a mainstay in Europe. This Provençal treatment, with golden raisins, garlic, and olives, gives sweetness, tang, and salt to the fleshy cooking greens. The varieties with multicolored stems are known as rainbow chard; although their vividness dims when cooked, they seem to be less tough than regular chard. ■

2 tablespoons olive oil
1 medium onion, finely chopped (1 cup)
1½ pounds Swiss chard (1½ bunches), center ribs discarded, leaves and stems separated, stems finely chopped, leaves coarsely chopped
¼ cup golden raisins
2 garlic cloves, finely chopped
8 Kalamata olives or other large brine-cured black olives, pitted and finely chopped
½ teaspoon salt
¼ teaspoon freshly ground black pepper
¼ cup pine nuts, lightly toasted (see Tips, page 938)

Heat oil in a 5-quart heavy pot over moderate heat. Add onion and cook, stirring, until softened, about 3 minutes. Add chard stems, raisins, and garlic, cover, and cook, stirring occasionally, until stems are tender, about 6 minutes. Stir in chard leaves, olives, salt, and pepper, cover, and cook, stirring occasionally, until leaves are wilted, about 3 minutes.

Remove lid and cook, stirring occasionally, until most of liquid chard gives off has evaporated and leaves are tender, about 4 minutes. Stir in pine nuts.

VARIATION

■ Substitute escarole, trimmed and chopped, for the Swiss chard. Cook the raisins and garlic until the raisins are plumped, then add all the escarole along with the olives, salt, and pepper.

Swiss Chard and Chickpeas

SERVES 4
ACTIVE TIME: 20 MINUTES ■ START TO FINISH: 20 MINUTES

■ With late-summer tomatoes and a squeeze of lemon, this quick, hearty, Armenian-inspired vegetable stew carries you into fall. It's a great accompaniment to roast chicken, roast pork, or pork chops; it is also a satisfying vegetarian main course. If you can't find Swiss chard, spinach is a good substitute. ■

3 tablespoons olive oil
2 small onions, thinly sliced
2 garlic cloves, thinly sliced
2 small tomatoes, cut into ¼-inch dice
2 cups rinsed canned chickpeas
1 pound Swiss chard (1 bunch), center ribs and stems discarded, leaves coarsely chopped
1 tablespoon fresh lemon juice
Salt and freshly ground black pepper

Heat oil in a 12-inch nonstick skillet over moderately low heat. Add onions and garlic and cook, stirring, until softened. Add tomatoes and chickpeas and cook, stirring, for 5 minutes. Add Swiss chard, cover, and cook until wilted, about 2 minutes. Stir in lemon juice and salt and pepper to taste.

Swiss Chard Gratin

SERVES 6

ACTIVE TIME: 1¼ HOURS ■ START TO FINISH: 1¾ HOURS

■ This is the sort of dish that helped give the city of Lyon its long-held reputation for solid home-style food. The recipe is from the New York chef Daniel Boulud, who grew up on a farm near Lyon and was inspired by his grandmother's cooking. ■

- 2 tablespoons unsalted butter, melted
- 1 cup coarse fresh bread crumbs
- 1 cup grated Tomme de Savoie or Gruyère (about 3 ounces)
- 1 garlic clove, finely chopped
- 1 tablespoon finely chopped mixed fresh herbs, preferably chives, tarragon, and flat-leaf parsley
- ⅛ teaspoon freshly grated nutmeg
- Salt and freshly ground black pepper
- 1 cup chicken stock or store-bought low-sodium broth
- ½ cup heavy cream
- 3 tablespoons unsalted butter
- 1 tablespoon all-purpose flour
- 1 medium onion, finely chopped (1 cup)
- 3 pounds Swiss chard (3 bunches), center ribs discarded, leaves and stems separated, both cut into 1-inch pieces
- 1 pound spinach, coarse stems discarded and leaves coarsely chopped

Toss melted butter with bread crumbs, cheese, garlic, herbs, half of nutmeg, and salt and pepper to taste in a bowl.

Bring stock to a boil in a small saucepan and boil until reduced by half. Add cream, remove from heat, and cover to keep warm.

Melt 1 tablespoon butter in a small heavy saucepan over moderate heat. Add flour and cook, whisking, for 1 minute to make a roux. Add stock mixture in a slow stream, whisking, and boil, whisking, for 1 minute. Season with salt and pepper and remove from heat.

Put a rack in middle of oven and preheat oven to 400°F. Butter a 12-inch oval gratin dish or 1-quart shallow baking dish.

Melt remaining 2 tablespoons butter in a wide 8-quart heavy pot over moderately low heat. Add onion and cook, stirring, until softened. Add chard stems, remaining nutmeg, and salt and pepper to taste and cook, stirring, until chard is tender but not browned, about 8 minutes. Increase heat to moderately high and add chard leaves and spinach by large handfuls, stirring, until all greens are wilted. Season with salt and pepper.

Transfer vegetables to a colander to drain well, pressing out liquid with back of a large spoon. (Be sure to drain as much liquid as possible from vegetables, so gratin isn't watery.) Toss vegetables with cream sauce and transfer to gratin dish, spreading evenly.

Top vegetables with bread crumb mixture and bake until gratin is bubbling and topping is golden, about 20 minutes.

COOK'S NOTE

■ The gratin can be assembled up to 4 hours ahead and refrigerated, covered. Bring to room temperature before baking.

Curried Greens with Golden Onion and Cashews

SERVES 4

ACTIVE TIME: 50 MINUTES ■ START TO FINISH: 50 MINUTES

■ This dish will turn an old favorite like roast chicken or grilled steak into a really interesting meal. One secret is the mixture of different greens—spinach, dandelion, and mustard. Each has its own character, and together they are full of nuance. Another secret is the spice blend. It might seem fussy—a teaspoon of this, a quarter teaspoon of that—but the seasonings round out the flavor beautifully, making all the difference. The spices we've used are easily found at the supermarket, and if you eliminate one or two of them, the dish isn't going to taste the same. This recipe was inspired by the cooking teacher and cookbook author Julie Sahni. ■

- 6 tablespoons olive oil
- 1 large onion, cut into 1/4-inch-wide wedges
- Salt
- 2 teaspoons curry powder
- 1 teaspoon ground coriander
- 1 teaspoon ground cumin
- 1 teaspoon mustard seeds
- 1/2 teaspoon ground cinnamon
- 1/4 teaspoon cayenne
- 1/2 cup coarsely chopped salted roasted cashews (4 ounces)
- 1 pound spinach, tough stems discarded, leaves coarsely chopped (6 cups)
- 3/4 pound mustard greens, stems and center ribs discarded, leaves coarsely chopped if large (5 cups)
- 3/4 pound dandelion greens, tough stems discarded, leaves coarsely chopped if large (4 cups)
- 1/2 cup water

Heat 3 tablespoons oil in a 10-inch heavy skillet over moderate heat. Add onion, season with salt, and cook, stirring occasionally, until onion is deep golden and some wedges are crisp, 15 to 20 minutes.

Meanwhile, stir together spices in a small bowl.

Add cashews to onion and cook, stirring occasionally, until nuts are one shade darker, about 3 minutes. Stir in 1 1/2 teaspoons spice mix and cook, stirring, until fragrant, about 30 seconds. Remove from heat.

Heat remaining 3 tablespoons oil in a 5-quart heavy pot over moderately high heat until hot but not smoking. Add remaining spice mix and cook, stirring, until fragrant, about 30 seconds. Immediately stir in spinach, mustard and dandelion greens, and water and cook, stirring occasionally, until most of liquid has evaporated and greens are tender, 3 to 5 minutes. Season with salt.

Serve greens sprinkled with onion mixture.

COOK'S NOTE

- The onion and cashew topping can be made up to 6 hours ahead and kept, covered, at room temperature.

Mashed Jerusalem Artichokes

SERVES 6

ACTIVE TIME: 35 MINUTES ■ START TO FINISH: 1 HOUR

■ You're in the mood to cook venison or maybe duck. This is what you make instead of the usual side of

Jerusalem Artichokes

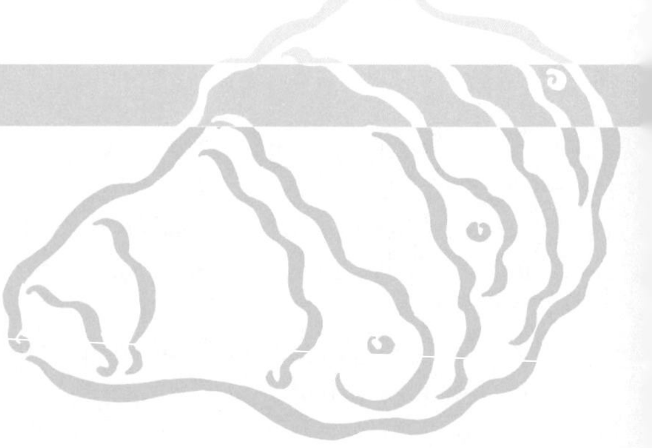

Neither native to Jerusalem nor an artichoke, this vegetable is a member of the sunflower family. The French explorers who first came across it in North America in the early 1600s thought its sweet, earthy flavor was similar to that of the artichoke. When it began to be cultivated in Europe, it became known as the plant that "turns to the sun." "Jerusalem" is generally thought to be an anglicized version of *girasole*, Italian for "sunflower." Jerusalem artichokes are sometimes more accurately called sunchokes; the term *Sunchokes* was actually trademarked in the 1960s by Frieda Caplan, the founder of Frieda's, Inc., a specialty produce purveyor in California.

The brown tubers resemble small, knobby potatoes or, in their gnarlier varieties, fresh ginger. They can be sautéed, roasted, boiled and mashed, sliced paper-thin and deep-fried, or cooked in soups. ("Palestinian soup" was popular in Victorian England.) Notwithstanding their reputation for being difficult to digest, Jerusalem artichokes are also delicious raw and provide a welcome crunch, like water chestnuts, in salads. At their best in fall and winter, they will keep in the refrigerator for about a week.

mashed potatoes, when you want texture and something to absorb the rich meat juices. Peeling three and a half pounds of Jerusalem artichokes is not fun, but you will be rewarded by their nutty, elusive flavor. ■

- 3½ pounds Jerusalem artichokes, peeled and cut into 1-inch pieces
- 1 pound boiling potatoes, peeled and cut into ¾-inch pieces
- 1 teaspoon salt
- 3 cups whole milk
- 3 tablespoons unsalted butter, softened
- Freshly ground black pepper

Combine artichokes, potatoes, salt, and milk in a 5-quart pot, add water to cover by 1 inch, and bring to a simmer. Simmer, uncovered, until vegetables are very tender, about 25 minutes.

Drain vegetables in a colander and return to pot. Using a potato masher, mash vegetables with butter and salt and pepper to taste until smooth.

COOK'S NOTE

■ The dish can be made up to 3 days ahead and refrigerated, covered. Bring to room temperature before reheating, covered, over low heat.

Poached Leeks with Warm Vinaigrette

SERVES 4

ACTIVE TIME: 30 MINUTES ■ START TO FINISH: 1½ HOURS

■ Leeks are most often used as an ingredient rather than as a vegetable in their own right. Not here. Bathed in a lovely warm vinaigrette and presented in halves, they are soft and sumptuous. Look for small to medium leeks in season. And don't screech to a halt when you see that we call for veal stock; it adds richness to this dish, but water will work well too. ■

- 8 medium leeks (2½ pounds total)
- 2½ cups Veal Stock (page 929) or store-bought broth, or water
- 2 tablespoons finely chopped shallots
- ¼ cup sherry vinegar
- 1 tablespoon Dijon mustard
- ¼ teaspoon dry mustard
- 6 tablespoons olive oil
- ¼ teaspoon salt, or to taste
- ¼ teaspoon freshly ground black pepper, or to taste

Put a rack in middle of oven and preheat oven to 400°F.

Trim off dark green tops of leeks, leaving pale green parts. Trim roots, leaving root ends intact. Halve leeks lengthwise and rinse well under cold water to remove any dirt. Drain and pat dry on paper towels.

Arrange leeks cut sides up in one layer in a 13-by-9-inch baking dish. Pour stock over them, cover tightly with foil, and bake until tender, about 1 hour.

With tongs, lift leeks from dish, letting excess stock drain into dish, and arrange on a platter. Cover to keep warm. Reserve ½ cup stock (save remainder for another use, if desired).

Combine shallots and vinegar in a 2-quart heavy saucepan, bring to a simmer, and simmer until reduced by half, 3 to 4 minutes. Whisk in reserved ½ cup stock and both mustards and bring to a simmer. Add oil in a slow stream, whisking, and simmer, whisking, for 1 minute. Season vinaigrette with salt and pepper.

Pour vinaigrette over leeks and serve warm.

Creamed Leeks

SERVES 4

ACTIVE TIME: 15 MINUTES ■ START TO FINISH: 1 HOUR

■ Leeks turn velvety when chopped and simmered in cream and stock. Serve this country dish as you would creamed spinach. It's delicious with roast beef, grilled steak, or baked chicken. ■

- 4 large leeks (about 2 pounds total; white and pale green parts only), halved lengthwise and chopped
- 2 tablespoons unsalted butter
- ½ cup heavy cream
- ⅓ cup chicken stock or store-bought low-sodium broth
- Pinch of freshly grated nutmeg, or to taste
- Salt
- Pinch of white pepper, or to taste

Wash leeks in a large bowl of cold water, then lift out and drain well. Heat butter in a 12-inch heavy skillet over moderate heat until foam subsides. Add leeks and stir to coat with butter. Add cream and stock and bring to a boil over high heat, stirring, then reduce heat to moderate and cook, uncovered, stirring occasionally, until leeks are tender and sauce is thickened, 10 to 15 minutes. Stir in nutmeg, salt to taste, and white pepper.

Grilled Leeks with Romesco Sauce

SERVES 4
ACTIVE TIME: 1 HOUR ■ START TO FINISH 1¼ HOURS

■ Every spring in the Catalan region of Spain, the leek-sized green onions called *calçots* are charred over open fires, then served with the hearty, rustic sauce called *romesco*, or a variation thereof. We've substituted leeks for the green onions here, but no matter which vegetable you decide to use, it will be an excuse for eating the sauce—an outstanding (and beautiful) concoction of chile, almonds, bread crumbs, and garlic. It's wonderful with anything grilled. New Mexico chiles are easier to obtain in this country than the traditional Catalan dried red chiles, and they give a similar mild heat. ■

- 1 dried New Mexico chile (¼ ounce; see page 561), stem, seeds, and ribs discarded
- ⅓ cup red wine vinegar
- ¾ cup olive oil, plus additional for brushing leeks
- ¼ cup skinned whole almonds
- 2 slices firm white sandwich bread, cut into ½-inch cubes
- 12 medium garlic cloves, peeled
- 1 cup coarsely chopped onion

LEEKS

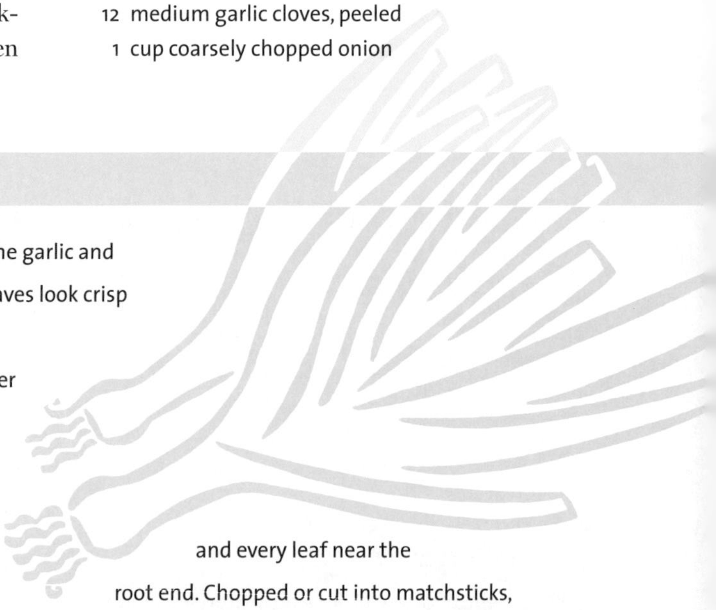

Leeks are the most refined and understated member of the garlic and onion family. When buying them, make sure the green leaves look crisp and the blanched white stems are firm.

Because of the way the leaves are formed, you'll never meet a leek that isn't dirty. *Gourmet* contributor William Woys Weaver, the author of the classic *Heirloom Vegetable Gardening,* explains that rain splashes dirt up onto the leaves, then washes it back down into the place where the leaves meet the stem (which is nothing more than lots of tightly bound leaves). As the plant grows, the dirt works its way deeper into the leaves. So don't cut corners when washing leeks. When a recipe calls for whole ones, trim the roots, keeping the ends of the leeks intact, and cut off the tough green parts at the point where the leaves turn pale. Peel off and discard the tough outer leaf layers, then split the leeks lengthwise, stopping one or two inches from the root end. Wash the halves under running water, fanning the layers of leaves to help remove sand and taking care to sluice water between each and every leaf near the root end. Chopped or cut into matchsticks, leeks are best cleaned in a large bowl of cold water after they are cut. Gently swish them around to make sure the sand drifts to the bottom of the bowl, then swoop them up from the water with your hands, leaving the sand behind, and transfer to a colander or sieve to drain. Repeat if the leeks are particularly dirty.

Leave leeks untrimmed until just before using. Wrapped in a damp kitchen towel and stored in a plastic bag, they'll keep for a couple of weeks in the refrigerator.

1 medium tomato, peeled (see Tips, page 940), seeded, and chopped
½ teaspoon sweet paprika, preferably Spanish smoked (see Glossary)
¼ teaspoon salt
12 medium leeks (3½ pounds total)

MAKE THE SAUCE: Tear chile into pieces and soak in vinegar until softened, 30 to 45 minutes.

Heat oil in a 10-inch heavy skillet over moderate heat until hot but not smoking. Add almonds and cook, stirring, until golden, about 1 minute. With a slotted spoon, transfer almonds to paper towels to drain. Toast bread cubes in oil remaining in skillet, turning once, until golden brown, about 2 minutes. With slotted spoon, transfer to paper towels to drain. Cook garlic in oil remaining in skillet, stirring, until golden, about 3 minutes. With slotted spoon, transfer garlic to a bowl. Cook onion in oil remaining in skillet, stirring, until golden, about 6 minutes. Add almonds, bread cubes, garlic, chile with vinegar, tomato, paprika, and salt, and simmer, stirring occasionally, for 2 minutes. (If desired, thin with water.)

Transfer mixture to a food processor and pulse until finely ground. Transfer sauce to a bowl and set aside, covered.

Prepare a charcoal or gas grill. If using a charcoal grill, open vents in bottom of grill, then light charcoal. Fire is hot when you can hold your hand above rack for just 1 to 2 seconds. If using a gas grill, preheat all burners on high, uncovered, for 10 minutes.

COOK THE LEEKS: Trim off dark green tops of leeks, leaving pale green parts. Trim roots, leaving root ends intact. Starting 2 inches from root end, halve each leek lengthwise through greens; leave root end intact. Wash leeks under cold water, separating layers to remove all grit.

Cook leeks in a 5-quart pot of boiling salted water (1 tablespoon salt per every 4 quarts water) until tender, 10 to 15 minutes. Drain well and pat dry. Brush leeks with oil.

Lightly oil grill rack. Grill leeks, uncovered, turning occasionally, until grill marks appear and leeks are hot, about 3 minutes total for a charcoal grill or 6 to 8 minutes total for a gas grill. Transfer to a serving platter.

Spoon some sauce over leeks and serve remainder on the side.

COOK'S NOTES

- The sauce can be made up to 1 week ahead and refrigerated, covered. Bring to room temperature before serving.
- The leeks can be grilled up to 1 day in advance and refrigerated, covered. Reheat on a baking sheet in a 350°F oven until heated through, about 10 minutes.
- The leeks can be grilled in an oiled well-seasoned large grill pan over moderately high heat, turning occasionally, until grill marks appear and the leeks are hot.

Savory Puréed Limas

SERVES 4
ACTIVE TIME: 10 MINUTES ■ START TO FINISH: 25 MINUTES

■ Serve this to people who profess to hate limas and you will change their image of the beans. Smooth, rich, and a beautiful celadon green, this is excellent with roast cod and slow-roasted tomatoes. ■

1¼ teaspoons salt
1 pound (3½ cups) frozen baby lima beans, not thawed
2 tablespoons unsalted butter
1½ teaspoons minced garlic
⅓ cup whole milk, or to taste
¼ teaspoon freshly grated nutmeg, or to taste
¼ teaspoon freshly ground black pepper

Bring 2 cups water and ¾ teaspoon salt to a boil in a 3-quart saucepan. Add lima beans and bring rapidly to a boil again, then reduce heat, cover, and simmer until beans are tender, 10 to 12 minutes.

Meanwhile, melt butter in a small saucepan over moderately low heat. Add garlic and cook, stirring, until pale golden, about 2 minutes. Remove from heat.

Drain beans and transfer to a food processor. Add garlic mixture, milk, nutmeg, pepper, and remaining ½ teaspoon salt and purée until smooth.

Mushrooms and Truffles

Mushrooms

The days when our shopping choices were limited to fresh or canned white button mushrooms are long gone. Today well-stocked supermarkets carry a selection of "exotics" such as shiitakes, chanterelles, and porcini, which are available practically year-round. (We refer to them as exotic rather than wild mushrooms because most of them are not truly wild anymore, but cultivated.)

Whether wild or cultivated, mushrooms are not quite as delicate as you may think. They do need circulating air, so we generally keep ours, unwashed, in paper bags on a refrigerator shelf (rather than in the vegetable crisper); they get slimy when kept in plastic.

To wash or not to wash is a controversial issue. Contrary to conventional wisdom, which holds that mushrooms should simply be wiped clean, we wash mushrooms in our test kitchens. Fresh close-capped mushrooms, which are naturally about 90 percent water, absorb very little additional water when washed, although it's probably not a good idea to let them soak. Drop them into a bowl of cool water and give them a good swish with your hands, letting any grit fall to the bottom of the bowl, then lift them out of the water and pat them dry with a cloth or paper towels. If they don't seem dirty, you can just give them a quick rinse and then dry them in the same way. If your mushrooms are open-gilled, simply wipe them clean with a damp paper towel or a soft brush and use them as soon as possible.

Sometimes our recipes specify dried mushrooms, which are generally more intensely flavored than their fresh counterparts. After soaking, we suggest rinsing them to remove any grit. (Strain the flavorful soaking liquid and incorporate it in the dish if possible.) And although some of the cultivated exotics may lose their color and shape when cooked, don't be tempted to serve them raw. They contain natural toxins (destroyed by cooking) that will cause indigestion.

These are the mushrooms we rely on the most:

CHANTERELLES Also called girolles, these frilly, lily-shaped orange or golden mushrooms are the darlings of chefs everywhere, because they taste as elegant as they look—delicately woodsy and fruity, with a hint of apricot.

CREMINI Cremini (sometimes labeled "Baby Bellas"), portobello, and white button mushrooms are essentially the same variety. According to Elizabeth Schneider's classic *Vegetables from Amaranth to Zucchini,* the cocoa-colored cremini, an immature portobello, is the reintroduction of a brown mushroom that was popular in the United States before the white strain was developed in the 1920s. It has a denser texture and richer flavor than the white buttons.

MORELS

In some regions of the United States — the Midwest and Appalachia, for instance — the whereabouts of morel patches are guarded family secrets and the spongy mushroom is the subject of many spring festivities (it's the state fungus of Minnesota). The flavor of morels is nutty and earthy, milder than that of most other wild mushrooms, and their honeycomb crevices and hollows have a great affinity for cream sauces. Cultivated morels are very clean, but always inspect wild ones carefully for sand, grit, and wildlife.

OYSTER MUSHROOMS

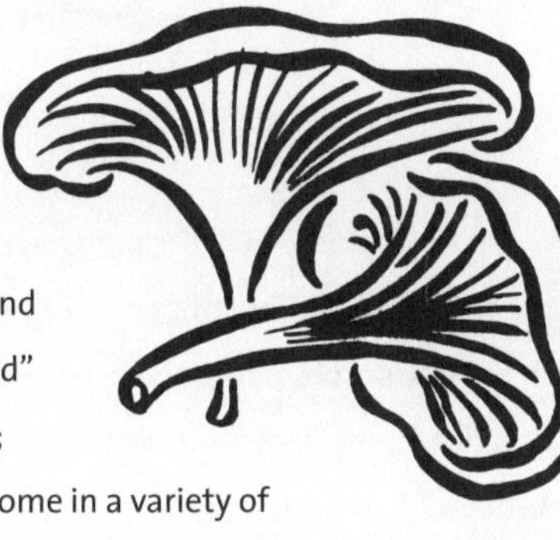

Oyster mushrooms, which have a very faint oceanic taste, are among the easiest and fastest-growing "wild" mushrooms to farm; consequently, they come in a variety of colors, shapes, and sizes. The ones that grow in clumps last longest and have a fleshy texture.

PORCINI Also known as cèpes or boletes, these succulent mushrooms, with their earthy, meaty flavor, are among the most popular of the exotic mushrooms.

The cap of a fresh porcini will have a creamy beige underside; as it gets older it darkens to deep, almost greenish brown. The brown portion is bitter, so trim it off before using.

PORTOBELLOS

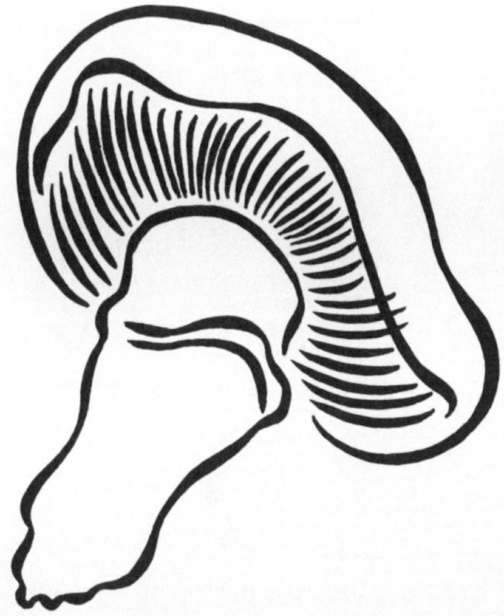

Also called portabellas, these meaty, firm-textured mushrooms were developed in Pennsylvania when mushroom farmers discovered that cremini grew large, broad caps if left to mature for a few more days.

SHIITAKES Although shiitake ("shee-*tah*-keh") mushrooms have been cultivated in Asia for more than a thousand years, they weren't farmed in the United States until the 1970s, when Malcolm Clark, a biologist and the president of Gourmet Mushrooms, in Sebastopol, California, pioneered production. Careful selection is key, he says, and bigger is not better. Look for small, firm, meaty shiitakes with caps that are curled under, not splayed open and flabby. The best shiitakes have a silvery veil of filaments over the gills, which indicates that their development was not rushed. Choose these, and you will be rewarded with a full, foresty flavor.

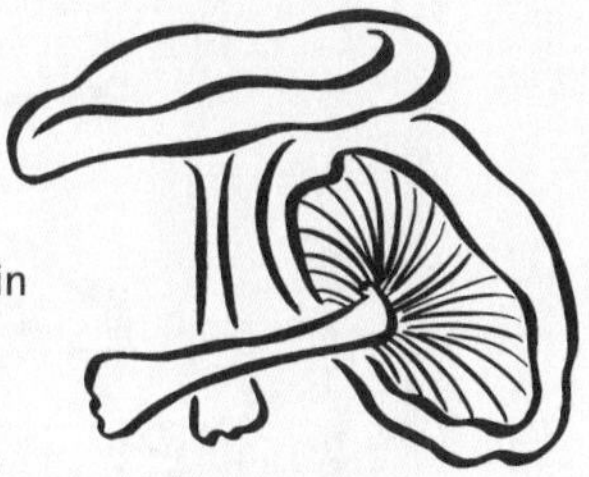

WHITE BUTTON MUSHROOMS These familiar standbys are plump, creamy white, and mild.

Truffles

A subterranean fungus that is attracted to the root systems of certain trees (oaks and willows produce the most aromatic specimens), truffles are practically mythologized, in part, perhaps, to justify their costliness.

BLACK TRUFFLES, harvested in the Périgord and Provence regions of France (as well as in Italy, Spain, and Portugal), have a dusty-looking, bumpy black exterior and a dark interior with white veins. (Often they have a nick in the surface so you can see the interior, especially early in the season.) Look for the black winter truffles (*Tuber melanosporum*) rather than the much less expensive black summer truffles (*T. aestivum*), for they are worlds apart in flavor and aroma. The summer ones, which are tan inside, taste light and mushroomy compared to the smoky, musky, almost loamy flavor of the winter variety.

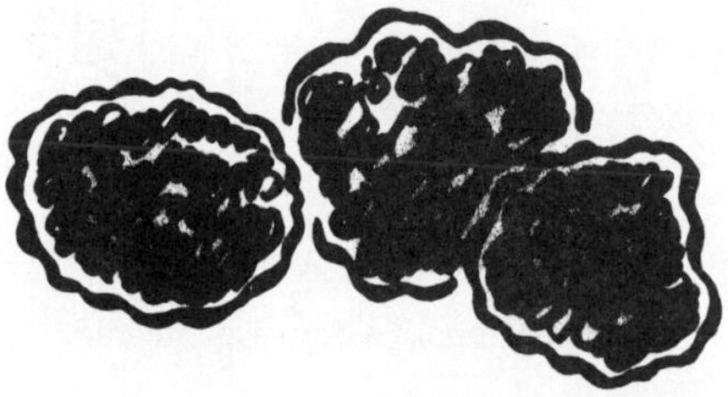

WHITE TRUFFLES (*T. magnatum*) are more delicate and mysterious than black truffles. Alba, in Italy's Piedmont region, is the heart of white truffledom, although some "Alba" truffles come from elsewhere, including other parts of central and northern Italy, Slovenia, and Istria. The exterior should be bland beige; the interior, pale with creamy veins.

How good a truffle is depends on growing conditions, which vary from year to year, and on how it is shipped and stored. There have been times when we've paid handsomely for a truffle, only to be disappointed by its lack of flavor and aroma. For consistency's sake, we sometimes turn to truffle paste or truffle oil, which are usually bolstered by synthesized chemical flavor essence. (Using enough real truffles to give flavor is prohibitively expensive, and if fresh truffles are added to oil, it will soon turn rancid.) Both the paste and the oil are highly concentrated, so use just the tiniest amount. Another option is canned or jarred truffles. Keep fresh truffles wrapped in paper towels in a tightly sealed jar in the refrigerator. Truffle oil, truffle paste, preserved truffles — and fresh ones, if you are feeling flush — are available at specialty foods shops and by mail from D'Artagnan and Urbani (see Sources).

Creamed Mushrooms with Chives

SERVES 6

ACTIVE TIME: 30 MINUTES ■ START TO FINISH: 30 MINUTES

■ Plain white mushrooms turn into comfort food par excellence. This makes a great side to roast beef or chicken, but you can also serve it on toast for a light main course. ■

- ½ stick (4 tablespoons) unsalted butter
- 2 pounds mushrooms, trimmed and quartered
- 1 medium onion, chopped (1 cup)
- ½ cup heavy cream
- ½ cup chicken stock or store-bought low-sodium broth
- 4 teaspoons fresh lemon juice, or to taste
- 3 tablespoons chopped fresh chives
- Salt and freshly ground black pepper

Heat butter in a 12-inch heavy skillet over moderate heat until foam subsides. Add mushrooms, increase heat to high, and cook, stirring occasionally, until liquid mushrooms give off has evaporated and mushrooms begin to brown, 10 to 15 minutes. Stir in onion and cook over moderate heat, stirring occasionally, until softened, about 5 minutes. Add cream, stock, and 4 teaspoons lemon juice, bring to a simmer, and simmer, stirring occasionally, until sauce is slightly thickened, about 10 minutes.

Stir in chives, salt and pepper to taste, and additional lemon juice, if desired.

Okra with Tomatoes and Ginger

SERVES 4 TO 6

ACTIVE TIME: 20 MINUTES ■ START TO FINISH: 30 MINUTES

■ Okra, generally thought to be native to Africa, was brought to the New World by slave traders, or perhaps even earlier by the Spanish and Portuguese, who have been eating it since Byzantine times. It is often considered the province of American southern cooks, but in fact it has been eaten for centuries in Arabia, Asia, and India. We've turned to the Indian subcontinent for inspiration: garlic, ginger, and red pepper flakes give this dish a bright heat. Much has been made of the fact that okra oozes a clear, viscous liquid, but frankly, it doesn't bother people who have grown up with it. And if you leave the okra whole and don't trim the little caps, the ooze factor won't be an issue. ■

- 2 garlic cloves, chopped
- 1 (2-by-1½-inch) piece peeled fresh ginger, chopped
- 2 tablespoons vegetable oil
- ⅛–¼ teaspoon red pepper flakes (to taste)
- 3 large tomatoes, cored and quartered
- ¾ teaspoon salt
- ¼ teaspoon freshly ground black pepper
- 1 pound small okra, untrimmed

Pulse garlic and ginger in a food processor until finely chopped, then transfer to a 12-inch heavy skillet (don't wash processor bowl). Add oil and red pepper flakes and cook over moderate heat, stirring, until fragrant, about 1 minute.

Pulse tomatoes with salt and pepper in processor until coarsely chopped, then stir into garlic mixture. Cook, uncovered, stirring occasionally, until slightly thickened, about 10 minutes.

Meanwhile, trim okra if necessary, leaving tops intact, being careful not to cut into pods. Stir okra into sauce and simmer, covered, until just tender, about about 10 minutes.

Roasted Okra

SERVES 4
ACTIVE TIME: 20 MINUTES ■ START TO FINISH: 20 MINUTES

■ A hot oven rids okra of any viscosity and renders it sweet, mellow, and very tender. You needn't trim young okra (the smaller the better, in this case). ■

- 2 tablespoons olive oil
- 1½ teaspoons dried oregano, crumbled
- ¼ teaspoon salt
- ⅛ teaspoon freshly ground black pepper
- 1 pound small okra, untrimmed

Put a rack in middle of oven and preheat oven to 500°F.

Stir together oil, oregano, salt, and pepper in a bowl, then toss okra in mixture. Spread okra on a large baking sheet with sides and roast, shaking sheet occasionally, until tender, 8 to 10 minutes.

Golden Creamed Onions

SERVES 10
ACTIVE TIME: 2 HOURS ■ START TO FINISH: 2 HOURS

■ Lightly caramelizing the onions before adding the cream gives this classic a whole new dimension. Don't limit the dish to the Thanksgiving table; it's just as delicious with roast beef, steak, or your Sunday night meat loaf. Note that we're not calling for pearl onions here, but for the slightly larger white boiling onions that are about the size of walnuts and are less labor-intensive. ■

- 3 pounds small white boiling onions
- 2 tablespoons unsalted butter
- 1 teaspoon sugar
- ¾ teaspoon salt
- 5 cups water
- ⅔ cup heavy cream
- Freshly ground black pepper
- ⅔ cup finely chopped fresh flat-leaf parsley

Blanch onions in a 5-quart pot of boiling water for 2 minutes. Drain in a colander and let cool until they can be handled, then peel.

Combine onions, butter, sugar, salt, and water in same pot, bring to a boil, and boil, uncovered, stirring occasionally, until most of liquid has evaporated, 40 to 45 minutes. Continue to cook onions over moderate heat, swirling them in the pot, until golden and beginning to brown, 5 to 10 minutes.

Add cream and boil until sauce is slightly thickened, about 1 minute. Season with salt and pepper to taste and stir in parsley.

COOK'S NOTE

■ The creamed onions, without the parsley, can be made up to 1 day ahead and refrigerated, covered. Reheat in a skillet over moderately low heat, stirring, until hot; thin the sauce with water if necessary. Stir in the parsley.

Fried Onion Rings

SERVES 4
ACTIVE TIME: 30 MINUTES ■ START TO FINISH: 30 MINUTES

■ You don't have to go to a steakhouse to get great onion rings—you can make them at home. And onion rings don't have to be a big project, either: you can fry them while you are cooking a juicy steak, or you can even make them as an hors d'oeuvre or a first course. The coating on these is golden, crisp, and not too thick. ■

- 6 cups vegetable oil for deep-frying
- 1 large onion (1 pound), cut crosswise into ¼-inch-thick slices
- 1 cup whole milk
- 1½ cups all-purpose flour
- ½ teaspoon salt

ACCOMPANIMENT: ketchup
SPECIAL EQUIPMENT: a deep-fat thermometer

Heat oil in a 4- to 5-quart wide heavy pot over moderate heat until it registers 370°F on thermometer.

Meanwhile, separate onion slices into rings. Pour milk into a bowl and combine flour and salt in a pie plate.

Know Your Onions

PEARL ONIONS

Broadly speaking, globe onions — as opposed to bunching onions, like leeks and scallions — are grouped as storage or sweet. Storage onions, which are the classic choice for cooking, have papery brown skin and are tinged with yellow inside. They are the pungent ones that can make you cry (when cut, their juices mingle with the air, forming new, eye-irritating compounds). Cured after harvest, they are suited to long-term storage. The new commercial hybrids, which are being bred sweeter and sweeter, don't keep as well as the old-fashioned varieties. Unless otherwise specified, storage onions are the ones we mean when we call for onions in a recipe. If using them raw, soak them in cold water after chopping to curb their harshness and make them crisp.

In Mexican and other Latin American recipes, we usually call for white onions, which are traditional in those countries. They have a sharper, cleaner flavor than yellow onions. Red onions are milder; their color gives them an edge when served raw in salads or cooked in kebabs. Pickled, they turn a beautiful shocking pink and get very crisp.

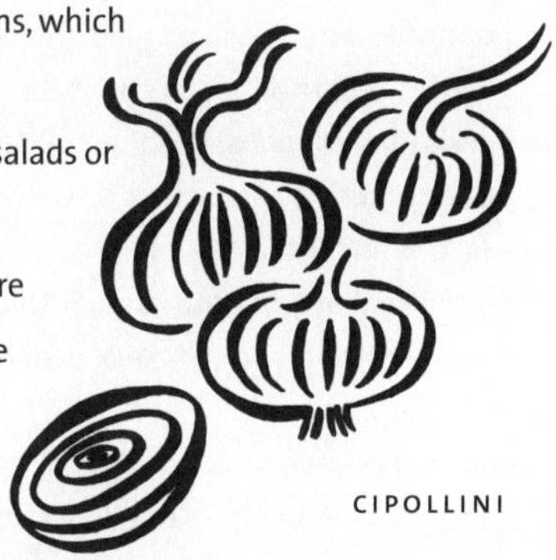

CIPOLLINI

Little onions such as pearl and boiling onions are all the same variety and are simply graded by size. *Cipollini,* which means "small onions" in Italian, refers to the distinctive small, flattened onions grown from Italian seed, which are mellower and richer-tasting than other little onions.

Sweet onions, once a seasonal, regional boutique crop, are now available year-round thanks to controlled-atmosphere storage. Domestic growing areas include Georgia, Texas, Washington, and Hawaii. Contrary to popular belief, "sweets" don't contain more sugar than storage onions, but they are milder because they have less pyruvic acid. Promotional claims that you "can eat them like an apple" aside, we prefer sweets that have a nice balance of sweetness and sharpness as well as some complexity, such as Vidalias (Georgia), Walla Wallas (Washington), and Mauis (Hawaii).

Over the years, satiny, bronze-skinned shallots (and other closely related look-alike varieties) have migrated from fancy food shops to supermarkets across the country, driven in some part, perhaps, by a burgeoning Asian population and a general interest in Asian food (according to Elizabeth Schneider's authoritative *Vegetables from Amaranth to Zucchini,* more shallots are grown in Southeast Asia than anywhere else). Their flavor is delicate, subtle, and intense all at once.

Dip 3 onion rings first in milk, then in flour, shaking off excess; repeat for a double coating and transfer to hot oil. Fry coated rings, stirring, until golden, about 2 minutes, then transfer with tongs to paper towels to drain. Coat and fry remaining rings in same manner (return oil to 370°F between batches). Serve immediately, with ketchup.

Scalloped Onions, Leeks, and Shallots

SERVES 8

ACTIVE TIME: 15 MINUTES ■ START TO FINISH: 1¼ HOURS

■ Combine the pungent directness of onions, the subtlety of leeks, and the sweet intensity of shallots and you get something nuanced and memorable. A bubbling-hot topping of bread crumbs and cheese takes it all home. This is especially delicious with ham, pork, or turkey. ■

- 2 pounds leeks (white and pale green parts only), halved lengthwise and chopped
- ½ stick (4 tablespoons) unsalted butter
- 3 pounds onions, halved lengthwise and cut crosswise into ¼-inch-thick slices
- ½ pound shallots, cut into ¼-inch-thick slices
- Salt and freshly ground black pepper
- ¼ cup heavy cream
- 1 cup coarse fresh bread crumbs
- 1 cup grated extra-sharp Cheddar (about 4 ounces)
- ¼ teaspoon paprika

Wash leeks well in a bowl of cold water; lift out and drain thoroughly.

Melt butter in a 7- to 8-quart heavy pot over moderate heat. Add onions, leeks, shallots, and salt and pepper to taste, cover, and cook, stirring occasionally, for 10 minutes. Reduce heat to moderately low and cook, covered, stirring occasionally, until vegetables are soft, 10 to 20 minutes more.

Remove lid and cook over moderate heat, stirring, until excess liquid has evaporated, 3 to 5 minutes.

Meanwhile, put a rack in middle of oven and preheat oven to 375°F.

Stir cream into onion mixture and transfer to a 2-quart shallow baking dish. Toss together bread crumbs and cheese in a small bowl and sprinkle evenly over onion mixture. Dust top with paprika. Bake until cheese is melted and sauce is bubbling, 20 to 30 minutes.

COOK'S NOTE

■ The onion mixture, without the cream or topping, can be made up to 2 days ahead and refrigerated, covered. Reheat in a heavy pot over moderately low heat, stirring occasionally, before proceeding.

Parsnip and Apple Purée

SERVES 4

ACTIVE TIME: 1 HOUR ■ START TO FINISH: 1 HOUR

■ Parsnips may be rather unprepossessing—pale, fleshy, and weedy-looking—but their appearance belies an elegant, complex, sweet flavor. They give wonderful body to this purée, which is outstanding with roast pork or venison. Parsnips are one of the oldest vegetables going, by the way. The food historian William Woys Weaver tells us that they were gathered from the wild in the Stone Age and were commonly found in the kitchen gardens of ancient Rome. ■

- 1½ pounds parsnips (about 6), peeled and coarsely chopped
- 2 tablespoons unsalted butter
- 1 cup finely chopped onion
- 2 Granny Smith apples, peeled, cored, and chopped
- ½ teaspoon salt
- ¼ teaspoon freshly ground black pepper
- ¼ cup sour cream, or to taste
- ⅛ teaspoon ground allspice, or to taste

Combine parsnips with water to cover in a saucepan, bring to a simmer, cover, and simmer until very tender, about 20 minutes.

Meanwhile, melt butter in a 10-inch heavy skillet over moderate heat. Add onion, apples, salt, and pepper and cook, stirring, until apples are tender, 5 to 10 minutes. Remove from heat.

With a slotted spoon, transfer parsnips to a food processor (reserve ¼ cup cooking liquid) and add apple mixture. Purée until smooth. With motor running, add sour cream, allspice, and salt and pepper to taste, then add enough cooking liquid, 1 tablespoon at a time, to thin purée to desired consistency.

COOK'S NOTE

- We specify Granny Smith apples here because they are not too sweet or juicy.

Minted Peas and Onions

SERVES 8

ACTIVE TIME: 30 MINUTES ■ START TO FINISH: 30 MINUTES

■ Garden-fresh peas have become almost a myth (by the time most of us get them, they are too starchy), so for consistency and ease, we prefer the frozen ones for this classic combination. We also use regular onions rather than the much smaller pearls; we like their texture here. ■

- 1/2 stick (4 tablespoons) unsalted butter
- 1 1/2 pounds onions, halved lengthwise and thinly sliced crosswise
- 2 (10-ounce) packages frozen green peas, thawed
- 1/4 cup finely chopped fresh mint
- 1/2 teaspoon salt
- 1/8 teaspoon freshly ground black pepper

Heat butter in a 12-inch heavy skillet over moderately low heat until foam subsides. Add onions, cover, and cook, stirring occasionally, until soft, about 8 minutes. Add peas, mint, salt, and pepper and cook, stirring, until peas are heated through.

Creamed Peas and Cucumbers with Dill

SERVES 6

ACTIVE TIME: 30 MINUTES ■ START TO FINISH: 30 MINUTES (DOES NOT INCLUDE SHELLING)

■ This recipe, of northern European ancestry, may sound peculiar, but it is really good. When cucumbers are cooked, they become tender and translucent. Their satiny texture is a nice foil for the sweet starchiness of the peas. Dill and a little lemon juice add a sprightly note. ■

- 2 tablespoons unsalted butter
- 1 pound cucumbers, peeled, quartered lengthwise, seeded, and cut into 1/2-inch pieces
- 1/2 teaspoon salt
- 1/8 teaspoon freshly ground black pepper
- 2 cups shelled fresh green peas or 1 (10-ounce) package frozen peas (not thawed)
- 1/3 cup water
- 1/3 cup heavy cream
- 3 tablespoons chopped fresh dill
- 1 1/2 teaspoons fresh lemon juice, or to taste

Heat butter in a 12-inch heavy skillet over moderately high heat until foam subsides. Add cucumbers, salt, and pepper and cook, stirring, for 5 minutes. Add peas and water, cover, and simmer for 5 minutes. Add cream and boil, uncovered, stirring occasionally, until peas are tender and liquid is slightly thickened, 3 minutes.

Stir in dill, lemon juice, and salt and pepper to taste.

Peas with Spinach and Shallots

SERVES 4

ACTIVE TIME: 15 MINUTES ■ START TO FINISH: 15 MINUTES (DOES NOT INCLUDE SHELLING)

■ Pairing peas with spinach and shallots yields a dish that's much more robust than its French counterpart, which traditionally combines peas and lettuce. ■

- 1 tablespoon unsalted butter
- 1 tablespoon vegetable oil
- 2 medium shallots, thinly sliced
- 2 garlic cloves, thinly sliced
- 2 cups shelled fresh green peas or 1 (10-ounce) package frozen peas (not thawed)
- 1/4 cup water
- 5 ounces baby spinach
- 3/4 teaspoon salt
- 1/4 teaspoon freshly ground black pepper

Melt butter with oil in a 12-inch nonstick skillet over moderate heat. Add shallots and garlic and cook, stirring, until soft, about 6 minutes. Stir in peas and water, cover, and cook, stirring occasionally, until peas are tender, about 5 minutes.

Stir in spinach, salt, and pepper and cook, tossing, until spinach is just wilted, about 1 minute.

Stir-Fried Pea Shoots

SERVES 4

ACTIVE TIME: 10 MINUTES ■ START TO FINISH: 10 MINUTES

■ Here's a celebration of something in season for a very short time. Pea shoots, which are the very essence of

Pea Shoots

Pea shoots are the tender, trailing leaves of a pea plant, long prized in China for their delicate texture and vivid pea flavor. Note, though, that there is a huge range in the size and heft of the leaves and stems of pea shoots: we've seen anything from a sprout (minus the root) to a large stem bearing the label. Although numbers 1, 2, and 3 in the illustrations are suitable for eating raw in a salad, only number 3 fits our idea of a perfect pea shoot. However, for stir-frying, number 4 (that is, more mature shoots) can be used.

green pea flavor, take well to stir-frying with garlic and hot red pepper. ■

- 3 tablespoons vegetable oil
- 3 garlic cloves, smashed
- 1/4 teaspoon red pepper flakes
- 1 pound pea shoots, coarse stems discarded
- Salt

Heat 1 tablespoon oil in a wok or 12-inch nonstick skillet over moderately high heat. Add 1 garlic clove and one third of red pepper flakes and stir-fry until garlic is golden, about 30 seconds. Add one third of pea shoots and stir-fry until wilted and tender, 2 to 3 minutes. With tongs, transfer to a serving dish, and cook remaining pea shoots in same manner, in 2 more batches. Season with salt to taste.

Snow Peas with Lemon Herb Butter

SERVES 6

ACTIVE TIME: 15 MINUTES ■ START TO FINISH: 15 MINUTES

■ Sweet, crunchy, and gloriously green, snow peas, so popular in Asian stir-fries, make a great side dish on their own. Try them with Cornish hens, for instance, or poussins. They are what the English, as well as the French, call *mangetouts* (literally, "eat all"). ■

- 1 1/2 tablespoons unsalted butter, softened
- 1 teaspoon finely grated lemon zest
- 1 teaspoon finely chopped fresh tarragon
- 1 teaspoon finely chopped fresh flat-leaf parsley
- 1/2 teaspoon salt
- 1/4 teaspoon freshly ground black pepper
- 1 pound snow peas, trimmed

Stir together butter, zest, tarragon, parsley, salt, and pepper in a small bowl.

Cook snow peas in a 5-quart pot of boiling salted water (1 tablespoon salt per every 4 quarts water) until crisp-tender, about 1 1/2 minutes; drain well. Transfer to a bowl, add lemon herb butter, and toss to coat.

Grilled Bell Peppers with Criolla Sauce

SERVES 6

ACTIVE TIME: 45 MINUTES ■ START TO FINISH: 45 MINUTES

■ Bell peppers, so often relegated to being a mere ingredient in a dish, shine when they stand on their own. Grilled to give them a smoky char, these are tossed with a South American vinaigrette called *criolla;* it's not terribly spicy, but it adds a little heat. Serve them with whatever else you put on the grill. ■

- 4 bell peppers of assorted colors (but not green)
- 2 medium tomatoes, finely chopped
- 1 medium white onion, finely chopped
- 1 serrano chile, minced (including seeds)
- 1 large garlic clove, minced
- 1 tablespoon minced fresh flat-leaf parsley
- 2 1/2 tablespoons olive oil
- 1 1/2 tablespoons red wine vinegar
- 1 teaspoon kosher salt

Prepare a charcoal or gas grill: If using a charcoal grill, open vents in bottom of grill, then light charcoal. Fire is hot when you can hold your hand 5 inches above rack for just 1 to 2 seconds. If using a gas grill, preheat all burners on high, covered, for 10 minutes.

Lightly oil grill rack. Grill peppers, uncovered, turning frequently with tongs, until skins are blackened, 10 to 12 minutes. Transfer peppers to a large bowl and cover tightly with plastic wrap. Let stand until cool enough to handle.

Peel peppers, then halve lengthwise; discard stems and seeds.

Stir together remaining ingredients in a bowl. Add peppers and toss gently.

COOK'S NOTES

- The peppers can also be roasted on the grates of gas burners over high heat; turn them with tongs. Or broil them on the rack of a broiler pan about 5 inches from the heat, turning occasionally, for about 15 minutes.
- The dish can be made up to 1 day ahead and refrigerated, covered. Bring to room temperature before serving.

Sweet-and-Savory Sautéed Bell Peppers

SERVES 4

ACTIVE TIME: 30 MINUTES ■ START TO FINISH: 35 MINUTES

■ This recipe exemplifies the Italian concept of *agrodolce*, sweet and sour. Avoid using green peppers, which would be too overpowering. This riotously colored side dish will bolster all sorts of grilled meats. Just add a loaf of crusty bread. ■

- 1 tablespoon unsalted butter
- 1 tablespoon olive oil
- 2 garlic cloves, thinly sliced
- 1 red bell pepper, cored, seeded, and cut into 1/4-inch-thick rings
- 1 yellow bell pepper, cored, seeded, and cut into 1/4-inch-thick rings
- 1 orange bell pepper, cored, seeded, and cut into 1/4-inch-thick rings
- 2 tablespoons golden raisins, soaked in 1/4 cup boiling water for 15 minutes
- 2 teaspoons drained capers, coarsely chopped
- 4 Kalamata or other brine-cured black olives, pitted and thinly sliced
- 2 tablespoons pine nuts, lightly toasted (see Tips, page 938)

Melt butter with oil in a 12-inch heavy skillet over moderate heat. Add garlic and cook, stirring, until softened, about 1 minute. Add peppers, increase heat to moderately high, and cook, stirring, for 1 minute. Add raisins, with their soaking liquid, capers, and olives, cover, and cook, stirring occasionally, until peppers are crisp-tender, 2 to 3 minutes. Stir in pine nuts.

Stuffed Bell Peppers

SERVES 8

ACTIVE TIME: 50 MINUTES ■ START TO FINISH: 2 HOURS

■ These peppers are not your typical Eastern European version: the bread stuffing is lightened with ricotta. Substantial and satisfying, this dish is pretty too, especially if you intersperse red, orange, and yellow peppers on a platter. Try them with lamb, roast chicken, or beef. ■

FOR FILLING

- 3 tablespoons olive oil
- 1 1/2 medium onions, chopped
- 3 anchovy fillets, rinsed, patted dry, and finely chopped
- 1 cup plus 2 tablespoons Toasted Bread Crumbs (recipe follows)
- 1 1/2 cups whole-milk ricotta
- 1/2 cup finely grated Parmigiano-Reggiano
- 3 tablespoons capers, rinsed, patted dry, and chopped
- 3 large eggs, lightly beaten
- 4 1/2 tablespoons finely chopped fresh flat-leaf parsley

FOR PEPPERS

- 4 small red, yellow, and/or orange bell peppers (1 1/2 pounds total)
- 1 tablespoon olive oil

MAKE THE FILLING: Heat oil in a 12-inch heavy skillet over moderate heat. Add onions and anchovies and cook, stirring frequently, until onions are golden, about 8 minutes (anchovies will dissolve). Transfer to a bowl and stir in bread crumbs, cheeses, capers, eggs, and parsley until well combined.

STUFF AND BAKE THE PEPPERS: Put a rack in middle of oven and preheat oven to 350°F. Oil a 13-by-9-inch baking dish.

Halve peppers lengthwise through stems and discard seeds and ribs. Stuff pepper halves with filling and arrange in baking dish. Add 1/2 cup water to dish and drizzle peppers with oil.

Bake, uncovered, until peppers are tender and filling is puffed, 50 to 60 minutes.

COOK'S NOTE

■ The peppers can be stuffed up to 1 day ahead and refrigerated, covered. Bring to room temperature before baking.

Toasted Bread Crumbs

MAKES ABOUT 2 CUPS

ACTIVE TIME: 10 MINUTES ■ START TO FINISH: 25 MINUTES

■ Far from being an afterthought, these bread crumbs are an art form that will change whatever you do with them. Their nutty texture and toasty flavor are nothing like store-bought. Make twice as much as you need, because they are delicious sprinkled on top of pasta (instead of Parmesan cheese) or any steamed vegetable. ■

- 3 cups fine fresh bread crumbs from a baguette or Italian loaf
- 1/4 cup extra-virgin olive oil
- Salt

Put a rack in middle of oven and preheat oven to 350°F.

Spread crumbs in a shallow baking pan and bake, stirring occasionally, until golden, 10 to 15 minutes. Transfer crumbs to a bowl, drizzle with oil, and stir until crumbs are coated. Season with salt to taste.

COOK'S NOTE

■ The crumbs can be made up to 1 day ahead and kept, covered, at room temperature.

Poblano Strips with Onion and Cream

Rajas con Crema

SERVES 6 TO 8

ACTIVE TIME: 1 HOUR ■ START TO FINISH: 1 HOUR

■ This traditional Mexican dish is a straightforward one to reproduce in an American kitchen, especially since poblano chiles are now available in many supermarkets. The roasted chile strips, called *rajas*, become deep and rich in flavor when cooked with onions and cream. This is one of Mexico's great culinary gifts to world cuisine. ■

- 2 pounds poblano chiles
- 3 tablespoons vegetable oil
- 1 medium white onion (8 ounces), halved lengthwise and cut lengthwise into 1/4-inch-thick slices
- Salt
- 1/3 cup *crema* (see Glossary), crème fraîche, or heavy cream

Roast, peel, and seed chiles (see page 560). Cut into 1/3-inch-wide strips.

Heat oil in a 12-inch heavy skillet over moderately low heat. Add onion and cook, stirring frequently, until softened, about 5 minutes. Add chiles and salt to taste and cook, stirring, for 5 minutes. Add *crema* and cook, stirring, for 2 minutes.

COOK'S NOTE

■ The *rajas* can be made up to 1 day ahead and refrigerated, covered. Reheat before serving.

Buttermilk Mashed Potatoes with Caramelized Shallots

SERVES 4

ACTIVE TIME: 15 MINUTES ■ START TO FINISH: 35 MINUTES

■ This recipe calls for only a smidgen of butter, relying instead on tangy buttermilk and, especially, browned shallots, which add a whole new dimension, almost a meatiness, to the rich yellow flesh of mashed Yukon Golds. ■

- 3/4 pound Yukon Gold potatoes
- 1/2 tablespoon unsalted butter
- 2 medium shallots, thinly sliced
- 1/2 cup well-shaken buttermilk
- Salt and freshly ground black pepper

Peel and quarter potatoes. Combine with cold well-salted water to cover by 1 inch in a 4-quart saucepan, bring to a simmer, and simmer until tender, about 20 minutes.

Meanwhile, melt butter in a small nonstick skillet over moderately high heat. Add shallots and cook, stirring frequently, until softened and deep golden, about 8 minutes.

Drain potatoes in a colander, return to pan, and coarsely mash with a potato masher. Stir in shallots, buttermilk, and salt and pepper to taste.

TO ROAST, PEEL, AND SEED CHILES

Lay each chile on its side on the grate of a gas burner (one or two per burner) and turn the flame to moderately high. Roast the chiles, turning them occasionally with tongs, until the skins blister all over, 4 to 6 minutes.

You can also roast the chiles on the rack of a broiler pan about 2 inches from the heat, turning them with tongs, until they blister, which will take 8 to 10 minutes. We prefer the stovetop method because it chars the skin without really cooking the chiles. The enclosed heat of the broiler cooks and softens the chile flesh too much.

Immediately transfer the chiles to a large bowl and cover tightly; let them steam for 20 minutes.

Gently scrape away the skins with a small knife (1) or rub them off with your fingers or a paper towel (the skins will cling to a paper towel and come right off).

To seed the chiles when you want to keep them whole for stuffing (for chiles rellenos, say), cut a lengthwise slit in each one with a small knife (2), then remove the seeds. Scissors work beautifully for this; snip through the small indentation just above the cluster of seeds (3); leave the stem attached, and don't snip too high, or the stem will come out with the seeds and the chile will collapse. If chopping the chiles into pieces or cutting them into strips for *rajas,* there is no need to be so finicky; simply cut open the chiles and remove the stems and seeds. Most recipes say to remove the veins, but if you have a mild batch of chiles, you might want to leave them in—they will provide a nice burst of heat.

1

2

3

After seeding the chiles, clean them with a paper towel or rinse them very briefly inside and out to remove any residual sticky seeds. (Longer rinsing would remove the flavorful oils.) Roasted chiles can be refrigerated, either before or after peeling, in a covered shallow bowl for up to one day.

Chile Peppers

Chile peppers are both very complicated and relatively simple. The complicated part comes from the fact that there are more than two thousand known varieties; the simplicity comes from the fact that, at least in the case of fresh chiles, you can often substitute one for another (as long as they have roughly similar heat levels) without significantly altering the recipe. That said, a few fresh chiles, notably the habanero, have such distinctive taste and heat that they have no real substitutes.

Dried chiles, in contrast, have more distinct flavors, so it is more important to use the particular variety called for in order to get the flavor we envision in the recipe. Fortunately, dried peppers of all kinds are now readily available in many supermarkets and by mail (see Sources).

Fresh Chiles

JALAPEÑO The chile that is most familiar to American cooks, the jalapeño is medium-hot to hot. It has thick flesh and is shaped like a bullet, measuring 2 to 3 inches long and ¾ to 1 inch in diameter. It may be green or red. When jalapeños are dried by smoking, they are known as chipotle chiles.

HABANERO A short, fat, lantern-shaped pepper 1 to 1½ inches long and 1¼ to 1¾ inches in diameter, the habanero is generally acknowledged as one of the hottest commercially available chile peppers in the world, thirty to fifty times hotter than the average jalapeño. It is grown primarily on the Yucatán Peninsula of Mexico, where it is very common. Ranging in color from yellow to red-orange to green to white, it has a floral flavor and an extreme nasal heat that is quite different from the flat back-of-the-throat heat of many other chile peppers.

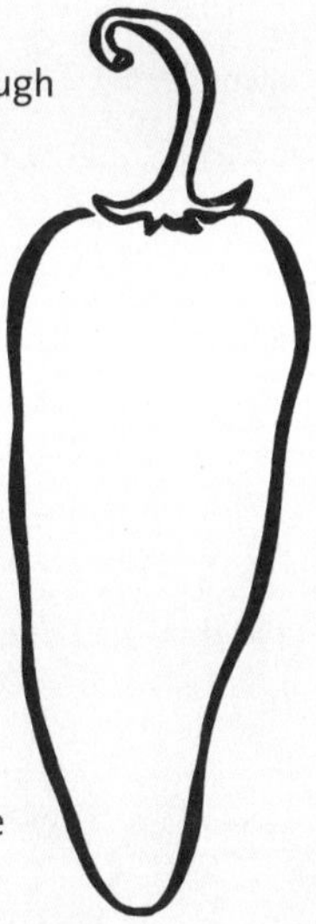

NEW MEXICO/ANAHEIM Although the characteristics of these two chiles differ slightly, they come from the same botanical parent and can be used interchangeably in recipes. Both are fairly mild long (6 to 8 inches) green chiles that turn red in the fall and are used in both green and red states. New Mexicos are grown extensively in northern Mexico, New Mexico, and Arizona, while Anaheims are grown in California.

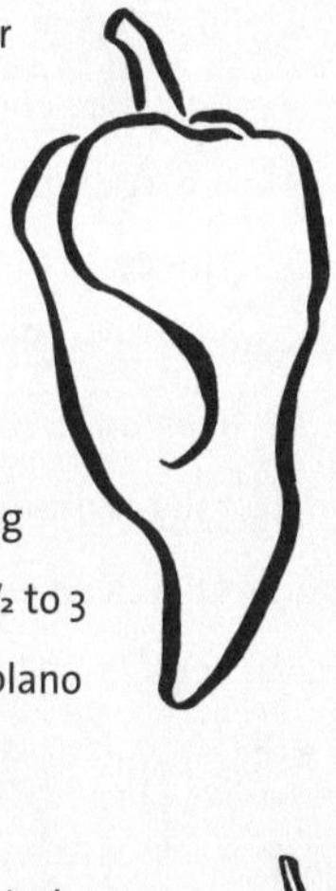

POBLANO One of the most popular chiles in Mexico, the poblano is red when ripe, but the green ones — a very dark green with a purple-black tinge — are far more common. Medium-hot to hot, this chile is thick-fleshed and has wide shoulders tapering to a point. It is 4 to 5 inches long and 2½ to 3 inches in diameter. When dried, the poblano is known as the ancho, or *mulato,* chile.

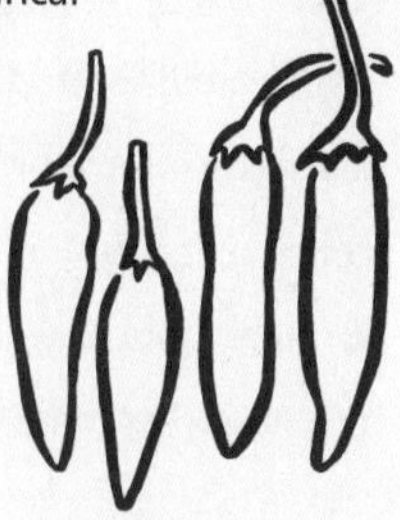

SERRANO This thick-fleshed, cylindrical chile is among the hottest commonly available in the United States. Usually seen when a bright dark green, it is scarlet when ripe. It measures 1 to 2 inches long and ½ to ¾ inch in diameter. In Mexico, the serrano is often called simply *chile verde,* "green chile."

SCOTCH BONNET Primarily grown in Jamaica, the Scotch bonnet is closely related to the habanero, with approximately the same heat level and a very similar aromatic, floral flavor. It also resembles the habanero in shape, but it is slightly smaller. It may be orange, red, or pale yellow.

THAI Thin, elongated, and slightly curved, little Thai chiles have a meaty texture and are very hot, with a long, lingering burn. They are usually about 1½ inches long and ½ inch in diameter, and they may be either green or red.

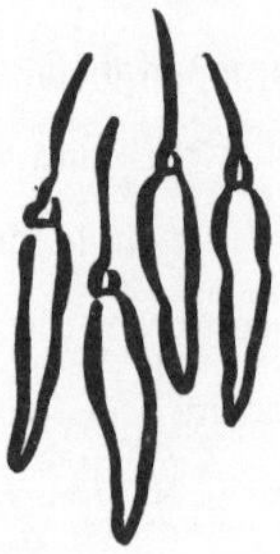

Dried Chiles

ANCHO This is the dried poblano chile, the most commonly used dried chile in Mexico. Wrinkled, with broad shoulders (the name means "wide" or "broad"), anchos are brick red to dark mahogany and medium-hot to hot, with a complex, sweet, raisiny flavor. Look for chiles that are still flexible and aromatic.

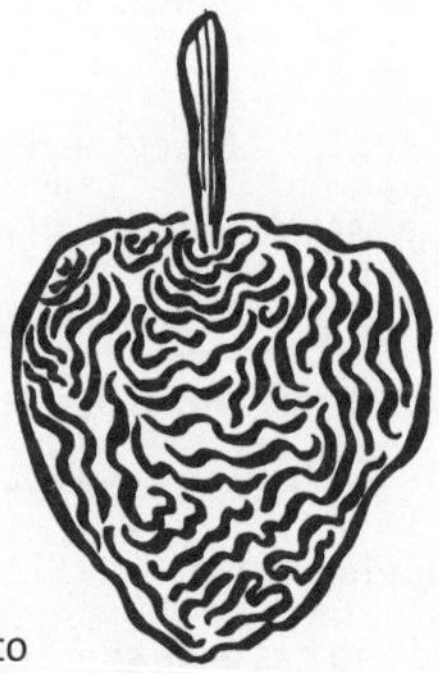

CHIPOTLE ("chi-*poht*-leh") Chipotles, which are dried and smoked jalapeños, have a unique, intense smoky flavor and a very consistent medium to hot heat level. Flat, wrinkled, and dark reddish brown, they are 1 to 1½ inches long. Chipotles are most readily available canned, packed in adobo sauce, a mixture of onions, tomatoes, vinegar, and spices, but you can also find them in the more traditional dried form.

CHILE DE ÁRBOL This is among the hottest of the dried chiles, with a searing, acidic heat and a sharp, somewhat astringent and smoky flavor. The smooth skin is brick red and the chile is about 3 inches long and ½ inch across at the widest point, with a distinctly tapered shape. Its name means "treelike," because of the woody stems of the plant.

GUAJILLO ("gwa-*hee*-oh") This shiny, burgundy-colored chile has mild to medium heat and a flavor that is rather straightforward, tart, and just a bit smoky. Elongated and tapering to a point, it comes in a variety of sizes but is most commonly 4 to 6 inches long and 1 to 1½ inches across.

PASILLA ("pas-*ee*-yah") Also known as *chile negro* ("black chile"), the pasilla is the dried *chilaca* chile. Dark brown and quite wrinkled (*pasilla* means "little raisin" in Spanish), it has an elongated, tapered shape and measures 5 to 6 inches long and ¾ to 1½ inches across. It is medium-hot to hot and has a deep, complex, long-lasting flavor, less sweet and more astringent than that of most dried chiles.

Mashed Potatoes with Six Variations

SERVES 4

ACTIVE TIME: 30 MINUTES ■ START TO FINISH: 40 MINUTES

■ Mashed potatoes serve as a wonderful bed for things—gravy, of course, but also the juices from steak, chicken, or mushrooms. And they are easy to make; we prefer to use an old-fashioned handheld masher, but you can use a ricer or food mill. (An electric mixer is too vigorous and will release too much starch, making the potatoes gluey. Under no circumstances use a food processor—you'll end up with library paste.) As for the main ingredient, in general, the better the potato, the better the result. We are very fond of Yukon Golds, which have great color and flavor. Russet potatoes, most often used for baking, work well too; we find that they need a little more salt. If you buy your spuds at a farmers market, have fun experimenting. Here you'll find some variations: goat cheese (great with lamb), olive oil (if the rest of your menu is Italian), roasted garlic or sour cream (good with anything), buttermilk (a viable low-fat version), and a combination of heavy cream and horseradish (if this is your last meal on earth). ■

- 2 pounds russet (baking) potatoes or boiling potatoes, such as Yukon Gold
- 3/4 cup whole milk
- 1/2 stick (4 tablespoons) unsalted butter, cut into tablespoons
- 1/2 teaspoon salt
- 1/4 teaspoon freshly ground black pepper

Peel potatoes and cut into 2-inch pieces. Combine with cold salted water (1 tablespoon salt per every 4 quarts water) to cover by 1 inch in a 5-quart pot, bring to a simmer, and simmer, uncovered, until tender, about 18 minutes.

Shortly before potatoes are done, bring milk just to a simmer in a small saucepan over moderate heat. Remove from heat.

Drain potatoes well in a colander, then return to pot. Add butter, milk, salt, and pepper and mash with a potato masher until well combined.

VARIATIONS

Here are six very different ways to alter our basic mashed potato recipe. We love them all.

- Add 1 cup crumbled goat cheese (about 4 ounces) to the potatoes along with the butter and milk and reduce the salt to 1/4 teaspoon.
- In place of the butter, use 1/4 cup extra-virgin olive oil.
- In place of the milk, use 3/4 cup heavy cream and 1/3 cup drained bottled horseradish.
- In place of the whole milk, use well-shaken buttermilk; heat the buttermilk but do not let it simmer.
- In place of 1/2 cup of the milk, use 1/2 cup sour cream, at room temperature.
- Add roasted garlic: Squeeze the pulp from 1 head of Roasted Garlic (page 935) into the potatoes before adding the butter and milk.

Mashed Potatoes and Rutabaga

Clapshot

SERVES 4 TO 6

ACTIVE TIME: 15 MINUTES ■ START TO FINISH: 45 MINUTES

■ "Everything about clapshot is good, including the smell and the color," the celebrated Scottish writer George Mackay Brown once wrote about the Orkney specialty. "Set the pot on the kitchen floor on top of last week's *Radio Times*, add a golden chunk of butter and a dash of milk, . . . and begin to mash." Peppery and nutty in flavor, rutabagas, or swedes, as they are called in Europe, are Scottish turnips, or "neeps" for short. Clapshot (the origin of the term is uncertain) is a traditional accompaniment to haggis, but don't wait until Burns Night (January 25) to enjoy it; clapshot goes with rich, flavorful meats such as duck, venison, even a grilled porterhouse.

Some of us like to use a Y-shaped peeler to remove the skin from a rutabaga; others prefer a sharp paring knife, lopping off one end to make a flat surface, then removing the skin in lengthwise strips. Look for medium rutabagas; the huge ones have woody cores that need to be cut out and discarded. ■

Potatoes

POTATOES

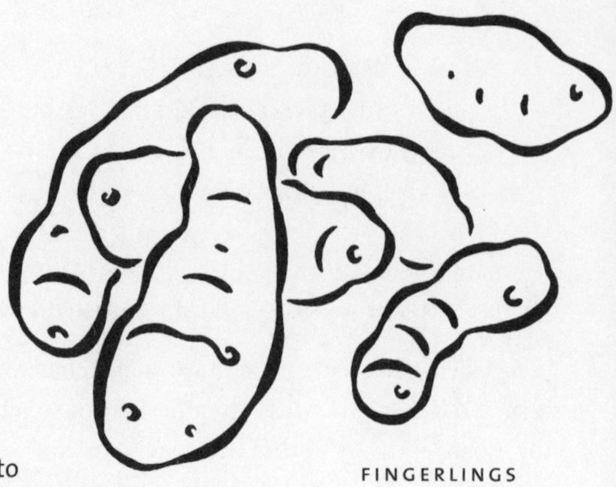

FINGERLINGS

A potato revolution has taken root in the United States. In supermarkets across the land, you'll see bins of hefty russets for baking, round red-skinned boilers, white "all-purpose" potatoes, yellow-fleshed Yukon Golds, and even small, knobby fingerlings, once found exclusively at farmers markets and specialty foods shops. The only thing you really have to remember is that all potatoes are not created equal. Varying starch and moisture content means that some varieties are better suited to baking and mashing, others to potato salad or french fries. When buying potatoes, avoid those that are tinged with green — that's a sign that they've been improperly exposed to light and thus contain solanine, a mildly toxic alkaloid.

Here are some of our favorites.

BOILING POTATOES Both white and red boiling potatoes have low starch and plenty of moisture. Much of that moisture stays with them once they've been boiled, which means that they hold together with waxy firmness if you cube them for potato salad. They take on the flavors around them while absorbing little dressing. They are also good when cut up and roasted: low starch means a higher amount of sugar, and since sugar caramelizes faster than starch, the result is beautifully brown and crisp. Because of their low starch content (and the type of starch they contain), boiling potatoes aren't as fluffy as russets for mashing or baking.

FINGERLINGS These oddly shaped, narrow little potatoes have great flavor and a firm, waxy texture. They can be roasted or boiled, but be aware that the peel can be bitter. We peel them before roasting or after boiling. Fingerlings may be any one of a number of heirloom potato varieties, meaning that they haven't been hybridized or bred for tough skin or long-term storage.

NEW POTATOES The term *new potatoes* refers to waxy low-starch spuds of any variety that are young and freshly dug from the leafy plant. (Mature potatoes are harvested after the plant dies.) They have a slightly nutty flavor that differs from one variety to another. New potatoes are crisp even when cooked because their water content is much higher than their starch content. They are great for boiling, and their thin, papery skins don't need to be peeled. Real new potatoes are classified by age, not size, and occasionally imposters — small mature potatoes — are sold as "new." One way to be sure that you are getting true new potatoes is to buy from a farm stand or farmers market in late spring or early summer. Another way of checking is the scratch test: if the potato's skin succumbs easily to a fingernail, it's a new potato.

RUSSETS The classic baking potatoes are russets: large, even oblongs with dark tweedy skins and fluffy white flesh. The proper name is Russet Burbank, after Luther Burbank, who developed the variety; they are sometimes called Idahos, although they are grown in other states as well. Their high starch content and low moisture cause russets to bake up light and dry. Those same qualities mean that they mash nicely (effortlessly absorbing vast amounts of butter and cream) and fry beautifully too. Because they don't hold their shape when cooked, they're not good for potato salad.

YUKON GOLDS The Yukon Gold, developed in 1981, was the first yellow-fleshed potato to hit the big time, and it has become incredibly popular. The name actually refers to the Yukon gold rush, implying that farmers who plant it will get high yields and plenty of cash, but it also suggests the color of the tuber. Yukon Golds have a medium starch content, so they're wonderfully versatile and full of flavor. We use them for practically everything. Another yellow-fleshed variety that is becoming more widespread is Yellow Finn.

- 1 pound rutabaga, peeled and cut into 1-inch pieces
- 2 pounds Yukon Gold or russet (baking) potatoes
- 1/4 cup whole milk
- 1/2 stick (4 tablespoons) unsalted butter
- 1/4 cup finely chopped fresh chives
- 1/2 teaspoon salt
- 1/4 teaspoon freshly ground black pepper

Cook rutabaga in a 4-quart saucepan of boiling well-salted water, uncovered, until very tender, about 15 minutes. With a slotted spoon, transfer to a colander to drain.

Meanwhile, peel potatoes and cut into 1-inch pieces. Simmer potatoes in same cooking water, uncovered, until very tender, about 20 minutes. Drain potatoes in colander.

Heat milk with butter in same saucepan over moderate heat until butter is melted. Remove from heat, add rutabaga and potatoes, and coarsely mash with a potato masher. Stir in chives, salt, and pepper.

COOK'S NOTE

- The clapshot can be made up to 1 day ahead and refrigerated, covered. Reheat in a heavy saucepan over low heat, stirring to prevent scorching; thin with milk if necessary.

VARIATION

- Substitute 1 pound celery root (celeriac) for the rutabaga. Peel with a sharp knife, then cut and cook in the same manner as the rutabaga.

Colcannon

Mashed Potatoes with Cabbage

SERVES 4 TO 6

ACTIVE TIME: 30 MINUTES ■ START TO FINISH: 30 MINUTES

■ The name *colcannon* comes from the Gaelic *càl ceannann* ("white-headed cabbage"), and along with champ, this is among Ireland's culinary treasures. In champ, potatoes are mashed with scallions or chives; in colcannon, they are lightened with tender wisps of cabbage. We like to eat this on its own, but it is also delicious with beef, pork, or fish—try it with cod or salmon. ■

- 2 pounds russet (baking) potatoes
- 1 cup whole milk
- 1 stick (8 tablespoons) unsalted butter, cut into tablespoons
- 1 pound green cabbage, cored and coarsely chopped (about 4 cups)
- 1/2 teaspoon salt
- 1/4 teaspoon freshly ground black pepper

Peel potatoes and cut into 2-inch pieces. Combine with cold salted water (1 tablespoon salt per every 4 quarts water) to cover by 1 inch in a 5-quart pot, bring to a simmer, and simmer, uncovered, until tender, about 15 minutes.

Meanwhile, combine milk, butter, cabbage, salt, and pepper in a 3-quart heavy saucepan, bring to a bare simmer, and cook, uncovered, stirring occasionally, until cabbage is tender, 10 to 15 minutes.

Drain potatoes well, then add to cabbage mixture and mash with a potato masher until well combined. Season with salt and pepper.

VARIATIONS

- To make champ, substitute 2 cups chopped scallion greens for the cabbage. Add to the pan with the butter and milk and proceed as directed.
- Substitute 1 1/2 pounds leeks for the cabbage. Cut off the dark green tops and trim the root ends, then halve the leeks lengthwise and chop. Wash well in a bowl of cold water, then lift out and drain. Add to the pan with the butter and milk and proceed as directed.

Sautéed Potato Balls

SERVES 8

ACTIVE TIME: 45 MINUTES ■ START TO FINISH: 45 MINUTES

■ These buttery little spheres are so elegant that they will make you yearn for a sterling silver chafing dish to put them in. Making them might seem like a fiddly chore, but it's nothing like it used to be when the potatoes were "turned"—carved—with a paring knife into little ovals. We think a melon baller does the trick nicely. Parboil the potatoes a day ahead and throw the lacy skeletons into the soup pot. Château potatoes, as they are called, are a classic accompaniment to châteaubriand, but don't feel constrained by that; they are superlative with practically everything. ■

- 4 pounds russet (baking) potatoes
- 3/4 stick (6 tablespoons) unsalted butter
- Salt

OPTIONAL GARNISH: finely chopped fresh flat-leaf parsley

SPECIAL EQUIPMENT: a 1¼-inch round or oval melon ball cutter

Peel potatoes and put in a bowl of cold water. Using melon ball cutter, scoop as many balls from potatoes as possible, transferring them to another bowl of cold water as you cut them.

Drain potato balls and cook in a 4-quart heavy saucepan of boiling well-salted water for 5 minutes. Drain in a colander and let air-dry for 2 minutes.

Heat butter in a 12-inch nonstick skillet over moderately high heat until foam subsides. Add potatoes and cook, shaking skillet frequently, until golden, 10 to 12 minutes. Season with salt and transfer to a serving bowl. Sprinkle with parsley, if desired.

COOK'S NOTE

- The potato balls can be parboiled up to 1 day ahead. Cool, then refrigerate, covered. Bring to room temperature before sautéing.

Rösti

Shredded Potato Cake

SERVES 2 TO 4

ACTIVE TIME: 10 MINUTES ■ START TO FINISH: 5 HOURS (INCLUDES CHILLING)

■ As any Swiss home cook will tell you, the secret to this dish—essentially mashed potatoes with a crust—is simmering the potatoes in their jackets and letting them chill for as long as a day or so before you grate and fry them. (In Switzerland, it's possible to buy already cooked potatoes.) The resulting potato cake will be crisp and golden brown on the outside and fluffy and tender inside. ■

- 1 pound medium yellow-fleshed potatoes, such as Yukon Gold, scrubbed
- Salt and freshly ground black pepper
- 2 tablespoons unsalted butter
- 1 tablespoon vegetable oil

Combine potatoes and well-salted water to cover by 2 inches in a 4-quart saucepan, bring to a simmer, and simmer, uncovered, until tender, 25 to 30 minutes. Drain and cool, then chill potatoes, covered, for at least 4 hours.

Peel potatoes. Using a box grater, coarsely shred into a large bowl. Season with salt and pepper, tossing with a fork. Heat 1 tablespoon butter and 1½ teaspoons oil in a 6-inch nonstick skillet over moderate heat until foam subsides. Add potatoes, spreading them evenly and pressing down with a rubber spatula to form an even cake. Reduce heat to moderately low and cook *rösti* until underside is golden brown, 10 to 12 minutes.

Carefully slide *rösti* onto a large plate. Invert another large plate over it and invert *rösti* onto it. Heat remaining 1 tablespoon butter and 1½ teaspoons oil in skillet over moderately low heat until foam subsides. Slide *rösti* back into skillet, browned side up, and cook until underside is golden brown, 10 to 12 minutes.

Slide *rösti* onto a serving plate and cut into wedges.

COOK'S NOTE

- The cooked (but not shredded) potatoes can be refrigerated for up to 2 days.

Grated Potato Pancake

Pommes Paillasson

SERVES 6

ACTIVE TIME: 20 MINUTES ■ START TO FINISH: 50 MINUTES

■ *Paillasson* ("*pay*-ah-sohn") is French for "straw mat," and although this potato pancake sounds similar to Rösti, it is quite different. Made from raw, not cooked, potatoes, it is much thinner and crisper, and inside, the woven strands of potato stay separate but become almost custardy in texture. Cut into wedges, the pancake makes a terrific bed for steak, chops, or sautéed chicken breasts, because the meat juices collect in the little pockets of the "straw." ■

2¼ pounds russet (baking) potatoes
5 tablespoons unsalted butter
½ teaspoon salt
½ teaspoon freshly ground black pepper

Peel potatoes. Grate in a food processor fitted with coarse shredding disk or on large teardrop-shaped holes of a box grater. Working in small batches, wrap potatoes in a kitchen towel and twist and squeeze tightly to wring out as much liquid as possible. Transfer to a bowl.

Heat 3 tablespoons butter in a 12-inch nonstick skillet over moderately high heat until foam subsides. While butter heats, toss potatoes with salt and pepper. Reduce heat to moderate, then immediately spread potatoes in skillet and press down on top once with a spatula. Cook potato cake until underside is golden brown, about 12 minutes.

Slide cake onto a large plate. Invert another large plate over it and invert cake onto it. Heat remaining 2 tablespoons butter in skillet over moderate heat until foam subsides. Slide cake back into skillet, browned side up, and cook until underside is golden brown, about 12 minutes more.

Slide cake onto a cutting board and cut into 6 wedges.

COOK'S NOTE

- You can make the potato cake up to 30 minutes ahead and set it aside at room temperature. Reheat on a baking sheet in the middle of a 450°F oven for about 5 minutes, then cut into wedges.

Potato Latkes

MAKES 12 TO 16 LATKES; SERVES 4
ACTIVE TIME: 45 MINUTES ■ START TO FINISH: 45 MINUTES

■ Latkes, the small potato pancakes served at Hanukkah (its name means "dedication" in Hebrew), are associated traditionally with olive oil, which symbolizes the rededication of the Temple in Jerusalem in 165 B.C. after the Maccabees, led by Judah, triumphed over the Syrians. They found just enough undefiled olive oil to light the menorah for one day, but legend holds that the supply lasted for eight days—enough time to make more consecrated oil. The potato wasn't available to Jewish cooks until Pizarro's conquest of Peru almost 1700 years later; in Israeli households today, doughnuts, not latkes, are the fried food of choice for Hanukkah.

We tested this recipe with russet potatoes (starchiest), Yukon Golds (medium starch), and boiling potatoes (the least starchy) and liked the flavor of them all, but we found that the starchier the potato, the crisper the latke. For thin, crisp latkes (as opposed to the more customary thick ones), be sure to wring out as much liquid as possible from the grated potatoes, and do not use matzo meal or flour as a filler. Because frying latkes is something of a juggling act—they are best hot from the pan—have them as a first course rather than a side dish, or make a whole meal of them. You can easily double this recipe for a crowd. ■

1 pound potatoes
½ cup finely chopped onion
1 large egg, lightly beaten
½ teaspoon salt
½–¾ cup olive oil
ACCOMPANIMENTS: sour cream and applesauce

Preheat oven to 250°F.

Peel potatoes. Coarsely grate on large teardrop-shaped holes of a box grater, then transfer to a large bowl of cold water. Soak potatoes for 2 minutes, then drain well.

Wrap grated potatoes and onion in a kitchen towel and twist and squeeze tightly to wring out as much liquid as possible. Transfer potato mixture to a bowl and stir in egg and salt.

Heat ¼ cup oil in a 12-inch nonstick skillet over moderately high heat until hot but not smoking. Working in batches of 4 latkes, spoon 2 tablespoons potato mixture per latke into skillet, flattening and spreading each one into a 3-inch round with a fork. Reduce heat to moderate and cook until undersides are browned, about 5 minutes. Turn latkes over and cook until undersides are browned, about 5 minutes more. Transfer to paper towels to drain and season with salt, then transfer to a wire rack set in a shallow baking pan and keep warm in oven while you cook remaining latkes. Add more oil to skillet as needed.

Serve with sour cream and applesauce.

COOK'S NOTES

- Soaking the grated potatoes briefly in water and then squeezing out the liquid helps keep the batter from turning brown.
- The latkes are best eaten right away but can be made up to 8 hours ahead, covered, and refrigerated. Reheat on a rack set over a baking sheet in a 350°F oven until hot, 5 to 10 minutes.

Roasted French Fries

SERVES 4
ACTIVE TIME: 15 MINUTES ■ START TO FINISH: 40 MINUTES

■ We all love french fries, but the real thing can be an undertaking. These oven-roasted fries are much easier and wonderfully crisp. ■

1½ pounds russet (baking) potatoes (3 large), scrubbed
¼ cup vegetable oil
½ teaspoon salt
¼ teaspoon freshly ground black pepper
ACCOMPANIMENT: ketchup and/or mayonnaise

Put a rack in lower third of oven and preheat oven to 500°F.

Cut potatoes lengthwise into ⅓-inch-thick slices, then cut into ⅓-inch-wide sticks. Immediately toss with oil, salt, and pepper in a large bowl, then spread sticks in one layer on a large baking sheet with sides.

Bake for 15 minutes. Loosen potatoes from bottom of pan with a metal spatula, turn them over, and spread out again. Bake until crisp and edges are golden brown, about 10 minutes more. Serve with ketchup and/or mayonnaise.

Golden Potato Wedges

SERVES 4
ACTIVE TIME: 15 MINUTES ■ START TO FINISH: 1 HOUR

■ Cutting potatoes lengthwise into wedges gives you more surface area to get crisp and golden. The potatoes turn tender and creamy inside. ■

2 pounds medium boiling potatoes, preferably Yukon Gold (6–8)
1½ tablespoons olive oil
½ teaspoon salt
⅛ teaspoon freshly ground black pepper

Put a rack in lower third of oven and preheat oven to 425°F. Oil a large baking sheet with sides.

Peel potatoes and cut each one lengthwise into 6 wedges. Toss potatoes with oil, salt, and pepper in a bowl, then arrange flat sides down in one layer on oiled baking sheet. Roast until undersides are golden, about 30 minutes.

Turn potatoes over onto other cut sides and continue roasting until undersides are golden and potatoes are tender, about 15 minutes more.

VARIATIONS

- Add 1 teaspoon finely chopped fresh rosemary to the potatoes before roasting.
- Add 3 garlic cloves, thinly sliced, to the potatoes before roasting.

Parsley-Leaf Potatoes

SERVES 8 TO 12
ACTIVE TIME: 15 MINUTES ■ START TO FINISH: 1 HOUR

■ A simple roast potato becomes a thing of beauty thanks to a decal of humble parsley. This makes a sophisticated side and is a great party trick. ■

¾ stick (6 tablespoons) unsalted butter, melted
8 russet (baking) potatoes, scrubbed
16 fresh flat-leaf parsley leaves
Salt

Put a rack in middle of oven and preheat oven to 450°F.

Pour butter onto one large or two small baking sheets with sides and tilt to coat bottoms. Working with 1 potato at a time, halve each potato diagonally lengthwise, then put a parsley leaf on cut side of each potato half, season with salt, and put cut sides down on baking sheet(s). Sprinkle potatoes with salt to taste and roast (do not turn over) until undersides are golden and potatoes are tender, about 45 minutes.

COOK'S NOTE

- The potatoes can be kept warm, turned cut sides up and loosely covered with foil, for about 30 minutes.

Potato Croquettes

Pommes Dauphine

SERVES 6

ACTIVE TIME: 50 MINUTES ■ START TO FINISH: 2 HOURS

■ We proudly present the most elegant french fries in the world: evenly golden and crisp on the outside, ethereally light on the inside. The procedure is somewhat involved, but perfectly straightforward: you simply blend dry mashed potatoes with cream-puff batter, which you can throw together in less than five minutes. The egg-rich batter causes the croquettes to puff up gloriously when cooked. These are a tour de force. ■

- 1½ pounds russet (baking) potatoes, scrubbed
- 3 tablespoons unsalted butter, cut into bits
- 1 teaspoon salt
- Pinch of freshly grated nutmeg
- ½ cup water
- ½ cup all-purpose flour
- 2–3 large eggs
- About 6 cups vegetable oil for deep-frying
- Coarse salt (optional)

SPECIAL EQUIPMENT: a ricer or food mill fitted with a medium disk; a deep-fat thermometer; a large pastry bag fitted with a ½-inch star tip

Put a rack in middle of oven and preheat oven to 425°F.

Prick potatoes with a fork. Bake on oven rack until soft, 50 minutes to 1 hour.

Remove from oven and reduce oven temperature to 300°F. Halve hot potatoes lengthwise, then scoop flesh into ricer or food mill set over a large bowl; discard potato skins. Force hot potato flesh through ricer into bowl.

Combine butter, salt, nutmeg, and water in a 2- to 3-quart heavy saucepan and bring to a boil over high heat, then reduce heat to moderate. Add flour all at once and cook, stirring vigorously with a wooden spoon, until mixture pulls away from sides of pan, 1 to 2 minutes. Remove pan from heat and cool slightly, about 3 minutes.

Add 2 eggs, one at a time, to flour mixture, beating well after each addition (batter will separate after addition of each egg, but will then become smooth). Batter should be glossy and just stiff enough to hold soft peaks and fall softly from a spoon; if it is too stiff, beat remaining egg in a small bowl and add to batter 1 teaspoon at a time, beating and then testing batter, until it reaches desired consistency. Add potatoes and beat until well combined.

Heat 2 inches oil in a 5- to 6-quart heavy pot until it registers 370°F on thermometer. Transfer potato mixture to pastry bag and pipe eight 2½-inch lengths directly into oil, using kitchen shears or a small knife to cut off each length of dough at tip of bag. Fry croquettes, turning occasionally with a slotted spoon, until crisp, golden, and cooked through, 2 to 3 minutes. Transfer to paper towels to drain and sprinkle with coarse salt, if using. Make more croquettes with remaining potato mixture in batches in same manner. (Return oil to 370°F between batches.) Transfer croquettes, once drained, to a rack set in a large sheet with sides to keep them crisp, and keep warm in oven until ready to serve.

COOK'S NOTES

- The potato batter can be made up to 1 day ahead and refrigerated, covered.
- The croquettes can be made up to 2 hours ahead and set aside, still on the rack in the pan, loosely covered with paper towels, at room temperature. Remove the paper towels and reheat in a 400°F oven until heated through and crisp, about 5 minutes.

Spicy French Fries

SERVES 4 TO 6
ACTIVE TIME: 40 MINUTES ■ START TO FINISH: 1 HOUR

■ These are fast and fun. ■

- 1/2 teaspoon salt
- 1/4 teaspoon cayenne
- 1/4 teaspoon paprika
- 1/4 teaspoon ground coriander
- About 8 cups vegetable oil for deep-frying
- 2 pounds medium russet (baking) potatoes (about 4), scrubbed

SPECIAL EQUIPMENT: a deep-fat thermometer

Stir together salt, cayenne, paprika, and coriander in a large bowl.

Heat 1 1/2 inches oil in a 5-quart heavy pot over moderate heat until it registers 325°F on thermometer. While oil is heating, cut potatoes lengthwise into 1/4-inch-thick slices, then cut into 1/4-inch-thick sticks.

Fry potatoes in 5 batches in hot oil for 1 1/2 minutes per batch (potatoes will not be golden) and transfer with a slotted spoon to paper towels to drain. (Return oil to 325°F between batches.)

Heat oil until it registers 350°F on thermometer. Refry potatoes, in 5 batches, until golden and crisp, about 5 minutes per batch, and transfer to clean paper towels to drain. (Return oil to 350°F between batches.) Toss fries in spice mixture.

Garlic-Roasted Potato Skins

SERVES 8
ACTIVE TIME: 30 MINUTES ■ START TO FINISH: 1 3/4 HOURS

■ Sometimes all you want from a baked potato is the crisp skin, and there's no reason on earth that you can't just cut to the chase. We leave a thin layer of potato on the skins and cut them so they form sturdy little scoops, just right for dip, such as the classic onion and sour cream. ■

- 3 pounds medium russet (baking) potatoes (about 6), scrubbed
- 1 small head garlic (about 2 inches in diameter)
- 3/4 stick (6 tablespoons) unsalted butter, softened
- 1 teaspoon salt
- 1/4 teaspoon freshly ground black pepper

Put racks in middle and lower third of oven and preheat oven to 350°F.

Prick potatoes with a fork. Cut off and discard top quarter of garlic head, then wrap garlic tightly in foil. Bake potatoes and garlic directly on rack in lower third of oven until potatoes are tender, 50 minutes to 1 hour. Remove potatoes from oven and cool on a rack for 15 minutes. Continue to bake garlic until very tender, about 15 minutes more (1 to 1 1/4 hours total). Transfer to rack, still wrapped in foil. Increase oven temperature to 425°F.

Halve potatoes lengthwise. Cut each half lengthwise and then crosswise in half to form short wedges. Scoop out potato flesh (reserve it for another use), leaving 1/4-inch-thick potato skins.

Squeeze garlic pulp into a small bowl; discard garlic skins. Add butter, salt, and pepper to garlic and mash to a paste with a fork.

Divide garlic paste among potato skins (about 1/2 teaspoon each), spreading it evenly. Arrange skins in one layer on a large baking sheet with sides and roast in middle of oven until golden and crisp, 20 to 25 minutes.

COOK'S NOTE

■ The potato skins can be spread with the garlic paste up to 1 day ahead and refrigerated, loosely covered with foil. Bring to room temperature before baking.

Twice-Baked Potatoes with Basil and Sour Cream

SERVES 8
ACTIVE TIME: 15 MINUTES ■ START TO FINISH: 1 3/4 HOURS

■ Lighter than the usual cheese-heavy stuffed potatoes and more manageable in size (we use Yukon Golds rather than brawny russets), these are perfect for entertaining. ■

8 medium yellow-fleshed potatoes, preferably Yukon Gold (2¾ pounds total), scrubbed
5 tablespoons unsalted butter, softened
½ cup milk
Salt and freshly ground black pepper
1 cup packed fresh basil leaves

ACCOMPANIMENT: ½ cup sour cream

Put a rack in middle of oven and preheat oven to 400°F.

Prick potatoes with a fork. Bake on a baking sheet with sides until tender, about 1 hour. Remove from oven (leave oven on).

When potatoes are just cool enough to handle, halve lengthwise. Leaving ¼-inch-thick shells, scoop flesh into a 3-quart saucepan. Using a potato masher, mash potatoes with 3 tablespoons butter. Stir in milk and salt and pepper to taste. Set aside, partially covered.

Return potato shells to baking sheet and brush insides with remaining 2 tablespoons butter, then season with salt and pepper. Bake until golden, about 20 minutes.

Meanwhile, cut basil into thin strips and stir about three quarters into warm mashed potatoes.

Spoon mashed potatoes into baked shells and bake until heated through, about 10 minutes. Serve each potato half topped with 1½ teaspoons sour cream and some of remaining basil.

COOK'S NOTE

- The mashed potatoes and shells can be prepared (but not baked) up to 1 day ahead and refrigerated, separately, covered. Reheat the mashed potatoes before proceeding.

Cheddar- and Garlic-Stuffed Potatoes

SERVES 4
ACTIVE TIME: 15 MINUTES ■ START TO FINISH: 1¾ HOURS

■ Potatoes have a blissful affinity for some of our favorite things: cheese, garlic, butter, and sour cream. ■

1 medium head garlic (about 2½ inches in diameter)
4 medium russet (baking) potatoes (2 pounds total), scrubbed
3 tablespoons unsalted butter, softened
⅓ cup sour cream
1½ cups coarsely grated Cheddar (about 6 ounces)
Salt and freshly ground black pepper

Put a rack in middle of oven and preheat oven to 400°F.

Cut off and discard top quarter of garlic head. Wrap garlic in foil. Prick potatoes with a fork. Bake potatoes and garlic on oven rack for 45 minutes. Remove garlic and let cool. Continue baking potatoes until tender, about 20 minutes more. (Leave oven on.)

Squeeze pulp from garlic cloves into a medium bowl and discard skin. Stir in butter, sour cream, and 1 cup Cheddar. Cutting lengthwise, slice off top quarter of each potato and discard. Leaving ¼-inch-thick shells, scoop flesh out of potatoes and add to cheese mixture. Mash with fork to combine. Season with salt and pepper and divide among shells.

Arrange potatoes in a small baking pan and sprinkle with remaining ½ cup Cheddar. Bake until heated through, 15 to 20 minutes.

Pommes Anna

SERVES 4
ACTIVE TIME: 25 MINUTES ■ START TO FINISH: 1½ HOURS

■ This French classic will be the centerpiece of any meal because it is such a beautiful thing to behold. Thinly sliced potatoes are layered with butter in a skillet and pressed down to form a compact pie. After baking, the pie is inverted like a tarte Tatin or an upside-down cake. It doesn't really matter how you arrange the overlapping potato slices; in the end, it will be pretty no matter what you do. ■

1½ pounds russet (baking) potatoes
½ stick (4 tablespoons) unsalted butter, melted
Salt and freshly ground black pepper

SPECIAL EQUIPMENT: a mandoline or other adjustable-blade slicer, such as a Japanese Benriner

Put a rack in middle of oven and preheat oven to 425°F.

Peel potatoes. Cut into 1/16-inch-thick slices with

slicer and transfer to a large bowl of cold water, then drain and pat dry with paper towels.

Generously brush bottom and sides of a 10-inch heavy ovenproof skillet, preferably nonstick, with some of butter. Arrange potato slices in skillet, overlapping slightly, in layers, brushing each layer with some of remaining butter and seasoning with salt and pepper. Cover top with a buttered round of foil, buttered side down, and press down firmly on potato cake. Bake for 30 minutes.

Remove foil and bake cake until potatoes are tender and top is golden, 25 to 30 minutes more.

Slide cake onto a cutting board and cut into wedges.

Gratin Dauphinois

SERVES 8
ACTIVE TIME: 30 MINUTES ■ START TO FINISH: 1¼ HOURS

■ This scalloped potato dish is part of our culinary repertoire, and we hope it will become part of yours too. There is something about the texture of the potatoes surrounded by creamy goodness and topped by golden brown cheese that wows people. It is perfect for a buffet supper or potluck; in our experience, it is the first thing to disappear. The technique of starting the potatoes in a saucepan of half-and-half and ending them in a buttered gratin dish comes from the masterful Jacques Pépin. ■

- 2½ pounds boiling potatoes, such as Yukon Gold
- 3½ cups half-and-half
- 2 large garlic cloves, minced
- 1 teaspoon salt
- ¼ teaspoon freshly ground black pepper
- ⅛ teaspoon freshly grated nutmeg
- ¾ cup coarsely grated Gruyère

SPECIAL EQUIPMENT: a mandoline or other adjustable-blade slicer, such as a Japanese Benriner

Put a rack in middle of oven and preheat oven to 400°F. Generously butter a 2½- to 3-quart gratin dish or other shallow baking dish.

Peel potatoes. Cut crosswise into 1/16-inch-thick slices with slicer and transfer to a 4-quart heavy saucepan. Add half-and-half, garlic, salt, and pepper and bring just to a boil over moderate heat.

Pour potato mixture into buttered dish, distributing potatoes evenly. Sprinkle nutmeg and cheese evenly over top. Bake until potatoes are tender and top is golden brown, 35 to 45 minutes. Let stand for 15 minutes before serving.

COOK'S NOTE

■ The gratin can be made up to 1 day ahead. Cool completely, then refrigerate, covered. Bring to room temperature before reheating, covered, in a 350°F oven.

Jansson's Temptation

Potato and Anchovy Gratin

SERVES 4 TO 6
ACTIVE TIME: 20 MINUTES ■ START TO FINISH: 1¼ HOURS

■ All things Scandinavian were the rage during the 1960s: think Danish Modern furniture, Marimekko prints, and . . . Jansson's Temptation. The pairing of potatoes and anchovies is an unlikely one to many Americans, but this classic Swedish late-night party snack (jokingly called "kick 'em out of the house food") is delicious. Don't be alarmed by the fact that we call for an entire can of anchovies; the cream tempers them, so they add a deep savoriness to the gratin. For the most authentic flavor, use Swedish anchovies, which are cured in a slightly sweet brine and are less salty and fishy than other types. The identity of Jansson (pronounced "*yahn*-son," by the way, not "*jan*-son") is lost in time, but the popularity of his namesake dish lives on. This recipe is from the Scandinavian cooking authority Beatrice Ojakangas. ■

- 1 (4½-ounce) can Swedish flat anchovy fillets (see Sources), drained and chopped, or 1 (2- to 3½-ounce) can other flat anchovy fillets, rinsed, patted dry, and chopped
- 1 large onion, halved lengthwise and cut lengthwise into ¼-inch-wide strips
- 1½ pounds russet (baking) potatoes
- ¾ teaspoon salt
- ¾ cup heavy cream

1 tablespoon unsalted butter, melted
¼ cup fine dry bread crumbs

Put a rack in middle of oven and preheat oven to 450°F. Butter a 2-quart gratin dish or other shallow baking dish.

Toss anchovies with onion in buttered dish. Peel potatoes and cut into sticks 2 inches long and ¼ inch thick. Arrange potatoes over anchovies and onions and sprinkle with salt. Pour cream evenly over potatoes.

Cover gratin tightly with foil and bake for 30 minutes.

Stir together butter and bread crumbs in a small bowl until well combined. Remove foil from gratin and sprinkle with crumb mixture. Bake, uncovered, until potatoes are tender and top is golden, 15 to 20 minutes more.

Sautéed Purslane with Garlic and Balsamic Vinegar

SERVES 4

ACTIVE TIME: 15 MINUTES ■ START TO FINISH: 15 MINUTES

■ With its tiny clusters of succulent, slightly tart leaves, purslane has long been common in kitchens all over the world, including India (where it probably originated), Turkey, and Greece. In the United States, it has morphed from a widespread garden pest into a fashionable green. In this recipe, it's mellowed by cooking and brightened by a splash of balsamic vinegar. It's also good raw in a salad bowl. Look for it at the farmers market in the height of summer—or in your own backyard. ■

2 tablespoons extra-virgin olive oil
2 garlic cloves, minced
1 pound purslane, stems thicker than ⅛ inch discarded
1 tablespoon balsamic vinegar
Salt and freshly ground black pepper

Heat oil in a 12-inch nonstick skillet over moderate heat. Add garlic and cook, stirring, until fragrant, about 1 minute. Add purslane and cook, tossing with tongs, until just wilted, 3 to 4 minutes. Stir in vinegar and season with salt and pepper.

Grilled Treviso Radicchio with Scamorza

SERVES 6 TO 8

ACTIVE TIME: 15 MINUTES ■ START TO FINISH: 40 MINUTES

■ Grilling tames the bitterness of radicchio and gives it a sweet, agreeable suppleness that's offset by a slightly smoky cheese such as scamorza, a cousin of mozzarella. We first had this dish in Milan years ago; we are happy to report that the long, narrow, loose-leafed kind of radicchio called Treviso has become more popular, and more widely available, here. ■

4 (9-inch-long) heads Treviso radicchio
¼ cup extra-virgin olive oil
Salt and freshly ground black pepper
1 cup coarsely grated scamorza or smoked mozzarella (about 3 ounces)
2½ tablespoons balsamic vinegar

Prepare a charcoal or gas grill: If using a charcoal grill, open vents in bottom of grill, then light charcoal. Fire is moderately hot when you can hold your hand 5 inches above rack for just 3 or 4 seconds. If using a gas grill, preheat all burners on high, covered, for 10 minutes.

Remove any loose outer leaves from radicchio. Trim bases, leaving heads intact, and quarter each head lengthwise. Brush radicchio lightly with oil and season with salt and pepper.

Lightly oil grill rack. Grill radicchio, covered with lid, turning every 10 minutes, until outer leaves are browned and hearts are tender, 25 to 30 minutes for a charcoal grill or 20 to 25 minutes for a gas grill.

To finish, sprinkle with cheese and grill, uncovered, until cheese begins to melt, about 2 minutes. Transfer radicchio to a platter and drizzle with vinegar.

COOK'S NOTE

- The radicchio (without the cheese) can also be cooked in batches in a hot well-seasoned ridged grill pan, covered, over moderate heat for 20 to 25 minutes. Transfer, cut sides up, to a baking sheet and keep warm in a 325°F oven. When all the radicchio is grilled, sprinkle the cheese over the cut sides and heat in the oven until the cheese melts.

Braised Radishes with Raspberry Vinegar

SERVES 4

ACTIVE TIME: 10 MINUTES ■ START TO FINISH: 30 MINUTES

■ When radishes are simmered until they are tender, they lose their redness and their bite is subdued; they taste like sweet little turnips. Adding raspberry vinegar to the cooked-down braising liquid plays up the sweetness of the radishes and gives them back a rosy blush of color. ■

- 1 pound radishes (without greens), trimmed
- 2½ tablespoons sugar
- ½ cup water
- ⅓ cup raspberry vinegar or red wine vinegar
- 1 tablespoon unsalted butter
- ½ teaspoon salt
- Freshly ground black pepper

GARNISH: 1 tablespoon chopped fresh chives

Separate radishes into two groups by size, for even cooking. Combine sugar, water, vinegar, butter, salt, and larger radishes in a 10-inch skillet or a saucepan just large enough to hold radishes in one layer, cover, and bring to a boil. Add smaller radishes, reduce heat, and simmer, covered, for 10 minutes. Remove lid and simmer, stirring occasionally, just until radishes are tender, 5 to 10 minutes more. With a slotted spoon, transfer radishes to a bowl, and cover to keep warm.

Boil braising liquid until slightly thickened and reduced to about ¼ cup, about 1½ minutes. Return radishes to skillet, add salt and pepper to taste, and swirl skillet to coat radishes thoroughly with glaze. Sprinkle with chives.

Sautéed Salsify with Garlic

SERVES 4

ACTIVE TIME: 15 MINUTES ■ START TO FINISH: 50 MINUTES

■ Salsify is a mild root vegetable that is harvested in late winter and early spring. Of southern European origin, it was widely used in Colonial American kitchen gardens, but by the mid-twentieth century its popularity had faded. What we particularly love about it is its texture, which is like that of extremely tender asparagus. Salsify is sometimes called "oyster plant," but to our palates it tastes more like a cross between asparagus and Jerusalem artichoke. Salsify and its close relative, scorzonera (often called black salsify), can be used interchangeably, although scorzonera is richer and meatier in flavor. Sautéed, they are both lovely with duck, venison, or other game. ■

1/3 cup fresh lemon juice
1 3/4 pounds salsify or scorzonera
1 tablespoon unsalted butter
1 1/2 teaspoons olive oil
1 garlic clove, minced
Salt and freshly ground black pepper

Stir together 3 cups cold water and lemon juice in a bowl. Peel salsify, transferring it to lemon water to keep it from browning. Cut each salsify diagonally into 1/4-inch-thick slices and return to bowl.

Drain salsify and cook in a 4-quart saucepan of boiling well-salted water until tender, about 25 minutes. Drain in a colander.

Heat butter and oil in a 12-inch nonstick skillet over moderately high heat until foam subsides. Add garlic and cook, stirring, until pale golden, about 30 seconds. Add salsify and salt and pepper to taste and cook, stirring, until heated through.

Riesling-Braised Sauerkraut and Apples

SERVES 6

ACTIVE TIME: 30 MINUTES ■ START TO FINISH: 2 1/2 HOURS

■ Pale gold Riesling, bacon, apple—this is the most sophisticated sauerkraut we've ever had. Not what you'd dress a hot dog with, but absolutely great with pork roast or meaty, juicy sausages. This recipe is from contributor Kay Rentschler. ■

4 cups drained sauerkraut (from 2 pounds packaged sauerkraut — not canned)
1 Granny Smith apple
1 McIntosh apple
3 tablespoons unsalted butter
1 cup finely chopped onion
1 cup finely chopped shallots
1 (1/2-ounce) piece slab bacon, rind discarded
1 cup dry Riesling
1 cup chicken stock or store-bought low-sodium broth
2 teaspoons minced fresh thyme
5 juniper berries (see Sources)
1/2 Turkish bay leaf or 1/4 California bay leaf
2 cups heavy cream (optional)
3 tablespoons apple schnapps (optional)
3/4 teaspoon salt
1/4 teaspoon freshly ground black pepper

Combine sauerkraut and cold water to cover by 1 inch in a large bowl and soak for 5 minutes; drain in a colander. Repeat soaking and draining once more, pressing on sauerkraut to squeeze out excess liquid.

Put a rack in middle of oven and preheat oven to 325°F.

Peel, quarter, and core apples. Cut into 1/4-inch-thick slices.

Melt butter in a 4- to 5-quart heavy ovenproof pot over moderate heat. Add onion and shallots and cook, stirring, until softened, 8 to 10 minutes. Add apples, bacon, wine, stock, thyme, juniper berries, and bay leaf and bring to a simmer. Stir in sauerkraut and cover pot with foil and then a lid.

Transfer to oven and braise until sauerkraut is tender, 1 to 1 1/2 hours. Discard bay leaf.

Meanwhile, combine cream and schnapps, if using, in a 2-quart heavy saucepan, bring to a simmer, and simmer until reduced to about 1 cup, about 40 minutes. Remove from heat.

Add hot cream mixture (if using), salt, and pepper to sauerkraut and stir well.

Edna Lewis's Creamed Scallions

SERVES 4 TO 6

ACTIVE TIME: 20 MINUTES ■ START TO FINISH: 20 MINUTES

■ In her cookbooks, Edna Lewis celebrates the country food she grew up with long ago in a small Virginia farming community founded by freed slaves. Instead of describing the soothing qualities of this dish or how much we love the fact that it takes only minutes to prepare, we thought Lewis's comments from her classic *In Pursuit of Flavor* would do the job much better: "Growing up, we would sow onion seed in the garden and then thin a lot of them out before their bulbs got too big. We chopped them up, sautéed them in bacon fat, poured in heavy cream, and ate them for breakfast.

This recipe is not quite as rich as that, but uses scallions in a way that tastes just as delicious. . . . I buy scallions that are about the size of a pencil, but if they are a little thicker, they still taste good." ■

- 2/3 cup heavy cream
- 1/4 teaspoon minced garlic
- 5 bunches scallions, sliced 1/2 inch thick
- 3 tablespoons cold water
- 1 tablespoon chopped fresh flat-leaf parsley
- Salt and freshly ground black pepper

Combine cream and garlic in a 10-inch skillet and bring to a boil. Lower heat and simmer briskly until cream is reduced by about half, about 7 minutes. Remove from heat.

Meanwhile, combine scallions with water in a 3-quart heavy saucepan, cover, and cook over moderately high heat until tender, 5 to 7 minutes.

Add cream mixture to scallions. Stir in parsley and salt and pepper to taste, reduce heat to moderate, and cook, stirring, until hot.

Scallions with Lemon Parsley Butter

SERVES 6 TO 8
ACTIVE TIME: 20 MINUTES ■ START TO FINISH: 20 MINUTES

■ Lighter, brighter, and prettier than traditional creamed onions, this dish is an easy way to get an onion fix. We treat the scallions like leeks, cooking them until tender and brushing them with a flavorful butter. ■

- 5 bunches scallions
- 2 tablespoons unsalted butter, softened
- 1 tablespoon minced fresh flat-leaf parsley
- 1/4 teaspoon finely grated lemon zest
- 1/2 teaspoon salt
- 1/8 teaspoon freshly ground black pepper

Trim roots from scallions, leaving ends intact, and remove any bruised outer leaves. Trim greens, leaving scallions 9 inches long.

Cook scallions in a deep 12-inch skillet of boiling well-salted water until just tender, 4 to 5 minutes.

Meanwhile, stir together butter, parsley, zest, salt, and pepper in a bowl until well blended.

With tongs, transfer scallions to a colander to drain. Arrange in a shallow serving dish and brush with lemon parsley butter.

COOK'S NOTE

■ The scallions can be made up to 1 day ahead and refrigerated, covered. Reheat in a microwave.

Spinach with Indian Fresh Cheese

Palak Paneer

SERVES 4
ACTIVE TIME: 2 HOURS ■ START TO FINISH: 3 HOURS (INCLUDES MAKING *PANEER* AND GHEE)

■ The North Indian specialty called *palak paneer* combines gently spiced cooked spinach with cubes of creamy fried *paneer*, freshly made cheese. This is an excellent vegetarian main course. For variety or convenience, substitute firm tofu for the cheese. ■

- 2 tablespoons coriander seeds, toasted (see Tips, page 939) and cooled
- 1 1/2 cups (7 1/2 ounces) pearl onions
- 1/2 teaspoon turmeric
- Paneer (recipe follows), cut into 1/2-inch cubes
- 1 pound spinach, coarse stems discarded
- 1/2 cup water
- 2 garlic cloves, finely chopped
- 2 teaspoons finely chopped peeled fresh ginger
- 6 tablespoons Ghee (recipe follows) or vegetable oil
- 1 teaspoon Indian red chile powder (see Sources)
- 1 teaspoon asafetida powder (see Glossary)
- 1 (3-inch) cinnamon stick
- 4 plum tomatoes, peeled (see Tips, page 940) and chopped
- Salt

SPECIAL EQUIPMENT: an electric coffee/spice grinder

Grind coriander seeds in coffee/spice grinder; set aside.

Blanch onions in a 1 1/2- to 2-quart saucepan of boiling water for 2 minutes; drain in a colander. When cool enough to handle, peel off papery outer skins and trim with a small knife, leaving root ends intact.

Stir together turmeric and 1½ cups water in a bowl, then stir in *paneer* and let stand for 20 minutes. Drain cheese in a sieve and gently pat dry.

Put spinach and water in a 4-quart saucepan, cover, and cook over moderately high heat until wilted and tender, about 2 minutes. Transfer spinach, without draining, to a food processor and coarsely purée.

Using flat side of a large heavy knife, mash garlic and ginger to a paste.

Heat ghee in a 12-inch nonstick skillet over moderately high heat until hot but not smoking. Brown *paneer* in 2 batches, gently turning to avoid breaking it up, 2 to 3 minutes per batch. With a slotted spoon, transfer cheese to a bowl. Add onions to skillet and cook, stirring, for 5 minutes. Reduce heat to moderate, add garlic paste, and cook, stirring, until fragrant, about 1 minute. Add ground coriander, chile powder, asafetida, and cinnamon stick and cook, stirring occasionally, until onions are tender, 4 to 6 minutes. Add tomatoes and spinach purée and simmer sauce, stirring occasionally, until thickened and almost all of liquid has evaporated, 2 to 4 minutes. Discard cinnamon stick. Gently stir in *paneer* and salt to taste.

Paneer

Indian Fresh Cheese

MAKES ABOUT ¾ POUND
ACTIVE TIME: 10 MINUTES ■ START TO FINISH: 1½ HOURS

■ The soft, fresh Indian cheese called *paneer* is made by curdling milk with an acid such as vinegar or lemon juice and separating the curds from the whey. It's very simple to do. ■

- 10 cups (2½ quarts) whole milk
- ⅓ cup fresh lemon juice

SPECIAL EQUIPMENT: cheesecloth

Bring milk to a full boil in a 6-quart heavy pot, stirring occasionally. Reduce heat to low and slowly stir in lemon juice. Cook until milk begins to separate, 1 to 2 minutes. Remove from heat and let milk stand for 10 minutes.

Pour mixture into a colander lined with a triple layer of cheesecloth and rinse cheese curds under gently running lukewarm water. Gather up edges of cheesecloth and twist gently to squeeze out as much water as possible, then transfer cheese, still in cheesecloth, to a bowl. Flatten cheese into a disk and weight with a bowl filled with water or a large can. Let *paneer* stand at room temperature for 1 hour, or until firm. Pour off any liquid that has accumulated in bowl.

COOK'S NOTE

■ *Paneer* keeps, wrapped well in plastic wrap and refrigerated, for up to 3 days.

Ghee

Indian Clarified Butter

MAKES ABOUT ¾ CUP
ACTIVE TIME: 20 MINUTES ■ START TO FINISH: 20 MINUTES

■ Clarified butter has a high smoke point (the stage at which it starts to smoke and taste acrid), making it useful for sautéing or frying; it also keeps for months. It's made by slowly melting butter until the water evaporates and the milk solids separate out and sink to the bottom of the pan. The froth is then skimmed and the clear (clarified) butter poured out, leaving the solids behind. For ghee, the butter is not skimmed; it is cooked until the milk solids turn light brown and the liquid becomes golden, translucent, and nutty in flavor. ■

- 2 sticks (½ pound) unsalted butter, cut into 1-inch pieces

SPECIAL EQUIPMENT: cheesecloth

Melt butter in a small heavy saucepan over moderate heat, then bring to a boil. Once foam completely covers butter, reduce heat to very low. Continue to cook butter, stirring occasionally, until a thin crust begins to form on surface and milky white solids fall to bottom of pan, about 8 minutes. Watching constantly and stirring occasionally to prevent burning, continue to cook until solids turn light brown and butter deepens to golden, turns translucent, and is fragrant, about 3 minutes. Remove ghee from heat and pour through a sieve lined with a triple layer of cheesecloth into a heatproof jar.

COOK'S NOTE

■ Ghee keeps, covered and refrigerated, for up to 2 months.

Buttered Baby Spinach

SERVES 6

ACTIVE TIME: 10 MINUTES ■ START TO FINISH: 10 MINUTES

■ Baby spinach is a godsend on a weeknight because it's such a great time-saver. It has already been trimmed, and the painstaking cleaning has been done for you (although it's a good idea to give it a quick rinse). It cooks up fast and becomes beautifully tender. ■

- ½ stick (4 tablespoons) unsalted butter
- 1½ pounds baby spinach
- Salt and freshly ground black pepper

Heat butter in a wide 6-quart heavy pot over moderate heat until foam subsides. Add spinach and cook, stirring, until just wilted and bright green, 2 to 3 minutes. Season with salt and pepper.

Sesame Spinach with Ginger and Garlic

SERVES 4

ACTIVE TIME: 15 MINUTES ■ START TO FINISH: 15 MINUTES

■ Garlic and ginger have become a part of everyday cooking in America. This all-purpose side dish is delicious with a rib eye, chicken breasts, or lamb chops. ■

- 1 tablespoon vegetable oil
- 2 garlic cloves, minced
- 2 teaspoons finely grated peeled fresh ginger
- 1½ pounds spinach (about 2 large bunches), coarse stems discarded
- 2 teaspoons sesame seeds, toasted (see Tips, page 939)
- Salt

Heat oil in a 6-quart heavy pot over moderate heat until hot but not smoking. Add garlic and ginger and cook, stirring, until fragrant and golden, about 30 seconds. Add spinach by the handful, stirring, and cook until just wilted and tender, 4 to 7 minutes (depending on maturity and type of spinach). Season with salt.

Serve spinach sprinkled with sesame seeds.

Creamed Spinach

SERVES 4

ACTIVE TIME: 15 MINUTES ■ START TO FINISH: 15 MINUTES

■ A little flour prevents the water in the greens from "weeping" in this old favorite, which is smoothed with cream. ■

- 1¼ pounds spinach (about 2 bunches), coarse stems discarded and leaves coarsely chopped
- 1 tablespoon unsalted butter
- 1 tablespoon all-purpose flour
- ⅔ cup heavy cream
- Salt and freshly ground black pepper

Steam spinach in a steamer rack set over boiling water, covered, until tender, about 1 minute. Drain well in a colander.

Melt butter in a 2- to 3-quart heavy saucepan over moderate heat. Add flour and cook, stirring, for 1 minute, to make a roux. Stir in cream and simmer, stirring constantly, for 2 minutes (sauce will be thick). Stir in spinach and season with salt and pepper.

Baked Breaded Acorn Squash

SERVES 4

ACTIVE TIME: 25 MINUTES ■ START TO FINISH: 45 MINUTES

■ It's hard to beat an acorn squash halved and roasted with butter and a little brown sugar, but it's also fun to do something different. After cutting an acorn squash into thin slices (leaving the skin on), we coat it with seasoned bread crumbs and bake it until it's crisp on the outside and tender within. Cooked this way, the skin of the squash turns beautifully soft. ■

- 1 cup fine dry bread crumbs
- ¾ teaspoon dried thyme, crumbled
- ½ teaspoon salt
- Freshly ground black pepper
- ½ stick (4 tablespoons) unsalted butter, melted
- 1 (1-pound) acorn squash, halved lengthwise, seeded, and cut lengthwise into ¼-inch-thick slices

Put a rack in upper third of oven and preheat oven to 375°F.

Stir together bread crumbs, thyme, salt, and pepper to taste in a shallow bowl. Put butter in another shallow bowl. Working in small batches, dip squash slices in butter, coat with bread crumbs, and arrange in one layer on a large baking sheet with sides. Bake squash until golden, about 20 minutes.

Maple Squash Purée

SERVES 6

ACTIVE TIME: 20 MINUTES ■ START TO FINISH: 35 MINUTES

■ Steamed and puréed butternut squash has great color and a gorgeous texture, almost like liquid velvet. This dish is very simple, very satisfying, and low in fat compared to any cream-based purée. (For tips on how to cut up and peel a butternut squash, see page 580.) ■

- 3½ pounds butternut squash, peeled, seeded, and cut into 1-inch pieces
- 2 tablespoons unsalted butter, cut into pieces
- ¼ cup pure maple syrup
- ½ teaspoon salt
- Freshly ground black pepper

Steam squash, covered, in a steamer rack set over boiling water until very tender, about 15 minutes.

Transfer squash to a food processor; reserve cooking liquid. Add butter, maple syrup, and salt to squash and purée, adding enough cooking liquid to reach desired consistency. Season with salt if necessary and pepper.

COOK'S NOTE

- The purée can be made up to 3 days ahead and refrigerated, covered. Add water as needed when reheating.

VARIATIONS

- Add ½ teaspoon finely grated peeled fresh ginger to the purée.
- Sprinkle ¼ pound (4 slices) bacon, cooked and crumbled, on top of the purée.

Roasted Butternut Squash and Spinach with Toasted Almond Dressing

SERVES 6

ACTIVE TIME: 20 MINUTES ■ START TO FINISH: 1¼ HOURS

■ With just five basic ingredients, this dish has an amazing complexity. If you want to add another layer of flavor, crumble Roquefort or Stilton on top. ■

- 1 (2- to 2¼-pound) butternut squash, peeled, seeded, and cut into ½-inch cubes (4 cups)
- 5½ tablespoons extra-virgin olive oil
- Salt and freshly ground black pepper
- ¾ cup (3½ ounces) whole almonds with skins, very coarsely chopped
- 2 teaspoons fresh lemon juice
- ½ pound spinach, stems discarded

Put a rack in middle of oven and preheat oven to 450°F.

Toss squash with 1½ tablespoons oil on a baking sheet with sides, then spread out in one layer. Season with salt and pepper and roast, stirring once halfway through roasting, until squash is just tender and pale golden, about 30 minutes. Cool on sheet on a rack until warm, about 15 minutes.

While squash cools, heat remaining 4 tablespoons (¼ cup) oil in a 10-inch heavy skillet over moderately low heat. Add almonds and cook, stirring constantly, until golden, about 3 minutes. Season with salt and pepper, pour almonds and oil into a fine-mesh sieve set over a large bowl, and cool until warm, about 10 minutes.

BUTTERNUT SQUASH

Butternut squash is a tried-and-true favorite in our kitchens — not a glamorous heirloom, perhaps, but dependable and valued for its smooth skin (it's easy to peel) and its sweet, creamy, deep orange flesh. When buying butternuts, look for ones with long necks; that's the most usable part of the squash for the least amount of work (the bulb is harder to peel and you have to deal with the seeds).

There are a couple of ways to go about peeling butternut or other winter squash. Some of us like to use two peelers: a regular swivel peeler for the long neck and a Y-shaped peeler for the bulb. Others prefer to cut the neck into slices, lay each slice on a cutting board, and pare off the peel with a sharp knife, then cut the bulb into wedges and peel.

To cut up a peeled butternut squash, follow these steps:

1. Place the squash on its side and cut through it crosswise just above the bulbous portion, where it meets the neck.

2. Cut the neck into rounds.

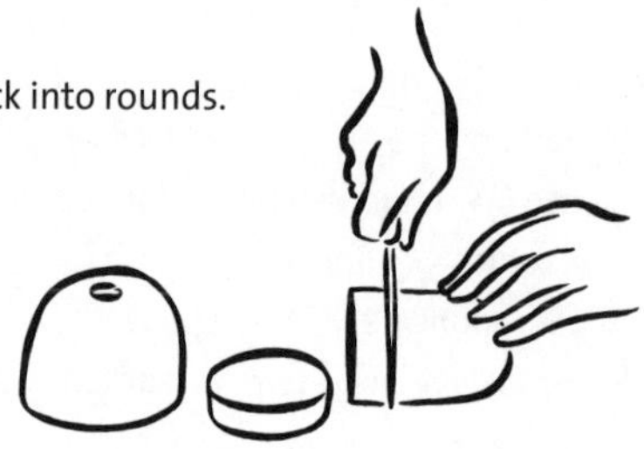

3. Place the rounds flat side down and cut each one into cubes.

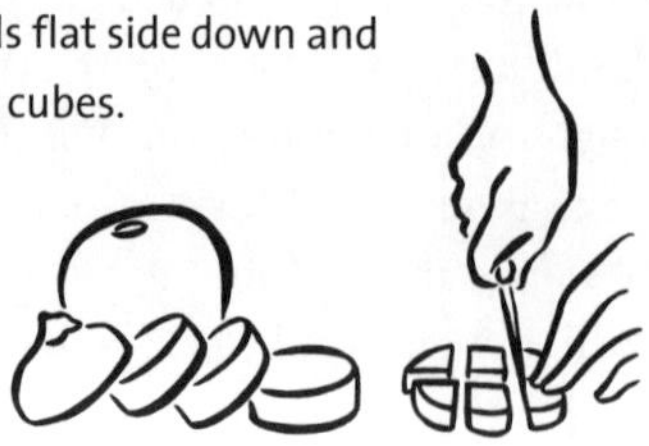

4. Remove the seeds from the bulbous section with a sharp spoon, then put the bulbous part flat side down and cut it in half vertically.

5. Lay one half on the side you just cut and slice it, then repeat with the other half.

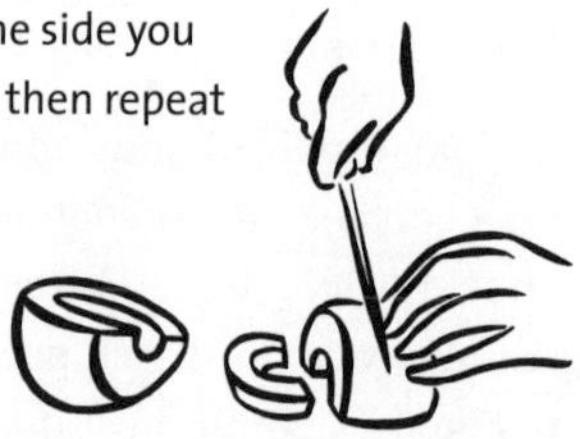

6. Place the slices flat side down and cut them into pieces.

Whisk lemon juice into cooled oil until well combined and season with salt and pepper. Add squash, spinach, and half of almonds and toss gently to coat.

Serve squash and spinach sprinkled with remaining almonds.

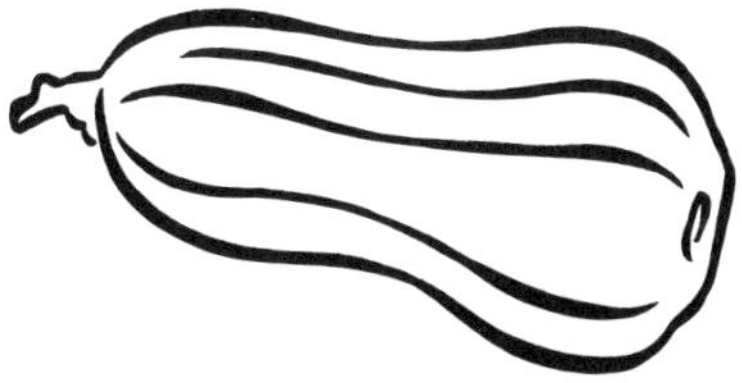

Roasted Squash and Green Beans with Sherry Soy Butter

SERVES 8 TO 10
ACTIVE TIME: 45 MINUTES ■ START TO FINISH: 1¾ HOURS

■ Butternut squash and green beans have different kinds of sweetness, and they both happen to go beautifully with the flavors of the mildly exotic sherry soy butter. This is a clever way to put two vegetables on the table at once, a boon at Thanksgiving as well as a great way to dress up a simple roast chicken. ■

- 2 pounds green beans, preferably *haricots verts*, trimmed
- 4 pounds butternut squash, halved lengthwise, peeled, seeded, and diagonally cut crosswise into 1½-inch-thick pieces
- 3 tablespoons olive oil
- ¼ teaspoon salt
- ¼ teaspoon freshly ground black pepper
- 1 stick (8 tablespoons) unsalted butter, cut into tablespoons, plus 1 tablespoon
- 1½ tablespoons sherry vinegar
- 1½ tablespoons soy sauce

Put a rack in middle of oven and preheat oven to 425°F.

Cook beans in 2 batches in a 4-quart saucepan of boiling well-salted water until just tender, 3 to 4 minutes per batch. Transfer with tongs to a bowl of ice and cold water to stop the cooking. When cool, drain beans and pat dry.

Toss squash with oil, salt, and pepper in a large bowl. Spread on a large baking sheet with sides and roast, turning occasionally, until golden brown and tender, about 40 minutes.

Meanwhile, melt 1 stick butter with vinegar and soy sauce in a small saucepan over moderately low heat, whisking until well blended, about 4 minutes. Season with salt and pepper and set aside.

Melt remaining 1 tablespoon butter.

Reduce oven temperature to 350°F. Push roasted squash to one side of baking sheet and add beans to other side. Drizzle beans with melted butter and roast, uncovered, stirring occasionally, for about 20 minutes, until beans are heated through.

Transfer roasted vegetables to a dish. Drizzle with sherry soy butter and toss gently.

COOK'S NOTE

■ The squash can be roasted up to 1 day ahead and refrigerated, covered. Bring to room temperature before reheating with beans.

Spaghetti Squash with Moroccan Spices

SERVES 4
ACTIVE TIME: 10 MINUTES ■ START TO FINISH: 25 MINUTES

■ This is one of the few recipes that works better in a microwave than a conventional oven. The mild-flavored squash gets its name from the fact that the interior, when cooked, separates into a glorious golden tangle of long spaghetti-like strands. That intriguing texture goes well with a Moroccan-inspired combination of supermarket spices. The larger the spaghetti squash, the thicker and more flavorful the strands. ■

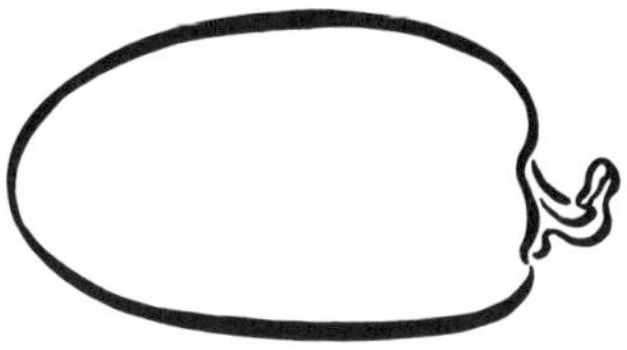

1 (3½- to 4-pound) spaghetti squash
½ stick (4 tablespoons) unsalted butter, cut into pieces
2 garlic cloves, minced
1 teaspoon ground cumin
½ teaspoon ground coriander
⅛ teaspoon cayenne
¾ teaspoon salt
2 tablespoons chopped fresh cilantro

Pierce squash about 1 inch deep all over with a small sharp knife to prevent bursting. Cook in an 800-watt microwave oven on high power (100 percent) for 6 to 7 minutes. Turn squash over and microwave until squash feels slightly soft when pressed, 8 to 10 minutes more. Cool squash for 5 minutes.

Meanwhile, melt butter in a small heavy saucepan over moderately high heat. Add garlic and cook, stirring, until golden, about 1 minute. Stir in spices and salt and remove from heat.

Carefully halve squash lengthwise (it will give off steam) and remove and discard seeds. Working over a bowl, scrape squash flesh with a fork, loosening and separating strands as you remove it from skin. Toss with spiced butter and cilantro.

COOK'S NOTE

- Alternatively, you can bake the squash in a preheated 350°F oven for 1 to 1¼ hours.

Summer Vegetable Succotash

SERVES 6
ACTIVE TIME: 40 MINUTES ■ START TO FINISH: 1 HOUR

■ We'll wager that for as long as there have been beans and corn, there has been succotash. This is one for the twenty-first century, using everything that is available in high summer, including potatoes and sweet little pattypan squash. Edamame (pronounced "ed-a-*mahm*-may"), or fresh soybeans (which are usually sold frozen), are not as starchy as the lima beans they replace here. Once the strict province of Japanese markets, they have recently become much more widely available. ■

1 pound small (1-inch-wide) yellow-fleshed potatoes, such as Yukon Gold
½ stick (4 tablespoons) unsalted butter
1 tablespoon vegetable oil, preferably corn oil
Salt and freshly ground black pepper
2 cups corn kernels (from 3 ears)
½ pound baby pattypan squash, trimmed and quartered
½ pound frozen shelled edamame (soybeans) or 1½ cups frozen baby lima beans, cooked according to package directions and cooled
¼ cup finely chopped red onion
¼ cup finely chopped fresh chives

Combine potatoes with cold well-salted water to cover by 1 inch in a 4-quart saucepan and bring to a boil, then reduce heat and simmer, uncovered, until potatoes are just tender, about 20 minutes. Drain and cool.

Cut potatoes into bite-sized pieces. Heat 1 tablespoon butter and oil in a well-seasoned 10-inch cast-iron skillet over high heat until foam subsides. Add potatoes, with salt and pepper to taste, and cook, turning once or twice, until nicely crusted, 8 to 10 minutes. Transfer to a large serving bowl.

Add remaining 3 tablespoons butter to skillet, add corn and squash, and cook over moderately high heat, stirring, until crisp-tender, about 5 minutes. Add edamame and cook, stirring, until heated through. Season with salt and pepper and stir into potatoes, along with onion and chives.

COOK'S NOTES

- If you can find edamame only in the pod, buy a 1-pound bag and shell them.
- The potatoes and edamame can be boiled (but not sautéed) up to 1 day ahead. Cool, then refrigerate, covered.

Maple Mashed Sweet Potatoes

SERVES 10
ACTIVE TIME: 15 MINUTES ■ START TO FINISH: 1½ HOURS

■ North meets South: a little maple syrup plays up the natural sweetness in sweet potatoes. ■

6 pounds sweet potatoes (about 5), scrubbed
1 stick (8 tablespoons) unsalted butter, melted
½ cup heavy cream, warmed
2 tablespoons pure maple syrup
1 teaspoon salt
½ teaspoon freshly ground black pepper

Put a rack in lower third of oven and preheat oven to 400°F. Line a baking sheet with sides with foil.

Prick potatoes with a fork. Bake on foil-lined baking sheet until very tender, about 1 hour.

When cool enough to handle, halve potatoes lengthwise and scoop flesh into a large bowl; discard skins. Mash potatoes with a potato masher or, for a smoother purée, force through a potato ricer into a bowl. Stir in butter, cream, syrup, salt, and pepper.

COOK'S NOTE

- The mashed sweet potatoes can be made up to 2 days ahead and refrigerated, covered. Reheat in a shallow baking dish, covered, in a 350°F oven.

Whipped Chipotle Sweet Potatoes

SERVES 8 TO 10
ACTIVE TIME: 10 MINUTES ■ START TO FINISH: 2¼ HOURS

■ The smoky heat of chipotle chiles is unexpected here, but as in so many spicy dishes, it's tempered by sweetness. This is just the thing to perk up the Thanksgiving table; it's also delicious with game. ■

5½ pounds sweet potatoes (about 4 large), scrubbed
1 tablespoon minced canned chipotle chiles in adobo (1½–2 chiles; see Glossary), mashed to a paste
3 tablespoons unsalted butter, cut into pieces, softened
1 teaspoon salt

SWEET POTATOES

Although our recipes call for common orange-fleshed sweet potatoes (such as the Beauregard, Jewel, and Garnet varieties), there is a vast array of sweet potatoes that goes far beyond the ones that grace almost every American Thanksgiving table. Consumption in the United States is very small compared to that in the rest of the world, where the harvest measures more than a hundred million metric tons a year. Take the boniato type: a mainstay from Mexico to Asia, it is dry and fluffy when roasted. The flesh can turn mauve-gray when cooked, but what it loses in appearance is made up for by a marvelous chestnutty flavor—terrific with game. Then there are what the vegetable expert Elizabeth Schneider characterizes as the "moist, white-fleshed types," which can turn pale yellow when roasted, delivering a delicate, squashlike flavor.

Sweet potatoes are not yams—not ever, no matter how they are labeled at the market. (In the 1930s, Louisiana sweet potato promoters decided to call their sweets yams to distinguish them from the drier, paler ones grown in other parts of the country.) The true yam, or *ñame* (pronounced "ny-*ah*-may"), a mainstay of Asian diets, originated in the Old World and was brought to Latin America by Portuguese slave traders during the Colonial period. Starchy, bland, and not related to the sweet potato or to your everyday russet in any way, yams can be found at Latino markets and some supermarkets.

Put a rack in middle of oven and preheat oven to 450°F. Line a baking sheet with sides with foil.

Prick potatoes with a fork. Bake on foil-lined baking sheet until very soft, 1 to 1½ hours. Set aside to cool slightly and reduce oven temperature to 350°F.

When cool enough to handle, halve potatoes lengthwise and scoop out flesh into a large bowl; discard skins. Add chile paste, butter, and salt and beat with an electric mixer just until smooth.

Butter a 2-quart shallow glass or ceramic baking dish and spread potato mixture in dish. Bake until hot, 20 to 25 minutes.

COOK'S NOTE

- The whipped potato mixture can be spread in the baking dish up to 1 day ahead and refrigerated, covered. Bring to room temperature before baking.

Sweet Potato and Parsnip Purée

SERVES 4
ACTIVE TIME: 10 MINUTES ■ START TO FINISH: 25 MINUTES

■ Two sweet, earthy vegetables come together here: the parsnips lighten up the sweet potatoes, and the sweet potatoes mellow the parsnips. For some of us, it wouldn't be Thanksgiving if this dish weren't on the table. ■

- 1¼ pounds sweet potatoes (2 small), peeled and cut into ½-inch pieces
- 1½ pounds parsnips (about 4), peeled and cut into ¼-inch-thick slices
- 3 tablespoons unsalted butter
- ¼ cup whole milk
- 3 tablespoons packed light brown sugar
- ½ teaspoon salt
- Freshly ground black pepper

Bring a 3½- to 4-quart saucepan of well-salted water to a boil. Add potatoes and parsnips and boil gently, uncovered, until tender, about 12 minutes. Drain well and transfer to a food processor.

Add butter and purée until smooth. Add milk, sugar, and salt and process until well blended. Season with pepper.

Sweet Potato Latkes

MAKES ABOUT 26 LATKES; SERVES 6
ACTIVE TIME: 30 MINUTES ■ START TO FINISH: 30 MINUTES

■ Jewish cooks often use sweet potatoes instead of regular potatoes for the customary Hanukkah fritters called latkes. ■

- 1 pound sweet potatoes, peeled and coarsely grated on large teardrop-shaped holes of a box grater
- 2 scallions, finely chopped
- ⅓ cup all-purpose flour
- 2 large eggs, lightly beaten
- 1 teaspoon salt
- ½ teaspoon freshly ground black pepper
- ¾ cup vegetable oil, or more as needed

Preheat oven to 250°F.

Stir together potatoes, scallions, flour, eggs, salt, and pepper in a bowl.

Heat oil in a deep 12-inch nonstick skillet over moderately high heat. Working in batches of 4 latkes, spoon 2 tablespoons potato mixture per latke into skillet, flattening and spreading each one into a 3-inch round with a slotted spatula. Reduce heat to moderate and cook latkes, turning once, until golden, about 3 minutes per batch. Transfer with spatula to paper towels to drain, then transfer to a rack set on a baking sheet with sides and keep warm in oven while you cook remaining latkes. Add more oil to skillet if needed.

Roasted Spiced Sweet Potatoes

SERVES 4 TO 6
ACTIVE TIME: 10 MINUTES ■ START TO FINISH: 45 MINUTES

■ We're not sure how we came up with the rather odd spice blend here, but it is sensational on rich, mellow sweet potatoes. Cutting the sweets into wedges before roasting speeds up the process. ■

- 1 teaspoon coriander seeds
- ½ teaspoon fennel seeds
- ½ teaspoon dried oregano
- ½ teaspoon red pepper flakes
- 1 teaspoon kosher salt
- 2 pounds medium sweet potatoes, scrubbed
- 3 tablespoons vegetable oil

SPECIAL EQUIPMENT: an electric coffee/spice grinder or a mortar and pestle

Put a rack in middle of oven and preheat oven to 425°F.

Coarsely grind coriander, fennel, oregano, and red pepper flakes in coffee/spice grinder or in mortar with pestle. Stir together spices and salt.

Cut potatoes lengthwise into 1-inch-thick wedges. Toss with oil and spices in a roasting pan and spread out in one layer. Roast for 20 minutes.

Turn wedges over with a spatula and roast until tender and slightly golden, 15 to 20 minutes more.

Roasted Cherry Tomatoes with Mint

SERVES 4

ACTIVE TIME: 5 MINUTES ■ START TO FINISH: 15 MINUTES

■ This is short and sweet—perfect any time you want to liven up a plate with a little acidity. If you buy cherry tomatoes on the vine, roast them that way; they'll be beautiful. ■

- 1 pint (12 ounces) cherry or grape tomatoes
- 1 tablespoon extra-virgin olive oil
- ¼ teaspoon salt
- ⅛ teaspoon freshly ground black pepper
- 2 teaspoons finely chopped fresh mint

Put a rack in middle of oven and preheat oven to 425°F.

Toss tomatoes with oil, salt, and pepper in a small baking pan. Roast until skins just begin to split, 5 to 10 minutes.

Sprinkle tomatoes with mint.

Crunchy Fried Green Tomatoes

SERVES 4

ACTIVE TIME: 20 MINUTES ■ START TO FINISH: 45 MINUTES

■ You can eat green tomatoes all summer long, but they are at their most practical in the early fall, when the days grow too short for them to ripen on the vine. Because they have a higher acidity than warm-weather tomatoes, they have an appealing tang, and they become almost custardy when cooked inside a mildly sweet cornflake crust. Pair them with Fresh Tomato Salsa (page 896) for a first course. ■

- 1¾ pounds green (unripe) tomatoes (4 medium)
- ½ cup all-purpose flour
- 1 teaspoon salt
- 1 teaspoon sugar
- ¾ teaspoon cayenne
- 1 large egg
- 1 tablespoon milk
- 4½ cups (6 ounces) cornflakes
- 3 tablespoons unsalted butter
- 3 tablespoons vegetable oil

Put a rack in middle of oven and preheat oven to 375°F.

Cut tomatoes into ½-inch-thick slices; discard end pieces. You should have about 12 slices. Whisk together flour, salt, sugar, and cayenne in a shallow bowl. Whisk together egg and milk in another shallow bowl. With your hands, coarsely crush cornflakes in a third shallow bowl.

Working with 1 slice at a time, dredge tomatoes in flour, shake off excess, dip in egg, letting excess drip off, and then coat with cornflakes, pressing to help them adhere. Arrange slices in one layer on a baking sheet.

Heat 1 tablespoon butter and 1 tablespoon oil in a 12-inch heavy skillet over moderate heat until foam subsides. Fry 4 tomato slices, turning once, until golden brown, about 6 minutes total (be careful not to let cornflakes burn). Transfer tomatoes to paper towels to drain. Fry remaining tomato slices in remaining butter and oil in 2 more batches in same manner, wiping out skillet with paper towels between batches. Arrange fried tomato slices in one layer on a clean baking sheet.

Bake fried tomatoes until tender and hot, about 4 minutes.

Tomato Gratin with Parmesan Crumbs

SERVES 4

ACTIVE TIME: 20 MINUTES ■ START TO FINISH: 35 MINUTES

■ This quick gratin shows off summer's greatest glory. ■

- 2 large tomatoes, preferably beefsteak, cored and cut into ½-inch-thick slices
- Salt and freshly ground black pepper
- 2 tablespoons finely chopped fresh basil
- 2 tablespoons extra-virgin olive oil
- 1 garlic clove, minced
- 1¼ cups coarse fresh bread crumbs from a baguette
- ⅓ cup finely grated Parmigiano-Reggiano

Put a rack in middle of oven and preheat oven to 500°F. Oil a 9-inch gratin dish or other shallow baking dish.

Arrange tomato slices, slightly overlapping, in gratin dish. Season with salt and pepper and sprinkle with basil.

Heat oil in a small skillet over moderate heat. Add garlic and cook, stirring, until fragrant, about 1 minute. Remove from heat and stir in bread crumbs, cheese, and salt and pepper to taste. Sprinkle over tomatoes.

Bake tomatoes until crumbs are golden, about 15 minutes.

Ratatouille

SERVES 8 TO 10

ACTIVE TIME: 40 MINUTES ■ START TO FINISH: 2 HOURS

■ For this Provençal eggplant and tomato stew, the vegetables can be cooked either together or separately. We prefer the latter method, which allows them to retain their character and does honor to every one. After you finally simmer them together, you'll find that you've created the very best kind of marriage—all the individual flavors are strengthened and lifted by their union. This recipe is adapted from that of Jacques Médecin, the famously charming and corrupt mayor of Nice in the mid-1960s. ■

- 2½ pounds tomatoes (4 large), peeled (see Tips, page 940) and coarsely chopped
- 8 large garlic cloves, thinly sliced
- 1 cup chopped fresh flat-leaf parsley
- 20 fresh basil leaves, torn in half
- 1 cup plus 2 tablespoons extra-virgin olive oil
- 1 (2-pound) eggplant, cut into 1-inch cubes
- 2¼ teaspoons salt
- 2 large onions (1½ pounds total), quartered lengthwise and thinly sliced lengthwise
- 3 assorted bell peppers (green, red, and/or yellow; 1½ pounds total), cored, seeded, and cut into 1-inch-wide pieces
- 4 medium zucchini (2 pounds total), quartered lengthwise and cut crosswise into ¾-inch-thick pieces
- ½ teaspoon freshly ground black pepper

Combine tomatoes, garlic, parsley, basil, and ⅓ cup oil in a 5-quart heavy pot, bring to a simmer, and simmer, covered, stirring occasionally, until tomatoes break down and sauce is slightly thickened, about 30 minutes.

While sauce is simmering, toss eggplant with ½ teaspoon salt in a large colander. Let stand in sink or on a deep platter for 30 minutes.

Meanwhile, heat 3 tablespoons oil in a 12-inch heavy skillet over moderate heat. Add onions with ¼ teaspoon salt and cook, stirring occasionally, until softened, 10 to 12 minutes. With a slotted spoon, transfer onions to a large bowl. Add 3 more tablespoons oil to skillet and cook bell peppers, with 1/4 teaspoon salt, stirring occasionally, until softened, about 10 minutes. With slotted spoon, transfer peppers to bowl with onions. Add 3 more tablespoons oil to skillet and cook zucchini, with 1/4 teaspoon salt, stirring occasionally, until softened, 8 to 10 minutes. With slotted spoon, transfer zucchini to bowl with other vegetables.

While zucchini is cooking, pat eggplant dry with paper towels. Add remaining oil (scant 1/4 cup) to skillet and cook eggplant over moderate heat, stirring occasionally, until softened, 10 to 12 minutes.

Add vegetables, remaining 1 teaspoon salt, and pepper to tomato sauce and simmer, covered, stirring occasionally, until vegetables are very tender, about 1 hour.

Season ratatouille with salt. Cool, uncovered, and serve warm or at room temperature.

COOK'S NOTE

- The ratatouille can be made up to 2 days ahead and refrigerated, covered. Bring to room temperature, or reheat, if desired.

Parsleyed Tomatoes with Pine Nuts

SERVES 6

ACTIVE TIME: 20 MINUTES ■ START TO FINISH: 50 MINUTES

■ Tomatoes stuffed with garlic and parsley and topped with toasted pine nuts are more substantial than those topped with bread crumbs. This is a terrific side for late summer, when the tomatoes are at their peak. ■

- 3 medium tomatoes (2 1/2 inches wide), halved crosswise and seeded
- Salt
- 5 tablespoons olive oil
- 1/3 cup pine nuts
- 3 tablespoons unsalted butter
- 3 garlic cloves, minced
- 1 cup minced fresh flat-leaf parsley
- Freshly ground black pepper

Sprinkle cut sides of tomatoes with salt. Drain cut sides down on a rack set over paper towels for 30 minutes.

Heat 4 tablespoons (1/4 cup) oil in a 12-inch heavy skillet over moderately high heat until hot but not smoking. Add tomato halves, cut sides down, and cook, turning once, until just softened but not browned, 3 to 4 minutes on each side. Transfer tomatoes, cut sides up, to a platter and cover to keep warm.

Add remaining 1 tablespoon oil to skillet and heat until hot but not smoking. Add pine nuts and cook, stirring, until golden, 1 to 2 minutes. Transfer to paper towels to drain. Add butter and garlic to skillet and cook over moderate heat, stirring, until light golden, about 1 minute. Add parsley and cook, stirring, for 1 minute. Season with salt and pepper and spoon mixture into tomatoes. Sprinkle with pine nuts.

Glazed Turnips with Scallion and Parsley

SERVES 4

ACTIVE TIME: 20 MINUTES ■ START TO FINISH: 1 HOUR

■ Peppery young turnips are cooked until just tender, then bathed in a glaze that enhances their natural sweetness. Try this with pork, lamb, or short ribs. ■

- 2 tablespoons unsalted butter
- 1 1/2 pounds turnips (about 4 medium), peeled and cut into 1-inch-thick wedges
- 1 1/4 cups chicken stock or store-bought low-sodium broth
- 1 teaspoon sugar
- 1/8 teaspoon salt
- 1 scallion, finely chopped
- 2 tablespoons finely chopped fresh flat-leaf parsley

Melt butter in a 4-quart heavy saucepan over moderately low heat. Add turnips, stirring until well coated. Add stock, sugar, and salt and bring to a boil, then reduce heat, cover, and simmer until turnips are tender, 30 to 40 minutes. Remove lid and boil, stirring occasionally, until liquid is reduced enough to glaze turnips, about 5 minutes more. Remove from heat and stir in scallion and parsley.

Creamed Turnips

SERVES 8
ACTIVE TIME: 50 MINUTES ■ START TO FINISH: 50 MINUTES

■ Turnips can be a little brusque in their bite. Here they are mellowed by a cream sauce. This is a delicious alternative to creamed onions. ■

- 3 pounds turnips (about 8 medium), peeled and cut into 1-inch pieces
- 2 cups whole milk
- 1/4 cup heavy cream
- 1 1/2 tablespoons unsalted butter
- 3/4 cup chopped shallots
- 1 1/2 teaspoons loosely packed fresh thyme leaves or 1/4 teaspoon dried thyme, crumbled
- 1/2 teaspoon salt
- 3 black peppercorns
- 3 whole cloves
- 1 Turkish bay leaf or 1/2 California bay leaf
- 1 1/2 tablespoons all-purpose flour
- 1/8 teaspoon white pepper
- 1/8 teaspoon freshly grated nutmeg

OPTIONAL GARNISH: chopped fresh flat-leaf parsley

Cook turnips in a 5-quart pot of boiling salted water (1 tablespoon salt per every 4 quarts water), uncovered, until tender, about 20 minutes; drain.

Meanwhile, bring milk and cream just to a simmer in a heavy saucepan, then reduce heat to low to keep hot.

Melt butter in a 4-quart heavy saucepan over moderately low heat. Add shallots and cook, stirring, until softened, about 5 minutes. Add thyme, salt, peppercorns, cloves, and bay leaf and cook, stirring, for 1 minute. Add flour and cook, stirring, for 3 minutes to make a roux. Whisk in hot milk mixture all at once and bring to a boil, whisking constantly. Reduce heat and simmer sauce, uncovered, whisking occasionally, for 15 minutes.

Pour sauce through a medium-mesh sieve into 5-quart heavy pot; discard solids. Stir in salt to taste, white pepper, and nutmeg.

Bring sauce to a simmer, add turnips, and cook, covered, over moderately low heat, stirring occasionally, until turnips are heated through, about 3 minutes. Serve sprinkled with parsley, if desired.

COOK'S NOTES

- The turnips can be boiled up to 1 day ahead and refrigerated, covered. Bring to room temperature before proceeding.
- The sauce can be made up to 1 day ahead and refrigerated, covered. Bring to a simmer, whisking, and if necessary thin with a little additional milk or water before proceeding.

Sautéed Watercress

SERVES 6 TO 8
ACTIVE TIME: 15 MINUTES ■ START TO FINISH: 20 MINUTES

■ Watercress has a life outside the salad bowl. A quick stint in the skillet tames its bite and gives it sophistication. It's perfect with lamb, a big juicy steak, or other rich meats. Three pounds of watercress seems like a vast amount, but it loses its bulk while cooking. ■

- 3 tablespoons olive oil
- 2 large garlic cloves, minced
- 3 pounds watercress (6 bunches), coarse stems discarded
- Salt and freshly ground black pepper

Heat oil in a 12-inch heavy skillet over moderately high heat until hot but not smoking. Add garlic and cook, stirring, until fragrant, about 30 seconds. Add watercress and stir until well combined. Cover and cook, stirring occasionally, until watercress is just wilted, 3 to 4 minutes. Season with salt and pepper.

Yuca Fries

SERVES 4 TO 6

ACTIVE TIME: 50 MINUTES ■ START TO FINISH: 50 MINUTES

■ These crisp, flaky fries are a great introduction to the bark-covered starchy root called yuca (pronounced "*yoo*-ka," and not to be confused with the spiky flowering plant called yucca), which has moved from Latino, Caribbean, and African markets into mainstream American supermarkets. It tastes very much like potato, but the flesh is denser and a little sweeter—wonderful with the nontraditional accompaniments suggested below. This recipe is from Leslie Glover Pendleton, a writer and former food editor at *Gourmet,* who introduced us to yuca in the early 1990s.■

- 1 pound fresh yuca (also called cassava) or frozen peeled yuca
- About 4 cups vegetable oil for deep-frying
- Coarse salt

ACCOMPANIMENTS: lemon wedges and barbecue sauce or ketchup

SPECIAL EQUIPMENT: a deep-fat thermometer

If using fresh yuca, trim ends and cut crosswise into 3-inch-long pieces, then peel, removing all waxy brown skin and pinkish layer underneath.

Combine (fresh or frozen) yuca with cold well-salted water to cover by 1 inch in a 3-quart saucepan and bring to a boil, then reduce heat and simmer briskly until yuca is tender when tested with a wooden pick, 15 to 20 minutes. With a slotted spoon, transfer it to a colander to cool slightly.

When cool enough to handle, gently pat yuca dry and cut lengthwise into 3/4-inch-wide wedges (discard thin, woody core).

Heat 2 inches oil in a 4-quart wide heavy saucepan over moderate heat until it registers 360°F on thermometer. Fry yuca in 3 batches, turning once, until golden brown, 3 to 4 minutes per batch. With slotted spoon, transfer to paper towels to drain. (Return oil to 360°F between batches.) Sprinkle fries with coarse salt and serve with lemon wedges and barbecue sauce or ketchup.

YUCA

Odds are you've had yuca before, but you may not have known it. A starchy root also known as cassava or manioc, it's the source of tapioca, long used as a pie-filling thickener and to make the pudding that people either love or loathe. When it is cooked and mashed, fresh yuca has an appealing waxy texture, somewhat like that of a new potato. It's available at ethnic markets and many supermarkets. Choose tubers that are free of mold, soft spots, or an ammonia smell. The flesh should be pure white, with no black veins. Often yuca is sold with one end lopped off and wrapped in plastic, so you can inspect the inside. Like much tropical produce, it spoils quickly. Use it within a few days or peel it, wrap it up well, and freeze it. (Frozen peeled yuca pieces are also available in some markets.) Yuca is always cooked; it is toxic if eaten raw.

Peeling yuca is simple. First, cut it into roughly three-inch lengths (1), then make a lengthwise slit through the bark and the thin pink layer underneath (2). (Some people use a sturdy Y-shaped peeler for this next step, but we usually stick with the knife.) Loosen these two outer layers by prying them away from the flesh with the knife; with the knife wedged between the outer layers and the flesh, continue to pry and peel your way around each piece (3).

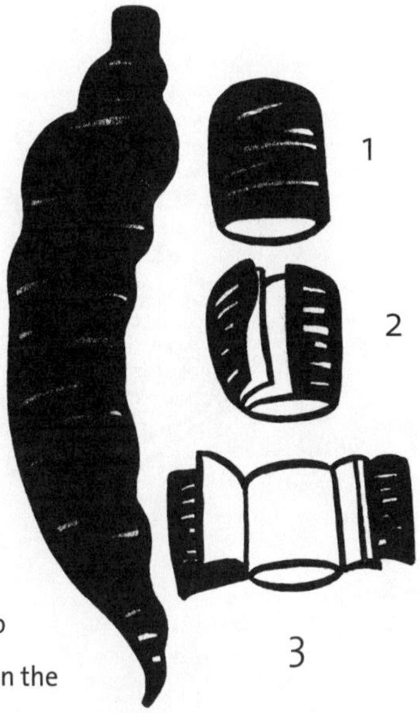

Cuban-Style Yuca with Garlic Lemon Oil

SERVES 4

ACTIVE TIME: 35 MINUTES ■ START TO FINISH: 35 MINUTES

■ Boiled yuca is delicious alongside broiled or grilled meats or poultry, a welcome change from boiled potatoes or a warm potato salad. This recipe is modeled after what is practically the national dish of Cuba, *yuca con mojo,* but a former colleague, Leslie Glover Pendleton, substituted olive oil and lemon juice for the more traditional lard and sour orange juice. ■

- 1 pound fresh yuca (also called cassava) or frozen peeled yuca (see page 589)
- 2 garlic cloves, minced
- 1/4 cup olive oil
- 1 tablespoon fresh lemon juice
- 1/4 teaspoon salt
- 1/4 teaspoon freshly ground black pepper

If using fresh yuca, trim ends and cut crosswise into 2-inch-long pieces, then peel, removing all waxy brown skin and pinkish layer underneath.

Combine (fresh or frozen) yuca with cold well-salted water to cover by 1 inch in a 3-quart saucepan and bring to a boil, then reduce heat and briskly simmer until yuca is tender when tested with a wooden pick, 15 to 20 minutes. With a slotted spoon, transfer it to a cutting board.

Combine garlic and oil in a 10-inch heavy skillet and heat over moderate heat, stirring, until garlic begins to sizzle, about 1 minute. Remove from heat and carefully stir in lemon juice, salt, and pepper.

While yuca is still warm, cut lengthwise into 3/4-inch-wide pieces (discard thin, woody core). Transfer to a platter and drizzle with sauce.

MANDOLINES AND OTHER SLICERS

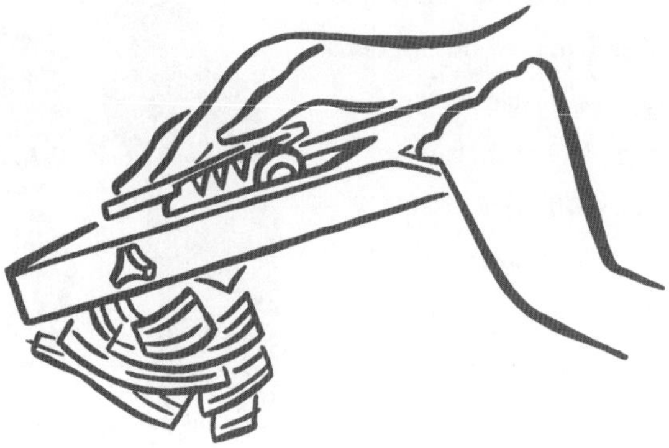

A mandoline is a piece of professional kitchen equipment that has trickled down to home cooks everywhere. It's a handy stainless steel device on hinged V-shaped legs that is used for cutting firm vegetables and other foods into perfectly uniform slices or strips. Depending on the blade attachment you use, you can produce paper-thin slices, matchsticks, even waffle-cut slices. A host of cheaper, smaller plastic knockoffs, including the Japanese Benriner (our personal favorite), work very well too, although you have to hold them up with one hand like an old-fashioned grater, and the blade assortment isn't as large. (Note: The blades of a slicer are very sharp, so always use the finger guard.)

Zucchini "Carpaccio"

SERVES 4 TO 6

ACTIVE TIME: 15 MINUTES ■ START TO FINISH: 15 MINUTES

■ Tender zucchini-like squashes ("summer," as opposed to "winter," squashes) are generally thought to have originated in the Americas and been taken to Europe by explorers. Zucchini wasn't popular in the United States until Italian immigrants brought it back again. This recipe was developed by a Florentine, Francesca Cianci, who cooked in New York City's Mezzaluna restaurant before returning home, and was published in *Red, White, and Greens,* by our longtime contributor and Italian cooking authority Faith Heller Willinger.

Even though zucchini is essentially a seasonless vegetable nowadays, for this dish you will need fresh young spring or summer zucchini. They should be small and have tight, unblemished skin. A little balsamic vinegar adds sweetness and depth; we used an inexpensive balsamic from the supermarket, but if you have a fancy one sitting around, so much the better. Arugula brings green pepperiness to this dish, and shavings of salty, nutty Parmigiano-Reggiano finish it off beautifully. ■

- 2 medium zucchini (¾ pound total)
- ⅓ cup coarsely chopped arugula
- 3 tablespoons extra-virgin olive oil
- 1 teaspoon balsamic vinegar (optional)
- Fine sea salt
- Freshly ground black pepper
- 1 (¼-pound) piece Parmigiano-Reggiano, for shaving

SPECIAL EQUIPMENT: a mandoline or other adjustable-blade slicer, such as a Japanese Benriner

With slicer, cut zucchini into 1/16-inch-thick rounds. Arrange slices in one layer, overlapping them slightly, on a large (18-by-12-inch) platter and sprinkle with arugula. Drizzle oil and vinegar (if using) over zucchini and season with sea salt and pepper. With a vegetable peeler, shave curls of cheese on top.

Grilled Summer Vegetables with Pesto

SERVES 4

ACTIVE TIME: 30 MINUTES ■ START TO FINISH: 1½ HOURS

■ Don't reserve pesto just for pasta. Because it is so rich, it can turn a plate of summer vegetables into a feast. ■

- 1 small eggplant, halved lengthwise
- 1 zucchini, halved lengthwise
- 1 yellow squash, halved lengthwise
- 1 red bell pepper, cored, seeded, and quartered lengthwise
- Salt and freshly ground black pepper
- 1 garlic clove
- 3 tablespoons olive oil or vegetable oil
- 1 tablespoon balsamic vinegar or red wine vinegar
- 1 tablespoon minced fresh oregano or ½ teaspoon dried oregano, crumbled
- 1 teaspoon fresh thyme leaves or ¼ teaspoon dried thyme, crumbled
- About 1 cup Pesto (page 889)

Arrange vegetables cut sides up in one layer in a large shallow baking dish and season with salt and pepper. Mince and mash garlic to a paste with a large heavy knife. Whisk garlic paste together with oil, vinegar, oregano, and thyme in a bowl and pour over vegetables. Cover vegetables and marinate at room temperature for at least 1 hour.

Prepare a charcoal or gas grill: If using a charcoal grill, open vents in bottom of grill, then light charcoal. Fire is moderately hot when you can hold your hand 5 inches above rack for just 3 to 4 seconds. If using a gas grill, preheat all burners on high, covered, for about 10 minutes.

Remove vegetables from marinade; discard marinade.

Lightly oil grill rack. Grill vegetables, turning once, until tender, 18 to 22 minutes total.

Cut zucchini, eggplant, and squash pieces crosswise in half. Serve vegetables with pesto.

COOK'S NOTE

■ The vegetables can marinate, covered and refrigerated, for up to 8 hours.

Zucchini and Carrots Julienne

SERVES 4
ACTIVE TIME: 30 MINUTES ■ START TO FINISH: 40 MINUTES

■ This will make you stop taking these two vegetables for granted. They steam in just a few minutes and are bright in flavor. You will, however, need a mandoline or other slicer with a julienne blade. ■

- 3/4 pound zucchini
- 1/2 pound carrots, peeled if desired
- 1 tablespoon unsalted butter
- 1 teaspoon fresh lemon juice, or to taste
- Salt and freshly ground black pepper

SPECIAL EQUIPMENT: a mandoline or other adjustable-blade slicer with a julienne cutter, such as a Japanese Benriner

Cut zucchini and carrots into 2-inch lengths. Working with one piece at a time, cut zucchini into julienne strips with slicer (be sure to use finger guard), turning zucchini to avoid core, then discard core. Cut carrots into julienne strips. Or use a sharp knife to slice vegetables.

Steam zucchini on a steamer rack set over boiling water, covered, until crisp-tender, 2 to 3 minutes; transfer to a bowl. Add carrots to steamer and steam, covered, until crisp-tender, about 3 minutes; transfer to bowl with zucchini.

Melt butter in a 12-inch heavy skillet over moderately low heat. Add vegetables and toss until coated and heated through. Stir in lemon juice and salt and pepper to taste.

COOK'S NOTE

■ You can steam the vegetables several hours in advance. Reheat them in the butter over moderately low heat just before serving.

HOW TO CUT HARD VEGETABLES INTO MATCHSTICKS

A mandoline or other vegetable slicer (see page 590) is perfect for producing thin, even matchsticks of a hard vegetable such as a carrot. If your slicer lacks a julienne attachment, you will need to stack thin slices of the vegetable two or three at a time and cut the slices into matchsticks with a large sharp knife. To julienne a hard round vegetable such as a turnip, cut it lengthwise in half first to make a flat surface, then slice away.

If you don't have a slicer, you'll have to resort to a sharp knife. To julienne carrots by hand, cut crosswise into pieces of the desired length (long, stout carrots will give you more to work with), then make a flat surface by cutting a thin strip from a long side of each piece. With the flat side down, cut each piece lengthwise into thin slices (about 1/8 inch thick). Then stack a few slices at a time and cut them lengthwise into strips of the same width.

Squash, Tomatoes, and Corn with Jack Cheese

SERVES 6 TO 8

ACTIVE TIME: 35 MINUTES ■ START TO FINISH: 35 MINUTES

■ This is our version of a New Mexican dish called *calabacitas con queso.* (*Calabaza* is Spanish for "squash"; *calabacitas* are little squash.) Yellow squash or zucchini are cut into small pieces and stewed with tomatoes, onion, and corn; grated Monterey Jack cheese melts into and thickens the juicy concoction. Served in wide, shallow bowls, this makes a flavorful bed for grilled chicken breasts. It also makes a terrific vegetarian main course. ■

- 3 tablespoons vegetable oil
- 1 medium onion, chopped
- 2 small garlic cloves, minced
- 2 large tomatoes (1½ pounds total), halved, seeded, and chopped
- 2 pounds yellow summer squash or zucchini, cut into ½-inch cubes
- 1½ cups corn kernels (from 3 ears)
- 2 cups coarsely grated Monterey Jack (about 6 ounces)
- ¾ teaspoon salt
- ¾ teaspoon freshly ground black pepper

Heat oil in a 12-inch heavy skillet over moderately low heat. Add onion and cook, stirring, until softened, about 5 minutes. Add garlic, tomatoes, squash, and corn, increase heat to moderate, and cook, stirring, until squash is tender, 10 to 12 minutes.

Reduce heat to low, stir in cheese, salt, and pepper, and simmer, covered, just until cheese is melted, about 30 seconds.

BREADS AND CRACKERS

There are two kinds of people in the world: those who bake bread and those who don't. If you're not a member of the former group, this chapter is aimed very much at seducing you into joining.

Nothing—absolutely nothing—smells as wonderful as baking bread. When that warm, welcoming aroma wraps itself around a house, it instantly creates a home. It is hard to think of anything else that offers such large rewards for so little effort.

During the sixty-three years that *Gourmet* has been on the newsstand, it has witnessed the fall and rise of the American bakery. When the magazine made its debut in the forties, no city in the United States was without a bakery. Back then one of the great joys of traveling was the opportunity to sample the vast array of regional breads that stretched across the country. Then, during the fifties, white bread—clean, uniform, perfect for sandwiches—moved in and muscled the mom-and-pop places out of business. For a long time the American bread situation was very sad.

Fortunately, people got tired of the same old stuff. One of the first gifts of the American food revolution was the return of the local loaf. But nobody will sell you rolls as good as those you can bake at home, and the best biscuits are always hot from the oven. Corn bread has never been much of a commercial product. And who ever heard of a store-bought popover?

We combed our files for these breads, along with crisps and crackers, scones and buns. Along the way we turned up the best breadsticks you'll ever taste. You'll also find extraordinary sweet breads in this chapter, including truly spectacular sticky buns, which took eight tries to perfect. As for our jelly doughnuts, we're so proud of these. Until you've tried them, still warm and glistening with powdered sugar, you have not truly lived.

Buttermilk Biscuits

MAKES TWELVE 2-INCH OR EIGHT 3-INCH BISCUITS
ACTIVE TIME: 10 MINUTES ■ START TO FINISH: 45 MINUTES (INCLUDES COOLING)

■ Biscuits are a classic breakfast bread in the American South, and buttermilk is a classic baking staple, adding flavor and acting as a tenderizer. The secret to light biscuits, though, can lie in the flour. Many southern cooks insist that you shouldn't bake biscuits with anything but White Lily. Indeed, this flour from Knoxville, Tennessee, makes superlative biscuits—light, airy foils for tupelo honey or fig preserves. White Lily is milled entirely from soft winter wheat, which is lower in protein than hard summer wheat. The flour is a supermarket item south of the Mason-Dixon Line, and it's becoming available in other parts of the country. But you don't need it to make a good biscuit; we tried this recipe with regular all-purpose flour and were happy with the texture of those biscuits as well. ■

2 cups White Lily flour (not self-rising) or all-purpose flour
2 teaspoons baking powder
½ teaspoon baking soda
½ teaspoon salt
1 stick (8 tablespoons) cold unsalted butter, cut into pieces
¾ cup well-shaken buttermilk, plus additional for brushing

SPECIAL EQUIPMENT: a 2- or 3-inch round cutter

Put a rack in middle of oven and preheat oven to 425°F. Lightly grease a baking sheet.

Sift together flour, baking powder, baking soda, and salt into a medium bowl. Blend in butter with your fingertips or a pastry blender until mixture resembles coarse meal. Add buttermilk and stir just until a dough forms.

Gather dough into a ball, turn out onto a lightly floured surface, and gently knead 6 times. Pat dough into a 10-inch round (½ inch thick). Cut out as many rounds as possible with lightly floured cutter, dipping it in flour before each cut, and invert rounds onto greased baking sheet, spacing them about 1½ inches apart. Gather scraps, pat out dough, and cut out more rounds in same manner.

Brush tops of rounds with buttermilk. Bake until biscuits are pale golden, 12 to 15 minutes. Transfer to a rack to cool and serve warm or at room temperature.

Cream Biscuits

MAKES TWELVE 2-INCH OR EIGHT 3-INCH BISCUITS
ACTIVE TIME: 10 MINUTES ■ START TO FINISH: 45 MINUTES (INCLUDES COOLING)

■ This biscuit dough is incredibly easy to make because you don't have to cut in the fat—it's already there in the cream. Although the White Lily flour suggested here (made from soft winter wheat, which has a low protein content) produces a very light biscuit, no one will be disappointed by the results of using regular all-purpose flour. ■

2 cups White Lily flour (not self-rising) or all-purpose flour
1 tablespoon baking powder
½ teaspoon salt
1¼ cups heavy cream, plus additional for brushing

SPECIAL EQUIPMENT: a 2- or 3-inch round cutter

Put a rack in middle of oven and preheat oven to 425°F. Lightly grease a baking sheet.

Sift together flour, baking powder, and salt into a medium bowl. Add cream and stir just until a dough forms.

Gather dough into a ball, turn out onto a lightly floured surface, and gently knead 6 times. Pat dough into a 10-inch round (½ inch thick). Cut out as many rounds as possible with lightly floured cutter, dipping it in flour before each cut, and invert rounds onto greased baking sheet, spacing them about 1½ inches apart. Gather scraps, pat out dough, and cut out more rounds in same manner.

Brush tops of rounds with cream. Bake until pale golden, 12 to 15 minutes. Transfer biscuits to a rack to cool and serve warm or at room temperature.

Cheddar Scallion Drop Biscuits

MAKES 12 BISCUITS
ACTIVE TIME: 15 MINUTES ■ START TO FINISH: 35 MINUTES

■ The glory of drop biscuits, with their craggy, crisp edges, is that you don't have to fuss with rolling out the dough—just mix and drop. These are as good with a bowl of chili as they are with scrambled eggs and bacon. ■

- 2¼ cups all-purpose flour
- 2½ teaspoons baking powder
- ¾ teaspoon baking soda
- 2 teaspoons sugar
- 1 teaspoon salt
- ¾ stick (6 tablespoons) cold unsalted butter, cut into ½-inch cubes
- 1½ cups coarsely grated Cheddar (about 6 ounces)
- 3 scallions, finely chopped
- 1 cup well-shaken buttermilk

Put a rack in middle of oven and preheat oven to 450°F. Butter a large baking sheet.

Whisk together flour, baking powder, baking soda, sugar, and salt in a medium bowl. Blend in butter with your fingertips or a pastry blender until mixture

Flour Facts

For nonbakers, flour can be a mysterious ingredient, but it's not really complicated at all. The main difference between flours is the amount of protein they contain. Bread flour has 13 to 14 grams per cup; all-purpose flour has about 11 grams per cup. Southern flours such as White Lily have less. When mixed with a liquid, the proteins form gluten, which helps give dough its elasticity. Therefore, flour with a high protein content, such as bread flour, will yield a resilient and elastic dough. All-purpose flour is a blend of many flours with varying levels of protein and is suitable for all types of baking.

Whole wheat flour contains both germ and bran, and it has less protein cup for cup than all-purpose flour milled from the same wheat. Although other grains — rye, millet, corn, oats, and buckwheat, for example — are ground into flour to make quick breads and pancakes, only wheat flour contains enough of the two proteins necessary to make gluten and thus a yeast bread that rises. Consequently, flours from these other grains are often blended with all-purpose flour to make a flavorful, well-leavened loaf.

As for the question of bleached versus unbleached flour, many professional bakers and pastry chefs strongly object to the chemical bleaches most millers use, maintaining that they alter the flour's flavor. But when one of our recipes calls for all-purpose flour, we've tested it with the bleached variety, because that's what most home cooks buy. If you choose to substitute an unbleached flour, such as King Arthur brand, be aware that your results could be different, because even though the protein content of the flour isn't affected by the bleaching process, millers tend to earmark higher-protein flour for the "unbleached" label. For doughs where strength is particularly important — pizza dough, for instance — we call for unbleached flour. It may be tempting to use whatever is in the pantry, but your results will be more successful if you go by what's called for in the recipe. (To find White Lily and King Arthur flour, see Sources.)

resembles coarse meal. Stir in Cheddar and scallions. Add buttermilk and stir until just combined.

Drop dough in 12 equal mounds about 2 inches apart onto buttered baking sheet. Bake until golden, 18 to 20 minutes. Serve warm.

Currant Tea Scones

MAKES 4 SCONES
ACTIVE TIME: 15 MINUTES ■ START TO FINISH: 1 HOUR (INCLUDES COOLING)

■ The scone originated in Scotland, and the first written reference to it comes in an early sixteenth-century translation of the *Aeneid* by the Scottish poet Gavin Douglas. The word is pronounced in various ways; early spellings imply that it rhymes with *swan,* but the pronunciation that rhymes with *stone* is much more prevalent today. Along with sandwiches and cake, currant scones, often served with clotted cream and strawberry jam, are a traditional accompaniment to afternoon tea, the light repast meant to tide one over until dinner. The currants are plumped, appropriately, in tea; almost any kind will do (Lipton's works fine), but avoid highly flavored or aromatic ones such as Lapsang souchong or mint. This recipe can easily be doubled. ■

- 2 tablespoons boiling water
- 1 tea bag, such as English Breakfast
- ½ cup dried currants
- 1 cup all-purpose flour
- 1½ teaspoons baking powder
- ½ teaspoon salt
- 2 tablespoons plus ½ teaspoon sugar
- ½ stick (4 tablespoons) cold unsalted butter, cut into ½-inch cubes
- 6 tablespoons half-and-half, plus additional for brushing

Put a rack in middle of oven and preheat oven to 400°F. Butter a small baking sheet.

Pour boiling water into a small cup, add tea bag, and steep for 2 minutes. Remove bag and squeeze excess liquid back into cup. Stir in currants.

Sift together flour, baking powder, salt, and 2 tablespoons sugar into a medium bowl. Add butter and blend with your fingertips or a pastry blender until mixture resembles coarse meal with small lumps of butter (roughly pea-sized). Add half-and-half and stir with a fork until a sticky dough forms. Stir in currant mixture.

Turn dough out onto a lightly floured surface and form into a 5-inch round. Transfer round to buttered baking sheet and brush lightly with half-and-half. Sprinkle dough with remaining ½ teaspoon sugar. Score into quarters, making ¼-inch-deep cuts with a sharp knife.

Bake scones until golden, 20 to 25 minutes. Transfer to a rack to cool. Serve warm or at room temperature, breaking scones along score marks.

Dried Apricot–Oatmeal Scones

MAKES 12 SCONES
ACTIVE TIME: 25 MINUTES ■ START TO FINISH: 1 HOUR (INCLUDES COOLING)

■ We'll bet that even people who don't like oatmeal for breakfast can't refuse one of these scones. The oatmeal adds body to the dough and gives the scones a slightly coarse texture. These have golden glints of dried apricots in them. You can substitute dried cherries or currants. ■

- 1⅔ cups all-purpose flour
- 6 tablespoons sugar, plus additional for sprinkling
- 1 tablespoon baking powder
- ¾ teaspoon baking soda
- ½ teaspoon salt
- 1⅓ cups old-fashioned rolled oats
- 1½ sticks (12 tablespoons) cold unsalted butter, cut into tablespoons
- Finely grated zest of 1 large navel orange
- ⅔ cup well-shaken buttermilk, plus additional for brushing
- ½ cup finely chopped dried apricots or dried cherries, or currants

SPECIAL EQUIPMENT: a 2¼-inch round cutter

Put a rack in middle of oven and preheat oven to 425°F. Lightly butter a large baking sheet.

Sift together flour, sugar, baking powder, baking

soda, and salt into a food processor. Add oats and pulse to mix. Add butter and pulse until mixture resembles coarse meal with small lumps of butter (roughly pea-sized), then transfer to a large bowl.

Stir together zest and buttermilk in a small bowl. Add fruit to flour mixture and toss, then add buttermilk, stirring with a fork just until a dough forms.

Turn dough out onto a lightly floured surface and gently knead 6 times. Pat dough into a 1-inch-thick round, dusting surface with more flour if necessary. Cut out as many scones as possible with floured cutter, dipping it in flour before each cut, and transfer scones to buttered baking sheet, spacing them about 1½ inches apart. Gather scraps into a ball, pat into a round, and cut out more scones in same manner.

Brush tops of scones with buttermilk and sprinkle lightly with sugar. Bake until golden brown, 15 to 18 minutes. Transfer to a rack and serve warm or at room temperature.

COOK'S NOTE

- The scones can be made up to 2 hours ahead and kept at room temperature.

Pumpkin Apple Bread

MAKES TWO 9-BY-5-INCH LOAVES
ACTIVE TIME: 30 MINUTES ■ START TO FINISH: 3 HOURS (INCLUDES COOLING)

■ Two fall favorites work their magic in this spicy bread with a streusel topping. The recipe is from Rebecca's Gourmet Bakery, in Cary, North Carolina. ■

FOR TOPPING

- 1 tablespoon all-purpose flour
- 5 tablespoons sugar
- 1 teaspoon ground cinnamon
- 1 tablespoon unsalted butter, softened

FOR BREAD

- 3 cups all-purpose flour
- ¾ teaspoon salt
- 2 teaspoons baking soda
- 1½ teaspoons ground cinnamon
- 1 teaspoon freshly grated nutmeg
- ¼ teaspoon ground cloves
- ¼ teaspoon ground allspice
- 1 (15-ounce) can solid-pack pumpkin
- ¾ cup vegetable oil
- 2¼ cups sugar
- 4 large eggs, lightly beaten
- 2 Granny Smith apples, peeled, cored, and chopped (2 cups)

MAKE THE TOPPING: Blend together flour, sugar, cinnamon, and butter in a small bowl with your fingertips until mixture resembles coarse meal.

MAKE THE BREAD: Put a rack in middle of oven and preheat oven to 350°F. Butter two 9-by-5-inch loaf pans.

Sift together flour, salt, baking soda, cinnamon, nutmeg, cloves, and allspice into a medium bowl. Whisk together pumpkin, oil, sugar, and eggs in a large bowl. Add flour mixture, stirring until well combined. Fold in apples.

Divide batter between buttered loaf pans. Sprinkle half of topping evenly over each loaf. Bake until a wooden pick or skewer inserted in center of bread comes out clean, 50 to 60 minutes.

Cool loaves in pans on a rack for 45 minutes, then turn out onto rack and cool completely, about 1 hour.

COOK'S NOTE

- The bread keeps, wrapped well in plastic wrap and foil and refrigerated, for up to 1 week. It can also be frozen for up to 1 month.

Coconut and Macadamia Nut Banana Bread

MAKES TWO 8½-BY-4½-INCH LOAVES
ACTIVE TIME: 35 MINUTES ■ START TO FINISH: 3 HOURS (INCLUDES COOLING)

■ There are plenty of banana bread recipes around, but this one is special. The addition of coconut and macadamia nuts plays up the tropical nature of the fruit, taking an old favorite to new heights. ■

2¼ cups all-purpose flour
¾ teaspoon baking powder
½ teaspoon baking soda
1 teaspoon salt
1½ sticks (12 tablespoons) unsalted butter, softened
1 cup packed light brown sugar
½ cup granulated sugar
3 large eggs
1½ teaspoons vanilla extract
1 tablespoon finely grated lemon zest
1⅓ cups mashed ripe bananas (about 3 large)
3 tablespoons sour cream
¾ cup (6 ounces) chopped macadamia nuts
1 cup (3 ounces) sweetened flaked coconut, lightly toasted (see Tips, page 939) and cooled

Put a rack in middle of oven and preheat oven to 350°F. Generously butter two 8½-by-4½-inch loaf pans and dust with flour, knocking out excess.

Sift together flour, baking powder, baking soda, and salt into a medium bowl. Beat together butter and sugars in a large bowl with an electric mixer at high speed until pale and fluffy, about 2 minutes. Reduce speed to medium and add eggs one at a time, beating well after each addition. Add vanilla, zest, bananas, and sour cream, beating until just combined. Reduce speed to low, add flour mixture, and mix until just combined. Stir in nuts and coconut.

Divide batter between buttered loaf pans and smooth tops. Bake until a wooden pick or skewer inserted in center of bread comes out clean, 45 to 50 minutes.

Remove bread from pans and cool completely, right side up, on rack.

COOK'S NOTE

■ The loaves can be kept, wrapped well in plastic wrap, for up to 1 day at room temperature.

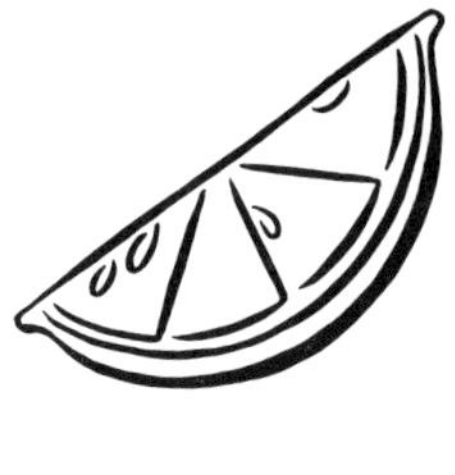

Skillet Corn Bread

SERVES 8
ACTIVE TIME: 10 MINUTES ■ START TO FINISH: 30 MINUTES

■ Our favorite corn bread is made from all cornmeal rather than the usual blend of cornmeal and white flour. Surprisingly light and very flavorful, it's reason enough to own a well-seasoned cast-iron skillet. (Nonstick pans produce anemic-looking, soft corn bread.) Susan Goff, the chef at Zinfandel, in Chicago, serves it with a wonderful buckwheat honey butter (see Cook's Note), but you can substitute another honey or maple syrup if you like. ■

1½ cups yellow cornmeal, preferably stone-ground
1 tablespoon sugar
¾ teaspoon baking soda
½ teaspoon salt
2 large eggs
1¾ cups well-shaken buttermilk
½ stick (4 tablespoons) unsalted butter, softened
SPECIAL EQUIPMENT: a well-seasoned 9- to 9½-inch cast-iron skillet

Put a rack in middle of oven and preheat oven to 425°F.

Heat skillet in oven for 10 minutes.

Meanwhile, stir together cornmeal, sugar, baking soda, and salt in a small bowl. Whisk together eggs and buttermilk in a medium bowl until blended.

Remove hot skillet from oven and add butter, swirling gently to coat bottom and sides of skillet (don't worry if butter begins to sizzle and brown around edges). Whisk hot butter into buttermilk mixture and return skillet to oven. Stir cornmeal into buttermilk mixture just until evenly moistened but still lumpy.

Scrape batter into hot skillet and bake until golden, 20 to 25 minutes. Turn out onto a rack to cool slightly (upside down). Serve warm.

COOK'S NOTE

■ To make buckwheat honey butter, combine 1 stick (8 tablespoons) softened unsalted butter with 2 tablespoons buckwheat honey.

Cheddar Jalapeño Corn Sticks

MAKES 14 CORN STICKS (OR ONE 9-INCH ROUND CORN BREAD)
ACTIVE TIME: 15 MINUTES ■ START TO FINISH: 40 MINUTES

■ We love what Cheddar does to the flavor and texture of corn bread. This combination of chiles and cheese is a great embellishment for an American classic. ■

1 cup yellow cornmeal
1 teaspoon sugar
½ teaspoon baking soda
½ teaspoon salt
1 cup well-shaken buttermilk
1 large egg
1 cup coarsely grated extra-sharp Cheddar (about 4 ounces)
¼ cup finely chopped scallions
1–2 tablespoons finely chopped drained pickled jalapeños (to taste)
½ stick (4 tablespoons) unsalted butter, melted
SPECIAL EQUIPMENT: 2 well-seasoned cast-iron corn stick pans, each with seven 5-by-1½-inch molds (see Cook's Note and Sources)

Put a rack in middle of oven and preheat oven to 425°F.

Heat pans in oven for 10 minutes.

Meanwhile, whisk together cornmeal, sugar, baking soda, and salt in a small bowl. Whisk together buttermilk and egg in a large bowl. Add cornmeal mixture, Cheddar, scallions, jalapeños, and 2 tablespoons butter, stirring until just combined.

Remove pans from oven and divide remaining 2 tablespoons butter among molds. Quickly divide batter among molds (about 3 tablespoons each). Bake until a wooden pick or skewer inserted in center of a corn stick comes out clean and tops are golden, 12 to 15 minutes.

Cool corn sticks in pans for 3 to 5 minutes, then remove from molds. Serve warm.

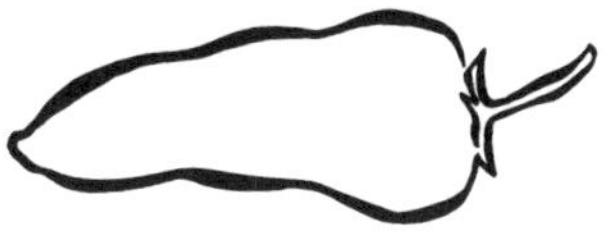

COOK'S NOTE

■ For corn bread, the batter can be baked in a well-seasoned 9- to 9½-inch cast-iron skillet. Heat the skillet in the oven for 10 minutes, add the 2 tablespoons butter, and pour in the batter. Bake for 15 to 20 minutes.

Irish Soda Bread

MAKES TWO 6-INCH ROUND LOAVES
ACTIVE TIME: 15 MINUTES ■ START TO FINISH: 3 HOURS (INCLUDES COOLING)

■ Soda bread is one of Ireland's greatest culinary legacies, and its appeal is enduring. You'll find this simple quick bread, chock-full of golden raisins and caraway, everywhere from the grandest of country house hotels to the most modest of village pubs, and in home kitchens all over the country. Because the principal leavening agent is baking soda, not yeast, this bread is great news for anyone pressed for time, although it's at its best when allowed to sit for a few hours before slicing. We could eat this every day—alongside eggs and bacon at breakfast, with smoked salmon and sweet butter for lunch, or with a pot of freshly made tea in the afternoon. ■

4 cups all-purpose flour
1½ teaspoons baking soda
1 teaspoon salt
1 tablespoon sugar
1½ tablespoons caraway seeds
1 cup golden raisins
1¾ cups well-shaken buttermilk
2 tablespoons unsalted butter, melted

Put a rack in middle of oven and preheat oven to 375°F. Butter and flour a large baking sheet, knocking off excess flour.

Sift together flour, baking soda, and salt into a large bowl. Stir in sugar, caraway seeds, and raisins. Add buttermilk and stir just until dough is evenly moistened but still lumpy.

Turn dough out onto a floured surface and gently knead with floured hands about 8 times, until slightly less sticky but still soft. Halve dough and form each half into a ball.

Pat out each ball into a domed 6-inch round on baking sheet, spacing them 4 inches apart. Cut a large ½-inch-deep X in top of each loaf with a sharp knife, then brush loaves with butter.

Bake until golden brown and bottoms sound hollow when tapped, 35 to 40 minutes. Cool on a rack for 2 hours before slicing.

COOK'S NOTE

- The bread keeps, wrapped in foil, for up to 3 days at room temperature.

Irish Brown Soda Bread

MAKES ONE 7-INCH ROUND LOAF
ACTIVE TIME: 20 MINUTES ■ START TO FINISH: 3 HOURS (INCLUDES COOLING)

■ "Brown bread," the most common kind of soda bread in Ireland, is a dark loaf made with wholemeal flour, and it's this version that we find most irresistible. Our whole wheat flour doesn't have the same character as Irish wholemeal flour, and if used alone it will not produce the proper flavor and texture. But this recipe, from the cookbook author Jeanne Lemlin, combines whole wheat flour with oats and wheat germ, which results in a loaf that's nearly identical to County Cork's best. And don't worry if your dough is almost a batter—it's supposed to be very wet. ■

- 1¼ cups unbleached all-purpose flour, plus additional for sprinkling
- 1 cup whole wheat flour
- ½ cup old-fashioned rolled oats
- ¼ cup toasted wheat germ
- 1½ teaspoons baking soda
- 1 teaspoon salt
- ½ stick (4 tablespoons) cold unsalted butter, cut into bits
- 1⅓ cups well-shaken buttermilk or plain yogurt

Put a rack in middle of oven and preheat oven to 425°F. Lightly flour a baking sheet.

Whisk together flours, oats, wheat germ, baking soda, and salt in a large bowl. Add butter and toss to coat with flour, then blend in butter with your fingertips or a pastry blender until mixture resembles coarse meal. Add buttermilk and stir until dough is evenly moistened but still lumpy.

Turn dough out onto a floured surface and knead for 1 minute, sprinkling lightly with additional flour to prevent sticking; dough should remain soft. Form dough into a ball and pat out into a 7-inch round on floured baking sheet. Sprinkle with flour and spread flour lightly over surface. Cut a shallow X in top of loaf with a sharp knife.

Bake bread until golden and bottom sounds hollow when tapped, 30 to 40 minutes. Cool on a rack for 2 hours before slicing.

Boston Brown Bread

MAKES 2 LOAVES
ACTIVE TIME: 20 MINUTES ■ START TO FINISH: 2½ HOURS (INCLUDES COOLING)

■ Baking soda breads of this kind used to be steamed in buttered molds with a cloth tied over the top, like an English steamed pudding. According to the food historian Anne Mendelson, from at least the 1880s recipes suggested using a small pail like the five-pound ones that lard was sold in, but at some point early in the twentieth century people changed over to one-pound baking powder cans (yes, one pound—baking powder must have been used lavishly by some). When vacuum-sealed coffee cans became popular, cooks switched to them, and even the commercial version came to be baked in molds shaped like cans.

Often paired with baked beans, this steamed bread is moist and sweet, with a molasses tang. It is also absolutely delicious with cream cheese. This recipe comes to us from Dorian Leigh Parker, a sometime contributor. ■

- 2 cups plus 2 tablespoons whole wheat flour
- ½ cup cornmeal
- ½ teaspoon salt
- ¾ cup molasses (not robust or blackstrap)
- 2 teaspoons baking soda, dissolved in 1 tablespoon hot water
- 2 cups well-shaken buttermilk
- 1 cup raisins

SPECIAL EQUIPMENT: two 13-ounce coffee cans (see Cook's Note); kitchen string; a 5- to 6-quart pot at least 7 inches deep

Generously butter coffee cans. Line bottom of each can with a round of wax paper and butter paper.

Sift together 2 cups flour, cornmeal, and salt into a large bowl. Heat molasses to lukewarm in a small saucepan. Remove from heat and stir in baking soda mixture and buttermilk. Add to flour mixture and stir until just combined. Toss raisins with remaining 2 tablespoons flour, shake off excess, and stir into batter.

Divide batter between coffee cans. Cover each can with a double thickness of foil, then tie foil securely onto each can with kitchen string. Put cans on a rack set into pot. Add enough boiling water to pot to reach halfway up sides of cans. Cover and steam bread at a simmer until a wooden pick or skewer inserted in center comes out clean, about 1 hour.

Transfer cans to a rack and cool loaves for 1 minute, then run a thin knife around each loaf, carefully slide bread out of cans, and cool, upright, on rack.

COOK'S NOTES

- If your coffee cans have a lip around the rim, remove it with a can opener.
- The bread keeps, wrapped well in plastic wrap, for up to 3 days at room temperature.

Classic Popovers

MAKES 6 LARGE OR 9 MEDIUM POPOVERS
ACTIVE TIME: 10 MINUTES ■ START TO FINISH: 1 1/4 HOURS

■ Popovers are incredibly easy to make, but they add an element of surprise to a simple meal—the "wow" quotient, we call it. Perhaps because of their dramatic height and irregular golden-brown tops, each one seems to have its own personality. ■

- 2 large eggs
- 3/4 cup whole milk
- 1/4 cup water
- 1 tablespoon unsalted butter, melted

- 3/4 cup plus 2 tablespoons all-purpose flour
- 1/2 teaspoon salt

SPECIAL EQUIPMENT: a popover pan with six (2/3-cup) cups or a muffin pan with twelve (1/2-cup) cups

Put a rack in lower third of oven and preheat oven to 375°F. Generously butter popover cups or 9 muffin cups.

Whisk together eggs, milk, and water in a medium bowl. Add butter, whisking. Add flour and salt and whisk until batter is well combined but still slightly lumpy.

Divide batter among popover or muffin cups. Bake until puffed and pale golden, about 45 minutes.

With a small sharp knife, cut a 1/2-inch slit in top of each popover to allow steam to escape. Bake until golden brown, about 10 minutes more. Serve immediately.

VARIATION

- GARLIC PARMESAN POPOVERS: Omit the butter. Mince and mash 1 large garlic clove to a paste with salt. Whisk into batter along with flour. Divide half of batter among popover or muffin cups, then sprinkle with 1/4 cup finely grated Parmigiano-Reggiano. Divide remaining batter among cups and sprinkle another 1/4 cup grated Parmesan over tops. Bake as directed above.

Buckwheat Pepper Crisps

MAKES ABOUT 60 CRACKERS
ACTIVE TIME: 1 HOUR ■ START TO FINISH: 2 HOURS

■ Try these paper-thin crisps with a rosé Champagne. Its flavor somehow makes the pepper taste spicier and the buckwheat sweeter. You can also make the crisps half the size and serve them with sour cream and caviar. ■

Vegetable-oil cooking spray (see Cook's Note)
3/4 cup all-purpose flour
1/4 cup buckwheat flour
1 tablespoon sugar
1 teaspoon baking powder
1 teaspoon salt
1 teaspoon freshly ground black pepper
1/2 stick (4 tablespoons) unsalted butter, softened
1 large egg, at room temperature
1 cup whole milk, at room temperature

Put a rack in middle of oven and preheat oven to 350°F. Spray two large baking sheets with cooking spray.

Whisk together flours, sugar, baking powder, salt, and pepper in a bowl.

Combine butter, egg, and milk in a blender and blend well. Add flour mixture and blend just until smooth. Transfer to a bowl.

Drop batter by level teaspoons (about 9 mounds) 4 inches apart onto a prepared baking sheet. With back of a spoon, spread each mound into a 3½- to 4-inch round.

Bake until golden in spots, 8 to 10 minutes. With a thin metal spatula, immediately transfer crisps to a rack to cool. Form more rounds on second baking sheet while first batch is baking. Continue to make and bake crisps, baking one sheet at a time. (Baking sheets should be cooled but not cleaned between batches.)

COOK'S NOTES

- Instead of using cooking spray, you can bake the crisps on nonstick baking sheets or baking sheets lined with reusable nonstick liners such as Silpats (see Sources).
- The crisps keep in an airtight container, layered between sheets of wax paper, for up to 2 weeks at room temperature.

Mustard and Cheese Crackers

MAKES ABOUT 60 CRACKERS
ACTIVE TIME: 25 MINUTES ■ START TO FINISH: 3 HOURS

■ There are loads of delicious cheese crackers in the world, but mustard in three forms—seeds, dry, and prepared—adds a piquant dimension to these. ■

1 stick (8 tablespoons) cold unsalted butter, cut into tablespoons
2 cups coarsely grated Swiss cheese (about 8 ounces)
1 cup all-purpose flour
2 teaspoons dry mustard
1½ teaspoons mustard seeds
1 teaspoon salt
3 tablespoons Dijon mustard
1 large egg yolk

Combine butter and cheese in a food processor and blend until almost smooth. Add remaining ingredients and pulse until just combined.

Turn dough out and divide between two sheets of wax paper. Form each half into an 8-inch log, using wax paper to help shape logs, and roll up in wax paper, then wrap in foil. Freeze until firm, 1½ to 2 hours.

Put racks in upper and lower thirds of oven and preheat oven to 350°F. Butter two large baking sheets.

Cut 1 log into ¼-inch-thick slices and arrange slices 1 inch apart on buttered baking sheets. Bake, switching position of sheets halfway through baking, until golden brown, 15 to 17 minutes total. With a spatula, transfer crackers to a rack to cool. Make more crackers in same manner with remaining dough.

COOK'S NOTES

- The dough can be frozen for up to 1 week.
- The crackers can be kept in an airtight container at room temperature for up to 3 days.

Salt and Pepper Grissini

MAKES 16 BREADSTICKS
ACTIVE TIME: 20 MINUTES ■ START TO FINISH: 1 HOUR (INCLUDES COOLING)

■ This is not a yeast dough, so these *grissini* (Italian for "breadsticks") are quick, easy, and very feasible to do at the last minute. They make an everyday meal—soup and salad, for instance—into something special. ■

1/4 cup rye flour
1/4 cup plus 1 tablespoon all-purpose flour
1/2 teaspoon baking powder
1/4 teaspoon baking soda

½ teaspoon sugar
1½–1¾ teaspoons kosher salt
¼ cup well-shaken buttermilk
1 teaspoon unsalted butter, melted and cooled
1 large egg white lightly beaten with 1 teaspoon water, for egg wash
1 teaspoon coarsely ground black pepper

SPECIAL EQUIPMENT: parchment paper

Put racks in upper and lower thirds of oven and preheat oven to 350°F. Line two large baking sheets with parchment.

Whisk together flours, baking powder, baking soda, sugar, and ¼ teaspoon salt in a medium bowl. Stir in buttermilk and butter with a fork until a dough forms. Transfer dough to a lightly floured surface and gently knead 5 or 6 times.

Form dough into a log and cut into 16 equal pieces. Roll each piece into a 10-inch-long rope (if dough sticks, lightly flour work surface) and arrange ½ inch apart on lined baking sheets.

Brush breadsticks with egg wash and sprinkle with remaining 1¼ to 1½ teaspoons salt (to taste) and pepper. Bake, switching position of sheets halfway through baking, until golden and crisp, 20 to 22 minutes total. Transfer to racks to cool.

COOK'S NOTE

- The *grissini* can be made up to 1 day ahead and kept in an airtight container at room temperature.

Seeded Breadsticks

MAKES 16 BREADSTICKS
ACTIVE TIME: 45 MINUTES ■ START TO FINISH: 2¼ HOURS (INCLUDES RISING AND COOLING TIMES)

■ We use peppery nigella seeds, sometimes mislabeled as black onion seeds, on these breadsticks. (They are what gives Armenian string cheese its distinctive flavor.) The flat, angular, jet-black seeds look striking, but you can use whatever seeds you have on hand: sesame, caraway, poppy, and/or toasted cumin seeds, for instance. ■

¾ cup warm milk (105°–115°F)
1 tablespoon olive oil
1 teaspoon sugar
1 teaspoon active dry yeast (from a ¼-ounce package)
1 cup whole wheat flour
1 cup all-purpose flour, plus additional for kneading
¾ teaspoon salt
Cornmeal for sprinkling
1 large egg white, lightly beaten
1 tablespoon nigella seeds (see Glossary) or mixed white and black sesame seeds
Kosher salt for sprinkling

Stir together milk, oil, sugar, and yeast in a large bowl until yeast is dissolved. Let stand until foamy, about 5 minutes. (If mixture does not foam, discard and start over with new yeast.)

Stir in both flours and salt until a dough forms.

Turn dough out onto a floured work surface and knead until smooth and elastic, 8 to 10 minutes, adding just enough additional flour to keep it from sticking. Transfer dough to a lightly oiled bowl and turn to coat with oil. Cover tightly with plastic wrap and let dough rise in a warm draft-free place until doubled in bulk, about 1 hour.

Grease two large baking sheets and sprinkle with cornmeal. Punch down dough and turn out onto work surface. Cut dough into 16 equal pieces. Roll each piece into a 15- to 16-inch-long rope and arrange 1 inch apart on prepared baking sheets. Let stand, uncovered, for 15 minutes.

Put racks in upper and lower thirds of oven and preheat oven to 400°F.

Brush breadsticks with egg white and sprinkle with seeds and kosher salt, pressing gently to help seasonings adhere. Bake, switching position of sheets halfway through baking, until golden brown, about 20 minutes total. Transfer to racks to cool.

COOK'S NOTE

- The cooled baked breadsticks can be frozen in sealable plastic bags for up to 1 week. Reheat in a 350°F oven until crisp.

Garlic Bread

SERVES 4 TO 6
ACTIVE TIME: 10 MINUTES ■ START TO FINISH: 30 MINUTES

■ Remember the simple pleasure of garlic bread? This retro accompaniment to Mom's spaghetti and meatballs has been cast aside in favor of focaccia and artisanal loaves, but we think it's about time for a comeback. Mother really did know best: this is a quick way to make something enticing out of basic supermarket ingredients. The secret to garlic bread that's neither too greasy nor too dry is having the correct proportion of butter to bread, so we give specific dimensions for the Italian loaf. If yours is a different size, you'll need to adjust the amount of garlic butter accordingly. ■

- 2 teaspoons finely chopped garlic
- Rounded ¼ teaspoon salt
- ½ stick (4 tablespoons) unsalted butter, softened
- 1 tablespoon extra-virgin olive oil
- 2 tablespoons finely chopped fresh flat-leaf parsley
- 1 (15-by-3½-inch) loaf Italian bread

Put a rack in middle of oven and preheat oven to 350°F.

Using a heavy knife, mince and mash garlic to a paste with salt. Stir together with butter and oil in a bowl until smooth. Stir in parsley.

Without cutting completely through bottom, cut bread diagonally into 1-inch-thick slices with a serrated knife. Spread garlic butter between slices.

Wrap loaf in foil and bake for 15 minutes. Open foil and bake for 5 minutes more.

COOK'S NOTES

- The bread can be spread with the garlic butter up to 8 hours ahead and refrigerated, wrapped in foil. Let stand at room temperature for 30 minutes before baking.
- For a brighter flavor, substitute 1 tablespoon finely chopped fresh basil for 1 tablespoon of the parsley.

Rosemary Focaccia

MAKES ONE 15-BY-10-BY-1-INCH FLATBREAD
ACTIVE TIME: 15 MINUTES ■ START TO FINISH: 3½ HOURS (INCLUDES RISING TIME)

■ Focaccia was popular in San Francisco first, but it was only a matter of time before the Genoese flatbread, topped with small pockets of flavorful olive oil and the delicate crunch of sea salt, became a runaway favorite in the rest of the country. This particular focaccia has a very nice crumb, striking just the right balance between chewiness and tenderness, with a golden, crisp outside and a moist inside. It's not hard to make and is extremely versatile. You might serve it as an accompaniment if you're having a hearty soup or stew for dinner—it's likely to become the most talked-about part of the meal. It's also thick enough to split in half so you can make sandwiches with it.

We strongly recommend using a stand mixer for this recipe. The dough is quite sticky, and a mixer will help you grapple with it. You can knead the dough by hand, but don't be tempted to add more flour than we specify, or the focaccia will be tough and dry. Whichever method you use, focaccia is best eaten on the day it's baked. ■

- 1⅔ cups warm water (105°–115°F)
- 1 (¼-ounce) package (2½ teaspoons) active dry yeast
- Pinch of sugar
- 5 cups unbleached all-purpose flour, plus additional for kneading
- ¼ cup plus 3 tablespoons extra-virgin olive oil
- 2½ teaspoons salt
- 1 tablespoon finely chopped fresh rosemary
- 1 teaspoon coarse sea salt

SPECIAL EQUIPMENT: a heavy-duty stand mixer with paddle attachment and dough hook

Stir together warm water, yeast, and sugar in mixer bowl until yeast is dissolved. Let stand until foamy, about 5 minutes. (If mixture doesn't foam, discard and start over with new yeast.)

Add flour, ¼ cup oil, and regular salt and beat with paddle attachment at medium speed until a dough forms. Switch to dough hook and knead dough at high speed until soft, smooth, and sticky, 3 to 4 minutes.

Turn dough out onto a lightly floured surface and knead in 1 to 2 tablespoons more flour. Knead dough for 1 minute longer (it will still be slightly sticky), then transfer to a lightly oiled large bowl and turn to coat with oil. Cover with plastic wrap and let rise in a warm draft-free place until doubled in bulk, 1 to 1½ hours.

Generously oil a 15-by-10-by-1-inch baking sheet and press dough evenly into pan. Cover completely with oiled plastic wrap and let rise in a warm draft-free place until doubled in bulk, about 1 hour.

Put a rack in middle of oven and preheat oven to 425°F.

Stir together rosemary and remaining 3 tablespoons oil in a small bowl or cup. Make shallow indentations all over top of dough with your fingertips, then brush with rosemary oil, letting it pool in indentations. Sprinkle sea salt evenly over focaccia.

Bake focaccia until golden, 20 to 25 minutes. Immediately invert a rack over pan and invert focaccia onto rack, then turn right side up. Serve warm or at room temperature.

COOK'S NOTE

- If the grains of your coarse sea salt are very large, you may want to crush them slightly before sprinkling over the focaccia.

Whole Wheat Pita Bread

MAKES EIGHT 6-INCH PITAS
ACTIVE TIME: 30 MINUTES ■ START TO FINISH: 3 HOURS (INCLUDES RISING TIME)

■ Why make your own pita when it's available at supermarkets throughout the land? One bite of these, fresh and warm from the oven, will tell you why. Try them with Tomato and Cucumber Salad (page 183) and a fresh mild goat cheese—a perfect meal for a hot summer's day. ■

- 1 (¼-ounce) package (2½ teaspoons) active dry yeast
- 1 teaspoon honey
- 1¼ cups warm water (105°–115°F)
- 2 cups bread flour or high-gluten flour, plus additional for kneading
- 1 cup whole wheat flour
- ¼ cup extra-virgin olive oil
- 1 teaspoon salt
- Cornmeal for sprinkling

Stir together yeast, honey, and ½ cup warm water in a large bowl until yeast is dissolved. Let stand until foamy, about 5 minutes. (If mixture doesn't foam, discard and start over with new yeast.)

Stir together flours in another bowl. Whisk ½ cup flour mixture into yeast mixture until smooth. Cover with plastic wrap and let rise in a warm draft-free place until doubled in bulk and bubbly, about 45 minutes.

Stir oil, salt, remaining ¾ cup warm water, and remaining flour mixture into yeast mixture until a dough forms.

Turn dough out onto a floured surface and knead, working in just enough additional flour to keep dough from sticking, until it is smooth and elastic, 8 to 10 minutes. Form dough into a ball, transfer to an oiled large bowl, and turn to coat with oil. Cover with plastic wrap and let rise in a warm draft-free place until doubled in bulk, about 1 hour.

Lightly sprinkle two baking sheets with cornmeal. Punch down dough and cut into 8 pieces. Form each piece into a ball. Flatten 1 ball, then roll out into a 6½- to 7-inch round on floured surface with a floured rolling pin. Transfer round to one baking sheet. Make 7 more rounds in same manner, arranging 4 of them on each baking sheet. Loosely cover pitas with two clean kitchen towels (not terry cloth) and let stand at room temperature for 30 minutes.

Put a rack in lower third of oven, remove other racks, and preheat oven to 500°F.

Transfer 4 pitas, one at a time, directly onto oven rack. Bake until just puffed and pale golden, about 2 minutes. Turn over with tongs and bake for 1 minute more. Cool pitas on a rack for 2 minutes, then stack and wrap loosely in a kitchen towel to keep warm. Bake remaining 4 pitas in same manner. Serve warm.

COOK'S NOTE

- The pitas can be baked up to 1 week ahead and frozen. Cool completely, then wrap well in foil, place in a sealable plastic bag, seal, and freeze. Thaw, still wrapped, before reheating. Heat, wrapped in foil, for 10 to 12 minutes in a 350°F oven.

Naan

Leavened Flatbread with Mixed Seeds

MAKES 4 LARGE FLATBREADS
ACTIVE TIME: 1 HOUR ■ START TO FINISH: 3½ HOURS
(INCLUDES RISING TIME)

■ The Indian leavened flatbread called naan doesn't require a traditional tandoor oven; a pizza stone works well. It doesn't need to be restricted to an Indian meal, either; it's delicious with leg of lamb or a vegetarian dish with a smidge of cumin or curry powder. ■

- 1 teaspoon active dry yeast
- ½ teaspoon sugar
- 1 tablespoon warm water (105°–115°F)
- 3–4 cups unbleached all-purpose flour
- ¼ teaspoon baking soda
- 1 teaspoon salt
- 2 teaspoons black poppy seeds
- ½ cup warm whole milk (105°–115°F)
- 1 cup plain whole-milk yogurt, at room temperature
- ⅓ cup finely chopped onion
- ½ stick (4 tablespoons) unsalted butter, melted
- 1 large egg, lightly beaten
- 1½ tablespoons mixed seeds, such as nigella seeds (see Glossary), sesame seeds, and/or white poppy seeds
- Kosher salt for sprinkling

SPECIAL EQUIPMENT: a pizza stone and a baker's peel (see Sources)

Stir together yeast, sugar, and water in a small bowl until yeast is dissolved. Let stand until foamy, about 5 minutes. (If mixture doesn't foam, discard and start over with new yeast.)

Sift together 2½ cups flour, baking soda, salt, and ½ teaspoon black poppy seeds into a large bowl. Stir together milk, yogurt, onion, and 2 tablespoons butter in another bowl. Make a well in center of flour mixture, then add yeast mixture, milk mixture, and egg and stir until a soft, sticky dough forms.

Turn dough out onto a lightly floured surface and knead for 10 minutes, adding just enough of remaining flour to prevent dough from sticking. Form dough into a ball, transfer to a lightly oiled large bowl, and turn to coat with oil. Cover with a kitchen towel (not terry cloth) and let rise in a warm draft-free place until doubled in bulk, about 2 hours.

Put pizza stone on oven floor if using a gas oven, lowest rack if using electric (remove other racks in either case), and preheat oven to highest setting (500°–550°F). Allow about 1 hour to preheat stone. Flour two baking sheets.

Turn dough out onto a lightly floured surface and cut into quarters. Roll out each quarter with a floured rolling pin into a ⅛-inch-thick oval about 12 inches long and 5 inches wide. Transfer to floured baking sheets, cover with kitchen towels, and let rest for 10 minutes.

Stir together remaining 1½ teaspoons black poppy seeds and mixed seeds in a small bowl.

Transfer 1 dough oval to well-floured peel. Brush top of oval with about ½ tablespoon of remaining butter and sprinkle with one quarter of seeds and some kosher salt. Line up far edge of peel with far edge of stone and tilt peel, jerking it gently to start dough moving. When edge of oval touches stone, quickly pull back peel to transfer loaf to stone (do not pull dough back). Bake until edges are golden brown and bread bubbles (top will be an uneven golden brown), 5 to 6 minutes. Keep naan warm, loosely covered with foil, while you bake remaining loaves, one at a time, in same manner; reflour peel as necessary to prevent dough from sticking.

COOK'S NOTE

■ The naans can be made 1 day ahead and cooled completely, then wrapped in plastic wrap and kept at room temperature. Reheat, uncovered, on a baking sheet in a 475°F oven until the bottoms are slightly crisp, about 2 minutes.

Portuguese White Cornmeal Bread

MAKES TWO 8-INCH ROUND LOAVES
ACTIVE TIME: 30 MINUTES ■ START TO FINISH: 4½ HOURS
(INCLUDES RISING AND COOLING TIMES)

■ This Portuguese classic, made with a mix of cornmeal and white flour, has a wonderfully tender, close texture. The small amount of white cornmeal gives it more substance than you'd get from a loaf made with just white flour. It is great for sandwiches or paired with a hearty bean soup, and it makes terrific toast. Buy your cornmeal from a store that has a high turnover and sniff it before using to make sure it isn't at all musty. ■

- 1 (¼-ounce) package (2½ teaspoons) active dry yeast
- 1 tablespoon sugar
- 2 cups warm water (105°–115°F)
- ½ stick (4 tablespoons) unsalted butter, melted and cooled
- 2½ teaspoons salt
- ½ cup white cornmeal, plus additional for sprinkling
- 5½–6 cups all-purpose flour
- 2 tablespoons whole milk

Stir together yeast, sugar, and ¼ cup warm water in a large bowl until yeast is dissolved. Let stand until foamy, about 5 minutes. (If mixture doesn't foam, discard and start over with new yeast.)

Add remaining 1¾ cups water, 2 tablespoons butter, salt, cornmeal, and 5½ cups flour and stir until a dough forms.

Turn dough out onto a lightly floured surface and knead, adding just enough additional flour to keep it from sticking, until smooth and elastic, 8 to 10 minutes. Transfer dough to a large buttered bowl and brush top lightly with some of remaining melted butter. Cover bowl with a kitchen towel (not terry cloth) and let dough rise in a warm draft-free place until doubled in bulk, about 1½ hours.

Brush two 9-inch metal pie plates with remaining butter and sprinkle with cornmeal. Turn dough out onto floured surface and knead 3 or 4 times to remove air. Halve dough, form each half into a 5-inch ball, and put in a pie plate (do not flatten). Cover each ball of dough loosely with a kitchen towel and let rise in a warm draft-free place until doubled in bulk, about 1 hour.

Put a rack in middle of oven and preheat oven to 350°F.

Gently brush loaves with milk. Cut a large ¼-inch-deep X in top of each with a sharp knife. Bake until loaves are golden brown and bottoms sound hollow when tapped, 55 to 60 minutes. Transfer loaves from pie plates to a rack and cool completely.

Swedish Rye Bread

Limpa

MAKES TWO 8-INCH LOAVES
ACTIVE TIME: 20 MINUTES ■ START TO FINISH: 3 HOURS
(INCLUDES RISING AND COOLING TIMES)

■ This rye bread, a popular offering on the smorgasbords of Minnesota and Wisconsin, has a clean-tasting combination of spiciness and sweetness that is characteristic of much of Scandinavian cooking. Great for toast, it's excellent for ham sandwiches and nontraditional Reubens as well. ■

- 2 (¼-ounce) packages (5 teaspoons) active dry yeast
- ½ cup warm water (105°–115°F)
- Pinch of sugar
- 1½ cups milk
- ⅓ cup molasses (not robust or blackstrap)
- ½ stick (4 tablespoons) unsalted butter, cut into pieces
- 1 tablespoon anise seeds
- 1 tablespoon caraway seeds (optional)
- 4 teaspoons salt
- 1½ teaspoons finely grated orange zest
- 2 cups rye flour
- 3¾–4½ cups unbleached all-purpose flour

Stir together yeast, warm water, and sugar in a small bowl until yeast is dissolved. Let stand until foamy, about 5 minutes. (If mixture doesn't foam, discard and start over with new yeast.)

Combine milk, molasses, and butter in a small saucepan and heat over low heat, stirring occasionally, until butter is melted. Remove from heat and cool to 105°–115°F.

Combine yeast mixture, milk mixture, anise seeds, caraway seeds (if using), salt, zest, rye flour, and 3¾ cups all-purpose flour in a large bowl and stir together until a dough forms. Turn dough out onto a floured surface and knead, adding as much remaining all-purpose flour as necessary to prevent it from sticking, until smooth and elastic, 8 to 10 minutes.

Transfer dough to a buttered large bowl and turn to coat with butter. Cover tightly with plastic wrap and let rise in a warm draft-free place until doubled in bulk, about 1½ hours.

Butter a large baking sheet. Punch down dough,

then turn out onto a floured surface and knead 3 or 4 times. Halve dough and form each half into a round loaf. Transfer loaves to baking sheet, arranging them 4 inches apart. Let rise, covered with kitchen towels (not terry cloth) in a warm draft-free place until almost doubled in bulk, about 1 hour.

Put a rack in middle of oven and preheat oven to 375°F.

Prick loaves all over with a fork in a decorative pattern. Bake until browned and bottoms sound hollow when tapped, 30 to 40 minutes. Transfer loaves to a rack to cool.

Braided Challah

MAKES 2 LARGE LOAVES
ACTIVE TIME: 1¼ HOURS ■ START TO FINISH: 6½ HOURS (INCLUDES RISING AND COOLING TIMES)

■ Challah is the traditional braided, round, or rectangular egg-enriched Jewish loaf that is blessed and served at Shabbat meals. The Dallas-based food writer Maxine Levy, who developed this recipe, suggests using thick slices for golden-brown French toast (see page 650); older slices make wonderful stuffings. On Rosh Hashanah, the advent of the Jewish New Year, she makes the same dough but coils it into large dome-shaped loaves, symbolic of the continuity of life. ■

FOR STARTER

- ¾ cup warm water (105°–115°F)
- 2 teaspoons sugar
- 1 tablespoon bread flour
- 2 (¼-ounce) packages (5 teaspoons) active dry yeast

FOR DOUGH

- ½ cup plus 1 tablespoon peanut oil
- ½ cup sugar
- 2 tablespoons kosher salt
- 4 teaspoons mild honey, preferably clover
- 3 extra-large eggs, at room temperature
- 2 extra-large egg yolks, at room temperature
- 1½ cups warm water (105°–115°F)
- 7¼ cups bread flour

FOR BAKING

- Vegetable shortening for greasing baking sheet
- Cornmeal for dusting
- 1 extra-large egg lightly beaten with 2 tablespoons sugar, for egg wash
- 1 tablespoon nigella seeds (optional; see Glossary)

SPECIAL EQUIPMENT: a 1-quart glass jar with a tight-fitting lid; a heavy-duty stand mixer with paddle attachment and dough hook; 2 long spatulas

MAKE THE STARTER: Rinse jar several times with hot water to warm it and drain well. Add warm water, sugar, flour, and yeast to jar and stir until yeast is dissolved. Cover with lid and let stand in a warm draft-free place until bubbles reach halfway up side of jar, about 10 minutes. (If mixture doesn't foam, discard and start over with new yeast.)

MAKE THE DOUGH: Warm mixer bowl and fit mixer with paddle attachment. Add oil, sugar, salt, honey, eggs, and yolks to bowl and beat together at medium speed until blended, about 1 minute. Add warm water and beat until sugar and salt are dissolved, about 30 seconds. Spread starter over batter with a rubber spatula. Add 2¾ cups flour and beat, scraping down sides of bowl, for 5 minutes.

Switch to dough hook. Add 4 cups flour and knead at low speed, scraping down sides of bowl, until dough is elastic and little blisters appear on surface, 8 to 10 minutes (dough will be very soft).

Transfer dough to a well-oiled large bowl, turn to coat with oil, and cover tightly with plastic wrap. Let rise in a warm draft-free place until doubled in bulk, about 2 hours.

Punch down dough, cover with plastic wrap, and let rise again until doubled in bulk, about 45 minutes.

Turn dough out onto a well-floured surface and knead in remaining ½ cup flour with floured hands. Let dough stand, covered with inverted bowl, for 10 minutes.

BRAID AND BAKE THE CHALLAH: Generously grease a large baking sheet with shortening and dust with cornmeal, knocking off excess.

Halve dough. Set one half aside, covered with inverted bowl. Divide other half into 3 equal pieces. Roll each piece on a lightly floured surface into a 12-inch-long rope (1½ to 2 inches wide). To form 3-rope braid, place ropes parallel to each other about

1 inch apart. Starting braid in center will create greatest height in center of loaf. Lift left rope and cross it over center of middle rope (1). Lift right rope and cross it over left (2). Lift bottom of middle rope and cross it over right rope and continue braiding to end of loaf (3). Flip braid over and turn so unbraided end is facing you. Continue as described until you reach end. Pinch ends of loaf together and tuck them under. Divide, roll, and braid remaining dough in same manner.

With long spatulas, transfer loaves carefully to prepared baking sheet, arranging them 5 inches apart. Brush loaves well with egg wash and sprinkle with nigella seeds, if using. Let loaves rise, uncovered, in a warm draft-free place for 30 minutes.

HOW TO BRAID CHALLAH

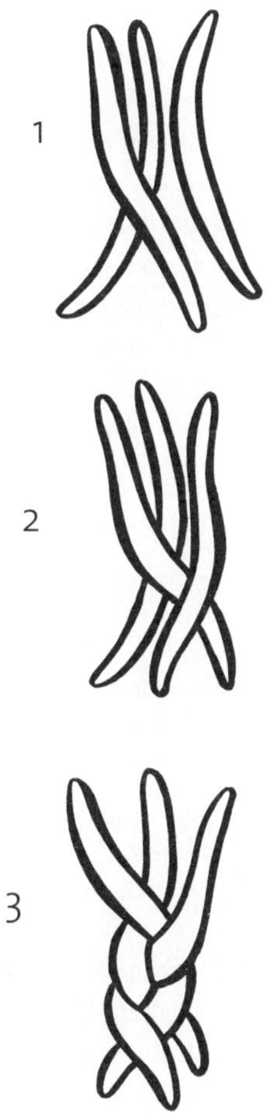

Put a rack in middle of oven and preheat oven to 375°F.

Bake loaves until deep golden and bottoms sound hollow when tapped, about 40 minutes. (If loaves begin to brown too quickly, cover with foil.) Transfer loaves to racks to cool completely.

Brioche Loaf

MAKES ONE 9-INCH LOAF
ACTIVE TIME: 40 MINUTES ■ START TO FINISH: 21 HOURS
(INCLUDES MAKING DOUGH AND COOLING BREAD)

■ Rich, buttery brioche is generally thought of as a small breakfast bread that wears a rakish topknot (see Classic Brioches, page 612), but it is very versatile when shaped into larger loaves. It makes delicious French toast and bread pudding, but also think of putting egg salad, lobster salad, or even a hamburger (square off the edges) between two slices of brioche toast. And a BLT with brioche is incomparable. This recipe is from our former executive food editor, the restaurateur Sally Darr. ■

Brioche Dough (recipe follows), chilled as directed
1 large egg yolk
1 tablespoon heavy cream

Butter a 9-by-5-inch loaf pan. Knead dough for 1 minute on a well-floured surface with floured hands. Form into a 9-inch log and transfer to pan. Cover loosely with plastic wrap and let rise in a warm draft-free place until dough has more than doubled in bulk and almost fills pan, about 2 hours.

Put a rack in middle of oven and preheat oven to 375°F.

Stir together yolk and cream in a small bowl, then brush onto loaf. Bake loaf until golden brown, about 35 minutes.

Cool bread in pan on a rack for 20 minutes, then turn out onto rack to cool completely, about 1 hour.

Brioche Dough

MAKES ABOUT 1¼ POUNDS
ACTIVE TIME: 45 MINUTES ■ START TO FINISH: 15½ HOURS
(INCLUDES RISING AND CHILLING TIMES)

■ You will need a heavy-duty stand mixer. We use a 4½-quart mixer and the whisk and dough hook attachments; if you have a larger model, use the whisk attachment throughout in order to work the dough properly. ■

FOR STARTER

- 1 teaspoon sugar
- ¼ cup warm milk or water (105°–115°F)
- 1 (¼-ounce) package (2½ teaspoons) active dry yeast
- ½ cup sifted all-purpose flour (sift before measuring)

FOR DOUGH

- 3 tablespoons sugar
- ½ teaspoon salt (¼ teaspoon if making Classic Brioches or Raisin Brioche Pastries)
- 1 tablespoon hot milk or water
- 3 large eggs
- 1½ cups sifted all-purpose flour, plus additional for dusting
- 1½ sticks (12 tablespoons) unsalted butter, cut into ½-inch-thick slices, well softened

SPECIAL EQUIPMENT: a heavy-duty stand mixer with whisk and dough hook (see headnote)

MAKE THE STARTER: Stir together sugar and milk in a small bowl. Stir in yeast and let stand until foamy, about 5 minutes. (If mixture doesn't foam, discard and start over with new yeast.)

Stir flour into yeast mixture, forming a soft dough. Cut a deep X in top. Cover with plastic wrap and let rise in a warm draft-free place for 1 hour.

MAKE THE DOUGH: Stir together sugar, salt, and hot milk in a small bowl until sugar and salt are dissolved. Fit mixer with whisk attachment and beat 2 eggs at medium-low speed until foamy. Add sugar mixture and beat until well combined. With motor running, add in order, beating well after each addition, ½ cup flour, remaining egg, ½ cup flour, about one quarter of butter, and remaining ½ cup flour. Continue to beat for 1 minute.

Switch to dough hook. Scrape starter onto dough with a rubber spatula and beat at medium-high speed until dough is smooth and elastic, about 6 minutes. Add remaining butter and beat until butter is incorporated, about 1 minute.

Lightly butter a large bowl and scrape dough into bowl with rubber spatula. Lightly dust dough with flour to prevent a crust from forming. Cover bowl with plastic wrap and let dough rise in a warm draft-free place until more than doubled in bulk, 2 to 3 hours.

Punch dough down and lightly dust with flour. Cover bowl with plastic wrap and refrigerate dough, punching it down after first hour, for at least 12 hours.

COOK'S NOTE

■ The dough can be refrigerated for up to 3 days. Punch it down once a day.

Bowl Scrapers

A bowl, or dough, scraper, made of slightly pliable plastic, is designed for a number of different tasks. Its curved edge makes it perfect for scraping the last remnant of a sticky brioche dough or cake batter from a mixing bowl onto a work surface or into a baking pan. It's also useful for pressing lumps out of a mixture while it is still in the bowl and for scraping thick purées through a sieve. The straight edge of the scraper is ideal for cleaning off a work surface or dividing and lifting dough.

Classic Brioches

MAKES 10 BRIOCHES
ACTIVE TIME: 1¼ HOURS ■ START TO FINISH: 18¼ HOURS
(INCLUDES MAKING DOUGH)

■ The sweet, buttery *brioche à tête,* baked in a cunning little fluted tin, is a familiar sight on French breakfast tables. Don't fret when you make the characteristic topknot, or head, for each brioche—the rising dough will camouflage any clumsiness. ■

About 2 tablespoons unsalted butter, melted
Brioche Dough (opposite page), chilled as directed
1 large egg yolk
1 tablespoon heavy cream

SPECIAL EQUIPMENT: 10 individual fluted brioche molds (3 inches across top; see Sources)

Brush butter onto bottoms and sides of brioche molds with a pastry brush. Arrange on a large baking sheet.

Knead dough for 1 minute on a well-floured surface with floured hands. Form into a 10-inch-long log and cut log into ten 1-inch pieces.

Pull off one quarter of dough from one piece (keep remaining pieces covered with plastic wrap) and form it into a small ball. Roll remainder of piece into a large ball on lightly floured surface and transfer to a buttered mold. Make a deep indentation in large ball by pressing a finger dipped in cold water down through center to bottom of mold. Pinch one end of small ball into a point and fit pointed end into indentation in large ball, pressing point down to bottom of mold to anchor it. Repeat with remaining pieces of dough.

Cover molds loosely with a sheet of plastic wrap and let dough rise in a warm draft-free place until doubled in bulk, about 1½ hours.

Put a rack in middle of oven and preheat oven to 400°F.

Stir together yolk and cream in a small bowl, then lightly brush onto brioches with pastry brush.

Bake brioches until golden brown, about 20 minutes. Cool in molds on a rack for 5 minutes, then turn out onto rack to cool completely.

Parker House Rolls

MAKES 20 ROLLS
ACTIVE TIME: 45 MINUTES ■ START TO FINISH: 3 HOURS (INCLUDES RISING TIME)

■ Even if you usually resort to store-bought rolls, do save this recipe for a rainy afternoon. These fabulous rolls, created in the 1870s at the Parker House Hotel in Boston (where, incidentally, Ho Chi Minh was once a busboy and Malcolm X a waiter), aren't hard to make, even if you're not an experienced baker. They are great with roast chicken or beef stew. You owe it to yourself. ■

3 tablespoons warm water (105°–115°F)
3 tablespoons sugar
1 (¼-ounce) package (2½ teaspoons) active dry yeast
1 stick (8 tablespoons) unsalted butter
1 cup whole milk
2 cups bread flour (not whole wheat)
1½ teaspoons salt
¾–1½ cups all-purpose flour

Stir together warm water, 1 tablespoon sugar, and yeast in a small bowl until yeast is dissolved. Let stand until foamy, about 5 minutes. (If mixture doesn't foam, discard and start over with new yeast.)

Melt ¾ stick (6 tablespoons) butter in a small saucepan. Add milk and heat until lukewarm. Pour into a large bowl, add yeast mixture, remaining 2 tablespoons sugar, bread flour, and salt, and stir with a wooden spoon until well combined. Stir in ¾ cup all-purpose flour, then, if necessary, add up to ½ cup more flour, 1 tablespoon at a time, to make a slightly sticky dough that forms a ball.

Turn dough out onto a lightly floured surface and knead, adding more all-purpose flour if dough is very sticky, until smooth and elastic but still slightly sticky, about 10 minutes. Form dough into a ball, put in a buttered large bowl, and turn to coat with butter. Cover with plastic wrap and let rise in a warm draft-free place until doubled in bulk, about 1 hour.

Butter a 13-by-9-inch baking pan. Divide dough into 20 equal pieces. Roll each one into a ball and arrange evenly in 4 rows of 5 in baking pan. Cover loosely with plastic wrap and let rise in a warm draft-free place until almost doubled in bulk, about 45 minutes.

Using a floured chopstick or edge of a ruler, make a deep crease down center of each row of rolls. Let rolls rise, loosely covered, for 15 minutes.

Put a rack in middle of oven and preheat oven to 375°F.

Melt remaining 2 tablespoons butter; cool slightly. Brush tops of rolls with butter and bake until golden, 20 to 25 minutes. Cool rolls in pan on a rack for 5 minutes, then turn out onto rack and cool, right side up, until warm.

COOK'S NOTE

- The rolls can be baked up to 1 day ahead. Cool completely, then wrap well in foil and keep at room temperature. Reheat in the foil in a 375°F oven for 15 to 20 minutes.

VARIATION

- CLOVERLEAF ROLLS: The cloverleaf shape is easy to form and gives these rolls a showy little fillip.

  After the dough has doubled in bulk, butter eighteen 1/3- to 1/2-cup muffin cups. Turn the dough out onto a lightly floured surface and divide it into thirds. Work with one portion at a time, keeping the remaining dough covered with plastic wrap. Cut off tablespoon-sized pieces of dough, form into balls, and put 3 balls in each buttered muffin cup.

  Let rise, loosely covered, in a warm draft-free place until almost doubled in bulk, 30 to 40 minutes.

  Preheat the oven to 400°F. Brush the rolls lightly with egg wash (1 large egg lightly beaten with 2 teaspoons water) and sprinkle with poppy and/or lightly toasted sesame seeds (see Tips, page 939). Bake until golden, 15 to 20 minutes. Cool as directed above.

Hamburger Buns

MAKES ABOUT 20 BUNS
ACTIVE TIME: 30 MINUTES ■ START TO FINISH: 5 1/2 HOURS (INCLUDES RISING TIME)

■ Once you taste these hamburger buns, you may never buy buns again. They're perfect, and they shouldn't be limited to burgers; try stuffing them with egg or chicken salad, or turkey and honey mustard. (They also make a terrific tomato sandwich, because they absorb the juices beautifully.) And they freeze well, so you can just pull them out of the freezer a few at a time. The recipe is from Joyce McClelland, from Terre Haute, Indiana, and has been handed down in her family for generations. You can also use this dough to make hot dog buns. ■

- 2 cups whole milk
- 1/4 cup warm water (105°–115°F)
- 2 (1/4-ounce) packages (5 teaspoons) active dry yeast
- 1/4 cup plus 1/2 teaspoon sugar
- 1/2 stick (4 tablespoons) unsalted butter, cut into tablespoons and softened
- 2 large eggs, lightly beaten
- 1 tablespoon salt
- 6–6 1/2 cups all-purpose flour

SPECIAL EQUIPMENT: a heavy-duty stand mixer with paddle attachment and dough hook (see Cook's Note); a 3-inch round cutter

Bring milk to a bare simmer in a small saucepan over moderate heat. Remove from heat. Let cool to 105°–115°F.

Meanwhile, stir together warm water, yeast, and 1/2 teaspoon sugar in mixer bowl until yeast is dissolved. Let stand until foamy, about 5 minutes. (If mixture doesn't foam, discard and start over with new yeast.)

Add butter and remaining 1/4 cup sugar to yeast mixture and mix with paddle attachment at low speed until just combined. Add warm milk and mix until butter is melted, then add eggs and mix until well combined. Add salt and 4 cups flour and mix, scraping down sides of bowl with a rubber spatula as necessary, until flour is just incorporated. Increase speed to medium and beat until well combined, about 1 minute.

Switch to dough hook and beat in 2 cups flour at medium speed, scraping down sides of bowl once or twice, until dough pulls away from sides of bowl, about 2 minutes; if necessary, add additional flour, 1 tablespoon at a time. Beat for 5 minutes more. (Dough will be sticky.)

Transfer dough to a lightly oiled large bowl and turn to coat with oil. Cover tightly with plastic wrap and let rise in a warm draft-free place until doubled in bulk, about 2 1/2 hours.

Butter two large baking sheets. Punch dough down. Turn out onto a lightly floured surface and roll out into a 14-inch round (about 1/2 inch thick) with a floured rolling pin. Cut out as many rounds as possible with floured cutter and transfer to buttered baking sheets, arranging them about 3 inches apart to allow for expansion. Gather and reroll scraps and cut out more buns in same manner.

Cover buns loosely with oiled plastic wrap and let rise in a warm draft-free place until they hold a finger mark when gently pressed, 1 1/2 to 2 hours.

Put racks in upper and lower thirds of oven and preheat oven to 375°F.

Bake buns, switching position of sheets halfway through baking, until tops are golden and bottoms are golden brown and sound hollow when tapped, 14 to 20 minutes. Transfer to racks to cool completely.

COOK'S NOTES

- If you don't have a stand mixer, stir the ingredients together in the same sequence in a large bowl with a wooden spoon until a dough forms. Turn the dough out onto a floured surface and knead, incorporating only enough flour to keep the dough from sticking, until smooth and elastic, 7 to 8 minutes.
- Once cooled, the baked buns can be frozen in a heavy-duty sealable plastic bag for up to 1 month.

Sopaipillas

MAKES ABOUT 36 SOPAIPILLAS
ACTIVE TIME: 1 1/2 HOURS ■ START TO FINISH: 2 1/2 HOURS (INCLUDES RISING TIME)

■ Almost anything you order in casual New Mexican restaurants comes with an earthy, vibrant side of "green" or "red" (chile, that is, used as a sauce or soup) along with another staple, the puffy, deep-fried bread called sopaipilla (pronounced "soap-ah-*pee*-yah"—the name means "sofa pillow"), which is served with warm honey. Visitors tend to tear off a corner of a sopaipilla and drizzle the honey inside; locals top the honey with a spoonful of chile. This recipe is a great one; it came from El Paragua restaurant, in Española, just north of Santa Fe. ■

- 1 (1/4-ounce) package (2 1/2 teaspoons) active dry yeast
- 1/4 cup warm water (105°–115°F)
- 2 tablespoons sugar
- 1 1/2 cups whole milk
- 3 tablespoons lard or vegetable shortening
- 2 teaspoons salt
- 1 cup whole wheat flour
- 3 1/2–4 cups all-purpose flour
- About 6 cups vegetable oil for deep-frying

ACCOMPANIMENT: warm honey
SPECIAL EQUIPMENT: an instant-read thermometer; 3 large trays; a deep-fat thermometer

Stir together yeast, warm water, and a pinch of sugar in a large bowl until yeast is dissolved. Let stand until foamy, about 5 minutes. (If mixture doesn't foam, discard and start over with new yeast.)

Combine milk, lard, salt, and remaining sugar in a 1-quart saucepan and heat over low heat just until milk registers 110°F on instant-read thermometer (lard does not need to be melted). Immediately stir milk mixture into yeast mixture. Stir in whole wheat flour and 3 cups all-purpose flour until just combined. Add 1/2 cup more all-purpose flour and stir until a stiff, sticky dough forms.

Turn dough out onto a lightly floured surface and knead with floured hands, kneading in just enough of remaining 1/2 cup flour to keep it from sticking, until dough is smooth and elastic, about 5 minutes. Transfer dough to a lightly oiled large bowl and turn to coat with oil. Cover with plastic wrap and let rise in a warm draft-free place for 1 hour.

Preheat oven to 300°F. Lightly flour trays.

Turn dough out onto a lightly floured surface and divide into thirds. Cover 2 pieces of dough with a kitchen towel (not terry cloth). Roll out remaining piece with a floured rolling pin into a 17-by-15-inch rectangle (1/8 inch thick). Trim edges with a sharp knife or a pizza wheel and cut into 12 rectangles roughly 5 inches by 4 inches. Arrange rectangles in one layer on one tray and cover with plastic wrap (refrigerate if not frying right away). Roll out, cut, and arrange remaining dough pieces on remaining trays in same manner.

Heat 2 inches oil in a 5-quart heavy pot over moderate heat until it registers 375°F on deep-fat thermometer. Fry dough rectangles in the same order they were cut in, 2 pieces at a time, turning over, until puffed and golden brown, about 1 minute per batch.

(Return oil to 375°F between batches.) Transfer sopaipillas to paper towels to drain, then keep warm on a baking sheet in oven. Serve immediately, with honey.

COOK'S NOTE

- The dough can be made up to 1 day ahead and allowed to rise, then covered with plastic wrap and refrigerated. Punch it down and let stand at room temperature for 15 minutes before proceeding.

Corn Fritters

MAKES ABOUT 45 FRITTERS
ACTIVE TIME: 45 MINUTES ■ START TO FINISH: 1¾ HOURS (INCLUDES STANDING TIME)

■ These free-form fried nuggets of corn flavor are delicious for breakfast with maple syrup or with deep, tangy sorghum, a type of molasses made from the stalks of sorghum, an ancient grain that's similar to millet. You might also serve the fritters as a savory side to ham or chicken. This recipe is from the late novelist and food writer Laurie Colwin. ■

2 cups all-purpose flour
Salt
2 cups water
¼ cup olive oil
1 large egg, separated
3⅓ cups corn kernels (from 6 large ears)
About 4 cups vegetable oil for deep-frying
1 garlic clove

SPECIAL EQUIPMENT: a 3- to 4-quart wide shallow saucepan; a deep-fat thermometer

Preheat oven to 200°F.

Stir together flour and a generous pinch of salt in a large bowl. Add water a little at a time, stirring, then stir in olive oil a little at a time. Add yolk and stir until batter is smooth.

Beat egg white with a whisk or handheld mixer in a small bowl until just stiff. Fold gently but thoroughly into batter. Let batter stand, covered, for 1 hour at room temperature.

Stir corn into batter. Pour 1¼ inches vegetable oil into pot, add garlic, and heat over moderately high heat until garlic turns golden; discard garlic and continue to heat oil. When it registers 375°F on thermometer, stir batter and, working in batches of 6, drop rounded tablespoons of batter into pot. Fry fritters, turning once, until golden and cooked through, 4 to 5 minutes per batch. With a slotted spoon, transfer to paper towels to drain and keep warm in oven. (Return oil to 375°F between batches.)

Stollen

MAKES ONE 12-INCH LOAF
ACTIVE TIME: 1 HOUR ■ START TO FINISH: 5½ HOURS (INCLUDES RISING AND COOLING TIMES)

■ In Germany, Christmas wouldn't be Christmas without stollen. This rich, fruit-studded bread is a labor of love, but it makes a fabulous gift. Or bake two loaves and save one for yourself—it keeps beautifully and is delicious toasted. Don't cut corners when it comes to the candied fruit. Try to avoid the kind sold in supermarkets, which smacks of preservatives; instead, splurge on the good stuff (see opposite page), full of a strong sugar syrup, because Christmas comes but once a year. The thick, batterlike sponge adds extra flavor to this bread. ■

FOR DRIED-FRUIT MIX
¼ cup glacéed (candied) cherries, halved
½ cup diced mixed glacéed (candied) fruits without cherries
½ cup raisins
½ cup dried currants
3 tablespoons dark rum

FOR SPONGE
1 (¼-ounce) package (2½ teaspoons) active dry yeast
¼ teaspoon granulated sugar
¾ cup warm milk (105°–115°F)
1 cup unbleached all-purpose flour

FOR DOUGH
2½ cups unbleached all-purpose flour
1 teaspoon salt
1 stick (8 tablespoons) unsalted butter, melted and cooled, plus 2 tablespoons melted butter

- 2 large eggs, lightly beaten
- ⅓ cup granulated sugar
- ½ cup sliced almonds, toasted (see Tips, page 938) and chopped

FOR BRUSHING AND GLAZE

- 2 tablespoons unsalted butter, melted
- 2 tablespoons confectioners' sugar

SPECIAL EQUIPMENT: a heavy-duty stand mixer with paddle attachment and dough hook

MAKE THE FRUIT MIX: Stir together all ingredients in a small bowl. Let stand at room temperature, stirring occasionally, for at least 2 hours.

MAKE THE SPONGE: Stir together yeast, sugar, and warm milk in mixer bowl until yeast is dissolved. Let stand until foamy, about 5 minutes. (If mixture doesn't foam, discard and start over with new yeast.)

Add flour to yeast mixture and beat with a wooden spoon until incorporated. Cover tightly with plastic wrap and let sponge rise in a warm draft-free place until doubled in bulk and blistering, about 45 minutes.

MAKE THE DOUGH: Add flour, salt, 8 tablespoons melted butter, eggs, and sugar to sponge and beat at medium speed with paddle attachment until incorporated. Switch to dough hook, add almonds and dried-fruit mixture, and beat at medium speed until dough is smooth and pulling away from sides of bowl, about 5 minutes. Beat for 5 minutes more (it will be a little sticky).

Put dough in a lightly oiled large bowl and turn to coat with oil. Cover tightly with plastic wrap and let rise in a warm draft-free place until doubled in bulk, about 1½ hours.

Punch down dough, turn out onto a lightly floured surface, and knead briefly. Roll out dough with an unfloured rolling pin into an oval about 12 inches long and 7 inches wide (1 inch thick).

Brush top of dough with remaining melted butter. Fold dough lengthwise in half so that bottom half extends about 1 inch beyond top half, and press folded edge lightly together with fingertips.

Generously butter a baking sheet. Arrange stollen diagonally on it. Cover loosely with plastic wrap and let rise in a warm draft-free place until doubled in bulk, about 1½ hours.

GLAZE AND BAKE THE STOLLEN: Put a rack in middle of oven and preheat oven to 350°F.

Brush stollen with melted butter. Bake until loaf is deep golden and bottom sounds hollow when tapped, 40 to 50 minutes. Transfer stollen to a rack to cool, then sprinkle with confectioners' sugar.

COOK'S NOTES

- The fruit mixture can be made up to 4 hours ahead and kept at room temperature. Oil your knife before cutting up the fruit—it's easier that way.
- The stollen will keep, wrapped well in foil, for up to 4 days at room temperature.

Glacéed Fruit

Vibrant with the jewel-like tones of stained glass, the candied fruits from a Manhattan outpost of Fauchon are expensive, but they're a whole lot cheaper than a trip to Paris. You can buy them by the piece. We also like the fruit from the Baker's Catalogue, and it is considerably less expensive. (See Sources for both.) The candied fruit found at supermarkets comes in a distant third. The best we can say about it is that it's available everywhere.

Hot Cross Buns

MAKES 24 BUNS
ACTIVE TIME: 1½ HOURS ■ START TO FINISH: 4 HOURS (INCLUDES RISING AND COOLING TIMES)

■ The English tradition of eating special sweet buns on Good Friday dates back to the sixteenth century, but the first mention of marking them with a symbolic cross comes in 1733, in *Poor Robin's Almanack*. They were presumably first simply docked with a knife; the practice of decorating them with pastry or icing came later. Hot cross buns are delicious plain or split, toasted, and spread with butter and jam. ■

- 1 cup warm milk (105°–115°F)
- 2 (1/4-ounce) packages (5 teaspoons) active dry yeast
- 1/2 cup plus 1 teaspoon granulated sugar
- 4 cups all-purpose flour
- 1 1/2 teaspoons ground allspice
- 1/2 teaspoon ground cinnamon
- 1 teaspoon salt
- 1 1/4 sticks (10 tablespoons) cold unsalted butter, cut into bits
- 2 large eggs
- 1 large egg yolk
- 1/2 cup dried currants
- 1/3 cup golden raisins
- 2 teaspoons finely grated orange zest
- 2 teaspoons finely grated lemon zest
- 3 tablespoons superfine sugar
- Basic Pastry Dough for a single-crust pie (page 790)

Stir together milk, yeast, and 1 teaspoon sugar in a small bowl until yeast is dissolved. Let stand until foamy, about 5 minutes. (If mixture doesn't foam, discard and start over with new yeast.)

Sift together flour, allspice, cinnamon, salt, and remaining 1/2 cup sugar into a large bowl. Blend in butter with your fingertips or a pastry blender until mixture resembles coarse meal. Lightly beat 1 egg with egg yolk in a small bowl. Make a well in center of flour mixture and pour in yeast and egg mixtures, then add currants, raisins, and zests and stir until a dough forms.

Transfer dough to a floured surface and knead with lightly floured hands until smooth and elastic, about 10 minutes. Transfer dough to an oiled large bowl and turn to coat with oil. Cover with plastic wrap and let rise in a warm draft-free place until doubled in bulk, about 1 1/2 hours.

Butter two baking sheets. Turn dough out onto a lightly floured surface and knead briefly. Halve dough and form each half into a 12-inch-long log. Cut each log crosswise into 12 equal pieces. Form each piece into a ball and arrange balls about 1 1/2 inches apart on buttered baking sheets. Let rise, loosely covered with plastic wrap, in a warm draft-free place until doubled in bulk, about 45 minutes.

Put racks in upper and lower thirds of oven and preheat oven to 400°F.

Lightly beat remaining egg with superfine sugar in a cup to make a glaze. Roll out pastry dough on lightly floured surface with a floured rolling pin into a 10-by-6-inch rectangle (1/8 inch thick). With a sharp knife, cut rectangle crosswise into forty-eight 1/8-inch-wide strips; discard extra dough.

Brush buns with egg glaze, arrange 2 pastry strips over center of each bun to form a cross, and trim ends of strips flush with bottoms of buns. Bake, switching position of sheets halfway through baking, until golden, about 12 minutes. Transfer buns to a rack to cool. Serve warm or at room temperature.

COOK'S NOTE

- Once cooled, the baked buns can be frozen, wrapped in foil, for up to 1 week. Thaw and then reheat, still in the foil packet, in a 350°F oven before serving.

Pecan Currant Sticky Buns

MAKES 12 BUNS
ACTIVE TIME: 45 MINUTES ■ START TO FINISH: 3 1/2 HOURS (INCLUDES RISING TIME)

■ These are perfection plus. They are a fantastic treat for special occasions. ■

FOR DOUGH

- 1 1/2 cups warm milk (105°–115°F)
- 2 (1/4-ounce) packages (5 teaspoons) active dry yeast
- 1/3 cup granulated sugar
- 5 1/4 cups all-purpose flour, plus additional for dusting
- 2 teaspoons salt
- 2 large eggs, at room temperature
- 1/2 stick (4 tablespoons) unsalted butter, softened

FOR FILLING

- 2/3 cup packed dark brown sugar
- 2/3 cup dried currants
- 2/3 cup chopped pecans
- 1 teaspoon ground cinnamon
- 1/2 stick (4 tablespoons) unsalted butter, softened

FOR SYRUP

- 1 stick (8 tablespoons) unsalted butter, cut into pieces
- 1/2 cup packed dark brown sugar
- 1/2 cup granulated sugar
- 2 tablespoons light corn syrup
- 1/4 cup heavy cream

SPECIAL EQUIPMENT: a heavy-duty stand mixer with dough hook; 2 muffin pans with 6 large (1-cup) cups each

MAKE THE DOUGH: Stir together 1/2 cup warm milk, yeast, and a pinch of sugar in a small bowl until yeast is dissolved. Let stand until foamy, about 5 minutes. (If mixture doesn't foam, discard and start over with new yeast.)

Put flour, remaining sugar, and salt in mixer bowl and mix with dough hook at low speed until combined. Whisk together remaining 1 cup milk and eggs in a small bowl, then add to dry ingredients, along with yeast mixture, and mix at medium speed until a very soft dough forms, about 2 minutes. Add butter and continue beating until dough is smooth and elastic, about 4 minutes (dough will be very sticky).

Rinse a large bowl with hot water, then put dough in wet bowl and cover tightly with plastic wrap. Let dough rise in a warm draft-free place until doubled in bulk, about 1 1/4 hours.

PREPARE THE FILLING: Stir together all ingredients except butter in a small bowl.

MAKE THE SYRUP: Butter muffin cups. Combine butter, sugars, corn syrup, and heavy cream in a 1-quart saucepan and heat over low heat, stirring, until butter is melted. Bring to a simmer and simmer, stirring, for 2 minutes. Spoon 2 tablespoons warm syrup into each muffin cup.

FILL AND FORM THE BUNS: Turn dough out onto a well-floured surface and dust with flour. Roll out into a 16-by-12-inch rectangle with a floured rolling pin. Turn dough if necessary so long side is nearest you. Brush off excess flour, then spread evenly with softened butter. Sprinkle filling evenly over dough. Beginning with long side near you, roll up dough to form a 16-inch-long log and press seam to seal.

Cut log crosswise into 12 rounds. Arrange buns cut sides up in muffin cups. Cover with oiled plastic wrap and let rise in a warm draft-free place until doubled in bulk, about 1 hour.

Put a rack in middle of oven and preheat oven to 350°F.

Bake buns until puffed and golden, 30 to 35 minutes. Cool in pan on a rack for 10 minutes, then invert buns onto rack and cool slightly.

Serve warm.

Raisin Brioche Pastries

MAKES 11 PASTRIES
ACTIVE TIME: 1 1/2 HOURS ■ START TO FINISH: 18 1/4 HOURS (INCLUDES MAKING DOUGH)

■ Along with croissants and *pains au chocolat,* these flat, spiral-shaped buns are ubiquitous in the morning bread basket that arrives after you order your *café crème* or espresso in Paris. Enriched with pastry cream and raisins, they deserve to be more popular on this side of the Atlantic. ■

FOR RAISINS
- 1 cup raisins
- 1 cup boiling water

FOR PASTRY CREAM
- 1 cup whole milk
- 3 large egg yolks
- 1/3 cup sugar
- 1 1/2 tablespoons cornstarch
- 1/2 teaspoon vanilla extract
- 1/2 tablespoon unsalted butter

Brioche Dough (page 612), chilled as directed

FOR GLAZE
- 1/4 cup apricot preserves
- 2 tablespoons water

PREPARE THE RAISINS: Soak raisins in boiling water until softened, about 10 minutes. Drain, pressing out excess liquid, and set aside.

MAKE THE PASTRY CREAM: Bring milk to a simmer in a 1 1/2-quart heavy saucepan. Whisk together yolks, sugar, and cornstarch in a medium bowl and gradually whisk in hot milk. Return mixture to pan and cook over moderately low heat, stirring with a wooden spoon, until mixture begins to boil. Simmer, stirring, until thickened and smooth, about 3 minutes.

Transfer to a clean bowl and stir in vanilla and butter. Cover surface with buttered round of wax paper, butter side down, and cool to room temperature. (Pastry cream will thicken as it cools.)

MAKE THE PASTRIES: Roll out brioche dough on a well-floured surface into an 18-by-11-inch rectangle. Turn dough if necessary so a short side is nearest you. Spread pastry cream evenly over dough, leaving a ½-inch border at top edge. Sprinkle raisins evenly over cream. Roll up dough, starting from short side nearest you, to make a log about 3½ inches in diameter. Moisten top edge with water and press to seal. Transfer roll to a cutting board or baking sheet, cover loosely with plastic wrap, and refrigerate until firm, at least 1 hour.

Butter two baking sheets. Cut chilled log into 11 equal slices and arrange about 2 inches apart on baking sheets. Let rise in a warm draft-free place, uncovered, for 1 hour. (Pastries will increase slightly in size and feel very tender to the touch.)

Put a rack in middle of oven and preheat oven to 425°F.

Bake pastries in 2 batches until tops are golden brown, 12 to 15 minutes per batch. Transfer pastries to a rack.

MAKE THE GLAZE: Combine preserves and water in a small saucepan, bring to a simmer, stirring, and simmer, stirring, for 1 minute. Pour through a sieve into a bowl, pressing on solids. Brush glaze lightly onto pastries.

COOK'S NOTE

- The uncut log can be refrigerated, well wrapped, for up to 8 hours. However, the pastries are best the day they are baked.

Buttery Croissants

MAKES 24 CROISSANTS
ACTIVE TIME: 2 HOURS ■ START TO FINISH: 19 HOURS (INCLUDES MAKING DOUGH)

■ Delicately crisp outside, light yet chewy inside, with enough sugar to accentuate the butter's sweetness, and just enough salt: in a word, perfect. This recipe is from the master baker Nancy Silverton, of Los Angeles's La Brea Bakery. ■

Croissant Dough (recipe follows), chilled as directed

SPECIAL EQUIPMENT: a ruler; a pastry brush; parchment paper; 2 or 3 garbage bags (unscented); a spray bottle filled with water

ROLL OUT AND CUT THE DOUGH: Cut dough in half. Wrap one half in plastic wrap and refrigerate. Roll out other half on a lightly floured surface into a 16-by-12-inch rectangle, dusting with flour as necessary and stretching corners to maintain shape. Brush off excess flour with pastry brush and trim edges with a sharp knife or pizza wheel.

Position dough with a short side nearest you and cut lengthwise in half. Transfer one half to a baking sheet and refrigerate. Cut remaining half crosswise into thirds, forming 3 rectangles. Cut each rectangle diagonally in half to make 2 triangles.

SHAPE THE CROISSANTS: Line two or three baking sheets with parchment paper. Holding short side (side opposite tip) of 1 dough triangle in one hand, stretch dough, tugging and sliding with other hand toward tip to elongate by about 50 percent (1). Return to work surface with short side of triangle nearest you. Beginning with short side, roll up triangle toward tip (2). Croissant should overlap 3 times, with tip sticking out from underneath; you may need to stretch dough while rolling (3). Put croissant tip side down on a parchment-lined baking sheet. Curve ends inward to make a crescent shape, if desired.

Make more croissants with remaining 5 triangles, then with remaining rolled-out dough, arranging them 2 inches apart on baking sheets. Repeat rolling, cutting, and shaping procedures with remaining dough.

HOW TO SHAPE CROISSANTS

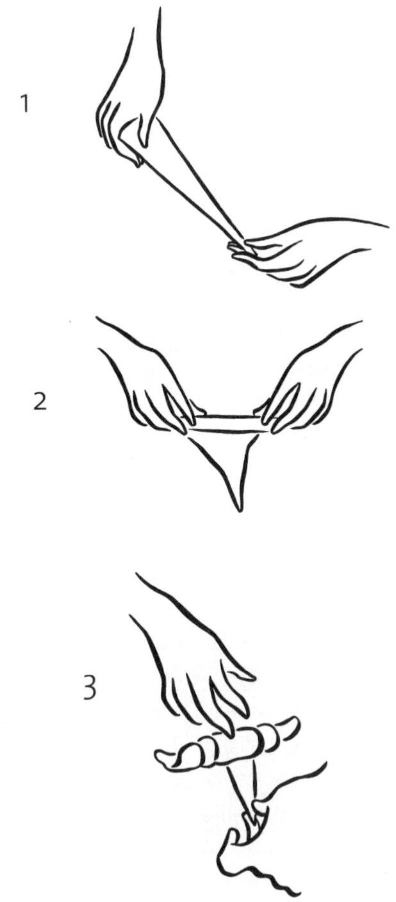

LET THE CROISSANTS RISE: Slide each baking sheet into a garbage bag, prop up top of bag with inverted glasses to keep it from touching croissants, and tuck open end under baking sheet. Let croissants rise until slightly puffy and spongy to the touch, 2 to 2½ hours.

BAKE THE CROISSANTS: Put racks in upper and lower thirds of oven and preheat oven to 425°F.

Remove baking sheets from bags. Or, if you have used three baking sheets, leave one covered while you bake the other two, then bake third sheet of croissants. Spritz inside of oven generously with spray bottle and immediately close door. Then put croissants in oven, quickly spritz again, and close door. Reduce oven temperature to 400°F and bake for 10 minutes without opening door.

Switch position of baking sheets, turning sheets around, reduce oven temperature to 375°F, and bake until croissants are deep golden, about 10 minutes more.

COOK'S NOTE

- Once cooled, the croissants can be frozen for up to 1 month. Freeze them, uncovered, on the baking sheets until firm, then wrap them snugly in foil and return to the freezer. To serve, remove foil and heat (without thawing) on a baking sheet in a 325°F oven for 5 to 10 minutes.

Croissant Dough

MAKES ABOUT 2¾ POUNDS
ACTIVE TIME: 1 HOUR ■ START TO FINISH: 14 HOURS (INCLUDES CHILLING)

■ The secret to a great croissant is the dough. Do not try to halve this recipe. Trust us: you will not have a problem getting rid of the twenty-four croissants it makes. ■

- 1½ cups warm whole milk (105°–110°F)
- ¼ cup packed light brown sugar
- 1 tablespoon plus ¼ teaspoon active dry yeast (from two ¼-ounce packages)
- 3¾–4½ cups unbleached all-purpose flour
- 1 tablespoon kosher salt
- 3 sticks (¾ pound) cold unsalted butter

SPECIAL EQUIPMENT: a heavy-duty stand mixer with dough hook; a ruler; a pastry brush

MAKE THE DOUGH: Stir together milk, brown sugar, and yeast in mixer bowl until yeast is dissolved. Let stand until foamy, about 5 minutes. (If mixture doesn't foam, discard and start over with new yeast.)

Add 3¾ cups flour and salt and mix with dough hook at low speed until dough is smooth and very soft, about 7 minutes. Transfer dough to a lightly floured work surface and knead for 2 minutes, adding more flour as necessary, a little at a time, to make a soft, slightly sticky dough. Form dough into a rectangle about 1½ inch thick and refrigerate, wrapped in plastic wrap, until cold, about 1 hour.

PREPARE AND SHAPE THE BUTTER: After dough has chilled, arrange butter sticks side by side on a work surface. Pound with a rolling pin to

soften slightly (butter should be malleable but still cold). Scrape butter into a block and put on a kitchen towel (not terry cloth), then cover with another towel. Pound and roll out, flipping towels over several times, until butter is a uniform 8-by-5-inch rectangle. Refrigerate, wrapped in towels, while you roll out dough.

ROLL OUT THE DOUGH: Unwrap dough and roll out on a lightly floured surface, dusting with flour as necessary and lifting and stretching dough (especially at corners) into a 16-by-10-inch rectangle. Position dough with a short side nearest you. Put butter in center of dough so that long sides of butter are parallel to short sides of dough (1). Fold as you would a letter: bottom third of dough up over butter, then top third down over dough (2). Brush off excess flour with pastry brush.

MAKE THE FIRST FOLD: Turn dough so a short side is nearest you, then flatten dough slightly by pressing down horizontally with rolling pin across dough at regular intervals, making uniform impressions. Roll out dough into a 15-by-10-inch rectangle, rolling just to but not over ends. Brush off any excess flour. Fold in thirds like a letter, as above, stretching corners to square off dough and forming a 10-by-5-inch rectangle. Refrigerate, wrapped in plastic wrap, for 1 hour.

MAKE THE REMAINING FOLDS: Make 3 more folds in same manner, refrigerating dough for 1 hour after each fold. (If any butter oozes out while rolling, sprinkle with flour to prevent sticking.) Wrap dough tightly in plastic wrap and refrigerate for at least 8 hours but no more than 18 (if refrigerated for longer, dough may not rise sufficiently when baked).

Sugar Doughnuts

MAKES ABOUT 18 DOUGHNUTS
ACTIVE TIME: 40 MINUTES ■ START TO FINISH: 40 MINUTES

■ There is nothing like a warm sugar doughnut. The cake type has the added advantage of being quicker to make than yeast doughnuts. Granulated sugar, rather than confectioners', works best on these, though you can also use cinnamon sugar. ■

- 3½ cups all-purpose flour
- 2 teaspoons baking powder
- ½ teaspoon baking soda
- 1½ teaspoons salt
- 2¼ cups sugar
- ¾ cup well-shaken buttermilk
- ½ stick (4 tablespoons) unsalted butter, melted
- 2 large eggs
- About 3 quarts vegetable oil for deep-frying

SPECIAL EQUIPMENT: a 3-inch doughnut cutter (or a 3-inch round cutter and a ½- to ¾-inch round cutter); a deep-fat thermometer

Sift together flour, baking powder, baking soda, and salt into a large bowl. Whisk together 1 cup sugar, buttermilk, butter, and eggs in another bowl, then add to flour and stir until a dough forms (dough will be sticky).

Turn dough out onto a well-floured surface and knead gently 8 times. Lightly flour, then roll out with a floured rolling pin into a 12-inch round (about ⅓ inch thick). Cut out as many doughnuts as possible with floured doughnut cutter, dipping it in flour before each cut (or cut out rounds with 3-inch cutter, then cut out centers with ½- to ¾-inch cutter) and transfer to lightly floured trays. Gather scraps once, reroll, and cut out more doughnuts in same manner.

Heat 3 inches oil in a 5-quart heavy pot until it registers 375°F on thermometer. Working in batches of 3, slide doughnuts into oil. Once each doughnut floats to surface, turn over and fry for 50 seconds, then turn again and fry for 50 seconds more. Transfer to paper towels to drain. (Return oil to 375°F between batches.) Let doughnuts cool slightly, then dredge in remaining 1¼ cups sugar.

COOK'S NOTE

- The doughnut holes can be cooked in the same manner as the doughnuts. Turn them occasionally until they are golden all over.

Viennese Jelly Doughnuts

MAKES ABOUT 16 DOUGHNUTS
ACTIVE TIME: 1 HOUR ■ START TO FINISH: 3 HOURS (INCLUDES RISING TIME)

■ Although the Viennese didn't invent coffee, they did make the coffeehouse into an art form. The first establishment of this kind was opened in the late sixteenth century by one Georg Kolschitzky. Legend has it that he subsidized a street vendor, the widow Krapf, to supply him with her fresh *Krapfen* every day. Today her sugary spheres are called jelly doughnuts, and we have the late longtime contributor Lillian Langseth-Christensen to thank for bringing the recipe to the pages of *Gourmet*. Light and not at all doughy, these little golden balloons sprinkled with confectioners' sugar typify the gemütlichkeit of the Viennese way of life. Langseth-Christensen usually filled her *Krapfen* with strawberry jam (we like raspberry too), but during Fasching, Vienna's indulgent party time before Lent, they are stuffed with apricot jam. ■

- 1 cup whole milk
- 2 tablespoons granulated sugar
- 1 teaspoon salt
- 1 (1/4-ounce) package (2 1/2 teaspoons) active dry yeast
- 2 tablespoons warm water (105°–115°F)
- 3 1/2–3 3/4 cups all-purpose flour, plus additional for dusting
- 2 tablespoons vegetable oil, plus about 10 cups for deep-frying
- 2 large eggs, lightly beaten
- About 1/2 cup strawberry, raspberry, or apricot jam
- Confectioners' sugar for dusting

SPECIAL EQUIPMENT: an instant-read thermometer; a 2-inch round cutter; a 2 1/2-inch round cutter; a deep-fat thermometer

MAKE THE DOUGH: Bring milk to a simmer in a 1-quart heavy saucepan. Remove from heat, add sugar and salt, and stir until dissolved. Cool to lukewarm (about 90°F).

While milk cools, stir together yeast and warm water in a small bowl until yeast is dissolved. Let stand until foamy, about 5 minutes. (If yeast doesn't foam, discard and start over with new yeast.)

Pour milk mixture into a large bowl. Add 2 1/2 cups flour, 2 tablespoons oil, eggs, and yeast mixture, stirring with a wooden spoon until a very soft dough forms. Spread 1 cup flour on work surface and transfer dough to it, scraping it from bowl with a rubber spatula. Knead dough, incorporating all of flour and adding just enough additional flour to keep dough from sticking, until smooth and elastic, 5 to 8 minutes.

Transfer dough to another large bowl and sprinkle lightly with flour. Cover with a clean kitchen towel (not terry cloth) and let rise in a warm draft-free place until doubled in bulk, about 1 1/2 hours.

FORM THE DOUGHNUTS: Turn dough out onto a floured surface. Roll out to a 1/2-inch thickness with a floured rolling pin. Cut out as many rounds as possible with 2-inch cutter. Stretch 1 round to 2 1/2 inches and put 1 teaspoon jam in center. Stretch another round to 2 1/2 inches, place over jam, and pinch edges of rounds firmly together (pinching will stretch doughnut to about 3 inches). Trim doughnut with 2 1/2-inch cutter, rotating cutter several times to help seal edges. Transfer doughnut to a floured kitchen towel and form more doughnuts in same manner. Reroll scraps only once to make more rounds (if dough shrinks back when rerolling scraps, let it stand for 10 minutes before proceeding).

Cover doughnuts with another kitchen towel and let rise in a warm draft-free place for 30 minutes.

FRY THE DOUGHNUTS: Heat 3 inches oil in a 4-quart deep heavy saucepan until it registers 375°F on deep-fat thermometer. Fry doughnuts in batches of 2, turning occasionally with a mesh skimmer or a slotted spoon, until puffed and golden brown, about 2 minutes per batch. Transfer to paper towels to drain. (Return oil to 375°F between batches.) Serve warm, dusted with confectioners' sugar.

BREAKFAST AND BRUNCH

Breakfast is the ultimate comfort meal. More a mood than a food, it is what we yearn for when we are feeling lonely or under the weather, at any time of day.

It is also the least adventurous meal. No matter how sophisticated we may be, when faced with the first flavors of the day, most of us cling to the kind of food we were raised on. Even audacious eaters—people who happily indulge in strange exotica every night—are very likely to climb out of bed early in the morning insisting on poached eggs.

For the committed cook, that makes breakfast the most relaxed of meals. You'll find wonderful pancakes in this chapter, and the best French toast any of us has ever tasted, along with great omelets and corned beef hash good enough to make a grown man cry. But that's only the beginning of our breakfast journey.

We've brought impressive huevos rancheros and terrific *migas* back from forays south of the border. We've also included frittatas and crêpes, matzo brei and blintzes, even warm lentil salad topped with fried eggs.

No true-blue American cookbook could possibly omit cereals, and you'll find them too, from crunchy homemade granola and soothingly healthful Birchermuesli to an extraordinary oatmeal brûlée, a dish so delicious we defy anyone to make it just once. You will also find a few dishes that came to our shores and insinuated themselves into the American breakfast landscape. While quiche Lorraine certainly didn't start its life as morning food, when it immigrated to this country, it quickly became an indispensable part of the brunch table. And although having pizza for breakfast would sound very strange in Italy, one version or another is being served in American cities every day of the year. We think ours is the best.

Blintzes and cheese puffs, hotcakes and muffins, sweet and savory meats—they're all here. We're hoping this chapter will expand your breakfast horizons, but if it doesn't, we'll certainly understand. Breakfast, after all, is the easygoing meal whose main purpose is to make people happy.

Maple Apricot Granola

MAKES ABOUT 10 CUPS
ACTIVE TIME: 20 MINUTES ■ START TO FINISH: 1 HOUR

■ This is a beautifully balanced blend of oats, seeds, nuts, and dried apricots. Add a little crystallized ginger for extra zing. ■

¼ cup flaxseeds
6 cups (18 ounces) old-fashioned rolled oats
2 cups (8 ounces) sliced almonds
1 cup (5 ounces) green (hulled) pumpkin seeds
½ cup (2½ ounces) hulled sunflower seeds (not roasted)
1 teaspoon salt
¾ cup vegetable oil
¾ cup pure maple syrup
2 cups (11 ounces) dried apricots, finely chopped
⅓ cup (2½ ounces) crystallized ginger, finely chopped (optional)
ACCOMPANIMENTS: plain yogurt or milk; honey or maple syrup
SPECIAL EQUIPMENT: an electric coffee/spice grinder

Put racks in upper and lower thirds of oven and preheat oven to 350°F.

Finely grind flaxseeds in coffee/spice grinder. Stir together with oats, almonds, pumpkin seeds, sunflower seeds, salt, oil, and syrup in a large bowl.

Spread mixture evenly on two large baking sheets with sides. Bake, stirring granola and switching position of sheets halfway through baking, until mixture is golden brown, about 30 minutes.

Cool granola completely on sheets on racks, then stir in apricots and ginger (if using). Serve with yogurt or milk and honey or syrup.

COOK'S NOTE

■ The granola can be kept in an airtight container at cool room temperature for up to 1 week. It can also be frozen for up to 1 month.

Birchermuesli

Uncooked Oats with Fruit and Nuts

MAKES 16 CUPS; SERVES 8 TO 10
ACTIVE TIME: 30 MINUTES ■ START TO FINISH: 8½ HOURS (INCLUDES SOAKING)

■ The secret to a delicious muesli lies in soaking the oats and dried fruits for eight hours before adding fresh fruit. That's how Dr. Bircher-Benner did it in Zurich back in 1887 at his "natural health" clinic, and it makes a huge difference. ■

1 lemon
3 navel oranges
1½ cups steel-cut oats, such as McCann's
3 cups old-fashioned rolled oats
⅓ cup coarsely chopped dried apricots
⅓ cup raisins
2 apples
2 firm but ripe pears
2 firm but ripe bananas
½ cup (3 ounces) hazelnuts, toasted (see Tips, page 938) and skinned
½ cup (2 ounces) sliced almonds, toasted
2 cups heavy cream or plain yogurt
ACCOMPANIMENT: honey

Finely grate zest from lemon and 1 orange. Squeeze juice from lemon and all oranges. Stir together oats, zests, and juices in a large bowl until well combined. Stir in apricots and raisins. Refrigerate, covered, for at least 8 hours.

Coarsely grate apples, pears, and bananas on large holes of a box grater, turning apples and pears as you go to avoid cores. Stir into muesli, along with hazelnuts, almonds, and cream. Serve with honey for drizzling.

COOK'S NOTE

■ The muesli, without the fresh fruit, nuts, or cream, can be refrigerated for up to 3 days.

Oatmeal Brûlée with Macerated Berries

SERVES 4
ACTIVE TIME: 25 MINUTES ■ START TO FINISH: 4 3/4 HOURS (INCLUDES MACERATING)

■ One of the great pleasures of a hotel experience is reacquainting yourself with the many possibilities of the most important meal of the day. This recipe from the Four Seasons Hotel in Vancouver turns the morning ritual of oatmeal into something special. It's topped with a thin layer of custard, sprinkled with sugar, and then caramelized. ■

- 3 1/4 cups water
- 1/4 cup plus 4 teaspoons granulated sugar
- 2 cups mixed berries, such as raspberries, blackberries, blueberries, and quartered strawberries
- 1/4 cup Champagne (optional)
- 1 tablespoon chopped fresh mint
- 1/2 cup very cold heavy cream
- 2 large eggs
- 3 tablespoons packed brown sugar
- 1/4 teaspoon salt
- 1 1/2 cups old-fashioned rolled oats

SPECIAL EQUIPMENT: a blowtorch

MACERATE THE BERRIES: Combine 1/4 cup water and 1/4 cup granulated sugar in a small saucepan and heat over moderately high heat, stirring, until sugar is dissolved. Remove from heat. Gently stir together berries, Champagne (if using), mint, and sugar syrup in a bowl. Cover and refrigerate, stirring occasionally, for at least 4 hours.

Put racks in upper and lower thirds of oven and preheat oven to 400°F.

MAKE THE CUSTARD: Whisk 1/4 cup cream in a small bowl until it just holds stiff peaks. Whisk together eggs, brown sugar, and remaining 1/4 cup cream in another small bowl, then gently whisk in whipped cream until smooth.

ASSEMBLE AND BAKE THE BRÛLÉES: Bring remaining 3 cups water and salt to a boil in a 2-quart heavy saucepan. Stir in oats and cook over moderate heat, stirring occasionally, until thickened and tender, about 5 minutes. Divide oatmeal among four flameproof soup plates or shallow bowls and smooth with back of a spoon. Pour custard over oatmeal. Put bowls on oven racks and bake, switching position halfway through baking, until set, about 12 minutes. (Or transfer oatmeal to a very shallow 2-quart baking dish and cover with custard. Bake in middle of oven until set, 12 to 15 minutes.)

Sprinkle 1 teaspoon remaining granulated sugar evenly over each custard. Caramelize topping on one bowl at a time with blowtorch, moving flame evenly back and forth, until sugar is melted and caramelized. With a slotted spoon, mound some berries in center of each brûlée, and serve remaining berries on the side.

COOK'S NOTE

■ The berries can macerate for up to 1 day.

Scrambled Eggs with Cream Cheese and Chives

SERVES 4
ACTIVE TIME: 15 MINUTES ■ START TO FINISH: 15 MINUTES

■ We love the way cream cheese enriches eggs and makes them creamier without announcing its presence. Instead of using chives in this recipe, you can coarsely chop a few leaves of baby spinach and scatter them over the cooking eggs. ■

- 8 large eggs
- 1 tablespoon minced fresh chives
- 1/4 teaspoon salt, or to taste
- 1/8 teaspoon freshly ground black pepper
- 2 ounces cream cheese, cut into bits, softened
- 1 tablespoon unsalted butter

GARNISH: 1 tablespoon minced fresh chives

Whisk together eggs, chives, salt, and pepper in a bowl, then stir in cream cheese.

Melt butter in a 10-inch nonstick skillet over moderate heat. Add egg mixture and cook, stirring, until just cooked through, 4 to 6 minutes. Serve eggs sprinkled with chives.

The Egg and Us

A truly amazing (and inexpensive) food, eggs make some of the simplest and most satisfying meals. (For a quick supper, for instance, try a fried egg on a heap of rice with a little tomatillo salsa and fresh cilantro.) The supermarket egg case, however, frequently confounds the average consumer. White or brown? What size? Organic or conventional? And what about the eggs enriched with the good-for-you fatty acids called omega-3s?

Let's start with color—that's easy. In terms of nutrition and culinary characteristics, color doesn't matter. The breed of chicken determines egg pigmentation. Brown eggs come from the Rhode Island Red, among other breeds. Eggs of the South American Araucana, which are increasingly available at farmers markets, range in color from pale blue and green to taupe and gray.

Size? Large eggs are the standard size in recipes, although you'll often see medium, extra-large, and jumbo eggs at the supermarket. If you need only two or three eggs for something, the difference is usually negligible. But what if you plan to make a génoise that requires five large eggs and all you can find are jumbo? Use this chart to figure out how many eggs to use:

Large		Medium	Extra-large	Jumbo
1 egg	=	1	1	1
2 eggs	=	2	2	2
3 eggs	=	3	3	2
4 eggs	=	5	4	3
5 eggs	=	6	4	4
6 eggs	=	7	5	5

Egg size primarily reflects the age of the hen—young hens lay smaller eggs—but the breed and weight of the bird also play a part. A hen starts laying when she reaches maturity, whether or not there's a rooster around; most egg farms these days have dispensed with the man of the house. (A tiny blood spot occasionally found on a yolk doesn't mean that the egg is fertilized; it's just a ruptured blood vessel that occurred when the hen was forming the egg. The egg is perfectly fine.)

Reams have been written about organic versus conventional foodstuffs. Politics aside, what's important to us is flavor, and in our experience that most often reflects not only freshness but also what "layers" eat. (Hens that are allowed to roam and scratch in the yard have a more varied diet, and their eggs are more flavorful.) There are also boutique eggs from hens fed a diet rich in the omega-3 fatty acids, which help build healthy eye, heart, and nerve cells. Omega-3 eggs may or may not be certified organic (and may or may not have great flavor), depending on the producer.

What about freshness? Stores generally have such a quick turnover, and eggs have such good keeping qualities, that you may never encounter a rotten egg. Fresh eggs will keep in the fridge for a good month after their sell-by date. (They should be stored in the carton on a bottom shelf, not in the refrigerator door, which tends to be warmer and more subject to temperature variations.)

Extreme freshness is not always desirable. For poaching, the fresher the egg, the stronger the yolk membrane and the thicker the white — it clings to the yolk and is easier to control in the simmering water. (The ropy chalazae, which are part of the white, anchor the yolk in place.) But a thick white also clings to the shell, making a very fresh egg difficult to peel; if you're making hard-boiled eggs, you're better off with eggs that are at least a week old.

Finally, we are all more aware of egg safety these days because salmonella (specifically *Salmonella enteritidis*) can be a problem, even in organic or free-range eggs. (The downside to happily roaming hens is that they can be exposed to wild birds, which carry salmonella.) So what is the risk, anyway? The statistics vary greatly, depending, for example, on whether eggs served in restaurants and food-service kitchens are taken into account. The Centers for Disease Control and Prevention document roughly 30,000 cases of salmonella a year (which may or may not be attributable to eggs), which represents one one-hundredth of 1 percent of the total U.S. population, and estimate that more than thirty-eight times that number of cases are not reported.

The risk of egg-borne salmonella is minimized by proper handling. Keep eggs cold until you cook them unless otherwise specified. Wash your hands and any utensils that come in contact with them. If you are preparing meals for young children, the elderly, pregnant women, or anyone with a compromised immune system, cook your eggs fully, which will kill the bacteria. As an alternative, you may be able to find pasteurized egg products (including eggs in the shell) at some markets. Be aware that pasteurized egg whites do not whip in the same way that unpasteurized eggs do; whipping may take up to three times as long.

Migas

Tortillas Scrambled with Bacon and Eggs

SERVES 2 TO 3

ACTIVE TIME: 25 MINUTES ■ START TO FINISH: 25 MINUTES

■ The dish called *migas* (literally, "crumbs"), which is popular in all the Southwest border states, is almost certainly related to Mexican *chilaquiles*, a homey concoction that uses leftover corn tortillas. For *migas*, economical cooks combine pieces of stale tortillas with eggs, bacon, tomatoes, chiles, cheese, and garlic to produce a satisfying brunch or light supper. This recipe is from Beatriz Esquivel, a bilingual teacher in Detroit, and appears in Marilyn Tausend and Miguel Ravago's *Cocina de la Familia*, a collection of Mexican-American family recipes. ■

- 2 thick bacon slices
- 3 tablespoons safflower or canola oil, plus more as needed
- 6 (6- to 7-inch) slightly dried leftover corn tortillas, torn into 1- to 1½-inch pieces (see Cook's Note)
- ½ cup finely chopped white onion
- 3 garlic cloves, minced
- 2 jalapeño chiles, seeded and finely chopped
- ½ red bell pepper, cored, seeded, and finely chopped (optional)
- 6 plum tomatoes, coarsely chopped
- ½ teaspoon ground cumin
- 4 large eggs, lightly beaten
- ½ cup coarsely grated Monterey Jack or white Cheddar
- Salt and freshly ground black pepper

Cook bacon in a small heavy skillet over moderate heat, turning occasionally, until crisp, 5 to 7 minutes. Transfer to paper towels to drain.

Heat oil in a 12-inch heavy skillet over moderately high heat until hot but not smoking. Fry tortilla pieces a handful at a time, turning them frequently, until pale golden, 2 to 3 minutes. Transfer to paper towels to drain.

Add onion, garlic, chiles, and bell pepper (if using) to skillet and cook, stirring, until onion is pale golden and chiles are tender, about 5 minutes (add a little more more oil to skillet if necessary). Crumble bacon and stir into vegetables, along with tomatoes and cumin. Cook, stirring, for 2 to 3 minutes. Add tortilla pieces and stir until well combined.

Pour eggs over tortilla mixture and stir in cheese and salt and pepper to taste. Cook over moderately high heat, stirring gently, until eggs are just set and cheese is melted, about 2 minutes.

COOK'S NOTES

- The eggs in this recipe are not fully cooked. If this is a concern, see page 629.
- You can dry fresh tortillas on a rack in a 300°F oven for 5 to 7 minutes.

Matzo Brei

SERVES 4

ACTIVE TIME: 5 MINUTES ■ START TO FINISH: 5 MINUTES

■ We couldn't imagine a breakfast chapter without matzo brei (*brei* rhymes with *fry*), one of the many ways Jewish cooks prepare the unleavened bread called matzo during Passover. Here is editor in chief Ruth Reichl's recipe. Everybody has a version, and they vary enormously. Reichl confesses that her secret, which she learned from her mother, is lots of butter. ■

- 4 matzos
- 4 large eggs
- 1 teaspoon salt, or to taste
- ¾ stick (6 tablespoons) unsalted butter

Crumble matzos into a large sieve placed over a bowl to catch crumbs, then hold sieve under cold running water until matzos are moist and softened but not completely disintegrated, about 15 seconds. Transfer to bowl with crumbs, add eggs and salt, and mix lightly with a fork.

Heat butter in a 10- to 12-inch skillet over moderately high heat until foam subsides. Add matzo mixture and cook, stirring constantly, until eggs are scrambled and matzo has begun to crisp, about 3 minutes.

COOK'S NOTE

- The eggs in this recipe are not fully cooked. If this is a concern, see page 629.

Cheese Omelet

SERVES 2

ACTIVE TIME: 10 MINUTES ■ START TO FINISH: 10 MINUTES

■ "Modern life is so hectic that sometimes we feel as if time is going up in smoke," wrote Édouard de Pomiane in 1930. "But we don't want that to happen to our steak or omelet, so let's hurry. Ten minutes is enough." Pomiane was a Pasteur Institute scientist who also lectured on nutrition, hosted a radio show, and wrote twenty-two cookbooks, among them *French Cooking in Ten Minutes*. Genuinely funny and utterly pragmatic, the book is for the most part as useful today as when it was written. This recipe makes one omelet; cut in half, it serves two people. Don't limit omelets to the morning hours; with a glass of wine, this one makes a great late supper after a movie, the opera, or a ball game. ■

- 1½ tablespoons unsalted butter
- 4 large eggs
- ¼ teaspoon salt
- ⅓ cup coarsely grated Gruyère or Cheddar

Heat butter in a 10-inch nonstick skillet over moderately high heat until foam subsides. Meanwhile, whisk together eggs and salt in a bowl.

Pour eggs into skillet and cook, stirring gently with a fork, until they begin to set. Spread eggs evenly in skillet and sprinkle with cheese. Reduce heat to low and cook until omelet is just set.

Holding skillet above a plate, tilt it until omelet begins to slide out and almost half is touching plate, then immediately invert skillet, as if trying to cover plate, to make omelet fold over itself. Cut in half and serve immediately.

COOK'S NOTE

■ The eggs in this recipe are not fully cooked. If this is a concern, see page 629.

VARIATION

■ In addition to the cheese, you can add 2 to 3 tablespoons of cooked mushrooms, chopped scallions, chopped peppers, diced cooked potatoes, chopped cooked ham, or chopped spinach.

Golden Egg-White Omelets with Spinach and Cheese

SERVES 4

ACTIVE TIME: 1¼ HOURS ■ START TO FINISH: 1½ HOURS

■ These are like no other egg-white omelets you have ever had. Most are rubbery and unappetizingly pallid, but golden bell pepper purée makes this version both tender and beautiful. You won't miss the yolks. This recipe is easily halved; use a smaller skillet for cooking the spinach filling. ■

- 2 medium yellow bell peppers, roasted (see Tips, page 941), peeled, seeded, and coarsely chopped
- 6 tablespoons water
- 1 small onion, finely chopped
- 1 tablespoon olive oil
- 2 (5-ounce) bags baby spinach, coarsely chopped
- 1½ teaspoons salt
- ½ teaspoon freshly ground black pepper
- 2 tablespoons all-purpose flour
- 12 large egg whites
- ¼ cup coarsely grated Gruyère

MAKE THE PEPPER PURÉE: Combine bell peppers and 2 tablespoons water in a blender and purée, scraping down sides of blender as necessary, until smooth.

PREPARE THE SPINACH: Cook onion in 1 teaspoon oil in a 12-inch nonstick skillet over moderate heat, stirring occasionally, until golden, about 5 minutes. Stir in spinach, ½ teaspoon salt, ¼ teaspoon pepper, and remaining 4 tablespoons (¼ cup) water and cook, stirring, until spinach is wilted, about 3 minutes. Transfer to a colander set over a bowl to drain and press on spinach to remove excess liquid.

MAKE THE OMELETS: Whisk together pepper purée and flour in a large bowl, then whisk in egg whites and remaining 1 teaspoon salt and ¼ teaspoon pepper until combined.

Heat ½ teaspoon oil in an 8-inch nonstick skillet over moderate heat until hot but not smoking. Pour ½ cup egg mixture into skillet and cook, lifting up cooked egg around edges occasionally to let uncooked egg flow underneath, until omelet is set but top is still slightly moist, about 2 minutes. Spoon one quarter of spinach over half of omelet and sprinkle with 1 tablespoon cheese. Using a heatproof plastic spatula, fold other half of omelet over filling and transfer to a plate. Keep warm, covered with foil.

Make 3 more omelets in same manner with remaining egg mixture, oil, spinach, and cheese.

COOK'S NOTES

- The egg whites in this recipe are not fully cooked. If this is a concern, see page 629.
- The pepper purée and spinach filling can be made up to 1 day ahead and refrigerated separately, covered. Reheat the spinach before making the omelets.

Tomato, Garlic, and Potato Frittata

SERVES 4

ACTIVE TIME: 15 MINUTES ■ START TO FINISH: 30 MINUTES

■ Garlic cooked until golden and sweet tomatoes make for a lusty frittata that is great for supper as well as breakfast or brunch. You don't have to worry about flipping this frittata so it cooks on the second side, but you do need an ovenproof skillet, since it is finished under the broiler. ■

- 6 large eggs
- 2 large egg whites
- 1/2 cup finely grated Parmigiano-Reggiano
- 1/3 cup thinly sliced fresh basil leaves
- 3/4 teaspoon salt
- 1/2 teaspoon freshly ground black pepper
- 4 garlic cloves, thinly sliced
- 3 tablespoons olive oil
- 1/2 pound boiling potatoes, peeled and cut into 1/4-inch dice
- 2 cups (6 ounces) grape tomatoes or halved cherry tomatoes

Whisk together eggs, whites, 1/4 cup Parmesan, basil, 1/2 teaspoon salt, and 1/4 teaspoon pepper in a large bowl.

Cook garlic in 1 tablespoon oil in a 10-inch nonstick ovenproof heavy skillet over moderate heat, stirring, until golden, about 1 minute. With a slotted spoon, transfer garlic to a small bowl.

Add potatoes to skillet, increase heat to moderately high, and cook, stirring occasionally, until just tender, about 6 minutes. With a slotted spoon, transfer to bowl with garlic.

Add 1 tablespoon oil and tomatoes to skillet and cook, stirring, until tomatoes begin to brown and skins split, about 4 minutes.

Preheat broiler. Add remaining 1 tablespoon oil, along with potatoes and garlic, to skillet, spreading potatoes evenly, and sprinkle with remaining 1/4 teaspoon each salt and pepper. Pour eggs over vegetables and cook, lifting up cooked egg around edges to let uncooked egg flow underneath, for 3 minutes. Reduce heat to moderate, cover, and cook for 5 minutes more (center will still be moist).

Remove lid and broil frittata 5 to 7 inches from heat until set, about 5 minutes. Sprinkle top evenly with remaining 1/4 cup cheese and broil until it melts and frittata is golden brown, 2 to 3 minutes more.

Slide onto a platter and cut into wedges.

Zucchini Frittata

SERVES 6 TO 8

ACTIVE TIME: 15 MINUTES ■ START TO FINISH: 25 MINUTES

■ Zucchini blossoms give this frittata a rustic elegance and enhance the squash flavor, but feel free to omit them. To lighten the texture, we use egg whites in addition to whole eggs. ■

- 7 large eggs
- 3 large egg whites
- 1/2 cup whole milk
- 5 ounces ricotta salata (see Glossary) or mild feta, finely crumbled (1 cup)
- 3/4 teaspoon salt
- 1/2 teaspoon freshly ground black pepper
- 1 tablespoon olive oil
- 2 medium zucchini (1–1 1/4 pounds total), quartered lengthwise and cut crosswise into 1/2-inch-thick slices
- 1 garlic clove, finely chopped

1½ teaspoons chopped fresh oregano
¼ cup finely grated Parmigiano-Reggiano
6 large zucchini blossoms, stem ends discarded if tough (optional)

Whisk together eggs, whites, milk, ricotta salata, ¼ teaspoon salt, and ¼ teaspoon pepper in a large bowl.

Preheat broiler. Heat oil in a 12-inch ovenproof nonstick skillet over moderate heat. Add zucchini and cook, stirring, until just tender, about 8 minutes. Add garlic, oregano, remaining ½ teaspoon salt, and remaining ¼ teaspoon pepper and cook, stirring, for 1 minute. Pour egg mixture over zucchini, increase heat to moderately high, and cook, lifting up cooked egg around edges occasionally to let uncooked egg flow underneath, for 3 to 5 minutes (center will still be moist).

Sprinkle frittata with Parmesan and arrange blossoms, if using, evenly on top, pressing them in lightly. Broil frittata about 6 inches from heat until set, puffed, and golden brown, about 3 minutes. Let cool for 5 minutes.

Loosen edges of frittata with a spatula and slide onto a platter. Serve warm or at room temperature, cut into wedges.

Kale and Potato Spanish Tortilla

SERVES 6
ACTIVE TIME: 1 HOUR ■ START TO FINISH: 1¾ HOURS

■ Unlike a Mexican tortilla, which is a flatbread, a Spanish tortilla is a potato-rich frittata. In the traditional Spanish style, we poach the potatoes in olive oil (only some of the oil is absorbed; the rest is drained off). And, as if eggs and potatoes weren't substantial enough, we've added greens to make this a meal. They add some color as well. ■

1 pound boiling potatoes
1 cup olive oil
1 large onion, chopped
1½ teaspoons salt
1 pound kale, tough center ribs discarded
7 large eggs

Peel potatoes and cut enough of them into ⅓-inch dice to measure 2¼ cups (discard any extra). Heat oil in a 10-inch nonstick skillet over moderate heat until hot but not smoking. Reduce heat to moderately low, add potatoes, onion, and 1 teaspoon salt, and cook, stirring occasionally, until potatoes are tender, about 20 minutes.

Meanwhile, cook kale in a 4- to 6-quart pot of boiling salted water (1 tablespoon salt per every 4 quarts water), uncovered, until wilted, 2 to 3 minutes. Drain, then immediately transfer to a bowl of cold water to stop the cooking. Drain again and squeeze handfuls of kale to extract excess moisture. Coarsely chop.

When potatoes are tender, add kale and cook, stirring occasionally, until tender, about 5 minutes. Drain vegetables in colander set over a bowl, reserving oil, and let cool for 10 minutes.

Lightly beat eggs in a large bowl. Stir in vegetables, 1 tablespoon reserved oil, and remaining ½ teaspoon salt.

Add 1 tablespoon reserved oil (save remainder for another use, if desired) to same skillet, then add egg mixture, cover, and cook over low heat until edges are set but center is still soft, about 12 minutes. Remove from heat and let stand, covered, for 15 minutes; eggs will continue to cook slightly.

Shake skillet gently to make sure tortilla is not sticking to it (if it is, loosen with a heatproof plastic spatula) and slide tortilla onto a large flat plate. Invert skillet over tortilla and, using pot holders to hold plate and skillet together tightly, flip it back into skillet. Round off edges of tortilla with plastic spatula and cook over low heat, covered, for 10 minutes more, or until cooked through. Slide tortilla onto a plate and serve warm, cut into wedges.

Baked Eggs and Mushrooms in Ham Crisps

SERVES 6

ACTIVE TIME: 45 MINUTES ■ START TO FINISH: 1 1/4 HOURS

■ Here the ham makes its own little container for the eggs, so you have two commonplace breakfast foods put together in a new, very appealing way. It's really easy to do. Be sure to let the person at the deli counter know you need slices of ham without holes, so the eggs don't leak out and stick. ■

- 2 tablespoons unsalted butter
- 3/4 pound mushrooms, trimmed and finely chopped
- 1/4 cup finely chopped shallots
- 1/2 teaspoon salt
- 1/4 teaspoon freshly ground black pepper
- 2 tablespoons crème fraîche or sour cream
- 1 tablespoon finely chopped fresh tarragon
- 12 thin slices (10 ounces) Black Forest or Virginia ham without any holes
- 12 large eggs

OPTIONAL GARNISH: fresh tarragon leaves

SPECIAL EQUIPMENT: a muffin pan with twelve (1/3- or 1/2-cup) cups

Put a rack in middle of oven and preheat oven to 400°F.

PREPARE THE MUSHROOMS: Melt butter in a large heavy skillet over moderately high heat. Add mushrooms, shallots, salt, and pepper and cook, stirring, until mushrooms are tender and liquid they give off has evaporated, about 10 minutes. Remove from heat and stir in crème fraîche and tarragon.

ASSEMBLE AND BAKE THE EGGS: Lightly oil muffin cups. Fit 1 slice of ham into each one (ends will hang over edges of cups). Divide mushrooms among cups and crack 1 egg into each. Bake until whites are set but yolks are still runny, about 15 minutes. Season eggs with salt and pepper and carefully remove crisps from muffin cups, using two spoons or small spatulas. Sprinkle with tarragon leaves, if desired.

COOK'S NOTE

■ The eggs in this recipe are not fully cooked. If this is a concern, see page 629.

Baked Eggs with Cream, Parmesan, and White Truffle

SERVES 4

ACTIVE TIME: 15 MINUTES ■ START TO FINISH: 30 MINUTES

■ After an early morning tour of the truffle market in Alba, Italy, we stopped at the little trattoria Osteria dell'Arco for what turned out to be decadence on a plate. Cream, eggs, truffles, a bit of cheese: it all goes to show that truffles are best when done very simply. Because white truffles don't travel well and can be very expensive, we used white truffle paste to turn baked eggs into something sublime. (For more about truffle paste, see Glossary.) ■

- 1/2 cup crème fraîche
- 2 tablespoons finely grated Parmigiano-Reggiano
- 1–2 teaspoons white truffle paste (to taste)
- 1/8 teaspoon salt, or to taste
- 1/8 teaspoon freshly ground black pepper, or to taste
- 4 large eggs

ACCOMPANIMENT: toasted Italian bread

SPECIAL EQUIPMENT: four 3-ounce ramekins

Put a rack in middle of oven and preheat oven to 400°F. Butter ramekins.

Stir together crème fraîche, cheese, truffle paste, salt, and pepper in a bowl, then divide among buttered ramekins. Break 1 egg into each ramekin. Put ramekins in a baking pan and fill pan with enough hot water to reach halfway up sides of ramekins.

Bake eggs until whites are barely set and yolks are still runny, 12 to 14 minutes. (Use a spoon to poke yolk and white gently; be aware that crème fraîche will rise to the top and make white appear less cooked than it is.) Serve with toasted bread.

COOK'S NOTE

■ The eggs in this recipe are not fully cooked. If this is a concern, see page 629.

Soft-Boiling Eggs

Soft-boiled eggs are one of the most underrated foods on the planet. Nothing is easier — or more satisfying.

Simply put eggs in a small saucepan, cover them with cold water, and bring to a boil. Turn the heat down (vigorously boiling water will cause the shells to crack) and simmer for 3 or 4 minutes, depending on how well cooked you like your yolks. Remember that the eggs will continue to cook a bit until you remove their tops, so consider that in your timing.

Salmon-Wrapped Poached Eggs

SERVES 8

ACTIVE TIME: 1 HOUR ■ START TO FINISH: 1 HOUR

■ This is our upscale, lightened take on eggs Benedict. We substitute buttery smoked salmon for Canadian bacon and a simple lemony sour cream sauce for the hollandaise. You might think the addition of avocado is over the top, but it complements the salmon, and a little tarragon perks the whole thing up. Poached eggs for a crowd are perfectly feasible if you cook them in a roasting pan straddling two burners and take the cooked eggs out of the simmering water in the order in which you put them in. If you don't have a friend to help you wrap the eggs in smoked salmon before they get cold, simply drape the salmon over the eggs. This is a perfect dish for a garden brunch. ■

FOR SAUCE

- ½ cup sour cream
- 2 teaspoons fresh lemon juice
- ¼ cup olive oil
- 1 tablespoon finely chopped fresh chives
- 1½ teaspoons chopped fresh tarragon
- ½ teaspoon kosher salt
- Freshly ground black pepper

FOR BRIOCHES AND EGGS

- 1 small red onion, thinly sliced
- 2 firm but ripe California avocados
- 1–2 tablespoons fresh lemon juice
- 6 individual brioches, topknots sliced off and discarded, each brioche cut horizontally into 3 (½-inch-thick) rounds and lightly toasted (see Cook's Note)
- Salt and freshly ground black pepper
- ¼ pound sorrel or arugula, coarse stems discarded
- 4 teaspoons distilled white vinegar
- 16 large eggs
- 1 pound thinly sliced smoked salmon

OPTIONAL GARNISH: chopped fresh chives

SPECIAL EQUIPMENT: a 17-by-11-inch flameproof baking pan

MAKE THE SAUCE: Whisk together sour cream and lemon juice in a small bowl. Add oil in a slow stream, whisking until well blended. (If necessary, add water 1½ teaspoons at a time to reach a thick yet spoonable consistency.) Stir in chives, tarragon, salt, and pepper to taste. Set aside.

PREPARE THE BRIOCHES: Soak onion in cold water to cover for 10 minutes. Drain and pat dry.

Halve, pit, and peel avocados. Cut crosswise into ¼-inch-thick slices and sprinkle slices with lemon juice. Put 2 brioche toasts on each of eight plates (you will have 2 extra toasts) and sprinkle with salt and pepper. Arrange a few sorrel leaves on each toast, then top with avocado and onion.

POACH THE EGGS: Butter baking pan, fill with 1¼ inches water, and stir in vinegar. Set pan over two burners and bring water to a simmer.

Break 1 egg into a cup and slide into water. Repeat with remaining eggs, adding them in rows so you can easily take them out in same order. Poach eggs at a bare simmer until whites are firm but yolks are still runny, 3 to 4 minutes. As they are cooked, transfer eggs with a slotted spoon to paper towels to drain. Season with salt and pepper.

Wrap each egg in a slice of salmon. Put a wrapped egg on top of each toast and drizzle sauce over salmon. Sprinkle with chives, if desired.

COOK'S NOTES

- If you can't get individual brioches, use a brioche or challah loaf. Cut it into eight ½-inch-thick slices and halve them diagonally.
- The eggs in this recipe are not fully cooked. If this is a concern, see page 629.

Poaching Eggs

The prospect of poaching an egg makes many people nervous — once the egg hits the water, their thinking goes, it's out of control. But a poaching egg is pretty good at taking care of itself, especially if you use the best and freshest eggs you can find, free-range and/or organic if possible. They cost more, but they're one of life's least expensive luxuries. The fresher the egg, the stronger the yolk membrane, which keeps the yolk together, and the thicker the white, the better it clings to the yolk. Add a little vinegar to the cooking water (acid makes the whites set faster). Then simply crack each egg into a cup or small dish and slip it into the barely simmering water.

Poached Eggs on Artichoke Bottoms with Mushrooms and White Truffle Cream

SERVES 4

ACTIVE TIME: 1 HOUR ■ START TO FINISH: 1 HOUR

■ Using artichoke bottoms as vessels for poached eggs and napping them with mushroom cream makes for an elegant, impressive presentation. We flavored the sauce with white truffle oil, a condiment that's often poorly used, but trust us: here it really works. ■

FOR ARTICHOKES

- 1 lemon, halved
- 4 large artichokes (10–12 ounces each)
- 1 tablespoon all-purpose flour
- 1 tablespoon olive oil
- 1 tablespoon salt
- 1 tablespoon fresh lemon juice

FOR SAUCE

- 3 small porcini or cremini mushrooms (3 ounces total)
- 1¼ cups heavy cream
- 1 tablespoon finely grated Parmigiano-Reggiano
- ½ teaspoon kosher salt
- ½ teaspoon white truffle oil (see Glossary)
- ¼ teaspoon freshly ground black pepper

FOR EGGS

- 1 teaspoon distilled white vinegar
- 4 large eggs
- Kosher salt and freshly ground black pepper

OPTIONAL GARNISH: finely chopped fresh flat-leaf parsley

PREPARE THE ARTICHOKES: Squeeze juice from 1 lemon half into a medium bowl of cold water, then drop lemon half into water. Cut off stem of 1 artichoke and trim ¼ inch from bottom end of stem to expose inner core. Trim sides of stem down to pale inner core, then rub with remaining lemon half. Drop stem into acidulated water. To trim artichokes, cut off top inch of artichoke with a serrated knife (see illustrations on page 518). Bend back outer leaves until they snap off close to base; remove and discard several more layers of leaves in same manner until you reach pale yellow leaves with pale green tips. With a sharp knife, cut off yellow leaves ½ inch above top of artichoke bottom. Trim dark green fibrous parts from base and sides of artichoke with a sharp paring knife. Rub artichoke bottom all over with lemon half and drop artichoke into acidulated water. Trim remaining artichokes and stems in same manner.

Put 2 quarts water in a 4-quart saucepan and whisk in flour (flour will help keep artichokes from discoloring). Whisk in oil, salt, and 1 tablespoon lemon juice and bring to a simmer. Add artichoke bottoms and stems and simmer, partially covered, until just tender, 15 to 20 minutes.

Remove artichokes with a slotted spoon; reserve cooking water. When artichokes are just cool enough to handle, cut a 1/4-inch slice from each bottom (reserve trimmings) so they will stand upright. Pull out all pointed inner leaves from each one and remove fuzzy choke (see page 518). Return artichokes to cooking water to keep warm. Cut reserved trimmings and stems into thin slices and reserve for sauce.

MAKE THE SAUCE: Trim mushrooms and thinly slice. Combine cream, mushrooms, cheese, and kosher salt in a small heavy saucepan, bring to a simmer, and simmer until sauce is slightly thickened and reduced to about 1 cup, about 10 minutes. Stir in truffle oil, kosher salt to taste, pepper, and sliced artichoke pieces. Keep sauce warm, covered.

POACH THE EGGS AND ASSEMBLE THE DISH: Butter bottom of a 2-quart heavy saucepan. Add 1 1/4 inches water and vinegar and bring to a simmer. Break 1 egg into a cup and slide into water. Repeat with remaining eggs, spacing them evenly, and poach at a bare simmer until whites are firm but yolks are still runny, 2 to 3 minutes.

As they are cooked, transfer eggs with a slotted spoon to paper towels to drain. Season with kosher salt and pepper.

Drain artichoke bottoms and put an egg in each one. Transfer to plates and spoon sauce over and around eggs. Sprinkle with parsley, if desired.

COOK'S NOTES

- The eggs in this recipe are not fully cooked. If this is a concern, see page 629.
- The artichoke bottoms and stems can be cooked up to 1 day ahead. Pour off half of the cooking water and replace it with cold water (to stop the artichokes from cooking further), then refrigerate artichokes in the water, uncovered. Reheat in the water before proceeding.

Huevos Rancheros

SERVES 4

ACTIVE TIME: 30 MINUTES ■ START TO FINISH: 30 MINUTES

■ Mexicans have a wealth of breakfast foods, and ranch-style eggs on tortillas is one dish that deserves to be in everyone's culinary repertoire. Huevos rancheros ("*way*-vohs ran-*cheh*-ros") are a simple way to get Mexican flavors—corn tortillas, fried eggs, an uncomplicated roasted tomato sauce, cilantro, a little crumbled fresh white cheese—on a plate. Don't be tempted to buy low-fat tortillas, which tend to toughen when cooked. We fry the tortillas in pairs to keep them moist. You want them with a nice toasty chew, not crisp. ■

- 1 pound plum tomatoes
- 1/4 large white onion, halved lengthwise
- 2 jalapeño chiles
- 2 garlic cloves
- 1 teaspoon salt
- 6 tablespoons vegetable oil
- 8 (5-inch) corn tortillas
- 8 large eggs
- Freshly ground black pepper
- 1/2 cup crumbled *queso fresco* (Mexican fresh white cheese), ricotta salata (see Glossary), or mild feta
- 2 tablespoons chopped fresh cilantro

MAKE THE SALSA: Heat a dry 10-inch well-seasoned cast-iron skillet over moderate heat until a bead of water dropped on its surface evaporates quickly. Add tomatoes, onion, and chiles and roast, turning occasionally with tongs, until charred on all sides, 10 to 15 minutes. Let cool slightly.

Core roasted tomatoes and transfer to a blender. Stem chiles and discard seeds from 1 chile, then transfer to blender. Add onion, garlic, and salt and purée until smooth.

FRY THE TORTILLAS: Put a rack in middle of oven and preheat oven to 200°F. Stack four ovenproof plates on oven rack to warm.

Heat 1 tablespoon oil in cleaned skillet over moderate heat until hot but not smoking. Stack 2 tortillas in skillet and cook for 25 to 30 seconds, then flip stack with tongs. Let second tortilla cook on bottom for 25 to 30 seconds while you turn top tortilla over with tongs. Flip stack again and repeat cooking and flipping process until both sides of both tortillas are cooked, 25 to 30 seconds per side. (Tortillas will soften and puff slightly, then deflate.) Wrap tortillas loosely in foil and keep warm in oven. Fry remaining tortillas in same manner, adding 1 tablespoon oil to skillet for each batch, and keep warm.

COOK THE EGGS: Heat remaining 2 tablespoons oil in cleaned skillet over moderate heat until hot but not smoking. Break 4 eggs into skillet and cook to desired doneness, 3 to 4 minutes for runny yolks. Keep warm, covered, while you cook the second batch. Season with salt and pepper.

To serve, spoon 3 tablespoons salsa onto each warmed plate and top with 2 tortillas, slightly overlapping them. With a spatula, transfer an egg to each tortilla, and top with some of remaining salsa. Sprinkle eggs with cheese and cilantro.

COOK'S NOTE

- The eggs in this recipe may not be fully cooked. If this is a concern, see page 629.

Fried Eggs and Asparagus with Parmesan

SERVES 2

ACTIVE TIME: 20 MINUTES ■ START TO FINISH: 25 MINUTES

■ Four very simple, very compatible ingredients: asparagus, eggs, butter, Parmigiano-Reggiano. Try this for brunch or a quick weeknight supper. ■

- 1½ pounds medium asparagus, trimmed and, if desired, peeled
- 2½ tablespoons unsalted butter
- Salt and freshly ground black pepper
- ⅔ cup finely grated Parmigiano-Reggiano
- 4 large eggs

SPECIAL EQUIPMENT: two 9½-inch oval gratin dishes (about 1½ inches deep)

Put a rack in upper third of oven and preheat oven to 425°F.

Cook asparagus in a large deep skillet of boiling well-salted water until crisp-tender, about 4 minutes. Transfer to paper towels to drain.

Generously butter gratin dishes using ½ tablespoon butter, then divide asparagus between them. Season with salt and pepper and sprinkle with half of cheese.

Heat remaining 2 tablespoons butter in a 10-inch nonstick skillet over moderately high heat until foam subsides. Fry eggs, seasoning with salt and pepper, until whites are barely set, about 2 minutes.

With a slotted spatula, carefully transfer 2 eggs to each gratin dish, placing them on top of asparagus. Sprinkle eggs with remaining cheese and drizzle with any butter remaining in skillet.

Bake until cheese is melted and eggs are cooked as desired, 4 to 5 minutes for runny yolks.

COOK'S NOTE

- The eggs in this recipe may not be fully cooked. If this is a concern, see page 629.

Fried Eggs over Warm Lentil Salad

SERVES 4

ACTIVE TIME: 40 MINUTES ■ START TO FINISH: 1 HOUR

■ We first had this combination of lentils, fried eggs, and lardons (crisp matchsticks of bacon) at the Ladurée tea salon in Paris. If you are not in love with lentils, you will be after you make this. Lentils are the quickest cooking of all the pulses because they don't require soaking. Easy to re-create at home, this dish makes a hearty breakfast, brunch, or supper. ■

- 2 leeks (white and pale green parts only), finely chopped
- ¾ cup lentils, preferably *lentilles du Puy* (French green lentils; see Glossary)
- 6 ounces thick-cut bacon (5 slices), cut crosswise into ¼-inch-thick strips
- 2 celery ribs, finely chopped
- 1 large carrot, finely chopped
- 2 tablespoons red wine vinegar, or to taste
- 1 tablespoon finely chopped fresh tarragon
- Salt and freshly ground black pepper
- 1 tablespoon olive oil
- 8 large eggs
- 1 cup baby spinach

Wash leeks in a bowl of cold water; lift out and drain well in a sieve.

Put lentils in a 2-quart saucepan, add cold water to cover by 2 inches, and bring to a simmer. Simmer, uncovered, until just tender, about 20 minutes.

Meanwhile, cook bacon in a 12-inch nonstick skillet over moderate heat, stirring, until crisp. With a slotted spoon, transfer to paper towels to drain. Add leeks, celery, and carrot to fat remaining in skillet and cook, stirring, until just tender, about 5 minutes. Add vinegar and boil until most of it has evaporated. Remove skillet from heat and stir in tarragon, half of bacon, and salt and pepper to taste. Transfer to a large bowl and cover to keep warm. Set skillet aside.

Drain lentils well and stir into vegetable mixture. Season with salt and pepper and keep warm, covered.

Wipe out skillet with paper towels. Add oil and heat over moderate heat until hot but not smoking. Break 4 eggs into skillet and fry until whites are just set but yolks are still runny, 3 to 4 minutes. Transfer to a platter, season with salt and pepper, and keep warm, covered, while you fry remaining 4 eggs.

Divide lentil salad among four plates. Top with spinach and eggs and scatter remaining bacon over.

COOK'S NOTE

- The eggs in this recipe are not fully cooked. If this is a concern, see page 629.

Breakfast Pizzas

SERVES 6

ACTIVE TIME: 40 MINUTES ■ START TO FINISH: 1 HOUR

■ These individual pizzas are a novel and easy way to serve up the traditional breakfast combination of ham, eggs, and biscuits. They're fun, and weekend guests love them. ■

- 1½ tablespoons unsalted butter
- 3 assorted (red, green, and/or yellow) bell peppers, cored, seeded, and cut into thin strips
- 1 onion, halved lengthwise and thinly sliced crosswise (1 cup)
- 1 cup finely diced (¼-inch) cooked ham (½ pound)
- 2 cups all-purpose flour
- 2 teaspoons baking powder
- 1 teaspoon salt
- 1 stick (8 tablespoons) cold unsalted butter, cut into bits
- ½ cup plus 2 tablespoons whole milk
- 2 cups coarsely grated Muenster or Monterey Jack (about 6 ounces)
- 6 large eggs
- Freshly ground black pepper

Melt butter in a large heavy skillet over moderate heat. Add bell peppers and onion and cook, stirring, until softened, about 6 minutes. Stir in ham and remove from heat.

Put racks in upper and lower thirds of oven and preheat oven to 425°F. Butter two large baking sheets.

Whisk together flour, baking powder, and salt in a medium bowl. Blend in butter with your fingertips or a pastry blender until mixture resembles coarse meal. Add milk and stir until mixture just forms a dough.

Gather dough into a ball and knead gently 6 times on a lightly floured surface. Cut into 6 equal pieces. Roll out each piece into a 7-inch round and form a ½-inch-high rim on each one by turning in edges of dough and pinching them until round measures 6 inches. Arrange 3 rounds on each buttered baking sheet.

Divide cheese among rounds and top with bell pepper mixture, making a well in center. Carefully crack an egg into each well.

Bake pizzas, switching position of sheets halfway through baking, until yolks are just set, 12 to 15 minutes. Season pizzas with salt and pepper.

COOK'S NOTES

- The bell pepper mixture can be made up to 1 day ahead and refrigerated, covered. Bring to room temperature before using.
- The eggs in this recipe are not fully cooked. If this is a concern, see page 629.

Eggs and Spinach on Buckwheat Crêpes

SERVES 4
ACTIVE TIME: 40 MINUTES ■ START TO FINISH: 1¼ HOURS
(INCLUDES MAKING BATTER)

■ In France, buckwheat flour is often used for savory crêpes. It's a little more substantial than white flour. We've used a classic technique: after cooking each crêpe on one side and flipping it over, we add the spinach and fold in the edges of the crêpe to form a square, leaving the spinach exposed in the center as a nest for a fried egg. The buckwheat crêpe becomes a dark brown frame for the green of the spinach and the yellow and white of the egg, making this a very pretty dish. ■

- 3 pounds spinach, coarse stems discarded
- 1 tablespoon unsalted butter
- Salt and freshly ground black pepper to taste
- Freshly grated nutmeg to taste
- Vegetable oil for brushing skillet
- Buckwheat Crêpe Batter (recipe follows), half reserved for another use
- 4 large eggs
- ¼ cup crème fraîche or sour cream

GARNISH: 1 tablespoon chopped fresh chives

Preheat oven to 200°F.

Wash spinach and drain in a colander. Steam spinach, with water clinging to leaves, in a large heavy pot, covered, over moderate heat, stirring occasionally, until wilted, about 3 minutes. Drain spinach in colander (set pot aside), pressing out as much liquid as possible with back of a large spoon.

Add butter to pot and melt over moderate heat, then add spinach, season with salt, pepper, and nutmeg, and cook, stirring, for 30 seconds. Set aside.

Brush a 12-inch nonstick skillet with oil and heat over moderately high heat until hot but not smoking, then remove from heat. Working quickly, stir batter and pour ¼ cup batter into skillet, tilting and rotating pan to cover bottom. (If batter sets before skillet is coated, reduce heat slightly for next crêpe.) Return skillet to heat and cook crêpe until underside is golden and top appears almost dry, about 1 minute. Loosen crêpe with a heatproof rubber spatula and flip over with your fingers. Put one quarter of spinach in center, then fold in edges of crêpe to form a square, leaving spinach in center exposed. Cook crêpe until bottom is golden, about 30 seconds. Slide crêpe onto a large baking sheet and keep warm in oven while you make 3 more crêpes in same manner.

Brush skillet lightly with oil and heat over moderate heat until hot but not smoking. Break eggs one at a time into skillet and cook until whites are set, about 2 minutes. Transfer crêpes to plates, top each with an egg and 1 tablespoon crème fraîche, and sprinkle with chives.

COOK'S NOTE

■ The eggs in this recipe are not fully cooked. If this is a concern, see page 629.

Buckwheat Crêpe Batter

MAKES ENOUGH BATTER FOR EIGHT 10-INCH CRÊPES
ACTIVE TIME: 10 MINUTES ■ START TO FINISH: 40 MINUTES

■ This recipe makes twice the amount of batter needed for the egg and spinach crêpes, but it cannot be halved successfully, so save the remaining portion for breakfast another day. With their nutty, tangy, sweet flavor, buckwheat crêpes are also delicious with a ham and cheese filling. ■

- 2 tablespoons unsalted butter
- ¾ cup plus 1 tablespoon buckwheat flour
- ⅓ cup all-purpose flour
- ½ teaspoon salt
- 1½ cups whole milk
- 3 large eggs

Cook butter in a small saucepan over moderately low heat until golden brown (bottom of pan will be covered with brown specks). Remove pan from heat and let cool slightly.

Sift together flours and salt into a large bowl. Whisk together milk, eggs, and brown butter in a medium bowl. Add to flour mixture and whisk until smooth. Refrigerate batter, covered, for 30 minutes before using.

COOK'S NOTE

- The batter keeps, covered in the refrigerator, for up to 2 days.

Blueberry Muffins

MAKES 12 MUFFINS
ACTIVE TIME: 35 MINUTES ■ START TO FINISH: 1¼ HOURS (INCLUDES COOLING)

■ Very tender and packed with berries, these are a summer Sunday morning tradition. ■

FOR BATTER

- ¾ stick (6 tablespoons) unsalted butter
- ⅓ cup whole milk
- 1 large egg
- 1 large egg yolk
- ¾ teaspoon vanilla extract
- 1½ cups all-purpose flour
- ¾ cup sugar
- 1½ teaspoons baking powder
- ¾ teaspoon salt
- 2 cups (12 ounces) blueberries

FOR TOPPING

- 3 tablespoons cold unsalted butter, cut into ½-inch cubes
- ½ cup all-purpose flour
- 3½ tablespoons sugar

SPECIAL EQUIPMENT: a muffin pan with twelve (⅓- to ½-cup) cups

MAKE THE BATTER: Put a rack in upper third of oven and preheat to 375°F. Generously butter muffin cups.

Melt butter in a small saucepan over moderately low heat; remove from heat. Whisk in milk, egg, yolk, and vanilla until well combined.

Whisk together flour, sugar, baking powder, and salt in a medium bowl. Add milk mixture and stir until just combined. Gently but thoroughly fold in blueberries.

Divide batter among muffin cups and spread evenly.

MAKE THE TOPPING AND BAKE THE MUFFINS: Combine all topping ingredients in a bowl and rub together with your fingertips until crumbly. Sprinkle evenly over batter in cups.

Bake until golden and crisp and a wooden pick or skewer inserted into center of a muffin comes out clean, 18 to 20 minutes. Cool in pan on a rack for 15 minutes, then run a knife around edges of muffin tops and carefully remove from cups. Serve warm or at room temperature.

Marion Cunningham's Raw-Apple Muffins

MAKES 20 MUFFINS
ACTIVE TIME: 35 MINUTES ■ START TO FINISH: 1½ HOURS (INCLUDES COOLING)

■ "Breakfast quick breads, puffy and delicious, gladden the heart," wrote Marion Cunningham in her *Breakfast Book*. Try her raw-apple muffins one morning and see. And even though there is nothing like a freshly baked muffin, these keep well, thanks to the moisture from the apples. ■

- 4 cups diced (¼-inch) peeled Granny Smith apples (1½ pounds)
- 1 cup sugar
- 2 large eggs
- ½ cup vegetable oil, preferably corn oil
- 2 teaspoons vanilla extract
- 2 cups all-purpose flour
- 2 teaspoons baking soda
- 2 teaspoons ground cinnamon
- 1 teaspoon salt
- 1 cup raisins
- 1 cup coarsely chopped walnuts (4 ounces)

SPECIAL EQUIPMENT: 2 muffin pans with twelve (⅓- to ½-cup) cups each

Put racks in upper and lower thirds of oven and preheat oven to 325°F. Generously butter 20 muffin cups.

Toss together apples and sugar in a large bowl. Whisk together eggs, oil, and vanilla in a small bowl.

With a fork, stir together flour, baking soda, cinnamon, and salt in another bowl. Stir egg mixture into apples, then add flour mixture and stir until just combined (batter will be stiff). Stir in raisins and walnuts.

Divide batter among muffin cups, filling each one two-thirds full. Bake, switching position of pans halfway through baking, until a wooden pick or skewer inserted into center of a muffin comes out clean, 25 to 30 minutes. Run a knife around edges of muffins and turn out onto a rack to cool.

Sour Cream–Bran Muffins

MAKES 12 MUFFINS
ACTIVE TIME: 30 MINUTES ■ START TO FINISH: 1¼ HOURS (INCLUDES COOLING)

■ These are the Rolls-Royces of bran muffins. Rich and raisiny, they taste nutty rather than good for you. Unlike most muffins, which are best when fresh, these get better with keeping. Be sure to buy unprocessed wheat bran (sometimes called miller's bran), not bran cereal, which has been processed and baked. Wheat bran is available at natural foods stores and many supermarkets. ■

- 1 stick (8 tablespoons) unsalted butter, softened
- ¼ cup packed light brown sugar
- 1 large egg, lightly beaten
- 1 cup sour cream
- ¼ cup robust molasses (not blackstrap)
- ½ cup raisins
- 1 cup all-purpose flour
- 1 teaspoon baking soda
- ¼ teaspoon salt
- 1 cup wheat bran (not cereal)

SPECIAL EQUIPMENT: a muffin pan with twelve (⅓- to ½-cup) cups

Put a rack in middle of oven and preheat oven to 400°F. Generously butter muffin cups.

Beat together butter and brown sugar in a large bowl with an electric mixer at high speed until pale and fluffy, 3 to 5 minutes. Beat in egg, sour cream, and molasses. Stir in raisins.

Whisk together flour, baking soda, salt, and bran in another bowl. Add to sour cream mixture and stir until just combined (batter will be lumpy). Spoon batter into muffin cups, filling them two-thirds full. Bake until golden brown and springy to the touch, 15 to 20 minutes. Turn muffins out onto a rack to cool.

COOK'S NOTE

■ These muffins improve in flavor if made 2 days ahead. Store in an airtight container at room temperature.

Morning Glory Muffins

MAKES ABOUT 30 MUFFINS
ACTIVE TIME: 35 MINUTES ■ START TO FINISH: 1¼ HOURS (INCLUDES COOLING)

■ The rise-and-shine brigade will love these little carrot cakes enriched with apples, coconut, and pecans. The recipe is from the Morning Glory Café, on Nantucket. The recipe can be easily halved if desired, although the muffins keep beautifully. ■

- 4 cups all-purpose flour
- 2½ cups sugar
- 4 teaspoons baking soda
- 4 teaspoons ground cinnamon
- 2 teaspoons salt
- 12 carrots, peeled, if desired, coarsely grated in food processor (4 cups)
- 1 cup raisins
- 1 cup chopped pecans (4 ounces)
- 1 cup sweetened flaked coconut
- 2 Granny Smith apples, peeled, cored, and coarsely grated with box grater
- 6 large eggs
- 2 cups vegetable oil
- 2 teaspoons vanilla extract

SPECIAL EQUIPMENT: 3 muffin pans, preferably nonstick, with twelve (⅓- to ½-cup) cups each

Put a rack in middle of oven and preheat oven to 350°F. Generously butter 30 muffin cups.

Whisk together flour, sugar, baking soda, cinnamon, and salt in a large bowl. Stir in carrots, raisins, pecans, coconut, and apples. Whisk together eggs, oil, and vanilla in another bowl, then add to flour mixture and stir until just combined.

Spoon batter into muffin cups, filling them to the top. Bake muffins, in batches if necessary, until springy to the touch, about 30 minutes per batch. Cool in pans for 5 minutes, then turn out onto a rack and cool to warm or room temperature.

COOK'S NOTE

- These muffins keep, stored in an airtight container at room temperature, for up to 2 days.

Cranberry Coffee Cake

SERVES 6 TO 8
ACTIVE TIME: 15 MINUTES ■ START TO FINISH: 1¾ HOURS (INCLUDES COOLING)

■ Although this coffee cake takes practically no time to prepare, it is anything but plain. Fresh or frozen cranberries are finely chopped in a food processor, then layered with the batter to form undulating ripples of fruit that offer a little hit of cranberry flavor in every bite. ■

- 2 cups (8 ounces) fresh or thawed frozen cranberries
- 1¾ cups granulated sugar
- 2 cups all-purpose flour
- 2 teaspoons baking powder
- ¾ teaspoon salt
- 1 stick (8 tablespoons) unsalted butter, softened
- 2 large eggs
- 1 teaspoon vanilla extract
- ½ cup whole milk

OPTIONAL GARNISH: confectioners' sugar

Put a rack in middle of oven and preheat oven to 350°F. Generously butter a 9-by-5-inch loaf pan.

Pulse cranberries with ½ cup sugar in a food processor until finely chopped; do not purée. Transfer to a sieve and let drain while you make batter.

Sift together flour, baking powder, and salt into a bowl. Combine butter and remaining 1¼ cups sugar in a large bowl and beat with an electric mixer at medium-high speed until pale and fluffy, about 3 minutes. Add eggs one at a time, beating well after each addition, then beat in vanilla. Reduce speed to low and add flour mixture and milk alternately in 3 batches, beginning and ending with flour mixture and mixing until just incorporated.

Spread one third of batter evenly in loaf pan. Spoon half of drained cranberries evenly over batter, leaving a ½-inch border on all sides. Top with another third of batter and remaining cranberries, then cover with remaining batter.

Bake until golden brown and a wooden pick or skewer inserted in center comes out clean, 50 minutes to 1 hour. Cool cake in pan on a rack for 30 minutes.

Invert cake onto rack. Serve warm or at room temperature, dusted with confectioners' sugar, if desired.

COOK'S NOTE

- The coffee cake can be made up to 1 day ahead and kept, covered, at room temperature. Reheat, covered, in a 350°F oven.

Blueberry Almond Coffee Cake

SERVES 8
ACTIVE TIME: 25 MINUTES ■ START TO FINISH: 1½ HOURS

■ If you are thinking of making muffins but want to avoid the bother of muffin tins, try this coffee cake. Pour the batter directly into a gratin or shallow baking dish and top it with the crunchy combination of fork-beaten egg white and sliced almonds. The result is a highly textured confection that contrasts crisp topping with tender cake. ■

- 2 cups all-purpose flour
- 2 teaspoons baking powder
- ¾ teaspoon salt
- 1 stick (8 tablespoons) unsalted butter, softened
- 1¼ cups plus 3 tablespoons sugar
- 2 large eggs
- 1 teaspoon vanilla extract or ¼ teaspoon almond extract
- ½ cup whole milk
- 2½ cups (15 ounces) blueberries
- ½ large egg white (see Cook's Note)
- 1 cup sliced almonds

Put a rack in middle of oven and preheat oven to 350°F. Butter a shallow (2¼-inch deep) 2- to 2½-quart baking dish.

Sift together flour, baking powder, and salt into a bowl. Combine butter and 1¼ cups sugar in a large bowl and beat with an electric mixer at medium-high speed until pale and fluffy, about 3 minutes. Beat in whole eggs one at a time, beating well after each addition, then beat in vanilla. Reduce speed to low and add flour mixture and milk alternately in batches, beginning and ending with flour mixture and mixing until just incorporated. Fold in berries. Spoon batter into baking dish and spread evenly.

In a small bowl, combine egg white, remaining 3 tablespoons sugar, and almonds, stirring to coat almonds. Spoon almond topping over batter.

Bake until golden brown and a wooden pick or skewer inserted in center comes out clean, 50 minutes to 1 hour. Cool in pan on a rack for 10 minutes. Invert cake onto rack, then invert again. Serve warm or at room temperature.

COOK'S NOTES

- To measure the half egg white, lightly beat an egg white with a fork in a measuring cup, then pour out half of it.
- The coffee cake can be made up to 1 day ahead and kept, covered, at room temperature. Reheat, covered, in a 350°F oven.

Coffee Coffee Cake with Espresso Glaze

SERVES 6 TO 8
ACTIVE TIME: 30 MINUTES ■ START TO FINISH: 2 HOURS (INCLUDES COOLING)

■ This coffee cake packs a wallop of joe. The recipe comes from a piece that Richard Sax, the late cookbook author and food columnist, wrote for *Gourmet* in the 1980s. Enjoy it anytime, with a glass of milk or, of course, a cup of coffee. ■

FOR CAKE

- 2 cups all-purpose flour
- 1 teaspoon baking powder
- ½ teaspoon baking soda
- ¼ teaspoon salt
- 1½ sticks (12 tablespoons) unsalted butter, softened
- 1 cup granulated sugar
- 2 large eggs
- 2 teaspoons vanilla extract
- 1 cup sour cream
- 2 tablespoons instant espresso powder, dissolved in 1 tablespoon hot water

FOR GLAZE

- 1½ teaspoons instant espresso powder
- 2–3 tablespoons strong brewed coffee
- ¾ cup confectioners' sugar, sifted

SPECIAL EQUIPMENT: an 8-inch (6-cup) Bundt pan

MAKE THE CAKE: Put a rack in middle of oven and preheat oven to 350°F. Generously butter Bundt pan.

Whisk together flour, baking powder, baking soda, and salt in a bowl.

Combine butter and sugar in a large bowl and beat with an electric mixer at medium speed until pale and fluffy, about 2 minutes. Add eggs one at a time, beating well after each addition, then beat in vanilla. Add flour mixture alternately with sour cream, beginning and ending with flour mixture and mixing until just incorporated.

Transfer about one third of batter to a small bowl. Add espresso mixture and stir until well combined. Spoon half of plain batter into Bundt pan and spread evenly. Top with coffee batter, spreading it evenly, and cover with remaining plain batter, spreading it evenly.

Bake until cake is golden and a wooden pick or skewer inserted in center comes out clean, 55 to 60 minutes. Cool in pan on a rack for 30 minutes, then invert onto rack to cool completely.

MAKE THE GLAZE: Stir together espresso powder and 2 tablespoons coffee in a bowl until powder is dissolved. Add confectioners' sugar and stir until well combined. If glaze is not pourable, thin with remaining coffee, as necessary.

Pour glaze over coffee cake and let cake stand until glaze is set, about 10 minutes, before serving.

COOK'S NOTES

- This recipe can be doubled and baked in a 10-inch (12-cup) Bundt pan. Increase the baking time to about 1 hour.

- The coffee cake can be made up to 1 day ahead and kept, covered, at room temperature. Reheat, covered, in a 350°F oven.

Streusel–Sour Cream Coffee Cakes

MAKES 18 INDIVIDUAL COFFEE CAKES
ACTIVE TIME: 30 MINUTES ■ START TO FINISH: 1½ HOURS (INCLUDES COOLING)

■ These individual orange-scented coffee cakes are baked with a classic streusel topping. Very soft and moist, they're perfect to serve to a group of morning stragglers, who can enjoy them after they amble downstairs for a casual breakfast or brunch. ■

- 2½ cups all-purpose flour
- 1 cup packed light brown sugar
- ¾ cup granulated sugar
- ½ teaspoon salt
- 2 sticks (½ pound) cold unsalted butter, cut into ½-inch cubes
- 1 teaspoon ground cinnamon
- 1½ cups (6 ounces) pecans, toasted (see Tips, page 938) and chopped
- 1 cup sour cream
- 1 large egg
- 1 large egg yolk
- 1 teaspoon vanilla extract
- 1 teaspoon baking soda
- 1½ teaspoons finely grated orange zest

SPECIAL EQUIPMENT: 2 muffin pans, with twelve (⅓- to ½-cup) cups each

Put a rack in middle of oven and preheat oven to 350°F. Generously butter 18 muffin cups; butter tops of pans as well.

Stir together flour, ¾ cup brown sugar, granulated sugar, and salt in a large bowl. Blend in 1½ sticks butter with your fingertips or a pastry blender until mixture resembles coarse meal, with some pea-sized lumps of butter.

Transfer ¾ cup of mixture to a medium bowl and blend in cinnamon, remaining ½ stick butter, and remaining ¼ cup brown sugar with your fingertips or pastry blender until crumbly. Stir in pecans. Refrigerate streusel topping for 15 minutes.

Whisk together sour cream, egg, yolk, vanilla, baking soda, and zest in a bowl. Stir into remaining flour mixture until just combined (batter will be stiff).

Divide batter among buttered muffin cups, filling them about two-thirds full. Sprinkle each with streusel topping and press it lightly into batter.

Bake until cakes are golden brown and a wooden pick or skewer inserted in center comes out clean, 20 to 25 minutes. Cool in pans on racks for 30 minutes.

Loosen cakes with a sharp small knife, then carefully remove from pans.

COOK'S NOTES

- The cakes can be made up to 1 day ahead and kept, covered, at room temperature. Reheat, covered, in a 350°F oven.
- The batter can also be baked in a 9- to 9½-inch (24-centimeter) springform pan. Increase the baking time to 1 to 1¼ hours.

Ruth's Pancakes

MAKES ABOUT 8 PANCAKES
ACTIVE TIME: 30 MINUTES ■ START TO FINISH: 30 MINUTES

■ If you need to pull out all the stops for an Extremely Special Breakfast, these pancakes from *Gourmet*'s editor in chief are for you. They are rich with butter, and the flavor is incomparable. ■

- 1 cup whole milk
- 2 large eggs
- 3 tablespoons plus ½ teaspoon vegetable oil
- 1 stick (8 tablespoons) unsalted butter, melted and cooled
- 1 cup all-purpose flour
- 4 teaspoons baking powder
- 4 teaspoons sugar
- 1 teaspoon salt

ACCOMPANIMENT: pure maple syrup

Whisk together milk, eggs, and 2 tablespoons vegetable oil in a medium bowl, then whisk in butter.

Stir together flour, baking powder, sugar, and salt in another medium bowl. Whisk in egg mixture until just combined.

Heat 1/2 teaspoon oil in a large nonstick skillet over moderate heat until hot but not smoking. Working in batches of 3 and adding 1/2 teaspoon more oil between batches, pour 1/3-cup measures of batter into skillet and cook until bubbles have formed on top and broken, about 2 minutes. Flip pancakes with a spatula and cook until undersides are golden, about 1 minute more. (Lower heat if pancakes brown too quickly.) Serve with maple syrup.

COOK'S NOTE

- These pancakes are best eaten in shifts, hot from the skillet, with the cook eating last, but if you really want to sit down together, you can keep the first batches warm on a baking sheet in a 200°F oven until all the pancakes are cooked.

Blueberry Syrup

MAKES ABOUT 1 CUP
ACTIVE TIME: 5 MINUTES ■ START TO FINISH: 5 MINUTES

■ Blueberries and maple trees both thrive in New England, and their flavors have an affinity for each other. Lemon juice cuts the sweetness and adds brightness to the blueberry-infused syrup. ■

- 1 cup (6 ounces) fresh or frozen blueberries
- 1/2 cup pure maple syrup
- 1 tablespoon fresh lemon juice

Cook berries in syrup in a small heavy saucepan over moderate heat, stirring occasionally, until they have burst, 3 to 6 minutes.

Pour syrup through a sieve into a heatproof pitcher, pressing on solids; discard solids. Stir in lemon juice.

COOK'S NOTE

- The syrup keeps, refrigerated in an airtight container, for up to 5 days. Reheat before serving.

Vanilla–Brown Sugar Syrup

MAKES ABOUT 1 1/2 CUPS
ACTIVE TIME: 10 MINUTES ■ START TO FINISH: 50 MINUTES

■ It's Sunday morning, you've got pancakes or waffles on the griddle, and you've run out of maple syrup. All is not lost—you can throw together this brown sugar syrup in no time flat from ingredients that are likely to be lurking in your pantry and fridge. ■

- 1 1/2 cups packed dark brown sugar
- 1 1/2 cups water
- 3 tablespoons unsalted butter
- 1/8 teaspoon salt
- 1 tablespoon fresh lemon juice
- 1/2 teaspoon vanilla extract

Combine brown sugar, water, butter, and salt in a 2-quart heavy saucepan and bring to a boil, stirring until sugar is dissolved. Boil until syrupy and reduced to about 1 1/2 cups, 12 to 15 minutes. Remove from heat and stir in lemon juice and vanilla, then let cool to warm or room temperature.

COOK'S NOTE

- The syrup keeps, refrigerated in an airtight container, for up to 2 weeks.

Whole-Grain Pancakes

SERVES 4 TO 5 (MAKES ABOUT TWENTY 3- TO 3 1/2-INCH PANCAKES)
ACTIVE TIME: 1 HOUR ■ START TO FINISH: 1 HOUR

■ We've always loved the nutty flavor and substantial texture of whole-grain pancakes. This recipe from our senior food editor, Kemp Minifie, produces light and tender cakes that will please even finicky eaters who usually insist on white flour. Pure maple syrup is de rigueur, of course, but if you find it a trifle too sweet, add a squeeze of lemon juice to round it out. We experimented with various brands of whole wheat flour and cornmeal (some stone-ground, some not), and the batters varied in thickness, but the resulting pancakes were all delicious. ■

- 1¼ cups whole wheat flour
- ⅓ cup cornmeal
- 1 tablespoon sugar
- 2 teaspoons baking powder
- 1 teaspoon salt
- 2 large eggs, separated
- ¼ cup vegetable oil, plus additional for brushing skillet
- 1½ cups whole milk, plus additional if needed

ACCOMPANIMENT: butter and pure maple syrup

Whisk together flour, cornmeal, sugar, baking powder, and salt in a large bowl. Whisk together yolks, oil, and 1½ cups milk in another bowl and add to flour mixture, whisking until smooth. Let batter stand for 5 minutes to allow flour to absorb liquid (batter will thicken).

If batter is too thick to fall easily from a spoon, stir in 1 to 2 tablespoons additional milk.

Beat egg whites in a large bowl with an electric mixer at moderately high speed until they just hold stiff peaks. With a whisk, gently but thoroughly fold into batter.

Brush a griddle or 12-inch nonstick skillet with oil and heat over moderately high heat until hot but not smoking. Reduce heat to moderate. Working in batches of 4, spoon 2 tablespoons batter per pancake (a heaping large serving spoon works well, or half fill a ¼-cup measure) into hot skillet, spreading it if necessary to form 3- to 3½-inch rounds. Cook pancakes until bubbles appear on surface, edges are set, and undersides are golden, 45 seconds to 1 minute. Flip pancakes with a metal spatula and cook until undersides are golden and pancakes are cooked through, 45 seconds to 1 minute. (Lower heat if pancakes brown too quickly before insides are cooked through.) Transfer pancakes to plates and serve with butter and syrup. Brush griddle with more oil between batches.

COOK'S NOTE

■ These pancakes are best eaten in shifts, hot from the skillet, with the cook eating last, but if you really want to sit down together, you can keep the first batches warm on a baking sheet in a 200°F oven until all the pancakes are cooked.

VARIATION

■ BLUEBERRY WHOLE-GRAIN PANCAKES: Fold 1½ cups (9 ounces) blueberries, preferably small ones, into the batter. Cook the pancakes for about 1½ minutes on each side. Flip pancakes a second time if necessary to cook through.

Gingerbread Pancakes

SERVES 4 (MAKES TEN TO TWELVE 4-INCH PANCAKES)
ACTIVE TIME: 25 MINUTES ■ START TO FINISH: 25 MINUTES

■ People associate gingerbread with Christmas, but there's no need to wait until then to indulge. These pancakes are a speedy alternative to gingerbread. Try serving them with strawberries or with maple syrup jazzed up with a little lemon juice. This recipe lends itself to creativity, so have fun: drizzle the batter into free-form gingerbread men for a special treat, or package the dry ingredients together with a copy of the recipe and give as a gift. ■

- 1 cup all-purpose flour
- 1 teaspoon baking powder
- ½ teaspoon baking soda
- ½ teaspoon salt
- 1 teaspoon ground ginger
- ½ teaspoon ground cinnamon
- ⅛ teaspoon ground cloves
- 3 tablespoons molasses (not robust or blackstrap)
- 1 large egg
- 1 cup sour cream
- 3 tablespoons whole milk
- 2 tablespoons melted butter, plus additional for brushing griddle

ACCOMPANIMENTS: sour cream and pure maple syrup

Preheat oven to 200°F.

Whisk together flour, baking powder, baking soda, salt, and spices in a medium bowl. Whisk together molasses, egg, sour cream, milk, and butter in a small bowl, then add to flour mixture and stir until just combined.

Heat a griddle or 12-inch heavy skillet over moderate heat until hot enough to make drops of water scatter over surface. Brush with butter. Working in batches of 4 to 6 (depending on size of griddle), drop ¼ cup batter per pancake onto griddle and cook until bubbles appear on surface and undersides are golden, 1 to 2 minutes. Flip pancakes with a spatula and cook until golden brown and cooked through, 1 to 2 minutes more. Transfer pancakes to a heatproof plate and keep warm in oven while you cook remaining batches.

Serve with sour cream and maple syrup.

Ricotta Hotcakes with Honeycomb Butter

SERVES 4 (MAKES ABOUT TWENTY 4-INCH PANCAKES)
ACTIVE TIME: 1 HOUR ■ START TO FINISH: 3¼ HOURS (INCLUDES CHILLING BUTTER)

■ Before we made a research trip to Sydney, Australia, everyone who had been there insisted that we go to Bill's and order the hotcakes. We fell in love with both the hotcakes and their topping. The honeycomb butter is made not from comb honey straight out of the hive but from a British-Australian candy known as honeycomb. The candy isn't commercially available in the United States, so we make our own—a simple process. The hotcakes are delicious by themselves, but the topping moves them into a whole new league. ■

FOR HONEYCOMB BUTTER

- ½ cup sugar
- 1 tablespoon light corn syrup
- 2 tablespoons water
- 1 tablespoon plus 1 teaspoon honey
- ⅛ teaspoon baking soda
- 1 stick (8 tablespoons) unsalted butter, softened
- Scant ¼ teaspoon salt

FOR HOTCAKES

- 1 cup whole-milk ricotta
- ¾ cup whole milk
- ⅓ cup cottage cheese
- 4 large eggs, separated
- 1 cup all-purpose flour
- 1¾ teaspoons baking powder
- ¼ teaspoon salt
- 2 tablespoons unsalted butter, melted

ACCOMPANIMENT: warm honey and sliced bananas

MAKE THE HONEYCOMB BUTTER: Combine sugar, corn syrup, water, and 1 teaspoon honey in a 2- to 3-quart heavy saucepan, cover, and bring to a boil over moderate heat, stirring occasionally until sugar is dissolved. Increase heat to moderately high and boil, uncovered, swirling pan occasionally, until mixture turns deep golden. Remove from heat and immediately stir in baking soda (mixture will foam up and look creamy). Pour onto a large sheet of foil. Let cool completely.

Peel foil from candy. Coarsely chop enough candy to measure ½ cup (you will have some left over). Blend butter, salt, and remaining 1 tablespoon honey in a food processor until smooth. Add chopped candy and blend until well combined. Transfer to a sheet of wax paper and shape into a 6-inch-long log. Refrigerate, tightly wrapped in wax paper, until firm, about 2 hours.

MAKE THE HOTCAKES: Preheat oven to 200°F.

Whisk together ricotta, milk, cottage cheese, and yolks in a medium bowl. Sift flour, baking powder, and salt over ricotta mixture and whisk until just combined.

Beat whites in a large bowl with an electric mixer until they just hold stiff peaks. Fold gently but thoroughly into batter.

Brush a 12-inch nonstick skillet with some melted butter and heat over moderate heat until hot but not smoking. Working in batches of 4, scoop ¼-cup measures of batter into skillet, spread to form 4-inch hotcakes, and cook until undersides are golden brown, 1 to 3 minutes. Flip with a spatula and cook until undersides are golden brown and hotcakes are cooked through, 1 to 2 minutes more. Transfer to an ovenproof platter and keep warm, covered with a kitchen towel, in oven while you make remaining batches, adding more butter to skillet as necessary.

While hotcakes are cooking, cut honeycomb butter diagonally into 20 slices.

Stack hotcakes on plates, interspersing them with slices of honeycomb butter. Serve with honey and bananas.

COOK'S NOTE

■ The honeycomb butter can be made up to 4 days ahead; wrap tightly in foil.

Puffed Apple Pancake

SERVES 4 TO 6
ACTIVE TIME: 25 MINUTES ■ START TO FINISH: 45 MINUTES

■ Here's a pancake and filling all in one. More custardy than cakelike, this is great for a ski weekend brunch or a Sunday night supper. Just add a side of sausages. ■

- 2 McIntosh or Granny Smith apples, peeled, cored, and sliced 1/4 inch thick
- 1 tablespoon fresh lemon juice
- 3 tablespoons packed light brown sugar
- 4 tablespoons granulated sugar
- 1/2 teaspoon ground cinnamon
- 1/8 teaspoon ground cloves
- 3 tablespoons unsalted butter
- 3/4 cup whole milk
- 3 large eggs
- 2/3 cup all-purpose flour
- Scant 1/4 teaspoon salt
- 1/2 teaspoon vanilla extract

OPTIONAL GARNISH: confectioners' sugar

Put a rack in middle of oven and preheat oven to 425°F.

Toss apples with lemon juice, brown sugar, 3 tablespoons granulated sugar, cinnamon, and cloves in a bowl.

Heat 1 1/2 tablespoons butter in a 10-inch ovenproof nonstick skillet over moderate heat until foam subsides. Add apples and cook, stirring occasionally, until just tender, about 4 minutes. Transfer apples and any liquid to a wide bowl and let cool.

Heat cleaned skillet in oven for 5 minutes. Combine milk, eggs, flour, remaining 1 tablespoon granulated sugar, salt, and vanilla in a blender and blend until smooth.

Remove skillet from oven. Melt remaining 1 1/2 tablespoons butter in skillet over moderately high heat, then pour batter into skillet. Spoon apple mixture evenly over top. Bake pancake until puffed and golden and a wooden pick or skewer inserted in center comes out clean, 15 to 20 minutes. Sprinkle with confectioners' sugar, if desired.

Cheese Blintzes

SERVES 4 TO 6 (MAKES 12 BLINTZES)
ACTIVE TIME: 1 HOUR ■ START TO FINISH: 1 HOUR

■ A blintz is an ultra-thin, delicate pancake that encloses a sweet or savory filling, rather like a crêpe. It's rolled into a cylinder or formed into a square packet, then sautéed until it's golden brown. Unlike a crêpe, a blintz pancake is cooked on only one side before filling. This combination of cottage cheese, farmer cheese (a dry type of cottage cheese), raisins, and a little lemon zest is great for brunch. ■

FOR BLINTZES
- 1/2 cup all-purpose flour
- 1/2 teaspoon salt
- 2 large eggs
- 2/3 cup whole milk
- 3/4 stick (6 tablespoons) unsalted butter, melted

FOR FILLING
- 1 (8-ounce) container small-curd cottage cheese (1 cup)
- 1 (8-ounce) container farmer cheese (1 cup)
- 1 large egg, lightly beaten
- 1/4 cup raisins
- 2 tablespoons sugar
- Pinch of salt
- 1/2 teaspoon vanilla extract
- 1/2 teaspoon finely grated lemon zest

OPTIONAL GARNISH: confectioners' sugar
ACCOMPANIMENT: Blueberry Syrup (page 646) or other fruit sauce
SPECIAL EQUIPMENT: a food mill fitted with a fine disk (optional)

MAKE THE BLINTZ BATTER: Combine flour, salt, eggs, milk, and 2 tablespoons melted butter in a blender or food processor and blend until smooth. Transfer to a bowl.

MAKE THE FILLING: Force cottage cheese and farmer cheese through food mill or a medium-mesh sieve into a medium bowl. Add egg, raisins, sugar, salt, vanilla, and zest and stir until well combined.

COOK THE BLINTZES: Heat a 7-inch crêpe pan or an 8-inch nonstick skillet over moderate heat until hot, then brush pan lightly with some of remaining melted butter. Half fill a 1/4-cup measure with batter, hold pan off heat, and pour in batter, immediately swirling and tilting pan to create an even thin layer. (If batter sets before pan is coated, reduce heat slightly for next blintz.) Return skillet to heat and cook blintz until underside is lightly browned, about 30 seconds. Loosen edge with a spatula and gently flip blintz (browned side up) onto a sheet of wax paper. Make more blintzes in same manner, brushing pan lightly with melted butter as needed. (You should have 12 blintzes.)

FILL THE BLINTZES: Spoon about 2 tablespoons filling across center of each blintz. Fold bottom flap up over filling, then fold over both sides and roll up blintz to form a cylinder.

Heat 1/2 tablespoon of remaining melted butter in a 12-inch skillet over moderate heat. Add half of blintzes seam sides down and cook, turning once with spatula, until golden brown, about 4 minutes total. Transfer to a platter and keep warm, covered. Heat 1/2 tablespoon more melted butter and brown remaining blintzes in same manner.

Sprinkle blintzes with confectioners' sugar, if desired, and serve with blueberry syrup.

Challah French Toast with Berry Sauce

SERVES 4

ACTIVE TIME: 20 MINUTES ■ START TO FINISH: 30 MINUTES

■ Berries make an appealing and tangy topping for French toast. We use the traditional Jewish egg bread called challah, but if you happen to have a brioche loaf, that is delicious as well. ■

FOR FRENCH TOAST

- 3 large eggs
- 1 cup whole milk
- 1 teaspoon granulated sugar
- 1/4 teaspoon salt
- 12 (1/2-inch-thick) slices challah (from a 1-pound loaf; not end slices)
- About 3 1/2 tablespoons unsalted butter

FOR BERRY SAUCE

- 3 cups mixed berries, such as blackberries, raspberries, and blueberries
- 1/3–1/2 cup granulated sugar (depending on sweetness of berries)
- 1 tablespoon fresh lemon juice

OPTIONAL GARNISH: confectioners' sugar

Put a rack in middle of oven and preheat oven to 350°F.

MAKE THE FRENCH TOAST: Whisk together eggs, milk, sugar, and salt in a bowl until blended. Pour into a large baking pan and add bread slices in one layer. Soak, turning once, until bread has absorbed all liquid but is not falling apart, 5 to 8 minutes.

MEANWHILE, MAKE THE BERRY SAUCE: Combine 1 1/2 cups berries, sugar, and lemon juice in a blender and purée. If you want to eliminate seeds, force purée through a fine-mesh sieve into a bowl. Transfer to a serving bowl and fold in remaining berries.

COOK THE FRENCH TOAST: Heat 1 1/2 tablespoons butter in a 12-inch heavy skillet or griddle over moderately high heat until foam subsides. With a slotted spatula, transfer 4 soaked bread slices to skillet and cook, turning once, until golden brown, about 2 minutes total. Transfer slices with a clean spatula to a large shallow baking pan. Cook remaining bread in 2 batches, adding more butter as needed.

Transfer French toast to oven and bake until cooked through, about 5 minutes. Dust with confectioners' sugar, if desired, and serve with berry sauce.

Baked French Toast

SERVES 6

ACTIVE TIME: 15 MINUTES ■ START TO FINISH: 2 1/4 HOURS (INCLUDES CHILLING)

■ The beauty of this recipe is that it's baked, not cooked on the stovetop, and you can put everything together the night before. In the morning, put the soaked bread in the oven, and by the time the juice is squeezed and the table is set, you'll have French toast, hot and sweet, baked to a golden crisp. ■

- 1 (13- to 14-inch-long) loaf soft supermarket Italian bread
- ½ stick (4 tablespoons) unsalted butter, softened
- 2 large eggs
- 1⅔ cups whole milk
- ¼ teaspoon salt
- 3 tablespoons sugar

ACCOMPANIMENT: pure maple syrup

Butter a 13-by-9-inch glass baking dish. Cut twelve 1-inch-thick diagonal slices from bread (reserve ends for another use). Generously butter one side of each slice and arrange slices buttered sides up in one layer in buttered dish, squeezing them slightly to fit if necessary.

Whisk together eggs, milk, and salt in a bowl until well combined, then pour evenly over bread. Refrigerate, covered, until bread has absorbed all of custard, at least 1 hour (time may vary depending on bread).

Put a rack in middle of oven and preheat oven to 425°F. Bring soaked bread to room temperature.

Sprinkle bread with sugar. Bake until bread is puffed and top is golden, 20 to 25 minutes. Serve immediately, with maple syrup.

COOK'S NOTE

■ The soaked bread can be refrigerated for up to 24 hours.

Crème Brûlée French Toast

SERVES 6

ACTIVE TIME: 15 MINUTES ■ START TO FINISH: 9 HOURS (INCLUDES CHILLING)

■ The owners of inns and bed-and-breakfasts are experts at making breakfast and brunch dishes that can be assembled in advance with a minimum of fuss. When you invert this French toast onto plates, it will have a lovely golden-brown caramel topping—and you don't even need syrup. Rich and Jackie Diehl, of the Inn at Sunrise Point, outside Camden, Maine, were happy to share the recipe, which they got from Barbara Furdyna, the owner of La Maison, a French country inn in Spring Lake, New Jersey. At La Maison, challah is often the bread of choice. We also tried the recipe with a baguette, leaving the crust on, and found it just as delicious. ■

- 1 stick (8 tablespoons) unsalted butter
- 1 cup packed brown sugar
- 2 tablespoons corn syrup
- 1 (8- to 9-inch) round country-style loaf
- 5 large eggs
- 1½ cups half-and-half
- 1 teaspoon vanilla extract
- 1 teaspoon Grand Marnier or other orange-flavored liqueur (optional)
- ¼ teaspoon salt

Melt butter with brown sugar and corn syrup in a small heavy saucepan over moderate heat, stirring until smooth. Pour into a 13-by-9-inch baking dish. Cut six 1-inch-thick slices from center portion of bread (reserve ends for another use) and trim off crusts. Arrange bread in one layer in baking dish, squeezing slices slightly to fit.

Whisk together eggs, half-and-half, vanilla, Grand Marnier (if using), and salt in a bowl until well combined and pour evenly over bread. Refrigerate, covered, for at least 8 hours.

Put a rack in middle of oven and preheat oven to 350°F. Bring soaked bread to room temperature.

Bake until toast is puffed and edges are pale golden, 35 to 40 minutes.

With a spatula, transfer French toast to plates, turning slices syrup side up.

COOK'S NOTE

■ The soaked bread can be refrigerated for up to 24 hours.

Santa Fe French Toast

SERVES 3 TO 4
ACTIVE TIME: 20 MINUTES ■ START TO FINISH: 25 MINUTES

■ It seems as if people have been making fun of the railroad for as long as we can remember, but no one jokes about the legendary French toast that used to be served on the Santa Fe line, brightening mornings all the way from Illinois to California. The train might have run late, but when indulging in a breakfast like this, who cared? ■

- 5 (3/4-inch-thick) slices firm white sandwich bread or challah, crusts discarded, slices cut diagonally in half
- 1 cup heavy cream
- 4 large eggs, lightly beaten
- 1/4 teaspoon salt
- About 4 cups vegetable oil for frying

GARNISH: confectioners' sugar
ACCOMPANIMENT: warm pure maple syrup or honey
SPECIAL EQUIPMENT: a deep-fat thermometer

Put a rack in middle of oven and preheat oven to 400°F.

Arrange bread in one layer in a large baking pan. Whisk together cream, eggs, and salt and pour over bread. Soak bread, turning once, until most of liquid is absorbed but bread is not falling apart, about 2 minutes. With a slotted spatula, carefully transfer soaked bread to a tray.

Heat 1/2 inch oil in a 12-inch heavy skillet over moderate heat until it registers 325°F on thermometer (see Cook's Note). Fry bread 3 or 4 pieces at a time, turning once, until golden brown and crisp, about 2 minutes per batch. (Return oil to 325°F between batches.) Transfer to paper towels to drain briefly, then arrange in one layer on a baking sheet.

Once all bread is fried, bake toast until puffed, about 4 minutes. Dust with confectioners' sugar and serve with syrup or honey.

COOK'S NOTE

■ To test the temperature of a shallow amount of oil, put the bulb in the oil (turn the thermometer facedown if using the flat metal type) and rest the other end of the thermometer on the edge of the skillet. Check the temperature frequently.

Buttermilk Waffles

MAKES TWELVE 4-INCH BELGIAN WAFFLES
OR TWENTY-FOUR 4-INCH STANDARD WAFFLES
ACTIVE TIME: 15 MINUTES ■ START TO FINISH: 35 MINUTES

■ "Brussels waffles," made on special waffle irons with large, deep grids and topped with strawberries and whipped cream, debuted at that city's World's Fair in 1960 and were introduced as Belgian waffles at the 1964 World's Fair in New York City. In Belgium the waffles are not relegated to the breakfast table but are considered an afternoon snack. To our mind, however, those deep crevices are ideal receptacles for butter and maple syrup. ■

- 3 cups all-purpose flour
- 1 tablespoon baking powder
- 3/4 teaspoon baking soda
- 1 teaspoon salt
- 3 1/4 cups well-shaken buttermilk
- 1 1/2 sticks (12 tablespoons) unsalted butter, melted and cooled
- 3 large eggs, lightly beaten
- Vegetable oil for brushing waffle iron, if necessary

ACCOMPANIMENT: butter and pure maple syrup
SPECIAL EQUIPMENT: a well-seasoned or nonstick Belgian or standard waffle iron

Preheat waffle iron. Put a rack in middle of oven and preheat oven to 200°F.

Whisk together flour, baking powder, baking soda, and salt in a large bowl. Add buttermilk, butter, and eggs and stir until smooth (batter will be thick).

Brush waffle iron lightly with vegetable oil, if necessary, and spoon batter into waffle iron, using 1/2 cup batter for each 4-inch-square Belgian waffle or 1/4 cup batter for each 4-inch-square standard waffle and spreading batter evenly. Cook according to manufacturer's instructions. Transfer waffle to a baking sheet and keep warm, uncovered, in oven. Make more waffles with remaining batter in same manner.

Serve with butter and maple syrup.

Pecan Waffles

SERVES 6
ACTIVE TIME: 35 MINUTES ■ START TO FINISH: 9 HOURS (INCLUDES CHILLING BATTER)

■ The beauty of these yeast waffles is that you make the batter the night before and pop it into the fridge. This gives the yeast time for a long, slow rise, which makes the waffles very light, crisp, and appealingly malty in flavor. ■

FOR WAFFLES

- 1 (1/4-ounce) package (2 1/2 teaspoons) active dry yeast
- 1/4 cup warm water (105°–115°F)
- 2 tablespoons plus 1 teaspoon sugar
- 6 large eggs
- 1 quart well-shaken buttermilk
- 1/3 cup vegetable oil
- 3 1/4 cups all-purpose flour
- 1 teaspoon baking powder
- 1 teaspoon baking soda
- 1/2 teaspoon salt
- 1 cup (4 ounces) pecans, toasted (see Tips, page 938) and finely chopped
- Vegetable oil for brushing waffle iron, if necessary

ACCOMPANIMENT: butter and pure maple syrup

SPECIAL EQUIPMENT: a well-seasoned or nonstick Belgian or standard waffle iron

MAKE THE BATTER: Stir together yeast, warm water, and 1 teaspoon sugar in a small bowl and let stand until foamy, about 5 minutes. (If mixture doesn't foam, discard and start over with new yeast.)

Whisk together eggs, buttermilk, and oil in a medium bowl. Sift together flour, baking powder, baking soda, salt, and remaining 2 tablespoons sugar into a large bowl. Add egg mixture and whisk until combined but still lumpy. Add yeast mixture and whisk until combined but still lumpy. Refrigerate, covered, for at least 8 hours.

COOK THE WAFFLES: Bring batter to room temperature, then stir in pecans. Meanwhile, preheat oven to 250°F and preheat waffle iron.

Brush waffle iron lightly with vegetable oil, if necessary, and spoon batter into iron, using 1/2 cup batter for each 4-inch-square Belgian waffle or 1/4 cup batter for each 4-inch-square standard waffle and spreading batter evenly. Cook according to manufacturer's instructions, then transfer directly onto oven rack to keep warm. (Don't stack waffles; they will stay crisp if kept in one layer.) Make more waffles with remaining batter in same manner.

Serve with butter and maple syrup.

COOK'S NOTES

- The batter can be refrigerated for up to 24 hours.
- The pecans can be toasted and chopped up to 1 day ahead. Store in an airtight container at room temperature.

Green Chile–Cheese Puff

SERVES 6
ACTIVE TIME: 20 MINUTES ■ START TO FINISH: 1 HOUR (INCLUDES ROASTING CHILES)

■ This dish, essentially a crustless quiche, is terrific for brunch. It's from the Bear Creek Lodge, in Victor, Montana, and it reflects the assimilation of Mexican ingredients into the American culinary tradition. Roasted poblano chiles cut the richness of the cheesy custard and give it an edge. ■

- 1/4 cup all-purpose flour
- 3/4 teaspoon salt, or to taste
- 1/2 teaspoon baking powder
- 6 large eggs
- 2 tablespoons unsalted butter, melted and cooled
- 1 cup cottage cheese
- 2 cups coarsely grated Monterey Jack (8 ounces)
- 3/4 pound poblano chiles (4 medium), roasted (see Tips, page 941), peeled, seeded, and cut into 1/2-inch dice

ACCOMPANIMENT: Fresh Tomato Salsa (page 896)

Put a rack in middle of oven and preheat oven to 350°F. Oil a 9-inch glass pie plate.

Sift together flour, salt, and baking powder into a small bowl. Beat eggs in a large bowl with an electric mixer at high speed until doubled in volume (about 3 minutes if using a stand mixer, about 12 minutes if using a handheld mixer). Add butter, flour mixture, and cheeses and beat well. Stir in chiles. Pour mixture into oiled pie plate.

Bake custard until top is puffed and golden brown and a wooden pick or skewer inserted in center comes out clean, 30 to 35 minutes. Serve immediately (it will fall slightly) with salsa.

COOK'S NOTE

- The chiles can be roasted, seeded, and peeled up to 1 day ahead and refrigerated, covered.

Quiche Lorraine

SERVES 6 TO 8
ACTIVE TIME: 40 MINUTES ■ START TO FINISH: 2¾ HOURS (INCLUDES MAKING PASTRY)

■ You may be surprised to learn that a true quiche Lorraine has no cheese to interfere with the flavor of what is essentially a delicate bacon-flavored custard in a flaky crust. Originating in the medieval region of western Europe called Lorraine, in what is now northeastern France, it has become a classic of French cuisine. ■

Basic Pastry Dough for a single-crust pie (page 790)
½ pound bacon (8 slices), cut crosswise into ½-inch-wide pieces
4 large eggs
2 large egg yolks
2 cups heavy cream
1 cup whole milk
1 teaspoon salt
⅛ teaspoon freshly grated nutmeg

Roll out dough on a lightly floured surface with a floured rolling pin into a 13-inch round. Fit into a 9½-inch deep-dish or 10-inch regular pie plate. Trim excess dough, leaving a ½-inch overhang. Turn edge under itself and crimp decoratively. Prick shell in several places with a fork and refrigerate, covered, for 30 minutes.

Put a rack in middle of oven and preheat oven to 375°F.

Line shell with foil and fill with pie weights, raw rice, or dried beans. Bake for 20 minutes. Remove foil and weights and bake shell until golden brown, about 10 minutes more. Transfer to a rack to cool. (Leave oven on.)

Meanwhile, cook bacon in a 12-inch heavy skillet over moderate heat, stirring occasionally, until crisp, about 8 minutes. With a slotted spoon, transfer to paper towels to drain.

Whisk together eggs, yolks, cream, and milk in a large bowl, then whisk in salt and nutmeg. Pour into baked pie shell and sprinkle with bacon.

Bake quiche until browned and puffed, 35 to 40 minutes (center will still be slightly wobbly but not liquid). If edges of shell are browning too quickly, cover with a pie shield or foil during last 10 minutes of baking.

Serve warm or at room temperature.

VARIATION

- SPINACH QUICHE LORRAINE: Bring ½ inch salted water to a boil in a large pot. Add 10 ounces spinach (coarse stems discarded), reduce heat, and simmer, covered, until wilted, 2 to 3 minutes. Drain in a colander and rinse under cold water to stop the cooking. Squeeze handfuls of spinach to remove excess water, then stir into the egg mixture.

Ultimate Quiche

SERVES 8
ACTIVE TIME: 30 MINUTES ■ START TO FINISH: 1¾ HOURS

■ Creamy and golden, tender of filling and flaky of crust: this quiche, from our executive food editor, Zanne Stewart, may change your life. Serve it on Christmas morning while presents are being opened, and its lush richness (Gruyère, crème fraîche, puff pastry) will tide everyone over until dinner. A salad turns it into a wonderful supper. ■

3/4 pound bacon (12 slices), cut crosswise into 3/4-inch-wide pieces
1 sheet frozen puff pastry (from a 17 1/4-ounce package), thawed
6 large eggs
2 (10-ounce) containers crème fraîche (2 1/4 cups)
1/2 teaspoon salt
1/8 teaspoon freshly grated nutmeg
1 cup coarsely grated Gruyère (about 4 ounces)

SPECIAL EQUIPMENT: an 8-inch deep-dish (2-inch-deep) fluted quiche pan with a removable bottom or a 9-inch ceramic quiche dish

Put a baking sheet on middle oven rack and preheat oven to 375°F.

Cook bacon in a 12-inch heavy skillet over moderate heat, stirring occasionally, until crisp, about 10 minutes. With a slotted spoon, transfer to paper towels to drain.

Roll out pastry on a lightly floured surface into a 13-inch square (because pastry sheet is a square, it is easier to roll it into a larger square, then trim it into a round). Fit pastry into quiche pan or dish and roll rolling pin over top to trim pastry flush with rim if using a metal pan, or trim with a knife if using a ceramic dish.

Whisk eggs in a medium bowl until well combined, then whisk in crème fraîche, salt, and nutmeg just until smooth. Pour filling through a fine-mesh sieve into pastry shell. Sprinkle bacon evenly over filling and top with Gruyère.

Bake quiche on heated baking sheet until center is set (it should not jiggle when shaken), 45 minutes to 1 hour. Transfer to a rack to cool to warm or room temperature.

If using quiche pan, remove rim of pan before serving.

Spinach and Cheese Strata

SERVES 6 TO 8
ACTIVE TIME: 30 MINUTES ■ START TO FINISH: 10 HOURS (INCLUDES CHILLING)

■ A strata is essentially a savory bread pudding. This one, with eggs, bread, greens, and cheese, makes a great brunch dish because it can be assembled the night before. Or you can put it together in the morning and bake it for Sunday night supper. ■

1 (10-ounce) package frozen spinach, thawed
3 tablespoons unsalted butter
1 large onion, finely chopped (1 1/2 cups)
1 teaspoon salt
1/2 teaspoon freshly ground black pepper
1/4 teaspoon freshly grated nutmeg
1/2 pound French or Italian bread, cut into 1-inch cubes (8 cups)
2 cups coarsely grated Gruyère (about 6 ounces)
1 cup finely grated Parmigiano-Reggiano (about 2 ounces)
2 3/4 cups whole milk
9 large eggs
2 tablespoons Dijon mustard

Squeeze handfuls of spinach to remove as much liquid as possible. Finely chop.

Melt butter in a large heavy skillet over moderate heat. Add onion and cook, stirring, until softened, 4 to 5 minutes. Add 1/2 teaspoon salt, 1/4 teaspoon pepper, and nutmeg and cook, stirring, for 1 minute. Stir in spinach, then remove from heat.

Butter a 3-quart gratin dish or other shallow baking dish. Spread one third of bread cubes in dish and top evenly with one third of spinach mixture. Sprinkle with one third of each cheese. Repeat layering twice, ending with cheeses.

Whisk together milk, eggs, mustard, remaining 1/2 teaspoon salt, and remaining 1/4 teaspoon pepper in a large bowl. Pour evenly over strata. Refrigerate, covered with plastic wrap, for at least 8 hours to allow bread to absorb custard.

Let strata stand at room temperature for 30 minutes. Put a rack in middle of oven and preheat oven to 350°F.

Bake strata, uncovered, until puffed, golden brown, and cooked through, 45 to 55 minutes. Let stand for 5 minutes before serving.

COOK'S NOTE

■ The strata can be refrigerated for up to 24 hours.

Grits and Cheddar Casserole

SERVES 6 TO 8
ACTIVE TIME: 40 MINUTES ■ START TO FINISH: 1¼ HOURS

■ Grits and cheese is an enduring classic in the American South. Grits are sometimes called hominy, especially in the Low Country of South Carolina and Georgia, but they shouldn't be confused with the big, starchy, dried corn kernels, also called hominy, that form the backbone of the New Mexican stew called posole. If anything, grits are more like polenta or porridge. In this recipe we beat the egg whites separately and fold them in to lighten the grits. Serve the casserole with ham or sausages for a truly wonderful breakfast or brunch. ■

- 6 cups water
- 1 teaspoon salt
- 1 cup regular grits (not stone-ground or quick-cooking)
- 2 tablespoons unsalted butter
- 3 large eggs, separated
- 2¼ cups grated sharp Cheddar (about 8 ounces)
- ¼ teaspoon cayenne, or to taste

Put a rack in middle of oven and preheat oven to 350°F. Butter a 2-quart soufflé dish or baking dish.

Bring water and salt to a boil in a large heavy saucepan over medium-high heat. Add grits in a thin stream, stirring constantly. Cover and simmer, stirring occasionally, until thickened, 15 to 20 minutes.

Remove grits from heat and beat in butter with a wooden spoon, then beat in yolks one at a time. Stir in 2 cups Cheddar and cayenne.

Beat egg whites in a bowl with an electric mixer until they just hold stiff peaks. Stir one quarter of whites into grits to lighten them, then gently but thoroughly fold in remaining whites.

Pour grits into buttered dish and smooth top. Sprinkle with remaining ¼ cup cheese.

Cover with foil and bake for 30 minutes. Uncover and continue to bake until bubbles form around edges, about 10 minutes more.

Grits with Tasso

SERVES 4
ACTIVE TIME: 1¼ HOURS ■ START TO FINISH: 1½ HOURS

■ At the heart of many a breakfast in the American South are stone-ground artisanal grits, which are coarser than supermarket grits and full of sweet cracked-corn flavor. They take longer to cook than ordinary grits, but the more they simmer, the creamier they become; they should be slightly loose but not too soupy. We've paired grits with tasso, the rich, smoky, tangy cured pork that's a Cajun specialty. Try this with fried eggs. ■

- 5½ cups water
- 1 teaspoon salt
- 1 cup white stone-ground grits
- ¼ pound tasso (Cajun smoked cured pork; see Sources) or country ham (see Sources), cut into ¼-inch dice
- ½ stick (4 tablespoons) unsalted butter
- Salt and freshly ground black pepper

Bring 4 cups water and salt to a boil in a 4-quart heavy saucepan. Add grits in a thin stream, stirring constantly, and return to a boil, stirring frequently. Reduce heat and simmer grits, uncovered, stirring occasionally, until very thick and most of water is absorbed, about 10 minutes.

Reduce heat further and gently simmer grits until cooked through, about 1 hour and 10 minutes, stirring frequently and adding remaining 1½ cups water ¼ cup at a time whenever grits become very thick. Add tasso, butter, and salt and pepper to taste and stir until butter is melted. Serve immediately.

Sweet and Spicy Bacon

SERVES 6
ACTIVE TIME: 10 MINUTES ■ START TO FINISH: 45 MINUTES

■ Bacon's smoky meatiness makes it one of life's most inexpensive luxuries (and a real temptation for many would-be vegetarians). In this recipe the bacon's smoke is given a little sweetness and spice. And we've put it in the oven to make the timing easy with whatever you've got cooking on the stovetop. (It's also less messy.)

- 1½ tablespoons packed brown sugar
- Rounded ¼ teaspoon cayenne
- Rounded ¼ teaspoon freshly ground black pepper
- 1 pound thick-cut bacon (12 slices)

Put a rack in middle of oven and preheat oven to 350°F.

Stir together brown sugar, cayenne, and black pepper in a small bowl.

Arrange bacon slices in one layer on rack of a large broiler pan. Bake for 20 minutes. Turn slices over and sprinkle evenly with spiced sugar. Continue baking until bacon is crisp and brown, 15 to 20 minutes more. Transfer to paper towels to drain.

Molasses-Cured Pork Shoulder Bacon

MAKES ABOUT 4½ POUNDS
ACTIVE TIME: 1¼ HOURS ■ START TO FINISH: 2 DAYS (INCLUDES CURING)

With just a kettle grill, a few ingredients, and a little patience, the cookbook author and sausage maker Bruce Aidells showed us how to make the real thing. Pork shoulder bacon may not get quite as crisp as belly bacon

Grits

The mass-produced grits found in every supermarket are made from processed corn kernels that are "degerminated"—divested of hull and nutritive germ—and ground by steel rollers, which heat up and in effect cook the corn, robbing it of much of its fragrance and flavor. There is a place for supermarket grits: they are easy to find, they cook relatively quickly, and their very blandness makes them a useful vehicle for butter, cheese, eggs sunny-side up, and gravies. Better supermarket grits than no grits at all. (Avoid the grits labeled "quick-cooking," though; the consistency is eerily reminiscent of baby food.)

Back in the eighties, small gristmills started cropping up, grinding grits to order for some enterprising southern chefs—Frank Stitt, from Birmingham, Alabama, and the late Bill Neal, from Chapel Hill, North Carolina, for instance—as well as for the artisanal foods supplier and cookbook author John Martin Taylor, known familiarly as Hoppin' John. These grits are made the way they were when every decent-sized southern town had its own mill: dried whole corn kernels are ground slowly between cool millstones, so that the nutritious germ and the sweet, deep, cracked-corn flavor are preserved, and then the coarsest bits of hull are sifted out. One forkful and you'll see the light. One forkful and you'll begin busily planning entire meals around an all-too-often-dismissed breakfast basic: shrimp and grits, panfried trout and grits, fried quail and grits.... You get the idea.

The downside to stone-ground grits is that they do take longer to cook—from forty minutes to an hour or so—and they must be stored in the freezer. Follow the directions on the back of the sack and don't rush the process; in our experience, the suggested cooking times are never long enough.

Two artisanal mills that we know and love are Logan Turnpike Mill, in the mountains of north Georgia (we order their grits from Hoppin' John's of Charleston, South Carolina), and Anson Mills, of Columbia, South Carolina (see Sources).

(see Cook's Note), but it has a great taste and meaty texture. Even if you have a thermometer for your grill, you'll still need an instant-read—the grill thermometer won't register low enough to monitor the cold-smoking. ■

- 1 (4- to 6-pound) boneless pork shoulder roast (Boston butt)
- 6 cups water
- 1 cup kosher salt
- 2/3 cup packed dark brown sugar
- 2½ tablespoons Instacure No. 1 (curing salts; see Sources)
- ½ cup molasses (not robust or blackstrap)
- 3 cups ice cubes
- ¼ cup coarsely ground black pepper (optional)

SPECIAL EQUIPMENT: a 1- to 2-gallon plastic storage tub or stainless steel bowl; a 22½-inch covered kettle grill with a hinged top rack; a 12-by-8-by-2-inch disposable aluminum roasting pan; 3 pounds hardwood sawdust (not from treated wood; see Sources); charcoal briquettes; a chimney starter; long metal tongs; an instant-read thermometer

Put pork fat side up on a work surface and halve horizontally with a large sharp knife.

Stir together water, salt, brown sugar, and Instacure in storage tub until salts and sugar are dissolved, about 3 minutes. Add molasses and stir until dissolved. Add ice and stir until cure is cold (it's fine if ice is not completely melted).

Add pork to cure and weight with a large plate to keep submerged. Cover tub with a lid or plastic wrap and refrigerate for 36 hours.

Rinse pork and pat dry; discard brine. Sprinkle pork evenly with pepper, if using.

SMOKE THE BACON: Open vents in bottom of grill and in lid; set lid aside. Remove top rack from grill and center disposable roasting pan on lower rack. Add 6 cups sawdust to pan.

Light 5 briquettes in chimney starter. When briquettes are completely covered with gray ash and glowing, transfer with tongs to sawdust, spacing them evenly. When sawdust begins to smolder, replace top rack and arrange pork pieces about 1 inch apart on rack. Cover grill with lid, then insert thermometer into a vent hole in lid to monitor temperature, which should be 80°–120°F. If temperature rises above 120°F, remove one or more briquettes or partially uncover grill until temperature falls. If temperature falls below 80°F, light more briquettes in the same manner and, if necessary, reignite sawdust.

Smoke pork for 8 hours, adding 1 cup sawdust to roasting pan every 1½ hours and stirring with tongs to ignite sawdust. Let pork cool completely, then refrigerate, wrapped in plastic wrap, until ready to use.

To cook, cut bacon crosswise into ⅛-inch-thick slices with a sharp knife. Fry in a heavy skillet over moderately low heat, turning, until browned. Transfer to paper towels to drain.

COOK'S NOTES

- ■ The preparation for traditional belly bacon is the same as for shoulder bacon, but the curing time is longer because belly is fattier. Halve a 6- to 8-pound pork belly crosswise and cure for 72 hours. Cold-smoke as above. Skinless, boneless pork belly can be ordered by mail from Niman Ranch (see Sources).
- ■ The bacon will keep, refrigerated, for up to 1 week. It can be frozen for up to 2 months.

Maple Mustard–Glazed Canadian Bacon

SERVES 6

ACTIVE TIME: 5 MINUTES ■ START TO FINISH: 10 MINUTES

■ This is perfect for a winter house party. If you like honey mustard, you'll love the maple mustard. Maple syrup works well with the intrinsic sweetness of the ham, and the mustard prevents it from being cloying. The glaze is excellent on ham and pork chops too. ■

- 1½ tablespoons Dijon mustard
- 2 teaspoons pure maple syrup
- Cayenne to taste
- ¾ pound thinly sliced Canadian bacon

Preheat broiler. Stir together mustard, syrup, and cayenne in a small bowl. Arrange bacon slices in one layer on rack of a broiler pan or a baking sheet with sides and brush top of each slice generously with glaze.

Broil bacon about 4 inches from heat, turning once, just until golden around edges, about 6 minutes total. Serve glazed sides up.

Corned Beef Hash

SERVES 4

ACTIVE TIME: 45 MINUTES ■ START TO FINISH: 45 MINUTES

■ You may think of this as a diner classic, but it's more than worth doing yourself. Red bell pepper adds color and flavor, and a little heavy cream brings it all together. We've baked eggs in the hash, but of course you can serve it plain. Pair it with a green salad and you've got dinner. ■

- 1 pound russet (baking) potatoes
- 1 (1-pound) piece cooked corned beef, cut into chunks
- 2 tablespoons unsalted butter
- 1 cup chopped onion
- 1 large red bell pepper, cored, seeded, and cut into 1/4-inch pieces
- Salt and freshly ground black pepper
- 1/4 cup heavy cream
- 4 large eggs

GARNISH: 1 tablespoon chopped fresh flat-leaf parsley

Peel potatoes and cut into 1/4-inch dice. Cook in a 2 1/2- to 3-quart saucepan of boiling well-salted water to cover until just tender, about 3 minutes; drain.

Pulse corned beef in a food processor until coarsely chopped.

Heat butter in a 12-inch nonstick skillet over moderately high heat until foam subsides. Add onion and bell pepper and cook, stirring, until lightly browned, about 5 minutes. Add potatoes and cook, stirring occasionally, until browned, about 5 minutes. Stir in corned beef, season with salt and pepper, and cook, stirring occasionally, until golden brown. Add cream and cook, stirring, for 1 minute.

Make 4 depressions in hash and break 1 egg into each. Reduce heat to moderately low and cook, covered, until eggs are cooked to desired doneness, 4 to 6 minutes. Season eggs with salt and pepper and sprinkle parsley over hash.

COOKIES, BARS, AND CONFECTIONS

Of all the chapters in this book, this was by far the easiest to put together. There were no arguments about which cookies to include. The reason is very simple: these are our favorites, and we bake them year in and year out. Our families wouldn't consider going through the holidays without them.

We knew, with very little discussion, that the adorable and delicious tiny chocolate chip cookies were going to be in this chapter, along with the rich, nutty Mexican tea cakes. Of course we had to include the lovely stained glass cookies, and we wouldn't dream of leaving out our elegant lemon thins, our delicate langues de chat, or our sophisticated Viennese vanilla crescents. A *Gourmet* book without pecan sablés, which dissolve into tender crumbs the minute you take a bite? Unthinkable. And if anyone on our staff professed a preference for anything but Katharine Hepburn's brownies, he or she would have been shouted off the floor. Unless, of course, it was for the utterly decadent cappuccino brownies, or the triple-chocolate fudge brownies, which take the brownie theme and up the ante.

The confections were also easy to choose. The candied grapefruit peel is superb, the molasses sponge candy is a fine old American classic, and we'll put our brown sugar fudge up against any in the nation.

This is a chapter for gift-givers and people-pleasers: armed with these recipes, you will surely be welcomed wherever you go.

Cookies

Tiny Chocolate Chip Cookies

MAKES ABOUT 12½ DOZEN COOKIES
ACTIVE TIME: 45 MINUTES ■ START TO FINISH: 45 MINUTES

■ The chocolate chip cookie is an American icon, but it's never been considered refined or particularly beautiful. Until now. When it's much smaller than usual, it's somehow elevated to petit-four status—exquisite and almost jewel-like. And as far as taste goes, the secret ingredient in superior chocolate chip cookies is a humble one: salt. It bumps up the flavor of the chocolate and brings everything into perfect balance. ■

- 1¼ sticks (10 tablespoons) unsalted butter, softened
- ⅔ cup packed light brown sugar
- ¾ teaspoon salt
- ½ teaspoon baking soda
- 1 large egg
- ½ teaspoon vanilla extract
- 1 cup all-purpose flour
- 1¼ cups (7½ ounces) semisweet chocolate chips

Put a rack in middle of oven and preheat oven to 400°F.

Beat together butter, sugar, salt, and baking soda in a large bowl with an electric mixer at medium speed until fluffy, about 3 minutes. Beat in egg and vanilla. Add flour and mix at low speed until just combined. Fold in chocolate chips.

Drop barely rounded ½ teaspoons of dough about 1½ inches apart onto ungreased baking sheets. Bake in batches until golden brown, 6 to 7 minutes per batch. Transfer cookies to racks to cool.

COOK'S NOTE

■ The cookies keep in an airtight container at room temperature for up to 4 days.

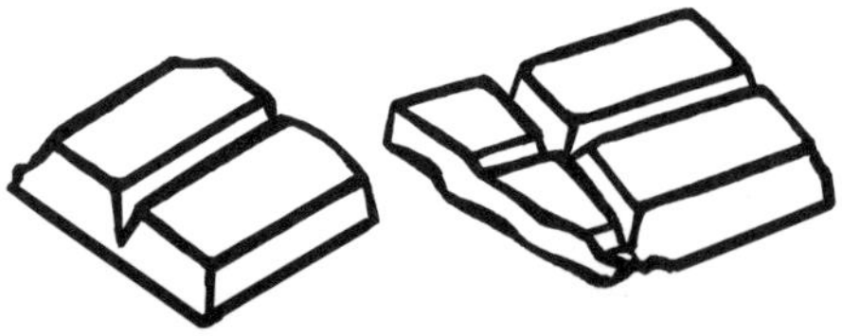

Chocolate Chunk Cookies with Pecans, Dried Apricots, and Dried Sour Cherries

MAKES ABOUT 3 DOZEN COOKIES
ACTIVE TIME: 30 MINUTES ■ START TO FINISH: 1½ HOURS (INCLUDES COOLING)

■ Use the best bittersweet chocolate you can find for this recipe. Dried cherries and apricots play up the fruitiness of good dark chocolate, and the apricots in particular offset the chocolate and pecans. ■

- 2½ cups all-purpose flour
- 1 teaspoon baking soda
- ½ teaspoon baking powder
- 1½ teaspoons salt
- 2 sticks (½ pound) unsalted butter, softened
- 1 cup granulated sugar
- ½ cup packed light brown sugar
- 2 large eggs
- 9 ounces good bittersweet (not unsweetened) or semisweet chocolate, cut into ½-inch pieces
- ¾ cup (4½ ounces) quartered dried apricots
- 1 cup (5 ounces) dried sour cherries
- 1 cup (4 ounces) coarsely chopped pecans

Put racks in upper and lower thirds of oven and preheat oven to 375°F.

Whisk together flour, baking soda, baking powder, and salt in a bowl.

Beat together butter and sugars in a large bowl with an electric mixer at high speed until fluffy, about 2 minutes. Add eggs one at a time, beating well after each addition. Beat in flour mixture at low speed until just combined. Stir in chocolate, apricots, cherries, and pecans.

Drop heaping tablespoons of dough about 2 inches apart onto ungreased baking sheets. Bake, switching position of sheets halfway through baking, until golden, about 12 minutes total. Cool cookies on sheets on racks for 5 minutes, then transfer to racks to cool.

COOK'S NOTE

■ The cookies keep in an airtight container at room temperature for up to 5 days.

Peanut Butter Cookies

MAKES ABOUT 4 DOZEN COOKIES
ACTIVE TIME: 45 MINUTES ■ START TO FINISH: 1¼ HOURS

■ Delicious and nutritious, the peanut is used to great effect in cuisines around the world. Here chunky peanut butter and brown sugar unite in one of its most beloved guises. The peanut, by the way, isn't a true nut but a legume, more closely related to black-eyed peas than to pecans or walnuts. And although it's often thought to be African in origin, as the culinary historian Jessica Harris explains in *Beyond Gumbo,* it was first cultivated in pre-Incan Peru and taken to Africa by Portuguese slave traders. ■

- 1 stick (8 tablespoons) unsalted butter, softened
- 1½ cups chunky peanut butter (not "natural-style")
- 1 cup packed light brown sugar
- 1 large egg
- 1¾ cups all-purpose flour
- 1 teaspoon baking powder
- ½ teaspoon salt

Put a rack in middle of oven and preheat oven to 350°F. Butter two large baking sheets.

Beat together butter, peanut butter, and sugar in a large bowl with an electric mixer at medium speed until fluffy, 2 to 3 minutes. Beat in egg. Add flour, baking powder, and salt and beat at low speed just until a dough forms.

Drop level tablespoons of dough about 1½ inches apart onto buttered baking sheets, then flatten with tines of a fork, making a crosshatch pattern, to 2½-inch rounds.

Bake in batches until slightly puffed, 12 to 15 minutes per batch. Cool cookies on baking sheets for 1 minute, then transfer to racks to cool completely.

COOK'S NOTE

■ The cookies keep in an airtight container at room temperature for up to 4 days.

BAKING SHEETS

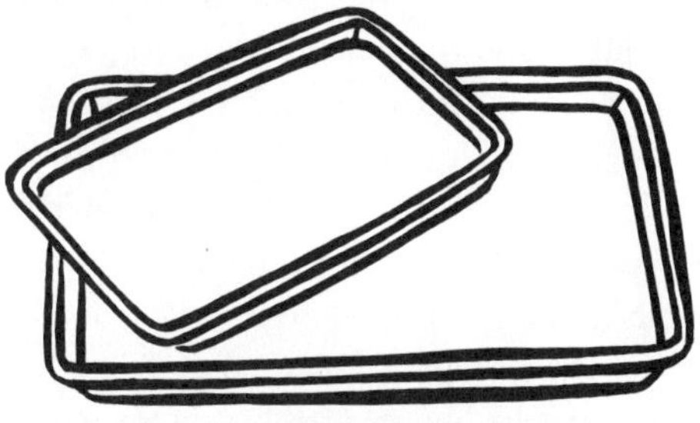

The rectangular baking pan with inch-high sides called a jelly-roll pan is often marketed as a cookie sheet because that's what many people use it for. It was originally designed, however, to contain and shape the batter for the thin sponge cake used in jelly rolls, those delectable, squishy pinwheels filled with jam or whipped cream. Every kitchen should have at least one of these pans, since they are perfect for toasting nuts and bread crumbs, roasting vegetables, and heating hors d'oeuvres. But if you love to make cookies, you might want to pick up a couple of proper baking sheets. They have only one or two lipped sides for handling, allowing you to slide the cookies quickly and easily from sheet to cooling rack. (It's always handy to have two— one sheet can be cooling while the next batch of cookies is in the oven.) We prefer medium-weight, light-colored (not nonstick) aluminum baking sheets. We especially like the solid aluminum pans made by Doughmakers, which have a pebble pattern that allows air to flow under baked goods so they brown more evenly. They are available at most cookware stores or directly from Doughmakers (see Sources). We are not huge fans of insulated cookie sheets; cookies tend to take longer to bake on them. Be aware that all pans do not cook in the same way, which is why we often give a range of baking times and/or a description of what the finished cookie should look like.

Oatmeal Cookies

MAKES ABOUT 2 DOZEN COOKIES
ACTIVE TIME: 25 MINUTES ■ START TO FINISH: 35 MINUTES

■ Whole grains have never tasted so good. This cookie is straightforward and dependable, with a great texture—crisp and chewy at the same time. We think it's perfect as is, but feel free to embellish it with raisins, dried cherries, or chocolate chips (see Cook's Note). ■

- 1¾ cups old-fashioned rolled oats
- ¾ cup all-purpose flour
- ¾ teaspoon ground cinnamon
- ½ teaspoon baking soda
- ½ teaspoon salt
- 1¼ sticks (10 tablespoons) unsalted butter, softened
- ⅓ cup packed light brown sugar
- ¼ cup granulated sugar
- 1 large egg
- ½ teaspoon vanilla extract

Put racks in upper and lower thirds of oven and preheat oven to 375°F. Butter two large baking sheets.

Stir together oats, flour, cinnamon, baking soda, and salt in a bowl.

Beat together butter, brown sugar, and granulated sugar in a large bowl with an electric mixer at medium speed until fluffy, about 3 minutes. Add egg and vanilla and beat until well combined. Add oat mixture and beat until just combined.

Drop heaping tablespoons of dough about 2 inches apart onto buttered baking sheets and flatten mounds slightly with moistened fingers. Bake cookies, switching position of sheets halfway through baking, until golden, about 12 minutes total. Transfer cookies to racks to cool.

COOK'S NOTES

- Add ½ to 1 cup raisins, dried cherries, or chocolate chips to the dough, if desired.
- The cookies keep in an airtight container at room temperature for up to 4 days.

Oatmeal–Trail Mix Cookies

MAKES ABOUT 2½ DOZEN COOKIES
ACTIVE TIME: 45 MINUTES ■ START TO FINISH: 1¼ HOURS

■ A sophisticated spin on gorp (good old raisins and peanuts, in hiker dialect), these hearty cookies are packed with coconut, chocolate chips, raisins, and roasted peanuts. Nearly a meal in themselves, they earn their keep in picnic baskets, backpacks, or lunch boxes. ■

- ½ stick (4 tablespoons) unsalted butter, softened
- ¼ cup vegetable shortening
- ½ cup packed light brown sugar
- ¼ cup granulated sugar
- 1 large egg
- ½ teaspoon baking soda, dissolved in 1 tablespoon warm water
- ½ cup plus 2 tablespoons all-purpose flour
- ¾ teaspoon salt
- ½ teaspoon vanilla extract
- 1½ cups old-fashioned rolled oats
- ½ cup sweetened flaked coconut
- 1 cup (6 ounces) semisweet chocolate chips
- ⅓ cup salted roasted peanuts
- ½ cup raisins

Put a rack in middle of oven and preheat oven to 375°F. Butter two large baking sheets.

Beat together butter, shortening, and sugars in a large bowl with an electric mixer at high speed until fluffy, about 2 minutes. Beat in egg, baking soda mixture, flour, salt, and vanilla until just combined. Stir in oats, coconut, chocolate chips, peanuts, and raisins until well combined.

Drop rounded tablespoons of dough about 4 inches apart onto buttered baking sheets, then flatten and spread each mound into a 3-inch round with a fork. Bake cookies in batches until golden, 8 to 10 minutes per batch. Transfer to racks to cool.

COOK'S NOTE

- The cookies keep in an airtight container at room temperature for up to 5 days.

Nonstick Baking Sheet Liners

Making delicate cookies is a whole new ball game if you use silicone-treated baking sheet liners. Their ultra-nonstick finish, valued by professional chefs for years, makes it easier to spread batter smoothly and evenly. Although they can be used for any kind of cookie, they are particularly helpful for wafer-thin ones such as Oat Lace Cookies (below), Cinnamon Chocolate Cigarettes (page 668), and Langues de Chat (page 682), which slide cleanly off the sheet. These liners are also terrific for making crackers or baked potato chips. One of the most commonly available brands is Silpat, which looks like a floppy plastic-coated burlap place mat. Nonstick baking sheet liners are found in cookware shops and even some supermarkets, or see Sources. They come in different sizes and can be reused almost endlessly. But don't put them in the dishwasher, don't slice on them, and be sure to let them cool completely flat before rolling them up for storage.

Oat Lace Cookies

MAKES ABOUT 1½ DOZEN COOKIES
ACTIVE TIME: 30 MINUTES ■ START TO FINISH: 1 HOUR

■ Because these cookies contain no flour, they are thin, lacy, and delicate. Toasting the oats before adding them to the batter burnishes their flavor. The cookies are special enough for dinner guests. ■

- 6 tablespoons quick-cooking rolled oats
- ½ stick (4 tablespoons) unsalted butter
- ¼ cup sugar
- 1 tablespoon heavy cream
- ⅛ teaspoon salt

SPECIAL EQUIPMENT: a nonstick baking sheet liner, such as a Silpat

Put a rack in middle of oven and preheat oven to 350°F. Line a large baking sheet with nonstick liner.

Spread oats in a thin layer on another baking sheet. Toast in oven until pale golden, about 10 minutes. Set aside.

Combine butter, sugar, cream, and salt in a small saucepan and heat over low heat, stirring, until butter is melted and sugar is dissolved. Stir in oats and remove from heat.

Spoon 2-teaspoon amounts of batter about 3 inches apart onto lined baking sheet. Bake cookies in batches until golden brown, about 10 minutes per batch.

Cool cookies completely on baking sheet on a rack.

COOK'S NOTE

■ The cookies keep, layered between sheets of wax or parchment paper, in an airtight container at room temperature for up to 4 days.

Brown Sugar–Ginger Crisps

MAKES ABOUT 7 DOZEN COOKIES
ACTIVE TIME: 25 MINUTES ■ START TO FINISH: 1¾ HOURS

■ These crisp, waferlike cookies have spicy candied ginger nuggets in every bite. ■

- 2 sticks (½ pound) unsalted butter, softened
- 1 cup packed light brown sugar
- 1 large egg yolk
- 1 teaspoon vanilla extract
- ½ cup (3 ounces) finely chopped crystallized ginger
- ¼ teaspoon ground ginger
- 1½ cups all-purpose flour
- ¾ teaspoon baking powder
- ½ teaspoon salt

Put a rack in middle of oven and preheat oven to 350°F.

Beat together butter and brown sugar in a large

bowl with a wooden spoon. Beat in yolk, vanilla, crystallized ginger, and ground ginger. Sift together flour, baking powder, and salt onto dough and stir until well combined.

Drop teaspoons of batter about 1½ inches apart onto ungreased baking sheets. Bake in batches until just golden, 10 to 15 minutes per batch. Cool cookies on sheets for 5 minutes, then transfer to racks to cool completely.

COOK'S NOTE

- The cookies keep in an airtight container at room temperature for up to 1 week.

Anzac Biscuits

MAKES ABOUT 2½ DOZEN COOKIES
ACTIVE TIME: 30 MINUTES ■ START TO FINISH: 1¼ HOURS

■ In Australia and other parts of the British Commonwealth, a biscuit is what Americans call a cookie. This one—a buttery, salty-sweet amalgam of hearty oatmeal, coconut, and treacle or golden syrup—was created by wives, mothers, and girlfriends concerned for the nutrition of their loved ones in the Australian and New Zealand Army Corps (ANZAC) during World War I. At first the cookies were called soldiers' biscuits, but after the landing on Gallipoli, on April 25, 1915, they were renamed Anzac biscuits. Note that there are no eggs to hold the dough together. Eggs were scarce during the war (many poultry farmers were in the armed forces), so a common binder was Lyle's Golden Syrup, a British sugarcane syrup that has the texture and color of honey but a subtle buttery flavor all its own. Anzac biscuits are still made Down Under today, both at home and commercially. Every year around April 25, they are sold to raise funds for the care of aged veterans. This version, from the Lodge Country House, in Seppeltsfield, South Australia, is more delicate than most, so we don't recommend shipping the cookies. Happily, Lyle's Golden Syrup is now available in the baking section of many supermarkets, or see Sources. ■

- 1 cup all-purpose flour
- 1 cup old-fashioned rolled oats
- 1 cup sugar
- ¾ cup sweetened flaked coconut
- ¾ teaspoon salt
- 1¼ sticks (10 tablespoons) unsalted butter
- 1 tablespoon Lyle's Golden Syrup
- 1½ teaspoons baking soda
- 2 tablespoons boiling water

Put racks in upper and lower thirds of oven and preheat oven to 300°F. Grease two large baking sheets.

Sift flour into a large bowl. Stir in oats, sugar, coconut, and salt.

Melt butter with syrup in a small saucepan over moderate heat, stirring until smooth. Remove from heat.

Stir together baking soda and boiling water in a small bowl, then stir into melted butter mixture. Stir into flour mixture until well combined (dough will be crumbly).

Arrange packed tablespoons of dough about 2 inches apart on greased baking sheets. Bake, switching position of sheets halfway through baking, until golden brown, about 20 minutes total. Cool cookies on sheets on racks for 5 minutes, then loosen cookies from sheets while still warm and transfer to racks to cool completely.

COOK'S NOTE

- The cookies keep in an airtight container at room temperature for up to 1 week.

Black-and-White Cookies

MAKES ABOUT 8 COOKIES
ACTIVE TIME: 25 MINUTES ■ START TO FINISH: 3 HOURS (INCLUDES COOLING)

■ For sheer showiness, it's hard to beat these big, rich, cakey disks, with their distinctive, invitingly iced tops: one half is chocolate and the other is vanilla. They are as emblematic of New York City as the Chrysler Building. ■

FOR COOKIES

- 1¼ cups all-purpose flour
- ½ teaspoon baking soda

- ½ teaspoon salt
- ⅓ cup well-shaken buttermilk
- ½ teaspoon vanilla extract
- 5⅓ tablespoons unsalted butter, softened
- ½ cup granulated sugar
- 1 large egg

FOR ICINGS

- 1½ cups confectioners' sugar
- 1 tablespoon light corn syrup
- 2 teaspoons fresh lemon juice
- ¼ teaspoon vanilla extract
- 1–2 tablespoons water
- ¼ cup unsweetened Dutch-process cocoa powder

MAKE THE COOKIES: Put a rack in middle of oven and preheat oven to 350°F. Butter a large baking sheet.

Whisk together flour, baking soda, and salt in a bowl. Stir together buttermilk and vanilla in a cup.

Beat together butter and sugar in a large bowl with an electric mixer at medium speed until pale and fluffy, about 3 minutes. Add egg, beating until well combined. Reduce speed to low and add flour mixture and buttermilk mixture alternately in batches, beginning and ending with flour mixture and beating until smooth (scrape down sides of bowl occasionally).

Spoon ¼-cup amounts of batter about 2 inches apart onto buttered baking sheet. Bake until tops are puffed and pale golden and cookies spring back when touched, 15 to 17 minutes. Transfer to a rack to cool.

MAKE THE ICINGS: Stir together confectioners' sugar, corn syrup, lemon juice, vanilla, and 1 tablespoon water in a small bowl until smooth. Transfer half of icing to another bowl and stir in cocoa, adding more water ½ teaspoon at a time to thin to same consistency as white icing.

ICE THE COOKIES: Turn cooled cookies upside down. With a small offset spatula, spread white icing over half of each cookie and then spread chocolate icing over other halves. Let cookies stand until icing is set, about 2 hours.

COOK'S NOTE

- The cookies keep in an airtight container at room temperature for up to 1 day.

Coconut Tuile Cones

MAKES ABOUT 8 CONES
ACTIVE TIME: 35 MINUTES ■ START TO FINISH: 2 HOURS (INCLUDES COOLING)

■ What's a cone doing in the cookie chapter? This one is nothing more than a tuile—the crisp, arched, paper-thin cookie named for the distinctive roof tiles seen in the South of France—rolled up. Fill the delicate coconut-flavored cones with your favorite ice cream and serve on a plate. If you prefer traditional tuiles ("tweels"), simply drape the warm cookies over a wine bottle and allow them to cool. (Normally tuiles are draped over a rolling pin to shape them, but because these are larger than usual, a wine bottle is more practical.) ■

- ½ stick (4 tablespoons) unsalted butter
- ¼ cup packed light brown sugar
- 3 tablespoons light corn syrup
- ¼ cup all-purpose flour
- ½ cup sweetened flaked coconut

Combine butter, brown sugar, and corn syrup in a 1½-quart saucepan and bring to a boil over moderate heat, stirring. Add flour and cook, stirring constantly, until batter is slightly thickened, about 1 minute. Stir in coconut. Cool to room temperature, about 45 minutes.

Put a rack in middle of oven and preheat oven to 375°F. Butter a baking sheet. Crumple foil to form a solid cone about 6 inches long and 3 inches across at the widest part for shaping cookies.

Drop two 1-tablespoon portions of batter 6 inches apart onto buttered baking sheet and pat each into a 5-inch round with your fingertips. Bake until golden, 6 to 8 minutes (cookies will spread to about 6 inches). Let cookies stand on baking sheet until just firm enough to hold their shape, about 2 minutes.

Gently loosen cookies from baking sheet, preferably with an offset spatula, and turn over so smooth sides are up. Roll one cookie onto foil cone and cool until cookie holds cone shape, about 15 seconds, then carefully slip off cone onto a rack to cool completely. Shape remaining cookie in same manner. (If cookies become too brittle to roll onto cone, return baking sheet to oven for a few seconds to soften.) Make and shape more cookies with remaining dough.

COOK'S NOTES

- The cookies keep in an airtight container at room temperature for up to 3 days.
- The cookies can also be shaped into cups: lay the cookies over inverted glasses and gently mold around the glasses.

Cinnamon Chocolate Cigarettes

MAKES ABOUT 2 DOZEN COOKIES
ACTIVE TIME: 45 MINUTES ■ START TO FINISH: 1¼ HOURS

■ The goal: a debonair dessert for a sophisticated, *noir*ish dinner party, circa 1940. Rum Currant Ice Cream (page 856), we thought, . . . and chocolate cigarettes. According to Bruce Healy and Paul Bugat's *French Cookie Book,* these "Russian cigarettes" were first sold in the 1920s with their own long cardboard holders, fashioned after the elegant ones favored by café society. (Many Russian aristocrats who had escaped the revolution were living the high life in Paris at that time.) The baked cookies, similar to tuiles but easier to work with, are rolled around a pencil while still warm to create their distinctive shape. If the cookies cool (and stiffen) too quickly, simply put the pan back in the oven to soften them again. ■

- 3 large egg whites
- ¾ cup confectioners' sugar
- ½ cup all-purpose flour
- 5⅓ tablespoons unsalted butter, melted
- ¼ teaspoon salt
- ¼ teaspoon ground cinnamon
- 4 ounces good bittersweet chocolate (not unsweetened), finely chopped

Put a rack in middle of oven and preheat oven to 350°F. Line a baking sheet with a nonstick liner, or butter baking sheet.

Whisk together egg whites, confectioners' sugar, flour, butter, salt, and cinnamon in a bowl until well combined. Working in batches of 4, drop level teaspoons of batter about 3 inches apart onto lined or buttered baking sheet, then spread each dollop of batter into a 3-inch round with a small offset spatula or back of a spoon (1).

Bake cookies until edges are golden, 6 to 8 minutes. Work quickly when forming cookies; they must be piping hot. Lift 1 cookie off sheet with a long flexible spatula, then roll it around a pencil or chopstick to form a narrow cylinder (2). Press pencil or chopstick against work surface, seam side down, for a few seconds to seal seam. Immediately slide cookie off pencil or chopstick onto a rack to cool. (If cookies become

HOW TO MAKE CIGARETTE COOKIES

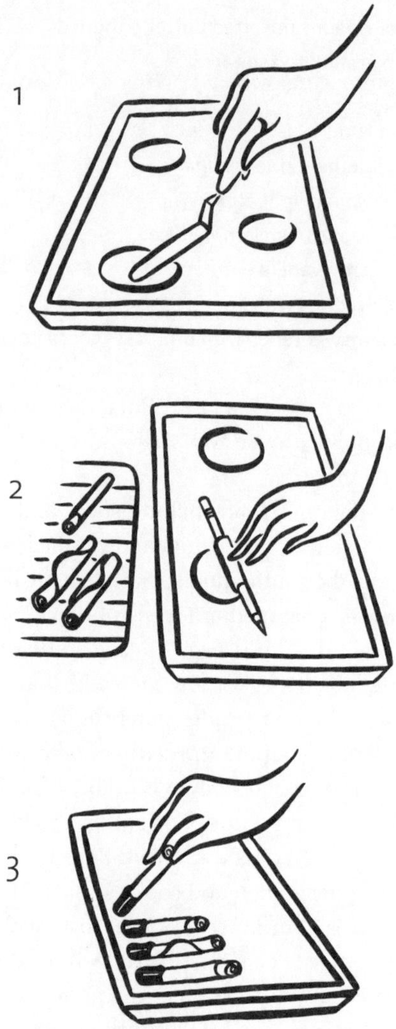

too brittle to roll, return to oven for 1 minute to soften.) Make more cigarettes with remaining batter in same manner. Cool completely.

Line a baking sheet with parchment or wax paper. Melt chocolate in a metal bowl set over a saucepan of barely simmering water, stirring occasionally until smooth. Remove bowl from heat. One at a time, dip 1/4 inch of one end of each cookie into melted chocolate (for the "ash"), letting excess drip off. For a professional look, scrape end on side of bowl to prevent a blob from forming. Place cookies on lined baking sheet (3). Let stand at room temperature until chocolate sets.

COOK'S NOTE

- The cookies keep in an airtight container at room temperature for up to 2 days.

Sugar Cookies

MAKES ABOUT 5½ DOZEN COOKIES
ACTIVE TIME: 40 MINUTES ■ START TO FINISH: 1 HOUR

■ Sugar cookies are taken seriously in the Midwest. They must remain plain and honest: they can have a delicate flavoring, such as vanilla or a trace of lemon, but they can't have nuts or extravagant ingredients. This classic recipe, from Cook's Café, in Brookings, South Dakota, was given to us by the late Helen Gustafson, tea maven at Alice Waters's Chez Panisse in Berkeley, California, and a culinary force in her own right. A native Minnesotan, she always said that a sugar cookie reminded her of a summer's day; all you needed was a front porch and a large glass pitcher of proper lemonade, the kind with visible lemon slices. We'd like to add that this cookie is perfect year-round. It lends a grace note to an afternoon cup of tea or a simple bowl of stewed fruit or ice cream. The inclusion of vegetable oil might seem odd at first glance, but it is actually a common ingredient in sugar cookies, keeping them wonderfully moist. ■

- 1 cup granulated sugar, plus additional for shaping and sprinkling cookies
- 1 cup confectioners' sugar
- 1 cup vegetable oil
- 2 large eggs, lightly beaten
- 1 teaspoon vanilla extract
- 1¼ teaspoons salt
- 1 teaspoon baking soda
- 1 teaspoon cream of tartar
- 4 cups all-purpose flour

Put a rack in middle of oven and preheat oven to 375°F.

Whisk together granulated sugar and confectioners' sugar in a large bowl. Whisk in oil, eggs, vanilla, salt, baking soda, and cream of tartar until combined. Add flour and stir until a dough forms; dough will be dry and slightly crumbly.

Form level tablespoons of dough into balls and arrange about 2 inches apart on ungreased baking sheets. Flatten balls with bottom of a glass dipped in granulated sugar (edges of cookies will crack), then sprinkle cookies with sugar.

Bake cookies in batches until set but still pale for chewy cookies, about 8 minutes per batch, or until pale golden for crisp cookies, about 10 minutes per batch. Transfer to racks to cool.

COOK'S NOTE

- The cookies keep in an airtight container at room temperature for up to 1 week; they will crisp up as they stand.

Spice Sugar Cookies

MAKES ABOUT 3 DOZEN COOKIES
ACTIVE TIME: 30 MINUTES ■ START TO FINISH: 2 HOURS (INCLUDES COOLING)

■ With their beautiful balance of spices and the earthy sweetness of molasses, these cookies are reminiscent of gingerbread men. They're always a hit at Christmastime—and on the hottest July day, with a tall glass of iced tea. ■

- 2 cups all-purpose flour
- 2 teaspoons baking soda
- 1 teaspoon ground cinnamon
- 1 teaspoon ground ginger
- 1/2 teaspoon ground cloves
- 1/4 teaspoon salt
- 3/4 cup vegetable shortening
- 1 cup packed light brown sugar
- 1 large egg, lightly beaten
- 1/4 cup molasses (not robust or blackstrap)
- Granulated sugar for dipping dough

Sift together flour, baking soda, cinnamon, ginger, cloves, and salt into a bowl. Beat together shortening and brown sugar in a large bowl with an electric mixer at medium speed until fluffy, about 1 minute. Reduce speed to low and beat in egg and molasses until just combined. Add flour mixture in 2 or 3 batches, blending well. Refrigerate dough, covered, until firm, at least 1 hour.

Put a rack in middle of oven and preheat oven to 375°F. Grease two large baking sheets.

Roll level tablespoons of dough into balls, dip one side of each ball into granulated sugar, and arrange balls, sugared sides up, about 3 inches apart on greased baking sheets.

Bake cookies in batches until puffed and cracked on top, 10 to 12 minutes per batch. Transfer to racks to cool.

COOK'S NOTES

- The dough can be refrigerated for up to 1 day.
- The cookies keep in an airtight container at room temperature for up to 1 week.

Lemon Thins

MAKES ABOUT 6 DOZEN COOKIES

ACTIVE TIME: 45 MINUTES ■ START TO FINISH: 1 3/4 HOURS

■ These, the ultimate lemon cookies, have pale yellow centers, golden, slightly crisp edges, and a bright citrus flavor that's pronounced without being puckery. It's the triple whammy of lemon zest, juice, and extract that makes them special. ■

- 1 1/2 cups all-purpose flour
- 1 1/2 teaspoons baking powder
- 1/2 teaspoon baking soda
- 1/2 teaspoon salt
- 1/2 cup vegetable shortening
- 2 tablespoons unsalted butter, softened
- 1 cup granulated sugar
- 1/2 teaspoon vanilla extract
- 1/2 teaspoon lemon extract
- 1 1/2 tablespoons finely grated lemon zest (from 2 lemons)
- 1/4 cup fresh lemon juice
- Confectioners' sugar for dusting

Put a rack in middle of oven and preheat oven to 350°F.

Sift together flour, baking powder, baking soda, and salt into a bowl.

Beat together shortening, butter, and granulated sugar in a large bowl with an electric mixer at medium speed for 1 minute. Beat in extracts, zest, and juice and continue to beat until smooth. Reduce speed to low and beat in flour mixture until well blended.

Roll heaping teaspoons of dough into balls and place about 2 inches apart on ungreased baking sheets, then flatten balls slightly with palm of your hand. Bake cookies in batches until edges are just golden, 8 to 10 minutes per batch. Immediately transfer cookies to racks to cool.

Sift confectioners' sugar lightly over cooled lemon thins before serving.

COOK'S NOTE

- The cookies keep in an airtight container at room temperature for up to 5 days.

Pfeffernüsse

German Spice Cookies

MAKES ABOUT 11 DOZEN COOKIES

ACTIVE TIME: 2 HOURS ■ START TO FINISH: 14 HOURS (INCLUDES CHILLING AND STANDING TIME)

■ The German word *Pfeffernüsse* ("*feff*-er-noose") translates literally as "pepper nuts." Although this version contains no pepper, these old-fashioned Christmas cookies are lavishly spiced with anise, clove, nutmeg, and molasses. They are at their best when made a day or so in advance—the flavor deepens and the cookies become soft. This recipe came to us from Anne Cody, of Southbury, Connecticut. She inherited it from her father, who emigrated from Germany in the late 1880s and was a baker's assistant in Brooklyn, New York. ■

FOR COOKIES

- ½ stick (4 tablespoons) unsalted butter, softened
- ¼ cup margarine, softened
- ¾ cup packed light brown sugar
- 1 large egg
- ½ cup molasses (not robust or blackstrap)
- 3 cups sifted all-purpose flour
- ¾ teaspoon salt
- 1½ teaspoons anise seeds
- ¼ teaspoon ground cloves
- ¼ teaspoon freshly grated nutmeg
- ¾ teaspoon baking soda
- 2 teaspoons hot water

FOR COATING

- 1 cup granulated sugar
- ½ cup water
- 2 cups confectioners' sugar

MAKE THE COOKIES: Beat together butter and margarine in a large bowl with an electric mixer at medium speed until smooth and creamy. Beat in brown sugar, egg, and molasses. Whisk together 1½ cups flour, salt, and spices in a medium bowl, then beat into molasses mixture. Dissolve baking soda in hot water, then beat into batter. Beat in remaining 1½ cups flour until incorporated. Refrigerate dough, wrapped in plastic wrap, for at least 8 hours.

Put racks in upper and lower thirds of oven and preheat oven to 350°F. Butter two large baking sheets.

Roll level teaspoons of dough into balls and arrange about 1½ inches apart on buttered baking sheets. Bake, switching position of sheets halfway through baking, until puffed and just set in center, 10 to 14 minutes total. Transfer cookies to racks to cool.

MAKE THE COATING: Combine granulated sugar and water in a 1-quart saucepan and bring to a boil, stirring until sugar is dissolved. Cool syrup completely.

Transfer syrup to a shallow bowl. Place sheets of wax paper under racks of cookies. Dip cooled cookies one at time in syrup to coat and return to racks to drain. Let stand at room temperature for 2 hours.

Sift confectioners' sugar into a paper bag. Shake a few cookies at a time in bag to coat, then lightly brush off excess sugar with your fingers.

COOK'S NOTE

- The cookies keep in an airtight container at room temperature for up to 4 days.

Chocolate Sambuca Crinkle Cookies

MAKES ABOUT 2½ DOZEN COOKIES
ACTIVE TIME: 30 MINUTES ■ START TO FINISH: 3 HOURS (INCLUDES CHILLING)

■ The chocolate crinkle is a great-looking cookie that's been around for a long time. Coated with confectioners' sugar before baking, it cracks its sugar-coated top while in the oven. We love the kick that sambuca gives this version, from reader Katy Macmaster. ■

- 1¼ cups all-purpose flour
- 1 tablespoon baking powder
- ½ teaspoon salt
- 12 ounces good bittersweet chocolate (not unsweetened), chopped
- ½ stick (4 tablespoons) unsalted butter
- 2 large eggs
- ½ cup walnuts, coarsely chopped
- ½ cup sambuca or other anise-flavored liqueur
- 2 tablespoons granulated sugar
- 1 cup confectioners' sugar

Sift together flour, baking powder, and salt into a bowl.

Melt chocolate with butter in a metal bowl set over a saucepan of simmering water, stirring until smooth. Remove from heat.

Lightly whisk together eggs, walnuts, sambuca, and granulated sugar in a large bowl. Stir in flour mixture and chocolate (dough will be loose). Refrigerate, covered, until firm, about 2 hours.

Put racks in upper and lower thirds of oven and preheat oven to 350°F. Lightly butter two baking sheets.

Sift confectioners' sugar onto a plate. One by one, roll heaping tablespoons of dough into balls, roll in confectioners' sugar to coat generously, and arrange balls about 2 inches apart on buttered baking sheets.

Bake, switching position of sheets halfway through baking, until cookies are puffed and cracked but centers are still a bit soft, 10 to 12 minutes. Transfer to racks to cool.

COOK'S NOTE

- The cookies keep in an airtight container at room temperature for up to 4 days.

Truffle Cookies

MAKES ABOUT 6 DOZEN COOKIES
ACTIVE TIME: 30 MINUTES ■ START TO FINISH: 3 HOURS (INCLUDES CHILLING)

■ Too much chocolate? Never. This is the fudgiest, most intense brownie you've ever had, morphed into a cookie. We have Ann Bolger, of East Lansing, Michigan, to thank for the recipe. ■

MELTDOWN

Melting chocolate isn't difficult, as long as you have patience and gentle heat. If you're dealing with a thick hunk of chocolate, use a serrated knife to chip off chunks, then chop them with a chef's knife. The process may seem laborious, but smaller pieces melt more quickly and evenly.

When you're ready to start melting, make sure your utensils are perfectly dry—a single drop of water will sabotage the chocolate by making it "seize" and become a recalcitrant mess. The two most popular melting methods are described here.

MICROWAVING: Put the chocolate, chopped or broken into small pieces, in a microwave-safe bowl and zap it at 50 percent power. (We use an 800-watt oven.) For 2 to 4 ounces of semisweet, bittersweet, or unsweetened chocolate, begin checking after 2½ minutes; for 5 to 8 ounces, begin checking after 3 minutes. Don't be fooled by how the chocolate looks at this point: it will appear intact, but a single stir with a rubber spatula will reveal that it's on its way to a molten state. If, after stirring, you still see unmelted bits, zap it again for 10- to 15-second intervals (still at 50 percent power) and stir after each interval. For milk chocolate, which is slightly more temperamental than its darker cousins, shorten the initial time by 30 seconds and the intervals to 5 to 10 seconds. And don't forget that chocolate scorches easily; if at any point the bowl feels hot, let it stand for about 1 minute to see if the residual heat will finish the job (be sure to stir the chocolate occasionally).

DOUBLE-BOILER ARRANGEMENT ON THE STOVETOP: If you are improvising a double boiler with a metal bowl set over a saucepan of water, select a bowl that is wide enough so the part holding the chocolate will sit completely within the mouth of the pan. Put the chopped chocolate in the bowl or double-boiler top and set it over gently simmering water. Make sure the water in the bottom pan isn't touching the bowl or top pan, and check the water occasionally—it shouldn't go above a bare simmer. Stir the chocolate frequently until melted and smooth.

- 4 ounces unsweetened chocolate, chopped
- ¾ stick (6 tablespoons) unsalted butter, cut into small pieces
- 2 cups (12 ounces) semisweet chocolate chips
- ½ cup all-purpose flour
- 2 tablespoons unsweetened cocoa powder (not Dutch-process)
- ¼ teaspoon baking powder
- ½ teaspoon salt
- 1 cup sugar
- 3 large eggs
- 1½ teaspoons vanilla extract

Melt unsweetened chocolate, butter, and 1 cup chocolate chips in a 1-quart heavy saucepan over low heat, stirring occasionally. Cool.

Whisk together flour, cocoa, baking powder, and salt in a bowl.

Beat together sugar, eggs, and vanilla in a large bowl with an electric mixer at medium speed until pale and frothy, about 2 minutes. Mix in melted chocolate mixture, then mix in flour mixture at low speed until well combined. Stir in remaining 1 cup chocolate chips. Refrigerate, covered, until dough is firm, about 2 hours.

Put a rack in middle of oven and preheat oven to 350°F.

With dampened hands, roll heaping teaspoons of dough into 1-inch balls and arrange 2 inches apart on ungreased baking sheets. Bake in batches until puffed and set, 10 to 12 minutes per batch (cookies will still be soft in center).

Cool cookies on baking sheet on a rack for 10 minutes, then transfer to racks to cool completely.

COOK'S NOTE

- The cookies keep in an airtight container at room temperature for up to 4 days.

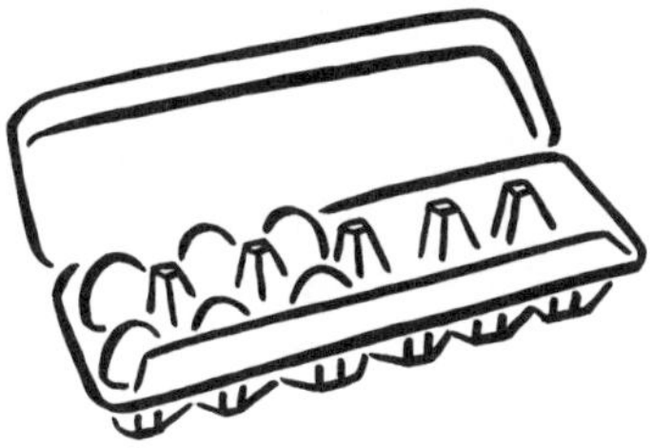

Mexican Tea Cakes

MAKES ABOUT 6 DOZEN COOKIES
ACTIVE TIME: 45 MINUTES ■ START TO FINISH: 8 HOURS (INCLUDES CHILLING)

■ Known by a variety of names, including Russian tea cakes, these exceptionally light yet very rich pecan cookies coated with powdered sugar are among our favorite holiday treats. We also love them during the heat of the summer, served with fresh berries or with a cup of tea in the middle of the afternoon. ■

- 2 sticks (½ pound) unsalted butter, softened
- 3 cups confectioners' sugar
- 1 teaspoon vanilla extract
- 2¼ cups all-purpose flour
- ¾ cup (3 ounces) very finely chopped pecans
- ¾ teaspoon salt

Beat together butter and ½ cup confectioners' sugar in a large bowl with an electric mixer at medium-high speed until pale and fluffy, about 4 minutes. Beat in vanilla. Add flour, pecans, and salt and mix at low speed until just combined. Refrigerate, covered, for at least 6 hours.

Put a rack in middle of oven and preheat oven to 375°F. Lightly butter two large baking sheets.

Let dough stand at room temperature until just pliable, about 15 minutes. Sift remaining 2½ cups confectioners' sugar into a large shallow bowl; set aside.

Roll level teaspoons of dough into ¾-inch balls and arrange about 2 inches apart on buttered baking sheets. Bake cookies in batches until bottoms are pale golden, 8 to 10 minutes per batch. Immediately transfer hot cookies, about 6 at a time, to confectioners' sugar, roll gently to coat well, and then transfer to racks to cool completely.

Roll cookies in confectioners' sugar again when cooled.

COOK'S NOTES

- The dough can be chilled for up to 2 days.
- The cookies keep in an airtight container at room temperature for up to 3 weeks.

Viennese Vanilla Crescents

MAKES ABOUT 8 DOZEN COOKIES
ACTIVE TIME: 1¾ HOURS ■ START TO FINISH: 4¾ HOURS (INCLUDES CHILLING) PLUS 1 DAY FOR VANILLA SUGAR

■ "From Vienna, city of music, laughter, and good food," wrote our longtime contributor Lillian Langseth-Christensen, "comes a cookie so delicate, so fragile, so meltingly good that it takes its place with the most famous of Vienna's justly famous pastries." She shared this recipe with us early on in *Gourmet*'s history. ■

- 3½ cups all-purpose flour
- ¼ cup confectioners' sugar
- ½ teaspoon salt
- 1 cup (5 ounces) skinned hazelnuts (see Tips, page 938)
- 3 sticks (¾ pound) cold unsalted butter, cut into tablespoons
- 2 cups Vanilla Confectioners' Sugar (recipe follows)

Pulse together flour, ¼ cup confectioners' sugar, salt, and hazelnuts in a food processor until nuts are finely ground. Add butter and pulse just until a dough forms. Turn dough out and form into a ball, then flatten into a disk and wrap in wax paper. Refrigerate for at least 2 hours.

Put a rack in middle of oven and preheat oven to 350°F.

Roll level tablespoons of dough into balls, then roll each one on a smooth surface into a 3-inch length with slightly tapered ends, rolling ends lightly to make them narrow. Bend lengths to form crescents and arrange about 1 inch apart on ungreased baking sheets.

Bake in batches until edges are pale golden, 10 to 15 minutes per batch.

While each batch of crescents is baking, sift enough vanilla confectioners' sugar onto a baking sheet with sides to cover bottom. Carefully transfer warm baked crescents to baking sheet and sprinkle with additional vanilla confectioners' sugar. Transfer cookies to racks to cool completely.

COOK'S NOTES

- The dough can be refrigerated for up to 1 day.
- The cookies keep, layered between sheets of wax or parchment paper, in an airtight container at room temperature for up to 5 days.

Vanilla Confectioners' Sugar

MAKES 2 CUPS
ACTIVE TIME: 5 MINUTES ■ START TO FINISH: 5 MINUTES PLUS 1 DAY TO ALLOW FLAVORS TO DEVELOP

■ This vanilla-scented sugar, terrific on Viennese Vanilla Crescents, can be used any time you want to enhance something with the delicate, enticing aroma and taste of vanilla. Try it sprinkled on fresh fruit or a simple cake. ■

- 2 cups confectioners' sugar
- 1 vanilla bean, halved lengthwise and chopped

Combine confectioners' sugar and vanilla bean in an airtight container and let stand, covered, for at least 24 hours. Sift before using.

COOK'S NOTE

- The sugar keeps indefinitely in an airtight container at room temperature.

Flourless Peanut Butter Cookies

MAKES ABOUT 4½ DOZEN COOKIES
ACTIVE TIME: 20 MINUTES ■ START TO FINISH: 1¼ HOURS

■ When this recipe came to us, we thought the absence of flour was an oversight. Nope. For the first time ever, the words *peanut butter* and *featherlight* seemed to go together, and if you don't believe us, one bite of these cookies will convince you. This is not the sort of peanut butter cookie to send off in a lunch box; it barely makes it from plate to palate, but its delicacy belies its rich, deep flavor. (If made with "natural-style" peanut butter, the cookies will be hard.) Amy Fritch, a reader from New York City, sent us the recipe. ■

- 1 cup creamy or chunky peanut butter
- 1 cup sugar
- 1 large egg, lightly beaten
- 1 teaspoon baking soda

Put a rack in middle of oven and preheat oven to 350°F. Lightly butter two large baking sheets.

Beat together peanut butter and sugar in a medium bowl with an electric mixer at medium speed until well combined, about 2 minutes. Beat in egg and baking soda until well combined.

Roll level teaspoons of dough into balls and arrange about 1 inch apart on buttered baking sheets. Flatten balls with tines of a fork, making a crosshatch pattern, to 1½-inch rounds.

Bake cookies in batches until puffed and pale golden, about 10 minutes per batch. Cool on baking sheets for 2 minutes, then transfer to racks to cool.

COOK'S NOTE

- The cookies keep in an airtight container at room temperature for up to 5 days.

Sesame Honey Lace Cookies

MAKES ABOUT 5 DOZEN COOKIES
ACTIVE TIME: 15 MINUTES ■ START TO FINISH: 1 HOUR

■ Brittle, fragile, and ultra-thin, these are part cookie, part confection, with the warm, toasty flavors of sesame and honey. They are a lovely way to end a Middle Eastern or Indian meal. ■

- 1 cup confectioners' sugar
- 3 tablespoons unsalted butter
- 3 tablespoons honey
- 2 tablespoons water
- 1 cup (6 ounces) sesame seeds
- ¼ cup all-purpose flour
- Pinch of salt

SPECIAL EQUIPMENT: parchment paper

Combine confectioners' sugar, butter, honey, and water in a 1- to 1½-quart heavy saucepan, bring to a boil over moderate heat, stirring, and boil for 1 minute. Remove pan from heat and stir in sesame seeds, flour, and salt until well combined. Cool dough to room temperature.

Put racks in upper and lower thirds of oven and preheat oven to 350°F. Line two large baking sheets with parchment paper.

Roll level ½-teaspoons of dough into balls and arrange about 1½ inches apart on lined baking sheets. Bake, switching position of sheets halfway through baking, until cookies are flat and golden, about 10 minutes. Slide cookies, on parchment, to racks to cool. Cool baking sheets and line with fresh parchment between batches.

COOK'S NOTE

- The cookies keep, layered between sheets of wax or parchment paper, in an airtight container at room temperature for up to 1 week.

Snowballs

MAKES ABOUT 2½ DOZEN COOKIES
ACTIVE TIME: 20 MINUTES ■ START TO FINISH: 1 HOUR

■ The macaroon, long a French specialty produced (especially during the 1700s) in convents, is a chewy cookie traditionally made of almond paste or ground almonds, or both, as well as sugar and egg whites. Sometimes coconut takes the place of almonds, as it does here. A surprise nugget of chocolate inside was inspired by a food editor's childhood devotion to Mounds bars. ■

- 2 cups (about 4 ounces) sweetened flaked coconut
- 1 cup (about 3 ounces) finely grated unsweetened coconut (see Sources)
- ⅔ cup granulated sugar
- ¼ teaspoon salt
- 2 large egg whites
- 2 teaspoons water
- About 30 (½-inch) squares good bittersweet chocolate (not unsweetened; cut from a 3½-ounce bar)
- About ½ cup confectioners' sugar for dusting

SPECIAL EQUIPMENT: parchment paper

Put a rack in middle of oven and preheat oven to 350°F. Line a large baking sheet with parchment.

Pulse sweetened and unsweetened coconut, granulated sugar, and salt together in a food processor until flaked coconut is finely chopped. Add whites and water and pulse until mixture is moistened and holds together when squeezed.

Roll level tablespoons of coconut mixture into balls with wet hands (you'll need to rinse your hands after every 3 or 4 balls). Make an indentation in center of each ball and insert a piece of chocolate, then pinch hole closed and reroll into a ball. Arrange balls about 1 inch apart on lined baking sheet.

Bake until bottoms are golden and balls are puffed but not colored, 13 to 15 minutes. Slide macaroons, on parchment, onto a rack to cool completely, then peel off paper. Dust macaroons lightly with confectioners' sugar just before serving.

COOK'S NOTE

- The macaroons keep in an airtight container at room temperature for up to 1 week.

Parisian Passover Coconut Macaroons

MAKES ABOUT 5 DOZEN COOKIES
ACTIVE TIME: 40 MINUTES ■ START TO FINISH: 1¼ HOURS

■ Some macaroons (such as the Snowballs on page 675) are wonderfully dense with coconut, but these, made with an Italian meringue, are ethereal, like coconut-flavored clouds. The recipe is from the cookbook author Faye Levy, who first tasted them at Sephardic bakeries in Paris. When baking these for Passover, dust the baking sheets with matzo cake meal; otherwise you can use flour. (For more about Italian meringue, see opposite page.) ■

Matzo cake meal for dusting
1¼ cups sugar
¾ cup water
3 large egg whites, at room temperature
3 cups (8 ounces) finely grated unsweetened coconut (see Sources)

SPECIAL EQUIPMENT: a candy thermometer; a stand mixer

Put a rack in middle of oven and preheat oven to 325°F. Grease two large baking sheets and dust with cake meal, knocking off excess.

Cook sugar and water in a small heavy saucepan over low heat, stirring, until sugar is dissolved. Boil syrup, without stirring, until it registers 238°F on thermometer.

Meanwhile, beat whites in stand mixer at low speed until stiff peaks form.

Beating constantly at high speed, gradually pour hot syrup in a thin stream down side of bowl into whites (be careful not to let syrup touch beaters when pouring, or it will spatter and harden). Continue to beat until meringue is cooled to room temperature. Stir in coconut.

Spoon rounded teaspoons of meringue into mounds about 1 inch apart on greased baking sheets. Shape mounds into pyramids with wet fingertips.

Bake macaroons in batches until just firm enough to be removed from baking sheet without losing their shape, about 12 minutes per batch. Carefully transfer to racks to cool. (Macaroons will firm as they cool.)

COOK'S NOTE

- The macaroons keep in an airtight container at room temperature for up to 1 week.

Chocolate Macaroons

MAKES ABOUT 4 DOZEN SANDWICH COOKIES
ACTIVE TIME: 1½ HOURS ■ START TO FINISH: 3½ HOURS (INCLUDES CHILLING)

■ The basis for this glorious, irresistible cookie—two airy almond macaroons sandwiched together with a rich ganache filling—is the chocolate and almond version from the luxurious Paris pastry shop Dalloyau, a favorite haunt of contributors Naomi Barry and Bettina McNulty. On one visit there they spied a billboard that read, *"Si je n'ai pas un chocolat avec mon café, je hurle,"* or "If I don't get a chocolate with my coffee, I scream." We find the sentiment enormously comforting. ■

FOR MACAROONS

1⅓ cups (7 ounces) skinned whole almonds
3½ cups confectioners' sugar
⅓ cup unsweetened Dutch-process cocoa powder
⅞ cup egg whites (from about 6 large eggs; see Cook's Note)

Pinch of salt
1 tablespoon granulated sugar

FOR GANACHE FILLING

½ cup heavy cream
2 teaspoons whole milk
2½ tablespoons unsweetened Dutch-process cocoa powder
4 ounces good bittersweet chocolate (not unsweetened), finely chopped
1 stick (8 tablespoons) unsalted butter, cut into ½-inch pieces

SPECIAL EQUIPMENT: parchment paper; a pastry bag fitted with a ¼-inch plain tip

MAKE THE MACAROONS: Put a rack in middle of oven and preheat oven to 400°F. Line two large baking sheets with parchment paper.

Pulse almonds with 2 cups confectioners' sugar in a food processor until finely ground (almost to a powder). Add cocoa and remaining 1½ cups confectioners' sugar and pulse until combined.

Beat egg whites with salt in a large bowl with an electric mixer at medium-high speed until they hold soft peaks. Add granulated sugar and beat until whites just hold stiff peaks. Gently but thoroughly fold in almond mixture in 3 batches (batter will be very soft).

Transfer batter to pastry bag and pipe 1-inch-wide mounds about 2 inches apart onto lined baking sheets. Bake macaroons in batches until tops are slightly cracked and appear dry but are still slightly soft to the touch, 8 to 10 minutes per batch. Transfer macaroons, still on parchment, to dampened kitchen towels and cool for 5 minutes, then peel from paper and cool completely on racks.

Italian Meringue

Beat hot sugar syrup into egg whites and you've got Italian meringue, the secret to Faye Levy's light-as-air macaroons (opposite page). The same process is used in making meringue buttercream (see pages 735, 743, and 746). It's not difficult to whip up a bowl of such glossy gorgeousness, but a certain amount of choreography is involved, because the egg whites and the sugar syrup must be at the right point at the same time: the whites at stiff peak stage when the syrup reaches 238°F on a candy thermometer. (You do have a little latitude, because the whites can sit while you wait for the syrup — but it doesn't work the other way around.) The worst of this patting-your-head-while-rubbing-your-stomach exercise can be overcome by using a stand mixer rather than a handheld one: you're free to keep an eye on both the boiling syrup and the egg whites while they are beating. Levy coordinates the process by starting to beat her whites on low speed rather than high, to give the syrup time to come up to temperature.

When combining the sugar syrup and the egg whites, the goal is to get the syrup into the whites, not onto the beaters, which will spatter it onto the sides of the bowl, where it will harden. The shape of the mixer bowl makes a difference too. We have two sizes of KitchenAid stand mixers in our test kitchens, but we prefer the smaller (4½-quart) one for this task; its sides are slightly flared, which gives you more room to maneuver. We cooked our syrup in a regular saucepan and poured it slowly down the side of the bowl, but if you have a saucepan with a spout, use it — you'll have even more control that way.

MEANWHILE, MAKE THE GANACHE FILLING: Bring cream and milk to a boil in a small heavy saucepan over moderate heat. Whisk in cocoa and remove from heat. Add chopped chocolate and butter and stir until smooth. Cool filling, then refrigerate, covered, until firm enough to hold its shape when spread, about 30 minutes.

Sandwich flat sides of macaroons together with ½ teaspoon filling per pair.

COOK'S NOTES

- While ⅞ cup egg whites may seem an odd measure, this amount gives the ideal texture and flavor. Measure the whites in a liquid-measuring cup.
- The macaroons can be made up to 1 day before you fill them. Refrigerate, layered between sheets of wax or parchment paper, in an airtight container.
- The filled macaroons keep, layered between sheets of wax or parchment paper in an airtight container and refrigerated, for up to 1 week.

Anise-Scented Fig and Date Swirls

MAKES ABOUT 4 DOZEN COOKIES
ACTIVE TIME: 1 HOUR ■ START TO FINISH: 6 HOURS (INCLUDES CHILLING)

■ As they bake, these pretty pinwheels fill your house with rich, warm scents. Figs and dates give a moist chewiness, and the anise elevates the cookies to something special. They're icebox cookies, which means that after you've formed the dough into a log, you can keep it in the refrigerator or the freezer and then slice and bake the cookies at your pleasure. ■

- 2 teaspoons anise seeds
- 1¾ cups all-purpose flour
- ¼ teaspoon baking powder
- ¼ teaspoon baking soda
- ¼ teaspoon salt
- 1 stick (8 tablespoons) unsalted butter, softened
- 4 ounces cream cheese, softened
- ½ cup plus 2 tablespoons granulated sugar
- 1 teaspoon vanilla extract
- 1 large egg yolk
- 1 cup (8 ounces) packed soft dried figs, stemmed and coarsely chopped
- 1 cup (7 ounces) packed pitted dates, coarsely chopped
- ⅓ cup water
- ¼ cup raw sugar, such as turbinado or Demerara

SPECIAL EQUIPMENT: an electric coffee/spice grinder

Finely grind anise seeds in coffee/spice grinder. Whisk together flour, anise, baking powder, baking soda, and salt in a bowl.

Beat together butter, cream cheese, and ½ cup granulated sugar in a large bowl with an electric mixer at medium speed until pale and fluffy, about 3 minutes. Beat in vanilla, then beat in yolk until well combined. Add flour mixture and mix at low speed until just combined.

Halve dough and form each half into a rectangle. Wrap each half in plastic wrap and refrigerate until firm, about 1 hour.

Meanwhile, to make the filling, combine figs, dates, water, and remaining 2 tablespoons granulated sugar in a blender or food processor and purée until almost smooth.

Roll out 1 piece of dough between two sheets of wax paper into a 9-by-7-inch rectangle. Remove top sheet of wax paper and drop half of fig mixture by spoonfuls onto dough, then gently spread in an even layer, leaving a ¼-inch border around edges. Starting with a long side and using wax paper as an aid, roll up dough jelly-roll style into a log. Roll log in raw sugar to coat completely and wrap in wax paper. Make another log in same manner and wrap in wax paper. Refrigerate logs until firm, at least 4 hours.

Put a rack in middle of oven and preheat oven to 350°F. Lightly butter two baking sheets.

Cut logs into ⅓-inch-thick slices and arrange slices about 2 inches apart on buttered baking sheets. Bake in batches until pale golden, 15 to 17 minutes per batch. Transfer cookies to racks to cool.

COOK'S NOTES

- The logs can be wrapped well with additional foil and refrigerated for up to 3 days or frozen for 2 months.
- The cookies keep, layered between sheets of wax or parchment paper, in an airtight container at room temperature for up to 1 week.

Pecan Sablés

MAKES ABOUT 2½ DOZEN COOKIES
ACTIVE TIME: 30 MINUTES ■ START TO FINISH: 2 HOURS (INCLUDES COOLING)

■ Pecans have a rich, buttery smoothness that is sublime with the texture of these cookies, which resemble shortbread. The name comes from the French word for "sand," which refers to the cookies' appealing crumbliness. To make them as good as they can be, use one of the European-style (higher-butterfat) butters, such as Keller's Plugrá or Land O' Lakes's Ultra Creamy (see page 780). Come November or December, if you can get your hands on some new-crop pecans from down South (see Sources), drop everything and put these together. ■

- ¾ cup (3 ounces) pecans, toasted (see Tips, page 938), plus about 32 pecan halves (3 ounces)
- ⅔ cup plus 2 tablespoons confectioners' sugar
- 1¼ cups all-purpose flour
- ½ teaspoon salt
- ¼ teaspoon baking powder
- 1 stick (8 tablespoons) unsalted butter, softened
- ½ teaspoon vanilla extract
- 1 large egg, separated

SPECIAL EQUIPMENT: a 2-inch round cookie cutter

Put a rack in middle of oven and preheat oven to 325°F. Butter two large baking sheets.

Pulse cooled toasted pecans with 2 tablespoons confectioners' sugar in a food processor until finely ground. Whisk together flour, salt, and baking powder in a bowl.

Beat together butter, remaining ⅔ cup confectioners' sugar, and vanilla in a large bowl with an electric mixer at high speed until pale and fluffy, about 3 minutes. Add egg yolk and beat well. Add flour and ground pecan mixtures and mix at low speed until just combined, 30 seconds to 1 minute. (Dough will be crumbly but will hold together when squeezed.)

Halve dough. Roll out one half between two sheets of wax paper to ¼ inch thick (about a 9-inch round). Cut out as many rounds as possible with cookie cutter and arrange about 2 inches apart on buttered baking sheets, reserving scraps. Roll out and cut remaining dough in same manner. Gather scraps, reroll, and cut in same manner.

Beat egg white until frothy and brush tops of rounds lightly with egg white. Put a pecan half on top of each round, then brush pecans lightly with egg white.

Bake cookies in batches until tops are pale golden, 15 to 20 minutes per batch. Cool cookies on sheets on racks for 2 minutes, then transfer to racks to cool completely.

COOK'S NOTE

■ The cookies keep in an airtight container at room temperature for up to 1 week.

Swedish Ginger Thins

MAKES ABOUT 13 DOZEN COOKIES
ACTIVE TIME: 2¼ HOURS ■ START TO FINISH: 4¼ HOURS (INCLUDES CHILLING)

■ These are the most refined Christmas cookies you'll ever meet. Thin, crisp, and elegant, they are ideal for a dinner party or the boss's present. And they are addictive as well, tending to disappear before your very eyes. Luckily, the dough is exceptionally easy to work with for such a delicate cookie, so making more isn't a hardship. The recipe came to us from reader Joyce Shinn, of Poway, California. ■

- ½ cup very cold heavy cream
- 1 stick (8 tablespoons) unsalted butter, softened
- 1 cup sugar
- ½ cup dark corn syrup
- 3 cups all-purpose flour
- 1½ teaspoons baking soda
- 1½ teaspoons ground cinnamon
- 1½ teaspoons ground ginger
- 1½ teaspoons ground cloves

OPTIONAL GARNISH: sliced almonds

SPECIAL EQUIPMENT: a pastry cloth; a rolling pin cover (see Sources); assorted 2- to 3-inch cookie cutters

Beat cream in a medium bowl with an electric mixer at medium speed until it just holds stiff peaks.

Beat butter and sugar in a large bowl at medium speed until pale and fluffy. Beat in corn syrup and whipped cream on low speed until cream is just incorporated. Sift in flour, baking soda, and spices and beat until well combined. Form dough into a disk, wrap in plastic wrap, and refrigerate until firm, at least 2 hours.

Put racks in upper and lower thirds of oven and preheat oven to 400°F.

Cut dough into quarters. Work with one quarter at a time, keeping remaining dough covered and refrigerated. Roll out dough as thin as possible (less than 1/8 inch thick and about 14 inches across) on lightly floured pastry cloth with a rolling pin fitted with cover. Cut out cookies with cutters and place about 1/2 inch apart on ungreased baking sheets, then top each with an almond slice, if desired. Reroll scraps and cut out more cookies.

Bake cookies in batches, switching position of sheets halfway through baking, until cookies puff and then collapse slightly, about 6 minutes per batch. Cool cookies on sheets for 1 minute, then transfer to racks to cool completely.

COOK'S NOTE

- The cookies keep in an airtight container at room temperature for up to 4 days.

Gingerbread Snowflakes

MAKES ABOUT 4 DOZEN COOKIES
ACTIVE TIME: 1½ HOURS ■ START TO FINISH: 2¼ HOURS (INCLUDES MAKING ICING)

■ Dark, crisp, and spicy, these are fabulous all-purpose Christmas cutout cookies that perfume the house while in the oven. Poke a hole in each cookie with a drinking straw before baking, then turn the children loose with decorating icing, and the tree will be trimmed in no time flat. ■

- 2/3 cup molasses (not robust or blackstrap)
- 2/3 cup packed dark brown sugar
- 1 tablespoon ground ginger
- 1½ teaspoons ground cinnamon
- ½ teaspoon ground allspice
- ½ teaspoon ground cloves
- 2 teaspoons baking soda
- 2 sticks (½ pound) unsalted butter, cut into tablespoons
- 1 large egg, lightly beaten
- ½ teaspoon salt
- 3¾–4 cups all-purpose flour
- Decorating Icing (recipe follows)

SPECIAL EQUIPMENT: assorted 2- to 3-inch cookie cutters (preferably snowflake-shaped; see Sources); an offset metal spatula; a pastry bag fitted with a 1/8- to ¼-inch plain tip (optional)

Put racks in upper and lower thirds of oven and preheat oven to 325°F. Butter two large baking sheets.

Combine molasses, brown sugar, and spices in a 4- to 5-quart heavy saucepan and bring to a boil over moderate heat, stirring occasionally. Remove from heat. Stir in baking soda (mixture will foam up), then stir in butter 3 pieces at a time, letting each addition melt before adding next. Add egg and stir until combined, then stir in salt and 3¾ cups flour.

Transfer dough to a lightly floured surface and knead, dusting with as much of remaining ¼ cup flour as needed to prevent sticking, until soft and easy to handle, 30 seconds to 1 minute. Halve dough, then wrap one half in plastic wrap and keep at room temperature.

Roll out remaining dough on lightly floured surface with a lightly floured rolling pin into a 14-inch round. Cut out as many cookies as possible with cutters and carefully transfer, preferably with an offset spatula, to buttered baking sheets, arranging them about 1 inch apart.

Bake cookies, switching position of sheets halfway through baking, until edges are slightly darker, 10 to 12 minutes (watch carefully toward end of baking, as cookies burn easily). Transfer to racks to cool completely. Make more cookies with remaining dough and scraps (reroll once).

Put icing in pastry bag, if using, and pipe decoratively onto cookies, or spread icing on cookies. Let stand until icing is set.

COOK'S NOTE

- The cookies keep in an airtight container at room temperature for up to 3 weeks.

Decorating Icing

MAKES ABOUT 3 CUPS
ACTIVE TIME: 10 MINUTES ■ START TO FINISH: 10 MINUTES

■ Egg whites act as a stabilizer in this icing, so it hardens on the decorated cookies. Because the whites are not cooked, we use powdered egg whites, such as Just Whites, which are available in the baking section of most supermarkets. ■

- 1 (1-pound) box confectioners' sugar
- 4 teaspoons powdered egg whites (not reconstituted)
- 1/3 cup water
- 1 tablespoon fresh lemon juice
- 1 teaspoon vanilla extract
- Food coloring (optional)

Beat together all ingredients except food coloring in a large bowl with an electric mixer at medium speed until just combined, about 1 minute. Increase speed to high and beat icing, occasionally scraping down sides of bowl, until it holds stiff peaks, about 3 minutes in a stand mixer, 4 to 5 minutes with a handheld mixer. Beat in food coloring, if using. If you plan to spread rather than pipe icing on cookies, stir in more water, 1 teaspoon at a time, to thin to desired consistency.

Stained Glass Teardrops

MAKES ABOUT 4 DOZEN COOKIES
ACTIVE TIME: 45 MINUTES ■ START TO FINISH: 3¼ HOURS (INCLUDES CHILLING)

■ The technique of crushing hard candy, sprinkling it into the center of cutout cookies, and then letting it melt during baking creates a stunning result worthy of Louis Comfort Tiffany—the cookies make great light-catching Christmas tree ornaments that are almost too pretty to eat. You can taste the "stained glass," so be sure to use good hard candy, either all one color or assorted. A nonstick baking sheet liner (see page 665) is a must if you want to make this recipe successfully. If you want to simplify and forgo the candy (and the baking sheet liner), you can make plain cutout cookies and decorate them as you wish. ■

- 2½ cups all-purpose flour
- 3/4 teaspoon salt
- 1½ sticks (12 tablespoons) unsalted butter, softened
- 3/4 cup sugar
- 1 large egg
- 1 teaspoon vanilla extract
- 6–8 ounces assorted fruit-flavored hard candies, such as sour balls

SPECIAL EQUIPMENT: a nonstick baking sheet liner, such as a Silpat; a 2- to 3-inch-wide teardrop-shaped cookie cutter; a 1- to 2-inch-wide teardrop-shaped cookie cutter (see Sources)

Whisk together flour and salt in a small bowl.

Beat together butter and sugar in a large bowl with an electric mixer at medium-high speed until pale and fluffy, about 3 minutes in a stand mixer (preferably fitted with paddle attachment) or 6 minutes with a handheld mixer. Beat in egg and vanilla. Add flour mixture and mix at low speed until just combined.

Divide dough into thirds, form into 5-inch disks, and wrap each disk in plastic wrap. Refrigerate until firm, at least 2 hours.

Separate candies by color and put in small heavy-duty sealable plastic bags. Seal bags, forcing out air, and coarsely crush candies by wrapping each bag in a kitchen towel and pounding it with a rolling pin.

Put a rack in middle of oven and preheat oven to 350°F. Line a large baking sheet with nonstick liner.

Roll out 1 piece of dough (keep remaining dough refrigerated) on a well-floured surface with floured rolling pin into a 9-inch round. Cut out as many cookies as possible with large cutter and transfer to lined baking sheet, arranging them about 1 inch apart. Cut out centers from cookies with small cutter and add to scraps. Spoon ½ to 1 teaspoon crushed candy, depending on size of cutout, into center of each cookie. If you want to use cookies as tree ornaments, make a hole with a drinking straw in top of each for hanging. Gather scraps and chill until firm enough to reroll, 10 to 15 minutes.

Bake cookies until edges are golden, 10 to 12 minutes. Cool cookies completely on baking sheet on a rack, then transfer to a plate or an airtight container. Make more cookies with remaining dough and scraps (reroll scraps only once) in same manner on cooled baking sheet.

COOK'S NOTES

- The dough can be refrigerated for up to 3 days.
- If the dough becomes too soft to roll out at any point, wrap in plastic wrap again and refrigerate until firm.
- The cookies keep, layered between sheets of wax or parchment paper, in an airtight container at room temperature for up to 1 week.

Date Walnut Rugelach

MAKES 4 DOZEN COOKIES
ACTIVE TIME: 1 HOUR ■ START TO FINISH: 3 HOURS (INCLUDES CHILLING)

■ Rugelach are an Eastern European Jewish tradition, especially at Hanukkah, when the cookies are a symbol of the cheesecakes or pancakes that Judith served to Holofernes, one of Nebuchadnezzar's generals. After the feasting, she took advantage of his drunken stupor and beheaded him, thus saving her besieged town. There are all sorts of variations on the theme; here, dates and nuts become almost jamlike in consistency when encased in the rich cream cheese dough. ■

FOR DOUGH

- 2 sticks (1/2 pound) cold unsalted butter, cut into tablespoons
- 1 (8-ounce) package cold cream cheese, quartered
- 1/4 cup sugar
- 3/4 teaspoon salt
- 2 cups all-purpose flour

FOR FILLING

- 8 ounces (1 1/3 cups) pitted dates, finely chopped
- 1/2 cup walnuts, finely chopped
- 1/2 cup sugar
- 1 teaspoon ground cinnamon
- 1/4 teaspoon vanilla extract
- 1/4 cup apricot jam, warmed, for brushing

MAKE THE DOUGH: Combine butter, cream cheese, sugar, salt, and flour in a food processor and pulse just until a dough forms. Do not overwork dough, or pastry will be tough.

Turn dough out onto a lightly floured surface and divide into 6 portions. With heel of your hand, smear each portion once or twice in a forward motion across work surface to help distribute fat. Form each portion into a ball, then flatten each ball into a 4-inch disk and wrap in plastic wrap. Refrigerate until firm, at least 1 hour.

MAKE THE FILLING: Toss together dates, walnuts, sugar, cinnamon, and vanilla in a bowl with your hands until well combined.

FORM AND BAKE THE RUGELACH: Put racks in upper and lower thirds of oven and preheat oven to 350°F.

Roll out 1 disk of dough (keep the others refrigerated) on a lightly floured surface with a floured rolling pin into an 8-inch round. Cut into 8 wedges, but keep round intact. Brush with 2 teaspoons jam. Sprinkle 1/3 cup filling in a ring around outer part of round, leaving a 1-inch border around edge, and gently press filling into dough. Working with 1 wedge at a time, fold outer edge of pastry over filling and roll up jelly-roll style, then fold sides under pastry to enclose filling. Transfer rugelach, pointed ends down, to an ungreased baking sheet, arranging them 1 inch apart, and make more rugelach in same manner.

Bake rugelach in batches, switching position of sheets halfway through baking, until golden, 15 to 20 minutes per batch. Transfer to racks to cool completely.

COOK'S NOTES

- The dough can be refrigerated for up to 1 day.
- The rugelach keep in an airtight container at room temperature for up to 3 days.

Langues de Chat

MAKES ABOUT 2 1/2 DOZEN COOKIES
ACTIVE TIME: 30 MINUTES ■ START TO FINISH: 1 HOUR

■ These long, crisp wafers, named for their resemblance to cats' tongues, are a favorite of Alice Waters, the cookbook author and chef-owner of Berkeley's Chez Panisse restaurant. Terrific on their own, the cookies also make a great accompaniment to a fruit dessert. Waters uses French orange-flower water (available at many supermarkets, or see Sources), distilled from the blossoms of bitter Seville oranges, because it has a milder, more delicate flavor than Middle Eastern brands do. ■

- 1 stick (8 tablespoons) unsalted butter, softened
- ½ cup sugar, plus additional for sprinkling
- 1 teaspoon orange-flower water
- ¼ teaspoon vanilla extract
- Pinch of salt
- 3 large egg whites, at room temperature
- ⅔ cup all-purpose flour

SPECIAL EQUIPMENT: a nonstick baking sheet liner, such as a Silpat (see page 665), or parchment paper; a pastry bag fitted with a ⅜-inch plain tip

Put a rack in middle of oven and preheat oven to 325°F. Line a large baking sheet with nonstick liner or parchment paper. If using parchment, anchor it to baking sheet by buttering edges of sheet before smoothing parchment over it.

Beat together butter and sugar in a medium bowl with an electric mixer at medium speed until pale and fluffy. Beat in orange-flower water, vanilla, and salt. Beat in whites on low speed (batter will look separated). Add flour in 3 batches, beating just until well combined; do not overmix.

Put batter in pastry bag and pipe out 6-inch-long strips (about ⅓ inch wide) 1½ inches apart (batter will spread during baking) on lined baking sheet, piping slightly more batter at each end. Bake until golden brown, 15 to 20 minutes. (Turn baking sheet if cookies are browning unevenly.) Immediately sprinkle hot cookies lightly with sugar and transfer to a rack to cool completely. Make more cookies in same manner, cooling baking sheet between batches.

COOK'S NOTE

- The cookies keep in an airtight container at room temperature for up to 1 week.

Pignoli Cookies

MAKES ABOUT 3½ DOZEN COOKIES
ACTIVE TIME: 40 MINUTES ■ START TO FINISH: 2 HOURS (INCLUDES COOLING)

■ Crisp on the outside and chewy within, pignoli cookies get their texture from pine nuts, almond paste, and egg whites. These cookies are extremely popular in Italy, but feel free to go global—try them after a Spanish, Mexican, or Middle Eastern meal, since those cuisines all use pine nuts as well. For this recipe, it's important to use canned almond paste (available in specialty foods shops and some supermarkets, or see Sources); the type sold in tubes is too crumbly and won't give the cookies the right consistency. And be sure to pick up almond paste, not marzipan, which is too sweet. ■

- 2 (8-ounce) cans almond paste (not marzipan), coarsely crumbled
- 1½ cups confectioners' sugar
- ½ teaspoon salt
- 2 large egg whites
- 2 tablespoons mild honey
- 1 cup (4½ ounces) pine nuts

SPECIAL EQUIPMENT: parchment paper; a stand mixer; a large pastry bag fitted with ½-inch plain tip (optional)

Put racks in upper and lower thirds of oven and preheat oven to 350°F. Line two baking sheets with parchment paper.

Pulse almond paste in a food processor until broken up into small bits. Add confectioners' sugar and salt and pulse until finely ground, about 1 minute.

Transfer almond mixture to bowl of mixer, add egg whites and honey, and beat at medium-high speed until smooth, about 5 minutes (batter will be very thick).

Spoon half of batter into pastry bag, if using, or a bowl, keeping remaining batter covered with a dampened paper towel. Pipe (or spoon) 1½-inch rounds about 1 inch apart onto lined baking sheets. Gently press half of pine nuts into tops of cookies.

Bake cookies, switching position of sheets halfway through baking, until golden, 12 to 15 minutes total. Slide cookies, on parchment, onto racks to cool completely. Make more cookies with remaining batter and pine nuts on cooled lined baking sheets.

When cookies are cool, peel off parchment.

COOK'S NOTE

- The cookies keep, layered between sheets of wax or parchment paper, in an airtight container at room temperature for up to 1 week.

Meringue Kisses

MAKES ABOUT 9 DOZEN KISSES
ACTIVE TIME: 1 HOUR ■ START TO FINISH: 4½ HOURS (INCLUDES COOLING)

■ These sweet, crisp meringues dissolve in the mouth like cotton candy. They are especially delicious with the Passion Fruit Fool on page 804. ■

- 8 large egg whites
- ⅛ teaspoon salt
- 2 cups superfine sugar

SPECIAL EQUIPMENT: parchment paper; a large pastry bag fitted with a ¼-inch plain tip

Put racks in upper and lower thirds of oven and preheat oven to 175°F. Line two large baking sheets with parchment paper.

Beat whites with salt in bowl of a stand mixer at high speed until they just hold stiff peaks (or make meringue in 2 batches with a handheld mixer). Gradually add sugar, beating at high speed until whites hold stiff, glossy peaks.

Spoon half of meringue into pastry bag and pipe 1-inch-wide kisses about ½ inch apart onto one baking sheet. Spoon remaining meringue into pastry bag and pipe more kisses onto second sheet in same manner. (All kisses will fit on two baking sheets.)

Bake meringues until crisp but still white, about 2 hours.

Turn off oven and cool meringues in oven for 1 hour, then cool completely on baking sheets on a rack.

COOK'S NOTE

■ The meringues keep in an airtight container at room temperature for up to 3 days.

Spritz Cookies

MAKES ABOUT 6 DOZEN COOKIES
ACTIVE TIME: 45 MINUTES ■ START TO FINISH: 1 HOUR

■ The word *spritz* comes from the German verb *spritzen,* which means "to squirt." These rich, almost-nothing-but-butter cookies are extruded through a cookie press to make all the traditional shapes: the letter S, bows, circles, ribbons. They aren't what we usually think of as frontier food, but this recipe is adapted from one by our contributor Carrie Young, who grew up on the North Dakota prairie. During the holidays, while her mother was waiting for the coal- and wood-fired oven to get hot enough to bake twelve loaves of bread at once, Carrie would bake batches of these cookies. If you don't have a cookie press, you can form this dough into balls and then use a fork to flatten and imprint them (see Cook's Note). ■

- 3½ cups all-purpose flour
- ½ teaspoon baking powder
- Rounded ½ teaspoon salt
- 3 sticks (¾ pound) unsalted butter, softened
- 1 cup sugar
- 1½ teaspoons vanilla extract
- ½ teaspoon almond extract
- 1 large egg, lightly beaten

SPECIAL EQUIPMENT: a cookie press fitted with a star, bow, circle, or ribbon plate (see Sources)

Put a rack in middle of oven and preheat oven to 350°F.

Sift together flour, baking powder, and salt.

Beat together butter, sugar, and extracts in a large bowl with an electric mixer at medium-high speed until pale and fluffy, about 3 minutes. Add egg and beat well. Add flour mixture and mix at low speed until just combined.

Quarter dough. Put 1 piece into cookie press and, holding press slightly above an ungreased baking sheet, squeeze out dough to form cookies (follow manufacturer's instructions), spacing them about 3 inches apart. Form more cookies on additional baking sheets with remaining dough in same manner.

Bake cookies in batches until edges are golden, 10 to 15 minutes per batch. Transfer to racks to cool.

COOK'S NOTES

■ If you don't have a cookie press, you can form the dough into 1½-inch balls, then flatten them to ⅓ to ½ inch thick on the baking sheets with the back of a fork, making a crosshatch design.

■ The cookies keep in an airtight container at room temperature for up to 3 weeks.

Cranberry Pistachio Biscotti

MAKES ABOUT 4 DOZEN COOKIES
ACTIVE TIME: 20 MINUTES ■ START TO FINISH: 2 HOURS

■ The word *biscotti* comes from a verb meaning "to cook twice," which refers to the way these cookies are made: first the dough is formed into a log and baked, then it's cut into slices and baked again until golden, crisp, and perfect for dipping into coffee or Vin Santo. Italian in origin, biscotti have become very popular in the United States. Perhaps it's the ultra-crunchy texture, or the fact that they are relatively low in fat compared to many American-style cookies. Here the sweetness of the pistachios and the tartness of the cranberries are absolutely great together. This recipe is adapted from one by the Italian baking expert Carol Field. ■

- 1⅓ cups (4 ounces) dried cranberries
- 2½ cups unbleached all-purpose flour
- 1 cup sugar
- ½ teaspoon baking soda
- ½ teaspoon baking powder
- ½ teaspoon salt
- 3 large eggs
- 1 teaspoon vanilla extract
- 1 cup (5 ounces) shelled salted natural pistachios (not dyed red)
- 1 large egg beaten with 1 teaspoon water, for egg wash

Soak cranberries in boiling water to cover in a small bowl until softened, about 10 minutes. Drain, then pat dry with paper towels.

Put a rack in middle of oven and preheat oven to 325°F. Butter and flour a large baking sheet, knocking off excess flour.

Whisk together flour, sugar, baking soda, baking powder, and salt in a large bowl. Add eggs and vanilla and beat with an electric mixer at medium speed just until a dough forms. Add cranberries and pistachios and mix at low speed.

Turn dough out onto a well-floured surface and knead several times. Halve dough. Using floured hands, form each half into a slightly flattened 13-by-2-inch log on baking sheet, spacing logs about 3 inches apart. Brush logs with egg wash.

Bake until golden, 25 to 30 minutes. Cool logs on baking sheet on a rack for 10 minutes. (Leave oven on.)

Transfer logs to a cutting board. With a serrated knife, cut diagonally into ½-inch-thick slices. Arrange slices cut sides down in one layer on baking sheet (it's fine if slices touch each other). Bake, turning once, until golden and crisp, 20 to 25 minutes. Transfer biscotti to racks to cool.

COOK'S NOTE

■ The biscotti keep in an airtight container at room temperature for up to 1 week.

Double Chocolate–Walnut Biscotti

MAKES ABOUT 2½ DOZEN COOKIES
ACTIVE TIME: 40 MINUTES ■ START TO FINISH: 2 HOURS

■ Plenty of deep, rich chocolate flavor makes these biscotti the perfect complement to a dessert that is slightly on the austere side—poached pears, for instance. ■

- 2 cups all-purpose flour
- ½ cup unsweetened cocoa powder
- 1 teaspoon baking soda
- 1 teaspoon salt
- ¾ stick (6 tablespoons) unsalted butter, softened
- 1 cup granulated sugar
- 2 large eggs
- 1 cup (3 ounces) walnuts, chopped
- ¾ cup semisweet chocolate chips
- 1 tablespoon confectioners' sugar

Put a rack in middle of oven and preheat oven to 350°F. Butter and flour a large baking sheet, knocking off excess flour.

Whisk together flour, cocoa, baking soda, and salt in a bowl. Beat together butter and granulated sugar in a large bowl with an electric mixer at high speed until combined, about 30 seconds. Add eggs and beat until well combined. Stir in flour mixture; dough will be stiff. Stir in walnuts and chocolate chips.

Halve dough. With floured hands, form dough into 2 slightly flattened 12-by-2-inch logs on baking sheet, about 3 inches apart. Sprinkle with confectioners' sugar.

Bake logs until slightly firm to the touch, about 35 minutes. Cool on baking sheet on a rack for 5 minutes. (Leave oven on.)

Transfer logs to a cutting board. With a serrated knife, cut diagonally into ¾-inch-thick slices. Arrange biscotti cut sides down on baking sheet. Bake until crisp, about 10 minutes. Transfer to racks to cool.

COOK'S NOTE

- The biscotti keep in an airtight container at room temperature for up to 1 week.

Almond Apricot Biscotti

MAKES ABOUT 4½ DOZEN COOKIES
ACTIVE TIME: 45 MINUTES ■ START TO FINISH: 2 HOURS

■ These out-of-the-ordinary biscotti are like cookies in consistency, much tenderer than the traditional crumbly Italian version. We prefer California dried apricots here (see Sources): their tangy, strong, unmistakable flavor is miles better than the generic fruity sweetness of apricots from Turkey. ■

- 2 cups all-purpose flour
- ¾ cup sugar
- 1½ teaspoons baking powder
- ½ teaspoon salt
- ½ stick (4 tablespoons) cold unsalted butter, cut into small pieces
- 1 large egg, lightly beaten
- ⅓ cup whole milk
- ½ teaspoon vanilla extract
- ¼ teaspoon almond extract
- 1 cup (5½ ounces) whole almonds with skins, toasted (see Tips, page 938)
- 1 cup (6 ounces) dried apricots, quartered
- 1 large egg yolk beaten with 1 tablespoon water, for egg wash

SPECIAL EQUIPMENT: parchment paper

Put a rack in middle of oven and preheat oven to 350°F. Line a baking sheet with parchment paper.

Whisk together flour, sugar, baking powder, and salt in a large bowl. Blend in butter with a pastry blender or your fingertips until mixture resembles coarse meal. Add egg, milk, and extracts, stirring with a fork until a soft dough forms. Knead in almonds.

Divide dough between two sheets of wax paper and shape each portion into a 5-inch disk. Put half of apricots in center of 1 disk and fold dough over to enclose them (use wax paper as an aid if necessary), then transfer to lined baking sheet; discard wax paper. Using wet hands, form dough into a 14-by-2½-inch log on one side of baking sheet. Make another log with remaining dough and apricots, placing it about 4 inches from first log.

Brush logs with egg wash. Bake until pale golden and firm, about 20 minutes. Cool on baking sheet on a rack for 20 minutes. Put a rack in upper third of oven and reduce oven temperature to 300°F.

Using two wide metal spatulas, carefully transfer baked logs to a cutting board. Cut logs diagonally into ½-inch-thick slices with a large heavy knife.

Line baking sheet with a clean sheet of parchment. Stand slices ½ inch apart on baking sheet and bake until dry, about 30 minutes (biscotti will harden as they cool). Transfer to racks to cool.

COOK'S NOTES

- To make smaller biscotti (and more of them), divide the dough into thirds and form into 3 logs, using one third of apricots for each.
- The biscotti keep, layered between sheets of wax or parchment paper, in an airtight container at room temperature for up to 2 weeks.

Madeleines

MAKES ABOUT 3 DOZEN COOKIES
ACTIVE TIME: 20 MINUTES ■ START TO FINISH: 40 MINUTES

■ This legendary cookie is really more like a tender, buttery, delicately flavored little cake. Madeleines are always baked in shell-shaped molds, and when they are turned out and served warm with a dusting of confectioners' sugar, your dinner guests will greet them with rapture. ■

1½ sticks (12 tablespoons) unsalted butter, melted and cooled, plus additional for brushing molds
1¼ cups sifted cake flour (not self-rising; sift before measuring)
½ teaspoon baking powder
¼ teaspoon salt
3 large eggs
1 teaspoon vanilla extract
⅔ cup granulated sugar
2 teaspoons finely grated lemon zest
Confectioners' sugar for dusting

SPECIAL EQUIPMENT: three madeleine pans with twelve 2-tablespoon molds each (see Sources)

Put racks in upper and lower thirds of oven and preheat oven to 350°F. Brush molds with melted butter.

Sift together flour, baking powder, and salt into a bowl. Set sifter aside.

Beat eggs in a large bowl with an electric mixer at high speed until light and foamy, about 30 seconds with a stand mixer, 2 minutes with a handheld mixer. Beat in vanilla. Gradually add granulated sugar, beating at high speed, then continue to beat until mixture is tripled in volume, about 3 minutes with stand mixer, 5 minutes with handheld mixer.

Sift flour mixture over egg in 3 to 5 batches, folding in each batch until just combined. Fold in zest and remaining 12 tablespoons (¾ cup) melted butter.

Spoon a rounded tablespoon of batter into each mold, filling it about two-thirds full. Bake (with 2 pans on one rack), switching position of pans halfway through baking, until golden around edges and a wooden pick or skewer inserted in centers comes out clean, 10 to 12 minutes total.

Invert madeleines onto a rack and dust scalloped sides with confectioners' sugar.

COOK'S NOTE

■ This batter is best baked as soon as it is made, but if you don't have three pans, you can bake the madeleines in batches.

Shortbread

MAKES 8 COOKIES
ACTIVE TIME: 10 MINUTES ■ START TO FINISH: 1 HOUR

■ In Scotland, shortbread is traditionally made in the form of a large round cake that is notched, some say, to symbolize the sun's rays. We like to serve it in smaller pieces, but it still shines a pale gold. Our crumbly, buttery shortbread cookies are rich in flavor and simple to make—and simpler still to enjoy, as a snack with a glass of iced tea, for dessert with ice cream, tucked into a picnic basket, or stashed in a cookie tin. Try jazzing them up with chopped toasted nuts—pecans, hazelnuts, or almonds, for instance. And because shortbread is all about the butter (there is just enough sugar and salt to enhance its flavor), use your favorite fine brand. (For more about butter, see page 780.) ■

1 stick (8 tablespoons) unsalted butter, softened
¼ cup superfine sugar
½ teaspoon vanilla extract
⅛ teaspoon salt
1 cup all-purpose flour
½ cup chopped toasted nuts (optional; see Tips, page 938)

Put a rack in middle of oven and preheat oven to 375°F.

Blend together butter, sugar, vanilla, and salt in a bowl with a fork until well combined. Sift flour over butter mixture and blend with fork until a soft dough forms.

Transfer dough to an ungreased baking sheet. With floured fingertips, pat into a 9-by-4½-inch rectangle. Crimp edges decoratively with tines of a fork and prick dough all over. Score dough crosswise with the back of a knife into 8 pieces. Sprinkle with nuts, if using, and press them gently into dough with your fingertips.

Bake shortbread until edges are golden, about 15 minutes. Cool on baking sheet on a rack for 10 minutes, then cut into slices (while still warm) with a sharp knife. Transfer to rack to cool completely.

COOK'S NOTE

■ The shortbread keeps in an airtight container at room temperature for up to 1 week.

Dark Chocolate Shortbread

MAKES 16 COOKIES
ACTIVE TIME: 15 MINUTES ■ START TO FINISH: 1 HOUR

■ Shortbread is a great cookie on its own, but for chocolate lovers, it's made even better by the addition of cocoa powder. Try pairing this with a vintage port after dinner. ■

- 1 stick (8 tablespoons) unsalted butter, softened
- 1/4 cup superfine sugar
- 1/2 teaspoon vanilla extract
- 1/8 teaspoon salt
- 3/4 cup all-purpose flour
- 1/4 cup unsweetened Dutch-process cocoa powder

Blend butter, sugar, vanilla, and salt in a bowl with a fork until well combined. Sift flour and cocoa over butter mixture and blend with fork just until a soft dough forms.

Divide dough in half. With floured fingertips, pat dough into 6- to 6½-inch rounds on an ungreased large baking sheet. Refrigerate, uncovered, until firm, about 30 minutes.

Put a rack in middle of oven and preheat oven to 375°F.

Prick dough all over with fork. Bake until centers are dry to the touch and edges are slightly darker, about 15 minutes. Cool on baking sheet on a rack for 10 minutes, then cut each shortbread into 8 wedges (while still warm) with a large heavy knife. Transfer to rack to cool completely.

COOK'S NOTE

■ The shortbread keeps, layered between sheets of wax or parchment paper, in an airtight container at room temperature for up to 1 week.

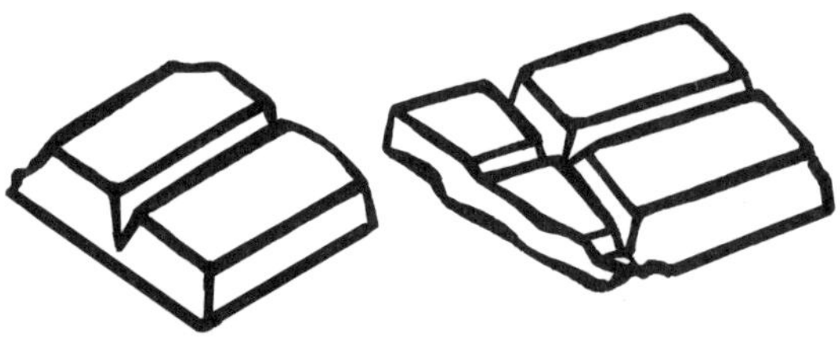

Bars

Katharine Hepburn's Brownies

MAKES 16 BROWNIES
ACTIVE TIME: 25 MINUTES ■ START TO FINISH: 1¾ HOURS

■ "There are as many brownie recipes as there are flowers in the meadow," the late novelist and food writer Laurie Colwin pointed out. Her favorite came from a friend who got it from a magazine article about Katharine Hepburn. It was, apparently, Hepburn's family's recipe, and it results in brownies that are on the fudgy side and a little slumped. "You can eat them out of the pan," Colwin admitted, "but it is so much nicer to pile them on a fancy plate. . . . If you want to smarten up your act you can put a square of brownie on a plate with a little blob of crème fraîche and a scattering of shaved chocolate." ■

- 1 stick (8 tablespoons) unsalted butter, cut into tablespoons
- 2 ounces unsweetened chocolate, chopped
- 1 cup sugar
- 2 large eggs
- 1/2 teaspoon vanilla extract
- 1/4 cup all-purpose flour
- 1/4 teaspoon salt
- 1 cup (3½ ounces) chopped walnuts (optional)

Put a rack in middle of oven and preheat oven to 325°F. Butter and flour an 8-inch square baking pan, knocking off excess flour.

Melt butter with chocolate in a 2- to 3-quart saucepan over low heat. Remove from heat and stir in sugar, eggs, and vanilla, then beat until well combined. Stir in flour and salt until just combined, then stir in walnuts, if using.

Pour batter into baking pan. Bake until a wooden pick or skewer inserted in center comes out clean, about 40 minutes.

Cool completely in pan on a rack, then cut into 16 bars.

COOK'S NOTE

- The brownies keep in an airtight container at room temperature for up to 5 days.

Cappuccino Brownies

MAKES 40 BROWNIES
ACTIVE TIME: 45 MINUTES ■ START TO FINISH: 12 HOURS (INCLUDES CHILLING)

■ More than brownies, these are an elegant, richly layered little dessert. A chocolate and espresso base supports a sweetened cream cheese layer (spiced with the barest hint of cinnamon) and a chocolate glaze. Pure pleasure. ■

FOR BROWNIE LAYER

- 8 ounces good bittersweet chocolate (not unsweetened), chopped
- 1½ sticks (12 tablespoons) unsalted butter, cut into pieces
- 2 tablespoons instant espresso powder, dissolved in 1½ teaspoons boiling water
- 1½ cups sugar
- 2 teaspoons vanilla extract
- 4 large eggs
- 1 cup all-purpose flour
- ½ teaspoon salt
- 1 cup (3½ ounces) walnuts, chopped

FOR CREAM CHEESE LAYER

- 8 ounces cream cheese, softened
- ¾ stick (6 tablespoons) unsalted butter, softened
- 1½ cups confectioners' sugar
- 1 teaspoon vanilla extract
- 1 teaspoon ground cinnamon

FOR GLAZE

- 6 ounces good bittersweet chocolate (not unsweetened), finely chopped
- 2 tablespoons unsalted butter
- ½ cup heavy cream
- 1½ tablespoons instant espresso powder, dissolved in 1 tablespoon boiling water

MAKE THE BROWNIE LAYER: Put a rack in middle of oven and preheat oven to 350°F. Butter and flour a 13-by-9-inch baking pan, knocking off excess flour.

Melt chocolate with butter and espresso mixture in a medium metal bowl set over a pan of barely simmering water, stirring until smooth. Remove bowl from heat and cool for 10 minutes.

Whisk sugar and vanilla into chocolate mixture, then add eggs one at a time, whisking until batter is smooth. Stir in flour and salt until just combined, then stir in walnuts.

Spread batter evenly in baking pan. Bake until a wooden pick or skewer inserted in center comes out with some crumbs adhering, 22 to 27 minutes. Cool completely in pan on a rack, at least 2 hours.

MAKE THE CREAM CHEESE LAYER: Beat together cream cheese and butter in a large bowl with an electric mixer on medium speed until light and fluffy. Sift in confectioners' sugar, then add vanilla and cinnamon and beat until well combined.

Spread cream cheese mixture evenly over cooled brownie layer. Refrigerate until firm, about 1 hour.

MAKE THE GLAZE: Combine all ingredients in a metal bowl set over a saucepan of barely simmering water and heat, stirring, until chocolate and butter are melted and glaze is smooth. Remove from heat and cool to room temperature, stirring occasionally, about 20 minutes.

Pour glaze over cream cheese layer, then spread evenly. Refrigerate brownies, covered, until very cold, about 8 hours or overnight. Cut into 40 bars and remove from pan while still cold. Serve chilled or at room temperature.

COOK'S NOTE

- The brownies keep in one layer in an airtight container, refrigerated, for up to 5 days.

Triple-Chocolate Fudge Brownies

MAKES 2 DOZEN BROWNIES
ACTIVE TIME: 20 MINUTES ■ START TO FINISH: 1¾ HOURS

■ The chocolate world is much bigger than it's ever been, with more variety and better quality. Here we've combined unsweetened, bittersweet, and semisweet chocolate for a dense, intense brownie with loads of complex flavor. (For more about chocolate, see page 741.) ■

- 6 ounces good bittersweet chocolate (not unsweetened), chopped
- 2 ounces unsweetened chocolate, chopped
- 1½ sticks (12 tablespoons) unsalted butter
- 1½ cups sugar
- 2 teaspoons vanilla extract
- 4 large eggs
- ¾ teaspoon salt
- 1 cup all-purpose flour
- 1 cup (6 ounces) semisweet chocolate chips

Put a rack in middle of oven and preheat oven to 350°F. Butter and flour a 13-by-9-inch baking pan, knocking off excess flour.

Melt bittersweet and unsweetened chocolates with butter in a medium metal bowl set over a pan of barely simmering water, stirring until smooth. Remove from heat and cool to lukewarm.

Stir sugar and vanilla into chocolate mixture, then add eggs one at a time, stirring well after each addition. Add salt and flour, stirring until just combined, then stir in chocolate chips.

Pour batter into baking pan and smooth top. Bake until a wooden pick or skewer inserted in center comes out with some moist crumbs adhering, 25 to 30 minutes. Cool completely in pan on a rack, then cut into 24 bars.

COOK'S NOTE

■ The brownies keep in an airtight container at room temperature for up to 3 days.

Turtle Brownies

MAKES 64 BROWNIES
ACTIVE TIME: 30 MINUTES ■ START TO FINISH: 5½ HOURS (INCLUDES CHILLING)

■ A brownie is an easy chocolate base for all sorts of luscious things. This version, a riff on the candy called turtles, sports a layer of pecan-studded chewy caramel. ■

FOR BROWNIE LAYER

- ¾ cup plus 2 tablespoons all-purpose flour
- ¼ teaspoon baking powder
- ½ teaspoon salt
- 4 ounces semisweet chocolate, chopped
- 1 ounce unsweetened chocolate, chopped
- 1 stick (8 tablespoons) unsalted butter, cut into pieces
- 1 cup packed brown sugar (light or dark)
- 1 teaspoon vanilla extract
- 2 large eggs

FOR CARAMEL-PECAN LAYER

- ¾ cup granulated sugar
- ⅓ cup light corn syrup
- 3 tablespoons water
- Pinch of salt
- ⅓ cup heavy cream
- 1 teaspoon vanilla extract
- 1½ cups (6 ounces) pecans

FOR DECORATION

- 2 ounces semisweet chocolate, very finely chopped

MAKE THE BROWNIE LAYER: Put a rack in middle of oven and preheat oven to 350°F. Butter and flour a 9-inch square baking pan, knocking off excess flour.

Whisk together flour, baking powder, and salt in a small bowl.

Melt chocolates and butter in a 2-quart heavy saucepan over low heat, stirring until smooth. Remove from heat and cool to lukewarm.

Stir brown sugar and vanilla into chocolate mixture. Add eggs one at a time, beating after each addition until mixture is glossy and smooth. Add flour mixture and stir until just combined.

Spread batter evenly in baking pan. Bake until a wooden pick or skewer inserted in center comes out clean, 30 to 35 minutes. Cool completely in pan on a rack.

MAKE THE CARAMEL-PECAN LAYER: Combine sugar, corn syrup, water, and salt in a 3-quart heavy saucepan and bring to a boil over moderate heat, stirring until sugar is dissolved. Boil, without stirring, until mixture turns a golden caramel color, about 10 minutes. Remove from heat and carefully add cream and vanilla (mixture will bubble and steam). Stir in pecans and immediately pour over brownie layer, spreading evenly. Cool completely in pan on rack.

DECORATE AND CUT THE BROWNIES: Melt chocolate in a metal bowl set over a saucepan of barely simmering water, stirring until smooth. Transfer to a small heavy-duty sealable plastic bag. Seal bag and snip off a tiny piece of one corner to form a small opening, then pipe chocolate decoratively over brownies.

Refrigerate brownies, loosely covered, until caramel and chocolate are firm, at least 4 hours.

Before serving, cut into 64 squares and remove from pan while cold, then bring to room temperature.

COOK'S NOTE

- The uncut brownies can be refrigerated in an airtight container for up to 1 week.

Lemon Bars

MAKES ABOUT 2 DOZEN BARS
ACTIVE TIME: 30 MINUTES ■ START TO FINISH: 5½ HOURS (INCLUDES CHILLING)

■ These bars are festive without being decorated. The lemon filling, sweet and citrus-sharp, joins a shortbread crust in a brilliant marriage. ■

FOR CRUST

- 1½ cups all-purpose flour
- 6 tablespoons granulated sugar
- 3/8 teaspoon salt
- 9 tablespoons cold unsalted butter, cut into ½-inch pieces

FOR FILLING

- 6 large eggs
- 2 cups granulated sugar
- ¼ cup all-purpose flour
- ¼ cup heavy cream
- 1 teaspoon finely grated lemon zest
- ¾ cup fresh lemon juice (from 3–5 lemons)
- ¼ teaspoon salt

Confectioners' sugar for sprinkling

MAKE THE CRUST: Put a rack in middle of oven and preheat oven to 350°F.

Pulse together flour, sugar, and salt in a food processor just until combined. Add butter and pulse until mixture resembles coarse, powdery meal. Press dough onto bottom of an ungreased 9-inch square baking pan. Bake until pale golden brown, about 20 minutes.

MEANWHILE, MAKE THE FILLING: Whisk together eggs, granulated sugar, flour, heavy cream, zest, juice, and salt in a bowl until combined.

BAKE THE BARS: When crust is baked, rewhisk lemon mixture and pour onto hot crust. Bake until just set, about 30 minutes. Transfer pan to a rack to cool.

Refrigerate bars, covered, until cold, at least 4 hours. Before serving, cut into bars and sprinkle with a thick layer of confectioners' sugar.

COOK'S NOTES

- The uncut bars can be refrigerated for up to 2 days.
- The bars keep, layered between sheets of wax or parchment paper, in an airtight container at cool room temperature for up to 1 day.

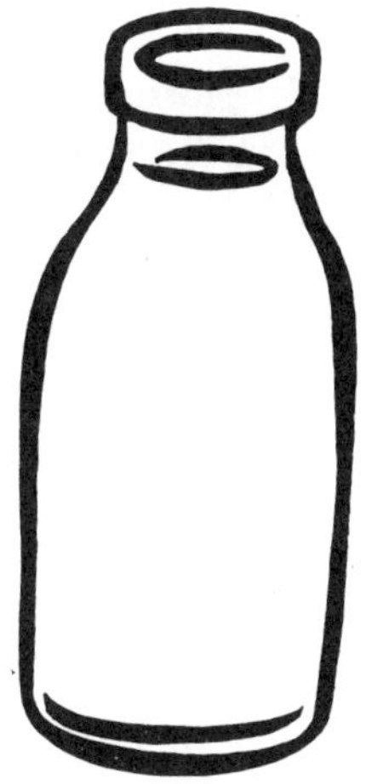

Cranberry Caramel Bars

MAKES 3 DOZEN BARS
ACTIVE TIME: 30 MINUTES ■ START TO FINISH: 2 HOURS

■ With their bracing tang, cranberries provide a tart counterpoint in sweets. Here a layer of buttery shortbread forms the base for cranberry- and pecan-laden caramel. These bars make a great dessert at holiday time, when you are feeding throngs of people. ■

FOR BASE

- 2 cups all-purpose flour
- 1/2 cup packed light brown sugar
- 1/2 teaspoon salt
- 1 1/2 sticks (12 tablespoons) cold unsalted butter, cut into 1/2-inch cubes

FOR TOPPING

- 2 sticks (1/2 pound) unsalted butter
- 1 2/3 cups granulated sugar
- 1/4 cup light corn syrup
- 1/2 teaspoon salt
- 1 1/2 cups fresh or frozen (not thawed) cranberries, coarsely chopped
- 1 teaspoon vanilla extract
- 3 cups (12 ounces) pecans, toasted (see Tips, page 938) and coarsely chopped

FOR DECORATION

- 2 ounces good bittersweet chocolate (not unsweetened), very finely chopped

SPECIAL EQUIPMENT: a candy thermometer

MAKE THE BASE: Put a rack in middle of oven and preheat oven to 350°F. Line a 15 1/2-by-10 1/2-inch baking sheet with sides with foil, leaving a 2-inch overhang on the two short sides. Butter all four sides but not bottom.

Combine flour, brown sugar, and salt in a food processor and pulse to blend. Add butter and pulse until mixture begins to form small (roughly pea-sized) lumps. Sprinkle into baking pan, then press down firmly with a metal spatula to form an even layer.

Bake until golden and firm to the touch, 15 to 17 minutes. Transfer pan to a rack.

MAKE THE TOPPING: Melt butter in a 3-quart heavy saucepan over moderate heat. Stir in sugar, corn syrup, and salt, increase heat to moderately high, and bring to a boil, stirring occasionally. Boil, stirring occasionally, until caramel registers 245°F on thermometer, about 8 minutes. Carefully stir in cranberries, then boil until caramel returns to 245°F. Remove from heat and stir in vanilla, then stir in pecans until well coated.

Working quickly, spread caramel topping over base, using a fork to distribute nuts and berries evenly. Cool completely.

CUT AND DECORATE THE BARS: Use foil to lift bars from pan and transfer to a cutting board. Cut into 36 bars.

Melt half of chocolate in a metal bowl set over a saucepan of barely simmering water, stirring until smooth. Remove from heat and add remaining chocolate, stirring until smooth. Transfer chocolate to a small heavy-duty sealable plastic bag. Seal bag and snip off a tiny piece of one corner to form a small opening, then pipe chocolate decoratively over bars.

Let stand at room temperature until chocolate sets, about 1 hour.

COOK'S NOTE

- The bars keep, layered between sheets of wax or parchment paper, in an airtight container at room temperature for up to 1 week.

Oatmeal Coconut Raspberry Bars

MAKES 2 DOZEN BARS

ACTIVE TIME: 20 MINUTES ■ START TO FINISH: 1 3/4 HOURS

■ Think of these deliciously chewy bars as sophisticated granola bars. Substantial and fruity, they travel beautifully, so pack them up and send them to far-flung loved ones. ■

- 1 1/2 cups (3 3/4 ounces) sweetened flaked coconut
- 1 1/4 cups all-purpose flour
- 3/4 cup packed light brown sugar
- 1/4 cup granulated sugar
- 1/2 teaspoon salt
- 1 1/2 sticks (12 tablespoons) cold unsalted butter, cut into pieces
- 1 1/2 cups old-fashioned rolled oats
- 3/4 cup seedless raspberry jam

Put a rack in middle of oven and preheat oven to 375°F. Butter a 13-by-9-inch baking pan.

Spread 3/4 cup coconut evenly on a baking sheet and toast in oven, stirring once, until golden, about 8 minutes. Cool on sheet on a rack.

Combine flour, sugars, and salt in a food processor and pulse to blend. Add butter and pulse just until a dough forms. Transfer to a bowl and knead in oats and toasted coconut until well combined.

Reserve 3/4 cup dough. Press remainder evenly

into bottom of buttered baking pan and spread jam over it. Crumble reserved dough evenly over jam, then sprinkle with remaining 3/4 cup (untoasted) coconut.

Bake until golden, 20 to 25 minutes. Cool completely in pan on rack.

Loosen bars from sides of pan with a sharp knife, then carefully lift out in one piece with a spatula and transfer to a cutting board. Cut into 24 bars.

COOK'S NOTE

- The bars keep in an airtight container at room temperature for up to 3 days.

Peanut Butter–Coconut Bars

MAKES 4 DOZEN BARS
ACTIVE TIME: 25 MINUTES ■ START TO FINISH: 1 3/4 HOURS

■ This is for the peanut butter lover who's in the mood for something a little different. ■

- 1 1/2 sticks (12 tablespoons) unsalted butter, softened
- 1 cup sugar
- 1 cup smooth peanut butter
- 1 large egg
- 1 teaspoon vanilla extract
- 1/2 teaspoon salt
- 2 cups all-purpose flour
- 2 cups (about 5 ounces) sweetened flaked coconut
- 1/2 cup finely chopped salted roasted peanuts

Put a rack in middle of oven and preheat oven to 350°F. Lightly butter a 15 1/2-by-10 1/2-inch baking sheet with sides.

Beat together butter and sugar in a large bowl with an electric mixer at medium speed until pale and fluffy, about 1 minute. Add peanut butter and beat until well combined. Beat in egg, vanilla, and salt. Add flour and beat until just combined, then stir in coconut.

Spread mixture evenly in baking pan. Sprinkle peanuts over top and gently press them into mixture so they adhere.

Bake until a wooden pick or skewer inserted in center comes out clean, 20 to 25 minutes. Cool completely in pan on a rack.

Cut into 24 bars, then cut each bar in half diagonally to form 2 triangles.

COOK'S NOTE

- The bars keep in an airtight container at room temperature for up to 5 days.

Date and Oat Bars

MAKES 3 DOZEN BARS
ACTIVE TIME: 30 MINUTES ■ START TO FINISH: 2 1/2 HOURS

■ Dates, with their deep, rich, nuanced flavor and texture, are a wonderful sweetener. Here a smidgen of orange zest adds brightness and lightness to a classic combo. ■

FOR FILLING

- 2 cups (11 ounces) packed pitted dates
- 3/4 cup water
- 1/4 cup packed light brown sugar
- 1/2 teaspoon vanilla extract
- 2 tablespoons unsalted butter

FOR DOUGH

- 1 1/4 cups quick-cooking rolled oats, plus 2 tablespoons for sprinkling
- 3/4 cup all-purpose flour
- 1/2 cup packed light brown sugar
- 3/4 teaspoon salt
- 1 1/2 sticks (12 tablespoons) unsalted butter, cut into 1/2-inch cubes
- 1/4 cup whole milk
- 1/2 teaspoon finely grated orange zest

MAKE THE FILLING: Pulse dates in a food processor until finely chopped.

Stir together dates and remaining filling ingredients in a 3-quart saucepan and bring to a simmer over moderate heat. Simmer, stirring, until mixture forms a thick paste, about 10 minutes. Cool to room temperature.

MAKE THE DOUGH: Put a rack in middle of oven and preheat oven to 350°F. Butter an 8-inch square baking pan.

Whisk together 1 1/4 cups oats, flour, sugar, and salt in a large bowl (or pulse in a food processor). Blend in butter with your fingertips or a pastry blender (or pulse) until mixture resembles coarse meal with some small (roughly pea-sized) lumps of butter. Add milk and zest and stir or pulse until a dough forms.

Spread half of dough evenly into buttered baking pan. Using an offset spatula or a spoon, carefully spread date filling over dough, then top filling with remaining dough, spreading it evenly. Sprinkle top with remaining 2 tablespoons oats.

Bake until golden brown, about 55 minutes. Cool completely in pan on a rack, then cut into 36 bars.

COOK'S NOTE

- The bars keep, layered between sheets of wax paper or parchment paper, in an airtight container at room temperature for up to 1 week.

Pecan Pie Bars

MAKES 2 DOZEN BARS

ACTIVE TIME: 25 MINUTES ■ START TO FINISH: 1½ HOURS

■ This is one of the world's greatest pies without the formality—or the forks. These bars are a snap to make (shortbread is easier than pie dough) and go anywhere in a picnic basket or backpack. ■

FOR BASE

- 1½ sticks (12 tablespoons) unsalted butter, cut into ½-inch pieces
- 2 cups all-purpose flour
- ½ cup packed light brown sugar
- ½ teaspoon salt

FOR TOPPING

- 2 cups (8 ounces) pecans
- 1 stick (8 tablespoons) unsalted butter
- 1 cup packed light brown sugar
- ⅓ cup honey
- 2 tablespoons heavy cream

MAKE THE SHORTBREAD BASE: Put a rack in middle of oven and preheat oven to 350°F.

Combine all ingredients in a food processor and pulse until mixture begins to form small lumps. Sprinkle mixture into an ungreased 13-by-9-inch baking pan and press evenly onto bottom with a metal spatula.

Bake shortbread until golden, about 20 minutes.

MEANWHILE, MAKE THE TOPPING: Coarsely chop pecans in food processor.

Melt butter in a 2-quart heavy saucepan over moderately low heat. Stir in brown sugar, honey, and cream and bring to a simmer, stirring. Simmer, stirring occasionally, for 1 minute, then stir in pecans. Remove from heat.

Pour pecan mixture over hot shortbread and spread evenly. Bake until bubbling, about 20 minutes.

Cool completely in pan on a rack, then cut into 24 bars.

COOK'S NOTE

- The bars keep, layered between sheets of wax or parchment paper, in an airtight container at room temperature for up to 5 days.

Mocha Toffee Cashew Bars

MAKES 4 DOZEN BARS

ACTIVE TIME: 20 MINUTES ■ START TO FINISH: 1½ HOURS

■ Like many bar cookies, this one is a layered affair: melted chocolate is spread over a baked espresso-flavored toffee base and topped with chopped roasted cashews. The result is an intense melding of flavors and textures, ideal with an espresso after a meal. ■

- 2 sticks (½ pound) unsalted butter, softened
- 1 cup packed light brown sugar
- 1 large egg yolk
- 1½ teaspoons vanilla extract
- 3 tablespoons instant espresso powder, dissolved in 2 tablespoons boiling water
- 2 cups all-purpose flour
- ½ teaspoon salt
- 8 ounces good bittersweet chocolate (not unsweetened), finely chopped
- ¾ cup (4 ounces) salted roasted cashews, chopped

Put a rack in middle of oven and preheat oven to 350°F.

Beat together butter and brown sugar in a large bowl with an electric mixer at medium-high speed until fluffy, about 3 minutes. Beat in yolk and vanilla, then gradually add espresso mixture, beating until well combined. Add flour and salt and mix at low speed until just combined.

Spread dough evenly in an ungreased 15½-by-10½-inch baking sheet with sides. Bake until top puffs slightly and sides pull away from edges of pan, 16 to 22 minutes. Watch carefully toward end of baking; base can burn easily.

Meanwhile, melt chocolate in a metal bowl set over a saucepan of barely simmering water, stirring occasionally. Remove bowl from heat.

Spread chocolate over warm base and immediately sprinkle with cashews. Cool completely in pan on a rack.

Cut into 48 bars and chill until chocolate is firm, at least 15 minutes.

COOK'S NOTE

- The bars keep, layered between sheets of wax or parchment paper in an airtight container and refrigerated, for up to 2 weeks. Serve cold.

Confections

Brown Sugar Fudge

MAKES 64 PIECES
ACTIVE TIME: 45 MINUTES ■ START TO FINISH: 1¼ HOURS

■ Another name for this kind of creamy caramel fudge is penuche ("puh-*noo*-chee"), derived from *panocha,* a Mexican raw sugar. We think the texture of this one is most unusual: the combination of confectioners' sugar and brown sugar results in a particularly smooth, lush, velvety quality. We adapted a recipe from Pinkie's Bakery, in Souris, Prince Edward Island; the writer Marialisa Calta brought it back from a trip to the Canadian Maritimes. ■

- ½ cup plus 2 tablespoons evaporated milk
- 2 cups (14 ounces) packed light brown sugar
- 1½ sticks (12 tablespoons) unsalted butter, cut into tablespoons
- ¼ teaspoon salt
- ½ teaspoon vanilla extract
- 1¾ cups confectioners' sugar

SPECIAL EQUIPMENT: a candy thermometer

Combine milk, brown sugar, butter, and salt in a 3-quart heavy saucepan and bring just to a boil over moderate heat, stirring until sugar is dissolved. Reduce heat to low and simmer, stirring frequently, until mixture registers 238°F on thermometer and a teaspoon of mixture dropped into a small bowl of cold water holds a soft ball when pressed between your fingers (this will take about 30 minutes).

Transfer to a heatproof bowl. Beat in vanilla with an electric mixer at medium speed, then add confectioners' sugar a little at a time, beating until fudge is thick and smooth, about 5 minutes.

Spread evenly in an ungreased 8-inch square baking pan. Refrigerate, uncovered, until firm enough to cut, about 30 minutes.

Cut fudge into 64 squares with a sharp paring knife.

COOK'S NOTES

- If desired, stir ¾ cup walnuts, lightly toasted (see Tips, page 938) and chopped, into the fudge before spreading it in the pan.
- The fudge keeps, layered between sheets of wax paper, in an airtight container and refrigerated for up to 5 days.

Chocolate Anise Bark

MAKES ABOUT 6 PIECES
ACTIVE TIME: 15 MINUTES ■ START TO FINISH: 45 MINUTES

■ Finish a meal with shards of dark chocolate dotted with nuts and dried fruit. The combination of chocolate and anise has spoken to us ever since we first had it at the Paris restaurant Arpège. A tin of this makes an impressive gift. ■

- 1 teaspoon anise seeds
- ⅓ cup dried sour cherries
- ⅓ cup dried apricots, coarsely chopped
- ⅓ cup salted roasted cashews, coarsely chopped
- 6 ounces good bittersweet chocolate (not unsweetened), finely chopped

SPECIAL EQUIPMENT: an electric coffee/spice grinder

Line a small baking sheet with foil and chill it.

Finely grind anise seeds in coffee/spice grinder. Stir together cherries, apricots, and cashews in a small bowl.

Melt chocolate in a small metal bowl set over a small saucepan of barely simmering water, stirring occasionally until smooth. Stir in anise and half of fruit mixture, then spoon chocolate onto center of chilled baking sheet. Spread with a rubber spatula into a roughly 10-by-5-inch rectangle. Sprinkle with remaining fruit and press lightly so it adheres.

Refrigerate until firm, about 30 minutes, then break into pieces.

COOK'S NOTE

- The bark keeps in an airtight container and refrigerated for up to 1 week.

Chocolate Truffles

MAKES ABOUT 5 DOZEN TRUFFLES
ACTIVE TIME: 1¼ HOURS ■ START TO FINISH: 2½ HOURS (INCLUDES CHILLING)

■ We are not alone in our belief that the cocoa-dusted chocolate truffles from La Maison du Chocolat, based in Paris, are the finest in the world. When Robert Linxe, the founder of the company, came to New York City, he showed us the technique (see below), and then we adapted his method for the home cook, eliminating his tempered-chocolate coating. We didn't even think about substituting a more widely available chocolate, though, for the Valrhona 56-percent cacao he used. Why mess with success? These are the ultimate valentine. ■

- 11 ounces Valrhona 56% cacao chocolate (see Sources), finely chopped
- 2/3 cup heavy cream
- 1/2 cup unsweetened Valrhona cocoa powder (see Sources)

TRUFFLE TIPS

When Robert Linxe showed us how to make what are arguably the world's best chocolate truffles, we took careful notes. Here are some tips for success from the master.

1. When heating the cream for the ganache, make sure your pan is small (to keep evaporation to a minimum) and heavy (to keep the cream from scorching).
2. Linxe boils his cream three times — he believes reboiling makes the ganache keep longer. If you do this, compensate for the extra evaporation by starting with a little more cream.
3. When piping, finish off each mound with a flick of the wrist to soften and angle the pointy tip.
4. The secret to a delicate coating of chocolate is to roll each truffle in a smear of melted chocolate in your hand. (Linxe always uses disposable gloves.)
5. A fork is the best tool for tossing truffles in cocoa powder.
6. Shake the truffles in a sieve to eliminate excess cocoa powder. *Voilà!* They will look like their namesakes, freshly dug from the earth.

SPECIAL EQUIPMENT: parchment paper; a pastry bag fitted with a 3/8-inch plain tip; plastic gloves

Put 8 ounces (3/4 cup) chocolate in a heatproof bowl. Bring cream just to a boil in a 1-quart heavy saucepan. Pour cream over chocolate, then mash any bigger pieces of chocolate with a wooden spoon and gently stir mixture with a whisk in concentric circles (do not beat, or you'll incorporate air), starting in center and working out to edges, until ganache is smooth. Let stand at room temperature until thick enough to hold a shape, about 1 hour.

Line two large baking sheets with parchment. Transfer ganache to pastry bag and pipe 1-inch mounds (3/4 inch high) onto sheets. Freeze until firm, about 15 minutes.

Meanwhile, melt remaining 3 ounces chocolate in a metal bowl set over a saucepan of barely simmering water, stirring occasionally until smooth.

Put cocoa powder in a small bowl. Wearing plastic gloves, smear some melted chocolate on a gloved hand. Gently rub each chilled truffle with chocolate, then gently toss truffles, a few at a time, in cocoa powder with a fork. Transfer truffles, a few at a time, to a sieve and gently shake off excess cocoa. Transfer coated truffles to a sheet of wax paper and refrigerate.

COOK'S NOTES

- Don't be tempted to double this recipe; make 2 batches instead.
- The truffles keep, layered between sheets of wax or parchment paper in an airtight container and refrigerated, for up to 2 weeks.

New Orleans Praline Pieces

MAKES ABOUT 16 CANDIES
ACTIVE TIME: 40 MINUTES ■ START TO FINISH: 1 1/2 HOURS

■ Our recipe for pecan-studded New Orleans pralines (pronounced "*prah*-leens") is true in all ways but form. Because its creamy texture is similar to that of fudge and it sets up quickly, we realized that the nut-filled syrup could be poured into a baking pan more easily than it could be spooned into the traditional patties. The result looks like a brittle bark, but it melts in your mouth. ■

3/4 cup granulated sugar
3/4 cup packed light brown sugar
1/2 cup heavy cream
2 tablespoons unsalted butter, cut into 1/2-inch cubes
1/4 teaspoon salt
1 1/4 cups (5 ounces) pecan pieces, toasted (see Tips, page 938)

SPECIAL EQUIPMENT: a candy thermometer

Butter a 9-inch square baking pan.

Sift granulated sugar through a sieve into a bowl to remove any lumps or large crystals, then rub brown sugar through sieve into bowl. Pour sugars into a 2 1/2- to 3-quart heavy saucepan, being careful not to get sugar on sides of pan. Add cream, butter, and salt and cook over very low heat, stirring frequently with a wooden spoon and washing down any sugar crystals on sides of pan with a pastry brush dipped in cold water, until sugar is dissolved, 10 to 15 minutes; do not let simmer.

Increase heat to moderately high and boil syrup, undisturbed, until it registers 236°F on thermometer and a teaspoon of syrup dropped into a small bowl of cold water holds a very soft ball when pressed between your fingers (this will take 3 to 6 minutes).

Remove pan from heat, leaving thermometer in place, and cool, undisturbed, until syrup registers 220°F, 1 to 3 minutes.

Stir syrup with clean dry wooden spoon until thickened and creamy, 1 to 2 minutes, then immediately stir in pecans. Working very fast (syrup hardens quickly), pour into baking pan, scraping sides of saucepan with wooden spoon.

Let candy harden at room temperature, about 45 minutes. Cut and break into 2-inch pieces.

COOK'S NOTE

- The praline pieces keep, layered between sheets of parchment or wax paper, in an airtight container in a cool, dry place for up to 3 days.

Molasses Sponge Candy

MAKES ABOUT 1 POUND
ACTIVE TIME: 25 MINUTES ■ START TO FINISH: 1¼ HOURS

■ Molasses gives almost anything a complex, rich flavor. Here it contrasts beautifully with the light honeycomb texture of this old-fashioned candy. That texture, by the way, is a great example of kitchen chemistry: when baking soda is added to the molasses syrup, it foams, resulting in the "sponge." Its tender crunch is delightful. ■

- 1½ cups sugar
- ⅓ cup water
- 3 tablespoons unsalted butter
- ¼ teaspoon cream of tartar
- ½ cup molasses (not robust or blackstrap)
- 2½ teaspoons baking soda

SPECIAL EQUIPMENT: a candy thermometer

Making Candy

Candy isn't hard to make, but precision is important. Measure ingredients and temperatures carefully and have everything you need at the ready. For most of our recipes you'll need a candy thermometer. Buy one that registers temperatures up to 320°F. It's a good idea to see if it's calibrated correctly before you use it: submerge it in a pan of water, bring the water to a boil, and let it boil for 10 minutes. The thermometer should read 212°F at sea level or one degree less for every five hundred feet above sea level.

When cooking a candy syrup to the right concentration, you might think it's never going to climb that last degree or so to the required temperature. Do not let your attention waver: all of a sudden the syrup will be ready, and then you must act quickly. It's reassuring to use what's called the cold-water test as well as the thermometer. Once the syrup reaches the required temperature, immediately drop a teaspoon of it into a little bowl of cold (not ice) water and gather the syrup between your fingers; you can identify the approximate temperature and/or stage of the syrup by the way it reacts in your hand. In general, the hotter the syrup is, the harder the finished candy will be. One last word of advice: don't try to make candy in humid weather; wait for a cool, dry day.

The Stages of Candy Syrup

SOFT BALL: At 234°–240°F, the syrup will form a soft ball between your fingers and will cool into soft but firm candy, such as fudge and pralines.

FIRM BALL: At 242°–248°F, the syrup will form a firm ball that holds its shape out of the water. This stage is used for chewy caramels.

HARD BALL: At 250°–268°F, the syrup will form a hard ball that is still pliable when removed from the water. This stage is usually used for taffy and sponge candy.

SOFT CRACK: At 270°–288°F, the syrup will form firm threads that can be bent when removed from the water. This stage is usually used for butterscotch.

HARD CRACK: At 290°–310°F, the syrup will form hard threads that break when removed from the water. This stage is usually used for nut brittles.

Line bottom and sides of a 13-by-9-inch baking pan with foil, leaving an inch overhang on either side, and butter foil.

Combine sugar, water, butter, and cream of tartar in a 3-quart deep heavy saucepan and bring to a boil over moderate heat, stirring until sugar is dissolved. Wash down any sugar crystals clinging to sides of pan with a pastry brush dipped in cold water. Boil, without stirring, until syrup registers 265°F on thermometer and a teaspoon of syrup dropped into a bowl of cold water holds a hard ball when pressed between your fingers (this will take about 10 minutes). Add molasses, without stirring, and continue to boil undisturbed until syrup registers 295°F and a teaspoon of syrup dropped into cold water forms hard threads (this will take 4 to 5 minutes). Remove pan from heat, sift baking soda over syrup, and whisk to incorporate (use caution: mixture will bubble vigorously).

Immediately pour syrup into baking pan. Cool completely. Use foil to lift candy from pan, then peel off foil and break candy into pieces.

COOK'S NOTE

- The candy keeps, layered between sheets of parchment or wax paper, in an airtight container at room temperature for up to 1 month.

Candied Grapefruit Peel

MAKES ABOUT 45 STRIPS
ACTIVE TIME: 45 MINUTES ■ START TO FINISH: 8¾ HOURS (INCLUDES DRYING)

■ Candied grapefruit peel should be in the repertoire of anyone cooking for the holidays—or at any time of the year. It's the perfect antidote to a rich meal, and all you need with it are cookies and espresso. If you're feeling ambitious, dip the candied peel (after tossing it in sugar) in melted dark chocolate. Or stir some chopped peel into ice cream or cake batter.

When candying grapefruit peel, you really need to keep only two things in mind. First, though blanching the peel five times may seem excessive, each go-round eliminates a little more bitterness and softens the peel. Second, keep an eye on the peel as it absorbs the sugar syrup and take it off the heat when a small amount of syrup still remains in the pan. If all of it is absorbed, the pan will immediately get too hot and the syrup will crystallize. ■

2 small grapefruit
1 cup granulated sugar
½ cup water
1 cup superfine sugar

Quarter grapefruit lengthwise and remove peel, including white pith, in one piece from each quarter. (Reserve fruit for another use.) Cut pieces of peel diagonally into ⅓-inch-wide strips.

Put peel in a 3-quart saucepan of cold water and slowly bring to a boil over moderate heat. Boil for 1 minute and drain. Repeat blanching procedure 4 times to remove bitterness.

Set a lightly oiled large rack in a shallow baking pan. Combine granulated sugar and water in a large heavy skillet and bring to a boil, stirring until sugar is dissolved. Add peel and boil, stirring, until most of syrup is absorbed, about 10 minutes.

Turn peel out onto rack, separating pieces. Dry, uncovered, at room temperature until only slightly sticky, 4 to 8 hours.

Toss a few pieces of peel at a time in superfine sugar and shake off excess.

COOK'S NOTES

- If the sugar syrup begins to crystallize on the peel, immediately turn the peel out of the skillet. It will still be good, but it will look different, and it won't need a sugar coating.
- The candied peel keeps in an airtight container at room temperature for up to 1 week, or refrigerated for up to 1 month. If the refrigerated peel becomes too moist, pat it dry and reroll in sugar.

CAKES

Cake is every cook's insurance policy.

For anybody who entertains, cake is the ace in the hole, the safety valve, the one sure thing. It is the dessert that makes any meal a party, the one that lifts the simplest dinner out of the ordinary. Cake also gives every hostess confidence: if you bake a cake early in the day, no matter what disaster may befall your meal, you know your guests will go home happy.

Because *Gourmet* has always focused on entertaining, we have published thousands of cake recipes over the years. We have loved every one of them, and choosing the forty-nine cakes for this chapter was agonizing. Just picking the nine chocolate cakes took months of testing and retesting, and we finally held bake-off contests between our favorites, so you can be sure that they are all very special. Coconut cakes were equally difficult to decide between; with great difficulty, we narrowed the selection down to five favorites. In the end common sense prevailed, and we chose the two fabulous but very different versions that you will find here.

Singling out the cheesecakes proved to be even more problematic. Cheesecakes are the most requested recipes, and we could easily have included a hundred. We pared the selection down to six essentials that are an indispensable part of our repertoire. Every one is unique and wonderful.

This chapter offers a wide range, from wedding cakes (both dark and light) to cupcakes, from easy upside-down cakes to a many-layered Dobostorte, the Hungarian classic that is filled with chocolate cream, topped with caramel, and so gorgeously delicious that you'll want to make it again and again. We have mousse cakes, pudding cakes, pound cakes, and cake rolls, and each of them is absolutely guaranteed to make any occasion at which it appears an unqualified success.

A Cake Primer

Although making a cake doesn't require lots of specialized equipment or hard-to-find ingredients, the right tools do help, and so does attention to detail. Baking, after all, is the most scientific of the culinary arts—and it's also one of the most rewarding. If you want to know more about successful cake-making techniques, some books we find useful are *The Cake Bible,* by Rose Levy Beranbaum; *The Simple Art of Perfect Baking,* by Flo Braker; *Baking with Julia,* by Dorie Greenspan; *How to Bake,* by Nick Malgieri; *The Art of Fine Baking,* by Paula Peck; *The Baker's Dozen Cookbook,* edited by Rick Rodgers; *Great Cakes,* by Carole Walter; and *The Secrets of Baking,* by Sherry Yard.

EQUIPMENT

The cake pans we use most frequently are round aluminum ones with straight sides, which make the cake easier to frost and more professional-looking, and a dull finish (pans with a bright, shiny finish or a dark nonstick finish will not give the same results as standard pans, so avoid them). A handheld electric mixer is fine for most cake batters and frostings, but sometimes you need a stand electric mixer. The widely available KitchenAid is our stand mixer of choice. However, although the paddle is designed for general blending, we prefer the whisk attachment both for blending and for beating as much air as possible into egg whites or a sponge cake batter.

INGREDIENTS

EGGS: Not only do eggs add richness and flavor, they are integral to a cake's leavening and structure. Freshness is vital, and size and temperature are also important. Be sure to use large eggs (if another size is all that's available, see the chart on page 628 for size equivalents). When separating eggs, get that last little bit of white out of the shell by running your clean thumb around the inside. It's only about a teaspoon's worth, but it adds up when you are dealing with thirteen eggs (for an angel food cake).

FLOUR: Probably the most common mistake in baking is failing to measure dry ingredients correctly. Many serious baking books suggest that you invest in a scale. Measuring dry ingredients by weight is fast, easy, and, most important, accurate (especially if you use metrics; the increments are smaller, so there's a smaller margin of error that way). However, until scales become commonplace in American kitchens, we'll stick with sturdy metal nested dry-measuring cups. When measuring flour (or something like cocoa powder), don't pack it into the cup. Spoon the flour in and level it off with a knife, not your finger. Using pitcher-shaped liquid-measuring cups for dry ingredients isn't a good idea because it's impossible to level the flour off without shaking the cup, which packs the flour, so you end up with more than you need.

Most of our recipes call for all-purpose flour, but some specify cake flour. It's lower in protein than most all-purpose flours, making for a finer, softer crumb. You'll notice that sometimes we call for sifted flour and sometimes we don't—it all depends on the recipe. There's a difference in weight, and therefore amount, of a cup of sifted flour and a cup of unsifted flour. (A cup of sifted flour weighs about 114 grams; a cup of unsifted weighs about 135 grams—approximately three quarters of an ounce more.) In general, people balk at sifting, but it can make a huge difference in the lightness of some finished cakes.

FLAVORINGS: Don't cut corners here. Good pure vanilla extract (see page 707) is worth every penny. If your jars of ground spices have been around forever, throw them out and buy new ones. And if you've never tasted freshly grated nutmeg, it will be a revelation.

Old-Fashioned Gingerbread

SERVES 9
ACTIVE TIME: 25 MINUTES ■ START TO FINISH: 1½ HOURS (INCLUDES COOLING)

■ For many of us, gingerbread carries with it the ineffable comfort and almost inexplicable delight of a well-loved childhood dessert. That goes a long way toward explaining why gingerbread, which has been around in more or less its present form for over three hundred years, has surged in popularity. This version delivers all the flavor and cozy appeal and is easy to make. ■

- 2 cups all-purpose flour
- 1 teaspoon baking soda
- 1½ teaspoons ground ginger
- 1 teaspoon ground cinnamon
- ¼ teaspoon ground cloves
- ½ teaspoon salt
- 1 stick (8 tablespoons) unsalted butter, softened
- ¾ cup packed light brown sugar
- 2 large eggs
- ½ cup molasses (not robust or blackstrap)
- ⅔ cup hot water

Put a rack in middle of oven and preheat oven to 350°F. Butter a 9-inch square baking pan.

Sift together flour, baking soda, spices, and salt into a bowl.

Beat together butter and brown sugar in a large bowl with an electric mixer at medium-high speed until pale and fluffy, 3 to 5 minutes. Add eggs one at a time, beating well after each addition, then beat in molasses (batter may look separated). Reduce speed to low and beat in flour mixture, then add water and mix until batter is smooth, about 1 minute.

Pour batter into baking pan. Bake until a wooden pick or skewer inserted in center of cake comes out clean, 35 to 40 minutes. Cool in pan on a rack for about 20 minutes and serve warm.

Lemon Pound Cake

SERVES 8 TO 10
ACTIVE TIME: 35 MINUTES ■ START TO FINISH: 3 HOURS (INCLUDES COOLING)

■ Pound cake, which originated in England, takes its name from the fact that in its early form it was made with one pound each of flour, eggs, sugar, and butter. Because it's a rich, substantial cake that's easy to make and keeps well, it is beloved by bakers of all levels of experience. Often pound cakes are baked in loaf pans, but we like the distinctive angled and ridged pattern (and even baking) provided by a kugelhopf pan, a tall, decorative tube pan named for the Austrian yeast bread traditionally baked in it. ■

FOR CAKE

- 2 cups cake flour (not self-rising)
- 1 teaspoon baking powder
- ½ teaspoon salt
- 2 sticks (½ pound) unsalted butter, softened
- 2 cups granulated sugar
- ¼ cup finely grated lemon zest
- 6 large eggs
- 1½ teaspoons vanilla extract
- ¼ cup whole milk
- ¼ cup fresh lemon juice

FOR GLAZE

- 1 cup plus 1 tablespoon confectioners' sugar
- 2 tablespoons fresh lemon juice

OPTIONAL ACCOMPANIMENT: strawberries

SPECIAL EQUIPMENT: a 2-quart kugelhopf pan

MAKE THE CAKE: Put a rack in middle of oven and preheat oven to 325°F. Butter and flour kugelhopf pan, knocking out excess flour.

Whisk together flour, baking powder, and salt in a bowl. Beat together butter, granulated sugar, and lemon zest in a large bowl with an electric mixer at medium speed until pale and fluffy, 2 to 3 minutes. Beat in eggs one at a time, beating well after each addition, then beat in vanilla. Reduce mixer speed to low and add flour mixture, then milk and lemon juice, alternately in 3 batches, beginning and ending with flour mixture, beating until just combined.

Spoon batter into pan and smooth top. Bake until cake is golden brown and a wooden pick or skewer inserted in center comes out clean, 45 to 55 minutes. Cool cake in pan on a rack for 15 minutes, then invert onto rack to cool completely.

MAKE THE GLAZE WHILE THE CAKE COOLS: Gradually whisk confectioners' sugar into lemon juice in a small bowl until smooth and thick.

When cake is cool, set rack over a baking sheet. Drizzle glaze over cake, letting it drip down sides.

Serve cake with strawberries, if desired.

COOK'S NOTE

- The cake can be made up to 1 day ahead and refrigerated, covered (let glaze set before covering). Bring to room temperature before serving.

Ginger Pound Cake

SERVES 12 TO 14
ACTIVE TIME: 45 MINUTES ■ START TO FINISH: 4 HOURS (INCLUDES COOLING)

■ Attention, ginger lovers: this is a very rich, buttery cake with plenty of unmistakable ginger flavor front and center. Unlike most such cakes, which rely solely on powdered ginger, this one also includes a hefty amount of grated fresh ginger. Mellowed by sweetness, it is a little piquant but not hot. Adapted from a recipe by the cookbook author Jean Anderson, it is particularly nice accompanied by fresh fruit or berries. ■

- 6 ounces fresh ginger, peeled
- 4 cups sifted cake flour (not self-rising; sift before measuring)
- 1 teaspoon baking powder
- 1½ teaspoons ground ginger
- ½ teaspoon salt
- ¼ teaspoon mace
- 4 sticks (1 pound) unsalted butter, softened
- 1 teaspoon finely grated orange zest
- 3 cups sugar
- 6 large eggs, left at room temperature for 30 minutes
- ¾ cup whole milk, at room temperature

ACCOMPANIMENTS: sliced peaches or raspberries and whipped cream

SPECIAL EQUIPMENT: a 10-inch (12-cup) tube pan (4 inches deep)

Put a rack in middle of oven and preheat oven to 300°F. Butter and flour tube pan, knocking out excess flour.

Grate enough fresh ginger on small holes of a box grater into a bowl to measure ⅓ cup; do not drain off ginger juice. Sift together flour, baking powder, ground ginger, salt, and mace into a bowl, then sift together again.

Beat butter and zest in a large bowl with an electric mixer at medium-high speed until pale and fluffy, about 5 minutes. Add sugar ¼ cup at a time, beating well after each addition. Add eggs one at a time, beating well after each addition. Add grated ginger, with its juice, and beat until well combined. Reduce speed to low and add flour mixture and milk alternately in 3 batches, beginning and ending with flour mixture and mixing until just combined after each addition.

Spoon batter into tube pan. Bake until a wooden pick or skewer inserted in center of cake comes out clean, 1½ to 1¾ hours. Cool cake in pan on a rack for 30 minutes, then invert onto rack to cool completely.

Serve cake with peaches or raspberries and whipped cream.

COOK'S NOTE

- The cake can be made up to 2 days ahead and kept, well wrapped in plastic wrap, at room temperature.

Apple Raisin Cake

SERVES 12 TO 16
ACTIVE TIME: 35 MINUTES ■ START TO FINISH: 2¾ HOURS (INCLUDES COOLING)

■ Cubes of apple create a pretty mosaic in this sweet, spicy Bundt cake. They also make it beautifully moist, which means this is a great keeper—it actually gets better as it ages. We call for Cortland or Empire apples, but any apple that holds its shape when cooked will do; try Golden Delicious (the cake will be a little sweeter) or Gala. Think of this as a snacking cake, perfect for that midafternoon cup of tea, or a child's lunch-box or after-school treat. It came to us by request from Ellen Wagner, a reader who first enjoyed it at Richardson's Canal House Inn, near Rochester, New York. ■

- 3 cups all-purpose flour
- 1 teaspoon baking soda
- 1/2 teaspoon salt
- 1 1/2 cups vegetable oil
- 3 large eggs
- 1 1/2 cups granulated sugar
- 1/2 cup packed light brown sugar
- 1 tablespoon ground cinnamon
- 1/2 teaspoon freshly grated nutmeg
- 1 tablespoon dark rum
- 1 teaspoon vanilla extract
- 3 Cortland or Empire apples, peeled, cored, and cut into 1/4-inch dice
- 1/2 cup raisins

SPECIAL EQUIPMENT: a 12-cup Bundt pan

Put a rack in middle of oven and preheat oven to 350°F. Butter and flour Bundt pan, knocking out excess flour.

Sift together flour, baking soda, and salt into a bowl.

Whisk together oil, eggs, sugars, cinnamon, nutmeg, rum, and vanilla in a large bowl until just combined. Fold in flour mixture until just combined, then fold in apples and raisins. Spoon batter into pan.

Bake until a wooden pick or skewer inserted in center of cake comes out clean, about 1 1/4 hours. Cool cake in pan on a rack for 10 minutes, then turn out onto rack to cool completely.

COOK'S NOTE

■ The cake can be kept in an airtight container at room temperature for up to 5 days.

Honey Cake

SERVES 8 TO 10
ACTIVE TIME: 30 MINUTES ■ START TO FINISH: 2 1/2 HOURS (INCLUDES COOLING)

■ Honey cake is traditionally served during Rosh Hashanah, the Jewish New Year celebration, when honey symbolizes the sweetness of the year to come. This dense cake becomes moister and more flavorful if allowed to mellow for a day or two after it's baked. Serve it as a snack with coffee or the way many Rosh Hashanah celebrants do: toasted and spread with a layer of fresh cream cheese, for breakfast. ■

- 1 3/4 cups all-purpose flour
- 3/4 teaspoon baking soda
- 1/2 teaspoon baking powder
- 3/4 teaspoon salt
- 1 teaspoon ground cinnamon
- 1/2 teaspoon ground ginger
- 1 cup honey, preferably buckwheat
- 2/3 cup vegetable oil
- 1/2 cup strong brewed coffee, at room temperature
- 2 large eggs
- 1/4 cup packed brown sugar
- 2 tablespoons whiskey or bourbon

Put a rack in middle of oven and preheat oven to 350°F. Oil a 9-by-5-inch loaf pan well and dust with flour, knocking out excess.

Whisk together flour, baking soda, baking powder, salt, cinnamon, and ginger in a medium bowl. Whisk together honey, oil, and coffee in another bowl until well combined.

Beat together eggs and brown sugar in a large bowl with an electric mixer at high speed for 3 minutes. Reduce speed to low, add honey mixture and whiskey, and mix until blended, about 1 minute. Add flour mixture and mix until just combined. Finish mixing batter with a rubber spatula, scraping bottom of bowl (batter will be thin).

Pour batter into loaf pan and bake for 30 minutes. Cover loosely with foil and continue to bake until cake begins to pull away from sides of pan and a wooden pick or skewer inserted in center comes out clean, about 30 minutes more. Cool on a rack for 1 hour.

Run a knife around sides of pan, then invert rack over pan and invert cake onto rack. Turn cake right side up and cool completely.

COOK'S NOTE

- The cake can be kept, tightly wrapped in plastic wrap or in an airtight container, at room temperature for up to 1 week.

Orange–Poppy Seed Cake

SERVES 10 TO 12
ACTIVE TIME: 1 HOUR ■ START TO FINISH: 2½ HOURS (INCLUDES COOLING)

■ This simple, unfrosted cake is just the thing to serve when you want a dessert that is satisfying but not too rich or fancy. The poppy seeds provide texture and a hint of nuttiness, while the cake's orange essence is enhanced by a brushing with warm Grand Marnier syrup. A slice is great all by itself, but we like it even better with fresh berries and a dollop of crème fraîche. ■

FOR CAKE

- 1¾ cups sifted cake flour (not self-rising; sift before measuring)
- 1 teaspoon baking soda
- ½ teaspoon baking powder
- ¾ teaspoon salt, plus a pinch
- ¼ cup poppy seeds
- 4 large eggs, separated
- ⅔ cup sour cream
- 2 teaspoons vanilla extract
- 1½ sticks (12 tablespoons) unsalted butter, softened
- 1¼ cups granulated sugar
- 2 teaspoons finely grated orange zest
- ¼ teaspoon cream of tartar

FOR SYRUP

- ⅔ cup fresh orange juice
- ¼ cup Grand Marnier or other orange-flavored liqueur
- 2 tablespoons granulated sugar

OPTIONAL GARNISH: confectioners' sugar

ACCOMPANIMENT: mixed berries and crème fraîche

SPECIAL EQUIPMENT: a 10-inch (26-centimeter) springform pan

MAKE THE CAKE: Put a rack in middle of oven and preheat oven to 350°F. Butter springform pan, then dust with flour, knocking out excess.

Sift together flour, baking soda, baking powder, and ¾ teaspoon salt into a medium bowl. Stir in poppy seeds. Whisk together yolks, sour cream, and vanilla in a small bowl.

Beat together butter, 1 cup sugar, and zest in a large bowl with an electric mixer at high speed until pale and fluffy, 2 to 3 minutes. Add flour and yolk mixtures alternately in batches, beginning and ending with flour and beating well after each addition.

Beat whites with pinch of salt in a large bowl with cleaned beaters until foamy. Add cream of tartar and beat until whites just hold soft peaks. Beat in remaining ¼ cup sugar 1 tablespoon at a time and continue to beat until meringue just holds stiff peaks.

Fold about one third of meringue into batter to lighten it, then gently but thoroughly fold in remaining meringue.

Pour batter into pan and smooth top. Bake until a wooden pick or skewer inserted in center of cake comes out clean, 40 to 50 minutes.

MEANWHILE, MAKE THE SYRUP: Combine orange juice, liqueur, and sugar in a small heavy saucepan and heat over moderately high heat, stirring, just until sugar is dissolved. Remove from heat.

FINISH THE CAKE: Transfer baked cake to a rack and immediately poke holes all over top with a wooden pick or skewer. Brush top of cake with half of syrup, letting some run down between cake and sides of pan, and let stand for 10 minutes.

Run a thin knife around edge of pan and remove side of pan. Invert cake onto rack and gently remove bottom of pan. Poke holes all over bottom of cake and brush with remaining syrup. Reinvert cake onto another rack and cool completely.

If desired, sift confectioners' sugar over cake just before serving. Serve with berries and crème fraîche.

COOK'S NOTE

- The cake can be made up to 1 day ahead and kept, well wrapped in plastic wrap or in a cake keeper, at room temperature.

Vanilla — Anything but Plain

Vanilla extract is an easily accessible form of the spice, but often we prefer using the whole bean (or sometimes just the tiny, soft, sticky black seeds within). When you buy whole vanilla beans, you are getting better quality and more complex flavor; the best beans are not the ones destined to be blended with alcohol, which is used to extract the hundreds of aroma and flavor compounds from beans.

And what are those "beans," anyway? They are the fruit of a climbing orchid (*Vanilla planifolia*) that is indigenous to Mexico and Central America. Aztec emperors drank vanilla mixed with chocolate, explains David Karp, a "fruit detective" and vanilla expert, and the Spanish took it to Europe, where it became popular as a flavoring, a medicine, and an aphrodisiac. Since the kinds of bees and birds that pollinated the pale greenish yellow vanilla flowers existed only in the New World (and are now largely extinct, along with much of the rain forest in which they lived), all supplies came from there until the 1840s, when Edmond Albius, a former slave on the Indian Ocean island of Réunion, discovered a practical method of hand pollination. Cultivation on nearby Madagascar soared after the French colonized the island in 1896.

Once vanilla flowers begin to open and have been pollinated by hand (in Madagascar, this takes place in May and June), they stay on the vine throughout the long growing season. Between the flower and the vine's stem is an ovary, about an inch in length, which develops into a green seedpod, or bean. In July and August of the following year, when the beans are six to eight inches long, they are harvested by hand. They have no fragrance when they are green; they must be cured and aged for months to gain their characteristic perfume and flavor.

The flavor of the beans grown in different regions varies, and each has a loyal following. Highly regarded Bourbon vanilla gets its name not from Kentucky's finest but from the fact that Réunion was once called Bourbon, after the French royal family; it is grown on that island, Madagascar, and the Comoros, all former French colonies. These beans have a woodsy, mellow, rich flavor and aroma, with sweet, delicately spicy backnotes. The Mexican beans we've had are just as flavorful and a little more robust-looking. Tahitian vanilla (claimed by some botanists to be a different species) has a more intoxicating floral aroma and flavor and tastes less like what we think of as vanilla.

The best vanilla beans are glossy, moist, and supple; their seeds are plentiful and easily scraped out. Avoid beans that are shriveled and that look like twigs. Experiment to see which kind you prefer, and brace yourself for sticker shock: at this writing, vanilla is one of the most expensive spices in the world (although prices are expected to decline within a few years as huge new plantings from China to Uganda begin to bear fruit). The upside? You get what you pay for.

As for vanilla extract, read labels carefully. View the words *vanilla flavoring* with skepticism. The chemical vanillin is naturally made by many plants other than vanilla orchids and is a by-product of the wood-pulp industry. The hallmark for genuine vanilla extract is "alcohol 35 percent." Again, you get what you pay for.

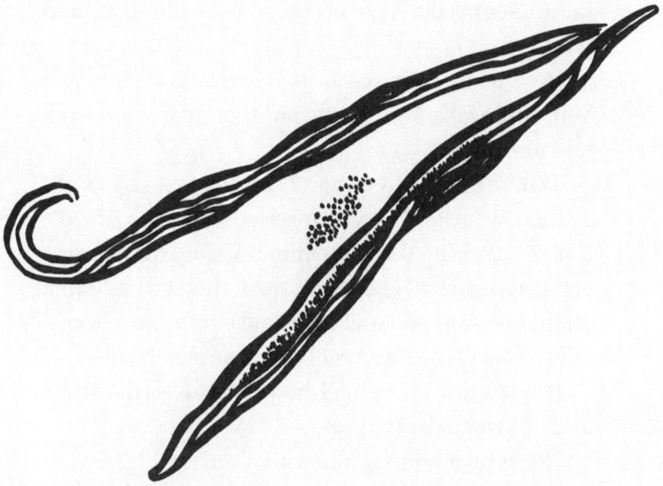

Lemon Semolina Cake with Raspberries and Whipped Cream

SERVES 6 TO 8
ACTIVE TIME: 30 MINUTES ■ START TO FINISH: 2 HOURS (INCLUDES COOLING)

■ Semolina, which is made from hard durum wheat and ground more coarsely than most flour, lends this lemony cake a pleasantly grainy texture. ■

- 12 blanched whole almonds
- 3 large eggs
- 3/4 cup superfine sugar
- 3/4 teaspoon finely grated lemon zest
- 1 tablespoon fresh lemon juice
- 1/2 cup plus 1 tablespoon semolina (see Sources)
- 1/2 cup very cold heavy cream
- 6 ounces (1 1/2 cups) raspberries

OPTIONAL GARNISH: confectioners' sugar
SPECIAL EQUIPMENT: an 8-by-2-inch round cake pan

Put a rack in middle of oven and preheat oven to 325°F. Grease cake pan, line bottom with a round of parchment or wax paper, and butter paper.

Pulse almonds in a food processor or an electric coffee/spice grinder until finely ground.

Separate eggs, putting yolks in a large bowl and whites in a slightly smaller one. Add sugar to yolks and beat with an electric mixer at high speed until very thick and pale, 2 to 3 minutes. Beat in zest and juice. Gently but thoroughly fold in almonds and semolina.

Beat whites with cleaned beaters until they just hold stiff peaks. Fold gently but thoroughly into yolk mixture.

Transfer batter to pan and smooth top. Bake until a wooden pick or skewer inserted in center of cake comes out clean, 25 to 30 minutes. Cool cake in pan on a rack for 10 minutes, then run a thin knife around edge of pan and invert cake onto rack. Carefully remove paper and cool cake completely.

Beat cream in a small bowl with electric mixer until it just holds stiff peaks.

Halve cake horizontally with a serrated knife (see page 727). Place bottom layer cut side up on a serving plate and spread cream evenly over it. Arrange raspberries on cream and top with remaining cake layer, cut side down.

Dust cake with confectioners' sugar, if desired.

VARIATION

■ You can fill the cake with sliced strawberries instead of raspberries and combine the whipped cream with a cup of bottled or homemade lemon curd (see page 876).

Walnut Spice Cake with Lemon Glaze

SERVES 10 TO 12
ACTIVE TIME: 45 MINUTES ■ START TO FINISH: 3 3/4 HOURS (INCLUDES COOLING)

■ Moist with sour cream, studded with chopped toasted walnuts, and aromatic with sweet spices, this cake makes a beautiful presentation when baked in a Bundt pan, and it keeps very well, so it can be made ahead. You can either spread the lemon glaze all over the cake, as we do here, or drizzle it generously in a pattern of your design. ■

FOR CAKE

- 2 cups all-purpose flour
- 1 teaspoon baking soda
- 1 teaspoon baking powder
- 1/2 teaspoon salt
- 1 1/2 teaspoons ground cinnamon
- 1 1/2 teaspoons ground allspice
- 1 1/2 teaspoons freshly grated nutmeg
- 2 sticks (1/2 pound) unsalted butter, softened
- 1 cup granulated sugar
- 3 large eggs, separated
- 1 teaspoon vanilla extract
- 1 1/4 cups sour cream
- 1 cup (3 1/2 ounces) walnuts, lightly toasted (see Tips, page 938) and finely chopped

FOR GLAZE

- 1 cup confectioners' sugar
- 4 teaspoons fresh lemon juice

SPECIAL EQUIPMENT: a 12-cup Bundt pan

MAKE THE CAKE: Put a rack in middle of oven and preheat oven to 350°F. Butter Bundt pan.

Sift together flour, baking soda, baking powder, salt, cinnamon, allspice, and nutmeg into a bowl.

Beat together butter and sugar in a large bowl with an electric mixer at medium-high speed until pale and fluffy, about 2 minutes in a stand mixer or about 4 minutes with a handheld mixer. Add egg yolks one at a time, beating well after each addition, then beat in vanilla. Reduce speed to low and add flour mixture and sour cream alternately in batches, beginning and ending with flour mixture and mixing well after each addition.

Beat egg whites in a large bowl with cleaned beaters until they just hold stiff peaks. Gently but thoroughly fold whites and walnuts into batter.

Spoon batter into buttered pan and smooth top. Bake until a wooden pick or skewer inserted in center of cake comes out clean, 40 to 50 minutes. Cool in pan on a rack for 10 minutes, then invert onto rack to cool completely.

MAKE THE GLAZE: Whisk together sugar and lemon juice in a small bowl until smooth. Transfer cake to a plate and spread on glaze with a spatula. Let stand until set, about 20 minutes.

COOK'S NOTES

- The cake, without the glaze, can be made up to 3 days ahead and kept, tightly wrapped in plastic wrap, at room temperature.
- The cake can be glazed up to 6 hours ahead and kept, loosely covered with plastic wrap, at room temperature (use wooden picks to keep the wrap from sticking to the glaze).

Passover Chocolate Nut Cake

SERVES 8 TO 10

ACTIVE TIME: 30 MINUTES ■ START TO FINISH: 3 HOURS (INCLUDES COOLING)

■ This elegant flourless chocolate cake relies on ground nuts for richness and body, making it perfect for the Passover holiday, when flour or leavening cannot be used. It's from contributor James Cohen, the former executive chef of the Lodge at Vail, in Colorado. ■

- 1 cup (3½ ounces) pecans
- 1 cup (5 ounces) hazelnuts
- 1 cup (5 ounces) almonds (with skins or without)
- 1 cup (3½ ounces) walnuts
- 7 ounces good bittersweet chocolate (not unsweetened), chopped
- ¾ cup sugar
- 8 large eggs, separated
- ½ teaspoon salt
- 1 teaspoon finely grated lemon zest
- 1 tablespoon finely grated orange zest

SPECIAL EQUIPMENT: a 9- to 9½-inch (24-centimeter) springform pan

Put a rack in middle of oven and preheat oven to 350°F. Lightly grease springform pan and line bottom with a round of parchment or wax paper.

Pulse nuts in batches in a food processor until finely ground (do not grind to a paste) and transfer to a bowl. Finely grind chocolate with 6 tablespoons sugar in processor and transfer to another bowl.

Beat yolks with salt in a large bowl with an electric mixer at medium-high speed until thick and pale, about 6 minutes. Beat in chocolate mixture, then beat in zests.

Beat egg whites with remaining 6 tablespoons sugar in a large bowl with cleaned beaters until whites hold soft peaks. Fold nuts and whites into yolk mixture alternately in batches until well combined.

Pour batter into pan. Bake until a wooden pick or skewer inserted in center of cake comes out clean, about 55 minutes.

Cool cake completely in pan on a rack before removing side of pan.

COOK'S NOTE

- The cake can be made up to 1 day ahead and kept, well wrapped in plastic wrap, at room temperature.

Almond Cake with Kirsch Cream and Lingonberry Preserves

SERVES 8 TO 10
ACTIVE TIME: 30 MINUTES ■ START TO FINISH: 2½ HOURS (INCLUDES COOLING)

■ There's a certain Scandinavian modesty about the look of this cake—it's low, topped very simply with whipped cream flavored with the cherry essence of kirsch and drizzled with lingonberry preserves—but inside it's rich, moist, and delicious. It's a keeper in two senses of the word: you'll want the recipe in your file forever, and the leftovers last beautifully. Make sure that you buy almond paste, not marzipan, which is too sweet; for this cake, we prefer Odense brand, in the tube, available in most supermarkets. ■

FOR CAKE
- 7 ounces almond paste (not marzipan; see Sources)
- 1 cup all-purpose flour
- 1 teaspoon baking powder
- ½ teaspoon salt
- 2 sticks (½ pound) unsalted butter, softened
- 1½ cups sugar
- 1 teaspoon vanilla extract
- 8 large eggs, left at room temperature for 30 minutes

FOR TOPPING
- 1½ cups very cold heavy cream
- 2 tablespoons kirsch
- 1 cup lingonberry preserves (see Sources)

SPECIAL EQUIPMENT: an 11-by-2½-inch (12-cup) springform tube pan with a decorative bottom or a 9-by-4-inch (12-cup) tube pan

MAKE THE CAKE: Put a rack in middle of oven and preheat oven to 325°F. Butter pan generously and dust with flour, knocking out excess.

Break almond paste into pieces and pulse in a food processor until very finely crumbled. Sift together flour, baking powder, and salt into a bowl.

Beat together butter and sugar in a large bowl with an electric mixer at high speed until pale and very fluffy, about 3 minutes. Add almond paste and vanilla and beat until well combined, about 2 minutes. Add eggs one at a time, beating well after each addition and occasionally scraping down sides of bowl with a rubber spatula. Reduce speed to low, add flour mixture, and mix for 30 seconds. Finish mixing batter by hand with spatula, scraping bottom of bowl.

Pour batter into tube pan and smooth top. Bake, turning pan around halfway through baking, until a wooden pick or skewer inserted in center of cake comes out clean and edges are beginning to pull away from pan, 55 minutes to 1 hour.

Cool cake completely in pan on a rack. (Cake may shrink and buckle slightly. Don't worry: this won't be visible once cake is inverted.) Run a thin knife around edges of pan and tube, invert a plate over pan, and invert cake onto plate.

JUST BEFORE SERVING, MAKE THE TOPPING: Beat together cream and kirsch in a chilled bowl with cleaned beaters at medium speed until soft peaks form.

To serve, spoon cream onto each slice of cake and drizzle with some of preserves.

COOK'S NOTE

■ The cake can be kept, well wrapped in plastic wrap, at cool room temperature for up to 3 days. It can also be frozen, wrapped in plastic wrap and foil, for up to 2 weeks. Thaw, without unwrapping, at room temperature.

Almond and Brown Butter Financiers

MAKES 4 DOZEN FINANCIERS
ACTIVE TIME: 45 MINUTES ■ START TO FINISH: 1½ HOURS (INCLUDES COOLING)

■ The flavor of these sophisticated little cakes comes from ground almonds, but it's intensified by the deep nuttiness of brown butter. They are rich and tender inside and have a wonderfully chewy outside. Financiers ("fin-nahn-see-*ays*") are often baked in ingot-shaped petit-four tins; you can also use narrow, pointed, shallow barquette tins (they remind us of canoes) or mini-muffin pans. The *Gourmet* contributor and cookbook author Faye Levy brought us this recipe. ■

- 1⅓ cups (5 ounces) slivered almonds
- 1¼ cups sugar
- ¾ cup all-purpose flour
- ½ teaspoon salt
- 8 large egg whites
- ¼ teaspoon almond extract
- 2 sticks (½ pound) unsalted butter

SPECIAL EQUIPMENT: twenty-four (4-inch) barquette tins (see Sources) or 2 mini-muffin pans, with twelve (1¾-inch) cups each

Put a rack in middle of oven and preheat oven to 400°F. Butter barquette tins or muffin pans.

Finely grind almonds with ¼ cup sugar in a food processor. Transfer to a large heavy saucepan and stir in remaining 1 cup sugar, then sift in flour and salt and stir until well combined. Add egg whites and almond extract and whisk to combine well. Set aside.

Cook butter in a 1- to 1½-quart heavy saucepan over moderately low heat until it is golden brown and has a nutty fragrance, about 15 minutes (bottom of pan will be covered with brown specks). Remove from heat.

Heat almond mixture over moderately low heat, whisking constantly, until just warm to the touch. Remove from heat and add browned butter in a slow stream, whisking constantly. Transfer batter to a 1-quart measuring cup or heatproof pitcher and let stand for 5 minutes.

Stir batter, then pour into buttered tins, or muffin pans, filling each three-fourths full. Set tins, if using, on baking sheets and bake financiers until firm to the touch and golden, 10 to 15 minutes. Turn out onto racks to cool completely. Let tins cool, then stir batter and make 24 more financiers in same manner.

COOK'S NOTE

■ The financiers can be kept in an airtight container at room temperature for 2 to 3 days.

Passover Sponge Cake with Apples

SERVES 8 TO 10
ACTIVE TIME: 30 MINUTES ■ START TO FINISH: 2½ HOURS (INCLUDES COOLING)

■ This ethereally light sponge cake combines matzo cake meal and potato starch and includes layers of sliced apples blended with cinnamon sugar. Be sure to use Golden Delicious apples, which keep their shape when baked and won't give off a lot of liquid. The result is a scrumptious cake appropriate for Passover, with warm cinnamon-flavored apples rippling through it. This recipe came to us from contributor Faye Levy. ■

- ½ cup matzo cake meal
- ¼ cup potato starch
- 6 large eggs, separated, left at room temperature for 30 minutes
- ¾ cup plus 1 tablespoon sugar
- 1 teaspoon finely grated lemon zest
- 1 teaspoon fresh lemon juice
- ¼ teaspoon salt
- 1½ teaspoons ground cinnamon
- 2 Golden Delicious apples

SPECIAL EQUIPMENT: a 9- to 9½-inch (24-centimeter) springform pan

Put a rack in middle of oven and preheat oven to 325°F.

Sift matzo meal with potato starch into a small bowl. Beat together yolks and ½ cup sugar in a large bowl with an electric mixer at high speed until pale and very thick, about 5 minutes. Beat in zest and juice.

Beat whites with salt in another large bowl with cleaned beaters at high speed until they hold soft peaks. Gradually beat in ¼ cup sugar and continue to beat until whites just hold stiff, glossy peaks.

Fold matzo-meal mixture into yolk mixture. Gently but thoroughly fold in whites in 3 batches.

Stir together remaining 1 tablespoon sugar and cinnamon. Peel, core, and thinly slice apples.

Spoon one third of batter into ungreased springform pan. Top with half of apple slices and sprinkle with half of cinnamon sugar. Repeat with another third of batter and remaining apples and cinnamon sugar. Gently spread remaining batter over apples and smooth top.

Bake cake until top is golden and firm and a wooden pick or skewer inserted in center comes out clean, about 1 hour. Cool in pan on a rack for 10 minutes, then loosen edge with a knife, remove side of pan, and cool cake completely.

COOK'S NOTE

- The cake can be made up to 2 days ahead and refrigerated, covered. Bring to room temperature before serving.

Measuring Egg Whites

If you measure the egg whites and whip them properly, you'll be well on your way to a successful angel food cake. Freshness is a factor too. Because an egg white is mostly water, you get more white per egg with fresh ones: the water hasn't yet begun to evaporate through the porous shell. Four fresh large Grade A eggs will yield about two tablespoons more whites than four that have been sitting around for a while. And, according to the food scientist Shirley Corriher, even though older, runnier whites whip up faster and give a little more volume when beaten, fresher, thicker whites produce a more stable foam. You are also less likely to break the yolk when separating a fresh egg—its telltale round, plump, "stand-up" shape means that the membrane corralling it is strong. An older yolk, flat and barely contained by its weakened membrane, breaks very easily.

Angel Food Cake

SERVES 8 TO 10
ACTIVE TIME: 20 MINUTES ■ START TO FINISH: $3\frac{1}{2}$ HOURS (INCLUDES COOLING)

This featherlight cake dates back to the 1870s, when it was considered a good way to use up egg whites. In those days, the whites were beaten to a fluff by spreading them out on a large platter or in a shallow bowl and whipping them to a foam with a fork, perforated spoon, or whisk. The fact that cooks considered this worth doing says volumes. Because it is naturally fat-free, angel food is often extolled as an alternative for cake lovers who are watching their diets. That's true, but we think this virtue pales beside the cake's sensational texture and delicate flavor—and the fact that it's an exceptional accompaniment to ice cream or fresh fruit.

FOR CAKE
- 1 cup cake flour (not self-rising)
- $1\frac{2}{3}$ cups sugar
- $1\frac{3}{4}$ cups egg whites (from about 13 large eggs)
- $\frac{1}{2}$ teaspoon salt
- 1 teaspoon cream of tartar
- $\frac{1}{2}$ teaspoon vanilla extract

FOR GLAZE
- 1 cup confectioners' sugar
- 2 tablespoons fresh lemon juice

OPTIONAL GARNISH: fresh raspberries and mint sprigs
SPECIAL EQUIPMENT: a 10-by-$4\frac{1}{2}$-inch (16-cup) tube pan, preferably with a removable bottom

MAKE THE CAKE: Put a rack in middle of oven and preheat oven to 300°F.

Sift flour 3 times, then sift together with $\frac{2}{3}$ cup sugar (see Cook's Note).

Beat egg whites in a large bowl with an electric mixer at medium-high speed until frothy. Add salt and cream of tartar and beat until whites barely form soft peaks. Beat in remaining 1 cup sugar 2 tablespoons at a time. Add vanilla and beat until whites hold soft peaks. Sift one quarter of flour mixture over whites and fold in gently but thoroughly, then sift and fold in remaining flour mixture in same manner.

Spoon batter into ungreased tube pan and smooth top. Rap pan on a hard surface twice to burst any air bubbles. Bake until cake is springy to the touch and a wooden pick or skewer inserted in center comes out clean, about 1¼ hours.

If pan has feet, invert it on a work surface; otherwise, invert it over neck of a long-necked bottle. Cool cake for 2 hours.

MAKE THE GLAZE: Stir together confectioners' sugar and lemon juice in a small bowl with a fork until smooth.

Run a thin knife in a sawing motion around edges of pan and tube to loosen cake. If using a two-piece pan, lift out cake with tube and invert onto a plate; or simply invert cake to unmold. Pour glaze over cake and let stand until glaze is set, about 10 minutes.

Garnish cake with raspberries and mint sprigs, if desired.

COOK'S NOTES

- The simplest way to do the sifting if you've got the space is on two sheets of wax paper. Sift the flour onto one sheet, then place the sifter on the other sheet and pour the flour into it for the second go-round.
- The unglazed cake can be made up to 1 day ahead and kept, covered, in the pan at room temperature.

Citrus Chiffon Cake

SERVES 12

ACTIVE TIME: 45 MINUTES ■ START TO FINISH: 2¾ HOURS (INCLUDES COOLING)

■ Cakes have been around for a long, long time, and it's not often that an entirely new approach to them shows up. So when a recipe for chiffon cake was announced on the Betty Crocker radio show in 1948 as "the cake discovery of the century," it was more than empty hype.

Though it was new to listeners, the cake, which was made with vegetable oil instead of solid fat, had been invented twenty years earlier by Harry Baker, a California insurance agent who baked the cakes for Hollywood restaurants. When General Mills finally bought the recipe from him, in 1947, and introduced it to the general public, it was a revelation.

Chiffon cakes have more than relative novelty to recommend them, though. The oil keeps them very moist, while the stiffly beaten egg whites folded into the batter just before baking ensure that they are light. With this version, we made a further innovation. Ordinarily the pan is not buttered and floured, but we discovered that if you do so, the cake develops a lovely delicate crust. When you cool this cake, don't follow the usual procedure and perch it on a bottle—if you do, it will fall out of the pan. Instead, cool it in the pan on a rack. ■

- 2¼ cups sifted cake flour (not self-rising; sift before measuring)
- 1½ cups granulated sugar
- 2 teaspoons baking powder
- 1 teaspoon salt
- 6 large eggs, separated
- 6 tablespoons canola oil
- 4 teaspoons finely grated orange zest
- 4 teaspoons finely grated lemon zest
- ¾ cup fresh orange juice
- 2 teaspoons vanilla extract
- 1 teaspoon cream of tartar

OPTIONAL GARNISH: confectioners' sugar

ACCOMPANIMENT: Citrus Syrup (recipe follows)

SPECIAL EQUIPMENT: a 10-inch (12-cup) tube pan

Put a rack in middle of oven and preheat oven to 350°F. Butter pan and dust with flour, knocking out excess.

Sift together flour, 1 cup sugar, baking powder, and salt into a large bowl. Whisk together yolks, oil, zests, orange juice, and vanilla in a medium bowl, then add to flour mixture and whisk until batter is smooth.

Beat whites with cream of tartar in a large bowl with an electric mixer at medium-high speed until they just hold soft peaks. Reduce speed to low and add remaining ½ cup sugar 2 tablespoons at a time, beating until whites just hold stiff, glossy peaks. Stir about one third of whites into batter to lighten it, then gently but thoroughly fold in remaining whites. Spoon batter into pan and smooth top (batter will reach top of pan).

Bake until cake is golden and a wooden pick or skewer inserted in center comes out clean, 50 minutes to 1 hour. Cool cake completely in pan on a rack.

Turn cake out of pan onto a serving plate. Dust with sifted confectioners' sugar and serve syrup on the side.

COOK'S NOTE

- The cake can be made up to 2 days ahead and kept in an airtight container at cool room temperature.

Citrus Syrup

MAKES ABOUT 2 CUPS
ACTIVE TIME: 15 MINUTES ■ START TO FINISH: 15 MINUTES

■ A classic simple syrup made with citrus juices instead of water, this is delicious drizzled over chiffon cake. It also works very nicely with fresh fruit salad. ■

- 1½ cups sugar
- 1 cup fresh orange juice
- 1 cup fresh lemon juice

Combine sugar and juices in a 1½-quart heavy saucepan, bring to a simmer, and simmer, stirring occasionally, until sugar dissolves. Continue to cook until syrup is slightly thickened and reduced to about 2 cups, about 10 minutes. Cool completely.

COOK'S NOTE

■ The syrup can be made up to 3 days ahead and refrigerated, covered.

Three-Milk Cake with Coconut and Fresh Fruit

Pastel de Tres Leches con Coco

SERVES 6
ACTIVE TIME: 1 HOUR ■ START TO FINISH: 5 HOURS (INCLUDES CHILLING)

■ The simple, light sponge cake technically called a génoise is made for soaking up delectable syrups. In this Latino classic, it's saturated with one made of "three milks"—sweetened condensed milk, whole milk, and heavy cream—after baking. You could even argue that this is *cuatro leches,* because coconut milk flavored with rum has been added to the mix, upping the wow factor. This recipe is adapted from the one served at Chicago's Adobo Grill. ■

FOR CAKE

- 1 stick (8 tablespoons) unsalted butter, cut into pieces
- ½ teaspoon vanilla extract
- ¼ cup all-purpose flour
- ¼ cup cornstarch
- ¼ teaspoon salt
- 5 large eggs
- ½ cup sugar

FOR MILK SYRUP

- 2 (14-ounce) cans sweetened condensed milk
- ½ cup heavy cream
- ½ cup whole milk
- ¼ cup well-stirred canned unsweetened coconut milk
- ⅓ cup light rum

ACCOMPANIMENTS: unsweetened whipped cream, chopped strawberries and kiwifruit, and toasted coconut

SPECIAL EQUIPMENT: two 8-inch square baking pans

MAKE THE CAKE: Put a rack in middle of oven and preheat oven to 350°F. Butter one baking pan and line bottom with a square of parchment or wax paper. Butter paper and dust with flour, knocking out excess.

Cook butter in a small saucepan over moderate heat, swirling pan occasionally, until golden brown, 5 to 7 minutes. Transfer to a heatproof bowl and let cool, then stir in vanilla.

Sift together flour, cornstarch, and salt into another bowl, then sift again.

Combine eggs and sugar in a mixer bowl or other large metal bowl set over a saucepan of simmering water (do not let bowl touch water) and heat, whisking constantly, until lukewarm. Remove bowl from pan and beat eggs with an electric mixer at high speed until thick, pale, and tripled in volume, about 6 minutes in a stand mixer or about 10 minutes with a handheld mixer. Sift half of flour mixture over eggs and fold in gently but thoroughly, then fold in remaining flour. Transfer ⅓ cup batter to a small bowl and fold butter into it until incorporated, then gently but thoroughly fold butter mixture into remaining batter.

Spread batter evenly in prepared pan. Bake until cake is springy to the touch and top is golden, 15 to 17 minutes.

MEANWHILE, MAKE THE MILK SYRUP: Whisk together all ingredients in a large glass measuring cup or a bowl with a spout until combined. Transfer ⅓ cup syrup to a small bowl and reserve, refrigerated, for garnish.

Cool cake in pan on a rack for 5 minutes, then prick all over with a skewer or wooden pick. Run a knife around edges of pan, then invert second baking pan over cake and flip cake into it. Remove paper and prick cake all over with skewer again.

Pour milk syrup over cake and gently press with a spatula to help saturate it. Refrigerate, covered with plastic wrap, until most of syrup has been absorbed, at least 4 hours.

Cut cake into 6 rectangles and transfer with spatula to plates. Drizzle reserved chilled syrup around it. Top with whipped cream and coconut and sprinkle top and plate with fruit.

COOK'S NOTE

- The syrup-soaked cake can be refrigerated for up to 2 days.

Sauternes-Soaked Cake with Candied Kumquats and Toasted Almonds

SERVES 10 TO 12
ACTIVE TIME: 1 HOUR ■ START TO FINISH: 2¾ HOURS (INCLUDES COOLING)

■ Kumquats are an underappreciated little winter fruit often thought of as having mainly decorative qualities. In fact, they have a distinctive, pleasantly tart citrus flavor that takes particularly well to candying in a sugar syrup, as we do here. (In contrast to most fruits, their rind is sweeter than their flesh.) The kumquat syrup from the candying is served on the side, and syrup made of sweet Sauternes wine is poured over the cake after it is baked. This works perfectly because the cake is a génoise, the sponge cake that was born to absorb syrup. Deceptively understated, this classy cake is extremely sophisticated, ideal for an important celebration such as an anniversary or a formal wintertime dinner party. If you like, you can make it in stages and assemble it just before serving. ■

FOR CAKE

- 1¼ cups cake flour (not self-rising)
- ⅛ teaspoon salt
- 5 large eggs
- ⅔ cup sugar
- 1 teaspoon vanilla extract
- 5 tablespoons unsalted butter, melted and cooled

FOR CANDIED KUMQUATS

- 1 cup water
- 1 cup sugar
- ⅛ teaspoon salt
- 3 cups kumquats (1 pound with leaves; see Sources), 1 whole kumquat reserved for syrup and remainder halved lengthwise (or quartered if large), leaves and seeds discarded

FOR SAUTERNES SYRUP

- 1½ cups Sauternes
- 6 tablespoons sugar
- Zest of reserved kumquat, removed with a vegetable peeler

FOR TOPPING

- 2 tablespoons sliced almonds, toasted (see Tips, page 938)

SPECIAL EQUIPMENT: a 10-by-2-inch round cake pan

MAKE THE CAKE: Put a rack in middle of oven and preheat oven to 350°F. Butter cake pan, line bottom with a round of parchment or wax paper, and butter paper.

Sift together flour and salt into a bowl.

Beat together eggs and sugar in a large bowl with an electric mixer at high speed until tripled in volume and thick enough to form a ribbon that takes 2 seconds to dissolve into batter when beater is lifted, 7 to 8 minutes with a stand mixer or 14 to 16 minutes with a handheld mixer. Beat in vanilla.

Sift flour mixture one third at a time over batter, folding it in gently but thoroughly with a rubber spatula. Stir together butter and about ¾ cup batter in a small bowl until combined, then gently but thoroughly fold butter mixture into batter.

Pour batter into cake pan and bake until a wooden pick or skewer inserted in center of cake comes out clean, 30 to 40 minutes.

MEANWHILE, MAKE THE CANDIED KUMQUATS: Combine water, sugar, and salt in a 2-quart heavy saucepan and bring to a boil, stirring until sugar is dissolved. Reduce heat and simmer, uncovered, for 2 minutes. Add halved kumquats and simmer, uncovered, stirring occasionally, until tender, 10 to 12 minutes. With a slotted spoon, transfer kumquats to a heatproof bowl. Boil syrup until reduced to about ¾ cup, 3 to 7 minutes. Pour syrup over kumquats.

When cake is done, transfer pan to a rack and run a thin knife around edge of pan. Cool for about 20 min-

Ribboning

The simple step of ribboning goes a long way toward ensuring the lightness and volume of a finished cake. When your egg mixture forms a ribbon that takes two seconds to dissolve into the batter when the beater is lifted, you are right where you want to be. It should drop in a wide, flat band that folds in on itself, as a heavy satin ribbon would. (If it falls in a thin column, keep beating.) Don't try to rush things: for the Sauternes-Soaked Cake (opposite page), for example, ribboning can take a good ten or fifteen minutes.

Ribboning is a sign that the sugar is completely dissolved and the eggs are well aerated, which will help them disperse evenly throughout the batter. A cake that hasn't been ribboned correctly won't rise as high as it should, and it may have a dense, rubbery layer on the bottom when baked. Volume is also lost if you let a ribboned mixture sit around before baking.

utes, then invert cake onto a platter with a lip and remove paper.

WHILE THE CAKE COOLS, MAKE THE SAUTERNES SYRUP: Combine Sauternes, sugar, and zest in a 1-quart heavy saucepan and bring to a boil, stirring until sugar is dissolved. Boil until reduced to about 1 cup, 5 to 8 minutes. Remove from heat and discard zest.

ASSEMBLE THE CAKE: Prick top of cake all over with a wooden pick or skewer. Brush or pour Sauternes syrup little by little evenly over cake, waiting for it to be absorbed after each addition. Cool cake for 1 hour.

With slotted spoon, mound kumquats on cake, then top with almonds. Serve remaining kumquat syrup on the side.

COOK'S NOTES

- The kumquats can be candied up to 3 days ahead and refrigerated, covered, in the syrup. Bring to room temperature before serving.
- The Sauternes syrup can be made up to 1 day ahead and refrigerated, covered.
- The cake can be baked up to 1 day ahead and kept, wrapped in plastic wrap, at room temperature.
- The cake can be soaked with the syrup up to 6 hours before serving and kept at room temperature, covered with an inverted large bowl or cake keeper.

Pineapple Upside-Down Cakes

MAKES 6 INDIVIDUAL CAKES
ACTIVE TIME: 20 MINUTES ■ START TO FINISH: 1½ HOURS

■ Pineapple upside-down cake zoomed to popularity shortly after the invention of canned pineapple in the early 1900s. In fact, when the Hawaiian Pineapple Company (now Dole Pineapple) sponsored a recipe contest in the mid-1920s, fully 2500 of the more than 60,000 recipes were for pineapple upside-down cake.

We've tweaked tradition by making single-serving upside-down cakes in muffin tins. Tender and buttery, these pineapple-infused cakes were requested by reader Linda Colehower after she tasted them at the Haliimaile General Store on Maui. ■

FOR PINEAPPLE LAYER

- ½ stick (4 tablespoons) unsalted butter, cut into pieces
- ⅓ cup packed dark brown sugar
- 6 (¼-inch-thick) slices fresh pineapple (about 3 inches wide), cored, or 6 canned pineapple slices in juice (from a 14-ounce can), drained

FOR CAKE

- 1½ cups cake flour (not self-rising)
- 2 teaspoons baking powder
- ½ teaspoon salt
- ½ cup whole milk
- 1 teaspoon vanilla extract
- ¾ stick (6 tablespoons) unsalted butter, softened
- ¾ cup granulated sugar
- 2 large egg yolks

SPECIAL EQUIPMENT: a nonstick muffin pan with six extra-large (1-cup) cups

Put a rack in middle of oven and preheat oven to 350°F.

MAKE THE PINEAPPLE LAYER: Melt butter in a 1½- to 2-quart heavy saucepan over moderately low heat. Add brown sugar and cook, whisking, until mixture is smooth, about 1 minute. Divide among muffin cups (about 1½ tablespoons per cup). Put 1 pineapple slice in each cup.

MAKE THE CAKE BATTER: Sift together flour, baking powder, and salt into a bowl. Whisk together milk and vanilla in a small bowl.

Beat butter with sugar in a large bowl with an electric mixer at medium speed until pale and fluffy, about 3 minutes. Add yolks one at a time, beating well after each addition. Reduce speed to low and add flour mixture and milk mixture alternately in 3 batches, beginning and ending with flour mixture and mixing until just combined.

BAKE THE CAKES: Divide batter evenly among cups. Bake until puffed and pale golden and a wooden pick or skewer inserted in center of a cake comes out with a few crumbs adhering, 25 to 30 minutes. Cool cakes in pan on a rack for 15 minutes, then loosen sides of cakes with a thin knife and invert onto rack to cool to warm or room temperature.

Rhubarb Anise Upside-Down Cake

SERVES 8

ACTIVE TIME: 30 MINUTES ■ START TO FINISH: 1½ HOURS

■ This pretty cake is a great way to use rhubarb, one of the first signs of spring. The flavor of the fruit is enhanced by a hint of anise—not what you might call an intuitive addition, but a wonderful, unexpected partner for the tartness of the rhubarb. We use a well-seasoned cast-iron skillet for this cake: it heats evenly and retains the heat. ■

FOR TOPPING

- ½ stick (4 tablespoons) unsalted butter
- ¾ cup packed light brown sugar
- 1½ pounds rhubarb stalks, trimmed and cut into 1-inch pieces (3 cups)

FOR CAKE

- 1 teaspoon anise seeds
- 1½ cups all-purpose flour
- 1½ teaspoons baking powder
- 1 teaspoon baking soda
- ½ teaspoon salt
- 1 stick (8 tablespoons) unsalted butter, softened
- ⅔ cup granulated sugar
- ½ teaspoon vanilla extract
- 2 large eggs
- ½ cup well-shaken buttermilk
- ¼ cup whole milk

SPECIAL EQUIPMENT: a well-seasoned 10-inch cast-iron or heavy ovenproof nonstick skillet (at least 2 inches deep); a mortar and pestle or an electric coffee/spice grinder

Put a rack in middle of oven and preheat oven to 350°F.

MAKE THE TOPPING: Heat butter in skillet over moderate heat until foam subsides. Reduce heat to low, sprinkle brown sugar evenly onto bottom of skillet, and cook, without stirring, for 3 minutes (not all sugar will be melted). Remove skillet from heat and arrange rhubarb decoratively, rounded sides down, in one layer on sugar mixture. Set aside.

MAKE THE CAKE BATTER: Finely grind anise seeds in mortar with pestle or in coffee/spice grinder. Sift together anise, flour, baking powder, baking soda, and salt into a bowl.

Beat together butter and sugar in a large bowl with an electric mixer at medium-high speed until pale and fluffy, about 1 minute. Beat in vanilla. Add eggs one at a time, beating well after each addition. Reduce speed to low and add flour mixture alternately in batches with buttermilk and milk, beginning and ending with flour mixture and mixing until just combined; do not overbeat.

BAKE THE CAKE: Spoon batter over rhubarb in skillet and spread it evenly, being careful not to disturb rhubarb. Bake cake until golden and a wooden pick or skewer inserted in center comes out clean, 40 to 45 minutes. Cool in skillet on a rack for 15 minutes.

Run a thin knife around edge of skillet. Wearing oven mitts, invert a plate over skillet and, keeping plate and skillet firmly pressed together, invert cake onto plate. Carefully lift skillet off cake and if necessary replace any fruit stuck to bottom of skillet. Serve cake warm or at room temperature.

Fresh Apricot Upside-Down Cake

SERVES 8

ACTIVE TIME: 15 MINUTES ■ START TO FINISH: 1¾ HOURS

■ For us, summer just wouldn't be summer without this twist on an old favorite, in which the lush flavors of caramel and apricots combine with the clean taste of a classic yellow cake. It is also a perfect dessert for those occasions when you don't have a lot of time to spend in the kitchen but want to present your guests with a slightly festive, wholly delicious home-baked dessert. ■

FOR TOPPING

- 1 stick (8 tablespoons) unsalted butter
- ¾ cup packed light brown sugar
- 10–11 small (2- to 2¼-inch-wide) apricots (1¼ pounds), halved lengthwise and pitted

FOR CAKE

- 1¾ cups all-purpose flour
- 1½ teaspoons baking powder
- ½ teaspoon baking soda
- ½ teaspoon salt
- 1 stick (8 tablespoons) unsalted butter, softened
- ¾ cup granulated sugar
- 1½ teaspoons vanilla extract
- ¼ teaspoon almond extract
- 2 large eggs, left at room temperature for 30 minutes
- ¾ cup well-shaken buttermilk

SPECIAL EQUIPMENT: a well-seasoned 10-inch cast-iron skillet or heavy ovenproof nonstick skillet (at least 2 inches deep)

Put a rack in middle of oven and preheat oven to 375°F.

MAKE THE TOPPING: Heat butter in skillet over moderate heat until foam subsides. Reduce heat to low, sprinkle brown sugar evenly over butter, and cook, without stirring, for 3 minutes (not all sugar will be melted). Remove skillet from heat and arrange apricot halves, cut sides down, close together on top of sugar mixture. Set aside.

MAKE THE CAKE BATTER: Sift together flour, baking powder, baking soda, and salt into a bowl.

Beat together butter, sugar, and extracts in a large bowl with an electric mixer at medium-high speed until pale and fluffy, about 3 minutes. Beat in eggs one at a time, then beat batter until creamy and doubled in volume, 2 to 3 minutes. Reduce speed to low and add flour mixture and buttermilk alternately in 3 batches, beginning and ending with flour and mixing just until combined.

BAKE THE CAKE: Gently spoon batter over apricots and spread evenly, being careful not to disturb fruit. Bake until cake is golden brown and springy to the touch and a wooden pick or skewer inserted in center comes out clean, 40 to 45 minutes. Cool in skillet on a rack for 15 minutes.

Run a thin knife around edge of skillet. Wearing oven mitts, invert a large plate over skillet and, keeping plate and skillet firmly pressed together, invert cake onto plate. Carefully lift skillet off cake and if necessary replace any fruit stuck to bottom of skillet. Serve warm or at room temperature.

Cranberry Cognac Trifle

SERVES 8 TO 12

ACTIVE TIME: 2½ HOURS ■ START TO FINISH: 13 HOURS (INCLUDES MAKING JAM, SYRUP, AND CUSTARD)

■ This exuberant dessert, a custardy, cakey, boozy mélange served in a deep bowl, dazzles the eye as well as the palate. It's the sum of many parts, each of which can be made several days ahead. Assemble the trifle the day before serving so the cake can absorb the custard and the flavors—bright, bracing cranberries mellowed by a splash of Cognac—can develop fully. ■

FOR CAKE LAYERS

- 6 large eggs, separated
- 6 large egg yolks
- 2¼ cups granulated sugar
- 6 tablespoons whole milk

1½ teaspoons vanilla extract
1½ cups all-purpose flour
¾ teaspoon salt

FOR ASSEMBLING TRIFLE

Cranberry Jam (recipe follows)
Cognac Syrup (recipe follows)
Rich Custard (recipe follows)

FOR CREAM TOPPING

1⅓ cups very cold heavy cream
¼ cup confectioners' sugar
2 tablespoons Cognac or other brandy
¼ teaspoon vanilla extract

SPECIAL EQUIPMENT: three 15-by-10-by-1-inch baking sheets; a 3½-quart straight-sided glass trifle or soufflé dish

MAKE THE CAKE LAYERS: Put a rack in middle of oven and preheat oven to 350°F. Butter baking sheets, line bottoms with parchment or wax paper, and butter paper. Dust pans with flour, knocking out excess.

Whisk together yolks, 1½ cups granulated sugar, milk, and vanilla in a large bowl until well combined. Whisk in flour and salt until smooth. (Batter will be thick.)

Beat whites in a large bowl with an electric mixer at medium speed until they hold soft peaks. Reduce speed to low and gradually mix in remaining ¾ cup sugar. Increase speed to high and beat until whites hold stiff, glossy peaks.

Fold about one third of whites into batter to lighten it, then gently but thoroughly fold in remaining whites. Divide batter among pans and spread evenly, then rap pans against work surface to burst any air bubbles. Bake one pan at a time until cake is pale golden and beginning to shrink around edges, 10 to 11 minutes per pan. Cool layers completely in pans on racks.

ASSEMBLE THE TRIFLE: Loosen edges of 1 cake layer with a knife. Lay a sheet of parchment or wax paper on top of layer and invert onto rack. Carefully peel off paper from cake. Put a new sheet of parchment or wax paper on inverted cake and reinvert onto work surface; peel off paper that is now on top. Repeat with remaining 2 layers.

Cut each layer crosswise in half with a serrated knife. Spread 3 half-layers with cranberry jam, then top with remaining plain layers. Cut each "sandwich" crosswise into ten ¾-inch-wide strips. Stand 1 strip on end in trifle dish with a cut side against glass and trim strip flush with top of dish. Using trimmed piece as a guide, cut remaining strips to fit dish; reserve trimmings. Brush strips on all sides with Cognac syrup and fit strips tightly all around sides of dish, with cut sides out. (If your dish is slightly narrower at the bottom than at the top, cut a few strips diagonally in half and use to fill any gaps.)

Brush trimmings with syrup and arrange one quarter of them in one layer in bottom of dish. Pour in 1 cup custard. Repeat layering trimmings and custard to fill dish, ending with custard. (You may have a small amount of custard left over.) Brush tops of strips around edges with syrup. Cover trifle with plastic wrap and refrigerate for at least 8 hours.

MAKE THE TOPPING: Just before serving, beat cream with confectioners' sugar, Cognac, and vanilla in a large bowl with electric mixer at medium speed until it holds soft peaks. Remove plastic wrap from trifle and mound cream on top.

COOK'S NOTES

- Resist the temptation to bake more than one cake layer at a time, or the layers will bake extremely unevenly.
- The layers can be baked up to 2 days before you assemble the trifle and refrigerated (cut them in half crosswise first, if desired), wrapped well in plastic wrap. They can also be frozen for up to 1 month.
- The trifle, without the topping, can be refrigerated for up to 1 day.

Cranberry Jam

MAKES ABOUT 2 CUPS
ACTIVE TIME: 15 MINUTES ■ START TO FINISH: 1 HOUR (INCUDES COOLING)

■ There's no need to reserve this jam exclusively for the trifle; make extra and enjoy it on toast. ■

1 vanilla bean, halved lengthwise
1 (12-ounce) bag (3½ cups) fresh or unthawed frozen cranberries
1½ cups sugar
½ cup fresh orange juice
½ cup water

SPECIAL EQUIPMENT: a food mill fitted with a fine disk

With tip of a sharp knife, scrape vanilla seeds from pod into a 2-quart heavy saucepan. Add pod and remaining ingredients and bring to a boil, stirring occasionally. Reduce heat and simmer, stirring occasionally, until thick, about 20 minutes (jam will continue to thicken as it cools).

Purée jam through food mill set over a bowl; discard skins and vanilla pod. Cool, stirring occasionally.

COOK'S NOTE

- The jam can be made up to 4 days ahead and refrigerated, covered.

Cognac Syrup

MAKES ABOUT 1½ CUPS
ACTIVE TIME: 5 MINUTES ■ START TO FINISH: 30 MINUTES (INCLUDES COOLING)

■ This heady syrup, an integral part of our trifle, brings a rich, almost caramel nuance to the party. ■

- 1 cup water
- ½ cup sugar
- 2 (4-inch) strips orange zest, removed with a vegetable peeler
- ⅔ cup Cognac or other brandy

Combine all ingredients in a 1-quart saucepan and bring to a boil, stirring until sugar is dissolved. Reduce heat and simmer for 5 minutes. Cool completely and discard zest.

COOK'S NOTE

- The syrup can be made up to 4 days ahead and refrigerated, covered.

Rich Custard

MAKES ABOUT 5 CUPS
ACTIVE TIME: 30 MINUTES ■ START TO FINISH: 1 HOUR (INCLUDES COOLING)

■ Custard for a trifle can be a tricky thing: if it's too thin, the dessert will be soupy, and if it's too thick, the cake won't absorb it. This one, thickened slightly with cornstarch, has just the right amount of body. ■

- ¾ cup sugar
- 3 tablespoons cornstarch
- Pinch of salt
- 4 cups whole milk
- 2 teaspoons finely grated orange zest
- 10 large egg yolks
- 1 teaspoon vanilla extract

SPECIAL EQUIPMENT: an instant-read thermometer

Whisk together ¼ cup sugar, cornstarch, and salt in a 2-quart heavy saucepan. Whisk in ¼ cup milk until smooth, then whisk in remaining milk and zest. Bring to a boil over moderate heat, whisking frequently.

Meanwhile, whisk together yolks and remaining ½ cup sugar in a large bowl. Gradually whisk in hot milk mixture, then pour mixture back into saucepan. Cook, stirring constantly, until mixture registers 170°F on thermometer, 3 to 4 minutes; do not let boil. Immediately pour custard through a fine-mesh sieve into a metal bowl set in a bowl of ice and cold water. Stir in vanilla. Cool, stirring frequently.

COOK'S NOTE

- The custard can be made up to 3 days ahead and refrigerated, its surface covered with wax paper and the bowl covered with plastic wrap.

Rhubarb Roulade

SERVES 6
ACTIVE TIME: 40 MINUTES ■ START TO FINISH: 1½ HOURS (INCLUDES COOLING)

■ A roulade is essentially an old-fashioned jelly roll: a thin cake layer rolled tightly around a filling while it is still warm. Tangy rhubarb cooked down to a thick deep-pink jam makes an eye-catching and flavorful swirl. ■

FOR CAKE

- 4 large eggs, separated
- 8 tablespoons granulated sugar
- 1 teaspoon vanilla extract
- ⅛ teaspoon salt
- ¾ cup all-purpose flour

FOR FILLING

1 pound rhubarb stalks, trimmed and finely chopped
½ cup granulated sugar

GARNISH: confectioners' sugar for dusting

ACCOMPANIMENT: lightly sweetened whipped cream

SPECIAL EQUIPMENT: a 15-by-10-by-1-inch baking sheet

MAKE THE CAKE: Put a rack in middle of oven and preheat oven to 350°F. Butter baking sheet and line with wax paper. Butter paper and dust with flour, knocking out excess.

Beat together yolks, 5 tablespoons sugar, and vanilla in a large bowl with an electric mixer at high speed until thick and pale, about 3 minutes.

Beat whites with salt in another large bowl with cleaned beaters until they just hold soft peaks. Add remaining 3 tablespoons granulated sugar a little at a time, beating until whites just hold stiff peaks.

Gently fold one third of flour and one third of whites into yolk mixture, then gently fold in remaining flour and whites in 2 more batches, making sure flour is thoroughly incorporated.

Spread batter evenly on lined sheet and bake until top is pale and dry to the touch, 10 to 12 minutes. Transfer sheet with cake to a rack, cover cake with a kitchen towel, and cool for 5 minutes.

MEANWHILE, MAKE THE FILLING: Combine rhubarb and sugar in a 12-inch nonstick skillet and cook over moderately high heat, stirring, until rhubarb is reduced to a thick purée, about 8 minutes. Spread filling on a plate and refrigerate for 5 minutes.

ASSEMBLE THE ROULADE: Remove towel and position cake with a short end nearest you. Spread rhubarb filling evenly over cake, leaving a 1-inch border on each short end. Put a platter next to far end of cake. Beginning with short side near you and using wax paper as an aid, roll up cake jelly-roll style. Carefully transfer roll seam side down to platter, using wax paper as an aid. Cool cake for 45 minutes.

Dust cake generously with confectioners' sugar. Slice with a serrated knife and serve with whipped cream.

COOK'S NOTE

- The rhubarb filling can be made up to 1 day ahead and refrigerated, covered.

Buttermilk Cupcakes

MAKES ABOUT 30

ACTIVE TIME: 30 MINUTES ■ START TO FINISH: 1½ HOURS (INCLUDES COOLING AND MAKING FROSTINGS)

■ Every cook needs one all-purpose cupcake recipe, perfect for a birthday party or bake sale. This is it. Buttermilk gives these delicious little cakes a well-rounded flavor. ■

3¼ cups plus 2 tablespoons sifted cake flour (not self-rising; sift before measuring)
1½ teaspoons baking powder
1½ teaspoons baking soda
1¼ teaspoons salt
1½ sticks (12 tablespoons) unsalted butter, softened
1½ cups sugar
1½ teaspoons vanilla extract
3 large eggs
1½ cups well-shaken buttermilk
Chocolate Cream Cheese Frosting (recipe follows)
Lemon Cream Cheese Frosting (recipe follows)

SPECIAL EQUIPMENT: two muffin pans with twelve (⅓- or ½-cup) cups each plus one pan with 6 cups; 30 paper muffin cup liners

Put racks in upper and lower thirds of oven and preheat oven to 350°F. Line muffin cups with paper liners.

Whisk together flour, baking powder, baking soda, and salt in a bowl.

Beat together butter and sugar in a large bowl with an electric mixer at high speed until pale and fluffy, 2 to 3 minutes. Beat in vanilla. Add eggs one at a time, beating well after each addition. Reduce speed to low, add buttermilk, and mix until just combined (mixture will look curdled). Add flour mixture in 3 batches, beating until just combined after each addition.

Divide batter among lined muffin cups, filling each about two-thirds full. Bake, switching position of pans halfway through baking, until cupcakes are golden and a wooden pick or skewer inserted in center of a cupcake comes out clean, 18 to 22 minutes total. Cool cupcakes in pans on racks for 5 minutes, then turn out onto racks to cool completely.

Spread half of cupcakes with chocolate frosting and remaining half with lemon frosting.

COOK'S NOTE

- The unfrosted cupcakes can be made up to 2 days ahead and kept in an airtight container at room temperature.

Chocolate and Lemon Cream Cheese Frostings

MAKES ABOUT 3¼ CUPS FROSTING (ENOUGH FOR 30 CUPCAKES)
ACTIVE TIME: 20 MINUTES ■ START TO FINISH: 35 MINUTES

■ These quick, simple frostings, yielding two flavors from one cream cheese base, will make cupcakes for a crowd a breeze. For a 9-inch layer cake, use the base to make either chocolate or lemon frosting; just double the flavoring amount. ■

3 ounces unsweetened chocolate, chopped
1 stick (8 tablespoons) plus 7 tablespoons unsalted butter, softened
8 ounces whipped cream cheese
3 cups confectioners' sugar
2 tablespoons plus 1 teaspoon fresh lemon juice

Melt chocolate in a metal bowl set over a saucepan of barely simmering water, stirring occasionally until smooth. Remove from heat and cool to room temperature.

Beat together butter, cream cheese, and confectioners' sugar in a large bowl with an electric mixer at low speed until light and fluffy, 5 to 8 minutes.

Transfer half of frosting to another bowl and stir in melted chocolate until well combined. Stir lemon juice into remaining frosting until well combined. (If frostings are too soft to spread easily, chill slightly before using.)

COOK'S NOTE

- The frostings can be made up to 2 days ahead and refrigerated, covered. Bring to room temperature and whisk until smooth before using.

Orange–Chocolate Chip Cupcakes with Chocolate Frosting

MAKES 12 CUPCAKES
ACTIVE TIME: 20 MINUTES ■ START TO FINISH: 1¾ HOURS (INCLUDES COOLING AND MAKING FROSTING)

■ Cupcakes once conjured up images of birthday parties for young children, but they are undergoing a renaissance among culinary trendsetters. ■

1 cup all-purpose flour
1½ teaspoons baking powder
⅛ teaspoon salt
5 tablespoons unsalted butter, softened
½ cup sugar
1 large egg
Finely grated zest of 1 orange
½ teaspoon vanilla extract
½ cup whole milk
½ cup mini semisweet chocolate chips
Chocolate Frosting (recipe follows)
SPECIAL EQUIPMENT: a muffin pan with twelve (⅓- to ½-cup) cups; 12 paper muffin cup liners

Put a rack in middle of oven and preheat oven to 350°F. Line muffin cups with paper liners.

Sift together flour, baking powder, and salt into a bowl.

Beat together butter and sugar in a large bowl with an electric mixer at medium-high speed until pale and fluffy, about 3 minutes. Beat in egg, zest, and vanilla. Reduce speed to low and add flour mixture and milk alternately in 3 batches, beginning and ending with flour mixture and beating just until incorporated. Fold in chips.

Divide batter among lined muffin cups. Bake until pale golden and a wooden pick or skewer inserted in center of a cupcake comes out clean, 20 to 25 minutes. Turn cupcakes out onto a rack to cool completely.

Spread frosting on cupcakes.

COOK'S NOTE

- The cupcakes can be made up to 1 day ahead and kept in an airtight container at room temperature.

Chocolate Frosting

MAKES ABOUT ½ CUP
ACTIVE TIME: 5 MINUTES ■ START TO FINISH: 35 MINUTES

■ This ganache frosting, made with heavy cream and semisweet chocolate chips, may seem thin compared to buttercream, but it spreads beautifully. If you want a slightly thicker ganache, let it stand at room temperature for up to thirty minutes, depending on the heat of your kitchen. ■

¾ cup mini semisweet chocolate chips
¼ cup heavy cream

Put chocolate chips in a small bowl. Bring cream to a simmer in a small heavy saucepan. Pour cream evenly over chocolate. Let stand for 1 minute to soften, then stir until smooth. If frosting is too loose to spread, let it sit at room temperature for 10 to 30 minutes, stirring occasionally; frosting will continue to thicken as it stands.

Blackberry Jam Cake with Caramel Icing

SERVES 12 TO 16
ACTIVE TIME: 40 MINUTES ■ START TO FINISH: 3½ HOURS (INCLUDES COOLING)

■ Every year for twenty years, *Gourmet*'s production director baked this cake for our mailroom manager on his birthday, so it has clearly stood the test of time. The blackberry jam not only adds a rather subtle sweet-tart flavor but also keeps the cake particularly moist. (Be sure to use jam, not an all-fruit product such as Polaner, or you will not get the proper texture and flavor.) Intriguingly spicy, the cake is finished off with an almost fudgelike caramel icing, called penuche, that is grainy before it melts on the tongue. This is an excellent dessert to take to a potluck or a casual dinner party, since it travels very well. ■

FOR CAKE

3 cups plus 1 tablespoon all-purpose flour
1¼ teaspoons salt
1½ teaspoons ground allspice
1½ teaspoons ground cloves
½ teaspoon ground cinnamon
2 sticks (½ pound) unsalted butter, softened
2 cups sugar
5 large eggs, lightly beaten
1 cup well-shaken buttermilk
1 teaspoon baking soda
1 cup seedless blackberry jam
1 cup chopped raisins or dates
1 cup (5 ounces) chopped pecans

FOR ICING

3 cups packed light brown sugar
1 cup evaporated milk
1 stick (8 tablespoons) unsalted butter

SPECIAL EQUIPMENT: a candy thermometer; an offset spatula

MAKE THE CAKE: Put a rack in middle of oven and preheat oven to 325°F. Butter a 13-by-9-inch baking pan, line bottom with parchment or wax paper, and butter paper.

Sift together 3 cups flour, salt, allspice, cloves, and cinnamon into a bowl.

Beat together butter and sugar in a large bowl with an electric mixer at high speed until pale and fluffy, 3 to 5 minutes. Add eggs and beat until well combined.

Stir together buttermilk and baking soda in a small bowl. Working in 3 batches, alternately add flour and buttermilk mixtures to butter mixture, beating well after each addition. Add jam and beat until well combined. Toss together raisins, pecans, and remaining 1 tablespoon flour in a bowl, then add to batter and stir until well combined.

Pour batter into baking pan. Bake until a wooden pick or skewer inserted in center of cake comes out clean, 55 to 60 minutes. Cool in pan on a rack for 15 minutes, then invert cake onto rack, remove paper, and cool completely.

MAKE THE ICING: Combine brown sugar, evaporated milk, and butter in a 3-quart saucepan and cook over moderately low heat, stirring, until sugar is dissolved. Cook, without stirring, washing down any sugar crystals clinging to side of pan with a pastry brush dipped in cold water, until caramel registers 238°F on thermometer, about 10 minutes. Immediately transfer to a heatproof bowl and beat with a handheld mixer at high speed until just thickened, pale, and spreadable, about 5 minutes.

Working very quickly, ice top of cake using offset spatula (icing will set after 15 minutes). If icing gets too hard to spread, dip spatula in hot water.

COOK'S NOTES

- The cake can also be made in two 9-inch round cake pans. Bake at 325°F for 40 to 45 minutes. Cool in the pans on a rack for 15 minutes, then invert onto the rack to cool completely. Transfer one layer, bottom side up, to a cake plate and ice it. Top with the remaining cake layer, right side up, and ice the top and sides of the cake.
- The cake is also good with cream cheese frosting in place of the caramel icing; see page 739.

All-Occasion Yellow Cake

MAKES ONE 13-BY-9-INCH CAKE OR TWO 8- OR 9-INCH ROUND CAKES
ACTIVE TIME: 15 MINUTES ■ START TO FINISH: 1¾ HOURS (INCLUDES COOLING)

■ One month, when we ran a story by the food historian Laura Shapiro about the pernicious effects of boxed cake mixes on the American home baker, we decided to provide a small object lesson on the virtues of baking from scratch. This basic all-purpose cake, developed in our test kitchens, is the result. Incredibly simple, it takes only about ten more minutes to prepare than a boxed mix, and the results are spectacularly better. It's very tender, with a light and airy crumb, and all the flavors—butter, eggs, sugar, and vanilla—are balanced and true. The cake is also the ultimate in versatility: it can be baked in a round or oblong cake pan, and whether layered or served as a sheet cake, it's wonderful with nearly any kind of frosting or topping, or it can be enjoyed on its own. It should be the cornerstone of every cake baker's repertoire. ■

- 2 cups cake flour (not self-rising)
- 2 teaspoons baking powder
- ½ teaspoon salt
- 1 stick (8 tablespoons) unsalted butter, softened
- 1 cup sugar
- 3 large eggs, left at room temperature for 30 minutes
- 1½ teaspoons vanilla extract
- ¾ cup whole milk

ACCOMPANIMENT: Chocolate Ganache Frosting or Seven-Minute Frosting (recipes follow)
SPECIAL EQUIPMENT: a 13-by-9-inch baking pan (not dark) or two 8- or 9-by-2-inch round cake pans

Put a rack in middle of oven and preheat oven to 350°F. Butter and flour baking pan or cake pans, knocking out excess.

Sift together flour, baking powder, and salt into a bowl.

Beat butter and sugar with an electric mixer (fitted with whisk attachment if using a stand mixer) at medium-high speed until pale and fluffy, 3 to 5 minutes. Beat in eggs one at a time, then beat in vanilla and beat until thoroughly blended, about 5 minutes. Reduce speed to low and add flour mixture and milk alternately in 3 batches, beginning and ending with flour mixture and mixing until batter is just smooth; do not overmix.

Spread batter evenly in pan(s). Bake until cake begins to pull away from sides of pan(s) and a wooden pick or skewer inserted in center comes out clean, 20 to 25 minutes (cake will still be pale in color, not golden brown). Cool for 5 minutes in pan(s) on a rack, then invert onto rack to cool completely.

Spread chocolate or seven-minute frosting on cake.

Chocolate Ganache Frosting

MAKES ABOUT 2 CUPS
ACTIVE TIME: 15 MINUTES ■ START TO FINISH: 2 HOURS

- ¾ pound good bittersweet chocolate (not unsweetened), finely chopped
- 1 cup heavy cream

Put chocolate in a heatproof medium bowl. Bring cream to a simmer in a 3- to 4-quart heavy saucepan, then pour over chocolate and whisk until smooth. Refrigerate, covered, stirring occasionally, until thickened but still spreadable, about 2 hours. (If ganache becomes too thick, let stand at room temperature, stirring once or twice, until slightly softened.)

COOK'S NOTE

- The ganache can be made up to 3 days ahead. Let stand at room temperature until soft enough to spread.

Seven-Minute Frosting

MAKES ABOUT 4 CUPS
ACTIVE TIME: 15 MINUTES ■ START TO FINISH: 15 MINUTES

- 2 large egg whites
- 1 cup sugar
- 1/4 cup water

Combine all ingredients in a metal bowl set over a saucepan of simmering water and beat with a handheld electric mixer at low speed until mixture is warm and sugar is dissolved. Increase speed to high and beat until frosting is thick and fluffy, about 7 minutes. Remove bowl from heat and beat until slightly cooled.

COOK'S NOTE

■ The egg whites in this recipe may not be fully cooked. If this is a concern, see page 629.

Golden Cake with Chocolate–Sour Cream Frosting

SERVES 12
ACTIVE TIME: 1 HOUR ■ START TO FINISH: 3 HOURS (INCLUDES COOLING AND MAKING FROSTING)

■ Very big and very beautiful, this classic four-layer cake is baked in two round cake pans, then split into four layers. The sour cream plays a dual role here: it adds richness to the cake, and its tang offsets the sweetness of the frosting. If you're looking for a delicious and very impressive birthday cake to serve to a large group, this is it. ■

- 3 1/2 cups cake flour (not self-rising)
- 1 tablespoon baking powder
- 3/4 teaspoon baking soda
- 1 teaspoon salt
- 2 sticks (1/2 pound) unsalted butter, softened
- 2 cups sugar
- 4 large eggs, left at room temperature for 30 minutes
- 2 teaspoons vanilla extract
- 2 cups sour cream
- Chocolate–Sour Cream Frosting (recipe follows)

OPTIONAL GARNISH: Brown Sugar Buttercream (page 743)
SPECIAL EQUIPMENT: two 9-by-2-inch round cake pans

Put a rack in middle of oven and preheat oven to 350°F. Butter cake pans and line bottoms with rounds of parchment or wax paper. Butter paper and dust pans with flour, knocking out excess.

Sift together flour, baking powder, baking soda, and salt into a bowl.

Beat together butter and sugar in a large bowl with an electric mixer at medium speed until pale and fluffy, about 3 minutes. Add eggs one at a time, beating well after each addition, then beat in vanilla. Reduce speed to low, add half of flour mixture, and mix until just blended. Add sour cream, mixing until just combined, then add remaining flour mixture and mix until smooth.

Divide batter between pans and smooth tops. Bake until cake is springy to the touch and a wooden pick or skewer inserted in center comes out clean, 30 to 40 minutes. Cool in pans on racks for 10 minutes, then invert onto racks, remove paper, and cool completely.

If necessary, trim tops of cooled cake layers with a long serrated knife to make them flat and level. Halve each layer horizontally with serrated knife (see page 727).

Put 1 cake layer on a cake plate and spread with 3/4 cup frosting. Top with remaining cake layers, using 3/4 cup frosting between each layer. Frost top and sides of cake with remaining frosting.

Pipe brown sugar buttercream decoratively on cake, if desired.

COOK'S NOTES

■ The cake layers can be made up to 1 day ahead and kept, well wrapped in plastic wrap, at room temperature.

■ The cake can be assembled up to 1 day ahead and refrigerated in a cake keeper or loosely covered with plastic wrap (use toothpicks to hold the wrap away from the frosting). Bring to room temperature before serving.

■ The batter can also be baked in a 13-by-9-inch pan for 50 to 55 minutes. It can also be used to make cupcakes; bake in thirty (1/3- or 1/2-cup) muffin cups for about 25 minutes.

Chocolate–Sour Cream Frosting

MAKES ABOUT 4 CUPS, ENOUGH FOR A FOUR-LAYER 9-INCH CAKE
ACTIVE TIME: 15 MINUTES ■ START TO FINISH: 30 MINUTES

■ This frosting couldn't be easier to make, or easier to work with. Use it on any yellow or white layer cake. ■

- 1¼ pounds good milk chocolate, finely chopped
- 10 ounces good semisweet chocolate, finely chopped
- 3 cups sour cream
- 2 teaspoons vanilla extract

Melt chocolates in a large metal bowl set over a saucepan of simmering water, stirring occasionally until smooth. Remove from heat and whisk in sour cream and vanilla. Cool to room temperature, stirring occasionally (frosting will thicken as it cools).

COOK'S NOTE

- Once frosting has cooled, spread it quickly, before it becomes too thick. If it does become stiff, reheat over simmering water, stirring, then cool again.

Carrot Cake with Cream Cheese Frosting

SERVES 10 TO 12
ACTIVE TIME: 45 MINUTES ■ START TO FINISH: 3 HOURS (INCLUDES COOLING)

■ Moist, rich, and dense, carrot cake is one of the most American of desserts, popular from one end of the country to the other. But there's always room for improvement: this version includes pineapple and coconut, which keep the cake extra-moist. The recipe, which came to us from reader Felix Papadakis, is one of the best we've ever tasted. ■

FOR CAKE

- About ¾ pound carrots
- 2 cups all-purpose flour
- 2 teaspoons baking powder
- 1½ teaspoons baking soda
- 1½ teaspoons salt
- 2 teaspoons ground cinnamon
- 2 cups granulated sugar
- 1½ cups vegetable oil
- 4 large eggs
- 1 (8-ounce) can crushed pineapple, drained
- 1 cup sweetened flaked coconut
- ½ cup chopped walnuts
- ⅔ cup raisins (optional)

FOR FROSTING

- 2 (8-ounce) packages cream cheese, softened
- 1 stick (8 tablespoons) unsalted butter, softened
- 1 teaspoon vanilla extract
- 2½ cups confectioners' sugar, sifted

SPECIAL EQUIPMENT: two 9-by-2-inch round cake pans

MAKE THE CAKE: Put a rack in middle of oven and preheat oven to 350°F. Butter and flour cake pans, knocking out excess flour.

Shred enough carrots on smallest teardrop holes of a box grater or with fine shredding disk in a food processor to measure 2 cups.

Sift together flour, baking powder, baking soda, salt, and cinnamon into a large bowl. Stir in sugar, oil, eggs, carrots, pineapple, coconut, walnuts, and raisins (if using).

Divide batter between cake pans and bake until a wooden pick or skewer inserted in center of cakes comes out clean, 35 to 45 minutes. Cool layers in pans on a rack for 5 minutes, then run a thin knife around edge of each pan and invert layers onto rack to cool completely.

MAKE THE FROSTING: Beat together cream cheese, butter, and vanilla in a large bowl with an electric mixer at medium-high speed until fluffy, about 2 minutes. Reduce speed to medium, add confectioners' sugar, and beat until frosting is smooth.

Place 1 cake layer bottom side up on a cake plate and spread with some of frosting. Place remaining cake layer right side up on top and spread remaining frosting over top and sides of cake.

COOK'S NOTES

- The cake layers can be made up to 1 day ahead and kept, well wrapped in plastic wrap, at room temperature.
- The frosting can be made up to 1 day ahead and refrigerated, covered. Bring to room temperature, then beat with an electric mixer at medium speed until smooth before frosting cake.

SPLITTING AND DECORATING A CAKE

Before a smidgen of frosting makes contact with your cake, be sure you have all the necessary tools clean and close at hand. (Any special equipment we mention is available at cookware shops and by mail from New York Cake & Baking Distributors; see Sources.) A long narrow offset spatula (see page 733) is extremely helpful for spreading wide swaths of frosting. If you plan to create a piped design, you'll need at least one good-sized pastry bag (or one for each color of frosting), the proper tips, and the couplers to attach them to the bags, which provide an extra measure of security. A cake-decorating turntable, similar to a lazy Susan, isn't essential for most cakes, but it does make smoothing the frosting on large cakes a breeze, and it certainly enables you to feel like a pro. If you do use a turntable, you'll also want a cardboard cake round (see Sources) to rest the cake on and two wide, rigid pancake turner–style spatulas to move it from turntable to cake plate.

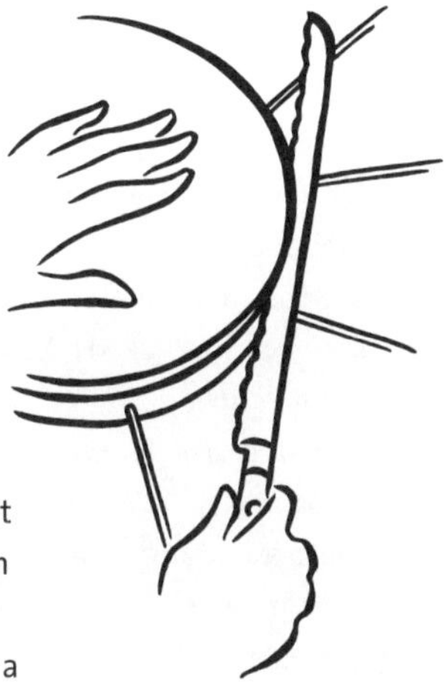

SPLITTING CAKE LAYERS: We try to avoid splitting cake layers — it is difficult to make them even, and once split, they are very fragile — but if you are going for a big four-layer cake, it makes sense. To do this, insert long wooden skewers horizontally into the cake halfway up the side in about eight places. Then rest an 11- to 12-inch knife (preferably serrated) on the sticks and use a long sawing motion to cut the cake layer in two. If your split cake layer is on the sturdy side, lift off the top half with two wide metal spatulas, so it doesn't crack or break. If it is more fragile, gently lift up one edge of the top half with a spatula and then carefully slip the removable bottom of a tart pan or a rimless baking sheet between the layers and lift off the layer. Bear in mind that frosting can cover a multitude of mishaps: if that top half cracks or breaks, gently piece it back together on top of the filling and frost.

PREPPING FOR FROSTING: Prepping a cake for frosting is a lot like getting a wall ready for painting: cake crumbs, like dust and grime, are the enemy. Once you have stacked your layers and lightly brushed them free of loose crumbs, apply what's called a crumb coating (think primer), a thin layer of frosting all over the top and sides, to seal any remaining crumbs in place. Chill the cake to firm up the frosting, then watch as your second coat goes on effortlessly. Put a generous amount of frosting on top and spread it until it begins to slump over the side, then go vertical. After spreading a small patch of frosting down the sides with a 6- to 8-inch narrow offset metal spatula, keep that hand still and slowly spin the turntable or turn the plate with the other, spreading the frosting smoothly and evenly.

PROTECTING YOUR CAKE: Once your masterpiece is finished, the best way to protect it is to keep it in a cake keeper. There's no better way to preserve both the decoration on the outside and the moisture on the inside. We love the elegance of a glass dome if your cake is staying put, but if it's going to travel, you'll do well to invest in a plastic version, preferably with handles.

Coconut Cake with Lime Curd

SERVES 10 TO 12
ACTIVE TIME: 1½ HOURS ■ START TO FINISH: 4 HOURS (INCLUDES CHILLING CURD)

■ Buttery and tender, this dramatic cake features three yellow cake layers sandwiched together with a tangy lime curd—the ideal complement to the sweet coconut frosting. ■

FOR LIME CURD FILLING

- 6 large egg yolks
- ¾ cup sugar
- ½ cup fresh lime juice
- 3 tablespoons heavy cream
- ¾ stick (6 tablespoons) cold unsalted butter, cut into tablespoons
- 2 teaspoons finely grated lime zest
- 1 cup sweetened flaked coconut

FOR CAKE LAYERS

- 3⅓ cups sifted cake flour (not self-rising; sift before measuring)
- 1 tablespoon baking powder
- 1 teaspoon salt
- 1 cup whole milk
- ½ cup water
- 1½ teaspoons vanilla extract
- 2½ sticks unsalted butter, softened
- 1¾ cups sugar
- 5 large eggs

FOR FROSTING

- 2 large egg whites
- 1½ cups sugar
- ½ cup water
- 1 tablespoon light corn syrup
- 1 teaspoon finely grated lime zest
- 1 teaspoon fresh lime juice

FOR TOPPING

- 2 cups sweetened flaked coconut

SPECIAL EQUIPMENT: three 9-by-2-inch round cake pans

MAKE THE LIME CURD: Whisk together yolks, sugar, lime juice (grate zest first and reserve), cream, and butter in a 1½- to 2-quart heavy saucepan and cook over low heat, whisking constantly, until curd is thick enough to hold marks of whisk and a few bubbles appear on surface, 5 to 7 minutes; do not let boil. Pour curd through a fine-mesh sieve into a medium bowl and stir in zest. Cover surface of curd with plastic wrap and refrigerate for at least 3 hours.

MAKE THE CAKE LAYERS: Put racks in middle and lower third of oven and preheat oven to 350°F. Butter cake pans and line bottom of each with a round of parchment or wax paper. Butter paper, then dust pans with flour, knocking out excess.

Whisk together flour, baking powder, and salt in a bowl. Stir together milk, water, and vanilla in a large glass measuring cup.

Beat butter in a large bowl with an electric mixer at medium speed for 1 minute, then add sugar in a slow steam and continue to beat until light and fluffy, about 2 minutes. Add eggs one at a time, beating well after each addition. Reduce speed to low and add flour and milk mixtures alternately in 3 batches, beginning and ending with flour mixture and mixing until just combined; do not overbeat.

Divide batter among pans and smooth tops. Place two pans in middle of oven and one pan in lower third (do not put top pans directly above bottom pan), and bake, switching position of pans halfway through baking, until a wooden pick or skewer inserted in center of cakes comes out clean, 25 to 30 minutes total. Run a thin knife around edges of pans, invert layers onto racks, remove paper, and cool completely.

ASSEMBLE THE CAKE LAYERS: Put 1 cake layer on a cake plate or platter. Spread evenly with half of lime curd and sprinkle with ½ cup coconut. Refrigerate for 15 minutes. Repeat layering with another cake layer, remaining lime curd, and remaining ½ cup coconut. Top with remaining cake layer and refrigerate for 15 minutes.

MAKE THE FROSTING: Combine all ingredients in a large metal bowl and beat with a handheld electric mixer until combined. Set bowl over a saucepan of boiling water and beat at high speed until frosting holds stiff, glossy peaks, about 7 minutes (depending on mixer and weather, this may take longer). Remove bowl from heat and beat frosting until cool and spreadable, about 8 minutes.

Frost cake. Gently press coconut onto top and sides of cake.

COOK'S NOTES

- The cake layers can be made up to 1 day ahead and kept, well wrapped in plastic wrap, at room temperature. They can also be frozen, wrapped in plastic wrap and foil, for up to 1 week. (Thaw, still wrapped, in the refrigerator for 1 day.)
- The lime curd can be refrigerated for up to 2 days.
- The cake can be layered with the curd up to 6 hours ahead and refrigerated; it can be frosted up to 2 hours ahead.

Coconut Cake with Raspberry Coulis

SERVES 10 TO 12
ACTIVE TIME: 1¼ HOURS ■ START TO FINISH: 4¾ HOURS (INCLUDES CHILLING PASTRY CREAM)

■ This coconut cake is subtler than our showstopping version with lime curd (see opposite page), but it's equally grand. The layers aren't as tall, so there is a higher proportion of custardy filling to cake. The recipe was requested by reader Lenn Curley, who enjoyed the cake at the Halekulani Hotel, in Honolulu. ■

FOR CAKE

- 1¼ cups sifted cake flour (not self-rising; sift before measuring)
- ⅓ cup plus 7 tablespoons sugar
- 1¼ teaspoons baking powder
- ¼ teaspoon salt
- ¼ cup vegetable oil
- ¼ cup water
- 1 large egg
- 4 large egg whites
- Pinch of cream of tartar

FOR PASTRY CREAM

- 1½ cups whole milk
- ¼ teaspoon salt
- 1 vanilla bean, halved lengthwise
- ⅓ cup plus 5 tablespoons sugar
- ¼ cup all-purpose flour
- 4 large egg yolks
- 1 cup sweetened flaked coconut
- 1¼ cups very cold heavy cream

FOR RASPBERRY COULIS

- 2 cups raspberries
- 1 cup sugar

FOR TOPPING

- 1½ cups sweetened flaked coconut

SPECIAL EQUIPMENT: a 9- to 9½-inch (24-centimeter) springform pan

MAKE THE CAKE: Put a rack in middle of oven and preheat oven to 350°F.

Stir together cake flour, ⅓ cup plus 1 tablespoon sugar, baking powder, and salt in a bowl. Whisk together oil, water, and egg in another bowl, then add to flour mixture and whisk until smooth.

Beat egg whites with cream of tartar in a large bowl with an electric mixer at medium-high speed until they barely hold soft peaks. Beat in remaining 6 tablespoons sugar 1 tablespoon at a time and continue beating until meringue holds stiff peaks.

Fold one third of meringue into batter to lighten it, then gently but thoroughly fold in remaining meringue.

Pour batter into ungreased springform pan. Bake until a wooden pick or skewer inserted in center of cake comes out clean, 20 to 25 minutes. Run a thin knife around edge of pan, then cool cake for 5 minutes. Remove side of pan and invert cake onto a rack. Gently remove bottom of pan and cool cake completely.

MEANWHILE, MAKE THE PASTRY CREAM: Bring milk and salt just to a simmer in a 2-quart saucepan over moderately high heat. Remove from heat and scrape seeds from vanilla bean into milk; discard pod.

Whisk together ⅓ cup plus 2 tablespoons sugar, flour, and yolks in a medium bowl (mixture will be very stiff). Whisk in one third of hot milk and whisk until smooth. Whisk yolk mixture into hot milk in saucepan, bring to a boil over moderate heat, and boil, whisking, for 1 minute. Transfer to a bowl and stir in coconut. Cover surface with wax paper and cool completely, then refrigerate for at least 3 hours.

Beat heavy cream with remaining 3 tablespoons sugar with cleaned beaters until it holds stiff peaks. Fold 1½ cups whipped cream into pastry cream; cover and refrigerate. Cover remaining whipped cream and refrigerate.

MAKE THE COULIS: Combine raspberries and

sugar in a blender and purée until smooth. Force through a fine-mesh sieve into a bowl, pressing hard on solids; discard solids.

ASSEMBLE THE CAKE: Cut cake horizontally into 3 layers with a serrated knife (see page 727). Place bottom layer cut side up on a cake stand or platter. Spread with half of pastry cream and top with middle cake layer. Spread with remaining pastry cream and top with third cake layer, cut side down. Spread reserved whipped cream on top and sides of cake. Gently press coconut onto top and sides.

Serve cake with coulis.

COOK'S NOTES

- The cake layers can be made up to 1 day ahead and kept, well wrapped in plastic wrap, at room temperature. They can also be frozen, wrapped in plastic wrap and foil, for up to 1 week. (Thaw, still wrapped, in the refrigerator for 1 day.)
- The pastry cream, without the whipped cream, can be refrigerated for up to 2 days.
- The raspberry coulis can be made up to 2 days ahead and refrigerated, covered.
- The cake can be assembled up to 6 hours ahead and refrigerated.

Nectarine Mousse Cake

SERVES 12 TO 14
ACTIVE TIME: 2 HOURS ■ START TO FINISH: 6 HOURS (INCLUDES CHILLING)

■ What you see is a rather beautiful pale pinkish orange mousse with a deeper orange glaze on top. What you get after slicing into it is a génoise saturated with peach schnapps or orange Muscat syrup. This outstanding cake, perfect for an engagement party or any other fancy frolic, is not difficult to make, and you will be *so* pleased with yourself. ■

FOR CAKE

- 2/3 cup all-purpose flour
- 1/2 teaspoon salt
- 1/4 cup Clarified Butter (page 935), melted and cooled slightly
- 1 teaspoon vanilla extract
- 4 large eggs
- 2/3 cup sugar

FOR MOUSSE

- 1 1/2 pounds nectarines
- 1/2 cup sugar
- 1/2 cup plus 2 tablespoons water
- 1/4 cup fresh lemon juice
- 2 tablespoons peach schnapps or orange Muscat, such as Essencia
- 1 1/2 tablespoons unflavored gelatin (from two 1/4-ounce envelopes)
- 1 1/2 cups very cold heavy cream

FOR SYRUP

- 1/4 cup sugar
- 1/4 cup water
- 1/4 cup peach schnapps or orange Muscat

FOR GLAZE

- 1 1/4 teaspoons unflavored gelatin (from a 1/4-ounce envelope)
- 6 tablespoons cold water
- 3/4 cup peach preserves or jam

SPECIAL EQUIPMENT: one 9- to 9 1/2-inch (24-centimeter) and one 10-inch (26-centimeter) springform pan, preferably nonstick

MAKE THE CAKE: Put a rack in middle of oven and preheat oven to 350°F. Butter bottom of 9-inch springform pan and line bottom with a round of parchment or wax paper. Butter paper and dust pan with flour, knocking out excess.

Sift together flour and salt onto a large sheet of wax paper. Stir together clarified butter and vanilla in a small bowl.

Whisk together eggs and sugar in a large metal bowl, then set bowl over a saucepan of barely simmering water and whisk until sugar is dissolved and mixture is warm, 2 to 3 minutes. Remove bowl from heat and beat mixture with an electric mixer at medium speed until tripled in volume and mixture forms a slowly dissolving ribbon when beaters are lifted, 10 to 15 minutes.

Fold flour mixture into egg mixture in 3 batches until just combined. Stir one quarter of egg mixture into butter, then quickly fold butter mixture into batter.

Pour batter into 9-inch springform pan and smooth top. Bake until top is golden and a wooden pick or skewer inserted in center of cake comes out clean, 25 to 30 minutes.

Cool cake in pan on a rack for 5 minutes, then remove side of pan and invert cake onto rack. Carefully remove bottom of pan and paper, reinvert cake, and cool completely.

MEANWHILE, BEGIN MAKING THE MOUSSE: Halve, pit, and chop nectarines. Combine with sugar and 1/2 cup water in a 3- to 4-quart heavy saucepan and bring to a boil. Reduce heat and simmer, uncovered, stirring occasionally, until fruit is tender, about 15 minutes.

Transfer mixture to a food processor or blender and purée until smooth (use caution). Force purée through a sieve into a large bowl.

Stir together lemon juice, schnapps, and remaining 2 tablespoons water in a 1- to 1 1/2-quart saucepan, sprinkle gelatin over mixture, and let soften for 1 minute. Heat over low heat, stirring, until gelatin is dissolved (mixture will look cloudy). Stir gelatin mixture into nectarine purée, mixing well. Cool to room temperature, stirring occasionally.

MAKE THE SYRUP: Bring sugar and water to a boil in another 1- to 1 1/2-quart heavy saucepan and stir until sugar is dissolved. Remove from heat and stir in schnapps. Cool to room temperature.

FINISH THE MOUSSE: Beat heavy cream in a large bowl with electric mixer at high speed until it just holds a soft shape (softer than soft peaks). Fold into nectarine purée.

ASSEMBLE THE CAKE: Invert bottom of 10-inch springform pan and then lock on side (this will make cutting cake easier).

Slice cake horizontally into 3 layers with a serrated knife (see page 727), keeping layers together. Invert entire cake so that bottom layer is on top, then invert layer now on top into 10-inch springform, centering it in pan. Brush layer with half of syrup and top with half of mousse. Cover mousse with second cake layer, brush with remaining syrup, and top with remaining mousse (mousse should completely cover top and sides of cake). Refrigerate cake, loosely covered with plastic wrap (use toothpicks to keep plastic from touching mousse), until mousse is set, at least 2 hours. Wrap third layer and set aside at room temperature.

GLAZE THE CAKE: Sprinkle gelatin over 3 tablespoons cold water in a small bowl and let soften for 1 minute.

Bring preserves and remaining 3 tablespoons water to a simmer in a small saucepan over low heat and stir until preserves are melted. Remove from heat and stir in gelatin mixture until dissolved. Cool slightly.

Pour warm glaze evenly over chilled cake, tilting cake if necessary to smooth top. Refrigerate for at least 1 hour.

GARNISH THE CAKE: Preheat oven to 350°F.

Grind remaining cake layer into fine crumbs in food processor. Spread crumbs evenly in a shallow baking pan and bake, stirring once or twice, until lightly toasted, about 10 minutes. Let cool.

Run a thin knife around edge of springform pan and remove side. Working over baking pan, coat sides of cake with toasted crumbs. Let cake stand at room temperature for 20 minutes before serving.

COOK'S NOTES

- The cake can be baked up to 1 day ahead. Cool completely, then wrap well in plastic wrap.
- The syrup can be made up to 2 weeks ahead and refrigerated, covered.
- The glazed cake can be refrigerated, still in the pan, for up to 1 day.

Fresh Banana Layer Cake

SERVES 8 TO 10
ACTIVE TIME: 45 MINUTES ■ START TO FINISH: 1 3/4 HOURS (INCLUDES COOLING)

■ A banana lover's dream. First very ripe bananas are mashed and folded into a yogurt cake batter, then the baked layers are spread with a thin layer of cream cheese frosting and sliced bananas are piled between them. Moist and suffused with banana flavor, this cake is a favorite with kids but sophisticated enough for any adult as well. Reader Connie Fuller alerted us to the cake; she first tasted it at Greg and Mary Sonnier's Gabrielle Restaurant, in New Orleans. ■

FOR CAKE LAYERS

- 2¼ cups sifted cake flour (not self-rising; sift before measuring)
- ¾ teaspoon baking soda
- ½ teaspoon baking powder
- ½ teaspoon salt
- 1 cup mashed very ripe bananas (about 2 large)
- ¼ cup plain yogurt or well-shaken buttermilk
- 1 teaspoon vanilla extract
- 1 stick (8 tablespoons) unsalted butter, softened
- 1 cup granulated sugar
- 2 large eggs

FOR FROSTING AND FILLING

- 8 ounces cream cheese, softened
- 1 stick (8 tablespoons) unsalted butter, softened
- 1 teaspoon vanilla extract
- Pinch of salt
- 3 cups confectioners' sugar, sifted
- 3–4 large, firm but ripe bananas

SPECIAL EQUIPMENT: three 8-by-2-inch round cake pans

MAKE THE CAKE LAYERS: Put racks in upper and lower thirds of oven and preheat oven to 350°F. Butter and flour cake pans, knocking out excess flour.

Sift together flour, baking soda, baking powder, and salt into a bowl. Whisk together mashed bananas, yogurt, and vanilla in a small bowl.

Beat together butter and sugar in a large bowl with an electric mixer at high speed until pale and fluffy, 2 to 3 minutes. Beat in eggs one at a time, beating well after each addition. Reduce speed to low and add flour and banana mixtures alternately in batches, beginning and ending with flour mixture and mixing after each addition until just combined; do not overmix.

Divide batter evenly among pans and smooth tops. Place two pans in middle of oven and one pan in bottom third (do not put top pans directly above bottom pan) and bake, switching position of pans halfway through baking, until layers are springy to the touch and a wooden pick or skewer inserted in center comes out clean, 18 to 22 minutes total.

Cool layers in pans on racks for 10 minutes. Run a thin knife around edges of pans and invert layers onto racks to cool completely.

MAKE THE FROSTING: Beat together cream cheese and butter in a large bowl with mixer at medium speed until pale and fluffy, 6 to 7 minutes. Beat in vanilla and salt. Beat in confectioners' sugar a little at a time, then continue to beat until smooth.

ASSEMBLE THE CAKE: Put a cake layer on a cake stand or platter and spread top with a thin coating of frosting. Cut enough bananas into ¼-inch-thick diagonal slices to cover cake and arrange in one layer, overlapping slightly. Top with second cake layer; spread with another thin coating of frosting and top with a layer of banana slices in same manner. Top with remaining cake layer and spread remaining frosting over top and sides of cake.

COOK'S NOTES

- The cake layers can be made up to 1 day ahead and kept, well wrapped in plastic wrap, at room temperature.
- The cake can be assembled up to 8 hours ahead and kept in a cake keeper at cool room temperature.

Lady Baltimore Cake

SERVES 12 TO 14
ACTIVE TIME: 1 HOUR ■ START TO FINISH: 3 HOURS (INCLUDES COOLING)

■ This stately grande dame, laden with nuts and chopped dried fruit, is an example of life imitating art. It originated in the kitchen of a fictional character, Mrs. Alicia Rhett Mayberry, who made the cake in Owen Wister's 1906 novel, *Lady Baltimore*. From there it quickly made its way into kitchens all over America. Our version is covered with a billowy meringue frosting that looks like marshmallow. ■

FOR CAKE LAYERS

- 3 cups all-purpose flour
- 1 tablespoon baking powder
- ½ teaspoon salt
- 2 sticks (½ pound) unsalted butter, softened
- 2 cups sugar
- 1 teaspoon vanilla extract
- ½ teaspoon almond extract
- 1 cup whole milk
- 7 large egg whites
- ¼ teaspoon cream of tartar
- Pinch of salt

FOR FILLING AND ICING

- 2 cups sugar
- 3/4 cup water
- 6 large egg whites
- Pinch of salt
- 2 teaspoons vanilla extract
- 3/4 cup (4 ounces) finely chopped dried figs
- 1½ cups (about 6 ounces) pecans, lightly toasted (see Tips, page 938) and finely chopped
- 3/4 cup raisins, chopped

OPTIONAL GARNISH: sliced dried figs and pecan halves

SPECIAL EQUIPMENT: three 9-by-2-inch round cake pans; a candy thermometer

MAKE THE CAKE LAYERS: Put a rack in middle of oven and preheat oven to 325°F. Butter cake pans and line bottoms with rounds of parchment or wax paper. Butter paper and dust pans with flour, knocking out excess.

Whisk together flour, baking powder, and salt in a bowl.

Beat together butter and sugar in a large bowl with an electric mixer at high speed until pale and fluffy, 1 to 2 minutes. Beat in extracts. Add flour mixture and milk alternately in batches, beating after each addition until just combined.

Beat whites, cream of tartar, and salt in a large bowl with cleaned beaters until whites just hold stiff peaks. Stir one third of whites into batter to lighten it, then gently but thoroughly fold in remaining whites.

Divide batter among pans and smooth tops. Bake, in batches if necessary, until a wooden pick or skewer inserted in center of cakes comes out clean, 25 to 35 minutes. Cool in pans on racks for 5 minutes, then turn out onto racks, remove paper, and cool completely.

MAKE THE FILLING AND ICING: Combine sugar and water in a small heavy saucepan, bring to a boil, and stir until sugar is dissolved. Boil until syrup registers 248°F on thermometer.

While syrup boils, beat whites and salt in a large bowl (preferably bowl of a stand mixer) with an electric mixer at high speed until whites hold soft peaks.

With mixer running, add hot syrup in a steady stream, being careful to avoid beaters and sides of bowl. Beat in vanilla, then beat icing until cool, about 15 minutes.

Transfer 3 cups icing to another bowl and fold in figs, pecans, and raisins to make filling. Set plain icing aside.

Place 1 cake layer bottom side up on a serving plate and spread half of fig filling on top. Place another cake layer right side up on filling and spread remaining filling on top. Place remaining cake layer right side up on filling. Frost top and sides of cake with reserved plain icing.

Garnish cake with dried figs and pecans, if desired.

COOK'S NOTES

- The cake layers can be made up to 1 week ahead and frozen, well wrapped in plastic wrap and foil. Thaw, still wrapped, overnight in the refrigerator.
- The cake can be assembled up to 8 hours ahead and kept in a cake keeper or loosely covered with plastic wrap (use toothpicks to keep the plastic wrap from sticking to the frosting) at room temperature.
- The egg whites in this filling and icing may not be fully cooked. If this is a concern, see page 629.

A FAVORITE TOOL

You can't have too many kinds (and sizes) of spatulas in a kitchen: flexible plastic or rubber ones for scraping bowls and folding egg whites into a batter; larger metal or plastic offset "pancake turner" models, both perforated and non-, to lift food out of pans or turn it over; and what are often called baking spatulas, which are metal, have long, narrow, rounded blades, and can be either straight or offset. This type is a workhorse in our test kitchens: the long offset version is a little longer than the diameter of a typical cake, which makes frosting fast and easy, and it is also great for removing cookies from a cookie sheet; the smaller version is indispensable for frosting cupcakes and cookies.

Chocolate Orange Dobostorte

SERVES 8

ACTIVE TIME: 3½ HOURS ■ START TO FINISH: 4 HOURS

■ A Dobostorte is a very distinctive Hungarian cake—tour de force is more like it—with a gleaming caramel top marked in wedges for ease of cutting. Beneath lie ultra-thin sponge cake layers and heavenly chocolate buttercream. This is a special cake for a special occasion. ■

FOR TORTE LAYERS

- 6 large eggs, separated
- ¾ cup sugar
- 2 teaspoons finely grated orange zest
- 1 teaspoon vanilla extract
- 1 cup plus 2 tablespoons sifted cake flour (not self-rising; sift before measuring)
- ¼ teaspoon salt, plus a pinch
- Pinch of cream of tartar

FOR ORANGE GLAZE

- ¾ cup (10 ounces) sweet orange marmalade
- 2 tablespoons water
- 2 tablespoons Grand Marnier or other orange-flavored liqueur

FOR FILLING

- Chocolate Buttercream (recipe follows)

FOR CARAMEL

- ¼ cup water
- ¾ cup sugar
- ¼ teaspoon cream of tartar

FOR GARNISH

- ¾ cup (3½ ounces) hazelnuts, toasted (see Tips, page 938), skinned, and finely chopped

SPECIAL EQUIPMENT: three 8-inch round cake pans

MAKE THE TORTE LAYERS: Put a rack in middle of oven and preheat oven to 350°F. Invert cake pans (layers will be baked on bottoms of pans) and butter bottoms and edges well. Dust with flour, knocking off excess.

Beat together yolks and ½ cup sugar in a large bowl with an electric mixer at high speed until mixture is thick and pale and forms a ribbon when beaters are lifted, 5 to 7 minutes. Beat in zest and vanilla. Sift together flour and ¼ teaspoon salt onto yolk mixture, then fold in gently but thoroughly.

Beat whites and pinch of salt in a large bowl with cleaned beaters at medium-high speed until foamy, then add cream of tartar and beat until whites just hold soft peaks. Add remaining ¼ cup sugar 1 tablespoon at a time, beating until whites just hold stiff peaks. Stir one third of whites into yolk mixture until just combined, then gently but thoroughly fold in remaining whites.

With a rubber spatula or a knife, spread ⅔ cup batter over each inverted pan bottom just to edges. Bake until just cooked through and just turning pale golden at edges, about 7 minutes. Cool layers on pans on racks for 2 minutes. (Leave oven on.)

With a long, thin knife, loosen each layer from pan and carefully transfer with a spatula to racks to cool completely. Cool pans completely and wipe clean with paper towels, then, working quickly, make 6 more layers in same manner, buttering and flouring pans between batches. (Batter should not stand any longer than necessary, because it will begin to lose volume.)

MAKE THE GLAZE: Heat marmalade with water in a small saucepan over moderate heat, stirring, until melted. Pour through a sieve into a bowl, pressing hard on solids; discard solids. Stir in liqueur.

ASSEMBLE THE TORTE: Reserve ⅓ cup chocolate buttercream at room temperature for finishing torte. Trim edges of torte layers if necessary so that layers are all the same size. Reserve best layer, wrapped in plastic wrap, for caramel top. Place one layer on a cake stand or large plate, using a small dab of buttercream to anchor it. Using a pastry brush, generously moisten cake layer with orange glaze. Refrigerate for 3 minutes.

Spread layer with 2 heaping tablespoons buttercream, top with a second layer, and moisten layer with orange glaze. Refrigerate for 3 minutes. Spread layer with 2 heaping tablespoons buttercream and continue to layer remaining torte layers (except reserved layer) in same manner, refrigerating the torte for 3 minutes after each layer. After spreading eighth layer with buttercream, spread remaining buttercream around sides of torte to coat. Refrigerate for 5 minutes to firm buttercream slightly.

MAKE THE CARAMEL TOP: Put reserved torte layer on a buttered rack set over a sheet of foil, and have a buttered sharp knife ready.

Combine water, sugar, and cream of tartar in a $1\frac{1}{2}$- to 2-quart heavy saucepan and cook over moderate heat, stirring and washing down sugar crystals clinging to sides of pan with cleaned pastry brush dipped in cold water, until sugar is dissolved. Bring to a boil and boil syrup, without stirring, until it is a deep golden caramel.

Immediately remove pan from heat, and as soon as it stops boiling, pour enough caramel over torte layer to coat thinly. Working very quickly, draw buttered knife through caramel down to torte to mark off 8 wedges, without cutting into torte layer. (The lines will make it easier to cut torte without shattering the hardened caramel. If caramel becomes too hard, heat knife blade over a burner.) Carefully loosen caramel-coated torte layer from rack with knife and cool completely.

FINISH THE TORTE: Place caramel-coated layer on top of torte. Using a small icing spatula or a dinner knife, fill gap between top two layers with some or all of reserved buttercream, smoothing it. Press nuts around sides of torte to cover buttercream.

COOK'S NOTES

- Be sure to spread the batter evenly, and take care not to overbake the layers. Do not use dark metal or nonstick pans.
- The glaze can be made up to 1 day ahead and refrigerated, covered.
- The torte, without the caramel top, can be assembled up to 1 day ahead and refrigerated, covered with an inverted bowl or in a cake keeper. Refrigerate the reserved torte layer, wrapped in plastic wrap, and the reserved buttercream, covered. Keep the nuts, covered, at room temperature. Bring the torte, torte layer, and buttercream to room temperature before proceeding.
- The torte can be fully assembled up to 4 hours ahead and refrigerated, covered with an inverted bowl or in a cake keeper. Bring to room temperature before serving.

Chocolate Buttercream

MAKES ABOUT $2\frac{3}{4}$ CUPS

ACTIVE TIME: 30 MINUTES ■ START TO FINISH: 30 MINUTES

■ This is known as a meringue buttercream, in short because it is based on egg whites, not the more classic yolks. That makes it much lighter—positively silky, in fact—and very easy to spread, a definite plus if you are making the many-layered Dobostorte. The chocolate flavor of this frosting is not intense but beautifully balanced. ■

- 4 ounces good bittersweet chocolate (not unsweetened), chopped
- $\frac{1}{4}$ cup water
- $\frac{1}{2}$ cup sugar
- 2 large egg whites
- Salt
- $\frac{1}{4}$ teaspoon cream of tartar
- 2 sticks ($\frac{1}{2}$ pound) unsalted butter, cut into tablespoons and softened
- $\frac{1}{3}$ cup unsweetened cocoa powder

SPECIAL EQUIPMENT: a candy thermometer

Melt chocolate in a metal bowl set over a saucepan of barely simmering water, stirring until smooth. Let cool.

Combine water and sugar in a $1\frac{1}{2}$-quart heavy saucepan and bring to a boil, stirring and washing down any sugar crystals clinging to sides of pan with a pastry brush dipped in cold water, until sugar is dissolved. Boil syrup, without stirring, until thermometer registers 248°F.

Meanwhile, beat whites with a pinch of salt in a large bowl with an electric mixer at medium-high speed until foamy. Add cream of tartar and continue beating until whites just hold stiff peaks.

Beating constantly, add hot syrup to whites in a slow stream, being careful to avoid beaters and sides of bowl. Reduce speed to medium and continue beating until meringue is completely cool, 7 to 10 minutes (it's important to cool meringue properly, or butter may melt).

Beat in butter one piece at a time, beating until incorporated after each addition. (If meringue is too warm and buttercream looks soupy after some of butter is added, chill bottom of bowl in a large bowl filled with ice water for a few seconds, then beat in remaining butter.) Continue beating until buttercream is smooth. (Mixture may look curdled before all butter is added, but it will come back together before beating is finished.) Sift cocoa powder onto buttercream and beat at low speed until combined. Increase speed to medium and beat in melted chocolate and a pinch of salt.

COOK'S NOTES

- The buttercream can be made up to 2 days ahead and refrigerated, covered. It can also be frozen in an airtight container for up to 1 month. Bring to room temperature (do not use a microwave) and beat with an electric mixer until smooth before using.
- The egg whites in this recipe may not be fully cooked. If this is a concern, see page 629.

Lemon Blackberry Wedding Cake

SERVES 50
ACTIVE TIME: 6 HOURS ■ START TO FINISH: 1 DAY (INCLUDES CHILLING)

■ If you want to make a wedding cake but are intimidated, this is the cake for you. The layers—from a pound cake batter with milk added—are very sturdy and forgiving, even when split. The cream cheese frosting couldn't be easier. And yet the result, layered with blackberries and garnished, perhaps with roses, couldn't be more of a showpiece, or more delicious. Although the thought of freezing your creation may be alarming, it's infinitely better to freeze the layers than to run the risk of having them dry out at room temperature. You will need a base for the assembled cake: this can be anything from a very large platter to a piece of wood covered with tulle. (For more on the mechanics of assembling a wedding cake, see page 738.) ■

FOR EACH BATCH OF BATTER (YOU WILL NEED TO MAKE TWO)

12 large eggs
¾ cup whole milk
2 tablespoons vanilla extract
6 cups cake flour (not self-rising)
1½ teaspoons salt
6 sticks (1½ pounds) unsalted butter, softened
3 cups sugar

FOR ASSEMBLY

Lemon Syrup (recipe follows)
2⅓ cups rose hip, rose fruit, or seedless blackberry jam (from three 12-ounce jars; see Sources)
Cream Cheese Frosting (recipe follows)
4 pints (8 cups) blackberries

GARNISH: blackberries and (optional) petals from 3 large organic, nontoxic roses

SPECIAL EQUIPMENT: one 12-by-2-inch round cake pan; one 9-by-2-inch round cake pan; one 6-by-2-inch round cake pan; 2 packages Magi-Cake strips (see Sources) or homemade foil strips (see page 738); a 5-quart stand mixer; a 12-inch serrated knife; four 11-inch cardboard cake rounds, four 8-inch cardboard cake rounds, and four 6-inch cardboard cake rounds, trimmed to 5-inch rounds (see Sources); a cake base (preferably a cake-decorating turntable) or large platter; five 8-inch plastic straws; a medium pastry bag fitted with a 3/16-inch plain tip

MAKE THE CAKE LAYERS: Put racks in upper and lower thirds of oven and preheat oven to 350°F. Grease cake pans and line bottom of each with a round of parchment or wax paper. Grease paper and dust pans with flour, knocking out excess. Wet Magi-Cake strips and fasten around pans, or attach homemade foil strips.

Whisk together eggs, milk, and vanilla in a medium bowl. Whisk together flour and salt in another bowl.

Beat together butter and sugar in bowl of stand mixer at medium speed until pale and fluffy, about 5 minutes. Reduce speed to low and add flour and egg mixtures alternately in 3 batches, ending with egg mixture and mixing until just incorporated.

Divide batter among pans, filling each one to 1 inch from top. Put 12-inch pan on upper rack and other pans on lower rack and bake for 20 minutes. (If you have a wall oven or other small oven, see Cook's Note.) Gently turn pans around and bake until a wooden pick or skewer inserted in center of cakes comes out of each with a few crumbs adhering, 10 to 20 minutes more, depending on cake size. Transfer each one as done to a rack to cool.

Cool layers slightly (9-inch and 6-inch layers for 10 minutes; 12-inch layer for 20 minutes), then invert onto racks. Peel off paper, turn cakes right side up, and cool completely.

Clean pans. Make a second batch of batter and bake and cool cakes in same manner.

ASSEMBLE THE CAKE LAYERS: Start with 12-inch layers. If necessary, trim top of each with long serrated knife to make it level, then cut horizontally in half (see page 727). Put each layer cut side up on an 11-inch cardboard round. Brush tops generously with syrup. Stir jam until smooth, then spread about 2/3 cup on one layer. Invert another layer (on cardboard) onto jam. Discard top cardboard round and spread about 2 1/2 cups frosting on top of layer. Scatter a layer of blackberries over to cover frosting. (If berries are 1 inch or larger, first halve them lengthwise.) Slide a third 12-inch layer, syrup side up, onto berries (discard cardboard) and press down gently. Spread about 2/3 cup jam on layer and invert last 12-inch layer (on cardboard) onto jam; discard cardboard.

Spoon 2 cups frosting onto top of 12-inch tier and cover cake with a thin coating. (This is called a crumb coating; see page 727.) Refrigerate tier while you work on remaining tiers.

Trim and halve 9-inch cakes similarly and put on 8-inch cardboard rounds. Brush cut sides generously with syrup. Assemble and crumb-coat 9-inch tier in same manner, using about 1/3 cup jam, 1 1/4 cups frosting, and more berries between layers, then crumb-coat with about 1 1/2 cups frosting. Refrigerate.

Repeat procedure to make 6-inch tier, using about 2 1/2 tablespoons jam, about 3/4 cup frosting, and more berries between layers, then crumb-coat with about 3/4 cup frosting. Refrigerate until frosting is firm.

Reserve 2 cups frosting for piping. Place 12-inch tier on cake base and frost top and sides. Frost remaining tiers. Refrigerate frosted tiers (do not stack) for at least 4 hours. If you won't be able to fit the assembled cake on its base into your refrigerator, stop here up to 1 day before assembling cake; cover each tier loosely with plastic wrap.

ASSEMBLE THE CAKE TIERS: Cut 3 straws in half. Insert one piece in center of 12-inch tier, all the way to bottom. Insert remaining pieces in a circle about 1 1/2 inches from center straw and trim straws level with top of tier. (Straws will support tiers.) Carefully put 9-inch tier (still on cardboard) in center of bottom tier. Cut remaining 2 straws in half and insert into middle tier in similar manner, with 1 piece in center and remaining pieces in a circle around it. Carefully put 6-inch tier (still on cardboard) in center of middle tier.

Fill in any gaps between tiers and any imperfections with some of reserved frosting, and transfer remainder to pastry bag. Pipe a decorative border around the bottom edge of each tier. Reserve remaining frosting for touch-ups if needed.

Bring cake to room temperature before serving; it can stand at cool room temperature for about 6 hours. Garnish cake with rose petals, if desired, and serve slices with blackberries.

COOK'S NOTES

- The cake layers can be baked up to 1 month ahead and frozen, well wrapped in foil and sealed in plastic bags. Thaw, still wrapped, overnight at room temperature before assembling the cake.
- The frosted tiers can be refrigerated for up to 24 hours.
- Wall ovens tend to be small (ours are about 19 inches wide, 15 inches high, and 17 1/2 inches deep). When using them, we found that the cakes cooked more evenly if we first baked the 12-inch cake alone on the middle rack, then baked the 6-inch and 9-inch layers together on the middle rack. If you do this, fill all the pans at the same time and leave the two smaller layers at room temperature while you bake the 12-inch one.

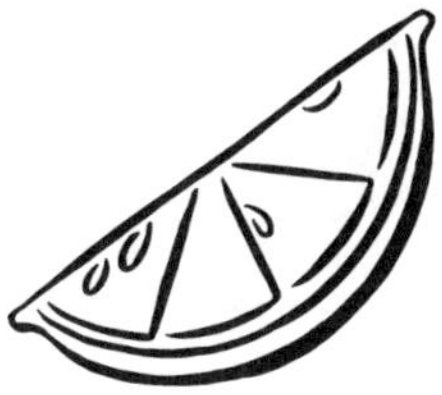

DECORATING A WEDDING CAKE

You don't need a degree in pastry arts, or architecture, to make a wedding cake. The Chocolate Cake with Orange Buttercream on page 744 is a very straightforward, high, three-layer cake, but its beauty and sophistication — its perfection in every detail — will take your breath away.

The recipe on page 736 for Lemon Blackberry Wedding Cake, an old-fashioned pound cake with cream cheese frosting and a filling of dark, winy blackberries, will produce a more traditional tiered wedding cake. Elegant, yes, but relatively simple to prepare, assemble, and decorate. What you need is a talent for organization and plenty of space in your refrigerator. Generous amounts of time, patience, and grace under pressure are nice too.

Because the layers of this cake are so high, we rely on Magi-Cake strips, which ensure that the cake layers bake to a level-topped finish and look professional. Without the strips, the layers will form a dome shape as they bake. The aluminum-coated fabric strips, dampened and wrapped around a pan, keep the pan cooler so the edges of the cake rise at the same rate as the center.

You can easily make cake strips yourself, using nothing more than foil, paper towels, scissors, and large paper clips: Tear off three different lengths of foil, equivalent to the circumference of each of the three cake pans. (Relax, we did the math: the 6-inch pan will require a 19-inch sheet of foil; the 9-inch pan, a 29-inch sheet; the 12-inch pan, a 38-inch sheet.) To make the strip for the 6-inch pan, dampen a length of paper towel (two connected sheets are just enough; they should be moist but not dripping) and fold it into a strip 1½ to 2 inches wide. Align one long side of the paper towel strip with one long side of the shortest sheet of foil (1) and fold the foil over it twice (2), trimming the excess width of foil sheet. After wrapping it snugly around the side of the pan (3), fasten it with a paper clip.

After baking and cooling the cake layers, assemble and frost each tier on a cardboard round as described in the recipe (a cake-decorating turntable will make this part much easier). Once everything is frosted and thoroughly chilled, it's time to build. The only tool you'll need is decidedly low-tech: plastic straws cut to size, to help support the cake tiers. Stacking the tiers on their cardboard rounds reinforces the structure, making this a very easy cake to put together. Then it's time to spackle any gaps between the tiers and cover up any other imperfections. Be sure to save some leftover frosting for last-minute touch-ups.

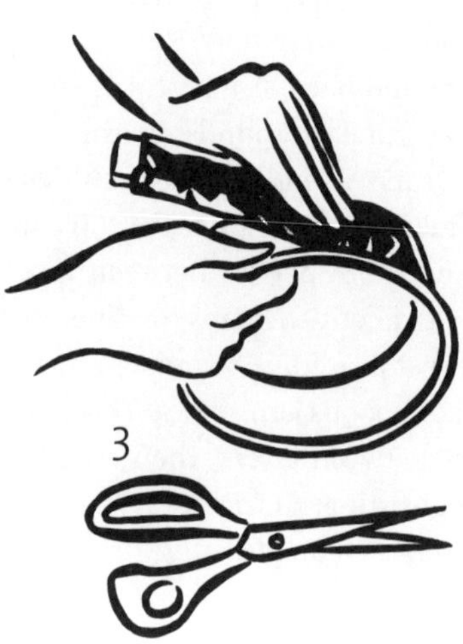

Lemon Syrup

MAKES ABOUT 4 CUPS
ACTIVE TIME: 20 MINUTES ■ START TO FINISH: 20 MINUTES

■ This lemon syrup can be flavored with rose water if you like. ■

- 2 cups fresh lemon juice (from 10–12 lemons)
- 2 cups sugar
- 1 cup water
- 1 teaspoon rose water (optional)

Stir together lemon juice, sugar, water, and rose water (if using) in a bowl until sugar is dissolved.

COOK'S NOTE

■ The syrup can be made up to 1 week ahead and refrigerated in an airtight container.

Cream Cheese Frosting

MAKES ABOUT 16 CUPS
ACTIVE TIME: 15 MINUTES ■ START TO FINISH: 15 MINUTES

■ The tang of the main ingredient in this supremely easy recipe really comes through; the frosting is not overly sweet. ■

- 12 (8-ounce) packages cream cheese, softened
- 6 sticks (1½ pounds) unsalted butter, softened
- 2 (1-pound) boxes confectioners' sugar (7½ cups)

SPECIAL EQUIPMENT: a stand mixer

Make frosting in 2 batches: Beat half of cream cheese in bowl of mixer at medium-high speed until smooth. Reduce speed to low, add half of butter and half of confectioners' sugar, and mix until sugar is incorporated. Increase speed to medium and beat for 1 minute. Transfer to a large bowl or other container. Repeat with remaining ingredients and add to first batch.

COOK'S NOTE

■ The frosting can be made up to 3 days ahead and refrigerated, covered. (You can ice the cake while the frosting is still cold.)

Flourless Chocolate Cake

SERVES 10 TO 12
ACTIVE TIME: 20 MINUTES ■ START TO FINISH: 2½ HOURS (INCLUDES COOLING)

■ The trick to a flourless cake is choosing what you'll use to provide the structure that flour supplies in a standard cake. Tortes, for example, typically rely on nuts or bread crumbs. This version is outstandingly dense and rich because, in addition to the structure the eggs give, it substitutes cocoa powder for the flour. The little secret (which there is no need to share with your guests) is that it is also one of the easiest of all cakes to put together. ■

- 8 ounces good bittersweet chocolate (not unsweetened), chopped
- 2 sticks (½ pound) unsalted butter
- 1½ cups sugar
- 6 large eggs
- 1 cup unsweetened cocoa powder, plus additional for dusting

SPECIAL EQUIPMENT: a 10-inch (26-centimeter) springform pan

Put a rack in middle of oven and preheat oven to 350°F. Butter pan, line bottom with a round of parchment or wax paper, and butter paper.

Melt chocolate with butter in a medium metal bowl set over a saucepan of barely simmering water, stirring until smooth. Remove bowl from heat and whisk in sugar. Add eggs one at a time, whisking well after each addition. Sift cocoa powder over chocolate and whisk until just combined.

Pour batter into pan. Bake until top has formed a thin crust and a wooden pick or skewer inserted in center of cake comes out with moist crumbs adhering, 35 to 40 minutes. Cool cake in pan on a rack for 10 minutes, then remove side of pan. Invert cake onto a plate and reinvert onto rack to cool completely.

Dust cake with cocoa powder before serving.

COOK'S NOTE

■ The cake can be made up to 3 days ahead and kept in an airtight container at room temperature.

Warm Chocolate-Raspberry Pudding Cake

SERVES 6 TO 8

ACTIVE TIME: 30 MINUTES ■ START TO FINISH: 1½ HOURS

■ Traditional pudding cakes are basically sponge puddings that separate into two layers as they bake—the top layer becomes a soft cake, the bottom a custardy sauce. This version uses a different approach. It starts out with a liquid bottom layer that is topped with a rather loose cake batter. Both are flavored with the classic combination of chocolate and raspberry. While they cook, the batter is transformed into a lovely, soft-textured cake and the bottom layer thickens. When the cake is inverted onto a cake plate a few minutes after it emerges from the oven, it is instantly bathed with a rich, creamy, oozy frosting. Although this cake is best served warm, it is also delicious at room temperature. ■

FOR FROSTING

- ½ cup seedless raspberry jam
- ½ cup heavy cream
- 3 ounces good bittersweet chocolate (not unsweetened), chopped

FOR CAKE BATTER

- ½ cup boiling water
- ⅓ cup plus 2 teaspoons unsweetened cocoa powder (not Dutch-process)
- ¼ cup whole milk
- ½ teaspoon vanilla extract
- ⅓ cup seedless raspberry jam
- 1 cup all-purpose flour
- ¾ teaspoon baking soda
- ¼ teaspoon salt
- 1 stick (8 tablespoons) unsalted butter, softened
- ⅓ cup packed light brown sugar
- ⅓ cup granulated sugar
- 2 large eggs

OPTIONAL GARNISH: raspberries

SPECIAL EQUIPMENT: a 9-by-2-inch round cake pan

Put a rack in middle of oven and preheat oven to 350°F. Generously butter cake pan.

MAKE THE FROSTING: Combine jam, cream, and chocolate in a small heavy saucepan and bring just to a simmer, stirring occasionally until smooth. Pour frosting into buttered cake pan.

MAKE THE CAKE BATTER: Whisk together boiling water and cocoa powder in a medium bowl until smooth, then whisk in milk, vanilla, and jam. Sift together flour, baking soda, and salt into another bowl.

Beat together butter and sugars in a large bowl with an electric mixer at medium-high speed until pale and fluffy. Add eggs one at a time, beating well after each addition. Add flour and cocoa mixtures alternately in batches, beginning and ending with flour mixture and beating on low speed until each addition is incorporated.

Spoon batter evenly over frosting and spread it to cover frosting completely. Bake until a wooden pick or skewer inserted in center of cake comes out clean (frosting on bottom will still be liquid), 30 to 40 minutes.

Cool cake in pan on a rack for 10 to 20 minutes.

Run a thin knife around edge of pan and twist pan gently back and forth on a flat surface to loosen cake. Invert a cake plate with a slight lip over pan and, holding pan and plate together with both hands, invert cake onto plate. (Frosting will cover sides of cake and run onto plate). Serve warm, garnished with raspberries, if desired.

COOK'S NOTE

■ The cake can be made up to 1 day ahead and cooled completely in the pan, then kept in the pan, covered, at room temperature. Reheat the cake, uncovered, in a 350°F oven for 15 minutes, then invert onto a plate as directed above.

Shopping for Chocolate

These days the array of fine semisweet and bittersweet chocolates available to the home baker is almost dizzying. However, we tend to rely on several brands that contain between 50 and 60 percent chocolate liquor (the official term for unsweetened chocolate, or cocoa solids). A higher percentage of chocolate liquor means a deeper chocolate flavor, so feel free to experiment if your palate leans toward darker chocolate — but be aware that your results may be more intense and less sweet than ours. Our favorites include Lindt (the regular bittersweet, not the 71 percent) and Ghirardelli, both available at supermarkets (Lindt is usually found in the candy aisle, Ghirardelli in the baking aisle), and Valrhona, available at specialty foods shops. (Note that the chocolate liquor percentage of Valrhona varies; it's marked on the package, unlike the supermarket brands.)

The flavor of chocolate also varies according to what cocoa beans are used, where they are grown, and how they are roasted. (Cocoa beans are a crop, and there are good years and bad years.) To complicate matters further, industry standards unhelpfully lump bittersweet and semisweet chocolates into the same category, and one boutique brand's bittersweet may be comparable to another's semisweet because the percentage of chocolate liquor is exactly the same. Generally, however, semisweet chocolate contains more sugar than bittersweet does. Also, although cooking chocolate and snacking chocolate are often interchangeable, don't automatically dismiss a chocolate for cooking if you don't like the way it tastes straight out of the package. You might be pleasantly surprised by its flavor when other ingredients come into play.

Cocoa powder is the finely ground, pressed substance left after cocoa butter has been extracted from chocolate liquor. In general, it's unwise to substitute American-style, or "natural," unsweetened cocoa (Hershey's regular or Ghirardelli) for European-style Dutch-process (Droste, Valrhona) or vice versa in baking, because the two kinds don't always behave the same way in a recipe. The Dutch-process technique was invented by a Dutchman, Conrad van Houten, in 1828. "Dutched" cocoa powder differs from regular in that an alkaline solution is added to the beans during roasting, mellowing their acidity. The result is reddish brown and milder-tasting. The chemical difference can be significant when it comes to baking: because regular cocoa powder is acidic, it must be combined with an alkaline ingredient such as baking soda to create bubbles of carbon dioxide, which cause leavening. Conversely, since Dutch-process cocoa is already alkalized, it needs to be combined with an acid, such as baking powder. If one of our recipes doesn't specify which kind of cocoa to use, either will be fine.

If you are interested in learning more about chocolate, we've found these books especially informative: Sophie and Michael Coe's *The True History of Chocolate*, Dorie Greenspan's *Chocolate Desserts by Pierre Hermé*, Alice Medrich's *Bittersweet*, and Maricel Presilla's *The New Taste of Chocolate*.

Individual Molten Chocolate Cakes

SERVES 6

ACTIVE TIME: 50 MINUTES ■ START TO FINISH: 1¼ HOURS

■ Crisp and cakey on the outside, gooey on the inside, molten chocolate cakes are sheer ecstasy. Present them to your lucky guests at the end of a sophisticated meal. If possible, use baba au rhum molds; if you use ramekins, the cakes will be slightly less molten and an indentation will form in the middle, but they will still taste terrific. After having one in Paris at La Bastide Odéon, where the *moelleux au chocolat* are served with pools of coffee *crème anglaise* and scoops of vanilla ice cream, reader Tia Cibani was hooked and requested the recipe. ■

FOR COFFEE *CRÈME ANGLAISE*

- 1¼ cups whole milk
- 4 teaspoons instant espresso powder
- 3 large egg yolks
- 2 tablespoons granulated sugar
- Pinch of salt

FOR CAKES

- Melted butter for brushing molds
- 6½ tablespoons granulated sugar, plus additional for dusting molds
- 7 tablespoons unsalted butter, cut into pieces
- 3½ ounces Lindt 71% bittersweet chocolate, chopped
- 3 large eggs
- ⅓ cup sifted all-purpose flour (sift before measuring)
- ⅛ teaspoon salt

GARNISH: confectioners' sugar

ACCOMPANIMENT: vanilla ice cream

SPECIAL EQUIPMENT: an instant-read thermometer; six 4-ounce nonstick baba au rhum molds (see Sources) or six 4-ounce ramekins

MAKE THE *CRÈME ANGLAISE:* Whisk together milk and espresso powder in a 1½-quart heavy saucepan and bring to a boil. Meanwhile, whisk together yolks, sugar, and salt in a medium bowl.

Slowly add hot milk to yolks, whisking constantly. Transfer custard to saucepan and cook over moderately low heat, stirring constantly with a wooden spoon, until it is thick enough to coat back of spoon and registers 170°F on thermometer; do not let boil.

Pour custard sauce through a fine-mesh sieve into a metal bowl. Put bowl into a larger bowl filled with ice and cold water and cool sauce, stirring occasionally. Refrigerate sauce, covered, until ready to use.

MAKE THE CAKES: Put a rack in middle of oven and preheat oven to 400°F. Brush molds with melted butter and dust with sugar, knocking out excess.

Melt butter and chocolate in a metal bowl set over a saucepan of barely simmering water, stirring occasionally until smooth. Remove bowl from pan and cool slightly.

Whisk together eggs and remaining 6½ tablespoons sugar in a medium bowl. Whisk in flour, melted chocolate mixture, and salt. Pour batter into molds, filling them about two-thirds full.

Put molds in a 9-inch square baking pan, or put ramekins on a baking sheet. Bake until outer ⅓ to ½ inch of cakes is set but centers are still moist, 10 to 12 minutes.

Holding one mold with a pot holder, run a knife around edge of cake to loosen it, then invert onto a plate. Unmold remaining cakes in same manner. Dust with confectioners' sugar and serve with *crème anglaise* and ice cream.

Devil's Food Cake with Brown Sugar Buttercream

SERVES 10

ACTIVE TIME: 1 HOUR ■ START TO FINISH: 2 HOURS (INCLUDES COOLING)

■ This is the ultimate chocolate birthday cake. Many people assume that this kind of chocolate cake is called "devil's food" because of its "sinfully rich" nature. In fact, it takes its name from the distinctive reddish brown color that results from the chemical reaction between the cocoa and the baking soda, which is used both to leaven the cake and to neutralize the natural acidity of the cocoa. (Be sure to use regular cocoa, not Dutch-process, or you will throw off the delicate balance in the recipe.) More important, though, this cake is particularly soft and deliciously moist. It's best when the layers are made ahead of time, which allows the flavors to intensify. You could use Chocolate Ganache Frosting (page 724) or Seven-Minute Frosting (page 725), but the brown sugar buttercream rounds out the chocolate flavor in an especially wonderful way. ■

- 1 cup boiling water
- 3/4 cup unsweetened cocoa powder (not Dutch-process)
- 1/2 cup whole milk
- 1 teaspoon vanilla extract
- 2 cups all-purpose flour
- 1 1/4 teaspoons baking soda
- 1/2 teaspoon salt
- 2 sticks (1/2 pound) unsalted butter, softened
- 1 1/4 cups packed dark brown sugar
- 3/4 cup granulated sugar
- 4 large eggs
- Brown Sugar Buttercream (recipe follows)

SPECIAL EQUIPMENT: three 8-by-2-inch round cake pans

Put racks in upper and lower thirds of oven and preheat oven to 350°F. Butter cake pans and line bottoms with rounds of parchment or wax paper. Butter paper and dust pans with flour, knocking out excess.

Whisk together boiling water and cocoa powder in a medium bowl until smooth, then whisk in milk and vanilla. Sift together flour, baking soda, and salt into another bowl.

Beat together butter and sugars in a large bowl with an electric mixer at medium speed until pale and fluffy. Add eggs one at a time, beating well after each addition. Beat in flour and cocoa mixtures alternately in 3 batches, beginning and ending with flour mixture (batter may look curdled).

Divide batter among pans and smooth tops. Place two pans in middle of oven and one pan in bottom (do not put top pans directly above bottom pan). Bake, switching position of pans halfway through baking, until a wooden pick or skewer inserted in center of cakes comes out clean and layers begin to pull away from sides of pans, 20 to 25 minutes.

Cool layers in pans on racks for 10 minutes, then invert onto racks, remove paper, and cool completely.

Put 1 cake layer right side up on a cake plate and spread with about 1 cup buttercream. Top with another layer, right side up, and spread with another cup buttercream. Top with remaining layer and frost top and sides of cake with remaining buttercream.

COOK'S NOTES

- The cake layers can be made up to 2 days ahead and kept, well wrapped in plastic wrap, at room temperature. They can also be frozen for up to 1 week. Thaw, still wrapped, in the refrigerator.
- The cake can be assembled up to 1 day ahead and refrigerated in a cake keeper or loosely covered with plastic wrap (use toothpicks to hold wrap away from frosting). Bring to room temperature before serving.
- The batter can also be baked in two 9-by-2-inch round cake pans for 25 to 30 minutes; in a 13-by-9-inch baking pan for 35 to 40 minutes; or in a 12-cup Bundt pan for 35 to 40 minutes. Or it can be used to make cupcakes: bake in twenty-four (1/3- or 1/2-cup) muffin cups for 20 to 25 minutes.

Brown Sugar Buttercream

MAKES ABOUT 3 1/2 CUPS, ENOUGH TO FROST A THREE-LAYER 8-INCH CAKE
ACTIVE TIME: 25 MINUTES ■ START TO FINISH: 55 MINUTES

■ This meringue-based buttercream (made with egg whites, not yolks) has brown sugar as a major component, which gives it a complex flavor. ■

- 3 large egg whites, left at room temperature for 30 minutes
- 1/8 teaspoon salt
- 1 cup packed dark brown sugar
- 1/2 cup water
- 1/2 teaspoon fresh lemon juice
- 3 sticks (3/4 pound) unsalted butter, cut into tablespoons and softened
- 2 teaspoons vanilla extract

SPECIAL EQUIPMENT: a candy thermometer

Combine egg whites and salt in a large bowl.

Stir together brown sugar and water in a small heavy saucepan and bring to a boil over moderately high heat, washing down sides of pan with a pastry brush dipped in cold water.

As soon as sugar syrup reaches a boil, start beating whites: with an electric mixer at medium-high speed, beat whites until frothy, then add lemon juice and beat at medium speed until whites just hold soft peaks. (Do not beat again until sugar syrup is ready.)

Meanwhile, continue boiling sugar syrup until it

reaches 238°–242°F on thermometer. Immediately remove from heat and pour into a heatproof 1-cup glass measuring cup. Slowly pour hot syrup in a thin stream down side of bowl into egg whites, beating constantly at high speed. Continue to beat meringue, scraping down sides of bowl with a rubber spatula as necessary, until cool to the touch, about 6 minutes. (It's important to cool meringue properly before proceeding.)

With mixer at medium speed, add butter one piece at a time, beating well after each addition until incorporated. (If meringue is too warm and buttercream looks soupy after some of butter is added, chill bottom of bowl in a larger bowl filled with ice and cold water for a few seconds, then continue to beat in remaining butter.) Continue beating until buttercream is smooth. (Mixture may look curdled before all of butter is added, but it will come back together before beating is finished.) Add vanilla and beat for 2 minutes more.

COOK'S NOTE

- The buttercream can be made up to 1 week ahead and refrigerated, covered. It can also be frozen in an airtight container for up to 1 month. Bring to room temperature (do not use a microwave) and beat with an electric mixer until smooth before using.

Chocolate Cake with Orange Buttercream

SERVES 20 TO 25

ACTIVE TIME: 2¼ HOURS ■ START TO FINISH: 11 HOURS (INCLUDES MAKING BUTTERCREAM AND CHILLING CAKE)

■ This is the perfect party cake—just right for a small family wedding or other fancy occasion. Layers of devil's food cake enriched with bittersweet chocolate are interspersed with a trufflelike ganache frosting, and the whole is enveloped by orange buttercream. ■

FOR CAKE LAYERS

- 1¾ cups boiling water
- 1¾ cups unsweetened cocoa powder (not Dutch-process)
- 4 ounces good bittersweet chocolate (not unsweetened), finely chopped
- 1 (8-ounce) container sour cream
- 4 teaspoons vanilla extract
- 3 cups all-purpose flour
- 2½ teaspoons baking soda
- 1 teaspoon salt
- 3¾ sticks unsalted butter, softened
- 1¾ cups granulated sugar
- ¾ cup packed light brown sugar
- 5 large eggs

FOR GANACHE

- 8 ounces good bittersweet chocolate (not unsweetened), finely chopped
- 2 tablespoons unsalted butter, softened
- 2 teaspoons finely grated orange zest
- 1 tablespoon Cointreau or other orange-flavored liqueur
- 1 cup heavy cream

FOR FROSTING

Orange Buttercream (recipe follows)

SPECIAL EQUIPMENT: three 9-by-2-inch round cake pans; a 4½- to 5-quart stand mixer; a cake stand; a pastry bag fitted with a ¼-inch plain tip

MAKE THE CAKE LAYERS: Put racks in middle and lower third of oven and preheat oven to 350°F. Butter cake pans and line bottoms with rounds of parchment or wax paper. Butter paper well and dust pans with flour, knocking out excess.

Add boiling water to cocoa in a medium bowl and whisk until smooth. Stir in chopped chocolate and let stand for 5 minutes, then stir until smooth. Cool for 20 minutes.

Whisk sour cream and vanilla into chocolate mixture. Sift together flour, baking soda, and salt into a bowl.

Beat together butter and sugars in bowl of mixer at high speed until pale and fluffy, about 3 minutes. Add eggs one at a time, beating well after each addition and scraping down sides of bowl with a spatula as needed. Reduce speed to low and add flour mixture and chocolate mixture alternately in 3 batches, beginning and ending with flour mixture and mixing until just combined. Finish mixing batter by hand with spatula, scraping bottom of bowl.

Divide batter among pans (about 3¾ cups in each) and smooth tops. Place two pans in middle of oven and one pan in bottom third (do not put top pans directly above bottom pan) and bake, switching position of pans halfway through baking, until a wooden pick or skewer inserted in center of cakes comes out with a few moist crumbs adhering, 30 to 40 minutes.

Run a thin knife around edges of pans. Invert racks over pans, then invert cakes onto racks. Carefully remove paper and cool layers completely.

MAKE THE GANACHE: Put chocolate, butter, zest, and liqueur in a metal bowl. Bring cream just to a boil in a small saucepan, then immediately pour into bowl and let stand for 5 minutes. Whisk until chocolate is melted and smooth. Refrigerate just until cool, 20 to 30 minutes.

ASSEMBLE AND FROST THE CAKE: Beat ganache with cleaned beaters just until light and fluffy; do not overbeat.

Reserve 2 cups buttercream for decorating. Put 1 cake layer on cake stand and spread top evenly with half of ganache. Cover with another cake layer and spread top with remaining ganache. Cover with remaining cake layer and frost top and sides of cake smoothly with a thin layer of buttercream (a crumb coating; see page 727). Refrigerate cake, uncovered, until buttercream is firm, about 30 minutes.

Generously frost top and sides of cake with remaining buttercream (reserving the 2 cups for decorating) and refrigerate, uncovered, until buttercream is firm, about 30 minutes.

Fill pastry bag with reserved buttercream and pipe a decorative border around top and bottom of cake. Refrigerate cake, covered with a large cake dome (or loosely covered with plastic wrap; use toothpicks to hold wrap away from frosting) for at least 6 hours.

Bring cake to room temperature (2 to 4 hours) before serving.

COOK'S NOTES

- The cake layers can be kept, well wrapped in plastic wrap, at cool room temperature for up to 2 days. They can also be frozen, wrapped in plastic wrap and foil, for up to 2 weeks; defrost the layers (without unwrapping) at room temperature.
- The decorated cake can be refrigerated for up to 1 day.

GANACHE

In the world of chocolate, nothing is quite as voluptuous as ganache, a concoction that at its simplest has only two ingredients: chocolate and cream. Nor is there a mixture quite so versatile. Depending on the temperature and the proportion of cream to chocolate, ganache can be as liquid as a sauce or as firm as fudge, with a range of textures in between.

Stir together equal proportions of finely chopped chocolate and hot cream until smooth and you've got a luxurious sauce that drapes like velvet over ice cream. Cool it to tepid and pour it over a cake and the ganache will enrobe the layers in a shiny glaze that hides many an imperfection. Cool it further and you've got the chocoholic's dream frosting. Chill it and scoop out roughly shaped bonbons to coat with unsweetened cocoa powder and you've made classic truffles. Things change when you double the proportion of cream: the resulting ganache will be quite liquid when warm, but chilled and whipped, it becomes an airy mousse, ideal for filling a cake.

The Hungarian Chocolate Mousse Cake Bars on page 749 provide a mini-tutorial in ganache. Coating the top cake layer is a dark bittersweet glaze that has a slightly higher ratio of chocolate to cream, making it a bit firmer than classic ganache. Holding the two cake layers together is whipped ganache, much paler in color than the glaze because of its higher proportion of cream and the air that's been incorporated.

Orange Buttercream

MAKES ABOUT 8 CUPS
ACTIVE TIME: 30 MINUTES ■ START TO FINISH: 2 HOURS

■ Meringue buttercreams are based on egg whites rather than egg yolks. They spread beautifully and hold up well. This one is flavored with orange curd. ■

FOR ORANGE CURD

- 5 large egg yolks
- 1/4 cup sugar
- 2 tablespoons finely grated orange zest
- 1/2 cup fresh orange juice
- 1/2 stick (4 tablespoons) unsalted butter, softened
- Pinch of salt
- 1 1/2 teaspoons fresh lemon juice

FOR BUTTERCREAM

- 1 1/4 cups sugar
- 1/2 cup water
- 5 large egg whites
- 1/2 teaspoon salt, plus a pinch
- 1/2 teaspoon cream of tartar
- 6 1/2 sticks unsalted butter, cut into tablespoons and softened

SPECIAL EQUIPMENT: a candy thermometer; a stand mixer

MAKE THE CURD: Whisk together yolks and sugar in a small heavy saucepan, then whisk in zest, orange juice, butter, and salt. Cook over moderately low heat, whisking, until mixture just reaches boiling point, 5 to 7 minutes. Pour through a fine-mesh sieve into a bowl, pressing on solids; discard solids. Whisk in lemon juice. Cover surface with wax paper and refrigerate until cold, at least 1 hour.

MAKE THE BUTTERCREAM: Bring sugar and water to a boil in a small heavy saucepan over moderately high heat, stirring and washing down any sugar crystals on side of pan with a pastry brush dipped in cold water, until sugar is dissolved. Boil syrup, without stirring, until it registers 248°F on thermometer.

Meanwhile, beat whites with pinch of salt in bowl of mixer until foamy, then beat in cream of tartar. Beat until whites just hold stiff peaks.

Slowly add hot syrup, being careful to avoid beaters and sides of bowl, beating constantly at medium speed, and continue to beat until completely cool, 15 to 20 minutes. (It is important to cool meringue properly before proceeding.)

Add butter one piece at a time, still beating at medium speed, until buttercream is thick and smooth (it will appear very thin at first, but as more butter is beaten in, it will thicken). Beat in curd and remaining 1/2 teaspoon salt.

COOK'S NOTE

■ The buttercream can be made up to 1 week ahead and refrigerated in an airtight container. It can also be frozen for up to 1 month. Bring to room temperature (do not use a microwave) and beat with an electric mixer until smooth before using.

Black Forest Cake

SERVES 10 TO 12
ACTIVE TIME: 1 HOUR ■ START TO FINISH: 3 HOURS (INCLUDES COOLING)

■ Rich, big, and positively bursting with flavor, this old-fashioned German favorite originated in Berlin in the 1930s. There the fulsome beauty is also known as a Schwarzwalder Kirschtorte (Schwarzwald being the Black Forest, and Kirsch referring to the lavish amount of cherry liqueur and sour cherries that fill the cake). We use good sour cherry (not Bing) jam or preserves. The chocolate flavor is not intense but light and well rounded, a perfect foil for the kirsch syrup, cherry filling, and fluffy whipped cream topping. ■

FOR CHOCOLATE SPONGE

- 5 ounces good bittersweet chocolate (not unsweetened), finely chopped
- 1 stick (8 tablespoons) unsalted butter, cut into tablespoons
- 2 tablespoons water
- 1/2 teaspoon vanilla extract
- 1/3 cup almonds
- 10 tablespoons sugar
- 8 large eggs, separated
- 1/2 cup all-purpose flour
- 6 zwieback toasts, ground into fine crumbs
- 1/2 cup unsweetened cocoa powder (not Dutch-process)
- 1/2 teaspoon salt

FOR KIRSCH SYRUP

- 1/3 cup water
- 1/3 cup sugar
- 1/4 cup kirsch

FOR CREAM FILLING AND TOPPING

- 3 cups very cold heavy cream
- 1/4 cup sugar

FOR CHERRY FILLING

- 1 1/4 cups (16 ounces) sour cherry jam or preserves

OPTIONAL GARNISH: chocolate curls

SPECIAL EQUIPMENT: a 10-inch (26-centimeter) springform pan

MAKE THE CHOCOLATE SPONGE: Put a rack in middle of oven and preheat oven to 375°F. Butter bottom of springform pan (leave pan sides unbuttered). Line bottom with a round of parchment or wax paper, then butter paper.

Melt chocolate and butter with water in a small metal bowl set over a saucepan of barely simmering water, stirring frequently until smooth. Cool to room temperature, then stir in vanilla.

Finely grind almonds with 4 tablespoons (1/4 cup) sugar in a food processor or blender (do not blend to a paste). Transfer to a large bowl, add yolks, and beat with an electric mixer (preferably a stand mixer fitted with whisk attachment) at medium-high speed until pale, very thick, and almost doubled in volume, about 5 minutes. Reduce speed to low and beat in chocolate mixture. Transfer to a large wide bowl to facilitate folding in beaten whites (cake may be heavy if you use a deep narrow bowl).

Beat egg whites in cleaned bowl with cleaned beaters at high speed just until soft peaks form. Gradually beat in remaining 6 tablespoons sugar and continue to beat until whites are barely stiff.

Whisk one quarter of whites into yolk mixture to lighten it, then gently but thoroughly fold in remaining whites. Whisk together flour, zwieback crumbs, cocoa, and salt in a small bowl, then gently but thoroughly fold into batter in 3 or 4 batches.

Pour batter into pan. Bake until a wooden pick or skewer inserted in center of cake comes out clean, 30 to 35 minutes. Cool cake in pan on a rack for 5 minutes, then run a thin knife around side of pan and remove side. Invert cake onto another rack and remove pan bottom and paper. Reinvert cake onto rack and cool completely.

WHEN THE CAKE IS ALMOST COOL, MAKE THE SYRUP: Combine water and sugar in a 1-quart heavy saucepan and heat over moderately high heat, stirring occasionally, until sugar is dissolved. Transfer to a small bowl and stir in kirsch. Cool to warm.

MAKE THE FILLING AND TOPPING AND ASSEMBLE THE CAKE: With a serrated knife, slice cake horizontally into 3 layers (see page 727).

Beat cream with sugar in a large bowl with electric mixer until just stiff.

Put bottom layer of cake on a serving plate and brush with one third of syrup. Spread half of jam over layer, then cover with a layer of cream (about 1 1/4 cups). Top with middle cake layer and cover with syrup, jam, and cream in same manner. Top with third cake layer, cut side down, and brush with remaining syrup. Spread top and sides of cake with remaining cream. Garnish with chocolate curls, if desired.

COOK'S NOTES

- The chocolate sponge can be made up to 1 day ahead and kept, well wrapped in plastic wrap, at room temperature.
- The syrup can be made up to 3 days ahead and refrigerated, covered.
- The cake can be assembled up to 2 hours ahead and refrigerated.

Inside-Out German Chocolate Cake

SERVES 12

ACTIVE TIME: 1½ HOURS ■ START TO FINISH: 4½ HOURS (INCLUDES CHILLING)

■ Unusual, brilliant, and absolutely delicious: German chocolate cake meets *dulce de leche,* the caramelized condensed milk that is one of Spain's great culinary gifts to the world. It gives great body to a cake that is further enriched with pecans and coconut. Unlike a conventional German chocolate cake, which is not frosted but rather topped with some of the filling, this one is enrobed with ganache. ■

FOR CAKE LAYERS

- 1½ cups sugar
- 1½ cups all-purpose flour
- ½ cup plus 1 tablespoon unsweetened Dutch-process cocoa powder
- ¾ teaspoon baking powder
- ¾ teaspoon baking soda
- ¾ teaspoon salt
- ¾ cup whole milk
- ¾ stick (6 tablespoons) unsalted butter, melted
- 1 large egg
- 1 large egg yolk
- ¾ teaspoon vanilla extract
- ⅛ teaspoon almond extract
- ¾ cup boiling water

FOR FILLING

- 7 ounces sweetened flaked coconut
- 1 cup (4 ounces) coarsely chopped pecans
- 1 (14-ounce) can sweetened condensed milk
- 1 tablespoon vanilla extract

FOR GLAZE

- 2½ sticks unsalted butter
- 10 ounces good semisweet chocolate, finely chopped
- 3 tablespoons light corn syrup

SPECIAL EQUIPMENT: three 9-inch round cake pans; a 9-inch deep-dish pie plate

MAKE THE CAKE LAYERS: Put racks in upper and lower thirds of oven and preheat oven to 350°F. Oil cake pans and line bottoms with rounds of parchment or wax paper.

Sift together sugar, flour, cocoa powder, baking powder, baking soda, and salt into a large bowl. Whisk together milk, butter, egg, yolk, and extracts in a medium bowl until just combined. Add egg mixture to flour mixture, beating with an electric mixer at low speed, then increase speed to high and beat for 1 minute. Reduce speed to low and mix in boiling water until just combined (batter will be thin).

Divide batter among cake pans and smooth tops. Place two pans in upper third of oven and one pan in bottom third (do not put top pans directly above bottom pan) and bake, switching position of pans and turning them around halfway through baking, until a wooden pick or skewer inserted in center of cakes comes out clean, 20 to 25 minutes total.

Transfer pans to racks to cool for 15 minutes. Reduce oven temperature to 325°F. Run a thin knife around edges of pans and invert layers onto racks, remove paper, and cool completely.

MAKE THE FILLING WHILE THE LAYERS COOL: Spread coconut on a baking sheet with sides and spread pecans on another sheet. Toast coconut in lower third and pecans in upper third of oven, stirring occasionally, until golden, 12 to 18 minutes. Transfer sheets to racks to cool. Put a rack in middle of oven and increase oven temperature to 425°F.

Pour condensed milk into pie plate and cover tightly with foil. Put pie plate in a larger baking pan, add enough boiling water to reach halfway up sides of pie plate, and bake for 45 minutes.

Add more boiling water as needed to reach halfway up sides of pie plate and bake, still covered, until milk is thick and brown, about 45 minutes more.

Remove pie plate from water bath. Stir coconut, pecans, and vanilla into baked milk and keep warm, covered with foil.

MEANWHILE, MAKE THE GLAZE: Melt butter in a 3-quart saucepan. Remove from heat, add chocolate and corn syrup, and whisk until chocolate is melted. Transfer 1 cup glaze to a bowl and set remaining glaze aside in pan. Refrigerate glaze in bowl, stirring occasionally, until thickened and spreadable, about 1 hour.

ASSEMBLE THE CAKE: For easier handling, put bottom cake layer upside down on a cardboard cake round or removable bottom of a tart or cake pan and place on a rack. Set rack over a baking pan, to catch excess glaze. Drop half of coconut filling by spoonfuls evenly over layer and gently spread with a wet spatula. Top with another cake layer and spread with remaining filling in same manner. Top with remaining cake layer. Spread chilled glaze evenly over top and sides of cake.

Heat reserved glaze in pan over low heat, stirring, until glossy and pourable, about 1 minute. Pour glaze evenly over top of cake, making sure it coats sides evenly. Shake rack gently to smooth glaze. Refrigerate cake until glaze is firm, about 1 hour.

Transfer cake to a plate before serving.

COOK'S NOTE

- The cake can be made up to 3 days ahead and refrigerated, covered. Bring to room temperature before serving.

Hungarian Chocolate Mousse Cake Bars

MAKES 30 BARS
ACTIVE TIME: 2 HOURS ■ START TO FINISH: 5 HOURS (INCLUDES CHILLING)

■ Reminiscent of a Sacher torte but known as *rigó jansci* in Hungary, these satisfying bars are an intense blend of apricot jam–moistened chocolate cake layers filled with chocolate mousse and whipped cream and glazed with bittersweet chocolate ganache. This is a convenient way to serve a serious chocolate mousse cake to a crowd. ■

FOR CAKE LAYERS
- 3 ounces good bittersweet chocolate (not unsweetened), chopped
- 1 stick (8 tablespoons) unsalted butter, softened
- 3/4 cup granulated sugar
- 6 large eggs, separated
- 1/3 cup cake flour (not self-rising)
- 1/3 cup unsweetened cocoa powder
- 1/4 teaspoon salt
- 1/4 teaspoon cream of tartar
- 2/3 cup apricot jam, melted and strained

FOR CHOCOLATE GLAZE
- 4 ounces good bittersweet chocolate (not unsweetened), finely chopped in a food processor
- 1/3 cup heavy cream

FOR CHOCOLATE MOUSSE FILLING
- 12 ounces good bittersweet chocolate (not unsweetened), finely chopped in a food processor
- 3 cups heavy cream

FOR WHIPPED CREAM FILLING
- 1 teaspoon unflavored gelatin (from a 1/4-ounce envelope)
- 2 tablespoons cold water
- 1 cup very cold heavy cream
- 2 tablespoons confectioners' sugar
- 1 teaspoon vanilla extract

SPECIAL EQUIPMENT: two 15-by-10-by-1-inch baking sheets

MAKE THE CAKE LAYERS: Put racks in upper and lower thirds of oven and preheat oven to 350°F. Butter baking sheets, line bottom and short sides of each sheet with a sheet of wax paper (paper may hang over ends), and butter paper. Dust sheets with flour, knocking out excess.

Melt chocolate in a small metal bowl set over a small saucepan of barely simmering water, stirring occasionally until smooth. Remove from heat.

Beat together butter and 1/2 cup granulated sugar in a large bowl with an electric mixer at medium speed until pale and fluffy, about 5 minutes. Beat in yolks one at a time, beating well after each addition. Beat in chocolate. Sift in flour, cocoa, and salt, reduce speed to low, and mix until well combined.

Beat egg whites with cream of tartar in another bowl with cleaned beaters at medium speed until they hold soft peaks. Gradually add remaining 1/4 cup sugar, and beat until whites just hold stiff peaks. Stir one quarter of whites into batter to lighten it, then gently but thoroughly fold in remaining whites.

Divide batter between sheets and carefully spread evenly (layers will be thin). Bake, switching position of sheets halfway through baking, until cake is set and firm to the touch, 14 to 18 minutes total.

Cool layers in sheets on racks for 10 minutes, then invert racks over sheets and flip layers onto them. Remove sheets and wax paper. Spread jam evenly over 1 warm layer and cool layers completely.

Transfer jam-coated layer to a baking sheet or tray lined with a sheet of parchment or wax paper.

MAKE THE GLAZE: Put chocolate in a small heatproof bowl. Bring cream just to a boil in a 3 1/2- to 4-quart saucepan and slowly pour over chocolate. Stir until smooth, then pour over plain cake layer and spread to coat top evenly. Let stand in a cool place until set, about 1 hour.

MAKE THE CHOCOLATE MOUSSE FILLING: Put chocolate in a large metal bowl. Bring cream just to a boil in a 3 1/2- to 4-quart saucepan and slowly pour over chocolate. Stir until smooth, then set bowl in a larger bowl of ice and cold water and stir occasionally until cold.

Remove bowl of mousse from ice bath and beat with electric mixer at medium speed until mousse just holds soft peaks. (If it becomes grainy, melt over a saucepan of barely simmering water and repeat chilling, then whipping.) Quickly spread over jam layer (mousse will stiffen as it stands) and refrigerate.

MAKE THE WHIPPED CREAM FILLING: Sprinkle gelatin over water in a small metal bowl and let soften for 1 minute. Put bowl over a small saucepan of boiling water and heat, stirring occasionally, until gelatin is dissolved. Remove pan from heat, leaving bowl over pan.

Beat cream with confectioners' sugar and vanilla in a medium bowl with cleaned beaters at medium speed until it holds a soft shape. Beat in warm gelatin mixture and continue beating until cream just holds stiff peaks. Spread evenly over top of mousse-coated layer.

ASSEMBLE THE CAKE: Cut glazed layer lengthwise into thirds, then cut each strip crosswise into 10 pieces. Reassemble bars on top of cream filling. Chill cake, uncovered, until glaze is firm, about 1 hour, then cover with plastic wrap and refrigerate until ready to serve.

Just before serving, cut cake into bars with a large knife, wiping it clean with a hot damp cloth between cuts.

COOK'S NOTE

- The cake can be refrigerated for up to 3 days.

Chocolate Roll with Cappuccino Cream

SERVES 8 TO 10
ACTIVE TIME: 1½ HOURS ■ START TO FINISH: 4 HOURS (INCLUDES CHILLING)

■ Eating a slice of this cake is like having a solid version of a particularly excellent mocha cappuccino, but with the advantage of a combination of various textures. Its tender crumb comes from the fact that it is really just a flourless chocolate soufflé base spread in a jelly-roll pan, baked quickly, filled with cappuccino cream, and rolled up. It was inspired by a chocolate roulade created by the cooking teacher and cookbook author Dione Lucas, the first famous TV chef in America. If you're looking for a simple *bûche de Noël,* this cake fills the bill perfectly, because as you roll it up it tends to crack, giving it a rustic, loglike appearance. ■

FOR CAKE

- 7 ounces good bittersweet chocolate (not unsweetened), chopped
- ¼ cup water
- 6 large eggs, separated
- ⅔ cup granulated sugar
- 1 teaspoon vanilla extract
- ¼ teaspoon salt
- ¼ teaspoon cream of tartar

FOR FILLING AND ROLLING CAKE

- 1 cup very cold heavy cream
- 1 tablespoon instant espresso powder
- ⅛ teaspoon ground cinnamon
- 5½ tablespoons confectioners' sugar
- 1½ tablespoons unsweetened cocoa powder

FOR GARNISH

- ⅓ cup very cold heavy cream
- 1 teaspoon instant espresso powder
- Pinch of ground cinnamon
- 1 tablespoon confectioners' sugar
- 5 chocolate-covered coffee beans (optional; see Sources)

SPECIAL EQUIPMENT: a 15-by-10-by-1-inch baking sheet; a pastry bag fitted with a small fluted tip

MAKE THE CAKE: Put a rack in middle of oven and preheat oven to 350°F. Lightly butter baking sheet, line with foil, and butter foil. Line foil with wax paper and butter paper.

Melt chocolate with water in a metal bowl set over a saucepan of barely simmering water, stirring until smooth. Remove bowl from heat and cool for 10 minutes.

Beat yolks with ⅓ cup sugar in a large bowl with an electric mixer at high speed until mixture is thick and pale and forms a ribbon when beaters are lifted, about 5 minutes. Beat in chocolate mixture and vanilla.

Beat egg whites with salt in another large bowl with cleaned beaters until frothy, then add cream of tartar and beat until whites hold soft peaks. Add remaining ⅓ cup sugar a little at a time, beating until whites just hold stiff peaks.

Stir one quarter of whites into chocolate mixture to lighten it, then gently but thoroughly fold in remaining whites. Pour batter into lined sheet and spread it evenly with a metal spatula. Bake until cake is puffed and just set, 12 to 15 minutes. Cool completely on sheet on a rack. (Cake will sink as it cools.)

MAKE THE FILLING WHILE THE CAKE COOLS: Beat cream with espresso powder and cinnamon in a medium bowl with electric mixer until it holds soft peaks. Add 4 tablespoons (1/4 cup) confectioners' sugar and beat until cream holds stiff peaks. Refrigerate filling, covered, for 10 minutes.

FILL AND ROLL THE CAKE: Stir together cocoa powder and remaining 1 1/2 tablespoons confectioners' sugar in a small bowl. Sift about half of mixture evenly over cake. Cover cake with a sheet of wax paper, invert a baking sheet over paper, and invert cake onto baking sheet. Carefully remove foil and wax paper. Spread filling on cake, leaving a 1-inch border on short ends and a 1/2-inch border on long sides. With a long side nearest you, and using wax paper as an aid, roll up cake jelly-roll style, keeping it wrapped in wax paper (cake will crack but will still hold together). Refrigerate cake, in wax paper, on baking sheet for at least 1 hour.

Transfer cake to a platter. Remove wax paper and trim ends on a diagonal. Sift remaining cocoa mixture over cake.

GARNISH THE CAKE: Beat cream with espresso powder, cinnamon, and confectioners' sugar in a small bowl until it just holds stiff peaks. Transfer to pastry bag and pipe decoratively on and around cake roll. Top with chocolate-covered coffee beans, if using.

COOK'S NOTE

- The rolled cake can be refrigerated for up to 1 day.

VARIATIONS

- For the filling, you can substitute the following for the espresso powder and cinnamon: 2 tablespoons Grand Marnier and 1 teaspoon finely grated orange zest; 2 tablespoons Cognac or other brandy and 1/2 teaspoon vanilla extract; or 2 tablespoons unsweetened cocoa powder and 1/2 teaspoon vanilla extract.

Three Cities of Spain Classic Cheesecake

SERVES 8 TO 10
ACTIVE TIME: 30 MINUTES ■ START TO FINISH: 9 1/2 HOURS (INCLUDES CHILLING)

■ Sometimes less really can be, if not exactly more, at least immensely rewarding. This cheesecake, which comes to us from Santa Fe's long-closed Three Cities of Spain coffeehouse, is a case in point. Although the filling contains only five ingredients and is very simple to make, it delivers all the decadently rich, creamy smoothness that has made cheesecake so popular. This cake has long been a favorite at *Gourmet*. ■

3 (8-ounce) packages cream cheese, softened
4 large eggs
1 cup plus 1 tablespoon sugar
2 teaspoons vanilla extract
Crumb Crust (recipe follows), made with graham crackers, in a 9- to 9 1/2-inch (24-centimeter) springform pan
1 pound sour cream

Put a rack in middle of oven and preheat oven to 350°F.

Beat cream cheese in a large bowl with an electric mixer at medium speed until fluffy. Reduce speed to low and add eggs one at a time, mixing well after each addition. Add 1 cup sugar and 1 teaspoon vanilla and mix until well combined, scraping down sides of bowl with a spatula as needed.

Put springform pan with crust on a baking sheet with sides, to catch any drips. Pour filling into crust. Bake until cake is set 3 inches from edges but center is still slightly wobbly, about 45 minutes. Cool in pan on a rack for 5 minutes. (Leave oven on.)

Stir together sour cream, remaining 1 tablespoon sugar, and remaining 1 teaspoon vanilla in a medium bowl. Drop spoonfuls of topping around edges of cake and then spread evenly over top. Bake cake for 10 minutes more.

Run a knife around top edge of cake to loosen it, then cool completely in pan on rack. (Cake will continue to set as it cools.)

Refrigerate cake, loosely covered, for at least 6 hours.

Remove side of pan, transfer cake to a plate, and bring to room temperature before serving.

COOK'S NOTE

- The cheesecake can be refrigerated for up to 3 days.

VARIATION

- CREAMY GINGER CHEESECAKE: Add 1/2 teaspoon ground ginger to the crust mixture. For the filling, reduce the sugar to 3/4 cup and pulse the sugar in a food processor with 1/2 cup (4 ounces) coarsely chopped crystallized ginger and 1 1/2 tablespoons grated peeled fresh ginger until both gingers are finely ground. Add to the cream cheese mixture along with the vanilla and proceed as directed.

Crumb Crust

MAKES ENOUGH FOR ONE 9 TO 9 1/2-INCH (24-CENTIMETER) CHEESECAKE
ACTIVE TIME: 10 MINUTES ■ START TO FINISH: 10 MINUTES

■ A crumb crust, whether of graham crackers, chocolate or vanilla wafers, or gingersnaps, is the classic base for cheesecake and key lime pie. ■

- 1 1/2 cups (about 5 ounces) finely ground graham crackers or cookies, such as chocolate or vanilla wafers or gingersnaps
- 5 tablespoons unsalted butter, melted
- 1/3 cup sugar
- 1/8 teaspoon salt

SPECIAL EQUIPMENT: a 9- to 9 1/2-inch (24-centimeter) springform pan

Invert bottom of springform pan (to make it easier to slide cake off bottom), then lock on side and butter pan.

Stir together all ingredients in a bowl. Press onto bottom and 1 inch up sides of buttered pan. Fill immediately or refrigerate for up to 2 hours.

Key Lime Cheesecake with Mango Ribbons

SERVES 8 TO 10
ACTIVE TIME: 1 HOUR ■ START TO FINISH: 8 HOURS (INCLUDES COOLING)

■ Unlike most cheesecakes, this one will not outweigh the main course. Thinner than the standard version, it is topped with a beautiful layer of very thinly sliced mango ribbons, and it manages to combine the tang and light texture of key lime pie with the ultimate creaminess of cheesecake. If you can't find fresh key limes, substitute bottled key lime juice, preferably Manhattan brand (see Sources). ■

FOR CRUST
- 1 1/4 cups graham cracker crumbs (from nine 4 3/4-by-2 1/4-inch crackers)
- 3 tablespoons sugar
- 1/2 stick (4 tablespoons) unsalted butter, melted

FOR FILLING
- 2 (8-ounce) packages cream cheese, softened
- 1 cup plus 2 tablespoons sugar
- 3/4 cup strained fresh key lime juice (from about 1 1/2 pounds key limes) or bottled key lime juice
- 1/2 cup sour cream
- 1/2 teaspoon vanilla extract
- 2 1/2 tablespoons all-purpose flour
- 1/4 teaspoon salt
- 3 large eggs

FOR TOPPING
- 2 large, firm but ripe mangoes
- 1 tablespoon strained fresh key lime juice or bottled juice
- 1/2 cup very cold heavy cream
- 1 tablespoon sugar

SPECIAL EQUIPMENT: a 9- to 9 1/2-inch (24-centimeter) springform pan; a mandoline or other adjustable-blade slicer, such as a Japanese Benriner

MAKE THE CRUST: Put a rack in middle of oven and preheat oven to 350°F. Invert bottom of springform pan (to make it easier to slide cake off bottom), then lock on side and butter pan.

Stir together crumbs, sugar, and butter in a bowl with a fork until well combined. Press evenly onto bottom and one third of the way up sides of pan.

Bake crust for 8 minutes. Transfer to a rack to cool. Reduce oven temperature to 325°F.

MAKE THE FILLING: Beat cream cheese in a large bowl with an electric mixer at medium speed until fluffy. Beat in sugar. Reduce speed to low, add lime juice, sour cream, and vanilla, and mix until smooth. Mix in flour and salt until just incorporated, scraping down sides of bowl with a spatula as needed. Add eggs and mix just until incorporated.

Pour filling into crust. Put cheesecake on a baking

sheet with sides and bake until just set in center, 1 hour to 1 hour and 10 minutes. Transfer to rack to cool completely. (Cake will continue to set as it cools.)

Run a thin knife around edge of cake and remove side of pan. With a large metal spatula, transfer cake to a serving plate.

MAKE THE TOPPING: Peel mangoes. Leaving fruit whole, slice mangos lengthwise very thinly (slightly less than 1/8 inch thick) with slicer (use caution—peeled mango will be slippery). Halve wider slices lengthwise. Gently toss mango slices with lime juice.

Beat cream with sugar in a small bowl with cleaned beaters at medium speed until it just holds stiff peaks. Spread over top of cheesecake. Bending and curling mango slices, arrange them decoratively over cream.

COOK'S NOTE

- The cheesecake, without the topping, can be made up to 1 day ahead and refrigerated, covered. Serve cold or bring to room temperature. Add the topping just before serving.

Pumpkin Cheesecake with Bourbon–Sour Cream Topping

SERVES 12 TO 14

ACTIVE TIME: 45 MINUTES ■ START TO FINISH: 10½ HOURS (INCLUDES CHILLING)

■ There comes a time when every Thanksgiving baker longs for a change from pumpkin pie. This cheesecake, neither too sweet nor too dense, is a great alternative. But there's no reason to save it for Thanksgiving—it can be made for any fall dinner or, in fact, all year round. If you're making this for a crowd that includes children, leave the bourbon out of both the filling and the sour cream topping, if you wish. ■

FOR CRUST

- ¾ cup graham cracker crumbs (from five 4¾-by-2¼-inch crackers)
- ½ cup pecans, finely chopped
- ¼ cup packed light brown sugar
- ¼ cup granulated sugar
- ½ stick (4 tablespoons) unsalted butter, melted and cooled

FOR FILLING

- 1½ cups canned solid-pack pumpkin
- 3 large eggs
- ½ cup packed light brown sugar
- 2 tablespoons heavy cream
- 1 teaspoon vanilla extract
- 1 tablespoon bourbon liqueur, such as Wild Turkey, or bourbon (optional)
- ½ cup granulated sugar
- 1 tablespoon cornstarch
- 1½ teaspoons ground cinnamon
- ½ teaspoon freshly grated nutmeg
- ½ teaspoon ground ginger
- ½ teaspoon salt
- 3 (8-ounce) packages cream cheese, softened

FOR TOPPING

- 2 cups (18 ounces) sour cream
- 2 tablespoons granulated sugar
- 1 tablespoon bourbon liqueur or bourbon (optional)

OPTIONAL GARNISH: pecan halves

SPECIAL EQUIPMENT: a 9- to 9½-inch (24-centimeter) springform pan

MAKE THE CRUST: Invert bottom of springform pan (to make it easier to slide cake off bottom), then lock on side and butter pan.

Stir together crumbs, pecans, sugars, and butter in a bowl until combined. Press crumb mixture into bottom and ½ inch up sides of pan. Chill crust for 1 hour.

MAKE THE FILLING: Put a rack in middle of oven and preheat oven to 350°F.

Whisk together pumpkin, eggs, brown sugar, cream, vanilla, and liqueur (if using) in a bowl until combined.

Stir together granulated sugar, cornstarch, cinnamon, nutmeg, ginger, and salt in a large bowl. Add cream cheese and beat with an electric mixer at high speed until creamy and smooth, about 3 minutes. Add pumpkin mixture and beat until smooth.

Pour filling into crust and smooth top. Put cheesecake on a baking sheet with sides and bake until center is just set, 50 to 60 minutes. Transfer to a rack and cool for 5 minutes. (Leave oven on.)

MAKE THE TOPPING: Whisk together sour cream, sugar, and liqueur (if using) in a bowl. Spread

Say Cheesecake

When we specify cream cheese in a recipe such as the cheesecake on page 751, we mean none other than Philadelphia brand. The more expensive artisanal varieties that you'll see in fancy foods shops won't give you the texture that you're after. Our cheesecake crusts range from none at all (the cake itself forms a skin while baking) to crumb crusts. We love the different textures and flavors that a good crumb crust imparts.

How do you prevent a cheesecake from cracking? Theories abound, but the most important thing to remember is not to overbake. (Souffléed cheesecakes are another matter entirely; they crack easily, and there's not much you can do.) We also find it helpful to run a knife around the edge of the cake as soon as it comes out of the oven. The cake will shrink as it cools, and if its sides are stuck to the pan, the surface will split open. Sometimes this happens no matter how painstaking you are. (In general, the magnitude of the rifts and fissures corresponds to the importance of the dinner party for which you've baked the cake.) You can camouflage the damage, however, by carefully spreading a thin layer of sour cream onto the chilled cake; leave it in the refrigerator overnight to set up, and it will look perfect.

Transferring a cheesecake from springform pan to serving plate is an easy matter if you turn the bottom of the pan over before you fill it, so the lip side is down; with the lip out of the way, the cake is also easier to cut. Speaking of which, to ensure clean slices, use a thin sharp knife and wipe it off between slices. Dipping the knife into hot water between slices can also be effective, but be especially careful to wipe it off before cutting so you don't add excess moisture to the pieces of cake.

We generally use a 9- to 9½-inch springform pan for cheesecakes; both sizes are often labeled "24 centimeters." Professional bakers treat their springform pans with TLC, and you should too. Always open a springform on a counter, not in midair, so it won't warp. (You don't want it to leak.) After you wash it, dry it right away — no amount of sour cream will camouflage that unmistakable rust taste. We pop ours in a low oven to ensure that they're completely dry, especially under the rolled lip.

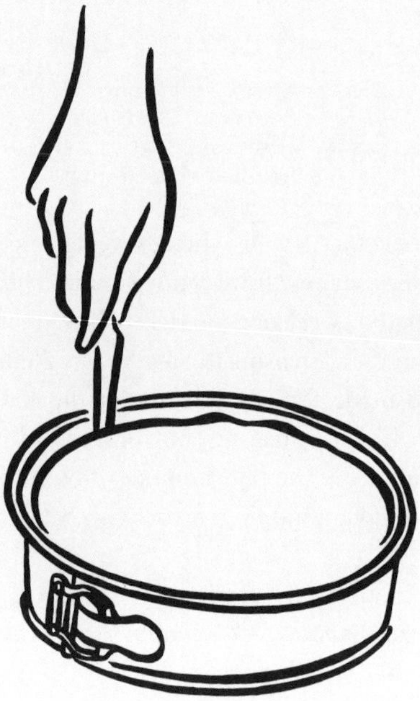

on top of cheesecake and bake for 5 minutes. Run a knife around edge of cake to loosen it, then cool completely in pan on rack, about 3 hours.

Refrigerate cheesecake, covered, for at least 4 hours.

Bring cheesecake to room temperature before serving. Garnish with pecans, if desired.

COOK'S NOTE

- The cheesecake can be refrigerated for up to 12 hours.

Russian Tea Room Cheesecake

SERVES 10

ACTIVE TIME: 30 MINUTES ■ START TO FINISH: 12 HOURS (INCLUDES CHILLING)

■ There are times when we want a cheesecake with a delicate texture and flavor. This, inspired by a cheesecake served for many years at the Russian Tea Room, in New York City, is our favorite for those occasions. Because beaten egg whites are folded into the batter just before baking, it is light, and the orange-flower water and lemon zest provide a subtle, gently aromatic flavor that perfectly matches the airy texture. ■

- 2½ (8-ounce) packages cream cheese, softened
- 1¼ sticks (10 tablespoons) unsalted butter, softened
- 1½ cups sugar
- 8 large eggs, separated
- 2 teaspoons finely grated lemon zest
- 2 tablespoons fresh lemon juice
- 1 teaspoon vanilla extract
- ½ teaspoon orange-flower water (see Sources)
- ½ teaspoon almond extract
- ¼ cup cornstarch

SPECIAL EQUIPMENT: parchment paper; a 10-inch (26-centimeter) springform pan

Put a rack in middle of oven and preheat oven to 350°F. Cut a 10-inch round and a 32-by-5-inch strip from parchment paper.

Invert bottom of springform pan (to make it easier to slide cake off bottom), then lock on side and butter bottom. Line bottom with round of parchment and butter round. Butter one side of parchment strip and press unbuttered side of strip against side of pan (strip will extend 2 inches above rim). Wrap outside of pan with a large sheet of heavy-duty foil (or a double layer of regular foil) to waterproof it.

Beat together cream cheese, butter, ¾ cup sugar, yolks, zest, juice, vanilla, orange-flower water, and almond extract in a large bowl with an electric mixer at medium speed until creamy, about 2 minutes with a stand mixer, 3 minutes with a handheld mixer. Reduce speed to low, add cornstarch, and mix until just combined.

Beat egg whites in another large bowl with cleaned beaters at medium speed until they just hold soft peaks. Beat in remaining ¾ cup sugar 1 tablespoon at a time, then increase speed to high and beat until meringue holds stiff, glossy peaks, about 2 minutes with stand mixer, 3 minutes with handheld mixer.

Fold one quarter of whites into cream cheese mixture to lighten it, then gently but thoroughly fold in remaining whites.

Pour batter into pan and gently smooth top. Put pan in a larger baking pan and add enough boiling water to reach halfway up sides of springform pan. Bake until top is golden but cake still trembles slightly when pan is shaken gently, 55 to 65 minutes. (Cheesecake will rise in oven, then fall slightly and set as it cools.) Run a knife around edge of cake to loosen it, then cool completely in pan on a rack.

Refrigerate cake, loosely covered, for at least 8 hours.

COOK'S NOTE

- The cheesecake can be refrigerated for up to 3 days.

Bananas Foster Cheesecake

SERVES 10 TO 12

ACTIVE TIME: 1 HOUR ■ START TO FINISH: 11 HOURS (INCLUDES CHILLING)

■ The famed flambéed dessert that was invented at Brennan's Restaurant, in New Orleans, is reborn (without the flame) in this layered cheesecake. The flavors of the banana liqueur and the rum that make bananas Foster so distinctive combine in one layer, banana liqueur is also folded into the cream cheese layer, and the cheesecake is topped with praline. This recipe came to us from contributor Jean Anderson after a trip to Café Vermilionville, in Lafayette, Louisiana.

FOR CRUST

- 1/2 stick (4 tablespoons) unsalted butter, melted
- 1 1/3 cups fine graham cracker crumbs (from ten 4 3/4-by-2 1/4-inch crackers)
- 2 tablespoons sugar
- 11–13 *savoiardi* (crisp Italian ladyfingers; see Sources), halved crosswise

FOR FILLING

- 1/4 cup sliced almonds
- 1/2 stick (4 tablespoons) unsalted butter
- 1/2 cup packed dark brown sugar
- 2 tablespoons banana liqueur
- 2 tablespoons dark rum
- 1/8 teaspoon ground cinnamon
- 1/2 teaspoon vanilla extract
- 4 medium, firm but ripe bananas

FOR CREAM CHEESE LAYER

- 5 large eggs
- 3 (8-ounce) packages cream cheese, softened
- 1 cup sugar
- 2 tablespoons banana liqueur
- 1 tablespoon vanilla extract

FOR PRALINE TOPPING

- 1 1/2 cups (6 ounces) pecans
- 2 sticks (1/2 pound) unsalted butter
- 1 cup packed dark brown sugar
- 1 1/2 tablespoons water

SPECIAL EQUIPMENT: a 10-inch (26-centimeter) springform pan

Put a rack in middle of oven and preheat oven to 350°F. Invert bottom of springform pan (to make it easier to slide cake off bottom), then lock on side and butter pan. Wrap outside of pan with a large sheet of heavy-duty foil (or a double layer of regular foil) to waterproof it.

MAKE THE CRUST: Stir together butter, graham cracker crumbs, and sugar in a bowl. Press crumb mixture evenly onto bottom of pan. Arrange ladyfingers upright, rounded edges on top and flat sides in, around sides of pan, pressing lightly into crust mixture to stabilize them.

MAKE THE FILLING: Spread almonds on a small baking sheet and toast until pale golden, about 5 minutes. Transfer sheet to a rack to cool. (Leave oven on.)

Melt butter with brown sugar in a 10- to 12-inch nonstick skillet over moderate heat, stirring until smooth. Stir in liqueur, rum, cinnamon, and vanilla and simmer, whisking, until sugar is dissolved, about 1 minute. Remove from heat.

Halve bananas crosswise and then cut lengthwise into 1/4-inch-thick slices. Add bananas to butter mixture and cook over moderately low heat, turning gently with a spatula, until just softened, 30 seconds to 1 minute. Remove from heat and sprinkle toasted almonds over bananas.

MAKE THE CREAM CHEESE LAYER: Whisk together eggs in a medium bowl until just combined. Beat together cream cheese and sugar in a large bowl with an electric mixer at medium-high speed until fluffy, about 3 minutes. Slowly add half of eggs and beat, scraping down sides of bowl as necessary, until combined. Slowly beat in remaining eggs, then beat in liqueur and vanilla.

Pour half of cream cheese mixture into crust. Bake for 10 minutes. Cool on a rack for 5 minutes. (Leave oven on.)

Gently spoon banana filling evenly over cream cheese layer, arranging bananas so they do not overlap. Pour remaining cream cheese mixture over filling, then put springform in a large baking pan. Add enough boiling water to reach halfway up sides of springform pan. Bake until filling is set in center and top is golden and firm, about 1 hour. Run a knife around edge of cake to loosen it, then cool completely in pan on rack.

Refrigerate cheesecake, loosely covered, for at least 8 hours.

MAKE THE PRALINE TOPPING: Put a rack in middle of oven and preheat oven to 350°F.

Spread pecans on a baking sheet and toast until one shade darker, about 5 minutes. Transfer sheet to a rack to cool.

Melt butter with brown sugar in a 2- to 2 1/2-quart heavy saucepan over moderate heat, stirring until smooth. Stir in water until incorporated. Stir in pecans, remove pan from heat, and cool to room temperature.

Serve cheesecake with praline topping spooned over slices.

COOK'S NOTE

- The cheesecake can be refrigerated for up to 3 days.

Chocolate Caramel Cheesecake

SERVES 8 TO 10
ACTIVE TIME: 45 MINUTES ■ START TO FINISH: 9 3/4 HOURS (INCLUDES CHILLING)

■ We love the combination of chocolate and caramel, perhaps because both contain a subdued edge of bitterness under their lush sweetness. Add some heavy cream, sour cream, eggs, and a bit of vanilla, and the result is this marvelous cheesecake, rich and intense but not too dense. The recipe is also delightfully simple. ■

- 1 cup sugar
- 3/4 cup heavy cream
- 8 ounces good bittersweet chocolate (not unsweetened), finely chopped
- 1/2 cup sour cream
- 3 (8-ounce) packages cream cheese, softened
- 4 large eggs
- 1 teaspoon vanilla extract
- Crumb Crust (page 752), made with chocolate wafer cookies, in a 9- to 9 1/2-inch (24-centimeter) springform pan

Put a rack in middle of oven and preheat oven to 350°F.

Cook sugar in a dry heavy 3 1/2- to 4-quart saucepan over moderately low heat, stirring slowly with a fork, until melted and pale golden. Continue to cook caramel, without stirring, swirling pan occasionally, until deep golden. Immediately remove from heat and carefully add heavy cream (mixture will vigorously steam and caramel will harden). Cook over moderately low heat, stirring, until caramel is dissolved. Remove from heat and whisk in chocolate until smooth. Stir in sour cream.

Beat cream cheese in a large bowl with an electric mixer at high speed until fluffy. Reduce speed to low and mix in chocolate mixture. Add eggs one at a time, mixing well after each addition and scraping down sides of bowl with a spatula as needed. Mix in vanilla.

Put springform pan with crust on a baking sheet with sides, to catch any drips. Pour filling into crust. Bake until cake is set 3 inches from edges but center is still slightly wobbly, about 55 minutes.

Run a thin knife around edge of cake to loosen it, then cool completely in springform pan on a rack. (Cake will continue to set as it cools.)

Refrigerate cake, loosely covered, for at least 6 hours.

Remove side of pan, transfer cake to a plate, and bring to room temperature before serving.

COOK'S NOTE

- The cheesecake can be refrigerated for up to 1 week.

PIES, TARTS, AND PASTRIES

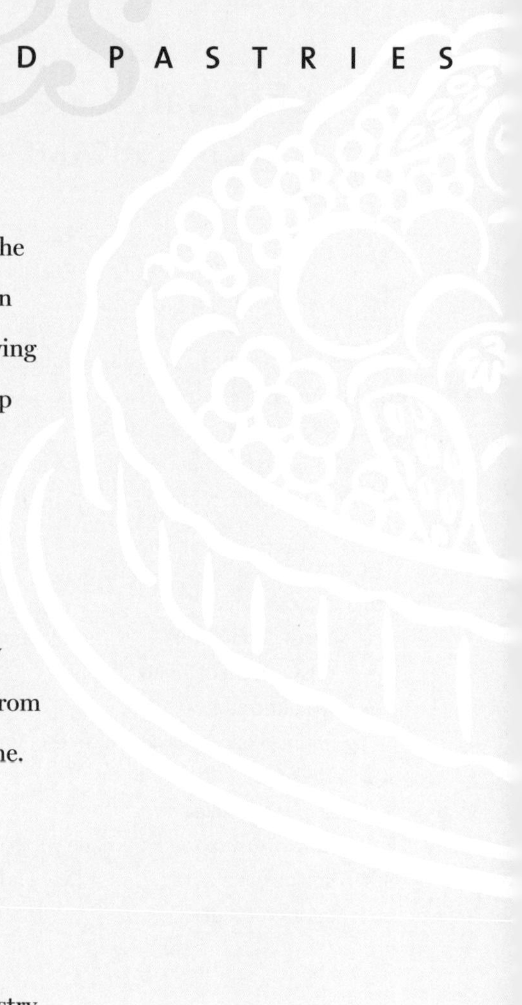

Pie people—and you know if you are one of us—would rather eat the plainest pie than the most elaborate dessert concoction. Offer us an honest piece of apple, a seductive slice of pecan pumpkin, or a serving of homely sweet potato, and as far as we're concerned, you can keep your precious pavlovas and your sophisticated soufflés.

We know that pie has never deserved its reputation as a temperamental creature; all it has ever wanted is to be handled with care. Besides, the food processor has taken the guesswork out of pastry dough and made the life of the pie maker remarkably carefree. We know too that the magical aroma which issues forth from any oven filled with pies makes a house smell like a well-loved home. And we know that the appearance of pie at the end of a meal is guaranteed to produce smiles.

This chapter is for the rest of you, the people who need to be convinced. We're so certain of the importance of pie that we offer recipes for every possible kind of pastry dough, from quick puff pastry to frozen butter pastry. We have also unlocked the secret of hand-stretched, paper-thin homemade strudel, and we tell you how to produce a perfect tarte Tatin. Here are recipes for simple pies (blueberry, cherry almond, peach), exotic tarts (apple and Calvados galette, red wine–poached pear and custard, roasted rhubarb with strawberry sauce), and a few fancy creations such as ice cream–filled profiteroles (so much easier than you would ever imagine) and a beautiful jalousie that allows a tantalizing glimpse of the filling. These are all the recipes you would possibly need to become a pie person too.

Pies

Apple Pie

SERVES 6 TO 8
ACTIVE TIME: 40 MINUTES ■ START TO FINISH: 5½ HOURS
(INCLUDES MAKING DOUGH AND COOLING)

■ The key to making a great apple pie is using a combination of apples: one variety might be sweet, another tart; another might hold its shape while still another disintegrates as it cooks. The result is a mélange of flavors and textures. Make this pie with tart apples such as Winesap and Granny Smith and sweet varieties like Fuji, Jonagold, Ida-Red, and Mutsu. Drape the top crust over the heaped apples in your pie dish; they'll settle during the baking process. ■

- 3 tablespoons all-purpose flour
- 1 teaspoon finely grated lemon zest
- ½ teaspoon ground cinnamon
- ¼ teaspoon ground allspice
- ⅛ teaspoon salt
- ⅔ cup plus 1 tablespoon sugar
- 2½ pounds apples, peeled, cored, and each cut into 10 wedges
- 1 tablespoon fresh lemon juice
- Basic Pastry Dough for a double-crust pie (page 790)
- 1 large egg, lightly beaten, for egg wash

Put a large baking sheet on middle oven rack and preheat oven to 425°F.

Whisk together flour, zest, cinnamon, allspice, salt, and ⅔ cup sugar in a large bowl. Gently toss with apples and lemon juice.

Roll out 1 piece of dough (keep remaining piece chilled) on a lightly floured surface with a lightly floured rolling pin into a 13-inch round. Fit it into a 9-inch pie plate. Trim edge, leaving a ½-inch overhang. Refrigerate shell while you roll out dough for top crust.

Roll out remaining piece of dough on lightly floured surface into an 11-inch round.

Spoon filling into shell. Cover pie with pastry round and trim with kitchen shears, leaving a ½-inch overhang. Press edges together, then crimp decoratively. Lightly brush top of pie with egg and sprinkle all over with remaining 1 tablespoon sugar. With a small sharp knife, cut 3 steam vents in top crust.

Bake pie on hot baking sheet for 20 minutes. Reduce oven temperature to 375°F and continue to bake until crust is golden and filling is bubbling, about 40 minutes more. Cool pie on a rack to warm or room temperature, 2 to 3 hours.

Blueberry Pie

SERVES 8
ACTIVE TIME: 40 MINUTES ■ START TO FINISH: 6 HOURS
(INCLUDES MAKING DOUGH AND COOLING)

■ In the middle of summer, when fresh blueberries are at their peak, there is nothing quite as satisfying as a pure fruit pie. Our version is unusual in that it uses both cornstarch and tapioca as thickeners; they work in different ways, and the resulting filling is juicy and not too firm. ■

- 1¼–1½ cups sugar, depending on sweetness of berries
- 3 tablespoons cornstarch
- 3 tablespoons quick-cooking tapioca
- 1 teaspoon finely grated lemon zest
- ¼ teaspoon salt
- 6¼ cups blueberries (from 3 pints)
- Basic Pastry Dough for a double-crust pie (page 790)

Line a large baking sheet with foil, put on middle oven rack, and preheat oven to 425°F.

Whisk together sugar, cornstarch, tapioca, lemon zest, and salt in a large bowl. Gently toss with blueberries.

Roll out 1 piece of dough (keep remaining piece chilled) on a lightly floured surface with a lightly floured rolling pin into a 13-inch round. Fit it into a 9-inch pie plate. Trim edge, leaving a ½-inch overhang. Refrigerate while you roll out dough for top crust.

Roll out remaining piece of dough on lightly floured surface into a 11-inch round.

Spoon filling into shell. Cover pie with pastry round and trim with kitchen shears, leaving a ½-inch overhang. Press edges together, then crimp decoratively. With a small sharp knife, cut 3 steam vents in top crust.

Bake pie on hot baking sheet for 30 minutes. Reduce oven temperature to 375°F and continue to bake until crust is golden brown and filling is bubbling, about 40 minutes more. Cool pie on a rack for at least 3 hours before serving.

Cherry Almond Pie

SERVES 6 TO 8
ACTIVE TIME: 1 HOUR ■ START TO FINISH: 4¼ HOURS (INCLUDES MAKING DOUGH AND COOLING)

■ Sour cherries are so intensely flavorful that when you can find them fresh in their short season, from late June to late July, it is well worth buying more than you can use at once, pitting them, and then freezing them to have on hand when the season ends. We've put a spin on the traditional combination of fruit and almond essence by flavoring the sour cherry filling with almond extract, then topping it with an almond-paste pastry lattice that you pipe through a pastry bag rather than roll out. This pie is as easy to make as it is beautiful. ■

Basic Pastry Dough for a single-crust pie (page 790)

FOR FILLING
- 2 tablespoons quick-cooking tapioca
- 5 cups (2 pounds) sour cherries, pitted
- 1–1½ teaspoons fresh lemon juice (to taste)
- ¼ teaspoon almond extract
- 1 cup sugar
- ½ teaspoon salt
- ⅛ teaspoon ground cloves

FOR ALMOND-PASTE LATTICE
- 2 tablespoons unsalted butter, softened
- ⅔ cup (7 ounces) almond paste (not marzipan; see Sources)
- ½ teaspoon finely grated lemon zest
- 2 large egg yolks
- ⅓ cup all-purpose flour
- 1 large egg yolk lightly beaten with 1 teaspoon water, for egg wash

SPECIAL EQUIPMENT: an electric coffee/spice grinder; a pastry bag fitted with a ¼-inch plain tip

Roll out dough on a lightly floured surface with a lightly floured rolling pin into a 13-inch round. Fit it into a 9-inch pie plate. Trim edge, leaving a ½-inch overhang. Crimp edge decoratively and refrigerate shell.

MAKE THE FILLING: Finely grind tapioca in coffee/spice grinder. Stir together cherries, lemon juice, almond extract, sugar, tapioca, salt, and cloves in a bowl until well combined. Let filling stand, stirring occasionally, for 15 minutes.

Put a rack in lower third of oven and preheat oven to 425°F.

MAKE THE LATTICE MIXTURE: Beat butter with almond paste and zest in a medium bowl with an

Pastry Cloths and Rolling Pin Covers

We rarely specify an old-fashioned pastry cloth and a rolling pin cover in our recipes, but they can be a boon. "Your dough is a perfect formula of wet and dry ingredients," says Carolynn Bridge, a veteran food stylist and the proprietor of New York City's Bridge Kitchenware. "You don't want to add any more flour than necessary when rolling it out, or you'll upset that ratio." Unlike a kitchen counter or a marble slab, the lightweight canvas cloth and cover absorb and hold flour, so that a dough incorporates only what it needs to keep from sticking as it's being rolled. Cloths and covers are available at many cookware shops and by mail from Bridge Kitchenware (see Sources). Be sure to wash them frequently to keep them fresh (we throw ours into the washing machine).

electric mixer at medium speed until well combined, about 1 minute. Add egg yolks one at a time, beating well after each addition. Beat in flour until well combined, about 1 minute. Transfer mixture to pastry bag.

ASSEMBLE AND BAKE THE PIE: Spoon filling into shell, pressing down gently to level it. Pipe almond-paste mixture over top, forming a lattice pattern of strips about 1 inch apart. Brush edge of shell with egg wash.

Bake pie for 25 minutes. Reduce oven temperature to 375°F and continue to bake until crust and lattice are golden brown and filling is bubbling, 20 to 25 minutes more. (If lattice and edges look too brown after a total of 40 minutes, cover loosely with foil.)

Cool pie on a rack for at least 2 hours before serving.

Lattice-Crust Peach Pie

SERVES 8 TO 10
ACTIVE TIME: 45 MINUTES ■ START TO FINISH: 5 HOURS (INCLUDES MAKING DOUGH AND COOLING)

■ When you can get ripe peaches fresh from the tree, the best thing to do is eat them out of hand. But once you've had your fill, slip the rest out of their skins and bake them into a pie that deepens the flavor. As much as we love this pie, though, we have to admit that we've included it partly for its light, crisp, flaky dough—which results from being made with lard. ■

FOR DOUGH
- 3 cups all-purpose flour
- 3/4 teaspoon salt
- 1 cup (8 ounces) cold lard, cut into bits
- 1 tablespoon fresh lemon juice
- 1/2 cup cold water

FOR FILLING
- 3 pounds peaches, peeled (see Tips, page 940), pitted, and sliced
- 1/4 cup fresh lemon juice, or to taste
- 5 tablespoons all-purpose flour
- 3/4 cup sugar
- 1/4 teaspoon salt
- Pinch of ground mace

FOR ASSEMBLY
- 2 tablespoons cold unsalted butter, cut into bits
- 1 large egg yolk lightly beaten with 1 tablespoon water, for egg wash

MAKE THE DOUGH: Blend together flour, salt, and lard in a medium bowl with your fingertips or a pastry blender until mixture resembles coarse meal. Gently stir in lemon juice and water with a fork until incorporated. Turn mixture out onto a lightly floured surface and divide into 4 portions. With heel of your hand, smear each portion once or twice in a forward motion to help distribute fat. Gather dough together, with a pastry scraper if you have one, then divide into 2 pieces, one slightly larger than the other. Shape each one into a disk, wrap in wax paper, and refrigerate for 30 minutes.

MAKE THE FILLING: Toss peaches with lemon juice in a large bowl. Stir together flour, sugar, salt, and mace in a small bowl, add to peaches, and toss until well combined. Set aside.

ASSEMBLE AND BAKE THE PIE: Put a rack in lower third of oven and preheat oven to 425°F.

Roll out larger disk of dough (keep remaining piece chilled) on a lightly floured surface with a lightly floured rolling pin into a 12-inch round. Fit it into a 10-inch pie plate. Trim edge, leaving a 1/2-inch overhang. Refrigerate shell while you roll out dough for lattice.

Roll out second disk of dough on lightly floured surface into an 11-inch round. Put on a baking sheet and refrigerate until firm enough to handle, about 5 minutes.

Spoon filling into shell, mounding it slightly in center. Dot with butter. Cut dough round into 3/4-inch-wide strips. Arrange half of strips over filling, placing them 3/4 inch apart. Arrange remaining strips perpendicular to first strips to form a simple lattice. Trim ends of strips flush with overhang of shell. Brush some of egg wash between ends of strips and overhang and press edges together. Fold overhang over strips and crimp decoratively, then brush with egg wash.

Bake pie for 20 minutes. Reduce oven temperature to 375°F and bake until crust is golden brown and filling is bubbling, 45 to 50 minutes more. Cool pie on a rack for at least 3 hours before serving.

Apricot Raspberry Pie

SERVES 8
ACTIVE TIME: 40 MINUTES ■ START TO FINISH: 5 HOURS (INCLUDES MAKING DOUGH AND COOLING)

■ This is a classic combination for people who appreciate a dessert that is not too sweet. And there's a notable bonus: neither fruit requires peeling, so this is one of the easiest fruit pies you can make. ■

- 1/4 cup cornstarch
- 1/4 teaspoon salt
- 1 1/4 cups sugar
- Basic Pastry Dough for a double-crust pie (page 790)
- 1 1/2 pounds firm but ripe apricots (8 large), pitted and cut into 1/2-inch-thick wedges
- 1 1/2 cups (6 ounces) raspberries
- 1 large egg, lightly beaten, for egg wash

Put a large baking sheet on middle oven rack and preheat oven to 450°F.

Whisk together cornstarch, salt, and 1 cup plus 2 tablespoons sugar in a large bowl.

Roll out 1 piece of dough (keep remaining piece chilled) on a lightly floured surface with a lightly floured rolling pin into a 13-inch round. Fit it into a 9-inch pie plate. Trim edge, leaving a 1/2-inch overhang. Refrigerate shell while you roll out dough for top crust.

Roll out remaining piece of dough on lightly floured surface into an 11-inch round.

Stir apricots into sugar mixture until combined. Gently stir in raspberries and spoon filling into shell. Cover pie with pastry round and trim with kitchen shears, leaving a 1/2-inch overhang. Press edges together, then crimp decoratively. Lightly brush top of pie with egg and sprinkle remaining 2 tablespoons sugar all over. With a small sharp knife, cut 3 steam vents in top crust.

Bake pie on hot baking sheet for 15 minutes. Reduce oven temperature to 375°F and continue to bake until crust is golden brown and filling is bubbling, about 45 minutes more. Cool pie on a rack for at least 2 hours before serving.

Three-Berry Pie with Vanilla Cream

SERVES 8
ACTIVE TIME: 40 MINUTES ■ START TO FINISH: 6 HOURS (INCLUDES MAKING DOUGH AND COOLING)

■ Sometimes known as jumbleberry pie, from the traditional term for a mixture of blackberries, raspberries, and blueberries, this spurts deep purple juice when you make the first cut. Topped with a soft cloud of vanilla cream, it is an irresistible dessert in the summertime. ■

- 1 cup granulated sugar
- 3 tablespoons cornstarch
- 2 tablespoons quick-cooking tapioca
- 1/4 teaspoon salt
- 3 cups (15 ounces) blackberries
- 2 cups (8 ounces) raspberries
- 2 cups (10 ounces) blueberries
- Basic Pastry Dough for a double-crust pie (page 790)
- 1 large egg, lightly beaten, for egg wash
- 1 tablespoon sanding (coarse) or granulated sugar

ACCOMPANIMENT: Vanilla Cream (recipe follows)

Put a large baking sheet on middle oven rack and preheat oven to 450°F.

Whisk together granulated sugar, cornstarch, tapioca, and salt in a large bowl. Toss with berries.

Roll out 1 piece of dough (keep remaining piece chilled) on a lightly floured surface with a lightly floured rolling pin into a 13-inch round. Fit it into a 9-inch pie plate. Trim edge, leaving a 1/2-inch overhang. Refrigerate shell while you roll out dough for top crust.

Roll out remaining piece of dough on lightly floured surface into an 11-inch round.

Spoon filling into shell. Cover pie with pastry round and trim with kitchen shears, leaving a 1/2-inch overhang. Press edges together, then crimp decoratively. Brush top of pie with egg and sprinkle all over with sanding sugar. With a small sharp knife, cut 3 steam vents in top crust.

Bake pie on hot baking sheet for 15 minutes. Reduce oven temperature to 375°F and continue to bake until crust is golden brown and filling is bubbling, about 45 minutes more. Cool pie on a rack for at least 3 hours before serving (filling will still be juicy).

Serve with vanilla cream.

Vanilla Cream

MAKES ABOUT 2 CUPS
ACTIVE TIME: 5 MINUTES ■ START TO FINISH: 5 MINUTES

- ½ vanilla bean, halved lengthwise, or 1 teaspoon vanilla extract
- 1 cup very cold heavy cream
- 2 tablespoons sugar

With tip of a knife, scrape seeds from vanilla bean into a medium bowl and add cream and sugar (or combine cream, sugar, and vanilla extract in bowl); discard pod. Beat with an electric mixer until cream just holds soft peaks.

COOK'S NOTE

■ The vanilla cream can be made up to 1 hour ahead and refrigerated, covered.

Lemon Meringue Pie

SERVES 8
ACTIVE TIME: 45 MINUTES ■ START TO FINISH: 6¾ HOURS (INCLUDES MAKING DOUGH AND CHILLING)

■ An American invention, a spectacular beauty, and a tour de force, lemon meringue pie is as much about texture as it is about taste. It required a daring imagination to think that a lemon custard rich with egg yolks could be sandwiched between a crisp, fragile crust and a mountain of frothy white meringue.

Of the many lemon meringue pies we have developed over the years, this is the best. One secret is to spread the meringue all the way to the edge of the shell when both the filling and the shell are hot, which keeps it from shrinking. We've also found that if you rush the cooling process by refrigerating the pie when it is still warm, the meringue will weep and bead, but if you follow the directions precisely, you will be rewarded with a stunning dessert that earns you a reputation as a master pie baker. ■

Basic Pastry Dough for a single-crust pie (page 790)

FOR FILLING
- 4 large egg yolks
- 1 cup sugar
- 4½ tablespoons cornstarch
- ¼ teaspoon salt
- 1 cup water
- ½ cup whole milk
- 1 tablespoon unsalted butter
- 2 teaspoons finely grated lemon zest
- ½ cup fresh lemon juice

FOR MERINGUE
- 6 large egg whites
- ½ teaspoon cream of tartar
- ¼ teaspoon salt
- ¾ cup sugar

MAKE THE PIE SHELL: Roll out dough on a lightly floured surface with a lightly floured rolling pin into a 13-inch round. Fit it into a 9-inch pie plate. Trim edge, leaving a ½-inch overhang, and crimp decoratively. Refrigerate for 30 minutes.

Put a rack in middle of oven and preheat oven to 375°F.

Lightly prick shell in several places with a fork. Line shell with foil and fill with pie weights, raw rice, or dried beans. Bake for 10 minutes. Carefully remove foil and weights and bake shell until golden, 12 to 15 minutes more. Transfer to a rack. Reduce oven temperature to 350°F.

MAKE THE FILLING: After you remove the foil and weights, whisk together egg yolks in a medium bowl. Whisk together sugar, cornstarch, and salt in a 2-quart heavy saucepan. Gradually add water and milk, whisking until cornstarch is dissolved. Bring to a boil over moderate heat, whisking until mixture begins to thicken. Gradually whisk about 1 cup milk mixture into yolks, then whisk yolk mixture into milk mixture. Simmer, whisking, for 3 minutes. Remove pan from heat and whisk in butter, zest, and juice until butter is melted and filling is smooth. Cover with a round of wax paper to keep warm.

MAKE THE MERINGUE: If pie shell has cooled, place it in oven just until warm. Beat egg whites, cream of tartar, and salt in a large bowl with an electric mixer at medium speed until whites hold soft peaks. At high speed, beat in sugar 1 tablespoon at a time, and continue to beat until meringue just holds stiff peaks.

ASSEMBLE AND BAKE THE PIE: Pour filling into warm shell. Spread meringue on top to very edge of pastry, covering filling completely. Draw meringue up into peaks with a spatula. Bake until meringue is golden, about 15 minutes.

Transfer pie to rack to cool to room temperature, about 2 hours, then refrigerate until cold, about 2 hours more.

Blind-Baking

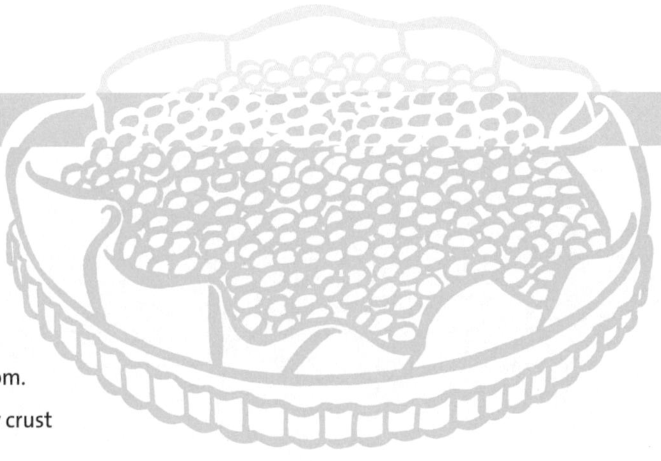

If you are making a single-crust pie, a tart that has a very loose filling, or one for which the filling will already be cooked, blind-baking — prebaking — the empty shell ensures that the crust will be evenly and thoroughly cooked, so it doesn't become soggy on the bottom. Blind-baking also prevents the sides of a very buttery pastry crust from slumping or shifting.

To make a crisp crust, refrigerate the unbaked pie or tart shell until firm, about 30 minutes, before lightly pricking it all over with a fork. Then line it with foil and fill the shell with weights so the bottom won't bubble up and set in billowy blisters as it bakes. (The pricking keeps it from puffing up once the weights and foil are removed.) Pie weights — metal or ceramic pellets made expressly for the job and available at cookware shops (see Sources) — aren't the only option for the task; raw rice or dried beans are a fine alternative. (If you use rice or beans, you can store and reuse them like pie weights; don't try to cook and eat them afterward.)

The actual blind-baking entails baking the shell until the sides are set, then removing the foil and weights and baking the shell until it is golden. When removing the foil and weights, play it safe and spoon the piping-hot weights into a bowl. If you attempt to lift out the foil complete with its load, the foil may tear.

A blind-baked shell is delicate, so handle it with great care. If you are not using it immediately, it will keep, loosely covered, for several hours at room temperature (not in the refrigerator — you don't want it to absorb any moisture or odors).

Key Lime Pie

SERVES 8
ACTIVE TIME: 20 MINUTES ■ START TO FINISH: 9 HOURS (INCLUDES CHILLING)

■ Once you've made this pie, you'll understand why it is found on so many restaurant menus: it is hard to think of another dessert that gives a cook such big rewards for such a small amount of work. ■

FOR CRUST

- 1¼ cups graham cracker crumbs (from nine 4¾-by-2¼-inch crackers)
- 2 tablespoons sugar
- 5 tablespoons unsalted butter, melted

FOR FILLING

- 1 (14-ounce) can sweetened condensed milk
- 4 large egg yolks
- 6 tablespoons fresh or bottled (preferably Manhattan brand) key lime juice

FOR TOPPING

- ¾ cup very cold heavy cream

MAKE THE CRUST: Put a rack in middle of oven and preheat oven to 350°F. Butter a 9-inch pie plate.

Stir together graham cracker crumbs, sugar, and butter in a bowl with a fork until well combined. Press crumb mixture evenly onto bottom and up sides of pie plate. Bake crust for 10 minutes. Transfer pie plate to a rack. (Leave oven on.)

MAKE THE FILLING AND BAKE THE PIE: Whisk together condensed milk and yolks in a bowl until well combined. Add juice and whisk until well combined (mixture will thicken slightly).

Pour filling into crust. Bake for 15 minutes. Cool pie completely on rack (filling will set as it cools).

Refrigerate pie, covered, for at least 8 hours.

JUST BEFORE SERVING, MAKE THE TOPPING: Beat cream in a medium bowl with an electric mixer until it just holds stiff peaks. Spread pie with cream or top each serving with a dollop.

COOK'S NOTE

■ The pie, without the topping, can be refrigerated for up to 24 hours.

Mincemeat Pie

SERVES 8
ACTIVE TIME: 1½ HOURS ■ START TO FINISH: 5¾ HOURS (INCLUDES MAKING DOUGH AND COOLING) PLUS 3 DAYS STANDING TIME FOR MINCEMEAT

■ The word rolls off the tongue, an instant holiday—even for those who have never tasted the real thing. If you're among the people who haven't tried mincemeat, this is the pie for you. Sweet and savory at the same time, it is a mixture of dried fruit and apples laced with brandy, spices, and lemon juice that perfumes your kitchen as it bakes and brings a medieval taste to your table. Our version contains no meat, but the suet is essential to achieve a classic mincemeat; it adds an earthy flavor that you won't notice until you leave it out. Try this pie once, and it is certain to become a holiday tradition at your house. ■

FOR MINCEMEAT

- 2 Granny Smith apples, peeled, cored, and finely chopped
- ⅔ cup golden raisins
- ⅔ cup dark raisins
- ⅔ cup dried currants
- ½ cup packed dark brown sugar
- 2 ounces beef suet (see Sources), shredded (½ cup), or ½ stick (4 tablespoons) unsalted butter, melted
- ¼ cup brandy
- 2 teaspoons finely grated lemon zest
- 2 teaspoons finely grated orange zest
- 2 tablespoons fresh lemon juice
- ½ teaspoon ground allspice
- ½ teaspoon freshly grated nutmeg

FOR CRUST

- Basic Pastry Dough for a double-crust pie (page 790)
- 1 large egg, lightly beaten, for egg wash
- 2 teaspoons granulated sugar

ACCOMPANIMENT: whipped cream or vanilla ice cream

MAKE THE MINCEMEAT: Stir together all ingredients. Refrigerate in an airtight container for at least 3 days to allow flavors to blend.

MAKE THE PIE: Put a large baking sheet on middle oven rack and preheat oven to 400°F.

Roll out 1 piece of dough (keep remaining piece chilled) on a lightly floured surface with a lightly floured rolling pin into a 13-inch round. Fit it into a 9-inch pie plate. Stir mincemeat, then spoon into shell. Refrigerate while you roll out dough for lattice.

Roll out remaining piece of dough on lightly floured surface into a 10-inch round. With a fluted pastry wheel or a knife, cut into ten 1-inch-wide strips. Arrange half of strips over filling, then arrange remaining strips perpendicular to first strips to form a simple lattice. Trim ends of strips and edge of bottom crust, leaving a ½-inch overhang. Press edges together and crimp decoratively. Brush lattice and edge with egg and sprinkle with sugar.

Bake until pastry is golden brown, 50 minutes to 1 hour. (If lattice and edge look too dark after 20 to 30 minutes, cover with foil.) Cool pie on a rack for 2 hours. Serve with whipped cream or ice cream.

COOK'S NOTES

- The mincemeat can be refrigerated for up to 3 months.
- The pie keeps, covered and refrigerated, for up to 4 days. Bring to room temperature or reheat in a low oven before serving.

Vinegar Pie

SERVES 8 TO 10
ACTIVE TIME: 1 HOUR ■ START TO FINISH: 6 HOURS (INCLUDES MAKING DOUGH AND COOLING)

■ Fans of lemon meringue and other citrus-based pies will adore this vigorously American delicacy, which we think originated in the Great Plains (although certain sources cite the South as its first home). These days the pie is a rarity, but it was once common; between 1947 and 1963, *Gourmet* published five variations on the theme. There is a good reason for that—we can't think of a more exciting use for a little bit of sugar, a couple of eggs, and some vinegar. ■

Quick Puff Pastry Dough (page 790)
2 large eggs
1 cup sugar
1 tablespoon all-purpose flour
1 cup cold water
2 tablespoons cider vinegar
Ground cinnamon for dusting

ACCOMPANIMENT: lightly sweetened whipped cream
SPECIAL EQUIPMENT: a 9-inch fluted tart pan with a removable bottom; an instant-read thermometer

MAKE THE PIE SHELL: Cut dough in half and reserve one half for another use (see Cook's Note). Roll out remaining dough on a lightly floured surface with a lightly floured rolling pin into a rough 12-inch round. Fit into tart pan. Trim edges, leaving a ½-inch overhang. Fold overhang inward and press against sides of pan to form a rim that extends ¼ inch above pan. Refrigerate for 30 minutes.

Put a rack in middle of oven and preheat oven to 400°F.

Lightly prick shell in several places with a fork. Line shell with foil and fill with pie weights, raw rice, or dried beans. Bake until edge is pale golden and sides are set, about 20 minutes. Carefully remove foil and weights and bake until bottom of shell is golden, 8 to 10 minutes more.

MEANWHILE, MAKE THE FILLING: Whisk together eggs and ¼ cup sugar in a medium bowl until well blended. Whisk together flour and remaining ¾ cup sugar in a 1-quart heavy saucepan, then whisk in water and vinegar. Bring to a boil, whisking until sugar is dissolved. Add to egg mixture in a slow stream, whisking constantly.

Pour filling back into saucepan and cook over moderate heat, stirring constantly with a wooden spoon, until filling coats back of spoon and registers 175°F on thermometer, 12 to 15 minutes; do not let boil. Immediately pour filling into a 2-cup glass measure. If pie shell is not ready, cover surface of filling with a round of wax paper.

BAKE THE PIE: Remove baked shell from oven and reduce oven temperature to 350°F. Pour filling into pie shell and cover edge of crust with a pie shield or foil to prevent overbrowning. Bake until filling is set, 15 to 20 minutes, then cool completely on a rack.

Before serving, remove rim of pan and dust pie evenly with cinnamon. Serve with whipped cream.

COOK'S NOTE

- The unused portion of the puff pastry can be frozen, well wrapped in plastic wrap, for up to 1 month.

Pumpkin Chiffon Pie with Gingersnap Crust

SERVES 10
ACTIVE TIME: 1 HOUR ■ START TO FINISH: 5 HOURS (INCLUDES CHILLING)

■ Our variation on the Thanksgiving classic is light instead of dense and piquant instead of overly sweet. Very tall and extremely light, it makes an impressive presentation. And because it must be prepared in advance so it can set properly, it is the perfect end to a holiday meal. ■

FOR CRUST

- 20 (2-inch) gingersnaps, finely ground
- ½ stick (4 tablespoons) unsalted butter, melted and cooled

FOR FILLING

- 3½ teaspoons unflavored gelatin (from two ¼-ounce envelopes)
- ¼ cup bourbon or brandy
- 6 large eggs, separated
- ¾ cup packed light brown sugar
- 2¼ cups solid-pack pumpkin (from one 29-ounce can or two 15-ounce cans)
- 1½ teaspoons ground cinnamon
- ¾ teaspoon ground ginger
- ¾ teaspoon freshly grated nutmeg
- ½ teaspoon salt
- ½ cup granulated sugar
- 1½ cups very cold heavy cream

OPTIONAL GARNISH: whipped cream and chopped crystallized ginger

SPECIAL EQUIPMENT: a 9- to 9½-inch (24-centimeter) springform pan; an instant-read thermometer

MAKE THE CRUST: Put a rack in middle of oven and preheat oven to 350°F. Invert bottom of springform pan (to make it easier to slide pie off bottom), then lock on side and butter pan.

Stir together gingersnap crumbs and butter in a bowl until crumbs are evenly moistened. Press onto bottom of springform pan. Bake until edges are golden brown, about 8 minutes (watch carefully toward end of baking; crust burns easily). Cool in pan on a rack.

MAKE THE FILLING: Sprinkle gelatin over bourbon in a small bowl and let soften for 1 minute.

Beat together yolks and brown sugar in a large bowl with an electric mixer at high speed until thick and pale, 3 to 5 minutes. Reduce speed to medium and mix in pumpkin, spices, and salt.

Transfer pumpkin mixture to a 4-quart heavy saucepan and cook over moderate heat, stirring constantly, until it registers 160°F on thermometer, about 6 minutes. Remove pan from heat, immediately add gelatin mixture, and stir until it is dissolved. Transfer to a large metal bowl set in a larger bowl of ice and cold water and cool, stirring occasionally, until mixture is the consistency of raw egg whites, about 15 minutes. Remove from ice bath.

Beat egg whites in another large bowl with cleaned beaters at high speed until frothy. Gradually add granulated sugar and beat until whites hold stiff, glossy peaks. Gently but thoroughly fold into pumpkin mixture.

Beat cream in another large bowl with cleaned beaters until it just holds stiff peaks. Gently but thoroughly fold into pumpkin mixture. Pour filling into springform pan and smooth top. Refrigerate, uncovered, for 1 hour, then cover and refrigerate until pie is set, at least 3 hours.

Before serving, run a thin knife around edge of pie and remove side of pan. Garnish with whipped cream and crystallized ginger, if desired.

COOK'S NOTES

- The egg whites in this recipe are not cooked. If this is a concern, see page 629.
- The pie can be refrigerated for up to 8 hours.

Pecan Pumpkin Pie

SERVE 8 TO 10
ACTIVE TIME: 45 MINUTES ■ START TO FINISH: 4½ HOURS (INCLUDES MAKING DOUGH AND COOLING)

■ The ideal solution for people who can't decide whether to bake pecan pie or pumpkin pie at Thanksgiving. For this combination classic, we've tempered a traditional pumpkin pie filling with a bit of sour cream and less sugar than usual so it forms a smooth custard layer on the bottom. We've covered it with a thin layer of traditional pecan pie filling zinged with a bit of lemon. The result does a little dance in your mouth, alternating between the smooth spiciness of the pumpkin and the sweet, sticky, caramelized pecan layer on top. ■

Basic Pastry Dough for a single-crust pie (page 790)

FOR PUMPKIN FILLING

- 3/4 cup canned solid-pack pumpkin
- 2 tablespoons packed light brown sugar
- 1 large egg, lightly beaten
- 2 tablespoons sour cream
- 1/8 teaspoon ground cinnamon
- 1/8 teaspoon freshly grated nutmeg
- Pinch of salt

FOR PECAN LAYER

- 3/4 cup light corn syrup
- 1/2 cup packed light brown sugar
- 3 large eggs, lightly beaten
- 3 tablespoons unsalted butter, melted and cooled
- 2 teaspoons vanilla extract
- 1/4 teaspoon finely grated lemon zest
- 1 1/2 teaspoons fresh lemon juice
- 1/4 teaspoon salt
- 1 1/3 cups (5 1/2 ounces) pecans, chopped if desired

MAKE THE PIE SHELL: Roll out dough on a lightly floured surface with a lightly floured rolling pin into a 13-inch round. Fit it into a 9-inch pie plate. Trim edge, leaving a 1/2-inch overhang, then fold overhang under and crimp edge decoratively. Refrigerate shell for 30 minutes.

Put a rack in middle of oven and preheat oven to 375°F.

Lightly prick shell in several places with a fork. Line shell with foil and fill with pie weights, raw rice, or dried beans. Bake for 20 minutes. Carefully remove foil and weights and bake shell until pale golden, 6 to 10 minutes more. Cool on a rack. (Leave oven on.)

MAKE THE PUMPKIN FILLING: Whisk together all ingredients in a bowl until smooth.

MAKE THE PECAN LAYER: Stir together corn syrup, brown sugar, eggs, butter, vanilla, zest, lemon juice, and salt in a bowl until well combined. Stir in pecans.

ASSEMBLE AND BAKE THE PIE: Spread pumpkin filling evenly in pie shell. Carefully spoon pecan mixture over it.

Bake until crust is golden and filling is puffed, about 35 minutes (center should still be slightly wobbly). Cool completely on rack.

COOK'S NOTE

■ The pie can be kept, uncovered, at cool room temperature for up to 4 hours. It can also be made up to 1 day ahead, cooled, and refrigerated, loosely covered. Reheat in a 350°F oven until the crust is crisp, about 15 minutes.

Sweet Potato Pie with Bourbon Cream

SERVES 6 TO 8

ACTIVE TIME: 45 MINUTES ■ START TO FINISH: 5 1/2 HOURS (INCLUDES MAKING DOUGH AND COOLING)

■ Because sweet potato pie looks so much like pumpkin pie, the two are often confused. One taste, however, will tell you the difference. Sweet potato pie is lighter and less dense than pumpkin, and its flavor is rounder and more complex. We roast the sweet potatoes instead of boiling them, which intensifies their flavor. ■

Basic Pastry Dough for a single-crust pie (page 790)

FOR FILLING

- 1 1/2 pounds sweet potatoes (4–5 medium)
- 2 large eggs
- 1/3 cup packed light brown sugar
- 1/4 teaspoon salt
- 1/4 teaspoon freshly grated nutmeg
- 1/2 cup whole milk
- 2 tablespoons heavy cream
- 2 tablespoons bourbon
- 1/2 teaspoon vanilla extract

FOR BOURBON CREAM

- 1/2 cup very cold heavy cream
- 1 tablespoon packed light brown sugar
- 1 teaspoon bourbon
- 1/4 teaspoon vanilla extract

MAKE THE PIE SHELL: Roll out dough on a lightly floured surface with a lightly floured rolling pin into a 13-inch round. Fit it into a 9-inch pie plate.

Trim edge, leaving a ½-inch overhang, then fold overhang under and crimp edge decoratively. Refrigerate for 30 minutes.

Put a rack in middle of oven and preheat oven to 375°F.

Lightly prick shell in several places with a fork. Line shell with foil and fill with pie weights, raw rice, or dried beans. Bake until pastry is set and beginning to brown around edge, about 15 minutes. Carefully remove foil and weights and bake until shell is pale golden all over, about 10 minutes more. Cool on a rack. Increase oven temperature to 400°F.

MAKE THE FILLING: Prick each sweet potato once with a fork. Roast on a foil-lined baking sheet with sides until tender, about 1 hour. Remove from oven and reduce oven temperature to 375°F.

Halve potatoes lengthwise. When they are cool enough to handle, peel, discarding skin, and cut away any eyes or dark spots. Purée potatoes in a food processor. Add eggs, brown sugar, salt, and nutmeg and blend until smooth. Add milk, cream, bourbon, and vanilla and pulse until just combined.

BAKE THE PIE: Pour filling into pie shell. Bake in middle of oven until filling 2 inches from edge is slightly puffed and center jiggles slightly when gently shaken, about 40 minutes. (If crust looks too brown after 20 minutes, cover edge with a pie shield or foil.) Cool pie on rack for about 1 hour.

MAKE THE BOURBON CREAM: Beat cream, brown sugar, bourbon, and vanilla in a small bowl with an electric mixer until cream just holds soft peaks. Place a spoonful of cream on center of each slice of pie and serve immediately.

Coconut Custard Pie

SERVES 6 TO 8

ACTIVE TIME: 1¼ HOURS ■ START TO FINISH: 6¾ HOURS (INCLUDES MAKING DOUGH AND COOLING)

■ Fans of coconut custard pie wax rhapsodic about its intense flavor and silken texture. We consider this recipe, with an easy puff pastry crust, to be the best we've tasted. It came to us in 1968 from contributor Lou Siebert Pappas, who, unable to duplicate her husband's favorite childhood custards satisfactorily, appealed to her father-in-law for help. He opened his confectionery in San Francisco shortly after the 1906 earthquake, and his recipe has never been equaled. ■

Quick Puff Pastry Dough (page 790)

FOR FILLING

- 5 large eggs
- ¾ cup plus 2 tablespoons sugar
- 2 cups whole milk
- ½ cup half-and-half
- 1 teaspoon vanilla extract
- ¼ teaspoon salt
- 1 cup sweetened flaked coconut

FOR TOPPING

- ½ cup fresh coconut shavings (cut with a vegetable peeler) or sweetened flaked coconut
- 1 cup very cold heavy cream
- 2 tablespoons sugar
- ½ teaspoon vanilla extract

MAKE THE PIE SHELL: Put a rack in middle of oven and preheat oven to 375°F.

Roll out dough on a floured surface with a floured rolling pin into a rough 16-inch square (because dough is already a rectangle, it's easier to roll it into a square, then trim it into a round). Fit it into a 10-inch pie plate. Trim edges, leaving a 1-inch overhang, then fold overhang under to form a rim (baked puff pastry will not hold a crimp).

Line pie shell with foil and fill with pie weights, raw rice, or dried beans. Bake until edge of pastry is set and pale golden, 17 to 20 minutes.

Carefully remove foil and weights and lightly prick bottom and sides of pie shell all over with a fork. Bake, lightly pricking shell again if any large air pockets form, until shell is golden all over, about 15 minutes more. Transfer to a rack. (Leave oven on.)

MEANWHILE, MAKE THE FILLING: Beat eggs in a large bowl with an electric mixer at medium speed until well combined. Beat in sugar, milk, half-and-half, vanilla, and salt. Stir in flaked coconut.

BAKE THE PIE: Pour filling into hot pie shell. Cover edge of pie shell with a pie shield or foil to prevent overbrowning. Bake until custard is set 2 inches from edge but still jiggles slightly in center, 30 to 40 minutes.

Cool pie completely on rack, about 1½ hours.

MEANWHILE, TOAST THE COCONUT: Reduce oven temperature to 350°F. Spread coconut on a baking sheet with sides and bake, stirring once, until pale golden, about 5 minutes (watch carefully—coconut burns easily). Cool on sheet on another rack.

JUST BEFORE SERVING, MAKE THE TOPPING: Beat cream with sugar and vanilla in a large bowl with electric mixer at medium speed until it just holds soft peaks. Spread cream over pie and sprinkle with toasted coconut.

Grapefruit and Coconut Angel Pie

SERVES 8
ACTIVE TIME: 1 HOUR ■ START TO FINISH: 7¾ HOURS (INCLUDES CHILLING)

■ When we considered omitting this pie from the book, we heard cries of outrage from its many fans on our staff. It may sound strange, but once you've tried it, you will bake it again and again. There is something extremely enticing about the way the sweet, crisp coconut meringue shell marries with the tart cream cheese and grapefruit filling. The fact that it looks like a fluffy white cloud is also part of its appeal. ■

FOR MERINGUE SHELL
- 4 large egg whites, left at room temperature for 30 minutes
- ¼ teaspoon salt
- ¼ teaspoon cream of tartar
- 1 cup sugar
- 1 cup sweetened flaked coconut
- 3 tablespoons unsalted butter, melted

FOR FILLING
- 5 medium grapefruit
- 2½ teaspoons unflavored gelatin (from one ¼-ounce envelope)
- 4 large egg yolks
- ½ cup sugar
- Pinch of salt
- 1 (8-ounce) package cream cheese, softened
- 1 cup very cold heavy cream

OPTIONAL GARNISH: grapefruit segments cut free from membranes

SPECIAL EQUIPMENT: a candy thermometer

MAKE THE MERINGUE SHELL: Put a rack in middle of oven and preheat oven to 250°F.

Beat whites with salt in a large bowl with an electric mixer at medium speed until foamy. Add cream of tartar and beat until whites hold soft peaks. Increase speed to high and beat in sugar a little at a time, then beat until meringue holds stiff, glossy peaks and sugar is dissolved, 5 to 7 minutes. Fold in coconut.

Brush a 10-inch pie plate with some of melted butter. Refrigerate until butter hardens, about 3 minutes, then brush with remaining melted butter.

Drop heaping tablespoons of meringue evenly around edge of pie plate, then spread meringue with back of spoon to form sides of shell. Spread remaining meringue evenly over bottom of pie plate.

Bake shell until firm and very pale golden, about 1¼ hours. Turn off oven and cool shell completely in oven with door propped slightly ajar, about 2 hours.

MAKE THE FILLING: With a sharp paring knife, cut peel and white pith from grapefruit. Working over a bowl, cut segments free from membranes. Cut segments into ½-inch pieces. Drain well in a sieve set over bowl, reserving juices. You should have 2 cups segments (reserve any extra for another use, if desired).

Sprinkle gelatin over ¼ cup reserved grapefruit juice in a small bowl and let soften for 1 minute.

Whisk together yolks and sugar in a 1-quart heavy saucepan, then add gelatin mixture, salt, and remaining reserved grapefruit juice. Cook mixture over moderate heat, whisking, until it registers 160°F on thermometer, about 3 minutes. Transfer to a metal bowl set in a larger bowl of ice and cold water and whisk constantly until thickened to consistency of raw egg whites but not set, about 3 minutes. Remove from bowl of ice water and reserve bowl of ice water.

Beat cream cheese in another metal bowl with electric mixer, scraping down sides of bowl as necessary, until light, fluffy, and smooth. Beat in yolk mixture a little at a time, then beat until smooth and well combined. Put bowl in bowl of ice water and beat until mixture is thickened and forms a ribbon when beaters are lifted, about 3 minutes. Remove from ice water.

Beat heavy cream in medium bowl with cleaned beaters until it holds stiff peaks. Whisk one quarter of whipped cream into cream cheese mixture to lighten it, then gently but thoroughly fold in remaining whipped cream. Gently fold in grapefruit segments.

Pour filling into shell and smooth top. Refrigerate pie, uncovered, until filling is completely set, 3 to 4 hours.

Serve garnished with grapefruit segments, if desired.

COOK'S NOTE

- The pie can be refrigerated for up to 8 hours. After 4 hours, cover it with plastic wrap or wax paper.

Grasshopper Pie

SERVES 6 TO 8
ACTIVE TIME: 20 MINUTES ■ START TO FINISH: 4½ HOURS (INCLUDES CHILLING)

■ First came the grasshopper cocktail, for which the essential ingredients are green (thus the grasshopper) crème de menthe, white crème de cacao, and cream. Then in the 1950s came the eponymous pie, which has a crust of either cookie or graham cracker crumbs and is served chilled. ■

FOR CRUST
- 1½ cups fine chocolate wafer crumbs (from about 30 cookies, such as Nabisco Famous Wafers)
- ½ stick (4 tablespoons) unsalted butter, melted

FOR FILLING
- 1¼ teaspoons unflavored gelatin (from one ¼-ounce envelope)
- 1⅓ cups very cold heavy cream
- ¼ cup sugar
- ¼ cup green crème de menthe
- ¼ cup white crème de cacao
- 4 large egg yolks

OPTIONAL GARNISH: grated mint-flavored chocolate
SPECIAL EQUIPMENT: an instant-read thermometer

MAKE THE CRUST: Put a rack in middle of oven and preheat oven to 425°F.

Stir together wafer crumbs and butter in a bowl with a fork until well combined. Press mixture evenly onto bottom and up sides of a 9-inch pie plate. Bake for 5 minutes. Cool completely on a rack.

MAKE THE FILLING: Sprinkle gelatin over ⅓ cup cream in a small metal bowl and let soften for 1 minute. Whisk in sugar, liqueurs, and yolks. Set bowl over a saucepan of simmering water and cook mixture, whisking constantly, until it registers 160°F on thermometer, about 2 minutes. Transfer bowl to a larger bowl of ice and cold water and stir mixture until cooled and thickened. Remove from ice bath.

Beat remaining 1 cup cream in a medium bowl with an electric mixer until it holds stiff peaks. Fold into liqueur mixture.

Pour filling into crust. Refrigerate until set, about 4 hours. Before serving, garnish pie with grated chocolate, if desired.

COOK'S NOTES

- The crust can be baked up to 1 day ahead and kept, covered, at room temperature.
- The pie can be refrigerated for up to 1 day.

Chocolate Cream Pie

SERVES 8 TO 10
ACTIVE TIME: 45 MINUTES ■ START TO FINISH: 9 HOURS (INCLUDES CHILLING)

■ If you're a fan of chocolate pudding but don't consider it fancy enough for company, this is the pie for you. A custard of bittersweet and unsweetened chocolate is spooned into a crust made of chocolate wafer crumbs. The result is adult and utterly pleasing. ■

FOR CRUST
- 1⅓ cups chocolate wafer crumbs (from about 26 cookies, such as Nabisco Famous Wafers)
- 5 tablespoons unsalted butter, melted
- ¼ cup sugar

FOR FILLING
- ⅔ cup sugar
- ¼ cup cornstarch

½ teaspoon salt
4 large egg yolks
3 cups whole milk
5 ounces good bittersweet chocolate (not unsweetened), chopped
2 ounces unsweetened chocolate, chopped
2 tablespoons unsalted butter, softened
1 teaspoon vanilla extract

FOR TOPPING
¾ cup very cold heavy cream
1 tablespoon sugar

OPTIONAL GARNISH: coarsely grated bittersweet chocolate

MAKE THE CRUST: Put a rack in middle of oven and preheat oven to 350°F. Butter a 9-inch pie plate.

Stir together crumbs, butter, and sugar in a bowl with a fork until well combined. Press mixture evenly onto bottom and up sides of pie plate. Bake crust until crisp, about 15 minutes. Cool completely on a rack.

MAKE THE FILLING: Whisk together sugar, cornstarch, salt, and yolks in a 3-quart heavy saucepan until well combined. Add milk in a slow stream, whisking constantly. Bring to a boil over moderate heat, whisking, then reduce heat and simmer, whisking, for 1 minute (filling will be thick).

Force filling through a fine-mesh sieve into a bowl; discard solids. Melt chocolates in a small metal bowl set over a saucepan of barely simmering water, stirring occasionally until smooth. Remove from heat. Whisk chocolate, butter, and vanilla into filling. Cover surface of filling with a buttered round of wax paper and cool completely, about 2 hours.

Spoon filling into crust and smooth top. Refrigerate, covered, for at least 6 hours.

JUST BEFORE SERVING, MAKE THE TOPPING: Beat cream with sugar in a bowl with an electric mixer until it just holds stiff peaks. Spoon on top of pie. Garnish with grated chocolate, if desired.

COOK'S NOTE

■ The pie, without the topping, can be refrigerated for up to 1 day.

Maple Syrup Pie

SERVES 8 TO 10
ACTIVE TIME: 25 MINUTES ■ START TO FINISH: 3½ HOURS (INCLUDES MAKING DOUGH AND COOLING)

■ Don't be tempted to forgo the cream with this very rich traditional French Canadian pie. It complements the dessert's silkiness and balances the sweetness. The recipe is a specialty of sugar shacks, the rustic Quebecois restaurants that open only in March and April to celebrate maple sugaring season. ■

Basic Pastry Dough for a single-crust pie (page 790)
1⅔ cups packed light brown sugar
2 large eggs, at room temperature
½ cup heavy cream
⅓ cup pure maple syrup, preferably dark amber
2 teaspoons unsalted butter, melted

ACCOMPANIMENT: crème fraîche or unsweetened whipped cream

Put a rack in lower third of oven and preheat oven to 350°F.

Roll out dough on a lightly floured surface with a lightly floured rolling pin into an 11-inch round. Fit it into an 8-inch pie plate. Trim edge, leaving a ½-inch overhang, then fold overhang under and crimp edge decoratively.

Whisk together brown sugar and eggs in a medium bowl until creamy. Add cream, syrup, and butter and whisk until smooth. Pour filling into pie shell.

Bake pie until pastry is golden and filling is puffed and looks dry but still trembles, 50 to 60 minutes. Cool completely on a rack (filling will set as pie cools).

Serve with crème fraîche or whipped cream.

COOK'S NOTE

■ If you don't have an 8-inch pie plate, you can use a 9-inch tart pan.

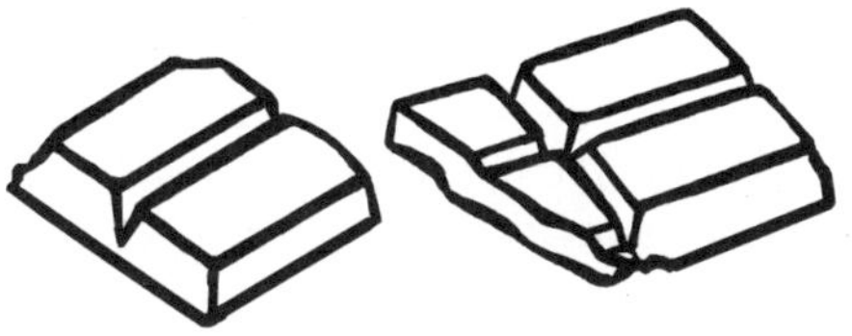

Tarts

Tarte Tatin

SERVES 8
ACTIVE TIME: 50 MINUTES ■ START TO FINISH: 1¾ HOURS

■ Butter and sugar melt together in the bottom of the pan to create a deep brown caramel glaze on the apples. Our old-fashioned cast-iron skillet did the job better than the traditional copper pan, and the Gala apple, a New Zealand hybrid of Kidd's Orange and Golden Delicious apples, brought the most flavor. A sheet of puff pastry baked on top of the apples becomes a flaky bottom crust when the tart is inverted. ■

- 1 sheet frozen puff pastry (from a 17¼-ounce package), thawed
- ½ stick (4 tablespoons) unsalted butter, softened
- ½ cup sugar
- 7–9 Gala apples (3–4 pounds total), peeled, quartered lengthwise, and cored

SPECIAL EQUIPMENT: a well-seasoned 10-inch cast-iron skillet

Put racks in middle and lower third of oven and preheat oven to 425°F.

Roll out pastry sheet on a lightly floured surface with a lightly floured rolling pin into a 10½-inch square. Brush off excess flour. Using a plate as a guide, cut out a 10-inch round with a sharp knife. Transfer to a baking sheet and refrigerate.

Spread butter thickly on bottom and sides of skillet and pour sugar evenly over bottom. Arrange as many apples as will fit in tight concentric circles in pan, standing them on end (apples will stick up above rim of skillet).

Cook apples over moderately high heat, without stirring, until juices are deep golden and bubbling, 18 to 25 minutes. (Don't worry if the juices color unevenly.)

Lay a sheet of foil on lower oven rack (to catch any drips) and put skillet on middle rack. Bake for 20 minutes (apples will settle slightly).

Remove skillet from oven and lay pastry round over apples. Bake until pastry is browned, 20 to 25 minutes. Transfer skillet to a rack to cool for at least 10 minutes.

Just before serving, invert a platter with a lip over skillet and, using pot holders to hold skillet and platter tightly together, invert tart onto platter. Replace any apples that stick to skillet. (Don't worry if there are caramelized black spots in apples.) Brush any caramel remaining in skillet over apples. Serve immediately.

COOK'S NOTE

■ The puff pastry round can be refrigerated for up to 1 day, covered with plastic wrap. Let stand at room temperature until just pliable, about 5 minutes, before topping tart.

Thin Apple Tarts

SERVES 4
ACTIVE TIME: 35 MINUTES ■ START TO FINISH: 1 HOUR

■ As long as you've got some puff pastry in the freezer and a few Granny Smiths in the fruit bowl, you can make these easy apple tarts. The only trick is slicing the apples uniformly thin, which you can accomplish easily with a mandoline or other manual slicer. Just wilt the apple slices in a buttery, lemony syrup, place them on the rounds of pastry, and bake them until they are golden. ■

- 2 small Granny Smith apples
- ½ cup water
- ½ cup sugar
- 2 tablespoons fresh lemon juice
- 2 tablespoons unsalted butter
- 1 sheet frozen puff pastry (from a 17¼-ounce package), thawed

SPECIAL EQUIPMENT: a mandoline or other manual slicer, such as a Japanese Benriner

Peel, core, and halve apples. Cut apple halves crosswise into 1⁄16-inch-thick slices with mandoline and transfer to a heatproof bowl.

Combine water, sugar, lemon juice, and butter in a

small saucepan and bring to a boil, stirring until sugar is dissolved. Pour over apples (set saucepan aside). Turn apples until slightly wilted, then drain in a colander set over a bowl; reserve liquid.

Put a rack in middle of oven and preheat oven to 425°F. Lightly butter a baking sheet.

Roll out pastry sheet on a lightly floured surface with a lightly floured rolling pin into a 12½-inch square. Using a plate or pot lid as a guide, cut out four 6-inch rounds. Transfer rounds to buttered baking sheet and top with apple slices, overlapping them. Bake tarts until pastry is golden brown, about 25 minutes.

Meanwhile, boil reserved liquid in same saucepan until reduced to about ⅓ cup. Remove from heat and cover to keep warm.

Brush warm syrup on baked tarts.

Apple and Calvados Galette

SERVES 8
ACTIVE TIME: 1 HOUR ■ START TO FINISH: 3¾ HOURS
(INCLUDES MAKING DOUGH AND APPLESAUCE)

■ This free-form tart makes baking virtually child's play. Sliced apples, Calvados, applesauce, and apple jelly deliver a multilayered wallop of apple flavor. The all-butter pastry dough is slightly less flaky than a dough made with a blend of butter and shortening or lard, but it is easy to work with and tastes delicious. ■

All-Butter Pastry Dough (recipe follows)
1¾ pounds Gala apples
2 teaspoons fresh lemon juice
⅓ cup plus 1½ teaspoons granulated sugar
Calvados Applesauce (recipe follows)
3 tablespoons unsalted butter, cut into ½-inch pieces
1½ tablespoons apple jelly
1 cup very cold heavy cream
1 tablespoon confectioners' sugar
1½ tablespoons Calvados
SPECIAL EQUIPMENT: a large baking sheet (at least 14 inches wide) or a half-sheet pan (not a jelly-roll pan); parchment paper

Line baking sheet with parchment. Roll out dough on a lightly floured surface with a lightly floured rolling pin into a rough 16-inch round. Carefully transfer to lined baking sheet and loosely fold in edges of dough as necessary to fit on sheet. Refrigerate, loosely covered with plastic wrap, for 30 minutes.

Put a rack in middle of oven and preheat oven to 425°F.

Peel and core apples, then cut into ⅛-inch-thick slices. Toss with lemon juice and ⅓ cup granulated sugar in a bowl.

Put baking sheet with dough on a work surface and unfold edges so pastry is flat. Spread applesauce over dough, leaving a 2-inch border. Top sauce with sliced apples, mounding them slightly. Fold edges of dough over filling, partially covering apples, pleating dough as necessary. Dot apples with butter. Brush edges of dough lightly with water and sprinkle with remaining 1½ teaspoons granulated sugar. Bake galette until pastry is golden and apples are tender, 40 to 45 minutes.

Meanwhile, melt apple jelly in a very small saucepan over moderately low heat, stirring. Remove from heat and keep warm.

Slide baked galette, on parchment, onto a rack and brush apples with melted jelly. Cool to warm or room temperature.

Beat cream and confectioners' sugar in a medium bowl with an electric mixer until cream just holds soft peaks, then beat in Calvados. Serve galette topped with dollops of cream.

COOK'S NOTE

■ The galette can be made up to 8 hours ahead and kept at room temperature. Make the Calvados cream just before serving.

All-Butter Pastry Dough

MAKES ENOUGH FOR A 12-INCH GALETTE OR A DOUBLE-CRUST 9-INCH PIE
ACTIVE TIME: 15 MINUTES ■ START TO FINISH: 1¼ HOURS (INCLUDES CHILLING)

■ Although this pastry is very good when made with regular butter, it positively shines when you use the richest butter possible, such as Keller's Plugrá or Land O' Lakes's Ultra Creamy. (For more about butter, see page 780.) ■

- 2½ cups all-purpose flour
- 2 teaspoons sugar
- ¾ teaspoon salt
- 2 sticks (½ pound) cold unsalted butter, cut into ½-inch cubes
- ½ cup plus 1–4 tablespoons ice water

Whisk together flour, sugar, and salt in a bowl (or pulse together in a food processor). Blend in butter with your fingertips or a pastry blender (or pulse) just until most of mixture resembles coarse meal with small (roughly pea-sized) lumps of butter. Drizzle ½ cup plus 1 tablespoon ice water evenly over mixture and gently stir with a fork (or pulse) until incorporated. Squeeze a small handful of dough: if it doesn't hold together, add more ice water 1 tablespoon at a time, stirring (or pulsing) until just incorporated, then test again. Do not overwork mixture, or pastry will be tough.

Turn dough out onto a lightly floured surface and divide into 8 portions. With heel of your hand, smear each portion once or twice in a forward motion to help distribute fat. Gather dough together, with a pastry scraper if you have one, and press into a ball. Flatten into a 6-inch disk if making a galette, or divide in half and shape into 2 disks if using for a pie. Wrap in plastic wrap and refrigerate until firm, at least 1 hour.

COOK'S NOTE

■ The dough can be refrigerated for up to 1 day. Let stand at room temperature for 20 minutes before rolling out.

Calvados Applesauce

MAKES ABOUT 1¼ CUPS
ACTIVE TIME: 30 MINUTES ■ START TO FINISH: 1 HOUR (INCLUDES COOLING)

■ This applesauce is also wonderful as a side for a crackling pork roast. ■

- 1 pound Gala apples, peeled, cored, and cut into 1-inch pieces
- ½ cup water
- ½ cup sugar
- ½ teaspoon finely grated lemon zest
- ⅛ teaspoon ground cinnamon
- 2 tablespoons Calvados

Combine apples, water, sugar, zest, and cinnamon in a 2-quart heavy saucepan and bring to a boil, stirring occasionally. Cover, reduce heat, and simmer for 15 minutes.

Remove lid and simmer until most of liquid has evaporated, 5 to 10 minutes. Add Calvados and simmer, stirring occasionally, for 1 minute. Remove from heat and mash apples with a potato masher or a fork to a chunky sauce. Cool.

COOK'S NOTE

■ The applesauce can be made up to 3 days ahead and refrigerated, covered.

Blueberry Tart

SERVES 8 TO 10
ACTIVE TIME: 45 MINUTES ■ START TO FINISH: 6¾ HOURS (INCLUDES CHILLING)

■ Blending fresh blueberries with cooked ones in a crisp butter-cookie crust results in a true-blue delight. Frozen berries can be used for the cooked portion of the filling in this recipe, which came from a former food editor, Leslie Glover Pendleton. ■

FOR CRUST

- 1¼ cups all-purpose flour
- ¼ cup sugar

¼ teaspoon salt
1 stick (8 tablespoons) cold unsalted butter, cut into bits
1 large egg yolk

FOR FILLING

1 tablespoon fresh lemon juice
½ cup sugar
¼ teaspoon ground cinnamon
Pinch of salt
8 cups blueberries (from 4 pints)
2½ teaspoons unflavored gelatin (from one ¼-ounce envelope)
3 tablespoons water
2 teaspoons vanilla extract

ACCOMPANIMENT: whipped cream

SPECIAL EQUIPMENT: an 11-inch fluted tart pan with a removable bottom

MAKE THE CRUST: Pulse together flour, sugar, salt, and butter in a food processor until mixture resembles coarse meal. Add yolk and pulse until dough begins to come together but is still crumbly.

Press dough evenly onto bottom and up sides of tart pan. Prick bottom of crust all over with a fork and refrigerate for 30 minutes.

Put a rack in middle of oven and preheat oven to 400°F.

Bake crust until golden, 15 to 20 minutes. Cool on a rack.

MAKE THE FILLING: Combine lemon juice, sugar, cinnamon, salt, and 3 cups berries in a 2-quart heavy saucepan, bring to a simmer, and simmer, stirring occasionally, for 10 minutes. Meanwhile, sprinkle gelatin over water in a small bowl and let soften.

Remove pan from heat and stir in gelatin mixture and vanilla. Transfer blueberry mixture to a metal bowl set in a bowl of ice and cold water and stir occasionally until thickened to the consistency of raw egg white but not set, about 10 minutes.

Fold in remaining 5 cups berries. Pour filling into crust and spread evenly. Refrigerate tart, loosely covered, until set, at least 4 hours.

Let tart stand at room temperature for 1 hour before removing rim of pan. Serve tart with whipped cream.

COOK'S NOTE

- The tart can be refrigerated for up to 1 day.

Berry Tart with Mascarpone Cream

SERVES 6 TO 8
ACTIVE TIME: 40 MINUTES ■ START TO FINISH: 3¼ HOURS (INCLUDES MAKING DOUGH AND COOLING)

■ This dessert is a tangy combination of vibrantly flavored fruit and velvety mascarpone sweetness. ■

Sweet Pastry Dough (page 791)
1 cup (8 ounces) mascarpone
⅓ cup very cold heavy cream
¼ cup sugar
1½ cups (8 ounces) small strawberries, quartered
1 cup (4 ounces) raspberries
1 cup (5 ounces) blueberries
1 cup (5 ounces) blackberries
2 tablespoons sweet orange marmalade
2 tablespoons dark berry liqueur, such as blueberry, blackberry, or crème de cassis

SPECIAL EQUIPMENT: a 9-inch fluted tart pan with a removable bottom

Overlap two sheets of wax paper on a work surface to form a 15-inch square. Place dough on paper and cover with two more sheets. Roll out dough into a 13-inch round. Transfer (with wax paper) to a baking sheet and refrigerate for 10 minutes.

Lift top sheets of wax paper from dough and gently replace on top (this will make it easy to remove paper later). Flip dough over and peel off and discard wax paper now on top. Carefully invert dough into tart pan and discard wax paper. Gently press dough into pan, then roll rolling pin over top of pan to trim edges of dough flush with rim. Refrigerate until firm, about 30 minutes.

Put a rack in middle of oven and preheat oven to 375°F.

Lightly prick shell in several places with a fork. Line shell with foil and fill with pie weights, raw rice, or dried beans. Bake for 20 minutes. Carefully remove foil and weights and bake shell until golden, about 10 minutes more. Cool completely on a rack.

Beat together mascarpone, cream, and sugar in a medium bowl with an electric mixer at high speed

until mixture holds stiff peaks, about 1 minute. Spoon mixture into shell and spread evenly.

Put berries in a large bowl. Combine marmalade and liqueur in a small saucepan, bring to a simmer, stirring, and simmer, stirring, until reduced to about 3 tablespoons, about 2 minutes. Pour mixture over berries and stir gently with a rubber spatula to coat evenly. Mound berries decoratively on mascarpone cream. Remove rim of pan before serving.

COOK'S NOTES

- The tart shell can be made up to 1 day ahead and kept, loosely covered, at room temperature.
- The tart can be assembled up to 2 hours ahead and refrigerated. Bring to room temperature before serving.

Frangipane Tart with Strawberries and Raspberries

SERVES 8

ACTIVE TIME: 1 HOUR ■ START TO FINISH: 3 3/4 HOURS (INCLUDES MAKING DOUGH AND COOLING)

■ Almonds and fresh berries are a brilliantly successful combination. Here frangipane, a rich, almond-scented pastry cream, is baked and covered with a mixture of berries. We recommend that you use fresh local berries. ■

Basic Pastry Dough for a tart shell (page 790)
3/4 stick (6 tablespoons) unsalted butter, softened
1/2 cup sugar
1 large egg
3/4 cup (3 ounces) skinned whole almonds, finely ground in a food processor
1/4 teaspoon almond extract
1 tablespoon amaretto (optional)
1 tablespoon all-purpose flour
1/8 teaspoon salt
2 cups (12 ounces) strawberries, hulled and cut lengthwise into 1/8-inch-thick slices
2 cups (8 ounces) raspberries
1/4 cup strawberry or raspberry jam, melted and strained

SPECIAL EQUIPMENT: a 10- or 11-inch fluted round tart pan or an 11-by-8-inch rectangular tart pan with a removable bottom

Roll out dough on a lightly floured surface with a lightly floured rolling pin into a 13-inch round or a 13-by-10-inch rectangle. Fit into tart pan, then roll rolling pin over top of pan to trim edges of dough flush with rim. Refrigerate for 1 hour.

Put a rack in middle of oven and preheat oven to 375°F.

Lightly prick dough in several places with a fork. Line shell with foil and fill with pie weights, raw rice, or dried beans. Bake for 15 minutes. Carefully remove foil and weights and bake shell until just golden, 5 to 10 minutes more. Cool on a rack. (Leave oven on.)

Beat together butter and sugar in a small bowl with an electric mixer at medium speed until pale and fluffy. Beat in egg, almonds, extract, amaretto (if using), flour, and salt. Spread frangipane evenly in bottom of shell.

Bake tart until frangipane is just golden, 20 to 25 minutes. (If crust looks too brown after 15 minutes, cover with a pie shield or loosely with foil.) Cool tart on rack for about 30 minutes.

Arrange overlapping strawberry slices and raspberries decoratively on frangipane. Brush gently with jam. (If jam is too thick, thin with hot water, 1 teaspoon at a time, as necessary.) Remove rim of pan before serving.

COOK'S NOTE

- The filled tart can be baked up to 12 hours ahead and kept, loosely covered, at room temperature.

Sour Cherry Crostata

SERVES 8
ACTIVE TIME: $1\frac{1}{2}$ HOURS ■ START TO FINISH: 5 HOURS (INCLUDES COOLING)

■ This tart features a pastry the Italians call *pasta frolla*. The dough is somewhat like a cookie dough. The lattice top is easy to make because it doesn't require weaving the strips, which melt into each other during baking. ■

FOR PASTRY

- $1\frac{1}{2}$ sticks (12 tablespoons) unsalted butter, softened
- $\frac{1}{3}$ cup plus 1 tablespoon sugar
- 1 large egg, lightly beaten
- 1 teaspoon vanilla extract
- $2\frac{1}{4}$ cups all-purpose flour
- $\frac{1}{2}$ teaspoon salt
- 2 teaspoons finely grated lemon zest

FOR FILLING

- 3 tablespoons unsalted butter, cut into pieces
- $5\frac{1}{4}$ cups fresh or frozen (not thawed) sour cherries ($1\frac{3}{4}$ pounds), pitted
- $\frac{3}{4}$ cup plus 1 tablespoon sugar
- 2 tablespoons cold water
- 3 tablespoons cornstarch

SPECIAL EQUIPMENT: a 9-inch fluted tart pan with a removable bottom

MAKE THE PASTRY: Beat together butter and $\frac{1}{3}$ cup sugar in a medium bowl with an electric mixer at medium speed until pale and fluffy, about 3 minutes. Reserve 1 tablespoon beaten egg, refrigerated, for egg wash, and beat remaining egg into butter mixture. Beat in vanilla. Reduce speed to low and mix in flour, salt, and zest until mixture just forms a dough.

Cut dough in half. Form each half into a 5- to 6-inch disk, wrap in plastic wrap, and refrigerate until firm, at least 30 minutes.

MEANWHILE, MAKE THE FILLING: Heat butter in a 12-inch nonstick skillet over moderate heat until foam subsides. Add cherries, with any juices, and sugar, bring to a simmer, and simmer, stirring, until sugar is dissolved and cherries exude their juice. Continue to simmer until cherries are tender but not falling apart, about 8 minutes. Stir together water and cornstarch in a cup to form a smooth thick paste, then stir into simmering filling and boil, stirring often, for 2 minutes.

Cool filling quickly by spreading it in a shallow baking pan and refrigerating it until lukewarm, about 15 minutes.

ASSEMBLE AND BAKE THE CROSTATA: Roll out 1 piece of dough (keep remaining piece chilled) between two sheets of wax paper into a 12-inch round. Remove top sheet of paper and invert dough into tart pan. Carefully peel off paper and fit dough into pan. Trim excess dough, leaving a $\frac{1}{2}$-inch overhang. Fold overhang in and press against sides of pan to reinforce sides. Refrigerate.

Roll out remaining dough in same manner. Remove top sheet of paper and cut dough into ten 1-inch-wide strips. Slide dough, still on wax paper, onto a baking sheet. Refrigerate strips until firm, about 5 minutes.

Line a large baking sheet with foil and put on middle oven rack. Preheat oven to 375°F.

Spread filling in chilled tart shell. Arrange 5 dough strips 1 inch apart across filling, pressing ends onto edge of tart shell. Arrange remaining 5 strips 1 inch apart diagonally across first strips to form a diamond-shaped lattice, pressing ends onto edge of tart shell. Trim edges of all strips flush with side of pan. Brush lattice with reserved beaten egg and sprinkle with remaining 1 tablespoon sugar.

Bake crostata on hot baking sheet until pastry is golden and filling is bubbling, about 1 hour. (If lattice and edges look too brown after 30 minutes, cover with a pie shield or loosely with foil.)

Cool crostata completely in pan on a rack, $1\frac{1}{2}$ to 2 hours.

COOK'S NOTE

■ The crostata is best the day it is baked, but it can be made up to 1 day ahead and kept, covered with foil, at room temperature.

Brandied Sour Cherry and Pear Tartlets

MAKES 16 TARTLETS
ACTIVE TIME: 1½ HOURS ■ START TO FINISH: 3½ HOURS (INCLUDES CHILLING DOUGH)

■ Packed with fruit and brandy flavor, the filling in these tarts is perfectly suited to a cold-weather dinner party. Serve with Eggnog Ice Cream (page 856) for a holiday celebration. ■

FOR PASTRY DOUGH

- 3½ cups all-purpose flour
- 1 teaspoon salt
- 2 sticks (½ pound) cold unsalted butter, cut into ½-inch cubes
- ½ cup cold vegetable shortening
- 3 tablespoons sugar
- ½ cup plus 1–2 tablespoons ice water
- 3 tablespoons whole milk

FOR FILLING

- 1½ pounds firm but ripe pears (about 3)
- 2 cups (10 ounces) dried sour cherries
- ½ cup brandy
- ½ cup water
- 3 tablespoons sugar
- 2 tablespoons cornstarch

SPECIAL EQUIPMENT: a 3½-inch fluted round cookie cutter; a small (½- to ¾-inch) decorative cutter (optional); a 4-inch fluted or plain round cookie cutter; sixteen 3¼- to 3½-by-5/8-inch round nonstick fluted tartlet pans

MAKE THE DOUGH: Combine flour, salt, butter, shortening, and 2 tablespoons sugar in a large bowl and blend together with your fingertips or a pastry blender just until most of mixture resembles coarse meal with some small (roughly pea-sized) lumps of butter. Drizzle ½ cup ice water evenly over dough and stir gently with a fork until incorporated. Squeeze a small handful of dough: if it doesn't hold together, add more ice water 1 tablespoon at a time, stirring until just incorporated, then test again. Do not overwork mixture, or pastry will be tough.

Turn dough out onto a lightly floured surface and divide into 8 portions. With heel of your hand, smear each portion once or twice in a forward motion to help distribute fat. Gather dough together, with a pastry

BUTTER

We've used thousands of pounds of butter in our test kitchens over the years, and we know one thing for a fact: you want to buy the best. After sampling more than twenty different brands of butter, we were astonished by the results. (Since salt, which is used as a preservative, can mask off flavors, we chose unsalted butters for our tasting.)

Most surprising? The way butter is wrapped may be more important than how it is made or shipped. Our favorites were all wrapped in foil. Paper, we found, does not protect the butter—and the flavor of paper-wrapped butter doesn't compare.

Freshness can often be a problem. While we always check the expiration date when buying milk, few of us think to look for dates on packages of butter. They are there, but they can be difficult to find and decipher. And if the butter has been mishandled during its complex distribution process, the date can be meaningless.

What to do? If you've never detected rancidity in the kind of butter you buy, stick with it. If it sometimes tastes odd, though, you might want to shop around. And if you see one of the higher-butterfat butters—Land O' Lakes's Ultra Creamy or Keller's Plugrá, for instance—which are becoming more available, treat yourself. More butterfat (thus less water) than the federal minimum of 80 percent will give your favorite piecrust a better texture and a richer flavor.

scraper if you have one, and divide into 2 pieces, one slightly larger than the other. Shape each one into a disk. Wrap in plastic wrap and refrigerate until firm, at least 1 hour.

MEANWHILE, MAKE THE FILLING: Peel, halve, and core pears. Cut into ¼-inch dice and stir together with remaining ingredients in a 3-quart heavy saucepan. Bring to a boil, stirring, then reduce heat and simmer, uncovered, stirring occasionally, until slightly thickened, about 10 minutes. Transfer filling to a shallow dish and cool to room temperature.

MAKE THE TARTLET TOPS: Roll out smaller disk of dough on a floured surface with a floured rolling pin into a 13-inch round, carefully lifting up dough and flouring surface as necessary to keep dough from sticking. Cut out as many rounds as possible (about 12) with 3½-inch fluted cutter and transfer them to a baking sheet lined with wax paper. Refrigerate rounds until firm, about 10 minutes. Gather dough scraps together and chill for 20 to 30 minutes, then reroll and cut additional 3½-inch rounds (reroll dough only once), for a total of 16; chill until firm.

Cut out shapes from rounds with decorative cutter or sharp paring knife, leaving at least a ½-inch border around edges; if desired, reserve cutout pieces for decoration. Brush tops lightly with milk. Lightly press reserved cutouts, if using, onto pastry rounds and brush lightly with milk. Sprinkle remaining 1 tablespoon sugar evenly over tops. Refrigerate.

MAKE THE TARTLET BOTTOMS: Roll out remaining disk of dough on floured surface into a 15-inch round, carefully lifting up dough and flouring surface as necessary to keep dough from sticking. Cut out as many rounds as possible (about 12) with 4-inch cutter. Gather dough scraps and refrigerate for 20 to 30 minutes.

Put a rack in middle of oven and preheat oven to 375°F.

While scraps are chilling, fit each 4-inch round into a tartlet pan (do not trim). When scraps are chilled, reroll and cut out additional 4-inch rounds (reroll dough only once), for a total of 16. Fit rounds into tart pans.

ASSEMBLE AND BAKE THE TARTLETS: Fill each tartlet with 3 tablespoons cooled filling. Brush edges of pastry lightly with milk. Place pastry

tops over filling and press each top lightly around edges to help seal; trim pastry if necessary.

Arrange tartlets on a large baking sheet. Bake until golden, 20 to 25 minutes. Transfer tartlets to a rack and cool for 10 minutes.

To remove tartlets from pans, cover one hand with a folded kitchen towel and invert tartlets onto towel one at a time, then reinvert onto a platter. Serve warm or at room temperature.

COOK'S NOTES

- The dough can be refrigerated for up to 1 day. Let stand at room temperature for about 20 minutes before rolling out.
- The filling can be made up to 1 day ahead. Cool, uncovered, then refrigerate, covered.
- The tartlets can be assembled up to 1 week ahead and frozen, wrapped well in plastic wrap. Do not thaw before baking. The baking time will be 10 to 15 minutes longer.
- The tartlets can be baked up to 1 day ahead and kept, loosely covered, at room temperature. Reheat in a 350°F oven until warm, 10 to 15 minutes.
- You can also use the recipe to make one 10-inch tart instead of the tartlets. Use a slightly larger cutter to make the cutouts in the top crust, if desired, and bake for 50 to 60 minutes.

Red Wine–Poached Pear and Custard Tart

SERVES 8 TO 10

ACTIVE TIME: 1 HOUR ■ START TO FINISH: 4 HOURS (INCLUDES MAKING DOUGH AND COOLING)

■ In late autumn, when the stone fruits of summer have disappeared and the leaves are turning red, this handsome tart comes into its own. The pears are bathed in red wine, giving them a deep burgundy hue, and then nestled in a vanilla- and cinnamon-scented custard. ■

Basic Pastry Dough for a tart shell (page 790)

FOR PEARS

1½ cups dry red wine
⅓ cup sugar
1 (2-inch) piece cinnamon stick
3 whole cloves
4 firm but ripe Bosc or Anjou pears (2 pounds total), peeled, halved, and cored

FOR FILLING

3 large eggs
⅔ cup sugar
1 teaspoon vanilla extract
¼ teaspoon salt
⅛ teaspoon ground cinnamon
¾ cup plus 2 tablespoons heavy cream

OPTIONAL GARNISH: 2 tablespoons slivered almonds, toasted (see Tips, page 938)

SPECIAL EQUIPMENT: a 10-inch fluted tart pan with a removable bottom

MAKE THE TART SHELL: Roll out dough on a lightly floured surface with a lightly floured rolling pin into a 13-inch round. Fit it into tart pan. Roll rolling pin over top of pan to trim dough flush with rim. Refrigerate for 30 minutes.

Put a rack in middle of oven and preheat oven to 375°F.

Lightly prick dough in several places with a fork. Line tart shell with foil and fill with pie weights, raw rice, or dried beans. Bake for 20 minutes. Carefully remove foil and weights and bake until shell is golden, about 10 minutes more. Cool completely on a rack.

MEANWHILE, POACH THE PEARS: Combine wine, sugar, cinnamon stick, and cloves in a 4- to 5-quart heavy pot and bring to a boil. Add pears and gently simmer over moderately low heat, turning and basting pears occasionally, until they are just tender, 15 to 20 minutes. With a slotted spoon, transfer pears to paper towels to drain and discard spices.

Boil pan juices until syrupy and reduced to about ½ cup, about 10 minutes. Pour syrup into a small bowl.

MAKE THE FILLING: Whisk together eggs, sugar, vanilla, salt, and cinnamon in a medium bowl until well blended. Whisk in cream.

ASSEMBLE AND BAKE THE TART: Arrange pears cut sides down in tart shell, wider ends out. Pour filling around them. Put on a baking sheet and bake until custard is puffed and golden, 40 to 50 minutes. Cool tart completely on rack.

Remove rim of pan and sprinkle tart with almonds, if desired. Brush some syrup over pears and serve, drizzling remaining syrup over tart wedges.

Caramelized Upside-Down Pear Tart

SERVES 6 TO 8
ACTIVE TIME: 20 MINUTES ■ START TO FINISH: 2½ HOURS (INCLUDES MAKING DOUGH)

■ In France the Tatin sisters were inspired to caramelize apples, cover them with puff pastry, and then turn the whole thing upside down, creating their now world-famous tart. Our colleague Betty Caldwell took the idea and gave it a modern twist, substituting pears for the apples and topping them with a classic pie dough. The result is dramatic—and delicious. ■

½ stick (4 tablespoons) unsalted butter
½ cup sugar
4 firm but ripe Bosc pears (2 pounds total), peeled, halved, and cored
½ teaspoon ground cinnamon
Basic Pastry Dough for a tart shell (page 790)

ACCOMPANIMENT: sweetened whipped cream or vanilla ice cream

SPECIAL EQUIPMENT: a 9- to 10-inch ovenproof nonstick skillet or well-seasoned cast-iron skillet

Heat butter in skillet over moderate heat until foam subsides. Stir in sugar (sugar will not dissolve yet). Arrange pears cut sides up in skillet, with wider ends out. Sprinkle cinnamon over pears and cook, without stirring, until sugar mixture becomes a deep golden caramel, 15 to 25 minutes (depending on skillet and stove). Remove from heat and cool pears completely in skillet.

Put a rack in middle of oven and preheat oven to 425°F.

Roll out dough on a lightly floured surface with a lightly floured rolling pin into a 9½- to 10½-inch round. Lay over pears in skillet and tuck edges in around pears.

Bake until pastry is golden brown, 30 to 35 minutes. Remove tart from oven and let stand for 5 minutes.

Wearing oven mitts, invert a rimmed serving plate slightly larger than skillet over tart and, keeping plate and skillet firmly pressed together, invert tart onto plate. Serve warm or at room temperature, with whipped cream or ice cream.

Plum Tart

SERVES 6 TO 8
ACTIVE TIME: 1½ HOURS ■ START TO FINISH: 4 HOURS (INCLUDES COOLING)

■ Italian prune plums, which are beloved by every baker for their rich purple-red color and the way they hold their shape when baked, turn up in markets in late August through mid-October. Because the plums only need to be halved and pitted and the dough is just pressed into the pan, this is a satisfying project for a novice baker. ■

FOR PASTRY DOUGH

- 1½ cups all-purpose flour
- 1 stick (8 tablespoons) plus 1 tablespoon cold unsalted butter, cut into ½-inch pieces
- ¼ cup sugar
- ½ teaspoon salt
- ½ teaspoon finely grated lemon zest
- 2 large egg yolks

FOR FILLING

- ½ cup sugar
- 2 tablespoons cornstarch
- 1¾ pounds small plums, preferably prune plums (about 26), halved and pitted
- 1½ teaspoons fresh lemon juice

ACCOMPANIMENT: crème fraîche or lightly sweetened sour cream

SPECIAL EQUIPMENT: a 9-inch fluted tart pan with a removable bottom

MAKE THE DOUGH: Combine flour, butter, sugar, salt, and zest in a food processor and pulse until mixture resembles coarse meal with some small (roughly pea-sized) lumps of butter. Add yolks and process just until incorporated and dough begins to clump.

Turn dough out onto a work surface and divide into 4 portions. Smear each portion once with heel of your hand in a forward motion to help distribute fat. Gather dough together, using a pastry scraper if you have one, form into a ball, and flatten into a disk.

Put dough in tart pan and pat out with floured fingertips into an even layer on bottom and up sides so it extends about ¼ inch above rim. Refrigerate until firm, about 30 minutes.

MEANWHILE, MAKE THE FILLING: Stir together sugar and cornstarch in a large bowl. Add plums and lemon juice and toss to coat. Let plums macerate at room temperature, stirring occasionally, until juicy, about 30 minutes.

ASSEMBLE AND BAKE THE TART: Put a rack in lower third of oven and preheat oven to 425°F.

Arrange plum halves skin sides down in tart shell in an overlapping decorative pattern. Halve any remaining plums lengthwise and randomly tuck in among plum halves. Pour all juices from bowl over plums.

Bake tart for 25 minutes. Reduce oven temperature to 375°F, cover tart loosely with foil, and bake until plums are tender and juices are bubbling and slightly thickened, about 40 minutes more. Brush warm juices over plums.

Cool tart completely on a rack, about 2 hours. (Juices will continue to thicken as tart cools.)

Remove rim of pan and serve tart with crème fraîche or sour cream.

COOK'S NOTES

- The unbaked tart shell can be refrigerated, covered, for up to 1 day.
- The plums can macerate for up to 1 day, covered and refrigerated. Stir well before arranging in the tart shell.

Mango Tart

SERVES 8

ACTIVE TIME: 35 MINUTES ■ START TO FINISH: 1 HOUR

■ This almost effortless tart is made with store-bought puff pastry and an easy filling of cream cheese, sugar, and sour cream. When you slice ripe mangoes thinly and drape the slices across the top, you create a stunning and fragrant showpiece. ■

- 1 sheet frozen puff pastry (from a 17¼-ounce package), thawed
- 1 large egg, lightly beaten
- 4 tablespoons sugar
- ½ cup sour cream
- ⅓ cup whipped cream cheese
- 1 teaspoon finely grated lime zest
- 2 large mangoes, peeled

OPTIONAL GARNISH: finely julienned lime zest, blanched briefly in boiling water

SPECIAL EQUIPMENT: a mandoline or other manual slicer, such as a Japanese Benriner (optional)

PREPARE THE PASTRY: Put a rack in lower third of oven and preheat oven to 400°F. Butter a baking sheet.

Unfold pastry sheet on buttered baking sheet, then turn over (to prevent it from splitting at creases while baking). Trim a very thin strip off each edge with a sharp knife and discard. Brush pastry lightly with egg (be careful not to let it drip down sides, or it might prevent pastry from rising evenly). Create a ¾-inch border all around by lightly scoring a line parallel to each side of pastry with knife (do not cut all the way through). Prick inner rectangle evenly with a fork, then sprinkle with 1 tablespoon sugar.

Bake pastry until puffed and golden brown, about 15 minutes. Transfer sheet to a rack and let cool.

MEANWHILE, MAKE THE CREAM AND CUT THE MANGOES: Whisk together sour cream, cream cheese, remaining 3 tablespoons sugar, and zest in a small bowl. Starting from flat sides, thinly slice mangoes lengthwise with mandoline or slicer or a sharp knife (be careful—peeled mango will be slippery). Halve wider slices lengthwise.

ASSEMBLE THE TART: Just before serving, spread cream mixture over inner rectangle of pastry. Top with mango slices, arranging them decoratively. Sprinkle with lime zest, if desired.

COOK'S NOTES

- Trimming the edges of the pastry allows the layers to separate so the pastry rises evenly as it bakes.
- The pastry can be baked up to 6 hours ahead and kept, loosely covered, at room temperature.
- The cream mixture can be made up to 6 hours ahead and refrigerated, covered.

Lemon Soufflé Tarts

SERVES 10 TO 12

ACTIVE TIME: 1¼ HOURS ■ START TO FINISH: 4½ HOURS (INCLUDES MAKING DOUGH AND COOLING)

■ A good demonstration of how to make a lot out of very little—in this case, just lemon, eggs, and sugar. The brilliance of these tarts lies in the balance between the tangy lemon soufflé filling and the sweet pastry crust. To achieve the ideal ratio of crust to filling, we make two small tarts rather than one large one. This festive dessert was brought to us by contributor Richard Condon, from Le Château du Domaine Saint-Martin, in the town of Vence in Provence. ■

- 2 recipes Sweet Pastry Dough (page 791)
- 5 large eggs, separated
- ¾ cup sugar
- 3 tablespoons finely grated lemon zest
- ¾ cup fresh lemon juice
- Pinch of salt

SPECIAL EQUIPMENT: two 8-inch fluted tart pans with removable bottoms; a candy thermometer

Put a rack in lower third of oven and preheat oven to 400°F.

Roll out half of dough on a lightly floured surface with a lightly floured rolling pin into a 10-inch round. Fit it into one tart pan. Trim excess dough, leaving a ½-inch overhang. Fold overhang inward and press against sides of pan to form a rim that extends ¼ inch above pan. Prick bottom of shell all over with a fork. Roll out remaining dough and fit into second tart pan in same manner. Refrigerate for 1 hour.

Line shells with foil and fill with pie weights, raw rice, or dried beans. Bake until edges are golden, about 10 minutes. Carefully remove foil and weights and bake shells until pale golden, 12 to 14 minutes longer. Cool completely on racks. Put a rack in middle of oven; leave oven on.

Beat together egg yolks and 1/2 cup sugar in a large bowl with an electric mixer at medium-high speed until mixture is thick and pale and forms a ribbon when beaters are lifted, about 5 minutes. Beat in zest and lemon juice. Transfer mixture to a 3-quart heavy saucepan and cook over moderately low heat, stirring constantly with a wooden spoon, until it registers 140°F on thermometer. Cook at 140°F, stirring constantly, for 3 minutes. Transfer to a large bowl, cover surface with a buttered round of wax paper (buttered side down), and cool to lukewarm.

Beat egg whites with salt in a large bowl with cleaned beaters until they just hold soft peaks. Beat in remaining 1/4 cup sugar 1 tablespoon at a time, and continue to beat until meringue holds stiff, glossy peaks. Stir one quarter of meringue into lemon mixture to lighten it, then gently but thoroughly fold in remaining meringue.

Transfer tart shells (in pans) to a baking sheet. Fill with lemon soufflé mixture, mounding it slightly.

Bake tarts until tops are golden and puffed, 10 to 12 minutes. Transfer to rack and cool completely.

Roasted Rhubarb Tarts with Strawberry Sauce

SERVES 6

ACTIVE TIME: 25 MINUTES ■ START TO FINISH: 1 HOUR

■ Rhubarb and strawberry are the first fruits of spring, and a winning combination. Here the rhubarb is roasted to deepen and sweeten its flavor, while frozen strawberries are simply puréed into sauce. Then we spread sweetened crème fraîche on crisp sugared rectangles of puff pastry, top them with the fruit, and drizzle them with the sauce. ■

- 1 sheet frozen puff pastry (from a 17¼-ounce package), thawed
- 1 pound rhubarb stalks, trimmed and cut into 1-inch pieces
- 8 tablespoons confectioners' sugar
- 1 (10-ounce) package frozen strawberries in heavy syrup, thawed
- 3/4 cup crème fraîche or sour cream

BAKE THE PASTRY: Put a rack in middle of oven and preheat oven to 425°F.

Roll out pastry sheet on a very lightly floured surface with a lightly floured rolling pin into a 12-inch square. Trim a very thin strip off each edge with a sharp knife and discard, then cut pastry into 6 rectangles (about 6 by 4 inches each). Arrange rectangles 1 to 2 inches apart on an ungreased baking sheet and lightly prick all over with a fork.

Bake until pastry is puffed and golden, 13 to 15 minutes. Cool on baking sheet on a rack. Reduce oven temperature to 375°F.

ROAST THE RHUBARB: Lightly oil a baking sheet with sides (preferably nonstick). Arrange rhubarb in one layer on baking sheet. Sift 2 tablespoons confectioners' sugar evenly over it.

Roast rhubarb until tender, 15 to 25 minutes. Cool on sheet on rack.

MEANWHILE, MAKE THE STRAWBERRY SAUCE AND CREAM FILLING: Purée strawberries, with syrup, in a food processor. Force purée through a fine-mesh sieve into a bowl; discard solids.

Sift 5 tablespoons confectioners' sugar over crème fraîche in a small bowl and whisk to combine.

ASSEMBLE THE TARTS: Divide baked pastry rectangles among six dessert plates. Sift remaining 1 tablespoon confectioners' sugar over pastry rectangles. Make a 3-inch lengthwise trough down the center of each rectangle by gently tapping with back of a teaspoon. Divide cream filling among troughs, top with rhubarb, and drizzle with strawberry sauce.

COOK'S NOTES

- The strawberry sauce and cream filling can be made up to 1 day ahead and refrigerated, covered.
- Trimming the edges of the pastry allows the layers to separate so the pastry rises evenly as it bakes.

Cranberry Walnut Tart

SERVES 8 TO 10
ACTIVE TIME: 45 MINUTES ■ START TO FINISH: 4½ HOURS (INCLUDES MAKING DOUGH AND COOLING)

■ This colorful addition to the Thanksgiving dessert spread was inspired by a walnut pie created by the late English food writer Jane Grigson and published in her 1971 classic, *Good Things.* We use fresh cranberries to brighten our version, which is made with a crumbly sweet pastry dough. ■

Sweet Pastry Dough (page 791)
3 large eggs
⅔ cup packed dark brown sugar
⅔ cup light corn syrup
½ stick (4 tablespoons) unsalted butter, melted and cooled
½ teaspoon salt
1 teaspoon vanilla extract
1¼ cups (7 ounces) chopped fresh cranberries
1 cup (4 ounces) chopped walnuts
SPECIAL EQUIPMENT: a 10- to 11-inch fluted tart pan with a removable bottom

Roll out dough on a floured surface with a floured rolling pin into a 13-inch round. Fit it into tart pan. Trim excess dough, leaving a ½-inch overhang, then fold overhang inward and press against sides of pan to reinforce sides. Refrigerate for 30 minutes.

Put a rack in lower third of oven and preheat oven to 425°F.

Lightly prick shell in several places with a fork. Line shell with foil and fill with pie weights, raw rice, or dried beans. Bake until edges are golden, about 15 minutes. Carefully remove foil and weights and bake shell until pale golden, 5 to 10 minutes more. Cool on a rack. Reduce oven temperature to 350°F.

Whisk together eggs, brown sugar, corn syrup, butter, salt, and vanilla in a medium bowl until smooth. Stir in cranberries and walnuts.

Pour filling into shell. Bake until golden, 40 to 45 minutes (if edges look too dark after 20 minutes, cover them with a pie shield or foil). Cool completely on rack. Remove rim of pan before serving.

COOK'S NOTES

- The tart can be made up to 1 day ahead and kept, covered, at room temperature.
- For a more unusual presentation, make the tart in a 11-by-8-inch fluted tart pan with a removable bottom.

Pecan Tart

SERVES 8
ACTIVE TIME: 45 MINUTES ■ START TO FINISH: 4 HOURS (INCLUDES MAKING DOUGH AND COOLING)

■ If you love pecan pie but sometimes find the heavy sweetness cloying, consider this lightened version. We've replaced much of the corn syrup with caramelized sugar and baked it into a tart instead of a pie, tinkering with the ratio of caramel filling to nuts, so the pecan flavor comes singing forth. ■

Basic Pastry Dough for a tart shell (page 790)
¾ cup sugar
1 cup light corn syrup
3 large eggs
Pinch of salt
2 tablespoons unsalted butter
1 teaspoon vanilla extract
1 teaspoon fresh lemon juice
1¾ cups (7 ounces) pecan halves
ACCOMPANIMENT: lightly whipped cream
SPECIAL EQUIPMENT: a 10-inch fluted tart pan with a removable bottom

Roll out dough on a lightly floured surface with a lightly floured rolling pin into a 15-inch round. Fit it into tart pan. Roll rolling pin over top of pan to trim dough flush with rim. Refrigerate for 30 minutes.

Put a rack in middle of oven and preheat oven to 375°F.

Lightly prick dough in several places with a fork. Line shell with foil and fill with pie weights, raw rice, or dried beans. Bake until edges are beginning to brown, about 20 minutes. Carefully remove foil and weights and bake until pale golden all over, 6 to 10 minutes more. Cool on a rack. (Leave oven on.)

Cook sugar in a dry heavy saucepan over moderately

low heat, stirring slowly with a fork, until melted and pale golden. Cook without stirring, swirling pan occasionally for even cooking, until caramel is deep golden. Add corn syrup and simmer (caramel will harden), stirring occasionally, until caramel is dissolved. Remove pan from heat and cool until mixture stops bubbling.

Whisk eggs with salt in a large bowl. Whisk caramel mixture into eggs in a slow stream, then whisk in butter, vanilla, and lemon juice and whisk until butter is melted. Spread pecans in bottom of tart shell and pour in filling, tapping down pecans as necessary to coat.

Bake tart until crust is golden and filling is puffed, 20 to 25 minutes. Cool on rack. Remove rim of pan and serve tart with whipped cream.

COOK'S NOTE

- The tart can be made up to 1 day ahead and refrigerated, covered. Reheat in a 375°F oven for about 15 minutes to recrisp the crust.

Raspberry Jam Tart with Almond Crumble

SERVES 8

ACTIVE TIME: 15 MINUTES ■ START TO FINISH: 45 MINUTES

■ A wonderful tart to make with children, this takes only a few minutes to put together. The almond-crumble pastry is a cross between a soft marzipan and a sugar cookie dough and is pressed into the tart pan rather than rolled out. Serve with whipped cream or vanilla ice cream. ■

- 2 cups (6 ounces) sliced almonds (with skins)
- 2/3 cup sugar
- 1 1/4 sticks (10 tablespoons) cold unsalted butter, cut into pieces
- 1 1/4 cups all-purpose flour
- Rounded 1/4 teaspoon salt
- 1 large egg, lightly beaten
- 1 cup (12 ounces) raspberry jam

SPECIAL EQUIPMENT: a 9-inch fluted tart pan with a removable bottom

Put a rack in middle of oven and preheat oven to 400°F.

Reserve 1/4 cup almonds in a small bowl for topping. Finely grind remaining 1 3/4 cups nuts with sugar in a food processor. Add butter, flour, and salt and process until mixture resembles sand.

Transfer 1 cup flour mixture to bowl of almonds. Add 2 tablespoons beaten egg (discard remainder) to remaining flour mixture and pulse until mixture begins to clump together. Transfer mixture to tart pan and press onto bottom and up sides of pan with floured fingers.

Bake tart shell for 15 minutes.

Meanwhile, stir raspberry jam in a small bowl to loosen it. Rub reserved almond mixture between your palms so it forms small clumps and drop them back into bowl.

Remove partially baked tart shell from oven and spread jam evenly over bottom. Scatter almond mixture over jam. Bake tart until topping is golden, about 15 minutes. Cool in pan on a rack.

Loosen rim of pan with a knife before removing.

COOK'S NOTE

- The tart can be made up to 1 day ahead and refrigerated, covered. Bring to room temperature before serving.

Linzertorte

SERVES 8 TO 10

ACTIVE TIME: 30 MINUTES ■ START TO FINISH: 3 3/4 HOURS (INCLUDES COOLING)

■ The easiest of the classic Viennese pastries, this is simply a buttery hazelnut dough filled with raspberry jam and topped with a lattice crust. Although the torte is rich and showy, it is the most forgiving of recipes: you can practically throw this dough around the kitchen and it will still come out perfect. Our linzertorte comes from *Gourmet's Old Vienna Cookbook*, written in 1958 by our longtime contributor Lillian Langseth-Christensen. ■

- 1⅓ cups (6½ ounces) hazelnuts, toasted (see Tips, page 938), skinned, and cooled
- 1¾ sticks (14 tablespoons) unsalted butter, softened
- ½ cup granulated sugar
- 3 large egg yolks
- 1 tablespoon finely grated lemon zest
- 2 cups all-purpose flour
- ¼ teaspoon salt
- 1⅓ cups (16 ounces) raspberry jam

GARNISH: confectioners' sugar

SPECIAL EQUIPMENT: a stand mixer with a paddle attachment; a 10-inch springform pan; parchment paper

Pulse nuts in a food processor until finely ground; do not grind to a paste.

Beat together butter and sugar in mixer bowl with paddle attachment at medium-high speed until pale and fluffy, about 2 minutes. Add yolks one at a time, beating until just combined, then beat in zest. Reduce speed to medium and beat in flour, salt, and ground nuts; dough will be stiff. Divide dough in half, form each half into a disk, and wrap disks in plastic wrap. Refrigerate until firm, at least 30 minutes.

Put a rack in middle of oven and preheat oven to 375°F. Line bottom of springform pan with a round of parchment paper.

Press 1 disk of dough evenly onto bottom and ¼ inch up sides of springform pan, using the back of a large spoon to smooth it if necessary. Spread jam evenly in crust.

Roll out remaining dough between two sheets of wax paper into a rough 10-inch round (½ inch thick). Remove top sheet of paper and cut dough into twelve ½-inch-wide strips. Arrange half of strips over jam, placing them about 1 inch apart and pressing ends onto edge of tart. Arrange remaining strips perpendicular to first strips to form a simple lattice. Crimp and seal edges with a fork.

Bake torte until lattice is lightly browned, about 35 minutes. Cool completely on a rack (about 2 hours).

Before serving, remove side of pan and dust edges of crust with confectioners' sugar.

COOK'S NOTE

- The torte (without the confectioners' sugar) can be made up to 2 days ahead and kept, covered, at room temperature.

Chocolate Tart

SERVES 8

ACTIVE TIME: 25 MINUTES ■ START TO FINISH: 2½ HOURS (INCLUDES CHILLING)

■ Filled with what is essentially a thick chocolate truffle cream, this tart is rescued from being too sweet by its almost savory wheatmeal crumb crust. The recipe is adapted from one created at Trattoria Garga, in Florence, which came from contributor Faith Heller Willinger. Wheatmeal biscuits are available in most supermarkets. ■

- 1 (7-ounce) package wheatmeal (digestive) biscuits, crushed (2 cups)
- 1 stick (8 tablespoons) unsalted butter, melted
- 3 tablespoons sugar
- 1 pound good bittersweet chocolate (not unsweetened), chopped
- 2 cups heavy cream
- 3 large egg yolks

SPECIAL EQUIPMENT: a 12-inch springform pan; an instant-read thermometer

Invert bottom of springform pan (to make it easier to slide tart off bottom), then lock on side. Stir together biscuit crumbs, butter, and sugar in a bowl until well combined. Press crust onto bottom of springform pan.

Melt chocolate in a metal bowl set over a saucepan of barely simmering water, stirring until smooth. Remove bowl from heat.

Bring cream to just under a boil in a 2- to 3-quart saucepan over moderate heat.

Meanwhile, lightly beat yolks in a medium bowl. Slowly add ½ cup hot cream to yolks, whisking constantly. Add yolk mixture to remaining cream and cook over moderate heat, whisking, until mixture registers 160°F on thermometer, about 2 minutes. Remove from heat and whisk in chocolate until smooth.

Pour filling into crust. Refrigerate, loosely covered, until set, at least 2 hours. Before serving, remove side of pan.

COOK'S NOTE

- The tart can be refrigerated for up to 1 day.

A Pastry Dough Primer

Despite what you may have heard, once you learn a few basic tips, making a pie or tart shell is not difficult. The process involves nothing more than combining a few ingredients in the right way.

Pastry chefs will tell you, "Keep it cold and keep it moving." Cool hands are a blessing but not a necessity as long as your fats — butter, vegetable shortening, or lard, or a combination — and water are cold. If the ingredients start to warm up while you're working them together, pop the bowl into the freezer for a few minutes to chill everything again. While using a food processor for mixing takes no time at all, be careful: you don't want to overwork the dough and end up with a tough crust. For that reason, some of us use the machine to cut in the fats and then transfer the mixture to a bowl so we can add the liquid by hand.

In most of our pastry doughs, we call for a final energetic blending of ingredients (a French technique called *fraisage*) to distribute the fat evenly and give the dough just enough structure to prevent it from cracking or tearing when it is rolled out and lifted. *Fraisage* is simple: using the heel of your hand, smear small portions of the crumbly mixture in one or two quick, short forward motions across the work surface. Then gather the dough together, preferably with a pastry scraper, and form it into a disk. It shouldn't be dry or wet or greasy, but it should be malleable. Don't be afraid to manhandle it a little, massaging it so that any cracks disappear. In most recipes, the dough is chilled thoroughly at this point, which gives the gluten in the flour time to relax and the fat time to firm up — another aid in making the dough easier to handle.

When you are rolling out the pastry, an offset spatula is handy for loosening the dough if it sticks (and also for sliding a finished tart off the bottom of the pan). To transfer the dough to a pie plate or tart pan, partially roll it onto the rolling pin, lift it off the work surface, and then unroll it over the top of the pan (1). With your fingertips, ease the dough onto the bottom of the pan without stretching it, and lightly pat it into the bottom and against the sides. Then trim the overhanging dough according to the directions in your recipe (2). Fold the overhang inward and press it against the side of the pan to form a sturdier edge (3).

We like pie plates made of glass or ceramic (they make the nicest presentation for serving) and tart pans made of shiny tinned steel, with removable bottoms. Tinned steel conducts heat well; you'll get a beautiful golden crust. A dark metal pan can bake too fast, resulting in an overly browned crust. A nonstick finish isn't necessary; pastry dough has enough butter in it to prevent sticking.

Placing the pie plate on a hot baking sheet when you put it into the oven not only protects your oven from spillovers but helps seal the bottom crust and prevent it from becoming wet. However, this tip applies only to uncooked single- or double-crust pies; blind-baked (prebaked) piecrusts might overbake on the sheet.

The edges of piecrusts that are blind-baked before the filling is added may become too brown before the filling is done. The usual solution is to crimp a ring of foil around the crust to protect it, but a pie shield (available at cookware shops and by mail; see Sources) is an easier — and reusable — solution. These come as a solid ring or a set of adjustable lengths.

1

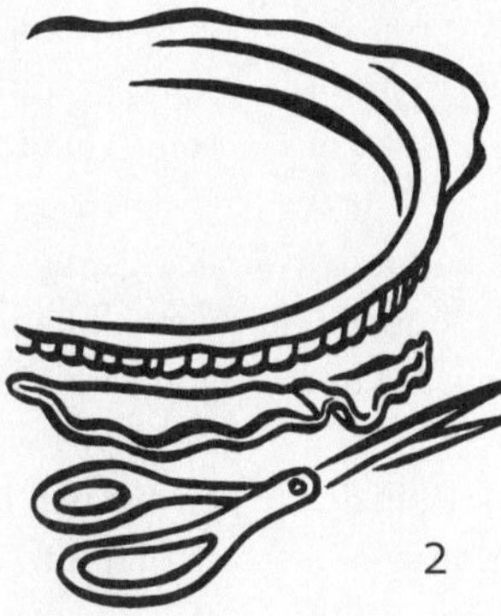

2

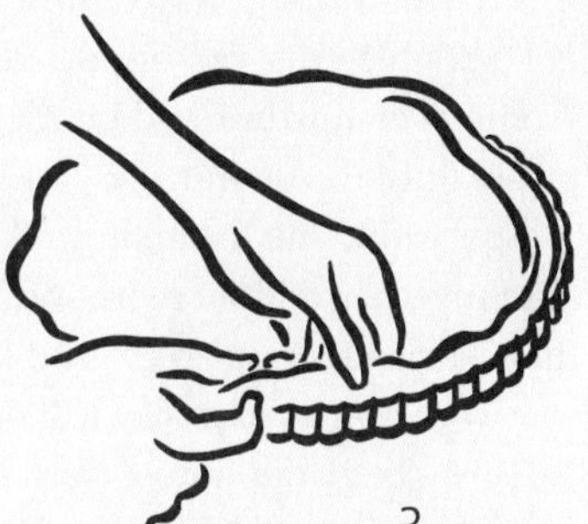

3

Basic Pastry Dough

MAKES ENOUGH FOR A SINGLE-CRUST 9-INCH PIE OR A 9- TO 11-INCH TART, OR FOR A DOUBLE-CRUST 9-INCH PIE
ACTIVE TIME: 10 MINUTES ■ START TO FINISH: 1¼ HOURS (INCLUDES CHILLING)

■ Our basic pastry recipe uses both butter, for flavor, and vegetable shortening, for flakiness. Be judicious when you are adding the ice water, since the amount of water in butter varies from brand to brand and season to season. If you add too much water, you'll probably need more flour, and your dough will be tough. ■

FOR A SINGLE-CRUST PIE OR A TART
- 1¼ cups all-purpose flour
- ¾ stick (6 tablespoons) cold unsalted butter, cut into ½-inch cubes
- 2 tablespoons cold vegetable shortening
- ¼ teaspoon salt
- 3–4 tablespoons ice water

FOR A DOUBLE-CRUST PIE
- 2½ cups all-purpose flour
- 1½ sticks (12 tablespoons) cold unsalted butter, cut into ½-inch cubes
- ¼ cup cold vegetable shortening
- ½ teaspoon salt
- 4–6 tablespoons ice water

Blend together flour, butter, shortening, and salt in a bowl with your fingertips or a pastry blender (or pulse in a food processor) just until mixture resembles coarse meal with some small (roughly pea-sized) lumps of butter. For a single-crust pie or a tart, drizzle 3 tablespoons ice water evenly over mixture and gently stir with a fork (or pulse) until incorporated. For a double-crust pie, drizzle 4 tablespoons ice water evenly over mixture and gently stir with a fork (or pulse) until incorporated.

Squeeze a small handful of dough: if it doesn't hold together, add more ice water ½ tablespoon at a time, stirring (or pulsing) until incorporated. Do not overwork dough, or pastry will be tough.

Turn dough out onto a work surface. For a single-crust pie or a tart, divide dough into 4 portions; for a double-crust pie, divide dough into 8 portions. With heel of your hand, smear each portion once or twice in a forward motion to help distribute fat. Gather all dough together, with a pastry scraper if you have one. For a single-crust pie or a tart, press into a ball, then flatten into a 5-inch disk. For a double-crust pie, divide dough in half, form each half into a ball, and then flatten each into a 5-inch disk. If dough is sticky, dust lightly with additional flour. Wrap each disk in plastic wrap and refrigerate until firm, at least 1 hour.

COOK'S NOTE

■ The dough can be refrigerated for up to 1 day.

Quick Puff Pastry Dough

MAKES ENOUGH FOR A SINGLE-CRUST 10-INCH PIE
ACTIVE TIME: 30 MINUTES ■ START TO FINISH: 3½ HOURS (INCLUDES CHILLING)

■ This recipe greatly simplifies the traditional technique for making puff pastry and shortens the preparation time. A basic pastry dough is spread with butter and then folded several times. The multilayered flaky crust is just right for any delicate filling. ■

- 2 cups all-purpose flour
- 1 teaspoon salt
- 1½ sticks (12 tablespoons) cold unsalted butter, cut into ½-inch cubes, plus 3 tablespoons butter cut into very thin slices
- 4–6 tablespoons ice water

Whisk together flour and salt in a large bowl. Blend half of butter cubes into flour with your fingertips or a pastry blender until mixture resembles coarse meal. Blend in remaining butter cubes in same manner until mixture resembles coarse meal with some small (roughly pea-sized) lumps of butter.

Drizzle 4 tablespoons ice water evenly over mixture and gently stir with a fork until incorporated. Squeeze a small handful of dough: if it doesn't hold together, add more ice water ½ tablespoon at a time, stirring until just incorporated. Do not overwork dough, or pastry will be tough. Gather dough into a ball, then flatten into a 5-inch square on a sheet of wax paper. Wrap in wax paper and refrigerate for 30 minutes.

Roll dough out on a floured surface with a floured rolling pin into a 13-by-11-inch rectangle. Position dough with a short side nearest you and place butter slices evenly over it. Fold dough into thirds like a letter: bottom third up and top third down. Turn dough so a short side is nearest you and roll it out into a 13-by-11-inch rectangle again, then fold into thirds once more. Brush off any excess flour, wrap dough in plastic wrap, and refrigerate for at least 3 hours.

COOK'S NOTE

- The dough can be refrigerated, wrapped in plastic wrap, for up to 1 day. It can also be frozen, well wrapped, for up to 1 month.

Sweet Pastry Dough

MAKES ENOUGH FOR AN 8- TO 11-INCH TART
ACTIVE TIME: 15 MINUTES ■ START TO FINISH: 1¼ HOURS (INCLUDES CHILLING)

- 1⅓ cups all-purpose flour
- 2 tablespoons sugar
- ¼ teaspoon salt
- 1 stick (8 tablespoons) cold unsalted butter, cut into ½-inch cubes
- 1 large egg yolk
- 1½ tablespoons ice water, plus additional if necessary

Whisk together flour, sugar, and salt in a large bowl (or pulse in a food processor). Blend in butter with your fingertips or a pastry blender (or pulse) until mixture resembles coarse meal with some small (roughly pea-sized) lumps of butter. Beat together yolk and water with a fork and stir into flour (or pulse) until incorporated.

Gently squeeze a small handful of dough: if it doesn't hold together, add more water ½ tablespoon at a time, stirring (or pulsing) after each addition. Do not overwork dough, or pastry will be tough.

Turn dough out onto a lightly floured surface and divide into 8 portions. With heel of your hand, smear each portion once in a forward motion to help distribute fat. Gather dough together and press into a ball, then flatten into a 5-inch disk. Wrap in plastic wrap and refrigerate until firm, at least 1 hour.

COOK'S NOTE

- The dough can be refrigerated for up to 2 days.

Pastries

Sautéed Dessert Crêpes

SERVES 4
ACTIVE TIME: 30 MINUTES ■ START TO FINISH: 30 MINUTES

■ Édouard de Pomiane was a scientist, radio commentator, and cookbook author who worked in Paris in the 1920s and '30s. He was first introduced to *Gourmet*'s readers by Elizabeth David, who called him her favorite cookbook author. In this recipe, adapted from his *French Cooking in Ten Minutes* (published in 1930), he reminds us how easy a crêpe can be. He sprinkles his crêpes with sugar, but you can embellish them with fruit, nuts, or whipped cream. ■

- 2 large eggs
- 6 tablespoons all-purpose flour
- ½ cup whole milk
- 1 tablespoon Cognac or other brandy
- Pinch of salt
- 1 (3-tablespoon) piece unsalted butter (cut from 1 stick, with wrapper still attached)
- 4 teaspoons sugar

OPTIONAL GARNISH: fresh strawberries
SPECIAL EQUIPMENT: a 7- to 8-inch well-seasoned crêpe pan or nonstick skillet

Whisk together eggs and flour in a medium bowl until smooth. Whisk in milk, then whisk in Cognac and salt.

Heat dry crêpe pan over moderately high heat until hot. Peel wrapper back slightly from butter and rub enough butter over bottom of pan to coat lightly. Pour about 1½ tablespoons batter into pan and tilt to coat bottom. (If batter sets before pan is coated, reduce heat slightly for next crêpe.) Cook until just set,

6 to 10 seconds, then jerk pan to loosen crêpe and flip crêpe with a spatula. Cook until just cooked through, about 20 seconds. Transfer crêpe to a plate and fold into quarters. Make 11 more crêpes in same manner, using about two thirds of remaining butter.

Heat remaining butter in a 12-inch heavy skillet over moderately high heat until foam subsides. Quickly arrange folded crêpes in skillet, overlapping them in a circle. Cook crêpes until golden on bottom, about 30 seconds, then invert onto a plate.

Serve crêpes sprinkled with sugar. Garnish with strawberries, if desired.

Profiteroles

SERVES 6
ACTIVE TIME 20 MINUTES ■ START TO FINISH: 1 HOUR

■ Because profiteroles are usually served in restaurants, they always seem as if they are fancy or complicated. In fact, nothing could be easier than these little pastry puffs, which can be filled with almost anything you can think of. As a savory, they're known as Yorkshire pudding or, with cheese, as *gougères*. As a dessert, they are spectacular filled with ice cream. For an absolute show-stopper, serve them with burnt orange ice cream and hot fudge sauce. All the components can be made in advance and assembled at the last minute. ■

- 3/4 stick (6 tablespoons) unsalted butter
- 3/4 cup water
- 1/4 teaspoon salt
- 3/4 cup all-purpose flour
- 3 large eggs

ACCOMPANIMENT: Burnt Orange Ice Cream (page 854) and Hot Fudge Sauce (page 874)

SPECIAL EQUIPMENT: a large pastry bag fitted with a 1/2-inch plain tip

Put racks in upper and lower thirds of oven and preheat oven to 425°F. Butter two large baking sheets.

Combine butter, water, and salt in a 2-quart heavy saucepan and bring to a boil over high heat, stirring until butter is melted. Reduce heat to moderate. Add flour all at once and cook, beating with a wooden spoon, until mixture pulls away from sides of pan and forms a ball, about 30 seconds. Transfer mixture to a bowl and let cool slightly. With an electric mixer at high speed, beat in eggs one at a time, beating well after each addition.

Transfer warm mixture to pastry bag and pipe 18 peaked mounds (each about 1 1/4 inches in diameter) about 1 inch apart onto each baking sheet. Bake profiteroles, switching position of sheets halfway through baking, until puffed and golden, 20 to 25 minutes total. Cool on a rack.

TO SERVE PROFITEROLES WITH ICE CREAM: Halve each profiterole horizontally with a serrated knife. Put a small scoop of ice cream in 6 profiteroles, set tops on ice cream, arrange profiteroles on a baking sheet, and place in the freezer while you assemble remaining profiteroles, working in batches of 6 and transferring them to freezer. Then arrange 6 profiteroles in each of six goblets or shallow bowls and top with hot fudge sauce.

COOK'S NOTE

■ The profiteroles can be baked up to 1 day ahead, cooled completely, and kept in an airtight container at room temperature. Reheat on a baking sheet in a 375°F oven to crisp them, about 5 minutes, then cool before filling.

Mocha Éclairs

MAKES 8 ÉCLAIRS
ACTIVE TIME: 50 MINUTES ■ START TO FINISH: 4 1/4 HOURS (INCLUDES MAKING FILLING)

■ A homemade éclair is infinitely better than one from a bakery. The secret is all in the timing. Although the components can be made ahead and none are complicated, an éclair tastes best when assembled an hour before serving. We've taken a classically crisp éclair pastry case, filled it with a rich mocha mousse, and spread a bittersweet chocolate glaze on top. ■

FOR ÉCLAIRS

- 1/2 stick (4 tablespoons) unsalted butter, cut into pieces
- 1/2 cup water
- 1/8 teaspoon salt

- ½ cup all-purpose flour
- 3 large eggs

FOR GLAZE

- 3 tablespoons heavy cream
- 1 ounce good bittersweet chocolate (not unsweetened), chopped

FOR ASSEMBLY

- Mocha Mousse Filling (recipe follows)

SPECIAL EQUIPMENT: a large pastry bag; a ¾-inch plain tip; a ⅜-inch plain tip

MAKE THE ÉCLAIRS: Put a rack in upper third of oven and preheat oven to 425°F. Butter a large baking sheet.

Combine butter, water, and salt in a 2-quart heavy saucepan and bring to a boil over high heat, stirring until butter is melted. Reduce heat to moderate. Add flour all at once and cook, beating with a wooden spoon, until mixture pulls away from sides of pan and forms a ball, about 15 seconds. Transfer mixture to a bowl and let cool slightly. With an electric mixer at high speed, beat in 2 eggs, one at a time, beating well after each addition. Lightly beat remaining egg in a small bowl and add 1 tablespoon beaten egg to batter. Batter should be stiff enough to just fall from spoon; add a little more egg if necessary.

Spoon batter into pastry bag fitted with ¾-inch tip and pipe eight 5-inch-long strips, about 1 inch wide, onto buttered baking sheet, spacing them about 2 inches apart.

Bake for 15 minutes. Reduce oven temperature to 400°F and continue to bake until éclairs are golden brown, puffed, and crisp, about 15 minutes more. Pierce side of each éclair with tip of a sharp knife and return éclairs to oven, propping door slightly ajar, for 5 minutes. Cool éclairs on a rack.

MAKE THE GLAZE: Bring cream just to a boil in a small saucepan. Put chocolate in a bowl, pour 2 tablespoons hot cream over it, and stir until smooth. If necessary, add enough of remaining cream to form a thick but pourable glaze.

ASSEMBLE THE ÉCLAIRS: Make 2 holes in bottom of each éclair at each end with a chopstick or similar instrument. Transfer mocha mousse filling to cleaned pastry bag fitted with ⅜-inch plain tip and pipe filling into éclairs through holes. Spread glaze over tops of éclairs with a small spatula. Refrigerate, uncovered, for 1 hour to set glaze.

COOK'S NOTE

- The éclairs, without the filling and glaze, can be made up to 1 day ahead, cooled completely, and kept in an airtight container at room temperature. Reheat them on a baking sheet in a 375°F oven to crisp them, about 5 minutes, then cool before filling.

Mocha Mousse Filling

MAKES ABOUT 1¼ CUPS
ACTIVE TIME: 15 MINUTES ■ START TO FINISH: 2¼ HOURS (INCLUDES CHILLING)

- 1 cup plus 2 tablespoons whole milk
- 3 tablespoons cornstarch
- Pinch of salt
- 3 large egg yolks
- 4½ tablespoons sugar
- 1 tablespoon instant espresso powder (see Sources)
- 1½ ounces good bittersweet chocolate (not unsweetened), finely chopped
- 1½ tablespoons unsalted butter, softened
- ¾ teaspoon vanilla extract
- ¼ cup very cold heavy cream

Whisk together ¼ cup milk, cornstarch, salt, and yolks in a medium bowl until smooth. Combine sugar, espresso powder, and remaining ¾ cup plus 2 tablespoons milk in a 1-quart heavy saucepan and bring to a boil, stirring, over moderate heat. Add to yolk mixture in a slow stream, whisking. Return mixture to saucepan and bring to a boil, whisking constantly, then boil, whisking, for 1 minute. (Lumps may form, but vigorous whisking will smooth mixture.)

Transfer to a bowl and whisk in chocolate, butter, and vanilla until smooth. Cover surface of filling with wax paper and refrigerate until cold, about 2 hours.

Beat cream in a small bowl with an electric mixer at medium speed just until it holds soft peaks. Whisk one quarter of cream into mocha filling to lighten it, then whisk in remaining cream.

COOK'S NOTE

- The filling can be made up to 1 day ahead and refrigerated, covered.

Prune and Walnut Turnovers

MAKES 16 PASTRIES
ACTIVE TIME: 1 HOUR ■ START TO FINISH: 2½ HOURS
(INCLUDES CHILLING DOUGH)

■ These will surprise you. Toasted nuts and prunes are ground until they become a smooth, intensely flavorful filling sparked by a hint of sherry. Wrapped inside the cream cheese pastry, it tastes like candy. These turnovers, which were brought to *Gourmet* by contributor Tatyana McWilliams, are wonderful embellished with a scoop of Prune Armagnac Ice Cream (page 858). ■

FOR DOUGH

- 2 sticks (½ pound) cold unsalted butter, cut into tablespoons
- 1 (8-ounce) package cold cream cheese, quartered
- ¼ cup sugar
- ¾ teaspoon salt
- 2 cups all-purpose flour
- 1 large egg yolk beaten with 1 tablespoon water, for egg wash

FOR FILLING

- ¾ cup (about 3 ounces) walnuts, toasted (see Tips, page 938)
- 1 cup (6 ounces) pitted prunes
- ¼ cup sugar
- ⅛ teaspoon ground cinnamon
- 1 tablespoon cream sherry or water

MAKE THE DOUGH: Combine butter, cream cheese, sugar, salt, and flour in a food processor and pulse just until a dough forms. Do not overwork, or pastry will be tough.

Turn dough out onto a lightly floured surface and divide into 6 portions. With heel of your hand, smear each portion once or twice in a forward motion to help distribute fat. Gather dough together, with a pastry scraper if you have one, and divide into quarters. Form each piece into a ball, then flatten each into a 4-inch disk. Wrap each disk in plastic wrap and refrigerate until firm, at least 1 hour.

MAKE THE FILLING: Combine walnuts, prunes, sugar, cinnamon, and sherry in cleaned food processor and pulse until nuts are finely chopped and filling becomes a thick paste.

FORM AND BAKE THE TURNOVERS: Put a rack in middle of oven and preheat oven to 375°F. Butter two large baking sheets.

Roll out 1 disk of dough (keep remaining dough chilled) on a lightly floured surface with a lightly floured rolling pin into a 9-inch square. Cut into 4 squares. Roll 1 tablespoon filling into a 2-inch-long log and lay diagonally across center of 1 dough square. Brush some egg wash along edges of dough, then fold dough over filling, forming a triangle. Pinch edges to seal. Make more turnovers in same manner with remaining dough and filling, arranging turnovers 1 inch apart on baking sheets.

Lightly brush tops of turnovers with egg wash. Cut 3 small steam vents in top of each turnover with a small sharp knife. Bake, in batches, until turnovers are golden, 15 to 20 minutes per batch. Transfer turnovers to rack to cool.

COOK'S NOTES

- ■ The dough can be refrigerated for up to 1 day.
- ■ The filling can be made up to 4 days ahead and refrigerated, covered.
- ■ The unbaked turnovers (without the egg-wash glaze) can be frozen, wrapped well in plastic wrap, for up to 2 weeks. Unwrap, thaw, and brush with egg wash before baking.

Quince, Apple, and Almond Jalousie

SERVES 6
ACTIVE TIME: 1¼ HOURS ■ START TO FINISH: 5½ HOURS
(INCLUDES MAKING DOUGH)

■ The name for this flaky pastry comes from the French term for a Venetian blind, which, like the dessert, has slits through which one can peek. The quinces give off a floral and citrusy perfume while cooking, which mingles with the mellow essence of the almonds. Make this in the fall, when quinces are in season and apples are at their best. You can find quinces at specialty produce markets, farmers markets, and some supermarkets. ■

- 2 medium quinces (about 1 pound total)
- 2½ cups water

1 cup plus 2 tablespoons sugar
2 Golden Delicious apples
½ cup (2 ounces) sliced almonds, toasted (see Tips, page 938)
⅛ teaspoon almond extract
Frozen Butter Pastry Dough (recipe follows)
1 large egg lightly beaten with 1 teaspoon water, for egg wash

ACCOMPANIMENT: whipped cream

Peel, quarter, and core quinces. Cut each quarter lengthwise into 5 slices. Bring water and 1 cup sugar to a boil in a 3-quart heavy saucepan and stir until sugar is dissolved. Add quinces and simmer, covered, for 2¼ hours.

Meanwhile, when mixture has simmered for 2 hours, peel, quarter, and core apples. Cut each quarter lengthwise into ¼-inch-thick wedges.

Stir apples into quince mixture and simmer, covered, until apples are crisp-tender, about 10 minutes. Remove pan from heat and stir in almonds and extract. Cool.

Drain quince mixture in a large sieve set over a bowl; reserve syrup. Transfer mixture to a bowl and stir in 3 tablespoons reserved syrup. Cover remaining syrup and set aside.

Roll each rectangle out on a lightly floured surface with a lightly floured rolling pin into a 12-by-8-inch rectangle. Transfer 1 rectangle to a floured large baking sheet. Spoon quince filling lengthwise down center, forming a 9-by-5-inch mound. Brush pastry around filling with some egg wash. Carefully drape remaining pastry rectangle lengthwise over filling and press gently to seal. Trim edges of pastry with a large sharp knife to make a 10-by-6-inch rectangle. Crimp edges, then make a decorative pattern of about 8 crosswise slits in pastry, exposing filling. Chill jalousie, loosely covered, for 30 minutes. Cover and refrigerate remaining egg wash.

Put a rack in middle of oven and preheat oven to 425°F.

Brush pastry evenly with egg wash and sprinkle with remaining 2 tablespoons sugar. Bake until deep golden, about 30 minutes. Cool on pan on a rack.

Serve jalousie warm or at room temperature, with reserved syrup and whipped cream.

COOK'S NOTE

- The filling can be made up to 3 days ahead and refrigerated, covered.

Frozen Butter Pastry Dough

MAKES ENOUGH FOR A 10-BY-6-INCH JALOUSIE OR A DOUBLE-CRUST 9-INCH PIE
ACTIVE TIME: 15 MINUTES ■ START FINISH: 2¾ HOURS (INCLUDES CHILLING)

■ Soft cake flour and plenty of icy cold butter are the secrets to the tenderest all-butter pastry. Handle it as little as you can; if you have a marble pastry board that you can chill in the refrigerator, all the better. ■

2¼ cups cake flour (not self-rising)
¼ teaspoon salt
2 sticks (½ pound) unsalted butter, frozen
½ cup plus 1–2 tablespoons ice water

Sift together flour and salt into a chilled large metal bowl. Set a grater in bowl and coarsely grate frozen butter into flour, gently lifting and tossing flour to coat butter. Refrigerate for 20 minutes.

Drizzle ½ cup ice water evenly over flour mixture and gently stir with a fork until just incorporated. Gently squeeze a small handful of dough: if it doesn't hold together, add more water ½ tablespoon at a time, stirring after each addition. Do not overwork dough, or pastry will be tough.

Turn dough out onto a lightly floured surface and divide into 8 portions. With heel of your hand, smear each portion once in a forward motion to help distribute fat. Gather dough together, with a pastry scraper if you have one, and divide in half. If making jalousie, form each piece into a 6-by-4-inch rectangle. Or, for a pie, form each piece into a ball, then flatten into a 5-inch disk. (Dough will not be smooth.) Wrap each piece in plastic wrap and refrigerate until firm, at least 2 hours.

COOK'S NOTE

- The dough can be refrigerated for up to 2 days.

Babas au Rhum

SERVES 8

ACTIVE TIME: 1¼ HOURS ■ START TO FINISH: 4¼ HOURS (INCLUDES RISING TIME)

■ Legend holds that this cake was invented by the eighteenth-century Polish king Stanislaw Leszczynski, who named it for his favorite literary hero, Ali Baba, from *A Thousand and One Nights*. The recipe has changed in every country and region that has laid claim to it, from Italy to Alsace, but it's always made with a yeast dough that is exceptionally wet and difficult to work with. This version, however—one of the first food-processor recipes to appear in the pages of *Gourmet*—is much easier. Baked in individual molds, the warm, light-textured cakes are dipped into a rum syrup, which keeps them flavorful and moist. ■

FOR BABAS

- 4 tablespoons warm whole milk (105°–110°F)
- 1⅛ teaspoons active dry yeast (from a ¼-ounce package)
- 1 tablespoon granulated sugar, plus a pinch
- 1 cup plus 1 tablespoon all-purpose flour
- 2 large eggs
- ⅜ teaspoon salt
- ¾ stick (6 tablespoons) unsalted butter, cut into tablespoons and softened

FOR RUM SYRUP

- ¾ cup granulated sugar
- 1½ cups water
- ¾ cup dark rum

FOR GLAZE

- ½ cup apricot jam
- 2 tablespoons dark rum

FOR RUM CREAM

- ¾ cup very cold heavy cream
- 3 tablespoons confectioners' sugar
- 1½ tablespoons dark rum

SPECIAL EQUIPMENT: eight 4-ounce baba au rhum molds (preferably nonstick; see Sources); a pastry bag fitted with a ½-inch plain tip

MAKE THE BABAS: Stir together 3 tablespoons warm milk, yeast, and pinch of sugar in a small bowl and let stand until foamy, about 5 minutes. (If mixture doesn't foam, discard and start over with new yeast.)

Stir 3 tablespoons flour into yeast mixture. Cover bowl with plastic wrap and let this sponge stand in a warm draft-free place until doubled in volume, 45 minutes to 1 hour.

Transfer sponge to a food processor, add eggs, remaining 1 tablespoon sugar, salt, remaining ¾ cup plus 2 tablespoons flour, and remaining 1 tablespoon milk, and blend until a very sticky dough forms, about 2 minutes. Add butter and pulse several times until incorporated.

Transfer dough to a lightly buttered bowl. Cover with plastic wrap and let rise in a warm draft-free place until doubled in volume, 45 minutes to 1 hour.

Lightly butter baba molds and put on a baking sheet. Stir down dough, then transfer to pastry bag. Pipe dough into molds, filling them one-third full. Let babas rise, loosely covered with plastic wrap, until dough reaches tops of molds, 30 to 45 minutes.

Put a rack in middle of oven and preheat oven to 450°F.

Put babas, on baking sheet, in oven and reduce temperature to 425°F. Bake until well browned, 12 to 14 minutes. Immediately unmold onto a rack. Cool for 20 minutes.

MEANWHILE, MAKE THE RUM SYRUP: Combine sugar and water in a 1- to 1½-quart heavy saucepan and bring to a simmer over moderate heat, stirring until sugar is dissolved. Simmer for 10 minutes. Remove from heat and stir in rum.

SOAK THE BABAS: Set the rack of babas over a baking pan. Dip warm babas in syrup one at a time for 10 seconds, then stand upright on rack. Spoon remaining syrup over babas, spooning syrup that collects in pan back over babas until well moistened.

MAKE THE GLAZE: Melt jam with rum in a small saucepan over moderate heat, stirring, then simmer for 1 minute. Pour glaze through a fine-mesh sieve into a small bowl; discard solids.

Brush tops and sides of babas with glaze.

MAKE THE RUM CREAM: Beat together cream, confectioners' sugar, and rum in a medium bowl with an electric mixer until cream just holds soft peaks.

Serve babas topped with rum cream.

COOK'S NOTES

- The syrup can be made up to 2 days ahead and refrigerated, covered. Reheat before soaking the babas.
- The babas can be baked, but not soaked, up to 1 week ahead and frozen, wrapped well in plastic wrap and foil. Thaw, still wrapped, at room temperature before soaking; you may need to soak frozen babas longer.

Baklava

MAKES ABOUT 24 PASTRIES
ACTIVE TIME: 1 HOUR ■ START TO FINISH: 14 HOURS (INCLUDES STANDING TIME)

Nearly every country in the eastern Mediterranean and the Middle East lays claim to this nut-filled phyllo pastry, and we've printed recipes from all of them. But this one, brought back from Crete by Doone Beal, a longtime contributor, is our favorite. It has the deep, spicy sweetness that you expect from good baklava, and the thick layer of chopped walnuts sandwiched between thin sheets of pastry. But the lemon mixed into the honey syrup adds just the right balancing note to all that sugar. Resist the urge to chop the nuts in a food processor, as that causes them to release more oil. Hand-chopping will produce a much lighter result. Baklava can be kept for a few days, and it doesn't need to be refrigerated, which means that it is a terrific make-ahead dessert.

FOR BAKLAVA

- 1 pound (4 cups) walnuts, finely chopped
- 1/3 cup sugar
- 1 teaspoon ground cinnamon
- 13 (17-by-12-inch) sheets phyllo (12 ounces), thawed if frozen
- 2 sticks (1/2 pound) unsalted butter, melted and cooled
- 24 whole cloves

FOR SYRUP

- 1/2 cup water
- 1 cup honey
- 1/2 cup sugar
- 1 tablespoon fresh lemon juice

SPECIAL EQUIPMENT: paper cupcake liners (optional)

MAKE THE BAKLAVA: Put a rack in middle of oven and preheat oven to 375°F.

Stir together walnuts, sugar, and cinnamon in a bowl.

Cut phyllo sheets crosswise in half with kitchen shears. Stack phyllo halves between two sheets of plastic wrap and cover with a kitchen towel. Lay 1 sheet on a work surface, keeping remaining sheets covered, and brush with some butter. Put sheet in bottom of a 13-by-9-inch metal baking pan. Top with 5 more sheets, buttering each one. Sprinkle 1/2 cup nut mixture over phyllo. Top with 2 more phyllo sheets, buttering them and arranging them so that nut mixture is completely covered. Repeat layering, topping each 1/2 cup nut mixture with 2 phyllo sheets, until all nut mixture is used. Top baklava with remaining phyllo sheets, buttering each of them and covering top evenly.

With a sharp knife, using a ruler as a guide, make 4 lengthwise cuts 1 3/4 inches apart to divide baklava into 5 strips. Make diagonal cuts 1 1/2 inches apart to divide baklava into about 24 diamonds (there will be irregular pieces at ends). Leaving white milky liquid in pan, pour remaining butter evenly over top. Press a clove into center of each diamond.

Put baklava in oven, reduce oven temperature to 325°F, and bake until golden, about 1 hour.

MEANWHILE, MAKE THE SYRUP: Combine all ingredients in a small saucepan and bring to a boil, stirring until sugar is dissolved. Reduce heat and simmer syrup until reduced to about 1 1/2 cups, about 5 minutes. Remove from heat and keep warm.

Pour warm syrup over hot baklava. Cool on a rack, then cover and let stand at room temperature for at least 12 hours to allow flavors to develop.

Serve baklava in paper cupcake liners, if desired.

COOK'S NOTE

- The baklava can be kept, covered, at room temperature for up to 5 days.

Roasted Apple Strudels

MAKES TWO 12-INCH STRUDELS; SERVES 12
ACTIVE TIME: 1½ HOURS ■ START TO FINISH: 4 HOURS

■ This is it: the original Viennese apple strudel recipe. You'll need to clear a table that's at least thirty-six inches square, remove all rings, bracelets, and watches, and be prepared to keep moving in order to shape a lump of dough into a sheet that's almost as thin as phyllo but slightly more substantial. You don't use a rolling pin, because you're stretching, not pressing, the dough. Using bread flour instead of all-purpose will give the dough more structure. This is a time-consuming project, but it's lots of fun, and the result is smooth, light, elastic, and entirely distinct from the phyllo dough that is often used as a substitute. ■

FOR FILLING

- 4 pounds Gala apples (9–10), peeled, cored, and cut into ¾-inch pieces
- ½ stick (4 tablespoons) unsalted butter, melted
- ½ cup granulated sugar
- 1 teaspoon finely grated lemon zest
- ¾ teaspoon ground cinnamon
- ¼ teaspoon salt
- 1 cup (5 ounces) golden raisins
- 1 tablespoon sweet white wine, such as ice wine or Tokay (optional)
- ½ cup (2 ounces) walnuts
- ⅓ cup fine fresh bread crumbs

FOR DOUGH

- 2 cups bread flour
- 1 tablespoon granulated sugar
- ½ teaspoon salt
- 1¼ sticks (10 tablespoons) unsalted butter, melted
- 1 large egg yolk
- ¾ cup lukewarm water
- About ½ cup all-purpose flour for dusting
- ¼ cup confectioners' sugar

SPECIAL EQUIPMENT: a stand mixer with a paddle attachment; parchment paper; a 36-inch round or square work table; a cotton sheet or tablecloth large enough to hang over edges of table

MAKE THE FILLING: Put a rack in middle of oven and preheat oven to 400°F.

Toss apples with butter, ¼ cup sugar, zest, ½ teaspoon cinnamon, and salt on a baking sheet with sides until well coated, then spread apples out. Roast, stirring occasionally, until apples are very tender and any liquid they release has evaporated, about 1¼ hours.

Transfer to a bowl and stir in raisins and wine (if using), then cool, stirring occasionally. Reduce oven temperature to 375°F.

MEANWHILE, MAKE THE DOUGH: Stir together bread flour, granulated sugar, and salt in bowl of mixer, then make a well in center and add 2 tablespoons butter, yolk, and water. Mix at medium-low speed with paddle until dough becomes silky and elastic, then forms a soft sticky ball and comes away from sides of bowl, 8 to 10 minutes.

Turn dough out onto a lightly floured surface and form into a ball. Lightly brush with some butter and let stand, covered with an inverted bowl, for 40 minutes.

STRETCH THE DOUGH: Line a baking sheet with sides with parchment paper.

Cover work table with sheet and rub all-purpose flour into it (it isn't necessary to flour overhanging edges of cloth). Put dough in center of table and stretch it into a 12-inch round with your fingers. Using floured backs of your wrists and hands, reach under dough and begin gently stretching and thinning dough from center out to edges, moving around table as you work and intermittently stretching thicker edges slightly. Gradually stretch dough paper-thin, into at least a 36-inch square (it will hang over edges of table), letting it rest for a few minutes whenever it resists stretching and occasionally reflouring hands; this will take about 20 minutes. (Try not to make any holes in the dough, but if you do, cut off thick edge from overhang and use it to patch them.) Let dough dry for 5 minutes.

ASSEMBLE THE STRUDELS: Combine walnuts, bread crumbs, remaining ¼ cup sugar, and remaining ¼ teaspoon cinnamon in a food processor and process until nuts are finely chopped.

Very gently brush dough with ⅓ cup butter and sprinkle evenly with walnut mixture. Mound apple filling in two 11-by-3-inch strips along side of dough closest to you, leaving a 3-inch space between mounds and 4-inch borders at sides and bottom. Fold side borders over filling and, holding sheet tautly to help you, roll up strudel, starting with bottom flap. Cut strudel into 2 pieces through center gap in filling and fold edges under strudels.

With a long metal spatula, transfer strudels to baking sheet, arranging them about 3 inches apart. Brush with remaining butter and dust generously with confectioners' sugar. Cut 3 or 4 steam vents in top of each strudel.

Bake strudels until golden, 40 to 45 minutes. Cool for 10 minutes on sheet on a rack, then transfer with spatula to rack and cool to warm or room temperature.

Cut strudels diagonally into 2-inch-thick slices with a serrated knife.

COOK'S NOTES

- The apple filling can be made up to 1 day ahead and refrigerated, covered. Bring to room temperature before proceeding.
- The strudels are best eaten the same day they're made, but they can be baked up to 1 day ahead and kept, covered, at room temperature. Reheat in a 350°F oven for 15 minutes.

FRUIT DESSERTS

Imagine this: You're in an orchard, surrounded by ripe peaches, whose scent hangs heavy in the air. You reach up, and a fuzzy globe falls into your hand. You take a bite, and the sweet, musky perfume fills your nostrils just as the soft flesh fills your mouth and a rush of peach juice spills down your throat. There is nothing to compare with the taste of fruit at its moment of ripe perfection. And when you are lucky enough to find it, you don't need to do a single thing but eat it just as it is.

These days, however, much of our fruit is not what it once was. Refrigeration, transportation, and science have all taken their toll. Thanks to them, we can now get almost anything we want at any time of the year, and while everyone agrees that a winter peach, picked hard and flown halfway round the world, bears no resemblance to a sun-warmed one that falls from the tree, we've been willing to accept that as the price of instant gratification.

At *Gourmet* we make every effort to eat fruit that is locally grown and served in its true season. In the summer we love to pile deep red strawberries on cream biscuits, add a few billows of whipped cream,

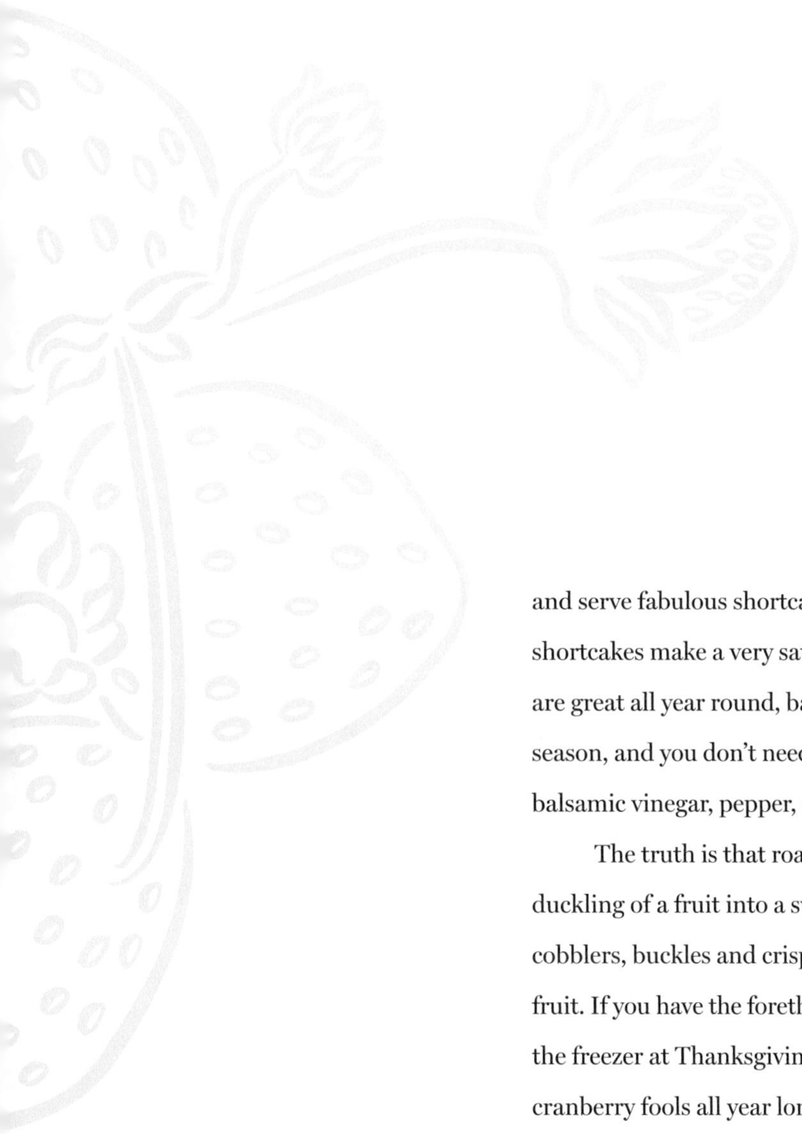

and serve fabulous shortcakes. In the middle of winter, orange shortcakes make a very satisfying substitute. Grapes with mascarpone are great all year round, bananas Foster are sophisticated in any season, and you don't need perfect pears to make roasted pears with balsamic vinegar, pepper, and honey taste really wonderful.

The truth is that roasting or baking can often turn an ugly duckling of a fruit into a swan. In this chapter, you'll find crumbles and cobblers, buckles and crisps. Almost all of them work well with frozen fruit. If you have the forethought to throw a few bags of cranberries into the freezer at Thanksgiving, you can make beautiful (and surprising) cranberry fools all year long.

We suggest that you support your local farmers and celebrate the produce they offer. Plenty of recipes here will showcase the incredible flavors of those fruits. But when the fields are bare, don't despair; we also have dozens of ideas to keep you eating fruit all through the slow season.

Baked Apples

SERVES 8

ACTIVE TIME: 15 MINUTES ■ START TO FINISH: 1½ HOURS

■ Nothing is simpler than baking a tart, crisp apple. We've topped this one with a dollop of crème fraîche and brandy sauce. ■

- 3 tablespoons cider vinegar
- 1 cup apple juice
- 3 tablespoons unsalted butter, cut into pieces
- ½ cup sugar
- 8 Gala or Golden Delicious apples
- 3 tablespoons brandy
- ½ cup crème fraîche

Put a rack in middle of oven and preheat oven to 350°F.

Combine vinegar, juice, butter, and sugar in a 13-by-9-inch baking dish. Cut off top ¾ inch of apples to make lids; set aside. Scoop out cores with a melon ball cutter, without cutting through bottoms, or use an apple corer, and replace lids. Put apples in baking dish and cover with foil.

Bake until apples are very tender but still intact, 1 to 1¼ hours.

Transfer apples to plates. Pour pan juices into a small saucepan, add brandy, and boil until reduced to about 1 cup. Set lids askew and fill apples with crème fraîche. Serve with sauce.

Baked Sliced Apples

SERVES 4

ACTIVE TIME: 25 MINUTES ■ START TO FINISH: 1½ HOURS

■ This one is all about kitchen chemistry. The apples are sliced and then put back together before baking; when served, anchored by a stick of cinnamon, they not only look different from ordinary baked apples, they taste different too. Baked whole, an apple becomes soft; sliced, it maintains its textural integrity. ■

- 4 large McIntosh apples
- 2 tablespoons fresh lemon juice
- ¼ cup packed light brown sugar
- 3 tablespoons unsalted butter, cut into bits
- 2 tablespoons light rum
- 4 (3-inch) cinnamon sticks

OPTIONAL GARNISH: organic apple or mint leaves

ACCOMPANIMENT: Calvados-flavored whipped cream (see Cook's Note)

Put a rack in middle of oven and preheat oven to 450°F.

Peel and core apples. Cut each one crosswise into ¼-inch-thick slices, keeping slices together, then reassemble slices to form whole apple. Brush with lemon juice. Put apples in a 9-inch glass pie plate and divide 2 tablespoons brown sugar, 2 tablespoons butter, and 1 tablespoon rum evenly among cavities. Sprinkle with remaining 2 tablespoons brown sugar, 1 tablespoon butter, and 1 tablespoon rum.

Bake apples, basting frequently with pan juices, for 25 minutes. Reduce oven temperature to 350°F, insert cinnamon sticks into cavities, and bake, basting frequently, until apples are tender and well browned and juices are thick and syrupy, about 20 minutes more.

Arrange apples on plates and spoon syrup over them. Garnish with apple or mint leaves, if desired, and serve with Calvados whipped cream.

COOK'S NOTE

■ To make Calvados-flavored whipped cream, beat 1 cup very cold heavy cream with 1 tablespoon confectioners' sugar until cream just holds soft peaks, then beat in 1½ tablespoons Calvados.

Bananas Foster

SERVES 4

ACTIVE TIME: 15 MINUTES ■ START TO FINISH: 15 MINUTES

■ New Orleans gave us, among other things, Cajun spice, jazz, zydeco, and Brennan's Restaurant, where this luscious ode to the banana was invented in 1951 in honor of Richard Foster, a patron and good friend of the owner, Owen Edward Brennan. Flambéing is not as hard—or scary—as it might seem: tilt the pan away from you and let the flames simmer down, but then carefully swirl the rum to keep them going. They will eventually die out, but you should allow them to burn for a couple of minutes to caramelize the banana liqueur, rum, sugar, and butter. ■

- 3 tablespoons unsalted butter
- 3/4 cup packed brown sugar
- Rounded 1/4 teaspoon ground cinnamon
- Scant 3 tablespoons banana liqueur
- 4 bananas, peeled, cut lengthwise in half, and halved crosswise
- 2 3/4 tablespoons dark rum
- 4 scoops vanilla ice cream

Melt butter in a 12-inch heavy skillet over moderate heat. Stir in sugar, cinnamon, and banana liqueur and cook for 3 minutes, stirring until sugar is dissolved. Place bananas in sauce and cook until soft and slightly browned, 3 to 4 minutes. Pour rum on top; do not stir into sauce. Allow rum to heat, then tilt pan and carefully ignite sauce with a match. Let sauce flame, swirling skillet to prolong flaming, until it dies out, 1 to 2 minutes. Remove from heat.

Place a scoop of ice cream in each of four dessert dishes. Lift bananas carefully out of skillet and place 4 pieces over each scoop of ice cream. Spoon hot sauce from pan over top. Serve immediately.

COOK'S NOTE

■ We like this with a squeeze of fresh lime to balance the sweetness.

Strawberries with Balsamic Vinegar

SERVES 4

ACTIVE TIME: 10 MINUTES ■ START TO FINISH: 40 MINUTES

■ Although this may sound strange, it is a classic in Modena, the home of *aceto balsamico.* The recipe calls for the best and oldest balsamic vinegar you can find, the kind that has been reduced over time to a thick, al-

most syrupy liquid imbued with the flavor of the many different wooden barrels in which it has aged. The vinegar alters the taste of the strawberries, emphasizing their sweetness and coaxing forth their elusive tartness as well. This recipe, which was brought to us by the Italian cooking expert Faith Heller Willinger, deserves the best berries you can find. ■

- 2 1/2 pints strawberries (about 2 pounds), hulled and halved lengthwise, or quartered if large
- 2 tablespoons aged balsamic vinegar (preferably *aceto balsamico tradizionale;* see Sources)
- 1 tablespoon sugar
- 1/4 teaspoon freshly ground black pepper, or to taste

ACCOMPANIMENT: unsweetened whipped cream or crème fraîche

Toss strawberries with vinegar, sugar, and pepper in a large bowl. Let stand at room temperature, tossing occasionally, for 30 minutes.

Toss strawberries again and serve with whipped cream or crème fraîche.

Cranberry Fool

SERVES 4

ACTIVE TIME: 25 MINUTES ■ START TO FINISH: 45 MINUTES (INCLUDES CHILLING)

■ Culinarily speaking, a fool is a chilled dessert made with whipped cream or thick custard blended with stewed or puréed fruit—traditionally, gooseberries, rhubarb, or raspberries. It's English in origin; one of the first known recipes appeared in Hannah Glasse's *Art of Cookery* in 1747. This version makes use of tart cranberries and Grand Marnier—a proper counterpoint to the sweetness of the cream. ■

- 1½ cups cranberries, picked over and rinsed
- ⅔ cup sugar
- ⅓ cup water
- 2 tablespoons Grand Marnier or other orange-flavored liqueur
- ⅔ cup very cold heavy cream

Combine cranberries, sugar, and water in a 1-quart saucepan and bring to a boil, stirring occasionally. Reduce heat and simmer, covered, for 5 minutes.

Transfer cranberry mixture to a food processor or blender, add liqueur, and purée (use caution). Force purée through a fine-mesh sieve into a medium metal bowl (discard solids), then set bowl in a larger bowl of ice and cold water. Let purée stand, stirring occasionally, until just cool, about 5 minutes.

Transfer ½ cup of cranberry purée to a small bowl. Beat cream in a medium bowl with an electric mixer until it holds soft peaks. Stir one quarter of whipped cream into remaining purée (in medium bowl), then gently but thoroughly fold in remaining whipped cream. Fold in reserved purée just until marbled through cream mixture.

Spoon fool into four stemmed glasses. Refrigerate for 20 minutes or freeze for 10 minutes before serving.

Passion Fruit Fool

SERVES 8
ACTIVE TIME: 15 MINUTES ■ START TO FINISH: 1¼ HOURS (INCLUDES CHILLING)

■ We've shaken things up a bit in this traditional English dessert by using passion fruit. Exploding with tangy, complex flavor, it is our favorite tropical fruit, and it has become more widely available (and affordable) in the form of frozen fruit pulp. This fool is terrific with the Meringue Kisses on page 684; dunk the kisses into the fool for a dessert version of chips and dip. ■

- 1 (14-ounce) package unsweetened passion fruit (*maracuyá*) purée, such as Goya or Palmas brand, thawed but cold (about 1½ cups; see Sources)
- 1 cup sugar, or to taste
- 2½ cups very cold heavy cream

Whisk purée with ⅔ cup sugar in a small bowl until sugar is dissolved.

Beat cream with remaining ⅓ cup sugar in a large bowl with an electric mixer until it just holds stiff peaks. Gently but thoroughly fold sweetened purée into cream. Refrigerate for at least 1 hour.

COOK'S NOTE

- The fool is best the day it is made. Gently refold if the fruit juices begin to separate from the cream.

VARIATIONS

- RASPBERRY, BLACKBERRY, OR STRAWBERRY FOOL: Use 1 pound fresh or thawed frozen berries, puréed, or 1½ cups unsweetened fruit purée, strained. Reduce the sugar to ½ cup and add 1 tablespoon fresh lemon juice to the purée. Use 1½ cups heavy cream. Serves 6.
- GUANABANA (SOURSOP) OR MANGO FOOL: Use 1 (14-ounce) package unsweetened guanabana purée (see Sources) or mango purée (1½ cups), thawed, or 2 mangoes (1½ pounds total), peeled, seeded, and puréed. Reduce the sugar to ½ cup and add 1 to 2 tablespoons fresh lime juice (to taste) to the purée. Use ¾ cup heavy cream. Serves 4 to 6.

Baked Figs with Grand Marnier and Whipped Cream

SERVES 6
ACTIVE TIME: 10 MINUTES ■ START TO FINISH: 50 MINUTES

■ Figs have two seasons, one in late summer through early fall, and a brief one in late May to early June. That's fortunate, because it means you can make this elegant but very simple dessert four months out of the year. ■

- 12 firm but ripe figs
- ⅓ cup plus 2 tablespoons sugar
- ½ cup water
- 5 tablespoons Grand Marnier or other orange-flavored liqueur
- 1 cup very cold heavy cream

Put a rack in middle of oven and preheat oven to 300°F. Butter a 9- to 10-inch flameproof gratin dish or ovenproof skillet.

With a fork, prick bottom of each fig several times. Stand figs upright in gratin dish and sprinkle with 1/3 cup sugar, then add water to dish.

Bake figs, basting twice with pan juices, until tender, about 30 minutes. Transfer dish to stovetop, add 4 tablespoons (1/4 cup) Grand Marnier, and bring to a boil over moderately high heat. Remove from heat and carefully ignite pan juices with a match, then let flames subside. Transfer figs to a shallow serving bowl. Pan juices should be syrupy; if juices are too thin, boil until syrupy and slightly thickened. Pour juices over figs.

Just before serving, beat cream, remaining 2 tablespoons sugar, and remaining 1 tablespoon liqueur in a medium bowl with an electric mixer until cream holds soft peaks. Serve figs warm or at room temperature, with cream.

Sambuca-Poached Figs with Ricotta and Pine Nuts

SERVES 4

ACTIVE TIME: 20 MINUTES ■ START TO FINISH: 25 MINUTES

■ The softness of gently poached figs, the crunch of pine nuts, and the rich creaminess of ricotta combine in this Italian classic. While sambuca is traditional, you can substitute another anise-flavored liqueur. Serve this dish as a fruit and cheese course all in one. ■

- 1 tablespoon olive oil
- 1/4 cup pine nuts
- Salt
- 3/4 cup sambuca
- 2 tablespoons sugar
- 12 firm but ripe purple figs
- 3/4 cup whole-milk ricotta, preferably fresh
- Freshly ground black pepper

Heat oil in a small skillet over moderately high heat until hot but not smoking. Add pine nuts and cook, stirring, until golden, about 2 minutes. Transfer to paper towels to drain, and season with salt.

Combine sambuca and sugar in a saucepan just large enough to hold figs upright and bring to a simmer, stirring until sugar is dissolved. Cut a very thin slice from bottom of each fig so it stands level and set figs in saucepan (figs will not be covered by liquid). Cover and poach at a bare simmer for 5 minutes. Cool figs slightly in liquid.

Season ricotta with salt and pepper. Mound ricotta on plates, set figs alongside, and drizzle some of poaching liquid over figs. Sprinkle with pine nuts.

Broiled Grapes in Mascarpone

SERVES 4

ACTIVE TIME: 10 MINUTES ■ START TO FINISH: 15 MINUTES

■ Grapes smothered in sour cream, topped with brown sugar, and baked were a big hit in the 1940s, when they were considered exceptionally sophisticated. We've improved on the recipe by using mascarpone, which takes heat much better than sour cream, and turbinado sugar, which caramelizes in a flash. The result is a dessert that is a bit like crème brûlée with a sweet-and-sour flavor and the surprise of hidden fruit. ■

- 3/4 pound small seedless red grapes, stemmed, halved if large (2 cups)
- 3/4 cup mascarpone
- 2 tablespoons Armagnac or Cognac
- 1/2 teaspoon vanilla extract
- 8 teaspoons turbinado sugar, such as Sugar in the Raw

SPECIAL EQUIPMENT: four 4-ounce gratin dishes or other shallow flameproof dishes

Preheat broiler. Divide grapes among gratin dishes, spreading them in a single layer. Whisk together mascarpone, Armagnac, and vanilla in a small bowl. Spoon over grapes, then gently spread to cover grapes. Sprinkle each dish with 2 teaspoons sugar.

Transfer dishes to a shallow baking pan and broil about 3 inches from heat until sugar melts and begins to caramelize, 2 to 3 minutes. (Watch carefully: sugar burns easily.) Cool for 5 minutes before serving.

Grapefruit Ambrosia

SERVES 4
ACTIVE TIME: 30 MINUTES ■ START TO FINISH: 45 MINUTES (INCLUDES CHILLING)

■ The festive southern dessert called ambrosia traditionally layers coconut and orange. We've added toasted pistachios, replaced the orange with grapefruit, and splashed in some bright red, tart Campari. The result is more refined than the original but retains its charm. ■

- 6 grapefruit, preferably 3 pink and 3 red
- 1 cup sweetened flaked coconut
- 2 tablespoons Campari
- 2 tablespoons sugar
- Pinch of salt
- ½ cup (2 ounces) salted shelled natural pistachios (not dyed red), toasted (see Tips, page 938) and coarsely chopped

With a sharp paring knife, cut peel and white pith from grapefruit, then cut segments free from membranes. Halve grapefruit segments crosswise and transfer to a medium bowl. Stir coconut, Campari, sugar, and salt into grapefruit. Refrigerate for at least 15 minutes.

Just before serving, stir nuts into ambrosia.

COOK'S NOTE

■ The ambrosia (without the nuts) can be refrigerated for up to 4 hours.

Honeydew in Rosemary Syrup

SERVES 4
ACTIVE TIME: 15 MINUTES ■ START TO FINISH: 1¾ HOURS (INCLUDES CHILLING AND STANDING TIME)

■ Whole peppercorns and aromatic rosemary ensure that the syrup for these melon balls is anything but cloying. You can also make this with cantaloupe, Persian melon, or casaba. ■

- ½ cup water
- ½ cup dry white wine
- ½ cup sugar
- 1 (3-inch) strip orange zest
- 1½ teaspoons chopped fresh rosemary
- 1 teaspoon black peppercorns
- 1 (5-pound) honeydew melon
- ¼ cup fresh orange juice

OPTIONAL GARNISH: fresh rosemary sprigs
SPECIAL EQUIPMENT: a melon ball cutter

Combine water, wine, sugar, zest, rosemary, and peppercorns in a 2-quart saucepan and bring to a boil, stirring until sugar is dissolved. Reduce heat and simmer, stirring occasionally, for 4 minutes. Pour syrup through a fine-mesh sieve into a small bowl, pressing hard on solids; discard solids. Refrigerate syrup until cold, about 30 minutes. Meanwhile, cut melon into balls with cutter and refrigerate.

Stir orange juice into syrup. Toss melon balls with syrup in a serving bowl and let stand for 1 hour at room temperature to allow flavors to develop.

Garnish with rosemary sprigs, if desired.

COOK'S NOTE

■ The syrup can be made up to 1 day ahead; cover it once it is chilled.

Cantaloupe in Port Jelly

SERVES 4
ACTIVE TIME: 20 MINUTES ■ START TO FINISH: 7½ HOURS (INCLUDES CHILLING)

■ This alluring, grown-up take on Jell-O marries the deep garnet color and intense flavor of ruby port with the fruity sweetness of fresh cantaloupe. ■

- 1½ teaspoons unflavored gelatin (from one ¼-ounce package)
- ¾ cup water
- ¼ cup sugar
- ¾ cup ruby port
- 1½ teaspoons strained fresh lemon juice
- ¼ large cantaloupe, seeded and cut into ¼-inch-thick wedges, rind discarded

Sprinkle gelatin over water in a 2-quart saucepan and let stand for 1 minute to soften. Heat gelatin mixture over moderate heat, stirring, until gelatin is dissolved, about 1 minute. Add sugar and port, bring to a simmer, stirring, and simmer, stirring occasionally, for 3 minutes. Remove pan from heat and stir in lemon juice. Cool to room temperature, about 1 hour.

Cut enough cantaloupe wedges crosswise into 1/4-inch pieces to measure 1 cup (reserve remainder for another use).

Divide melon among four 8-ounce ramekins or dessert bowls and pour port gelatin over it. Refrigerate, covered, until jelly is set, at least 6 hours.

COOK'S NOTE

- The desserts can be refrigerated for up to 1 day.

Roasted Nectarines with Caramel Sauce

SERVES 6

ACTIVE TIME: 30 MINUTES ■ START TO FINISH: 50 MINUTES

■ We love this dessert with vanilla ice cream or a little whipped cream. Roasting some of the nectarines concentrates their flavor, and puréeing the others and adding them to the caramel sauce ensures that the dessert is not too sweet. ■

- 2 pounds nectarines (7–8), halved and pitted
- Pinch of salt
- 3/4 cup sugar
- 1/2 cup heavy cream
- 1 teaspoon fresh lemon juice

OPTIONAL GARNISH: raspberries and fresh mint sprigs

Put a rack in middle of oven and preheat oven to 375°F.

Put 12 nectarine halves cut sides down in a glass baking dish just large enough to hold them in one layer. Roast until softened, about 20 minutes.

Meanwhile, chop remaining nectarine halves. Cook in a small nonstick skillet over moderate heat, stirring frequently, until very soft, about 10 minutes. Transfer to a blender or food processor, add salt, and purée.

Melt sugar in a small heavy saucepan over moderate heat, stirring with a fork. Cook, swirling pan occasionally, until sugar becomes a golden caramel. Carefully but quickly stir in cream, nectarine purée, and lemon juice (caramel will harden and steam vigorously) with a wooden spoon and stir until sauce is smooth, about

PEACHES AND NECTARINES

Peaches and nectarines can be freely substituted for each other in recipes, but that doesn't mean they are twins. Although the two fruits resemble each other closely and have been consistently crossbred over the years, the nectarine is actually a subspecies of the peach (one differing gene makes peaches fuzzy and nectarines smooth-skinned). Nectarines, depending on the variety, usually have a sharper, clearer, more intense taste. According to Al and Rebecca Courchesne, of Frog Hollow Farm in Brentwood, California — producers of what are possibly the most delicious peaches and nectarines in the world — tannins in the nectarines' skin contribute to their zing; peaches have fewer tannins. The texture is subtly different as well: nectarines are usually firmer and meatier.

2 minutes. Remove from heat and cover to keep warm.

Put 2 roasted nectarine halves cut sides up in each of six small bowls. Top each serving with about 2 tablespoons caramel sauce. Garnish with raspberries and mint sprigs, if desired.

Fresh Orange Slices with Candied Zest and Pistachios

SERVES 4

ACTIVE TIME: 20 MINUTES ■ START TO FINISH: 45 MINUTES

■ Serve this dessert at the end of a Moroccan or Caribbean meal. Fresh-tasting, with just the right amount of sweetness and crunch, it's colorful and easy to prepare. ■

- 4 navel oranges
- 1/3 cup sugar
- 2/3 cup water
- 1/4 cup Grand Marnier or other orange-flavored liqueur
- 3 tablespoons shelled natural pistachios (not dyed red), chopped

Remove zest from 2 oranges in long, wide strips with a vegetable peeler. Remove any white pith from zest with a small knife and cut zest into matchsticks. Combine zest with water to cover in a small heavy saucepan, bring to a simmer, and simmer for 10 minutes. Drain in a sieve.

With a sharp paring knife, cut a slice from top and bottom of each orange to expose flesh. Stand each orange on a cutting board and cut away peel, with pith, in wide strips from top to bottom. Cut oranges crosswise into 1/4-inch-thick slices and arrange on four dessert plates.

Combine zest, sugar, and 2/3 cup water in small saucepan, bring to a simmer over moderately low heat, and simmer, uncovered, until zest is translucent and syrup is thickened, about 15 minutes. Add liqueur and simmer for 1 minute.

Using a slotted spoon, arrange candied zest decoratively on and around orange slices. Top with syrup and pistachios.

Caramelized Oranges

SERVES 6

ACTIVE TIME: 25 MINUTES ■ START TO FINISH: 35 MINUTES

■ Oranges and caramel sauce are a near-perfect combination, especially in winter. The nutty, sweet flavor of the warm caramel provides a deep contrast to the juicy citrus. ■

- 9 medium navel oranges
- 1/2 cup sugar
- 1/2 cup water
- 1 tablespoon unsalted butter

Squeeze enough juice from 3 oranges to measure 1 cup.

Combine sugar and water in a 1 1/2-quart heavy saucepan and bring to a boil over moderate heat, stirring until sugar is dissolved. Boil without stirring, washing down sides of pan with a pastry brush dipped in cold water to remove any sugar crystals, until caramel begins to turn golden brown around edges, 8 to 10 minutes. Tilt pan away from you and carefully add orange juice (caramel will harden and steam vigorously). Simmer, stirring, until caramel is completely dissolved, about 2 minutes. Remove from heat.

With a sharp paring knife, cut peel and white pith from remaining 6 oranges, then cut each orange crosswise into thirds.

Heat 1 teaspoon butter in a 12-inch nonstick skillet over moderately high heat until hot but not smoking. Add 6 orange slices and cook, turning once, until golden, 4 to 6 minutes total. Transfer to a plate. Cook remaining orange slices in remaining butter in same manner, wiping out skillet between batches if necessary.

Return all oranges slices to skillet, add caramel sauce, and cook over moderate heat until heated through, about 1 minute. Serve oranges with sauce.

Roasted Pears with Hazelnut Syrup and Candied Hazelnuts

SERVES 6

ACTIVE TIME: 35 MINUTES ■ START TO FINISH: 1¼ HOURS

■ This combination of sugar-dusted roasted pears and hazelnuts is simple to put together, and the syrup and nuts can be prepared up to two days ahead, making it a good choice for a dinner party (it can easily be doubled). Serve it with the cookies of your choice. ■

- 1 cup water
- 1¼ cups sugar
- ¾ cup (4 ounces) hazelnuts, toasted (see Tips, page 938), skinned, and coarsely chopped
- 1 tablespoon unsalted butter, cut into small pieces
- 6 firm but ripe Bosc pears with stems
- 3 tablespoons Cognac or other brandy
- 2 tablespoons fresh lemon juice, or to taste
- 1 teaspoon vanilla extract

Put a rack in middle of oven and preheat oven to 350°F. Lightly butter a 13-by-9-inch baking pan.

Combine water and 1 cup sugar in a 1- to 2-quart heavy saucepan and bring to a boil over moderately high heat, stirring until sugar is dissolved. Stir nuts into syrup and simmer for 1 minute. With a slotted spoon, transfer nuts to baking pan, spreading them out into one layer; transfer remaining syrup to a bowl and reserve.

Bake nuts until golden brown, about 15 minutes. Add butter to nuts, toss to coat and to separate nuts, and, with a spatula, transfer nuts to a plate to cool (they will crisp as they cool). Leave oven on.

Lightly butter a 12-by-2½-inch round casserole dish. Trim a very thin slice from bottom of each pear with a sharp knife so pears stand upright. Dip and roll each pear in reserved syrup to coat completely and transfer to casserole dish, standing pears upright. Sprinkle with remaining ¼ cup sugar. Add Cognac, lemon juice, and vanilla to remaining reserved syrup and pour down side of casserole.

Roast pears, uncovered, until bottoms are tender when pierced with a knife, about 30 minutes.

Arrange pears on a serving platter. Spoon syrup around them and sprinkle with candied nuts. Serve warm or at room temperature.

COOK'S NOTE

■ The nuts can be candied up to 2 days ahead and kept in an airtight container in a cool, dry place. Cover and refrigerate the sugar syrup.

Balsamic-Roasted Pears with Pepper and Honey

SERVES 4

ACTIVE TIME: 10 MINUTES ■ START TO FINISH: 40 MINUTES

■ Pears surrounded by chunks of cheese and served with a dish of honey are a very Italian ending to a meal. This recipe embellishes the idea by roasting the pears with vinegar to sharpen the flavor, setting them beside Manchego, a mild sheep's milk cheese, and drizzling honey across the top. A little black pepper adds sparkle. ■

- 2 tablespoons unsalted butter
- 2 firm but ripe Bosc pears, halved lengthwise and cored
- 3 tablespoons balsamic vinegar
- ¼ pound Manchego or mild fresh goat cheese, cut into 4 pieces, at room temperature
- ¼ cup honey
- Freshly ground black pepper

Put a rack in middle of oven and preheat oven to 400°F.

Put butter in an 8-inch square baking dish and melt in oven, about 3 minutes.

Arrange pears cut sides down in one layer in dish. Roast until tender, about 20 minutes.

Pour vinegar over pears and roast for 5 minutes more.

Transfer pears, cut sides down, to serving plates and spoon some of juices from baking dish over them. Arrange cheese next to pears, drizzle pears and cheese with honey, and sprinkle with pepper.

Asian Pears with Vanilla-Poached Kumquats

SERVES 6
ACTIVE TIME: 20 MINUTES ■ START TO FINISH: 2 1/2 HOURS (INCLUDES CHILLING)

■ The edgy, slightly bitter sweetness of the poached kumquats sets off the pears beautifully. This is the perfect close to any meal with Asian overtones. ■

- 1/2 cup water
- 3 tablespoons fresh lime juice
- 1/2 vanilla bean, halved lengthwise
- 1/2 cup sugar
- Pinch of salt
- 1/2 pound kumquats (about 20), ends trimmed, fruit cut into 1/3-inch-thick slices and seeded
- 4 large Asian pears, peeled, halved, cored, and cut lengthwise into 1/4-inch-thick slices

Combine water and lime juice in a small heavy saucepan. Scrape seeds from vanilla bean into pan, then add pod, sugar, and salt. Bring to a boil, stirring until sugar is dissolved. Reduce heat and simmer for 3 minutes. Add kumquats, cover, and simmer until they just begin to soften, 3 to 4 minutes.

Put pears in a heatproof bowl. Pour kumquats and syrup over pears and toss gently. Cool, then refrigerate, covered, for at least 2 hours.

COOK'S NOTE

■ The fruit can be refrigerated for up to 1 day.

PEARS

BOSC PEAR

ASIAN PEAR

There are two main types of pears, European and Asian. Most of the European types, such as Bosc, Bartlett, Comice, and Anjou, start out firm and ripen off the tree to a juicy, buttery softness. Bartlett and Comice are perhaps the best choices for eating out of hand, but we tend to cook more with Bosc, because its denser flesh seems to stand up better to heat. To ripen European pears, put them in a paper bag at room temperature.

Asian pears combine the familiar flavor and juiciness of a ripe Bartlett with the crisp crunch of an apple. They are meant to be eaten when ripe but firm and can be enjoyed right off the tree. Most of the Asian pears we see are grown in California's Central Valley, but a handful of farms on the East Coast also grow them. Although they will last at room temperature for about a week, they keep best in a paper bag in the refrigerator. Serve them chilled, when they are at their most refreshing. For the Asian Pears with Vanilla-Poached Kumquats, look for an extremely fragrant variety of Asian pear, such as the Shinseiki, which is crunchy, juicy, and aromatic, or the more popular, highly floral Twentieth Century.

Prosecco and Summer Fruit Terrine

SERVES 8

ACTIVE TIME: 15 MINUTES ■ START TO FINISH: 6¼ HOURS (INCLUDES CHILLING)

■ As cool and elegant as a Florentine paperweight, this terrine suspends fruit in a light aspic made of Prosecco, the Italian version of Champagne. It looks as refreshing as it tastes, making it the perfect dessert for a hot afternoon. Be sure to use a *frizzante* Prosecco rather than the still (*tranquillo*) style. ■

- 4 cups mixed fruit, such as berries, thinly sliced peeled peaches (see Tips, page 940), and halved seedless grapes
- 2¾ teaspoons unflavored gelatin (from two ¼-ounce envelopes)
- 2 cups Prosecco
- ½ cup sugar
- 2 teaspoons fresh lemon juice

Arrange fruit in a 1½-quart glass, ceramic, or nonstick terrine or loaf pan.

Sprinkle gelatin over ¼ cup Prosecco in a small bowl and let stand for 1 minute to soften.

Meanwhile, combine 1 cup Prosecco and sugar in a 1-quart saucepan and bring to a boil, stirring until sugar is dissolved. Remove from heat, add gelatin mixture, and stir until gelatin dissolves. Stir in remaining ¾ cup Prosecco and lemon juice, then transfer to a metal bowl set in a larger bowl of ice and cold water. Cool mixture, stirring occasionally, just to room temperature.

Slowly pour Prosecco mixture over fruit. Refrigerate, covered, until firm, at least 6 hours.

To unmold, dip pan in a larger pan of hot water for 3 to 5 seconds to loosen terrine. Invert a serving plate over terrine and invert terrine onto plate.

COOK'S NOTE

■ The terrine can be refrigerated for up to 3 days; unmold just before serving.

Grilled Tropical Fruit with Rum Sauce

SERVES 8

ACTIVE TIME: 1 HOUR ■ START TO FINISH: 1¼ HOURS

■ Grilling fruit just enough to heat it through enhances its inherent sweetness, deepens its flavor, and gives it a little smoky char. A sprinkling of chili powder adds a bit of heat, while a sweet rum sauce lends a final tropical touch. ■

FOR SAUCE

- ⅔ cup dark rum
- ¼ cup boiling water
- 1 teaspoon vanilla extract
- 2 cups sugar
- 1 tablespoon unsalted butter

FOR GRILLED FRUIT

- 1 firm but ripe mango
- 1 papaya, peeled, halved, and seeded
- ½ pineapple, peeled and cored
- 12 small firm but ripe finger bananas or 6 small regular bananas
- 1 tablespoon chili powder

ACCOMPANIMENT: vanilla ice cream

OPTIONAL GARNISH: toasted fresh coconut shavings or toasted sweetened flaked coconut (see Tips, page 939)

MAKE THE SAUCE: Stir together rum, boiling water, and vanilla in a small bowl. Cook sugar in a 3-quart heavy saucepan over moderately low heat, stirring slowly with a fork, until melted and pale golden. Continue to cook caramel without stirring, swirling pan, until deep golden. Remove pan from heat and carefully stir in rum mixture (caramel will harden and steam vigorously). Removing pan from flame should prevent rum from igniting; if it does ignite, simply allow flames to burn out on their own. Return sauce to heat and simmer, stirring, until smooth. Remove pan from heat and, when bubbling subsides, stir in butter. Cool to room temperature.

GRILL THE FRUIT: Prepare a charcoal or gas grill: If using a charcoal grill, open vents in bottom of grill, then light charcoal. Fire is medium-hot when you can hold your hand 5 inches above rack for just

3 to 4 seconds. If using a gas grill, preheat on high, covered, for 10 minutes, then reduce heat to moderate.

Peel mango, then stand it upright and cut a lengthwise slice from each broad side of fruit to remove flesh (be careful: peeled mango will be slippery); discard pit. Cut each papaya half lengthwise into thirds.

Stand pineapple upright and cut lengthwise into 1/2-inch-thick slices. Peel bananas and halve lengthwise. Sprinkle all fruit lightly on one side with chili powder.

Lightly oil grill rack. Grill fruit, uncovered, turning once, until grill marks form on both sides, 2 minutes total. Transfer to a cutting board and slice into serving pieces.

To serve, put 3 scoops ice cream into each of eight dishes and top with grilled fruit and sauce. Garnish with coconut, if desired.

COOK'S NOTE

- The rum sauce can be made up to 2 days ahead and refrigerated, covered. If the cold sauce is too thick, bring to room temperature before serving.

Apple Crisp

SERVES 8 TO 10
ACTIVE TIME: 30 MINUTES ■ START TO FINISH: 1 3/4 HOURS

■ When the chef Claire Archibald was at Café Azul, in Portland, Oregon, she created this recipe, using Yellow Transparent apples because they have great flavor and do not turn into mush as they bake. We've substituted Macouns, Fujis, and Jonagolds, and the result is a butter-rich, nutty crisp that is quite simply the finest we've ever had. ■

FOR TOPPING

- 2 1/3 cups all-purpose flour
- 3/4 cup packed dark brown sugar
- 1/4 cup granulated sugar
- 3/8 teaspoon ground cinnamon
- 3/8 teaspoon salt
- 2 sticks (1/2 pound) unsalted butter, cut into tablespoons, softened
- 1 1/3 cups (5 ounces) pecans, toasted (see Tips, page 938) and chopped

FOR FILLING

- 1/2 cup granulated sugar
- 1/2 teaspoon ground cinnamon
- 5 pounds Macoun, Fuji, or Jonagold apples
- 2 tablespoons fresh lemon juice
- Finely grated zest of 1 navel orange

Put a rack in middle of oven and preheat oven to 375°F. Lightly butter a shallow 3 1/2- to 4-quart baking dish.

MAKE THE TOPPING: Combine flour, sugars, cinnamon, and salt in a food processor and blend until well combined. Add butter and pulse until mixture forms large clumps. Transfer to a bowl and work in pecans with your fingertips.

MAKE THE FILLING: Whisk together sugar and cinnamon in a large bowl. Peel, quarter, and core apples, then cut into 1/2-inch-thick slices. Add apples, lemon juice, and orange zest to sugar mixture and toss until well combined.

ASSEMBLE AND BAKE THE CRISP: Spread apples in buttered baking dish. Crumble topping evenly over them. Bake until topping is golden brown, about 1 hour. Cool to warm.

Strawberry Rhubarb Crumble

SERVES 8
ACTIVE TIME: 30 MINUTES ■ START TO FINISH: 1 1/2 HOURS

■ Here is a delightfully simple option for strawberry-rhubarb pie lovers. Old-fashioned rolled oats lend a homey and decidedly nutty flavor to the sharp edge of the fruit. ■

FOR FILLING

- 2 pounds strawberries, hulled and halved (6 cups)
- 1 1/2 pounds rhubarb stalks, trimmed and cut into 1/2-inch-thick slices (4 1/2 cups)
- 1–1 1/4 cups granulated sugar, depending on sweetness of strawberries
- 3 tablespoons cornstarch

1 tablespoon fresh lemon juice
1/8 teaspoon salt

FOR TOPPING

1 1/4 cups old-fashioned rolled oats
3/4 cup all-purpose flour
3/4 cup packed light brown sugar
1/4 teaspoon salt
1 1/2 sticks (12 tablespoons) unsalted butter, cut into 1/2-inch pieces, slightly softened

Put a rack in middle of oven and preheat oven to 425°F.

MAKE THE FILLING: Gently stir together all ingredients in a large bowl. Spoon mixture into a shallow 3-quart baking dish.

MAKE THE TOPPING: Stir together oats, flour, brown sugar, and salt in a medium bowl. Blend in butter with your fingertips until mixture forms small clumps.

ASSEMBLE AND BAKE THE CRUMBLE: Crumble topping evenly over filling. Bake until fruit is bubbling and topping is golden, 40 to 50 minutes. Cool slightly on a rack and serve warm.

Strawberry Shortcake

SERVES 8
ACTIVE TIME: 20 MINUTES ■ START TO FINISH: 1 3/4 HOURS (INCLUDES MAKING BISCUITS)

■ To honor this American classic, you really should make it only during strawberry season: nothing compares to freshly picked berries. Mashing them just enough to bring out their juice without crushing them into a pulp is one of the secrets to this recipe, which came from the father of our senior food editor Kemp Minifie. Brushing the biscuits with cream before baking gives them a sheen. ■

3 pints strawberries (2 1/4 pounds), hulled and quartered
1/3 cup granulated sugar, or to taste
1 cup very cold heavy cream
1/3 cup sour cream
1 1/2 tablespoons confectioners' sugar, or to taste
1/2–1 teaspoon vanilla extract (to taste)
8 Cream Biscuits (recipe follows)

Gently mash strawberries with granulated sugar in a large bowl with a potato masher just until berries release their juices, being careful not to crush them to

Rhubarb

Greeted with joy at the end of winter, these beautiful red stalks are a vegetable but are almost always treated like a fruit. Although rhubarb is very tart, think of this as an asset rather than a liability, and refrain from adding too much sugar. Like lemon, rhubarb is best when slightly sour. Field-grown stalks are firmer and more intensely flavored than the hothouse kinds, which come to market earlier. No matter where it's grown, rhubarb is usually sold without the leaves, which contain toxic levels of oxalic acid and should never be eaten.

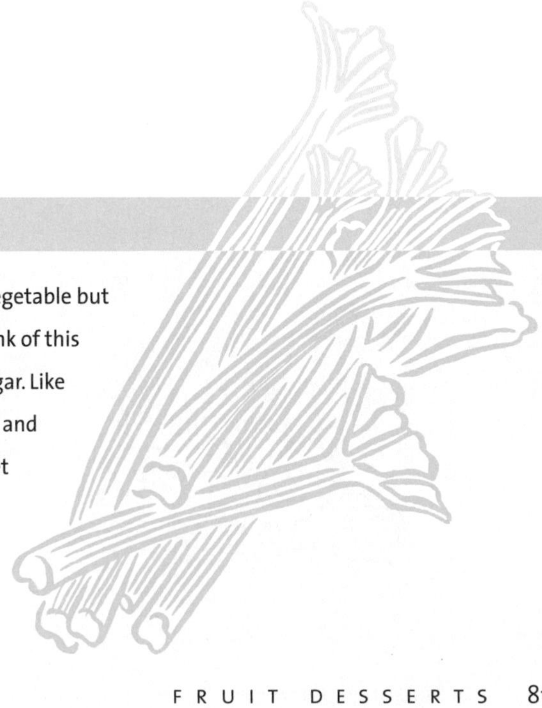

a pulp. Let stand at room temperature, stirring occasionally, for 1 hour.

Beat heavy cream, sour cream, and confectioners' sugar in a medium bowl with an electric mixer until cream holds soft peaks. Beat in vanilla.

Split biscuits with a fork and arrange bottom halves on eight plates. Spoon strawberry mixture over them. Top with some whipped cream and arrange biscuit tops on cream. Serve remaining cream on the side.

Cream Biscuits

MAKES 8 BISCUITS
ACTIVE TIME: 10 MINUTES ■ START TO FINISH: 45 MINUTES

■ Although the White Lily flour suggested in this recipe produces a very light biscuit, no one will be disappointed by the results with regular all-purpose flour. ■

- 2 cups White Lily (see Sources) or all-purpose flour
- 1 tablespoon baking powder
- ½ teaspoon salt
- 1¼ cups heavy cream, plus additional for brushing

SPECIAL EQUIPMENT: a 3-inch round cutter

Put a rack in middle of oven and preheat oven to 425°F. Lightly butter a baking sheet.

Sift together flour, baking powder, and salt into a medium bowl. Add cream and stir just until a dough forms. Gather dough into a ball and gently knead 6 times on a lightly floured surface.

Pat dough into a 10-inch round (½ inch thick). Cut out as many rounds as possible with lightly floured cutter and invert rounds onto buttered baking sheet. Gather scraps, pat out dough, and cut out more rounds in same manner, for a total of 8 rounds.

Brush tops of rounds with cream and bake until pale golden, 15 to 20 minutes. Transfer biscuits to a rack to cool.

Berries with Orange and Sour Cream Shortcake

SERVES 6
ACTIVE TIME: 25 MINUTES ■ START TO FINISH: 4½ HOURS (INCLUDES MACERATING)

■ Creamy yet light, the drop biscuits for this shortcake require no rolling. We top them with a colorful assortment of fresh berries. ■

FOR BERRIES
- 3 cups (13 ounces) blackberries
- 9 tablespoons granulated sugar
- 3 cups (12 ounces) raspberries
- 3 cups (15 ounces) blueberries

FOR BISCUITS
- 1½ cups all-purpose flour
- 1½ teaspoons baking powder
- Rounded ¼ teaspoon baking soda
- Rounded ¼ teaspoon salt
- 2½ tablespoons granulated sugar
- ¾ stick (6 tablespoons) cold unsalted butter, cut into bits
- ¾ teaspoon finely grated orange zest
- 6 tablespoons sour cream
- ½ cup whole milk

FOR CREAM
- 1 cup very cold heavy cream
- 2 tablespoons confectioners' sugar

MACERATE THE BERRIES: Gently mash 1½ cups blackberries with 3 tablespoons sugar in a medium bowl with a potato masher. Stir in remaining 1½ cups blackberries. Mash raspberries with 3 tablespoons sugar in another bowl. Mash blueberries with remaining 3 tablespoons sugar in a third bowl. Let berries stand at room temperature for 4 hours.

MAKE THE BISCUITS: Put a rack in middle of oven and preheat oven to 425°F. Butter a baking sheet.

Whisk together flour, baking powder, baking soda, salt, and sugar in a large bowl. Blend in butter with your fingertips until mixture resembles coarse meal. Whisk together zest, sour cream, and milk in a small bowl. Add to flour mixture and stir just until a soft, sticky dough forms.

Drop dough into 6 mounds about 1 inch apart on buttered baking sheet. Bake until pale golden, 12 to 15 minutes. Transfer biscuits to a rack to cool.

ASSEMBLE THE SHORTCAKES: Beat cream and confectioners' sugar in a large bowl with an electric mixer until cream holds soft peaks.

Split biscuits with a fork and arrange bottom halves on six plates. Spoon berry mixtures over them. Top with some whipped cream and arrange biscuit tops on cream. Serve remaining cream on the side.

COOK'S NOTES

- The berry mixtures can be made up to 1 day ahead and refrigerated, covered. Bring to room temperature before serving.
- The biscuits can be made up to 4 hours ahead and kept in an airtight container at room temperature.

Fruit Crumble

SERVES 6

ACTIVE TIME: 15 MINUTES ■ START TO FINISH: 50 MINUTES

■ Make this with either a jumble of fresh, in-season fruits or just one. Cooks who think they're pastry-impaired will find this foolproof. ■

- 3/4 cup all-purpose flour
- 3/4 cup sugar
- 1/2 cup (2 ounces) sliced almonds
- 1/4 teaspoon salt
- 1 stick (8 tablespoons) cold unsalted butter, cut into 1/2-inch cubes
- 2 pounds plums, peaches, nectarines, or apricots, or a combination, pitted and cut into 1/2-inch-thick wedges

ACCOMPANIMENT: vanilla ice cream

Put a rack in middle of oven and preheat oven to 425°F. Butter a 9 1/2-inch deep-dish glass pie plate.

Combine flour, sugar, almonds, and salt in a food processor and pulse until nuts are coarsely chopped. Add butter and pulse until mixture begins to clump.

Spread fruit in pie plate and sprinkle topping over it.

Bake crumble until fruit is tender and topping is golden brown, 25 to 30 minutes. Cool slightly on a rack.

Serve warm, with ice cream.

Blackberry Cobbler

SERVES 8

ACTIVE TIME: 30 MINUTES ■ START TO FINISH: 1 1/4 HOURS

■ Next time you're going to visit a friend for a weekend in the summer, tuck this recipe into your pocket. There is no better hostess gift than to whip it up when the kitchen is free. Juicy blackberries are topped with drop biscuits—it's so easy to make that it won't create a mess, and it has all the down-home goodness of traditional American baking. The recipe, which comes from the mother of contributor Kathryn Stewart, is just as good made with blueberries. ■

- 3 tablespoons cornstarch
- 1/3 cup cold water
- 1 3/4–2 cups sugar
- 1 1/2 tablespoons fresh lemon juice
- 6 cups blackberries or blueberries (from 3 pints), picked over, rinsed, and drained well
- 1 1/2 cups all-purpose flour
- 1 1/2 teaspoons baking powder
- 3/4 teaspoon salt
- 8 tablespoons (1 stick) plus 1 tablespoon cold unsalted butter, cut into bits
- 1/3 cup boiling water

ACCOMPANIMENT: vanilla ice cream

Put a rack in middle of oven and preheat oven to 400°F. Line a baking sheet with foil.

Stir together cornstarch and cold water in a large bowl until cornstarch is completely dissolved. Add 1 to 1 1/4 cups sugar, depending on sweetness of berries, lemon juice, and berries and combine gently but thoroughly. Transfer berry mixture to a 10-inch well-seasoned cast-iron skillet or other ovenproof skillet (wrap handle in foil if necessary); set aside.

Combine flour, baking powder, salt, and remaining 3/4 cup sugar in a food processor and pulse to blend. Add butter and pulse until mixture resembles coarse meal. Transfer mixture to a medium bowl, add boiling water, and stir just until a dough forms.

Bring blackberry mixture to a boil on top of stove, stirring. Carefully drop 8 large spoonfuls of dough onto fruit. Set skillet on foil-lined baking sheet and bake until topping is golden, 30 to 35 minutes. Cool slightly on a rack and serve warm, with vanilla ice cream.

Blueberry and Nectarine Buckle

SERVES 8 TO 10
ACTIVE TIME: 40 MINUTES ■ START TO FINISH: 2 HOURS

■ Slump, grunt, pandowdy, buckle—they're all great words. Slumps and grunts, should you be wondering, are both steamed cakes that resemble puddings. A pandowdy always has fruit baked beneath a crust. But we like buckles best. They begin with a simple cake batter into which you fold fruit, then you cover the top with a generous streusel so thick that it causes the cake to buckle beneath its weight as it bakes. The result is a lovely warm dessert that is especially nice for brunch. ■

FOR TOPPING
- 1/2 stick (4 tablespoons) cold unsalted butter, cut into bits
- 1/2 cup sugar
- 1/3 cup all-purpose flour
- 1/2 teaspoon ground cinnamon
- 1/2 teaspoon freshly grated nutmeg

FOR BATTER
- 1 1/3 cups all-purpose flour
- 1/4 teaspoon baking powder
- 1/2 teaspoon salt
- 1 1/2 sticks (12 tablespoons) unsalted butter, softened
- 3/4 cup sugar
- 1 teaspoon vanilla extract
- 3 large eggs
- 2 cups (12 ounces) blueberries, picked over and rinsed
- 2 nectarines (9 ounces total), pitted and cut into 1-inch wedges

ACCOMPANIMENT: whipped cream or vanilla ice cream

MAKE THE TOPPING: Blend together all ingredients in a small bowl with your fingertips until mixture forms large clumps. Refrigerate.

Put a rack in middle of oven and preheat oven to 350°F. Generously butter a 10-by-2-inch round cake pan or 2-quart baking dish.

MAKE THE BATTER: Stir together flour, baking powder, and salt in a small bowl.

Beat together butter and sugar in a large bowl with an electric mixer at medium speed until pale and fluffy. Beat in vanilla. Add eggs one at a time, beating well after each addition. Stir in flour mixture until just combined. Fold in blueberries and nectarines.

ASSEMBLE AND BAKE THE BUCKLE: Spread batter in buttered pan and sprinkle topping evenly over it. Bake buckle until a wooden pick or skewer inserted in center comes out clean and topping is crisp and golden, 55 to 60 minutes. Serve warm, with whipped cream or ice cream.

Plum and Almond Crisp

SERVES 8
ACTIVE TIME: 20 MINUTES ■ START TO FINISH: 1 3/4 HOURS

■ Prune plums are a boon to any baker. They need no peeling, they slice in a trice, and when topped with a nutty crumble and baked in a hot oven, they bubble up into a glorious dessert. ■

- 1/2 cup packed light brown sugar
- 2 tablespoons cornstarch
- 1/2 teaspoon ground cinnamon
- 2 1/2 pounds plums, preferably prune plums, quartered and pitted
- 2 tablespoons fresh lemon juice
- 2 tablespoons unsalted butter, cut into bits
- 1 cup granulated sugar
- 3/4 cup all-purpose flour
- 1/2 teaspoon salt
- 3/4 cup (3 ounces) sliced almonds
- 1 large egg, lightly beaten

Put a rack in middle of oven and preheat oven to 375°F.

Whisk together brown sugar, cornstarch, and cinnamon in a large bowl. Add plums, lemon juice, and butter and toss well. Spoon into a shallow 3-quart baking dish.

Combine granulated sugar, flour, salt, and 1/2 cup almonds in a food processor and pulse until almonds are finely ground. Add egg and pulse until well combined. Spoon batter over plum mixture and lift up some plum wedges so they show through. Sprinkle remaining 1/4 cup almonds over top.

Bake crisp until golden and bubbling, 50 to 55 minutes. Cool on a rack and serve warm or at room temperature.

Cherry Clafouti

SERVES 6

ACTIVE TIME: 30 MINUTES ■ START TO FINISH: 1½ HOURS

■ Halfway between custard and cake, this traditional dessert will bring the French countryside to your table with its subtle richness. Sour cherries peep out of the easy, eggy batter; we have removed the pits, but if you want to do things the French way (and, incidentally, save some time), leave them in place and simply serve the clafouti with a warning. ■

- 1¼ pounds fresh sour cherries, pitted, or 1 pound frozen sour cherries, thawed and drained
- ½ cup plus 1 tablespoon granulated sugar
- 4 large eggs
- 1 cup whole milk
- ½ cup all-purpose flour
- ¼ teaspoon salt
- 3 tablespoons unsalted butter, melted and cooled
- 2 tablespoons kirsch
- ½ teaspoon vanilla extract
- ⅛ teaspoon almond extract

GARNISH: confectioners' sugar

Put a rack in middle of oven and preheat oven to 400°F. Butter a shallow 2-quart baking dish.

Toss cherries with 1 tablespoon sugar and spread evenly in baking dish.

Combine eggs, milk, flour, salt, butter, kirsch, extracts, and remaining 1/2 cup sugar in a blender and blend until smooth. Pour batter over cherries.

Bake clafouti until puffed and golden, 35 to 45 minutes.

Cool slightly on a rack (clafouti will sink as it cools) and serve warm, dusted with confectioners' sugar.

Banana Fritters

SERVES 4

ACTIVE TIME: 30 MINUTES ■ START TO FINISH: 30 MINUTES

■ Bananas soaked in sugar syrup, rolled in cornflakes, fried until crisp, and served hot with a rum-lime sauce are simultaneously smooth and crisp, sweet and tart. These fritters are the specialty of reader Marguerite Hannon. ■

- 1 cup sugar
- 1 cup water
- 4 cups cornflakes
- 4 firm but ripe bananas
- About 5 cups vegetable oil for deep-frying
- ¼ cup light rum
- 1½ tablespoons fresh lime juice

SPECIAL EQUIPMENT: a deep-fat thermometer

Combine sugar and water in a 1-quart heavy saucepan and heat over moderate heat, stirring occasionally, until sugar is dissolved. Transfer syrup to a medium heatproof bowl and cool slightly, about 5 minutes.

Meanwhile, pulse cornflakes in a food processor until some small pieces remain (not until finely ground). Transfer to a large shallow bowl.

Peel bananas and cut crosswise into 1½-inch pieces. Soak half of bananas in sugar syrup for 10 minutes; set remaining bananas aside.

Heat 1 inch oil in a deep 12-inch skillet over moderate heat until it registers 375°F on thermometer. With a slotted spoon, remove first batch of bananas from syrup and add to cornflakes. Add remaining bananas to sugar syrup to soak for 10 minutes.

Roll soaked bananas in cornflakes and arrange on a wax paper–lined tray. With slotted spoon, gently lower coated bananas into oil and fry, turning occasionally, until golden brown, 1 to 2 minutes. With slotted spoon, transfer fried bananas to paper towels to drain. Coat and fry remaining bananas in same manner. (Return oil to 375°F between batches.)

Pour remaining sugar syrup through a fine-mesh sieve into a small heavy saucepan. Bring to a boil over moderately high heat and boil until reduced to about ¾ cup, about 5 minutes. Remove from heat and stir in rum and lime juice. Serve alongside bananas for dipping.

Varenikis

Apricot and Walnut Dumplings

SERVES 4 TO 6
ACTIVE TIME: 1¼ HOURS ■ START TO FINISH: 2 HOURS (INCLUDES MAKING DOUGH)

■ These wonderful little dessert dumplings are not well known outside the Ukraine, but they deserve a wider audience. Imagine biting into ravioli and discovering that they are filled with sweet brandied fruit and nuts. Imagine buttery, spicy crumbs spilling across the top and each bite dancing into your mouth, tasting just a little different from the one before. Then you'll understand why, having made these sweet, floppy pockets of pasta once, you will surely make them again. ■

- ¼ cup water
- 6 tablespoons sugar
- 2 tablespoons apricot brandy (optional)
- 6 ounces (1 cup) dried apricots, preferably California (see Sources)
- ½ cup (2 ounces) walnuts, finely chopped
- Vareniki Dough (page 242)
- 1 stick (8 tablespoons) unsalted butter
- ½ cup coarse fresh bread crumbs
- Salt
- ¼ teaspoon ground cinnamon

To make the filling, combine water and 4 tablespoons (¼ cup) sugar in a small saucepan and bring to a boil, stirring until sugar is dissolved. Remove from heat and stir in brandy, if using.

Finely chop apricots in a food processor. Add sugar syrup and pulse until just combined; do not purée. Transfer to a bowl and stir in ¼ cup walnuts. Let cool.

Halve dough. Roll out 1 piece (keep remaining dough wrapped) on a lightly floured surface with a lightly floured rolling pin into a 15-inch round. Trim dough to a 13-inch square. Cut lengthwise into 4 strips, then cut each strip crosswise into quarters, to make sixteen 3¼-inch-squares.

Put 1 slightly rounded teaspoon filling in center of each square. Moisten edges of 1 square with water, fold diagonally in half to form a triangle, and press edges firmly together to seal. Overlap bottom points of triangle and press to seal (dumpling will look like a pointed hat). Transfer *vareniki* to a flour-dusted kitchen towel and repeat with remaining squares, then make more dumplings with remaining dough and filling.

Bring a large pot of lightly salted water to a boil. Add *varenikis* and cook until tender, about 15 minutes.

Meanwhile, melt 2 tablespoons butter in a small skillet over moderate heat. Add bread crumbs and remaining ¼ cup walnuts and cook, stirring frequently, until golden, 2 to 3 minutes. Remove from heat and season lightly with salt.

Stir together cinnamon and remaining 2 tablespoons sugar in a cup. Sprinkle 2 teaspoons cinnamon sugar over crumb mixture and toss well.

Just before *varenikis* are cooked, melt remaining 6 tablespoons butter.

Drizzle about 2 tablespoons melted butter on a warmed serving platter. With a slotted spoon, transfer *varenikis* to platter and drizzle with remaining butter.

Sprinkle with bread crumb mixture and remaining cinnamon sugar to taste and serve hot.

COOK'S NOTE

■ The filled *varenikis* can be frozen for up to 1 month. Freeze in one layer on a tray until firm, about 2 hours, then transfer to sealable plastic bags and freeze. Thaw before cooking.

Rhubarb Charlotte

SERVES 6
ACTIVE TIME: 45 MINUTES ■ START TO FINISH: 24 HOURS (INCLUDES CHILLING)

■ Charlottes, which are named for Queen Charlotte, the wife of King George III of England, are adorable little mousses surrounded by ladyfingers and baked in slant-sided molds. We are particularly fond of this one. In addition to its delicate flavor, the rhubarb contributes so much natural pectin that this mousse needs no gelatin to hold its shape. Like all charlottes, this is a beautiful creature, and because it needs to be chilled for twenty-four hours before it can be served, it is a natural make-ahead party dessert. ■

- 2¼ pounds rhubarb stalks, trimmed
- 1 cup granulated sugar
- 1½ tablespoons fresh lemon juice
- 37 (3-by-1-inch) soft ladyfingers
- 2 tablespoons kirsch
- ¾ cup very cold heavy cream
- 3 tablespoons confectioners' sugar

SPECIAL EQUIPMENT: a 6-cup charlotte mold (see Sources)

Cut enough rhubarb into ¼-inch-thick slices to measure 6 cups (reserve remainder for another use). Combine rhubarb, granulated sugar, and lemon juice in a large heavy saucepan and cook over moderately high heat, stirring occasionally, until rhubarb begins to release its juices. Reduce heat and simmer, stirring occasionally, until rhubarb falls apart and is reduced to about 2 cups, 25 to 30 minutes. Let cool.

Brush flat sides of ladyfingers with kirsch. Lightly oil mold and line with two 24-inch-long sheets of plastic wrap, crisscrossing them and letting excess hang over sides. Line sides and bottom of mold with ladyfingers, flat sides facing in, trimming bottom ones to fit snugly; reserve remaining ladyfingers.

Beat together cream and confectioners' sugar in a medium bowl with an electric mixer until cream just holds stiff peaks. Spoon half of rhubarb into mold and smooth top. Spoon half of cream over rhubarb and smooth top. Cover cream with a layer of ladyfingers. Repeat layering with remaining rhubarb, cream, and ladyfingers.

Fold plastic wrap over to cover charlotte and weight with a flat-bottomed dish that just fits inside mold. Set a 2-pound weight in dish and refrigerate charlotte for 24 hours.

Remove weight and dish. Unfold plastic wrap, invert a platter over mold, and invert charlotte onto platter, using plastic wrap to release it; peel off plastic wrap.

Chocolate Cherry Charlottes

SERVES 6
ACTIVE TIME: 1 HOUR ■ START TO FINISH: 3½ HOURS (INCLUDES FREEZING)

■ Freezing the chocolate filling for these individual charlottes before baking them prevents the chocolate from overcooking or burning in the oven. ■

- ⅔ cup dried sour cherries
- ¼ cup kirsch
- 2 tablespoons sugar
- 2–3 drops almond extract (to taste)
- ½ cup heavy cream
- 3½ ounces good bittersweet chocolate (not unsweetened), chopped
- Pinch of salt
- 7 tablespoons unsalted butter, softened
- 1½ loaves challah or large brioche (about 1½ pounds total), cut into ½-inch-thick slices

ACCOMPANIMENT: lightly sweetened whipped cream

SPECIAL EQUIPMENT: a 2-inch round cookie cutter; six 5- to 6-ounce charlotte molds (see Sources) or ramekins

Combine cherries, kirsch, and sugar in a small saucepan and bring to a boil, stirring occasionally. Remove from heat, cover, and let stand for 15 minutes. Stir in almond extract.

Combine cream, chocolate, and salt in a small heavy saucepan and heat over low heat, stirring, until chocolate is melted and smooth. Remove from heat and add 1 tablespoon butter, stirring until incorporated. Stir in cooled cherries, with any liquid.

Transfer filling to a metal bowl and freeze, stirring occasionally, until firm but not frozen solid, about 2½ hours.

Put a rack in middle of oven and preheat oven to 350°F.

Cut 12 rounds from bread slices with cookie cutter, reserving trimmings. With a bread knife, cut forty-two 2-by-1½-inch rectangles from trimmings and remaining slices. Spread one side of each round and rectangle with some of remaining 6 tablespoons butter. Put 1 round, buttered side down, in bottom of each mold. Using 5 to 7 rectangles per mold, line sides (buttered sides against mold), arranging rectangles vertically and slightly overlapping; press gently so they adhere. Trim any overhang flush with rims of molds.

Divide filling among molds. Top with remaining 6 bread rounds, buttered sides up, and press gently so they fit inside bread rims.

Put molds on a baking sheet and bake until bread is golden, about 25 minutes. Cool for 5 minutes, then invert a plate over each charlotte and invert charlotte onto plate. Serve warm, with whipped cream.

Chocolate Prune Pavé with Armagnac Crème Anglaise and Candied Orange Zest

SERVES 12

ACTIVE TIME: 1½ HOURS ■ START TO FINISH: 10½ HOURS (INCLUDES CHILLING AND MAKING ZEST)

■ This is really candy disguised as cake, an intense amalgamation of prunes, Armagnac, cream, and a full pound of chocolate. Embellished with candied orange zest, it's absolutely spectacular. The name, which comes from the French word for paving stone, is generally applied to a dense chocolate cake. ■

- ½ pound pitted prunes
- ¼ cup Armagnac
- 1 pound good bittersweet chocolate (not unsweetened), chopped
- 1½ cups heavy cream
- 2 cups Armagnac Crème Anglaise (page 876)
- Candied Orange Zest (recipe follows)

Lightly oil an 8½-by-4½-inch loaf pan and line with a sheet of plastic wrap.

Purée prunes with Armagnac in a food processor. Force purée through a medium-mesh sieve into a small bowl, scraping purée from bottom of sieve with a rubber spatula as necessary.

Melt chocolate with cream in a 2-quart heavy saucepan over moderately low heat, stirring until smooth. Remove from heat.

Combine chocolate and prune mixtures in cleaned food processor bowl and blend until smooth. Scrape into loaf pan and smooth top. Rap pan on counter once or twice to settle mixture. Cover top of pavé with plastic wrap and refrigerate for at least 8 hours.

To serve, remove plastic wrap from top and invert pavé onto a platter. Remove remaining plastic wrap and let pavé stand at room temperature for 1 hour.

Cut pavé into thin slices with a knife dipped in hot water and dried before each slice and arrange on plates. Spoon crème anglaise around pavé and sprinkle with candied zest.

COOK'S NOTE

■ The pavé can be refrigerated for up to 3 days.

Candied Orange Zest

MAKES ABOUT ½ CUP

ACTIVE TIME: 30 MINUTES ■ START TO FINISH: 1 HOUR

- 2 large navel oranges
- ⅔ cup Cointreau or other orange-flavored liqueur

With a swivel-bladed peeler, remove zest from oranges in long, wide strips. With a paring knife, cut any white pith from zest. Cut enough zest into thin strips to measure ⅔ cup. (Reserve remaining zest for another use, if desired.)

Combine zest and Cointreau in a 1-quart heavy saucepan, bring to a simmer over moderately low heat, and simmer until liquid has just evaporated and zest is translucent, 15 to 18 minutes.

Spread zest out on a sheet of wax paper, separate strands with a fork, and cool.

COOK'S NOTE

■ The candied zest keeps, layered between sheets of wax paper, in an airtight container at room temperature for up to 2 days.

Chilled Sour Cherry Soup

SERVES 4

ACTIVE TIME: 25 MINUTES ■ START TO FINISH: 3 HOURS (INCLUDES CHILLING)

■ Soup for dessert? Why not, when it's a romantic bowl of deep red soup filled with the fresh, elusive flavor of cherries. We adapted this from a recipe in George Lang's *The Cuisine of Hungary.* It is very beautiful when drizzled with sour cream. ■

- 3 cups plus 2 tablespoons cold water
- 3/4 cup sugar
- 1/2 teaspoon finely grated lemon zest
- 1/4 teaspoon ground cinnamon
- 1 1/4 pounds fresh sour cherries, pitted, or 1 pound frozen sour cherries (not thawed)
- 2 tablespoons cornstarch
- 3 tablespoons sour cream
- 1 1/2 tablespoons heavy cream

Combine 3 cups water, sugar, zest, and cinnamon in a 3-quart heavy saucepan, bring to a boil, stirring to dissolve sugar, and boil for 2 minutes. Add cherries, bring back to a boil, and boil for 2 minutes.

Whisk cornstarch together with remaining 2 tablespoons cold water in a small cup, then whisk into boiling cherry mixture. Simmer, whisking, until slightly thickened, about 2 minutes. Remove from heat and cool soup completely, uncovered, then refrigerate, covered, for at least 2 hours.

Just before serving, whisk together sour cream and heavy cream in a small bowl. Ladle soup into four bowls and drizzle with cream mixture.

COOK'S NOTE

■ The soup can be refrigerated for up to 2 days.

PUDDINGS, CUSTARDS, MOUSSES, AND SOUFFLÉS

Pudding is a very silly word that instantly conjures up old English nursery rhymes. Indeed, flipping through the pages of this chapter, you might be forgiven for thinking that it is the most childlike part of the book. Certainly sticky toffee pudding would make any child wild with joy, and chocolate pudding is the essence of childhood served in a bowl. And what could be more innocent than a sedate rice pudding?

But keep turning the pages and you'll soon find that sophisticated desserts also reside here—soufflés, for instance, which may be the most misunderstood recipes of all time. They are so showy and impressive that they've fooled the world into thinking that they're difficult. They are not. We offer them in several sizes and several

flavors: Grand Marnier, chocolate, coffee. . . . And there is *Gourmet*'s famous apricot soufflé, which all by itself is worth the price of this book.

An entire family of custard concoctions also lives here. They go from A (almond flan with summer fruit) to Z (zabaglione), with stops along the alphabet for crème caramel, panna cotta, and maple pumpkin pots de crème. They're a useful lot when you have last-minute guests; they're rich, lovable, and easy to make, and most of them require only the kind of ingredients you're likely to have on hand.

Old-Fashioned Chocolate Pudding

SERVES 4

ACTIVE TIME: 20 MINUTES ■ START TO FINISH: 2 1/2 HOURS (INCLUDES CHILLING)

■ Chocolate pudding should be a food group all its own, and if you adored the boxed variety as a child (who didn't?), you'll be bowled over by this luxuriant blend of semisweet chocolate and unsweetened cocoa powder. Be sure to use the best semisweet chocolate you can find. ■

- 1/4 cup sugar
- 1/4 cup unsweetened cocoa powder (not Dutch-process)
- 2 tablespoons cornstarch
- Pinch of salt
- 2 cups whole milk
- 1 large egg
- 4 ounces good semisweet chocolate, finely chopped

ACCOMPANIMENT: lightly sweetened whipped cream

SPECIAL EQUIPMENT: four 6-ounce ramekins or custard cups

Whisk together sugar, cocoa powder, cornstarch, and salt in a 2-quart heavy saucepan, then gradually whisk in milk. Bring to a boil, whisking constantly, and boil, whisking, until pudding is thick, 3 to 5 minutes. Remove from heat.

Immediately beat egg lightly in a medium heatproof bowl, then very gradually add hot pudding to egg, whisking constantly. Whisk in chocolate until smooth.

Pour pudding into ramekins or custard cups and cover surface of each with wax paper to prevent a skin from forming. Refrigerate, covered, until cold, at least 2 hours.

Serve pudding with whipped cream.

COOK'S NOTE

■ The pudding can be refrigerated for up to 1 day.

Old Plymouth Indian Meal Pudding

SERVES 8

ACTIVE TIME: 20 MINUTES ■ START TO FINISH: 2 3/4 HOURS

■ Indian meal—early Colonial slang for cornmeal—combined with molasses is one of our nation's oldest, greatest, and most undersung culinary combinations. Hardly fancy, this sweet pudding makes a soothing warm dessert on a frigid night; splashed with milk and reheated in the microwave the next morning, it does double duty for breakfast. The recipe is adapted from one in the *Country Kitchen Cookbook,* published by the Friends of the South County Museum of Narragansett, Rhode Island. We love it drizzled with heavy cream or topped with vanilla ice cream. ■

- 4 1/2 cups whole milk
- 1/2 cup cornmeal (preferably Quaker)
- 1/2 cup molasses (not robust or blackstrap)
- 1/2 teaspoon ground cinnamon
- 1/2 teaspoon salt
- 2 large eggs
- 1/4 cup sugar

ACCOMPANIMENT: heavy cream or vanilla ice cream

Put a rack in middle of oven and preheat oven to 350°F.

Bring 2 cups milk just to a simmer in a 2- to 3-quart heavy saucepan over moderate heat. Gradually stir in cornmeal and cook, stirring constantly, until thickened, about 1 minute. Transfer to a large heatproof bowl and cool to warm, about 5 minutes, then stir in molasses, cinnamon, and salt.

Whisk eggs with sugar in a small bowl, then whisk in 2 cups milk. Whisk egg mixture into cornmeal mixture. Transfer to an 8-inch square baking dish or other 2-quart shallow baking dish.

Bake pudding, uncovered, for 30 minutes. Pour remaining 1/2 cup milk on top of pudding (do not stir). Bake, uncovered, for 1 1/2 hours more.

Cool pudding on a rack for 20 minutes and serve warm, with cream or ice cream.

COOK'S NOTE

- The pudding can be made up to 1 day ahead. Cool completely, uncovered, then refrigerate, covered. Reheat, covered with foil, in a 350°F oven until heated through, about 20 minutes.

Black-Bottom Caramel Pudding

SERVES 6

ACTIVE TIME: 20 MINUTES ■ START TO FINISH: 3½ HOURS (INCLUDES CHILLING)

■ Deconstruct a chocolate-covered caramel candy and the result is this: silky layers of chocolate and caramel pudding served in a glass. It's easy to make, but do keep an eye on the caramel as it nears the end of cooking—it can go from the deep amber you want to the burn you don't want in the blink of an eye. ■

- ¾ cup plus 2 tablespoons sugar
- ¼ cup water
- 1 cup heavy cream
- 3 cups whole milk
- ¼ cup cornstarch
- 2 large eggs
- 1½ teaspoons vanilla extract
- ¼ teaspoon salt
- 2 ounces good bittersweet chocolate (not unsweetened), finely chopped

OPTIONAL GARNISH: unsweetened whipped cream and finely chopped chocolate wafer cookies or grated bittersweet chocolate

Combine sugar and water in a 3-quart heavy saucepan and bring to a boil over high heat, stirring with a fork until sugar is dissolved. Boil, without stirring, washing down sugar crystals clinging to sides of pan with a pastry brush dipped in cold water, until caramel is pale golden, 4 to 5 minutes. Continue to cook without stirring, swirling pan occasionally, until caramel turns a deep amber, 1 to 2 minutes. Remove from heat and carefully add cream in a slow stream (mixture will bubble vigorously and steam). Return to low heat and cook, whisking, until smooth. Remove from heat.

Stir together ½ cup milk and cornstarch in a small bowl until smooth. Beat eggs with vanilla and salt in another small bowl. Put chocolate in a third small bowl.

Stir remaining 2½ cups milk into caramel and bring to a simmer, whisking occasionally. Stir cornstarch mixture, then whisk into caramel and bring to a boil, whisking. Reduce heat and simmer, whisking, for 2 minutes. Remove from heat.

Immediately whisk about 1 cup hot caramel mixture into egg mixture until well blended, then whisk egg mixture back into caramel. Continue whisking, off heat, for 1 minute.

Immediately whisk ½ cup hot caramel pudding into chopped chocolate, stirring until smooth. Spoon chocolate pudding into six 8-ounce parfait glasses or other footed glasses, then top with caramel pudding. Refrigerate until set, at least 3 hours.

Serve garnished with whipped cream and sprinkled with chopped cookies or grated chocolate, if desired.

COOK'S NOTE

- The pudding can be refrigerated, covered with plastic wrap, for up to 3 days.

Tapioca Pudding

SERVES 8

ACTIVE TIME: 1 HOUR ■ START TO FINISH: 1½ HOURS

■ A sensory delight, tapioca manages to be both creamy smooth and wonderfully textured at the same time. We're particularly fond of this version, which we adapted from a recipe created at the Kenwood Restaurant, in Sonoma Valley, California, because it produces a very light pudding. When shopping, note that the size of tapioca pearls varies widely. What one brand calls small another brand might call large, so don't pay too much attention to the label. You want pearls that are one eighth to three sixteenths of an inch in diameter. ■

- 1/3 cup pearl (preferably 1/8- to 3/16-inch) tapioca (not quick-cooking)
- 2 cups whole milk
- 1/3 cup plus 1 tablespoon sugar
- 1/8 teaspoon salt, plus a pinch
- 2 large eggs, separated
- 1 teaspoon vanilla extract
- 1/2 cup very cold heavy cream

SPECIAL EQUIPMENT: an instant-read thermometer

Soak tapioca in 1 cup water for 10 minutes to soften it, then drain in a sieve (do not rinse).

Combine milk, 1/3 cup sugar, and 1/8 teaspoon salt in a 2-quart heavy saucepan and bring to a simmer over moderate heat, stirring with a flat wooden spatula until sugar is dissolved. Stir in tapioca and simmer, stirring constantly, until mixture is thickened and tapioca is completely translucent, 20 to 30 minutes (if you notice any scorching or brown flecks, immediately transfer tapioca to a clean saucepan and continue cooking over slightly lower heat). Remove tapioca mixture from heat.

Prepare a large bowl of ice and cold water and set aside.

Whisk together yolks and vanilla in a small bowl, then gradually add 1/2 cup hot tapioca mixture, whisking constantly. Whisk yolk mixture into tapioca in saucepan and cook over moderate heat, stirring constantly, until tapioca is thickened and registers 175°F on thermometer, 2 to 3 minutes. Immediately transfer tapioca to a metal bowl and set in bowl of ice and cold water. Cool, stirring occasionally, for about 5 minutes.

Beat whites with pinch of salt in a small bowl with an electric mixer until they just hold soft peaks. Add remaining 1 tablespoon sugar and beat until whites hold stiff peaks. Beat cream in another small bowl until it just holds soft peaks. Gently but thoroughly fold whites and then cream into tapioca. Serve at room temperature or chilled.

COOK'S NOTES

- The pudding can be made up to 1 day ahead and refrigerated, covered.
- The egg whites in this recipe are not cooked. If this is a concern, we recommend using powdered egg whites, such as Just Whites, reconstituted according to the manufacturer's directions, or packaged liquid egg whites (see opposite page).

Warm Tapioca Pudding with Rhubarb

SERVES 4

ACTIVE TIME: 30 MINUTES ■ START TO FINISH: 1 1/4 HOURS

■ Tapioca pudding grows up when it is topped with a tart layer of rosy rhubarb. The secret here is the pinch of pepper, which imparts a definite aura of mystery. ■

- 8 1/3 cups water
- 1/3 cup plus 5 tablespoons sugar
- 1/2 teaspoon salt, plus a pinch
- 2/3 cup pearl (preferably 1/8- to 3/16-inch) tapioca (not quick-cooking)
- 1/2 pound rhubarb stalks, trimmed and thinly sliced (1 3/4 cups)
- 1/8 teaspoon freshly ground black pepper
- 1 teaspoon fresh lemon juice
- 1/4 cup half-and half
- 1/8 teaspoon vanilla extract

Combine 8 cups water, 3 tablespoons sugar, and 1/2 teaspoon salt in a 3- to 4-quart heavy saucepan and bring to a boil. Add tapioca in a steady stream, stirring constantly. Reduce heat and simmer briskly, uncovered, stirring occasionally, until tapioca is almost completely translucent, 35 to 50 minutes, depending on size of tapioca.

Meanwhile, combine 1 1/4 cups rhubarb, 1/3 cup sugar, pinch of salt, pepper, and remaining 1/3 cup water in a 2-quart heavy saucepan, bring to a simmer, and simmer, uncovered, stirring occasionally, until rhubarb is just tender, about 8 minutes.

Purée rhubarb mixture in a food processor until smooth (use caution). Reserve 1/4 cup, and return remainder to saucepan. Stir in remaining 1/2 cup raw rhubarb and simmer, stirring occasionally, until it is tender, about 5 minutes. Stir in lemon juice and transfer to a shallow bowl.

Drain tapioca in a sieve and transfer to cleaned 2-quart heavy saucepan. Stir in half-and-half, remaining 2 tablespoons sugar, vanilla, and reserved 1/4 cup rhubarb purée and bring to a simmer, stirring occasionally until sugar is dissolved. Cool slightly.

Divide tapioca among four dessert bowls and top with rhubarb. Serve warm.

Packaged Liquid Egg Whites

Using packaged liquid egg whites is more convenient than separating eggs (especially when you don't want to deal with leftover yolks), and packaged whites are safer too, since they are pasteurized to kill most bacteria. Measuring is a snap — although egg sizes vary, two tablespoons of liquid whites are roughly equivalent to one egg white. Any pasteurized whites will work for most recipes, but if you need to whip them for a meringue or an angel food cake, we recommend Eggology brand egg whites; unlike many others on the market, they contain no traces of egg yolk (which hinders foaming).

Best Rice Pudding

SERVES 6 TO 8

ACTIVE TIME: 40 MINUTES ■ START TO FINISH: 1 HOUR

■ How could a dessert so delicious actually be good for you? This one, served warm so that the aromas of vanilla, lemon, and cinnamon are still swirling in the air, is wholesome enough to put on the table for dinner in a pinch. ■

- 2 cups water
- 2 tablespoons unsalted butter
- Rounded 1/4 teaspoon salt
- 1/2 teaspoon finely grated lemon zest
- 1 cup long-grain white rice
- 4 cups whole milk
- 1/2 cup sugar
- 1/2 vanilla bean, halved lengthwise
- 1 cup raisins
- Ground cinnamon

Combine water, butter, salt, and zest in a 2-quart heavy saucepan and bring to a boil. Stir in rice and return to a boil, then cover and simmer over very low heat until water is absorbed, about 15 minutes.

Combine milk, sugar, and vanilla bean in a 3-quart heavy saucepan and bring just to a simmer over low heat. Add rice mixture and raisins and simmer, uncovered, stirring frequently, until most of milk is absorbed and rice is creamy, about 20 minutes. Transfer pudding to a bowl; discard vanilla bean. Dust with cinnamon and cool until just warm before serving.

Dried Cherry and Raisin Rice Pudding

SERVES 6

ACTIVE TIME: 15 MINUTES ■ START TO FINISH: 3 1/2 HOURS (INCLUDES CHILLING)

■ Kissed with cardamom and studded with dried fruit, this cool, light rice pudding is made with low-fat milk and egg whites. Nobody will notice the missing calories. ■

- 1 cup water
- 1/4 teaspoon salt
- 1/2 cup long-grain white rice
- 3 cups 1% milk
- 1/3 cup sugar
- 1 large egg
- 2 large egg whites
- 1 teaspoon vanilla extract
- 1/8 teaspoon ground cardamom
- Pinch of salt
- 1/3 cup golden raisins
- 1/3 cup dried sour cherries

SPECIAL EQUIPMENT: an instant-read thermometer

Bring water with salt to a boil in a 2-quart heavy saucepan. Stir in rice, cover pan, reduce heat to low, and cook until water is absorbed, about 15 minutes.

Stir in milk and sugar and cook over very low heat, covered, until mixture resembles a thick soup, 50 minutes to 1 hour. Remove from heat.

Whisk together egg, egg whites, vanilla, cardamom, and salt in a medium bowl. Whisk in about 1 cup hot rice mixture, then stir mixture into remaining rice. Cook over low heat, whisking constantly, until pudding registers 170°F on thermometer, 1 to 2 minutes; do not let boil. Remove from heat and stir in raisins and cherries.

Transfer pudding to a 2-quart dish or six 8-ounce ramekins. Cover surface with wax paper and refrigerate until cool but not cold, 1 to 2 hours.

Sticky Rice with Mango

SERVES 6
ACTIVE TIME: 40 MINUTES ■ START TO FINISH: 8 HOURS (INCLUDES SOAKING RICE)

■ The chewy texture of Thai sticky rice (see page 253) provides a wonderful counterpoint to the silky, tart mango, the richly sweet coconut milk, and the crunchy sesame seeds. ■

- 1½ cups (12 ounces) Thai sticky rice (see Sources)
- 1⅓ cups well-stirred canned unsweetened coconut milk
- ⅓ cup plus 3 tablespoons sugar
- ¼ teaspoon salt
- 1 tablespoon sesame seeds, lightly toasted (see Tips, page 939)
- 1 large firm but ripe mango, peeled, pitted, and cut into thin slices (at least 24)

Wash rice in several changes of cold water until water is clear. Soak rice in cold water to cover for at least 6 hours.

Drain rice well in a medium-mesh sieve. Set sieve over a deep 3-quart saucepan of simmering water (sieve should not touch water). Cover pan with a kitchen towel and then a lid and fold edges of towel up over lid (so towel won't burn). Steam until rice is tender, 30 to 40 minutes (check water level in pan occasionally and add more water if necessary).

Meanwhile, combine 1 cup coconut milk, ⅓ cup sugar, and salt in a 1- to 1½-quart saucepan and bring to a boil, stirring until sugar is dissolved. Remove from heat and cover to keep warm.

Transfer cooked rice to a bowl and stir in coconut milk mixture. Let stand, covered, until coconut milk mixture is absorbed, about 30 minutes.

Meanwhile, combine remaining ⅓ cup coconut milk and 3 tablespoons sugar in cleaned 1- to 1½-quart saucepan, bring to a simmer, and simmer, stirring occasionally, for 1 minute. Transfer sauce to a small bowl and cool until slightly thickened, about 15 minutes.

To serve, mound ¼-cup servings of sticky rice on dessert plates. Drizzle with sauce and sprinkle with sesame seeds. Divide mango slices among plates.

COOK'S NOTES

- The rice can soak for up to 12 hours.
- The rice with coconut milk can stand, covered, at room temperature for up to 2 hours.
- The coconut sauce can be made up to 1 day ahead and refrigerated, covered.

Chocolate Bread Pudding

SERVES 6
ACTIVE TIME: 15 MINUTES ■ START TO FINISH: 2 HOURS

■ An American take on the classic European bread and chocolate—not to mention a splendid way to use up stale bread. In making this custardy dessert, we get the best results with a soft supermarket Italian loaf (without seeds, of course) rather than something crusty or fancy. ■

- 4 cups cubed (¾ inch) day-old Italian bread
- ½ stick (4 tablespoons) unsalted butter, melted
- 4 ounces unsweetened chocolate, finely chopped
- 2 cups whole milk
- 1 cup heavy cream
- 2 large eggs
- 1 cup sugar
- 1 teaspoon vanilla extract
- ⅛ teaspoon salt

ACCOMPANIMENT: whipped cream

Toss bread with butter in a large bowl.

Put chocolate in a heatproof bowl. Bring milk and

cream to a simmer in a 2-quart heavy saucepan and pour over chocolate. Let stand for 2 minutes, then whisk until smooth. Add eggs, sugar, vanilla, and salt and whisk until well combined. Pour custard over bread. Cover pudding loosely with plastic wrap, then place a smaller bowl or plate on top and weight with a heavy can. Let pudding stand for 1 hour so bread absorbs custard.

Put a rack in middle of oven and preheat oven to 350°F. Butter an 8-inch square baking pan.

Transfer pudding to pan. Bake until just set but center still trembles slightly, 40 to 45 minutes; do not overbake (custard will continue to set as it cools). Serve warm or at room temperature, with whipped cream.

COOK'S NOTE

- If you don't have day-old bread on hand, you can dry out a 12-inch Italian loaf in a 350°F oven for 10 minutes.

Toasted Bread-and-Butter Pudding

SERVES 10 TO 12
ACTIVE TIME: 30 MINUTES ■ START TO FINISH: 2 HOURS (INCLUDES MAKING CARAMEL SAUCE)

■ Two things lift this out of ordinary bread-pudding territory. The first is toasting the bread, which deepens the flavor. The second is using challah, the braided egg bread, which adds a richness all its own. ■

3½ tablespoons unsalted butter, well softened
12 (½-inch-thick) slices challah or firm white sandwich bread, crusts removed
3 cups half-and-half
4 large eggs
½ cup sugar
1 teaspoon vanilla extract
¼ teaspoon salt
ACCOMPANIMENT: Caramel Sauce (page 873)

Put a rack in middle of oven and preheat oven to 350°F. Butter a 3-quart shallow baking dish.

Butter both sides of bread and arrange in one layer on a large baking sheet. Bake, turning once, until lightly toasted, 15 to 20 minutes. Cool on a rack. (Leave oven on.)

Whisk together half-and-half, eggs, sugar, vanilla, and salt in a medium bowl until sugar is dissolved. Halve toasted bread slices diagonally and arrange triangles in rows, overlapping slightly, in buttered baking dish. Pour custard evenly over toast and let stand for 15 minutes.

Put baking dish in a larger baking pan and add enough boiling water to reach halfway up sides of baking dish. Bake until custard is set 2 to 3 inches from edges but still trembles in center, 50 to 60 minutes (custard will continue to set as it cools). Serve warm, with caramel sauce.

Raspberry Summer Pudding

SERVES 6
ACTIVE TIME: 45 MINUTES ■ START TO FINISH: 13 HOURS (INCLUDES CHILLING)

■ There is nothing more beautiful than this traditional English dessert, which is as brilliant as a sunset on a plate. Very simple to make, it has a fresh, bright berry flavor to match its deep red color. ■

10 (½-inch-thick) slices firm white sandwich bread, such as *pain de mie* or Pullman loaf, crusts removed, 6 slices halved crosswise
3 cups (18 ounces) raspberries
1 cup (6 ounces) strawberries, hulled and sliced
⅓ cup sugar, or to taste
¼ cup framboise or other raspberry-flavored liqueur
GARNISH: raspberries, sliced strawberries, and (optional) whipped cream
SPECIAL EQUIPMENT: a 1-quart charlotte mold (see Sources); a 5-inch round of stiff cardboard

Line charlotte mold with plastic wrap. Trim 1 whole bread slice into a round to fit in bottom of mold and reserve. Arrange halved slices, overlapping slightly, around sides of mold, then press bread round into bottom.

Combine raspberries, strawberries, sugar, and framboise in a 2-quart saucepan and bring to a simmer over moderate heat, stirring. Cover and simmer, stirring occasionally, until fruit is crushed and has given off liquid and sugar is dissolved, about 3 minutes. Pour fruit into a medium-mesh sieve set over a bowl and let drain for 5 minutes; reserve fruit and syrup separately. (You should have about 1 cup syrup.)

Spoon half of fruit into mold. Top with 1 slice of remaining bread, trimming it as necessary. Spoon remaining fruit into mold and ladle about 1/3 cup syrup over it. Top with enough of remaining 2 slices of bread, cut into pieces as necessary, to cover top completely. Cover bread with plastic wrap and top with cardboard round, then weight pudding evenly with a 2-pound weight. Refrigerate for at least 12 hours. Refrigerate remaining syrup, covered.

Just before serving, remove weight, cardboard, and top piece of plastic wrap, invert a large round serving plate with a lip over mold, and invert pudding onto plate; remove plastic wrap. Spoon reserved syrup a little at a time over top and sides of pudding. Decorate top with fruit and serve, with whipped cream if desired.

COOK'S NOTE

- The pudding can be refrigerated in the mold for up to 36 hours.

Sticky Toffee Pudding with Toffee Sauce

SERVES 6
ACTIVE TIME: 45 MINUTES ■ START TO FINISH: 1 1/2 HOURS

■ Rich with dates and brown sugar and topped with a caramel-like sauce, this dark pudding is what many of us prefer to plum pudding at the holidays. It's an English classic and one of the desserts that most of our staff members would name among their top ten. This spectacular version, which comes from Chewton Glen, a country-house hotel near London, calls for Lyle's Golden Syrup. Although it sounds esoteric, most American supermarkets have it on their shelves. ■

FOR PUDDING
- 2 cups (10 ounces) pitted dates
- 2 2/3 cups water
- 3/4 stick (6 tablespoons) unsalted butter, softened
- 1/3 cup packed dark brown sugar
- 3 large eggs
- 1 1/2 teaspoons vanilla extract
- 1 3/4 cups self-rising flour (not cake flour)
- 1 1/2 teaspoons baking soda

FOR SAUCE
- 1 cup heavy cream
- 1 stick (8 tablespoons) unsalted butter
- 1/2 cup packed dark brown sugar
- 1 tablespoon Lyle's Golden Syrup (see Sources)

SPECIAL EQUIPMENT: six 8-ounce ramekins

MAKE THE PUDDING: Put a rack in middle of oven and preheat oven to 400°F. Butter and flour ramekins, knocking out excess flour.

Combine dates and water in a 1- to 2-quart saucepan and bring to a boil. Transfer dates (with water) to a heatproof bowl and cool to room temperature.

Beat butter and brown sugar in a medium bowl with an electric mixer at medium-high speed until pale and fluffy, about 1 minute. Add eggs one at a time, beating well after each addition, then beat in vanilla. Mix in flour.

Purée cooled date mixture with baking soda in a food processor until just combined. Add to batter and stir until just combined. Divide batter among ramekins.

Put ramekins on a baking sheet and bake until a wooden pick or skewer inserted in center of a pudding comes out clean, 20 to 30 minutes. Cool puddings in ramekins on a rack for 10 minutes.

WHILE THE PUDDINGS COOL, MAKE THE SAUCE: Combine cream, butter, brown sugar, and syrup in a 1- to 2-quart heavy saucepan and bring to a boil, stirring. Boil until sauce is reduced to about 1 1/3 cups and thick enough to coat back of a wooden spoon, 3 to 5 minutes.

Run a sharp knife around edge of each ramekin and transfer puddings one by one, right side up, to dessert plates. Serve warm with sauce.

COOK'S NOTE

- The puddings can be baked, cooled, and unmolded up to 1 day ahead and stored in an airtight container at room temperature. Reheat, wrapped in foil, in a 350°F oven until heated through, about 15 minutes.

Fig Pudding with Rum Butter

SERVES 10
ACTIVE TIME: 1 HOUR ■ START TO FINISH: 4 HOURS

■ This is the figgy pudding you're always reading about in Dickens, the one that the Victorians sat down to every Christmas. It's dense, filled with spices and figs and bread crumbs, and enlivened with grated orange rind. Do note that the intense flavor comes from suet, so this is not the dessert to serve to vegetarians. ■

FOR PUDDING

- 1¾ cups whole milk
- 1 pound dried Calimyrna figs, stemmed and chopped (2 cups packed)
- 1½ cups all-purpose flour
- 2½ teaspoons baking powder
- 1 teaspoon ground cinnamon
- 1 teaspoon freshly grated nutmeg
- ¾ teaspoon salt
- 3 cups cold shredded beef suet (12 ounces; see Sources)
- 1 cup sugar
- 3 large eggs
- 1½ cups fresh white bread crumbs
- 2 tablespoons finely grated orange zest

FOR RUM BUTTER

- 2 sticks (½ pound) unsalted butter, softened
- 1 cup packed light brown sugar
- ⅛ teaspoon freshly grated nutmeg
- ¼ cup dark rum

SPECIAL EQUIPMENT: a 2-quart decorative pudding mold with a lid

PREPARE THE PUDDING: Combine milk and figs in a 2-quart heavy saucepan, bring just to a simmer, and simmer gently over low heat, uncovered, stirring occasionally, for 20 minutes. Transfer to a shallow dish and cool completely, about 1 hour.

Generously butter mold. Sift together flour, baking powder, cinnamon, nutmeg, and salt into a medium bowl.

Beat suet and sugar in a large bowl with an electric mixer at medium speed until fluffy, about 3 minutes with a stand mixer, 6 minutes with a handheld mixer. Add eggs one at a time, beating well after each addition. Reduce speed to low and mix in bread crumbs and orange zest. Add flour mixture in batches alternately with fig mixture, mixing well after each addition.

Pour mixture into buttered mold and fit with lid. Put mold in a large pot and add enough boiling water to reach halfway up sides of mold. Cover pot with a lid and steam pudding over moderately low heat for 2 hours. (Replenish water if necessary.)

Remove mold from pot and cool pudding in mold on a rack, still covered with lid, for 20 minutes.

MEANWHILE, MAKE THE RUM BUTTER: Beat together butter, sugar, and nutmeg in a medium bowl with electric mixer until fluffy, about 1 minute. Beat in rum 1 tablespoon at a time until incorporated.

Remove lid from pudding, invert a serving plate over mold, and invert pudding onto plate. Serve warm with rum butter.

COOK'S NOTES

- The pudding can be prepared (but not steamed) up to 1 day ahead. Pour it into the buttered mold, cover with the lid, and refrigerate.
- The steamed pudding can be cooled on a plate, then returned to the mold and refrigerated, covered, for up to 2 days. To reheat, steam as above until heated through (a metal skewer inserted into the pudding for 10 seconds and then removed should be hot to the touch all the way along the inserted portion), about 1½ hours.

Chocolate Espresso Pots de Crème

SERVES 8
ACTIVE TIME: 30 MINUTES ■ START TO FINISH: 5½ HOURS (INCLUDES CHILLING)

■ Intensely flavorful and velvety, this dessert is one that no chocolate lover could possibly resist. We've replaced the whole eggs in the classic French pudding with egg yolks, making it even richer and smoother. We've also added a touch of espresso to temper the sweetness. In France these are made in little white lidded dishes, but ramekins or custard cups will do just as well. ■

- 6 ounces good bittersweet chocolate (not unsweetened), finely chopped
- 1⅓ cups heavy cream
- ⅔ cup whole milk
- 1½–2 teaspoons instant espresso powder, to taste
- Salt
- 6 large egg yolks
- 2 tablespoons sugar

OPTIONAL GARNISH: bittersweet chocolate curls (see Cook's Note) and chocolate-covered espresso beans (see Sources)

SPECIAL EQUIPMENT: 8 pot de crème cups or 4- to 5-ounce ramekins

Put chocolate in a small heatproof bowl. Combine cream, milk, espresso powder, and a pinch of salt in a 2-quart heavy saucepan and bring just to a boil, stirring until espresso powder is dissolved. Pour over chocolate, then whisk gently until chocolate is melted and mixture is smooth.

Whisk together yolks, sugar, and a pinch of salt in a medium bowl. Add warm chocolate mixture in a slow stream, whisking constantly. Pour custard through a fine-mesh sieve into a 1-quart glass measuring cup and let cool to room temperature (to prevent condensation from diluting pots de crème when covered), stirring occasionally, about 15 minutes.

Put a rack in middle of oven and preheat oven to 300°F.

Line bottom of a baking pan large enough to hold pot de crème cups with a folded kitchen towel and arrange cups on towel. Divide custard among cups and add enough boiling water to baking pan to reach halfway up sides of cups. (If cups have lids, do not use during baking.) Cover pan tightly with foil and poke a few holes in foil with a skewer. Bake until custards are set around edges but still tremble slightly in centers, 30 to 35 minutes.

With tongs, transfer cups to a rack to cool completely, uncovered, about 1 hour. Refrigerate, covered, until cold, at least 3 hours.

Serve garnished with chocolate curls and chocolate-covered espresso beans, if desired.

COOK'S NOTES

- The pots de crème can be refrigerated for up to 2 days.
- To make chocolate curls, shave curls from a block of room-temperature chocolate with a vegetable peeler.

Maple Pumpkin Pots de Crème

SERVES 10
ACTIVE TIME: 30 MINUTES ■ START TO FINISH: 3 HOURS (INCLUDES CHILLING)

■ The perfect marriage of maple and pumpkin, this custard is an elegant alternative to pumpkin pie. Or serve it along with the traditional parade of Thanksgiving desserts. Be sure to use only pure maple syrup. Grade A Dark Amber and Grade B syrup (see Sources) have a more intense flavor than Fancy Grade. ■

- 1 cup heavy cream
- ¾ cup whole milk
- ¾ cup pure maple syrup
- ½ cup canned solid-pack pumpkin
- 7 large egg yolks
- ½ teaspoon ground cinnamon
- ⅛ teaspoon freshly grated nutmeg
- ⅛ teaspoon salt

SPECIAL EQUIPMENT: ten 2- to 3-ounce ramekins or custard cups

Put a rack in middle of oven and preheat oven to 325°F.

Whisk together cream, milk, syrup, and pumpkin in a 1½-quart heavy saucepan and bring just to a simmer over moderate heat.

Meanwhile, whisk together yolks, cinnamon, nutmeg, and salt in a medium bowl.

Add hot pumpkin mixture to yolks in a slow stream, whisking constantly. Pour custard through a fine-mesh sieve into a large glass measuring cup, then divide among ramekins (you may have some custard left over if using smaller ramekins). Arrange ramekins in a large baking pan and add enough boiling water to pan to reach halfway up sides of ramekins. Cover pan tightly with foil and bake until a knife inserted in center of a custard comes out clean, 35 to 40 minutes.

With tongs, transfer custards to a rack to cool completely. Refrigerate, covered, until cold, at least 2 hours.

COOK'S NOTE

- The pots de crème can be refrigerated for up to 2 days.

Crème Caramel

SERVES 8

ACTIVE TIME: 20 MINUTES ■ START TO FINISH: 4 HOURS (INCLUDES CHILLING)

■ Make this once and you'll understand why so many countries have a version of this dish—and why so many claim it as their own. This is kitchen magic at its best: a few eggs, cream, milk, and sugar stirred into a silky custard that comes to the table floating on a sauce the color of topaz. ■

1½ cups sugar
1½ cups heavy cream
1½ cups whole milk
⅛ teaspoon salt
3 large eggs
3 large egg yolks
¾ teaspoon vanilla extract

SPECIAL EQUIPMENT: a 10-inch glass pie plate (1–1½ inches deep); an 11- to 14-inch round serving plate with a slight lip

Put a rack in middle of oven and preheat oven to 350°F.

Cook 1 cup sugar in a dry large nonstick skillet over moderate heat, swirling and shaking pan to help sugar melt evenly, until sugar melts and becomes a deep golden caramel. Immediately pour caramel into pie plate and tilt plate to coat bottom and sides evenly.

Combine cream, milk, salt, and remaining ½ cup sugar in a 3-quart heavy saucepan and bring to a simmer; remove from heat.

Whisk eggs, yolks, and vanilla together in a medium bowl, then slowly add hot cream mixture, whisking constantly. Pour custard through a fine-mesh sieve into pie plate.

Put pie plate in a baking pan and add enough boiling water to pan to reach halfway up sides of pie plate. Bake custard until it is set but still trembles slightly, 40 to 45 minutes (custard will continue to set as it cools). Remove pie plate from water and cool completely on a rack.

Cover custard loosely with plastic wrap and refrigerate for at least 2 hours.

Run a thin knife around edge of crème caramel and rotate pie plate back and forth to make sure crème is loosened. Invert serving plate on top of pie plate, then invert crème caramel onto serving plate (caramel will run out to edges of plate).

COOK'S NOTE

- The crème caramel can be refrigerated in the pie plate for up to 1 day.

Almond Flan with Summer Fruit

SERVES 6
ACTIVE TIME: 30 MINUTES ■ START TO FINISH: 5¾ HOURS (INCLUDES COOLING)

■ In Spain, the name for crème caramel is flan. In this one, the flavor of almonds is added to the mix and the custard is embellished with fruit. ■

1¾ cups sugar
¼ cup water
3 cups whole milk
1 cup heavy cream
5 large eggs
5 large egg yolks
¼ teaspoon salt
½–¾ teaspoon almond extract (to taste)
½ teaspoon vanilla extract
ACCOMPANIMENT: berries or sliced peaches or nectarines

Put a rack in middle of oven and preheat oven to 325°F.

Set out a 9-by-5-inch loaf pan. Combine ¾ cup sugar and water in a 1- to 1½-quart heavy saucepan and cook over moderate heat, stirring, until sugar is dissolved. Bring to a boil and boil, brushing down sides of pan with a pastry brush dipped in cold water, until syrup begins to turn golden, about 5 minutes. Continue to boil, swirling pan, until caramel is golden, about 2 minutes more, then immediately pour into loaf pan and tilt pan to coat bottom and ½ inch up sides (use caution, as pan will get very hot). Let caramel harden.

Bring milk and cream to a bare simmer in a 2-quart heavy saucepan over moderate heat.

Meanwhile, whisk together eggs, yolks, salt, and remaining 1 cup sugar in a large bowl. Add hot milk mixture in a slow stream, whisking constantly, then stir in almond and vanilla extracts. Pour custard through a fine-mesh sieve into loaf pan and cover pan with a double layer of foil.

Put loaf pan in a larger baking pan and pour enough boiling water into baking pan to reach halfway up sides of loaf pan. Bake until a knife inserted 1 inch from edge of flan comes out clean but center still trembles, about 1¼ hours (flan will continue to set as it cools). Remove loaf pan from water, remove foil, and cool completely on a rack.

Cover custard loosely with plastic wrap and refrigerate for at least 3 hours. Run a thin knife around sides of loaf pan, invert a platter over pan, and invert flan onto platter. Surround with fruit.

COOK'S NOTE

■ The flan can be made up to 1 day ahead and refrigerated in the loaf pan, covered.

Classic Zabaglione

SERVES 6
ACTIVE TIME: 10 MINUTES ■ START TO FINISH: 10 MINUTES

■ Restaurants all over Italy serve this Marsala-scented dessert for two reasons. One is that it makes delicious clouds of custard. The other is that it gives the cook the opportunity to walk around the dining room whipping the custard by hand in a copper bowl. We've simplified the process, mixing it over hot water in the kitchen—less dramatic, but no less delicious. ■

6 large egg yolks
½ cup sugar
¼ cup dry Marsala wine
ACCOMPANIMENT: fresh berries
SPECIAL EQUIPMENT: an instant-read thermometer

Put thermometer in a cup of hot water, to expedite taking temperature of custard.

Beat together all ingredients in a small deep metal bowl with a whisk or a handheld electric mixer until well combined. Set bowl over a saucepan of barely simmering water and beat until mixture triples in volume and registers 140°F on thermometer, about 5 minutes. Then beat for 3 minutes more, keeping temperature at 140°F. Serve immediately, with fresh berries.

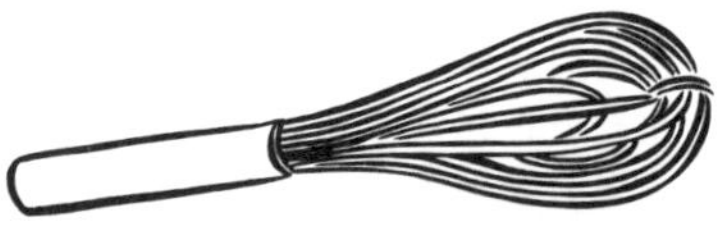

Classic Crème Brûlée

SERVES 6
ACTIVE TIME: 20 MINUTES ■ START TO FINISH: 5 HOURS (INCLUDES CHILLING)

■ Legend holds that this subtly flavored, delicate custard, whose name translates literally as burned cream, originated at the University of Cambridge, in England. Indeed, nearly every individual college, whether it is Christ's College, Trinity College (where the hardened sugar cover is broken with the aid of a perfectly weighted sterling silver hammer), or King's College, lays claim to having invented it. The silken vanilla-scented custard is covered with a layer of sugar, which becomes a brittle sheet of caramel. Burning the sugar evenly can be a challenge the first time out, and though you can accomplish it with a broiler, we find that a small blowtorch specifically designed for kitchen use works best. We prefer turbinado sugar, a slightly refined sugar, for the topping, because it melts easily and forms a crisp, easily shattered cover. ■

- 3 cups heavy cream
- 1 vanilla bean, halved lengthwise, or 1½ teaspoons vanilla extract
- 6 large egg yolks
- ⅓ cup granulated sugar
- Pinch of salt
- 3 tablespoons turbinado sugar, such as Sugar in the Raw

SPECIAL EQUIPMENT: six 5-ounce flameproof ramekins; a small blowtorch (see Sources)

Put a rack in middle of oven and preheat oven to 325°F.

Pour cream into a 2-quart heavy saucepan. Using tip of a knife, scrape seeds from vanilla bean, if using, into cream and add pod (if using vanilla extract, do not add it yet). Heat cream over moderate heat until hot but not boiling; remove from heat and discard pod.

Whisk together yolks, granulated sugar, and salt in a medium bowl until well combined. Add hot cream in a slow stream, whisking constantly until combined. Pour custard through a fine-mesh sieve into a bowl and whisk in vanilla extract, if using. Ladle custard into ramekins.

Arrange ramekins in a roasting pan and add enough boiling water to pan to reach halfway up sides of ramekins. Bake until custards are just set, 25 to 30 minutes. With tongs, transfer custards to a rack to cool, then refrigerate, uncovered, for at least 4 hours.

Just before serving, sprinkle turbinado sugar evenly over custards. Move blowtorch flame evenly back and forth close to sugar until sugar is caramelized. Let stand until sugar is hardened, 3 to 5 minutes.

COOK'S NOTE

■ The custards can be refrigerated for up to 2 days (cover after the first 4 hours). Pat the tops gently with paper towels before sprinkling with turbinado sugar and caramelizing.

VARIATION

■ COFFEE CRÈME BRÛLÉE: Stir 1½ tablespoons instant espresso powder into the hot cream and proceed as directed.

Panna Cotta

SERVES 8
ACTIVE TIME: 15 MINUTES ■ START TO FINISH: 4¾ HOURS (INCLUDES CHILLING)

■ *Panna cotta* means "cooked cream" in Italian, and that's exactly what this dessert is: an eggless cream custard that's set with a little gelatin and chilled. It looks and tastes wonderful with red summer fruits such as raspberries, strawberries, and sweet cherries. You'll need to make it at least four hours in advance so it can set. Our version is adapted from one served at the Maples Inn, in Bar Harbor, Maine. ■

2¾ teaspoons unflavored gelatin (from two ¼-ounce envelopes)
2 tablespoons cold water
2 cups heavy cream
1 cup half-and-half
⅓ cup sugar
1½ teaspoons vanilla extract

SPECIAL EQUIPMENT: eight 3-ounce ramekins

Lightly oil ramekins. Sprinkle gelatin over water in a small bowl and let stand for about 1 minute to soften.

Combine cream, half-and-half, and sugar in a 2- to 3-quart heavy saucepan and bring just to a boil over moderately high heat, stirring until sugar is dissolved. Remove from heat and stir 1 cup cream mixture into gelatin mixture, then stir cream and gelatin mixture back into cream. Stir in vanilla.

Divide cream mixture among ramekins and let cool to room temperature, about 30 minutes, then refrigerate, covered, until panna cotta is set, at least 4 hours.

One at a time, dip ramekins into a bowl of hot water for 3 seconds, then run a thin flexible knife around edge of ramekin, tilting it so panna cotta pulls away from sides. Invert ramekin onto center of a small plate, holding ramekin and plate at a 45-degree angle so panna cotta slips out.

COOK'S NOTE

- The panna cotta can be refrigerated in the ramekins for up to 1 day.

Burnt Orange Panna Cotta

SERVE 6

ACTIVE TIME: 30 MINUTES ■ START TO FINISH: 9½ HOURS (INCLUDES CHILLING)

■ Light as air, this panna cotta combines the sparkle of orange caramel and the tanginess of sour cream. Topped with a fresh orange sauce, it makes an unusual and utterly irresistible dessert. ■

1½ teaspoons unflavored gelatin (from one ¼-ounce envelope)
2 tablespoons whole milk
¼ cup confectioners' sugar
⅛ teaspoon salt
1½ cups heavy cream
¼ cup granulated sugar
2½ teaspoons finely grated orange zest
¼ cup fresh orange juice
¾ cup sour cream
2 navel oranges

SPECIAL EQUIPMENT: six 4-ounce metal molds or ramekins

Lightly oil molds or ramekins. Sprinkle gelatin over milk in a small bowl and let stand for about 1 minute to soften. Whisk together confectioners' sugar, salt, and 1 cup cream in another small bowl.

Heat granulated sugar in a dry small heavy saucepan over moderate heat, without stirring, until it begins to melt. Continue to cook, stirring occasionally with a fork, until melted into a golden caramel. Stir in 1½ teaspoons zest and cook, stirring, until zest is fragrant, 30 seconds to 1 minute. Stir cream mixture and carefully add to caramel (it will bubble and harden). Cook over moderately low heat, stirring, until caramel is dissolved. Add gelatin mixture and remaining 1 teaspoon zest and stir until gelatin is dissolved. Stir in orange juice, remove from heat, and let stand just until cooled to room temperature.

Pour caramel mixture through a fine-mesh sieve into a medium bowl.

Beat remaining ½ cup heavy cream in a small bowl with an electric mixer until it just holds soft peaks. Whisk sour cream in another small bowl until smooth. Fold whipped cream into sour cream, then fold into caramel mixture until well combined.

Spoon into molds and refrigerate, covered, until firm, at least 8 hours.

One at a time, dip molds into a bowl of hot water for 3 seconds, then run a thin flexible knife around edge of mold, tilting mold so panna cotta pulls away from sides. Invert mold onto center of a dessert plate, holding mold and plate at a 45-degree angle so panna cotta slips out. Let panna cotta stand at room temperature for 20 minutes.

Meanwhile, remove peel and white pith from oranges with a sharp paring knife. Holding oranges over a bowl to catch juices, cut segments free from membranes and transfer segments to a cutting board.

Squeeze juice from membranes into bowl. Coarsely chop orange segments and add them to juice.

Just before serving, spoon oranges and juice over panna cotta.

COOK'S NOTE

- The panna cotta can be refrigerated in the molds for up to 1 day.

Tiramisù

SERVES 6
ACTIVE TIME: 25 MINUTES ■ START TO FINISH: 6½ HOURS (INCLUDES CHILLING)

■ This Italian dessert, whose name means "pull me up," swept across America in the 1970s and has stayed on menus ever since. Though many restaurants serve pallid versions, this wonderful mélange of mascarpone, Marsala, cake, and espresso, from Wendy Artin, an American artist living in Rome, will remind you of the reason for its enduring popularity. Ladyfingers are standard, but we've found that the Italian version, called *savoiardi,* are exceptionally good at absorbing the espresso, becoming tasty and tender without falling apart. Look for them at Italian markets and specialty foods shops, or see Sources. ■

3 large eggs, separated
¾ cup sugar
1 (8-ounce) container (1 scant cup) mascarpone
Pinch of salt
½ cup very cold heavy cream
2 cups brewed espresso or very strong brewed coffee, cooled to room temperature
2 tablespoons sweet Marsala wine
18 *savoiardi* (crisp Italian ladyfingers)
¼ cup good bittersweet chocolate shavings (not unsweetened; shavings made with a vegetable peeler) or 2 tablespoons unsweetened cocoa powder

Beat together yolks and ½ cup sugar in a large bowl with an electric mixer at medium speed until thick and pale, about 2 minutes. Beat in mascarpone until just combined.

Beat whites and salt in another bowl with cleaned beaters until whites just hold soft peaks. Add remaining ¼ cup sugar a little at a time, beating, then continue to beat until whites just hold stiff peaks.

Beat cream in another bowl with cleaned beaters until it just holds soft peaks. Gently but thoroughly fold cream into mascarpone mixture, then fold in whites.

Stir together espresso and Marsala in a shallow bowl. Dip 1 ladyfinger in espresso mixture, soaking it for about 4 seconds on each side, and transfer to an 8-inch square glass baking dish (1-quart capacity). Repeat with 8 more ladyfingers, trimming them as needed to fit snugly in bottom of dish. Spread half of mascarpone mixture evenly over ladyfingers. Make another layer in same manner with remaining ladyfingers and mascarpone mixture. Refrigerate tiramisù, covered, for at least 6 hours.

Just before serving, sprinkle with chocolate.

COOK'S NOTES

- The eggs in this recipe are not cooked. If this is a concern, see page 629.
- The tiramisù can be refrigerated for up to 1 day.

Coeurs à la Crème with Blackberries

SERVES 6
ACTIVE TIME: 15 MINUTES ■ START TO FINISH: 5 HOURS (INCLUDES CHILLING)

■ If you've ever wondered about those pretty heart-shaped porcelain molds you see in cookware stores, wonder no more: they're made specifically for this thoroughly romantic dessert, which is like cheesecake in texture and not overly sweet. This version was adapted from a recipe by the author Suzanne Rodriguez. ■

FOR *COEURS À LA CRÈME*

- ¾ pound cream cheese, softened
- 1 (8-ounce) container sour cream
- 3 tablespoons confectioners' sugar, or to taste
- Pinch of salt
- ½ teaspoon vanilla extract
- ½ teaspoon fresh lemon juice

FOR TOPPING

- 1 pint (11 ounces) blackberries
- 1 tablespoon granulated sugar
- 1 tablespoon crème de cassis (black currant liqueur; optional)
- ½ teaspoon fresh lemon juice

SPECIAL EQUIPMENT: six ⅓-cup ceramic *coeur à la crème* molds (see Sources); cheesecloth

MAKE THE *COEURS*: Beat together cream cheese, sour cream, confectioners' sugar, salt, vanilla, and lemon juice in a large bowl with an electric mixer until smooth. Force mixture through a fine sieve into a bowl.

Line each mold with a single layer of dampened cheesecloth. Divide cheese mixture among molds and smooth tops. Fold overhanging cheesecloth over tops and press down lightly. Arrange molds in a shallow pan or dish (to catch drips) and refrigerate, covered, for at least 4 hours.

MAKE THE TOPPING: Mash half of blackberries with sugar in a small bowl. Stir in remaining whole berries, cassis (if using), and lemon juice. Let berries macerate, stirring occasionally, for 20 minutes.

Unfold cheesecloth, unmold *coeurs* onto plates, and carefully peel off cheesecloth. Let stand at room temperature for 20 minutes.

Spoon topping over *coeurs*.

COOK'S NOTE

- The *coeurs* can be refrigerated in the molds, covered, for up to 2 days.

Chocolate Mousse

SERVES 8

ACTIVE TIME: 45 MINUTES ■ START TO FINISH: 7 HOURS (INCLUDES CHILLING)

■ Chocolate mousse was the first classic French dessert that many of us tasted. And no matter how often we may have eaten it since, a well-made mousse still has all the rich allure of that first bite. This version has another advantage: it is made with cooked eggs, not raw ones. Use your favorite bittersweet chocolate here; some premium brands, with a higher percentage of cocoa solids, will result in a slightly denser mousse. ■

- 2 cups very cold heavy cream
- 4 large egg yolks
- 3 tablespoons sugar
- Pinch of salt
- 1 teaspoon vanilla extract
- 7 ounces good bittersweet chocolate (not unsweetened), chopped

ACCOMPANIMENT: lightly sweetened whipped cream

SPECIAL EQUIPMENT: an instant-read thermometer

Heat ¾ cup cream in a 1-quart heavy saucepan until hot but not boiling; remove from heat.

Whisk together yolks, sugar, and salt in a metal bowl until well combined, then add hot cream in a slow stream, whisking until combined. Transfer mixture to saucepan and cook over moderately low heat, stirring constantly, until it registers 160°F on thermometer. Pour custard through a fine-mesh sieve into a small bowl and stir in vanilla.

Melt chocolate in a large metal bowl set over a pan of barely simmering water, stirring frequently. Whisk custard into chocolate until smooth. Let cool.

Beat remaining 1¼ cups cream in a large bowl with an electric mixer until it just holds stiff peaks. Whisk one quarter of cream into chocolate custard to lighten it, then gently but thoroughly fold in remaining cream.

Spoon mousse into eight 6-ounce stemmed glasses or ramekins. Refrigerate, covered, for at least 6 hours.

Let mousse stand at room temperature for about 20 minutes before serving, with whipped cream.

COOK'S NOTE

- The mousse can be refrigerated for up to 1 day.

VARIATIONS

- ESPRESSO CHOCOLATE MOUSSE: Dissolve 2 teaspoons instant espresso powder in the hot cream; omit the vanilla extract.
- ORANGE-FLAVORED CHOCOLATE MOUSSE: Whisk 3 tablespoons Grand Marnier or other orange-flavored liqueur into the strained custard.
- COGNAC-FLAVORED CHOCOLATE MOUSSE: Whisk 2 tablespoons Cognac into the strained custard.

Lemon Parfaits

SERVES 8
ACTIVE TIME: 45 MINUTES ■ START TO FINISH: 2¾ HOURS (INCLUDES CHILLING)

■ Sally Tager, a *Gourmet* contributor, once said that for every chocolate fanatic there is an equally enthusiastic lemon fanatic. Her lemon mousse custard demonstrates why. We like to serve it well chilled, in short-stemmed parfait glasses. ■

1 tablespoon finely grated lemon zest
½ cup strained fresh lemon juice
3 large eggs, separated
1 cup granulated sugar
Pinch of cream of tartar
Pinch of salt
1 cup very cold heavy cream
3 tablespoons confectioners' sugar

OPTIONAL GARNISH: slivered lemon zest
SPECIAL EQUIPMENT: an instant-read thermometer

Whisk together lemon zest, juice, egg yolks, and ½ cup granulated sugar in a 1- to 1½-quart heavy saucepan until well combined. Cook over moderate heat, whisking constantly, until mixture thickens and registers 160°–170°F on thermometer, about 5 minutes; do not let boil. Transfer to a large heatproof bowl and let cool.

Beat egg whites, cream of tartar, and salt in a large bowl with an electric mixer at medium speed until whites hold soft peaks. Beat in remaining ½ cup sugar 1 tablespoon at a time, then beat at high speed until meringue holds stiff, glossy peaks, about 1 minute with a stand mixer or 2 minutes with a handheld mixer. Fold meringue into lemon mixture.

Beat cream in a large bowl with cleaned beaters until it holds soft peaks. Add confectioners' sugar and beat at medium-high speed until cream holds stiff peaks.

Fold whipped cream into lemon mixture and divide among eight 8-ounce stemmed glasses. Freeze, covered with plastic wrap, for at least 2 hours.

Serve garnished with lemon zest, if desired.

COOK'S NOTES

- The parfaits can be frozen for up to 1 day. Transfer to the refrigerator 30 minutes to 1 hour before serving to soften slightly.
- The egg whites in this recipe are not cooked. If this is a concern, we recommend using powdered egg whites, such as Just Whites, reconstituted according to the manufacturer's directions, or packaged liquid egg whites (see page 827).

Crème Citron

Chilled Lemon-Wine Mousse with Raspberries

SERVES 4

ACTIVE TIME: 15 MINUTES ■ START TO FINISH: 1¾ HOURS (INCLUDES CHILLING)

■ Dry white wine adds an unusually mellow acidity that complements and lightens the lemon juice in this mousse, a summer favorite of ours. It comes from an old family recipe that was passed down to us by Hélène Ellaway via *Gourmet* reader Kasia Foch. ■

- 2 large eggs
- ½ cup sugar
- ½ cup dry white wine
- 3 tablespoons fresh lemon juice
- 2 teaspoons finely grated lemon zest
- ½ cup very cold heavy cream
- 1½ cups (about 6 ounces) raspberries

SPECIAL EQUIPMENT: an instant-read thermometer

Beat eggs in a medium bowl with an electric mixer at moderately high speed to blend. Add sugar a little at a time, beating at moderately high speed, then beat for 3 minutes more. Add wine and lemon juice and beat until just combined.

Transfer mixture to a 2-quart heavy saucepan and cook over moderately low heat, stirring constantly with a wooden spoon, until custard is thick enough to coat back of spoon and registers 170°F on thermometer, about 5 minutes; do not let boil. Transfer to a large bowl and stir in zest. Cover surface with wax paper and refrigerate until cold, about 30 minutes.

Beat cream in a small bowl with cleaned beaters until it just holds stiff peaks. Fold into custard.

Layer mousse and berries alternately in several layers in four wineglasses and refrigerate until cold, about 1 hour.

COOK'S NOTE

■ The custard can be refrigerated, covered, for up to 1 day.

Chocolate Soufflé

SERVES 4

ACTIVE TIME: 20 MINUTES ■ START TO FINISH: 45 MINUTES

■ Here is a chocolate dessert that we dream about: made with only four ingredients, it is exceptionally flavorful, thanks to the top-quality chocolate. We got the best taste—rich, complex, and lingering—from Valrhona chocolate, which can be found at specialty foods shops (or see Sources). According to Maricel Presilla, the author of *The New Taste of Chocolate,* Valrhona has a high cacao content (60 to 70 percent) and is a blend of the best beans. Callebaut, another good brand that we generally like very much, proved disappointing in this recipe. We omitted the milk that goes into most chocolate soufflés, and the result is a puffier, crisper texture outside and a lighter, airier consistency inside. ■

- ⅓ cup sugar, plus additional for coating soufflé dish
- 5 ounces good bittersweet chocolate (not unsweetened), chopped
- 3 large eggs, separated, left at room temperature for 30 minutes
- 3 large egg whites, left at room temperature for 30 minutes
- Pinch of salt

ACCOMPANIMENT: lightly sweetened whipped cream

SPECIAL EQUIPMENT: a 5½- to 6-cup soufflé dish

Put a rack in middle of oven and preheat oven to 375°F. Generously butter soufflé dish and coat with sugar, knocking out excess.

Melt chocolate in a metal bowl set over a saucepan of barely simmering water, stirring occasionally until smooth. Remove bowl from heat and stir in yolks (mixture will stiffen).

Beat 6 whites with salt in a large bowl with an electric mixer at medium speed until they just hold soft peaks. Add 1/3 cup sugar a little at a time, then beat at high speed until meringue just holds stiff peaks. Stir about 1 cup meringue into chocolate mixture to lighten it, then gently but thoroughly fold mixture into remaining meringue.

Spoon into soufflé dish and run the tip of your thumb around inside edge of dish (this will help soufflé rise evenly). Bake until puffed and crusted on top but still trembling in center, 24 to 26 minutes. Serve immediately, with whipped cream.

COOK'S NOTE

- The soufflé can be assembled up to 30 minutes before baking. Keep, covered with an inverted large bowl (do not let the bowl touch the soufflé), at room temperature.

Coffee Soufflés with Chocolate Sauce

SERVES 4

ACTIVE TIME: 50 MINUTES ■ START TO FINISH: 1 HOUR

■ Individual soufflés can turn an ordinary dinner party into something magical. And there's a secret: they are not difficult to make. This recipe showcases the celestial combination of fine bittersweet chocolate and coffee. ■

FOR CHOCOLATE SAUCE

- 1/4 cup water
- 3 ounces good bittersweet chocolate (not unsweetened), chopped
- 1/4 teaspoon vanilla extract
- 1/8 teaspoon ground cinnamon

FOR SOUFFLÉS

- 1 cup whole milk
- 4 teaspoons cornstarch
- 4 teaspoons instant coffee granules (not espresso powder)
- 8 tablespoons granulated sugar, plus 2 tablespoons for coating ramekins
- 1 teaspoon vanilla extract
- 6 large egg whites, left at room temperature for 30 minutes
- 1/2 teaspoon cream of tartar
- Pinch of salt

GARNISH: confectioners' sugar

SPECIAL EQUIPMENT: four 6-ounce ramekins

MAKE THE CHOCOLATE SAUCE: Combine all ingredients in a small saucepan and cook, whisking, over moderately low heat until smooth and thick, about 2 minutes. Remove from heat and cool to warm.

MAKE THE SOUFFLÉS: Whisk together milk, cornstarch, coffee granules, and 2 tablespoons granulated sugar in a 1- to 2-quart heavy saucepan until smooth. Cook, whisking, over moderate heat until soufflé base boils and thickens, 1 to 2 minutes. Transfer to a heatproof large bowl and stir in vanilla. Cover surface of soufflé base with a round of wax paper to prevent a skin from forming, then cool to warm.

Put a rack in lower third of oven and preheat oven to 400°F. Lightly oil ramekins and coat each with 1 1/2 teaspoons granulated sugar, knocking out any excess.

Beat egg whites with cream of tartar and salt in a large bowl with an electric mixer at medium speed until whites just hold soft peaks. Gradually add remaining 6 tablespoons granulated sugar, then beat at high speed until whites hold stiff peaks. Stir one quarter of whites into soufflé base to lighten it, then gently but thoroughly fold in remaining whites.

Spoon mixture into ramekins, mounding it slightly. Arrange on a baking sheet and bake until soufflés are puffed and golden brown, about 15 minutes.

Lightly dust soufflés with confectioners' sugar and serve immediately, with chocolate sauce.

COOK'S NOTES

- The sauce can be made up to 2 days ahead and kept, covered, at room temperature. Reheat before serving.
- The soufflé base can be made up to 1 day ahead and refrigerated, covered. Bring to room temperature before proceeding.

Making a Soufflé

There's much to be said for the ability to fashion something truly glorious from practically nothing. In a resourceful cook's world, soufflés belong in that category. Take the Chocolate Soufflé on page 840, for instance: eggs, sugar, chocolate, and, if you're prone to gilding the lily, a little whipped cream.

A soufflé isn't as capricious as you might think, although admittedly it holds a certain element of suspense: it's going to taste good no matter what it looks like, but will it fulfill its potential — that is, rise to its most impressive height?

Essentially, you have only a few things to keep in mind.

THE FLAVOR OF THE BASE MUST BE RELATIVELY INTENSE, since it will be diluted by the beaten egg whites.

BEATING THE EGG WHITES PROPERLY is also key. Air, in the form of tiny bubbles, is trapped in the egg foam; as the soufflé bakes, the air expands, causing the soufflé to puff dramatically. (When the soufflé cools, the air contracts, making the soufflé fall.) The trick is to know when to stop beating: the whites must stay elastic so the air bubbles can expand without bursting. Adding the sugar at the right time — not before the whites hit the soft-peak stage — gives the foam stability.

FOLDING is also important. First, stir about a cup of meringue into the base to lighten it; the two mixtures will combine more readily that way. Many cookbooks tell you then to add the remaining whites to the base. We sometimes do it the other way around; as long as you are gentle and fold quickly, you shouldn't have a problem. To fold, scrape the base into the remaining foam, then cut down toward the center, turning the bowl with your other hand as you continue rhythmically to cut down and lift up some of the foam from the bottom of the bowl.

Apricot Soufflés with Vanilla Rum Crème Anglaise

SERVES 6

ACTIVE TIME: 20 MINUTES ■ START TO FINISH: 1¾ HOURS

■ This was the signature dessert at La Tulipe, the Greenwich Village restaurant founded by Sally Darr, a former *Gourmet* food editor. No wonder so many people were devastated when the restaurant closed: many of us think that if we could eat only one dessert for the rest of our lives, it would be this delightfully tart soufflé with sweet custard sauce melting gently into the puffed top. But if you don't make this with California apricots, which are much zingier in flavor and darker in color than the Turkish variety, you won't understand what all the fuss is about. ■

- 6 ounces (about 1½ cups) dried California apricots (see Sources)
- 1½ cups water
- ¾ cup sugar, plus additional for coating ramekins
- 1 tablespoon fresh lemon juice
- 1 tablespoon dark rum (optional)
- ½ teaspoon vanilla extract
- Salt
- 5 large egg whites, left at room temperature for 30 minutes
- ¼ teaspoon cream of tartar

ACCOMPANIMENT: Vanilla Rum Crème Anglaise (recipe follows)

SPECIAL EQUIPMENT: six 6-ounce ramekins

Combine apricots, water, and ½ cup sugar in a 1- to 2-quart heavy saucepan and bring to a simmer, then reduce heat and simmer, covered, until apricots are tender, about 20 minutes. Transfer to a food processor and purée until very smooth (use caution).

Transfer purée to a large bowl and stir in lemon juice, rum (if using), vanilla, and a pinch of salt. Cool completely.

Put a rack in middle of oven and preheat oven to 350°F. Generously butter ramekins and coat with sugar, knocking out excess.

Beat whites with a pinch of salt in a large bowl with an electric mixer at medium speed until foamy. Add cream of tartar and beat until whites hold soft peaks. Beat in remaining ¼ cup sugar a little at a time, then beat meringue at high speed until it just holds stiff peaks. Whisk one quarter of meringue into purée to lighten it, then gently but thoroughly fold in remaining meringue.

Ladle mixture into ramekins and arrange ramekins on a baking sheet. Bake until soufflés are puffed, golden brown, and just set in center, 25 to 30 minutes. Transfer ramekins to a rack. Using two forks, gently pull open center of each soufflé and pour some crème anglaise into each opening. Serve immediately.

COOK'S NOTES

- The purée can be made up to 2 days ahead and refrigerated, covered. Bring to room temperature before proceeding.
- To cool the purée quickly, spread it in a shallow pan and refrigerate until completely cool.

DRIED APRICOTS

We've been fans of California dried apricots for years—their tangy, strong, unmistakable flavor comes through loud and clear. We prefer them to the very sweet but insipid Turkish varieties. Unfortunately, the California fruits are becoming rarer because the growers can't compete with Turkish suppliers, who can sell their apricots for half the price. Turkish apricots, often labeled "Mediterranean," are smaller and dried whole, after the pits have been slipped out. The California kind, perhaps because they are larger and might not dry as well whole, are always cut in half before they are pitted. These days, California 'cots are available at some specialty foods shops and by mail. If you are going to eat them out of hand, splurge on tangy, tender-fleshed Blenheims, such as the "extra-fancies" from the Apricot Farm. They are the best of the best (see Sources).

Vanilla Rum Crème Anglaise

MAKES ABOUT 2¼ CUPS
ACTIVE TIME: 10 MINUTES ■ START TO FINISH: 2½ HOURS (INCLUDES CHILLING)

■ This sauce is also superb served over poached fresh fruit. ■

- 2 cups half-and-half
- ½ vanilla bean, halved lengthwise
- 5 large egg yolks
- ¼ cup sugar
- Pinch of salt
- 1 tablespoon dark rum, or to taste

SPECIAL EQUIPMENT: an instant-read thermometer

Combine half-and-half and vanilla bean in a 1- to 2-quart heavy saucepan and bring just to a boil. Remove pan from heat. Remove bean and, using tip of a knife, scrape seeds from bean into half-and-half; reserve pod for another use, if desired.

Whisk together yolks, sugar, and salt in a medium bowl. Add hot half-and-half in a steady stream, whisking constantly. Return custard to pan and cook over moderately low heat, stirring constantly with a wooden spoon, until sauce is thickened and registers 170°F on thermometer, about 3 minutes; do not let boil. Pour sauce through a fine-mesh sieve into a heatproof bowl and cool, stirring occasionally, for 15 minutes.

Stir rum into sauce. Refrigerate, covered, until very cold, at least 2 hours.

COOK'S NOTE

■ The sauce can be refrigerated for up to 2 days.

Grand Marnier Soufflé

SERVES 6
ACTIVE TIME: 20 MINUTES ■ START TO FINISH: 2 HOURS

■ Elegant in its simplicity, with a delicate Grand Marnier flavor, this soufflé is a bit of an anomaly. Baked in a low gratin dish rather than a high-sided soufflé mold, it does not puff up as high as a conventional soufflé, and it has the consistency of a light, airy pudding. ■

- ⅔ cup sugar, plus additional for coating gratin dish
- 1⅓ cups whole milk
- 1 stick (8 tablespoons) unsalted butter
- ½ cup all-purpose flour
- 4 large eggs, separated, left at room temperature for 30 minutes
- ½ cup Grand Marnier
- 4 large egg whites, left at room temperature for 30 minutes
- ½ teaspoon salt
- ½ teaspoon cream of tartar

SPECIAL EQUIPMENT: a 16-inch-long gratin dish

Put a rack in middle of oven and preheat oven to 400°F. Butter gratin dish and sprinkle with sugar, knocking out excess.

Bring milk just to a simmer in a small saucepan. Remove from heat.

Melt butter in a 2- to 3-quart saucepan over low heat. Stir in flour and cook, stirring, for 5 minutes to make a roux. Remove pan from heat and add milk in a steady stream, whisking constantly, then add remaining ⅔ cup sugar, whisking vigorously. Cook mixture over low heat, whisking, until smooth, about 2 minutes.

Remove pan from heat and add yolks one at a time, whisking after each addition until incorporated. Slowly whisk in Grand Marnier. Cover mixture with a buttered round of wax paper and cool to room temperature.

Beat 8 whites with salt in a large bowl with an electric mixer at medium speed until frothy. Add cream of tartar, increase speed to high, and beat until whites hold stiff peaks. Stir one quarter of whites into yolk mixture to lighten it, then gently but thoroughly fold mixture into remaining whites.

Reserve 1 cup of mixture and transfer remainder to gratin dish. Mound reserved mixture in center. Bake soufflé until puffed and golden, 25 to 30 minutes. Serve immediately.

Snow Eggs with Pistachio Custard and Chocolate Drizzle

SERVES 8
ACTIVE TIME: 2 HOURS ■ START TO FINISH: 10½ HOURS (INCLUDES CHILLING)

■ In France, lightly poached ovals of meringue in custard sauce are known as *oeufs à la neige* ("eggs in snow"). In Liguria, they are called *sciumette* ("little sponges"). Although we've named our spin on this classic recipe snow eggs, we might just as well have given it the fanciful title ships on the sea, since the meringues float in a pale green pistachio custard sauce. ■

- ½ cup plus 2 tablespoons (2½ ounces) shelled unsalted natural pistachios (not dyed red; preferably raw)
- 1 cup sugar
- 4 cups whole milk
- 4 large eggs, separated
- 1 teaspoon fresh lemon juice
- Salt
- 3 drops almond extract
- 2 ounces good bittersweet chocolate (not unsweetened), finely chopped

SPECIAL EQUIPMENT: an instant-read thermometer

Put a rack in middle of oven and preheat oven to 350°F.

Blanch nuts in a saucepan of boiling water for 2 minutes. Drain in a colander and transfer to a bowl of ice and cold water to stop the cooking; drain again. Peel off skins and pat nuts dry.

Spread nuts in one layer in a shallow baking pan. Bake until dry and lightly toasted, about 7 minutes. Let cool. Coarsely chop 2 tablespoons nuts; leave remaining nuts whole.

MAKE THE PISTACHIO CREAM: Finely grind whole pistachios with 2 tablespoons sugar in a food processor. Add 3 tablespoons milk and process to a paste. Add 5 tablespoons milk and process to blend. Transfer pistachio cream to a small bowl, cover, and refrigerate for 8 hours to allow flavors to develop.

MAKE THE "EGGS": Whisk together 2 tablespoons sugar and remaining 3½ cups milk in a deep 12-inch skillet and bring just to a bare simmer; milk should steam but not bubble.

Meanwhile, beat whites, lemon juice, and a pinch of salt in a large bowl with an electric mixer at medium speed until whites just hold soft peaks. Gradually beat in ½ cup plus 2 tablespoons sugar, then beat at medium-high speed until meringue just holds stiff peaks.

Using an oval ice cream scoop or soupspoon, form 8 meringue "eggs" and gently drop them into skillet of milk (keep milk at a bare simmer). Poach meringues until set on bottom, about 2 minutes, then carefully turn over and poach until set throughout, about 2 minutes more. With a slotted spoon, transfer to a shallow baking pan lined with plastic wrap and make 8 more meringues in same manner.

MAKE THE CUSTARD: Pour poaching liquid through a fine-mesh sieve into a large glass measuring cup or bowl. Whisk together yolks, remaining 2 tablespoons sugar, and a pinch of salt in a 2-quart heavy saucepan, then slowly add poaching liquid, whisking constantly. Cook over moderately low heat, stirring constantly with a wooden spoon, until custard is thick enough to coat back of spoon and registers 170°–175°F on thermometer; do not let boil.

Pour custard into a medium metal bowl and stir in pistachio cream and almond extract. Set bowl in a larger bowl of ice and cold water and cool custard, stirring occasionally. Pour custard through fine-mesh sieve into a medium bowl, pressing on solids; discard solids.

ASSEMBLE THE DESSERT: Melt chocolate in a small metal bowl set over a small saucepan of barely simmering water, stirring occasionally until smooth.

Pour custard into eight shallow bowls or rimmed plates and arrange meringues on top. Drizzle chocolate over meringues and custard and sprinkle with chopped pistachios.

COOK'S NOTES

■ Using raw, not roasted, pistachios gives the custard the best color and truest pistachio flavor.

- The meringue "eggs" and custard can be made up to 5 hours ahead and refrigerated separately, covered. Bring to room temperature before serving.
- The egg whites in this recipe are not fully cooked. If this is a concern, we recommend using powdered egg whites, such as Just Whites, reconstituted according to the manufacturer's directions, or packaged liquid egg whites (see page 827).

Pavlovas with Kiwis

SERVES 6

ACTIVE TIME: 40 MINUTES ■ START TO FINISH: 2 HOURS

■ With billows of soft whipped cream, crunchy meringue, and smooth kiwifruits, these pavlovas feel like a miracle in the mouth, slipping smoothly from one sensation to another. The vinegar in the meringue makes it crispy outside while it stays chewy within. Although this Australian classic will be welcomed wherever it goes, its ruffly white beauty makes it the perfect production for a bridal shower. ■

- 4 large egg whites, left at room temperature for 30 minutes
- 1/4 teaspoon salt
- 1/8 teaspoon cream of tartar
- 1 cup granulated sugar
- 1 tablespoon distilled white vinegar
- 1 tablespoon cornstarch
- 1 teaspoon vanilla extract
- 1 1/2 cups very cold heavy cream
- 2 tablespoons confectioners' sugar (optional)
- 4 kiwifruits, peeled, quartered lengthwise, and cut crosswise into 1/8-inch-thick slices

ACCOMPANIMENT: Kir Royale Sorbet (page 861) or 1 quart store-bought fruit sorbet

Put a rack in lower third of oven and preheat oven to 250°F. Line a baking sheet with parchment paper or foil.

Beat egg whites, salt, and cream of tartar in a large bowl with an electric mixer at medium speed until whites just hold soft peaks. Add the granulated sugar a little at a time, beating at low speed, then beat at high speed until meringue holds stiff, glossy peaks, about 2 minutes. Beat in vinegar, cornstarch, and vanilla.

With back of a spoon, spread meringue into six 3 1/2-inch rounds on baking sheet, making a slight depression in center of each (to hold fruit). Bake until crisp on outside but soft in middle, about 1 hour.

Carefully peel parchment from meringues and cool meringues on a rack for at least 20 minutes.

Beat cream with confectioners' sugar, if using, in a large bowl until it just holds stiff peaks. Serve meringues topped with whipped cream, kiwis, and sorbet.

COOK'S NOTE

- The meringues can be stored in an airtight container at room temperature for up to 1 day.

Making Meringue

A meringue is nothing more than egg whites beaten with sugar. The ratio of sugar to egg whites, along with the way you combine the sugar and whites, determine the kind of meringue you make — a smooth, glossy mixture to fold into a soufflé, a cloudlike topping for a lemon pie, or crisp baked shapes for a *dacquoise*.

There are three traditional methods for making meringues. For a classic (cold) meringue, the type we rely on most often, the sugar is gradually added to the egg whites as they are beaten, without being heated. For an Italian meringue, a hot sugar syrup is added to the whites as they are beaten (see page 677). For a Swiss meringue, the sort most often used for frosting, the whites and sugar are warmed together to dissolve the sugar before being beaten. Our tips for making a successful meringue follow.

AVOID MAKING MERINGUE ON A HUMID DAY. Because meringues have a high sugar content and sugar absorbs moisture from the air, they can become very soft if made on a humid or rainy day.

MAKE SURE YOUR UTENSILS AND BOWL ARE SQUEAKY CLEAN. The minutest trace of fat (especially from an egg yolk) can doom a meringue. It impedes foaming and drastically reduces the volume of beaten whites.

USE FRESH EGGS. They will give you a stronger, more stable meringue. Older, runnier egg whites beat up faster, but they aren't as stable and may collapse when you add other ingredients.

HAVE THE EGG WHITES AT ROOM TEMPERATURE. They will beat up faster that way. Separate the eggs while they are cold (it's easier to separate cold eggs) and leave the whites out on the kitchen counter for thirty minutes. Or, if you're in a hurry, set the bowl of whites in a larger bowl of warm water.

SEPARATE THE EGGS CAREFULLY. Since even the tiniest bit of yolk can ruin a meringue, separate each egg into two small bowls first; after you make sure that the yolk is unbroken, pour the white into the bowl you will use for beating. If you break a yolk, discard the white, even if it looks pure, and wash the bowl before proceeding. And use your thumb to remove that last little bit of white from the shell; it's not much, but it adds up in volume.

ADD THE SUGAR AT THE RIGHT TIME. Sugar (as well as the mildly acidic cream of tartar) gives a meringue stability. If you add the sugar too early, you will have to beat the whites longer to get good volume. If you add it too late, the whites will get too dry and lose their elasticity. Beat the whites at medium speed until they just hold soft peaks before you start adding the sugar. Add the sugar gradually, then beat the meringue on high speed until it forms stiff, glossy peaks, which will usually take about two minutes. Add any flavorings, such as vanilla, after you reach the stiff-peak stage; if it is added with the sugar, vanilla will tint the sugar, and thus the meringue, brown.

Dacquoise

SERVES 8 TO 10
ACTIVE TIME: 1¼ HOURS ■ START TO FINISH: 5½ HOURS (INCLUDES CHILLING)

■ There is perhaps no more elegant meringue confection than the *dacquoise,* a favorite in restaurants and pâtisseries all over Paris. Our version layers baked almond meringue with a rich coffee buttercream and is garnished with sliced almonds and a dusting of confectioners' sugar. ■

FOR ALMOND MERINGUE

- 1¼ cups (7 ounces) skinned whole almonds
- ¾ cup plus 2 tablespoons granulated sugar
- 1 tablespoon cornstarch
- 6 large egg whites, left at room temperature for 30 minutes
- ¼ teaspoon cream of tartar
- ¼ teaspoon salt

FOR COFFEE BUTTERCREAM

- 6 large egg yolks
- 1 cup granulated sugar
- ½ cup heavy cream
- 2 tablespoons instant espresso powder
- ¼ teaspoon salt
- 2½ sticks unsalted butter, cut into tablespoons, softened

GARNISH: 1 cup (4 ounces) sliced almonds, toasted (see Tips, page 938), and confectioners' sugar

SPECIAL EQUIPMENT: parchment paper; a stand mixer; an offset spatula; an instant-read thermometer

MAKE THE MERINGUE LAYERS: Put racks in upper and lower thirds of oven and preheat oven to 250°F. Line two large baking sheets with parchment paper. Using a springform pan or a plate as a guide, draw two 8½-inch circles on one sheet and a third circle on second sheet. Flip paper over (circles will show through).

Pulse nuts with 2 tablespoons sugar in a food processor until finely ground. Add cornstarch and pulse until combined.

Beat egg whites in stand mixer at medium-high speed until foamy. Add cream of tartar and salt and beat until whites just hold soft peaks. Reduce speed to low and add remaining ¾ cup sugar a little at a time. Increase speed to high and beat until meringue just holds stiff, glossy peaks. Transfer to a large bowl and gently but thoroughly fold in almond mixture.

Divide meringue evenly among parchment circles and spread with offset spatula to fill circles evenly; make a decorative swirl in top of one circle. Bake meringues, switching position of sheets halfway through baking, until just firm, dry, and pale golden, 1½ to 1¾ hours total. (If centers are still soft when meringues are golden, turn off oven and let meringues cool in oven.) Slide meringues, still on parchment, onto racks to cool, about 1 hour (they will continue to firm as they cool).

WHILE THE MERINGUES COOL, MAKE THE BUTTERCREAM: Beat yolks with ½ cup sugar in cleaned bowl of mixer at high speed until thick and pale, about 4 minutes.

Meanwhile, combine cream and remaining ½ cup sugar in a 2-quart heavy saucepan and bring to a boil, whisking until sugar is dissolved. Remove from heat. Add half of hot cream to yolks in a slow stream, beating. Pour yolk mixture into saucepan with cream and whisk in espresso powder and salt. Cook over moderate heat, stirring constantly with a wooden spoon, until custard registers 170°F on thermometer, 3 to 4 minutes; do not let boil.

Transfer mixture to cleaned bowl and beat with cleaned beaters at medium-high speed until completely cooled, about 6 minutes. At high speed, beat in butter 1 tablespoon at a time, beating well after each addition. Cover buttercream and refrigerate until firm enough to spread, at least 30 minutes. (If buttercream gets too hard or separates after chilling, beat at high speed until smooth and spreadable.)

ASSEMBLE THE *DACQUOISE:* Carefully remove meringues from parchment. Reserving swirled one for top, put 1 meringue smooth side down on a plate and spread evenly with about 1 cup buttercream. Top with another meringue, smooth side down, and press gently so that buttercream spreads to edges. Spread with another cup of buttercream and top with reserved meringue, smooth side down, pressing gently so that buttercream spreads to edges (you will have some buttercream left over). Press almonds onto sides of *dacquoise.*

Chill *dacquoise,* loosely covered with plastic wrap, until buttercream is firm, at least 2 hours.

Just before serving, dust *dacquoise* with confectioners' sugar. Cut into slices with a serrated knife, using a sawing motion.

COOK'S NOTES

- The meringue layers can be made up to 1 day ahead and kept in an airtight container at room temperature.
- The buttercream can be refrigerated for up to 2 days. Allow to soften slightly at room temperature (do not use a microwave) and beat with an electric mixer at high speed before using.
- The *dacquoise* can be refrigerated for up to 12 hours.

FROZEN DESSERTS AND SWEET SAUCES

Once upon a time ice cream was something you bought by the pint—usually flavored with vanilla, chocolate, or strawberry—or, sometimes, hand-churned at home in a laborious process requiring rock salt, water, and very strong arms. Making ice cream was a nostalgic activity primarily reserved for summer holidays.

All that changed when premium ice creams came on the market. Americans suddenly discovered that all ice creams are not created equal. Now there were issues of butterfat and additives to consider and a range of flavors that became wildly imaginative. People who cooked began to contemplate the virtues of making their own.

When they tried it, they discovered the wonder of freshness. Ice cream may keep for a very long time, but it changes while it waits, and it never tastes as good as ice cream fresh from the churn. The time of the home ice cream maker was upon us, and *Gourmet* responded by publishing recipes by the dozen. Here is the best of the lot, wonderful flavors like burnt orange and lemon meringue and the oddly fabulous Grape-Nuts ice cream. Not content to leave good enough alone, we devised two terrific cookies that turn even ordinary ice cream into superb ice cream sandwiches.

As time went on, we began experimenting with the form, discovering sneaky shortcuts like cream cheese ice cream and the sheer pleasure of fresh fruit sorbets with interesting flavors like roasted apricot. We concocted grainy granitas and smooth sherbets and an incredibly sophisticated cappuccino gelato.

In this chapter you will also find some of our favorite and most festive party desserts: chocolate-raspberry baked Alaskas, a stunning marriage of hot and cold, and watermelon sorbet with chocolate seeds that will fool anyone into thinking it's a sedate slice of fruit. There are also the madly improbable crispy macadamia-nut fried ice cream balls.

What does this prove? Just this: even if you can't take the heat, you can still be in the kitchen.

Frozen Desserts

Vanilla Bean Ice Cream

MAKES ABOUT 1 QUART
ACTIVE TIME: 20 MINUTES ■ START TO FINISH: 7 HOURS
(INCLUDES CHILLING AND FREEZING)

■ Vanilla ice cream fans are purists. This recipe delivers. The seeds are scraped out of three whole vanilla beans, and the pods are then added as well for luxurious, powerful vanilla flavor. ■

- 2 cups heavy cream
- 1 cup whole milk
- 3/4 cup sugar
- 1/8 teaspoon salt
- 3 vanilla beans, halved lengthwise
- 2 large eggs

SPECIAL EQUIPMENT: an instant-read thermometer; an ice cream maker

Combine cream, milk, sugar, and salt in a 2- to 3-quart heavy saucepan. With tip of a knife, scrape seeds from vanilla beans into cream mixture, then drop in pods. Bring just to a boil, stirring occasionally.

Meanwhile, whisk eggs in a large metal bowl. Add hot cream mixture in a slow stream, whisking constantly, then pour mixture into saucepan and cook over moderately low heat, stirring constantly with a wooden spoon, until custard is thick enough to coat back of spoon and registers 170°–175°F on thermometer; do not let boil.

Pour custard through a fine-mesh sieve into cleaned metal bowl; discard pods. Cool to room temperature, stirring occasionally, then refrigerate, covered, until cold, at least 3 hours.

Freeze custard in ice cream maker. Transfer to an airtight container and put in freezer to harden.

COOK'S NOTES

- If you can't find vanilla beans, add 1 1/2 teaspoons vanilla extract to the custard.
- The custard can be refrigerated for up to 24 hours.
- The ice cream can be made up to 1 week ahead.

Chocolate Velvet Ice Cream

MAKES ABOUT 1 QUART
ACTIVE TIME: 30 MINUTES ■ START TO FINISH: 7 HOURS
(INCLUDES CHILLING AND FREEZING)

■ A very serious version of the all-time American favorite. The combination of bittersweet chocolate and cocoa powder is the secret to its intensity. ■

- 3/4 cup plus 2 tablespoons sugar
- 1/2 cup unsweetened Dutch-process cocoa powder
- 1/4 teaspoon salt
- 1 1/2 cups heavy cream
- 1 cup whole milk
- 3 large egg yolks
- 6 ounces good bittersweet chocolate (not unsweetened), finely chopped

SPECIAL EQUIPMENT: an instant-read thermometer; an ice cream maker

Whisk together sugar, cocoa powder, and salt in a 2- to 3-quart heavy saucepan until combined, then whisk in cream and milk. Bring mixture just to a boil, stirring occasionally.

Meanwhile, beat yolks in a large metal bowl until smooth. Add hot cream mixture in a slow stream, whisking constantly, and pour back into pan. Cook over moderately low heat, stirring constantly with a wooden spoon, until custard is thick enough to coat back of spoon and registers 170°F on thermometer; do not let boil. Remove pan from heat and add chocolate, whisking until melted.

Pour custard through a fine-mesh sieve into cleaned metal bowl. Cool to room temperature, stirring occasionally, then refrigerate, covered, until cold, at least 3 hours. (Custard will get very thick.)

Beat custard with an electric mixer at medium-high speed until it is thick and holds very soft peaks, 2 to 4 minutes. Freeze in ice cream maker. Transfer to an airtight container and put in freezer to harden.

COOK'S NOTES

- The custard can be refrigerated for up to 24 hours.
- The ice cream can be made up to 1 week ahead.

Cream of the Crop

Cream is categorized by the amount of milk fat it contains. The more milk fat it has, the easier it is to whip. But, we wondered as we compared labels, if so-called whipping cream has less milk fat than heavy cream, why is it marketed specifically for whipping? According to the Center for Dairy Research at the University of Wisconsin in Madison, the high milk-fat content of heavy cream means that it can be overbeaten in a flash, turning to butter before your very eyes. Whipping cream, with its slightly lower fat content, is more forgiving ("almost idiot-proof," said our source).

HALF-AND-HALF: This mixture of cream and milk must contain at least 10.5 percent but no more than 18 percent milk fat. It's best used in coffee and anytime you want something with more body than milk but lighter than light cream. Because of its low fat content, it can't be whipped.

LIGHT CREAM: Sometimes called coffee cream, this contains anything from 18 to 30 percent milk fat. It also may contain stabilizers and emulsifiers.

WHIPPING CREAM: This may also be labeled "light whipping cream." It has between 30 and 36 percent milk fat.

HEAVY CREAM: With at least 36 percent milk fat, heavy cream whips up faster than whipping cream, and it is firmer and more stable when whipped.

TIPS ON WHIPPING: Perhaps the most important factor to consider when you are whipping cream (along with the cream's milk-fat content) is temperature. Everything should be cold: the cream, the beaters, and the bowl — pop them into the freezer for fifteen minutes or so beforehand. If possible, even the kitchen should be cool (at any rate, don't work near the stove). The cream should be as fresh as can be, and if you have a choice between pasteurized and ultra-pasteurized, choose the former. Ultra-pasteurized cream, which contains stabilizers and emulsifiers, has a much longer shelf life than pasteurized cream, but because it has been heated to a higher temperature, it tends to be less fresh-tasting. It also takes longer to whip, and the volume isn't as great.

Raspberry Ice Cream

MAKES ABOUT 1½ QUARTS
ACTIVE TIME: 30 MINUTES ■ START TO FINISH: 7 HOURS
(INCLUDES CHILLING AND FREEZING)

■ This tastes like summer on a spoon. And it can be made all year round: when we were testing this recipe, we found, to our surprise, that frozen raspberries in heavy syrup offer a much more intense flavor experience than fresh berries do. ■

- 2 (10-ounce) boxes frozen raspberries in heavy syrup, thawed
- 2 teaspoons fresh lemon juice
- ½ cup sugar
- 1½ teaspoons cornstarch
- 1¼ cups whole milk
- 2 large egg yolks
- Pinch of salt
- ¼ teaspoon vanilla extract
- 1 cup heavy cream

SPECIAL EQUIPMENT: an ice cream maker

Combine raspberries with their syrup and lemon juice in a food processor and purée. Force through a fine-mesh sieve into a large metal bowl, pressing hard on solids; discard solids. Set aside.

Whisk together sugar and cornstarch in a medium bowl, then whisk in milk, yolks, and salt. Transfer to a 2½- to 3-quart heavy saucepan and cook over moderate heat, whisking, until custard just reaches a boil. Reduce heat and simmer, whisking, for 1 minute (custard will look curdled). Pour custard through fine-mesh sieve into cleaned metal bowl, then stir in vanilla. Cool to room temperature, stirring occasionally.

Stir berry purée and cream into custard. Refrigerate, covered, until cold, at least 2 hours.

Freeze custard in ice cream maker. Transfer to an airtight container and put in freezer to harden.

COOK'S NOTES

- The custard can be refrigerated for up to 24 hours.
- The ice cream can be made up to 1 week ahead.

Burnt Orange Ice Cream

MAKES ABOUT 1½ QUARTS
ACTIVE TIME: 40 MINUTES ■ START TO FINISH: 7¾ HOURS
(INCLUDES CHILLING AND FREEZING)

■ The orange in this ice cream isn't really "burnt"—it's caramelized in a pan along with sugar. The process is quite easy, and the results are definitely worth it: a frozen confection suffused with the sweet-bitter flavor of caramel tinged with orange. This ice cream is great on its own but also makes a fabulous filling for profiteroles (page 792). ■

- 1½ cups heavy cream
- 1½ cups whole milk
- 2 tablespoons finely grated orange zest (from 3 large navel oranges)
- ¾ cup sugar
- ½ cup strained fresh orange juice
- 6 large egg yolks
- ¼ teaspoon salt
- ½ teaspoon vanilla extract

SPECIAL EQUIPMENT: an instant-read thermometer; an ice cream maker

Combine cream, milk, and zest in a 2- to 3-quart heavy saucepan and bring just to a boil. Remove pan from heat, cover, and let stand for 30 minutes.

Combine ½ cup sugar and orange juice in another 2- to 3-quart heavy saucepan and bring to a boil over moderately high heat, stirring until sugar is dissolved. Boil, without stirring, swirling pan occasionally, until syrup becomes a deep golden caramel. Remove pan from heat, carefully add ½ cup cream mixture (mixture will bubble and steam), and whisk until smooth. Add remaining cream mixture in a steady stream, whisking. Cook caramel mixture over very low heat, whisking, until caramel has dissolved and mixture is hot. Remove from heat.

Whisk together yolks, remaining ¼ cup sugar, and salt in a medium metal bowl. Add hot caramel mixture in a slow stream, whisking constantly. Return mixture to saucepan and cook over moderately low heat, stirring constantly with a wooden spoon, until custard is thick enough to coat back of spoon and registers 170°F on thermometer; do not let boil.

Pour custard through a fine-mesh sieve into cleaned metal bowl and stir in vanilla. Cool to room temperature, then refrigerate, covered, until cold, at least 3 hours.

Freeze custard in ice cream maker. Transfer to an airtight container and put in freezer to harden.

COOK'S NOTES

- The custard can be refrigerated for up to 24 hours.
- The ice cream can be made up to 1 week ahead.

Cream Cheese Ice Cream

MAKES ABOUT 1 QUART
ACTIVE TIME: 5 MINUTES ■ START TO FINISH: 3½ HOURS (INCLUDES FREEZING)

■ The perfect recipe for anyone who thinks that making ice cream is complicated, this delightful shortcut came to us from the French chef Michel Richard, of Citronelle, in Washington, D.C., who was fascinated by American cream cheese. This ice cream is rich, creamy, and tangy—absolutely unlike anything you can buy in the store. ■

- 1 (8-ounce) package cream cheese, softened
- 1 cup whole milk
- 1 tablespoon fresh lemon juice
- ¾ cup sugar
- ⅛ teaspoon salt
- ½ cup heavy cream
- ½ teaspoon vanilla extract

SPECIAL EQUIPMENT: an ice cream maker

Combine cream cheese, milk, lemon juice, sugar, and salt in a blender and blend until smooth. Transfer to a bowl and stir in cream and vanilla. Chill completely.

Freeze mixture in ice cream maker. Transfer to an airtight container and put in freezer to harden.

Let ice cream soften for 5 minutes before serving.

COOK'S NOTE

- The ice cream can be made up to 1 week ahead.

Strawberry Cheesecake Ice Cream

MAKES ABOUT 1 QUART
ACTIVE TIME: 10 MINUTES ■ START TO FINISH: 4 HOURS (INCLUDES FREEZING)

■ Cheesecake aficionados will be thrilled with the consistency of this ice cream, a cool marriage of strawberries and cream cheese. Be sure to use locally grown strawberries; the big, woody berries that are available all year round won't do here. ■

- 1 pint (12 ounces) strawberries, hulled and coarsely chopped
- 1 (8-ounce) package cream cheese, softened
- ¾ cup sugar
- 1 cup whole milk
- 1 tablespoon fresh lemon juice
- ⅛ teaspoon salt
- ½ cup heavy cream

SPECIAL EQUIPMENT: an ice cream maker

Combine strawberries, cream cheese, sugar, milk, lemon juice, and salt in a blender and purée just until smooth. Transfer to a bowl and stir in cream. Chill completely.

Freeze mixture in ice cream maker. Transfer to an airtight container and put in freezer to harden.

COOK'S NOTE

- The ice cream can be made up to 1 week ahead.

Rum Currant Ice Cream

MAKES ABOUT 1 QUART
ACTIVE TIME: 15 MINUTES ■ START TO FINISH: 10½ HOURS
(INCLUDES CHILLING AND FREEZING)

■ The concept of plumping raisins in rum or another liquor is a very old one. Rum raisin ice cream became popular back in the 1970s. With a nod to Häagen Dazs, we've modernized it by replacing the raisins with dried currants, which are a bit sharper-tasting. The rum gives this dessert a soft texture. ■

- 1/3 cup dark rum
- 3/4 cup dried currants
- 2 cups heavy cream
- 1 cup half-and-half
- 1/8 teaspoon salt
- 2 large eggs
- 3/4 cup packed light brown sugar

SPECIAL EQUIPMENT: an instant-read thermometer; an ice cream maker

Heat rum in a small saucepan until just warm. Remove from heat, add currants, and let stand, covered, for 1 hour.

Combine cream, half-and-half, and salt in a 2-quart heavy saucepan and bring just to a boil.

Meanwhile, whisk together eggs and brown sugar in a large metal bowl. Add hot cream mixture in a slow stream, whisking constantly, then pour into saucepan and cook over moderately low heat, stirring constantly with a wooden spoon, until custard is thick enough to coat back of spoon and registers 170°–175°F on thermometer; do not let boil.

Pour custard through a fine-mesh sieve into cleaned metal bowl. Add rum and currants. Cool completely, stirring occasionally, then refrigerate, covered, until cold, at least 3 hours.

Freeze custard in ice cream maker. Transfer ice cream to an airtight container and put in freezer to harden, at least 6 hours.

COOK'S NOTES

- The custard can be refrigerated for up to 24 hours.
- The ice cream can be made up to 1 week ahead.

Eggnog Ice Cream

MAKES ABOUT 1 QUART
ACTIVE TIME: 20 MINUTES ■ START TO FINISH: 8 HOURS
(INCLUDES CHILLING AND FREEZING)

■ Here's an easy way to bring a touch of holiday tradition to a meal. The ice cream also makes an excellent topping for a slice of mincemeat pie. ■

- 1 cup whole milk
- 1/4 teaspoon salt
- 7 large egg yolks
- 2/3 cup sugar
- 2 cups heavy cream
- 2 tablespoons dark rum
- 2 tablespoons Cognac or other brandy
- 1 teaspoon vanilla extract
- 1/4 teaspoon freshly grated nutmeg

SPECIAL EQUIPMENT: an instant-read thermometer; an ice cream maker

Bring milk and salt just to a boil in a 2- to 3-quart heavy saucepan over moderate heat. Remove from heat.

Meanwhile, whisk together yolks and sugar in a large metal bowl. Add hot milk in a slow stream, whisking constantly. Return custard to pan and cook, whisking constantly, over low heat until custard thickens and registers 170°F on thermometer, about 10 minutes; do not let boil.

Pour custard through a fine-mesh sieve into cleaned metal bowl. Stir in cream, rum, Cognac, vanilla, and nutmeg. Cool completely, stirring occasionally, then refrigerate, covered, until cold, at least 3 hours.

Freeze custard in ice cream maker. Transfer to an airtight container and put in freezer to harden.

COOK'S NOTES

- The custard can be refrigerated for up to 24 hours.
- The ice cream can be made up to 1 week ahead.

Grape-Nuts Ice Cream

MAKES ABOUT 1½ QUARTS
ACTIVE TIME: 20 MINUTES ■ START TO FINISH: 7 HOURS
(INCLUDES CHILLING AND FREEZING)

■ Odd-sounding, yes, but ice cream fans line up in droves for this Yankee delicacy, which is served all over New England every summer. *Gourmet* contributors Jane and Michael Stern discovered it on one of their journeys. Reminiscent of butter pecan ice cream, it combines a very rich egg yolk and cream base with Grape-Nuts, which impart a welcome crunchy note. ■

- 6 large egg yolks
- ⅔ cup sugar
- 3 cups heavy cream
- ¼ teaspoon salt
- 1 cup Grape-Nuts
- 1½ teaspoons vanilla extract

SPECIAL EQUIPMENT: an instant-read thermometer; an ice cream maker

Beat together yolks and sugar in a large metal bowl with an electric mixer at high speed until pale yellow and thick, 1 to 2 minutes.

Heat 2 cups cream in a 3-quart heavy saucepan over moderate heat until warm. Add warm cream to yolk mixture in a slow steam, whisking constantly. Pour back into pan and cook, stirring constantly with a wooden spoon, until custard is thick enough to coat back of spoon and registers 170°F on thermometer; do not let boil.

Pour custard through a fine-mesh sieve into cleaned metal bowl. Stir in salt and remaining 1 cup cream. Cool custard to room temperature, stirring occasionally, then refrigerate, covered, until cold, at least 3 hours.

Stir cereal and vanilla into custard. Freeze custard in ice cream maker. Transfer to an airtight container and put in freezer to harden.

COOK'S NOTES

- The custard (without the cereal and vanilla) can be refrigerated for up to 24 hours.
- The ice cream can be made up to 1 week ahead.

Lemon Meringue Ice Cream

MAKES ABOUT 1½ QUARTS
ACTIVE TIME: 40 MINUTES ■ START TO FINISH: 8 HOURS
(INCLUDES CHILLING AND FREEZING)

■ Fans of lemon meringue pie will be enchanted by this icy version of the classic. The meringue is baked, broken into bits, and scattered through the tart frozen custard, waiting to leap out and surprise the tongue with its crispness. The bits soften and blend into the custard after two days or so, but even when the texture is uniform, this ice cream remains pure pleasure. ■

FOR MERINGUE

- 2 large egg whites
- ⅛ teaspoon salt
- ⅓ cup sugar

FOR ICE CREAM

- 1½ cups heavy cream
- 1 cup whole milk
- ¾ cup sugar
- 4 teaspoons finely grated lemon zest
- ⅛ teaspoon salt
- 6 large egg yolks
- ⅔ cup fresh lemon juice

SPECIAL EQUIPMENT: parchment paper; an instant-read thermometer; an ice cream maker

MAKE THE MERINGUE: Put a rack in middle of oven and preheat oven to 250°F. Line a baking sheet with parchment paper.

Beat whites and salt in a medium bowl with an electric mixer at medium speed until whites hold soft peaks. Add sugar 1 tablespoon at a time, beating at medium speed, then beat at high speed until meringue holds stiff, glossy peaks, about 1 minute. Spread meringue into a 9-inch round on parchment-lined baking sheet.

Bake until firm to the touch, about 1 hour. Turn off oven and let meringue stand in oven for 1 hour. Transfer meringue, on parchment, to a rack to cool completely.

Peel off parchment and, working over a bowl, break meringue into ½- to 1-inch pieces.

MAKE THE ICE CREAM: Combine cream, milk, sugar, zest, and salt in a 2- to 3-quart heavy saucepan and bring just to a boil, stirring occasionally.

Meanwhile, whisk yolks in a medium metal bowl until smooth. Add hot cream mixture to yolks in a slow stream, whisking constantly, then pour back into pan. Cook custard over moderately low heat, stirring constantly with a wooden spoon, until custard is thick enough to coat back of spoon and registers 170°F on thermometer; do not let boil.

Pour custard through a fine-mesh sieve into cleaned metal bowl and stir in lemon juice. Cool custard to room temperature, then refrigerate, covered, until cold, at least 3 hours.

Freeze custard in ice cream maker. Transfer ice cream to a bowl and fold in meringue, then transfer to an airtight container and put in freezer to harden, at least 4 hours.

COOK'S NOTES

- The meringue can be made up to 3 days ahead and kept in an airtight container in a cool, dry place.
- The custard can be refrigerated for up to 24 hours.
- The ice cream can be made up to 1 week ahead.

Maple Walnut Ice Cream

MAKES ABOUT 1½ QUARTS
ACTIVE TIME: 35 MINUTES ■ START TO FINISH: 7½ HOURS (INCLUDES CHILLING AND FREEZING)

■ To get the full impact of maple flavor, seek out Grade B syrup, which is less refined and far more powerful than the easier-to-find Grade A. (Don't even think about making this with "pancake syrup.") The novelist Ann Patchett, a *Gourmet* contributor, brought us this old-fashioned dessert from a vacation at the Keeper's House, an inn on Isle au Haut, Maine. ■

1 cup Grade B maple syrup (see Sources)
2 cups heavy cream
1 cup whole milk
¼ teaspoon salt
2 large eggs
⅓ cup walnuts, toasted (see Tips, page 938) and chopped

SPECIAL EQUIPMENT: an instant-read thermometer; an ice cream maker

Boil syrup in a 2-quart heavy saucepan over moderately high heat until reduced to ¾ cup, 5 to 10 minutes.

Stir cream, milk, and salt into syrup and bring to a boil over moderate heat.

Meanwhile, whisk eggs in a large metal bowl. Add hot cream mixture in a slow stream, whisking constantly, then pour into saucepan and cook over moderately low heat, stirring constantly with a wooden spoon, until custard is thick enough to coat back of spoon and registers 170°–175°F on thermometer, 1 to 2 minutes; do not let boil.

Pour custard through a fine-mesh sieve into cleaned metal bowl. Cool to room temperature, stirring occasionally, then refrigerate, covered, until cold, at least 3 hours.

Freeze custard in ice cream maker until soft-frozen. With motor running, add nuts, and continue churning ice cream until frozen. Transfer to an airtight container and put in freezer to harden.

COOK'S NOTES

- The custard can be refrigerated for up to 24 hours.
- The ice cream can be made up to 1 week ahead.

Prune Armagnac Ice Cream

MAKES ABOUT 1 QUART
ACTIVE TIME: 30 MINUTES ■ START TO FINISH: 2 DAYS (INCLUDES MACERATING PRUNES, CHILLING, AND FREEZING)

■ In Gascony, land of foie gras, prunes, and potent Armagnac brandy, this elegant ice cream has become a new tradition. The brandy prevents the ice cream from being too sweet and keeps it slightly soft, with a consistency closer to that of gelato than of ice cream. This recipe comes from the Mapotel de France in the lovely Gascon town of Auch, via *Gourmet* reader Robert Willis. ■

¾ cup (about 6 ounces) pitted prunes
⅓ cup Armagnac

2 cups heavy cream
1 cup half-and-half
¼ teaspoon salt
½ vanilla bean, halved lengthwise
6 large egg yolks
½ cup sugar

SPECIAL EQUIPMENT: an instant-read thermometer; an ice cream maker

Pack prunes into a ½-pint jar and add Armagnac; it should just cover them. Cover jar and let prunes macerate at room temperature for at least 12 hours.

Combine cream, half-and-half, and salt in a 2- to 3-quart heavy saucepan. With tip of a knife, scrape seeds from vanilla bean into cream mixture, then drop in pod. Bring mixture just to a boil and remove from heat.

Whisk together yolks and sugar in a medium metal bowl. Add hot cream mixture in a slow stream, whisking constantly, then pour into saucepan and cook over moderately low heat, stirring constantly with a wooden spoon, until custard is thick enough to coat back of spoon and registers 170°F on thermometer; do not let boil.

Pour custard through a fine-mesh sieve into cleaned metal bowl; discard pod. Cool to room temperature, stirring occasionally, then refrigerate, covered, until cold, at least 3 hours.

Pulse prunes with macerating liquid in a food processor to a thick, slightly chunky purée. Add about 1 cup cold custard and pulse just until well combined, then whisk mixture into remaining custard.

Freeze custard in ice cream maker. Transfer to an airtight container and put in freezer to harden.

COOK'S NOTES

- The prunes can macerate at room temperature for up to 1 week.
- The custard (without the prune purée) can be refrigerated for up to 24 hours.
- The ice cream can be made up to 1 week ahead.

Cappuccino Gelato

MAKES ABOUT 1 QUART
ACTIVE TIME: 30 MINUTES ■ START TO FINISH: 7½ HOURS (INCLUDES CHILLING AND FREEZING)

■ Traditionally, eggs provide the creaminess of Italy's version of ice cream, popular from Milan in the north to Palermo in the south. Our egg-free rendition is light in texture and long on flavor. ■

2½ cups whole milk
2½ tablespoons instant espresso powder
2 tablespoons cornstarch
½ cup plus 2½ tablespoons sugar
⅛ teaspoon salt

SPECIAL EQUIPMENT: an ice cream maker

Whisk ¼ cup milk into espresso powder in a small bowl, whisking until powder is dissolved. Stir ¼ cup milk into cornstarch in another small bowl, stirring until cornstarch is dissolved.

Combine sugar, salt, and remaining 2 cups milk in a 3-quart heavy saucepan and bring just to a boil over moderately high heat, stirring until sugar is dissolved. Stir cornstarch mixture again, then whisk into milk mixture and simmer, whisking, for 2 minutes. Whisk in espresso mixture.

Transfer mixture to a metal bowl and cool to room temperature, stirring occasionally, then cover surface with a round of wax paper and refrigerate until cold, at least 3 hours.

Freeze mixture in ice cream maker. Transfer to an airtight container and put in freezer to harden.

COOK'S NOTES

- The gelato mixture can be refrigerated for up to 24 hours before freezing.
- The gelato can be made up to 1 week ahead.

Italian Lemon Ice

MAKES ABOUT 1 QUART
ACTIVE TIME: 15 MINUTES ■ START TO FINISH: 6½ HOURS
(INCLUDES CHILLING AND FREEZING)

■ The simplest and most refreshing dessert we know, this Italian classic is basically lemonade frozen to a wonderful slush. It's just the thing to have on hand during the dog days of summer. (If you use a Microplane rasp to grate the lemon zest, be sure to measure a *packed* tablespoon.) ■

- 1½ cups water
- 1 cup plus 2 tablespoons sugar
- 1 tablespoon finely grated fresh lemon zest
- 1 cup fresh lemon juice
- Pinch of salt

SPECIAL EQUIPMENT: an ice cream maker

Bring water and sugar to a boil in a 1-quart heavy saucepan, stirring until sugar is dissolved. Remove from heat and stir in zest, juice, and salt. Transfer to a metal bowl and cool syrup to room temperature. Refrigerate syrup, covered, for at least 1 hour.

Freeze syrup in ice cream maker. Transfer to an airtight container and freeze until firm, about 2 hours.

COOK'S NOTES

- The syrup can be refrigerated for up to 1 day.
- The frozen lemon ice keeps for 3 days. Let it sit at room temperature for 5 to 10 minutes before serving.

Lemon Buttermilk Sherbet

MAKES ABOUT 1 QUART
ACTIVE TIME: 15 MINUTES ■ START TO FINISH: 5¾ HOURS
(INCLUDES CHILLING AND FREEZING)

■ Lemony, sweet, and refreshingly tart, this sherbet has a silky texture. The flavor of the buttermilk is virtually undetectable, but it plays up the lemon. We've been serving this much-requested dessert for decades, and it's still as fresh as it was in 1968, when we created it for William Taber, who asked for a recipe "just like Mom's." ■

- 2 cups well-shaken buttermilk
- ¾ cup light corn syrup
- 2 teaspoons packed finely grated lemon zest (from 3 medium lemons)
- ¼ cup fresh lemon juice
- ¼ cup sugar

SPECIAL EQUIPMENT: an ice cream maker

Stir together buttermilk, corn syrup, zest, juice, and sugar in a bowl until sugar is dissolved. Refrigerate, covered, until cold, at least 2 hours.

Freeze mixture in ice cream maker. Transfer to an airtight container and put in freezer to harden.

COOK'S NOTES

- The buttermilk mixture can be refrigerated for up to 24 hours.
- The sherbet can be made up to 1 week ahead.

Green Apple Sorbet

MAKES ABOUT 5 CUPS
ACTIVE TIME: 15 MINUTES ■ START TO FINISH: 4¾ HOURS
(INCLUDES CHILLING AND FREEZING)

■ The Vitamin C tablet in this subtly tart sorbet is not intended to help you fend off a cold; the ascorbic acid prevents the apple juice from oxidizing and turning brown, so it keeps the sorbet a lovely cool green in color. ■

- 2/3 cup sugar
- 1/3 cup water
- 1 (1000-milligram) tablet vitamin C
- 6 Granny Smith apples (2 2/3 pounds total), cut into 1-inch wedges

SPECIAL EQUIPMENT: an electric juice extractor; an ice cream maker

Bring sugar and water to a simmer in a small heavy saucepan, stirring until sugar is dissolved. Remove from heat.

Crush vitamin C tablet to a powder in a mortar with a pestle or with the back of a spoon, and place in a 1-quart bowl or other container that will fit under spout of electric juicer. Juice apples into container. Spoon off foam and stir in sugar syrup. Refrigerate, covered, until cold, at least 1 hour.

Freeze juice mixture in ice cream maker. Transfer to an airtight container and put in freezer to harden.

COOK'S NOTES

- It's not necessary to peel or seed the apples before putting them in the juicer.
- The juice mixture can be refrigerated for up to 24 hours.
- The sorbet can be made up to 1 week ahead.

Roasted Apricot Sorbet

MAKES ABOUT 3 CUPS
ACTIVE TIME: 20 MINUTES ■ START TO FINISH: 7 HOURS (INCLUDES CHILLING AND FREEZING)

■ Apricots and almonds have a natural affinity. To further intensify the flavor, we roast the apricots and add a purée of dried apricots to the blend. The result is a sorbet of deep color and enormous fruit flavor. ■

- 3/4 cup sugar
- 1/2 cup water
- 1/3 cup dried apricots, chopped
- 1 1/4 pounds firm but ripe apricots (7 large)
- 2 tablespoons fresh lemon juice
- 1/8 teaspoon almond extract

SPECIAL EQUIPMENT: an ice cream maker

Put a rack in middle of oven and preheat oven to 350°F.

Combine sugar, water, and dried apricots in a 3-quart heavy saucepan and bring to a boil over moderate heat, stirring until sugar is dissolved. Remove from heat and let stand until apricots are softened, about 1 hour.

Meanwhile, put whole fresh apricots in a small roasting pan and roast until soft, about 1 hour. Cool in pan, then peel, halve, and pit when cool enough to handle.

Combine dried apricot mixture, roasted apricots, lemon juice, and almond extract in a blender and purée until very smooth, 1 1/2 to 2 minutes. Force purée through a fine-mesh sieve into a bowl, pressing hard on solids; discard solids. Refrigerate purée, covered, until cold, at least 2 hours.

Freeze purée in ice cream maker. Transfer to an airtight container and put in freezer to harden.

COOK'S NOTES

- The purée can be refrigerated for up to 8 hours.
- The sorbet can be made up to 1 week ahead.

Kir Royale Sorbet

MAKES ABOUT 1 QUART
ACTIVE TIME: 10 MINUTES ■ START TO FINISH: 5 HOURS (INCLUDES CHILLING AND FREEZING)

■ Kir royale was invented in the 1940s as a celebratory aperitif. It's a gorgeous drink, lightly sweetened by cassis, a syrup made of black currants. Often a single raspberry is dropped into the glass as a finishing touch. We think this sorbet is even prettier than the drink—and twice as invigorating. ■

- 2/3 cup sugar
- 2/3 cup water
- 2 1/2 cups (about 12 ounces) raspberries
- 1 cup Champagne or other sparkling white wine
- 1/4 cup crème de cassis
- 1 1/2 tablespoons fresh lemon juice

SPECIAL EQUIPMENT: an ice cream maker

Combine sugar and water in a 1-quart heavy saucepan and bring to a boil, stirring until sugar is dissolved. Remove from heat and cool to room temperature.

Purée raspberries with Champagne, crème de cassis, and sugar syrup in a blender. Force purée through a fine-mesh sieve into a bowl, pressing hard on solids; discard solids. Stir in lemon juice. Refrigerate purée, covered, until cold, at least 1 hour.

Freeze purée in ice cream maker. Transfer to an airtight container and put in freezer to harden.

COOK'S NOTES

- The purée can be refrigerated for up to 24 hours.
- The sorbet can be made up to 1 week ahead.

Cosmopolitan Sorbet

MAKES ABOUT 1 QUART
ACTIVE TIME: 20 MINUTES ■ START TO FINISH: 6 HOURS (INCLUDES CHILLING AND FREEZING)

■ The shell-pink cosmopolitan, better known as the cosmo, took urbane young martini drinkers by storm in the late 1990s, showing up everywhere. Our frozen version, intensely colored thanks to the cranberries, is a beautiful thing during the holidays. ■

- 2 cups sugar
- 2 cups water
- 5⅓ cups (1½ pounds) fresh or frozen (not thawed) cranberries
- ¼ cup vodka
- ¼ cup fresh lime juice
- 2 tablespoons Cointreau or other orange-flavored liqueur

SPECIAL EQUIPMENT: an ice cream maker

Bring sugar and water to a boil in a 3-quart heavy saucepan, stirring until sugar is dissolved. Add cranberries and simmer, uncovered, until berries have burst, 8 to 10 minutes.

Drain mixture in a large sieve set over a medium bowl and gently press on solids to extract liquid without forcing pulp through; discard solids. Cool syrup to room temperature, then refrigerate, covered, until cold, at least 1 hour.

Stir vodka, lime juice, and Cointreau into syrup. Freeze mixture in ice cream maker. Transfer to an airtight container and put in freezer to harden.

COOK'S NOTES

- The cranberry syrup can be refrigerated for up to 24 hours.
- The sorbet can be made up to 1 week ahead.

Grapefruit and Campari Granita

MAKES ABOUT 7 CUPS
ACTIVE TIME: 20 MINUTES ■ START TO FINISH: 4½ HOURS (INCLUDES FREEZING)

■ The round, crystalline flakes of ice in a properly made granita melt slowly on the palate. The result is a cold snap of concentrated flavor. Created from just four ingredients, this one showcases the time-honored Italian combination of Campari and grapefruit juice. ■

- 1⅓ cups sugar
- 1 cup water
- 3 cups fresh pink grapefruit juice with some pulp (from 4 pink grapefruits)
- ¼ cup Campari

OPTIONAL GARNISH: 3-inch-long strips of grapefruit zest (removed with a vegetable peeler)

Bring sugar and water to a boil in a 2-quart saucepan, stirring until sugar is dissolved. Remove from heat and cool syrup to room temperature.

Stir grapefruit juice and Campari into syrup. Freeze in a 13-by-9-inch metal baking pan, stirring and crushing lumps of ice with a fork every 30 minutes, until mixture is firm but not frozen hard, 3 to 4 hours.

Before serving, scrape granita with a fork to lighten texture. Garnish with grapefruit zest, if desired.

COOK'S NOTE

- Though the consistency of granita is best the day it's made, the granita can be prepared up to 1 day ahead. Scrape it with a fork to lighten it before serving.

Coffee Granita

MAKES ABOUT 3¾ CUPS
ACTIVE TIME: 15 MINUTES ■ START TO FINISH: 2¼ HOURS (INCLUDES FREEZING)

■ One bite and you can imagine yourself happily ensconced in Rome's Caffè Greco, from which this recipe originally came. Behind its simplicity lies a secret weapon—vanilla extract, which has a softening effect and mellows the bitter punch of the espresso. ■

2 cups hot espresso or very strong coffee
½ cup sugar
2 teaspoons vanilla extract
ACCOMPANIMENT: lightly sweetened whipped cream

Stir together coffee and sugar in a small bowl until sugar is dissolved, then stir in vanilla. Pour into an 8-inch square baking pan (1-quart capacity), let cool, then freeze, stirring every 30 minutes, until slushy, about 1½ hours.

Transfer mixture to a bowl and stir vigorously with a fork until slightly smoother and more uniform in texture, about 30 seconds. Freeze until firm enough to scoop, about 30 minutes more.

Serve in bowls, topped with whipped cream.

COOK'S NOTE

- Though the consistency of granita is best the day it's made, it can be prepared up to 1 day ahead. Scrape it with a fork to lighten it before serving.

GRANITA

It's easy to make granita—the basic tools are a freezer, a metal pan, and a fork. Your goal is to create large, granular ice crystals, which is why you don't want to churn the dessert, as you would sorbet. Ice will form near the sides of the pan first; scrape it down and stir it into the rest of the granita, then repeat the action occasionally until the whole mixture is firm. Another thing that affects the iciness is the amount of sugar added. Granita contains relatively little sugar compared to sorbet or gelato.

When you are ready to serve your granita, drag the fork repeatedly across the surface to lighten and fluff it up.

Strawberry Margarita Ice Pops

MAKES 8 ICE POPS
ACTIVE TIME: 10 MINUTES ■ START TO FINISH: 1 DAY (INCLUDES FREEZING)

■ Cocktails on a stick—cool, beautiful, and lots of fun—are almost guaranteed to get a summer party off to the right start. If you want to make nonalcoholic pops, simply substitute fresh orange juice for the tequila; although they won't produce the same effect, they'll be even prettier. ■

1¼ pounds strawberries, hulled and halved
⅓ cup white tequila
½ cup superfine sugar
1 tablespoon fresh lime juice
SPECIAL EQUIPMENT: eight ⅓-cup ice pop molds and eight wooden sticks

Combine all ingredients in a blender and purée until smooth. Force mixture through a fine-mesh sieve into a large glass measuring cup or a bowl, pressing on solids; discard solids.

Pour into molds and add sticks. Freeze for at least 24 hours.

COOK'S NOTE

- The ice pops can be made up to 1 week ahead.

Frozen Terrine

SERVES 10 TO 12
ACTIVE TIME: 20 MINUTES ■ START TO FINISH: 8½ HOURS (INCLUDES FREEZING)

■ You can use any combination of high-quality store-bought ice cream or sorbet for this terrine, or you can make your own. Slice it at the table and serve topped with fresh fruit or a fruit sauce. ■

6 pints ice cream and/or sorbet (2 pints each of 3 flavors), slightly softened in refrigerator
SPECIAL EQUIPMENT: a 12-by-4½-by-3-inch loaf pan (see Sources) or an 8-cup mold

Line loaf pan with three pieces of plastic wrap (one lengthwise and two crosswise), leaving at least a 2-inch overhang on all sides. Freeze pan for 10 minutes.

Mash first 2 pints ice cream or sorbet in a bowl with a spoon until spreadable but not melted. Mash 2 pints of second flavor in another bowl, then mash third flavor in same manner.

Evenly spread 1¾ cups of first flavor in bottom of loaf pan, preferably using a small offset metal spatula. Top with 1¾ cups of second flavor and half of third flavor. (If ice cream or sorbet becomes too soft for spreading, freeze for 10 minutes between layering.) Repeat layering with another 1¾ cups of first flavor, 1¾ cups of second flavor, and all of remaining third flavor (pan will be full; you will have about ½ cup left over from each of the first two flavors). Cover top of terrine with plastic wrap overhang, then wrap pan with more plastic wrap.

Freeze until terrine is hard, at least 8 hours.

To serve, unwrap pan, then open overhang and invert pan onto a chilled serving platter. Wet a kitchen towel with hot water, quickly wring it dry, and drape over pan for 30 seconds. Lift off pan and peel off plastic wrap. Slice terrine with a knife dipped in hot water and dried between each cut.

COOK'S NOTE

- The terrine can be frozen for up to 3 days.

Cherry Tortoni

SERVES 10
ACTIVE TIME: 1 HOUR ■ START TO FINISH: 5 HOURS (INCLUDES FREEZING)

■ During the 1950s, every Italian-American restaurant offered tortoni, a creamy frozen mousse rich with almonds, amaretti, and Marsala, as a way to end a meal. Although it went out of fashion long ago, we yearned to taste it once again. We've embellished our version with sour cherries, bringing bright color and tart flavor to the mix. ■

FOR CHERRIES
2¼ cups fresh or frozen (not thawed) pitted sour cherries (about 1 pound fresh cherries or ¾ pound frozen cherries)
½ cup sugar

2 tablespoons Disaronno amaretto or other almond-flavored liqueur
1½ teaspoons cornstarch
1 tablespoon cold water

FOR CRUST

1½ cups (6 ounces) sliced almonds, toasted (see Tips, page 938) and cooled
1¼ cups fine vanilla wafer crumbs (from about 40 wafers)
½ stick (4 tablespoons) unsalted butter, melted

FOR FILLING

4 large egg whites
½ teaspoon cream of tartar
Pinch of salt
½ cup sugar
1⅓ cups very cold heavy cream
2 tablespoons sweet Marsala or sweet sherry
¾ cup coarsely ground amaretti (Italian almond macaroons; from about twenty 1-inch cookies)

SPECIAL EQUIPMENT: a 9- to 9½-inch (24-centimeter) springform pan; an instant-read thermometer

COOK THE CHERRIES: If using frozen cherries, thaw, reserving juices. Combine cherries (and juice), sugar, and liqueur in a 2- to 3-quart heavy saucepan, bring to a simmer, and simmer, uncovered, stirring occasionally, until cherries are soft, about 5 minutes. Whisk cornstarch and water together in a small cup until combined, then whisk into cherry mixture and boil, stirring, for 1 minute.

Transfer to a shallow bowl and refrigerate, uncovered, for 1 hour.

MAKE THE CRUST: Invert bottom of springform pan, then lock on side and butter pan.

Pulse 1 cup almonds in a food processor until finely ground (be careful not to pulse to a paste). Transfer to a bowl and stir in wafer crumbs and butter with a fork until well combined. Pat crumb mixture evenly onto bottom and 1½ inches up side of springform pan. Freeze while you make filling.

MAKE THE FILLING AND ASSEMBLE THE TORTONI: Combine egg whites, cream of tartar, salt, and sugar in a medium metal bowl. Set over a saucepan of simmering water and beat with a handheld electric mixer at medium-high speed until meringue just holds soft peaks and registers 170°F on thermometer, about 5 minutes. Remove bowl from saucepan and continue to beat until meringue just holds stiff peaks.

Beat cream with Marsala in a medium bowl with cleaned beaters at medium speed until it just holds stiff peaks. Gently but thoroughly fold in ground amaretti and half of meringue. Fold in remaining meringue. Pour filling into springform pan and smooth top.

Drain cherries in a sieve set over a bowl, reserving juices. Scatter cherries evenly over top of tortoni, then swirl into tortoni with tip of a sharp knife for a marbled effect. Sprinkle top of tortoni with remaining ½ cup almonds. Freeze, loosely covered, until firm, at least 4 hours. Refrigerate juices, covered.

Let tortoni stand in pan at room temperature for 10 minutes to soften slightly before serving. Carefully remove side of pan, cut tortoni into wedges, and serve with cherry juices.

COOK'S NOTE

- The tortoni can be frozen and the cherry juices refrigerated for up to 1 week.

Raspberry Semifreddo Torte

SERVES 10
ACTIVE TIME: 15 MINUTES ■ START TO FINISH: 4¾ HOURS (INCLUDES FREEZING)

■ Essentially an Italian raspberry ice cream cake, this is an elegant and remarkably easy dessert. The crust is made with store-bought shortbread, and the filling is a frozen custard mousse that does not require an ice cream maker. The raspberries, folded into the custard, freeze into little nuggets of pure flavor. ■

FOR CRUST

- 2 (5⅓-ounce) boxes shortbread
- ½ cup (3 ounces) whole almonds with skins, toasted (see Tips, page 938) and cooled

FOR FILLING

- 2 large eggs
- ½ cup plus 1 tablespoon sugar
- Pinch of salt
- 1½ cups (6 ounces) raspberries
- 1 cup very cold heavy cream

SPECIAL EQUIPMENT: a 9- to 9½-inch (24-centimeter) springform pan; an instant-read thermometer

MAKE THE CRUST: Put a rack in middle of oven and preheat oven to 350°F. Invert bottom of springform pan, then lock on side and butter pan.

Break shortbread into pieces and pulse with nuts in a food processor until finely ground. Press mixture firmly over bottom and 1¼ inches up side of springform pan. Bake crust for 10 minutes. Cool on a rack.

MAKE THE FILLING AND ASSEMBLE THE TORTE: Beat eggs, ½ cup sugar, and salt in a metal bowl with a handheld electric mixer at medium-high speed until doubled in volume, about 5 minutes. Set bowl over a saucepan filled with 1 inch of simmering water and beat custard until it registers 140°F on thermometer, about 5 minutes. Continue beating custard over heat for 3 minutes more. Remove bowl from heat and refrigerate custard, uncovered, until cool, about 10 minutes.

Toss raspberries with remaining 1 tablespoon sugar in a large fine-mesh sieve set over a bowl. Force berries through sieve, pressing on solids; discard solids. Fold raspberries into cooled custard.

Beat cream in a medium bowl with cleaned beaters until it just holds stiff peaks. Fold gently into raspberry mixture.

Spoon filling into crust and smooth top. Wrap pan in foil and freeze for at least 4 hours. (Filling will be firm but not frozen solid.)

Before serving, run a thin knife around edge of torte and remove side of pan.

COOK'S NOTE

- The torte can be frozen for up to 2 days.

Dark Chocolate–Caramel Ice Cream Sandwiches

MAKES ABOUT 18 SANDWICHES
ACTIVE TIME: 1¼ HOURS ■ START TO FINISH: 7¾ HOURS (INCLUDES CHILLING AND FREEZING)

■ These are the most satisfying ice cream sandwiches any of us has ever tasted. The caramel ice cream, filled with tiny chunks of bittersweet chocolate, was created by *Gourmet* contributor Sally Tager and will remind you of a chocolate-covered toffee candy bar that has been softened and chilled. The dark, rich cookies are also wonderful with Vanilla Bean Ice Cream (page 852) or, come to think of it, just about any ice cream you care to use. This is a recipe you'll find yourself turning to again and again. ■

FOR COOKIES

- ¾ cup all-purpose flour
- ¾ cup unsweetened cocoa powder
- ½ teaspoon baking soda
- ½ teaspoon salt
- 1½ sticks (12 tablespoons) unsalted butter, softened
- 1 cup sugar
- 2 large eggs
- 1 teaspoon vanilla extract

FOR ICE CREAM

- ¾ cup sugar
- 1½ cups whole milk
- 3 large egg yolks
- ¼ teaspoon salt
- 1 tablespoon cornstarch
- 1½ cups heavy cream
- 1½ teaspoons vanilla extract
- 3 ounces good bittersweet chocolate (not unsweetened), finely chopped

SPECIAL EQUIPMENT: an ice cream maker

MAKE THE COOKIES: Put a rack in middle of oven and preheat oven to 375°F.

Whisk together flour, cocoa, baking soda, and salt in a medium bowl.

Beat together butter and sugar in a large bowl with an electric mixer at medium-high speed until pale and fluffy, 2 to 3 minutes. Beat in eggs and vanilla until combined. Add flour mixture and mix just until combined.

Drop level tablespoons of dough about 2 inches apart onto ungreased baking sheets (you should have about 36 cookies). Bake, in batches, until cookies are puffed and set, about 12 minutes per batch. Transfer with a metal spatula to a rack to cool.

WHILE THE COOKIES COOL, MAKE THE ICE CREAM: Cook sugar in a dry large heavy skillet over moderately high heat, stirring constantly with a fork, until completely melted and a deep golden caramel color. Immediately remove skillet from heat and, stirring caramel to prevent further darkening, carefully pour milk down side of skillet (caramel will harden and steam vigorously). Return to moderate heat and cook, stirring, until caramel is dissolved, about 5 minutes (some milk solids may rise to surface of caramel). Remove skillet from heat.

Whisk together yolks, salt, and cornstarch in a medium metal bowl. Add caramel in a slow stream, whisking constantly. Transfer to a 3- to 4-quart heavy saucepan and bring to a boil over moderate heat, whisking constantly. Continue to boil, whisking constantly, for 2 minutes. Pour custard through a fine-mesh sieve into cleaned metal bowl and cool to room temperature, stirring occasionally.

Whisk cream and vanilla into custard. Cover and refrigerate until cold, at least 3 hours.

Freeze custard in ice cream maker. Transfer to a bowl and stir in chocolate, then transfer to an airtight container and put in freezer to harden.

TO ASSEMBLE THE SANDWICHES: Place a scant 1/4 cup ice cream on flat side of a cookie, top with a second cookie, flat side down, and gently press to spread filling to edges. Wrap sandwich in plastic wrap and put in freezer. Make more sandwiches in same manner and freeze for at least 1 hour.

Let sandwiches stand at room temperature for 5 minutes to soften filling slightly before serving.

COOK'S NOTES

- The cookies can be stored in an airtight container at room temperature for up to 2 days.
- The custard for the ice cream can be chilled for up to 24 hours.
- The sandwiches can be frozen for up to 1 week. Before serving, transfer to the refrigerator to soften slightly.

Gingersnap Ice Cream Sandwiches

MAKES 18 SANDWICHES
ACTIVE TIME: 35 MINUTES ■ START TO FINISH: 2½ HOURS

■ An ideal way to make ice cream into finger food, our sweet-spicy gingerbread cookies never get hard, even when frozen. They're delicious paired with lemon or chocolate ice cream—provided you can keep yourself from eating them straight out of the oven. ■

FOR COOKIES

- 2 cups all-purpose flour
- 1½ teaspoons baking soda
- ½ teaspoon salt
- 1 teaspoon ground cinnamon
- 2 teaspoons ground ginger
- ⅛ teaspoon ground cloves
- 1½ sticks (12 tablespoons) unsalted butter, softened
- ¾ cup packed dark brown sugar
- ¼ cup granulated sugar
- 1 large egg
- ¼ cup molasses (not robust or blackstrap)
- ⅓ cup turbinado sugar, such as Sugar in the Raw

FOR FILLING

- 1½ quarts ice cream

SPECIAL EQUIPMENT: parchment paper

MAKE THE COOKIES: Sift together flour, baking soda, salt, cinnamon, ginger, and cloves into a bowl.

Beat together butter, brown sugar, and granulated sugar in a large bowl with an electric mixer at medium-high speed until pale and fluffy, about 3 minutes. Beat in egg and molasses until well blended. Add flour mixture all at once and mix on low speed until just combined.

Wrap dough in plastic wrap and refrigerate until firm enough to handle, about 30 minutes.

Put racks in upper and lower thirds of oven and preheat oven to 375°F. Line two baking sheets with parchment paper.

Roll dough into 1½-inch balls (you should have 36), then roll each ball in turbinado sugar. Arrange balls about 1½ inches apart on lined baking sheets.

Bake, switching position of sheets halfway through baking, until edges are browned and tops are cracked, 13 to 15 minutes total. Let cookies stand on sheet for 1 minute, then transfer with a metal spatula to a rack to cool completely.

ASSEMBLE THE SANDWICHES: Place ⅓ cup ice cream on flat side of a cookie, top with a second cookie, flat side down, and gently press to spread filling to edges. Wrap sandwich in plastic wrap and put in freezer. Make more sandwiches in same manner and freeze for at least 1 hour.

Let sandwiches stand at room temperature for 5 minutes to soften filling slightly before serving.

COOK'S NOTES

- The cookies can be stored in an airtight container at room temperature for up to 1 week.
- The sandwiches can be frozen for up to 1 week. Before serving, transfer to the refrigerator to soften slightly.

Coffee Almond Ice Cream Cake with Dark Chocolate Sauce

SERVES 6 TO 8

ACTIVE TIME: 50 MINUTES ■ START TO FINISH: 6½ HOURS (INCLUDES FREEZING AND MAKING SAUCE)

■ Ice cream cakes are easy on the host because they are made well in advance. This one combines the crackle of chocolate wafer crumbs and Italian almond macaroon crumbs with the smooth richness of coffee ice cream. ■

- 1½ cups fine chocolate wafer crumbs (from about 30 wafers)
- ½ stick (4 tablespoons) unsalted butter, melted
- 1½ pints coffee ice cream, slightly softened
- 1½ cups very cold heavy cream
- 1 teaspoon vanilla extract
- 1½ cups crushed amaretti (Italian almond macaroons; from about forty 1-inch cookies)
- ½ cup (2 ounces) sliced almonds, toasted (see Tips, page 938)

ACCOMPANIMENT: Dark Chocolate Sauce (page 873)

SPECIAL EQUIPMENT: a 2½-inch-deep 8-inch (20-centimeter) springform pan

Invert bottom of springform pan, then lock on side and lightly oil pan.

Stir together chocolate wafer crumbs and butter in a bowl with a fork until well combined. Pat onto bottom and 1 inch up side of springform pan. Freeze crust until firm, about 30 minutes.

Spread ice cream evenly in crust and freeze until firm, about 30 minutes.

Beat cream and vanilla in a large bowl with an electric mixer until cream holds stiff peaks. Fold in amaretti. Spread mixture over ice cream and smooth top. Sprinkle with almonds. Freeze cake until top is firm, 30 to 45 minutes.

Cover cake with plastic wrap and then foil and freeze for at least 4 hours.

Before serving, wrap a warm dampened kitchen towel around pan, then remove side of pan and transfer cake to a serving plate. Let soften for 20 minutes in refrigerator.

Cut cake into wedges with a knife dipped in hot water and dried between each cut. Serve with chocolate sauce.

COOK'S NOTE

- The ice cream cake can be frozen for up to 8 hours.

Tiramisù Ice Cream Cake

SERVES 8

ACTIVE TIME: 1¼ HOURS ■ START TO FINISH: 12 HOURS (INCLUDES CHILLING AND FREEZING)

■ An interpretation of the classic Italian blend of espresso, mascarpone, and liqueur-soaked cake, this is one of our most requested recipes. The layered terrine makes a very pretty party dessert and can be made well ahead of time. ■

FOR MASCARPONE ICE CREAM

- 2 large eggs
- ½ cup sugar
- ½ teaspoon vanilla extract
- 1 (17½-ounce) container mascarpone (about 2 cups)
- Pinch of salt

FOR ESPRESSO ICE CREAM

- 2 large eggs
- ½ cup sugar
- 1 teaspoon vanilla extract
- 1½ cups heavy cream
- ½ cup whole milk
- ¼ cup instant espresso powder, dissolved in 3 tablespoons boiling water

FOR ASSEMBLING

- 1 (10- to 12-ounce) frozen pound cake, thawed
- 3 tablespoons dark rum
- 2 tablespoons Kahlúa
- 2 ounces good bittersweet chocolate (not unsweetened), coarsely grated

ACCOMPANIMENT: Mocha Fudge Sauce (page 875)

SPECIAL EQUIPMENT: an ice cream maker

MAKE THE MASCARPONE ICE CREAM: Beat together eggs and sugar in a medium bowl with an electric mixer at high speed until very thick and pale, about 3 minutes. Beat in vanilla, mascarpone, and salt. Refrigerate, covered, until cold, about 1 hour.

Freeze mascarpone mixture in ice cream maker. Transfer to an airtight container and put in freezer.

MAKE THE ESPRESSO ICE CREAM: Beat together eggs and sugar in a medium bowl with electric mixer at high speed until very thick and pale, about 3 minutes. Beat in vanilla, cream, milk, and espresso mixture. Refrigerate, covered, until cold, about 2 hours.

Freeze espresso mixture in ice cream maker. Transfer to an airtight container and put in freezer.

MEANWHILE, TOAST THE CAKE: Put a rack in middle of oven and preheat oven to 350°F.

Cut pound cake into ¼-inch-thick slices. Arrange in one layer on two baking sheets. Bake until pale golden, 10 to 12 minutes.

Stir together rum and Kahlúa. Brush warm cake slices on both sides with Kahlúa mixture, then transfer to a rack to cool.

ASSEMBLE THE CAKE: Line a 9¼-by-5¼-inch loaf pan lengthwise with two 18-inch-long sheets of plastic wrap, overlapping them slightly in center of pan and letting excess hang over all sides.

Arrange one row of cake slices, overlapping slightly, down center of pan. Spread half of mascarpone ice cream evenly over them. Sprinkle ¼ cup grated chocolate over ice cream and arrange another layer of cake slices, overlapping slightly, to cover chocolate. Spoon all of espresso ice cream into pan, spread it evenly, and sprinkle with ¼ cup chocolate. Top with another layer of cake slices and spread with remaining mascarpone ice cream. Arrange any remaining cake slices on top, pressing down firmly (pan will be filled to just above rim). Fold plastic wrap over top of cake.

Freeze cake for at least 8 hours.

Lift plastic wrap off top of cake, invert cake onto a platter, and remove and discard plastic wrap. Sprinkle with remaining chocolate and serve with mocha fudge sauce.

COOK'S NOTES

- The eggs in the ice creams are not cooked. If this is a concern, see page 629.
- The cake can be frozen for up to 2 days.

Peach Praline Bombes with Peach Syrup

SERVES 6
ACTIVE TIME: 2 HOURS ■ START TO FINISH: 14½ HOURS
(INCLUDES CHILLING AND FREEZING)

■ Nothing is as good as a perfectly ripe peach—except, perhaps, these individual bombes, which begin with the very best and ripest peaches and take them to new heights. Frozen layers of peach ice cream filled with a whipped cream and praline center (in a pinch, you can use crumbled amaretti; see Cook's Note) are topped with a drizzle of fresh peach syrup. ■

FOR PEACH ICE CREAM

- 2 pounds very ripe peaches
- 2 tablespoons fresh lemon juice
- ¾ cup sugar
- 1½ cups heavy cream
- 5 large egg yolks
- ¼ teaspoon salt
- ½ teaspoon vanilla extract
- ¼ teaspoon almond extract

FOR ALMOND PRALINE FILLING

- ⅓ cup sugar
- 3 tablespoons water
- ⅓ cup skinned whole almonds, lightly toasted (see Tips, page 938) and coarsely chopped
- ⅔ cup very cold heavy cream
- ½ teaspoon vanilla extract

FOR PEACH SYRUP

- 1½ pounds very ripe peaches
- ½ cup sugar
- 1 teaspoon fresh lemon juice

GARNISH: peach slices

SPECIAL EQUIPMENT: an instant-read thermometer; an ice cream maker; six 8- to 9-ounce paper cups

MAKE THE PEACH CUSTARD FOR THE ICE CREAM: Slice (unpeeled) peaches ¼ inch thick, then toss with lemon juice and ¼ cup sugar in a medium bowl. Let stand for 30 minutes.

Meanwhile, bring cream just to a boil in a 2-quart heavy saucepan.

Whisk together yolks, remaining ½ cup sugar, and salt in a medium metal bowl. Add cream in a slow stream, whisking constantly, then pour into saucepan and cook over moderately low heat, stirring constantly with a wooden spoon, until custard is thick enough to coat back of spoon and registers 170°F on thermometer; do not let boil. Pour through a very fine-mesh sieve into cleaned metal bowl and cool, stirring occasionally.

Purée peaches, with their liquid, in batches, in a blender until very smooth. Force through very fine-mesh sieve into custard, pressing hard on solids; discard solids. Whisk in extracts and refrigerate, covered, until cold, 2 to 3 hours. (Do not chill for longer than 3 hours, or custard will discolor.)

MEANWHILE, MAKE THE PRALINE: Lightly butter a small baking sheet or a sheet of foil.

Bring sugar and water to a boil in a small heavy saucepan, stirring until sugar is dissolved. Boil syrup without stirring, washing down any sugar crystals on sides of pan with a pastry brush dipped in cold water, until syrup turns a golden caramel. Remove from heat and stir in almonds. Immediately pour praline onto baking sheet. Cool completely.

Break praline into pieces. Pulse in a food processor until finely ground but with some small pieces remaining.

FREEZE THE ICE CREAM: Freeze peach custard in ice cream maker. Transfer to a bowl and put in freezer.

ASSEMBLE THE BOMBES: Beat cream in a medium bowl with an electric mixer until it just holds stiff peaks. Fold in vanilla and crushed praline.

Spoon about ½ cup ice cream into one paper cup and spread it evenly over bottom and about two thirds of the way up sides of cup, forming a well. Spoon a rounded ¼ cup praline filling into well, top with another ¼ cup ice cream, and spread ice cream evenly to cover filling. Cover cup tightly with foil and put in freezer. Make 5 more bombes in same manner. Freeze bombes for at least 8 hours.

MEANWHILE, MAKE THE PEACH SYRUP: Chop (unpeeled) peaches. Combine with sugar in a 3- to 4-quart saucepan and bring to a boil over moderate heat, covered, stirring occasionally, until sugar is dissolved. Reduce heat and simmer, covered, until peaches are very soft and have given off some liquid, about 15 minutes.

Pour peach mixture through a fine-mesh sieve into

a bowl, pressing on solids; discard solids. Stir in lemon juice and cool syrup. Refrigerate, covered, until cold.

To serve, carefully tear paper cups off bombes and invert bombes onto plates. Halve each with a sharp knife so filling shows. Let stand for about 5 minutes to soften slightly, then garnish with peach slices and drizzle about 2 tablespoons peach syrup around each serving.

COOK'S NOTES

- The bombes can be frozen for up to 2 days.
- The peach syrup can be refrigerated for up to 3 days.
- You can substitute ⅔ cup crushed amaretti (Italian almond macaroons) for the almond praline in the filling; this will result in a stronger almond flavor.

Watermelon Sorbet with Chocolate Seeds

SERVES 4

ACTIVE TIME: 40 MINUTES ■ START TO FINISH: 11 HOURS (INCLUDES CHILLING AND FREEZING)

■ This stunning trompe l'oeil creation of bright red sorbet with chocolate "seeds" looks exactly like a slice of watermelon. The fruit itself is puréed into sorbet, then studded with chocolate and spooned into the frozen rind. (Be aware that if you buy a long, narrow watermelon, you'll end up with more slices than if you have a fatter, rounder one.) ■

- 1 (3½- to 4-pound) piece watermelon (one quarter of a large watermelon that has been halved lengthwise and crosswise)
- 1 cup sugar
- ¼ cup fresh lime juice
- 2 tablespoons sambuca or other anise-flavored liqueur (optional)
- 1½ ounces good bittersweet chocolate (not unsweetened), chopped

SPECIAL EQUIPMENT: an ice cream maker

Cut watermelon into 1-inch-thick semicircular slices. Remove flesh, reserving rinds. Coarsely chop flesh and discard seeds.

Purée enough watermelon flesh in a blender to yield 5 cups. Transfer to a medium bowl. Heat 1 cup purée with sugar in a saucepan over moderate heat, stirring, until sugar is dissolved. Stir into remaining purée, along with lime juice and liqueur (if using). Refrigerate purée, covered, until cold, at least 4 hours.

Meanwhile, lay reserved rind slices on their sides on two foil-lined baking sheets and cover tightly with plastic wrap. Freeze until frozen hard, at least 2 hours.

Line a baking sheet or a tray with parchment or wax paper. Melt chocolate in a small metal bowl set over a small saucepan of barely simmering water, then remove bowl from heat. Transfer chocolate to a small sealable plastic bag and seal bag. Snip off tip of one bottom corner of bag to form a tiny hole and pipe chocolate into ⅓- to ½-inch ovals (resembling watermelon seeds) onto prepared baking sheet. Freeze chocolate "seeds" on baking sheet until very firm, about 30 minutes.

Working quickly, peel "seeds" from paper into a small bowl; keep frozen.

Freeze watermelon purée in ice cream maker until frozen to a thick slush. Add three quarters of chocolate "seeds" and continue to freeze until frozen.

Working quickly, fill frozen watermelon rinds, still on baking sheets, with sorbet, smoothing with a rubber spatula. Arrange remaining chocolate "seeds" realistically on slices and smooth sorbet again. Cover with plastic wrap and freeze until very firm, about 6 hours.

COOK'S NOTES

- If your freezer is too narrow to accommodate a regular baking sheet, divide the rinds between smaller trays.
- If you want to serve the sorbet on its own, just omit the directions for freezing rinds.
- The purée can be refrigerated for up to 8 hours.
- The dessert can be frozen, wrapped well in plastic wrap, for up to 3 days.

Individual Chocolate-Raspberry Baked Alaskas

SERVES 6
ACTIVE TIME: 1¼ HOURS ■ START TO FINISH: 6 HOURS
(INCLUDES MAKING ICE CREAM)

■ We've always been charmed by the notion of cold ice cream covered by hot meringue. And there's certainly something thrilling about baking ice cream in the oven. But every time we tried baked Alaska, we thought it sounded better than it tasted. When we set out to improve the recipe, we found an easy solution. Our individual Alaskas offer the perfect ratio of ice cream to meringue—and eliminate the messy step of cutting the cake. ■

FOR CAKE AND ICE CREAM

- 4 ounces good bittersweet chocolate (not unsweetened), chopped
- 1 stick (8 tablespoons) unsalted butter, cut into tablespoons
- ¾ cup sugar
- 3 large eggs
- ⅛ teaspoon salt
- ½ cup unsweetened cocoa powder
- Raspberry Ice Cream (page 854), slightly softened

FOR MERINGUE

- 8 large egg whites, left at room temperature for 30 minutes
- Pinch of salt
- 1½ cups sugar

SPECIAL EQUIPMENT: six 8-ounce shallow gratin dishes

MAKE THE CAKE: Put a rack in middle of oven and preheat oven to 375°F. Butter an 8-inch square baking pan, line bottom with parchment or wax paper, and butter paper.

Melt chocolate and butter in a medium metal bowl set over a saucepan of barely simmering water, stirring until smooth. Remove bowl from pan and whisk in sugar. Whisk in eggs and salt, then sift cocoa over top and whisk until just combined.

Pour batter into baking pan and spread it evenly. Bake until a wooden pick or skewer inserted in center comes out with a few crumbs adhering, 20 to 25 minutes. Cool cake in pan on a rack for 5 minutes, then invert onto rack, peel off paper, and cool completely.

Cut cake into 6 equal pieces. Arrange 1 piece in each gratin dish, trimming as necessary to fit. Top each piece of cake with a large scoop of ice cream (about ½ cup). Freeze, covered, just until ice cream is hard, about 25 minutes (do not let ice cream become rock hard unless making ahead; see Cook's Note).

JUST BEFORE SERVING, MAKE THE MERINGUE: Put a rack in middle of oven and preheat oven to 450°F.

Beat egg whites and salt in a large bowl with an electric mixer at medium speed until whites just hold soft peaks. Add sugar a little at a time, beating at high speed, and continue beating until meringue just holds stiff, glossy peaks, about 5 minutes with a stand mixer or 12 minutes with a handheld mixer.

BAKE THE MERINGUE: Remove gratin dishes from freezer, mound meringue over ice cream and cake, and spread to edges of gratin dishes. Put on a baking sheet and bake until meringue is golden brown, about 6 minutes. Serve immediately.

COOK'S NOTES

- The ice cream and cake can be frozen in the gratin dishes for up to 1 day. Let soften at room temperature for 15 minutes before covering with the meringue.
- The egg whites in this recipe will not be fully cooked. If this is a concern, we recommend using powdered egg whites, such as Just Whites, reconstituted according to the manufacturer's directions, or packaged liquid egg whites (see page 827).

Crispy Macadamia-Nut Fried Ice Cream Balls

MAKES 12 BALLS; SERVES 4 TO 6
ACTIVE TIME: 1 HOUR ■ START TO FINISH: 9 HOURS
(INCLUDES FREEZING AND MAKING SAUCE)

■ Intrigued by the idea of fried ice cream? The trick is to freeze the ice cream balls very hard, cover them with a protective layer of nuts, and freeze them again. Then repeat the process with crushed cornflakes, and then repeat it again. Snug in their nut and cereal coats, the balls deep-fry into crisp hot-and-cold confections that will reliably bring dinner-table conversation to a gratifying halt. ■

- 1 quart super-premium vanilla ice cream
- 1½ cups (7 ounces) macadamia nuts, toasted (see Tips, page 938) and finely chopped
- 6 cups (7 ounces) cornflakes
- 3 large eggs
- About 6 cups vegetable oil for deep-frying
- Confectioners' sugar for dusting

ACCOMPANIMENT: Chocolate Caramel Sauce (page 874)
SPECIAL EQUIPMENT: a 1-ounce ice cream scoop (1½ inches in diameter); a deep-fat thermometer

Line a baking sheet with sides with wax paper and put in freezer for 5 minutes.

Scoop out 12 ice cream balls with ice cream scoop and transfer to baking sheet. Cover with plastic wrap and freeze balls until very hard, at least 3 hours and up to 8.

Put nuts in a shallow bowl. Roll balls in nuts until well coated, pressing lightly so nuts adhere, and transfer back to baking sheet. Cover and freeze balls until very hard, at least 1 hour and up to 8.

Put cornflakes in a sealable plastic bag and roughly crush with a rolling pin. Transfer to a shallow bowl. Lightly beat eggs in another shallow bowl. Dip balls in egg, letting excess drip off, then roll in cornflakes to coat. Return to baking sheet, cover, and freeze balls for at least 1 hour and up to 8 hours. (Reserve remaining egg and cornflakes; refrigerate egg.)

Repeat dipping and coating procedure with reserved egg and cornflakes. Return balls to baking sheet, cover, and freeze until very hard, at least 3 hours and up to 8.

Heat 2 inches oil in a 3-quart heavy saucepan over moderate heat until it registers 375°F on thermometer. Working in batches of 2 or 3, fry balls, turning them occasionally, until golden and crisp, 20 to 30 seconds per batch. With a slotted spoon, transfer balls to paper towels to drain. (Return oil to 375°F between batches.)

Dust ice cream balls with confectioners' sugar and serve immediately, with sauce.

Sweet Sauces

Dark Chocolate Sauce

MAKES ABOUT 3 CUPS
ACTIVE TIME: 15 MINUTES ■ START TO FINISH: 20 MINUTES

■ Bittersweet and unsweetened chocolates are mellowed by the almond edge of amaretto. Wonderful with ice cream cake, this is an easy-to-prepare sauce that's terrific to have on hand in your refrigerator; serve it with everything from store-bought ice cream to fresh strawberries. ■

- 1½ cups heavy cream
- ⅔ cup packed dark brown sugar
- 4 ounces good bittersweet chocolate (not unsweetened), finely chopped
- 3 ounces unsweetened chocolate, finely chopped
- ½ stick (4 tablespoons) unsalted butter, softened
- 3–4 tablespoons Disaronno amaretto or other almond-flavored liqueur (to taste)

Combine cream and sugar in a 2-quart heavy saucepan and bring to a boil over moderately high heat, whisking until sugar is dissolved. Remove from heat, add chocolates, and whisk until melted. Add butter and amaretto and whisk until sauce is smooth. Let cool slightly before serving.

COOK'S NOTE

■ The cooled sauce can be refrigerated in an airtight container for up to 1 week. Reheat in a double boiler, stirring occasionally, or in a microwave.

Caramel Sauce

MAKES ABOUT ¾ CUP
ACTIVE TIME: 15 MINUTES ■ START TO FINISH: 15 MINUTES

■ Caramel sauce is made by cooking sugar just shy of its burning point. Keep a close watch on the sugar to monitor its color, which can vary from light golden, when it has a very slightly nutty flavor, to a darker brown, which is much deeper in flavor. Adding cream and a bit of butter makes the sauce lush. Its applications go far beyond ice cream—a drizzle dresses up almost any kind of fruit pie or tart. ■

- 2/3 cup sugar
- 1/2 cup heavy cream
- 1 tablespoon unsalted butter

Cook sugar in a dry heavy saucepan over moderately low heat, stirring slowly with a fork, until melted and pale golden. Then cook caramel without stirring, swirling pan, until deep golden. Remove pan from heat. Carefully pour cream down side of pan (mixture will bubble and steam vigorously), then return to heat and simmer, stirring, until hardened caramel is completely dissolved. Add butter and cook, stirring, until just incorporated. Remove from heat and serve warm.

COOK'S NOTE

- The cooled sauce can be refrigerated in an airtight container for up to 1 week. Reheat over low heat, stirring occasionally, or in a microwave.

Chocolate Caramel Sauce

MAKES ABOUT 1 1/4 CUPS
ACTIVE TIME: 15 MINUTES ■ START TO FINISH: 15 MINUTES

■ The best of both worlds: caramel sauce infused with bittersweet chocolate. ■

- 1/2 cup sugar
- 3/4 cup heavy cream
- 6 ounces good bittersweet chocolate (not unsweetened), finely chopped
- 1/8 teaspoon salt
- 1/2 teaspoon vanilla extract

Cook sugar in a dry heavy saucepan over moderately low heat, stirring slowly with a fork, until melted and pale golden, then cook caramel, swirling pan, until deep golden. Remove pan from heat. Carefully pour cream down side of pan (mixture will bubble and steam vigorously), then return to heat and simmer, stirring, until hardened caramel is dissolved. Add chocolate and salt and cook over low heat, whisking, until chocolate is melted and sauce is smooth. Whisk in vanilla.

Serve sauce warm or at room temperature.

COOK'S NOTE

- The cooled sauce can be refrigerated in an airtight container for up to 1 week. Reheat in a double boiler, stirring occasionally, or in a microwave.

Hot Fudge Sauce

MAKES ABOUT 2 CUPS
ACTIVE TIME: 20 MINUTES ■ START TO FINISH: 30 MINUTES

■ This is the kind of sauce that firms up when it hits cold ice cream. In theory, it will last for a week in the refrigerator, but it's so delicious simply eaten with a spoon that none of us has ever managed to keep it around that long. ■

- 1/4 cup unsweetened Dutch-process cocoa powder
- 1/3 cup packed dark brown sugar
- 1/2 cup light corn syrup
- 2/3 cup heavy cream
- 1/4 teaspoon salt
- 6 ounces good bittersweet chocolate (not unsweetened), finely chopped
- 2 tablespoons unsalted butter, cut into 1/2 tablespoons
- 1 teaspoon vanilla extract

Stir together cocoa powder, brown sugar, corn syrup, cream, salt, and half of chocolate in a 1 1/2- to 2-quart heavy saucepan and cook over moderate heat, stirring, until chocolate is melted. Cook mixture at a low boil, stirring occasionally, for 5 minutes.

Remove pan from heat, add remaining chocolate, butter, and vanilla, and stir until smooth. Cool slightly before serving.

COOK'S NOTE

- The cooled sauce can be refrigerated in an airtight container for up to 1 week. Reheat over low heat, stirring.

Mocha Fudge Sauce

MAKES ABOUT 2 CUPS
ACTIVE TIME: 15 MINUTES ■ START TO FINISH: 15 MINUTES

■ An easy alternative to classic hot fudge, this is the sauce for people who like the taste of chocolate tempered with coffee. It's also the one to make when the chocolate you have on hand is unsweetened. ■

1 cup packed dark brown sugar
1/2 cup light corn syrup
1 1/2 tablespoons instant espresso powder
3 ounces unsweetened chocolate, finely chopped
1/2 cup heavy cream
2 1/2 tablespoons Kahlúa, or to taste
Pinch of salt

Combine brown sugar, corn syrup, and espresso powder in a small heavy saucepan and bring to a boil over moderate heat, stirring until sugar is dissolved. Remove pan from heat and stir in chocolate until melted. Stir in cream, Kahlúa, and salt. Serve warm or at room temperature.

COOK'S NOTE

- The cooled sauce can be refrigerated in an airtight container for up to 1 week. Reheat in a double boiler, stirring occasionally, or in a microwave.

Strawberry Sauce

MAKES ABOUT 2 1/2 CUPS
ACTIVE TIME: 15 MINUTES ■ START TO FINISH: 2 1/4 HOURS (INCLUDES CHILLING)

■ In strawberry season, this vibrant sauce turns fresh fruit or store-bought pound cake into an instant party dessert. Quick to make, it's also a good use for those burstingly ripe strawberries that will not last the day. ■

1/4 cup sugar
1/2 cup water
Zest of 1 small orange, removed in thin strips with a vegetable peeler
2 pints strawberries, hulled and sliced
1 1/2 tablespoons fresh lemon juice, or to taste
1 1/2 tablespoons Grand Marnier or other orange-flavored liqueur, or to taste (optional)

Combine sugar, water, and zest in a 1- to 1 1/2-quart heavy saucepan and bring to a boil over moderately high heat, stirring until sugar is dissolved. Boil, stirring occasionally, for 5 minutes. Remove zest with fork and discard it. Cool syrup completely.

Purée strawberries in a blender or food processor. Force through a fine-mesh sieve into a medium bowl, pressing hard on solids; discard solids.

Add syrup, lemon juice, and Grand Marnier (if using) to strawberry purée and stir until well combined. Refrigerate sauce, covered, for 2 hours to allow flavors to develop.

Stir in additional lemon juice and Grand Marnier (if using) to taste.

Serve chilled or at room temperature.

COOK'S NOTE

- The sauce can be refrigerated, covered, for up to 3 days.

Raspberry Sauce

MAKES ABOUT 1 CUP
ACTIVE TIME: 10 MINUTES ■ START TO FINISH: 10 MINUTES

■ We always keep frozen raspberries on hand, ready to purée into this versatile sauce, which is as happy poured over a piece of chocolate cake as it is spooned onto a fresh fruit salad. ■

- 1 (10-ounce) package frozen raspberries in syrup, thawed
- 2 tablespoons sugar
- 1 teaspoon fresh lemon juice, or to taste

Combine raspberries, with their syrup, sugar, and lemon juice in a blender or food processor and purée. Pour mixture through a fine-mesh sieve into a bowl, pressing hard on solids; discard solids.

Serve chilled or at room temperature.

COOK'S NOTES

- ■ The sauce can be refrigerated, covered, for up to 3 days.
- ■ You can also make the sauce with fresh raspberries: use 2½ cups raspberries and ¼ cup sugar.

Vanilla Crème Anglaise

MAKES ABOUT 2 CUPS
ACTIVE TIME: 25 MINUTES ■ START TO FINISH: 1½ HOURS (INCLUDES CHILLING)

■ On its own, this plain, simple custard sauce is delicious. For special occasions, dress it up with Calvados, Armagnac, or Grand Marnier. ■

- ½ vanilla bean, halved lengthwise
- 2 cups half-and-half
- 2 large eggs
- ½ cup sugar

SPECIAL EQUIPMENT: an instant-read thermometer

With tip of a paring knife, scrape seeds from vanilla bean into a heavy 3-quart saucepan, then add pod. Add half-and-half and bring just to a boil. Remove from heat.

Whisk together eggs and sugar in a medium bowl until well combined. Add hot half-and-half mixture in a slow stream, whisking constantly, then return to saucepan and cook over moderately low heat, stirring constantly with a wooden spoon, until custard is thickened and registers 175°F on thermometer; do not let boil.

Pour custard sauce through a fine-mesh sieve into a metal bowl; discard solids. Set bowl in a larger bowl of ice and cold water and stir sauce until cool. Refrigerate, covered, until cold, at least 1 hour.

COOK'S NOTE

■ The sauce can be refrigerated, covered, for up to 2 days.

VARIATION

■ ARMAGNAC, CALVADOS, OR GRAND MARNIER CRÈME ANGLAISE: Use 1 whole vanilla bean, halved lengthwise, and add it and a pinch of salt to half-and-half. Proceed as directed. Add 2 tablespoons Armagnac, Calvados, or Grand Marnier to the chilled sauce and stir until combined.

Lemon Curd

MAKES ABOUT 3 CUPS
ACTIVE TIME: 15 MINUTES ■ START TO FINISH: 1 HOUR (INCLUDES CHILLING)

■ With its sunny yellow brightness, vivid flavor, and smoothly appealing texture, this is the easiest kind of custard—and the most versatile. Fold it into whipped cream for an instant mousse, slather it on muffins, or spread it in a baked pastry shell and top with berries for a speedy tart. ■

- 1 tablespoon plus 2 teaspoons finely grated lemon zest
- 1 cup fresh lemon juice
- 1⅓ cups sugar
- 4 large eggs
- Pinch of salt

1¾ sticks (14 tablespoons) unsalted butter, cut into tablespoons

Whisk together zest, juice, sugar, eggs, and salt in a 2-quart heavy saucepan. Add butter and cook over moderately low heat, whisking constantly, until curd is thick enough to hold marks of whisk and first bubbles appear on surface, about 10 minutes.

Immediately force curd through a fine-mesh sieve into a bowl; discard solids. Cool to room temperature, stirring occasionally, then refrigerate in an airtight container until cold.

COOK'S NOTE

- The lemon curd can be refrigerated, covered, for up to 1 week.

SAUCES AND SALSAS

Sauce is one of the things that separates the great cooks from the good ones.

Reading that, you might expect us to be talking about complex French sauces that take days to make. In the old days, that might have been the case. But you won't find complicated concoctions in this chapter, nor recipes requiring sleight of hand or years of experience. What you will find are sprightly salsas with the ability to perk up anything from fried eggs to grilled pork, barbecue sauces that encourage ordinary cuts of meat to break out in song, and a Stilton sauce that makes just about anything taste better. Quick hollandaise, whipped up in the blender, can make plain Jane green vegetables sparkle, and a little English mint sauce will do wonders for a lamb chop. Along with pesto, polonaise, and tapenade, we've included a range of French sauces, from aïoli to velouté.

On the theory that many of these sauces are quick fixes that you will want in your repertoire to jazz up a weekday meal, we have also included compound butters. Top a perfectly plain piece of meat with Roquefort butter and you turn it into something special.

You don't have to be a trained French chef to be a modern sauce master. All you need is a few favorite recipes and a little imagination. The recipes are here; you'll have to supply the imagination.

Béchamel Sauce

MAKES ABOUT 2 CUPS
ACTIVE TIME: 30 MINUTES ■ START TO FINISH: 30 MINUTES

■ This mother of all white sauces is named for the marquis de Béchameil, a bon vivant and financier during the time of Louis XIV. It's used as a basis for other sauces—Mornay and Cheddar (see variations), for example—and as a component in dishes such as croquettes, gratins, and the all-American, love-it-or-hate-it classic creamed chipped beef on toast. The secret to success lies in the simmering, which further cooks the roux (the mixture of flour and fat that acts as thickener), changing its character and flavor and making the finished sauce satiny. ■

- 2 tablespoons unsalted butter
- 1 tablespoon finely chopped onion
- 2 tablespoons all-purpose flour
- 2 cups whole milk
- 1/4 teaspoon salt
- White pepper to taste

Melt butter in a heavy 1½- to 2-quart saucepan over moderately low heat. Add onion and cook, stirring, until softened, about 2 minutes. Add flour and cook, whisking, for 3 minutes to make a roux. Add milk in a steady stream, whisking constantly, and cook, whisking, until thick and smooth. Whisk in salt and pepper, then simmer sauce, whisking frequently, until thickened to desired consistency, 10 to 15 minutes.

Pour sauce through a fine-mesh sieve into a bowl; discard solids. If not serving sauce immediately, cover surface with a buttered round of wax paper, buttered side down, to prevent a skin from forming.

COOK'S NOTE

■ The sauce can be made up to 1 day ahead. Cool, covered with the wax paper round, then refrigerate, tightly covered. You may need to thin it with a little milk when reheating.

VARIATIONS

■ MORNAY SAUCE: Pour the sauce through a fine-mesh sieve into a 1½- to 2-quart saucepan and return to a simmer. Remove from the heat, whisk in 2/3 cup grated Gruyère, or 1/3 cup grated Gruyère plus 1/3 cup finely grated Parmigiano-Reggiano, and whisk until the cheese is melted.

■ CHEDDAR SAUCE: Pour the sauce through a fine-mesh sieve into a 1½- to 2-quart saucepan and return to a simmer. Remove from the heat, whisk in 2/3 cup grated extra-sharp Cheddar, and whisk until the cheese is melted.

Velouté Sauce

MAKES ABOUT 2½ CUPS
ACTIVE TIME: 20 MINUTES ■ START TO FINISH: 40 MINUTES, PLUS ADDITIONAL TIME FOR MAKING STOCK

■ A velouté, named for its velvety consistency, is essentially a béchamel sauce made with stock instead of milk. Spoon this over poached skinless, boneless chicken breasts, pop them under the broiler briefly to glaze, and dinner will seem much fancier than it really is. ■

- 3 cups Chicken, Veal, or Fish Stock (page 928, 929, or 930; do not used canned broth)
- 3 tablespoons unsalted butter
- 1 tablespoon finely chopped onion
- 1/4 cup all-purpose flour
- 1/4 cup finely chopped mushroom stems (optional)
- 2 (5-inch) fresh parsley stems (without leaves)
- 1 (4-inch) fresh thyme sprig
- 1/2 Turkish bay leaf or 1/4 California bay leaf
- 2 white peppercorns
- Salt

Bring stock to a simmer in a 1½- to 2-quart saucepan. Keep warm, covered.

Melt butter in a 1½- to 2-quart heavy saucepan over moderate heat. Add onion and cook, stirring, until softened, about 2 minutes. Reduce heat to low, add flour, and cook, stirring, for 3 minutes to make a roux. Remove from heat and add warm stock in a slow stream, whisking constantly to prevent lumps. Add mushroom stems (if using), parsley stems, thyme, bay leaf, and peppercorns, return to heat, and simmer sauce, stirring occasionally and skimming froth, until thickened, about 20 minutes.

Pour sauce through a fine-mesh sieve into a bowl; discard solids. Season with salt. If not serving sauce immediately, cover surface with a buttered round of wax paper, buttered side down, to prevent a skin from forming.

COOK'S NOTE

- The sauce can be made up to 1 day ahead. Cool, covered with the wax paper round, then refrigerate. Skim any skin from top and reheat before serving; you may need to thin the sauce with a little stock or water when reheating.

Portobello Vegetarian Gravy

MAKES ABOUT 3½ CUPS
ACTIVE TIME: 45 MINUTES ■ START TO FINISH: 2¼ HOURS (INCLUDES MAKING STOCK)

■ Here deep flavor and color come from the well-browned vegetables as well as the portobello mushrooms in the vegetable stock. Use this as you would any gravy—over rice or potatoes, say. It makes a fine alternative to turkey gravy during the holidays. Even diehard carnivores won't miss the meat. ■

- 3 cups Vegetable Stock (page 930; do not use canned broth)
- ½ stick (4 tablespoons) unsalted butter
- ⅓ cup all-purpose flour
- ¼ cup heavy cream
- ½ teaspoon salt
- ¼ teaspoon freshly ground black pepper

Bring stock to a simmer in a 1½- to 2-quart saucepan. Keep warm, covered.

Melt butter in a 1½-quart heavy saucepan over moderate heat. Add flour and cook, whisking, for 2 to 3 minutes to make a roux. Add stock in a fast stream, whisking constantly to prevent lumps, and bring to a boil, whisking. Reduce heat and simmer, whisking frequently, until thickened to desired consistency, 6 to 8 minutes.

Stir in cream, salt, and pepper.

COOK'S NOTE

- The gravy can be made up to 3 days ahead. Cool, uncovered, then refrigerate, covered.

White Bordelaise Sauce

MAKES ABOUT 1 CUP
ACTIVE TIME: 1 HOUR ■ START TO FINISH: 5½ HOURS (INCLUDES MAKING STOCK)

■ A traditional bordelaise sauce is made with red wine and beef marrow. This version is lighter yet still earthy. It's from Laurent Manrique, a native of Gascony and the chef at San Francisco's Campton Place Restaurant. He serves the sauce with roasted monkfish, but it is delicious with any roasted fish—cod, for example—or with roast chicken. ■

- 1 tablespoon olive oil
- 1 small onion, thinly sliced
- 4 garlic cloves
- 1 cup dry white wine
- ½ cup white port
- ½ Turkish bay leaf or ¼ California bay leaf
- 2 cups Chicken Stock (page 928; do not use canned broth)
- 1 cup veal demi-glace (see Sources)

Heat oil in a 3-quart heavy saucepan over moderately high heat until hot but not smoking. Reduce heat to moderate, add onion and garlic, and cook, stirring, until onion is softened, about 2 minutes. Stir in white wine, port, and bay leaf, bring to a boil, and boil until liquid is reduced to about 2 tablespoons, about 8 minutes.

Stir in chicken stock and boil until liquid is reduced to about 1 cup, about 18 minutes. Add demi-glace and boil, stirring occasionally, until liquid is reduced to about 1 cup again, about 10 minutes.

Pour sauce through a fine-mesh sieve into a sauceboat or bowl, pressing on solids; discard solids.

COOK'S NOTE

- The sauce can be made up to 2 days ahead. Cool completely, uncovered, then refrigerate, covered.

Beurre Blanc

White Butter Sauce

MAKES ABOUT 2/3 CUP
ACTIVE TIME: 25 MINUTES ■ START TO FINISH: 30 MINUTES

■ Back in the late 1970s and early 1980s, this sleek, smooth butter sauce supplanted flour-based sauces, which were suddenly dismissed as "hopelessly old-fashioned." A decade later, of course, the Food Police came down on butter sauces like a ton of bricks. Well, we don't play favorites—there is room in our hearts for both. This French classic is unbeatable on seafood or poached chicken breasts. ■

- 1/4 cup dry white wine
- 1/4 cup white wine vinegar
- 2 tablespoons minced shallots
- 1 tablespoon cold water
- 1 stick (8 tablespoons) cold unsalted butter, cut into 1/2-inch cubes
- 1/2 teaspoon salt
- 1/8 teaspoon white pepper

Combine wine, vinegar, and shallots in a small heavy saucepan, bring to a simmer over moderately high heat, and simmer until liquid is reduced by about half, about 6 minutes. Remove from heat and stir in water. Return to heat, then reduce heat to low and whisk in butter one piece at a time, adding each new piece before previous one has completely melted and lifting pan from heat occasionally to cool mixture (this will take about 12 minutes). (Sauce must not get hot enough to separate; it should be the consistency of hollandaise.)

If desired, pour sauce through a fine-mesh sieve into a bowl, pressing on solids; discard solids. Whisk in salt and pepper and serve immediately.

COOK'S NOTE

■ The vinegar–white wine reduction can be made up to 1 hour ahead.

White Butter Sauce with Cream

Beurre Nantais

MAKES ABOUT 3/4 CUP
ACTIVE TIME: 10 MINUTES ■ START TO FINISH: 10 MINUTES

■ We thought up a new word when we tasted this sauce: it's a basic *beurre blanc* that's been "velvetized" with cream. It's traditionally served with fish, but we also like it over steak or vegetables. ■

- 2 tablespoons dry white wine
- 2 tablespoons white wine vinegar
- 1 tablespoon finely chopped shallot
- 3 tablespoons heavy cream
- 1 stick (8 tablespoons) cold unsalted butter, cut into 1/2-inch cubes
- 1/8 teaspoon fresh lemon juice
- Salt and white pepper

Combine wine, vinegar, and shallot in a small heavy saucepan, bring to a simmer over moderate heat, and simmer until liquid is reduced to about 1 tablespoon, about 5 minutes. Add cream and simmer until slightly thickened, about 2 minutes. Add butter a few pieces at a time, whisking and adding more before previous pieces are fully incorporated (mixture will be creamy and pale).

Remove pan from heat and pour sauce through a fine-mesh sieve into a bowl, pressing on solids; discard solids. Stir in lemon juice and season with salt and pepper. Serve immediately.

COOK'S NOTE

■ The vinegar–white wine reduction can be made up to 1 hour ahead.

Brown Butter Sauce with Lemon

Beurre Meunière

MAKES ABOUT ¼ CUP
ACTIVE TIME: 10 MINUTES ■ START TO FINISH: 10 MINUTES

■ This sauce enhances the natural sweetness in foods; try it on steamed cauliflower or asparagus or with sautéed fish. It's simple to make, but somewhat deceptively so: the precipitous slide from golden brown butter to burned butter can happen in an instant, so don't even think about walking away from the stove. Ideally, the sauce should be served while it is foaming (courtesy of the lemon juice), for a little drama at the table. ■

- ½ stick (4 tablespoons) unsalted butter, cut into bits
- 1½ teaspoons fresh lemon juice
- ⅛ teaspoon salt, or to taste
- Freshly ground black pepper
- 1 tablespoon chopped fresh flat-leaf parsley

Melt butter in a small heavy skillet over moderately low heat, then simmer until golden brown with a nutty aroma, about 5 minutes. Remove skillet from heat and immediately add lemon juice, salt, and pepper to taste, swirling skillet to incorporate (butter will foam). Add parsley and additional salt to taste, if desired. Serve immediately.

Hollandaise Sauce

MAKES ABOUT 1 CUP
ACTIVE TIME: 20 MINUTES ■ START TO FINISH: 20 MINUTES

■ Hollandaise is one of the world's great sauces. It is very rich, true, but it's also light: because it's an emulsion, like mayonnaise, it has an airiness that a lemon butter sauce doesn't have. Hollandaise is also the most voluptuous of sauces: look at the way it drapes over eggs Benedict, gently steamed asparagus, or broccoli. ■

- 2 sticks (½ pound) unsalted butter
- 3 large egg yolks
- 1 tablespoon fresh lemon juice
- 1 tablespoon water
- ¼ teaspoon salt
- ⅛ teaspoon white pepper

Melt butter in a 1-quart heavy saucepan over moderate heat. Remove pan from heat and let stand for 3 minutes. Skim foam from top of butter.

Whisk together yolks, lemon juice, and water in another 1-quart heavy saucepan until frothy. Set pan over low heat and whisk constantly and vigorously until yolks are pale yellow and slightly thickened (you should be able to draw whisk through yolks and see bottom of pan before yolks flow back together), 3 to 4 minutes.

Remove pan from heat and gradually whisk in melted butter: drop by drop for first third of butter, then 1 teaspoon at a time for second third and 1 tablespoon at a time for final third, leaving milky solids in bottom of pan. Whisk in salt and white pepper.

COOK'S NOTES

- If the yolks overcook, they will curdle (scramble). If you detect the slightest bit of curdling, immediately place the saucepan in a large bowl of ice and cold water and whisk to cool the yolks slightly, then continue with the recipe. (If you have more than just a little bit of curdled yolk, it is best to start over.)
- The sauce can be made up to 1 hour ahead. Cover the pan with plastic wrap and place in a 4-quart saucepan of warm water (135°F; if the water is too hot, it will curdle the sauce). If the sauce thickens while sitting, whisk in 1 to 2 tablespoons warm water.
- The yolks in this recipe are not fully cooked. If this is a concern, see page 629.

VARIATIONS

- MALTAISE SAUCE: This sauce is usually served with asparagus. Replace the water with 1 tablespoon fresh orange juice (if available, use blood-orange juice). Whisk in 1 teaspoon finely grated orange zest and 1 additional tablespoon orange juice along with the salt and pepper at the end.
- BLENDER HOLLANDAISE: This version is denser than regular hollandaise. Prepare the butter as described above. Combine the yolks, lemon juice, and water in a blender and blend for 2 seconds. With the blender running at medium speed (if the speed is too high, the

sauce will splatter), add half of the melted butter in a slow stream through the hole in the lid. Add 1 tablespoon warm water to thin the sauce, then continue slowly adding the remaining butter (leaving the milky solids in the bottom of the pan). Thin the sauce to the desired consistency by whisking in additional warm water (1 to 2 tablespoons), then whisk in the salt and pepper.

Béarnaise Sauce

MAKES ABOUT 1 CUP
ACTIVE TIME: 20 MINUTES ■ START TO FINISH: 30 MINUTES

■ Béarnaise turns a plate of simple vegetables or grilled or broiled meat into a special occasion. Because it is so rich, it's best suited to lean cuts of meat—filet mignon or beef tenderloin, for instance, or small, tender noisettes of lamb. Using the higher amount of butter will mute the tarragon flavor as well as the acidity of the white wine and vinegar. ■

- 1/3 cup dry white wine
- 1/3 cup white wine vinegar
- 2 tablespoons finely chopped shallots
- 6 (6-inch) fresh tarragon sprigs, leaves removed and finely chopped, stems coarsely chopped
- 8 black peppercorns
- 1 1/2–2 sticks (12–16 tablespoons) unsalted butter
- 3 large egg yolks
- 1/4 teaspoon salt

Combine wine, vinegar, shallots, tarragon stems, and peppercorns in a 1-quart heavy saucepan, bring to a boil over moderately high heat, and boil until reduced to about 1/4 cup, about 8 minutes. Remove from heat and cool for 5 minutes.

Pour mixture through a fine-mesh sieve into a small bowl, pressing on solids; discard solids. You should have 2 tablespoons strained reduction; if you have less, add enough water to make 2 tablespoons.

Melt butter in another 1-quart heavy saucepan over moderate heat. Remove pan from heat and let stand for 3 minutes. Skim foam from top of butter.

Whisk together reduction and yolks in cleaned 1-quart heavy saucepan until frothy. Set pan over low heat and whisk constantly and vigorously until yolks are pale yellow and slightly thickened (you should be able to draw whisk through yolks and see bottom of pan before yolks flow back together), 3 to 4 minutes.

Remove pan from heat and gradually whisk in melted butter: drop by drop for first third of butter, then 1 teaspoon at a time for second third and 1 tablespoon at a time for final third, leaving milky solids in bottom of pan. Whisk in tarragon leaves and salt.

COOK'S NOTES

- The béarnaise can be made up to 1 hour ahead. Cover the pan with plastic wrap and place in a 4-quart saucepan of warm water (135°F; if the water is too hot, it will curdle the sauce). If the sauce thickens while sitting, whisk in 1 to 2 tablespoons warm water.
- The yolks in this recipe are not fully cooked. If this is a concern, see page 629.

VARIATION

- BLENDER BÉARNAISE: This version is denser than regular béarnaise. Prepare the reduction and butter as described above. Combine the reduction and yolks in a blender and blend for 2 seconds. With the blender running at medium speed (if the speed is too high, the sauce will splatter), add half of the melted butter in a slow stream through the hole in the lid. Add 1 tablespoon warm water to thin the sauce, then continue slowly adding the remaining butter (leaving the milky solids in the bottom of the pan). Thin the sauce to the desired consistency by whisking in additional warm water (1 to 2 tablespoons), then whisk in the tarragon leaves and salt.

Stilton Sauce

MAKES ABOUT 2 CUPS
ACTIVE TIME: 15 MINUTES ■ START TO FINISH: 40 MINUTES

■ This *makes* a dinner party. Serve it with lean cuts such as filet mignons or a whole beef tenderloin roast, or instead of Mornay sauce over cauliflower. ■

- 1/2 pound Stilton or Roquefort, softened
- 1 stick (8 tablespoons) unsalted butter, softened
- 1 1/2 cups dry white wine

1 cup heavy cream
4 teaspoons finely chopped fresh flat-leaf parsley

Stir together cheese and butter in a bowl until smooth.

Boil wine in a 1-quart saucepan until reduced to about 2 tablespoons, about 15 minutes. Add cream and boil until liquid is reduced by about half, about 8 minutes.

Reduce heat to moderately low and whisk in cheese mixture a little at a time, then whisk in parsley.

COOK'S NOTE

- The sauce, without the parsley, can be made up to 1 day ahead. Cool, covered with wax paper, then refrigerate, tightly covered. Reheat over moderately high heat, whisking constantly. Whisk in parsley.

Avgolemono

Egg and Lemon Sauce

MAKES ABOUT 2½ CUPS
ACTIVE TIME: 20 MINUTES ■ START TO FINISH: 20 MINUTES

■ The applications of this Greek specialty (pronounced "ahv-go-*leh*-mo-no") extend far beyond the Aegean Sea. It's lighter, brothier, and more versatile than hollandaise. Although it's a little too brothy for eggs Benedict (it would make the English muffins soggy), it's delicious poured over steamed asparagus or broccoli. And it's really nice with a piece of fish. ■

2 cups chicken stock or store-bought low-sodium broth
3 large eggs
1 large egg white
¼ cup fresh lemon juice
½ teaspoon salt

Heat stock in a small saucepan until hot; keep warm.

Combine eggs, egg white, lemon juice, and salt in top of a double boiler or a metal bowl and beat (off heat) with an electric mixer at high speed until frothy, about 3 minutes. Add 1 cup hot stock in a stream, beating, then stir in remaining 1 cup stock. Set over simmering water and cook sauce, whisking, until slightly thickened, 8 to 10 minutes. Serve immediately.

COOK'S NOTE

- The eggs in this recipe may not be fully cooked. If this is a concern, see page 629.

Tartar Sauce

MAKES ABOUT 1½ CUPS
ACTIVE TIME: 20 MINUTES ■ START TO FINISH: 20 MINUTES

■ If you've never had homemade tartar sauce, this will be a revelation. We know that this recipe contains tiny amounts of lots of ingredients, but be patient: each one carries its own weight. A classic accompaniment to fried seafood, this is also great with cold poached salmon. ■

1 cup mayonnaise
1½ tablespoons finely chopped dill pickle
1½ tablespoons finely chopped sweet pickle relish
2 tablespoons finely chopped onion
1½ teaspoons finely chopped capers
Yolk of 1 hard-boiled large egg, finely chopped
¼ cup finely chopped fresh flat-leaf parsley
2 teaspoons finely chopped fresh dill (optional)
2½ teaspoons finely chopped fresh tarragon or ½ teaspoon dried tarragon, crumbled
2½ teaspoons finely chopped fresh chervil or ½ teaspoon dried chervil, crumbled
¾ teaspoon Dijon mustard
Salt and freshly ground black pepper to taste

Stir together all ingredients in a small bowl until well combined.

COOK'S NOTE

- The tartar sauce can be made up to 1 day ahead and refrigerated, covered.

Mayonnaise

MAKES ABOUT 1 CUP

ACTIVE TIME: 10 MINUTES ■ START TO FINISH: 10 MINUTES

■ Homemade mayonnaise has a silkiness, an elegance, that you won't find in any commercial preparation. It's versatile, too: you can spread it on a sandwich or make a dip, of course, but slightly thinned, it comes into its own as a sauce (see the following recipes for some flavoring suggestions). And it can also become a puffed, golden topping for broiled fish or chicken. This kind of sauce has been around since antiquity; the Roman epicure Apicius wrote about sauces made with eggs and oil in the first century A.D.

Making mayonnaise by hand isn't hard, but patience, constant whisking, and attention to detail are the keys to success. We like to add a little mustard, which helps the sauce emulsify properly and adds piquancy. A quick word about the oil: make sure it's fresh. ■

- 1 large egg yolk, left at room temperature for 30 minutes
- 1/2 teaspoon Dijon mustard
- 1/4 teaspoon salt
- 3/4 cup olive or vegetable oil, or a combination
- 1 teaspoon white wine vinegar
- 1 1/2 teaspoons fresh lemon juice
- 1/4 teaspoon white pepper

Whisk together yolk, mustard, and salt in a small bowl until well combined. Add about 1/4 cup oil drop by drop, whisking constantly until mixture begins to thicken. Whisk in vinegar and lemon juice until combined, then add remaining 1/2 cup oil in a very slow, thin stream, whisking constantly until well blended. If at any time it appears that oil is not being incorporated, stop the stream of oil and whisk mixture vigorously until it is smooth, then continue adding oil. Whisk in salt to taste and white pepper. Refrigerate, the surface covered with plastic wrap, until ready to use.

COOK'S NOTES

- The egg yolk in this recipe (and the following mayonnaise recipes) is not cooked. If this is a concern, see page 629.
- The mayonnaise keeps, covered and refrigerated, for up to 2 days.
- If using the mayonnaise as a sauce instead of a spread or dip, thin it to the desired consistency with a little water, adding 1/2 teaspoon at a time.

Horseradish Mayonnaise

■ This makes the best roast beef sandwich ever. It's also delicious as a dip for crudités or, slightly thinned, as a sauce for salmon. (For more about horseradish, see page 893.) ■

- 1 large egg yolk, left at room temperature for 30 minutes
- 1/4 teaspoon salt
- 2–3 teaspoons fresh lemon juice (to taste)
- 3/4 cup olive or vegetable oil, or a combination
- 2–3 tablespoons drained bottled horseradish (to taste)
- 1 tablespoon minced pimiento-stuffed olives (8 small)
- 1/4 teaspoon white or freshly ground black pepper

Whisk yolk, salt, and 1 teaspoon lemon juice in a bowl until well combined. Following procedure for Mayonnaise, add about 1/4 cup oil drop by drop, whisking constantly, until mixture begins to thicken. Whisk in another 1 teaspoon lemon juice until combined, then add remaining 1/2 cup oil in a very slow, thin stream, as directed. Whisk in 2 tablespoons horseradish, olives, and pepper, then add up to 1 teaspoon more lemon juice and 1 tablespoon more horseradish to taste, if desired. Refrigerate, the surface covered with plastic wrap, for at least 1 hour to allow the flavors to develop, then season with salt if necessary and refrigerate until ready to use. (Makes about 1 1/4 cups.)

Mustard Mayonnaise

■ Great on a steak sandwich or as a sauce for chicken or salmon. This mayonnaise makes a terrific dip as well. ■

- 1 large egg yolk, left at room temperature for 30 minutes
- 1/2 teaspoon Dijon mustard

- 1/4 teaspoon salt
- 1 tablespoon fresh lemon juice
- 3/4 cup olive or vegetable oil, or a combination
- 1 tablespoon whole-grain mustard
- 1/8 teaspoon freshly ground black pepper

Whisk together yolk, Dijon mustard, salt, and 1 teaspoon lemon juice, as directed for Mayonnaise. Following procedure, add 1/4 cup oil drop by drop, whisking constantly, until mixture begins to thicken. Whisk in remaining 2 teaspoons lemon juice until combined, then add remaining 1/2 cup oil in a very slow, thin stream, as directed. Whisk in whole-grain mustard and pepper. Refrigerate, the surface covered with plastic wrap, for at least 1 hour to allow the flavors to develop, then season with salt if necessary and refrigerate until ready to use. (Makes about 1 cup.)

Curry Mayonnaise

■ Lime juice adds a bright dimension to this mayonnaise, and cayenne gives it a little kick. Serve it with cold poached chicken or instead of cocktail or tartar sauce with cold seafood. ■

- 1 large egg yolk, left at room temperature for 30 minutes
- 3/4 cup olive or vegetable oil, or a combination
- 1 tablespoon fresh lime juice
- 2 teaspoons curry powder
- 1/4 teaspoon salt
- 1/8 teaspoon cayenne

Whisk yolk in a bowl. Following procedure for Mayonnaise, add 1/4 cup oil drop by drop, whisking constantly, until mixture begins to thicken. Whisk in 1 1/2 teaspoons lime juice until combined, then add remaining 1/2 cup oil in a very slow thin stream, as directed. Whisk in remaining 1 1/2 teaspoons lime juice, curry powder, salt, and cayenne. Refrigerate, the surface covered with plastic wrap, for at least 1 hour to allow the flavors to develop, then season with salt if necessary and refrigerate until ready to use. (Makes about 1 cup.)

Blender Mayonnaise

MAKES ABOUT 1 CUP
ACTIVE TIME: 5 MINUTES ■ START TO FINISH: 5 MINUTES

■ If blenders had existed in the days of Escoffier and his crowd, they would have used them. ■

- 1 large egg, left at room temperature for 30 minutes
- 1 tablespoon fresh lemon juice
- 1 teaspoon Dijon mustard
- 1/4 teaspoon salt
- 1/4 teaspoon white pepper
- 1 cup olive or vegetable oil, or a combination

Blend egg, lemon juice, mustard, salt, and pepper in a blender until combined. With blender running, add oil in a very slow, thin stream, blending until mayonnaise is thickened and smooth. Transfer to a bowl and refrigerate, the surface covered with plastic wrap, until ready to use.

Green Mayonnaise

MAKES ABOUT 1 CUP
ACTIVE TIME: 15 MINUTES ■ START TO FINISH: 2 1/4 HOURS (INCLUDES CHILLING)

■ The full flavor and aroma of fresh herbs create a wonderful synergy in a homemade mayonnaise or brighten up the store-bought kind. ■

- 3 tablespoons chopped fresh flat-leaf parsley
- 2 tablespoons chopped fresh chives
- 1 1/2 tablespoons chopped fresh tarragon
- 1 tablespoon chopped fresh chervil (optional)
- 2 teaspoons chopped fresh dill
- 1 tablespoon fresh lemon juice
- 1 cup mayonnaise (store-bought or homemade)
- 1/4 teaspoon salt
- 1/4 teaspoon freshly ground black pepper

Combine parsley, chives, tarragon, chervil (if using), and dill in a blender, add lemon juice and 1/2 cup mayonnaise, and pulse until herbs are puréed. Add remaining 1/2 cup mayonnaise, salt, and pepper and blend well. Transfer to a bowl and refrigerate, the surface covered with plastic wrap, for at least 2 hours to allow the flavors to blend.

Making Aïoli

The intense, sublime sauce called aïoli (pronounced "eye-*oh*-lee"), a classic of the Provençal kitchen, is the essence of simplicity, but it's not simple to make. It's a lot of work, frankly—not the fiddly, fussy kind, though, but relaxed and mellow. We recommend that you use a large mortar (about eight inches in diameter; it should hold two cups) and a large pestle. Such a mortar isn't easy to find; most cookware shops carry smaller ones, suitable for grinding spices but not much else. Large marble ones can be ordered by mail from Dean & DeLuca; the apothecary-style bisque ones carried by Sur La Table are nice too. Of course you can use a large glass or ceramic bowl, but in that case you'll need a wooden pestle, not one made of lava or marble. Sur La Table sells those as well, as does the Spanish Table (see Sources).

We find it easier to pulverize the garlic to a smooth paste with a little of the oil and salt in a blender than to pound it by hand in the mortar; the technique works especially well if you are making aïoli for a crowd. Then transfer the paste to the mortar.

This is when you need to switch to Mediterranean time: it takes about fifteen minutes to work the rest of the olive oil slowly into the garlic paste (switch hands halfway through so you don't get tired). You can't rush the process, and you won't want to once you see the aïoli starting to come together in a gorgeous green emulsion (the color comes from the olive oil). Patience is critical; adding too much oil at one time will cause the emulsion to break, and there's no saving it once that happens. If you like making risotto, you are going to love making aïoli.

The garlic you buy is crucial: it needs to be as fresh as possible. Look for solid heads with tight, papery skins. If the cloves have little green sprouts inside, they're too old—even if you pick the bitter green bits out, the garlic will still be too strong. Coarse salt helps break down the garlic and enhances the flavor. We're partial to sea salt here, but additive-free kosher salt is fine too. We also recommend a good extra-virgin olive oil with a fruity taste and aroma. And make sure that both garlic and oil are at room temperature, or you're going to have trouble with the emulsion.

Eggless Aïoli

MAKES ABOUT 1 CUP
ACTIVE TIME: 25 MINUTES ■ START TO FINISH: 25 MINUTES

■ *Le grand aïoli* is one of the renowned communal summer events in the South of France. The Provençal cooking authority Georgeanne Brennan tells us that the occasion might be a Sunday afternoon gathering for family or friends or a festival on a village green. Aïoli—a thick, rich, garlicky sauce—is the main attraction, supported by a delicious cast of poached salt cod, hard-boiled eggs, steamed shellfish, crudités, and cooked vegetables (roasted beets and onions, steamed artichokes, boiled potatoes, and green beans, for example) for dipping. Normally the aïoli is made with an egg yolk or a whole egg to help along the emulsion, but here we've made an eggless version, in which the flavor of the garlic is more robust. Purity has its downside, however; the eggless sauce is notoriously tricky to make (see opposite page for more information). So we've given you the option of a quick aïoli, whizzed up in a blender with an egg. ■

- 1/4 cup coarsely chopped very fresh garlic, at room temperature
- 1 teaspoon coarse sea salt or kosher salt
- 1 cup extra-virgin olive oil, at room temperature

SPECIAL EQUIPMENT: a large mortar and pestle

Combine garlic, salt, and 2 tablespoons oil in a blender and blend at high speed until smooth and creamy, about 2 minutes. Transfer to mortar. Very slowly add remaining 3/4 cup plus 2 tablespoons oil, 1 to 2 teaspoons at a time, stirring and mashing constantly and vigorously with pestle; this will take about 15 minutes (aïoli will separate if oil is added too quickly). Mixture will become very thick and glossy. Transfer to a bowl.

Quick Aïoli

MAKES ABOUT 1 CUP
ACTIVE TIME: 10 MINUTES ■ START TO FINISH: 10 MINUTES

■ Aïoli makes a wonderful sauce for vegetables, but it's also delicious with grilled fish or roast leg of lamb. This speedy blender recipe is for all the immediate-gratification types out there (and sometimes they are us). When making aïoli entirely in the blender, you must add whole eggs or egg yolks in order to hold the emulsion together. The consistency is creamier and more like mayonnaise than the eggless rendition. ■

- 1/4 cup coarsely chopped very fresh garlic, at room temperature
- 1 teaspoon coarse sea salt or kosher salt
- 1 cup extra-virgin olive oil, at room temperature
- 1 large egg or 2 large egg yolks, left at room temperature for 30 minutes

Combine garlic, salt, and 2 tablespoons oil in a blender and blend at high speed until smooth and creamy, about 2 minutes. Add egg or yolks and, with motor running, very slowly add remaining 3/4 cup plus 2 tablespoons oil in a thin, steady stream, blending until aïoli is thick. This will take about 2 minutes. Transfer to a bowl.

COOK'S NOTES

- The eggs in this recipe are not cooked. If this is a concern, see page 629.
- The aïoli can be refrigerated, covered, for up to 2 days.

Pesto

MAKES ABOUT 1 1/3 CUPS
ACTIVE TIME: 15 MINUTES ■ START TO FINISH: 15 MINUTES

■ This gutsy, vibrant sauce from Genoa is best made with standard sweet (Genoese) basil. We swear by the food processor method for preparing it, as opposed to the time-honored mortar and pestle (the word *pesto* refers to that kitchen tool), because everyone we know makes vast quantities at the height of the basil season. A dollop of undiluted pesto is delicious stirred into minestrone or served over corn on the cob, boiled potatoes, or a platter of hot tender green beans, but the secret to serving it over pasta lies in diluting it with a little pasta cooking water, which enables the cheese to melt and the sauce to coat the pasta more easily (see Cook's Note). ■

- 3 large garlic cloves
- 1/2 cup pine nuts
- 2/3 cup coarsely grated Parmigiano-Reggiano
- 1 teaspoon salt
- 1/2 teaspoon freshly ground black pepper
- 3 cups loosely packed fresh basil leaves
- 2/3 cup extra-virgin olive oil

With the food processor running, drop in garlic and finely chop. Stop motor and add nuts, cheese, salt, pepper, and basil, then process until finely chopped. With motor running, add oil, blending until incorporated but not completely smooth.

COOK'S NOTES

- The pesto keeps, refrigerated, the surface covered with plastic wrap, for up to 1 week.
- The pesto can be frozen in an airtight container for up to 2 months. If you are planning to freeze it, omit the cheese when preparing the recipe, then stir it into the thawed sauce before serving.
- For pasta with pesto: Put 2/3 cup pesto in a large bowl. Cook 1 pound linguine or spaghetti until al dente, then whisk about 1/3 cup of the pasta cooking water into the pesto. Add the drained pasta to the pesto, along with salt and pepper to taste, and toss well. Serve with additional grated Parmigiano-Reggiano.

Salsa Verde

MAKES ABOUT 1/2 CUP
ACTIVE TIME: 15 MINUTES ■ START TO FINISH: 15 MINUTES

■ Uncooked green sauces (of which pesto may be the most famous) have been made in Italy for centuries and are incredibly versatile. Based on various green herbs, they add a jazzy accompaniment to plain poached meats or steamed vegetables. Try this one with any leftover roast or steak—it will spark the eye as well as the palate. Note the tiny amount of anchovy paste in the recipe. It's our secret weapon in many dishes because it grounds lots of other flavors (try it in salad dressing or spaghetti sauce). Think of it as a bass note; you'd miss it if it weren't there. ■

- 1 tablespoon fresh lemon juice
- 1/8 teaspoon anchovy paste
- 3 tablespoons extra-virgin olive oil
- 1 tablespoon chopped shallot
- 1 tablespoon drained capers, chopped
- 2 tablespoons chopped fresh flat-leaf parsley
- Salt and freshly ground black pepper

Whisk together lemon juice, anchovy paste, and oil in a small bowl until blended. Stir in shallot, capers, and parsley and season with salt and pepper.

Tapenade

MAKES ABOUT 2 CUPS
ACTIVE TIME: 15 MINUTES ■ START TO FINISH: 15 MINUTES

■ There are many different versions of this Mediterranean olive paste, but they all have one thing in common: good, meaty olives. Garlic adds a piquant roughness and capers add a salty tang. Put this out when serving aperitifs, along with toasted slices of French bread and goat cheese. It will also bring a plain grilled chicken breast or piece of fish to life. ■

- 2 cups pitted brine-cured black olives, such as Kalamata
- 3 garlic cloves
- 1 tablespoon small capers, drained
- 1/3 cup extra-virgin olive oil

Combine olives, garlic, and capers in a food processor and blend until a smooth paste forms, about 3 minutes. With motor running, add olive oil in a steady stream and pulse until well combined.

COOK'S NOTE

- The tapenade keeps, refrigerated in an airtight container, for up to 2 weeks.

Green Olive and Almond Tapenade

MAKES ABOUT 1½ CUPS
ACTIVE TIME: 15 MINUTES ■ START TO FINISH: 25 MINUTES

■ Olives gradually ripen from green to purple to black over the course of about six months. Green olives, picked in late August or September in the Mediterranean, are a natural combination with almonds, which are harvested then too. This tapenade, from reader Amy Sue Keck, of San Diego, is delicious smeared on grilled toasts at cocktail time. Or serve it with carrot sticks or toasted pita wedges. ■

- 1½ cups brine-cured green olives, pitted
- ½ cup loosely packed fresh flat-leaf parsley leaves
- ¼ cup slivered almonds, toasted (see Tips, page 938)
- 2 tablespoons fresh lemon juice
- ⅔ cup extra-virgin olive oil

Combine olives, parsley, almonds, and lemon juice in a food processor and pulse, scraping down sides of bowl occasionally, until mixture is finely chopped. With motor running, add oil in a steady stream, blending to form a paste.

COOK'S NOTE

■ The tapenade keeps, refrigerated in an airtight container, for up to 5 days. The light film of oil that rises to the surface can simply be stirred back in.

Tahini Sauce

MAKES ABOUT 1⅓ CUPS
ACTIVE TIME: 20 MINUTES ■ START TO FINISH: 20 MINUTES

■ This beautifully smooth sauce made with tahini tastes rich without relying on mayonnaise or cream—that's why it's so popular in street food such as Falafel Pitas (page 182). It's also excellent drizzled over a salad of tomatoes and cucumber or as an accompaniment for kebabs or crudités. ■

TAHINI

Rich, creamy tahini, a staple of Middle Eastern cooking, is a paste made of sesame seeds. All tahini separates when it sits—the oil rises to the top and the dense paste settles to the bottom—so you must stir it before you use it. (If instead you skimmed the top layer away, the tahini would be dry and unspreadable.) We have found that tahini can go off, so buy it from a place with a high turnover, such as a Middle Eastern market or natural foods store.

- 2 garlic cloves
- ½ teaspoon fine sea salt, or to taste
- ½ cup well-stirred tahini (Middle Eastern sesame paste)
- ⅓ cup fresh lemon juice
- ¼ cup water
- ¼ cup olive oil
- 1 tablespoon finely chopped fresh cilantro
- 1 tablespoon finely chopped fresh flat-leaf parsley
- ¼ teaspoon ground cumin

Using a large heavy knife, mince garlic, then mash to a paste with salt. Whisk together garlic paste and remaining ingredients in a medium bowl until well combined.

COOK'S NOTE

■ The sauce can be made up to 1 day ahead and refrigerated, covered. Bring to room temperature before serving.

Cocktail Sauce

MAKES ABOUT 1 CUP
ACTIVE TIME: 10 MINUTES ■ START TO FINISH: 10 MINUTES

■ Orange zest and juice give this a rounder, slightly sweeter flavor than most other cocktail sauces. It's delicious dabbed onto the usual suspects—shrimp, oysters, clams, and an occasional saltine. ■

3/4 cup ketchup
1/4 teaspoon finely grated orange zest
1/4 cup fresh orange juice
1–1 1/2 tablespoons fresh lemon juice (to taste)
3 tablespoons drained bottled horseradish
1/4 teaspoon Tabasco

Stir together all ingredients in a small bowl until well combined.

COOK'S NOTE

- The sauce can be made up to 1 day ahead and refrigerated, covered.

Tomato Ketchup

MAKES ABOUT 2 CUPS
ACTIVE TIME: 20 MINUTES ▪ START TO FINISH: 3 1/4 HOURS (INCLUDES CHILLING)

▪ As the food historian Andrew Smith tells us in *Pure Ketchup: A History of America's National Condiment,* ketchup emerged during the late eighteenth century from a non–tomato-based "culinary crucible of salted, pickled, and fermented foods from ancient Europe and exotic Southeast Asia." In the mid-1800s, Isabella Beeton offered three ketchup recipes in her enormously influential *Book of Household Management,* and in 1878 Marion Cabell Tyree published sixteen in *Housekeeping in Old Virginia.* Today we don't normally think of ketchup as something you make at home, but it's easier than you might think, and absolutely delicious. ▪

1 (28- to 32-ounce) can whole tomatoes in purée
2 tablespoons olive oil
1 medium onion, chopped
1 tablespoon tomato paste
2/3 cup dark brown sugar
1/2 cup cider vinegar
1/2 teaspoon salt

Purée tomatoes in a blender until smooth.

Heat oil in a 4-quart heavy saucepan over moderate heat until hot but not smoking. Add onion and cook, stirring, until softened, about 8 minutes. Stir in puréed tomatoes, tomato paste, brown sugar, vinegar, and salt and simmer, stirring more frequently as cooking progresses to prevent sticking, until very thick, about 1 hour.

Purée ketchup in 2 batches in blender (use caution) until smooth. Refrigerate, covered, for at least 2 hours to allow flavors to develop.

COOK'S NOTE

- The ketchup keeps, refrigerated in an airtight container, for up to 1 month.

Cranberry Ketchup

MAKES ABOUT 3 CUPS
ACTIVE TIME: 35 MINUTES ▪ START TO FINISH: 2 HOURS (INCLUDES COOLING)

▪ This began as a holiday treat for us; now it's a year-round staple. It makes a great condiment for roast turkey (and turkey burgers), chicken, duck, and pork. ▪

1 medium onion, chopped
2 cups water
3 1/2 cups (1 pound) fresh or frozen (not thawed) cranberries
1 (2-by-1/2-inch) strip orange zest
1/2 cup plus 2 tablespoons packed light brown sugar
1/2 cup granulated sugar
1/2 teaspoon Chinese Five-Spice Powder (page 932, or store-bought)
1 1/2 teaspoons salt

Combine onion and water in a 3- to 4-quart heavy saucepan, bring to a simmer, and simmer, uncovered, until onion is tender, 10 to 15 minutes.

Add cranberries and zest and simmer, uncovered, until berries burst, about 10 minutes. Discard zest.

Purée cranberry mixture in a food processor, then force through a large sieve back into saucepan; discard solids. Stir in sugars, five-spice powder, and salt and simmer, stirring occasionally, for 5 minutes. Cool completely.

COOK'S NOTE

- The ketchup keeps, refrigerated in an airtight container, for up to 1 month.

English Mint Sauce

MAKES ABOUT 1⅓ CUPS
ACTIVE TIME: 10 MINUTES ■ START TO FINISH: 2¼ HOURS
(INCLUDES STEEPING)

■ Invite a few friends over for a Sunday lunch in June. Serve this with pink slices of roast leg of lamb, boiled new potatoes, and peas and you will have those friends for life. If you have a choice between spearmint and peppermint, go with the spearmint—it's mellower than peppermint. ■

- 1 cup packed fresh mint leaves, chopped
- 2 tablespoons sugar, or to taste
- ½ cup boiling water
- ½ cup malt vinegar or cider vinegar

Stir together mint, sugar, and boiling water in a small heatproof bowl until sugar is dissolved. Stir in vinegar. Let sauce stand at room temperature for 1 to 2 hours to allow flavors to develop.

COOK'S NOTE

■ The sauce keeps, covered and refrigerated, for up to 2 weeks.

Whipped Horseradish Cream

MAKES ABOUT 2 CUPS
ACTIVE TIME: 15 MINUTES ■ START TO FINISH: 1¼ HOURS
(INCLUDES CHILLING)

■ This makes an ethereal condiment for lamb or beef. If you are using fresh horseradish, be aware that its heat varies. Bottled horseradish is more consistent, but it can turn an unappetizing shade of brown after a few months in the refrigerator, so buy a fresh bottle. ■

- 3–4 tablespoons grated peeled fresh horseradish or bottled horseradish (to taste)
- 2 teaspoons cider vinegar
- 1 teaspoon honey
- 1 cup very cold heavy cream
- ¼ teaspoon salt
- ¼ teaspoon freshly ground black pepper

Stir together 3 tablespoons horseradish, vinegar, and honey in a small bowl.

Beat heavy cream in a large bowl with an electric mixer until it holds soft peaks. Gently whisk in horseradish mixture, salt, and pepper.

Taste cream, then add up to 1 tablespoon more

HORSERADISH

The pungency and intense aroma of horseradish come from a highly volatile oil that is released as soon as the flesh of the root is grated, so grate it just before using. If you are serving it in a vinegary mixture or sauce, the vinegar will stabilize the pungency, maintaining the strong taste. A number of horseradish strains are cultivated commercially, and some pack more of a wallop than others; unfortunately, there's no way to tell by looking. You might find a greater variety to sample, though, in springtime, at Passover, when horseradish has a place on the seder plate (as a symbol of the bitter lot of Jews held in captivity in Egypt) and alongside the holiday gefilte fish and brisket.

If you decide to grate fresh horseradish in the food processor, remove the lid carefully and keep your face away from the spout so the fumes won't funnel straight up into your eyes and nose.

We usually call for bottled horseradish in our recipes because we know we consistently get more bang for the buck, so to speak. And it's available year-round.

horseradish, if desired. Refrigerate, covered, for 1 hour to allow flavors to develop.

COOK'S NOTE

- The horseradish cream can be made up to 1 day ahead. Whip again before serving.

Maple Mustard Sauce

MAKES 3/4 CUP
ACTIVE TIME: 5 MINUTES ■ START TO FINISH: 5 MINUTES

■ Stunningly simple, and delicious with ham. Pure maple syrup is the secret (avoid anything with corn syrup in it). The sauce doesn't have a strong maple flavor, but rather a deep, sweet undertone. ■

1/2 cup Dijon mustard
1/4 cup pure maple syrup

Stir together mustard and syrup in a small bowl until well combined.

COOK'S NOTE

- The sauce can be made up to 2 days ahead and refrigerated, covered. Bring to room temperature before serving.

Maître d'Hôtel Butter

MAKES ABOUT 1/2 CUP
ACTIVE TIME: 15 MINUTES ■ START TO FINISH: 1 1/4 HOURS (INCLUDES CHILLING)

■ Compound butter—butter creamed with various flavorings—is a classic French accompaniment used to top everything from broiled steak to steamed vegetables. Because it's virtually an instant sauce, it is invaluable in the kitchen and adds finesse to weeknight suppers. This one is reason enough for a steak. ■

1 stick (8 tablespoons) unsalted butter, softened
1/4 teaspoon finely grated lemon zest
1 tablespoon fresh lemon juice
2 tablespoons chopped fresh flat-leaf parsley
1/2 teaspoon salt

Mash together butter and all other ingredients in a medium bowl with a fork until well combined.

Transfer butter to a sheet of wax paper and roll into a 6-inch-long log, wrapping with wax paper. Refrigerate for at least 1 hour to allow flavors to develop.

COOK'S NOTE

- This and the following butters keep, covered and refrigerated, for up to 2 days. They can also be frozen, wrapped in wax paper and then in foil, for up to 1 month; simply cut off frozen slices whenever the need arises.

Marchand de Vin Butter

■ "Wine merchant's" butter is traditionally served with steak, but it's great with chicken or even salmon. ■

1 cup dry red wine
3 tablespoons minced shallots
1 stick (8 tablespoons) unsalted butter, softened
1 teaspoon minced fresh flat-leaf parsley
1/2 teaspoon salt
1/4 teaspoon freshly ground black pepper

Combine wine and shallots in a small heavy saucepan, bring to a boil, and boil until wine is reduced to about 1/4 cup, 12 to 15 minutes. Cool completely.

Mash together butter, parsley, salt, and pepper in a medium bowl with a fork. Mash in wine mixture 1 tablespoon at a time, then proceed as directed in Maître d'Hôtel Butter.

Anchovy Butter

■ The anchovies don't taste at all fishy here; instead they add depth and flavor. Delicious with veal, seafood, or lamb chops, this butter also takes grilled chicken galloping off in a new direction. ■

1 garlic clove
1/8 teaspoon salt

1 stick (8 tablespoons) unsalted butter, softened
2 teaspoons drained capers, rinsed and minced
2 flat anchovy fillets, minced and mashed to a paste
1½ teaspoons fresh lemon juice
Rounded ⅛ teaspoon freshly ground black pepper

Using a large heavy knife, mince garlic and mash to a paste with salt, then proceed as directed in Maître d'Hôtel Butter.

Lemon Mustard Butter

This will brighten up broiled or grilled chicken and fish.

1 stick (8 tablespoons) unsalted butter, softened
2 tablespoons Dijon mustard
1½ tablespoons fresh lemon juice, or to taste
½ teaspoon salt
¼ teaspoon freshly ground black pepper

Proceed as directed in Maître d'Hôtel Butter.

Porcini Butter

Dried porcini mushrooms impart a delicate yet foresty flavor to this butter. Serve with grilled meats, chicken, or fish.

½ cup (¼ ounce) dried porcini mushrooms
½ cup boiling water
1 garlic clove, finely chopped
1 stick (8 tablespoons) unsalted butter, softened
¼ teaspoon salt

Soak porcini in boiling water in a small bowl for 20 minutes. Lift out of soaking liquid, squeeze excess liquid back into bowl (reserve liquid), and rinse porcini well to remove any grit. Finely chop porcini.

Pour soaking liquid through a fine-mesh sieve lined with a dampened paper towel into a small saucepan. Add porcini and garlic and simmer until liquid is reduced to about 1 tablespoon, about 2 minutes. Cool completely, then proceed as directed in Maître d'Hôtel Butter.

Roquefort Butter

The butter mellows the cheese and makes it even more luscious. Try this on top of something lean, like beef tenderloin or a grilled chicken breast, or on steamed vegetables, or just spread it on a slice of rye bread.

1 stick (8 tablespoons) unsalted butter, softened
4–6 tablespoons crumbled Roquefort (to taste)

Proceed as directed in Maître d'Hôtel Butter.

Polonaise Topping

MAKES ABOUT ⅔ CUP
ACTIVE TIME: 15 MINUTES ■ START TO FINISH: 15 MINUTES

These bread crumbs cooked in butter "in the manner of Poland" add richness and texture to steamed cauliflower, asparagus, broccoli, carrots, or green beans.

5 tablespoons unsalted butter
⅓ cup fresh bread crumbs, lightly toasted (see Cook's Note)
2 hard-boiled large eggs, finely chopped
2 tablespoons finely chopped fresh flat-leaf parsley
Salt and freshly ground black pepper

Heat butter in a 10-inch skillet over moderately high heat until foam subsides. Add bread crumbs and cook, stirring, until golden brown. Remove from heat and stir in egg, parsley, and salt and pepper to taste.

COOK'S NOTE

To lightly toast bread crumbs, spread them on a small baking sheet and toast in a 250°F oven, stirring once, until they are dry, about 8 minutes.

Fresh Tomato Salsa

MAKES ABOUT 1½ CUPS
ACTIVE TIME: 15 MINUTES ■ START TO FINISH: 15 MINUTES

■ Salsa has become part of the American culinary repertoire. For those who have had only store-bought processed salsa, though, the taste of this fresh, uncooked version will be eye-opening. We use plum tomatoes because they're less juicy than regular tomatoes, but if you don't mind a runnier salsa, substitute good ripe beefsteaks. White onion, rather than yellow, is traditionally used in Mexican cooking because it has a sharper, cleaner, brighter flavor, especially raw. ■

- ½ pound plum tomatoes, halved crosswise, seeded if desired
- 2 serrano chiles, minced (including seeds)
- ½ cup finely chopped white onion
- ¼ cup chopped fresh cilantro
- 1 teaspoon kosher salt, or to taste
- 3 tablespoons water

Finely chop tomatoes. Transfer to a bowl, along with any juices. Stir in remaining ingredients.

COOK'S NOTE

■ The salsa can be made up to 6 hours ahead and refrigerated, covered. Bring to room temperature before serving.

Strawberry Salsa

MAKES ABOUT 1¼ CUPS
ACTIVE TIME: 15 MINUTES ■ START TO FINISH: 15 MINUTES

■ This salsa will make you think of strawberries in a whole new way. It's not overly fruity; the sweetness is there, but tartness is too, and the onion and cilantro take it down a savory road. Use large, firm strawberries from the supermarket, not the smaller, more delicate ones from the farmers market, for this recipe. It's delicious with sliced avocados or with cream cheese or goat cheese instead of pepper jelly. It's also good with roast chicken or pork. ■

- 1 cup finely chopped strawberries
- ¼ cup finely chopped white onion
- 1 serrano or jalapeño chile, seeded and finely chopped
- 2 tablespoons finely chopped fresh cilantro
- ½ teaspoon fresh lime juice
- ¼ teaspoon salt
- ½ teaspoon sugar (optional)

Stir together all ingredients in a bowl.

COOK'S NOTE

■ The salsa can be made up to 4 hours ahead and refrigerated, covered. Bring to room temperature before serving.

Georgian Salsa

MAKES ABOUT 2 CUPS
ACTIVE TIME: 20 MINUTES ■ START TO FINISH: 20 MINUTES

■ Halfway around the world from the Peach Tree State is another Georgia, a rich, fertile land that lies at the crossroads of East and West. Lush culinary treasures (including peaches) have lured travelers, merchants, and invaders there for more than two thousand years. One of the intriguing things about spice blends in the Republic of Georgia (fenugreek and coriander seeds are two common ingredients) is how similar they are to some Indian masalas, or spice mixtures. The food historian Darra Goldstein tells us that, in general, Georgian food does seem to be more influenced by India than by Asia.

A woman named Gulisa Lataria, who runs a guesthouse in Tbilisi, gave Goldstein this recipe for *ajika*, a fiery salsa made from herbs and chiles. It's dark and complex, with body from the red bell pepper. The heat of the chiles enhances the fragrant spices without overwhelming them. This salsa is the proper accompaniment to the pork stew on page 485, but it can also liven up grilled meats and poultry. ■

- 1 teaspoon coriander seeds
- ½ teaspoon fenugreek seeds
- ½ cup loosely packed fresh cilantro sprigs
- ¼ cup loosely packed fresh basil leaves
- 2 garlic cloves

1 large red bell pepper, cored, seeded, and cut into 1-inch pieces
4 jalapeño chiles, preferably red, stemmed and halved, seeded if desired
2 teaspoons red wine vinegar
½ teaspoon kosher salt

SPECIAL EQUIPMENT: a mortar and pestle or an electric coffee/spice grinder

Finely grind coriander and fenugreek seeds in mortar with pestle or in coffee/spice grinder.

Combine cilantro, basil, and garlic in a food processor and pulse until finely chopped. Add bell pepper and jalapeños and pulse until finely chopped. Add vinegar, coriander mixture, and salt and blend until just combined.

COOK'S NOTE

- The salsa keeps, refrigerated in an airtight container, for up to 4 days.

FENUGREEK

If you've ever walked into an Indian spice shop, chances are you've smelled fenugreek, one of the predominant aromas in many chutneys and curries. One species is also used extensively in the cooking of the Republic of Georgia, as in the salsa on the opposite page. Fenugreek's Georgian name, *utskho suneli,* translates as "a strange and fragrant smell from far away." Its English name comes from the Latin *fenum Graecum,* literally, "Greek hay"; in classical times, the legume was grown for fodder. Look for whole fenugreek seeds at Indian markets, specialty foods shops, and some supermarkets, or order it already ground from Penzeys (see Sources).

Papaya Pineapple Salsa

MAKES ABOUT 2¼ CUPS
ACTIVE TIME: 20 MINUTES ■ START TO FINISH: 20 MINUTES

■ The sweet-tart acidity of pineapple balances out the creamy, dense taste of papaya. Look for the small (one-pound) Hawaiian papayas labeled "strawberry," or for larger papayas from Mexico and Southeast Asia, all of which tend to have deep pink flesh. Their color is a nice contrast to the yellow pineapple. This salsa, which is not too sweet, is delicious with lamb, fish, pork—and tortilla chips. The recipe can easily be doubled if you are serving a crowd. ■

2 pounds firm but ripe papayas (preferably pink-fleshed), peeled, seeded, and cut into ¼-inch dice
¼ small pineapple, peeled, cored, and cut into ¼-inch dice (¾ cup)
1 scallion, finely chopped
½ small garlic clove, minced
1 tablespoon fresh lime juice
¼ teaspoon salt
⅛ teaspoon freshly ground black pepper

Stir together all ingredients in a large bowl.

COOK'S NOTE

- The salsa can be made up to 2 hours ahead and refrigerated, covered.

Pineapple Habanero Salsa

MAKES ABOUT 2 CUPS
ACTIVE TIME: 25 MINUTES ■ START TO FINISH: 1 HOUR

■ This taste of the Caribbean is wonderful with ham, smoked pork chops, or pork tenderloin. We prefer the acid tang of regular pineapple to the "extra-sweet" ones for this recipe. ■

- ½ pineapple, peeled (rind reserved), cored, and coarsely chopped (2 cups)
- 2 tablespoons fresh lime juice, or to taste
- 1 tablespoon molasses (not robust or blackstrap)
- 3 scallions, finely chopped
- ¼–½ teaspoon minced seeded habanero or Scotch bonnet chile (see Glossary; to taste)
- 1 teaspoon chopped fresh thyme
- ¾ teaspoon salt
- ¼ teaspoon ground allspice

With your hands, squeeze 2 tablespoons juice from reserved pineapple rind into a large bowl; discard rind. Add remaining ingredients and toss well. Let stand, stirring occasionally, for 30 minutes to blend flavors.

COOK'S NOTE

- The salsa can be made up to 1 day ahead and refrigerated, covered. Bring to room temperature before serving.

Tomato Barbecue Sauce

MAKES ABOUT 2 CUPS
ACTIVE TIME: 15 MINUTES ■ START TO FINISH: 1 HOUR (INCLUDES COOLING)

■ There are probably as many barbecue sauces as there are backyards in America. What makes this one so interesting are the layers of flavor created by different acids (orange juice, cider vinegar, Worcestershire sauce), different sweeteners (brown sugar, sautéed onion, ketchup, tomato paste), and different sources of heat (ancho chile, ginger, dry mustard, black pepper). Lightly brush chicken or ribs with it toward the end of grilling (not before, or the sugars will char) and serve the rest of the sauce on the side. ■

- 1 dried ancho chile (optional; see Glossary)
- 1 tablespoon vegetable oil
- 1 large onion, minced
- 2 garlic cloves, minced
- 1 (½-inch) piece peeled fresh ginger, minced
- ½ cup packed dark brown sugar
- ¼ cup soy sauce
- ¼ cup fresh orange juice
- ¼ cup cider vinegar
- ¼ cup Worcestershire sauce
- 1 cup ketchup
- 1 tablespoon tomato paste
- 2 teaspoons dry mustard
- ½ teaspoon freshly ground black pepper

If using chile, heat a dry heavy skillet, preferably cast-iron, over moderately high heat until hot. Toast chile, turning and pressing with tongs, until slightly darker, about 1 minute. Remove stem and, if desired, seeds. Soak chile in hot water to cover until softened, about 5 minutes. Lift out and coarsely chop.

Heat oil in a 2-quart heavy saucepan over moderate heat. Add onion and cook, stirring, until softened, about 2 minutes. Add garlic and ginger and cook, stirring, for 3 minutes. Add remaining ingredients (including chile, if using), bring to a simmer, and simmer, stirring occasionally, for 5 minutes.

Pour sauce through a sieve into a bowl, pressing on solids; discard solids. Cool to room temperature.

COOK'S NOTES

- The barbecue sauce keeps, covered and refrigerated, for up to 2 weeks.
- Keep the sauce for serving separate from the basting sauce to avoid possible bacterial contamination from uncooked meat.

Coffee Bourbon Barbecue Sauce

MAKES ABOUT 1 CUP
ACTIVE TIME: 5 MINUTES ■ START TO FINISH: 25 MINUTES

■ Deep-flavored, rich-tasting . . . fabulous with steak, chicken, or pork. ■

- 1 cup strong brewed coffee
- ½ cup bourbon
- ½ cup packed light brown sugar
- ½ cup soy sauce
- 2 tablespoons cider vinegar
- 1 teaspoon Worcestershire sauce

Combine all ingredients in a 2½- to 3-quart heavy saucepan, bring to a simmer, and simmer, uncovered, stirring occasionally, until reduced to about 1 cup, 15 to 20 minutes (sauce will be thin). Cool to room temperature.

COOK'S NOTE

- Brush the meat with the sauce toward the end of grilling (not before, or the sugars will char).

Asian Barbecue Sauce

MAKES ABOUT 1 CUP
ACTIVE TIME: 15 MINUTES ■ START TO FINISH: 30 MINUTES

■ This sauce incorporates different elements from different Asian cuisines: the hoisin sauce and five-spice powder, for instance, are Chinese, and the use of a caramel base, which provides a deep, mellow flavor, is primarily Vietnamese. Put this together in the time it takes to fire up the grill, then slather it on chicken or shrimp. ■

- 6 tablespoons hoisin sauce
- 2 tablespoons rice vinegar (not seasoned)
- 1 tablespoon Asian fish sauce
- 1 tablespoon soy sauce
- 1 tablespoon honey
- ⅓ cup minced shallots
- 2 garlic cloves, minced
- 1 tablespoon minced peeled fresh ginger
- ⅛ teaspoon Chinese Five-Spice Powder (page 932, or store-bought)
- ⅓ cup sugar

Stir together all ingredients except sugar in a small bowl.

Cook sugar in a dry small heavy saucepan over moderate heat, without stirring, until it begins to melt. Continue to cook, stirring occasionally with a fork, until sugar is melted into a deep golden caramel. Tilt pan away from you and carefully pour in hoisin mixture (caramel will harden and steam vigorously). Cook over moderately low heat, stirring, until caramel is dissolved and sauce is thickened, 6 to 8 minutes. Cool to room temperature.

COOK'S NOTES

- The sauce keeps, covered and refrigerated, for up to 2 weeks.
- Brush the meat with the sauce toward the end of cooking (not before, or the sugar will char).
- If you'd like to serve some of this sauce on the side, double the recipe. Keep the sauce for serving separate from the sauce for basting to avoid possible bacterial contamination from uncooked meat.

Teriyaki Glaze

MAKES ABOUT ¾ CUP
ACTIVE TIME: 5 MINUTES ■ START TO FINISH: 30 MINUTES

■ Teriyaki sauce—sweet, salty, and glossy—is one of the most popular Japanese flavorings. Depending on its thickness, it can be used as a marinade, a glaze, or, in America, a sauce. This one—authentic and dead simple—works best as a glaze, brushed onto chicken, beef, or a rich, oily fish such as salmon two or three times while broiling. ■

- ½ cup soy sauce
- ½ cup sake or dry sherry
- ⅔ cup mirin (Japanese sweet rice wine)
- 2 tablespoons sugar

Combine all ingredients in a 2-quart heavy saucepan and bring to a boil, then reduce heat to moderately low and simmer until reduced to about ¾ cup, about 15 minutes.

Pour into a shallow bowl to cool to room temperature.

COOK'S NOTE

- The glaze keeps, refrigerated in an airtight container, for up to 5 days.

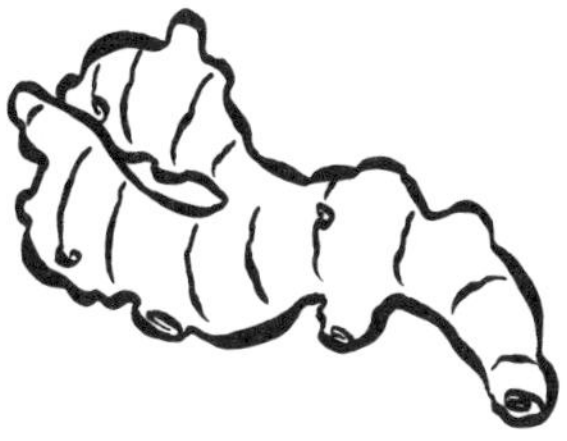

RELISHES, CHUTNEYS, PICKLES, AND PRESERVES

Stop! Don't turn the page! Before you decide that this chapter has nothing to interest you, hear us out. We know that you are probably not the kind of person who spends the summer months putting up preserves against the coming cold weather. We are aware that your survival does not depend on the ability to pickle a cucumber or sterilize a jar properly.

Honestly, if that was all we had to offer, we would not urge you to linger in this chapter. But aren't you intrigued by the prospect of apricot jam so spectacular that your friends will beg you to give them a jar? Can you really turn your back on a sour cherry preserve that makes the taste of summer linger all year long? And surely you are interested in a grape jam so good it makes the most ordinary peanut butter and jelly sandwich sing. Each of the preserves you will find in this chapter is extraordinary, fruit cooked down to its very essence until it has become a jam that honors the flavor of the fruit without adding undue sweetness.

Beyond these delicious fruit jams, most of this chapter has very little to do with sterile jars and water baths. Preserving was a laborious task in days past, but refrigeration changed all that. Many of these recipes enable you to save the fruits of the season simply by cooking them down and storing them in your refrigerator. And some, like the wonderful quick plum preserves, are the perfect rescue plan for those times when the fruit is so fragrant you buy more than you can use. It's a solution that produces remarkable results in very little time.

While many of these recipes are tried-and-true American classics—corn relish, green tomato pickles, mint jelly—many are newcomers on the national culinary scene. Among them you'll find fresh chutneys to add real character to any Indian dish that you serve and Moroccan-style preserved lemons with the sort of zest that makes a lackluster meal suddenly start to sparkle.

Although this might seem like the most old-fashioned group of recipes in the book, it is also a sign that everything old eventually becomes new again. Farmers markets are starting to sprout on city sidewalks all across the country, and these recipes, which might very well have been left out of a cookbook of the seventies or eighties, now seem absolutely essential. In a time when we are finally learning what it means to eat with the seasons, it's good to know how to store the fruits of summer to lighten up the winter kitchen.

Corn Relish

MAKES ABOUT 6 CUPS
ACTIVE TIME: 40 MINUTES ■ START TO FINISH: 2¾ HOURS (INCLUDES COOLING)

■ Pure Americana. The keen flavors add snap to a chicken or pork dinner. We like to make this in late August or September, when the charms of corn on the cob have begun to pall. ■

- 4 cups corn kernels (from about 8 ears)
- 1½ cups chopped green bell peppers (1½ large)
- 1½ cups chopped celery (3 ribs)
- 1½ cups chopped onion (1 large)
- 2½ cups distilled white vinegar
- 1¼ cups sugar
- ¼ cup water
- 2 teaspoons dry mustard
- 2 teaspoons salt, or to taste
- 2 teaspoons turmeric
- 2 teaspoons celery seeds

Combine ingredients in a 4-quart saucepan and bring to a boil, then reduce heat and simmer, uncovered, stirring occasionally, for 15 minutes. Transfer relish to a bowl. Cool, uncovered, for about 2 hours.

Serve relish chilled or at room temperature.

COOK'S NOTE

■ The relish keeps, refrigerated in an airtight container, for up to 1 month.

Hot Red Pepper Relish

MAKES ABOUT 3 CUPS
ACTIVE TIME: 15 MINUTES ■ START TO FINISH: 2¼ HOURS (INCLUDES COOLING)

■ This is not a southern-style red pepper jelly (although as a topping for cream cheese on a cracker, it's a satisfying stand-in) but a revved-up, chunky relish that's great with steak or lamb chops or on a turkey sandwich. And it's a real supermarket recipe, since no special chiles are required; red pepper flakes provide the heat. ■

- 2 pounds red bell peppers, cored, seeded, and finely chopped (4 cups)
- 2 medium onions, chopped (2 cups)
- 2 cups cider vinegar
- ¾ cup sugar
- 2 teaspoons mustard seeds
- 1½ teaspoons salt
- 1 teaspoon red pepper flakes, or to taste

Combine all ingredients in a 3-quart heavy saucepan, bring to a simmer, and simmer, uncovered, stirring occasionally, until reduced to about 3 cups, about 1 hour.

Transfer relish to a bowl and cool, uncovered, for about 1 hour.

Serve relish chilled or at room temperature.

COOK'S NOTE

■ The relish keeps, refrigerated in an airtight container, for up to 1 month.

Ashkenazic Haroseth

Fruit and Nut Spread

MAKES ABOUT 2 CUPS
ACTIVE TIME: 10 MINUTES ■ START TO FINISH: 10 MINUTES, PLUS 1 DAY FOR FLAVORS TO DEVELOP

■ The fruit and nut condiment made of chopped apples or dates and nuts is served at virtually every Passover seder around the globe. According to Joan Nathan, the author of *Jewish Cooking in America*, it probably came into the Passover service during the Greco-Roman period and symbolizes the mortar that enslaved Jews were forced to work with in Egypt. Ashkenazic haroseth, from the Eastern European tradition, uses a large proportion of apple. Sephardic versions, from the Jewish tradition of Spain, Portugal, and the Levant, use dates or a smaller proportion of apple. Some families make enough haroseth to last the entire week of Passover, to be enjoyed as a snack with matzo. ■

2 McIntosh apples, peeled, cored, and coarsely chopped
2/3 cup Passover wine, such as Concord grape Manischewitz
1/2 cup coarsely chopped walnuts or almonds
1/4 teaspoon ground cinnamon
Pinch of salt

ACCOMPANIMENT: matzos

Combine all ingredients in a bowl. Refrigerate, covered, for 24 hours. Serve with matzos.

Jellied Cranberry Sauce

SERVES 8
ACTIVE TIME: 20 MINUTES ■ START TO FINISH: 2½ HOURS (INCLUDES CHILLING)

■ You might be sentimental about the jellied cranberry sauce that slides so neatly out of its can, but it pales in comparison to the real thing. With only four ingredients, this sauce is the essence of cranberry. Intensely flavored and gorgeously garnet in hue, it sparkles in the mouth, a Thanksgiving icon. ■

4 (12-ounce) bags (12 cups) fresh or frozen cranberries, thawed if frozen, picked over
3 cups sugar
3¼ cups cold water
5 teaspoons unflavored gelatin (from two ¼-ounce envelopes)

SPECIAL EQUIPMENT: a large fine-mesh sieve or four 15-inch squares cheesecloth; a 1-quart nonreactive decorative mold

Stir together cranberries, sugar, and 3 cups water in a 3-quart heavy saucepan, bring to a simmer, and simmer, uncovered, stirring occasionally, until all berries have burst, about 15 minutes. Pour mixture into sieve set over a heatproof bowl or into a colander lined with layered cheesecloth and set over bowl and let stand until all juices have drained through, about 10 minutes. You should have 3 cups juice; press on solids if necessary to release more juice, then discard solids.

Stir together gelatin and remaining ¼ cup water in a medium bowl and let stand for 1 minute to soften. Bring 1 cup cranberry liquid to a simmer in a small saucepan, stir in gelatin mixture, and stir until gelatin dissolves. Return to medium bowl and add remaining cranberry liquid. Stir well and pour into mold. Refrigerate until set, at least 2 hours.

To unmold sauce, set mold in a larger bowl of hot water for 5 seconds to loosen it, then invert a serving plate over mold and invert mold onto plate. Carefully remove mold.

COOK'S NOTE

■ The sauce can be refrigerated in the mold, covered with plastic wrap, for up to 2 days.

Spicy Cranberry Relish

MAKES ABOUT 2½ CUPS
ACTIVE TIME: 10 MINUTES ■ START TO FINISH: 2¼ HOURS (INCLUDES CHILLING)

■ We're big fans of the recipe for raw cranberry relish on the back of the Ocean Spray bag, but there are times when we need more zing. We get that by using serrano chile. Its fresh, clear heat and the lime's tang give the raw cranberries a new friskiness. ■

1 lime
1 (12-ounce) bag (3 cups) fresh cranberries, picked over
1 medium red onion, chopped
½ cup sugar
1–2 teaspoons minced serrano chile (including seeds)

Finely grate 1 teaspoon zest from lime. Halve lime and squeeze enough juice to measure 2 tablespoons.

Combine cranberries with zest, juice, onion, sugar, and chile, to taste, in a food processor and pulse until finely chopped. Transfer to a bowl, cover, and refrigerate, stirring occasionally, for at least 2 hours to allow flavors to develop.

COOK'S NOTE

■ The relish keeps, refrigerated in an airtight container, for up to 1 week.

Cranberry and Pickled Beet Relish

MAKES ABOUT 3 CUPS
ACTIVE TIME: 25 MINUTES ■ START TO FINISH: 2 HOURS (INCLUDES COOLING)

■ More savory than sweet, this relish is a natural for the Thanksgiving table, but it's also delicious with beef or game. ■

- 1/2 cup red wine vinegar
- 1/2 cup water
- 2/3 cup sugar
- 1 (12-ounce) bag (3 cups) fresh or frozen (not thawed) cranberries, picked over
- 1 (16-ounce) jar sliced pickled beets, drained and quartered

Combine vinegar, water, and sugar in a 2-quart heavy saucepan and bring to a boil, stirring until sugar is dissolved. Add cranberries and simmer, uncovered, stirring occasionally, until berries have burst and mixture is thick, about 20 minutes. Stir in beets, remove from heat, and cool.

Serve relish chilled or at room temperature.

COOK'S NOTE

■ The relish keeps, refrigerated in an airtight container, for up to 4 days.

Cranberry, Shallot, and Dried Cherry Compote

MAKES ABOUT 3 CUPS
ACTIVE TIME: 1 1/4 HOURS ■ START TO FINISH: 3 HOURS (INCLUDES COOLING)

■ Some people spread this compote on a turkey sandwich; others simply eat it by the spoonful. Dried sour cherries give body—almost a meaty texture—to the combination, and shallots sweeten the two tart red fruits. ■

- 1/2 pound small (1-inch-diameter) shallots or pearl onions, preferably red, unpeeled
- 1 tablespoon unsalted butter or vegetable oil
- 3/4 cup sugar
- 8 tablespoons white wine vinegar
- 1 cup dry white wine
- 1/2 teaspoon salt
- 1 cup (5 ounces) dried sour cherries
- 2 cups fresh or frozen (not thawed) cranberries, picked over
- 1/2 cup water

Blanch shallots (or onions) in a 3-quart saucepan of boiling water for 1 minute; drain. Peel shallots and separate into cloves if necessary.

Melt butter (or heat oil) in a 3-quart heavy saucepan over moderate heat. Add shallots and cook, stirring, for 1 minute. Add sugar and 1 tablespoon vinegar and cook, stirring frequently, until sugar syrup turns a golden caramel, 15 to 20 minutes. Add wine, remaining 1/4 cup plus 3 tablespoons vinegar, and salt and boil for 1 minute (use caution, as mixture will bubble up). Add cherries and simmer, uncovered, stirring occasionally, until shallots are tender and liquid is syrupy, about 45 minutes.

Add cranberries and water and boil, uncovered, over moderate heat, stirring occasionally, until cranberries burst, about 10 minutes. Transfer compote to a bowl and cool.

Serve at room temperature.

COOK'S NOTE

■ The compote keeps, refrigerated in an airtight container, for up to 5 days.

Bell Pepper and Dried Apricot Chutney

MAKES ABOUT 2¼ CUPS
ACTIVE TIME: 15 MINUTES ■ START TO FINISH: 1¼ HOURS, PLUS AT LEAST 2 HOURS FOR FLAVORS TO DEVELOP

■ Choosing an orange bell pepper for this chutney gives it a kissed-by-the-sun glow, but a red or yellow bell pepper is just as sweet and beautiful. Don't use a green bell pepper, though; its flavor would be too overbearing in this recipe. This is terrific on poultry (including the Thanksgiving turkey), lamb, and pork. ■

- 1 medium onion, chopped
- 1 orange, yellow, or red bell pepper, cored, seeded, and cut into ½-inch pieces
- 1 cup (6 ounces) dried apricots, cut into quarters
- ½ cup water
- ¾ cup cider vinegar
- ¼ cup plus 1 tablespoon sugar
- 1½ teaspoons curry powder, preferably Madras
- ¼ teaspoon salt

Combine all ingredients in a 2-quart heavy saucepan and bring to a boil, stirring occasionally. Reduce heat, cover, and simmer, stirring occasionally, until chutney is thickened but still saucy, about 50 minutes.

Transfer chutney to a bowl. Cool, uncovered, then cover and refrigerate, stirring occasionally, for at least 2 hours to allow flavors to develop.

COOK'S NOTE

■ The chutney keeps, refrigerated in an airtight container, for up to 1 week.

Tomato Chutney

MAKES ABOUT 3 CUPS
ACTIVE TIME: 15 MINUTES ■ START TO FINISH: 1¼ HOURS

■ This chutney is wonderful with cheese in every way, shape, and form. We first tasted it with a molten cheese fondue at Ballymaloe House, a Georgian manor turned hotel in southwestern Ireland, but we love it with grilled cheese sandwiches, cream cheese and crackers, and (always a party favorite) Brie wrapped in pastry. It's a great condiment for meats as well. ■

- 1 (28- to 32-ounce) can whole tomatoes in juice, drained and chopped
- 1 large onion, chopped
- Zest of 1 lemon, removed with a vegetable peeler and minced
- ½ cup sugar
- ½ cup cider vinegar
- ⅓ cup dried currants
- 1½ teaspoons mustard seeds
- ½ teaspoon salt
- ¼ teaspoon cayenne
- ¼ teaspoon ground allspice
- ¼ teaspoon ground cinnamon

SPECIAL EQUIPMENT: a 5- to 6-quart heavy pot at least 9½ inches in diameter

Combine all ingredients in pot and cook, uncovered, over moderate heat, stirring occasionally, for 30 minutes.

Reduce heat to low and simmer, stirring occasionally, until chutney is thickened and reduced to about 3 cups, about 30 minutes more.

Transfer chutney to a bowl to cool, uncovered, then refrigerate, covered.

COOK'S NOTE

■ The chutney keeps, refrigerated in an airtight container, for up to 1 month.

Watermelon Rind Chutney

MAKES ABOUT 3 CUPS
ACTIVE TIME: 45 MINUTES ■ START TO FINISH: 2 HOURS, PLUS 1 DAY FOR FLAVORS TO DEVELOP

■ Using every inch of a watermelon, rind and all, is a great way to practice the age-old maxim "Waste not, want not." This tangy, spicy chutney is a spin on the watermelon rind pickles popular in the American South, a classic accompaniment to ham and biscuits. One of the nice things about this chutney, though, is that the watermelon rind is finely cubed, so it can be easily incorporated in a sandwich or served with cream cheese and crackers as an hors d'oeuvre. And because it is not preserved (like the pickles), you can put it together relatively quickly. ■

- 1 (8-pound) piece watermelon
- 1½ cups cider vinegar
- 1½ cups water
- 2 cups sugar
- ¼ cup minced peeled fresh ginger
- 2 tablespoons minced small hot green chile, such as Thai or serrano (including seeds)
- 1½ tablespoons minced garlic
- 1 teaspoon salt
- ½ teaspoon black peppercorns, coarsely crushed with side of a large knife

Remove watermelon from rind; reserve fruit for another use. Scrape and discard any remaining pink flesh from rind, then cut rind crosswise into 2-inch-wide pieces. Remove green peel with a Y-shaped vegetable peeler or sharp knife and discard. Cut rind into ½-inch cubes (you will have 5 to 6 cups).

Combine rind and remaining ingredients in a 4-quart heavy saucepan and bring to a boil over moderate heat, stirring until sugar is dissolved. Reduce heat and simmer, uncovered, stirring occasionally, until rind is tender and translucent and liquid is syrupy, 45 to 55 minutes.

Transfer chutney to a bowl to cool, uncovered, then refrigerate, covered, for 1 day to allow flavors to mellow.

COOK'S NOTE

■ The chutney keeps, refrigerated in an airtight container, for up to 1 month.

Mango Chutney

MAKES ABOUT 3¾ CUPS
ACTIVE TIME: 15 MINUTES ■ START TO FINISH: 2 HOURS, PLUS AT LEAST 1 DAY FOR FLAVORS TO DEVELOP

■ This sweet, tangy chutney has a great texture because the mango is left in chunks, not cooked down into a thick jam. It is not overly spiced; the flavors are beautifully balanced so that you can taste the ripe, rich fruit. Try this with practically anything, from lamb to a grilled cheese sandwich. ■

CUTTING UP A MANGO

The best way of getting at the sweet, rich flesh of a mango is to stand the unpeeled fruit on end and slice off the two wide "fillets" on either side of the flat pit. To avoid waste, don't be afraid to cut as close to the pit as possible. For the Mango Chutney, crosshatch the two fillets down to but not through the skin, making 1-inch squares (1), then turn the fillets inside out and cut off the chunks of flesh (2).

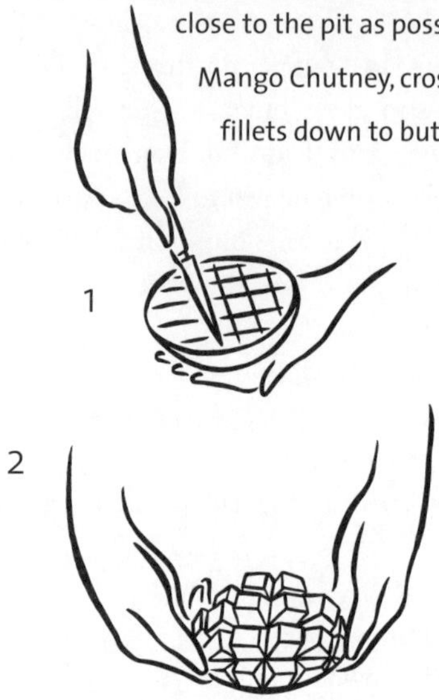

- 3 large firm but ripe mangoes (3 pounds total), peeled, pitted, and cut into 1-inch chunks (4 cups)
- ½ cup fresh orange juice
- ⅓ cup fresh lime juice
- ½ cup cider vinegar
- ½ cup packed dark brown sugar
- 1 (3-inch) cinnamon stick
- 1 garlic clove, smashed
- 1 teaspoon mustard seeds
- 1 teaspoon red pepper flakes
- ¾ teaspoon salt
- ½ teaspoon coriander seeds
- ½ teaspoon cumin seeds
- ¼ teaspoon fennel seeds

Chill two small plates for testing chutney.

Combine all ingredients in a 3-quart heavy saucepan and bring to a boil, stirring frequently. Reduce heat and simmer, skimming any foam and stirring frequently as chutney thickens, until chutney tests done, 30 to 35 minutes: Begin testing for doneness at 30 minutes; remove saucepan from heat while testing. Drop a spoonful of chutney onto a chilled plate. Refrigerate for 1 minute, then tilt plate; chutney should remain in a mound and not run.

Transfer chutney to a bowl to cool, uncovered, then refrigerate, covered, for at least 1 day to allow flavors to develop.

COOK'S NOTE

- The chutney keeps, refrigerated in an airtight container, for up to 1 month.

Mint Chutney

MAKES ABOUT 2 CUPS
ACTIVE TIME: 30 MINUTES ■ START TO FINISH: 2½ HOURS (INCLUDES CHILLING)

■ The word *chutney* derives from the Hindi *chatni* ("condiment" or "spice"). Mint and cilantro give this one pizzazz, and unsweetened grated coconut (available in natural foods stores), toasted with spices and then ground, lends it body. It is delicious with lamb, chicken, scallops, shrimp, or grilled fish. ■

MANGOES

Life in our test kitchens is the richer for fruit detective David Karp. Clad in neatly pressed khakis, well-worn boots, and a pith helmet (protection against heatstroke as well as falling fruit and tree limbs), he travels the world looking for and writing about fruit. One day Karp arrived with crates of gorgeous mangoes from the International Mango Festival, held each July at Fairchild Tropical Botanic Garden, in Coral Gables, Florida. Unlike most of the mangoes available in the United States, which are imported from Mexico, Latin America, and the Caribbean and tend to disappoint, these were a revelation.

According to Karp, mangoes theoretically ship well, but imported fruits are usually picked very underripe and treated in a hot water bath to kill insects, a combination that often results in mushy texture and pallid flavor. To enjoy mangoes at their best, he suggests searching out the ones that come from southern Florida, which are in season from late May until August. They are available primarily at local roadside stands and ethnic markets, as well as from a few mail-order sources (see Sources).

Ataulfo mangoes (marketed as "Champagne") and mangoes labeled "Mexican" and "Haitian" are all of the Tommy Atkins variety. This type is the Red Delicious of the mango world, Karp says, fibrous and mediocre. The Kent mango, with smooth, deep orange flesh and a rich, creamy flavor, is arguably the finest commercial variety. Keitt, which often has green skin, is another good one. If you see either variety in your market, snap them up. Even if they are imported, they'll be better than Tommy Atkinses.

When shopping for mangoes, look for plump, firm fruits with a heady fragrance. Color is not a great indicator of quality; in fact, red fruits are often of the unimpressive Atkins variety. "Mangoes, like pears, are harvested firm and ripened off the tree," says Karp. "If picked ripe, they often decay near the pit. They're best ripened at room temperature, and they are ready to eat when they give slightly to gentle pressure at the bottom."

2 tablespoons vegetable oil
3 serrano chiles, seeded and coarsely chopped
1 tablespoon fennel seeds
1 teaspoon cumin seeds
1 teaspoon coriander seeds
1/3 cup unsweetened finely grated coconut
1 1/2 cups coarsely chopped fresh mint
1 1/4 cups coarsely chopped fresh cilantro
3/4 cup plain yogurt
1/4 cup (1 ounce) slivered almonds, lightly toasted (see Tips, page 938)
1–2 tablespoons white wine vinegar (to taste)
2–3 tablespoons fresh lemon juice (to taste)
1 teaspoon sugar
1 teaspoon salt

Heat oil in a small heavy skillet over moderate heat until hot but not smoking. Add chiles, fennel, cumin and coriander seeds, and coconut and cook, stirring, until coconut is golden, about 3 minutes (watch carefully, as spices burn easily). Transfer spice mixture to a blender, add remaining ingredients, and blend, scraping down sides occasionally, until smooth.

Transfer chutney to a bowl and refrigerate, covered, until cold, about 2 hours.

COOK'S NOTE

- The chutney keeps, refrigerated in an airtight container, for up to 2 days.

Moroccan-Style Preserved Lemons

MAKES 48 PIECES
ACTIVE TIME: 15 MINUTES ■ START TO FINISH: 5 DAYS (INCLUDES MARINATING)

■ Preserved lemons are perhaps most at home in Moroccan dishes, but we love their complex, bright flavor and aroma in all kinds of soups, stews, and salads. They take very little time to put together and keep forever in the fridge. We've adapted the Mediterranean food authority Paula Wolfert's quick method and made it even faster by blanching the lemons first. Save the pulp for bloody Marys or anything else enlivened by a little lemon juice and salt. If you manage to find Meyer lemons (see page 919), this is a great way to capture their unforgettable taste and perfume. ■

2 1/2–3 pounds lemons (10–12)
2/3 cup kosher salt
1/4 cup olive oil
SPECIAL EQUIPMENT: a 6-cup jar with a tight-fitting lid

Blanch 6 lemons in boiling water for 5 minutes; drain. When cool enough to handle, cut each lemon into 8 wedges and discard seeds. Toss with kosher salt in a bowl, then pack, along with salt, into jar.

Squeeze enough juice from remaining lemons to measure 1 cup. Add enough juice to jar to cover lemons and screw on lid. Let lemons stand at room temperature, shaking gently once a day, for 5 days.

Add oil to lemons and refrigerate.

COOK'S NOTE

- The preserved lemons keep, refrigerated, for up to 1 year.

Quick Dilled Cucumber Pickles

SERVES 6
ACTIVE TIME: 10 MINUTES ■ START TO FINISH: 30 MINUTES

■ These pickles, like many condiments, can really make a meal. They're sweet-tart, not sour. The main seasoning is dill, and horseradish adds some zing. Serve them with cheese, hearty rye or whole-grain bread, and good beer and you've got a simple, satisfying hors d'oeuvre or light supper. They are also wonderful with sausages or on a sandwich. ■

2 seedless cucumbers (usually plastic wrapped), scrubbed and cut into 1/8-inch-thick slices
2 teaspoons kosher salt
1/2 cup cider vinegar
1/4 cup sugar
1 tablespoon dry mustard
2 teaspoons drained bottled horseradish
1 tablespoon chopped fresh dill

Toss cucumbers with salt in a bowl and let stand for 15 minutes. Rinse and drain cucumbers and pat dry with paper towels.

Whisk together vinegar, sugar, mustard, horseradish, and dill in a bowl until sugar is dissolved. Stir in cucumbers and let stand for at least 5 minutes.

COOK'S NOTE

- The pickles keep, covered and refrigerated, for up to 4 hours.

Sichuan Pickled Cucumbers

MAKES ABOUT 6 CUPS
ACTIVE TIME: 20 MINUTES ■ START TO FINISH: 4 HOURS (INCLUDES MARINATING)

■ Asians are the masters of quick pickles like this one. Crunchy, juicy, and irresistible, it gets its toasted flavor from Asian sesame oil and its tongue-tingling, lemony bite from Sichuan peppercorns. These are not, in fact, true peppercorns but rather the dried pods of the prickly ash, which is distantly related to citrus fruits. Because there is a tiny chance they may carry citrus canker (highly destructive to citrus groves), the peppercorns have long been banned for import, although they've managed to reach market shelves in all sorts of circuitous ways. As of this writing, though, the USDA has revised the ban to allow Sichuan peppercorns that have been heat-treated (at a temperature of 140°F for at least ten minutes) into the country. ■

- 2 pounds small Kirby (pickling) cucumbers or 1 seedless cucumber (usually plastic wrapped)
- 4 teaspoons salt
- 3 tablespoons sugar
- 2 tablespoons rice vinegar (not seasoned)
- 1/3 cup Asian sesame oil
- 1 (1-inch) piece peeled fresh ginger, finely grated
- 8 (1-inch-long) dried hot chiles, seeded
- 1 teaspoon Sichuan peppercorns (optional)

If using Kirby cucumbers, halve each one lengthwise, then cut each half lengthwise into 3 wedges and seed wedges. If using a seedless cucumber, cut it crosswise into 2-inch sections, then cut each section lengthwise into 8 wedges and remove seeds. Toss cucumbers with salt in a bowl and let stand for 20 minutes.

Drain cucumbers in a colander, rinse under cold water, and pat dry. Stir together sugar and vinegar in a medium bowl until sugar is dissolved. Add cucumbers, tossing to coat.

Heat sesame oil in a wok or small deep skillet over moderately high heat until just smoking. Stir-fry ginger, chiles, and peppercorns, if using, until spices are fragrant and chiles are very dark, about 1 minute. Remove from heat and cool completely.

Pour spiced oil over cucumbers and toss well. Marinate cucumbers at room temperature for 3 hours before serving.

COOK'S NOTE

- The cucumbers can marinate, covered and refrigerated, for up to 4 days; stir occasionally. The longer the cucumbers marinate, the spicier they will be.

Pickled Carrot Sticks

MAKES ABOUT 4 CUPS
ACTIVE TIME: 20 MINUTES ■ START TO FINISH: 20 MINUTES, PLUS AT LEAST 1 DAY FOR FLAVORS TO DEVELOP

■ Our lives wouldn't be the same without these pickled carrots. They're a great snack, straight out of the fridge, for schoolchildren and work-weary adults. They're also a terrific addition to any picnic basket and a beautiful and highly popular element on the Thanksgiving Day relish tray. ■

- 1 pound carrots, cut into 3½-inch (⅓-inch-thick) sticks
- 1¼ cups water
- 1 cup cider vinegar
- ¼ cup sugar
- 2 garlic cloves, lightly crushed
- 1½ tablespoons dill seed
- 1½ tablespoons salt

Blanch carrots in a 4-quart saucepan of boiling well-salted water for 1 minute; drain in a colander and rinse under cold water to stop the cooking. Transfer to a heatproof bowl.

Combine water, vinegar, sugar, garlic, dill seed, and salt in same saucepan and bring to a boil. Reduce heat and simmer for 2 minutes. Pour mixture over carrots. Cool carrots, uncovered, then refrigerate, covered, for at least 1 day to allow flavors to develop.

COOK'S NOTE

- The carrots keep, refrigerated in an airtight container, for up to 1 month.

Bread-and-Butter Pickles

MAKES 6 PINTS
ACTIVE TIME: 1¼ HOURS ■ START TO FINISH: 5½ HOURS, PLUS 1 WEEK FOR FLAVORS TO DEVELOP

■ These pickles, around since the turn of the twentieth century and among our very favorites, are true to their name in several ways. The food historian William Woys Weaver suspects the name derives from a German-American recipe, because it looks like a translation of *butterbrot gepoeckeltes,* or "sandwich pickles," which is, after all, what they are. And if you look up *bread-and-butter* in the dictionary, you'll find that the definitions include "being as basic as the earning of one's livelihood" and "reliable." These are. Most bread-and-butter pickle recipes include sugar, but we use maple syrup, which gives a mellower, more rounded sweetness. ■

- 4 pounds Kirby (pickling) cucumbers, scrubbed and cut into ¼-inch-thick slices
- 2 large onions (1½ pounds total), halved lengthwise and cut crosswise into ¼-inch-thick slices
- ¼ cup plus 1½ teaspoons canning salt (see Sources)
- 4 cups crushed ice
- 2¼ cups cider vinegar
- 1 cup pure maple syrup, preferably Grade A dark amber
- ¾ cup water
- 1 tablespoon mustard seeds
- 1 tablespoon pickling spices
- 1 teaspoon turmeric
- ½ teaspoon red pepper flakes

SPECIAL EQUIPMENT: six 1-pint canning jars with lids and screw bands

Toss cucumbers and onions with ¼ cup canning salt and crushed ice in a large bowl. Set a plate directly on vegetables and place a 5-pound weight on top (a bag of sugar in a sealed plastic bag works well). Let stand at room temperature for 4 hours. (This draws out excess water from vegetables while preserving their crispness.)

Sterilize jars and lids and wash screw bands following procedure on page 913.

Combine vinegar, syrup, water, mustard seeds, pickling spices, turmeric, red pepper flakes, and remaining 1½ teaspoons canning salt in a 3-quart saucepan and bring to a boil, then reduce heat and simmer, uncovered, for 10 minutes.

Drain jars upside down on a clean kitchen towel for 1 minute, then invert.

Drain vegetables in a colander, then pack firmly into jars. Fill jars with hot brine, leaving a ¼-inch space at top, and run a thin knife between vegetables and sides of jars to eliminate air bubbles.

Seal, process, and cool filled jars following procedure on page 913, boiling cucumbers in jars for 20 minutes (see Cook's Note).

Let pickles stand for at least 1 week to allow flavors to develop.

COOK'S NOTE

- If you have a jar that is partially full, do not process it. Instead, cover it with the lid and screw band and refrigerate. Use this jar first.

Green Tomato Pickles

MAKES 6 QUARTS
ACTIVE TIME: 30 MINUTES ■ START TO FINISH: 30 MINUTES, PLUS AT LEAST 1 MONTH FOR FLAVORS TO DEVELOP

■ As Fannie Flagg (or anyone who has seen the box-office hit based on her novel) would tell you, a platter of fried green tomatoes is a beautiful thing. But green tomatoes aren't limited to frying, nor to the American South. These refrigerator pickles, with their tart flavor and firm texture, are based on the traditional delicatessen green tomato pickles that the cookbook author Joyce Goldstein, who contributed the recipe, remembers from her Brooklyn childhood. ■

- 9 tablespoons kosher salt
- 2 tablespoons pickling spices
- 12 fresh dill sprigs
- 12 garlic cloves, lightly crushed
- 6 (2-inch-long) dried hot red chiles
- 6 pounds firm green tomatoes, halved crosswise, or quartered if large

SPECIAL EQUIPMENT: six 1-quart canning jars with lids and screw bands

Sterilize jars and lids and wash screw bands following procedure on page 913.

Drain jars upside down on a clean kitchen towel for 1 minute, then invert. Put 1½ tablespoons kosher salt, 1 teaspoon pickling spices, 2 dill sprigs, 2 garlic cloves, and 1 chile in each jar, then pack each jar with as many tomatoes as will fit. Fill jars with hot water, leaving ¼-inch space at top. Wipe rims of jars with a dampened cloth. Seal jars with lids and screw bands.

Refrigerate pickles for 1 month to allow flavors to develop.

Tricolor Pickled Peppers

MAKES 6 PINTS
ACTIVE TIME: 2 HOURS ■ START TO FINISH: 3 HOURS, PLUS AT LEAST 1 WEEK FOR FLAVORS TO DEVELOP

■ Roasted bell peppers are terrific, but pickling them in vinegar adds piquancy and tartness, taking them to a whole new level. This is just the sort of thing you want to do with peppers in midsummer, when they are cheap and abundant at the farmers market. We love these on an antipasto platter or piled into a hero sandwich. Because they are so beautiful, they also make a stunning gift. ■

- 9 pounds mixed red, yellow, and orange bell peppers, quartered lengthwise, cored, and seeded
- 3½ cups white balsamic vinegar
- 1¾ cups water
- ¼ cup sugar
- 2 tablespoons canning salt (see Sources)
- 12 garlic cloves, peeled
- 1 teaspoon black peppercorns
- 6 (2-inch) sprigs fresh rosemary

SPECIAL EQUIPMENT: six 1-pint canning jars with lids and screw bands

Preheat broiler. Arrange peppers, in batches, skin sides up on a broiler pan and broil about 4 inches from heat until skins are blistered and lightly charred, 4 to 6 minutes per batch. Transfer peppers to a large bowl, cover, and let steam until cool. Peel peppers and separate by color.

Sterilize jars and lids and wash screw bands following procedure on page 913.

Combine vinegar, water, sugar, canning salt, garlic, and peppercorns in a 3-quart saucepan and bring to a boil. Reduce heat and simmer, uncovered, for 10 minutes.

Drain jars upside down on a clean kitchen towel for 1 minute, then invert. Fill jars with pepper quarters, alternating colors. Tuck 2 garlic cloves (from pickling liquid) and 1 rosemary sprig into one side of each jar. Fill jars with pickling liquid, leaving ¼-inch space at top, then run a thin knife between vegetables and sides of jars to eliminate air bubbles.

Seal, process, and cool filled jars following procedure on page 913, boiling peppers in jars for 20 minutes (see Cook's Note).

Let peppers stand for at least 1 week to allow flavors to develop.

COOK'S NOTE

■ If you have a jar that is partially full, do not process it. Instead, cover it with the lid and screw band and refrigerate. Use this jar first.

Preserving and Pickling

Put-up fruits and vegetables, like chicken stock and bread, are not something you make, exactly; they are something you *do*. To us, the key to integrating canning into our home kitchens these days is working in small batches. We rarely prepare more than eight pints (that's about four or five pounds of fruits or vegetables) of anything at a time. Otherwise, it turns into a daunting weekend project. Working in small batches also makes it easier to can a wider selection of fruits and vegetables.

Because produce comes from nature, each batch of jam or preserves is going to be a little different. That's part of the beauty of homemade. Always start with really fresh produce, as perfect as you can find. It should be ripe but firm. Cut out any blemishes or bruised spots; microorganisms multiply so fast on decaying areas that processing might not be able to destroy them all.

Making jams and preserves can be fraught with anxiety: Will it set? Will it set *enough*? The trick is in the balance of fruit, sugar, and pectin, a natural substance that is found in varying degrees in fruits and causes the cooked-down mass to jell. Many older recipes use equal amounts of sugar and fruit, but then you end up with something that's very sweet, and you don't really taste the fruit. We're not fans of the no-sugar school of preserving, either, because sugar, like salt, brings out flavor. And without sugar, you have to cook the fruit down too much in order for it to thicken. You lose the freshness, and the result can taste caramelized.

Pickling is another area of canning where proportions — in this case, of the brine — are all-important. The mixture acts as a preservative and adds flavor and crispness to the pickles. The one specialty ingredient you'll need is canning, or pickling, salt (see Sources), a fine-grained salt with none of the additives found in table salt, which would cloud the brine.

Equipment for Preserving and Pickling

When cooking jams and preserves, you'll have the best results with a 5- to 6-quart heavy pot. It should be wide, so the liquid evaporates quickly. (Stockpots, which are tall and narrow to encourage slow evaporation, are not suitable.)

Many recipes recommend a candy thermometer for testing the doneness of jellies, jams, and preserves, but we have found them unreliable. We prefer the visual certainty of the chilled-plate method: a spoonful of hot jam, brought to room temperature by quick chilling on a cold plate in the refrigerator for a minute, stays in a mound even when the plate is tilted.

The high-acid foods of this chapter require little in the way of specialty equipment. (Low-acid foods such as corn, beans, and most other vegetables call for a steam-pressure canner.) You will need a boiling-water canner, but it's easy enough to rig one up with an 8- to 10-quart pot and a rack to keep the glass jars away from direct heat (or you can use two folded kitchen towels to pad the bottom). You'll also need some canning jars with lids and screw bands. The jars and screw bands may be used more than once, but you must use new lids each time. If using wire-bailed jars and rubber rings (still sold, but not approved by the USDA), follow the manufacturer's instructions. A wide canning funnel comes in handy as well. Supplies are available at many hardware stores and by mail from Home

Canning Supply and Specialties (see Sources). Alltrista Corporation publishes the *Ball Blue Book of Preserving,* which is full of great information, and has a help line.

Sterilizing Jars

Wash jars, lids, and screw bands in hot, soapy water, then rinse well. Dry the screw bands.

Put the empty jars on a rack in a boiling-water canner or an 8- to 10-quart deep pot and add enough water to cover by 2 inches. Cover the pot with a lid, bring to a boil, and boil for 10 minutes. Remove the pot from the heat, leaving the jars in the water and the lid in place. Heat the lids in water to cover in a small saucepan until a thermometer registers 180°F (do not let boil); remove the pan from the heat and cover with a lid. Keep the jars and lids submerged in the hot water until ready to use.

Sealing, Processing, and Storing Jars

Wipe off the rims of filled jars with a clean, damp kitchen towel, then firmly screw on the lids with the screw bands.

Put the sealed jars on the rack in the boiling-water canner or 8- to 10-quart pot and add enough water to cover by 2 inches. Bring to a boil, covered. Boil jams, preserves, chutneys, or fruit preserves for 10 minutes (for ½-pint jars), pickles for 20 minutes (for pint jars), or as directed in the recipe. With tongs, transfer the jars to a towel-lined surface to cool. The preserves will thicken as they cool, and the jars will seal; if you hear a ping, it signals that the vacuum formed at the top of the cooling preserves has made the lid concave. You may or may not be around to hear the ping—some jars make the sound soon after you remove them from the water, while others in the same batch may take a few hours. The important thing is concave lids.

After the jars have cooled for 12 to 24 hours, press the center of each lid to check that it's concave, then remove the screw band and try to lift off the lid with your fingertips. If you can't, the lid has a good seal. Replace the screw band. Put any jars that haven't sealed properly in the refrigerator and use them first. Store the other jars in a cool, dark, dry place. Light and heat hasten deterioration, and dampness will result in rusting and corrosion of the lids.

Commonsense Canning Tips

- Always label your canning jars with the date they were processed and identify what's inside. If looking at those rows of gleaming jars doesn't give you a sense of accomplishment, we don't know what will. According to the *Ball Blue Book of Preserving,* the bible of home canners, properly canned food will keep indefinitely, but after about a year, chemical changes that affect taste, color, and texture do happen.
- Before using, check each jar again to make sure the lid is concave, signifying that the vacuum seal is still present. If you can remove the lids without having to pry them off with a can opener, do not use the contents. Other signs of spoilage include mold, cloudiness, seepage, yeast growth, fermentation, and (yikes!) spurting liquid when the jar is opened. The *Ball Blue Book* says, in essence, when in doubt, throw it out—carefully, to prevent any possible contamination from *botulinum* toxin. You don't want people or pets to come into contact with the contents of the suspect jars. And thoroughly wash (or discard) any sponges, dishcloths, or kitchen towels that might have been contaminated.
- Now that we've scared the living daylights out of you, relax. Home cooks have been canning food for centuries. Even if you didn't survive your high school science lab, you can make preserves your grandmother would be proud of.

DRIED LONG PEPPERS

Combine water and remaining ingredients in a 3-quart saucepan and bring to a boil, stirring until sugar is dissolved. Reduce heat and simmer, uncovered, stirring occasionally, for 15 minutes.

Immediately pour pickling liquid over plums. Cool plums completely, uncovered, then screw on lid with screw band and refrigerate for at least 1 day to allow flavors to develop.

COOK'S NOTE

■ The plums keep, refrigerated, for up to 1 month.

Spicy Pickled Plums

SERVES 8 AS A CONDIMENT
ACTIVE TIME: 20 MINUTES ■ START TO FINISH: 2 HOURS, PLUS AT LEAST 1 DAY FOR FLAVORS TO DEVELOP

■ Aside from being delicious, these plums have real presence on a plate. Their blush of color next to a lamb chop or slices of roast pork in midwinter is welcome. (You can slip off the skins before eating, if you like.) They are also wonderful as an hors d'oeuvre, served with slices of mild goat cheese on crackers. The seasonings are subtle but unusual: warm, sweet star anise; a touch of heat from chiles de árbol; and sharp, sweet long peppers—a pungent dried spice that predated the use of black peppercorns in Asia, India, and Europe. ■

- 2 pounds firm but ripe red or black plums
- 2 cups water
- 2½ cups sugar
- 1¼ cups red wine vinegar
- 3 dried chiles de árbol (see Glossary)
- 3 star anise
- 3 (1-inch-long) dried long peppers (see Sources) or 1 (3-inch) piece peeled fresh ginger, cut into ½-inch-thick slices

SPECIAL EQUIPMENT: a 4-quart canning jar with lid and screw band

With a sharp paring knife, make 4 to 6 evenly spaced lengthwise slits from top to bottom in each plum. Put plums in jar.

Mint Jelly

MAKES ABOUT 4 CUPS
ACTIVE TIME: 25 MINUTES ■ START TO FINISH: 1½ HOURS, PLUS AT LEAST 1 DAY FOR JELLY TO SET

■ With a lovely soft set, this mint jelly almost becomes a sauce when it mixes with lamb juices on a plate. We call for an optional two drops of green food coloring (to brighten what would otherwise be the palest shade of green), but the color will not be anything like the Day-Glo green of commercial mint jelly. And the flavor is incomparable. ■

- 1 cup finely chopped fresh mint
- 1¾ cups cold water
- 3½ cups sugar
- 2 tablespoons cider vinegar
- 1 tablespoon strained fresh lemon juice
- 2 drops green food coloring (optional)
- 1 (3-ounce) pouch liquid pectin

SPECIAL EQUIPMENT: four ½-pint canning jars with lids and screw bands; fine cheesecloth or a kitchen towel (not terry cloth); a wide 5- to 6-quart heavy pot at least 9½ inches in diameter (see page 912)

Sterilize jars and lids and wash screw bands following procedure on page 913.

Combine mint and water in a 2-quart heavy saucepan and bring to a boil, covered, over moderately low heat. Remove from heat and let stand, covered, for 15 minutes.

Pour mixture through a cheesecloth- (or towel-) lined fine-mesh sieve into pot. Firmly squeeze mint in cheesecloth to extract all liquid, then discard mint. Add sugar, vinegar, lemon juice, and food coloring, if using, to pot and bring to a rolling boil, stirring constantly. Stir in pectin, return to a rolling boil, and boil for 1 minute. Skim foam from surface. Remove from heat.

Drain jars upside down on a clean kitchen towel for 1 minute, then invert. Ladle jelly into jars, leaving 1/4-inch space at top.

Seal, process, and cool filled jars following procedure on page 913, boiling jelly in jars for 10 minutes (see Cook's Note).

Let jelly stand for at least 1 day to set.

COOK'S NOTE

- If you have a jar that is partially full, do not process it. Instead, cover it with the lid and screw band and refrigerate. Use this jar first.

Garlic and Rosemary Jelly

MAKES ABOUT 4 CUPS

ACTIVE TIME: 50 MINUTES ■ START TO FINISH: 2 HOURS, PLUS AT LEAST 1 DAY FOR FLAVORS TO DEVELOP

■ Rosemary plays up the mellow sweetness of the garlic. Give this savory jelly a quick stir—the garlic drifts to the bottom of the jar—before dabbing it on a slice of roast lamb (it's a great alternative to mint jelly) or roast pork. Or stir it into the pan juices to finish a meat sauce. ■

- 1 3/4 cups dry white wine
- 1/4 cup white wine vinegar
- 1/3 cup finely chopped garlic (15 large cloves)
- 4 (4-inch) fresh rosemary sprigs
- 3 1/2 cups sugar
- 1 (3-ounce) pouch liquid pectin

SPECIAL EQUIPMENT: four 1/2-pint canning jars with lids and screw bands; a wide 5- to 6-quart heavy pot at least 9 1/2 inches in diameter (see page 912)

Sterilize jars and lids and wash screw bands following procedure on page 913.

Stir together wine, vinegar, garlic, rosemary, and sugar in pot and bring to a rolling boil over high heat, stirring constantly. Quickly stir in pectin and bring mixture back to a rolling boil. Boil, stirring constantly, for 1 minute, then remove from heat. Pour jelly through a fine-mesh sieve into a large glass measure; reserve garlic and rosemary.

Drain jars upside down on a clean kitchen towel for 1 minute, then invert. Distribute garlic and rosemary evenly among jars. Skim off any foam from jelly, then immediately pour jelly into jars, leaving 1/4-inch space at top.

Seal, process, and cool filled jars following procedure on page 913, boiling jelly for 10 minutes (see Cook's Note).

Let jelly stand for at least 1 day to allow flavors to develop. Stir to distribute garlic before using.

COOK'S NOTE

- If you have a jar that is partially full, do not process it. Instead, cover it with the lid and screw band and refrigerate. Use this jar first.

Garlic–Ancho Chile Jam

MAKES ABOUT 1 CUP

ACTIVE TIME: 20 MINUTES ■ START TO FINISH: 1 1/4 HOURS

■ Bread isn't just for butter anymore—not when you've got this savory spread made from mellow roasted garlic and ancho chiles, which have an earthy, sweet heat. A little of this jam also rounds out a meat or wine reduction sauce. The recipe is adapted from one belonging to Robert del Grande, of Café Annie, in Houston. ■

- 2 medium heads garlic (2 inches in diameter)
- 3 tablespoons olive oil
- 2 ounces dried ancho chiles (see Glossary), stemmed, seeded, and ribs discarded
- 2 tablespoons cider vinegar
- 2 tablespoons mild honey
- Salt

Put a rack in middle of oven and preheat oven to 400°F.

Cut off tops of garlic heads to expose cloves and discard tops. Rub each head with 1½ teaspoons oil. Wrap heads together in foil and roast until tender, about 45 minutes. Cool to warm.

While garlic is roasting, toast chiles in a dry heavy skillet over moderate heat, turning occasionally, until fragrant and a shade darker, about 1 minute. Soak chiles in a small bowl of hot water to cover until softened, about 20 minutes; drain.

Squeeze garlic from skins into a food processor. Add chiles, vinegar, honey, remaining 2 tablespoons oil, and salt to taste and purée. Force purée through a medium-mesh sieve into a bowl.

Serve jam warm or at room temperature.

COOK'S NOTE

- The jam keeps, refrigerated in an airtight container, for up to 5 days. Bring to room temperature before serving.

Apple Butter

MAKES ABOUT 4 CUPS
ACTIVE TIME: 2¼ HOURS ■ START TO FINISH: 2½ HOURS, PLUS AT LEAST 1 DAY FOR FLAVORS TO DEVELOP

■ This tastes like a crisp fall day in New England. We used McIntosh apples, but any flavorful, juicy, sweet-tart apple—Northern Spy, Empire, Cortland, or Macoun, for instance—will do. Let your farmers market be your guide. ■

- 4 tart flavorful apples, such as McIntosh, peeled, cored, and cut into 8 wedges each
- 1½ cups unfiltered apple cider
- 2 tablespoons fresh lemon juice
- ½ cup packed dark brown sugar
- 1 teaspoon ground cinnamon
- ¼ teaspoon ground allspice

SPECIAL EQUIPMENT: four ½-pint canning jars with lids and screw bands; a wide 5- to 6-quart heavy pot at least 9½ inches in diameter (see page 912); a food mill fitted with a fine disk

Sterilize jars and lids and wash screw bands following procedure on page 913.

Chill two small plates for testing butter. Combine all ingredients in pot, cover, and bring to a boil over moderate heat, then reduce heat and simmer, uncovered, stirring occasionally, until apples are tender, about 15 minutes.

Purée mixture in food mill set over a large bowl, then return purée to pot. Simmer over moderately low heat, stirring and scraping bottom of pan frequently (stir constantly and adjust heat toward end of cooking to prevent scorching), until butter is very thick and tests done, 1¼ to 1¾ hours. Begin testing for doneness at 1¼ hours; remove pot from heat while testing. Drop a spoonful of apple butter onto a chilled plate and refrigerate for 1 minute, then tilt plate; butter should remain in a mound and not run.

Drain jars upside down on a clean kitchen towel for 1 minute, then invert. Ladle apple butter into jars, leaving ¼-inch space at top. Run a thin knife between apple butter and sides of jars to eliminate air bubbles.

Seal, process, and cool filled jars following procedure on page 913, boiling apple butter in jars for 10 minutes (see Cook's Note).

Let apple butter stand for at least 1 day to allow flavors to develop.

COOK'S NOTE

- If you have a jar that is partially full, do not process it. Instead, cover it with the lid and screw band and refrigerate. Use this jar first.

Tangy Apricot Jam

MAKES ABOUT 8 CUPS
ACTIVE TIME: 2 HOURS ■ START TO FINISH: 10 HOURS, PLUS AT LEAST 1 DAY FOR FLAVORS TO DEVELOP

■ Really good apricots are the key to this jam. They should have a rich, musky fragrance, and the fruit's intense sweetness should be balanced by a welcome tinge of sourness, or acidity. If all you get is sweetness, you lose the magic. Look for local varieties; no matter where you live, they will be picked riper and are less likely to have suffered from rough handling. Note that we add a little almond extract. Apricots, like other stone fruits, are closely related to almonds, and the flavors have a great affinity for each other. ■

- 5 pounds firm but ripe fresh apricots, quartered and pitted
- 4½ cups sugar
- ⅓ cup fresh lemon juice
- 1 (1¾-ounce) box powdered pectin
- ½ teaspoon almond extract

SPECIAL EQUIPMENT: eight ½-pint canning jars with lids and screw bands; a wide 5- to 6-quart heavy pot at least 9½ inches in diameter (see page 912)

Toss apricots with 4 cups sugar in a large bowl. Refrigerate, covered, for at least 8 hours.

Sterilize jars and lids and wash screw bands following procedure on page 913.

Chill two small plates for testing jam. Transfer apricot mixture (sugar will not be completely dissolved) to pot and stir in lemon juice. Bring to a boil over moderate heat. Boil, stirring frequently and skimming off foam, for 20 minutes. Then reduce heat and cook at a slow boil, skimming occasionally and stirring frequently as jam thickens (to prevent scorching), until jam tests done, 35 minutes to 1 hour more: Begin testing for doneness at 35 minutes; remove pot from heat while testing. Drop a spoonful of jam onto a chilled plate and refrigerate for 1 minute, then tilt plate; jam should remain in a mound and not run.

Meanwhile, whisk together pectin and remaining ½ cup sugar in a small bowl. Stir almond extract into jam, then gradually add pectin mixture, whisking constantly. Return jam to a rolling boil and boil for 1 minute. Remove from heat.

Drain jars upside down on a clean kitchen towel for 1 minute, then invert. Ladle jam into jars, leaving ¼-inch space at top. Run a thin knife between jam and sides of jars to eliminate air bubbles.

Seal, process, and cool filled jars following procedure on page 913, boiling jam in jars for 10 minutes (see Cook's Note).

Let jam stand for at least 1 day to allow flavors to develop.

COOK'S NOTES

- The apricot-sugar mixture can be refrigerated for up to 24 hours.
- If you have a jar that is partially full, do not process it. Instead, cover it with the lid and screw band and refrigerate. Use this jar first.

Concord Grape Jam

MAKES ABOUT 7 CUPS
ACTIVE TIME: 2¾ HOURS ■ START TO FINISH: 2¾ HOURS, PLUS AT LEAST 1 DAY FOR FLAVORS TO DEVELOP

■ This is the most delicious grape jam we've ever had: deep, rich, and not too sweet. One taste will convince you forevermore that making something from scratch is worth the effort. The idea of peeling grapes may sound daunting, but the skins slip right off. You don't need to add pectin to help the jam set, because grapes have plenty of their own. ■

- 5 pounds Concord grapes, stemmed
- 5 cups sugar
- 3 tablespoons fresh lemon juice

SPECIAL EQUIPMENT: seven ½-pint canning jars with lids and screw bands; a wide 5- to 6-quart heavy pot at least 9½ inches in diameter (see page 912); a food mill fitted with a fine disk

Sterilize jars and lids and wash screw bands following procedure on page 913.

Chill two small plates for testing jam. Slip skins from grapes, reserving skins. Purée skins with 1 cup

sugar in a food processor, then transfer to pot. Stir in lemon juice, grapes, and remaining 4 cups sugar and bring to a boil over moderate heat. Boil, stirring frequently and skimming off foam, for 20 minutes.

Force jam through food mill into a large bowl; discard seeds and solids. Return jam to pot and cook at a slow boil, skimming off foam occasionally and stirring frequently to prevent scorching as jam thickens, until jam tests done, 35 minutes to 1 hour: Begin testing for doneness at 35 minutes; remove pot from heat while testing. Drop a spoonful of jam onto a chilled plate and refrigerate for 1 minute, then tilt plate; jam should remain in a mound and not run.

Drain jars upside down on a clean kitchen towel for 1 minute, then invert. Ladle jam into jars, leaving ¼-inch space at top. Run a thin knife between jam and sides of jars to eliminate air bubbles.

Seal, process, and cool filled jars following procedure on page 913, boiling jam in jars for 10 minutes (see Cook's Note).

Let jam stand for at least 1 day to allow flavors to develop.

COOK'S NOTE

- If you have a jar that is partially full, do not process it. Instead, cover it with the lid and screw band and refrigerate. Use this jar first.

Meyer Lemon Marmalade

MAKES ABOUT 6 CUPS
ACTIVE TIME: 1¼ HOURS ■ START TO FINISH: 25¼ HOURS (INCLUDES SOAKING LEMONS), PLUS 1 DAY FOR FLAVORS TO DEVELOP

■ Meyer lemons, a specialty citrus hybrid that's grown in California, have a complex flavor and a haunting fragrance. The good news is that they are becoming more widely available. The bad news is that they are perishable and aren't in the market for long. (For more about Meyer lemons, see opposite page.) The beauty of this flavorful marmalade is that it gives you a way to enjoy them year-round. ■

1½ pounds Meyer lemons
4 cups water
4 cups sugar

SPECIAL EQUIPMENT: cheesecloth; kitchen string; a wide 5- to 6-quart heavy pot at least 9½ inches in diameter (see page 912); six ½-pint canning jars with lids and screw bands

Halve lemons crosswise and remove seeds, reserving them (they provide pectin). Tie seeds in a cheesecloth bag. Quarter each lemon half and thinly slice crosswise. Combine lemons with bag of seeds and water in pot and let stand, covered, at room temperature for 24 hours.

Sterilize jars and lids and wash screw bands following procedure on page 913.

Chill two small plates for testing marmalade. Bring lemon mixture to a boil over moderate heat. Reduce heat and simmer, uncovered, until reduced to about 4 cups, about 45 minutes.

Stir in sugar and boil over moderate heat, stirring occasionally and skimming off any foam, until marmalade tests done, about 15 minutes: Begin testing for doneness at 10 minutes; remove pot from heat while testing. Drop a spoonful of marmalade onto a chilled plate and refrigerate for 1 minute, then tilt plate; marmalade should remain in a mound and not run.

Drain jars on a clean kitchen towel for 1 minute, then invert. Ladle hot marmalade into jars, leaving ¼-inch space at top, then run a thin knife between marmalade and sides of jars to eliminate air bubbles; discard cheesecloth bag.

Seal, process, and cool filled jars following procedure on page 913, boiling marmalade in jars for 10 minutes (see Cook's Note).

Let marmalade stand for at least 1 day to allow flavor to develop.

COOK'S NOTE

- If you have a jar that is partially full, do not process it. Instead, cover it with the lid and screw band and refrigerate. Use this jar first.

Meyer Lemons

The Meyer lemon has achieved cult status for its juicy, flavorful pulp and incomparable scent. Rounder than more conventional lemon varieties, it has a smooth, thin yellow rind that deepens to orange-yellow as it ripens. In markets, you might mistake it for a small orange. Its pulp has a higher sugar content than a regular lemon, with just the right amount of acidity to balance the sweetness, and it is almost seedless.

The fruit expert David Karp tells us that the Meyer was introduced to the United States by another renowned plant explorer, Frank Meyer of the USDA, who discovered the tree growing in pots near Peking in 1908. At that time, Karp says, lemons were indigenous to India and exotic and scarce in China; the trees fetched up to ten dollars each, a lot of money then. American botanists always suspected that the Meyer was a hybrid, and recently a researcher at the University of California at Riverside determined that its female parent is almost certainly a sweet orange, and the male a lemon or citron.

In 1918, Frank Meyer disappeared mysteriously from a Yangtze steamer. In the years that followed, the tree that bears his name became a fixture in the backyards of California cooks and gardeners. Commercially, the fruit didn't catch on, because it's too delicate to survive handling and storage, unlike regular lemons, which are "cured" at a set temperature and humidity and often gassed with ethylene in order to yield juicy yellow fruit months after harvest. According to Karp, another obstacle to the Meyer's success was that in the 1940s, it was found to carry a virus devastating to other citrus trees. As a result, it was banned from California growing areas until twenty years later, when scientists developed a virus-free strain.

The Meyer began to move into the mainstream in the 1980s, when California chefs, notably Lindsey Shere, then pastry chef at Chez Panisse, in Berkeley, latched on to the fruit's complex, almost floral flavor and aroma, which combine lemon, orange, and just the barest hint of lime. The Meyer is extraordinary in dishes that showcase its nuances — soufflés and tarts, for instance — and it makes great marmalade (opposite page) and preserved lemons (page 908).

Meyer lemons have a dedicated following but remain a niche item. Look for them in specialty foods shops during winter months. They are also available by mail-order from Snow's Citrus Court (see Sources) from November through January.

Nectarine Preserves with Basil

MAKES ABOUT 8 CUPS
ACTIVE TIME: 1½ HOURS ■ START TO FINISH: 3 HOURS, PLUS AT LEAST 1 DAY FOR FLAVORS TO DEVELOP

■ Nectarines—named for the nectar quaffed on Olympus—are a smooth-skinned variety of peach with their own unique flavor. Compared to a peach's muskier, more complex sweetness, they have a clearer, acidic quality. The warm sunniness of basil complements the fruit, adding a little spice and perfume. These preserves are wonderful for breakfast, slathered on hot buttered toast or swirled into yogurt, and delicious with sliced ham for supper. ■

- 4 cups sugar
- ¼ cup fresh lemon juice
- ¼ cup water
- 1 cup loosely packed fresh basil sprigs, plus 8 small sprigs
- 5 pounds nectarines or peaches, peeled (see Tips, page 940), pitted, and cut into 8 wedges each
- 1 (1¾-ounce) box plus 2 tablespoons lower-sugar powdered pectin

SPECIAL EQUIPMENT: eight ½-pint canning jars with lids and screw bands; a wide 5- to 6-quart heavy pot at least 9½ inches in diameter (see page 912); a candy thermometer

Sterilize jars and lids and wash screw bands following procedure on page 913.

Combine sugar, lemon juice, water, and 1 cup basil in pot and bring to a boil, stirring until sugar is dissolved. Reduce heat and simmer, uncovered, until thick and syrupy, about 25 minutes. With a slotted spoon, remove and discard basil.

Add nectarines to syrup, bring to a rolling boil over moderately high heat, and boil, uncovered, stirring frequently, for 5 minutes. Remove from heat. With slotted spoon, transfer nectarines to a sieve set over a bowl to catch juice. Drain nectarines for 5 minutes; set aside. Add juice from bowl to juice in pot.

Drain jars upside down on a clean kitchen towel for 1 minute, then invert. Using slotted spoon, divide nectarines among jars. Tuck a basil sprig into one side of each jar.

Return juice in pot to a rolling boil, skimming off any foam. Boil until juice registers 220°–224°F on thermometer, 7 to 10 minutes. Gradually add pectin, whisking constantly. Return juice to a rolling boil and boil, skimming off any foam, for 1 minute. Remove from heat.

Ladle juice into jars, leaving ¼-inch space at top, then run a thin knife between fruit and sides of jars to eliminate air bubbles.

Seal, process, and cool filled jars following procedure on page 913, boiling preserves in jars for 10 minutes (see Cook's Note).

Let preserves stand for at least 1 day to allow flavors to develop.

COOK'S NOTE

■ If you have a jar that is partially full, do not process it. Instead, cover it with the lid and screw band and refrigerate. Use this jar first.

Quick Plum Preserves

MAKES ABOUT 2½ CUPS
ACTIVE TIME: 45 MINUTES ■ START TO FINISH: 2 HOURS (INCLUDES COOLING)

■ If you are afraid of making jams or preserves, this is the recipe for you, because the preserves are made in a small batch and simply stored in the refrigerator—no need to worry about sterilizing jars or processing them in a water bath. Serve with yogurt or toast or spoon over vanilla ice cream. ■

- 2 pounds firm but ripe red, black, or prune plums, halved, pitted, and coarsely chopped
- ½ cup sugar
- ½ cup water
- 1 (3-inch) cinnamon stick

Stir together plums, sugar, water, and cinnamon stick in a 2-quart heavy saucepan. Bring to a simmer and simmer, uncovered, stirring frequently to prevent sticking as mixture thickens, until thickened and reduced to about $2\frac{1}{2}$ cups, 45 minutes to 1 hour.

Transfer preserves to a bowl and discard cinnamon stick. Cool, uncovered, then refrigerate, covered.

COOK'S NOTE

- The preserves keep, refrigerated in an airtight container, for up to 1 month.

Plum Butter

MAKES ABOUT 5 CUPS
ACTIVE TIME: 2 HOURS ■ START TO FINISH: 3 HOURS, PLUS AT LEAST 1 DAY FOR FLAVORS TO DEVELOP

■ Plums are cooked down into a beautiful thick spread in order to concentrate their elusive, delicate flavor. ■

- 1 vanilla bean, halved lengthwise
- 4 pounds ripe plums, pitted and cut into $\frac{1}{2}$-inch-thick wedges
- 3 cups sugar
- $\frac{1}{4}$ cup fresh lemon juice

SPECIAL EQUIPMENT: five $\frac{1}{2}$-pint canning jars with lids and screw bands; a wide 5- to 6-quart heavy pot at least $9\frac{1}{2}$ inches in diameter (see page 912); a food mill fitted with a fine disk

Sterilize jars and lids and wash screw bands following procedure on page 913.

Chill two small plates for testing butter. Scrape seeds from vanilla bean into pot. Add pod, then add plums, sugar, and lemon juice. Slowly bring to a rolling boil over moderate heat (this will take about 15 minutes), stirring frequently. Boil, uncovered, stirring frequently, until plums are tender, about 5 minutes.

Remove and discard vanilla pod. Force plums, with liquid, in batches through food mill set over a bowl. Transfer purée to pot and simmer, uncovered, over moderately low heat, stirring and scraping bottom of pan frequently (stir constantly and adjust heat toward end of cooking to prevent scorching), until butter is very thick and tests done, $1\frac{1}{2}$ to 2 hours: Begin testing for doneness at $1\frac{1}{2}$ hours; remove pot from heat while testing. Drop a spoonful of plum butter onto a chilled plate and refrigerate for 1 minute, then tilt plate; butter should remain in a mound and not run.

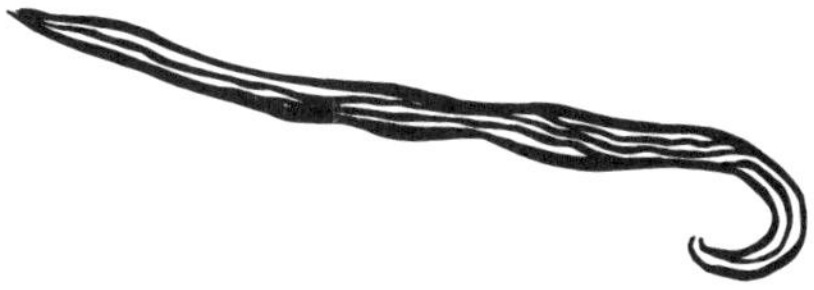

Drain jars upside down on a clean kitchen towel for 1 minute, then invert. Ladle plum butter into jars, leaving $\frac{1}{4}$-inch space at top. Run a thin knife between plum butter and sides of jars to eliminate air bubbles.

Seal, process, and cool filled jars following procedure on page 913, boiling plum butter in jars for 10 minutes (see Cook's Note).

Let plum butter stand for at least 1 day to allow flavors to develop.

COOK'S NOTE

- If you have a jar that is partially full, do not process it. Instead, cover it with the lid and screw band and refrigerate. Use this jar first.

Sour Cherry Preserves

MAKES ABOUT 8 CUPS
ACTIVE TIME: $2\frac{1}{4}$ HOURS ■ START TO FINISH: $10\frac{1}{2}$ HOURS, PLUS AT LEAST 1 DAY FOR FLAVORS TO DEVELOP

■ Sour cherries have a vibrant, sophisticated tartness and depth of flavor. Their season is fleeting, though, and they aren't quite as common as sweet varieties at farmers markets. Being more perishable, they're most often frozen, dried, or canned right after harvest. If you are lucky enough to find them, buy a big sack and preserve them so you can enjoy their incomparable charms later in the year. For the best color, choose true-red sour cherries. Darker varieties will make darker (though still delicious) preserves. The fruit is steeped overnight in sugar, which deepens the flavor and helps them stay plump. Kernels from the cherry pits, tied in a cheesecloth bag, add an almond note. ■

PITTING CHERRIES

A small sharp knife will do the trick, but a cherry pitter, which looks a bit like a hole punch, is more efficient. Either tool works on sweet as well as sour cherries, of course, but because sour cherries are so soft, you can just use your fingers: working over a bowl to catch the juices, squeeze the pits out through the stem ends. Pitted cherries freeze well for six months or so. Spread them on paper towel–lined baking sheets and freeze them; then, when they're frozen hard, double-bag them in heavy-duty sealable plastic bags and tuck them back into the freezer. If your winter plans for them include compotes and sauces, where it's not important to keep them whole, simply double-bag the pitted fresh cherries without freezing them individually first.

- 4 pounds sour cherries, stemmed and pitted, 3 tablespoons pits reserved
- 5 cups sugar
- $\frac{1}{3}$ cup fresh lemon juice
- 1 ($1\frac{3}{4}$-ounce) box plus 3 tablespoons lower-sugar powdered pectin

SPECIAL EQUIPMENT: a cherry pitter (optional); cheesecloth; kitchen string; eight $\frac{1}{2}$-pint canning jars with lids and screw bands; a wide 5- to 6-quart heavy pot at least $9\frac{1}{2}$ inches in diameter (see page 912); a candy thermometer

Toss together cherries, sugar, and lemon juice in a large bowl.

Wrap reserved cherry pits in a paper towel and crack them with a rolling pin or pestle just enough so you can extract inner white kernels. Discard outer shells and tie white kernels in a cheesecloth bag. Stir bag into cherry mixture and refrigerate, covered, for at least 8 hours.

Sterilize jars and lids and wash screw bands following procedure on page 913.

Pour cherries, with liquid and cheesecloth bag (sugar will not be completely dissolved), into pot. Bring to a rolling boil over moderate heat and boil, uncovered, stirring frequently, for 5 minutes. Remove from heat. With a slotted spoon, transfer cherries to a sieve set over a bowl to catch juice. Drain cherries for 5 minutes; set aside. Add juice from bowl to juice in pot.

Drain jars upside down on a clean kitchen towel for 1 minute, then invert. Using slotted spoon, divide cherries among jars.

Return juice in pot to a rolling boil, skimming off any foam. Boil until juice registers 220°–224°F on thermometer, 7 to 10 minutes. Discard cheesecloth bag. Gradually add pectin, whisking constantly. Return juice to a rolling boil and boil, skimming off any foam, for 1 minute.

Ladle juice into jars, leaving $\frac{1}{4}$-inch space at top, then run a thin knife between fruit and sides of jars to eliminate air bubbles.

Seal, process, and cool filled jars following procedure on page 913, boiling preserves in jars for 10 minutes (see Cook's Note).

Let preserves stand for at least 1 day to allow flavors to develop.

COOK'S NOTE

- If you have a jar that is partially full, do not process it. Instead, cover it with the lid and screw band and refrigerate. Use this jar first.

Quick Strawberry Jam

MAKES ABOUT $1\frac{1}{4}$ CUPS
ACTIVE TIME: 10 MINUTES ■ START TO FINISH: 40 MINUTES

■ There is nothing like homemade jam on hot buttered toast. And there is nothing like immediate gratification—this jam is ready to eat in no time. ■

- 1 pound strawberries, rinsed, hulled, and halved
- $\frac{2}{3}$–$\frac{3}{4}$ cup sugar, depending on sweetness of berries
- 2 tablespoons powdered pectin
- 2 teaspoons fresh lemon juice

Mash strawberries in a large bowl with a potato masher or a fork. Transfer to a 12-inch nonstick skillet and stir in sugar, pectin, and lemon juice. Bring to a boil over moderate heat and boil, stirring occasionally, until slightly thickened, about 5 minutes.

Transfer jam to a bowl and cool, then refrigerate, covered, until ready to serve.

COOK'S NOTE

- The jam keeps, refrigerated in an airtight container, for up to 2 weeks.

Strawberry Jam

MAKES ABOUT 4 CUPS
ACTIVE TIME: 1¼ HOURS ■ START TO FINISH: 1½ HOURS, PLUS AT LEAST 1 DAY FOR FLAVORS TO DEVELOP

■ This soft strawberry jam, from longtime contributor Caroline Bates, who inherited the recipe from her mother, is summer captured in a jar. The flavor depends on having berries that are fully sweet, completely ripe yet firm, and without a trace of white near the stem. Such berries have less pectin than underripe ones, so the jam will be loose. (Out of season, frozen organic strawberries make a delicious substitute; see Cook's Note.) Just spoon it out of the jar and drizzle on fresh, hot biscuits. ■

CHOOSING STRAWBERRIES

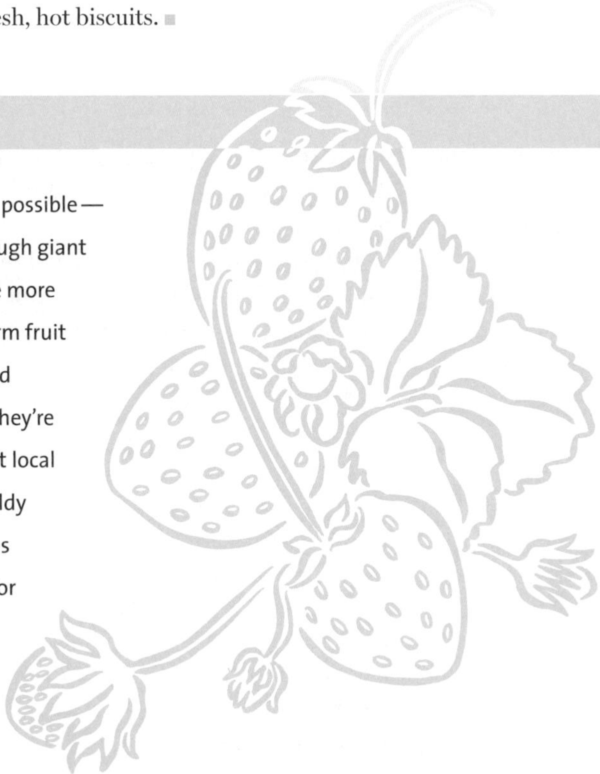

We recommend seeking out local strawberries in season whenever possible—those that have had to travel the least always taste the best. Although giant commercially raised berries fetch high prices, small ones often have more flavor. When shopping for or picking fresh berries, choose plump, firm fruit with even coloring; those with green or white shoulders haven't had ample time to ripen. Look for berries that have a heady fragrance. They're at their most aromatic and flavorful at room temperature, but most local berries need to be refrigerated if they're to be kept. Discard any moldy berries, as mold spreads quickly and can ruin an entire batch. Berries that are merely soft, wrinkled, or "deflated," however, can be used for preserves or pies without loss of quality.

We've had good luck keeping picked-over berries in their cardboard carton tucked inside a paper bag and refrigerated; they keep for about five days with minimum loss to spoilage. Alternatively, if you have room in your refrigerator, store them in a single layer on a baking sheet or in a shallow baking dish lined with paper towels. Don't wash the berries until you're ready to use them, and leave their green caps on until you've dried them, so they don't get waterlogged. Because of their high water content, strawberries can't be frozen as successfully as cherries or blueberries, but frozen berries are fine if you want to make wintertime smoothies.

3 pounds ripe strawberries (4½ pints), rinsed and hulled
4 cups sugar
⅓ cup fresh lemon juice

SPECIAL EQUIPMENT: four ½-pint canning jars with lids and screw bands; a wide 5- to 6-quart heavy nonreactive pot at least 9½ inches in diameter (see page 912)

Sterilize jars and lids and wash screw bands following procedure on page 913.

Chill two small plates for testing jam. Using a potato masher, crush strawberries lightly with sugar in pot, then bring to a boil over moderate heat and boil, stirring and skimming off foam frequently, for 10 minutes.

Add lemon juice and cook at a slow boil, skimming and stirring frequently, until jam tests done, 20 to 40 minutes: Begin testing for doneness at 20 minutes; remove pot from heat while testing. Drop a spoonful of jam onto a chilled plate and refrigerate for 1 minute, then tilt plate; jam should remain in a soft mound and run slightly.

Drain jars upside down on a clean kitchen towel for 1 minute, then invert. Ladle jam into jars, leaving ¼-inch space at top. Run a thin knife between jam and sides of jars to eliminate air bubbles.

Seal, process, and cool filled jars following procedure on page 913, boiling jam in jars for 10 minutes (see Cook's Note).

Let jam stand for at least 1 day to allow flavors to develop.

COOK'S NOTES

- This jam can also be made with 3 pounds frozen organic strawberries (five 10-ounce bags), thawed.
- If you have a jar that is partially full, do not process it. Instead, cover it with the lid and screw band and refrigerate. Use this jar first.

Raspberry Jam

MAKES ABOUT 8 CUPS
ACTIVE TIME: 2 HOURS ■ START TO FINISH: 3½ HOURS, PLUS AT LEAST 1 DAY FOR FLAVORS TO DEVELOP

■ If you are lucky enough to have a raspberry patch that is overflowing (or know someone who does), and you have already gorged on them, you owe it to yourself to make jam. Big, juicy, ripe raspberries will give you something rich and profound. ■

4 pounds ripe raspberries
4½ cups sugar
¼ cup fresh lemon juice
1 (1¾-ounce) box powdered pectin

SPECIAL EQUIPMENT: eight ½-pint canning jars with lids and screw bands; a wide 5- to 6-quart heavy pot at least 9½ inches in diameter (see page 912)

Toss raspberries with 4 cups sugar and lemon juice in a large bowl. Let stand at room temperature, stirring occasionally, until juicy, about 1½ hours.

Sterilize jars and lids and wash screw bands following procedure on page 913.

Chill two small plates for testing jam. Transfer raspberry mixture (sugar will not be completely dissolved) to pot and bring to a boil over moderate heat. Boil, stirring frequently and skimming off foam, for 20 minutes. Then reduce heat and cook at a slow boil, skimming occasionally and stirring frequently to prevent scorching as jam thickens, until jam tests done, 35 minutes to 1 hour: Begin testing for doneness at 35 minutes; remove pot from heat while testing. Drop a spoonful of jam onto a chilled plate and refrigerate for 1 minute, then tilt plate; jam should remain in a mound and not run.

Meanwhile, whisk together pectin and remaining 1/2 cup sugar in a small bowl. Gradually add pectin mixture to jam, whisking constantly. Return jam to a rolling boil and boil for 1 minute. Remove from heat.

Drain jars upside down on a clean kitchen towel for 1 minute, then invert. Ladle jam into jars, leaving 1/4-inch space at top. Run a thin knife between jam and sides of jars to eliminate air bubbles.

Seal, process, and cool filled jars following procedure on page 913, boiling jam in jars for 10 minutes (see Cook's Note).

Let jam stand for at least 1 day to allow flavors to develop.

COOK'S NOTE

- If you have a jar that is partially full, do not process it. Instead, cover it with the lid and screw band and refrigerate. Use this jar first.

BASICS

This is the most important chapter in the book. These are the secrets hidden in many of our dishes, a few fundamental recipes whose only purpose is to make food taste better.

Armed with a freezer filled with containers of stock, anyone can put a delicious dinner on the table in a matter of minutes—and cooks who have mixed their own fresh seasonings will never again settle for store-bought blends.

These are the basic building blocks of great cooking. Remarkably, not one of them is hard to master.

1 LITRE
900
800
700
600
500ml
400
300
200
100
4 CUPS
3 ½
3 CUPS
2½
2 CUPS
1½
1 CUP
½

Chicken Stock

MAKES ABOUT 10 CUPS
ACTIVE TIME: 30 MINUTES ■ START TO FINISH: 4½ HOURS

■ Chicken stock isn't something you make, it is something you *do*. So one Saturday morning throw this stock on the back burner while you tend to chores, and you'll reap the benefits for weeks to come. ■

- 1 (3- to 3½-pound) chicken, cut into 8 pieces, neck and giblets (except liver) reserved
- 4 quarts cold water
- 2 onions, unpeeled, halved
- 2 whole cloves
- 4 garlic cloves, unpeeled
- 1 celery rib, halved
- 2 carrots, halved
- 1 teaspoon salt
- 6 long fresh parsley sprigs
- 8 black peppercorns
- ½ teaspoon dried thyme, crumbled
- 1 Turkish bay leaf or ½ California bay leaf

Put chicken pieces (including neck and giblets) in an 8-quart stockpot, add cold water, and bring to a boil, skimming froth. Add remaining ingredients and simmer, uncovered, skimming froth occasionally, for 3 hours.

Pour stock through a fine-mesh sieve into a large bowl; discard solids. If using stock right away, skim off and discard fat. If not, cool stock completely, uncovered, then refrigerate, covered, until cold. Scrape congealed fat from chilled stock.

COOK'S NOTE

■ The stock can be refrigerated for up to 1 week or frozen for up to 3 months.

VARIATION

■ CHICKEN STOCK WITH GINGER: Add two ¼-inch-thick slices fresh ginger with the other ingredients and proceed as directed above.

Beef Stock

MAKES ABOUT 8 CUPS
ACTIVE TIME: 30 MINUTES ■ START TO FINISH: 6½ HOURS

■ Beef stock is no more difficult to make than chicken stock, and just a small amount of it can be used to great effect in all sorts of dishes. There's no real substitution for it in Onion Soup Gratinée (page 114), which gets tremendous body (and a beautiful sheen) from all the natural gelatin in the beef and veal shanks; the rich, smooth beefy taste is incomparable. Beef stock is often called brown stock, because the bones and vegetables are roasted in a hot oven (spread out in a large pan so they have room to brown all over), which caramelizes the proteins on the surface to add color and flavor. ■

- 2 pounds meaty beef shanks, sawed crosswise into 1-inch slices by the butcher
- 2 pounds meaty veal shanks, sawed crosswise into 1-inch slices by the butcher
- 2 onions, unpeeled, quartered
- 1 carrot, quartered
- 4 fresh parsley sprigs
- 1 fresh thyme sprig
- 1 Turkish bay leaf or ½ California bay leaf
- 4 quarts cold water
- 2 celery ribs, quartered
- 1½ teaspoons salt

SPECIAL EQUIPMENT: cheesecloth; kitchen string

Put a rack in middle of oven and preheat oven to 450°F.

Spread beef shanks, veal shanks, onions, and carrot in a large roasting pan. Roast in oven, turning occasionally, until well browned, about 1 hour.

Meanwhile, wrap parsley, thyme, and bay leaf in cheesecloth and tie into a bundle with string to make a bouquet garni.

With a slotted spoon, transfer meat and vegetables to a 6- to 8-quart stockpot. Set roasting pan across two burners, add 2 cups water to roasting pan, then deglaze by boiling over high heat, stirring and scraping up brown bits, for about 2 minutes. Add liquid to pot, along with remaining 3½ quarts water, celery, salt, and bouquet garni, bring to a boil, and skim froth. Reduce heat and simmer gently, uncovered, skimming froth occasionally, until stock is reduced to about 8 cups, 3 to 5 hours.

Pour stock through a fine-mesh sieve into a bowl, pressing hard on solids; discard solids. If using right away, skim off and discard fat. If not, cool stock completely, uncovered, then refrigerate, covered, until cold. Scrape congealed fat from chilled stock.

COOK'S NOTE

- The stock can be refrigerated for up to 1 week or frozen for up to 3 months.

Veal Stock

MAKES ABOUT 8 CUPS
ACTIVE TIME: 1½ HOURS ■ START TO FINISH: 18 HOURS (INCLUDES CHILLING)

■ Veal stock, one of the great wonders of the culinary world, amplifies other flavors without imposing its own, as chicken and beef stock do. It's loaded with natural gelatin, which gives body and substance—not heaviness—to a sauce, and you need to use only a small amount to make magic. Frozen in ice cube trays and then sealed in a plastic bag, it will keep for months in the freezer. Add a couple of cubes to the pan juices of a roast chicken and the stock will round out the flavor beautifully. This recipe is adapted from that of the writer Michael Ruhlman. It is considered a brown veal stock because the veal bones are browned first; white veal stocks do not include this step. ■

- 5 pounds veal knuckle bones
- 4 quarts plus 1 cup water
- 2 large leeks, cut into 1-inch pieces
- ½ pound carrots, cut into 1-inch pieces
- ½ pound onions, cut into 1-inch pieces
- 2 celery ribs, cut into 1-inch pieces
- 1 tablespoon tomato paste
- 2 fresh thyme sprigs
- 2 large fresh parsley sprigs
- 1 Turkish bay leaf or ½ California bay leaf
- 1½ teaspoons black peppercorns

SPECIAL EQUIPMENT: an instant-read thermometer; a heat diffuser (optional)

Put a rack in middle of oven and preheat oven to 450°F. Oil a large roasting pan.

Arrange veal bones in one layer in oiled roasting pan and roast, turning once or twice, until browned, 30 to 45 minutes.

With tongs, transfer bones to a tall narrow 7- to 8-quart stockpot and add 4 quarts water. (Leave oven on.) Discard fat from roasting pan, then immediately add ½ cup water to hot pan, stirring and scraping up brown bits, and add to stockpot. Bring liquid to a bare simmer (about 190°F on thermometer) and cook slowly (if necessary, use a heat diffuser), skimming froth frequently during first hour, for about 8 hours.

Meanwhile, wash leeks in a bowl of cold water; lift out and drain well. Oil roasting pan again and spread leeks, carrots, onions, and celery in one layer in pan. Roast, stirring once or twice, until vegetables are golden brown, 30 to 35 minutes.

Transfer vegetables to a bowl and immediately add remaining ½ cup water to hot pan, stirring and scraping up brown bits, then add to stockpot. Cool vegetables, then refrigerate, covered.

After stock has cooked for 8 hours, add roasted vegetables and remaining ingredients to stockpot and cook for about 2 hours more.

With tongs, remove bones from stock and discard. Pour stock in batches through a large fine-mesh sieve into a 4-quart saucepan; discard solids. Cool stock, uncovered, then refrigerate, covered, until cold. Scrape congealed fat from chilled stock.

If you have more than 8 cups stock, simmer it, skimming froth, to reduce. If you have less, add water to make 8 cups. If not using stock right away, cool completely, uncovered, then refrigerate, covered.

COOK'S NOTE

- The stock can be refrigerated for up to 1 week or frozen for up to 3 months.

Fish Stock

MAKES ABOUT 6 CUPS
ACTIVE TIME: 15 MINUTES ■ START TO FINISH: 45 MINUTES

■ Of all the stocks, fish stock is the quickest to make. This one, from Melissa Kelly, the chef-owner of Primo, in Rockland, Maine, uses fennel to great effect and is very straightforward. ■

- 2 pounds bones and trimmings of white fish, such as halibut, snapper, flounder, and/or bass, chopped
- 1 large onion, sliced
- 1 medium fennel bulb, stalks trimmed flush with bulb, bulb coarsely chopped
- 24 fresh parsley sprigs
- 1/4 cup fresh lemon juice
- 1 teaspoon salt
- 7 cups cold water
- 1 cup dry white wine

Generously butter bottom and sides of a 4- to 6-quart heavy pot. Put fish bones and trimmings, onion, fennel, parsley sprigs, lemon juice, and salt in buttered pot and cook, covered, over moderate heat for 5 minutes. Add water and wine and bring to a boil, skimming off froth. Reduce heat and simmer, uncovered, for 20 minutes.

Pour stock through a fine-mesh sieve into a large bowl; discard solids. If not using stock right away, cool completely, uncovered, then refrigerate, covered.

COOK'S NOTE

■ The stock can be refrigerated for up to 2 days or frozen for up to 3 months.

Vegetable Stock

MAKES ABOUT 8 CUPS
ACTIVE TIME: 30 MINUTES ■ START TO FINISH: 2 HOURS

■ This stock is very well rounded and full of flavor. Once you've tasted it, you'll realize that the key to making a great vegetable stock is getting the proportions right, so that one vegetable—tomato, pepper, or carrot, for instance—doesn't overpower the others. ■

- 1/2 pound portobello mushrooms, caps and stems cut into 1-inch pieces
- 1 pound shallots, unpeeled, quartered
- 1 pound carrots, cut into 2-inch pieces
- 2 red bell peppers, cored, seeded, and cut into 1-inch pieces
- 6 fresh parsley sprigs
- 5 fresh thyme sprigs
- 4 garlic cloves, coarsely chopped
- 2 tablespoons olive oil
- 1 cup dry white wine
- 2 Turkish bay leaves or 1 California bay leaf
- 1 cup canned crushed tomatoes
- 8 cups water
- 1 teaspoon salt
- Freshly ground black pepper

Put a rack in middle of oven and preheat oven to 425°F.

Toss together mushrooms, shallots, carrots, bell peppers, parsley and thyme sprigs, garlic, and oil in a large roasting pan. Roast vegetables, turning occasionally, until golden, 30 to 40 minutes.

With a slotted spoon, transfer vegetables to a tall narrow 6-quart stockpot. Set roasting pan across two burners, add wine, and deglaze pan by boiling over moderate heat, stirring and scraping up brown bits, for 2 minutes. Transfer wine to stockpot and add bay leaves, tomatoes, and water. Bring to a boil, then reduce heat and simmer, uncovered, stirring occasionally, for 45 minutes.

Pour stock through a large fine-mesh sieve into a large bowl, pressing on solids; discard solids. Stir in salt and pepper to taste. Skim off fat. If not using stock right away, cool completely, uncovered, then refrigerate, covered.

COOK'S NOTE

- The stock can be refrigerated for up to 1 week or frozen for up to 3 months.

Lemon Pepper Seasoning

MAKES ABOUT 1½ TABLESPOONS
ACTIVE TIME: 10 MINUTES ■ START TO FINISH: 10 MINUTES

■ Fresh lemon zest puts this in a different league from store-bought lemon pepper: it's a boon to any home cook. Pat it onto a chicken before roasting or sprinkle it over vegetables after cooking. ■

- 1 lemon
- 1 teaspoon black peppercorns
- 1½ teaspoons coarse sea salt or kosher salt

SPECIAL EQUIPMENT: an electric coffee/spice grinder

Remove zest from lemon in strips with a vegetable peeler and cut away any white pith from strips with a paring knife. Coarsely chop enough zest to measure 1 tablespoon.

Grind zest, peppercorns, and salt in coffee/spice grinder until zest is finely chopped.

COOK'S NOTE

- The lemon pepper keeps, refrigerated in an airtight container, for up to 2 weeks.

Herbes de Provence

MAKES ABOUT ¼ CUP
ACTIVE TIME: 5 MINUTES ■ START TO FINISH: 5 MINUTES

■ Thyme, rosemary, and savory grow wild in the garigue, the low, open scrubland of Provence. Those woody herbs, along with any other herbs that catch the cook's eye, form the basis for this important seasoning, used in chicken, lamb, beef, and tomato dishes. If the bottles or tins of dried herbs in your kitchen cupboard are old, splurge on new ones for this recipe, or the blend will taste stale and musty. Or dry your own herbs by hanging bunches of them upside down in the kitchen. It's a great look, and inspirational too. ■

- 2 tablespoons dried thyme
- 2 teaspoons dried basil
- 2 teaspoons dried summer savory
- 2 teaspoons dried rosemary
- 1 teaspoon dried marjoram
- ½ Turkish bay leaf or ¼ California bay leaf, finely crushed

Crumble thyme, basil, savory, rosemary, and marjoram into a small bowl. Add bay leaf and mix well.

COOK'S NOTE

- The herbes de Provence keep in an airtight container in a cool, dark place for up to 6 months.

Quatre-Épices

Four-Spice Mix

MAKES ABOUT ⅓ CUP
ACTIVE TIME: 10 MINUTES ■ START TO FINISH: 10 MINUTES

■ Thanks to the Romans (and through them, the Greeks) and the Arabs, spices were used very early on in France. A mixture called *épices à foison*, "spices in abundance," in fact, appears in Taillevent's *Le Viandier*, which dates from the late fourteenth century and was the best-known cookbook of its time. Seasoning with spices started to decline in France in the early seventeenth century, but quatre-épices ("four spices") is still used in pâtés, sausages, and sauces. Although French chefs tend to prepare their own, a fairly standard blend consists of white peppercorns, nutmeg, cloves, and dried ginger. ■

3 tablespoons white peppercorns
1 whole nutmeg, coarsely crushed with bottom of a heavy skillet
12 whole cloves
1 tablespoon ground ginger

SPECIAL EQUIPMENT: an electric coffee/spice grinder

Finely grind peppercorns, nutmeg, and cloves in coffee/spice grinder, then shake through a fine-mesh sieve into a bowl. Stir in ginger.

COOK'S NOTE

■ Quatre-épices keeps in an airtight container in a cool, dark place for up to 6 months.

Chinese Five-Spice Powder

MAKES ABOUT ¼ CUP
ACTIVE TIME: 15 MINUTES ■ START TO FINISH: 45 MINUTES

■ There is neither a set formula for the composition of five-spice powder nor a limit to the number of its components, although it usually contains Sichuan peppercorns, star anise, and fennel seeds. The number five has fundamental significance in Chinese culture, and in the kitchen a balance of five flavors—salty, sour, sweet, pungent, and bitter—is beneficial both medicinally and culinarily. Use five-spice powder to flavor braises and meat or poultry that is going to be roasted or grilled. ■

1 tablespoon Sichuan peppercorns (see Glossary) or 1½ teaspoons *sansho* (Japanese pepper)
8 star anise
6 whole cloves
1 (1½-inch) piece cinnamon stick, coarsely crushed
1 tablespoon fennel seeds
1 teaspoon black peppercorns

SPECIAL EQUIPMENT: an electric coffee/spice grinder

Put a rack in middle of oven and preheat oven to 250°F.

Spread Sichuan peppercorns (if using; do not add *sansho* yet), star anise, cloves, cinnamon, and fennel seeds in a small shallow baking pan and toast in oven for 20 minutes. Cool to room temperature.

Add *sansho* (if using) and black peppercorns to spices and grind to a powder in coffee/spice grinder, then shake through a fine-mesh sieve into a bowl.

COOK'S NOTE

■ The Chinese five-spice powder keeps in an airtight container in a cool, dark place for up to 6 months.

Garam Masala

MAKES ABOUT 3 TABLESPOONS
ACTIVE TIME: 10 MINUTES ■ START TO FINISH: 10 MINUTES

■ Garam masala, the classic ground spice blend of northern India, has many interpretations. Although ready-made versions can be found at Indian markets, they sometimes contain fillers and are not fresh, so we encourage you to make your own. The spices below are all available at the supermarket, and you can whirl them in an electric coffee/spice grinder in no time flat. This recipe, from the Indian cooking authority Madhur Jaffrey, makes more than you need for the Indian Baked Rice on page 258, but use what's left over to give everyday meals a boost. It's delicious worked into ground beef for burgers or rubbed onto skinless, boneless chicken breasts. ■

1 tablespoon cardamom seeds (from about 55 green or white pods)
1 (2-inch) piece cinnamon stick, broken into pieces
1 teaspoon cumin seeds
1 teaspoon whole cloves
¾ teaspoon black peppercorns
¼ nutmeg

SPECIAL EQUIPMENT: an electric coffee/spice grinder

Grind all ingredients to a powder in coffee/spice grinder.

COOK'S NOTE

■ The garam masala keeps in an airtight container in a cool, dark place for up to 1 month.

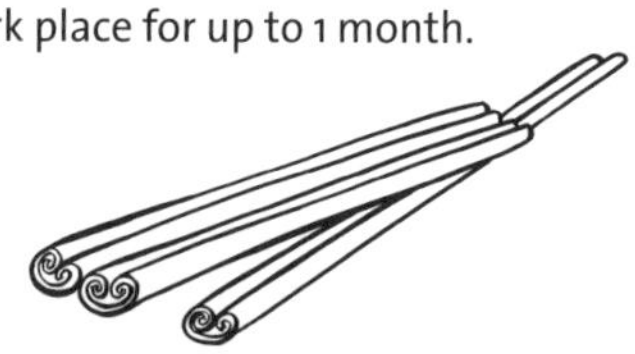

Ras el Hanout

Moroccan Spice Blend

MAKES ABOUT ¼ CUP
ACTIVE TIME: 15 MINUTES ■ START TO FINISH: 15 MINUTES

■ We use this sophisticated spice blend (its Arabic name means "the best the shop has to offer") in the Individual B'stillas on page 374, but it's also great rubbed on chicken, lamb, or beef or stirred into couscous or rice. In Morocco and other parts of North Africa, you might find more exotic versions, which may include ash berries, chufa nuts, grains of paradise, orris root, monk's pepper, cubebs, dried rosebuds, or the potentially toxic belladonna and cantharides (Spanish fly), but our mix of supermarket spices works just fine. ■

- 8 cardamom pods
- 1 teaspoon fennel seeds
- ½ teaspoon anise seeds
- 8 allspice berries
- 8 whole cloves
- 15 black peppercorns
- 1 (3-inch) cinnamon stick, broken in half
- 1 tablespoon sesame seeds
- 1 teaspoon coriander seeds
- ½ teaspoon cumin seeds
- Pinch of red pepper flakes
- Pinch of ground mace
- 1 tablespoon ground ginger
- 1 teaspoon freshly grated nutmeg

SPECIAL EQUIPMENT: an electric coffee/spice grinder

Remove seeds from cardamom pods and discard pods. Combine cardamom seeds, fennel seeds, anise seeds, allspice, cloves, peppercorns, cinnamon stick, sesame seeds, coriander seeds, cumin seeds, and red pepper flakes in coffee/spice grinder and finely grind.

Transfer to a small bowl, add mace, ginger, and nutmeg, and stir until well combined.

COOK'S NOTE

■ The *ras el hanout* keeps in an airtight container in a cool, dark place for up to 6 months.

Spice Paste

MAKES ABOUT ¼ CUP
ACTIVE TIME: 10 MINUTES ■ START TO FINISH: 10 MINUTES

■ This will add a spicy richness to skirt steak, pork tenderloin, or chicken. Rub the meat all over with the paste and marinate it, refrigerated, in a large sealable plastic bag for at least six hours, or up to one day, before grilling. ■

- 3 garlic cloves
- 1½ teaspoons kosher salt
- 1½ teaspoons paprika
- 1½ teaspoons ground cumin
- 1½ teaspoons ground coriander
- 1 teaspoon freshly ground black pepper
- ½ teaspoon ground cinnamon
- Pinch of ground cloves
- 1 tablespoon olive oil

With a large heavy knife, mince garlic and mash to a paste with kosher salt. Stir together spices in a bowl, then stir in mashed garlic and oil until a paste forms.

Jerk Marinade

MAKES ABOUT 1½ CUPS
ACTIVE TIME: 15 MINUTES ■ START TO FINISH: 15 MINUTES

■ True jerk seasoning, a spicy, wet paste of Scotch bonnet chiles, allspice, thyme, garlic, black pepper, onion, nutmeg, and cinnamon, originated in Jamaica, where it's traditionally used on chicken and pork. Happily, it has migrated all over the Caribbean and the United States. The inclusion of soy sauce may seem odd at first glance, but according to Jessica Harris, the Atlantic Rim cooking authority, there is a fair-sized Chinese community in Jamaica with deep roots. If you want more of a calypso kick, ratchet up the chiles. ■

3 scallions, chopped
4 large garlic cloves, chopped
1 small onion, chopped
4–5 Scotch bonnet or habanero chiles (see Glossary), stemmed, halved, and seeded (to taste)
¼ cup fresh lime juice
2 tablespoons soy sauce
3 tablespoons olive oil
1½ tablespoons salt
1 tablespoon packed brown sugar
1 tablespoon loosely packed fresh thyme leaves
2 teaspoons ground allspice
2 teaspoons freshly ground black pepper
¾ teaspoon freshly grated nutmeg
½ teaspoon ground cinnamon

Combine all ingredients in a blender and blend until smooth.

Thai Green Curry Paste

MAKES ABOUT ⅔ CUP
ACTIVE TIME: 25 MINUTES ■ START TO FINISH: 25 MINUTES

■ This staple of the Thai kitchen adds a bright, clear heat to seafood, meat, or poultry. Although good commercial green curry pastes are available, homemade is fresher, and you have control over how hot you want it to be. ■

1 teaspoon cumin seeds
1 teaspoon coriander seeds
1 fresh Thai (see Glossary), serrano, or jalapeño chile, seeded if desired and chopped
1 lemongrass stalk (see Glossary), tough outer leaves discarded, lower 2 inches of stalk thinly sliced
4 large garlic cloves
⅔ cup chopped shallots
1 (1-inch) piece fresh ginger, peeled and chopped
1 teaspoon salt
¾ cup chopped fresh cilantro (including roots if attached)
½ teaspoon Asian shrimp paste (see Sources)
1 tablespoon fresh lime juice

SPECIAL EQUIPMENT: a mortar and pestle or an electric coffee/spice grinder

Toast seeds in a dry small skillet over moderately high heat, stirring, until several shades darker and fragrant, 1 to 2 minutes. Grind toasted seeds to a powder in mortar with pestle or in coffee/spice grinder.

Combine chile, lemongrass, garlic, shallots, ginger, and salt in a food processor and blend until finely chopped. Add ground seeds, cilantro, shrimp paste, and lime juice and blend until a paste forms.

COOK'S NOTES

■ The curry paste keeps, covered and refrigerated, for up to 2 weeks.
■ To make a delicious curry dish, pour 1 teaspoon oil into a wok or skillet, add 2 tablespoons curry paste, and stir over moderately high heat, stirring, until fragrant, about 1 minute. Add one 13- to 14-ounce can unsweetened coconut milk, well stirred, in a slow stream, stirring, and bring to a boil. Add 1 pound shellfish or cut-up meat, poultry, or fish and simmer until cooked through. Serve with cooked rice.

Confit Garlic Cloves

MAKES ABOUT ½ CUP
ACTIVE TIME: 35 MINUTES ■ START TO FINISH: 1½ HOURS (INCLUDES COOLING)

■ These garlic cloves are submerged in olive oil and cooked so slowly that they stay whole but turn soft enough to fall apart when touched. Put on a pizza, they melt into the pie. This confit is also delicious on country bread, mashed potatoes, or blended with mayonnaise for roast beef or pork sandwiches. ■

½ cup peeled garlic cloves (about 24)
About ½ cup olive oil

Put garlic in a small heavy saucepan and add enough oil to cover garlic. Bring just to a simmer, reduce heat, and cook at a bare simmer until garlic is tender, about 25 minutes. Let garlic cool in oil.

COOK'S NOTE

■ The confit garlic keeps, in the oil, for up to 2 weeks, covered and refrigerated.

Roasted Garlic

MAKES ABOUT 3 TABLESPOONS
ACTIVE TIME: 5 MINUTES ■ START TO FINISH: 1¼ HOURS

■ Nothing could be simpler than roasting a head of garlic. It softens and caramelizes until it's surprisingly sweet and spreadable, ready to add dimension to all sorts of things—pot roast, for instance, or slices of crusty bread, as well as the Pissaladière on page 70. ■

1 medium head garlic
1 tablespoon olive oil

Put a rack in middle of oven and preheat oven to 350°F.

Remove papery outer skin from garlic without separating cloves. Put garlic on a sheet of aluminum foil and spoon oil over it, then wrap garlic in foil. Roast until soft, about 1 hour.

Carefully unwrap garlic to cool slightly before squeezing out pulp.

Clarified Butter

■ Sometimes called drawn butter, clarified butter is slowly melted until any water evaporates and the milk solids separate out and sink to the bottom of the pan. Then the froth is skimmed off and the clear (clarified) butter is carefully removed, leaving the solids, which could burn, behind. The beauty of clarified butter is that it has a higher smoke point than regular butter and so can be used to sauté at higher temperatures. For best results, clarify at least one stick of butter at a time. ■

Unsalted butter, cut into 1-inch pieces

Melt butter in a heavy saucepan over low heat. Remove from heat and let stand for 3 minutes.

Skim froth and slowly pour butter into a measuring cup, leaving milky solids in bottom of pan (discard them).

COOK'S NOTES

- A stick (8 tablespoons) of butter will yield 5 to 6 tablespoons clarified butter.
- Clarified butter keeps, refrigerated in an airtight container, for up to 1 month.

TIPS AND TECHNIQUES

GLOSSARY

SOURCES

INDEX

TIPS AND TECHNIQUES

USING SALT AND PEPPER

When we call for salt in our recipes without specifying the kind, we tested the recipes with regular table salt. We don't recommend substituting another kind of salt, such as kosher salt or sea salt, in these instances, because the texture of various salts can differ significantly, and therefore the amounts when measured by volume also differ.

When we call for ground black or white pepper, we mean freshly ground peppercorns from a pepper mill, not ground pepper from a jar. Like other spices, pepper is far more aromatic and flavorful when freshly ground. If you use white pepper frequently, you might want to invest in a second pepper mill.

TO MEASURE LIQUIDS AND FLOUR

Use the appropriate measuring cup for each ingredient: measure liquids in glass or clear plastic liquid-measuring cups and dry ingredients in nesting dry-measuring cups (usually made of metal or plastic) that can be leveled off with a knife.

Spoon flour (don't scoop it) into a dry-measuring cup, letting it mound slightly on top, then level it off with the straight edge of a knife. Don't be tempted to tap or shake the cup to level the flour, because that will increase the amount the cup holds.

Do not sift flour before measuring it unless the recipe tells you to. If sifted flour is called for (as it is in many recipes using cake flour), sift the flour before spooning it into a dry-measuring cup. (Many brands say "presifted" on the label; disregard this.)

CHOOSING AND MEASURING PANS

Measure skillets and baking pans across the top, not across the bottom.

When we call for a baking sheet with sides, we mean an old-fashioned jelly-roll or cookie pan. They range in depth from about 1/2 inch to 1 inch.

Use light-colored metal pans for baking unless otherwise specified. If you use dark metal pans, including nonstick ones, your baked goods will probably brown more and the cooking times may be shorter.

TO TOAST NUTS

Spread nuts out in a baking sheet with sides and toast them in the middle of a preheated 350°F oven until they are golden and aromatic, 5 to 10 minutes. If the nuts are dark to begin with, like almonds with skins and hazelnuts, you may need to cut one open to check the interior color.

Recipes using hazelnuts often specify rubbing off any loose skins after toasting. To do this, wrap the nuts while they are still hot in a clean kitchen towel and rub them together to flake off the papery brown skins. Patches of skin often remain on the nuts, and that is not a problem. Occasionally we've even encountered hazelnuts that won't part with any of their skin, no matter how much they are rubbed.

TO TOAST SEEDS

You can toast most seeds either in a dry heavy skillet or on a baking sheet in a preheated 350°F oven. One exception to the rule is sunflower seeds: they are best when toasted in the oven. Some seeds, such as mustard seeds, pop when cooked on top of the stove, so it is best to toast them in a skillet with a pan lid to cover it if necessary. Be sure to shake the skillet to keep the seeds moving.

TO TOAST COCONUT

Spread the flaked coconut evenly in a baking sheet with sides and toast it in the middle of a preheated 350°F oven, stirring occasionally, until golden, 10 to 12 minutes. Cool it in the pan on a rack, stirring occasionally.

TO TOAST SPICES

Toast spices (these will usually be whole) in a dry heavy skillet over moderate heat, stirring, until they are fragrant and a shade or two darker, no more than a few minutes.

TO MAKE FRESH BREAD CRUMBS

Tear bread into 1-inch pieces. Pulse them in a food processor until they are coarsely chopped, for coarse crumbs, or finely ground, for fine crumbs. Because brands of bread vary, it's difficult to give exact equivalents. Use the following approximate yields as a guide.

- To get 1 cup of coarse crumbs, use 2 slices of firm white sandwich bread or a 4-inch-long piece of baguette (with any tough bottom crust removed).
- To get 1 cup of fine crumbs, use about 3 slices of firm white sandwich bread or a 5-inch-long piece of baguette (with any tough bottom crust removed).

You will probably have leftovers, which freeze beautifully. For example, one slice of Pepperidge Farm sandwich bread will yield a scant half cup of fine crumbs, so we suggest you use two slices; that way, you will get a full half cup of crumbs with some left over.

TO MAKE DRIED BREAD CRUMBS

Spread fresh crumbs in a baking sheet with sides and bake them in the middle of a preheated 250°F oven, stirring once, until they are dry and very pale golden, about 10 minutes for fine crumbs or 15 minutes for coarse crumbs. Cool the crumbs in the pan on a rack.

- To get 1 cup of dried coarse crumbs, use 1¼ cups of fresh coarse crumbs.
- To get 1 cup of dried fine crumbs, use 1⅓ cups of fine fresh crumbs.

TO GRATE CHEESE

The volume measure (cups) of grated cheeses can differ depending on a number of variables, including the kind of cheese and its temperature, the choice of grater, and the way the cheese is put into the measuring cup (loosely or firmly). Weight is a more precise measure, but since many people do not have kitchen scales, we usually give just the cup measure. For measures of 1 cup or more, we give the weight as well, to provide you with a guide to how much you'll need to buy for these larger volumes. For the recipes in this book, assume, unless we tell you otherwise, that the cheese is cold from the refrigerator (since room-temperature cheese, being slightly softer, packs down more in the cup).

To coarsely grate firm cheeses such as Cheddar and Gruyère, use the large (1/4-inch) teardrop-shaped holes of a box or other handheld grater, then loosely pack the cheese in dry-measuring cups. The shredding disk of a food processor produces thicker shreds of cheese and can give you a slightly different cup–weight ratio, as can purchased pregrated cheese.

To finely grate Parmigiano-Reggiano and similar cheeses, use the small (1/8-inch) teardrop-shaped holes (not the ragged-edged holes) of a box or other handheld grater, such as a rotary grater, unless otherwise specified in the recipe. Be aware that graters with different-shaped holes, the Microplane rasp, and pregrated cheese result in significantly different volumes.

TO PREPARE PRODUCE

Wash and dry all produce before you use it. Before chopping herbs, remove the leaves or fronds from the stems; the exception is cilantro, which has tender stems.

To wash greens, submerge them in a large bowl or a sink full of cold water and agitate them with your hands to loosen any dirt. Lift them from the water and transfer them to a salad spinner. If a noticeable amount of dirt is visible in the wash water, wash the greens again in clean water (spinach, arugula, and basil often need two or three washings). When spinning greens dry in a salad spinner, spin them several times, stopping to pour off the collected water occasionally and redistribute the greens in the basket. Alternatively, you can drain the washed greens well in a colander and then pat them dry with a kitchen towel.

TO PEEL FRESH TOMATOES OR PEACHES

Using a very sharp paring knife and being careful not to cut deeply into the flesh, cut an X through the skin in the bottom of each tomato or peach. Have a large pot of boiling water and a bowl of ice and cold water ready. Working in batches of 2 or 3, lower the tomatoes or peaches one by one into the boiling water with a slotted spoon, or carefully drop them in. Keep them immersed in the boiling water for 10 seconds, then transfer them to the ice water with the slotted spoon. (Barely ripe or out-of-season tomatoes or peaches will take 15 to 20 seconds.) When they are cool enough to handle, pull or slip off the skins, beginning at the X, using the paring knife to remove any stubborn spots.

TO SEED TOMATOES

Cut each tomato horizontally in half, then squeeze the halves gently, cut sides down, to extract the seeds.

TO HANDLE CHILES

Wear protective gloves when handling chiles, and avoid touching your face, particularly your eyes.

TO ROAST AND PEEL BELL PEPPERS OR POBLANO CHILES

If you are using a gas stove, lay the bell peppers or chiles on their sides on the burner grates and turn the flames on high. Char the peppers or chiles, turning them with tongs, until the skins are blackened on all sides, 3 to 8 minutes.

If you are using a (preheated) broiler, put the peppers or chiles on the rack of the broiler pan and broil about 2 inches from the heat, turning them frequently, until the skins are blistered and charred, about 5 minutes for chiles and about 15 minutes for bell peppers.

Transfer the roasted peppers or chiles to a bowl, cover it, and let them stand until they are cool enough to handle. Peel them, then cut off the stems and remove and discard the seeds and ribs.

TO ZEST CITRUS FRUITS

Remove the colored part of the rind only; avoid the bitter white pith. For strips, use a vegetable peeler; we prefer the swivel-bladed kind. Peelers vary in how deeply they cut, so some strips may include some white pith. If so, turn each strip over and trim away any pith with a small sharp knife. For grated zest, we prefer to use the rasplike Microplane zester, which results in fluffier zest—so if you use one, pack the zest to measure it.

TO SALT WATER FOR COOKING

When salting water for cooking, use 1 tablespoon of table salt for every 4 quarts of water.

TO PREPARE A WATER BATH FOR BAKING

Put your filled pan in a larger pan and add enough boiling water to the larger pan to reach halfway up the sides of the smaller pan. When using large shallow pans, you'll find it easier to add the hot water once the pans are in the oven.

GLOSSARY

For information about obtaining the following ingredients, see Sources.

ACHIOTE ("ah-chee-*o*-teh")—Also called annatto, bright brick-red achiote, harvested from a tropical shrub, lends a subtle, earthy flavor and aroma to many South American dishes. It has been used as a dye and a natural food coloring for centuries. The seeds are sold whole, crushed, or in a paste. Avoid dull brown seeds; they are too old. Keep achiote in a cool, dry, dark place.

ALEPPO CHILE PEPPER FLAKES—These dried flakes of a Syrian chile, which are often called simply Aleppo pepper, are relatively mild compared to regular red pepper flakes but give depth and a fruity sweetness to many Middle Eastern dishes. **Maras** or **Urfa pepper flakes** are a good alternative.

ANAHEIM/NEW MEXICO CHILES—Although the characteristics of these two fresh chiles differ slightly, they come from the same botanical parent and can be used interchangeably in recipes. Both are fairly mild and six to eight inches long. They are used in both their green and red states (the latter is a little sweeter). Dried and crushed New Mexico chiles are called *chile caribe.* New Mexicos are grown extensively in northern Mexico, New Mexico, and Arizona; Anaheims are grown in California.

ANCHO CHILE—The dried form of the poblano chile, this is the most commonly used chile in Mexico. Its name means "wide" or "broad," which describes its shoulders. Brick red to dark mahogany in color, it is wrinkled and medium-hot to hot, with a complex, sweet, raisiny flavor. Look for anchos that are pliable and aromatic.

AREPA FLOUR ("ah-*reh*-pa")—*Arepa* flour is made from corn (usually white but sometimes yellow) that has been dried, cracked, precooked with steam, pressed into flakes, then ground. It's used extensively in Venezuela and Colombia for the round corn cakes called *arepas.* Unlike Mexican *masa,* it is not treated with mineral lime, and it has a more neutral, less earthy flavor. One common brand is Masarepa Blanca. Store *arepa* flour in double sealable plastic bags in the refrigerator.

ASAFETIDA ("as-a-feh-*tee*-dah")—Like Asian fish sauce, shrimp paste, and anchovies, asafetida gives balance and depth to a dish when used judiciously. This extremely stinky spice, used mostly in India, comes from the dried gum resin of giant fennel plants. (It's also said to be one of the secret ingredients in Worcestershire sauce.) Asafetida is sold as both a finely ground powder and a resinous lump, but we prefer to use the powder because it's easier to deal with. (If you use a lump, break off tiny chunks and grind it.) Keep both forms of asafetida in a sealed airtight container in a cool, dry, dark place or in the freezer. There is no substitute for this herb; if you can't find it, leave it out. The dish won't taste as balanced, but it will still be delicious.

ASIAN CHILI PASTE—Lots of different Asian chili pastes are available; they vary in thickness, but they are all hot, so use them sparingly. Luckily, they keep forever, stored in their jars in the refrigerator. Some pastes come in cans; if that's what you can find, transfer the paste to a small jar and refrigerate it.

ASIAN CHILI SAUCE—The seasonings in this sauce—a blend of chiles, vinegar, salt, and sugar that might also include tomato, dried shrimp, garlic, and/or ginger—depend on the country of origin and range from mildly to very hot and from thin to thick. In general, Southeast Asian chili sauces are sweeter and more garlicky than Chinese and Korean ones. A good all-purpose chili sauce is Sriracha, named for the town in southern Thailand where it was first produced. It is hot but not as hot as ***sambal oelek***. Sriracha often comes in a handy squirt bottle; store it and other chili sauces in the refrigerator next to the Tabasco, where they will keep indefinitely.

BLACK MUSTARD SEEDS—*See* **mustard seeds.**

BLACK SESAME SEEDS—Unlike white sesame seeds, which are used in all sorts of dishes throughout Asia and the Middle East, black sesame seeds tend to be reserved for garnishes and coatings in Chinese and Japanese cooking. They look a little like **nigella seeds** (which are sometimes mislabeled "black sesame seeds"), so taste them: they should have the characteristic mild, nutty flavor of sesame. Black sesame seeds can be kept in a cool, dry, dark place or the freezer for about six months.

BONITO FLAKES (*katsuobushi*)—Paper-thin shavings of dried bonito (a fish related to mackerel and tuna) have been used as a smoky-salty seasoning in Japan since the fifteenth century. Along with kelp, dried bonito is an integral component of *dashi*, the simple sea stock that is the basis of many Japanese dishes. Dried bonito flakes come in cellophane packages. Stored in an airtight container in a cool, dry, dark place, they will keep almost indefinitely.

BROWN MUSTARD SEEDS—*See* **mustard seeds.**

BUCKWHEAT FLOUR—This flour, which contains no gluten, is milled from the triangular seeds of the buckwheat plant, which is not a true cereal grain but is related to sorrel and rhubarb. It is used to make the little Russian pancakes called blini, as well as crêpes in France, noodles in Japan and Korea, and the Italian noodles called *pizzoccheri,* a specialty of Lombardy. Stored in double sealable plastic bags in the refrigerator or freezer, it will keep almost indefinitely.

CALABAZA—This large tan or greenish pumpkin, sometimes called Caribbean or West Indian pumpkin or Cuban squash, is usually sold cut into pieces so you can see the flesh. Look for a fine-grained texture and golden to deep orange flesh. The flavor is mild and sweet. Butternut squash is an able stand-in.

CHANA DAL—A variety of dried small Indian chickpeas also known as Bengal gram beans, *chana dal* are always sold hulled and split. The beans look more like yellow split peas than what we think of as chickpeas (garbanzos). Carefully pick over and wash the *chana dal* before cooking. Soaking isn't necessary.

CHAYOTE ("chai-*oh*-teh")—Also called *mirliton* (in Louisiana) or *christophene* (in the Caribbean), chayote is a member of the enormous gourd/squash family. It has crisp, mild flesh like that of a cucumber or very firm squash and is about the size and shape of a pear. Chayote is usually cooked, although it can be eaten raw in salads. It is sometimes peeled before it is used.

CHILE DE ÁRBOL—This small, reddish orange dried Mexican chile is descriptively named for the "treelike" plant on which it grows. Closely related to the cayenne chile, it has a searing, very straightforward heat.

CHINESE FERMENTED BLACK BEANS—Not the turtle beans you see in black bean soup or burritos, these are black soybeans that have been steamed, then fermented with salt and spices, especially ginger. They come in plastic packages; after opening, transfer them to a tightly sealed jar or double sealable plastic bags (they are very pungent) and store them in a cool, dry, dark place or the freezer. They'll keep almost indefinitely.

CHINESE HOT BEAN SAUCE—Sometimes labeled "hot bean paste," this seasoning is made from fermented soybeans (one of the oldest flavorings in China) and hot chiles. Two brands that we like are Lee Kum Kee and Koon Chun, both from Hong Kong. Stored in the refrigerator after opening, a jar of hot bean sauce will keep indefinitely.

CHINESE RICE WINE—Made from fermented glutinous rice, millet, and yeast, this alcoholic beverage is usually aged for ten years or more and is used for drinking as well as for marinades and sauces. Shaoxing is China's most renowned rice wine; it's been made for more than two thousand years. Chinese rice wine is drier than the Japanese rice wine called **sake**, which can be substituted in many recipes. Medium-dry sherry and Scotch are other good substitutes.

CHIPOTLE CHILE—When cherry-red ripe jalapeños are smoked and dried, they are called chipotles ("chi-*pote*-lehs"); the name comes from the Aztec *chilli poctli,* meaning "smoked chile." Their ripeness in their former incarnation helps explain the sweetness underneath the savor, and the smokiness partially obscures their heat. They are sold dried as well as canned in a tomato-based sauce called adobo, which takes the flavor in a different, more piquant direction. After using part of a can of chipotles in adobo, transfer the remaining portion to a glass jar and store it in the refrigerator. It keeps almost indefinitely.

CHORIZO—*See* **Mexican chorizo, Spanish chorizo,** and **chouriço.**

CHOURIÇO—The Portuguese version of **Spanish chorizo.**

COTIJA ("co-*tee*-hah")—Sometimes called *queso anejado* ("aged cheese"), this firm white cow's milk cheese from Mexico and elsewhere in Latin America has a lovely acidity and pungency. It's crumbled over salads, soups, stews, and tacos. Feta, another white cheese that crumbles nicely, is a good substitute. *Cotija* keeps in the refrigerator for about two weeks.

CREMA—This tangy cultured cream from Mexico and Central America can be thin or almost as thick as crème fraîche, which is usually a good substitute.

CURRY LEAVES—Spicy and citrusy, these dark green, aromatic fresh leaves (often sold on the stem) from a small deciduous tree are widely used in the cooking of southern India. Sealed in a plastic bag, they will keep for about two weeks in the refrigerator or about a month in the freezer. Dried leaves can sometimes be found in ethnic markets, but they are nothing like their fresh counterpart.

DRIED BONITO FLAKES—*See* **bonito flakes.**

EDAMAME ("ed-ah-*mah*-may")—A Japanese treat, edamame are young, tender green soybeans that are boiled and often eaten straight from the pod. Both frozen edamame in the pod and frozen shelled edamame are now widely available.

FLEUR DE SEL—The most famous sea salt from France's Brittany region, *fleur de sel* adds not just flavor but a spiky crunch to food. As opposed to *sel gris*, which acquires its distinctive color when salt crystals sink to the gray earth at the bottom of the salt ponds, *fleur de sel* consists of lightweight white crystals that float to the ponds' surface and are skimmed off. Because of its relative scarcity, *fleur de sel* is expensive, but a little goes a long way: it's generally reserved for seasoning a finished dish.

GALANGAL—This rhizome, cultivated throughout Southeast Asia, Indonesia, and India, resembles ginger but is thicker and pinkish near the base. Its flavor is like that of young ("spring") ginger, but it is more piquant, with notes of pepper and cardamom, and it is more fragrant. Galangal is sold fresh or frozen; it's also available dried (in slices), but we don't recommend using the dried. If that's all you can find, simply leave it out of the recipe. Fresh galangal can be kept in a sealable plastic bag in the refrigerator for about two weeks and can be frozen for up to three months.

GUAJILLO CHILE ("gwa-*hee*-yo")—This shiny, burgundy-colored dried chile has mild to medium heat and a flavor that is rather direct, tart, and just a bit smoky. Elongated and tapering to a point, it is sold in a variety of sizes but is usually four to six inches long and an inch to an inch and a half across.

GYOZA SKINS—These round wrappers (sold fresh or frozen) are used for the Japanese dumplings called gyoza. Made from a wheat dough similar to that used for wonton wrappers, they are an adaptation from Chinese cuisine. Whereas Chinese dumplings are usually steamed or boiled, gyoza are panfried, then steamed. Thaw the skins, still wrapped in plastic, in the refrigerator.

HABANERO CHILE—One of the hottest commercially available chiles in the world, the habanero is a short, fat, lantern-shaped pepper with a floral flavor and an intense nasal heat. It is related to the **Scotch bonnet chile** but is slightly bigger. Habaneros may be pale or dark green, yellow, or red-orange.

HARISSA—This searingly hot chili sauce is common to North Africa, especially Tunisia. It's used both in cooking and as a condiment. An opened jar keeps in the refrigerator almost indefinitely.

JUNIPER BERRIES—Juniper, with its refreshing woodsy fragrance, has long been used to flavor gin. The dried berries are also used in marinades and brines and have a great affinity for venison and other game, as well as pork.

KAFFIR LIME LEAVES—These glossy, bright green leaves (sometimes called *bai makroot*) give many Southeast Asian dishes a distinctive citrus tang and floral aroma. Fresh leaves are becoming more readily available, since they are now grown in Florida and California. They keep for about a week refrigerated in a plastic bag and for months frozen. The leaves are also available dried, but we don't recommend buying them; they will not deliver the fragrance and flavor of fresh or frozen leaves, and they can't be thinly sliced.

KONBU—Also called kombu, this dried kelp is an essential ingredient of the subtle Japanese sea stock called *dashi*. Dark olive green in color, it is two and a half to twelve inches in width and can be several yards long. Dried sheets are cut and folded into cellophane packages. Don't wash off the white salt residue that coats konbu; simply wipe it lightly with a damp cloth or paper towel before using. As with any dried product, humidity is detrimental; keep konbu tightly wrapped in plastic or in an airtight container in a cool, dry, dark place, where it will last for about a year.

LACINATO KALE—This dark leafy green is also known as *cavolo nero* ("black cabbage"), Tuscan kale, dinosaur kale, black kale, or flat black cabbage. The flavor is rich, sweet, and almost meaty. Regular kale can be substituted.

LEMONGRASS—A dramatic tropical grass with long, blade-shaped leaves, lemongrass gives a clean lemon aroma and flavor to the cuisines of Southeast Asia. Only the lower six inches or so of the interior stalk are used; before slicing it, remove two or three of the dry, fibrous outer layers (use them, along with the tops, for making tea or stock). Lemongrass is generally used fresh (sliced paper-thin) or chopped fine and pounded into pastes. Avoid dried lemongrass. The herb keeps, wrapped in plastic, in the refrigerator for two weeks; frozen, it keeps for several months.

LENTILLES DU PUY (French green lentils)—These small green lentils from Le Puy, France, are prized for their delicate flavor. They also hold their shape better than other varieties do. Regular lentils can be substituted for French green lentils, though the outcome won't have the same finesse.

MARAS PEPPER FLAKES—These mildly hot, brightly flavored pepper flakes are an essential pantry item for cooks in Turkey and the Middle East. **Urfa pepper flakes** can be substituted.

MERGUEZ—When Algeria became a French colony in the 1800s, these small, spicy, coarsely ground, crumbly lamb or beef sausages (which are commonly available fresh and only rarely seen dried) made their way back to France and on to Spain and Portugal. Now they appear in the cuisines of those European countries as well as in the cooking of North Africa. Hot Italian sausage can be substituted.

MEXICAN CHORIZO—Unlike **Spanish chorizo**, which is a cured sausage, this fresh pork sausage must be cooked before it is eaten. Crumbly and rich with chiles, it is not generally a good substitute for the Spanish variety.

MEXICAN OREGANO—Not a true oregano at all, this plant is actually related to lemon verbena. However, the leaves taste like common oregano and lack the bitterness so often found in that herb. Mexican oregano is most commonly sold dried but is becoming more widely available fresh.

MIRIN—This syrupy, golden Japanese cooking wine, made from glutinous rice, adds sweetness and flavor to many Japanese dishes. Look for *hon-mirin* (naturally brewed) rather than *aji-mirin*, which contains additives such as corn syrup and salt. Kept in a cool, dry, dark place, it lasts for months.

MISO—The fermented soybean pastes called *miso* are a protein-rich staple of Japanese and Korean kitchens, used in dressings, soups, sauces, marinades, and grilled foods. Miso comes in various strengths and colors. White miso (*shiro miso*), which is actually pale yellow or golden, is the mellowest; yellow miso (*shinshu miso*), which ranges from pale yellow to yellowish brown, is the most versatile; the darkest, headiest miso (*hatcho miso*), which looks like chocolate fudge, is pungent and almost meaty in flavor. The lighter-flavored misos are all-purpose. Use strongly flavored misos only when they are specifically called for. Miso keeps in the refrigerator for several weeks.

MUSTARD SEEDS—There are three common types of mustard seeds: black, brown, and yellow. The colors refer to the hulls; inside, all three are pale yellow. Black seeds are the hottest; yellow, the mildest. True black seeds are difficult to find; brown seeds, more suitable for high-yield harvesting, are often labeled "black." Mustard seeds should be kept in a cool, dry, dark place or in the freezer.

NEW MEXICO CHILES—*See* **Anaheim chiles.**

NIGELLA SEEDS—Often mistaken for (and incorrectly labeled as) onion seeds or black sesame seeds, these peppery black seeds are from *Nigella sativa*, a near relative of the garden plant called love-in-a-mist. They are an important seasoning in India (where they are called *kalonji*), Turkey, Russia, and the Middle East. Keep nigella seeds in a cool, dry, dark place or in the freezer.

NORI—Sometimes called laver (Latin for "water plant"), nori is a dried seaweed that is used to wrap sushi and is crumbled or shredded for garnish. It comes in cellophane packages of large flat sheets, strips, or broken-up pieces. Nori should always be toasted until crisp before you use it; otherwise, it is tough and flavorless. Many brands now come already toasted and are labeled as such. Tightly wrapped and stored in a cool, dry, dark place, nori lasts almost indefinitely.

PASILLA CHILE ("pah-*see*-yah")—*Pasilla* means "little raisin" in Spanish, a reference to the dark brown color and wrinkled texture of this dried chile. About five or six inches long and three quarters of an inch to an inch and a half across, it is medium-hot to hot and has a deep, complex flavor.

PICKLED GINGER—Paper-thin, translucent slices of peeled ginger that are pickled in salt, sugar, and vinegar are used primarily as a condiment for sushi. They range in color from beige to delicate pink. Pickled ginger comes in small glass jars, plastic containers found in the refrigerated case, or in vacuum-packed packages on the shelf in Japanese markets. Do not confuse it with the bright red slivered ginger called *kizami shoga* or *beni shoga*, which is a salty, pungent pickled ginger. Kept in the refrigerator, pickled ginger lasts almost indefinitely.

POBLANO CHILE—Medium-hot to hot, the poblano is thick-fleshed, with wide shoulders tapering to a point. Those commonly found in the market are dark green with a purplish black tinge and four to five inches long. When dried, the poblano is known as an **ancho chile**.

POMEGRANATE MOLASSES—This thick, dark syrup made from pomegranate juice carries a concentrated boost of fruity tart flavor. It is often used in Middle Eastern cuisines. It keeps indefinitely in a cool, dry, dark place.

PORCINI—Known most commonly by their Italian name, these thick-capped, meaty mushrooms are also called by their French name, *cèpes*. They are usually bought dried, in cellophane packages. (Reconstitute them by soaking them in hot water.) Cultivated fresh porcini are starting to appear in markets, especially during fall and winter.

QUESO FRESCO ("*keh*-so *fres*-co")—Mild and salty, this crumbly fresh cow's milk cheese from Mexico and elsewhere in Latin America is similar to **ricotta salata** (which can be substituted), not creamy like young goat cheese or briny like feta. Because it's relatively low in fat, it doesn't melt; it softens into a dish, imparting a gentle richness. The terms *queso fresco* and *queso blanco* are often used interchangeably; almost every country in Latin America has a different name for the cheese, depending on how mature (firm) it is. *Queso fresco* keeps in the refrigerator for about one week.

RICE STICK NOODLES—The most widely available rice-flour noodles, these thin off-white noodles are usually sold dried and turn a brighter white when cooked. Despite the name, they are not stick-straight but are generally gathered together into wide, wiry skeins. Rice sticks are usually softened in water before use. Another kind of dried rice stick noodle is flat and about the width of fettuccine but much longer. This shape is most often used in Thai and other Southeast Asian cuisines. Soften the noodles in water before you use them.

RICE VINEGAR—Many specialized Asian rice vinegars are available in Asian markets, but when we call for rice vinegar in our recipes, we mean the white kind found in supermarkets. You'll often find it labeled "seasoned" (meaning that it contains salt and sugar; it is often used to season sushi rice) or not (meaning that it contains no additives).

RICOTTA SALATA—Like traditional feta, this salty Sicilian cheese is made from sheep's milk, but it is milder and nuttier. Smooth and soft, it is aged for a minimum of three months. It keeps for up to three weeks in the refrigerator.

SAKE ("sah-keh")—This colorless alcoholic beverage is used frequently in Japanese cooking as well as for drinking. Sake is commonly referred to as rice wine because it is fermented from rice, a grain, but it's technically closer to beer. It is not carbonated, though, and it does taste more like wine. It is generally a little higher in alcohol content than wine is.

SAKE KASU ("sah-keh kah-soo")—The lees (solids) that remain after sake is made from fermented rice mash make up *sake kasu.* They are pressed into sheets and used in fish marinades, where they act as both a preservative and a heady flavoring agent. *Sake kasu* is whitish in color, with a consistency like that of Play-Doh. It comes in a thick flat sheet in a cellophane package and keeps in the refrigerator for six months.

SALT COD—Packed in salt and dried to preserve it, salt cod is usually sold in plastic bags or wooden boxes. Buy it in plastic bags if you can; it's helpful to see what you're getting. The whiter the cod, the better the quality. Look for thick pieces that feel firm yet give slightly when squeezed. Before you cook the fish, you must soak it in water for a day or more to rehydrate it and remove most of its salt. The amount of salt can vary greatly—a light film or coating is fine, but if there is too much, the fish will take several days to rehydrate.

SAMBAL OELEK—This Indonesian chili sauce, used throughout Southeast Asia as a condiment, is coarse, since it includes the seeds from the chiles, yet thin in consistency. Red to orange and very hot, it comes in a jar and keeps indefinitely in the refrigerator. If you can't find *sambal oelek,* any other nonsweet Asian chili sauce will work.

SANSHO—This ground spice is also known as Japanese pepper, although it is not a true peppercorn at all but instead related to **Sichuan peppercorns.** Both are the seedpods of varieties of the prickly ash.

SCOTCH BONNET CHILE—Like its close relative the **habanero,** the Scotch bonnet is one of the hottest chiles in the world. It looks like the **habanero** but is slightly smaller. It has a floral, somewhat smoky flavor, and it may be pale yellow-green, orange, or red.

SHISO LEAVES—Also called perilla, this aromatic herb with serrated, rounded leaves is a member of the mint family. Fresh green *shiso* leaves are used primarily as a garnish, either whole or chopped, or are incorporated, chopped, into sushi. Red or purple *shiso,* a variant of the same species, is used mostly for making pickled plums and in some confections. The leaves wilt quickly, so wrap them in a damp paper towel, keep them refrigerated, and use them within a day or so.

SICHUAN PEPPERCORNS—Unrelated to black and white peppercorns, this aromatic, tongue-tingling spice, which comes from south-central China, is made from the dried pods of the prickly ash, although inferior brands will include the seeds too. It is different from the "Szechwan seasoning" or "Szechwan-style pepper blend" (neither of which contains Sichuan peppercorns) sometimes found in supermarket spice racks. Until recently banned from import by the U.S. Department of Agriculture because of the small chance that they may carry a canker destructive to citrus trees, Sichuan peppercorns are hard to find but can sometimes be seen in Chinese markets. As of this writing, the federal government has revised the ban to allow Sichuan peppercorns that have been heat-treated (at a temperature of 140°F for at least ten minutes) into the United States. Until heat-treated Sichuan peppercorns are more widely available, we suggest substituting a blend of ***sansho*** and black peppercorns.

Spanish chorizo—This famous, rust-red cured Spanish sausage is made from pork, garlic, and a generous quantity of Spanish smoked paprika. Do not substitute **Mexican chorizo,** which is a fresh pork sausage. Spanish chorizo keeps for up to six months at room temperature (scrape off any mold that forms) or in the refrigerator.

Spanish smoked paprika (*pimentón de la Véra*)—In the remote Extremadura region of Spain, deep-flavored paprika chiles aren't dried in the sun, as they are in Hungary, but roasted over smoldering oak fires before being ground to a velvety powder. We like La Chinata brand, which comes in three strengths: sweet, bittersweet, and hot.

sumac—A Middle Eastern spice, sumac comes from the tart berries of the Silician, or elm-leafed, sumac tree. The berries are dried and ground to a purplish red powder.

sushi rice—In Japan, the term *sushi rice* means cooked rice that has been seasoned with vinegar, sugar, and salt and is ready for use in a sushi preparation. In the United States, the term generally applies to the raw rice, which is usually labeled as such. True Japanese varieties are not imported to this country, but good Japanese-style rice is grown here.

tamarind—Tamarind's complex fruity-sour taste has made it a staple in the cuisines of India, Southeast Asia, the Caribbean, and Latin America, where it is used as an acid, much as we use lemon or lime. The pulp found in the long reddish brown seedpods comes in several forms; most common are the pliable pressed blocks of pulp and the smooth, jellylike concentrate that comes in a jar. Tamarind trees, which reach a height of nearly eighty feet, are indigenous to eastern Africa but grow in tropical climates all over the world. To use a block of tamarind pulp, break off a chunk, soften it in some warm water (work it with your fingers to loosen it), and force it through a sieve. Discard the fibers and seeds and use the collected brown liquid or purée. Once you have opened tamarind blocks, double-bag them in sealable plastic bags and store in a cool, dry, dark place; keep the concentrate in the refrigerator.

THAI CHILES—There are many varieties of fresh Thai chiles, but the one most often seen in the United States is the small (one-half- to one-inch-long) hot "bird pepper," or *prik khee nu* (which means "mouse-dropping chile"). Green, or unripe, chiles are generally sharper in flavor than red ones. Bird peppers are often sold dried here; fresh ones are becoming more widely available.

THAI CURRY PASTE—Pungent, complex Southeast Asian curry pastes are categorized by color as well as heat. The two we use most often are red curry pastes, which are highly versatile, and green curry pastes, which are more herbal in flavor, generally hotter, and more specialized. Store-bought curry pastes come in jars, plastic tubs, or cans. After opening, keep them either in the freezer (remove them from their jars or cans and put them in plastic containers) or in the refrigerator (a thin film of vegetable oil will make them last longer; pour off the oil before you use the paste). Refrigerated, curry pastes keep almost indefinitely.

TOMATILLOS—These tart fruits, native to Mexico and Guatemala, are sometimes referred to as Mexican green tomatoes, but they are only distantly related to backyard beefsteaks. When fresh, tomatillos are enclosed in a papery husk; pull it off before you use the fruit and rinse the tomatillo under warm water if it's sticky. Husked whole tomatillos are also available canned.

URAD DAL—Commonly called black lentils but more closely related to mung beans, these are also known as *urd,* or black gram beans. You'll see these dried beans in the market in three forms: whole (about the size of a BB), with black skins; split, with their skins; and split, without their skins, when they are ivory in color.

URFA PEPPER FLAKES—Like **Maras pepper flakes,** these warm, darkly sweet pepper flakes are essential to many Middle Eastern dishes. One can be substituted for the other.

WAKAME ("wah-*kah*-meh")—This mild, deep green, leafy seaweed, common to Japanese waters, turns up in many Japanese dishes—miso soup, for instance. It is sold dried and must be soaked before you use it. It is most commonly found in plastic or paper packages. Kept tightly wrapped in plastic or in an airtight container in a cool, dry, dark place, it lasts for about a year.

WASABI ("wah-*sah*-bee")—This pungent green rhizome is often called Japanese horseradish, but it is not related to true horseradish. Most of what's sold in this country is ground western horseradish with or without ground mustard and sometimes a bit of true wasabi. It comes in either powder or paste form. Wasabi powder is mixed with water much as dry mustard is; let it sit for about ten minutes to allow the flavor to bloom. True wasabi is slowly becoming available; it is slightly sweeter and more herbal than our "wasabi."

WHITE MISO—*See* **miso.**

WHITE TRUFFLE OIL, WHITE TRUFFLE PASTE—Because fresh truffles are costly and can be disappointing in flavor, we sometimes turn to truffle paste or truffle oil for consistency's sake. These are usually bolstered by synthesized chemical flavor essence. Both are highly concentrated, so use just the tiniest amount. The paste, once opened, should be kept in the refrigerator; check the expiration date on the box. Store the oil in the refrigerator, like other oils you use infrequently.

SOURCES

To contact specific sources, see the directory on page 963. Items are listed alphabetically by key word.

Ingredients and Cooking Supplies

ACHIOTE (annatto seeds)—Latino markets, the spice section of some supermarkets, and Kitchen/Market

ALEPPO CHILE PEPPER FLAKES—*See* **chiles**

ALMOND PASTE
canned—Specialty foods shops, some supermarkets, and Sweet Celebrations
in tubes—Most supermarkets (Odense brand)
Be sure to buy almond paste, not marzipan, which is too sweet.

AMARETTI (Italian almond macaroons)—Italian markets, specialty foods shops, upscale supermarkets, and Formaggio Kitchen

ANCHOVY FILLETS, SWEDISH FLAT—Scandinavian and some other specialty foods shops and Scandia Food & Gifts

ANDOUILLE SAUSAGE—*See* **sausage**

APRICOTS, DRIED CALIFORNIA—Some specialty foods shops and the Apricot Farm

AREPA FLOUR—*See* **flour**

ASAFETIDA—Indian markets, some specialty foods shops, and Kalustyan's (we like the Vandevi brand)

ASIAN PEARS—Specialty produce markets, some supermarkets and farmers markets, Melissa's/World Variety Produce, and Frieda's

BAHARAT SPICE MIX—Middle Eastern markets and Formaggio Kitchen

BALSAMIC VINEGAR, AGED (*aceto balsamico tradizionale*)—Many specialty foods shops and Dean & DeLuca

BARLEY—Natural foods stores and supermarkets

BASIL, THAI—Southeast Asian markets, some specialty produce markets, and farmers markets

BEAN SAUCE, CHINESE HOT (sometimes labeled "hot bean paste")—Asian markets, EthnicGrocer.com, and Uwajimaya

BEAN THREAD NOODLES—*See* **noodles**

BEEF SUET—*See* **suet, beef**

BLACK BEANS, CHINESE FERMENTED—Asian markets, EthnicGrocer.com, and Uwajimaya

BLACK MUSTARD SEEDS—*See* **mustard seeds**

BLACK SESAME SEEDS—*See* **sesame seeds, black**

BONITO FLAKES, DRIED (*katsuobushi*)—Japanese markets and Uwajimaya

BRAN, UNPROCESSED WHEAT—Natural foods stores, some specialty foods shops and supermarkets, and the Birkett Mills

BUCKWHEAT FLOUR—*See* **flour**

BUFFALO

ground—Butcher shops, upscale supermarkets such as Whole Foods, some regular supermarkets, Jackson Hole Buffalo Meat Company (4-pound minimum), and Arrowhead Buffalo Meats (5-pound minimum)

prime rib roast—Butcher shops and Wild Idea Buffalo Company, Jackson Hole Buffalo Meat Company, Arrowhead Buffalo Meats, and D'Artagnan

BULGUR—Middle Eastern markets, natural foods stores, many supermarkets, and EthnicGrocer.com (where it is labeled "cracked wheat")

BUTTER, HIGHER-BUTTERFAT—Specialty foods shops, many supermarkets, and natural foods stores (brands include Keller's European-Style Plugrá, Land O' Lakes Ultra Creamy, and Organic Valley European Style)

CALABAZA—Caribbean, Latino, and West African markets and, increasingly, supermarkets

CAMPANELLE—*See* **pasta**

CANNING SALT—*See* **salt**

CARDAMOM SEEDS—Indian markets, specialty foods shops, many supermarkets, and Penzeys Spices

CAVIAR

Caspian—Specialty foods shops and Caviar Russe

farm-raised domestic—Stolt Sea Farm California (Sterling Classic white sturgeon) and Sunburst Trout Company (rainbow trout caviar)

salmon—Seafood stores, specialty foods shops, some supermarkets, and Yarra Valley Salmon

CHANA DAL—*See* **dal, chana and urad**

CHAYOTE—Latino markets and some specialty produce shops and supermarkets

CHEESES, ARTISANAL—Specialty cheese shops such as Murray's Cheese Shop, Formaggio Kitchen, and Artisanal Cheese Center

CHESTNUTS, BOTTLED WHOLE COOKED—Specialty foods shops, some supermarkets, and Dean & DeLuca

CHILES

Aleppo, dried flakes—Middle Eastern markets, some specialty foods shops, and Kalustyan's

ancho—Mexican markets, many supermarkets, and Chile Today–Hot Tamale

chile de árbol—Latino markets and Chile Today–Hot Tamale

chipotle—Latino markets, many supermarkets, and Chile Today–Hot Tamale

chipotle in adobo—Latino markets, many supermarkets, and Chile Today–Hot Tamale

guajillo—Latino markets, specialty foods shops, some supermarkets, and Chile Today–Hot Tamale

habanero—Latino markets, specialty produce markets, and some supermarkets

New Mexico—Some Latino markets and (dried chiles only) the Chile Shop

New Mexico red, crushed (caribe)—Southwestern markets, Los Chileros de Nuevo Mexico, and the Chile Shop

pasilla—Latino markets, specialty foods shops, some supermarkets, and Chile Today–Hot Tamale

poblano—Latino markets, specialty produce markets, and many supermarkets

Scotch bonnet—Latino markets, specialty produce markets, and some supermarkets

serrano—Specialty foods shops, some supermarkets, and Kitchen/Market

Thai—Asian markets, specialty produce shops, some supermarkets, and Temple of Thai

CHILE POWDER, INDIAN RED—Indian markets, some Asian markets, and Kalustyan's

CHILI PASTE, ASIAN—Asian markets, some specialty foods shops, and EthnicGrocer.com

CHOCOLATE, VALRHONA 56% CACAO—Specialty foods shops and New York Cake & Baking Distributors

CHORIZO

Mexican—Mexican and other Latino markets, many supermarkets, and Kitchen/Market

Spanish chorizo or *Portuguese chouriço*—Latino markets, some specialty foods shops and supermarkets (look for Goya brand), Citarella (Palacios brand), La Tienda, and the Spanish Table

CLEMENTINES, UNSPRAYED OR CERTIFIED ORGANIC—Some farmers markets, specialty produce markets, supermarkets, and Polito Family Farms

COCOA POWDER, UNSWEETENED VALRHONA—Specialty foods shops and New York Cake & Baking Distributors

COCONUT, UNSWEETENED GRATED—Natural foods stores, some supermarkets, and Kalustyan's

COFFEE BEANS, CHOCOLATE-COVERED—Specialty coffee stores, specialty foods shops, and Formaggio Kitchen

COTIJA—Mexican and other Latino markets and the Cheese Supply

COUNTRY HAM—*See* **ham**

CRABS

Dungeness, fresh live—Fish markets on the West Coast, high-quality fish stores elsewhere in the United States, and Pacific Seafood Company

Dungeness, frozen cooked—Pacific Seafood Company

CRAWFISH, LIVE—Some seafood shops and Louisiana Crawfish Company

CREMA—Mexican and other Latino markets and La Tienda

CREOLE MUSTARD—*See* **mustard, creole**

CURRY LEAVES—Indian and Asian markets

CURRY PASTE, THAI (red and green)—Asian markets, many supermarkets and specialty foods shops, Temple of Thai, and Uwajimaya

DAL, CHANA AND URAD—Indian markets and Kalustyan's

DEMI-GLACE, VEAL—Some specialty foods shops and More Than Gourmet

DUCK BREASTS
magrets, boneless breast halves with skin—Butcher shops, some upscale supermarkets, D'Artagnan, and Hudson Valley Foie Gras
Muscovy breast halves—Butcher shops, some specialty foods shops, and D'Artagnan

DUCK LEGS (confit and fresh)—Butcher shops, some specialty foods shops, and D'Artagnan

EDAMAME—Asian markets, specialty foods shops, natural foods stores, and many supermarkets (frozen); some farmers markets (fresh)

ELDERFLOWER CONCENTRATE—Some specialty foods shops and Dean & DeLuca

ESCARGOTS
canned—Zabar's
shells—Often sold with canned snails, or separately at some specialty foods shops and cookware shops

ESPRESSO POWDER, INSTANT—Specialty foods shops, some supermarkets, and the Baker's Catalogue

FENUGREEK
ground—Indian markets, specialty foods shops, and Penzeys Spices
seeds—Indian markets, specialty foods shops, and some supermarkets

FIG PRESERVES—Some specialty foods shops and supermarkets, Maison Glass, and the Lee Bros. Boiled Peanuts Catalogue

FISH SAUCE, ASIAN (Vietnamese *nuoc mam* and Thai *naam pla*)—Asian markets, many supermarkets, some specialty foods shops, and EthnicGrocer.com

FIVE-SPICE POWDER, CHINESE—Asian markets, specialty foods shops, and EthnicGrocer.com

FLEUR DE SEL—*See* **salt**

FLOUR (*See also* **semolina**)
arepa, white—Latino markets and EthnicGrocer.com
buckwheat—Natural foods stores, some supermarkets, and the Birkett Mills
high-gluten all-purpose—The Baker's Catalogue
King Arthur—Many supermarkets and the Baker's Catalogue
rye—Natural foods stores, some supermarkets, and the Baker's Catalogue
White Lily—Southern supermarkets, some specialty foods shops, and direct from the White Lily Foods Company

FOIE GRAS, COOKED PURE-GOOSE MEDALLIONS—Citarella

GALANGAL—Southeast Asian markets, some specialty produce markets, Temple of Thai, Melissa's/World Variety Produce, and Uwajimaya

GINGER, PICKLED—Japanese markets, many supermarkets, and Uwajimaya

GLACÉED (CANDIED) FRUIT, MIXED—Fauchon and the Baker's Catalogue

GOAT CHEESE, COACH FARM—Many specialty foods shops, Murray's Cheese Shop, and Formaggio Kitchen

GOOSE FAT, RENDERED AND CANNED—Some butcher shops and specialty foods shops and Citarella

GRITS, STONE-GROUND—Some specialty foods shops, Hoppin' John's, and Anson Mills

GUANABANA (SOURSOP), FROZEN—Latino markets and some supermarkets (look for Goya or La Fe brand)

GUANCIALE—Salumeria Biellese and Niman Ranch

GUINEA HENS—Many butcher shops and D'Artagnan

GYOZA SKINS—Asian markets, specialty foods shops, some supermarkets, and Uwajimaya

HAM

Serrano—Specialty foods shops, some butcher shops, La Tienda, and the Spanish Table

Virginia country—Some specialty foods shops and Edwards

HARISSA—Middle Eastern markets, specialty foods shops, and Kalustyan's

HIBISCUS FLOWERS, ORGANIC—Latino and Caribbean markets, natural foods stores, and MexGrocer.com

INSTACURE NO. 1—*See* **salt**

ISRAELI COUSCOUS—Middle Eastern markets, specialty foods shops, and Kalustyan's

JICAMA—Latino and Asian markets, specialty produce markets, many supermarkets, Melissa's/World Variety Produce, and Frieda's

JUNIPER BERRIES—Many supermarkets, specialty foods shops, and Penzeys Spices

KAFFIR LIME LEAVES—Asian markets, some specialty produce markets, and Uwajimaya

KEY LIME JUICE—Some specialty foods shops (look for Manhattan Key Lime)

KONBU (dried kelp; also labeled "kombu")—Japanese markets and Uwajimaya

KUMQUATS—Specialty produce markets, some supermarkets, Melissa's/World Variety Produce, and Frieda's

LACINATO KALE—Some supermarkets, specialty produce markets, natural foods stores, and Radicchio.com

LAKE PERCH—*See* **perch, lake**

LEMONGRASS—Asian markets, specialty produce stores, some supermarkets and farmers markets, and Temple of Thai

LENTILS

lentilles du Puy (French green lentils)—Specialty foods shops, natural foods stores, some supermarkets, and Dean & DeLuca

red—Some natural foods stores and supermarkets, and Kalustyan's

LINGONBERRY PRESERVES—Upscale supermarkets and Scandia Food & Gifts

LONG PEPPER, DRIED—Some Southeast Asian markets and Adriana's Caravan

LYLE'S GOLDEN SYRUP—Specialty foods shops, some supermarkets, and Oakville Grocery

MANGOES (domestically raised)—Robert Is Here and Pine Island Nursery

MAPLE SUGAR, GRANULATED—Some specialty foods shops and farmers markets, the Baker's Catalogue, and La Cuisine

MAPLE SYRUP, GRADE B—The Baker's Catalogue and Dakin Farm

MARAS PEPPER FLAKES—*See* **pepper flakes, Maras and Urfa**

MARIGOLD, DRIED—Aphrodisia

MERGUEZ—*See* **sausage**

MEYER LEMONS—Specialty produce stores, upscale supermarkets, and Snow's Citrus Court

MIRIN—Japanese and some other Asian markets, natural foods stores, many supermarkets, and Uwajimaya

MISO—Japanese and some Asian markets, natural foods stores, many supermarkets, and Uwajimaya

MUSHROOMS

morels, dried—Specialty foods shops, Marché aux Delices, and D'Artagnan

morels, fresh—Some specialty foods shops and Marché aux Delices (available late March through July)

porcini, dried—Specialty foods shops, some supermarkets, and Marché aux Delices

porcini bouillon cubes—Specialty foods shops and Salumeria Italiana

MUSTARD, CREOLE—Many supermarkets and Louisiana Crawfish Company

MUSTARD SEEDS, BLACK—Indian markets and Kalustyan's

NIGELLA SEEDS (may be labeled *kalonji* or mislabeled "black onion seeds")—Middle Eastern markets, Indian markets, and Kalustyan's

NOODLES (*See also* **pasta**)

Asian wheat or *buckwheat*—Asian markets and Uwajimaya

bean thread (cellophane)—Asian markets and Uwajimaya

rice, fresh—Asian markets

rice stick—Asian markets, some supermarkets, and EthnicGrocer.com

soba—Japanese markets, natural foods stores, some supermarkets, Uwajimaya, and EthnicGrocer.com

udon—Japanese markets, natural foods stores, some supermarkets, and Uwajimaya

NORI (dried laver)—Asian markets, natural foods stores, some supermarkets, and Uwajimaya

OCTOPUS, FROZEN CLEANED—Many seafood stores, some supermarkets (you may have to order a few days ahead), and Freshfish4u.com

OLIVE OIL, ALZIARI—Formaggio Kitchen and Zingerman's

ORANGE-FLOWER WATER, FRENCH—The bar aisle (next to the Rose's Lime Juice and bitters) or bakery aisle (A. Monteux brand) of some supermarkets, and Kalustyan's

ORECCHIETTE—*See* **pasta**

OREGANO, MEXICAN—Latino markets, specialty foods shops, many supermarkets, and Kitchen/Market

PALM SUGAR—Asian markets and Uwajimaya

PANKO—Asian markets, specialty foods shops, many supermarkets (often near the fish counter) and fish stores, and Uwajimaya

PAPRIKA

Hungarian—Specialty foods shops, some supermarkets, and Penzeys Spices

Spanish smoked—Specialty foods shops, La Tienda, and the Spanish Table

PASSION-FRUIT PULP, FROZEN—Latino markets and some supermarkets (look for Goya or La Fe brand)

PASTA

campanelle—Italian markets and supermarkets (Barilla brand)

orecchiette—Italian markets and supermarkets (Barilla brand)

perciatelli—Italian markets, specialty foods shops, and EthnicGrocer.com (De Cecco brand)

tagliarelle—Many specialty foods shops and Dean & DeLuca (Cipriani brand)

PECANS, NEW-CROP—Southern roadside stands, Ellis Bros. Pecans, and Pearson Farm

PEPPER FLAKES, MARAS AND URFA—Middle Eastern markets and Formaggio Kitchen

PEPPER SAUCE, SCOTCH BONNET—Caribbean and Latino markets, some specialty foods shops, and Mo Hotta–Mo Betta (ask for Walkerswood brand Jamaican Scotch bonnet pepper sauce)

PEPPERCORNS

black—Specialty foods shops, many supermarkets, and Zingerman's

Sichuan—*See* **Sichuan peppercorns**

white—Specialty foods shops and Zingerman's

PERCH, LAKE—Many seafood stores and Freshfish4u.com

PERCIATELLI—*See* **pasta**

PHEASANT—Butcher shops, some farmers markets and specialty foods shops, and D'Artagnan

PICHOLINE OLIVES—Specialty foods shops, upscale supermarkets, and Kalustyan's

PICKLED GINGER—*See* **ginger, pickled**

POMEGRANATE MOLASSES—Middle Eastern markets and Sadaf

PORCINI BOUILLON CUBES—*See* **mushrooms**

PORK BELLY—Butcher shops, some supermarkets, and Karl Ehmer Quality Meats

PORK CHOPS, SMOKED—Butcher shops, some supermarkets, Nueske's, and Karl Ehmer Quality Meats

PORTUGUESE CHOURIÇO—*See* **chorizo**

POUSSINS—Butcher shops, some specialty foods shops, and D'Artagnan

QUAIL—Butcher shops, specialty foods shops, some upscale supermarkets, Cavendish Game Birds, and D'Artagnan

QUAIL EGGS—Chinese markets, many specialty foods shops, and D'Artagnan

QUESO FRESCO—Mexican and other Latino markets and Mozzarella Company

QUINCES—Specialty produce markets, farmers markets, and some supermarkets

QUINOA—Natural foods stores, many supermarkets, and EthnicGrocer.com

RABBIT—Butcher shops, many supermarkets, and D'Artagnan

RAS EL HANOUT—Middle Eastern markets, some specialty foods shops, and Formaggio Kitchen

RICE

black (Forbidden)—Asian markets, specialty foods shops, Lotus Foods, and Kalustyan's

Carolina Gold—Some specialty foods shops, some supermarkets, Charleston Favorites, and the Lee Bros. Boiled Peanuts Catalogue

Japanese short-grain—Japanese markets, some specialty foods shops, and Uwajimaya

Spanish short-grain (such as SOS or Calasparra)—Some Latino markets, La Tienda, and the Spanish Table

sushi—Japanese markets, some specialty foods shops and supermarkets, and Uwajimaya

Thai jasmine—Asian markets, natural foods stores, and Uwajimaya

Thai sticky—Asian markets, some specialty foods shops, and Uwajimaya

RICE NOODLES—See **noodles**

RICE VINEGAR—Asian markets, most supermarkets, and Uwajimaya

RICE WINE, CHINESE—Asian markets, some specialty foods shops and supermarkets, and EthnicGrocer.com

RICOTTA SALATA—Cheese shops, Italian markets, many specialty foods shops, and Murray's Cheese Shop

ROSE HIP OR ROSE FRUIT JAM—Natural foods stores and some supermarkets

ROSE WATER—The bar or bakery aisle of supermarkets (A. Monteux brand) and New York Cake & Baking Distributors

SAKE—Wine shops and liquor stores

SAKE KASU—Japanese markets and Uwajimaya

SALSIFY/SCORZONERA—Specialty produce markets and some farmers markets

SALT
canning—Hardware stores, some supermarkets, and Home Canning Supply and Specialties
fleur de sel—Specialty foods shops and Zabar's
Instacure No. 1 (curing salts)—The Sausage Maker

SALT COD—Seafood stores, some supermarkets, and La Tienda

SAMBAL OELEK—Asian markets and Uwajimaya

SANSHO—Asian markets and Adriana's Caravan

SAUSAGE (*See also* **chorizo**)
andouille (Cajun smoked)—Specialty foods shops and CajunGrocer.com
garlic pork—Some butcher shops and specialty foods shops and D'Artagnan
merguez—Specialty foods shops and D'Artagnan

SAVOIARDI (crisp Italian ladyfingers)—Italian markets, specialty foods shops, Salumeria Italiana, and Formaggio Kitchen

SAWDUST, HARDWOOD—The Sausage Maker

SCALLOP SHELLS—Some cookware stores and Bridge Kitchenware

SEAFOOD BOIL SPICES, CAJUN—Some fish stores and Louisiana Crawfish Company (Zatarain's brand)

SEAFOOD GLAZE—Some supermarkets, specialty foods shops, and More Than Gourmet (ask for Glace de Fruits de Mer Gold)

SEMOLINA (sometimes labeled "semolina flour"; resembles fine yellow cornmeal)—Italian markets, natural foods stores, specialty foods shops, some supermarkets, and Dean & DeLuca

SERRANO HAM—*See* **ham**

SESAME OIL
Asian—Asian markets, many specialty foods shops and supermarkets, and EthnicGrocer.com
Japanese—Japanese markets and Uwajimaya

SESAME SEEDS, BLACK—Asian markets, specialty foods shops, some supermarkets, and Uwajimaya

SHISO LEAVES (also labeled "perilla")—Japanese markets, some specialty produce markets, and Sushi Foods Co.

SHRIMP PASTE, ASIAN—Asian markets, some specialty foods shops and supermarkets, and Uwajimaya

SICHUAN PEPPERCORNS—Some Asian markets

SOBA NOODLES—*See* **noodles**

SOY SAUCE, DARK (black or mushroom)—Asian markets and EthnicGrocer.com

SQUAB—Butcher shops (usually by special order), some specialty foods shops and farmers markets, and D'Artagnan

SUET, BEEF—Butcher shops (ask the butcher to shred it for you)

SUMAC, GROUND—Middle Eastern markets and Formaggio Kitchen

SUMMER SAVORY, DRIED—Specialty foods shops and many supermarkets

SUSHI RICE—*See* **rice**

TAGLIARELLE—*See* **pasta**

TAMARIND
block—Indian markets, some Asian markets, and Kalustyan's
concentrate—Indian and Latino markets and Kalustyan's

TASSO (Cajun cured smoked pork)—Some butcher shops and specialty foods shops and CajunGrocer.com

TATSOI—Specialty produce markets and some farmers markets and supermarkets

TOFU, PLAIN BAKED—Asian markets and EthnicGrocer.com

TOMATILLOS

canned—Latino markets, some supermarkets, and Kitchen/Market

fresh—Specialty foods shops, many supermarkets, and Frieda's

TRUFFLE BUTTER, BLACK—Specialty foods shops and D'Artagnan

TRUFFLE PASTE AND OIL, WHITE—Specialty foods shops and Urbani Truffles USA

TRUFFLES, JARRED FRESH BLACK WINTER OR CANNED BLACK WINTER—Many specialty foods shops, Urbani Truffles USA, and D'Artagnan

UDON NOODLES—*See* **noodles**

URAD DAL—*See* **dal, chana and urad**

URFA PEPPER FLAKES—*See* **pepper flakes, Maras and Urfa**

VANILLA BEANS

Bourbon—Specialty foods shops and the Vanilla Company; also sold in supermarkets (avoid dry, shriveled beans)

Mexican—Specialty foods shops, Zingerman's, and the Vanilla Company

Tahitian—Specialty foods shops and the Vanilla Company

VEAL DEMI-GLACE—*See* **demi-glace, veal**

WAKAME—Japanese markets, natural foods stores, and Uwajimaya

WALNUT OIL—Specialty foods shops, some supermarkets, Oakville Grocery, and Dean & DeLuca

WASABI PASTE AND POWDER—Asian markets, specialty foods shops, some supermarkets, and Uwajimaya

WHEAT BERRIES—Natural foods stores, Middle Eastern markets, and Kalustyan's

WOOD CHIPS (apple, cherry, or hickory)—Hardware stores, specialty foods shops, some supermarkets, and C. M. International

YUCA, FRESH OR FROZEN (sometimes labeled "cassava")—Latino markets and some supermarkets and Frieda's

ZUCCHINI BLOSSOMS—Farmers markets, specialty produce markets, and some supermarkets

Kitchenware

BABA AU RHUM MOLDS (4-ounce, preferably nonstick)—Some cookware shops and Bridge Kitchenware

BAKER'S PEEL and BAKING (PIZZA) STONE—The Baker's Catalogue

BAKING SHEET LINERS (such as Silpat brand)—Cookware shops and Bridge Kitchenware

BAKING SHEETS, SOLID ALUMINUM WITH PEBBLE PATTERN—Some cookware shops and Doughmakers

BALL BLUE BOOK OF PRESERVING—Alltrista Corporation and Home Canning Supply and Specialties

BARQUETTE TINS (4-INCH)—Some cookware shops and Sur La Table

BEAN POT OR FAGIOLIERA (5-QUART)—La Cuisine (Prial brand)

BENRINER SLICER, JAPANESE—Asian markets, cookware shops, and Uwajimaya

BLOWTORCH, SMALL—Cookware shops and Chef's Catalog (ask for the BonJour Crème Brûlée torch)

BRIOCHE MOLDS, INDIVIDUAL FLUTED (3 inches across top)—Specialty bakeware shops and Bridge Kitchenware

CAKE PANS (springform, round, square, tube, Bundt, loaf, kugelhopf)—Bakeware shops, Bridge Kitchenware, and New York Cake & Baking Distributors

CAKE ROUNDS, CARDBOARD—Cookware shops and New York Cake & Baking Distributors

CANNING SUPPLIES (jars with lids and screw bands and wide-mouth funnels)—Many supermarkets, Wal-Mart, Kmart, Target, hardware stores, and Home Canning Supply and Specialties

CHARLOTTE MOLDS

- *1-quart*—Broadway Panhandler and Bridge Kitchenware
- *5- to 6-cup*—Broadway Panhandler and Bridge Kitchenware
- *5- to 6-ounce*—Many kitchenware shops and Broadway Panhandler
- *4-ounce*—Many kitchenware shops and Bridge Kitchenware

CHEESE IMPLEMENTS—Cookware stores, cheese shops, and Artisanal Cheese Center

CHERRY PITTER—Cookware shops, some hardware stores, Bridge Kitchenware, and Chef's Catalog

COEUR À LA CRÈME MOLDS, CERAMIC (⅓-cup)—Many cookware shops and Zabar's

COOKIE CUTTERS (assorted, snowflake, and teardrop)—Some bakeware shops and Sweet Celebrations

COOKIE PRESS—Cookware shops and Williams-Sonoma

CORN-STICK PANS, CAST-IRON (with seven 5-by-1½-inch molds)—Bridge Kitchenware

COUSCOUSSIÈRE—Many cookware shops and Broadway Panhandler

CUSTARD CUPS OR RAMEKINS (2- to 3-ounce)—Cookware shops

FISH POACHER (24-inch)—Cookware shops and Zabar's

ICE SHAVER—Asian markets and PureEarth

JULIENNE PEELER (KUHN RIKON BRAND)—Some cookware shops and Chef's Catalog

LEMON AND LIME PRESSES—Many kitchenware shops, La Cuisine, Sur La Table, and Williams-Sonoma

LOAF PANS (12-by-4½-by-3-inch)—Cookware stores and Bridge Kitchenware (pan size may vary slightly)

MADELEINE PANS, MINIATURE (with twenty ½-inch molds)—Many cookware shops and Bridge Kitchenware

MAGI-CAKE STRIPS—Some specialty bakeware shops and New York Cake & Baking Distributors

MELON BALL CUTTER, OLIVE-SHAPED—Cookware shops and Bridge Kitchenware

MOLCAJETE Y TEJOLOTE—Many Mexican markets, Kitchen/Market, and the CMC Company

MORTAR AND PESTLE—Specialty foods shops, Dean & DeLuca, Sur La Table, and the Spanish Table

NEEDLE, CARPET, DARNING, OR UPHOLSTERY—Sewing supply shops and some housewares stores

PAELLA PAN (17-inch)—Cookware shops, Bridge Kitchenware, and the Spanish Table

PASTRY CLOTHS AND ROLLING PIN COVERS—Bridge Kitchenware

PECTIN, LIQUID AND POWDERED—Supermarkets and Home Canning Supply and Specialties

PIE SHIELDS—Cookware shops and New York Cake & Baking Distributors

PIE WEIGHTS—Cookware shops and New York Cake & Baking Distributors

POT DE CRÈME CUPS—Bridge Kitchenware

SPAETZLE MAKER—Many cookware stores and Bridge Kitchenware

TAGINE—Berber Trading Company

TARTLET PANS—Specialty bakeware shops and Bridge Kitchenware

TERRINES (various sizes)—Bridge Kitchenware

TORTILLA PRESS—Many Latino markets and Kitchen/Market

Adriana's Caravan
Retail store and mail-order catalog
78 Grand Central Terminal
New York, NY 10017
800-316-0820 (toll-free)
www.adrianascaravan.com

Alltrista Corporation
P.O. Box 2005
Muncie, IN 47307
800-392-2575 (toll-free)
www.homecanning.com

Anson Mills
Retail store
1922-C Gervais Street
Columbia, SC 29201
803-467-4122
www.ansonmills.com

Aphrodisia
Retail store and mail-order catalog
264 Bleecker Street
New York, NY 10014
212-989-6440

The Apricot Farm
Retail store and mail-order catalog
420 Lucy Brown Lane
San Juan Bautista, CA 95045
800-233-4413 (toll-free)
www.apricot-farm.com

Arrowhead Buffalo Meats
9120 State Road 521
Sunbury, OH 43074
877-328-2833 (toll-free)
www.arrowheadsteaks.com

Artisanal Cheese Center
Retail store and mail-order catalog
500 West 37th Street
New York, NY 10018
877-797-1200 (toll-free)
www.artisanalcheese.com

The Baker's Catalogue
Retail store and mail-order catalog
133 Route 5 South
Norwich, VT 05055
800-827-6836 (toll-free)
www.kingarthurflour.com

Berber Trading Company
Retail store
8865 SW 132nd Street
Miami, FL 33176
877-277-7227 (toll-free)
www.tagines.com

The Birkett Mills
Retail store
163 Main Street
Penn Yan, NY 14527
315-536-3311
Mail-order catalog
P.O. Box 440
Penn Yan, NY 14527
315-536-3311
www.thebirkettmills.com

Bridge Kitchenware
Retail store and mail-order catalog
214 East 52nd Street
New York, NY 10022
800-274-3435 (toll-free outside New York City)
or 212-688-4220
www.bridgekitchenware.com

Broadway Panhandler
Retail store
477 Broome Street
New York, NY 10013
866-266-5927 (toll-free) *or* 212-966-3434
www.broadwaypanhandler.com

www.CajunGrocer.com
888-272-9347 (toll-free)

Cavendish Game Birds
396 Woodbury Road
Springfield, VT 05156
802-885-5339
www.vermontquail.com

Caviar Russe
Retail store
538 Madison Avenue
New York, NY 10022
800-692-2842 (toll-free) *or* 212-980-5908
www.caviarrusse.com

Charleston Favorites
Retail store
1023 Wappo Road, Suite B-28
Charleston, SC 29407
800-538-0003 (toll-free)
Mail-order catalog
P.O. Box 31883
Charleston, SC 29417
800-538-0003 (toll-free)
www.charlestonfavorites.com

The Cheese Supply
P.O. Box 515
Vashon, WA 98070
866-205-6376 (toll-free)
www.cheesesupply.com

Chef's Catalog
Mail-order catalog
P.O. Box 650589
Dallas, TX 75265
800-884-2433 (toll-free)
www.chefscatalog.com

The Chile Shop
Retail store and mail-order catalog
109 East Water Street
Santa Fe, NM 87501
505-983-6080
www.thechileshop.com

Chile Today–Hot Tamale
Mail-order catalog
31 Richboynton Road
Dover, NJ 07801
800-468-7377 (toll-free)
www.chiletoday.com

Citarella
Retail store
2135 Broadway
New York, NY 10023
212-874-0383
www.citarella.com

C. M. International
Mail-order catalog
P.O. Box 60220
Colorado Springs, CO 80960
888-563-0227 (toll-free)
www.cameronsmoker.com

The CMC Company
Mail-order catalog
P.O. Drawer 322
Avalon, NJ 08202
800-262-2780 (toll-free)
www.thecmccompany.com

D'Artagnan
Mail-order catalog
280 Wilson Avenue
Newark, NJ 07105
800-327-8246 (toll-free)
www.dartagnan.com

Dakin Farm
Retail store and mail-order catalog
5797 Route 7
Ferrisburgh, VT 05456
800-993-2546 (toll-free)
www.dakinfarm.com

Dean & DeLuca
Retail store
560 Broadway
New York, NY 10012
212-226-6800
Mail-order catalog
2526 E. 36th Street, North Circle
Wichita, KS 67219
800-221-7714 (toll-free)
www.deandeluca.com

Doughmakers
888-386-8517 (toll-free)
www.doughmakers.com
Order from www.thebakersplace.com.

Edwards
Retail store
11381 Rolfe Highway
Surry, VA 23883
757-294-3688
Mail-order catalog
P.O. Box 25
Surry, VA 23883
800-222-4267 (toll-free)
www.vatraditions.com

Ellis Bros. Pecans
Retail store and mail-order catalog
1315 Tippettville Road
Vienna, GA 31092
800-635-0616 (toll-free)
www.werenuts.com

www.EthnicGrocer.com

Fauchon
Retail store
442 Park Avenue
New York, NY 10022
212-308-5919
Mail-order catalog
3502 Borden Avenue
Long Island City, NY 11101
718-752-1240

Formaggio Kitchen
Retail store and mail-order catalog
244 Huron Avenue
Cambridge, MA 02138
888-212-3224 (toll-free)
www.formaggiokitchen.com

www.Freshfish4u.com
877-474-3474 (toll-free)

Frieda's
Mail-order catalog
P.O. Box 58488
Los Angeles, CA 90058
800-241-1771 (toll-free)
www.friedas.com

Home Canning Supply and Specialties
Mail-order catalog
P.O. Box 1153
Ramona, CA 92065
800-354-4070 (toll-free)
www.homecanningsupply.com

HOPPIN' JOHN'S
800-828-4412 (toll-free)
www.hoppinjohns.com

HUDSON VALLEY FOIE GRAS
877-289-3643 (toll-free)
www.hudsonvalleyfoiegras.com

JACKSON HOLE BUFFALO MEAT COMPANY
Mail-order catalog
P.O. Box 1770
Jackson, WY 83001
800-543-6328 (toll-free)
www.jhbuffalomeat.com

KALUSTYAN'S
Retail store
123 Lexington Avenue
New York, NY 10016
800-352-3451 (toll-free)
www.kalustyans.com

KARL EHMER QUALITY MEATS
Retail store
63-35 Fresh Pond Road
Ridgewood, NY 11385
800-487-5275 (toll-free)
www.karlehmer.com

KITCHEN/MARKET
Retail store and mail-order catalog
218 Eighth Avenue
New York, NY 10011
888-468-4433 (toll-free)
www.kitchenmarket.com

LA CUISINE
Retail store
323 Cameron Street
Alexandria, VA 22314
800-521-1176 (toll-free)
www.lacuisineus.com

LA TIENDA
Retail store and mail-order catalog
3701 Rochambeau Drive
Williamsburg, VA 23188
888-472-1022 (toll-free)
www.tienda.com

THE LEE BROS. BOILED PEANUTS CATALOGUE
Mail-order catalog
P.O. Box 315
Charleston, SC 29402
843-720-8890
www.boiledpeanuts.com

LOS CHILEROS DE NUEVO MEXICO
888-328-2445 (toll-free) *or* 505-471-6967
www.888eatchile.com

LOTUS FOODS
866-972-6879 (toll-free)
www.lotusfoods.com

LOUISIANA CRAWFISH COMPANY
888-522-7292 (toll-free)
www.lacrawfish.com

MAISON GLASS
800-822-5564 (toll-free) *or* 212-755-3316
www.maisonglass.com

MARCHÉ AUX DELICES
888-547-5471 (toll-free)
www.auxdelices.com

MELISSA'S/WORLD VARIETY PRODUCE
800-588-0151 (toll-free)
www.melissas.com

WWW.MEXGROCER.COM
877-463-9476 (toll-free)

Mo Hotta–Mo Betta
Mail-order catalog
P.O. Box 1026
Savannah, GA 31402
800-462-3220 (toll-free)
www.mohotta.com

More Than Gourmet
800-860-9385 (toll-free)
www.morethangourmet.com

Mozzarella Company
Retail store and mail-order catalog
2944 Elm Street
Dallas, TX 75226
800-798-2954 (toll-free) *or* 214-741-4072
www.mozzco.com

Murray's Cheese Shop
Retail store
257 Bleecker Street
New York, NY 10014
888-692-4339 (toll-free)
www.murrayscheese.com

New York Cake & Baking Distributors
Retail store
56 West 22nd Street
New York, NY 10010
800-942-2539 (toll-free)
www.nycake.com

Niman Ranch
1025 East 12th Street
Oakland, CA 94606
510-808-0340
www.nimanranch.com

Nueske's
Retail store
W17878 Business Highway 29 East
Wittenberg, WI 54499
715-253-2226
Mail-order catalog
Rural Route 2, P.O. Box D
Wittenberg, WI 54499
800-392-2266 (toll-free)
www.nueskes.com

Oakville Grocery
Retail store
7856 St. Helena Highway
Oakville, CA 94562
707-944-8802
800-973-6324 (toll-free)
www.oakvillegrocery.com

Pacific Seafood Company
Retail store
3380 SE Powell Boulevard
Portland, OR 97202
503-233-4894
www.pacseafood.com

PEARSON FARM

Retail store and mail-order catalog

11022 Highway 341
Fort Valley, GA 31030
888-423-7374 (toll-free)
www.pearsonfarm.com

PENZEYS SPICES

Retail store

19300 West Janecek Court
Brookfield, WI 53045
262-785-7637

Mail-order catalog

P.O. Box 924
Brookfield, WI 53008
800-741-7787 (toll-free)
www.penzeys.com

PINE ISLAND NURSERY

Retail store

16300 SW 184th Street
Miami, FL 33187
305-233-5501
www.tropicalfruitnursery.com

POLITO FAMILY FARMS

Farm store (call first)

11920 Betsworth Road
Valley Center, CA 92082
760-749-1636

PUREEARTH

352 Friendship Court SW
Marietta, GA 30064
800-669-1376 (toll-free)
www.pure-earth.com

WWW.RADICCHIO.COM

831-758-1957

ROBERT IS HERE

Retail store and mail-order catalog

19200 SW 344th Street
Homestead, FL 33034
305-246-1592
www.robertishere.com

SADAF

Mail-order catalog

2828 South Alameda Street
Los Angeles, CA 90058
800-852-4050 (toll-free)
www.sadaf.com

SALUMERIA BIELLESE

Retail store

376–378 Eighth Avenue
New York, NY 10001
212-736-7376
www.salumeriabiellese.com

SALUMERIA ITALIANA

Retail store

151 Richmond Street
Boston, MA 02109
800-400-5916 (toll-free)
www.salumeriaitaliana.com

The Sausage Maker
Mail-order catalog
1500 Clinton Street
Building 123
Buffalo, NY 14206
888-490-8525 (toll-free)
www.sausagemaker.com

Scandia Food & Gifts
Retail store and mail-order catalog
30 High Street
Norwalk, CT 06851
203-838-2087
www.scandiafood.com

Snow's Citrus Court
P.O. Box 1316
Newcastle, CA 95658
916-663-1884
www.vfr.net/~snow

The Spanish Table
Retail store
1427 Western Avenue
Seattle, WA 98101
206-682-2827
www.spanishtable.com

Stolt Sea Farm California
Informational brochure
9149 East Levee Road
Elverta, CA 95626
800-525-0333 (toll-free)
www.stoltseafarm.com *or* www.sterlingcaviar.com

Sunburst Trout Company
Retail store and mail-order catalog
128 Raceway Place
Canton, NC 28716
800-673-3051 (toll-free)
www.sunbursttrout.com

Sur La Table
Retail store
Pike Place Market
84 Pine Street
Seattle, WA 98101
206-448-2244
Mail-order catalog
P.O. Box 34707
Seattle, WA 98124
800-243-0852 (toll-free)
www.surlatable.com

Sushi Foods Co.
888-817-8744 (toll-free)
www.sushifoods.com

Sweet Celebrations
Retail store
14276 Plymouth Avenue
Burnsville, MN 55337
952-435-3377
Mail-order catalog
P.O. Box 39426
Edina, MN 55439
800-328-6722 (toll-free)
www.sweetc.com

Temple of Thai
877-811-8773 (toll-free)
www.templeofthai.com

Urbani Truffles USA
380 Meadowbrook Road
North Wales, PA 19454
215-699-8780
www.urbanitruffles.com

Uwajimaya
Retail store
600 Fifth Avenue South, Suite 100
Seattle, WA 98104
800-889-1928 (toll-free)
www.uwajimaya.com

The Vanilla Company
Mail-order catalog
P.O. Box 3206
Santa Cruz, CA 95063
800-757-7511 (toll-free)
www.vanilla.com

The White Lily Foods Company

Mail-order catalog

218 East Depot Avenue
Knoxville, TN 37917
800-264-5459 (toll-free)
www.whitelily.com

Wild Idea Buffalo Company

Mail-order catalog

P.O. Box 1209
Rapid City, SD 57709
866-658-6137 (toll-free)
www.wildideabuffalo.com

Williams-Sonoma

Mail-order catalog

3250 Van Ness Avenue
San Francisco, CA 94109
800-541-1262 (toll-free)
www.williams-sonoma.com

Yarra Valley Salmon

Retail store

Corti Bros.
5810 Folsom Boulevard
Sacramento, CA 95819
800-509-3663 (toll-free)

Zabar's

Retail store and mail-order catalog

2245 Broadway
New York, NY 10024
800-697-6301 (toll-free outside New York City)
or 212-496-1234
www.zabars.com

Zingerman's

Retail store and mail-order catalog

422 Detroit Street
Ann Arbor, MI 48104
888-636-8162 (toll-free)
www.zingermans.com

INDEX

A

B

C

D

E

F

G

H

I

J

K

L

M

N

O

P

Q

R

S

T

U

V

W

Y

Z

PERMISSIONS

Grateful acknowledgment is made to the following for permission to reprint recipes previously published in *Gourmet*.

"Green Apple Salad with Grilled Beef" from *Pleasures of the Vietnamese Table* by Mai Pham, published in *Gourmet*, July 2001. Copyright © 2001 by Mai Pham. Used by permission of Dystel and Goderich Literary Management.

"Curried Noodles with Vegetables," "Mu Shu Vegetables with Pork," "Stir-Fried Pepper Beef," and "Mock Mandarin Pancakes" by Nina Simonds, originally published in *Gourmet*, September 1994. Copyright © 1994 by Nina Simonds. Used by permission.

"Risotto with Porcini" by Elizabeth Schneider, originally published in *Gourmet*, October 1984. Copyright © 1984 by Elizabeth Schneider. Used by permission.

"Escarole, Sausage, and White Bean Stew" from *American Brasserie* by Rick Tramonto, Gale Gand, and Julia Moskin, published in *Gourmet*, October 1998. Copyright © 2002 by Rick Tramonto, Gale Gand, and Julia Moskin. All rights reserved. Reproduced here by permission of Wiley Publishing, Inc.

"Pan-Roasted Mahimahi with Butter and Lime" from *Great Fish, Quick* by Leslie Revsin, published in *Gourmet*, October 1998. Copyright © 1997 by Leslie Revsin. Used by permission.

"Halibut with Spicy Asian Vinaigrette and Wasabi Cream" by Patricia Perry, originally published in *Gourmet*, August 2000. Copyright © 2000 by Patricia Perry. Used by permission.

"Baked Bay Scallops," by Sally Darr, originally published in *Gourmet*, November 1992. Copyright © 1992 by Sally Darr. Used by permission.

"Shrimp in Adobo Sauce" by Elisabeth Lambert Ortiz, originally published in *Gourmet*, January 1985. Copyright © 1985 by Elisabeth Lambert Ortiz.

"Emeril's Barbecued Shrimp with Mini Buttermilk Biscuits" from *Emeril's New New Orleans Cooking* by Emeril Lagasse and Jesse Tirsch, published in *Gourmet*, April 1993. Copyright © 1993 by Emeril Lagasse. Reprinted by permission of HarperCollins Publishers Inc.

"Stuffed Squid" from *Pani Caliatu* by Susan Lord and Danilo Baroncini, published in *Gourmet*, January 2004. Copyright © 1999 by Susan Lord and Danilo Baroncini. Used by permission.

"Duck Legs and Carrots" from *Nose to Tail Eating* by Fergus Henderson, published in *Gourmet*, October 2002. Copyright © 2000 by Fergus Henderson. Used by permission of Lutyens and Rubenstein.

"Roast Loin of Pork with Braised Red Cabbage and Port Wine Sauce" from *The Food of Campanile* by Mark Peel and Nancy Silverton, published in *Gourmet*, October 1997. Copyright © 1997 by Mark Peel and Nancy Silverton. Used by permission.

"Zucchini Carpaccio" from *Red, White, and Greens: The Italian Way with Vegetables* by Faith Heller Willinger, published in *Gourmet*, June 1996. Copyright © 1996 by Faith Heller Willinger. Used by permission.

"Corn Fritters," by Laurie Colwin, originally published in *Gourmet*, August 1993. Copyright © 1993 by Laurie Colwin. Reprinted by permission of Donadio & Olson, Inc.

"Migas (Tortillas Scrambled with Bacon and Eggs)" from *Cocina de la Familia* by Marilyn Tausend, published in *Gourmet*, July 1998. Copyright © 1997 by Marilyn Tausend. Reprinted by permission of Simon & Schuster Adult Publishing Group.

"Cheese Omelet" and "Sautéed Dessert Crêpes," from *French Cooking in Ten Minutes* by Édouard de Pomiane, translated by Philip Hyman and Mary Hyman, published in *Gourmet*, March 2001. Translation copyright © 1977 by Farrar, Straus & Giroux, Inc. Reprinted by permission of Farrar, Straus & Giroux, LLC, and Faber and Faber, Ltd.

"Parisian Passover Coconut Macaroons" and "Passover Sponge Cake with Apples" from *1,000 Jewish Recipes* by Faye Levy, published in *Gourmet*, April 2000. Copyright © 2000 by Faye Levy. All rights reserved. Reproduced here by permission of Wiley Publishing, Inc.

"Strawberry Jam" by Caroline Bates, originally published in *Gourmet*, September 1999. Copyright © 1999 by Caroline Bates. Used by permission.